P9-DOF-213

DICTIONARY OF
AMERICAN BIOGRAPHY

American Council of Learned Societies

American Philosophical Society, Philadelphia, Pennsylvania

American Academy of Arts and Sciences, Cambridge, Massachusetts

American Antiquarian Society, Worcester, Massachusetts

American Oriental Society, New Haven, Connecticut

American Numismatic Society, New York, New York

American Philological Association, Swarthmore, Pennsylvania

Archeological Institute of America, New York, New York

Society of Biblical Literature and Exegesis, Haverford, Pennsylvania

Modern Language Association of America, New York, New York

American Historical Association, Washington, District of Columbia

American Economic Association, Evanston, Illinois

American Philosophical Association, Middletown, Connecticut

American Anthropological Association, Chicago, Illinois

American Political Science Association, Evanston, Illinois

Bibliographical Society of America, Albany, New York

Association of American Geographers, Minneapolis, Minnesota

American Sociological Society, Washington, District of Columbia

American Society of International Law, Washington, District of Columbia

College Art Association of America, New York, New York

History of Science, South Hadley, Massachusetts

Linguistic Society of America, Washington, District of Columbia

Mediaeval Academy of America, Cambridge, Massachusetts

Population Association of America, Washington, District of Columbia

~ Dictionary of ~

American Biography

PUBLISHED UNDER THE AUSPICES OF

American Council of Learned Societies

EDITED BY

Dumas Malone

Mills — Oglesby

VOLUME XIII

NEW HANOVER COUNTY
DISCARDED
201 CHESTNUT STREET
New Hanover County Public Library
from
New Hanover County Public Library

NEW YORK

Charles Scribner's Sons

MCMXLIII

Prompted solely by a desire for public service the New York Times Company and its President, Mr. Adolph S. Ochs, have made possible the preparation of the manuscript of the Dictionary of American Biography through a subvention of more than $500,000 and with the understanding that the entire responsibility for the contents of the volumes rests with the American Council of Learned Societies.

COPYRIGHT, 1934, BY

AMERICAN COUNCIL OF LEARNED SOCIETIES

———

Printed in the United States of America

The Dictionary of American Biography is published under the auspices of the American Council of Learned Societies and under the direction of a Committee of Management which consists of J. Franklin Jameson, *Chairman*, John H. Finley, Dumas Malone, Frederic L. Paxson, Iphigene Ochs Sulzberger, Carl Van Doren, Charles Warren.

The editorial staff consists of Dumas Malone, *Editor*; Harris E. Starr, *Associate Editor*; George H. Genzmer, Eleanor R. Dobson, Mildred B. Palmer, Katharine Elizabeth Crane, *Assistant Editors*.

The American Council of Learned Societies consists of the following societies:

American Philosophical Society
American Academy of Arts and Sciences
American Antiquarian Society
American Oriental Society
American Philological Association
Archaeological Institute of America
Society of Biblical Literature and Exegesis
Modern Language Association of America
American Historical Association

American Economic Association
American Philosophical Association
American Anthropological Association
American Political Science Association
Bibliographical Society of America
American Sociological Society
History of Science Society
Linguistic Society of America
Mediaeval Academy of America

CONTRIBUTORS TO VOLUME XIII

Charles G. Abbot	C. G. A.	Sarah G. Bowerman	S. G. B.
Willis J. Abbot	W. J. A.	Walter Russell Bowie	W. R. B.
Thomas P. Abernethy	T. P. A.	Julian P. Boyd	J. P. B.
Adeline Adams	A. A.	William K. Boyd	W. K. B.
James Truslow Adams	J. T. A.	William L. Boyden	W. L. B.
Daniel Dulany Addison	D. D. A.	William Bridgwater	W. B—r.
Nelson F. Adkins	N. F. A.	Crane Brinton	C. B—n.
Cyrus Adler	C. A.	Ruth Lee Briscoe	R. L. B.
Robert Greenhalgh Albion	R. G. A.	Robert Bruce	R. B.
Carroll S. Alden	C. S. A.	Solon J. Buck	S. J. B.
John Lincoln Alger	J. L. A.	John W. Buckham	J. W. B.
Harold M. Anderson	H. M. A.	Charles W. Burr	C. W. B.
Neal L. Anderson	N. L. A.	Huntington Cairns	H. Ca—s.
John Clark Archer	J. C. A—h—r.	Robert G. Caldwell	R. G. C—l.
Percy M. Ashburn	P. M. A.	Earnest Elmo Calkins	E. E. Ca—s.
Astley P. C. Ashhurst	A. P. C. A.	Lester J. Cappon	L. J. C.
Clifford W. Ashley	C. W. A.	Harry J. Carman	H. J. C.
Frederick W. Ashley	F. W. A.	William S. Carpenter	W. S. C.
Albert W. Atwood	A. W. A.	Charles Joseph Chamberlain	C. J. C.
Warren O. Ault	W. O. A.	Charles E. Chapman	C. E. C.
Joseph Cullen Ayer	J. C. Ay—r.	Edward P. Cheyney	E. P. C.
William F. Badè	W. F. B.	Francis A. Christie	F. A. C.
Edward M. Bailey	E. M. B.	Robert C. Clark	R. C. C.
Roland H. Bainton	R. H. B.	Rudolf A. Clemen	R. A. C.
Horace B. Baker	H. B. B.	Ernest W. Clement	E. W. C.
Ray Palmer Baker	R. P. B.	Harry Clemons	H. Cl—s.
Hayes Baker-Crothers	H. B–C.	Oral Sumner Coad	O. S. C.
Thomas S. Barclay	T. S. B.	Collier Cobb	C. C.
Lewellys F. Barker	L. F. B.	Frederick W. Coburn	F. W. C.
Gilbert H. Barnes	G. H. B.	Robert P. Tristram Coffin	R. P. T. C.
Claribel R. Barnett	C. R. B.	Fannie L. Gwinner Cole	F. L. G. C.
Adriaan J. Barnouw	A. J. B—w.	Rossetter G. Cole	R. G. C—e.
Allen J. Barthold	A. J. B—d.	Christopher B. Coleman	C. B. C.
Clarence Bartlett	C. B—t.	John R. Commons	J. R. C.
George A. Barton	G. A. B.	Robert Spencer Cotterill	R. S. C.
Robert Duncan Bass	R. D. B.	George S. Cottman	G. S. C.
Frances Bates	F. B.	Theodore S. Cox	T. S. C.
William G. Bean	W. G. B.	Katharine Elizabeth Crane	K. E. C.
W. J. Bender	W. J. B.	Verner W. Crane	V. W. C.
Orval Bennett	O. B.	Abigail Curlee	A. C.
Adolph B. Benson	A. B. B.	Edward E. Curtis	E. E. Cu—s.
Percy W. Bidwell	P. W. B.	Robert E. Cushman	R. E. C.
Alan Rogers Blackmer	A. R. B.	Arthur B. Darling	A. B. D.
Helen C. Boatfield	H. C. B.	Donald Davidson	D. D.
Ernest Ludlow Bogart	E. L. B.	Arthur Powell Davis	A. P. D.
Charles K. Bolton	C. K. B.	Richard E. Day	R. E. D.
Milledge Louis Bonham, Jr.	M. L. B., Jr.	Charles A. Dinsmore	C. A. D.
Witt Bowden	W. B—n.	Roland B. Dixon	R. B. D.
George F. Bowerman	G. F. B.	Eleanor Robinette Dobson	E. R. D.

Contributors to Volume XIII

William Howe Downes	W. H. D—s.
Donald Marquand Dozer	D. M. D.
Stella M. Drumm	S. M. D.
Louise B. Dunbar	L. B. D.
Waldo H. Dunn	W. H. D—n.
Lionel C. Durel	L. C. D.
George B. Dutton	G. B. D.
Edward Dwight Eaton	E. D. E.
Walter Prichard Eaton	W. P. E.
Edwin Francis Edgett	E. F. E.
Granville D. Edwards	G. D. E.
Martin Egan	M. E—n.
Luther P. Eisenhart	L. P. E.
Thompson C. Elliott	T. C. E.
Elizabeth Breckenridge Ellis	E. B. E.
Milton Ellis	M. E—s.
Barnett A. Elzas	B. A. E.
John Norris Evans	J. N. E.
Paul D. Evans	P. D. E.
John O. Evjen	J. O. E.
Charles Fairman	C. F.
Paul Patton Faris	P. P. F.
Hallie Farmer	H. F—r.
Oscar W. Firkins	O. W. F.
Daniel Moore Fisk	D. M. F.
Edward Fitch	E. F.
John E. Flitcroft	J. E. F.
Henry Wilder Foote	H. W. F.
Allyn B. Forbes	A. B. F.
Amelia C. Ford	A. C. F.
Hughell E. W. Fosbroke	H. E. W. F.
Harold N. Fowler	H. N. F.
L. Webster Fox	L. W. F.
Philip Franklin	P. F.
Joseph C. W. Frazer	J. C. W. F.
John H. Frederick	J. H. F.
John C. French	J. C. F.
Herbert Friedmann	H. F—n.
Claude M. Fuess	C. M. F.
John F. Fulton	J. F. F.
Franklin DeR. Furman	F. DeR. F.
Caroline E. Furness	C. E. F.
Herbert P. Gallinger	H. P. G.
Gilbert J. Garraghan	G. J. G.
Curtis W. Garrison	C. W. G.
F. Lynwood Garrison	F. L. G.
Samuel W. Geiser	S. W. G.
George Harvey Genzmer	G. H. G.
W. J. Ghent	W. J. G.
George W. Goler	G. W. G.
Cardinal Goodwin	C. G.
Colin B. Goodykoontz	C. B. G—z.
Armistead Churchill Gordon, Jr.	A. C. G., Jr.
Kenneth M. Gould	K. M. G.
Louis H. Gray	L. H. G.
John N. Greely	J. N. G.
Edwin L. Green	E. L. G.
Gurney C. Gue	G. C. G.
Charles Burton Gulick	C. B. G.
Charles W. Hackett	C. W. H.
Le Roy R. Hafen	L. R. H.
Philip M. Hamer	P. M. H.
J. G. deR. Hamilton	J. G. deR. H.
William A. Hammond	W. A. H.
Alvin F. Harlow	A. F. H.
George M. Harper	G. M. H.
Albert Bushnell Hart	A. B. H.
Freeman H. Hart	F. H. H.
Mary Bronson Hartt	M. B. H.
Margaret Harwood	M. H.
Daniel C. Haskell	D. C. H.
Stephen J. Herben	S. J. H.
Frederick C. Hicks	F. C. H.
Granville Hicks	G. H.
John Donald Hicks	J. D. H.
Frederick W. Hodge	F. W. H.
Raymond Holden	R. H.
John Haynes Holmes	J. H. H.
Oliver W. Holmes	O. W. H.
A. Van Doren Honeyman	A. V–D. H.
Stephen Henry Horgan	S. H. H.
Walter Hough	W. H.
John Tasker Howard	J. T. H.
G. Evans Hubbard	G. E. H.
Arthur W. Hummel	A. W. H.
Louis C. Hunter	L. C. H.
Augustus E. Ingram	A. E. I.
Ray W. Irwin	R. W. I.
Asher Isaacs	A. I.
Edith J. R. Isaacs	E. J. R. I.
Joseph Jackson	J. J.
Alfred P. James	A. P. J.
Smith Ely Jelliffe	S. E. J.
Howard Mumford Jones	H. M. J.
H. Donaldson Jordan	H. D. J.
James R. Joy	J. R. J.
Louis C. Karpinski	L. C. K.
Delbert Kay	D. K.
Louise Phelps Kellogg	L. P. K.
Rayner W. Kelsey	R. W. K.
Roland G. Kent	R. G. K.
John Kieran	J. K.
Fiske Kimball	F. K.
John A. Krout	J. A. K.
L. B. Krueger	L. B. K.
Leonard W. Labaree	L. W. L.
John W. Lang	J. W. L.
Herbert S. Langfeld	H. S. L.
Alexander S. Langsdorf	A. S. L.
Conrad H. Lanza	C. H. L.
Stephen Leacock	S. L.
Max Lerner	M. L.
Charles Lee Lewis	C. L. L.
Frederic Thomas Lewis	F. T. L.
George M. Lewis	G. M. L.

Contributors to Volume XIII

W. Lee Lewis	W. L. L.	Leigh Page	L. P.
Arnold J. Lien	A. J. L.	Scott H. Paradise	S. H. P.
Anna Lane Lingelbach	A. L. L.	John I. Parcel	J. I. P.
Ella Lonn	E. L.	Stanley M. Pargellis	S. M. P.
Harry Miller Lydenberg	H. M. L.	John C. Parish	J. C. P.
Virginia MacAdam	V. M.	Charles W. Parker	C. W. P.
Helen McAfee	H. M.	Henry Bamford Parkes	H. B. P.
N. E. McClure	N. E. M.	John Jay Parry	J. J. P.
Roger P. McCutcheon	R. P. M.	Edward L. Parsons	E. L. P.
W. J. McGlothlin	W. J. M.	James W. Patton	J. W. P.
R. Tait McKenzie	R. T. M.	Charles O. Paullin	C. O. P.
John McNaugher	J. M.	Frederic Logan Paxson	F. L. P.
John H. T. McPherson	J. H. T. M.	C. C. Pearson	C. C. P.
James C. Malin	J. C. M.	James H. Peeling	J. H. P.
W. C. Mallalieu	W. C. M.	Dexter Perkins	D. P—s.
Arthur T. Mann	A. T. M.	Frederick T. Persons	F. T. P.
H. A. Marmer	H. A. M.	A. Everett Peterson	A. E. P.
Frederick H. Martens	F. H. M.	Robert H. Pfeiffer	R. H. P.
Lawrence Martin	L. M.	James M. Phalen	J. M. P.
Shailer Mathews	S. M—s.	David Philipson	D. P—n.
Robert Douthat Meade	R. D. M.	Paul Chrisler Phillips	P. C. P.
Albert B. Meredith	A. B. M—h.	David deSola Pool	D. deS. P.
Newton D. Mereness	N. D. M.	Arthur Pope	A. P.
Robert L. Meriwether	R. L. M.	Jermain G. Porter	J. G. P.
George P. Merrill	G. P. M.	Charles Shirley Potts	C. S. P.
Frank J. Metcalf	F. J. M.	Arthur Chilton Powell	A. C. P.
Perry Miller	P. M.	Edward Preble	E. P.
Edwin Mims, Jr.	E. M., Jr.	Herbert I. Priestley	H. I. P.
Broadus Mitchell	B. M.	Leon C. Prince	L. C. P.
Stewart Mitchell	S. M—l.	Richard J. Purcell	R. J. P.
Wilmot B. Mitchell	W. B. M.	Arthur Hobson Quinn	A. H. Q.
Carl W. Mitman	C. W. M.	Lowell Joseph Ragatz	L. J. R.
Conrad Henry Moehlman	C. H. M.	Charles W. Ramsdell	C. W. R.
E. V. Moffett	E. V. M.	George H. Ramsey	G. H. R.
John R. Mohler	J. R. M.	James G. Randall	J. G. R.
Raymond Moley	R. M.	Daniel S. Rankin	D. S. R.
Frank Monaghan	F. M—n.	Albert G. Rau	A. G. R.
Fulmer Mood	F. M-d.	P. O. Ray	P. O. R.
Robert E. Moody	R. E. M.	Thomas T. Read	T. T. R.
Albert B. Moore	A. B. M—e.	Herbert S. Reichle	H. S. R.
Austin L. Moore	A. L. M.	Charles Dudley Rhodes	C. D. R.
Charles Moore	C. M.	Leon B. Richardson	L. B. R.
Samuel Eliot Morison	S. E. M.	Robert E. Riegel	R. E. R.
Richard B. Morris	R. B. M.	James Alexander Robertson	J. A. R.
Jarvis M. Morse	J. M. M.	Burr Arthur Robinson	B. A. R.
Josiah Morse	J. M—e.	J. Magnus Rohne	J. M. R.
Donald H. Mugridge	D. H. M.	James H. Ropes	J. H. R.
David Saville Muzzey	D. S. M.	Lois K. M. Rosenberry	L. K. M. R.
H. Edward Nettles	H. E. N.	Victor Rosewater	V. R.
Allan Nevins	A. N.	Frank Edward Ross	F. E. R.
Lyman C. Newell	L. C. N.	Henry Kalloch Rowe	H. K. R.
A. R. Newsome	A. R. N.	Joseph L. Rubin	J. L. R.
Robert Hastings Nichols	R. H. N.	Durward V. Sandifer	D. V. S.
Joe L. Norris	J. L. N.	George Henry Sargent	G. H. S.
Alexander D. Noyes	A. D. N.	Max Savelle	M. S.
Hermon M. Noyes	H. M. N.	Joseph Schafer	J. S.
Ellis P. Oberholtzer	E. P. O.	Herbert W. Schneider	H. W. S—d—r.
John Chadwick Oliver	J. C. O.	H. W. Schoenberger	H. W. S—g—r.

Contributors to Volume XIII

Carl F. Schreiber	C. F. S.		Olin F. Tower	O. F. T.
Hamilton Schuyler	H. S.		Milton Haight Turk	M. H. T—k.
Franklin D. Scott	F. D. S.		Alonzo H. Tuttle	A. H. T.
Roy W. Sellars	R. W. S.		Roland Greene Usher	R. G. U.
Robert Francis Seybolt	R. F. S.		George B. Utley	G. B. U.
George Dudley Seymour	G. D. S.		William T. Utter	W. T. U.
Robert Shafer	R. S.		Irene Van Fossen	I. V–F.
Robert K. Shaw	R. K. S.		S. C. Vestal	S. C. V.
William Bristol Shaw	W. B. S.		Henry R. Viets	H. R. V.
Jay J. Sherman	J. J. S.		Harold G. Villard	H. G. V.
Guy Emery Shipler	G. E. S.		Oswald Garrison Villard	O. G. V.
Fred W. Shipman	F. W. S.		Eugene M. Violette	E. M. V.
Lester B. Shippee	L. B. S.		Buz M. Walker	B. M. W.
Wilbur H. Siebert	W. H. S—t.		Alexander J. Wall	A. J. W.
Francis Butler Simkins	F. B. S.		James J. Walsh	J. J. W.
Charles P. Sisson	C. P. S.		Frederic A. Washburn	F. A. W.
Clarence R. Skinner	C. R. S.		W. Randall Waterman	W. R. W.
David Eugene Smith	D. E. S.		Luther Allan Weigle	L. A. W.
Edward Conrad Smith	E. C. S.		Theodore H. Weisenburg	T. H. W.
William E. Smith	W. E. S—h.		Francis P. Weisenburger	F. P. W.
William Roy Smith	W. R. S.		Allan Westcott	A. W.
Herbert Weir Smyth	H. W. S—h.		Arthur P. Whitaker	A. P. W.
W. E. Snyder	W. E. S—r.		Melvin J. White	M. J. W.
M. E. Spalding	M. E. S.		William A. White	W. A. W.
E. Wilder Spaulding	E. W. S.		Mary T. Whitley	M. T. W.
Thomas M. Spaulding	T. M. S.		Henry F. Wickham	H. F. W.
Harris Elwood Starr	H. E. S.		Jeanne Elizabeth Wier	J. E. W.
Bertha Monica Stearns	B. M. S.		Clarence Russell Williams	C. R. W—s.
George W. Stephens	G. W. S.		Mary Wilhelmine Williams	M. W. W.
Wendell H. Stephenson	W. H. S—n.		Stanley T. Williams	S. T. W.
Wayne E. Stevens	W. E. S—s.		Charles C. Williamson	C. C. W.
Witmer Stone	W. S.		Francis T. Williamson	F. T. W.
William W. Sweet	W. W. S.		James Southall Wilson	J. S. W.
Henry O. Swindler	H. O. S.		Harry A. Wolfson	H. A. W.
Charles S. Sydnor	C. S. S.		Helen Sumner Woodbury	H. S. W.
C. R. Walther Thomas	C. R. W. T.		Maude H. Woodfin	M. H. W.
David Y. Thomas	D. Y. T.		Carl R. Woodward	C. R. W—d.
Milton Halsey Thomas	M. H. T—s.		Walter C. Woodward	W. C. W.
Frederic L. Thompson	F. L. T.		Robert H. Woody	R. H. W
Herbert Thoms	H. T.		Helen Wright	H. W.
Irving L. Thomson	I. L. T.		Walter L. Wright, Jr.	W. L. W., Jr.
J. Monroe Thorington	J. M. T.		Lawrence C. Wroth	L. C. W.
Edward Larocque Tinker	E. L. T.		Donovan Yeuell	D. Y.

DICTIONARY OF
AMERICAN BIOGRAPHY

——

Mills — Oglesby

MILLS, ANSON (Aug. 31, 1834–Nov. 5, 1924), soldier and inventor, was born on a farm near Thorntown, Ind., where his father, James P. Mills, a descendant of a Philadelphian of Penn's time, had taken up land about 1830. There he had married Sarah Kenworthy, also of Quaker ancestry, whose family came to North Carolina in the eighteenth century. Anson Mills's boyhood was spent on the farm, where he became a practical carpenter and weaver, as well as farmer. He entered West Point in 1855, but was unprepared to carry the course and was discharged early in 1857. His next four years were spent in Texas, where, during his work as a surveyor, he made the original plat of the city of El Paso and gave the place its name. When the Civil War broke out, he cast one of the two anti-secession votes recorded in the county, and started for Washington. In June 1861 he received an antedated commission (May 14, 1861) as first lieutenant in a regular infantry regiment just organized.

His first battle was Shiloh, and until the end of the war he was in the field in the West, under Buell, Rosecrans, and Thomas, fighting in the Murfreesboro, Chickamauga, Atlanta, and Nashville campaigns. He was promoted to captain in 1863. On Oct. 13, 1868, he was married to Hannah Cassel, daughter of William C. Cassel, of Zanesville, Ohio. From 1865 to 1893 practically all of his service was on the frontier, involving much Indian fighting, notably the Rosebud campaign of 1876. He was transferred to the cavalry in 1871, was promoted to major in 1878, to lieutenant-colonel in 1890, and to colonel in 1892.

As early as 1866 he had patented a cartridge belt which was much more satisfactory than the regulation box. It had certain faults, however, which he hoped to obviate by weaving the whole belt in one piece, without sewing. For years he worked to perfect this invention. Later, in writing of his wife, he said: "I purchased foot-power lathes, drills, etc., to develop models of my various patents in belts and equipment. I installed them in one of her best rooms in each succeeding one of perhaps twenty posts, soiling the carpets with grease, filings and shavings, which would have driven most wives mad" (*My Story*, p. 126). All difficulties were finally overcome, and the belt was adopted by the United States Army, the requirements of which in those days, however, were small. The war with Spain caused Mills and his associates to expand their factory so as to produce a thousand belts a day, but the early termination of the war "put us in a practically bankrupt condition, a hundred thousand belts on hand and no market for them, and a large indebtedness" (*Ibid.*, p. 322). Some of the belts were disposed of by presenting them to two Canadian regiments preparing to leave for the war in South Africa, and by June 1901 orders were received for equipping three thousand British troops. The success of the belt was assured. Military and hunting equipment of all sorts is now manufactured under Mills's patents. Mills himself, however, sold out his interest in 1905, having seen his invention a success and having made a fortune in his old age.

In 1894 he was designated as the American member of the International Boundary Commission, charged with settling cases involving the boundary with Mexico. He continued as commissioner until 1914, although he had been appointed brigadier-general in 1897 and placed on the retired list. His autobiography, *My Story,* was privately printed in 1918. He died in Washington, where he had made his home since 1894.

[In addition to the autobiography (in which the date of birth is apparently a misprint), see F. B. Heitman, *Hist. Reg. and Dict. U. S. Army* (1903), I, 713; *Who's Who in America,* 1924–25; *Washington Post,* Nov. 6, 1924, *Evening Star* (Washington), Nov. 5, 1924.]

T. M. S.

MILLS, BENJAMIN (Jan. 12, 1779–Dec. 6, 1831), Kentucky legislator and jurist, was born in Worcester County, Md., but when quite young he was taken by his family to Washington, Pa., where he spent his youth. After the usual elementary education he studied medicine but postponed its practice for teaching and was for a time at the head of Washington Academy (now Washington and Jefferson College). He removed with his father to Bourbon County, Ky., where, abandoning medicine, he studied law and began practice in Paris about 1805. He represented Bourbon County in the state House of Representatives for six terms, 1806, 1809, 1813, 1814, 1815, and 1816. His repeated election to the House indicated the unusual measure of public confidence that he enjoyed. During the later period he was a member of the committee on courts of justice. In 1816 he was a candidate before the legislature for the United States Senate but was defeated by a few votes. In 1817 he was appointed judge of the Montgomery circuit court and the next year was transferred to the Fayette circuit at the request of the Fayette bar.

In 1820 with his appointment as associate justice of the court of appeals, he entered on the most important phase of his career, a phase that was disastrous to his personal fortunes and popularity. The relief laws passed by the legislature to aid those who had suffered by the collapse of state banks were declared unconstitutional by the court in 1823, and this action resulted in the dissolution of the court by the angry legislature and the creation of a new court. There ensued in Kentucky the notorious "court contest" around which Kentucky politics centered for a decade. Mills and his two colleagues refused to give up their positions or to recognize the validity of the action of the legislature. Since the relief laws were popular in Kentucky he was severely denounced for his attitude. In the end the old court was sustained but he had worn himself out and had lost his usefulness as a jurist. In December 1828 he resigned. He was immediately reappointed by the governor, but the Senate refused to confirm him. He continued to reside in Frankfort, however, and devoted himself to the practice of law. He died of apoplexy. He was known for his extensive charities which were quite often beyond his means,

was a member of the Presbyterian Church, for a long time one of its elders, and was one of the founders of the American Bible Society. His grandson was Benjamin Fay Mills [*q.v.*].

[Shane MSS., II cc4, Wis. Hist. Lib.; Lewis and R. H. Collins, *Hist. of Ky.,* revised ed. (2 vols., 1874); H. Levin, *The Lawyers and Lawmakers of Ky.* (1897); W. H. Perrin, J. H. Battle, and G. C. Kniffin, *Kentucky* (1886); A. M. Stickles, *The Critical Court Struggle in Ky.* (1929); *Ky. Gazette* (Lexington), Dec. 8, 1831; *Focus* (Louisville), Dec. 8, 1831.]

R. S. C.

MILLS, BENJAMIN FAY (June 4, 1857–May 1, 1916), evangelist and liberal religious leader, was born at Rahway, N. J. His father, Thornton A. Mills, son of Benjamin Mills [*q.v.*] of Kentucky, was a Presbyterian minister who became moderator of the General Assembly of the Presbyterian Church in the United States of America; his mother, Anna (Cook) Mills, had been a missionary in India. He prepared for college at Phillips Academy, Andover, and was graduated with the degree of A.B. from Lake Forest University in 1879. Ordained to the Congregational ministry in 1878, he had brief pastorates in villages of Dakota and New York, and in 1884 became minister of the Congregational church at West Rutland, Vt. His pastorate here was characterized by a revival of religious interest which attracted the attention of neighboring ministers; as a result he was invited to conduct a two-week series of evangelistic meetings at Middlebury. The community and college were deeply stirred, and more than three hundred people professed conversion.

In May 1886 he resigned his pastorate to devote himself to itinerant, interdenominational evangelism. His culture and training caused him to be welcomed as an evangelist of a new type; and for ten years, in city after city, his work met with extraordinary success. Toward the end of this period, under the influence of Prof. George D. Herron [*q.v.*] of Grinnell College, he began to develop a social interpretation of the gospel which led him to question the worth of individual, personal evangelism. This attitude of mind appeared in his address before the World's Parliament of Religions at Chicago in 1893. In 1895 he accepted for one year a pastorate at Albany, N. Y., in order that he might study in the state library; thence he went to Boston and began to preach his new social gospel in Music Hall and the Hollis Street Theatre, under the auspices of a committee headed by Edward Everett Hale [*q.v.*]. In 1897 he definitely withdrew from the evangelical ministry and from evangelistic work. He said that he did this, "first, because I despaired of the possibility of a genuine, widespread awakening and inspiration of the church; second, because of a social vision, by which I came to conceive of Christ as the Saviour of the social organization rather than of individuals; and third, because of the universal viewpoint which came to me through my study of the great books of all ages and nations, through which the Bible ceased to be to me the exclusively inspired Word of God" (*Advance,* June 24, 1915, p. 1251).

After two years in Boston, Mills was for four years (1899–1903) minister of the First Unitarian Church of Oakland, Cal. He then removed to Los Angeles and devoted himself to lecturing on liberal religion and the conduct of life in a sort of itinerant ministry similar to that of his evangelistic period. He was founder and minister (1904–11) of the Los Angeles Fellowship; and founder and leader (1911–14) of the Chicago Fellowship. These were independent religious organizations based upon principles which he formulated thus: "Absolute Trust as the Fixed Attitude of Mind, and Perfect Love as the Unvarying Practice of the Life" (*Ibid.*). He chose as motto the comprehensive question, "What is the Loving Thing to Do?" the answer to which he believed would solve all practical questions. He finally came to feel that these principles, though true, fall short of a genuine gospel and give insufficient impulse to right living. In 1915 he experienced a reconversion to the Christian faith, and sought readmission to its ministry. He was received into the Chicago Presbytery and began again to conduct evangelistic meetings in various cities. He died at Grand Rapids, Mich., survived by his wife, Mary Russell (Hill) Mills, to whom he was married on Oct. 31, 1879, by three sons, and three daughters.

Mills published, in his evangelistic period, *Power from On High* (1890); *A Message to Mothers* (1892); *Victory Through Surrender* (1892); *God's World, and Other Sermons* (1893); and in his non-evangelical period, *Twentieth Century Religion* (copr. 1898, 1899), and *The Divine Adventure* (1905). He published a brief spiritual autobiography in a series of articles entitled, "Why I Return to the Church," which appeared in three numbers of *The Advance,* beginning June 24, 1915.

[Besides the series of articles mentioned above, see the following: "The Passing of B. Fay Mills," in *Advance,* May 11, 1916; *Congregationalist,* Aug. 19, 1915, May 25, 1916; *Christian Advocate,* Sept. 23, 1897; *North Shore Leader* (Chicago), May 5, 1916; J. J. Francis and C. B. Morrell, *Mills Meetings Memorial Vol.* (1892).]   L. A. W.

MILLS, CHARLES KARSNER (Dec. 4, 1845–May 28, 1931), neurologist, was born in Philadelphia, the son of James and Lavinia Ann (Fitzgerald) Mills. He graduated from Central High School in 1864, having served in the Union army during the Civil War. In a series of articles entitled "The Military History of the Falls of Schuylkill," published in the *Weekly Forecast,* a suburban paper, Mar. 13–Oct. 16, 1913, he gave a complete account of the emergency campaigns of 1862 and 1863 in which he took part. For several years after he finished his high-school course he was engaged in teaching. He then began the study of medicine, graduating from the medical department of the University of Pennsylvania in 1869. In 1871 he received the degree of Ph.D.

After a few years of general practice he became interested in nervous and mental diseases, in which he subsequently specialized. In 1874 he was made chief of the clinic for nervous diseases in the University Hospital, and in 1877 he was appointed neurologist to the Philadelphia Hospital. In the latter year he became lecturer on electrotherapeutics in the University of Pennsylvania, and was connected with that institution until his death, being successively lecturer in neuropsychiatry, professor of mental diseases, and professor of neurology in charge of the department. His work in this last position was so meritorious that the "Philadelphia school of neurology" which he created, was known all over the scientific world. In 1915 he was made emeritus professor of neurology. From 1883 to 1898 he was professor of nervous and mental diseases in the Philadelphia Polyclinic, of which he was one of the founders. In 1914 he organized a graduate course in the wards of the Philadelphia General Hospital, and later became professor of neurology in the Graduate Medical School of the University of Pennsylvania, which position he held until a few years before his death. He was also professor of nervous diseases in the Woman's Medical College of Pennsylvania (1891–1902), and was connected with many hospitals in both the city and the state. He took an active part in the proceedings of the American Neurological Association from its establishment until his death, was elected president in 1887, and again in 1924 on the fiftieth anniversary of its organization. In 1883 he founded the Philadelphia Neurological Society.

Mills wrote extensively on many subjects. His neurologic contributions alone number 345, his predominant interest being in cerebral localization and the philosophy of neurology. His bibliography covers such subjects as neurologic surgery, cerebral morphology, vasomotor and trophic diseases, hydrophobia, multiple neuritis,

poliomyelitis, myotonia and athetoid spasm, surface thermometry, electrotherapeutics, problems
in electrical potential, hypnotism, hysteria, neu-
rasthenia, psychotherapeutics, mental overwork,
Swedish movements and systemized therapeutic
exercises, occupational neuroses, localization of
tumors of the brain by Roentgen exploration, the
treatment of aphasia by training, disorders of
pantomime (a forerunner of subsequent work on
apraxia), the symptomatology of lenticular lesions, intradural root anastomosis, insanity in
children and adults, criminal lunacy and the
medico-legal aspects of nervous diseases and insanity. In 1898 he published *The Nervous System and Its Diseases,* undoubtedly the most scholarly contribution on diseases of the brain and
cranial nerves which had appeared up to that
time in the American literature of the subject.
He wrote a great deal on medical biography and
history, and even produced some poetry in his
younger days. Among his biographical sketches
are *Benjamin Rush and American Psychiatry*
(1886); *Isaac Ray, the Great Alienist* (1888),
and a tribute to his friend of many years, Dr. S.
Weir Mitchell. His historical papers include
"History of Medical Jurisprudence in Philadelphia," in F. P. Henry's *The Standard History of
the Medical Profession in Philadelphia* (1897);
Neurology in Philadelphia from 1874 to 1904
(1904); *Historical Memoranda Concerning the
Philadelphia Hospital for the Insane* (1909);
and *The Philadelphia Almshouse and the Philadelphia Hospital from 1854 to 1908* (1909). His
longest poem, *The Schuylkill, a Centennial Poem
by M. K. C.,* was published in book form in 1876.
He was a witness in the Guiteau, Thaw, and
other important cases, and was highly esteemed
in the realm of medical jurisprudence. On Nov.
6, 1873, he married Clara Elizabeth, daughter of
Charles Wilson and Harriet (Friel) Peale of
Philadelphia. He was survived by a daughter
and three sons.

[*Semi-centennial Vol. of the Am. Neurological Asso.,
1875–1924* (1924) contains bibliog. of Mills publications; for further data see T. H. Weisenburg in
Archives of Neurology and Psychiatry, July 1931;
Jour. Am. Medic. Asso., June 13, 1931; *Jour. of Nervous and Mental Disease,* Nov. 1931; *Who's Who in
America,* 1930–31; *Public Ledger* (Phila.), May 28,
1931.]   T. H. W.

MILLS, CLARK (Dec. 13, 1810–Jan. 12,
1883), sculptor, pioneer bronze founder, was
born in Onondaga County, N. Y. At the age of
five, upon his father's death, he was placed with
an uncle, from whom he ran away eight years
later because of real or fancied ill-treatment.
Thereafter he made his own way. He worked
as a farmhand, at scant wages not always paid;
at times he attended school in winter. He hauled
lumber in Syracuse, but when oxen were supplied instead of horses, he found life too slow
and went to work on the canal. Later, while cutting cedar posts in a swamp, he froze his feet
and for months could wear no shoes. Seeking
lighter labor, he worked with a cabinet-maker,
at first for instruction, afterward for board. He
spent two years as millwright's apprentice, for a
time was employed in plaster and cement mills,
and then drifted to New Orleans, La. After a
year there he passed to Charleston, S. C., where
he worked in stucco until 1835. In that year he
began modeling busts in clay. His experiences
from 1828 to 1835 had developed all his native
hardihood, versatility, and inventiveness. He
next discovered a new method of taking casts
from the living face, which gained him considerable work in portraiture, then he studied marble-cutting. In Carolina marble he carved a bust
of John C. Calhoun. It was bought by the city
council of Charleston and in 1846 won for Mills
a gold medal, grandiloquently inscribed in Latin
and in English. He was offered means for study
abroad by certain well-to-do men of the city but
he declined because of work offered at home.
John S. Preston, who had befriended the sculptor Powers, invited him to Columbia, S. C.,
where he made ten busts, to be cut in marble after further study in art. William C. Preston suggested that before going abroad, Mills should
see the statuary in Washington, D. C., and paid
the expenses of the round trip; he also gave
Mills orders for two busts, those of Webster and
of Crittenden. On his travels Mills stopped at
Richmond, Va., and there studied Houdon's
"Washington," the first statue he had ever seen.
As to Greenough's "Washington," in the guise
of the Olympian Zeus, he pronounced the anatomy perfect, but the treatment lacking in historical truth. He resolved that should he himself
have a statue to make, "the world should find
fault for his giving too much truth, and not for
want of it" (*Round Table,* May 14, 1864, p. 340).

His opportunity came in 1848, when Cave
Johnson, president of the Jackson monument
committee, proposed that before going to Europe
the young man should make a design for an
equestrian monument to General Jackson. Mills
had never seen either Jackson or an equestrian
statue and at first refused. Nevertheless, the
thought took possession of him and after nine
months of study he produced a small model in
which the hind feet of the horse came well under
the center of the group, thus giving a lifelike
effect of perfect balance entirely satisfactory to
the committee. A contract for twelve thousand

dollars was made, the committee to furnish the bronze. After two years of strenuous labor, the full-size plaster model was finished; for the bronze, Congress appropriated cannon captured by Jackson. Then appeared the true magnitude of the task. The industry of bronze casting was almost unknown in the United States and never before had so large a piece been undertaken in the country. After seemingly insuperable difficulties had been overcome, largely through the resourcefulness and pertinacity of the sculptor, the pioneer equestrian statue emerged in bronze. Dedicated in January 1853, on the thirty-eighth anniversary of the battle of New Orleans, it still stands in Lafayette Square across from the White House in Washington, indulgently viewed by sophisticates who perceive its lack of sculptural dignity, but perhaps overlook its pioneer importance. Congress now voted to Mills an additional twenty thousand dollars, doubtless well earned; it also awarded him a fifty-thousand-dollar contract for an equestrian statue of Washington for the capital city and in 1860 commissioned him to cast in bronze Crawford's colossal "Liberty" for the Capitol dome. The city of New Orleans ordered a replica of the "Jackson." With these projects assured, Mills bought land three miles from Washington and there erected a suitable studio and foundry. A gale wrecked the studio, a fire destroyed the foundry, but both were soon rebuilt. The New Orleans replica was dedicated in 1856, the "Washington" in 1860, and the "Liberty" in 1863. The "Washington" lacks interest and is without even such unity of design as may be descried in the "Jackson," a third replica of which was erected in Nashville, Tenn., in 1880. Other works by Mills are numerous portrait busts; the Corcoran Gallery owns his "Calhoun" and his "Washington." His final undertaking was an enormous design for a Lincoln monument, to include thirty-six heroic figures, equestrian and pedestrian. The project fell into oblivion after his death at Washington in 1883. He was survived by a widow, two sons, and a step-daughter. One of his sons, Theodore Augustus, was a sculptor of talent who died in 1916.

[Lorado Taft, The Hist. of Am. Sculpture (1930); Chas. E. Fairman, Art and Artists of the Capitol (1927); "Mr. Clark Mills, the Sculptor," Round Table, May 14, 1864; "Sculpture at the Capital," Ibid., Sept. 8, 1866; H. T. Tuckerman, Book of the Artists (1867); Leila Mechlin, "Art Life in Washington," Records of the Columbia Hist. Soc., Wash., D. C., vol. XXIV (1922); W. O. Hart, "Clark Mills," Ibid.; Am. Art Rev., vol. II (1881), p. 131; Frank Leslie's Illustrated Newspaper, Mar. 3, 1860; Evening Star (Wash., D. C.), Jan. 12, 1883; Washington Post, Jan. 13, 15, 1883.]
A. A.

MILLS, CYRUS TAGGART (May 4, 1819–Apr. 20, 1884), missionary, educator, and business man, was born in Paris, N. Y., youngest of the three sons of William and Mary Mills. He grew up in the midst of the poverty which was common among families on the frontier during the early part of the nineteenth century. Although he was inadequately prepared for college when he entered Williams, and was obliged to work his way through, he graduated in 1844, seventh in a class of thirty-three. The influence of Mark Hopkins [q.v.] was a force that Mills delighted to acknowledge throughout his life. From Williams College he went to the Union Theological Seminary, New York, worked his way through there, and graduated in 1847. At some time during his period of preparation he became interested in missionary work in India, and took up the study of Tamil while in the theological seminary. On Feb. 2, 1848, he was ordained by the Third Presbytery of New York and on Sept. 11 he married Susan Lincoln Tolman [see Mills, Susan Lincoln Tolman]. The two sailed almost immediately for India, under appointment of the American Board of Commissioners for Foreign Missions.

Full of enthusiasm, the young couple landed in Ceylon and Mills took charge of Batticotta Seminary, an institution devoted to training native teachers and preachers. His administration was successful and he established an enviable reputation among both his colleagues and the natives of the community; but the climate was enervating and the environment was unhealthful. A constitution none too rugged at any time was soon undermined by the diseases common to that section, and after six years of arduous labor he and his wife returned to the United States. Then followed four years of recuperation, agitation on behalf of foreign missionary work, pastoral labors in Berkshire, N. Y. (1856–58), business ventures, and, finally, determination to undertake again the work in foreign fields. This time he and his wife went to the Hawaiian Islands, and in 1860 took charge of Oahu College near Honolulu. He found the college dependent on the American Board for support, but put it on a self-supporting basis during the four years he remained in charge. Obviously his business acumen had not deserted him, though his body had not fully recuperated from the ravages of disease contracted in India. His health failed again and in 1864 he returned to the United States, spent a year at Ware, Mass., and in 1865 settled in California. From Mary Atkins he bought a school for young ladies at Benicia and devoted his energies to administering it. His missionary zeal was tinctured, however, with a penchant for business venture, and within a few years he acquired about sixty acres of land in what was then called Brooklyn, five miles south of Oakland and east of the southern end of San Francisco Bay. On this new site he erected a modern building with accommodations for about one hundred and twenty-five women, and in 1871 moved the school from Benicia, giving the name of Mills Seminary to the new institution.

The transfer brought heavy financial obligations. About one hundred and sixty thousand dollars had been spent, approximately eighty thousand of which remained unpaid. To the task of canceling this obligation he now turned his attention. He had invested in lands in the southern part of California, and while looking after his property there, a few years before his death, he was induced to make another venture. The country around Pomona interested him, the need for water attracted his attention, and in 1882, with M. L. Wicks, he formed a company to supply the town with water, which soon became the Pomona Land & Water Company, of which Mills was president until his death. From his various financial investments and from gifts he paid off the obligations with the exception of seven thousand dollars, about forty thousand dollars being contributed from his own private funds.

He was a hard worker, patient and persevering in the tasks he assigned himself, keenly interested in the development of the community in which he lived, and judicious in his financial investments. Recognizing his limitations in purely educational matters he wisely sought the advice of his wife, and frequently her decision could be seen behind his action in connection with campus administration. He died in Oakland, Cal.

[In Memoriam: Rev. Cyrus Taggart Mills, D.D. (n.d.), which appeared at the time of his death, gives the most complete account; see also Reports of the Am. Board of Commissioners for Foreign Missions, 1849–54, 1861–64; R. A. Keep, Fourscore Years: A Hist. of Mills Coll. (1931); The Friend (Honolulu), Nov. 1860, July 1864, June 1884; Hawaiian Gazette, June 1891; San Francisco Morning Call and San Francisco Evening Bulletin, Apr. 21, 1884; Oakland Times, Apr. 21 and 24, 1884; Oakland Tribune, Apr. 21, 23, 26, and 29, 1884.]   C. G.

MILLS, DARIUS OGDEN (Sept. 5, 1825–Jan. 3, 1910), merchant, banker, and philanthropist, was born in North Salem, Westchester County, N. Y., his parents being James and Hannah (Ogden) Mills. The Mills family was of North-of-England origin, and had come to America before the Revolution. Darius' father was unfortunate in local investments, and at the age of seventeen, after an elementary education at excellent private schools in the neighborhood of

his home, the boy was obliged to go to work. As a clerk in New York City, he showed aptitude for the mercantile and banking business and in 1847, when he was but twenty-two years old, he became on invitation of a cousin, cashier of the Merchants' Bank of Erie County, Buffalo, N. Y., with a percentage share in the institution's profits.

Discovery of gold in California in 1848 started an exodus of young Eastern business men to the Pacific Coast. Two of Mills's brothers had equipped a sailing ship with merchandise and had embarked for San Francisco by the Cape Horn route. Mills himself hesitated long, but at the end of 1848 set forth for the same destination by way of the Isthmus. He went as a passenger, provided with the necessary money to engage in merchandising or banking, or both. Unable to obtain passage from Panama to San Francisco—previous north-bound vessels having been deserted by their crews in the "gold rush" from the California port and tied up in that harbor—Mills turned to the West coast of South America, and at Callao was able to charter a bark. Arriving at San Francisco in June 1849, he at once bought merchandise and proceeded to establish a trading business; first, temporarily, at Stockton; then, and permanently, at Sacramento.

His undertaking, which comprised not only buying of gold dust and selling of goods, but dealing in New York exchange, proved highly profitable. After a brief visit to the East at the end of 1849, he returned to Sacramento, establishing there in 1850 the Bank of D. O. Mills & Company, which thereafter led in the business activities of the city. During the following decade he accumulated a large fortune. In 1864 he was active in organizing the Bank of California at San Francisco, of which he was president until July 1873. Two years later, however, as a result of business conditions following the panic of 1873 and also of the rash policies of his successor in the institution's presidency, W. C. Ralston, the Bank of California was forced to suspend payments, and Mills was called back to his old office. Through his endeavors, barely a month after the bank had closed, it resumed business and entered on a career of prolonged prosperity. During his residence on the Pacific Coast, he had been an organizer and important benefactor of such Californian enterprises as the San Francisco Protestant Orphan Asylum, St. Luke's Hospital, and the University of California, of which he long acted as regent and treasurer. He also contributed largely to the Lick Observatory, of which he was trustee, and in behalf of which he personally equipped and sent

Mills

Mills

to South America in 1903 an astronomical expedition to study solar phenomena. In March 1878 he definitely retired from active business on the Pacific Coast, though retaining large investments in that section.

Residing thereafter in New York City, he became investor and director in many of the large Eastern banking, railway, and industrial concerns. He was active in philanthropic enterprises, notably in the construction, during 1888 and afterward, of the "Mills hotels." These embodied a pioneer attempt to provide household accommodations at a low cost but with modern equipment, for people of small means. In them a bed in a private room was obtainable for twenty cents a night, and wholesome meals could be secured at prices ranging from five to fifteen cents. They were so carefully managed that, despite the small charges, they returned to the owner a slight surplus over interest, taxes, maintenance, and depreciation. Mills was connected with other enterprises for providing shelter and credit at low rates and with numerous public charities; he was also a generous contributor to the Metropolitan Museum of Art and the New York Botanical Garden.

Personally, he was a man of quick and positive decision on financial problems and of strong executive capacity. He never courted publicity, and was sometimes described as retiring in manner; but he possessed a quiet urbanity in social conversation, which displayed itself in his numerous visits to the country houses of well-known Englishmen, and in his contacts with British statesmen and royalty. During his later years he spent much time in foreign travel, increasing in his European visits his collections of books and paintings. He was married, Sept. 5, 1854, to Jane Templeton Cunningham, and was survived by two children.

[J. T. Scharf, *Hist. of Westchester County, N. Y.* (1886), II, 509–13; *Lick Observatory Bull., No. 173* (vol. V, 1908–10); Henry Clews, *Fifty Years in Wall Street* (1908); *Who's Who in America*, 1908–09; *Cosmopolitan*, July 1902; *Outlook*, Jan. 15, 1910; *N. Y. Tribune*, Jan. 5, 1910.]   A.D.N.

MILLS, ELIJAH HUNT (Dec. 1, 1776–May 5, 1829), congressman and lawyer, was born in Chesterfield, Hampshire County, Mass., the son of the Rev. Benjamin and Mary (Hunt) Mills. After the death of his mother in 1779 and of his father in 1785, he was adopted by his maternal uncle, Elijah Hunt of Northampton. Graduating from Williams College in 1797, he devoted himself to the study of law, in 1803 was admitted to the bar at Northampton, and became one of the most prominent lawyers in western Massachusetts. From 1804 to 1814 he occupied

the position of town clerk and in the latter year was appointed advocate (district attorney) for Hampshire County. In 1823 he and Samuel Howe opened a law school in Northampton. The number of students is reported to have ranged from ten to fifteen, many of them coming from the South. The instruction was by lectures, recitations, moot courts, and discussion, written and oral, of legal questions. There is no record of the continuance of the school after 1830. Entering political life as a Federalist, Mills became one of the active leaders of this party in western Massachusetts. He was elected to the Massachusetts House of Representatives in 1811 and served through 1814. From 1815 to 1819 he served two terms in the United States House of Representatives. In 1819 he was elected to the Massachusetts House of Representatives of which body he was made speaker in May 1820. He had occupied this position less than two weeks when he was elected to the United States Senate for the remainder of the term of Prentiss Mellen (resigned) ending Mar. 3, 1821, and for the next full term. He failed of reëlection and was succeeded in 1827 by Webster. He returned to Northampton where he died on May 5, 1829, at the age of fifty-two, having suffered much from ill-health during the period of his service in the Senate.

Mills took an active part in the Federalist opposition to the War of 1812. He was one of the committee appointed by the Hampshire County Convention of 1809 to prepare an address protesting against the Embargo. In the convention of delegates from the towns of the three river counties of Massachusetts held in Northampton, July 1812, he was a member of the committee which prepared a memorial to President Madison urging the immediate negotiation of peace. He was author (*Hampshire Gazette*, May 13, 1829) of the "Address of the House of Representatives to the People of Massachusetts" (*Niles' Weekly Register*, Aug. 29, 1812), adopted June 26, 1812, a severe arraignment of the war which urged opposition to it by all constitutional means. A Fourth of July address delivered by Mills at Northampton in 1813 was less restrained: "The rights of commerce, and the constitutional privileges of New England must be ransomed from the grasp of usurpation; 'Peaceably if you can, forcibly if you must'" (*An Oration Pronounced at Northampton*, 1813, p. 23). As a member of Congress, however, his Federalism became more subdued and his career while inconspicuous was characterized by moderation and intelligence. Acquaintance with leading men in the opposite party led him to qualify

7

earlier judgments. His legal training gave him a particular interest in constitutional questions and he occasionally took the floor in support of his views. He was a strong advocate of a national system of bankruptcy. In support of the commercial interest of Massachusetts he opposed the tariff of 1824. He was twice married: in 1802 to Sarah Hunt who died in the same year, and in 1804 to Harriette Blake. He had seven children by his second wife.

[Calvin Durfee, *Williams Biog. Annals* (1871); Solomon Clark, *Antiquities, Historicals and Grads. of Northampton* (1882); *Proc. of a Convention . . . Holden at Northampton, the 14th and 15th of July, 1812* (1812); *Columbian Centinel* (Boston), Sept. 1804, Jan.–June 1820, May 1829, May 13, 1829; *Hampshire Gazette* (Northampton, Mass.), Feb.–Nov. 1800, Jan. 1825, May 1829; letters in the possession of the Mass. Hist. Soc.]
L. C. H.

MILLS, HIRAM FRANCIS (Nov. 1, 1836– Oct. 4, 1921), hydraulic and sanitary engineer, was born at Bangor, Me., the son of Preserved Brayton and Jane (Lunt) Mills. In 1856 he was graduated from Rensselaer Polytechnic Institute. During the next twelve years, while he was serving an apprenticeship under several distinguished engineers, he assisted in the construction of the Bergen Tunnel and the Hoosac Tunnel; he erected dams on the Deerfield River and on the Penobscot River; and he conducted various studies in connection with water-power developments at Cohoes, N. Y., and North Billerica, Mass. In 1868 he opened his own office in Boston, where he soon attained a high place in his profession. Although he was consulted by many corporations and municipalities throughout the United States and Mexico, his principal work was done in Massachusetts, where he became chief engineer of the Essex Company, of Lawrence, and of the Locks and Canals Company, of Lowell.

At Lowell he undertook a series of experiments on the flow of water in natural and artificial channels which led to the perfection of the piezometer and advanced materially the development of the turbine. Owing to the pressure of other duties, however, he early abandoned his interest in this phase of hydraulics, and his conclusions were not systematized until the posthumous publication of *Flow of Water in Pipes* (1923). As consulting engineer to the Boston Metropolitan Water and Sewerage Board, he was chiefly responsible for the design of the water supply, drainage, and sewerage systems of the areas under its jurisdiction. Possibly because his father was a physician, he had always been interested in epidemiology. When the Massachusetts State Board of Health was organized in 1886, he therefore accepted the chairmanship of the committee on water supply and sewerage, a position which he held for twenty-eight years. Much of the success of the Board was due to his efforts, for he not only standardized methods of sampling and analysis but he also initiated far-reaching experiments on the purification of water and sewage. From these investigations emerged the great experiment station at Lawrence, which has long been recognized as the foremost in America, if not in the world. As a result of the studies completed under his direction, the death rate from typhoid throughout Massachusetts was reduced eight-ninths. Since Mills had always been skeptical of the theory of self-purification of streams by rapid flow which was popular in his day, he constructed at Lawrence a slow-sand filter which, because of its obvious efficiency, marked the beginning of a new era in municipal engineering. Absorbed as he was in his professional activities, he nevertheless wrote numerous articles, brochures, and memoirs in his special field. Among these, his contributions to the *Proceedings* (vol. XIV, 1879) of the American Academy of Arts and Sciences, of which he was a fellow, the *Journal of the Franklin Institute* (February 1870), the *Transactions of the American Society of Civil Engineers* (April 1885, November 1893), and the *Journal of the New England Water Works Association* (March 1887, September 1894), are especially significant.

Although Mills, who was inclined to be a recluse and a mystic, shrank from publicity of any kind, he dedicated his life wholeheartedly to the welfare of the community. To the cause of education he devoted no inconsiderable share of his energy, serving on a number of local boards and on important committees at both the Lawrence Scientific School of Harvard University and the Massachusetts Institute of Technology. He was a successful man of affairs, director and president of several corporations; and he accumulated a fortune which enabled him to remember in his will the institutions to which he was especially devoted and to found, at Harvard University, the Elizabeth Worcester Mills Fund for cancer research in memory of his wife, Elizabeth Worcester, whom he married Oct. 8, 1873, and who died Mar. 23, 1917. His name is also perpetuated by foundations in Lawrence and Lowell. His death occurred in Hingham, Mass.

[H. B. Nason, *Biog. Record Officers and Grads. Rensselaer Polytechnic Inst.* (1887); R. A. Hale, in *Trans. Am. Soc. Civil Engineers*, vol. LXXXVII (1924); *Who's Who in America*, 1920–21; *Boston Herald*, Oct. 6, 1921; *Flow of Water in Pipes* (1923), mentioned above, which contains personal notes on Mills by J. R. Freeman.]
R. P. B.

MILLS, LAWRENCE HEYWORTH
(1837–Jan. 29, 1918), Iranian scholar, was born
in New York City, the son of Philo L. and Elizabeth Caroline (Kane) Mills. He was probably
descended from Peter van der Meulen, of Amsterdam, who emigrated from Leyden to New
England in the second half of the seventeenth
century, settled in Windsor, Conn., and changed
his name to Mills. Lawrence was educated at
the University of the City of New York (A.B.
1858; A.M. 1863) and the Protestant Episcopal
Theological Seminary in Virginia (B.D. 1861).
He married Maria Bowen Swann, daughter of
Robert Paige Swann of Leesburg, Va., and had
three sons and one daughter. Ordered deacon
in 1861 and priested in the following year, he
was successively curate (1861–64) and rector
(1864–67) of St. Ann's, Brooklyn, and then
(1867–70) rector of St. John's, Hartford, Conn.

After 1872 he made his permanent residence
outside the United States. From 1873 to 1877
he was associate rector of the American Episcopal Church in Florence, and then went to Germany, where he studied Vedic and Iranian under Rudolf von Roth and laid the foundation of
his entire later career. By 1883 his studies of
the Avesta had won such distinction that he was
requested by F. Max Müller to complete the
translation of the texts left unfinished at that
time by James Darmesteter. This work appeared
at Oxford in 1887 as Volume XXXI of *The
Sacred Books of the East,* and in the same year
Mills settled in Oxford. In 1897 a group of his
English and Indian friends established for him
a chair of "Zend Philology" at the University,
the first full professorship of its kind. This he
held until his death, when the position automatically ceased.

Mills was a prolific writer. His publications
include more than a hundred papers and nearly
a dozen books. The latter, besides the transla-
tion already mentioned, were: *A Study of the
Five Zarathushtrian (Zoroastrian) Gâthâs, with
Texts and Translations* (Leipzig, 1894); *The
Ancient Manuscript of the Yasna with its Pahlavi
Translation (A.D. 1323) Generally Quoted as
J 2, Reproduced in Facsimile* (Oxford, 1893);
*The Gâthâs of Zarathushtra (Zoroaster) in
Metre and Rhythm* (Oxford, 1900); *Zaraθûstra,
Philo, the Achaemenids, and Israel* (2 parts,
Leipzig, 1905–06); *Avesta Eschatology Com-
pared with the Books of Daniel and Revelations
[!]* (Chicago, 1908); *The Yasna of the Avesta
. . . A Study of Yasna I* (Leipzig, 1910); *Our
Own Religion in Ancient Persia* (Chicago,
1913); *A Dictionary of the Gâthic Language of
the Zend Avesta* (Leipzig, 1913); *An Expo-*

*sition of the Lore of the Avesta in Catechetical
Dialogue* (Bombay, 1916); *The Creed of Za-
rathushtra* (Bombay, 1916); and *The Funda-
mental and Dominant Presence of Zoroastrian
Thought in the Jewish Exilic, Christian and
Muhammadan Religions, and in the Greek and
Gnostic Philosophies with Their Modern Suc-
cessors* (Bombay, 1917).

Mills's work was practically restricted to that
portion of the Avesta known as the Yasna, and
especially to its Gāthās, a group of seventeen
hymns in an archaic dialect traditionally ascribed to Zoroaster himself. He gives, in original and translation, both the Avesta text and its
Oriental versions; and this is of value as a convenient assemblage of all the native material.
The worth of his translations, on the other hand,
is diminished by excessive reliance on Zoroastrian tradition, as is his exegesis. In his enthusiasm for the Gāthās he sought to find borrow-
ings from Persia in the Old Testament that are
by no means certain; and he was far from adequately equipped either in comparative linguis-
tics or in comparative religion. To these shortcomings he added a style of curious involution
and obscurity, so that it was not strange that his
work excited little attention in circles of strict
scholarship.

Mills was never attached to any of the Oxford Colleges, even as honorary fellow, and his
life was rather isolated. He imagined himself,
apparently quite without reason, the victim of
jealousy on the part of Continental Iranists and
of ingratitude on the part of some of his pupils.
Theologically, as might be expected from his
Virginia training, he was a pronounced Evangelical or Low Churchman, with tendencies toward the "Broad Church" point of view.

[*Biog. Cat. of the Chancellors, Professors and Graduates of the Dept. of Arts and Science of the Univ. of
the City of New York* (1894); Paul Carus, "Professor Mills, the Zendavesta Scholar," *Open Court,* Aug.
1905; *Monist,* Apr. 1918; *Jour. Royal Asiatic Soc.,*
Jan. 1919; *Who's Who* (British), 1917; *N. Y. Times,*
Feb. 1, 1918; H. R. Stiles, *The Hist. and Geneals. of
Ancient Windsor,* vol. II (1893); personal acquaintance.] L. H. G.

MILLS, ROBERT (Aug. 12, 1781–Mar. 3,
1855), architect, engineer, was born in Charleston, S. C., the son of William Mills, a Scotchman, who came to America from Dundee in
1770 and married Anne Taylor, "a lady of ancient and honorable Carolina lineage." Robert
received his early education at the College of
Charleston and was unique among Americans
at that early day in resolving to secure regular
training for the career of a professional architect. Of the professionals then or previously ac-

tive in the United States as architects, James Hoban, William Thornton, George Hadfield, and Benjamin H. Latrobe were British born; L'Enfant, Hallet, Mangin, and Godefroy were Frenchmen. James Hoban [q.v.], who had learned building and drawing as a boy in the school of the Dublin Society of Arts and had designed and built the South Carolina state capitol at Columbia, had won the competition for the President's House in Washington and had been established there since 1792. To him young Mills repaired in 1800 for his initiation. On his journey northward he saw the newly completed capitol at Richmond, modeled by Jefferson on the Maison Carrée. "The location of the building is on a high eminence and commands an extensive prospect," he wrote later; "I remember the impression it made on my mind when first I came in view of it coming from the South. It gave me an idea of the position and effect of those Greek temples which are the admiration of the world" (autobiographical fragment, Dimitry papers). From honest Hoban, who on occasion contracted for buildings as well as designed them, he learned the rudiments of construction, and of draftsmanship and rendering.

He was eager, however, to go beyond the somewhat obsolete academism of the Irish builder architect and found his opportunity when he came to the attention of Thomas Jefferson [q.v.], pioneer of the Roman revival and encourager of American talents. He was taken into Jefferson's family at "Monticello" in 1803. The house, which Jefferson had given its first Palladian impress before the Revolution, was then being remodeled on more classical lines, suggested in part by those of the Hôtel de Salm. Here Mills had the benefit of Jefferson's collection of architectural books, then unrivaled in America. During his stay he made an admirable tinted drawing in elevation of the front of the house as Jefferson's design of 1796 would bring it to completion—a drawing which has sometimes misled his biographers to consider Mills as the architect of a house begun before he was born and redesigned when he was but fifteen years of age. Mills also made a drawing from the design of Jefferson for a rebuilding of "Shadwell," never executed. This drawing (preserved like the other in the Coolidge Collection of the Massachusetts Historical Society, and bearing the inscription "T. Jefferson, Arch't. R. Mills, Del't, 1803") shows a version of Jefferson's favorite *villa rotonda* type, having a high central dome, with many other features to which he was attached, such as the oval salon, octagonal bows, and alcove bedrooms (F. Kimball, *Thomas Jefferson, Architect,* 1916).

Besides teaching Mills what he could, Jefferson recommended him to the others from whom he could best learn. To Charles Bulfinch [q.v.] who had seen the monuments of Paris under Jefferson's guidance and had followed his route in southern France, he had given Mills an introduction on the young student's tour of the northern states in 1802. He now advised him to attach himself to Benjamin H. Latrobe [q.v.], who had the fine foreign training of Cockerell and Smeaton. Latrobe, the first of the newcomers to succeed in establishing himself in professional architectural practise as it is known today, had been appointed by Jefferson as surveyor of the public buildings of the United States. From 1803 to 1808 Mills was in Latrobe's office as a draftsman and clerk. Some of his first experience was on the Chesapeake & Delaware Canal. In 1807 he was supervising for his employer the erection of the Bank of Philadelphia, a vaulted edifice in the Gothic style. From Latrobe, the father of the Greek revival in America, he imbibed not only his knowledge of Greek forms, but his principles of professional practice and his scientific engineering skill.

Early in the period of his training Mills began to make designs for buildings independently. In 1802, when only twenty-one, he submitted a plan for South Carolina College which secured a half share of the prize, the other half going to Edward Clark who become the contractor for the building, Rutledge College, since rebuilt. In 1804 he designed the Congregational Church in Charleston, the "Circular" church, in which he adopted for the first time in America the auditorium type of plan suited for the preaching service. A design for a penitentiary for South Carolina, from this period, did not come to execution.

In 1808 he established himself in independent practice in Philadelphia, where he remained until 1817. Among his first designs here was that for a row of houses still standing on Ninth Street between Locust and Walnut. In 1809 he also designed Washington Hall. In 1810 he submitted a design for the State House at Harrisburg, still preserved there, from which was erected, with some modifications, the building which stood until late in the nineteenth century. A semicircular portico of Ionic columns adorned the principal front, with balancing outbuildings. Over the center rose a tall drum surrounded by a peristyle and crowned by a low Roman dome (contemporary engraving by J. L. Frederick for *The Casket*). The Unitarian Church in Philadelphia, of octagonal form, was begun in 1811 and dedicated Feb. 14, 1813; and Dr. Stoughton's Church, circular, seating four thousand, was executed at the same period. In 1812 Mills rebuilt for municipal offices the wings of the old State House (Independence Hall), since restored to nearly their original aspect. In the same year he had a share in the design of the remarkable Upper Ferry Bridge (burned in 1838), a single timber arch of 360 feet span, much the longest in the world at that day. The Gothic house built by John Dorsey, one of Mills's principal patrons, is presumed to have been from his design, as is the picturesque Burlington County prison in New Jersey, still standing.

Commissions for a number of buildings in Richmond came to him after he won the competition for the Monumental Church which memorialized the victims of the theatre fire of Dec. 26, 1811. In this church, still standing, Mills again used the octagonal form, with a portico of Egyptian columns. The Wickham house (now the Valentine Museum), also from 1812, has a salon bowed toward the garden and a richly designed central circular staircase. In 1814 he gave a design for the Court House, with which Godefroy [q.v.] was also concerned. The building was destroyed many years ago. The Brockenbrough house, afterwards occupied by Jefferson Davis as the "White House of the Confederacy," and the lovely Archer house (recently demolished) were likewise from this time.

The citizens of Baltimore were the first to undertake an important public monument to Washington. A competition was instituted in 1814, in which many of the leading architects of the time took part. Joseph Ramée, later the designer of Union College in Schenectady, proposed a great Roman triumphal arch; Mills, a tall Greek column. The latter was chosen. The corner stone was laid in Mount Vernon Place, on July 4, 1815, and the monument, crowned by a figure of Washington by Causici, was completed in 1829. The design was the first of the colossal Greek Doric type, preceding the Wellington columns in London and Dublin. Other commissions in Baltimore followed, and Mills took up his residence there in 1817. During his stay of three years he designed the First Baptist Church ("Round Top"), a smaller model of the Roman Pantheon, with a portico of six columns, and St. John's Evangelical Episcopal Church, with three aisles (both buildings illustrated on the margins of the Poppleton plat of Baltimore). He was also made president and chief engineer of the water-works company.

The great prize of the profession in these years was the building for the Bank of the United States in Philadelphia, for which a competition was advertised in July 1818. Mills submitted two distinct sets of designs, with additional variants. All of his façades extended the full width of the plot, permitting a variety of effects: a long Doric colonnade with terminal masses; a six-column portico with flanking wings of the same order. For the central banking room Mills proposed a simple rotunda, or a square with flanking apses screened by columns. The design submitted by Latrobe was preferred, however, and executed, with some modifications, by Strickland.

In 1820 Mills returned to Charleston to become a member of the Board of Public Works of his native state. He is referred to in public documents of that period as "State Engineer and Architect," and as "Civil and Military Engineer of the State." South Carolina had entered on an extensive scheme of internal improvements, with annual appropriations exceeding $100,000, spent chiefly on roads and on river and canal development. To his interest in the latter subject Mills had already testified in his *Treatise on Inland Navigation,* published in 1820 before his departure from Baltimore. Extensive works were built under his direction on the Saluda, Broad, and Catawba rivers, with numerous locks, and the rivers and bays were connected by several canals. By 1826 he could write "We now have an inland navigation equal to 2,370 miles" (*Statistics of South Carolina,* p. 301). The Board of Public Works had charge also of the public buildings of the state and the districts, for which appropriations ranged from $50,000 to $80,000 annually. Those erected from 1820 to 1830 were on designs made by Mills or revised by him. They included, in 1822, the court houses at Kingstree, Newberry, Yorkville, and Greenville, the jails at Union, Spartanburg, Lancaster, and Yorkville. Among the buildings undertaken, one of the more notable was the fireproof Record Building in Charleston, begun in 1822. It is of great simplicity, with porticos of four Greek Doric columns on each front. Others in Charleston included a wing of the prison, planned on the principle of solitary confinement, and several powder magazines. The Baptist Church, of the temple type, was also his work. Special importance attaches to his designs, still preserved, for the State Hospital for the Insane at Columbia, of which the central portion was erected in 1822. At a period very early in the development of modern ideas in the care of the insane, this building was not a prison but a hospital: fireproof, with all its rooms and wards having southern exposure to a garden court, and with a roof garden over the whole structure. (The building is discussed in its institutional aspects by Dr. J. W. Babcock in the *Handbook of South Carolina*, 1st ed., 1907, and in vol. III, pp. 587–613, of *The Institutional Care of the Insane in the United States and Canada*, 1916, ed. by H. M. Hurd.) The façade showed a portico of six Greek Doric columns at the principal story.

Mills's manuscript designs reveal his authorship of certain houses in Columbia, both the first Ainslee Hall, about 1830 (now Chicora College for Women), and the second (now the center building of the Presbyterian Theological Seminary). At Camden, S. C., his work comprised the Presbyterian Church, the DeKalb monument—a squat obelisk on a pedestal—of which the corner stone was laid by Lafayette in 1825, and the Court House (1826), which was of the full hexastyle temple form. While in Charleston Mills issued a number of valuable publications relative to his native state: *Internal Improvement of South Carolina* (1822); a most accurate *Atlas of the State of South Carolina* (1825); and *Statistics of South Carolina, Including a View of Its . . . History* (1826).

In 1824 designs were invited for the Bunker Hill Monument, and Mills submitted one not unlike that for the monument in Baltimore, a great Greek Doric column, surmounted by a tripod and banded with military trophies. He states in sketches of his life that he proposed an obelisk form, doubtless as an alternative, and considered that his idea had been adopted in the executed work. The simple obelisk actually erected was the work of Solomon Willard.

With the cessation of state appropriations for public works in 1830 Mills removed to Washington. A stanch Jacksonian as he had been a stanch Jeffersonian, he had hopes of federal employment, which were not to be disappointed. His first recorded project in the capital was one for a Potomac bridge, advocated by President Jackson (W. B. Bryan, *A History of the National Capital*, vol. II, 1916, p. 250). Soon he was receiving various governmental commissions, such as those for the custom houses at New Bedford, and Newburyport, Mass., New London, and Middletown, Conn.—buildings solid and of Tuscan simplicity. On July 6, 1836, he was appointed "Architect of Public Buildings," a position which he held for fifteen years. During his tenure of this office there fell to him three of the principal buildings of the nineteenth century in Washington: the Treasury, the Patent Office, and the Post Office. For the Treasury, of which he built the Fifteenth Street front (1836–

39), he adopted the motive of a long unbroken colonnade, in which he used the Ionic order of the Erechtheum. It is a façade of great impressiveness. Although the sandstone in which it was first executed suffered badly from exposure, the recent replacement with granite followed faithfully the original lines and still preserves the design of Mills. For the central feature of the front of the Patent Office (1836–40) he used his favorite portico of the Greek Doric, but this time with the eight columns and the proportions of the Parthenon, happily situated on a fine vista. For the old Post Office (begun 1839) which fronts it, he recurred to academic forms, with pilasters above a tall basement.

The crowning success of his life was his victory in competition for the design of the Washington Monument at the capital. This project, which antedated even the formation of the national government, was revived in 1833 by the formation of the Washington National Monument Association; funds were solicited by popular subscription, and designs were invited by advertisement in 1836. That of Mills, officially adopted, proposed an obelisk six hundred feet in height, surrounded at the base by a circular colonnaded building with a portico at the principal face, surmounted by the figure of Washington in a triumphal chariot. The order was to be a very massive Doric. Subscriptions came slowly, and the corner stone was not laid until 1848. After a good beginning the work languished for lack of funds and was suspended in 1855, the year of Mills's death, when the shaft had reached a height of 152 feet. In spite of the efforts of the Association it could not be resumed, and it was not until after many years and much controversy that, in 1878, Congress made possible the continuance of construction, and the obelisk itself was carried to completion in 1884 at a height of 555 feet. It was then the highest of human structures. In it the simplicity and grandeur of the form were matched with the character of the subject.

Much further work for the government and some for other clients fell to Mills as architect of public buildings. No less than eight of the Marine Hospitals were from his designs (some of which he published in 1837), as were the jail in Washington (1839), the court house in Alexandria (1838), and the Library at South Carolina College (1838). The chief work of his later incumbency was in remodeling the heating, ventilating, and lighting systems of the Capitol, and in correcting the acoustic defects of the old Hall of Representatives. In 1850 he was called on by the Senate Committee on Public Buildings for designs for the enlargement of the Capitol, and submitted plans for the north and south wings as well as for an enlargement of the dome, employing masonry construction (Glenn Brown, *History of the United States Capitol,* vol. II, 1902, plate 137). Although this scheme was reported favorably by the committee, a competition was instituted, and Mills was directed to prepare the working plans, "utilizing the four sets of drawings which had been submitted for what he might find them to be worth" (*Ibid.,* II, 117). He doubtless had but little stomach for this task, and being past seventy, soon relinquished it, retiring from public office in 1851. Thomas U. Walter [q.v.], who had been one of the competitors, was then chosen as the architect. During his years in Washington Mills had continued his activity in publication with *The American Pharos, or Lighthouse Guide* (1832), and a *Guide to the Capitol of the United States,* which first appeared in 1834 and was frequently reprinted. As late as 1853 he published a report on waterworks for the city of Washington.

Mills was a humanitarian, a reformer, a man of broad and prophetic vision. In matters of institutional care, whether of the insane, the criminal, or the poor, he was able by his profession to contribute to a more enlightened treatment. He saw clearly the hygienic, the social, and, in less degree, the economic problems of his native state, was an advocate of the drainage of its lowlands, and of the abolition of slavery through colonization of the blacks. He early urged the introduction of railroads and the advantages of trunk lines, including a transcontinental road, although he took no recorded part in the actual establishment of the railroads, his engineering work falling within the period of canal transportation. In architecture he stands as the first native-born professional, and as one of the chief exponents of the Greek revival. His works now appear a little stereotyped, a little arid, but very sober, very competent, very dignified—contributing to that austere tradition still so powerful in American architectural style.

He was married in 1808 to Eliza Barnwell Smith, daughter of General Smith of "Hackwood Park," Frederick County, Va. Of his four daughters, all of whom married, two left issue: Mary, wife of Alexander Dimitry [q.v.], an officer in the American diplomatic service, and Sarah, wife of Dr. John Evans. Mills was a member of the Society of Artists organized in Philadelphia in 1810, and its first secretary. According to an old Washington lady who knew him in her youth, he was "a man of strikingly strong features, of evidently studious hab-

its, with an air of deep absorption or abstraction; a man of unusual dignity and reserve, yet affable and kindly. He was of simple and correct taste in dress, and his presence was always an interesting one to everybody." She speaks of his regular attendance at the Presbyterian Church and of his one vice, the intemperate use of snuff (Gallagher memoranda). His portrait, drawn by St. Memin, has been several times reproduced.

[A number of drawings and other papers of Mills have been preserved among his descendants in New Orleans. A memorandum book and about eighty "Miscellaneous Papers" as well as certain documents in the Jefferson Papers, are in the MSS. Div. Lib. of Cong. Other documents are in the office of the Supt. of the U. S. Capitol, the archives of S. C., the Hist. Soc. of Pa., and the Mass. Hist. Soc. Autobiographical sketches by Mills, preserved in part in manuscript, formed the basis of the notice in Wm. Dunlap's *Hist. of the Rise and Progress of the Arts of Design in the U. S.* (1834), vol. II, upon which were based the accounts in *The Dict. of Architecture Issued by the Architectural Pub. Soc.* (1848–92), vol. IV, and in P. A. Planat's *Encyclopédie de l'Architecture* (1888–95), vol. V. The skilful wording of Mills's manuscript, itself not overstepping the truth, has given rise to exaggerated claims as to his share in certain enterprises. Some of these occur in an article by his grandson, C. P. Dimitry [q.v.], in the New Orleans *Daily Picayune,* May 26, 1895, which has been frequently used by later writers, notably Glenn Brown in the biographical sketch of Mills in his *Hist. of the U. S. Capitol,* vol. II (1902). This work, like the *Doc. Hist. of the U. S. Capitol* (1904), includes many official papers. A valuable notice by C. C. Wilson, *Robert Mills, Architect* (1919), corrects many misconceptions, and offers new material, particularly on his works in South Carolina. Extensive documentary research has been undertaken by Mrs. H. M. Pierce Gallagher, and is in part embodied in well-illustrated papers published in the *Architectural Record,* Apr., May, 1929. See also Montgomery Schuyler, "The Old Greek Revival," pt. 2, *Am. Architect,* Dec. 21, 1910, which is inaccurate in some details; and obituary in the *Daily National Intelligencer* (Washington), Mar. 5, 1855.]   F.K.

MILLS, ROBERT (Mar. 9, 1809–Apr. 13, 1888), merchant and planter, the fourth child of Adam and Janet (Graham) Mills, was born in Todd County, Ky. On May 15, 1826, he entered Cumberland College (now George Peabody College for Teachers), where he studied until the following May. When he was twenty-one he set out for Texas to join an elder brother, Andrew G. Mills, in merchandizing at Brazoria. Since Andrew was a sea-faring man, the management of the business devolved upon Robert. The firm supplied planters and other merchants of the Brazos and Colorado valleys with necessities bartered for pelts and cotton, and extended its trade area even across the Rio Grande. Trains of burros returned to Mexico laden with goods in exchange for specie and bars of Mexican silver, which Robert stacked like stovewood in the counting room. He and Andrew fought in the battle of Velasco against the Mexicans on June 26, 1832. After Andrew's death in 1835, Robert and his younger brother, David G. Mills, conducted the firm, first as R. Mills & Company, later as R. & D. G. Mills. About 1849 Mills, realizing that the Brazos would never be navigable, removed to Galveston. The next year he became a partner of Mills, McDowell & Company of New York and of McDowell, Mills & Company of New Orleans. From 1850 till 1863 John William Jockusch, the Prussian consul at Galveston, was a third partner. Their ships and steamboats plied the rivers of Texas and the ocean, transporting cotton and sugar to the markets of the world. In 1852 Mills was president and director of the Galveston and Brazos navigation company that hoped to connect these two points by an intercoastal canal. From the beginning he performed the double function of merchant and banker, dealing in exchange and advancing credit to customers. In the absence of banks, R. & D. G. Mills countersigned the questionable notes of the Northern Bank of Mississippi at Holly Springs. Between twenty-five and five hundred thousand dollars of this money were reported to have circulated as readily as gold in Texas and in New Orleans. The suspension in 1852 of the affiliated houses in New York and New Orleans sent "Mills's money" below par for only one day in Galveston. In 1859 the supreme court of Texas decided that the partnership had violated no statute in reissuing these notes and remitted a fine of one hundred thousand dollars, assessed against the firm in 1857 by the district court of Galveston (23 *Texas Reports*, 295–309). While Robert was building up the commission and banking business in Texas, David was equally successful in operating their plantations. By 1860 the brothers had four sugar and cotton plantations, "Low Wood," "Bynum," "Palo Alto," and "Warren," embracing approximately 3,300 acres in cultivation and 100,000 acres of unimproved land. They owned another 100,000 acres scattered over the state. They were also the largest slaveholders in Texas; they emancipated about eight hundred slaves in 1865. Though reputed to have been worth between three and five million dollars before the Civil War, R. & D. G. Mills in 1873 were bankrupt. Thereupon Robert surrendered to his creditors his plate, carriages, and his mansion, though he might have claimed the protection of the homestead law. His declining years were embittered by inactivity, poverty, and dependence upon relatives. He died in Galveston, where he was buried from Trinity Church. He married Elizabeth McNeel, who died with their first-born child.

[Records of Brazoria County, Angleton, Tex.; tax assessor's rolls, Comptroller's Department, Austin; manuscript census of 1850 and 1860, Bureau of Census, Washington, D. C., and State Library, Austin; correspondence with Bruce R. Payne, Ballinger Mills, Julius W. Jockusch, and Henry A. Perry; J. H. Brown, *Hist. of Texas,* vol. I (copr. 1892), pp. 187, 228; W. M. Gouge, *The Fiscal Hist. of Texas* (1852); A. J. Strobel, *The Old Plantations and their Owners of Brazoria County* (1926); *Southwestern Hist. Quart.,* July 1923; *Democratic Telegraph and Texas Register* (Houston), Aug. 14, 1850; Jan. 17, 1851, Jan. 30, 1852, Mar. 26, 1853, Feb. 11, 25, Mar. 7, Oct. 28, Nov. 4, 11, 1857. Jan. 13, July 7, 1858; *Semi-Weekly Journal* (Galveston), Dec. 24, Mar. 22, 1850, Oct. 15, 1852; *State Gazette* (Austin), Feb. 7, 1852, Jan. 24, 31, 1857; *Galveston Tri-Weekly News* (Houston), June 1, 1864; *Washington American* (Tex.), Apr. 19, 1856; *Galveston Daily News,* Apr. 14, 15, 19, 22, 1888; *Austin Weekly Statesman,* Apr. 15, 19, 1888.]   A. C.

MILLS, ROGER QUARLES (Mar. 30, 1832– Sept. 2, 1911), representative and senator from Texas, was born in Todd County, Ky. His parents were Tabitha (Daniel) and Charles Henley Mills, a planter. His grandfather was Charles Mills of Hanover County, Va. At the age of seventeen he went to Palestine, Tex., where he studied law in the office of a brother-in-law, Reuben A. Reeves. Admitted to the bar in 1852 by act of legislature, he began practice in Corsicana. His marriage on Jan. 7, 1858, to Caroline R. Jones, the daughter of a large ranch owner, added substantially to his prestige in the community. In 1859 and 1860 he represented Navarro County in the state legislature, where he became known as an eloquent advocate of secession. He entered the Confederate army early in 1861 and remained in it to the end of the war. At Oak Hills, Mo., in August 1861 he fought as a private in the ranks of the 3rd Texas Cavalry. From 1862 to the end of the war, he was colonel of the 10th Texas Infantry and was called upon more than once to command the brigade with which it served. At Missionary Ridge and again at Atlanta he was severely wounded. The official records show that his reputation for courage was well earned (*War of the Rebellion: Official Records (Army),* 1 ser., vol. XXXI, pt. 2, 1890, p. 750).

The years that followed the war were lean for the young lawyer at Corsicana, but in 1872, when the state Democratic convention met in his home town, he gained a nomination as congressman at large which at the time was equivalent to an election. Year after year he was returned by his admiring fellow citizens, serving in the House of Representatives from Mar. 4, 1873, until his resignation on Mar. 28, 1892. In 1877 he was one of the most outspoken opponents of the Electoral Commission, which he regarded as a device to steal a fairly won election. Nevertheless, he was a generous opponent and

Mills

in 1884 came to the aid of McKinley whose seat was being contested, an act which the Ohio congressman never forgot. Mills belonged to the picturesque group, called at first in derision and, as the years went on, in growing affection, "The Confederate Brigadiers." Their political philosophy, like their manners, was old fashioned, and they usually favored economy and lower taxes. In 1887 he was in a strategic position to advocate his favorite views. Seniority had brought him the chairmanship of the ways and means committee at the moment when Cleveland had made a tariff for revenue the central theme of an exciting presidential contest. The Mills bill provided for the reduction of tariff on manufactured articles and placed lumber, wool, salt, and other raw materials on the free list. The bill, after a bitter debate, passed the Democratic House, but was, of course, promptly shelved by the Republican Senate. During the campaign of 1888 he was in great demand as a speaker. A speech in New York City on July 4, 1888, especially, aroused national attention (*Speeches of Hon. Thomas B. Reed . . . and Hon. Roger Q. Mills*, 1888; see *Nation*, July 12, 1888). Before a popular audience he was always at his best, earnest, simple, and eloquent; in running debate, especially under the stinging satire of opponents like Reed of Maine, he sometimes lost his temper, and his language was not always remarkable for moderation. In two essays printed in *Both Sides of the Tariff Question,* copr. 1889, he explained his point of view in a mood that was calmer though no less effective.

In 1891, largely on account of his opposition to free silver, he was defeated for the speakership by a younger man, Charles Frederick Crisp of Georgia, but his prestige in Texas was still sufficient to obtain his election to the Senate, where he served from March 1892 to March 1899. He was a close friend of President Cleveland and a supporter of his policies. His opposition to prohibition in 1887 and his dislike for free silver had already made him many enemies, among them the powerful ex-governor, James Hogg. The age of the Confederate brigadiers had passed, and in 1899, when Mills came up for reëlection, he was passed over in favor of Governor Culberson. He spent his remaining years in Corsicana. At the time of his death the discovery of oil had made the old senator a wealthy man.

[Unpublished thesis by Durell Carothers in the Lib. of Rice Institute; *War of the Rebellion: Official Records (Army)*, 1 ser., vols. XXII, pt. 1, XXIII, XXX, pt. 2; L. E. Daniell, *Personnel of the Texas State Government* (1892); *The Encyc. of the New West*, ed. by W. S. Speer and J. H. Brown (1881); *Biog. Dir. of*

Mills

Am. Cong. (1928); *Dallas Morning News,* Sept. 3, 1911; *Galveston Daily News,* Sept. 3, 1911.]

R. G. C—l.

MILLS, SAMUEL JOHN (Apr. 21, 1783–June 16, 1818), Congregational clergyman, was the son of Samuel John and Esther (Robbins) Mills. His father was long pastor of the church at Torringford, Conn., in which town the younger Samuel was born. His original purpose was to be a farmer, but his religious experiences finally impelled him to enter the ministry. He became much concerned about his spiritual welfare in the revival of 1798, and for two years thereafter felt convinced that he would go to hell. In the autumn of 1801, however, his mother's piety enabled him to rejoice in God's perfections without considering his own future destiny, and he afterwards realized that this was his conversion. Immediately the idea came to him of going abroad to preach the gospel to the heathen, the first time probably that such an enterprise had been seriously considered in the United States.

Accordingly, in 1801, he sold a farm which had been bequeathed to him by his grandmother, and entered Morris Academy, Litchfield. In 1806 he became a student at Williams College, where, during his first year, he was a leader in a religious revival. He proposed to several of his friends that they should become foreign missionaries and secured from them a favorable response. Graduating in 1809, he spent a few months at Yale, in the hope of enlisting supporters of the missionary project there, but his stay was fruitless save for his discovery of Henry Obookiah, a native of the Sandwich Islands, who had recently found his way to New Haven. Early in 1810 he proceeded to Andover Theological Seminary taking Obookiah with him; Obookiah was converted soon afterwards, and his conversion resulted in the foundation a few years later of the Foreign Mission School at Cornwall, Mass. While in the seminary Mills talked about missions incessantly. In June 1810, he and three of his friends presented a paper to the General Association of Massachusetts, in which they declared their desire to go as missionaries to the heathen and asked for counsel. As a result the American Board of Commissioners for Foreign Missions was formed, which in 1812 sent out ten missionaries to Calcutta, and by 1820 had eighty-one missionaries under its charge.

On his graduation from Andover in 1812, Mills was licensed to preach and was sent by the Connecticut and Massachusetts Home Missionary societies on a tour of the country beyond the

15

Alleghanies, from Cincinnati to New Orleans, in company with John F. Schermerhorn; in 1814–15 he made a second and more extensive journey with Daniel Smith. They preached the gospel, distributed Bibles and tracts, promoted the formation of Bible societies, and collected information about the religious and moral condition of the inhabitants. They endured great hardships and were sometimes in danger of their lives from starvation, Indians, and flooded rivers. In collaboration with Schermerhorn he published in 1814 *A Correct View of That Part of the United States Which Lies West of the Allegany Mountains, with Regard to Religion and Morals,* and with Smith, in 1815, *Report of a Missionary Tour through That Part of the United States Which Lies West of the Allegany Mountains.* On June 21, 1815, Mills was ordained at Newburyport, Mass. During the next two years he resided at Albany, New York, Philadelphia, and Washington; and in these years he was the instigator and the chief organizer of the American Bible Society, of the United Foreign Missionary Society (formed by the Presbyterian and Dutch Reformed churches), and of a school for training negro preachers. He also spent some months visiting the poor in the city of New York, and distributing Bibles and tracts. He planned a missionary tour of South America, and hoped finally to accompany Obookiah to the Sandwich Islands.

He became particularly interested in the negroes, however, and when the American Colonization Society was formed in 1817 he at once offered his services. With Ebenezer Burgess he was dispatched to Africa to find suitable territory for purchase. They set out for England in November and were almost wrecked in a storm in which their ship was deserted by the captain, but finally made port at St. Malo. After consulting with the leaders of the English anti-slavery movement they sailed in February 1818 for Sierra Leone, where they spent three months negotiating with a number of native chiefs, and selecting territory for the future colony of Liberia. On the return voyage, begun May 22, 1818, Mills caught a chill, died of fever, and was buried at sea.

Few men with such slender natural endowments have accomplished more. He was quite undistinguished as a scholar, writer, or preacher; he was slow of tongue, inert in manner, and unimpressive in personality. Nevertheless, he was a good judge of men, and had considerable ability as an organizer. His unquenchable ardor and tireless energy made him the father of foreign missionary work in the United States, and the chief creator of four important philanthropic institutions.

[Samuel Orcutt, *Hist. of Torrington, Conn.* (1878); Calvin Durfee, *Williams Biog. Annals* (1871); *Gen. Cat. Theol. Sem., Andover, Mass., 1808–1908* (n.d.); Gardiner Spring, *Memoirs of the Rev. Samuel J. Mills* (1820); W. B. Sprague, *Annals Am. Pulpit,* vol. II (1857); E. G. Stryker, *Missionary Annals: A Story of One Short Life* (copr. 1888); T. C. Richards, *Samuel J. Mills, Missionary Pathfinder, Pioneer, and Promoter* (1906); *Conn. Courant* (Hartford), Sept. 8, 1818; *Conn. Jour.* (New Haven), Sept. 22, 1818.]
H. B. P.

MILLS, SUSAN LINCOLN TOLMAN (Nov. 18, 1826–Dec. 12, 1912), missionary and educator, was the third in a family of six children, five of whom were girls. On her father's side she was descended from Thomas Tolman, a native of England, who settled in Dorchester, Mass., in 1630. In 1835 her parents, John and Elizabeth (Nichols) Tolman, moved from Enosburg, Vt., her birthplace, to Ware, Mass., where she received her early education. She entered Mount Holyoke Seminary (now Mount Holyoke College) in 1842, and graduated in 1845. During the next three years she taught at that institution under the direction of Mary Lyon [*q.v.*] and on Sept. 11, 1848, she married Rev. Cyrus Taggart Mills [*q.v.*].

During the years from 1848 to 1884 she assisted her husband in missionary and educational work. Their first engagement was at Batticotta Seminary in Ceylon, India, an institution devoted to the education of native teachers and preachers. Besides helping in administering the affairs of the seminary, she also supervised the work of several day schools. After six years, which sorely taxed their health, they returned to the United States. With improvement in health came the old urge for foreign service, and in 1860 they went to the Hawaiian Islands. Cyrus Mills became president of Oahu College in Honolulu, and his wife taught English and natural sciences. During the four years of their sojourn she established an enviable reputation among the young people of the school and of the community by her wholesome advice and her cheerful disposition. Returning to the United States in 1864 they settled in California the following year, and purchased a young ladies' seminary from Mary Atkins at Benicia.

The acquisition of this school opened the field to which Mrs. Mills dedicated the remainder of her active life—the "Christian education" of young women. Benicia was not the most desirable place for such a school, however, and they acquired about sixty acres of land five miles south of Oakland and just east of the south end of San Francisco Bay, erected a comfortable building which would accommodate about one hundred and twenty-five students, and moved to the new site in 1871. Mills Seminary—for this was the name given to the school at that time—was favorably regarded from the very beginning. In 1877 the property was deeded to a board of trustees. When Cyrus Mills died in 1884, his wife was appointed to the board in his place and was practically in charge of the institution until Homer B. Sprague assumed the duties of president in the autumn of 1885. In the meantime a four years' college course was added to the curriculum, a college charter was secured from the state of California, and Mills Seminary became Mills College. In 1890 Mrs. Mills became president, and during the nineteen years she held the office she proved an efficient executive. In 1901 she transferred property to the trustees valued at about $200,000, which was to be administered by the board for the benefit of the college. Beginning in 1906, the seminary classes were eliminated, one each year, and the institution was devoted entirely to the higher education of young women. Mrs. Mills retired from the presidency in 1909, but as president emeritus she continued to exercise considerable influence over the administration of the college. The growth of the institution while under her charge, together with the addition of the college curriculum, is ample justification for recognizing her as the founder of Mills College. She died at Oakland, Cal.

[C. K. Wittenmyer, ed., *The Susan Lincoln Mills Memory Book* (1915); R. A. Keep, *Fourscore Years: A Hist. of Mills Coll.* (1931); *Who's Who in America, 1912–13*; *San Francisco Examiner,* Dec. 13, 1912.]

C. G.

MILLSPAUGH, CHARLES FREDERICK (June 20, 1854–Sept. 15, 1923), botanist, was born at Ithaca, N. Y., the son of John Hill Millspaugh, an artist, and Marion (Cornell) Millspaugh, sister of Ezra Cornell [*q.v.*]. At an early age he took great interest in sports and natural history. While still a boy he became acquainted with Louis Agassiz and began a long friendship which had much to do with shaping his subsequent career. On Sept. 19, 1877, he married Mary Louisa Spaulding, who died in 1907, and in 1910 he married Clara Isobel Mitchell.

He studied at Cornell University, 1871–73, then at the New York Homeopathic Medical College and Hospital, where he received the degree of M.D. in 1881. From 1881 to 1890 he practised medicine at Binghamton, N. Y., and then for one year at Waverly, N. Y. During this time he became interested in botany and made a special study of plants used in medicine,

preparing a monumental two-volume work, illustrated by himself with 180 colored plates, which was published in 1887 under the title, *American Medicinal Plants*. His skill as an artist, which he attributed to early instruction from his father, added to the value of this work, which brought him so prominently before the botanical fraternity that in 1891 he was called to the chair of botany in the University of West Virginia. Here he published a "Preliminary Catalogue of the Flora of West Virginia" (*Annual Report of the West Virginia Agricultural Experiment Station,* 1892, pp. 315–537), and began to specialize in the *Euphorbiaceae,* contributing a number of papers on this subject to various journals between 1890 and 1915.

After the World's Columbian Exposition (1893), he became curator of botany at the Field Museum of Natural History, Chicago, a position which he held until his death. He built up the herbarium, both by purchases and by his own collecting, until it became one of the largest and probably the most thoroughly catalogued and the most safely housed of all herbaria. He made many collecting trips to Mexico, Yucatan, the Bahamas, and the West Indies, besides expeditions in the United States and a journey around the world. Nearly forty papers were published as a result of these collections. As a museum curator he was particularly successful; he watched the visitors, noting which displays attracted most attention, then developed others along similar lines. His labels, striking and efficient, are models which other museums might well copy. Glass flowers, and plants made of a combination of glass and wax, formed an interesting and instructive part of the botanical exhibit. He was an excellent lecturer and in this capacity his services were in great demand and brought prestige to the Museum. He was a professorial lecturer in botany at the University of Chicago, professor of medical botany in the Chicago Homœpathic Medical College, a fellow of the American Association for the Advancement of Science, of the Faculdad de Medicina, Mexico, and of the Faculdad de Medicina, Brazil, and was president of the Wild Flower Preservation Society for several years.

In person, he was a man of unusually fine appearance. He was athletic, and a good tennis player even at an age when most men are too slow for such sport. Throughout his public career he was prominent socially. His distinguished appearance made a good first impression which improved with acquaintance. His extensive travels, wide information, and knowledge of the world developed contacts which brought invitations to yacht cruises among the Antilles, where so much of his collecting was done. A few years before his death he went to Santa Catalina Island to rest after a serious operation, but while there studied the flora of the island and, in collaboration with L. W. Nuttall, prepared an extensive paper.

Chief among his publications, in addition to those already mentioned, were the following: "Contribution to the Coastal and Plain Flora of Yucatan" (*Field Museum Publications, Botanical Series I*, 1895, 1896, 1898); "*Plantae Yucatanae*" (*Ibid., Series III*, 1903, 1904); "Flora of West Virginia" (*Ibid., Series I*, 1896), with L. W. Nuttall; "The Living Flora of West Virginia" (*West Virginia Geological Survey Reports*, 5A, 1913); "Flora of Santa Catalina Island" (*Field Museum Publications, Botanical Series V*, 1923), with Nuttall.

[E. E. Sherff, in *Bot. Gazette*, Apr. 1924; *Who's Who in America*, 1922–23; *Cornell Alumni News*, Oct. 11, 1923; *Chicago Daily Tribune*, Sept. 17, 1923; complete list of Millspaugh's publications at the Field Museum.]   C. J. C.

MILMORE, MARTIN (Sept. 14, 1844–July 21, 1883), sculptor, was born in Sligo, County Sligo, Ireland, of excellent Irish stock. After the death of his father, a schoolmaster, in 1851, the widowed mother with her four young sons came to the United States and settled in Boston. Martin and his brother Joseph were educated at the Brimmer School and the Latin School, while in addition Martin had art lessons at the Lowell Institute for seven years. Joseph, the eldest son, was early obliged to go to work. At first a cabinet-maker's assistant, he later became a proficient stone-cutter, with a recognized talent for sculpture. From this brother Martin, while still in school, received lessons in wood-carving, which determined him to become a sculptor. His earliest effort was a bust of himself, made by the aid of a mirror. Wishing to study modeling in clay, he presented himself at the newly built studio of Thomas Ball [*q.v.*], during the first hour after that sculptor had taken possession. Ball did not give lessons, but, touched by the lad's disappointment, gave him a work room and materials, in return for which the boy agreed to keep the studio clean and attend to the fires. The close association thus begun lasted from 1860 to 1864, when Milmore set up his own studio.

In the early sixties Ball was building up, bowlful by bowlful, the plaster model of his famous equestrian statue of Washington, and Milmore as observer and helper was initiated into many branches of the sculptor's craft. While still

with Ball he produced a little figure called "Devotion," ordered for the Sanitary Fair of 1863, and a high relief, "Phosphor," of which he sold the original and two replicas. In 1864, through the purchaser of one of the replicas, he received a commission for three granite figures for the Boston Horticultural Hall: "Ceres," over twelve feet high, "Flora" and "Pomona," each eight feet high. The "Ceres" he modeled in plaster, after the manner of Ball in the Washington equestrian. He spent two years on these figures, his brother Joseph assisting him in the cutting. In 1865 came his much praised bust of Charles Sumner, presented by the Massachusetts legislature to George William Curtis and now in the Senate wing of the Capitol, Washington, D. C.

Milmore's growing fame was established in 1867 when the City of Boston accepted his design for the Roxbury Soldiers' Monument, Forest Hills Cemetery. An excellent piece of work for its day, it has as its chief feature the seven-foot bronze statue of a soldier resting on his gun and contemplating the graves of his fallen comrades. The success of this monument paved the way for the most significant undertaking of Milmore's career, the Soldiers' and Sailors' Monument erected on Boston Common in 1877, which became the prototype of numerous Civil War memorials throughout the land. In Milmore's design an extensive granite base, with bronze panels on its sides and symbolic bronze figures at four piers, supports at its center a high shaft crowned by a bronze figure of "Liberty." Now outmoded, the monument remains a sincere and dignified effort. To model the sculpture, he went to Rome, where he spent studious years from 1870 to 1875. During his stay he made portrait busts of Pope Pius IX, Wendell Phillips, and Ralph Waldo Emerson. "Milmore was a picturesque figure," wrote one of his contemporaries, "somewhat of the Edwin Booth type, with long dark hair and large dark eyes. He affected the artistic (as all of us artists used to, more or less), wearing a broad-brimmed soft black hat, and a cloak. His appearance was striking, and he knew it." (Daniel Chester French, to the writer of this sketch, Feb. 7, 1931.)

Other busts by Milmore are Lincoln, Grant, Daniel Webster, Cardinal McCloskey, and George Ticknor, the last-mentioned now owned by the Boston Public Library. At West Point, N. Y., is his bronze statue of Gen. Sylvanus Thayer. At Erie, Pa., Keene, N. H., Charlestown, Mass., and Fitchburg, Mass., are typical Civil War monuments from his hand. His brother Joseph, a sculptor of scarcely less talent than himself, was his constant collaborator; the great granite Sphinx commemorating the Union dead, at Mount Auburn Cemetery, Cambridge, Mass., is their joint work. Martin Milmore's monuments were among the best of their time, yet were not good enough to have a truly vitalizing influence on American monumental art. T. H. Bartlett, an informed if acrimonious critic, writing in the eighties, found them better in intention than in execution, while Lorado Taft (*post*, p. 255) writes: "Milmore stands for good workmanship rather than for poetic expression. Few, if any, of his productions seem inspired. . . . There is nothing epic in his grasp of war subjects, nothing lyric in his treatment of gentler themes. . . . But we find throughout good honest construction, adequate modelling, and, rarest of all, a sense of the monumental in line and mass."

Milmore died, unmarried, at Boston Highlands, aged thirty-eight. His grave in Forest Hills Cemetery, Roxbury, is marked by one of the most famous pieces of sculpture in the United States—"Death and the Young Sculptor," by Daniel Chester French.

[C. R. Post, "Martin Milmore," in *Art Studies, Medieval, Renaissance, and Modern* (1925), vol. III; H. T. Tuckerman, *Book of the Artists* (1867), incorrect as to place of birth; "New Monument in Boston," *Art Journal* (N. Y.), Oct. 1877; obituaries of Martin and Joseph Milmore in *Am. Architect and Building News*, Aug. 18, 1883, and Jan. 30, 1886; Justin Winsor, *The Memorial Hist. of Boston*, vol. III (1881); Lorado Taft, *The Hist. of Am. Sculpture* (rev. ed., 1930); C. E. Fairman, *Art and Artists of the Capitol of the U. S. A.* (1927); Thomas Ball, *My Threescore Years and Ten* (1891); *Boston Evening Transcript*, July 23, 1883.]   A.A.

MILNER, JOHN TURNER (Sept. 29, 1826– Aug. 18, 1898), civil engineer, industrialist, was born in Pike County, Ga., the son of Willis Jay and Elizabeth (Turner) Milner. His parents were pioneer settlers of Georgia, the Milners being Virginians and the Turners North Carolinians. John's early youth was spent on a farm which his father ran in addition to his activities as a railroad contractor, builder, and miner. The boy received a simple schooling and at the age of ten was working in his father's gold mines in Lumpkin County. In the years immediately following he gained from his father some practical insight into railroad construction. He matriculated at the University of Georgia in 1843 and made a brilliant record until ill health forced him to leave at the end of his third year.

Railroads were then new and construction work was in no small measure a matter of empiricism. What young Milner had learned by actual experience he combined with his scientific training and within two years became principal assistant in building the Macon & Western Railroad. This activity was pioneering of a sort, but

far more alluring was the gold rush of 1849, which Milner joined, journeying to California by the overland route. After arriving he abandoned mining, however, to become city surveyor of San José, then the capital of the new territory. Returning to Georgia in 1854, he soon removed to Alabama, where he built the Montgomery & West Point Railroad. Meanwhile, a number of enterprising citizens who had tapped the coal and iron deposits of the state were proclaiming the urgent need of a railroad to make accessible the rich mineral resources north of the Black Belt. Persistent argument before a cotton-growing legislature finally resulted, in 1858, in an appropriation for a reconnoissance through the region, and Milner was appointed to undertake the survey. His *Report of the Chief Engineer . . . of the South & North Alabama Railroad Company* (1859) was far-reaching in its ultimate effects. Although construction was suspended during the Civil War, his proposals were eventually followed and his predictions substantiated. He projected the road from Decatur, Ga., to Elyton, Ala., through the richest coal and iron region. By analogy with the state-owned Western & Atlantic of Georgia, he showed how the iron industry would be stimulated to the advantage of the railroad and the state as a whole, and he discussed the value of slave labor, which he declared to be more reliable and cheaper than white. With aid from the Confederacy the railroad was built part way into the mineral region; Milner and Frank Gilmer, a partner, were also granted a subsidy to aid them in erecting the Oxmoor furnaces, in order to provide war materials.

When work on the South & North Alabama Railroad was resumed after the war, Milner made an agreement with the rival Alabama & Chattanooga Railroad concerning the location of the crossing of the two, so that both might benefit from the sale of land where a new city would presumably arise. A site near Village Creek was selected; and both roads were surveyed and located toward it. The Carpet-baggers, who controlled both the legislature and the Alabama & Chattanooga, broke the agreement, however, and diverted the direction of the road toward Elyton, on land in the vicinity of which they had taken sixty-day options, thereby hoping to ruin Milner, who had invested heavily in the district first chosen. Milner, however, by his tactics in surveying kept his opponents in such doubt as to where he would actually locate the crossing that they did not dare take up the options, and on the minute the sixty days expired the land was purchased by a Montgomery banker, Josiah Morris, for Milner and his friends. They formed the Elyton Land Company, which, in 1871, founded Birmingham. The following year the Louisville & Nashville Railroad took over the South & North, and Milner retired from railroading.

Subsequently, he organized the Newcastle Coal & Iron Company (1873) and was connected with the Experimental Coke & Iron Company, which was instrumental in producing the first coke pig iron in Birmingham in 1876. This same year he wrote a pamphlet, *Alabama: As It Was, As It Is, and As It Will Be,* setting forth somewhat enthusiastically the resources and industrial possibilities of the state. His Milner Coal & Railroad Company, established in 1879, he sold a decade later at a profit of over $200,000. On Dec. 30, 1855, he married Flora J. Caldwell of Greenville, Ala., by whom he had one son and three daughters. From 1888 to 1896 he served as state senator from Jefferson County. He was a member of the Presbyterian Church. He died at his Newcastle home from a paralytic stroke at the age of seventy-two.

[The best sketch of Milner is found in T. M. Owen, *Hist. of Ala. and Dict. of Ala. Biog.* (1921), vol. IV; an obituary is in *The Age-Herald* (Birmingham), Aug. 19, 1898; Ethel Armes, *The Story of Coal and Iron in Ala.* (1910), contains a detailed account of his work with the South & North Railroad and excerpts from his writings; contemporary and inaccurate sketch of his career, with special reference to the rise of Birmingham, is published in *Jefferson County and Birmingham, Ala., Hist. and Biog.* (1887), J. W. Du Bose, ed.]
L. J. C.

MILNER, MOSES EMBREE [See CALIFORNIA JOE, 1829–1876].

MILNER, THOMAS PICTON [See PICTON, THOMAS, 1822–1891].

MILROY, ROBERT HUSTON (June 11, 1816–Mar. 29, 1890), soldier and Indian agent, was born in Washington County, Ind., the son of Samuel and Martha (Huston) Milroy. He came of fighting stock being, it was claimed, a descendant of Robert Bruce through his great-grandfather, John McElroy, who fled from Scotland, changed his name to Milroy, and later settled near Carlisle, Pa. Robert Milroy's immediate ancestors were Indian fighters, and his father contributed stoutly to the upbuilding of the young state of Indiana. The son fully sustained the family reputation. The Milroys removed from Washington County to Carroll County, Ind., when he was ten years old. In 1840 he entered Norwich University in Vermont and graduated in 1843 with the degrees of Bachelor of Arts and Master of Military Science. In the Mexican War he raised a voluntary company in Carroll County. Mustered into service on June 20, 1846, at New Albany, he was mustered out at New Orleans on June 16, 1847. On May 17, 1849, he was married to Mary Jane Armitage of Alexandria, Pa., who bore him seven children. He took a law course at the University of Indiana, where he received the degree of Bachelor of Laws in 1850, was admitted to the bar, and began practice at Delphi, Ind. In 1850 he was elected a delegate from Carroll County to the state's second constitutional convention as, by an interesting coincidence, his father had been sent to the first one. He was appointed to the bench of the 8th judicial circuit, but resigned, removed to Rensselaer, Ind., in 1854 and took up the practice of law.

In Indiana he is best known as a soldier of the Civil War. At the first call for troops he proceeded to raise a voluntary company in Rensselaer. Of this he was made captain but on Apr. 27, 1861, was mustered into the three months' service as colonel of the 9th Regiment of Indiana Volunteers. At the expiration of this term of service he reënlisted for the three years' service with the same rank, but on Sept. 3 of that year was promoted brigadier-general, and on Nov. 29, 1862, major-general of volunteers. Much of his field service was in western Virginia, where his measures to suppress guerrilla warfare were so drastic that the Confederates offered a large reward for him, dead or alive. As major-general he commanded the second division of the VIII Army Corps, being stationed at Winchester, Va., when Lee made his movement northward toward Pennsylvania. He engaged the Confederate army till driven back with losses so disastrous that they were afterward the subject of military investigation, but he was finally exonerated. He claimed that his retarding of Lee's forces enabled Meade to prepare for Gettysburg. He remained in the service till the end of the war.

After the war he occupied positions of trust and responsibility. He was one of the trustees of the Wabash and Erie Canal. In 1872 he became superintendent of Indian affairs in the state of Washington, and from 1875 to 1885 he was Indian agent with headquarters at Olympia, where he died. Twenty years later a bronze statue of heroic size was erected at his old home, Rensselaer, where it still perpetuates his memory. Personally, he was of fine, athletic appearance, fully six feet and two inches in height; he had piercing black eyes; and these, together with an aquiline nose and long silver hair, gained for him the sobriquet of the "Gray Eagle." Carl Schurz wrote that "he lived on a footing of very democratic comradeship with his men. The most extraordinary stories were told of his discussing with his subordinates what was to be done, of his permitting them to take amazing liberties with the orders to be executed. . . . But he did good service, was respected and liked by all" (*The Reminiscences of Carl Schurz*, II, 1907, p. 388).

[*Norwich University* (3 vols., 1911); T. A. Wylie, *Ind. University* (1890); F. B. Heitman, *Hist. Register and Dict. of the U. S. Army* (1903); *War of the Rebellion: Official Records* (*Army*), 1 ser., XXI, 3 ser., II, III; 4 ser., II; T. B. Helm, *Hist. of Carroll County, Ind.* (1882); J. H. Stewart, *Recollections of the Early Settlement of Carroll County* (1872), pp. 38, 47, 170.]
G. S. C.

MILTON, JOHN (Apr. 20, 1807–Apr. 1, 1865), governor of Florida, was born in Jefferson County, Ga., the son of Elizabeth (Robinson) and Homer Virgil Milton, a planter and an officer in the War of 1812. His great-grandfather, John Milton, emigrated from England and, about 1730, settled in Halifax County, N. C., from which his grandfather, also John Milton, removed to Georgia, where as first secretary of state he saved the records from the British and in 1789 received two votes of the Georgia electors for the presidency. The boy was educated in the academy at Louisville, Ga. He studied law in the office of Roger L. Gamble of Louisville and after admission to the bar began the practice of his profession at that place. In two years he removed to Columbus, Ga., and a little later to Mobile, Ala. His law practice continued at this place and at New Orleans until 1846 with a two years' interruption, when he served as a captain of Mobile volunteers in the Seminole War. In 1846 he removed to Florida, settling down on his plantation near Marianna, in Jackson County, where he made his home until his death. He was a Democratic elector in 1848 and in 1849 was elected to the state Senate.

His claim to remembrance rests on his record as war governor of Florida. He was inaugurated governor in 1861 and began his term inauspiciously by denouncing the state secession convention for assuming legislative functions and by refusing to recognize the executive council that the convention had created to limit the governor's powers. During his term as governor his time was so taken up with military affairs that he had scant opportunity to show his ability in any other field. He was an earnest advocate of war-time prohibition both because he deplored drunkenness and because he wished corn to be conserved for other purposes. He approved, if he did not originate, the Florida law providing for the issue of paper money se-

cured by the public land of the state. While not hesitating at times to assert the doctrine of state rights with such vigor as to cause Secretary Benjamin moments of acute distress, the records indicate that on the whole he gave the Confederacy a greater measure of cooperation than was usual among Southern governors. He resisted the recruiting of cavalry in the state on the ground that Florida topography was not suitable for cavalry activities. He differed from the Confederate military authorities in regard to the abandonment of certain Florida ports and the defense of others. Particularly he insisted on the defense of Apalachicola, and, unable to obtain Confederate cooperation to that end, he proposed to Alabama and Georgia a joint defense of the port. He constantly, though vainly, urged that the Confederacy give him charge of military affairs in Florida and more than once hinted to Davis that he would rather be a Confederate brigadier-general than a civilian governor. Failing in all these things, he did his utmost to raise troops for the Confederacy and to keep them supplied with clothing and hospital supplies. He met the Confederate requisitions for money promptly and, throughout the war, received Confederate money for taxes to the practical exclusion of the Florida paper itself. He was vigorous in the use of the militia for the defense of the state and is entitled to credit for the fact that Florida was the only Southern state whose capital remained uncaptured at the end of the war. It must be conceded, however, that the security of Florida during the war may have been due less to defensive measures than to its lack of importance. As the fortunes of the Confederacy ebbed the governor remained defiant, opposed all peace proposals that left the independence of the Confederacy unrecognized, and, upon the collapse of the Southern cause, his mind gave way and he destroyed his own life. He was married twice: first, on Dec. 9, 1826, to Susan Amanda Cobb, of Cobbham, Ga., and, after her death in 1840, to Caroline Howze of Marion, Ala.

[Papers in the supreme court library of the state house at Tallahassee; date of birth and other information from W. H. Milton, Marianna, Fla.; extract from Sarah L. Jones, *Life in the South* (1863), in *Fla. Hist. Soc. Quart.*, July 1909; *War of the Rebellion: Official Records* (*Army*), esp. 1 ser. VI, LII, pt. 2; R. H. Rerick, *Memoirs of Fla.* (1902), vol. I; W. W. Davis, *The Civil War and Reconstruction in Fla.* (1913); *Makers of America* (1909, Fla. ed.), vol. I, pp. 148–153.]
R. S. C.

MINER, ALONZO AMES (Aug. 17, 1814–June 14, 1895), Universalist clergyman, president of Tufts College, was born in Lempster, a small village in Sullivan County, N. H., the second of the five children of Benajah Ames and Amanda (Carey) Miner. He was a descendant of Thomas Miner (or Minor) who emigrated to Charlestown, Mass., in 1629, removed to Hingham in 1636, and later joined the younger Winthrop's colony at New London, Conn. Alonzo's parents had rebelled against the strict Calvinism of their time, thus becoming marked people in their community. The boy therefore grew up in the atmosphere of theological debate and early acquired an intense interest in all the issues of his day. His education was somewhat irregular and informal, due partly to the lack of advantages in the sparsely populated country, and more to the fact that a serious accident made him a semi-invalid in his early years. He attended schools in Lempster, Hopkinton, Lebanon, and Franklin, N. H., and in Cavendish, Vt. Much of his study, however, was carried on alone, with the advice and direction of clergymen.

At the age of twenty he was taken into partnership by the principal of the school at Chester, Vt., and a year later he was called to become head of the academy at Unity, N. Y., where he remained for four years. On Aug. 24, 1836, he married Maria S. Perley, whom he had known since childhood, and who now became preceptress at the academy. There were no children. Teaching, however, was only a stepping-stone to his chosen life work. When he was twenty-five years of age, he became a Universalist preacher, conducting services in various small rural communities in the neighborhood, and in 1839 he was ordained.

His first full-time pastorate was in Methuen, Mass., where he quickly earned a name for himself as a public defender of his faith by engaging in frequent debates with orthodox preachers. From Methuen, he was called to a pastorate in Lowell, Mass. Here he became a public man in the ordinary sense of the term, for he began championing public causes and soon found himself in the midst of great discussions and struggles. First, he became a passionate upholder of the temperance movement, taking the extreme stand of absolute abstinence, which in those days was unpopular, and pleading that the church should espouse the cause. Next, in 1843, he was drawn into the anti-slavery movement and threw himself with characteristic abandon into the effort to free the slaves. His love for the church, however, was so strong that he found a double battle on his hands, for he was also opposed to the extreme reformers such as Garrison who advocated "Come-Outism" to church members. His debates on this subject attracted large crowds and gave him a high reputation as a

good logician and fearless fighter. In 1848, he was called to the pastorate of the School Street Church, the Second Universalist Society of Boston, as an associate of Hosea Ballou, 1771–1852 [q.v.]. With this church he remained for forty-three years, rounding out a life of distinguished service in many fields.

In 1862, he became president of Tufts College, largely because the college was in financial difficulties, and because his administrative genius, it was believed, would be adequate to the need. He served without salary, devoting heroic efforts to raising money, teaching classes, and carrying on his work as minister of the church. Through his contacts with men of means and influence, he was able finally to pull the college through its crisis, not only adding largely to the endowment, but also increasing its equipment and faculty. He resigned from the presidency of the college in 1874, and resumed his full-time connection with the church, maintaining, however, his interest in educational institutions, serving as trustee of the college, and being active in promoting the development of Dean Academy in Massachusetts and Goddard Seminary in Vermont. He died in Boston, after a short illness, in his eighty-first year.

[L. L. Selleck, *One Branch of the Miner Family* (1928); G. H. Emerson, *Life of Alonzo Ames Miner* (1896); A. B. Start, *Hist. of Tufts Coll.* (1896); G. H. Emerson, in *Sketches of Successful New Hampshire Men* (1882), ed. by J. B. Clarke; *Boston Daily Advertiser*, June 15, 1895.]   C. R. S.

MINER, CHARLES (Feb. 1, 1780–Oct. 26, 1865), editor, congressman, the son of Seth and Anna (Charlton) Miner and a descendant of Thomas Miner (or Minor) who came to Massachusetts from Somersetshire about 1629, was born in Norwich, Conn. His father was a printer, and after attending the schools near his home Charles worked for some time at his father's trade in New London. During the winter of 1798–99 he studied surveying, and on Feb. 8, 1799, set out for the Wyoming Valley in Pennsylvania to take charge of preparing his father's lands, held under the Connecticut claim, for settlement. In 1802 he joined his brother Asher at Wilkes-Barre in publishing the *Luzerne Federalist and Susquehannah Intelligencer*.

In 1804 Charles Miner bought his brother's interest, becoming sole proprietor of the paper, which he published until 1809 and again in 1810–11. On Feb. 1, 1811, he began the publication of a new journal, the *Gleaner and Luzerne Intelligencer*, which gained a considerable reputation and became something of a political power. During these years he wrote a series of humorous sketches for the columns of his paper, later collected in book form under the title *Essays from the Desk of Poor Robert the Scribe* (1815). In one of them, "Who'll Turn Grindstone?", which appeared in the *Luzerne Federalist,* Sept. 7, 1810, he originated the phrase "to have an axe to grind," which has since come to have a very definite meaning in American speech. He also wrote and published "The Ballad of James Bird," which was circulated widely. In May 1806 he was chosen a member of the first borough council of Wilkes-Barre and in October 1807 was elected a member of the Pennsylvania House of Representatives in which he served till 1809. He was elected again in 1812.

In 1816 he sold the *Gleaner* and went to Philadelphia to become editor and part owner of the *True American,* a daily paper. The next year, unable to stand city life, he returned to Wilkes-Barre, and in July 1817 bought the *Chester and Delaware Federalist* at West Chester, Pa., to which place he removed his family. He soon changed this paper's name to the *Village Record,* under which title it was for years one of the best-known provincial weeklies in the United States. He was elected as a Federalist representative from Pennsylvania to the Nineteenth and Twentieth congresses (Mar. 4, 1825–Mar. 3, 1829) but was not a candidate for reëlection in 1828 because of increasing deafness and the need of his services at home. He resumed the post of editor and publisher of the *Village Record* but in 1832 sold the paper and returned to Wilkes-Barre, retiring to private life. During the next few years he spent a great deal of time and effort in writing his *History of Wyoming* (1845), a standard work dealing with the massacre of July 3, 1778, and the long-disputed land claims of Connecticut and Pennsylvania. It was based on original investigations and interviews with old residents.

While in Congress he became the close personal friend of the leading men of the times, including President Adams, Henry Clay, and others, who continued to correspond with him on political questions after his retirement. He was opposed to slavery, and on May 13, 1826, offered a series of resolutions in the House of Representatives in favor of its abolition in the District of Columbia and its eventual extinction in the United States. These were not favorably received by the House, but he persistently pressed the question throughout the term of his service. He endeavored to popularize silk-growing in the United States, was one of the first to plant mulberry trees and to undertake the raising of silk worms, and drew up and introduced into Congress the first resolutions on silk-culture. He

was an early promoter of the anthracite coal trade in Pennsylvania and of canals as a part of internal improvement. With three others he leased the Mauch Chunk mine from the Lehigh Coal Mine Company, and in 1814 was a member of the firm of Hillhouse, Miner & Cist which was responsible for sending the first boatload of anthracite down the Schuylkill River to Philadelphia. Although this first load was very hard to sell, Miner through his writings did much to introduce anthracite and popularize its use. He married Letitia Wright on Jan. 16, 1804, and was the father of ten children, of whom only three survived him. One of his daughters was the mother of Charlton T. Lewis [*q.v.*]. He died at his home, "The Retreat," near Wilkes-Barre, at the age of eighty-five. Although he was a man of varied activities his reputation rests upon the fact that he was one of the most original and influential of the Pennsylvania editors of the first part of the nineteenth century.

[C. F. and E. M. T. Richardson, *Charles Miner: A Pa. Pioneer* (1916); J. T. Sharf and Thompson Westcott, *Hist. of Phila.* (1884), I, 578; *Biog. Dir. Am. Cong.* (1928); O. J. Harvey, *A Hist. of Lodge No. 61, F. and A. M., Wilkesbarre, Pa.* (1897); *Proc. and Colls. Wyoming Hist. and Geol. Soc., 1922,* vol. XVIII (1923).]

J.H.F.

MINER, MYRTILLA (Mar. 4, 1815–Dec. 17, 1864), promoter of negro education, was born in Brookfield, N. Y., to which place her father's family had come from Norwich, Conn. That portion of New York State was then a wilderness, the Miners were very poor, and there were no educational opportunities for the children. Myrtilla, though physically frail, was possessed by a desire for learning. She disliked house and farm work and, after teaching herself to read, borrowed books, or purchased them with money earned by picking hops. She wrote naïvely and with no satisfactory result to Hon. William H. Seward, governor of New York, asking for advice about securing an education. At fifteen, she was teaching a country school, which she was soon obliged to leave because of "spinal trouble." Recovering partially, she secured admission to a school in Clinton, N. Y., promising to pay her expenses when she was able to teach. Often ill, she studied in bed and after a year secured a position in a public school of Rochester, N. Y. From there she went to a school in Providence, R. I., and then to Newton Institute, a school for planters' daughters at Whitesville, Miss. The milder climate benefited her health but her first sight of negro slavery shocked her profoundly. She came to believe that in education lay the salvation of the negro, and asked for permission to instruct the slaves on one of the plantations, but was told that it was a criminal offense in Mississippi to teach a slave to read. After two years there, she returned North, very ill again. During her illness she made a vow that if she recovered she would devote herself to the cause of the slaves.

When she regained a measure of health, without money or influence, she determined to start a normal school for colored girls in Washington, D. C., a stronghold of aristocratic, pro-slavery feeling, Frederick Douglass [q.v.], negro philanthropist, whom she consulted, knowing the difficulties, discouraged her. She begged money, paper, almost anything, and on Dec. 3, 1851, in a small apartment, opened her normal school for free colored girls. The school had six students at the start, fifteen after a month, forty after two months. With her teaching, she carried on a continuous campaign for funds. In 1853, through the kindness of Thomas Williamson and Samuel Rhoads of the Society of Friends of Philadelphia, who loaned $2,000 and consented to act as trustees, and of Harriet Beecher Stowe, who gave $1,000 of her earnings from *Uncle Tom's Cabin,* she was able to purchase for $4,000 three acres between N Street and New Hampshire Avenue, with a small house, barn, and orchard. In March 1854 the school was moved to this location, which was then on the outskirts of the city. The house was often attacked and threatened, but a high fence, a dog, and the sight of the mistress and her assistant practising with a revolver in the yard warned off intruders. By 1856 the school was placed under trustees, one of whom was Johns Hopkins [q.v.]. Printed solicitations for funds aroused public antagonism and Walter Lenox, a former mayor of Washington, wrote an article, which appeared in the *National Intelligencer* (May 6, 1857), attacking the school and all attempts at negro education as aids in the abolition movement. The institution was several times under other management, or temporarily closed, on account of Miss Miner's poor health.

In 1861 she went to California, where she supported herself by practising clairvoyance and magnetic healing. An accident in which she was thrown from a carriage was followed by symptoms of tuberculosis, to which she was probably always predisposed. She returned to Washington by steamer, arriving there only a few days before her death, which occurred at the home of her friend, Mrs. Nancy M. Johnson. Her funeral was conducted by Rev. William Henry Channing [q.v.] of the Unitarian Church and she was buried at Oak Hill Cemetery, Georgetown. Her work did not lapse, however; on

Mar. 3, 1863, Congress incorporated the Institution for the Education of Colored Youth in the District of Columbia. In 1871 it was joined with Howard University, but separated in 1876, and in 1879 as the Miner Normal School (now Miner Teachers' College) it became part of the public school system of the District.

[E. M. O'Connor, *Myrtilla Miner: A Memoir* (1885); G. S. Wormley, "Myrtilla Miner," in *Jour. of Negro Hist.,* Oct. 1920; *Washington Daily Times,* Dec. 20, 1864, Washington *Daily Morning Chronicle,* Dec. 19, 1864.]

S. G. B.

MING, JOHN JOSEPH (Sept. 20, 1838–June 17, 1910), Roman Catholic priest and sociologist, was born in Gyswyl, Unterwalden, Switzerland. On completion of a classical course in the Benedictine College of Engelburg, he entered the Society of Jesus (Sept. 7, 1856) and passed through the various cycles of the novitiate, juniorate, teaching apprenticeship, and the study of theology in the Jesuit institutions of Aachen and Maria-Laach, Switzerland. On Sept. 13, 1868, he was ordained. Honored with a preachership at Kreuzberg, a center for pilgrimages, he was soon assigned, after completion of a rigid tertianship, to the chair of theology at the seminary of the prince-bishop of Görz in Austria. In 1872 when the German government expelled the Jesuits, Ming accompanied a number of his brethren to the United States—men whose scholarship incidentally improved the Society's institutions of higher learning in this country.

After two years of parochial work, Ming taught theology in the archdiocesan Seminary of St. Francis near Milwaukee. Soon the Society required his services, and he lectured in sociology and philosophy in various Jesuit institutions—Springhill College in Alabama, Canisius College in Buffalo, N. Y., Campion College at Prairie du Chien, Wis., and finally at St. Louis University, where he remained twenty-one years. An inspiring teacher of sound scholarship and conservative tone, he gained recognition especially in the Mid-West as a Catholic pioneer in the sociological field. A laborious writer, he found time to contribute a number of articles to *America,* the *Messenger of the Sacred Heart,* and the *Catholic Encyclopedia,* as well as to write a score of sound essays on economic and social subjects for the *American Catholic Quarterly Review,* which in Ming's day was probably the most erudite of Catholic publications. His brochure on *The Temporal Sovereignty of the Holy See* (1892) has been widely quoted. His scholarship is evinced in such volumes as *The Data of Modern Ethics Examined* (1894), *The Characteristics and the Religion of*

Minor

Modern Socialism (1908), and *Morality of Modern Socialism* (1909). At the time of his death, at Saint Stanislaus' Jesuit Home, Parma, Ohio, he was gathering material for a book on labor problems.

[*America*, July 2, 1910; *Am. Cath. Who's Who* (1911); *The Cath. Encyc. and Its Makers* (1917); *Cleveland Plain Dealer*, June 18, 1910; materials from the archives at Woodstock, Md.] R. J. P.

MINOR, BENJAMIN BLAKE (Oct. 21, 1818–Aug. 1, 1905), editor, lawyer, educator, was born at Tappahannock, Essex County, Va., the eldest child of Dr. Hubbard Taylor and Jane (Blake) Minor. His grandfather, Thomas Minor, Jr., of Spotsylvania County, a substantial planter, served as an officer through the Revolution, while his great-grandfather, James Taylor, Jr., of Caroline County, fought in the French and Indian War, and was a distinguished member of the House of Burgesses, of the Virginia Conventions of 1775 and 1776, of the first Virginia Senate, and of the convention which ratified the federal Constitution. His mother's father was a successful plantation owner and merchant whose vessels traded as far as the West Indies.

Benjamin Minor received his early education in private schools in Essex County. At the age of twelve, he entered the classical academy of Thomas Hanson in Fredericksburg. He was admitted in 1834 to the junior class of Bristol College, a mechanical institution near Philadelphia, and in 1835 matriculated at the University of Virginia, which he attended until 1837, taking diplomas in several "schools," but no degree. In 1838–39 he attended the College of William and Mary, studying "moral philosophy and political economy" under President Thomas R. Dew [*q.v.*] and law under Judge N. Beverley Tucker. In 1839 he received the degree of LL.B. Too young to practise, he spent the next year in the office of the clerk of the circuit court of Fredericksburg and also visited sessions of the legislature in Richmond. He began the practice of law in Petersburg in October 1840, and took a part in the exciting presidential campaign of Harrison and Tyler. In the spring of the next year he opened his office in Richmond. On May 26, 1842, he was married, in Columbia, Tenn., to Virginia Maury Otey, daughter of James Hervey Otey, Protestant Episcopal Bishop of Tennessee.

His editorial career began the year after his marriage. Thomas W. White, proprietor of the *Southern Literary Messenger*, died Jan. 19, 1843, and in the *Messenger* for August of that year Minor was announced as the new editor

and proprietor. From the beginning he conducted the magazine with vigor and definiteness of purpose. He had no experience as an editor and the somewhat amateurish air which had marked the *Messenger* under White's ownership was not discarded; but the journal now reflected a more positive and energetic personality. Minor determined from the beginning to identify it with Southern writers and Southern views, and though he continued to publish articles from other sections, his policy succeeded in making the magazine strongly provincial. He attempted to reopen relations with the *Messenger's* most distinguished editor and in April 1845 announced that "E. A. Poe, Esq.," would contribute "monthly a *critique raisonnée* of the most important forthcoming works"; but the only products of Poe's pen that appeared during Minor's editorship were a revised form of "The Raven" (March 1845) and "The Literary Life of Thingum Bob, Esq.," in December 1844. Perhaps the most noteworthy article printed in the *Messenger* in this period was "Paper on the Gulf Stream and Currents of the Sea," by Lieut. Matthew Fontaine Maury [*q.v.*], in July 1844. In November 1845, the editor announced the purchase from William Gilmore Simms [*q.v.*] of the *Southern and Western Monthly Magazine and Review,* which was merged with the *Messenger* in January 1846 under the title of the *Southern and Western Literary Messenger and Review.* The issue for October 1847 was the last to appear under Minor's editorship; in that year he sold the magazine to young John R. Thompson [*q.v.*] and accepted the principalship of the Virginia Female Institute of Staunton, Va.

After one session in this school he returned in 1848 to Richmond, where he resumed the practice of the law and founded the Home School for Young Ladies. On July 4, 1860, he was elected president of the University of Missouri and professor of moral and political science there. The institution was closed by the provisional government in March 1862, and President Minor, forced to retire, remained in Columbia until 1865, maintaining himself during the Civil War by teaching a boys' school and giving public lectures. In 1865 he opened a school for girls in St. Louis, but after four years disposed of it and engaged in life insurance and public lecturing until 1889 when he returned to Richmond to remain for the remainder of his life. He was one of the founders of the Richmond Male Orphan Asylum. While practising law he edited *Decisions of Cases in Virginia by the High Court of Chancery, by George Wythe, with a Memoir of the Author* (1852) and a new edition of Hening and Munford's *Virginia Reports*. He was the author of *The Southern Literary Messenger, 1834–1864* (1905). A deeply religious and patriotic man, he devoted much time in his latter years to the activities of historical and patriotic societies and the Episcopal church. He died in Richmond and was buried in Hollywood Cemetery.

[["Sketch of Author" in Minor's *The So. Lit. Messenger, 1834–1864* (1905); L. G. Tyler, *Encyc. of Va. Biog.* (1915), vol. III; J. B. Minor, *The Minor Family of Va.* (1923); F. L. Mott, *A Hist. of Am. Mags.* (1930); *Times Dispatch* (Richmond), Aug. 2, 1905; *News Leader* (Richmond), Aug. 1, 1905; autobiog. article in *Evening Journal* (Richmond), Aug. 1, 1905.]

J. S. W.

MINOR, JOHN BARBEE (June 2, 1813–July 29, 1895), teacher of law and author of legal works, brother of Lucian Minor [*q.v.*], was the ninth and youngest child of Lancelot and Mary Overton (Tompkins) Minor, and a descendant of Maindort Doodes, a Dutch mariner, and his son Doodes Minor, who were naturalized in Virginia in 1673. He was born at "Minor's Folly," Louisa County, Va., and after attending local schools and spending a year at Kenyon College, Gambier, Ohio, in 1831 he entered the University of Virginia. Augmenting his slender resources by tutoring, he remained three years, received diplomas from several academic schools, and graduated in law. Admitted to the bar, he practised about six years in Buchanan, Botetourt County, demonstrating his industry, painstaking care, and veneration for the common law, qualities which were to distinguish him later.

Returning to Charlottesville, he continued practice until 1845, when, at thirty-two, despite strong opposition because of his youth and comparative obscurity, he was appointed professor of law in the University of Virginia, the fourth to occupy that chair. He immediately raised the law school's standards and made graduation more difficult; the enrollment steadily increased. Like his predecessors, he taught the law unaided, from 1845 to 1851 and again during the Civil War. His system of instruction was that of searching analysis, based on the methods of Hale and Blackstone. Exquisite in diction, remarkably clear in exposition, wealthy in illustration, rising almost to eloquence, his lectures aroused the enthusiasm of the most indifferent of his students and stimulated the dullest minds. His zealous and almost fanatical love for the common law led him to oppose every contemplated change therein—his only defect, perhaps, as a teacher and author. Preëminent in legal education, he established the high position of the law school of the University of Virginia among American law schools. Originally a Union man, deeming secession neither wise nor warranted under the Constitution, he supported Virginia's course, however, as "necessary revolution," her only possible self-respecting reply to Lincoln's call for troops. In March 1865 when Sheridan passed through Charlottesville from his devastating Valley campaign, Minor, aided by Prof. Socrates Maupin, secured safe-guards from the Union commanders, thereby saving the University from pillage and possible destruction. After Appomattox, again with Maupin, he borrowed money on his personal credit to prepare for the session of 1865–66. From 1870 until his death he conducted a private summer law class —an early experiment in summer instruction. In 1875 he began publication of the *Institutes of Common and Statute Law* (1875–95), a monumental contribution to American jurisprudence. An outgrowth of blackboard analyses of his courses in common and statute law, it went through many editions, was cited in all American courts, and still remains an authority. He was also the author of *The Virginia Report 1799–1800* (1850) and an *Exposition of the Law of Crimes and Punishments* (1894).

Despite honorary degrees he preferred to be called simply "Mr. Minor," abjuring even the title "Professor" because of its misuse. His energy was amazing and his industry untiring. Although he was strong-tempered and positive to dogmatism, his character was mellowed with gentleness. He was deeply religious, intolerantly hating moral obliquity but having compassion for the transgressor. Long a vestryman in the Episcopal church, he held family prayers daily, superintended an ante-bellum Sunday school for slaves, taught a students' Bible class, and powerfully championed the temperance movement. Six feet tall and well proportioned, he had a dignity of presence that was the embodiment of strength, wisdom, and virtue. He married: first, Martha Macon Davis; following her death, Anne Jacqueline Fisher Colston; and after the latter's death, Ellen Temple Hill. He had three children by his first wife, and five by the second, one of whom was Raleigh Colston Minor [*q.v.*]. On a bust presented by alumni to the University of Virginia a few weeks before he died, after fifty years of service, is inscribed: "He Taught the Law and the Reason Thereof."

[J. B. Minor, *The Minor Family of Va.* (1923); P. A. Bruce, *Hist. of the Univ. of Va. 1819–1919* (5 vols., 1920–22); P. B. Barringer and J. M. Garnett, eds., *Univ. of Va.* (1904), vol. I; *Va. Law Reg.*, Nov. 1895; *The Green Bag*, Sept. 1895; *Report of . . . Va. State Bar Asso.*, vol. IX (1896); *The Alumni Bull. of the*

Univ. of Va., July 1895, Feb. 1896; Univ. of Va. Mag., Nov. 1895; The Richmond Dispatch, July 30, 1895.]
T. S. C.

MINOR, LUCIAN (Apr. 24, 1802–July 8, 1858), temperance advocate, was born in Louisa County, Va., the son of Lancelot and Mary (Tompkins) Minor and the brother of John Barbee Minor [q.v.]. Plain Dutch ancestors, important and interesting Virginia family connections, and the simple atmosphere of a Piedmont farmer's home were his birthright. His earliest education was at the simple, rigorous school conducted by his father. Being poor in health as well as in purse the lad, for a while, drove the mail to Fredericksburg. Then he attended the Nelsons' classical school nearby and later taught school. A few months spent in studying law at the College of William and Mary enabled him to graduate in 1823. After a year or two in Alabama he settled as a lawyer in his home county. From 1828 to 1852 he was commonwealth's attorney for the county. The rough-and-tumble of law practice and of politics, however, did not appeal to him; he was modest, sternly moral, incapable of flattery or intrigue, and a poor judge of men; he liked to formulate his ideas independently and to state them with frankness in language suited to cultured ears. Accordingly in 1834 he toured New England on foot, making eager, keen, and unprejudiced observations and seeking the acquaintance of distinguished men, among whom Francis Wayland impressed him most favorably. In "Letters from New England" published in the Southern Literary Messenger (Nov. 1834–Apr. 1835) he set down his observations with literary skill and taste. Many years later parts of the journal on which the letters were based were printed by Lowell in the Atlantic Monthly ("A Virginian in New England Thirty-five Years Ago," Sept.–Dec. 1870, June 1871). He was impressed by New England's superiority in public spirit, social and civic organization, and comforts of living. In 1835 appeared also his Address of Education ... before the Institute of Education at Hampden-Sidney College (also printed in Southern Literary Messenger, Dec. 1835) in which he frankly pointed out the pauperizing tendencies of the Virginia public school system.

In 1830 he had spoken before a local temperance society to advocate wine and beer as substitutes for ardent spirits; in 1834 at the Charlottesville convention of temperance advocates he spoke out for total abstinence, having become convinced that this was the necessary basis of any broad temperance reform movement. There-

after the movement interested him most. In the extensive organization of the Sons of Temperance of the United States he was an enthusiastic officer, lecturer, and editorial supervisor; for it he wrote Reasons for Abolishing the Liquor Traffic (1853), 30,000 copies of which were distributed; and to him the order erected a monument in Williamsburg. Though he did not originate the Virginia prohibitory movement of the '40's and '50's, he prepared its legislative papers, served as chairman of its central committee, came nearest to effecting an organization of the counties behind it, and published in the Southern Literary Messenger of July 1850 "The Temperance Reformation in Virginia," a brief history of the movement. This activity was grounded on considerations of humanity and statesmanship rather than on religion, for until his latest years the practices of professed Christians deterred him from any examination of their principles. In 1855 he became professor of law in the College of William and Mary. Though his distinguished younger brother, John Barbee Minor [q.v.], believed him capable of rivaling Story and Tucker, his actual law writing was slight: an article on the civil duties of justices of the peace in John A. G. Davis' Treatise on Criminal Law (1838), a one-volume edition of Hening and Munford's Reports (1857), and an edition of the first three volumes of Call's Reports (1854). He was married on May 4, 1846, to Lavinia Callis Price. They had four children.

[J. R. Lowell, "A Virginian in New England," Atlantic Monthly, Aug. 1870, with autobiographical fragment and early journal; "Vita" in A. J. Morrison, Six Addresses on the State of Letters and Science in Va. (1917); Southern Literary Messenger, Sept. 1858; J. B. Minor, The Minor Family in Va. (copr. 1923); C. C. Pearson, unpublished manuscript "Liquor and Anti-Liquor in Va.," in possession of author; John B. Minor, Manuscript Sketch of Lucian Minor in private possession; information from Mrs. Farrell D. Minor, Beaumont, Texas.]
C. C. P.

MINOR, RALEIGH COLSTON (Jan. 24, 1869–June 14, 1923), author, publicist, teacher of law, was born at the University of Virginia, the son of John Barbee Minor [q.v.] and Anne Jacqueline Fisher (Colston). After studying under tutors and in private schools, he entered the University of Virginia in 1883 at the age of fourteen. He received his baccalaureate degree at eighteen, his master's degree one year later, and graduated in law in 1890. Following admission to the bar, he practised in Richmond for three years and then returned to the University of Virginia as assistant professor of law, being a colleague of his father. After the latter's death the son, in 1895, became adjunct professor and in 1899 was made professor. He taught for three decades, the overlapping teaching careers of father and son covering a period of seventy-eight years, a unique record of unbroken family service in the same school of the same university. His principal subjects were real property, constitutional law, conflict of laws, and international law. His book on *The Law of Real Property* appeared in 1908. Although based on the second volume of his father's *Institutes,* it was none the less an original work and became an outstanding authority in Virginia. In 1910, collaborating with Prof. John Wurts of Yale, he published a smaller edition dealing less with Virginia law and hence more suitable for use in other localities. He stands as one of America's three pioneers in the field of private international law or, as Justice Story named it, the conflict of laws. In 1901, at the age of thirty-two, he achieved international recognition by the publication of his *Conflict of Laws,* an American legal classic, which materially clarified the existing chaotic condition of that difficult branch of jurisprudence, and placed subsequent writers on the subject largely in his debt. For more than fifteen years, in addition to his classes in the University of Virginia, he delivered lectures on conflict of laws at Georgetown University. His last writing was *A Republic of Nations* (1918). Impressed by the tremendous failure of public opinion as a preventive of war and recognizing that any world tribunal would have jurisdiction over justiciable disputes only, whereas war results primarily from political questions, he deemed that the path to permanent peace lies in the formation of a union of nations to which its members would relinquish for joint administration their war-breeding political powers—the regulation of international commerce, the acquisition of territory, and the treatment of aliens. Written before the Armistice, his book was a thoughtful humanitarian's unequivocal and forward-looking contribution toward the solution of a baffling problem. Minor was also the author of *The Law of Tax Titles in Virginia* (1898) and *Notes on the Science of Government and the Relations of the States to the United States* (1913). A tranquil scholar and an imperturbable teacher, perhaps too calm and placid, he exacted a high standard of proficiency from his students, who respected him for his learning and loved him for his character. Courageous and happy in disposition, stanch and unyielding in principle, unworldly in viewpoint, he was an idealist as a writer, a teacher, and a man. An Episcopalian, he had a broad and tolerant religious outlook. He was modest to the extreme, although possessed of a marked yet unconscious

dignity. In 1897 he married Natalie Embra Venable, a daughter of Charles Scott Venable, a colonel in the Confederate army and professor of mathematics in the University of Virginia; two children were born to them. Devoted to the University, Minor labored actively for its advancement but steadfastly opposed co-education, coördination, and the general tendency to make it a standardized state university. The institution, indeed, was almost a part of him; there he was born and educated, there as childhood playmates he and his wife first met, there he spent his happy married life, there distinction came to him, there he died and is buried.

[J. B. Minor, *The Minor Family of Va.* (1923); P. A. Bruce, *Hist. of the Univ. of Va., 1819–1919,* vols. IV, V (1921–22); P. B. Barringer and J. M. Garnett, *Univ. of Va.* (1904), vol. II; *Univ. of Va. Alumni News,* June 1923; *Va. Law Rev.,* Dec. 1923, Feb. 1926; *Proc. . . . Va. State Bar Asso.,* vol. XXXV (1923); *Richmond Times-Dispatch,* June 15, 1923.]   T. S. C.

MINOR, ROBERT CRANNELL (Apr. 30, 1839–Aug. 3, 1904), landscape painter, born in New York, the son of Israel and Charlotte (Crannell) Minor, was a descendant of Thomas Minor (or Miner) who came to New England in 1629. Upon leaving school Robert worked for his father, who was a coal dealer, but after a brief experience he found that he had no taste for business, and decided to take up painting. He studied for two years under Alfred C. Howland in New York, then went to Antwerp, where he continued his training under H. Boulanger and Joseph Van Luppen. From Antwerp he turned to Paris, and after three years of experimentation there, joined the artists' colony at Barbizon, where he was fortunate enough to become the disciple of that brilliant colorist, Narcisse Diaz. This relationship proved to be the turning-point in his career; it determined the direction in which his work was to develop, and he became an avowed Barbizon man. Before returning to the United States he spent two years painting landscapes in the south of England. He exhibited "The Silent Lake" at the Paris Salon of 1872, and several landscapes at the Royal Academy and the Grosvenor Gallery in London. Most of his English subjects were found in the Wold of Kent. So many of his works had appeared in the current exhibitions in America during his long absence that he found himself already well known when he returned and set up his easel in the old University Building, Washington Square, New York. In the exhibition of the Society of American Artists, 1878, he had several pictures, among them "The Studio of Corot," which was a delicate early-morning effect not wholly unlike the work of Corot himself. He was made a National Academician in 1897; and served as president of the Salmagundi Club in 1898. While a student in Antwerp he had been vice-president of the Société Artistique et Littéraire; and he was a member of several other artistic associations. His New York clubs were the Lotos and the National Arts. The Lotos Club purchased one of his paintings from the National Academy Exhibition of 1896.

One of his favorite sketching grounds for several seasons was Keene Valley in the Adirondacks, and other places in northern New York attracted him for a time, but his final choice was Waterford, Conn., not far from New London, where he did much of his best and ripest work, and where he died. He had married Isabel Smith in 1860, and a son and a daughter survived him. Soon after his death a collection of 109 of his pictures were exhibited and sold at the American Art Galleries, New York (1905), bringing a total of $35,190. Emerson McMillin bought nine works, including "The End of Summer," for which he paid $1,200. This noble composition, with its fine old trees and luminous sky, reminds the observer in a vague way of both Ruysdael and Rousseau. McMillin was also the owner of "Sunrise," while "Eventide" belongs to the Corcoran Gallery, Washington, D. C. No American landscapist, with the possible exception of George Inness, has drawn so much inspiration from the Fontainebleau group of French masters as Minor. His body of work forms a handsome memorial to the great tradition of French nineteenth-century landscape painting. He had thoroughly assimilated the ways and means of his master, Diaz, had much of the same instinctive sense of color, and composed with the same pictorial dignity and distinction.

[*Biog. Sketches of Am. Artists* (Mich. State Lib., 1924); *Am. Art Annual*, 1905–06; Wm. Cothren, *Hist. of Ancient Woodbury, Conn.* (1854), I; *Who's Who in America*, 1903–05; Cat. of sale exhibit of R. C. Minor's works, 1905; *The Private Coll. of Foreign and Am. Paintings formed by E. McMillin* (1913); *Catalogue of the Thos. B. Clarke Coll. of Am. Pictures* (1891); *N. Y. Evening Mail*, Mar. 8, 1878; *N. Y. Times*, Aug. 4, 5, 1904.]   W. H. D—s.

MINOR, VIRGINIA LOUISA (Mar. 27, 1824–Aug. 14, 1894), woman suffragist, was born in Goochland County, Va., the daughter of Warner and Maria (Timberlake) Minor. Her father, a first cousin of Lucian and John B. Minor [*qq.v.*], was a descendant of Maindort Doodes, a Dutch mariner, and his son, Doodes Minor, who became naturalized citizens of Virginia in 1673. Except for a short period of study in the academy for young ladies at Charlottes-

ville, Va., the greater part of her education was received at home. She was noted in these early years, as she continued to be, for her personal charm and beauty. On Aug. 31, 1843, she was married to Francis Minor, a relative, who was a graduate of Princeton and the University of Virginia, and a lawyer by profession. For a year they lived in Mississippi and then moved to St. Louis. During the Civil War Mrs. Minor was actively engaged in welfare and relief work among the sick and wounded in the hospitals of the St. Louis area. To the depression and sorrow which the war brought to her, was added, in 1866, the grief occasioned by the accidental death of her only child, Francis Gilmer, then fourteen years of age.

She had long been keenly interested in politics and public affairs, and soon after the war she became active in the movement to raise the status of women in America. She was convinced that the extension of the suffrage to women was essential to the accomplishment of this object, which conviction was enthusiastically shared by her husband. In 1866 she launched the woman-suffrage movement in Missouri, and early in the following year she took a leading part in the organization of the Woman Suffrage Association of Missouri—the first organization in the world to make its exclusive aim that of enfranchising women—of which she was elected president. At the woman-suffrage convention held at St. Louis in 1869, she made a militant speech, urging women no longer to submit to their inferior condition. A set of resolutions, drafted by her husband, asserting the right of woman suffrage under the national Constitution was adopted. On Oct. 15, 1872, as "a native-born, free white citizen of the United States, and of the State of Missouri, . . . over the age of twenty-one years," she made her famous claim to the right to vote and presented herself for registration. Reese Happersett, the registrar of voters, refused to place her name on the list because "she was not a 'male' citizen, but a woman." In association with her husband (since the status of a woman under the common law made it impossible for her to bring suit independently of him), she sued for damages in the circuit court at St. Louis. The decision was against the plaintiffs. On appeal to the supreme court of Missouri, the court unanimously upheld the decision. The case was carried to the Supreme Court of the United States, and Francis Minor was one of the attorneys who presented arguments. In giving the unanimous opinion of the court in upholding the Missouri decisions, Chief Justice Waite centered his elaborate argument around two main propositions; first, that "if the courts can consider any question settled, this is one"; and second, that "the Constitution of the United States does not confer the right of suffrage upon any one" (21 *Wallace,* 177, 178). While the congenitally feeble legal case was lost, the publicity accompanying it no doubt contributed to the victory which came later. In 1889 she appeared before the Senate committee on woman suffrage to reiterate her stock arguments. Her last office was an honorary vice-presidency of the Interstate Woman Suffrage Convention, held at Kansas City in 1892. Two years later she was buried in Bellefontaine cemetery in St. Louis with religious solemnity but, of her own choice, without an officiating clergyman, since she had long regarded the clergy as hostile to the great mission of her life.

[E. C. Stanton, S. B. Anthony, and M. J. Gage, *Hist. of Woman Suffrage,* vol. II (1882); Wm. Hyde and H. L. Conard, *Encyc. of the Hist. of St. Louis* (1899), vol. IV; M. S. Scott, "Hist. of Woman Suffrage in Mo.," in *Mo. Hist. Rev.,* Apr.–July 1920; *Minor vs. Happersett,* 53 *Mo.,* 58, and 21 *Wallace,* 162 (1874); *The St. Louis Republic,* Aug. 16, 1894, p. 7; J. B. Minor, *The Minor Family of Va.* (copr. 1923); unpublished family genealogy by Minor Meriwether.]
A. J. L.

MINOT, CHARLES SEDGWICK (Dec. 23, 1852–Nov. 19, 1914), biologist and educator, was the son of William Minot, "a well-to-do Boston lawyer," and Katharine Maria Sedgwick, grand-daughter of Theodore Sedgwick and a descendant of Jonathan Edwards. "He was born not merely a Bostonian, but a legendary Bostonian" (Porter, *post,* p. 467). Forsaking the legal traditions of his family, at the age of sixteen, he appeared before the Boston Society of Natural History with descriptions of new species of butterflies, and had elected to study at the Massachusetts Institute of Technology where entrance was easy and the curriculum congenial. With the Technology B.S. in 1872, he could enter the graduate school of Harvard College as a candidate for the S.D. degree in natural history. That degree he obtained in 1878 after six years of very independent studies. Part of this time was spent as the first research pupil of his lifelong friend, Henry P. Bowditch, in the physiological laboratory of the Harvard Medical School; and part abroad with Ludwig, Leuckart, and His at Leipzig, Semper at Würzburg, and Ranvier at Paris. Publications in British, French, and German journals, divided between reports of physiological experiments and studies of the miscroscopic structure of invertebrates, served as his doctor's thesis. He had acquired new insight into the aims of the naturalist and the method of science.

Two years later, minor appointments in the Harvard Medical School were "procured for him with some difficulty" (Eliot, *post,* p. 89), for he was not a doctor of medicine, and agreed with Semper that doctors are "spoilt zoologists." He remained on the Harvard faculty until his death. Medical education in America had reached its lowest ebb, but the tide was turning. Minot, eager for improvement, said of American schools, "there prevails the miserable delusion that they are good." He was a reformer. Though reserved and aristocratic, "he pursued his ends with clear-sighted intensity and indomitable persistence," often finding it "hard to see that his opponent had some reason on his side" (Eliot, *post,* p. 91). Limiting his investigations to human embryology, Minot published in 1892 a monumental *résumé* of that subject— *Human Embryology,* 815 pages—which soon appeared in German translation. Through his *Laboratory Text-book of Embryology* (1903; 2nd ed. 1910) he introduced the general use of pig embryos as the best laboratory substitute for those of man. He invented widely used forms of microtomes, and made a large and very methodical collection of prepared sections of embryos—the prototype of similar collections in other universities. His plan for a great embryological institute at Harvard led quite directly to the founding of the Carnegie Laboratory of Embryology in Baltimore. His prolonged studies comprehended in *The Problem of Age, Growth, and Death* (New York, 1908; Japanese translation, Tokyo, 1915) were a search into the fundamental nature of senility. His recognition of a special type of "sinusoidal" circulation, in which the blood bathes closely the glandular substance, proves to be of fundamental importance. "Not only by his original researches, by his masterly books and by his fine addresses and lectures, but in countless other ways he helped his fellow-workers in science" (Cattell, *post,* p. 59); and in recognition thereof he received a full professorship at Harvard (1892) and honorary doctorates from Yale, Oxford, Toronto, and St. Andrews. He was married, on June 1, 1889, to Lucy Fosdick of Groton, Mass. He died without issue. In Mall's critical judgment "Minot has done more than any other American to add dignity to the career of anatomy."

[Biographical sketches of Minot, by his associates, and minutes concerning him, include the following: Frederic T. Lewis, *Boston Medic. and Surgic. Jour.,* Dec. 10, 1914, pp. 911–14; Henry H. Donaldson, *Science,* Dec. 25, 1914, pp. 926–27; Minute by Prof. Cattell for the Am. Asso. for the Advancement of Science, *Science,* Jan. 8, 1915, p. 59; Minute by Professor Huntington for the Am. Asso. of Anatomists, *Anatomical Record,* Jan. 1915, pp. 42–43; C. Frank Allen, *Technology Rev.,* Jan. 1915, pp. 91–95; Henry H. Donaldson and Charles W. Eliot, Addresses before the Boston Soc. of Natural Hist., Mar. 17, 1915, in the *Proceedings*, vol. XXXV, pp. 79–93, portrait, President Eliot's address being also in *Science*, May 14, 1915, pp. 701–04; John L. Bremer, *Harvard Grads'. Mag.*, Mar. 1915, pp. 374–78; W. T. Porter, *Boston Medic. and Surgic. Jour.*, Apr. 1, 1915, pp. 467–70; Frederic T. Lewis, *Anatomical Record*, Jan. 1916, pp. 133–64, portrait and bibliography; W. T. Councilman, *Proc. Am. Acad. Arts and Sci.*, vol. LIII, Sept. 1918, pp. 840–47; Edward S. Morse, *Nat. Acad. Sci. Biog. Memoirs*, vol. IX (1920), pp. 263–85, portrait and bibliography.]   F. T. L.

MINOT, GEORGE RICHARDS (Dec. 22, 1758–Jan. 2, 1802), jurist and historian, was born in Boston, Mass., the youngest of the ten children of Stephen Minot, a Boston merchant, A. B. Harvard, 1730, and Sarah Clark, daughter of Jonas Clark, of Boston. The Minots were early associated with Dorchester, George Minot, son to Thomas Minot of Saffron Walden, in Essex, England, having emigrated to Massachusetts and been admitted freeman of the town in 1634. According to the Rev. James Freeman, who wrote a memoir of the historian, Minot's father was "educated" and his mother "affectionate," and the "intermediate ancestors were gentlemen of respectable characters." The chief influence on his youth seems to have been the good example of his brother, Francis, who died in 1774, at the age of twenty-eight. In 1767 Minot entered the South Latin School in Boston, where his diligence, discretion, and decorum soon made him the favorite pupil of his teacher, John Lovell. In July 1774 he matriculated at Harvard and attracted the attention of his tutor, John Wadsworth, by his amiable manners and his love of books. When Wadsworth died in 1777 at the early age of thirty-seven, Minot established a reputation as a public speaker with the funeral oration he was selected to deliver. As a consequence, he was chosen to pronounce the valedictory address at the time he took his "second-degree" (A.M.) in July 1781. Years later, Minot noted in his Journal for January 1800, on the occasion of his speech on the death of Washington: "A whole edition of my Eulogy sold in a day."

On receiving his degree of A.B. in July 1778, Minot entered the law office of William Tudor, through whose influence he was appointed in 1781 clerk of the Massachusetts House of Representatives in the first Great and General Court which met after the adoption of the new constitution in 1780. From Jan. 9 to Feb. 7, 1788, he served as secretary of the convention called to consider the ratification of the Federal Constitution. As a result of his conspicuous success in both these offices, he was appointed judge of probate for the County of Suffolk in January 1792. He had already made his mark as the his-

torian of Shays's Rebellion. *The History of the Insurrection in Massachusetts in the Year Seventeen Hundred and Eighty-Six and the Rebellion Consequent Thereon* was first published in Worcester in 1788. A second edition was brought out in Boston in 1810. The reception of this volume encouraged Minot to begin a continuation of the history of Massachusetts from the point at which Thomas Hutchinson had left off. The first volume of his *Continuation of the History of the Province of Massachusetts Bay, from the Year 1748* was published at Boston in February 1798—four introductory chapters containing a survey of the period from 1630 to the Treaty of Aix-la-Chapelle. A second volume, carrying events through 1765, was published posthumously in June 1803. John Adams, who was "not satisfied with Hutchinson, though his work is valuable" (quoted, Freeman, *post,* p. 101), praised Minot's performance in a letter written from Philadelphia, Feb. 28, 1798. Just as he was completing his second volume, Minot died suddenly in Boston.

Besides being a member of the Amicable Fire Society and president of the Massachusetts Charitable Fire Society, Minot was one of the original ten members of the Massachusetts Historical Society, founded in 1791, and served the organization as librarian, 1793–95, and treasurer, 1796–99. Although his politics took color from his associates and circumstances, his history of Shays's Rebellion is by no means unreasonably hostile. His style was modeled on what already in college had become his favorite reading: Robertson, and Burke's contributions to the *Annual Register.* New methods of scholarship were to supplant his *Continuation* by the middle of the nineteenth century, and he did not live to cover that portion of the history of Massachusetts which he could have narrated at first hand. The reproduction of his portrait (*Proceedings of the Massachusetts Historical Society,* 1 ser., vol. I, 1879, facing p. 42) shows Minot to have been a man of distinguished, if not handsome, appearance, the only fault of whose character, according to a friend, was "a temper by nature irascible" (Freeman, *post,* p. 88). The eulogy John Quincy Adams delivered before the Massachusetts Charitable Fire Society, May 28, 1802, was long and enthusiastic. For ten years (1789–99) he was in almost constant correspondence with Fisher Ames. Minot married Mary Speakman, by whom he had one son, George Richards Minot, and a daughter.

[Jas. Freeman, "Character of the Hon. Geo. Richards Minot . . .," and notes and selections from Minot's journal, *Mass. Hist. Soc. Colls.,* 1 ser. VIII (1802); *New-Eng. Hist. and Geneal. Reg.,* Apr., July 1847; the

Mass. Gazette (Boston), Feb. 8, 1788; the *Polyanthos* (Boston), Mar. 1806; the *Boston Gazette*, Jan. 4, 7, 1802; the *Columbian Centinel and Mass. Federalist*, Jan. 6, 20, 1802.]   S. M—l.

MINTO, WALTER (Dec. 5, 1753–Oct. 21, 1796), mathematician, was born in Cowdenham, County Merse, Scotland. His family was of Spanish origin and had once had rank but his parents were very poor. He was given a sufficiently good schooling, however, and was attending the University of Edinburgh at the age of fifteen. Hume was then teaching there. At the wishes of his parents and friends he studied theology, living during this time with a Mr. Watson in Perthshire, and occupying his leisure time with writing verse and humorous articles for the magazines. He planned to go to Italy as a pilgrim, begging his way, but Hume recommended him as tutor to two boys, the sons of George Johnstone, formerly the governor of West Florida and member of the British Parliament, and Minto sailed for Italy with the boys. There they established themselves in the home of Giuseppe Slop, a professor of astronomy in the University of Pisa. On Mar. 13, 1781, William Herschel discovered the planet Uranus and Minto was in Pisa when the exciting discovery was announced in the papers of Florence. He reported that in May 1781 he and the Italian professor saw the planet "in an excellent reflecting telescope." Two years later Minto published his treatise, *Researches into Some Parts of the Theory of the Planets* (London, 1783), containing mathematical formulae dealing with the determination of astronomical magnitudes and also observational data concerning the new planet made by a number of observers. At the time the treatise was written the new planet had not been named Uranus and Minto suggested the name Minerva "because, being a telescopic star, it may be said to denote the modesty of the Goddess of Wisdom."

Following his return to Edinburgh he became a teacher of mathematics. He had considerable correspondence with the philosophers of England, wrote several papers on astronomy, and collaborated with D. S. Erskine, Earl of Buchan, in *An Account of the Life, Writings, and Inventions of John Napier of Merchiston* (Edinburgh, 1787), supporting Napier's claim as the inventor of logarithms. Having warmly supported the cause of American independence, in 1786 he sailed for America and soon afterward became the principal of Erasmus Hall at Flatbush, Long Island. In 1787 he was called to the College of New Jersey to succeed Ashbel Green [*q.v.*] as professor of mathematics and

natural philosophy. His fellow countryman, Dr. John Witherspoon, was president of the college and Minto had heard favorably of the institution. He was given a salary of £200 per year, including room and board in Nassau Hall. His inaugural oration, "On the Progress and Importance of the Mathematical Sciences," presented on the evening before the annual commencement in 1788, was subsequently published. Shortly after his arrival President Witherspoon wrote to the Earl of Buchan expressing his approval of Minto. He became treasurer of the college and wrote his textbook of mathematics, which was in manuscript at the time of his death. He was married to Mary Skelton of Princeton. They had no children. He died in October 1796, at the age of forty-two, and was buried in the Princeton cemetery.

[The principal source is the article, "Walter Minto, LL.D.," in the *Princeton Mag.*, Mar. 1850. See also V. L. Collins, *President Witherspoon, a Biog.* (1925), vol. II; and J. F. Hageman, *Hist. of Princeton and its Institutions* (2 vols., 1879).]   L. P. E.

MINTURN, ROBERT BOWNE (Nov. 16, 1805–Jan. 9, 1866), merchant, was born to the purple in New York social and commercial circles and went even farther in both fields, winning general respect for his philanthropic as well as his business success. His grandfather, the elder William Minturn, had moved a profitable business from Newport to New York. His father, William Minturn, Jr., who married Sarah Bowne, was a partner in the firm of Minturn, Champlin & Company, which was prominent until its failure at the close of the War of 1812. Robert was forced to go into business at thirteen upon the death of his father. In 1825 he became the partner of Charles Green, whom he had served as clerk, and in 1829 he entered the counting-house of Fish, Grinnell & Company, a connection probably traceable to the marriage of his sister Sarah to Henry Grinnell in 1822. This firm had been established about 1815 by Preserved Fish and Joseph Grinnell [*qq.v.*] from New Bedford. Starting as commission merchants for whale oil, the firm expanded into the management of transatlantic packets, ship-owning, and general commerce. By 1832 the two original partners retired and the firm was reorganized as Grinnell, Minturn & Company, Minturn joining with Joseph Grinnell's younger brothers, Moses Hicks and Henry [*qq.v.*].

Under its new name the firm attained a secure position as one of the greatest of the New York commercial houses, ranking with the Griswolds, Howlands, and Lows. "All is fish that gets into their nets," wrote Scoville about 1860 (*post*, I,

Minty — Minuit

p. 100). In Latin America they were behind the Howlands, though their Cuban business was so extensive that Minturn sent his son to Spain to learn the language. In China they competed successfully with the houses of Griswold and Low which virtually specialized in that trade. They did a great deal of business with England and extended their influence into almost all parts of the world. They seem to have shared with the Welds of Boston the honor of being the greatest American ship-owners of the day. Their blue and white or red and white swallowtail house flags flew over more than fifty vessels, including regular packet lines to Liverpool and London as well as some of the finest clippers of the day. They owned the *North Wind* and *Sea Serpent* and above all, the greatest of the clippers, Donald McKay's *Flying Cloud*.

Minturn's fortune was estimated at $200,000 as early as 1846. He and his partners were more public spirited than many of the other New York merchants of the day. He himself served as commissioner of emigration to improve the condition of the incoming foreigners and was instrumental in founding the Association for Improving the Condition of the Poor, and St. Luke's Hospital. His wife was Anna Mary Wendell, the daughter of John Lansing Wendell of Albany, whom he married on June 2, 1835. She has been credited with the idea of establishing Central Park and he supported her in the project. At first a Whig, Minturn was later a Republican and was first president of the Union League Club. He has been described, like others of his family, as dark, tall, and handsome. George William Curtis pictured him as "gentle, just and generous; modest, humane and sagacious; his sense of responsibility growing with his increasing fortune, until his devoted life was that of a humble almoner of the Divine bounty" (*Harper's Weekly*, Jan. 27, 1866). He died suddenly of paralysis at his New York home.

[The sources for Minturn's biography are fragmentary. See R. B. Minturn, Jr., *Memoir of Robert Bowne Minturn* (1871); J. A. Scoville, *The Old Merchants of N. Y. City* (4 vols., 1863–66); *The Diary of Philip Hone* (2 vols., 1927), ed. by Allan Nevins; Henry Hall, *America's Successful Men of Affairs*, vol. I (1895); L. H. Weeks, *Prominent Families of N. Y.*, vol. I (1897); F. G. Griswold, *The House Flags of the Merchants of N. Y., 1800–1860* (1926); O. T. Howe and F. C. Matthews, *Am. Clipper Ships* (2 vols., 1927); M. Y. Beach, *Wealth and Pedigree of the Wealthy Citizens of N. Y.* (1846); *N. Y. Times, N. Y. Tribune*, Jan. 10, 1866.]   R. G. A.

MINTY, ROBERT HORATIO GEORGE (Dec. 4, 1831–Aug. 24, 1906), soldier, railroad official, was born in County Mayo, Ireland, son of a British officer. He served under his father as ensign in the British army (1849–53) in Africa, Honduras, and the West Indies. In 1853 he emigrated to Michigan and upon the outbreak of the Civil War entered military service. Within a few months he had been commissioned major, 2nd Michigan Cavalry, lieutenant-colonel, 3rd Michigan Cavalry, and colonel, 4th Michigan Cavalry (July 31, 1862). During 1863–64 he brilliantly commanded a cavalry unit known as the Sabre Brigade (*Battles and Leaders of the Civil War*, vol. IV, 1888, p. 413) and led a division in General Kilpatrick's raid around the city of Atlanta, being promoted brigadier-general of volunteers in 1864. Subsequently, in Wilson's final raids through Alabama and Georgia, he commanded a division in the march upon Macon (*Ibid.*, p. 761). A noteworthy incident of his service during this period was his participation in the capture of President Jefferson Davis, and the latter's confinement at Fortress Monroe.

Minty received the brevets of brigadier-general and major-general of volunteers (Mar. 13, 1865) for gallant and meritorious services, and on two different occasions received the thanks of Congress. He declined proffer of a majority in the regular army and was mustered out of the military service, Aug. 15, 1865. Of his services and character, Gen. James H. Wilson wrote: "He was an educated soldier of great intelligence and enterprise. . . . He was in every respect a modest and obedient officer, an excellent disciplinarian, and as good a leader as Murat himself" (*Under the Old Flag*, 1912, II, pp. 171–72). After the close of the war he became general manager of the Elizabethtown and Paducah Railroad, making his home at Elizabethtown, Ky., and later was connected in various capacities with railroad administration in the West and Southwest. He passed away in 1906 at Jerome, Ariz., and was interred at Ogden, Utah. Twice married, he was survived by his second wife, Laura Abbott Minty, to whom he had been married at Maysville, Ky., on May 14, 1871, and by three children.

[See H. M. Cist, *The Army of the Cumberland* (1882); J. G. Vale, *Minty and the Cavalry* (1886); J. C. O'Connell, *The Irish in the Revolution and the Civil War* (1903); *Hist. Colls., Pioneer Soc. of the State of Mich.*, vol. XXVI (1896); *Detroit Free Press*, Oct. 9, 1896. Information as to certain facts was supplied by Minty's son, Courtney Abbott Minty, Tucson, Ariz.]   C. D. R.

MINUIT, PETER (1580–1638), director-general of New Netherland and governor of New Sweden, was born at Wesel, then in the Duchy of Cleves. The spelling Minnewit reflects the Dutch pronunciation of his name. He himself gave it the sound of the French *minuit*,

33

and he bore a bat, as an emblem of midnight, in his coat of arms (Memorandum book of Arend van Buchel, *Rijksarchief,* The Hague). Moreover, in the earliest Dutch record that refers to him, he is called not Peter but Pierre Minuit. He was therefore probably of French or Walloon descent, but in his letters he employed the Dutch language, which he wrote without fault except for occasional lapses into German orthography. According to the Rev. Jonas Michaëlius, Minuit served as a deacon in the Dutch Church at Wesel. In the civil records of Wesel it is recorded on Apr. 15, 1625, that he had left for foreign parts. The capture of Wesel by the Spaniards in the previous year had probably driven him to Holland. From there he sailed for the Dutch colony of New Netherland, perhaps on the same ship with Willem Verhulst, the Company's provisional director of the new settlement. He is mentioned in 1625 among the members of the Director's Council, but he must have returned to Holland before the end of the year, for he was on board *Het Meeuwtje* (The Little Gull), which sailed from The Texel on Jan. 9, 1626, and arrived at the mouth of the Hudson on May 4, 1626.

Minuit returned to Manhattan in a minor capacity, possibly that of supercargo. Verhulst, at that time, was still at the head of the colony. On Sept. 23, 1626, however, the latter was sent back to Holland, having been deposed by the Council of New Netherland, which appointed Peter Minuit his successor. Minuit had evidently not intended to stay in Manhattan, for he had left his wife in Holland; it was only after his appointment that he sent for her to join him. He was the first to be officially designated as director-general. One of his first acts in his new capacity was the purchase of Manhattan Island from the Indian sachems for trinkets valued at sixty gilders ($24). By this transaction the accomplished fact of occupation acquired a semblance of legality which the West India Company was eager to lend to its enterprise. Little is known about Minuit's administration, owing to the disappearance of the Company's records. When the fort was completed according to Crijn Fredericksen's plans, Minuit made New Amsterdam the rallying point of the isolated settlements north and south of Manhattan; he brought eight families down the river from Fort Orange, leaving a garrison there of sixteen men under Bastiaen Jansen Krol, and ordered Fort Nassau on the South River, near the present site of Gloucester, N. J., to be evacuated and the garrison to be transferred to New Amsterdam. When, in 1628, the Rev. Jonas Michaëlius began church services in the fort, Minuit and his brother-in-law Jan Huyghen, the Company's storekeeper, consented to serve as elders. In 1627 he started diplomatic relations with Governor Bradford and opened trade with the Plymouth colonists. The peaceful relations with his English neighbor lasted longer than those with the Dutch Reformed ministers, who, instead of trying to mediate in the quarrel between Minuit and the secretary, Johan van Remunde, stirred up the fire of discord.

In 1631 the Amsterdam Chamber of the West India Company recalled the director-general for examination. Minuit, together with Remunde, sailed in the *Eendracht* (Concord), a fitting conveyance for the pair. Minuit's examination lasted for several months and resulted in his dismissal from the Company's service, whereas Johan van Remunde was allowed to return to his post. In 1635 Minuit was living in Emmerich, in the Duchy of Cleves, as appears from a letter of Samuel Blommaert, a director of the West India Company, to the Swedish chancellor Axel Oxenstierna, recommending him as the very man to conduct successfully an expedition that was to plant a Swedish colony on Delaware Bay. In January 1637, at a meeting at The Hague between Blommaert, Minuit, and Spiering, a representative of Swedish interests in Holland, it was decided to establish a Swedish company for the purpose of trading to the American coast from Florida to Terra Nova and of establishing a colony there. The capital needed was fixed at 24,000 guilders, one-eighth of which was supplied by Minuit himself.

Late in the fall of 1637, Minuit sailed from Göteborg in the *Key of Calmar,* which was accompanied by the yacht *The Griffin.* In March 1638 they arrived at the mouth of the South River, or Delaware. They sailed up the Minquas Kill, concluded on Mar. 29 a contract with the chiefs of the Indians, who sold them a tract of land on the right bank of the Delaware, and Minuit, having erected the arms of the Queen of Sweden, in the presence of the sachems, gave the country the name of New Sweden. He christened the Minquas Kill the Elbe, and here he built Fort Christina, on the site of the present city of Wilmington. Willem Kieft, his successor at New Amsterdam, sent Minuit a protest which the latter ignored. As soon as Fort Christina was completed, Minuit left Måns Kling in charge of it and sailed in the *Key of Calmar* for the island of St. Christopher. Here he exchanged his cargo for tobacco. While he was paying a visit to the captain of *Het Vliegende Hert* (The Flying Stag), a Rotterdam merchantman, a hurricane swept the coast and the ship was lost in the storm. Thus Minuit's career came to a sudden end. If we must believe Michaëlius, he was "a slippery fellow who, under the painted mask of honesty, was a compound of all iniquity and wickedness." But in view of Blommaert's high opinion of his protégé, there is reason to believe that what the dominie took for a mask was the man's own face. He was, perhaps, not over-scrupulous, and a man of coarser fiber than the scholarly preacher, but courage, self-reliance, determination, and shrewdness were not lacking in his nature.

[*Documents Relating to New Netherland, 1624–26,* in the Henry E. Huntington Library (1924) and *N. Y. State Lib. Van Rensselaer Bowier Manuscripts* (1908), trans. and ed. by A. J. F. van Laer; E. B. O'Callaghan, *Documents Relative to the Colonial Hist. of the State of N. Y.,* vol. I (1856); *Ecclesiastical Records: State of N. Y.,* vol. I (1901); *Narratives of New Netherland, 1609–64* (1909), ed. by J. Franklin Jameson; *Narratives of Early Pa., West N. J., and Del., 1630–1707* (1912), ed. by A. C. Myers; I. N. P. Stokes, *The Iconography of Manhattan Island* (6 vols., 1915–28); G. W. Kernkamp, "Brieven van Samuel Blommaert aan den Zweedschen Rijkskanselier Axel Oxenstierna, 1635–1641," *Bijdragen en Mededeelingen van het Historisch Genootschap,* vol. XXIX (1908); Albert Eekhof, *Jonas Michaëlius, Founder of the Church in New Netherland* (Leyden, 1926); L. P. Boer, "Peter Minuit," *N. Y. Geneal. and Biog. Record,* Jan. 1928; Friedrich Kapp, "Peter Minnewit aus Wesel," *Historische Zeitschrift,* vol. XV (1866); Amandus Johnson, *The Swedish Settlements on the Delaware* (1911), vol. I.]
A. J. B—w.

MIRÓ, ESTEBAN RODRÍGUEZ (1744–1795), Spanish governor of Louisiana, was born in Catalonia. He entered the Spanish army as a cadet at the age of sixteen and took part in the campaign of 1762 against Portugal. During the American Revolution he served in the West Florida campaigns as first aide-de-camp to Bernardo de Gálvez [*q.v.*], and was rewarded with promotion to the rank of colonel and command of the regular Louisiana regiment. When Gálvez left Louisiana in 1782, Miró was made acting governor. Upon Gálvez's promotion to viceroy of New Spain, Miró's appointment was made permanent by a commission dated Aug. 19, 1785. The commandants of Mobile and Pensacola and the governor of Natchez were subordinated to him. In 1789 he was promoted to the rank of brigadier-general. On the retirement of the intendant of Louisiana, Martin Navarro, the intendancy was combined with the governorship (May 10, 1788), and Miró discharged the duties of both offices until Dec. 30, 1791, when he was succeeded by the Baron de Carondelet [*q.v.*]. Returning to Spain, he defended himself successfully against various charges, one of which was that, under cover of the intrigue with James Wilkinson [*q.v.*], he had for several years made an annual profit of $2,000 by the purchase of

Kentucky tobacco (Archivo Histórico Nacional, Madrid, *Consejo de Indias, residencia* of Miró). He was promoted to the rank of *mariscal de campo* shortly before his death, which occurred in Spain.

His administration was filled with alarms caused by disputes with the United States and its frontiersmen. His conduct with respect to these was not so aggressive, independent, or venal as it has sometimes been described. Toward the Southern Indians, whom he sought to control through Alexander McGillivray [*q.v.*] and Panton, Leslie & Company, his policy was purely defensive. In the Bourbon County episode (1785) and in his relations with the Georgia land companies (1790–91) he earnestly sought to avoid a rupture. His notorious intrigue with James Wilkinson was begun on the initiative of the latter and carried on (as were all his important affairs) under minute directions from Madrid. His encouragement of foreign immigration and partial opening of the Mississippi to the Western Americans was due not to bribery but to an explicit royal order of 1788. He gave Louisiana a mild and beneficent administration, encouraging commerce and agriculture, opposing the establishment of the Inquisition, and making every effort to restore New Orleans after the great fire of 1788. The construction of several notable public buildings was begun at this time.

His influence with the people of lower Louisiana was increased by his marriage to Céleste Eléonore Elizabeth Macarty, sprightly daughter of a wealthy creole family. In 1787 he asked that his salary of 4,000 pesos be increased, complaining that the high prices and lavish style of living at New Orleans had consumed most of her dowry of 16,000 pesos as well as his own savings. He spoke French and had some knowledge of English. It was rumored that his secretary did all his work for him, and in 1787 he thought it proper voluntarily to assure the colonial secretary that the rumor was unfounded. Vicente Folch, commandant of Mobile and Pensacola, was his nephew.

[Charles Gayarré, *Hist. of La.: The Spanish Domination* (1854), vol. III; Grace King, *Creole Families of New Orleans* (1921); *La. Hist. Quart.,* Jan., Oct. 1919; A. P. Whitaker, *The Spanish-American Frontier, 1783–1795* (1927); Alcée Fortier, *A Hist. of La.* (1904), vol. II; documents on Miró's relations to Spanish-American intrigues, in *Am. Hist. Rev.,* July 1904, Oct. 1909, Jan. 1910.]
A. P. W.

MITCHEL, JOHN (Nov. 3, 1815–Mar. 20, 1875), journalist, Irish nationalist, the son of the Rev. John and Mary (Haslett) Mitchel, was born at Camnish, County Londonderry, Ireland.

Mitchel

He is said to have graduated from Trinity College in 1834. After a brief period as a bank clerk he entered a solicitor's office and studied law. On Feb. 3, 1837, he married Jane Verner, and in 1840 he began to practise law in Newry. He did not become active in politics until 1845 when he joined the Young Ireland movement, a protest against O'Connell's policy of non-resistance. In the same year he became a member of the staff of the *Nation,* but in time he became dissatisfied, and when, in January 1847, the Irish Confederation was formed he founded the *United Irishmen* to advocate armed resistance to England and the repeal of the Union. He was arrested and in May 1848 a packed jury found him guilty of treason-felony and he was sentenced to fourteen years transportation. His remarkable speech from the dock was the culminating point in his career. After he had spent some months in Bermuda his failing health caused his transfer to Van Diemen's Land, from which he and his family, who had joined him in 1851, escaped in 1853. He was enthusiastically welcomed in San Francisco on Oct. 9, 1853, receiving a similar reception in New York on Nov. 29. Within two weeks he had conceived the plan of a newspaper. This was the *Citizen,* dedicated to the cause of Irish freedom, which began publication in New York on Jan. 7, 1854. The paper quickly attained a circulation of 50,000, but Mitchel's bluntness soon arrested its growth. In his controversy with Henry Ward Beecher [q.v.] he launched a bitter fight against the abolitionists and imprudently announced himself in favor of slavery. By writing against the temporal power of the pope he alienated a large group of Catholic readers and at the same time he antagonized the members of the Know-Nothing party. In the face of these disputes his enthusiasm for America sensibly diminished.

In 1854 he twice visited Virginia. His cordial receptions there determined him to settle in the South, and at the end of the year he gave up the *Citizen* and in the following spring settled on a farm at Tuckaleechee Cove, thirty-two miles from Knoxville, Tenn. He busied himself with farming and with extensive lecture tours. In the fall of 1856 he moved to Knoxville, where one year later he began to publish the *Southern Citizen,* an extremist paper devoted to the slavery interests. It survived almost two years; the second year it was published in Washington. In the midst of these labors Mitchel was still interested in Irish freedom, and when, in 1859, it appeared that France might declare war on Great Britain, he hastened to Paris. This was an idle quest, but in July 1860 he moved his family to Paris and became the French correspondent for several papers, among them the *Charleston Standard.* Late in 1862 he returned to New York, succeeded in reaching Virginia, and there his three sons joined the Confederate army while he edited the *Richmond Enquirer* and served on the ambulance committee of the Confederate army. In the spring of 1864 he broke his connections with Jefferson Davis and became editor of the *Examiner.* Early in 1865 he went to New York as editor of the *Daily News,* a Democratic paper actively opposed to the Grant administration. For his violent writings he was imprisoned more than four months in Fortress Monroe; from this imprisonment he never recovered his mental or physical powers. He spent the winter of 1865–66 in Paris as a Fenian agent, returning to Richmond to engage in literary work. He again returned to New York as editor of the *Irish Citizen,* published from Oct. 19, 1867, to July 27, 1872. Here he fought Grant and criticized the Fenian movement, which diminished the paper's circulation. During the winter of 1872–73 he wrote a series of articles attacking J. A. Froude's views on the Irish. He returned to Ireland for the last time in 1875. There, as a last gesture of defiance to the British government, he accepted election to Parliament, shortly after which he died.

During the period of his exile from Ireland Mitchel confessed that he was "truly dead and a ghost"; following his conviction in 1848 he did not actively participate, with one small exception, in any important Irish movement. He had much love of Ireland, but a far greater hatred of England, and his desire for vengeance against England motivated him throughout his life. His intense nationalism prevented his feeling any spirit of kinship with other men working in similar causes; for liberty in the abstract and humanity at large he cared nothing; Socialists he termed "worse than wild beasts," and for Communists, "unhappy creatures," he recommended "grape and cannister." He was neither poet nor dreamer, merely a hard-headed patriot who sought to combat British force with Irish violence. His present influence in Ireland is explained by the eloquence of his writings, especially his *Jail Journal* (1854) and *The Crusade of the Period: and Last Conquest of Ireland (Perhaps)* (1873).

[The standard biography is Wm. Dillon, *Life of John Mitchel* (2 vols., 1888). Consult also: the biography and lengthy bibliography in the *Dict. Nat. Biog.*; Émile Montégut, *John Mitchel: A Study of Irish Nationalism* (English translation, Dublin, 1915); P. S. O'Hegarty, *John Mitchel, an Appreciation* (Dublin, 1915); Ida A. Taylor, *Revolutionary Types* (London, 1904); and the *Sun* (N. Y.), Mar. 22, 1875.] F. M—n.

MITCHEL, JOHN PURROY (July 19, 1879–July 6, 1918), lawyer, mayor of New York City, was born and reared in Fordham, N. Y. He came of fighting Irish stock. His paternal grandfather was John Mitchel [*q.v.*]; his father, James Mitchel, served on the staff of Stonewall Jackson, then after the war moved his family to New York, where he served the city as fire marshal. The family of his mother, Mary Purroy, were prominent in anti-Tammany circles. Mitchel was educated in the public schools, pursued academic studies at St. John's College, and graduated from Columbia in 1899, having achieved a distinguished record in oratory and debate. In 1901 he graduated with honors from the New York Law School. His brief career at the bar, begun in partnership with George V. Mullan, was merely a prelude to spectacular political achievements. He first attracted public attention in 1906 through an appointment by Corporation Counsel Ellison as special investigator of the office of Borough President of Manhattan, John F. Ahearn. A political admirer described him at this time as "a gosling with the fuzz on him—lean, lank, long-necked and embarrassed. . . . But you ought to have seen him pitch in!" (*Collier's,* Aug. 25, 1917, p. 41). "Young Torquemada," as he was soon called, was also empowered to investigate Borough President Louis Haffen of the Bronx. His work was reviewed by Governor Hughes, who removed both officials. In 1909, as running-mate of Gaynor, he was elected president of the Board of Aldermen and served as acting mayor of the city during the chief executive's prolonged illness. In recognition of the exceptional administrative talent which Mitchel had demonstrated, President Wilson in May 1913 appointed him collector of the Port of New York, but the anti-Tammany forces drafted him almost at once as their candidate for the mayoralty, and he received the public support of the President (*New York Times,* July 31, 1913). Running on the issue of civic reform as a Fusion party candidate against McCall, he was elected by a plurality of 121,209 votes (*Ibid.,* Nov. 6, 1913).

Entering office at the age of thirty-four, Mitchel was the youngest mayor in the history of the city. To this position he brought youthful vigor, nervous energy, practical idealism, and the manner and appearance of the cultivated gentleman in politics. He at once embarked upon a serious program of municipal reform and ignored party ties in making numerous appointments. He maintained that an administration must stand or fall on the record of the police department and selected for the post of police com-

missioner his friend, Arthur Woods, who performed the duties of the office with distinction. He promoted active executive control by employing to advantage the agencies of the chamberlain and the commissioner of accounts. A champion of home-rule, he fought to eliminate the inequalities of the state tax quotas and instituted a program of tax relief for the city. Opposing any increase in the huge funded debt of the city, he had the new commitments cut appreciably, and in the economic depression at the outbreak of the World War, he formed a citizens' committee, with Judge Gary as chairman, which studied the unemployment problem, raised a modest relief fund, and established workshops. Long before the United States was drawn into the war, he sought to lend all the weight of his official influence to promote military preparedness. He consistently opposed volunteer armies, condemned pacifism, and advocated universal military training. He served in the officers' training camp at Plattsburg during the summers of 1915 and 1916. During the summer of 1917 he officiated as host at the receptions to the numerous allied missions which came to the United States.

Despite an engaging personality, an unquestioned honesty of purpose, and a record of creditable achievement, Mitchel and his administration became increasingly unpopular. He was looked upon by many as undemocratic, the associate of captains of industry and the companion of wealthy society. "Too much Fifth Avenue, too little First Avenue," expressed a popular feeling. His administration was charged with inadequate supervision of real-estate purchases. Mitchel was personally responsible for the introduction by way of experiment in the public schools of the plan of vocational training and industrial education conducted in Gary, Ind. The crude manner with which the plan was introduced enflamed popular indignation, and the assumption by many of the people that it was a deliberate scheme to train the masses for menial labor aroused them against the system. But the most serious cause of Mitchel's subsequent defeat was the sensational "charities controversy." Charges were raised by Fusion reform officials against the secretary of the state board of charities, and an investigation by the Fusion charities' commissioner revealed that certain Catholic and Protestant institutions were being grossly mismanaged. Both Catholics and Protestants resented the investigation, and despite the fact that Mitchel was himself a Catholic, strong religious feeling was aroused. It was also discovered that the Fusion police department had been for some time tapping wires on private telephone conversations. Finally, in his campaign for reëlection against John F. Hylan, Mitchel wrapped himself in a mantle of patriotism and denounced his opponent as pro-German and possessing a "yellow streak" (*New York Times,* Oct. 28, 29, 1917). These insubstantial issues did not strengthen him with the German- and Irish-American voters.

Mitchel was defeated for the Republican nomination by W. M. Bennett with a bare majority of 224 votes in a bitterly fought contest (*New York Times,* Sept. 27, 1917), and in the November election, despite a huge campaign fund, he was crushed by the Tammany ticket. Although clearly disappointed, he lost no time in joining the aviation corps. He had virtually completed his training for service at the front, when, at Gerstner Field, Lake Charles, La., on July 6, 1918, he fell from a single-seater scout plane at a height of about five hundred feet. An investigation revealed that his safety belt had been unfastened at the time of the accident. He was survived by his widow, Olive Child Mitchel, the daughter of Franklin D. Child of New York, whom he had married on Apr. 3, 1909.

[Wm. Dillon, *Life of John Mitchel* (2 vols., 1888), for the Mitchel family background; H. L. McBain, "John Purroy Mitchel," *Nat. Municipal Rev.,* Sept. 1918; Chas. A. Beard, "John Purroy Mitchel," *Survey,* July 13, 1918; "John Purroy Mitchel: His Chief Contribution to City Government," *Survey,* Aug. 3, 1918; *John Purroy Mitchel, 1879–1918: In Memoriam* (1918), pub. by the Class of 1899, Columbia; D. F. Malone, "John Purroy Mitchel," *World's Work,* Feb. 1914; Julian Street, "New York's Fighting Mayor," *Collier's,* Aug. 25, 1917; O. G. Villard, "John Purroy Mitchel," *Nation,* July 13, 1918; Emanie M. Sachs, "Being Human: a Great Mayor and What Happened to Him," *Century,* Feb. 1926; *Speech made by Hon. John Purroy Mitchel, . . . at the Dinner of the Committee of 107 at the Aldine Club, Monday, Apr. 12, 1915* (1915); *Speech of Hon. John Purroy Mitchel, at the Dinner of the Committee of 107 at the Hotel Astor, Tuesday, May 2, 1916* (1916); Eda Amberg and William H. Allen, *Civic Lessons from Mayor Mitchel's Defeat* (1921); *N. Y. Times,* Jan. 25, 30, Sept. 8, 1915; Jan. 22, 27, Mar. 4, June 28, 1916; and New York press for July 7, 1918.]   R. B. M.

MITCHEL, ORMSBY MacKNIGHT (July 28, 1809–Oct. 30, 1862), astronomer, Union soldier, was the son of John and Elizabeth (MacAlister) Mitchel, both of Scotch-Irish descent. Some five years before his birth his parents moved from Virginia to Union County, Ky., settling at what is now Morganfield. Here, in the rudest surroundings, Ormsby MacKnight, the youngest child of a large family, was born. Two or three years later the father died. After vainly trying to win a livelihood from the plantation, the widow moved with her children to Lebanon, Ohio, not far from Cincinnati.

It was in this center of education and trade that Mitchel received his early schooling. When about fourteen years of age he started to support himself, working as a clerk in Xenia. A little later, having seen a notice of a pending examination for entrance to the United States Military Academy, he determined to apply for an appointment, which through influential family friends in Washington he secured. Reporting for examination June 1, 1825, he was admitted, and graduated fifteenth in his class of forty-six, in 1829. His love for mathematics, derived from his father, resulted in such marked proficiency that upon graduation he was detailed as assistant professor at the Academy. There he met a young widow, Louisa (Clark) Trask, who was living with her father, Judge Clark, at Cornwall-on-the-Hudson. In the summer of 1831 they were married. After brief service at Fort Marion, St. Augustine, Fla., Mitchel resigned his commission in 1832, and moved to Cincinnati. While teaching at West Point he had studied law; he was now admitted to the bar and became the partner of E. D. Mansfield [*q.v.*]. Neither partner really cared for the law, however, and before long Mansfield became a journalist and Mitchel drifted back into teaching. The Cincinnati College, founded in 1819, was reëstablished in 1835, and the year following he was appointed to its faculty as professor of mathematics, philosophy, and astronomy. In 1836–37 he was also chief engineer of the Little Miami Railroad.

Thus began in the most casual way the career that was to give Mitchel a permanent place in the annals of American science. In his teaching of astronomy he became enthusiastic himself on the subject and aroused so great an interest in his students and their friends that he was persuaded to give a short course of public lectures. In his diary he wrote of this venture: "On the first evening my audience was respectable, on the second evening my house was filled, and on the third it was overflowing" (Mitchel, *post,* p. 51). On the platform he showed himself to be a gifted orator, and invitations to speak in several of the larger cities came to him. A member of one of his audiences wrote: "In New York the music hall is thronged night after night to hear his impassioned eloquence poured in an unbroken flow of 'thoughts that breathe and words that burn' on the excited thousands" (Porter, *post,* p. 8). This magical gift of oratory, together with indomitable energy and perseverance, enabled Mitchel to carry to completion a scheme which at first seemed chimerical. In 1825 John Quincy Adams had endeavored to persuade Congress to found a national observatory, but without avail. In 1843, however, Mitchel's lectures on celestial phenomena roused his audience to such a pitch of enthusiasm that they provided him with means to erect "the first astronomical establishment worthy of the name" in the United States (Clerke, *post,* p. 8). Moreover, his lectures in other parts of the country had no small part in stimulating the interest which resulted in the establishment, at very nearly the same time, of the Harvard Observatory and the Naval Observatory at Washington.

The Cincinnati Astronomical Society had been founded in 1842, and in 1845 there was erected on one of the hills outside the city the second largest telescope in the world, and by far the largest on the Western continent. In 1846 Mitchel began the publication of the *Sidereal Messenger,* which he conducted until October 1848—the first magazine ever devoted to a popular exposition of astronomy. In 1846, also, he was offered the Rumford professorship at Harvard, but declined it, since he felt obliged to direct the Cincinnati Observatory for at least ten years. During this period he took great interest in the establishment of the Dudley Observatory at Albany, and in fact furnished the plans for it; when, therefore, in 1859 he was asked to become its director, he accepted.

His astronomical work was practically ended, however. Soon after the outbreak of the Civil War the President appointed him a brigadier-general of volunteers (Aug. 9, 1861), and he was assigned to command the Department of the Ohio. Later the departments of the Ohio and the Cumberland were united, and Mitchel served under Gen. D. C. Buell [*q.v.*]. In April 1862 he made the memorable dash from Shelbyville, Tenn., to Huntsville, Ala., surprising and capturing the city without firing a gun, and thus getting control of the Memphis & Charleston Railroad. For this brilliant exploit the thanks of the War Department were telegraphed to him and he was promoted to be major-general of volunteers. His relations with Buell, who found his discipline lax and his control of his troops unsatisfactory, grew increasingly strained, however; and in the summer of 1862 he tendered his resignation. It was not accepted, but in the fall (Sept. 17) he was transferred to the command of the Department of the South and the X Army Corps, with headquarters at Hilton Head, S. C. Before he could organize the work there he was stricken with yellow fever, and died at Beaufort on Oct. 30. He was the author of two books published during his lifetime: *Planetary and Stellar Worlds* (1848) and *Popular Astronomy*

(1860). A posthumous volume, *The Astronomy of the Bible,* was copyrighted in 1863.

[F. A. Mitchel, *Ormsby MacKnight Mitchel, Astronomer and General* (1887), a biography by his son; J. G. Porter, *Hist. Sketch of the Cincinnati Observatory, 1843–93* (1893); G. W. Cullum, *Biog. Reg. Officers and Grads. U. S. Mil. Acad.* (3rd ed., 1891), vol. I; *Proc. Cincinnati Astron. Soc. in Commemoration of Prof. Ormsby M. Mitchel* (1862); A. M. Clerke, *A Pop. Hist. of Astronomy during the Nineteenth Century* (1887); *Battles and Leaders of the Civil War* (4 vols., 1887–88), esp. vol. II; *War of the Rebellion: Official Records* (*Army*), 1 ser. IV, VII, X (pt. 1), XIV, XVI; *Evening Star* (Washington), Nov. 5, 1862.]
J.G.P.

MITCHELL, ALEXANDER (Oct. 18, 1817–Apr. 19, 1887), banker, financier, congressman, and railroad builder, was born in Ellon, Aberdeenshire, Scotland, and died in New York City. His parents were John and Margaret (Lendrum) Mitchell. The father, a well-to-do farmer, was the son of an emigrant from the north of England; the mother was of pure Scottish descent. At twenty-two, Alexander Mitchell came to America as secretary of the Wisconsin Marine & Fire Insurance Company, with headquarters at Milwaukee. The guiding spirit behind this organization was George Smith [*q.v.*], also a Scotchman, who had obtained the charter from the Wisconsin territorial legislature in February 1839, ostensibly to do an insurance business. Shortly after its organization, however, the company began doing a full-fledged banking business under a clause in its charter which authorized it to receive money on deposit and issue certificates therefor. Various efforts were made to repeal the charter, but were frustrated, largely through the strategy and astuteness of Alexander Mitchell, who maintained that a court at law, rather than the legislature, should determine whether or not the corporation was usurping powers not conferred upon it in the charter. Despite the hostile attitude of the legislature at almost every session, the institution continued to thrive and flourish during the forties. By Dec. 1, 1852, the certificates of deposit outstanding totaled $1,470,235, which went a long way toward meeting the currency needs of the Northwest.

Soon after Wisconsin was admitted as a state in 1848, the attorney-general commenced proceedings by *quo warranto* to test the legality of the charter. This was the correct legal procedure, and there is no question but that the charter would have been revoked had a truce not been declared. In 1852 Wisconsin passed its free-banking law, and it is generally understood that Mitchell had agreed that if the free-banking law were ratified by a vote of the people at the November election, the Wisconsin Marine &

Fire Insurance Company would be reorganized under the laws of the state. The law was approved by the people, and in January 1853 the Wisconsin Marine & Fire Insurance Company became a state bank, with Alexander Mitchell as president. In 1854, Mitchell bought Smith's holdings and became the principal owner. At the outbreak of the Civil War the free banks in Wisconsin faced financial ruin. In 1861 about two-thirds of the collateral placed in trust with the state treasurer to safeguard the interests of the noteholder were the bonds of seceding states. Alexander Mitchell is commonly credited with the execution of a scheme whereby approximately a million dollars' worth of Wisconsin war bonds were assigned to the solvent banks and substituted for the depreciated Southern bonds. As a result, more than two-thirds of the 110 banks in the state remained in good standing. He was the first president of the Wisconsin Bankers' Association.

It was as a railroad builder, however, that Mitchell rendered his greatest contribution to society. During the fifties, most of the railroads which now cross Wisconsin were substantially completed, but they were without tributary or connecting lines, and their revenues were insufficient to pay operating expenses. In 1863 the Milwaukee & St. Paul Railway Company was organized and got a continuous road from Milwaukee to La Crosse by welding together several hitherto unconnected lines. It failed to pay running expenses and the interest on the mortgage debt, and the bondholders were about to foreclose in the spring of 1865. Mitchell was the only director who opposed this policy and maintained that with proper management the road could be made to pay its way. He accepted the challenge to take the presidency and was elected to that office in 1865. Within a year the road was again on a paying basis. At that time it comprised in all about 270 miles. When Mitchell died in 1887, the corporation, whose name had been changed in 1874 to the Chicago, Milwaukee & St. Paul Railway Company, owned and operated over 5,000 miles of railway, covering Wisconsin, northern Illinois, Minnesota, Iowa, and South Dakota. Mitchell, South Dakota, was named in Mitchell's honor.

In politics he was originally a Whig; in the late fifties he became a Republican and a loyal supporter of Lincoln; later he championed the Reconstruction policies of Andrew Johnson and became a Democrat. An unsuccessful candidate in 1868, he was elected to Congress in 1870 and again in 1872. In 1877 he was nominated by the Wisconsin Democrats for governor, but refused to run. He was married, Oct. 7, 1841, to Martha Reed. He left the bulk of his fortune to his only son, John L. Mitchell, who represented Wisconsin in the United States Senate from 1893 to 1899.

[J. J Knox, *A Hist. of Banking in the U. S.* (1900), pp. 740–46; A. M. Thomson, *A Political Hist. of Wis.* (1900), pp. 304–06; E. B. Usher, *Wisconsin, Its Story and Biog.* (1914), VII, 2012–19, III, 471–81; *Milwaukee Sentinel,* Apr. 20, 1887; *Chicago Tribune,* Apr. 24, 1887; J. D. Butler, "Alexander Mitchell," in *Wis. Hist. Soc. Colls.,* XI (1888), 442; *Proc. Am. Soc. Civil Engineers,* vol. XIII (1887); *Biog. Dir. Am. Cong.* (1928).]

L. B. K.

MITCHELL, DAVID BRYDIE (Oct. 22, 1766–Apr. 22, 1837), governor of Georgia and agent of the United States to the Creek Indians, was born near Muthill, Perthshire, Scotland, the son of John Mitchell. His uncle, David Brydie, a successful physician, served both as soldier and surgeon in the American Revolution, took part under General Screven in the skirmish near Midway, and, captured by the British after the fall of Savannah, died on a prison ship, leaving his estate to his nephew who in 1783 arrived in Savannah to claim it. The youth of seventeen was charmed with the new life. He made friends rapidly, studied law in the office of William Stephens, and in 1795 was elected attorney-general. He was sent to the state House of Representatives, opposed the fraudulent Yazoo scheme, and gained a popular favor that made him major-general of the Georgia militia about 1804 and governor of the state from 1809 to 1813 and again from 1815 to 1817. His messages and activities as governor show him as a liberal supporter of internal improvements, education, road building, and, especially frontier defense. He signed the first Georgia law against dueling though he himself had, at least once, been involved in such an affair. He foresaw the dangers of Indian attack and induced the General Assembly to devote $30,000 to a series of frontier forts and provision of arms. The necessity for such preparations was even more apparent when the Fort Mims massacre of 1813 vindicated his judgment as to the danger.

He resigned as governor on Nov. 4, 1817, to accept an appointment by President Monroe as Indian agent to the Creek nation. The Indian situation in Georgia at the time was most difficult. The white people were growing restless over the prospect of the erection of a permanent Indian territory covering a large part of the most desirable section of the state. Pressure brought to bear on the Indians produced a strained situation, which the War of 1812 enhanced. The president selected Mitchell for the delicate position of Indian agent on account of his skilful conduct of Indian relations while he was governor. He brought to conclusion on Jan. 22, 1818, a treaty in which the Creeks ceded to Georgia about 1,500,000 acres of land in two sections where the demand was greatest. His agency was terminated in 1821 by a charge brought by Gov. John Clark [*q.v.*] that he was concerned in the smuggling into the vicinity of a number of African slaves. He denied those charges and others concerning his administration of Indian affairs, but the president decided that the evidence was clearly against him (*Niles' Weekly Register,* Apr. 15, 1820, Apr. 21, 1821). He retired to Milledgeville, where he died. The state legislature provided for the erection of a marble tomb to his memory.

[A few letters in Lib. of Cong.; W. J. Northen, *Men of Mark in Ga.,* vol. II (1910); L. L. Knight, *Georgia's Landmarks* (2 vols. 1913–14); George White, *Hist. Colls. of Ga.* (1855); Clark Howell, *Hist. of Ga.* (1926), vol. I; *Daily Georgian* (Savannah), Apr. 28, 1837.]   J. H. T. M.

MITCHELL, DAVID DAWSON (July 31, 1806–May 23, 1861), fur-trader, soldier, superintendent of Indian Affairs, was born in Louisa County, Va. He was a man of culture as well as ability. Entering the fur trade at St. Louis in 1828 as a clerk in the employ of the American Fur Company, he was first assigned to the "Ioway Outfit" and in 1830 was transferred to the "Upper Missouri Outfit," with which he remained during the rest of his fur-trading career. He built Fort Mackenzie in 1832, amidst dangers and difficulties that appeared insurmountable. His battles with the Indians marked him as a leader of great courage and resource. As a tribute to his meritorious service the fort built by Leclerc in 1833 was named Fort Mitchell. In 1835 he became a partner in the establishment, but after his marriage in 1840 to Martha Eliza Berry—daughter of Maj. Taylor Berry, a retired army officer, landowner, and speculator —he settled down in St. Louis. Six children were born of this marriage. He was appointed superintendent of Indian Affairs, central division, in September 1841, and held this office, with one interval, almost continuously until 1853.

At the beginning of the Mexican War he entered the volunteer service as lieutenant-colonel of the 2nd Missouri Regiment, organized and commanded by Sterling Price [*q.v.*]. He afterwards served under Col. Alexander Doniphan [*q.v.*], and was conspicuous in the battles of Brazito and Sacramento; Doniphan's report

commended him for bravery. When money was needed to purchase army supplies for the campaign to open communication with General Wool, Mitchell, being a handsome and conspicuous officer, flattered the notorious gambling-house queen, Señora Tules, by escorting her to a fandango in Santa Fé, and borrowed from her a large sum of money for the use of the army. He led the advance in the subsequent campaign, taking Chihuahua and then marching on to join Zachary Taylor near Saltillo. On Feb. 10, 1847, shortly before the battle of Sacramento, Mitchell impressed into service some traders, their men, wagons, teams, and equipment. Although he was acting under orders from Colonel Doniphan, his superior officer, a final judgment of $95,000 was rendered against him after the war on account of this incident. Upon the recommendation of the Secretary of the Treasury, made Feb. 27, 1851, Congress voted to pay the judgment in his behalf.

Mitchell remained in the army for several years after the war, and was again made superintendent of Indian Affairs in 1851. Early in 1855 he promoted the organization of a corporation known as the Missouri and California Overland Mail and Transportation Company, which he served as president for several years. He was a second to Gov. Benjamin Gratz Brown [*q.v.*] in the famous Brown-Reynolds duel of 1856. In 1858 he supplied the United States government with a large number of mules for the Utah Military Expedition.

[Pierre Chouteau Maffitt Collection, Fort Tecumseh letter book (1830–32); Fort Union letter book, all MSS. in Mo. Hist. Soc.; U. S. Commissioner of Indian Affairs, *Ann. Reports,* 1842–53; W. E. Connelley, *Doniphan's Expedition and the Conquest of N. Mex. and Cal.* (1907); St. Louis city directories; Susan Shelby Magoffin, *Down the Santa Fé Trail* (1926) ed. by Stella M. Drumm; *Mo. and Cal. Overland Mail and Transportation Company, Charter, Memorial, Addresses,* etc. (1856); *Sen. Doc. 53,* 32 Cong., 1 Sess.; *House Doc. 281,* 37 Cong., 2 Sess.; H. M. Chittenden, *The Am. Fur Trade of the Far West* (1902); *Missouri Republican,* May 24 and 25, 1861; W. B. Stevens, *The Brown-Reynolds Duel* (1911).]   S. M. D.

MITCHELL, DONALD GRANT (Apr. 12, 1822–Dec. 15, 1908), agriculturist, landscape gardener, and author, better known as Ik Marvel, was born in Norwich, Conn., the son of the Rev. Alfred Mitchell, a Congregational minister, and Lucretia Mumford Woodbridge. He was the grandson of Stephen Mix Mitchell [*q.v.*]. His father died in 1831, his mother in 1839. A tubercular tendency inherited from the Woodbridges proved fatal to six of the nine children of his parents before 1846, and he himself overcame the disease only by good fortune. He prepared for college at John Hall's school, El-

Mitchell

lington, Conn., then entered Yale, where in his last year he was an editor of the *Yale Literary Magazine*. As a student he was alert and independent. Graduating in 1841, he retired to an ancestral farm in Salem township, New London County, Conn., where, after the manner of his father, he indulged his love for rural things and continued his literary work. In 1843 the New York Agricultural Society awarded him a silver medal for plans of farm buildings. In the autumn of 1844 he went as clerk to Joel W. White, consul to Liverpool, and remained in the consular office until January 1845, when failing health necessitated retirement to the milder climate of the island of Jersey. After resting for two months on the sands of St. Aubin's Bay he traveled from March 1845 to August 1846 over the British Isles and the Continent, much of the time on foot. This outdoor life so far overcame his pulmonary weakness that he returned to America in September 1846 in comparatively good health.

From 1846 to 1855 Mitchell's life was unsettled. From Washington, D. C., he wrote for the *Morning Courier and New York Enquirer* over the signature Ik Marvel, a name by which he later came to be well known. In New York under the guidance of John Osborne Sargent [*q.v.*] he read law "after a fashion," but for the most part engaged in literary work. His first volume, *Fresh Gleanings* (1847), is a good record of his European travel. In June 1848 he went to Paris and wrote a series of thirty letters for the *Courier and Enquirer* on the progress of the revolution of that year. Upon his return to Sargent's office he wrote his second book, *The Battle Summer* (1850), which treats of aspects of the revolution prior to those described in his newspaper correspondence. A projected sequel was never written. During 1850 he edited the *Lorgnette*, a journal designed to satirize the follies of New York society. His *Reveries of a Bachelor* (1850) was immediately popular. Fourteen thousand copies were sold within a year. It was followed in 1851 by *Dream Life*, which sold almost as well. On May 31, 1853, he married Mary Frances Pringle, of Charleston, S. C., and went to Venice as United States consul. Resigning the Venetian consulate in February 1854 he resided in Paris until May 1855, when he returned to America.

In June 1855 he purchased a two-hundred-acre farm, later increased to 360 acres, near New Haven, Conn., and named it "Edgewood." His natural taste, cultivated by his residence abroad, recoiled from the ugliness of much in American life, and he set himself the task of arousing his countrymen to a sense of beauty in farming,

home building, and town planning. "Edgewood" became an object lesson to pilgrims from all over America, and his series of Edgewood books propagated his gospel. "We gratefully acknowledge that you have laid the foundation for scientific and beautiful park building throughout this country," said Christopher Clarke in 1904 when he presented a silver cup to Mitchell on behalf of the New England Association of Park Superintendents.

Mitchell was strikingly handsome and had a rare sense of humor. By temperament retiring and reserved, he was a delightful companion when once he gave his confidence. Calm and judicious, he was never an extremist. "Good example will do very much in way of reform," he once wrote, "more, in most instances, than any zeal of impeachment." He always maintained a modest and apologetic attitude toward his own literary efforts, although he made a place for himself in American letters. He used the English language in its purest forms, achieving his effects by sincerity and simplicity rather than by display. Occasionally he tried his hand at a bit of verse, such as in his "To Torquatus" in *Scribner's Magazine*, March 1891. He contributed to the leading American periodicals from 1842 to 1897. His books, in addition to those already named, are: *Fudge Doings* (1855); *My Farm of Edgewood* (1863); *Seven Stories* (1864); *Wet Days at Edgewood* (1865); *Doctor Johns* (1866); *Rural Studies* (1867, republished as *Out-of-Town Places*, 1884); *About Old Story Tellers* (1877); *Woodbridge Record* (1883); *Daniel Tyler* (1883); *Bound Together* (1884); *English Lands, Letters and Kings* (4 vols., 1889–97), and *American Lands and Letters* (2 vols., 1897–99). The Edgewood edition of his *Works* in fifteen volumes was published in 1907.

[The history of Mitchell's genealogy is given in his own *Woodbridge Record*. Waldo H. Dunn, *The Life of Donald G. Mitchell, Ik Marvel* (1922), is based upon original documents and contains an extensive bibliography.]   W. H. D—n.

MITCHELL, EDWARD CUSHING (Sept. 20, 1829–Feb. 27, 1900), college president, Old Testament scholar, grandson of Nahum Mitchell [*q.v.*], was descended from Experience Mitchell, one of the Pilgrim passengers on the ship *Anne* in 1623. His father, Silvanus Lazell Mitchell, a graduate of Harvard, married Lucia Whitman, and in the Old Colony village of East Bridgewater, Mass., Edward C. Mitchell was born. At the age of sixteen he matriculated at Waterville (later Colby) College in Maine, where he was graduated in the class of 1849. There he made lasting friendships which influenced his character; and during the same period a deepening religious feeling decided him to enter the ministry. He had qualities suited to that profession. He possessed the dignity and courtly presence of a gentleman of the old school, yet was approachable and friendly. His family had joined in the Unitarian secession from the old Puritanism, and were disappointed that he should enter the Baptist ministry, but his own conviction of duty was not moved. After college he went to the Newton Theological Institution, where he followed the three years' course, graduating in 1853, and remained a year for post-graduate study. He was ordained at Calais, Me., in 1854, and became minister of the Baptist church at that place, serving for two years. He then served brief pastorates at Brockport, N. Y., 1857–58, and Rockford, Ill., 1858–63.

For years he had been a diligent student of the Bible, and in 1863 he was invited to become professor of Biblical literature in Shurtleff College, Alton, Ill., where he remained until 1870. He then held the chair of Hebrew and Old Testament literature in the Baptist Union Theological Seminary, Chicago, from 1870 to 1877. While on leave of absence in Europe, 1876–77, he acted as professor of Hebrew in Regent's Park College, London, a Baptist institution, temporarily filling a vacancy created by the death of one of the faculty. He then crossed the Channel to Paris, where he was president of the Baptist Theological Seminary, 1878–82. Returning to Chicago, he was editor of the *Present Age,* 1883–84, then, in 1884–85, president of Roger Williams University, an institution for negroes, at Nashville, Tenn. In 1886–87 he supplied the pulpit of a Baptist church at Neponset, Mass., and in 1887 he found in New Orleans the work to which he gave the rest of his life—the presidency of Leland University, another school for the higher education of negroes. During his thirteen years in this position he enhanced the reputation of the institution in the South, made friends for the college and for himself, and exerted a remarkable influence over the colored people in Louisiana.

In 1884, soon after his return from Europe, Mitchell gave a series of lectures on the Lowell Institute platform in Boston on "Biblical Science and Modern Discovery." During the same period he delivered lecture courses in Worcester and Brooklyn and at the School of Hebrew at Morgan Park, Ill. He had previously published the results of his diligent study in a *Critical Handbook of the New Testament* (1879; 2nd American edition 1895), and while in Paris had issued a French edition of this work under the title *Les Sources du Nouveau Testament* (1882). He also revised Benjamin Davies' *Compendious and Complete Hebrew and Chaldee Lexicon to the Old Testament* (1879), edited *Gesenius' Hebrew Grammar* (1880), and wrote *An Elementary Hebrew Grammar and Reading Book* (1884). He was married twice. By his first wife, Maria (Morton) Mitchell, he had two sons and a daughter. His second wife, Marcia (Savage) Mitchell, was "Lady Principal" of Leland University while he was president.

[*Watchman,* Mar. 15, 1900; alumni records, Newton Theol. Inst.; Nahum Mitchell, *Hist. of the Early Settlement of Bridgewater in Plymouth Colony, Mass.* (1897); *Daily Picayune* (New Orleans), Mar. 1, 1900; catalogues of institutions mentioned.]   H. K. R.

MITCHELL, EDWARD PAGE (Mar. 24, 1852–Jan. 22, 1927), editor, came from a family which in America traces to Experience Mitchell, a passenger in 1623 on the ship *Anne* from Leyden, the third vessel to bring settlers to Plymouth, and his wife Jane Cook. He was born in Bath, Me., son of Edward H. and his wife Frances A. Page Mitchell. His background was the New England of theologians, soldiers, teachers, sailors, merchants, farmers; his boyhood environment that of the rigid Sabbatarians of the time tempered by the sympathetic understanding of a father intellectually curious and naturally enterprising. He inherited a sturdy frame, tall stature, natural dignity of bearing; his mind was equipped for the most serious and the most whimsical exercises. Eight years after his birth the family moved from Bath to New York City, where Mitchell attended Grammar School 35 and George W. Clarke's Mount Washington Collegiate Institute, watched the troops pass on to the front in the Civil War, saw some of the most violent phases of the Draft Riots, and absorbed an understanding of the city which endured throughout his life. His earliest published writings were a series of letters descriptive of Southern life written at fourteen to the Bath (Maine) *Times* from the Gen. Bryan Grimes plantation on the Tar River, North Carolina, which his father leased in an unsuccessful cotton speculation. They reveal acute comprehension and unexpected power of observation; yet their author had no intention of making a literary career when, a conditioned sub-freshman, he entered Bowdoin College with the class of 1871. His purpose was to practise medicine. As a student he excelled in the humanities; he was the author of the college song "Phi Chi," still sung by all Bowdoin men; he taught school in the long vacation; he was suspended for participation in a hazing. But he was graduated A.B. and later became an Overseer of the college.

It was the necessity of earning money to pay for his education in medicine that took Mitchell to Edward Stanwood, assistant editor of the Boston *Advertiser,* from whom in 1871 he obtained work as a reporter. His career in Boston was cut short by an impairment of his sight, but he was with the *Advertiser* long enough to cover fires and horse races, to meet, among others, Edward Everett Hale, John Fiske, Oliver Wendell Holmes, John Boyle O'Reilly, and others of equal flavor, to get the smell of ink; and newspaper life engulfed him. He retired to Bath for treatment of his eyes, and there in the course of his recovery he wrote, when just past twenty, an imaginative tale, "The Tachypomp," in pseudo-scientific style. The story was published in *Scribner's Monthly* (March 1874) and it stood the test of time so well that forty years later (May 1913) the *Century* republished it as one of the "specimens of the characteristic fiction read by an earlier generation." Mitchell might have become an eminent fiction writer, but journalism claimed him, and when, in 1873, the Dingley brothers offered him, on probation, a place on their Lewiston, Maine, *Journal,* he accepted fifteen dollars a week and with skill and pleasure performed the arduous and multifarious tasks of a country newspaper man. Among his duties were those of exchange editor, and in this capacity he first became acquainted with the New York *Sun.* In 1874 his wage was increased to twenty dollars a week when he married (Oct. 29, 1874) Annie Sewall Welch; twenty-five dollars was later refused him. But his success in fiction emboldened him to submit manuscripts to the *Sun,* and Charles Anderson Dana recognized his talent. Thus on Oct. 1, 1875, at the latter's invitation, Mitchell joined the staff of the paper to work directly under Dana. From that day until his death, he lived for the *Sun,* and from the beginning of his service until the end he possessed the unquestioning confidence of the paper's successive proprietors.

For fifty-two years, in the anonymity of the newspaper, Mitchell used his well-stored mind, his genius for wit, his capacity for exposition, and his faculty for denunciation for the sustenance of policies he believed would best serve the interests of America, for the exposure of men and schemes he held to be fraudulent, and for the amusement of the readers of the newspaper. Men he appraised for himself; in the detection of shams and pretenders he was uncanny; and he was as tolerant of amiable weakness as he was relentless in the exposure of evil design. Newspaper purpose and policy never swerved his mind from the search for fact: in the *Sun's*

campaign against the Whiskey Ring the zeal which sought every incriminating circumstance was as energetically employed to detect and expose the false accuser; the pen that defined the attempt of Cleveland to reëstablish the monarchy in Hawaii as "this policy of infamy" was inked to praise unreservedly that Executive when he used the army to protect the mails in the railroad strikes of 1894 and when in the Venezuela crisis of 1895 he asserted the Monroe Doctrine. In the final and successful effort to make possible the Panama Canal his contribution to the contest drew forth from Philippe Bunau-Varilla, in his capacity of minister plenipotentiary from the Republic of Panama, a telegram (Feb. 24, 1904) reading: "The last battle is fought and the victory complete. I shall always remember that I owe it to the victory of 1902 in which you took the most eminent share" (*Memoirs, post,* p. 340). In the campaign to prevent the entrance of the United States into the League of Nations, Mitchell again demonstrated his skill in argumentation. His historical knowledge, his fertility of resource, his appraisal of public opinion, all were exercised with tremendous energy, and, in his opinion, the outcome of that struggle was a supreme victory for American institutions and independence. It was his last great battle and was fought by a man convinced of the justice of his cause.

From an ill-defined but authoritative official status perhaps best described as that of chief editorial writer, Mitchell became editor of the *Sun* on July 20, 1903, under the ownership of William M. Laffan. On Laffan's death, Nov. 19, 1909, at the latter's wish, he assumed the office of president of The Sun Printing and Publishing Association to hold it until the property was sold. When William C. Reick became owner and president, Dec. 17, 1911, Mitchell again gave all his time to the editorship. He was continued in this by Frank Munsey when Munsey became proprietor, June 30, 1916, and held that post under the Munsey management until 1920 when, to conserve his health, he sought less arduous duties, and by vote of the stockholders on motion of Munsey, was retained for life as a permanent member of the staff. On the death of Munsey, Dec. 22, 1925, his successor, William T. Dewart, induced Mitchell to accept a directorship of the *Sun* and the *Evening Telegram,* and his counsel and pen were thereafter used as occasion suggested in the product of the newspapers until his death; he was in consultation with his associates within a few days of his passing. Professional tribute to his place in journalism was paid at an Amen Corner dinner in

New York City given in his honor, Jan. 7, 1922, at which several hundred newspaper editors from all parts of the United States were present.

Annie Sewall Welch Mitchell died Dec. 13, 1909, having borne four sons. The family home was in Glen Ridge, N. J., a residential borough Mitchell did much to establish. On July 22, 1912, Mitchell married Ada M. Burroughs, of Brooklyn, by whom he had one son, Burroughs. After his second marriage he made his home at Watchapey Farm, Charlestown, R. I., where his property included part of the battlefield on which his ancestors fought King Philip. His death occurred in the Mohican Hotel, New London, Conn., and his body was interred in the family plot in Glen Ridge, Jan. 25, 1927. He was a member of no church and was independent in politics.

[The principal source of information concerning Mitchell is his *Memoirs of an Editor* (1924). Other sources include F. M. O'Brien, *The Story of The Sun* (ed. 1928); *Lit. Digest*, Feb. 12, 1927; *Outlook*, Feb. 2, 1927; *Who's Who in America*, 1926–27; and files and records of The Sun Printing and Publishing Association.]   H. M. A.

MITCHELL, ELISHA (Aug. 19, 1793–June 27, 1857), geologist, botanist, was born in Washington, Litchfield County, Conn., the son of Abner and Phoebe (Eliot) Mitchell. His father, a farmer, was descended from Matthew Mitchell who came to Massachusetts from Yorkshire in 1635 and two years later settled at Wethersfield, Conn.; his mother was a grand-daughter of the Rev. Jared Eliot [*q.v.*], a man distinguished in his day for the successful pursuit of knowledge in many branches of science. In Mitchell's commanding presence, great bodily vigor, quaint humor, and liberal philanthropy, he bore a marked resemblance to this great-grandfather. In boyhood he showed an insatiable desire for knowledge and a special interest in objective science, which were encouraged by his schoolmaster, the Rev. Azel Backus [*q.v.*], then head of a classical school in Litchfield County. At Yale, where he was a classmate of Denison Olmsted [*q.v.*], Mitchell was marked by the "dignity of his bearing, his handsome face, the originality of the views he set forth, the humor with which he enlivened his arguments, and the evident intimacy of his acquaintance with great English authors" (Phillips, "Sketch," *post*, pp. 9–10). He graduated at the head of his class in 1813. After a term or two as usher in the school of Dr. Eigenbrodt, Jamaica, Long Island, and about a year in charge of a girls' school at New London, Conn., he was appointed a tutor at Yale in 1816. During the following year, recommended by Rev. Sereno E. Dwight of New Haven,

chaplain of the United States Senate, to Judge William Gaston [*q.v.*], member of Congress from North Carolina and trustee of the University, Mitchell and Denison Olmsted were called to professorships in the University of North Carolina at Chapel Hill, Mitchell being chosen professor of mathematics and natural philosophy, and Olmsted, professor of chemistry, geology, and mineralogy. Mitchell studied for a short time at Andover Theological Seminary and on Dec. 30, 1817, received a license to preach, then removed to North Carolina, where he entered upon his professorial duties at Chapel Hill in January 1818. Here he continued for the remaining thirty-nine years of his life. He married Maria Sybil North, daughter of Dr. Elisha North [*q.v.*], of New London, Nov. 19, 1819, and had three sons and four daughters. In August 1821, at Hillsborough, N. C., he was ordained to the ministry by the Presbytery of Orange. Four years later, when Olmsted accepted a professorship at Yale, Mitchell succeeded him in the chair of chemistry, geology, and mineralogy.

Even while professor of mathematics, he had made frequent botanical excursions through the country around Chapel Hill; and after the change in his professorship he extended and multiplied the excursions, "so that when he died he was known in almost every part of North Carolina, and he left no one behind him better acquainted with its mountains, valleys, and plains; its birds, beasts, bugs, fishes, and shells; its trees, flowers, vines, and mosses; its rocks, stones, sands, clays, and marls" (*Memoir, post*, p. 8). He contributed accounts of his observations to Silliman's *American Journal of Science* and other periodicals, wrote "Agricultural Speculations" for *Papers on Agricultural Subjects . . . Published by Order of the Board of Agriculture of North Carolina* (vol. I, 1825); in 1827 published part III of the "Report on the Geology of North Carolina" (*Ibid.*, vol. III); and in 1842, *Elements of Geology*, accompanied by a geological map of North Carolina. Perhaps his best work was that printed privately for the use of his students— manuals of natural history, botany, zoölogy, and mineralogy. His chief claim to distinction, however, is that he was the first to measure the height of the mountain now called Mitchell's Peak or Mount Mitchell, the highest peak in the United States east of the Rockies. Accompanied by his daughter, he first explored the region in 1835, and visited it several times thereafter, revising his measurements. To settle a controversy with Thomas L. Clingman [*q.v.*] who had measured the peak in 1844 and claimed priority, asserting that Mitchell had measured not the highest, but a lesser peak, the latter made a fifth expedition to the mountains in 1857. Equipped with improved instruments and accompanied by his son, he set about his task in the middle of June. On the 27th, with the work half done, he started to cross the mountain alone to the home of former guides on the Caney River. Overtaken by a storm, he slipped down a steep bank, fell into a creek, and was drowned. His body was recovered ten days later from a pool at the place now called Mitchell's Falls. Buried at Asheville, it was removed in June of the following year and reinterred with formal ceremonies on the top of Mount Mitchell.

[Charles Phillips, *A Memoir of the Rev. Elisha Mitchell* (1858) and "Sketch of Elisha Mitchell" in *Jour. Elisha Mitchell Sci. Soc., 1883–84* (1884); *N. C. Univ. Mag.,* Mar. 1858; Wm. Cothren, *Hist. of Ancient Woodbury* (2 vols., 1854–72); Collier Cobb, in *Appleton's Pop. Sci. Mo.,* Oct. 1896; S. A. Ashe, *Biog. Hist. of N. C.,* vol. I (1905); K. P. Battle, *Hist. of the Univ. of N. C.* (2 vols., 1907–12); "Diary of a Geological Tour in 1827 and 1828," ed. by K. P. Battle, in *Univ. of N. C. James Sprunt Hist. Monograph No. 6* (1905); F. B. Dexter, *Biog. Sketches Grads. Yale Coll.,* vol. VI (1912); *Geneal. of the Descendants of John Eliot* (1905); *N. C. Standard* (Raleigh), July 15, 1857.]
C. C.

MITCHELL, GEORGE EDWARD (Mar. 3, 1781–June 28, 1832), physician, soldier, congressman, was born at Head of Elk (later called Elkton), Cecil County, Md., one of a family of eight children. His father, Dr. Abraham Mitchell, moved to Cecil County from Lancaster County, Pa., some time before 1767. His mother, Mary Thompson Mitchell, was the daughter of a physician. The son studied medicine in his father's office and afterward attended the University of Pennsylvania, where he graduated from the medical department in 1805. Back again in Elkton, in partnership with his father, he became interested in politics. He was elected to the Maryland House of Delegates, session of 1808–09, where he vigorously supported the Jefferson administration. He declined reëlection to the General Assembly but was elected a member of the state executive council, on which he served as president from 1809 to 1812.

In January 1809 he had declined a commission as captain of light dragoons in the regular army, but at the outbreak of the War of 1812 he resigned from the executive council and on May 1, 1812, was appointed major of the 3rd Maryland Artillery and recruited a company of volunteers in Cecil County. On Mar. 3, 1813, he was promoted to the rank of lieutenant-colonel. He was wounded at the capture of York, Canada, and also fought at Fort George, in the spring of 1813. During the summer and fall he was in command of Fort Niagara. His most brilliant exploit was at Fort Oswego, N. Y., in the following year. In April 1814, while on the march from Sacketts Harbor to Buffalo, he was met at Batavia by General J. J. Brown, who had ridden forty miles during the night to reach him, and was ordered to Fort Oswego, at the mouth of the Oswego River. Twelve miles up the river, at Great Falls (now Fulton), there was an important depot of naval stores, the loss of which would have seriously crippled the American forces on Lake Ontario. To defend this was his real object. Marching at the rate of fifty miles a day, Mitchell with about three hundred men reached Fort Oswego on Apr. 30, 1814. They found the walls of the fort rotting, and some of the cannon useless. Pitching all the tents available near the town of Oswego, across the river, to make a show of force, the little company withdrew into the fort, repairing its defenses as best they could. On the morning of May 5th eight British ships with 222 guns appeared in the harbor, saw the tents near the town, and attacked the fort. They were repulsed but the next day landed a party and were met in the open field by Mitchell's much smaller force. After two hours' fighting, the Americans retreated to a position farther up the river, determined to save the stores at all costs. On May 7th, however, the British withdrew. For his gallantry Mitchell was brevetted colonel, and during the closing months of the war commanded the center of the Army of the Niagara. After peace was declared, the Maryland General Assembly passed a series of resolutions in his honor and presented him with a sword. He was placed in charge of the 4th military department and retained his commission until June 1, 1821, when he retired to his estate, "Fair Hill," which he had inherited from his father.

In 1822 Mitchell was elected without opposition as a Democrat to the Eighteenth Congress and was reëlected in 1824. He wrote and introduced the resolution in January 1824 inviting Lafayette to America. When the latter arrived in Washington he proposed the resolution inviting him to a seat in Congress and was made chairman of the congressional reception committee. A friendship was established between Lafayette and Mitchell which lasted to the end of their lives. He was not a candidate for Congress in 1826, but was elected in 1828 and again in 1830. He was an unsuccessful candidate for governor of Maryland in 1829. He died at Washington, June 28, 1832, while attending Congress, and was buried in the Congressional Cemetery.

He had married, on May 28, 1816, Mary Hooper of Dorchester County, Md., by whom he had seven children.

[*Biog. Dir. Am. Cong.* (1928); Geo. Johnston, *Hist. of Cecil County, Md.* (1881); *Daily Nat. Intelligencer* (Wash., D. C.), June 30, 1832.]   I. L. T.

MITCHELL, HENRY (Sept. 16, 1830–Dec. 1, 1902), hydrographer, engineer, the son of William Mitchell, 1791–1869 [*q.v.*], and Lydia (Coleman) Mitchell, came of Quaker stock long settled in America. He was born and reared in Nantucket, Mass., at a time when whaling furnished the basis of the prosperity there and Nantucket whalers were ranging the seas from the Arctic to the Antarctic. The nature of its industry fostered in the island community the study of navigation, including mathematics and astronomy. Mitchell's education was obtained in private schools and also at home, where his immediate family furnished good examples and excellent instructors. His mother had been a teacher prior to her marriage; his sister, Maria Mitchell [*q.v.*], twelve years his senior, was busily engaged at home in her astronomical labors; while his father, a teacher and later a bank official and one of the overseers of Harvard College, was an able astronomer who enjoyed a wide acquaintance among American men of science.

In 1849 Mitchell entered the Coast Survey. At first assigned to triangulation, he was later transferred to hydrographic work, in which field his abilities soon became manifest. After serving several years in junior capacities, he was assigned to make tide and current investigations in various harbors of the North Atlantic states. The results of his researches are embodied in numerous papers which appeared principally in the annual reports of the Coast Survey between the years 1854 and 1888. In these investigations his attention was directed particularly to the study of the tidal régime as related to hydrographic features, and he was successful in elucidating the complex of forces and factors at work in maintaining or changing shore lines and channels. His principal publications are: *Tides and Tidal Phenomena* (1868); "On the Reclamation of Tide Lands and Its Relation to Navigation" (Coast Survey *Report,* 1869); "On a Physical Survey of the Delaware River in Front of Philadelphia" (*Ibid.,* 1878); "Physical Hydrography of the Gulf of Maine" (*Ibid.,* 1879); "On the Circulation of the Sea through New York Harbor" (*Ibid.,* 1886); *The Under-Run of the Hudson* (1888).

Recognized as the leading hydrographer in America, he was drafted into the service of various government commissions. In 1868 he was sent to Europe to report on hydrographic and engineering progress, and while there he made an inspection of the Suez Canal, his report, entitled "The Coast of Egypt and the Suez Canal," appearing in the *North American Review* for October 1869. He was consulting engineer for various harbors. In 1874 he was appointed a member of the commission on the construction of an interoceanic ship canal to make an inspection and investigation of proposed routes. That same year he was appointed by President Grant a member of the board of engineers to survey the mouth of the Mississippi River, and in 1879 President Hayes appointed him a member of the Mississippi River commission. His scientific attainments likewise received wide recognition. He was elected to membership in various scientific societies; in 1867 Harvard conferred upon him the degree of M.A., in 1869 he was appointed professor of physical hydrography at the Massachusetts Institute of Technology, and in 1875 was made a member of the National Academy of Sciences.

In 1888, after thirty-nine years' service, he resigned from the Coast Survey. The following year he was offered the superintendency of the Survey by President Harrison, but his health did not permit him to assume the burdens of the office. He thereafter lived a quiet, studious life, and with his wife and daughter spent his summers at Nantucket and his winters near Boston. During this period he wrote a biographical sketch of Maria Mitchell (*Proceedings of the American Academy of Arts and Sciences,* vol. XXV, 1890), and one of Ferdinand de Lesseps (*Ibid.,* vol. XXXI, 1896). Mitchell was married three times: first, to Mary Dawes of Boston, who died twelve years later; second, in 1873, to Margaret Hayward, who died in 1875, about five months after the birth of a daughter, his only child; and third, two years later, to his deceased wife's elder sister, Mary Hayward, who died in March 1902. Mitchell's death occurred about nine months thereafter, at the home of his daughter in New York City.

[*Vital Records of Nantucket, Mass. to the Year 1850,* vol. II (1926); *Who's Who in America,* 1901–02; *N. Y. Times,* Dec. 2, 1902; official records Coast and Geodetic Survey; family records.]   H. A. M.

MITCHELL, HINCKLEY GILBERT THOMAS (Feb. 22, 1846–May 19, 1920), Methodist Episcopal clergyman, scholar, was born in Lee, Oneida County, N. Y. His father, James, was the descendant of a colonial New England line; the ancestry of his mother, Sarah Gilbert (Thomas), was partly Welsh and partly

German. Until the age of sixteen he lived in the vicinity of his birthplace (after 1857 on a farm near Prospect), working on the farm and attending the district school, where his thirst for knowledge and his religious feelings were awakened. During the winter of 1862–63 he attended the Seminary at Falley where, in 1864, he joined the Methodist church in fulfilment of a vow. From 1867 to 1869, after finishing his preparation for college, he taught school and worked as a bookkeeper. In preparation for the ministry he entered Wesleyan University in 1869 (A.B. 1873), and Boston University School of Theology in 1873 (S.T.B. 1876). He then studied Semitic languages (chiefly Hebrew under Franz Delitzsch) at Leipzig, 1876–78, where he obtained the degree of Ph.D. in 1879. His dissertation, "Final Constructions in Biblical Hebrew," was later reprinted in the *Journal of Biblical Literature* (vol. XXXIV, 1915).

In the fall of 1879 he became pastor of the Methodist Church in Bearytown (or Fayette), N. Y.; during his incumbency of ten months he was married, June 29, 1880, at Springfield, Mass., to Alice Stanford of Alton, Ill., whom he had met at Leipzig. He taught Latin and Hebrew at Wesleyan University, 1880–83, and from 1883 to 1905 occupied the chair of Hebrew in Boston University School of Theology. From 1882 to 1888 he served as secretary of the Society of Biblical Literature and as editor of its *Journal*. He spent the months from March to September 1888 in Jerusalem and in 1891–92 studied in Leipzig and Paris. In 1901–02 he was director of the American School of Oriental Research in Jerusalem. In the meantime he had been championing in his classes the critical study of the Old Testament and in 1895 he was charged with "Unitarian" tendencies on account of his denial of the Mosaic authorship of the Pentateuch. During the next ten years he became a theological storm center in the Methodist Church. The Methodist bishops warned him in 1899; in 1905 they refused to confirm his reappointment in Boston University, and his chair was given to Prof. Albert C. Knudson. After devoting the years 1906–08 to literary work and the year 1909 to travel in Europe, he was appointed to the chair of Hebrew in Tufts College, which he held to the day of his death. After 1915 he also taught the New Testament.

He wrote the following books: *Hebrew Lessons* (1884); *Amos* (1893); *Isaiah 1–12* (1897); *The World before Abraham* (1901); *Genesis* (1909); *A Critical and Exegetical Commentary on Haggai and Zechariah* (1912); *The Ethics of the Old Testament* (1912). He translated

Charles Piepenbring's *Theology of the Old Testament* (1893) and edited *Tales Told in Palestine* (1904), collected by J. E. Hanauer. He was a contributor to the *Harvard Theological Review*, the *American Journal of Theology*, the *Old Testament and Semitic Studies in Memory of William Rainey Harper* (2 vols., 1908), and the *Journal of Biblical Literature*. He left an unfinished autobiography, *For the Benefit of My Creditors* (1922), which was published after his death. As a scholar he was painstaking, accurate, and conscientious, though not brilliant; as a man he was devout and rigidly loyal to his ideals.

[The fullest source is Mitchell's autobiography, *For the Benefit of My Creditors* (1922); see also: *Who's Who in American Methodism* (1916); for his difficulty with the bishops see *Current Lit.*, Jan. 1906, *Outlook*, Dec. 16, 1905; *Independent*, Nov. 16, 1905; for obituaries, *Jour. of Biblical Lit.*, vol. XL (1921), pp. v–vi, and *Boston Evening Transcript*, May 20, 1920. Mitchell never used the "Thomas" in his name, although it appears in *Who's Who in America*, 1912–13–1920–21.]
R. H. P.

MITCHELL, ISAAC (c. 1759–Nov. 26, 1812), newspaper editor, and novelist, was born in the vicinity of Albany, N. Y. He first appears as editor of the *American Farmer and Dutchess County Advertiser,* a newspaper established at Poughkeepsie, Jan. 8, 1799, under his guidance. In November 1801 he transferred his services to a rival publication, the *Guardian,* in which he purchased an interest, and in June 1802 renamed it the *Political Barometer.* Four years later this paper again changed hands, and Mitchell became editor of the *Republican Crisis* in Albany. In 1812 he returned to Poughkeepsie, where he bought out the *Republican Herald* and began to issue the *Northern Politician.* After a few months, however, he contracted typhus fever, of which he died.

The distinction due him is derived from the bizarre specimen of early American fiction which he wrote and printed over his signature in weekly installments in the *Political Barometer,* beginning with the issue of June 5, 1804, and concluding with that of Oct. 30, 1804. In its original version Mitchell's story has the title, "Alonzo and Melissa, a Tale." On Dec. 2, 1810, a copyright for the publication of the story in book form was obtained in the name of Joseph Nelson "as proprietor" of the *Political Barometer.* That paper advertised, Sept. 25, 1811, "A New Novel, *The Asylum or Alonzo and Melissa,* will be ready for delivery to subscribers and others on Monday next," while on Oct. 2, 1811, the *Republican Herald* of Poughkeepsie advertised: "New Novel just published by Joseph Nelson ... *The Asylum or Alonzo and Melissa,* An American Tale founded on fact by I. Mitchell. In two volumes." The first book contains a preface, a lengthy dissertation on novel writing in general, and an episode with little bearing on the main story, which is unfolded in the second book. This edition of Mitchell's novel was never reprinted. (Copies are in the Library of Congress, the Harvard University Library, and the Poughkeepsie Public Library.)

In the same year, 1811, there appeared at Plattsburg, N. Y., an extraordinary example of plagiarism, a one-volume novel entitled *Alonzo and Melissa or The Unfeeling Father,* of which Daniel Jackson, Jr. (b. May 31, 1790), a teacher at Plattsburg Academy, claimed to be author and proprietor. Jackson's story, a continuous narrative without chapter divisions, is identical, except for a few verbal substitutions with Isaac Mitchell's newspaper story in the *Political Barometer* of 1804. (Jackson, in one instance, substituted "permit" where Mitchell used "suffer.") The chief change Jackson made was in the title. Only one copy of Jackson's 1811 edition is now known to exist (in the possession of the Huntington Library in California), but from its second edition in 1824, the pirated novel became a "best seller." It enjoyed a period of phenomenal popularity extending to 1876, during which it was reprinted at least eleven times.

Why copyright claims were not brought against Daniel Jackson was an unsolved problem until the recent discovery of obituary notices in the *Northern Politician* of Poughkeepsie which show that Joseph Nelson, proprietor of the *Political Barometer* and of the copyright of Mitchell's novel, died Nov. 3, 1812 (*Northern Politician,* Nov. 11, 1812), and Isaac Mitchell himself, some three weeks later.

[Mitchell's obituary in the *Northern Politician,* Dec. 2, 1812; a group of controversial letters on the authorship of *Alonzo and Melissa* is in the *N. Y. Times Sat. Rev. of Books,* June 4, 11, Sept. 3, 17, 1904; Jan. 21, 28, Mar. 4, 1905. See also N. Y. *Evening Post,* Dec. 10, 31, 1904; Feb. 3, 1905; the *Nation* (N. Y.), Dec. 8, 1904; Feb. 2, 1905; Feb. 25, 1909; *Booknotes* (Providence, R. I.), Jan. 14, Feb. 11, Mar. 25, 1905. See also Edmund Platt, *The Eagle's Hist. of Poughkeepsie* (1905); Frank Hasbrouck, *The Hist. of Dutchess County, N. Y.* (1909). The Poughkeepsie Public Library has partial files of the *Political Barometer,* the *Northern Politician,* the *Poughkeepsie Journal,* the *Republican Herald.* For records of the marriage and death of Mitchell's daughter, Aurelia, see Helen W. Reynolds, *Notices of Marriages and Deaths 1778–1825* (Colls. Dutchess County Hist. Soc., 1930). L. D. Loshe, *The Early Am. Novel* (1907, repr. 1930), gives an outline of *Alonzo and Melissa* with a critical appraisal of its importance. E. L. Pearson, *Queer Books* (1928), has a picture of the title-page of Jackson's 1811 edition.]   D. S. R.

MITCHELL, JAMES TYNDALE (Nov. 9, 1834–July 4, 1915), jurist, was the son of Edward P. Mitchell, a merchant of St. Louis, and Elizabeth (Tyndale) Mitchell, member of a Philadelphia family. He was born on his grandfather's farm near Belleville, Ill. At seven he was sent to school in Philadelphia, whither his parents later moved. After attending the Zane Street Grammar School and Central High School in Philadelphia, he entered Harvard College and received the degree of A.B. in 1855. In 1860 he graduated from the law department of the University of Pennsylvania, having previously read law in the office of George W. Biddle and having already been admitted, in 1857, to the Philadelphia bar. His public career began in 1860, when he became assistant city solicitor of Philadelphia. In 1863 he became editor of the *American Law Register.* His editorial work for this journal (1863–88) and for the *Weekly Notes of Cases* (1875–99) covered more than a third of a century. From 1865 to 1873 he served as librarian of the Law Association of Philadelphia. On Dec. 4, 1871, he was elected judge of the district court of the city and county of Philadelphia. In January 1875, under the new state constitution, he became judge of common pleas of Court No. 2 of Philadelphia. He served in this capacity until elected an associate justice of the supreme court of Pennsylvania in 1888, and in this court he served as associate justice till 1903 and as chief justice from 1903 till the expiration of his term in 1910. He was then appointed prothonotary of the supreme court, and this post he held till his death in Philadelphia in 1915.

During his service on the supreme court Mitchell participated in 11,580 cases. He wrote 1,008 opinions, including thirty-four dissenting opinions. In initiating change and shaping policy, this vast amount of judicial work had little significance. Mitchell was once described as "a brake upon the wheels of progress," a man little inclined "to change the ancient ways of the law," imbued with "a tenacious love of the things which time had hallowed" (F. S. Brown, in *Legal Intelligencer,* Jan. 7, 1916, p. 12). His principal positive influence was in connection with legal procedure. In this field he was recognized as an authority and published *Motions and Rules at Common Law According to the Practice of the Courts of Philadelphia County* (1879). His opinions did much to clarify and to standardize the relations of the courts to each other, to juries, and to the bar. In addition to his editorial work for legal journals, he collaborated with Henry Flanders in editing and publishing under official auspices *The Statutes at Large of Pennsylvania from 1682 to 1801* (16 vols., 1896–1911). His ventures in the field of history included *The District Court of the City and County of Philadelphia* (1875). His interest in history was further attested by his active official connection with the Pennsylvania Historical Society for more than half a century, and by his extensive collection of autographs and manuscripts. He never married.

[The best biography is the laudatory but detailed account by H. L. Carson in *Pa. Mag. of Hist. and Biog.*, Jan. 1916. See also: *Pittsburg Legal Jour.*, July 17, 1909; J. H. Martin, *Martin's Bench and Bar of Phila.* (1883); *Pa. Bar Asso.: Reception and Banquet Tendered to James Tyndale Mitchell . . . Nov. 3, 1907* (1908); and S. W. Pennypacker, *The Autobiog. of a Pennsylvanian* (1918). Mitchell's judicial opinions are scattered through 124–226 *Pa. Reports.* Some of his letters are indexed in the collections of the Pa. Hist. Soc.; and the Society has thirty-four boxes of Mitchell papers.]
W. B—n.

MITCHELL, JOHN (d. 1768), physician, botanist, author, and maker of one map, was born probably in the British Isles, though one contemporary understood that he was a native of Virginia (Kalm, *post*, I, p. 384; Martin, in Miller, *post*, pp. 349–50). He could not have emigrated to Virginia until 1721 or 1725 at the earliest. He received his first instruction in botany from Dr. Charles Alston, of the University of Edinburgh (Thatcher, *post*, April 1931, p. 132; January 1932, p. 50), and perhaps held the degree of M.D., but whether from that institution or another is uncertain. He was the physician of the poor of Christ Church Parish in Middlesex County, Va., for some time following 1735, and received his compensation in tobacco; he was made justice of the peace in that county in 1738. He may have been a Quaker. He knew or corresponded with John Bartram, Benjamin Franklin, Cadwallader Colden, Carl von Linné (Linnæus), J. F. Grovenius, Peter Collinson, Pehr Kalm, John Clark, Alexander Munro, the Earl of Bute, and many others, including the Duke of Argyle with whom he traveled in Scotland in 1749. He lived at Urbanna, Va., and practised his profession successfully there and nearby for eleven years following 1735, yet he himself had to leave America in 1746 because of persistent ill health. On the voyage home his ship was attacked by a French privateer and he lost valuable botanical collections, diaries, and medical notes, some of which were irreparably damaged before being returned to him.

He resided chiefly in or near London after leaving Virginia. His versatility is indicated by his writings, which include, in addition to a number of professional letters, a discussion of the principles of botany and zoölogy, written in 1738 (*Acta Physico-Medica Academiæ Cæsareæ . . . Ephemerides . . . Germaniæ*, vol. VIII, Nürnberg, 1748; reprinted as *D. Johannis Mitchell Dissertatio Brevis de Principiis Botanicorum et Zoologorum*, 1769); an account of the opossum

(1745; *MS.* No. I 468, archives of the Royal Society, first printed in 1932, see *Virginia Magazine of History*, October 1932, pp. 338–46); "An Essay upon the Causes of the Different Colours of People in Different Climates" (*Philosophical Transactions of the Royal Society*, vol. XLIII, 1746); "An Account of the Preparation and Uses of the Various Kinds of Potash" (*Ibid.*, vol. XLV, 1750); "A Letter . . . Concerning the Force of Electrical Cohesion" (*Ibid.*, vol. LI, pt. 1, 1760); and "Remarks on the Journal of Batts and Fallam in their Discovery of the Western Parts of Virginia in 1671" (probably written between 1755 and 1760; first printed by Berthold Fernow in *The Ohio Valley in Colonial Days*, 1890, pp. 230–40). He is also generally credited with being the author of two anonymous books on contemporary problems: *The Contest in America between Great Britain and France* (1757), and *The Present State of Great Britain and North America* (1767). With less certainty, a work entitled *American Husbandry* (1775) has been attributed to him, and, with still less plausibility, *A New and Complete History of America*, of which three volumes appeared in 1756 (Carrier, *post*). His reputation in medicine is established because his method of treating yellow fever, as practised after his death by Dr. Benjamin Rush of Philadelphia, is thought to have saved more than six thousand lives in that city during the epidemic of 1793. Mitchell's letters to Cadwallader Colden and Benjamin Franklin describing this method, which was the result of experience in Virginia epidemics in 1737, 1741, and 1742, were published, wholly or in part, in the *Philadelphia Medical Museum* (vol. I, 1805), and the *American Medical and Philosophical Register* (October 1813 and January 1814). As a botanist Mitchell collected and described many plants and introduced many into the permanent flora of the British Isles, although not all the new genera and species which he proposed turned out to be really new. An American partridge berry, *Mitchella repens*, was named for him. In 1747 he was elected a fellow of the Royal Society. In 1751–53 he aspired to be postmaster general of the American Colonies.

His most important work, however, was the great map which he commenced to make in 1750 and published five years later. He was intimate with George Dunk, Earl of Halifax, in or before 1753. Through this intimacy he doubtless secured access to the great depot of American manuscript maps and geographical materials in the archives of the Board of Trade and obtained the opportunity to compile his *Map of the Brit-*

Mitchell

ish and French Dominions in North America with the Roads, Distances, Limits, and Extent of the Settlements, scale 1 : 2,000,000. It was published at London, under the auspices of the board, shortly after Feb. 13, 1755. Twenty years later the fourth English edition appeared, with the title simplified by the substitution of the words British Colonies for the words British and French Dominions. In the intervening years the map had been printed at least five times in England; it was also translated and printed eight times in France, twice in The Netherlands, and twice in unacknowledged plagiarism by Antonio Zatta in Italy. There was also a full-scale French reproduction of two parts of the map during the American Revolution. Portions of the map were copied twice in Spain. Its quality and timeliness were attested further by more than a score of small-scale, simplified plagiarisms published in England between 1755 and 1782, including such well-known maps as those of Jean Palairet; none of these acknowledged indebtedness to Mitchell. The whole map and different portions of it have since been reproduced in the publications of half a dozen historical and geographical societies in the United States and Canada, and officially by the British Foreign Office, the Province of Ontario, the Province of Quebec, the Dominion of Canada (1910 and 1926), the states of Maine, Massachusetts, Maryland, and Virginia, and (at intervals from 1829 to 1933) by the government of the United States of America.

The map is thought to have been in use in the British House of Commons during the debate on the Quebec Act of 1774; it is known to have hung in the halls of Congress in 1802 and several times subsequently. It was used in the peace negotiations at the end of the American Revolution, in the discussion of British land grants in the Ohio and Mississippi valleys, and in scores of controversies involving the boundary lines existing at the time of its publication. Great Britain and the United States agreed to its official status in the Convention of Sept. 29, 1827; the King of The Netherlands made one of his conclusions, albeit an erroneous one, after using it in 1831; it exerted substantial influence in the negotiation and ratification of the Webster-Ashburton treaty of 1842, and serious argument was based upon it by Great Britain before the Court of Arbitration at The Hague in 1910 in connection with the North Atlantic Coast Fisheries Arbitration. It was submitted in evidence before the Law Lords of the British Privy Council in 1926 in the appeal of Price Brothers & Company, Limited, from a judgment of the su-

preme court of Canada, and in 1926–27 in the Canada-Newfoundland (Labrador) boundary case. It was used as evidence before the Supreme Court of the United States in 1926 in the Wisconsin-Michigan boundary case, in 1926–27 in the Great Lakes level case, and in 1932 in the New Jersey-Delaware boundary case. Without serious doubt Mitchell's is the most important map in American history.

[A. F. Pollard, in Dict. Nat. Biog., XXXVIII (1894), 70; Lyman Carrier, "Dr. John Mitchell, Naturalist, Cartographer, and Historian," Ann. Report Am. Hist. Asso. for 1918, vol. I (1921), pp. 201–19, and article in Jour. Am. Soc. of Agronomy, May 1919; Lawrence Martin, "Mitchell's Map" in Hunter Miller, Treaties and Other International Acts, III (1933), 328–51, "Mitchell's Map" (unpublished book), and notes and articles in various publications of the Library of Congress, 1926–33; Herbert Thatcher, "Dr. Mitchell, M.D., F.R.S., of Virginia," chapters at irregular intervals in Va. Mag. of Hist. and Biog., beginning Apr. 1931; biographical references in each of the works cited above; see also Pehr Kalm, En Resa til Norra America, I (1753), 384; Joseph Lucas, Kalm's Account of His Visit to England (1892), pp. 31–32. Among the famous, or important, or annotated copies of Mitchell's map which have survived and been identified are the "King George Map" and the "Record Office Map" (in the British Museum and the Colonial Office at London, respectively), John Jay's Mitchell (N. Y. Hist. Soc.), the Steuben-Webster Mitchell, and the "Sheet which contains the Bay of Passamaquoddy," sent by Benjamin Franklin to Thomas Jefferson when the latter was secretary of state (both maps in Dept. of State, Washington, D. C.), and d'Aranda's transcription of the Franklin red-line map (Archivo Histórico Nacional, Madrid). The most comprehensive collection of original printed editions of Mitchell's map, together with facsimiles, photostats of annotated copies, etc., is that in the Lib. of Cong.]   L. M.

MITCHELL, JOHN (Feb. 4, 1870–Sept. 9, 1919), labor leader, was born in Braidwood, Ill. His father, Robert Mitchell, was a Civil War veteran and a coal miner. John's mother, Martha (Halley) Mitchell, died when he was two and a half years old. His father was killed when John was six and he was brought up by his stepmother, a devout Presbyterian. His early education was gained from a few weeks a season at the district school. He went into the mines at the age of twelve, although the state law put the limit at thirteen. Faced by the industrial depression of 1886–87 he set out on two tramping trips to Colorado and Wyoming mines but returned to Illinois as penniless as he left. In 1885 he joined the Knights of Labor, but in the strike of 1888 in Spring Valley, which lasted a year and resulted in a twenty per cent. reduction in wages, he learned the need of a separate miners' union. Later, in 1890, when pressure from below brought the Knights and the trade union together in this industry to form the United Mine Workers of America, Mitchell joined the local branch. On June 1, 1891, he was married to Katherine O'Rourke, the daughter of a miner.

He joined in the many discussions with fellow workers on the remedies for unemployment and low wages, reading law for a year and studying social and economic problems.

In 1894 Mitchell was one of 125,000 men who obeyed the call of the weak national United Mine Workers of America to strike and was discharged at its end. Obtaining work in a near-by camp he was found by an old acquaintance who picked the youthful miner to be secretary-treasurer of the sub-district. Mitchell's willingness to serve at a time when the organization was still weak conduced to his advancement and in 1897 he became a member of the State Executive Board. That year he had an active part in the first victorious national strike called by the union. Elected a delegate to the national convention of the union, he was elected vice-president, and in September 1898, almost by accident, he stepped into the vacant presidency. In the anthracite coal fields of Pennsylvania in 1902 he brought together 150,000 English and non-English mine workers, who by a five months' strike won from the consolidated owners an advance of wages, a reduction of hours, and an arbitration agreement which was continued and strengthened after that time. He thus, at the age of thirty-two, became the leader of the first successful organization of immigrant labor from eastern and southern Europe, speaking more than a dozen languages and hitherto despised and exploited by the English-speaking laborers and their employers. He sought out the possible leaders of the many nationalities, trained them in the principles of united action, and won the support of public opinion, business men, and especially of Catholic priests. He himself in time accepted the Catholic faith.

Physically Mitchell was slight and wiry. He had a sober, thoughtful appearance which was enhanced by the long ministerial black coat he wore. He was recognized as distinctly conservative. In this position he was fortunately aided by the recovery of business prosperity, after 1898, and the resulting ability of employers to grant better terms of employment. It was the depression in the bituminous coal fields, after 1904, and the failure of several strikes against a falling market, that led to his defeat by the bituminous mine workers in 1907. Yet he retained the devotion of the anthracite workers. He was the least hurried of labor leaders. His ability to wait for his opponents to involve themselves in contradictions, and then his ability to state the issue in moderate but clear and convincing terms, so evident at the conference called by President Roosevelt, at which Mitchell was bitterly assailed

by the employers who had refused to confer until national pressure was brought to bear, caused Roosevelt to say of him: "There was only one man in the room who behaved like a gentleman, and that man was not I." It was in 1902, when he had organized and conducted the anthracite strike, that he became a national figure and achieved the name, bestowed by his admirers, of "the greatest labor leader the country ever saw."

Mitchell's presidency of the union ended in 1908, after which he lectured on trade unionism. He then became head of the trade-agreement department of the National Civic Federation, from which he resigned in 1911 on account of a resolution of the United Mine Workers calling for his resignation either from the union or from the Civic Federation. In 1915 he was appointed chairman of the New York state industrial commission, a position which he held until his death in New York City in September 1919. He had published in 1903 *Organized Labor,* showing his interest in the reconciliation of the ideals of labor and capital through the recognition of the union. In 1913 he published *The Wage Earner and His Problems,* which gave in familiar terms the purposes of unions and the human needs they meet. This book had a part in creating and fashioning the forces of national thought and action on the labor problem.

[A complete bibliography is contained in Elsie Glück's excellent and complete study *John Mitchell, Miner—Labor's Bargain with the Gilded Age* (1929) which is based on study of original sources. See also an article by his secretary, Elizabeth C. Morris, "John Mitchell, the Leader and the Man," *Independent,* Dec. 25, 1902; W. E. Weyl, "John Mitchell, the Man the Miners Trust," *Outlook,* Mar. 24, 1906; *Who's Who in America,* 1918–19.]   J. R. C.

MITCHELL, JOHN AMES (Jan. 17, 1845–June 29, 1918), artist, novelist, and editor, was born in New York City, the son of Asa and Harriet (Ames) Mitchell. Early in life he showed an aptitude for drawing. He attended Phillips Exeter Academy and the Lawrence Scientific School at Harvard, aiming toward an architectural career. Later he studied architecture in Boston and from 1867 to 1870 at the École des Beaux-Arts in Paris. In 1876, after following the profession for a few years in Boston, he returned to Paris, this time to study painting at the Atelier Julien. Here he developed an interest in studies in black and white and succeeded so well that some of his etchings were published in *L'Art.* In 1880 he returned to New York to work as an illustrator. He believed that there ought to be some American medium for the publication of line work by Americans, a belief confirmed by the fact that a zinc process for the reproduction of black and white had recently been developed. With this much to go on, with a ten-thousand-dollar legacy as capital, and against the advice of friends, he founded *Life,* with Edward S. Martin as literary editor. The first issue appeared Jan. 4, 1883. At the outset the young founder had some difficulty finding enough illustrators to keep up with his ideas but he soon gathered about him a number of promising young men, among them Francis Gilbert Attwood of the *Harvard Lampoon,* Oliver Herford, and Charles Dana Gibson. The editor himself contributed cartoons and editorials.

As an editor Mitchell had very decided opinions and was not afraid to express them. He was an outspoken opponent of modern medicine and fought the use of serum in the cure of any disease. He contended that sanitation, not vaccination, had reduced the scourge of smallpox, and he was opposed to the use of dogs, which he loved, in medical vivisection. Owing to his outspoken policy he was frequently involving his magazine in libel suits, one of the chief being that brought by the theatrical producers, Klaw and Erlanger, who objected to a cartoon run in *Life* after the Iroquois Theatre fire in Chicago in 1903. In this as in many cases the jury returned a verdict in favor of the weekly. The success of *Life* was due largely to Mitchell's quick ability to divine and anticipate the trends in American popular thought and to give expression to them in the form of humor. His belief that humor should depend not upon old hackneyed jokes but upon topics of current interest led to an emphasis on politics. It was said that politicians of the nineties and early nineteen hundreds feared *Life's* cartoons more than its editorials. When Mitchell had well established his magazine he began writing novels. His best known were *Amos Judd* (1895) and *The Pines of Lory* (1901). His other works include: *The Summer School of Philosophy at Mt. Desert* (1881), illustrated by the author; *A Romance of the Moon* (1886); *The Last American* (1889); *Life's Fairy Tales* (1892); *That First Affair* (1896); *Gloria Victis* (1897); *The Villa Claudia* (1904); *The Silent War* (1906), and *Pandora's Box* (1911).

Although Mitchell was a great lover of dogs he was an even greater lover of children. It was this interest which prompted him to establish "Life's Fresh Air Fund," which made possible the establishment of summer camps for poor city children. Mitchell's last two campaigns were the result of the war: one a bitter anti-German battle resulting from the torpedoing of the *Lusitania* and the other a movement to raise funds

for French war orphans. Through *Life* he collected more than two hundred thousand dollars for the latter purpose and in 1918 subscribers to the magazine were supporting 2,800 French children. Mitchell retained until his death a controlling interest in *Life* and had a hand in passing upon all material published in it. He died of apoplexy at his summer home in Ridgefield, Conn., survived by his wife, Mary Mott Mitchell. During his life he was a member of the National Institute of Arts and Letters.

[Jubilee number of *Life,* Jan. 1893; Sinclair Lewis, "John Ames Mitchell," *Book News Monthly,* Mar. 1912; E. S. Martin, "John Ames Mitchell, 1845–1918," *Harvard Grads.' Mag.,* Sept. 1918; *Am. Mag.,* June 1911; *Life,* July 18, 1918; *N. Y. Times,* June 30, 1918.]   R.H.

MITCHELL, JOHN HIPPLE (June 22, 1835–Dec. 8, 1905), lawyer, United States senator from Oregon, son of John Hipple and Jemima Mitchell, was born in Washington County, Pa. His father took him at the age of five to a farm in the neighboring Butler County where he attended a rural school. At seventeen he began teaching during the winter while in the other months of the year he studied at Butler Academy and afterward also at Witherspoon Institute. He then read law and was admitted to its practice in 1857 at Butler, Pa. In this period of his life he was married to Sadie Hoon whom he left behind with their two children when he went to California in 1860. He remained for only a short time in California, then went on to Portland, Ore., arriving in July 1860. Here, under the name of Mitchell, he took up the practice of law, during his first year was appointed city attorney, and in his second year was elected a member of the city council. With the outbreak of the Civil War he supported the Unionist cause, helped to defeat the movement to form at that time a "Pacific Coast Republic," and in 1862 was elected to the state Senate as a candidate of the Unionist party. Reëlected to that body in 1864, he was made its president and in 1866 came within one vote of being elected United States senator, an election won in 1872 against Henry W. Corbett. In the meantime, he had built up a lucrative law practice, associated, 1862–83, with Joseph N. Dolph and aided by his connection with Ben Holladay, who dominated river and railroad transportation in Oregon, and whose interests in the Oregon legislature Mitchell defended. During the senatorial campaign of 1872 the Corbett faction quoted him as having boasted: "Whatever is Ben Holladay's politics, is my politics, and whatever Ben Holladay wants, I want" (Joseph Gaston,

Portland, Its History and Builders, 1911, I, p. 561).

After his election as senator in 1872 the Democratic opposition brought up against him his Pennsylvania "past" in an effort to prevent him from taking his seat. In 1862 he had married Mattie Price of Oregon City without securing a divorce from his first wife. There were six children in his Oregon family. He was charged with having deserted his family in Pennsylvania, with financial dishonesty, with bigamy, and with living under an assumed name, charges which the Senate committee on privileges and elections decided (June 27, 1874) did not merit investigation. Mitchell, however, felt compelled to make reply to this attack in a public letter in which he protested his innocence (*Oregon State Journal,* June 7, 1873). He did, however, secure a divorce from his first wife and legalize the change in his name by an act of the Multnomah county court in 1874. The story of his private life continued to come up in succeeding campaigns, but more detrimental to his political success was the opposition of the Corbett group and of Harvey W. Scott, editor of the Portland *Morning Oregonian* and a rival for the leadership of the Republican party in the state, who came to oppose bitterly Mitchell's successive attempts to be reëlected United States senator. (For Scott's version of the beginning of this feud see the *Oregonian,* Dec. 14, 1905, p. 8.) The attacks in the *Oregonian* became more virulent after Mitchell had caused Scott's removal in 1876 as customs' collector at Portland. In 1878 a Democratic majority in the legislature brought about the election of James H. Slater to succeed him as senator, and in 1882, unable to secure his own election, he threw his vote to his law partner, Dolph, who was ultimately elected.

The regular legislative session of 1885 adjourned without the election of a senator, but at a called session Mitchell was a second time elected, Nov. 18, 1885. Seventeen Democrats voted for him after the *Oregonian* had printed facsimile letters written by Mitchell, showing marital infidelity, and charged that his conduct in the United States Senate had been "as grossly mercenary and corrupt" as his private life had been immoral (*Oregonian,* Nov. 16, 1885). Later it was charged that he had bought the votes necessary to his election with money furnished by the Southern Pacific Railroad (Joseph Gaston, *The Centennial History of Oregon,* 1912, I, pp. 665–68). He had, however, a large and devoted following and he was reëlected in 1891 without Republican opposition. He failed of reëlection in

1897 because his stand on the money question had satisfied neither gold nor silver men. In 1901 he was for the fourth time elected United States senator. In July 1905 he was convicted in the United States district court on an indictment of having received fees for expediting the land claims of clients before the United States Land Commissioner, a charge that the evidence, as presented by special prosecutor Francis J. Heney, seemed amply to sustain. (Full stenographic report of the trial, *Oregonian,* June–July, 1905.) His death came pending an appeal. The Senate departed from its usual custom in honoring a deceased member by refusing either to adjourn or to send a delegation to attend his funeral.

Mitchell was the most popular political leader of his generation in Oregon. Possessed of an impressive physical presence and considerable power as a public speaker, as well as being adept in the politician's art, he drew thousands of devoted followers. His friends were rewarded with office and he secured generous appropriations for light-houses, for the improvement of rivers and harbors, and for public buildings throughout Oregon. He was also adroit in championing the popular will on questions of public interest. He supported the interstate commerce, the Sherman silver purchase, and Chinese exclusion acts in the Senate; gave his approval to the "Oregon system" of initiative, referendum, and direct primary; supported woman's suffrage, and made capital of the opposition of the *Oregonian* by representing himself as the candidate of the people against the conservative and business interests.

[H. W. Scott, *Hist. of the Ore. Country* (1924), vols. I, IV, and V, and *Hist. of Portland* (1890); *Who's Who in America,* 1903–05; *Morning Oregonian,* Jan. 17, 1898, Dec. 9, 1905; *Oregon State Jour.,* Dec. 16, 1905.]
R. C. C.

MITCHELL, JOHN KEARSLEY (May 12, 1793–Apr. 4, 1858), physician, chemist, and physiologist, was born in Shepherdstown, Jefferson County, Va. (now in W. Va.). His father, Alexander, a Scotch physician belonging to an Ayrshire family of prosperous farming folk, had settled in America some years before and had married Elizabeth Kearsley, of a Pennsylvania family. He died when he was thirty-six years old. When eight years of age John, whose mother also had died, was sent to his father's people in Scotland, to receive his schooling at Ayr and his academic degree from the University of Edinburgh. He returned to Virginia, and in 1816 began the study of medicine, first under a preceptor in Jefferson County and then under Dr. Nathaniel Chapman in the University of Pennsylvania, where he was graduated M.D. in 1819. His health at this time was not good—he had had several hemorrhages from the lungs while a medical student—and he became a ship's surgeon. He continued in this position for three years, making voyages to Canton and Calcutta. In 1822 he began practice in Philadelphia and in the same year married Sarah Matilda Henry, daughter of Alexander Henry. He had nine children, of whom Silas Weir Mitchell [q.v.] was the third. In 1824 he lectured on the institutes of medicine and physiology in the Philadelphia Medical Institute, and later (1833–38), on chemistry in the Franklin Institute. In 1841 he was elected to the chair of theory and practice of medicine in the Jefferson Medical College, Philadelphia, which position he held till his death. He was also visiting physician to the Pennsylvania Hospital and to the city hospital. In 1856 he had an apoplexy which left him with a residual hemiplegia and a slight difficulty in articulation, but without mental defect. He died of pneumonia.

Mitchell wrote a great deal on medical subjects. He was strongly of the opinion that rheumatism was a disease of the spinal cord and had considerable success by local treatment of the spine. He was the first to describe the spinal arthropathies. He was an early writer on osmosis and on the liquefaction of carbonic acid gas. He was much interested in mesmerism and wrote about it. He described the cure of muscular cramps and spasm by the application of a tourniquet to the middle of the forearm, a procedure he had learned in Japan. In 1849 he published a volume containing six lectures, *On the Cryptogamous Origin of Malarious and Epidemical Fevers,* in which, on *a priori* grounds, he maintained the parasitic origin of these diseases. In addition to his scientific interests, he had a definite trend toward literature, and in 1839 published *Indecision, a Tale of the Far West, and Other Poems.* The book does not show great genius, but does prove the author had definite poetic instincts. He was very fond of music and had an excellent tenor voice. Weir Mitchell derived his literary and scientific genius from his father but did not possess his musical ability.

[S. H. Dickson, *The Late Prof. J. K. Mitchell; Inaugural Lecture, Jefferson Medic. Coll.* (1858); F. H. Garrison, *An Intro. to the Hist. of Medicine* (1929); *Trans. Medic. Soc., State of Pa.,* n.s. IV (1859); *Boston Medic. and Surgic. Jour.,* Aug. 8, 1849; *Charleston Medic. Jour.,* Jan. 1858; *Medic. and Surgic. Reporter,* May 1858; *North Am. Medico-Chirurgical Rev.,* May 1858; *Daily News* (Phila.), Apr. 6, 1858.] C.W.B.

MITCHELL, JONATHAN (1624–July 9, 1668), Congregational clergyman, the fifth son of Matthew and Susan (Butterfield) Mitchell, was born in the parish of Halifax, Yorkshire, England. He was brought by his parents to America in 1635, graduated from Harvard in 1647, and was ordained on Aug. 21, 1650. The year previous he had received a call to succeed Hooker at Hartford, but because of a prior commitment he became pastor of the church at Cambridge, Mass., as successor to Thomas Shepard, whose widow, Margaret (Boradel) Shepard, he married on Nov. 19, 1650. In May of the same year he became and continued for the rest of his life to be a fellow of Harvard. Cotton Mather says that "his *Sermons* ... were admirably *Well-studied.* ... And when he came to Utter what he had Prepared, his Utterance had had such a becoming *Tuneableness,* and *Vivacity,* to set it off, as was indeed Inimitable; though many of our Eminent Preachers, that were in his Time Students at the *Colledge,* did essay to Imitate him" (*Magnalia,* Bk. IV, ch. iv, §9). "Such *Holiness* and *Patience,* and sweet *Condescension,* were his *Incomparable* Abilities accompanied withal, that Good Men, who otherwise differed from him, would still speak of him with Reverence" (*Ibid.,* §14). In the course of his career he came to differ with Henry Dunster, the president of Harvard, under whom he had been trained, and who "was unaccountably fallen into the Briars of Antipædobaptism; and being briar'd in the Scruples of that Perswasion" (*Ibid.,* §10). A remonstrance cost Dunster the presidency of the college, but did not disturb the friendship of the two men.

Mitchell *"was a Circle, whereof the Center was at* Cambridge, *and the Circumference took in more than all* New England" (*Ibid.,* §13). His most outstanding achievement was the adoption by the Synod of 1662 of the "Half-Way Covenant," of which he was a leading advocate, an attempt to meet the problem which arose because of declining religious enthusiasm. The requisite for church membership in the earlier period had been a personal experience of religion, but many could not meet the test, so it was proposed to relax the standard half way. In accord with previous usage only the regenerate should be admitted to the Lord's Supper, but the children of those who did not dissent from the doctrine of the church, and were not scandalous in life, might be brought to baptism. Thus the good standing of the unregenerate parents received a partial recognition and there was a greater chance of retaining the children within the fold, for "The Lord hath not set up

Churches onley that *a few old Christians* may keep one another warm while they live, and then carry away the Church into the cold grave with them when they dye" (*A Defence of the Answer and Arguments of the Synod*, 1664, p. 45). The Half-Way Covenant was an incongruous combination of two conceptions of the church, as an ark of salvation comprising all in the parish, and as a community of the saints, composed only of the converted. The whole compromise was swept away by the revival of Jonathan Edwards.

Mitchell lived to be but forty-three or forty-four. In spite of exercise he could not free himself from "an ill Habit of Body. Of extream Lean he soon grew extream Fat; and in an *extream* hot Season a *Fever* arrested him" (Mather, *op. cit.*, §16). Several of his sermons were published after his death under the title: *A Discourse of the Glory to which God Hath Called Believers by Jesus Christ* (London, 1677).

[A brief biography with a complete bibliography is contained in J. L. Sibley, *Biog. Sketches of the Grads. of Harvard Univ.* (1873), I, 141–57. The primary source is the life by Cotton Mather, in *Magnalia Christi Americana* (1702). There is a sketch of his connection with the Half-Way Covenant in W. Walker, *The Creeds and Platforms of Congregationalism* (1893), ch. xi, together with the text of the "Preface to the Result of 1662," which is "probably from the pen of Jonathan Mitchell," pp. 301 ff. The theological aspects of Mitchell's relation to the Half-Way Covenant are more fully discussed by F. H. Foster in *A Genetic Hist. of the New England Theol.* (1907). For family genealogy and sketch of Mitchell see Wm. Cothren, *Hist. of Ancient Woodbury, Conn.*, vol. II (1872).]

R. H. B.

MITCHELL, LUCY MYERS WRIGHT (Mar. 20, 1845–Mar. 10, 1888), historian of ancient art, was born at Urumiah, Persia, the eldest child of the Rev. Austin Hazen Wright, M.D., and Catherine A. (Myers) Wright. Her paternal ancestors, of English stock, came to New England between 1630 and 1640 and were among the first settlers of Hartford, Vt., where her father was born. Her mother, of German and New England descent, went in 1843 to Urumiah to teach in the school of the mission of which Dr. Wright was in charge. There they were married in 1844, and there four daughters and a son were born and passed their early years. The father was a scholarly linguist, and the children constantly heard foreign languages spoken. In 1860 the family came to America, and a little later Lucy entered Mount Holyoke Seminary; but in 1864, at her own request, returned with her father to Persia. After his sudden death, in 1865, she came to America and in 1867 was married to Samuel S. Mitchell of Morristown, N. J. She and her husband went as missionaries to Syria, but the failure of his health forced them to leave that country, and the rest of her life

was passed almost continuously in Europe. She spoke Syriac, Arabic, French, German, and Italian, and until 1873 was interested chiefly in philological researches. She prepared a dictionary of modern Syriac, which was not published; the manuscript became the property of Cambridge University, England.

In 1873 she began those studies in classical archeology which resulted in her becoming one of the foremost archeologists of her time. Her husband, who was a painter of considerable ability, rendered her valuable assistance with pen and pencil and discriminating criticism. In Rome (1876–78) she gave parlor lectures to ladies on Greek and Roman sculpture, taking her hearers also to the museums. Many of the leading archeologists of Europe aided and encouraged her in her work; she was granted special opportunities in museums and libraries; and in 1884 she was made a regular member of the Imperial German Archeological Institute, an honor which had been bestowed upon only one other woman. In Berlin (1884–86), as part of her preparation for a work on Greek vases and vase-paintings, she began the study of ancient and modern Greek and of the art of photography, making excellent progress in all these pursuits. In the winter of 1886–87, however, it became apparent that she was suffering from renal and cardiac disease, and after a long struggle for life at Montreux and Lausanne she died at Lausanne early in 1888.

Lucy Mitchell was tall and fair, with a cordial and responsive expression and manner which gained her friends at once. She was of an earnest and intense temperament, but modest and retiring, and was happiest when serving others. Her one book is *A History of Ancient Sculpture* with its accompanying volume of plates entitled *Selections from Ancient Sculpture* (1883). Without claiming great originality she made full use of the discoveries which had been made and published up to that time, and added sound observations of her own. The book was highly praised by competent critics, and, in spite of subsequent discoveries, remains a scholarly and eminently readable presentation of its subject, a work which will always be of value. Her other published writings comprise articles, for the most part on Greek art, in the *Century Magazine* and the *New York Times*.

[T. D. Seymour in the *Critic*, Apr. 14, 1888; *N. Y. Times*, Apr. 3, 1888; obituary notice of Prof. John Henry Wright in *Harvard Grads. Mag.*, Mar. 1909.]

H. N. F.

MITCHELL, MARGARET JULIA (June 14, 1837–Mar. 22, 1918), actress, affectionately known as "Maggie Mitchell" to play-goers of four decades, created in the title rôle of *Fanchon the Cricket* a dramatic miniature of such delicacy, faithfulness, charm, and subtle power, that it must rank among the finer traditions of the stage. She was born in New York City. Her elder half-sisters, Mary and Emma Mitchell, were early on the stage, and when she was twelve, Maggie herself became so ambitious to act that her mother placed her under the tutelage of a veteran English player. On June 2, 1851, she made her first appearance at Burton's Chambers Street Theatre as little Julia in *The Soldier's Daughter*. Her playing won her an engagement for the ensuing season at the Bowery Theatre, where she played boy parts, dancing between the acts. Here she scored her first real hit some months later as Oliver Twist. After winning favor in New York and Boston with the James M. Robinson company, she began to star. During nomad years she ranged principally up and down the Ohio and the Mississippi in such light plays as *A Middy Ashore, The Pet of the Petticoats, The Daughter of the Regiment,* and *Our Maggie.* She was a favorite everywhere, especially in the South, and in 1857 she was the principal attraction at Burton's Theatre, New York.

In 1860 she appeared in New Orleans in the title rôle of *Fanchon the Cricket,* a play adapted for her from George Sand's *La Petite Fadette,* which was to bring her wealth and a unique place in the hearts of the people. Until then she had been but one of many clever American comediennes. After appearing with brilliant success in the South and in Boston, where the play was given with an all-star cast, on the night of June 9, 1862, she opened at Laura Keene's little theatre, rechristened the New Olympic, in New York. It is said that after the last rousing curtain-call, she walked off the stage, famous. The play ran for six weeks, and during twenty succeeding years, never staled with the public. In temperament and physique she fitted the part, that of a sprite-like child, grand-daughter to a reputed witch, herself a trifle "touched by the moon." The actress was a little creature, winsome and piquant rather than beautiful, and animated with an electric energy which followed Fanchon through her lightning changes of mood. From skipping about the scene, laughing spontaneously, she dropped to sudden mysterious melancholy or flashed into elfin rages. It was "one of those perfect bits of acting before which even the chronic fault-finder is dumb" (Phelps, *post*, p. 402). The grace of her fantastic shadow-dances inspired verses

by Emerson. In later life she played with ability many other parts, notably Jane Eyre, which the poet Longfellow urged her to repeat in England, Pauline in *The Lady of Lyons,* Mignon, and Parthenia in *Ingomar.* But it is her Fanchon which will be remembered.

Maggie Mitchell was apparently married three times. Her first marriage, said to have taken place in the fifties, ended in divorce. On Oct. 15, 1868, she was happily married at Troy, N. Y., to her manager, Henry Paddock, of Cleveland, by whom she had two children, who survived her. In 1892 she left the stage, retiring to Elberon, N. J. Paddock having died, she married again before 1909, Charles Abbott, formerly her leading man, whose legal name seems to have been Mace, for she was buried as Margaret Julia Mace. After this marriage she made her home in New York, where she died of apoplexy in 1918.

[T. Allston Brown, *A Hist. of the N. Y. Stage* (1903), vols. I and III; J. N. Ireland, *Records of the N. Y. Stage from 1750 to 1860* (1867); J. B. Clapp and E. F. Edgett, *Players of the Present,* pt. 1 (1899), pt. 2 (1900); H. P. Phelps, *Players of a Century* (1880); F. E. McKay and C. E. L. Wingate, *Famous Am. Actors of Today* (1896); *Who's Who in America,* 1916–17; *Galaxy,* Aug. 1868; *Dramatic Mirror,* Apr. 6, 1918; *N. Y. Times, N. Y. Tribune,* Mar. 23, 1918.]
M.B.H.

MITCHELL, MARIA (Aug. 1, 1818–June 28 1889), astronomer and teacher, was the sister of Henry [*q.v.*] and the daughter of William Mitchell, 1791–1869 [*q.v.*], and Lydia (Coleman) Mitchell, both of Quaker ancestry. She was born on the island of Nantucket, which had been for more than a century the principal seat of the whaling industry. Its captains undertook long voyages on uncharted and perilous seas, and were perforce expert navigators and commanders of men. During their long absences their wives shouldered the family responsibilities alone and thus acquired an unusual freedom of action and independence of judgment, while their Quaker training made them simple and genuine. Born into such a community, Maria Mitchell was endowed with some of its finest traits, a keen intellect, a strong character, and a nature simple and truthful. Her father was deeply interested in astronomy and with plain equipment kept up continuous observations of the sky. He made a business of rating chronometers which were brought him by returning captains. He often called upon his children for assistance, and Maria, who was the third in a family of ten, began at an early age to be his special helper. She excelled in arithmetic and often worked out formulas which she did not understand. She also learned to use her father's

Mitchell

instruments, at first to help him but later for her own pleasure. Her education was carried on in the schools of Nantucket where her teachers encouraged her love of mathematical studies, but before long she outstripped them and began working by herself.

While she was still young, an excellent opportunity came for her to cultivate her talent. She was appointed librarian of the town Atheneum, and as her hours were not confining she had abundant leisure for private study. She found the scientific shelves well stocked with books on mathematical subjects, and read such difficult works as Laplace's *Mécanique Céleste,* annotated by Bowditch, and Gauss's *Theoria Motus* in the original Latin. Having in addition to her intellectual tastes a strong interest in young people, she gladly acted as guide to their reading and often formed helpful friendships with them. Both she and her father, through their interest in astronomy, were brought into contact with eminent scientific men in Boston and the vicinity whose friendship proved most valuable.

Her free evenings were spent with the telescope exploring the sky, and she observed among other objects the positions of several comets and worked out their orbits. On one eventful evening in October 1847 she discovered a new comet. It was announced by her father to their friends in Boston who in turn communicated it to astronomers in Europe, then the distributing center for astronomical information. The discovery brought her a gold medal from the king of Denmark, offered several years earlier, in order to stimulate an interest in astronomy, to any one who should discover a comet previously unknown. This unusual and picturesque achievement brought her friendly recognition from other astronomers and scientific men. She was elected to membership in several learned societies, among them the American Academy of Arts and Sciences (honorary member, 1848; later fellow), was appointed a computer for the *American Ephemeris and Nautical Almanac,* and was presented with an excellent telescope by a group of American women, the use of which enlarged her observing program. Women of intellectual ambitions pointed to her work as an example of what a woman could accomplish as a scholar when given opportunity and encouragement. She was received everywhere as a person of distinction and ranked in the public eye with such progressive women as Julia Ward Howe, Lucy Stone, and Mary A. Livermore [*qq.v.*], in whose projects she was deeply interested. In 1857–58 she traveled

abroad with the purpose of visiting observatories and meeting scientific men, taking with her many letters of introduction. The resulting contacts greatly enriched her experience.

After the death of her mother in 1861 she and her father removed to Lynn, Mass. In succeeding years she followed with interest the plans and fortunes of Vassar College, the new enterprise for the advanced education of women which was announced to the world in 1861, but she was quite surprised when its founder, Matthew Vassar, invited her to become its first professor of astronomy. Since she had no experience as a teacher she hesitated to accept; but, encouraged by her father, she yielded and in 1865, at the age of forty-seven, took up the duties of a professor in a new and untried institution. She was the only member of the faculty widely known both at home and abroad, and her name at once inspired confidence in the college and indicated its purpose of maintaining a high standard of scholarship. Her uncompromising support of this ideal was of inestimable value in the early days of Vassar, when its inadequate endowment made it dependent for its existence upon the approval of a somewhat unsympathetic public. She had a powerful influence upon her students, not only in their intellectual development but in preparation for their later usefulness in society. She mingled in their social life and her simplicity and wit made her gatherings in the observatory ever memorable. Her strength of character, her genuineness, her kindly human interest made her an impressive personality. In 1869 her scientific attainments brought her election as a member of the American Philosophical Society, while her position as an educator was recognized by institutions other than Vassar, several of which conferred honorary degrees upon her. She died at Lynn, in her seventy-first year. In 1922 a bust of her was unveiled in the Hall of Fame of New York University.

[Phebe Mitchell Kendall, *Maria Mitchell: Life, Letters, and Journals* (1896); Mary W. Whitney, "Life and Work of Maria Mitchell," in *Papers Read before the Asso. for the Advancement of Women: 18th Women's Cong., Toronto, Can., Oct. 1890* (1891); "Maria Mitchell," in *Sidereal Messenger,* IX (1890), 49; Henry Mitchell, "Maria Mitchell," in *Proc. Am. Acad. Arts and Sci.,* vol. XXV (1890); M. K. Babbitt, *Maria Mitchell as Her Students Knew Her* (1912); *Boston Transcript,* June 28, 1889; J. M. Taylor and E. H. Haight, *Vassar* (1915); other references in accounts of the beginnings of Vassar College.]   C.E.F.

MITCHELL, NAHUM (Feb. 12, 1769–Aug. 1, 1853), jurist, author, composer, and congressman, was born at East Bridgewater, Mass. Through his father, Cushing Mitchell, who married Jennet Orr of East Bridgewater, he was fourth in descent from Experience Mitchell, of London, who arrived at Plymouth in the *Anne* in 1623. Nahum prepared for college under the Hon. Beza Hayward of Bridgewater, and entered Harvard in July 1785, receiving the degree of A.B. in 1789. In the meantime he had "kept" school at Weston, Bridgewater, and Plymouth. In the autumn of 1789 he began to read law with Judge John Davis, 1761–1847 [*q.v.*], then living at Plymouth. Admitted to the bar on Nov. 24, 1792, he began practice at East Bridgewater. Six years later he was first elected to the state House of Representatives, of which he remained a member until 1802. For one term (1803–05) he represented the Plymouth district in Congress as a Federalist, and subsequently served again in the state House of Representatives (1809–10, 1812–13). He was state senator from Plymouth County (1813–14), member of the governor's council (1814–21) and treasurer of Massachusetts (1821–26). From 1812 to 1821 he sat as a justice of the circuit court of common pleas, serving as chief justice during the last two years. He was on commissions to establish the boundaries with Rhode Island and Connecticut in 1801 and 1823, respectively. In 1827 he was chosen chairman of the commissioners in charge of the route for the Boston & Albany Railroad. In 1839–40, as a representative from Boston, he sat in the Massachusetts General Court for the last time.

In spite of his almost constant service to the commonwealth, Mitchell found time to build up an "honorable practice" at law. In his leisure he grew trees, studied music, and compiled facts of local history. He presided over the first temperance society of his native town, helped to found and endow there in 1799 the Plymouth County Academy, as a trustee of which he served for fifty-four years, and sponsored, as president, Bridgewater's first lyceum (1827). The variety and extent of his interests and his duties make the description of him as a man "exact and methodical in his habits; of untiring industry; and of a remarkably even temper" seem eminently fitting.

His interest in music led him to assist Bartholomew Brown and others in compiling *The Columbian and European Harmony: or Bridgewater Collection of Sacred Music* (1802). The third edition, 1810, carried the title: *Templi Carmina . . . or The Bridgewater Collection of Sacred Music,* and later editions were generally known simply as "The Bridgewater Collection." It was widely used in New England churches and had no little influence in determining the character of church music in that field. Some

of the compositions were the work of Mitchell himself.

Meanwhile, he had been carefully collecting material for his *History of the Early Settlement of Bridgewater, in Plymouth County, Massachusetts* (1840), an excellent work of its kind, on which he was engaged at intervals for over forty years. In its first form it was published as "A Description of Bridgewater" in the *Collections of the Massachusetts Historical Society* (2 ser., vol. VII, 1818), of which society he was elected a member the same year. From 1835 to 1836 he served as its librarian and from 1839 to 1844, as treasurer. A reprint in facsimile of the *History* was brought out at Bridgewater in 1897, and contains as a frontispiece a reproduction of the portrait of Mitchell painted in 1837 by Bass Otis of Boston. According to a fellow member of the Massachusetts Historical Society, Ellis Ames, Mitchell's "antiquarian and genealogical knowledge was copious and exact" (*Proceedings,* April 1854, p. 561).

"Economical and unassuming in manner," Mitchell, with his "genial face, his tall, erect, dignified person and elastic step," was a familiar sight about Plymouth County for years. On Aug. 1, 1853, already well past eighty-four, he set out for Plymouth, in the heat of midsummer, in order to join in the celebration of the embarkation of the Pilgrims from Delft Haven for America. After arriving he discovered that his pocketbook, containing one hundred and fifty dollars and some valuable papers, was missing, and stooping to look for it, fainted. He died later in the day and was buried at East Bridgewater. In 1794 he had married Nabby, daughter of Silvanus Lazell, by whom he had five children, three girls and two boys.

[*Proc. Mass. Hist. Soc.,* Apr. 1854; *New-Eng. Hist. and Geneal. Reg.,* July 1847, July 1864; F. J. Metcalf, *Am. Writers and Compilers of Sacred Music* (copr. 1925); *Biog. Dir. Am. Cong.* (1928); *The Mass. Reg.,* 1802–26; *Fleet's Reg. and Pocket Almanac* (1799); *Daily Herald* (Newburyport, Mass.), Aug. 3, 1853.]

S. M—l.

MITCHELL, NATHANIEL (1753–Feb. 21, 1814), governor of Delaware, Revolutionary soldier, was born near Laurel, Sussex County, Del., the son of James and Margaret (Dagworthy) Mitchell. His long and respectable record as an officer in the Revolutionary War commenced in 1775, when he was raised to the rank of captain and transferred to Col. Samuel Patterson's Delaware Battalion of the "Flying Camp." The next year he was again transferred (Jan. 20, 1777), this time to Col. William Grayson's Additional Continental Regiment, and on Dec. 23 of the same year was raised to the rank of major. Mitchell remained in the Continental Line to the end of active fighting. His regiment was consolidated, April 1779, with Col. Nathaniel Gist's Additional Continental Regiment, and later in the year he was made brigade-major and inspector to Gen. Peter Muhlenberg, serving only part time in this capacity, however. While campaigning under Lafayette in Virginia during the latter part of 1780, he was sent to Petersburg to obtain intelligence of the enemy and collect stores. During the campaign he was captured and made prisoner of war, being paroled on May 10, 1781. By resolution of Congress his detachment had been disbanded Jan. 1, but he did not know it, and his petition for pay from that date was unsuccessful (*Journals of the Continental Congress, 1774–1789*, XXI, 1039–40; *Papers of the Continental Congress, Letters, M 78*, vol. XVI, no. 243, MSS., Library of Congress).

Mitchell then probably retired to his home at Laurel. From 1786 until the date of his death, he held offices in Delaware almost continuously, but without special distinction. His political career began with his election as delegate to the Continental Congress. He presented his credentials on Jan. 18, 1787, and appeared on Feb. 1 of the following year with credentials of reelection (*Journals of the Continental Congress*, no. 1, vol. XXXVIII, MSS., Library of Congress). It was probably no descent from being delegate to the enfeebled Congress to the position of prothonotary of Sussex County, to which he was appointed in the fall of 1788; this office he held until 1805 (Conrad, *post*, II, 689). On Jan. 15 of that year he became governor of Delaware, having been elected over Joseph Haslet in 1804 by a very small majority, and served until 1808. From 1808 to 1810 he was a member of the Delaware House of Representatives, and from Jan. 2, 1810, to May 1812, of the state Senate (*Journal of the House of Representatives of the State of Delaware*, 1808–11; *Journal of the Senate of Delaware*, 1808–11, 1812–14). His wife was Hannah Morris Mitchell, daughter of Anthony C. Morris (*The Mitchell Family Magazine*, January 1917, p. 79); they had one son, Theodore. Mitchell died in Laurel and is buried at Christ Church.

[In addition to the above references, see H. C. Conrad, *Hist. of the State of Del.* (3 vols., 1908); H. H. Bellas, "A Hist. of the Delaware State Soc. of the Cincinnati," in the *Papers of the Hist. Soc. of Del.*, no. 13 (1895), which is inaccurate with respect to some of the dates.]   C. W. G.

MITCHELL, ROBERT BYINGTON (Apr. 4, 1823–Jan. 26, 1882), soldier, governor of New Mexico Territory, was born in Mansfield, Rich-land County, Ohio, of Scotch-Irish parents. Whether he graduated at Kenyon College, Ohio, or Washington College, Pa., is a controverted matter; neither school has a record of his attendance. He studied law in the office of John K. Miller at Mount Vernon, Ohio, was admitted to the bar, and began practice at Mansfield. In the Mexican War he served as first lieutenant in the 2nd Ohio Infantry. Later he resumed the practice of law, and in 1855 was elected Democratic mayor of Mount Gilead. In the same year he was married to Jennie, daughter of Henry St. John of Tiffin, Ohio.

A business trip to Kansas Territory in 1855 convinced Mitchell that it offered opportunities for advancement; accordingly in October 1856 he migrated thither and settled at Paris, Linn County. Throughout the Kansas struggle he was a conservative, law-and-order Free-State man. He was elected to the lower house of the territorial legislature in 1857 and was reëlected a year later. In 1858 he was a delegate to the Leavenworth constitutional convention. The following year he was appointed treasurer of the territory, serving until it became a state in 1861. When the Republican party supplanted the Free-State organization in 1859, he returned to the Democratic party, and was appointed delegate to the Charleston convention in 1860.

After brief service as adjutant on the staff of Gov. Charles Robinson [*q.v.*], Mitchell was commissioned colonel of the 2nd Kansas Volunteer Infantry. At the battle of Wilson's Creek he was severely wounded, but recovered and was transferred to a cavalry regiment. On Apr. 8, 1862, President Lincoln commissioned him brigadier-general, and at the battle of Perryville, Ky., he commanded the 9th Division. He was then stationed at Nashville for several months. As chief of cavalry in the Army of the Cumberland he made commendable contributions to Union successes in southeastern Tennessee in 1863. Severe wounds incapacitated him temporarily for field service, and Secretary Stanton ordered him to Washington for court-martial duty. Early in 1864 he was assigned to the district of Nebraska Territory in the department of Kansas. A year later he was transferred to the district of North Kansas, and when the two divisions of the state were combined, June 28, 1865, he was appointed to the command. Throughout the war he had the reputation of being a shrewd and energetic commander.

Late in 1865 President Johnson nominated Mitchell to be governor of New Mexico Territory. The nomination was confirmed Jan. 15, 1866, and he took office on the 16th of the following July. He soon quarreled with the legislature and his removal was requested. He was accused of making a vacancy appointment of delegate to Congress, of remaining in Washington during an entire session of the assembly, of removing officials appointed by the secretary during his absence, and of usurpation of power. In 1868 the organic act was amended to abrogate the governor's absolute veto. Mitchell relinquished the office in 1869 and returned to Kansas. In 1872 he was nominated for Congress by Liberal Republicans and Democrats, but was defeated. Subsequently, he removed to Washington, D. C., where he died.

[A sketch of his career, published in the La Cygne *Weekly Jour.*, Apr. 26, May 3, 1895, was reprinted in *Kan. Hist. Colls.*, XVI (1923–25); material relating to his Civil War career is in *War of the Rebellion: Official Records (Army)*; for resolutions of the New Mexico legislature consult *House Misc. Docs.* 64 and 94, 40 Cong., 2 Sess. See also D. W. Wilder, *The Annals of Kansas* (1886); H. H. Bancroft, *Hist. of Ariz. and New Mex.* (1889); R. E. Twitchell, *The Leading Facts of New Mex. Hist.*, vol. II (1912); *Harper's Weekly*, Apr. 4, 1863; *Evening Star* (Washington), Jan. 28, 1882.]   W. H. S—n.

MITCHELL, SAMUEL AUGUSTUS (Mar. 20, 1792–Dec. 18, 1868), geographer, publisher of geographical works, was the youngest son of William and Mary (Alton) Mitchell. His father came to America from Scotland when he was a lad of twelve, learned the clothier's trade, and settled in Bristol, Conn., about 1773. Samuel Mitchell was born at Bristol and died in Philadelphia. In August 1815 he married Rhoda Ann Fuller. Possessing literary as well as business talent, he devoted his early life to teaching, but, becoming dissatisfied with the treatment of geography in the textbooks then in use, transferred his attention to writing and publishing geographical works. Forty years of his life, in Philadelphia, were given over to preparing textbooks, maps, and geographical manuals, the demand for which became so great that, at one time, more than 400,000 copies were sold annually. More than 250 persons were employed in the manufacture of these books, and every effort was made to include in them the results of the latest geographical discoveries.

In 1831 he published *A New American Atlas* and the same year issued separate maps of several sections of the United States, following these by maps of the settled portions of the various territories. In 1832 appeared *Mitchell's Traveller's Guide through the United States*; it contained the latest information on stage, canal, and steamboat routes, and was reëdited annually for more than twenty years. In 1834 a series of "Tourist's Pocket Maps" of the different states was begun, supplemented in 1836 by *Reference and Distance Map of the United States*. Keeping an eye on current events, Mitchell issued in 1846 a *Map of Mexico* and *Mitchell's New Map of Texas, Oregon and California*, and in 1847, *Map of the Seat of War*; while in 1849 there came from the press *Description of Oregon and California . . . with a Map*, and in 1861, at the outbreak of the Civil War, a *Map of the United States and Territories*, on which the various fortifications then existing were displayed. In the meantime, among other works, he had published *Mitchell's Compendium of the Internal Improvements of the United States* (1835); *A General View of the World Comprising a Physical, Political, and Statistical Account of Its Grand Divisions* (1842); *An Accurate Synopsis of the Sixth Census of the United States* (1843); *A General View of the United States* (1846), and in 1847, *A New Universal Atlas*, which went through many editions. He had early conceived the idea of a system of school geographies adapted to the progressively developing capacities of the student, and issued, among others: *Mitchell's School Geography . . . Illustrated by an Atlas of Sixteen Maps* (1839); *Mitchell's Geographical Reader* (1840); *Mitchell's Primary Geography* (1840); *A Key to the Study of the Maps Comprising Mitchell's School Atlas* (1841), later entitled *Mitchell's Geographical Question Book*; *Mitchell's Ancient Atlas* (1844); *Mitchell's Ancient Geography* (1845); *Mitchell's Biblical and Sabbath School Geography* (1849); *Intermediate or Secondary Geography* (1850). In this group may also be included *Mitchell's Atlas of Outline Maps* (1839), and *Key for Exercise on Mitchell's Series of Outline Maps* (1842). Most of these works went through many successive editions, some of them, in revised form, being reissued after the beginning of the twentieth century.

Many of Mitchell's earlier maps were engraved by J. H. Young, and compare favorably with the contemporary work of John Arrowsmith the younger, distinguished English mapmaker. Mitchell entered the field of cartography at an opportune moment, when national expansion, following the expeditions of Lewis and Clark, Pike, and others, stimulated an interest in the newer parts of the country and created a market for travel maps and guidebooks. He remains an outstanding figure in the development of American geography; he placed his subject accurately and popularly before the students of his day, and met the demand for maps with all the resources at his command.

[S. A. Allibone, *A Critical Dict. of English Lit. and Brit. and Am. Authors* (1870), II, 1328; *Bristol, Conn.* (1907); *Commemorative Biog. Record of Hartford County, Conn.* (1901); *Geneal. of Some Descendants of Edward Fuller* (1905); *Press* (Phila.), Dec. 19, 1868; Philadelphia directories; information from Hist. Soc. of Pa. and Conn. Hist. Soc.]   J.M.T.

MITCHELL, SILAS WEIR (Feb. 15, 1829–Jan. 4, 1914), physician, neurologist, poet, and novelist, was born in Philadelphia, Pa., the son of John Kearsley Mitchell [*q.v.*] and Sarah Matilda (Henry). He attended the "University Grammar School" at Fourth and Arch Streets, the descendant of the old Academy of Philadelphia from which the University of Pennsylvania sprang, and in 1844 entered the College Department of the University, remaining until illness compelled his withdrawal during his senior year. In 1906 he was granted the degree of bachelor of arts as of the class of 1848. In 1850 he graduated from the Jefferson Medical College, in which his father was a professor, and then spent a year abroad, studying chiefly with Claude Bernard, the physiologist, and Charles Phillippe Robin, the microscopist. Returning in the fall of 1851, he encountered heavy professional and family responsibility on account of the failing health of his father, whose assistant he became. He had very positive interest in research and was elected a member of the Academy of Natural Sciences of Philadelphia in 1853. His first paper, "Observations on the Generation of Uric Acid and Its Crystalline Forms," was published in the *American Journal of the Medical Sciences* in July 1852. In 1858 he read a paper before the biological section of the Academy of Natural Sciences, entitled "Observations on the Blood Crystals of the Sturgeon," which was published in the *Proceedings* of that year. This subject interested him through life and ended in the great work on the crystalography of hemoglobin published in 1909 by E. T. Reichert and A. P. Brown, in whose investigations Mitchell had a part. His next important contribution was "Researches upon the Venom of the Rattlesnake," which appeared in *Smithsonian Contributions to Knowledge* (vol. XII, 1860). He was the first to point out that snake venom is a double, not a single, poison. Hideyo Noguchi's great work, done many years later, had its origin in Mitchell's early researches.

Early in the Civil War he was appointed an acting assistant surgeon in the Union army, and improved the opportunity to study nerve wounds and diseases afforded by the Turner's Lane Hospital, Philadelphia. G. R. Moorehouse and W. W. Keen were associated with him in his army work. In collaboration with them he published two important studies: *Gunshot Wounds and Other Injuries of Nerves* (1864) and *Reflex Paralysis* (1864). The former was amplified and reissued in 1872 under the title *Injuries of Nerves and Their Consequences*. This work received immediate recognition and wide acclaim. It is an important contribution to knowledge of the peripheral nerves, both from the point of view of the symptomatology of peripheral nerve injuries and that of the treatment of such injuries.

The wide scope of Mitchell's investigations makes it difficult to classify, or, at least, to list, all his contributions. From the end of the Civil War to 1870 he wrote articles on toxicology, peripheral nerve paralyses, the physiology of the cerebellum, opium and its effects, and other subjects. From 1870 to 1878 he published thirty-four neurological articles, among them "Influence of Nerve Lesions on the Local Temperature" (*Archives of Scientific and Practical Medicine*, vol. I, 1873), "On the Spasmodic Diseases of Stumps" (*Philadelphia Medical Times*, Feb. 13, 1875), and "On a Rare Vaso-motor Neurosis of the Extremities and on the Maladies with Which It May Be Confounded" (*American Journal of the Medical Sciences*, July 1878). His description of this rare neurosis, erythromelalgia, is a masterpiece. He was the first to describe it adequately, and it has been named "Weir Mitchell's disease." In 1874 he called attention to a new clinical entity, post-paralytic chorea. His researches on the physiology of the cerebellum mark him as an experimental investigator of the first rank. They were carried on from 1863 to 1869, but he did not begin publishing his results until April of the latter year (*American Journal of the Medical Sciences*).

In 1871 appeared his *Wear and Tear,* a book calling attention to the inability or indisposition of Americans to play, and the increase in nervous disorders that was likely to follow. The book had a wide sale and made a deep impression. It was followed in 1873 and 1875 respectively by two articles on rest in the treatment of the neuralgia of locomotor ataxia (*American Journal of the Medical Sciences*, July 1873), and on rest in the treatment of disease (*A Series of American Clinical Lectures*, edited by E. C. Seguin, vol. I, no. 4, 1875). These were really preparations for his therapeutically important work *Fat and Blood*, which appeared in 1877. In this volume Mitchell advocated rest, overfeeding, massage, electrotherapy, and physiotherapy in the treatment of functional nervous disorders. These methods were viewed at first with skepticism, but, because of the success which followed Mitchell's use of them, they soon came to be regarded as important aids in treating nervous disorders. The demonstration of their value was one of his most significant contributions to medicine, and they have become known as the "Weir Mitchell Rest Cure." The book went through many editions, and was translated into French, German, Italian, and Russian. In 1881 he published a volume entitled *Lectures on the Diseases of the Nervous System, Especially in Women,* and in 1897, *Clinical Lessons on Nervous Diseases,* works which contain many original and valuable observations. Mitchell was a very keen clinician, and pointed out the seasonal relations of chorea, pre-hemiplegic and post-hemiplegic pains, the disorders of sleep, and the faulty reference of sensations of pain. His "Physiological Studies on the Knee-jerk" (*Medical News,* Feb. 13, 20, 1886), in collaboration with Morris Lewis, is still one of the best treatments of this subject.

Mitchell's contributions to medical literature covered many different fields. In all he wrote 119 neurological, and fifty-two pharmacological, physiological, and toxicological papers. Besides those already mentioned these included studies on the nerve supply to the skin, spinal arthropathies, neurotomy, the cremaster reflex, hysteria, tendon and muscle jerks, facial tics, sleep, and sciatica. To the knowledge of many of these subjects he made original contributions. Mitchell was a fine combination of the practitioner and investigator in medicine. Many of his original investigations were made in clinical subjects, but his studies of snake venom and of the functions of the cerebellum indicate that he was also a laboratory student of the first rank. He was never satisfied unless he was engaged in research of some sort. He was made a professor in the Philadelphia Polyclinic and College for Graduates in Medicine, but the hospital with which his name is most intimately associated is the Philadelphia Orthopædic Hospital and Infirmary for Nervous Diseases. To this institution he devoted over forty years of service, and under his influence it became a center for the treatment of nervous disorders. Here many came to study with him and here he gave most of his instruction. He was a member of numerous societies, American and foreign, and the recipient of many honors.

Mitchell did not, however, limit himself to medical interests; he became distinguished also in the field of literature. His first creative work was in verse. As early as 1856 he had made a collection of his poems which, upon the advice of Dr. Oliver Wendell Holmes, he did not publish, and his initial volume of verse, *The Hill of*

Stones, did not appear until 1882. His most important early poems are to be found in *A Psalm of Deaths, and Other Poems* (1890); *Francis Drake—A Tragedy of the Sea* (1893), in which he included his vivid dramatic narratives; and *The Mother and Other Poems* (1893), containing in the title poem one of his most appealing lyrics. In 1896, *Collected Poems* was published, and in 1901 *Selections from the Poems of S. Weir Mitchell* was issued in London. The last included his finest effort in verse, "Ode on a Lycian Tomb," inspired by the death of his only daughter, and written with a restraint and a distinction of phrase which make it one of the outstanding elegies in American literature. His ability was revealed also in his metrical adaptation of one of the most exquisite of Middle English poems, *Pearl* (1906), a father's symbolic vision of a little daughter in Paradise. Mitchell's last volume of verse, *The Comfort of the Hills,* appeared in 1909, and a definitive edition of his poetical works, *Complete Poems,* in 1914.

He began his career as a writer of fiction with "The Case of George Dedlow," published anonymously in the *Atlantic Monthly* as the leading article for July 1866. This satire on spiritualism, in which a soldier whose arms and legs have been amputated sees them revived at a seance, was so realistic that contributions were sent to the author under the impression that George Dedlow was a real person. The story is also of great interest because it portrays the real feelings of a soldier upon entering a battle, antedating the work of Stephen Crane [*q.v.*] by nearly thirty years. After three novelettes, published in one volume in 1880, the first two of which, "Hephzibah Guinness" and "Thee and You," dealt with life in Philadelphia in the early nineteenth century, Mitchell returned to the Civil War period in his first long novels, *In War Time* (1885), which appeared originally as a serial in the *Atlantic Monthly* (January to December 1884), and *Roland Blake* (1886). In the former, which has for its background the army hospital in Philadelphia, he portrays a number of characters, notable among whom is Dr. Ezra Wendell, the earliest of the writer's profound studies in human weakness. *Roland Blake,* so far as the hero, a Union soldier, is concerned, is a portrait of valor and mysticism; but the greatest character in the story, Octopia Darnell, who absorbs without mercy the emotional lives of those she dominates, is the first of the abnormal women in the depiction of whom Mitchell was unrivaled in his time.

Roland Blake represents in itself the two forms of fiction in which Mitchell was to excel—the novel of psychology and the historical romance. *Far in the Forest,* a dramatic story of the woodland region of Pennsylvania, appeared in 1889, and in *Characteristics* (1891), Mitchell created a different form of fiction, one in which the story consists largely of the conversations of a group of people whose center is Owen North, a physician. This conversation reproduces the flavor of the Saturday evening gatherings at the author's home. *When All the Woods Are Green* (1894) was based on Mitchell's summer experiences in Canada, and, while a favorite with those who love fishing as did he, has less framework than the most of his fiction. His great historical novel of the Revolution, *Hugh Wynne, Free Quaker,* first appeared in the *Century Magazine* (November 1896–October 1897) and was published separately in 1898. Mitchell spent seven years of study in preparation for the work, but the composition took but six weeks. While the hero is fictitious, Edward Wynne, an ancestor of the second Mrs. Mitchell, came over with Penn in 1682, and the story has the atmosphere of reality. Mitchell knew Philadelphia's history well, and his portrayal of life there in war time, and especially his portraiture of Washington, Hamilton, Rush, and others, give the book an unrivaled position among the romances of the Revolution.

His next work, *The Adventures of François* (1899), which had also appeared in the *Century Magazine* (January–September 1898), is a novel of the French Revolution, and its hero, a foundling and a thief "of whom Nature meant to make a gentleman," is one of Mitchell's most vivid portraits. His preparation as usual was thorough, and in his description of the seamy side of Paris life he showed the effect of his close study of the methods of the great realist Defoe, of whose works he possessed a complete collection, including a number of first editions. *The Autobiography of a Quack* (1900), an expansion of a story published in the *Atlantic Monthly* (October and November 1867), was followed by *Dr. North and His Friends* (1900), a sequel to *Characteristics,* in which the same group of characters appear, and, in addition, Sybil Maywood, probably the first example of dual personality in American literature. As early as 1888 Mitchell had published a scientific account of a woman living in a state of double consciousness (*Transactions of the College of Physicians of Philadelphia,* vol. X). *Circumstance* (1901), a story laid in Philadelphia immediately after the Civil War, contains another of his remarkable studies of women in Lucretia Hunter, the adventuress. In 1903 he published *Little Stories,* a collection

of tales notable for their compression and dramatic quality. "A Consultation" could have been written by no one else. The same may be said of *Constance Trescott* (1905), perhaps the most truly organized of all his novels. The account of Constance's revenge for the murder of her husband has seldom been equaled in modern fiction.

In 1907 Mitchell again revivified the past of Philadelphia in *The Red City,* giving a picture of the national capital when the struggle between Democrats and Federalists made Washington's administration a hotbed of intrigue. Washington the statesman is painted as accurately as Washington the soldier had been in *Hugh Wynne,* and the yellow-fever epidemic of 1793 is depicted with the skill which the knowledge of the physician made possible. *John Sherwood, Inn Master* (1911), while not on the same high level, contains an interesting study of insanity, while his last novel, *Westways* (1913), is one of his best. Here the Civil War is described from the point of view of a surgeon with Doubleday's Pennsylvania troops, the forces that held the center against Pickett's charge at Gettysburg.

Mitchell's own selection of his most significant work reveals his sound critical judgment. In a personal letter (to one of the writers of this article), he said: "Of course Hugh Wynne is regarded as the book which is likely to have any continuous life—let us say, the immortality of a decade. But François is the book of my affections and the only novel with which I can find no fault is *Constance Trescott.*" To these must be added, however, as of special excellence, *Roland Blake, The Red City,* and *Westways,* pictures of life in great moments of the Republic, and *Characteristics* and *Dr. North* for their originality of form.

In 1858 Mitchell married Mary Middleton Elwyn, daughter of Alfred Langdon Elwyn of Philadelphia, who died in 1862 leaving two sons, John Kearsley, who became associated with his father in his profession, and Langdon Elwyn, playwright and poet. In 1875, Mitchell married Mary Cadwalader, daughter of Gen. Thomas Cadwalader of Philadelphia. It was in memory of their daughter that the "Ode on a Lycian Tomb" was written. While he never accepted public office, in a strict sense, he was constantly called upon for advice and help in progressive civic movements in Philadelphia. He preferred to limit his official duties to such semi-public offices as his trusteeship of the University of Pennsylvania, which began in 1875. Here he worked with Provost William Pepper in the development of the school of medicine and the foundation of the department of hygiene. Among his honorary degrees were the M.D. *honoris causa,* from the University of Bologna in 1888, and an LL.D. from Edinburgh in 1895. In 1902, upon the foundation of the Franklin Inn, the writers' club of Philadelphia, he became its first president, remaining in office till his death. It was in such associations, but more especially at his own residence at 1524 Walnut Street, where he was at home every Saturday evening to his friends, that he shone in repartee and presided over "the best talk in Philadelphia."

George Meredith, who read *Roland Blake* three times, said, "It has a kind of nobility about it," and this comment remains the best characterization of its author. He met financial loss after the failure of the Real Estate Trust Company, of which he was a director, with the same courage that had animated him in his early days of struggle. Liberal, tolerant, with a readiness to help younger men and accord them full credit for their achievement, a patrician to the finger tips, Weir Mitchell wore his many honors with the ease of those to whom great achievement brings no change of character.

[In 1894 *A Catalogue of the Scientific and Literary Work of S. Weir Mitchell,* containing an analytical bibliography of his publications from 1852, was printed under his direction. Additional items were added in MS., bringing the record up to 1907, and two copies were deposited in the library of the University of Pennsylvania. Neither this list nor that given in the only biography, *Weir Mitchell, His Life and Letters* (1929), by Anna Robeson Burr, is in all cases accurate. Appreciations of his character and achievements, read at the memorial meeting in Philadelphia, by Talcott Williams, Dr. William H. Welch, and Owen Wister, were published in 1914 under title of *S. Weir Mitchell, M.D., LL.D., F.R.S., 1829–1914—Memorial Addresses and Resolutions.* See also C. W. Burr, *S. Weir Mitchell, Physician, Man of Science, Man of Letters, Man of Affairs* (1920); *Proceedings of the Mitchell Memorial Meeting of the Phila. Psychiatric Soc.,* Dec. 13, 1929, containing "S. Weir Mitchell, Poet and Novelist," by F. E. Schelling, and "S. Weir Mitchell, Physician," by C. W. Burr; *Gen. Mag. and Hist. Chronicle of the Univ. of Pa.,* Apr. 1930; A. H. Quinn, "Weir Mitchell, Artist, Pioneer and Patrician," the *Century,* Jan. 1930; *Public Ledger* (Phila), Jan. 5, 1914.]   C. W. B.
A. H. Q.

MITCHELL, STEPHEN MIX (Dec. 9, 1743–Sept. 30, 1835), jurist and statesman, was born at Wethersfield, Conn., the son of James Mitchell, a merchant and West-Indian trader who had emigrated about 1730 from Paisley, Scotland. Stephen was the only child of his father's second marriage. His mother, Rebecca, a first cousin of Jonathan Edwards, was a daughter of the Rev. Stephen Mix (Harvard, 1690), a native of New Haven and pastor of the First Church of Wethersfield. Prepared for college by the aid of a private tutor, Stephen entered Yale where he graduated with the class of 1763. He continued his studies there as a Berkeley scholar for the next three years. In the fall of 1766 he

began a three years' service as tutor at the college, and while carrying on his work as a teacher, he studied law under the direction of the elder Jared Ingersoll. On Aug. 2, 1769, he was married to Hannah Grant of Newtown, Conn., whose father had left her a large fortune. He was admitted to the bar in 1770 and practised first at Newtown, thereafter at Wethersfield, until in May 1779 he was made associate judge of the Hartford county court. He began here a judicial career which lasted with but one interruption (1793–95) until his retirement from the bench in 1814. In May 1790, after eleven years as associate judge, he was placed at the head of the county court. As an Assistant, 1784–85 and 1787–93, he was a member of the supreme court of errors. In October 1795 he was raised to the superior court of the state and when in 1807 the powers of a supreme court were transferred from the Council to his tribunal, he was made chief justice. This office he held until 1814 when he retired under the age limit. As a jurist he was less distinguished for deep learning and brilliance than for impartiality in the conduct of judicial proceedings; he was much more interested in justice than in the intricacies of the law. Not given to words, he wrote few of the opinions of his court, preferring to concur with, or dissent from, those of his associates.

During his service on the bench and in the interim from 1793 to 1795 Mitchell held numerous legislative positions. During the Revolution, from 1778 to 1783, he served in the lower house of the Connecticut legislature. In 1784 he was transferred to the Council where, except for 1786, he sat until 1793 when he was chosen to fill the unexpired term of Roger Sherman in the United States Senate. He retired from this post in 1795 to take his place in the superior court of his state. He had meanwhile been chosen to represent Connecticut in the Continental Congress from 1783 to 1788. Here he was partially responsible for securing Connecticut's title to the Western Reserve. In 1818 he served in the state constitutional convention. Throughout his life he was a staunch Federalist. In 1814 he retired to Wethersfield where he spent his last score of years. He was a benevolent patriarch with abundant white hair, clean-shaven face, and aquiline nose, a venerable figure dressed in knee breeches, woolen hose, and a long coat with capacious pockets, trudging about his farm with the aid of a great oaken staff or riding through the village in a low chariot specially constructed for him. He died in 1835 having outlived his wife and all but four of his eleven children. His six sons all graduated from Yale. The youngest was the father of Donald Grant Mitchell [q.v.], "Ik Marvel," whose descendants possess an admirable portrait of the Judge done by Samuel F. B. Morse in 1827. Another by the same painter is owned by the Connecticut Historical Society at Hartford.

[F. B. Dexter, *Biog. Sketches of the Grads. of Yale Coll.*, vol. III (1903) ; E. E. and E. M. Salisbury, *Family Hists. and Geneals.*, vol. I (1892) ; H. R. Stiles, *The Hist. of Ancient Wethersfield, Conn.*, vol. II (1904) ; 13 *Conn. Reports*, App. ; *Biog. Dir. Am. Cong.* (1928) ; "The Supreme Court of Conn.," *Green Bag*, Oct. 1890 ; *Columbian Reg.* (New Haven, Conn.), Oct. 10, 1835.]   P. D. E.

MITCHELL, THOMAS DUCHÉ (1791–May 13, 1865), physician, was born in Philadelphia, of a family of proved "respectability and morality," established there for four generations. He received his English and classical education at Carson Academy, and the Friends' Academy. After spending almost a year in the drug store and chemical laboratory of Dr. Adam Seybert [q.v.], where he acquired his taste for chemistry, he took up the study of medicine under the preceptorship of a Dr. Parrish, with whom he continued for three years. In the meantime he attended lectures in the medical department of the University of Pennsylvania, receiving his degree there in 1812. He began the publication of papers on medical subjects while yet an undergraduate and the year of his graduation he was appointed professor of animal and vegetable physiology in St. John's College, Philadelphia. In 1813 he was appointed physician to the Philadelphia Lazaretto, which position he held for three years. From 1822 to 1831 he practised in Frankford, Pa.

In 1819 he published a small volume entitled, *Medical Chemistry; or a Compendious View of the Various Substances Employed in the Practice of Medicine.* The following year he was offered the professorship of chemistry in Ohio University at Athens, Ohio, but declined it. He was an early advocate of total abstinence from alcohol, and in 1826 he attempted to form a total-abstinence temperance society at Frankford, but was unsuccessful. Apparently, too few of his contemporaries shared his views. In 1831 he accepted the chair of chemistry at Miami University, but before the end of the year went to a similar position in the Medical College of Ohio.

In 1832 he published his *Elements of Chemical Philosophy,* a volume of about 600 octavo pages, and his *Hints on the Connexion of Labor with Study, as a Preventive of Diseases Peculiar to Students,* a duodecimo. In 1832–33 he was co-editor of the *Western Medical Gazette.* He went to Louisville, Ky., in 1837 as professor of chem-

istry at the Medical Institute, but a month later, accepted a similar position in Transylvania University, Lexington. In 1839 he was transferred to the chair of materia medica and therapeutics, which he held until 1849, teaching obstetrics, also, in the session of 1845–46. In 1849 he became professor of theory and practice of medicine, obstetrics, and medical jurisprudence, at the Philadelphia College of Medicine. In 1850 he published his *Materia Medica and Therapeutics* (revised edition, 1857), an octavo of 750 pages, and also edited John Eberle's *A Treatise on the Diseases and Physical Education of Children,* to which he added notes and about 200 pages of new material. In 1857 he became professor of materia medica in Jefferson Medical College. At the time of his death he left unpublished a work of 600 pages on the "Fevers of the United States." He was the biographer of John Eberle [q.v.] in Samuel D. Gross's *Lives of Eminent American Physicians* (1861), and a frequent contributor to medical periodicals.

[Sketch by "Cato" in *Boston Medic. and Surgic. Jour.*, Dec. 10, 1851 ; August Schachner in H. A. Kelly and W. L. Burrage, *Am. Medic. Biogs.* (1920) ; Robert Peter, *The Hist. of the Medic. Dept. of Transylvania Univ.* (1905), being Filson Club Pub. No. 20 ; Otto Juettner, *Daniel Drake and His Followers* (1909) ; the *Press* (Phila.), May 17, 1865.]   P. M. A.

MITCHELL, WILLIAM (Dec. 20, 1791–Apr. 1, 1869), amateur astronomer, was born in Nantucket, Mass., the son of Peleg and Lydia (Cartwright) Mitchell, and a lineal descendant of several of the first settlers of the island, including Peter Folger [q.v.], the grandfather of Benjamin Franklin. Peleg Mitchell was the grandson of Richard who emigrated to Rhode Island in 1708. The Mitchells, like many other residents of Nantucket, belonged to the Society of Friends. They were in comfortable circumstances until the War of 1812, when their income, hitherto derived from whaling ventures, was greatly reduced. William was a natural student, with a scientific mind, and an innate fondness for astronomy. The strict discipline of the times, however, prevented his having any love for school or his teachers. He prepared for Harvard College but he did not enter, and at fifteen years of age he undertook to learn the cooper's trade. He was married, Dec. 10, 1812, to Lydia Coleman of Nantucket. They had ten children, two of whom, Maria and Henry [qq.v.], gained distinction in the scientific world. Giving up cooperage and work in an oil factory for the more congenial occupation of teaching school, Mitchell became, in 1827, master of the first free school of Nantucket. In 1830 he became secretary of the Phoenix Marine Insurance Company, and from 1837 until 1861 he was cashier of the Pacific Bank. His kind and sympathetic character, his love of peace, and his other sterling traits, won for him the affection of his pupils and of all with whom he came in contact. He was president of the Nantucket Atheneum for more than thirty years; a delegate to the Massachusetts constitutional convention of 1820; state senator in 1845; and a member of the council of Gov. George N. Briggs [q.v.] in 1848 and 1849. Astronomy was his favorite diversion. He had several telescopes and made observations of star positions for the United States Coast Survey and for his own use in rating chronometers for the Nantucket fleet of ninety-two whaleships. A scientific atmosphere pervaded his home and neighborhood, a fact somewhat remarkable when the isolated position of the island is considered. He was held in high esteem by scientific men of the day. Professors William Cranch Bond and George P. Bond [qq.v.], the first two directors of the Harvard Observatory, were his intimate friends. He was a member of the visiting committee of the Harvard College observatory from 1848 to 1865, its chairman after 1855, and an overseer of Harvard University from 1857 to 1865. The honorary degree of master of arts was conferred upon him by Brown University in 1848, and by Harvard in 1860. He was a fellow of the American Academy of Arts and Sciences and a member of the American Association for the Advancement of Science. After the death of his wife in 1861 he moved to Lynn, Mass. In 1865, when his daughter, Maria, became head of the Astronomical Department of Vassar College he went to Poughkeepsie to live. There he died.

[*Vital Records of Nantucket, Mass. to the Year 1850*, vols. II (1926), IV (1927); L. S. Hinchman, *Early Settlers of Nantucket* (2nd ed., 1901); *Proc. Am. Acad. Arts and Sciences*, vols. II (1852), VIII (1873); E. S. Holden, *Memorials of William Cranch Bond and of His Son George Phillips Bond* (1897); Phebe Mitchell Kendall, *Maria Mitchell: Life, Letters, and Journals* (1896); *The Am. Ann. Cyc. and Register of Important Events of the Year 1869*; original letters of William Mitchell filed in Memorial House of Nantucket Maria Mitchell Association.]   M. H.

MITCHELL, WILLIAM (1798–May 11, 1856), actor, dramatist, manager, was of British birth and peculiarly a product of the English theatres. He was born at Billquay in the County of Durham, England, and after fifteen years as actor and stage manager in the provincial and in London theatres, he came to America with his family in 1836, making his American début at the National Theatre, New York, on Aug. 29, as Grimes in *The Man with the Carpet Bag* and as Jem Baggs in *The Wandering Minstrel*, the latter a play in which he had been received with great favor in London. Both of these plays were given as afterpieces to a performance of *The Merchant of Venice*, with Junius Brutus Booth as Shylock. He continued to act in New York with varying degrees of popularity until on Dec. 9, 1839, he took over the management of the hitherto unlucky Olympic Theatre on Broadway between Howard and Grand Streets, and then began what was to prove one of the most amazing series of seasons of managerial triumphs in the history of the New York, and indeed of the American, stage. His opening pieces were *His First Champagne, No!* and *High Life Below Stairs*, and thenceforth for almost ten years the words Mitchell's Olympic represented a diversified form of theatrical entertainment that has never been duplicated. His preliminary announcement read that his purpose was the production of "vaudevilles, burlettas, extravaganzas, farces, etc., the evening performances beginning at seven o'clock, and the prices being extremely low, 50 cents for the boxes, and 25 cents for pit seats."

As manager and actor Mitchell seemed to know exactly what the public of his day liked. Contemporary records testify to his great popularity, and permanent chronicles of the theatre emphasize and record it in phrases that would seem to be exaggerative were they not unanimous. Ireland says that "his various amusing burlesques and travesties, and his inimitable personation of Dickens's *Manager Crummles* raised him to the very summit of popular favor and insured for him an extraordinary patronage for several years" (*post*, p. 192). Odell records the fact that "he is one of the most interesting figures in our stage history; the world today laughs at his antics, in sheer envy of those who were fortunate enough to have laughed with him" (*post*, IV, p. 137). Among the most sensational of his productions was a burlesque of *Hamlet*, with Mitchell himself singing comic songs in the title character; and a burlesque of Fanny Elssler, who was then all the rage, was extremely popular. Mitchell's Olympic was a fashionable resort as well as a place of popular entertainment, but as inevitably happens its patronage eventually decreased, and its eleventh and last season came to a sudden close on Mar. 9, 1850, when Mitchell retired permanently from its management and from public life. He left a gap in the New York theatre, for the position and reputation of Mitchell's Olympic rightly deserved to be described as unique. Little is remembered, however, of Mitchell as an actor, so completely is his fame eclipsed by his theatre and his part in its direction. It was not simply the Olympic Theatre, it was Mitchell's Olympic. Joseph Jefferson (*Autobiography*, p. 107) describes him as "a manager of rare ability," but says nothing of his acting. Since his object was the laughter of the moment, and since he invariably portrayed grotesque characters, there was doubtless more rough comedy than artistic finesse in his impersonations. A long period of ill health intervened between his retirement from management and his death six years afterward.

[Sources include: *The Autobiography of Joseph Jefferson* (1889); J. N. Ireland, *Records of the N. Y. Stage* (1867), vol. II; T. Allston Brown, *A Hist. of the N. Y. Stage* (1903), vol. I; Arthur Hornblow, *A Hist. of the Theatre in America* (1919), vol. II; G. C. D. Odell, *Annals of the N. Y. Stage*, vol. IV (1928), vol. V (1931); the *New World*, July 11, 1840; *N. Y. Times*, *N. Y. Herald*, *N. Y. Daily Tribune*, May 13, 1856. Although several sources give May 12, 1856, as the date of Mitchell's death, the death notice in the *N. Y. Daily Tribune*, May 13, 1856, states that he died on Sunday, May 11.]   E. F. E.

MITCHELL, WILLIAM (Feb. 24, 1801–Oct. 6, 1886), jurist, the son of Edward and Cornelia (Anderson) Mitchell, was born in New York City. His grandfather, William Mitchell, was a stationer in Coleraine, Ireland, near Belfast. His father emigrated in 1791 and for many years was pastor of the Society of United Christians (Universalist) in New York City. His mother was a native of New York City, a descendant of Peter Andresson to whom a grant of land in the city of New Amsterdam was made in 1645 by the Dutch West India Company. William prepared for college at the school of Joseph Nelson, a blind teacher. He was at the head of his class and received from Nelson as a testimonial of esteem a rare copy of Quintilian. In 1820 he graduated with high honors from Columbia College, where he excelled in mathematics and classics. To the end of his life Greek and Latin authors continued to be his recreation from professional studies. His Commencement oration, delivered in Latin, was entitled, *"De Julii Caesaris vita et nece."* On June 2, 1841, he was married to Mary Penfold Berrien of New York City, a descendant of Cornelius Jansen Berrien who came to Long Island about 1670 from Rotterdam.

He studied law in the office of William Slosson and was admitted as attorney at law in 1823, solicitor in chancery in 1824, counselor at law in 1826, and counselor in chancery in 1827. In 1832 he published an edition of Blackstone's *Commentaries* with special references to American cases, which was one of the early efforts to correlate American decisions with English common law. He is said to have been too modest to acknowledge his editorship so he attributed the work to "A Member of the New York Bar." He

was made master in chancery in 1840 and was elected justice of the state supreme court for the 1st judicial district in 1849. In 1854 he became the presiding justice of the court and continued in that position until he retired in 1857, with the exception of the year 1856 when he was a member of the court of appeals. He was so learned and just in his decisions that, after his retirement from the bench in 1857, the court often chose him as referee in important cases, and individuals brought cases to him for trial and decision. He continued to hold his court regularly throughout the later years of his life. He served two terms as vice-president of the New York bar association. At the time of his death he had been a member of the New York bar sixty-three years and was said to be its oldest member. He died on a visit to his son at Morristown, N. J.

[Information from Cornelius von Erden Mitchell, a grandson, New York City; B. D. Silliman, "Memorial of Wm. Mitchell," *Asso. of the Bar of the City of N. Y. . . . Report . . . 1887* (n.d.); "In Memoriam," by J. A. Flack in the general minutes of the supreme court for Oct. general term, 1886; *N. Y. Times*, and *N. Y. Tribune*, Oct. 7, 1886.]   D. V. S.

MITCHELL, WILLIAM (Nov. 19, 1832–Aug. 21, 1900), judge, was the son of John and Mary (Henderson) Mitchell, both natives of Scotland. He was born in Welland County, Ontario. After a preparatory education in the local schools he matriculated at Jefferson College, Canonsburg, Pa., where he was graduated in 1853. At college he formed a friendship with Eugene M. Wilson, with whose father, Edgar C. Wilson of Morgantown, Va. (now W. Va.), he read law after a brief period of teaching. He was admitted to the bar in the circuit court of Virginia in 1857. On Sept. 3, 1857, he was married to Mrs. Jane (Hanway) Smith, the daughter of John Hanway of Morgantown. Almost immediately he went to the pioneer town of Winona, Minn., to practise with the younger Wilson until the latter removed to Minneapolis. A partnership with Daniel S. Norton, which was terminated by Norton's election to the United States Senate, was followed by one with William H. Yale. In 1859–60 Mitchell was a member of the second state legislature of Minnesota. He was interested in railroads, became president of the Winona & Saint Peter Railroad Co., and later was president of the Winona Savings Bank. His first wife died in 1867, leaving three daughters. On July 11, 1872, he was married to Mrs. Frances (Merritt) Smith of Chicago, the daughter of Jacob M. Merritt. They had one son, William DeWitt Mitchell.

Mitchell's real career began when he became

judge of the 3rd judicial district in 1874, to which position he was reëlected in 1880. His reputation as a sound lawyer and impartial judge made him one of the most respected members of the Minnesota bench and was the cause of his designation as temporary judge of the supreme court sitting on a case in which two of the regular justices had been previously connected as counsel. In 1881, shortly after his second election, he was appointed by Gov. John S. Pillsbury to one of the two newly created positions on the supreme bench. In 1882 he was elected for the regular term and twice thereafter reëlected, so that his service in this capacity extended from the spring of 1881 to December 1899, when he filed his last opinion. In 1898 he accepted nomination by the Democratic and Populist parties but was not indorsed by the Republicans, as he had been at the three previous elections. His Republican opponent was elected by a small majority, much to the regret of most of the bar. During the years he was an associate justice of the supreme court of Minnesota there were relatively few issues of great public significance that came before it for adjudication; it was, however, a period during which he had occasion to read many opinions that vitally affected the body of common law in Minnesota. The soundness of his reasoning, balanced between respect for past judicial dicta and a recognition that new times and new forces demanded modification of old formulae, drew the attention of lawyers and legal writers in all parts of the country. Sometime after Mitchell's death, Dean Woodruff of the College of Law in Cornell University wrote: "It has seemed to me, as I have read Judge Mitchell's opinions, that he belongs in the group with Chief Justice Shaw of Massachusetts, Chief Justice Gibson of Pennsylvania, and the few others who mark the highest achievement of our state courts. His mind was a quick solvent for the most refractory and opaque material of legal contention" (*Minnesota Law Review, post*, p. 386). He was an indefatigable worker and student. His opinions, and they averaged one every three days for the nineteen years on the bench, showed familiarity not only with contemporary decisions but a real knowledge of the history of the law. Coke, Littleton, or Blackstone were as often on his lips as the names of the foremost American jurists. "To him the common law was a living, growing organism" (*Minnesota Law Review, post*, p. 385) although he regarded precedent as a leader and not a master.

Without bitterness at his defeat he turned, for the remaining few months of his life, to private practice, for he had accumulated no fortune on which to retire. He declined to be considered for appointment as chief justice of Puerto Rico. In 1891 he had been nominated by President Harrison for the circuit court of appeals, but his name was withdrawn before action by the Senate. It was, however, probably no loss to legal development that he was left to carry on his invaluable work in a state court, whatever might have been his gratification at holding the more conspicuous position. He died at Lake Alexandria, Minn.

[*Great Amer. Lawyers*, ed. by W. D. Lewis, vol. VIII (1909); *Minn. Law Review*, May 1920; *Biog. and Hist. Cat. of Washington and Jefferson College* (1889); *Hist. of Winona County* (1883); *Progressive Men of Minn.*, ed. by M. D. Shutter and J. S. McLain (1897); *Portrait and Biog. Record of Winona County* (1895); *U. S. Biog. Dict. and Portrait Gallery* (Minn. vol., 1879); *Minnesotian* (Saint Paul), Mar. 2, 1860; *Daily Pioneer Press* (St. Paul), Nov. 2, 1898, Aug. 22, 1900; information in regard to date of birth and certain other matters from Hon. W. D. Mitchell.]
L.B.S.

MITCHILL, SAMUEL LATHAM (Aug. 20, 1764–Sept. 7, 1831), physician, United States senator and representative, promoter of science, was born of Quaker parents, Robert and Mary (Latham) Mitchill, at North Hempstead, L. I. He was the grandson of Robert Mitchill who came to America about 1694. His uncle, Dr. Samuel Latham, taught him the elementary principles of medicine while he was receiving his classical education; he studied for three years with Dr. Samuel Bard [*q.v.*] in New York City, and in 1783 went to Edinburgh, where in 1786 he graduated from the University with the degree of M.D. Returning to New York, he was licensed to practise medicine and commenced the study of law. In 1788 he was appointed one of the commissioners to negotiate with the Six Nations for the purchase of lands in western New York, and in 1791 he was a member of the state legislature.

His scientific career began in 1792, with his appointment to the chair of natural history, chemistry, and agriculture at Columbia College; from 1793 to 1795 he was professor of botany also. In Edinburgh he had studied chemistry under Joseph Black, and he now began to teach the new or antiphlogistic chemistry recently promulgated by Lavoisier, in defense of whose theories he carried on a controversy for some years with Joseph Priestley [*q.v.*] and others. In 1801 he published *Explanation of the Synopsis of Chemical Nomenclature and Arrangement*. He was among the early analysts of the Saratoga spring waters and his work on the salts in these waters attracted public attention to mineral springs in general. His theory of the septic ac-

Mitchill

tion of a substance he called "septon," though fanciful and erroneous, was an incentive to the study of sanitary chemistry and hygiene and was one of the factors that led Davy to investigate problems in nitrous oxide. He made many contributions to problems in industrial chemistry, conspicuously those relating to gunpowder, soap, and disinfectants. In 1800 and soon afterwards he published papers on the "non-action" of nitric acid on silver, tin, and copper, on the history of muriate of soda, on the presence of soda, magnesia, and lime in the ocean, and on the use of ocean water for washing without the aid of soap. He collected minerals, displayed specimens in his lectures, and deposited them in a museum at the college for the use of future teachers. He also studied fertilizers and was greatly interested in the agricultural devolopment of his native state. In 1796, under the auspices of the Society for the Promotion of Agriculture, Arts, and Manufactures, which he had helped to found, he made a mineralogical exploration of the banks of the Hudson River, a pioneer piece of geological research. With Edward Miller [q.v.] and Elihu H. Smith he established, in 1797, the *Medical Repository,* which soon became a medium for scientific contributions of all kinds. Of this journal he was principal editor for twenty-three years. He was again a member of the New York legislature in 1798, and gave sturdy support to the act granting Livingston and Fulton a monopoly of steam navigation in the waters of New York. Through his marriage, June 23, 1799, to Catherine, daughter of Samuel Akerly and widow of William Cock, he came into the possession of comfortable means. There were no children.

He resigned his professorship at Columbia in 1801 to accept a seat in Congress, sitting in the House until 1804; in the Senate, 1804–09; and in the House again from 1810 to 1813. In 1810 he served a third term in the New York legislature. At Washington, he advocated the establishment of quarantine laws and made several reports on matters connected with the Library of Congress, and one urging the exploration of the Louisiana Purchase. During the War of 1812 he served on a commission to supervise the construction of a steam war-vessel, and with other citizens of New York labored for several days digging trenches for the defense of the city. In 1807, upon the organization of the College of Physicians and Surgeons in New York, he was chosen professor of chemistry, and the next year was transferred to the chair of natural history, which he held until 1820, when he became professor of botany and ma-

teria medica. Resigning with the rest of the faculty in 1826, he joined his colleagues J. W. Francis, David Hosack, W. J. MacNeven, and Valentine Mott [qq.v.] in forming the Rutgers Medical College, of which he was vice-president during the four years of its existence. For two decades he was a physician to the New York Hospital. He helped to found the New York Literary and Philosophical Society in 1814, and in 1817 was principal founder of the Lyceum of Natural History, forerunner of the New York Academy of Sciences. He was surgeon general of the state militia in 1818.

Throughout his life he wrote prolifically, contributing paper after paper to the transactions of the many societies to which he belonged, to literary journals, and especially to his own *Medical Repository.* His most notable contributions included papers on the fishes of New York (*Transactions of the Literary and Philosophical Society* and *Medical Repository,* 1815); "A Sketch of the Mineralogical History of New York" (*Medical Repository,* 1797, 1800, 1802); "A Discourse . . . Embracing a Concise and Comprehensive Account of the Writings which Illustrate the Botanical History of North and South America" (*Collections of the New York Historical Society,* vol. II, 1814); papers on the origin of the Indians, Indian poetry, and Indian antiquities (*Transactions and Collections of the American Antiquarian Society,* vol. I, 1820). To the New York edition of Thomas Bewick's *General History of Quadrupeds* (1804) he contributed notes on American animals. He was frequently called upon to deliver addresses, notably at celebrations in 1823 and 1825 of steps in the completion of the Erie Canal, of which he had been an enthusiastic supporter. Other discourses worthy of mention are *The Life, Precepts, and Exploits of Tammany*; the *Famous Indian Chief* (1795), chiefly an exposition of political mythology; and *A Discourse on the Character and Services of Thomas Jefferson, More Especially as a Promoter of Natural and Physical Science* (1826). It has been said with considerable truth that Mitchill "supported the Republican party because Jefferson was its leader and supported Jefferson because he was a philosopher" (Henry Adams, *History of the United States,* vol. I, 1889, p. 111), but his attachment to republican ideas is manifested in his endeavor to establish "Fredonia" as a name for the United States.

Characterized variously by contemporaries as "a living encyclopedia" and "a chaos of knowledge," Mitchill is perhaps "remembered more for the goodness of his heart than the strength of his head." His investigations resulted in no epoch-making discoveries, his theories were often erroneous, but through the sincerity of his interest, the extent of his learning, and the simple amiability of his character, he won renown both at home and abroad as a man of science and was able to exert a pronounced influence in the promotion of scientific inquiry and in the practical application of scientific principles to life.

[Mitchill himself published *Some of the Memorable Events and Occurences in the Life of Samuel L. Mitchill, of New York, from 1786 to 1821* (n.d.); see also: *Harper's Mag.*, Apr. 1879; James Herring and J. B. Longacre, *The Nat. Portrait Gallery of Distinguished Americans*, vol. I (1834); J. W. Francis, *Old New York* (1858); *Reminiscences of Samuel Latham Mitchill* (1859), repr. in S. D. Gross, *Lives of Eminent Am. Phys. and Surg.* (1861), and abridged in H. A. Kelly and W. L. Burrage, *Am. Medic. Biogs.* (1920); Félix Pascalis-Ouvière, *Eulogy on the Life and Character of the Hon. Samuel Latham Mitchill* (1831); E. A. and G. L. Duyckinck, *Cyc. of Am. Lit.* (1875), vol. I; C. R. Hall, in *Jour. Chem. Educ.*, Mar. 1928, in *N. Y. Hist.*, Apr. 1933, and "An American Scientist—Samuel Latham Mitchill" (1933), doctor's thesis at Columbia Univ.; E. F. Smith, *Chem. in America* (1914), and *Samuel Latham Mitchill* (1922), repr. from *Jour. Indus. & Engineering Chem.*, June 1922; W. J. Youmans, *Pioneers of Science in America* (1896); B. F. Thompson, *Hist. of L. I.* (1839); H. L. Fairchild, *A Hist. of the N. Y. Acad. of Sci.* (1887); G. B. Goode, *The Beginnings of Am. Sci.: the Third Century* (1888); F. L. Mott, *A Hist. of Am. Mags.* (1930); list (incomplete) of Mitchill's scientific papers in Royal Soc. of London, *Cat. of Sci. Papers* (1800–1863), vol. IV (1879).]   L. C. N.

MITTEN, THOMAS EUGENE (Mar. 31, 1864–Oct. 1, 1929), street-railway official, was born at Brighton, Sussex, England, the son of George and Jane (Lucke) Mitten. His parents emigrated to the United States in 1877 and settled on a farm near Goodland, Newton County, Ind. In the next seven years on the farm Thomas acquired a working knowledge of telegraphy from the Goodland station agent and at the end of that period became a telegraph operator and station agent at Wyndham (now Swanington), Ind., for the Chicago & Eastern Illinois Railroad. In 1887 he became local agent at Attica, Ind., for the same railroad and from 1890 to 1893 he held various minor positions with the Denver & Rio Grande Railroad and the Rio Grande Western Railroad. He then became general superintendent of the Denver, Lakewood & Golden Railroad, a suburban line, parts of which were electrified under his direction. His opportunity to enter the electric street-railway industry came in 1896 when he was made assistant superintendent and later general superintendent of the street-railway system of Milwaukee, Wis. He left this position in 1901 to become general superintendent of the International Railway Company, operating electric lines in and around Buffalo, N. Y., and for a year, 1904–05, was

general manager of the system. In 1905 he went to Chicago to accept the presidency of the Chicago City Railway Company. He resigned this position in 1911 to become director and general supervisor of the physical properties of the lines of the Philadelphia Rapid Transit Company, then practically bankrupt. In June of this same year he was elected chairman of the executive committee and later president of the company, which post he held until February 1923 when he resigned, retaining, however, the chairmanship of the board of directors and of the executive committee. He had gained a reputation for interesting himself in the problems of labor and of turning labor into capital through the cooperation of men and management. One of his first projects in connection with the affairs of the Philadelphia Rapid Transit Company was the formation of the so-called "Mitten Co-Operative Plan," which gave employees a voice in matters affecting wages and working conditions, made employees stockholders of the company, and gave them representation on the board of directors. He also organized the Mitten Men and Management Bank and Trust Company.

The independent transit corporations in the city of Philadelphia Mitten brought under the control of Mitten Management, Incorporated, a company capitalized at $10,000 and incorporated under the laws of Delaware. In 1924 the company took over the operation of the Philadelphia Rapid Transit Company. Under Mitten management the Transit Company failed to submit annual reports to the city comptroller called for by the company's contract with the city and in July 1929 Mayor Mackey ordered an investigation of the accounts. As a result of the audit conducted by Milo R. Maltbie, revealing tremendous expenditures for the operation of the Transit Company, the city comptroller filed suit on Dec. 1, 1929, for an accounting of transit finances. Meanwhile, on Oct. 1, Mitten was drowned in Big Log Cabin Pond on his estate, "Sunnyland," about twelve miles from Milford in Pike County, Pa. In April 1931 the Transit Company was ordered into receivership. Judge Harry S. McDevitt of the Philadelphia court of common pleas, in making the order, condemned the Mitten Management as "'a colossal conspiracy against the taxpayers" (*New York Times*, Apr. 12, 1931). The bulk of Mitten's estate, which by the terms of a will drawn up a few days before his death, was to have been largely used in furthering friendly relations between capital and labor, was absorbed in the settlement of claims of the Philadelphia Rapid Transit Company against Mitten Management.

Mitten was married in 1887 to Kate M. Warner of Fowler, Ind. In 1904 he was married to Ruth Bissell of Lockport, N. Y., who divorced him in Paris in 1926.

[*Who's Who in America*, 1928–29; *Am. Mag.*, Mar. 1930, Nov. 1922; *World's Work*, July 1922, Mar. 1929; *Outlook*, Apr. 12, 1922, Mar. 30, 1927; *Collier's*, Feb. 7, 1920, Dec. 9, 1922; *Lit. Digest*, Apr. 1, 1922, Oct. 2, 1926; *Nat. Municipal Rev.*, Apr. 1932, pp. 252–53; and newspaper accounts of Mitten's affairs and the investigation of Mitten Management, especially the *N. Y. Times*, Mar. 16, 17, 1922, July 20, Aug. 29, Oct. 2, 3, 8, 9, 16, Dec. 1, 1929, Aug. 17, Sept. 17, 1930, Apr. 12, May 14, 15, July 17, Nov. 4, 1931, July 1, Aug. 3, 4, 1932.]
                    J. H. F.

MIXTER, SAMUEL JASON (May 10, 1855–Jan. 19, 1926), surgeon, was born in Hardwick, Mass., to William and Mary (Ruggles) Mixter. He was a descendant of Isaac Mixter (or Mixter), born in Suffolk County, England, who sailed from Ipswich for America on the *Elizabeth,* Apr. 10, 1634. Through Mary Ruggles his mother, he traced his ancestry to Gov. Thomas Prence of Plymouth Colony and to Elder William Brewster. Some of his ancestors were successful farmers and storekeepers; others were prominent in the business and political life of their communities. He received his early education in schools at Amherst and Boston, graduated as a bachelor of science from the Massachusetts Institute of Technology in 1875, and as a doctor of medicine from Harvard in 1879. In 1879 he became a surgical house officer at the Massachusetts General Hospital, and on Aug. 12 of this same year married Wilhelmina Galloupe, descended from John Gallop who came to America on the *Mary and John* in 1630, and was one of the earliest grantees of land in Boston. Soon after, they went to Vienna, where Mixter studied surgery, anatomy, and microscopic pathology. In 1882 he became assistant demonstrator of anatomy at the Harvard Medical School and in 1887 demonstrator. The Warren Museum of that institution possesses specimens prepared by him which testify to his skill and careful craftsmanship.

In 1886 he was appointed to the staff of the Massachusetts General Hospital, a connection which lasted to the end of his life. He was surgeon to out-patients, 1886 to 1894; visiting surgeon, 1894 to 1911; chief of West Surgical Service, 1911 to 1915; and on the board of consultation, 1915 to 1926. At one time or another he was upon the staff of other hospitals but his life work centered at the Massachusetts General. Here his surgical colleagues were C. B. Porter, H. H. A. Beach, J. Collins Warren [*q.v.*], Arthur T. Cabot [*q.v.*], John Homans, Maurice H. Richardson [*q.v.*], John W. Elliott,

and Francis B. Harrington. Even in such a group he was conspicuous. His knowledge of anatomy and pathology, his skilled surgical technique, his courage and sound judgment, and his resourceful mind made him a notably successful surgeon. His modification of the Abbe operation for the cure of trigeminal neuralgia was one of his outstanding contributions to neurological surgery and this operation was well known until superseded by section of the sensory root of the nerve. He was particularly interested and successful in surgery of the œsophagus. Some of the best known of the many instruments which he invented are those which he used in his œsophageal operations. He perfected the technique of skin grafting and devised special instruments for this purpose. The "Mixter colostomy" is one of the recognized procedures in intestinal obstruction. He made numerous contributions to medical literature, dealing particularly with unusual cases and original surgical methods, and delivered scholarly addresses on other subjects before some of the larger surgical societies of the country. To his interest in the practical problems of the hospital was due the reclaiming of surgical gauze at the Massachusetts General Hospital, by a process which has been of great economic value to hospitals all over the country. He was president of the American Surgical Association in 1917 and the first president of the New England Surgical Society.

Mixter was a friendly person; his greetings, invariably cheerful and happy. His physical appearance, even in his later years, was that of a man of robust health. He always dressed carefully and generally wore a flower in his buttonhole; his mobile face lighted and his eyes twinkled as he talked to his friends. He was a keen sportsman. No year was complete for him unless it contained its proper share of hunting and fishing. During the later part of his life the large Mixter farm at Hardwick came under his care. There he developed and perfected a herd of Guernsey cattle, which, at the time of its dispersal, was the largest and probably the best in the United States. He saw active service during the World War and returned a lieutenant-colonel in the Medical Reserve Corps. He died at Grand Junction, Tenn., where he happened to be when taken ill with pneumonia.

[Private family records; *Boston Medic. and Surgic. Jour.*, May 13, 1926; *Surgery, Gynecology and Obstetrics*, Nov. 1927; Records Mass. Soc. of Mayflower Descendants; H. A. Kelly and W. L. Burrage, *Dict. of Am. Medic. Biog.* (1928); *Mass. General Hospital, Memorial and Hist. Vol.* (1921); *Index Medicus*; *Who's Who in America*, 1926–27; J. C. Warren and A. P. Gould, *The International Text-book of Surgery by American and British Authors,* 2 vols. (1899–1900);

Boston Evening Transcript, Jan. 20, 1926 ; W. S. Bickham, *Operative Surgery* (1924), vol. V.]   F. A. W.

MODJESKA, HELENA (Oct. 12, 1840–Apr. 8, 1909), Polish-American actress, was born in Cracow, Poland. Her father, Michael Opid, was a music teacher, born in the Polish mountains. He died early, and his widow had to put all her children to work. Little Helena, who saw and was greatly moved by her first play at seven, from the first aspired to the stage. While still in her teens she was married to her guardian, a man much older than herself, named Gustav Modrzejewski, and by him she had one son. With his aid she secured a small place in the provincial theatre, and in 1863 she acted in Germany. Two years later she returned to Cracow where her talents were hailed and she became a favorite. In 1867 Dumas *fils* invited her to Paris, to play Marguerite Gauthier, but she refused the challenge, feeling she was not yet ready. Her first husband, meanwhile, had died, and in 1868 she married Charles Bozenta Chlapowski, a member of the Polish aristocracy, and joined the company at the Imperial Theatre in Warsaw. There she remained, the reigning actress of the nation, until 1876. That year the nationalistic views of her husband and herself made life in Warsaw difficult, under Russian régime, and with her husband, her son, and a group of Poles she journeyed to America.

The party visited the Philadelphia Exposition and then moved on to California, where it was proposed to found a Polish colony in what was supposed to be an earthly Paradise. A large ranch was purchased and the colonists lighted their Polish cigarettes, climbed into their hammocks, and proceeded to enjoy the climate. But, alas! oranges are not grown and marketed without labor, and the colonists knew little about labor. Their money was soon gone. Modjeska (as she abbreviated her name for America) learned to speak English in six months, at the suggestion of Edwin Booth, and went to San Francisco, where John McCullough, then managing the famous California Theatre, gave her a chance, in 1877, to appear in *Adrienne Lecouvreur.* In spite of her foreign accent (which she never wholly lost, though it soon became but a piquant sauce to her acting), the public welcomed her, and it was immediately apparent that she had a future career on the American stage. She was signed for a two-year tour in a repertoire of plays, making her New York début Dec. 22, 1877. In 1878 she revisited Poland, where she was warmly welcomed, but after a limited engagement there, she came back to America. In 1880 she went to London and acted

for the rest of the year in that city, in English. She then again returned to the United States, which thereafter became definitely the country of her adoption. Her husband became a citizen and purchased a ranch outside Santa Anna, Cal. Madame Modjeska for many years toured the country in a wide range of parts, though in 1882 and 1884 she again visited both Poland and London.

In 1882, in Warsaw, she produced Ibsen's *Doll's House,* under the title *Nora,* and with the "happy ending" then used on the Continent, in spite of the author's objections. This play she brought back to America and produced in Louisville, Ky., in 1883, probably the first production of Ibsen in English—certainly the first in America. It attracted no attention—as, indeed, it did not deserve to, with the whole point removed by the botched, sentimental ending. In 1889–90 she played a joint engagement with Edwin Booth, but by this time both actors were past their prime, and the union was less successful than it would have been ten years earlier. In 1892 she produced an American play, *Countess Roudine,* by Paul Kester and Minnie Maddern Fiske. At the World's Fair in 1893, Modjeska delivered a speech attacking the Russian government and was thereafter forbidden to enter Russian territory. Illness in 1895 caused her temporary retirement, but she reappeared in 1897. In 1900–01 she produced *King John,* and in 1902 made a "farewell tour" with Louis James. In 1905, at the Metropolitan Opera House, New York, a testimonial performance was given for her benefit. She attempted a brief tour in 1907, but was too frail to continue. She died Apr. 8, 1909, at Bay Island, East Newport, on the coast south of Los Angeles, and her body was taken by her husband, who had always acted as her manager, to Cracow for burial. Neither he nor she was practical in business matters, and though her earlier tours had made her much money, her last days were passed in comparative poverty, cheerfully endured (William Winter, *The Wallet of Time,* vol. I, p. 366).

Modjeska was of slim, aristocratic, and graceful figure, with a face interesting, expressive, and gracious, rather than conventionally beautiful. In Polish she had a repertoire of over a hundred rôles. In English she played nine heroines of Shakespeare, from Juliet and Rosalind to Cleopatra, and such well-known parts as Adrienne Lecouvreur, Camille, Julie de Martemar in *Richelieu* (which she created in America), Ibsen's Nora, Mary Stuart, Frou-Frou, and several more. Her personal preference, from girlhood, had been for Shakespeare, and she was essentially a poetic actress. She excelled not so much in sweep or profundity of emotion as in the depiction of womanly grace and charm, in piquant archness and especially in scenes where she impersonated a fine woman displaying affection, or suffering for it. Her technique was carefully studied, and she was conscious mistress of her effects. "Her movements," according to William Winter, "always graceful, were sometimes electrical in their rapidity and long and sinuous reach" (*The Wallet of Time,* I, p. 370). Although her technique was masterful, and her intellectual grasp of all her characters sure and steady, her hold on the public lay more, perhaps, in her personality, with its gleams of humor, its graceful dignity, its womanly sweetness, and always an indefinable atmosphere of poetic elevation. She even imparted those qualities to Camille and Magda, and possibly not wholly unintentionally. But in Viola, Rosalind, Queen Katherine, and similar rôles, the effect was exactly right, and her impersonations of such parts were long dwelt upon affectionately by those who saw them.

[William Winter, *The Wallet of Time,* vol. I (1913); L. C. Strang, *Famous Actresses of the Day in America* (1899); Brander Matthews and Laurence Hutton, *Actors and Actresses of Great Britain and the U. S.,* vol. V (1886); *Who's Who in America,* 1901–02; T. A. Brown, *A Hist. of the N. Y. Stage* (1903), vols. II and III; J. B. Clapp and E. F. Edgett, *Players of the Present,* pt. 2 (1900); *Los Angeles Daily Times,* Apr. 9, 1909.]   W. P. E.

MOELLER, HENRY (Dec. 11, 1849–Jan. 5, 1925), Roman Catholic prelate, was the son of Bernard and Teresa (Witte) Moeller, who emigrated from Westphalia about 1845. Born in Cincinnati, Ohio, he was educated there in St. Joseph's German parochial school and St. Francis Xavier's College. His father, a bricklayer and building contractor, provided well for the education of his six children: the only daughter joined the Sisters of Charity at Mount St. Joseph on the Ohio; one son, Ferdinand, became a Jesuit; and another, Bernard, a distinguished secular priest of Cincinnati. Henry was sent by Archbishop Purcell to the American College at Rome in 1869, and there, according to the rector, F. S. Chatard, passed with honors an examination for the doctorate in divinity seven years later. Ordained by Archbishop Lenti at the church of St. John Lateran, Rome, June 10, 1876, he returned to Ohio and was assigned to St. Patrick's Church, Bellefontaine. During the next two years he taught in Mount St. Mary's Seminary, Cincinnati, then, after a few months as secretary to Bishop Chatard of Vincennes, became secretary to Archbishop William Henry Elder [*q.v.*], whom he assisted in the financial

reorganization of the Cincinnati archdiocese. In 1886 he was made chancellor in recognition of his unusual administrative skill. Fourteen years later, the Holy Father named him to the see of Columbus, for which he was consecrated by Archbishop Elder in St. Peter's Cathedral, Cincinnati, on Aug. 25, 1900. Here again his business ability was tested, for this diocese had been in such poor financial condition that its dissolution had been considered.

On the request of Elder for a coadjutor, the suffragan bishops failed to decide between Moeller and C. P. Maes [*q.v.*] of Covington for the nomination and sent both names to Rome. Moeller was selected, Apr. 27, 1903, as coadjutor *cum jure successionis* with the title of Archbishop of Aeropolis. Hence, upon the death of Elder in 1904, he automatically succeeded to the see, Oct. 31, 1904, and received the pallium in his cathedral at the hands of Cardinal Gibbons, Feb. 15, 1905.

Archbishop Moeller assumed direction of a well-organized, conservative diocese which had practically settled the old financial tangle bequeathed by Archbishop Purcell. During his tenure he accomplished a great deal: the number of priests and churches was increased; Mount St. Mary's Seminary was erected at Norwood; the new St. Francis Xavier College was established by the Jesuits with the archbishop's active support; the Fenwick Club was built; the Sisters of St. Ursula, the cloistered nuns of the Second Order of St. Dominic, and the Dominican Nuns of St. Catherine de Ricci were introduced into the diocese; St. Rita's School for the Deaf was established; diocesan charities were centrally organized under a Bureau of Catholic Charities; and parochial and secondary schools were raised to a standard which other dioceses sought to emulate. Moeller was deeply concerned with Catholic education and the National Catholic Educational Association. He was heartily interested in the National Catholic Welfare Council, and in 1922, with Bishop Schrembs of Cleveland, went to Rome in order to protect its threatened existence. His mission was evidently successful, for the reorganized National Catholic Welfare Conference was continued under the same management and given papal approbation. Two years later he was appointed an assistant to the pontifical throne. Chairman of the committee of the hierarchy on missions, president of the board of the Catholic Students' Mission Crusade, and an organizer of the languishing National Councils of Catholic Men and of Catholic Women, he was a recognized power in Catholic circles.

At his funeral mass, celebrated by Cardinal Hayes of New York, he was eulogized by Archbishop Glennon of St. Louis as an active priest of forceful character.

[J. H. Lamott, *Hist. of the Archdiocese of Cincinnati* (1921); *Am. Cath. Who's Who* (1911); *Who's Who in America*, 1924–25; annual Cath. directories; files of the *Catholic Telegraph* (the diocesan organ); Nat. Cath. Welfare Conference News Service, Jan. 6, 19, 1925; the *Sun* (Baltimore), Jan. 7, and *Cincinnati Enquirer*, Jan. 6, 1925; note on death of Moeller's sister, Sister Henrietta Maria, in *N. Y. Times*, Mar. 6, 1932.]   R. J. P.

MOFFAT, DAVID HALLIDAY (July 22, 1839–Mar. 18, 1911), capitalist, was born at Washingtonville, Orange County, N. Y. His parents were David Halliday and Katherine (Gregg) Moffat (*Who's Who in America*, 1910–11). After a common-school education he started work as a bank messenger in New York City (1851), and rose to the position of assistant teller. In 1855 he joined a brother at Des Moines, Iowa, and the following year became teller of the Bank of Nebraska at Omaha. When the bank closed in 1860, Moffat and a partner drove a wagonload of books and stationery to the new mining center at Denver. There they opened a store which soon handled also groceries, newspapers, and wall paper, contained the post office, and held the agency for the Western Union Telegraph Company. In 1861 Moffat returned East and on Dec. 11 married a boyhood sweetheart, Fannie A. Buckhout of Mechanicsville, N. Y., taking her to Colorado with him. In 1865 he became cashier of the First National Bank, Denver, and fifteen years later, president. This connection identified him thoroughly with the affairs of Denver and of Colorado and made him an influential citizen, so that a history of Moffat henceforward is almost a history of the city and state in which he lived. He invested widely in mining properties during and after the latter seventies. Among his best-known mines were the "Little Pittsburgh," "Robert E. Lee," and "Maid of Erin," and he was particularly interested in the regions of Leadville, Cripple Creek, and Creede. He was adjutant-general of the Colorado militia in 1865 and territorial treasurer, 1874–76. He helped organize the Denver Clearing House in 1885, was part owner of the *Denver Times* until 1902, was a director and sometime president of the Denver water company which built the Cheesman dam, was interested in the Denver Tramway Company during the nineties and later; and was an incorporator and director of the Central Colorado Power Company. He was also a large owner of Colorado farming lands and Denver real estate.

Moffat was one of the men who realized that Denver's future importance depended largely on the adequacy of its transportational facilities. He saw Denver as a railroad center, with roads radiating in every direction. When it became certain that the Union Pacific would not touch the town he became one of the backers of the Denver & Pacific, of which he was treasurer and John Evans president (*First Annual Report . . . of the Denver and Pacific . . .*, 1869, *passim*). He was a factor in the affairs of the Boulder Valley Railroad, built to Boulder; of the Denver, South Park & Pacific, opened between Denver and Leadville; and of the Denver & New Orleans, making connections to the Gulf. The last two of these roads are now parts of the Colorado & Southern. Moffat was also a director of the Denver & Rio Grande from 1883, and president from 1884 to 1891 (*Sixth Annual Report . . . of the Denver and Rio Grande*, p. 2). His most lucrative road was the Florence & Cripple Creek, built in the middle nineties to connect the Cripple Creek mines with the main line of the Denver & Rio Grande, but the best known was the Denver, Northwestern & Pacific, still called "the Moffat road." It was chartered in 1902 to create a direct route from Denver to Salt Lake City. The main difficulty encountered in building it was a tunnel at Long's Peak. Moffat planned a two and a half mile tunnel, but when it was completed it was six miles long. The chief promoter spent a considerable share of his personal fortune on the construction of the road, but by 1908 had been able to complete only 211 miles of a scenic line rising to 11,600 feet, as far as Steamboat Springs. His efforts to raise money in the East were blocked by E. H. Harriman [*q.v.*], who preferred not to have new competition. Moffat died in 1911, while on a trip to New York to finance the road. After his death the line became the Denver & Salt Lake, and the tunnel was completed in 1926 by means of public taxation.

[E. C. McMechen, *The Moffat Tunnel of Colo.* (2 vols., 1927); W. F. Stone, *Hist. of Colo.* (4 vols., 1918); J. C. Smiley, *Hist. of Denver* (1901); H. H. Bancroft, *Hist. of Nev., Colo., and Wyo.* (1890); *Hist. of the City of Denver, Arapahoe County, and Colo.* (1880); Frank Hall, *Hist. of the State of Colo.*, vol. III (1891); *Who's Who in America*, 1910–11; *Denver Republican* and *Rocky Mountain News*, Mar. 19, 1911; W. C. Williams, "Colorado's Great Tunnel," in *Rev. of Revs.* (N. Y.), Oct. 1922; G. F. Paul, "The Six-Mile Moffat Tunnel," in *Sci. American*, Apr. 1926; M. M. Rice, "Tunneling the Rockies," in *Rev. of Revs.* (N. Y.), Sept. 1926; Arthur Chapman, "Colorado Tears Down Her Mountains," in *World's Work*, Aug. 1927.]   R. E. R.

MOFFAT, JAMES CLEMENT (May 30, 1811–June 7, 1890), church historian, was born in Scotland, at Glencree. His father was David Douglas Moffat, his mother was Margaret Clement. Most of his early education he gave himself. From his tenth year to his sixteenth he was a shepherd-boy, and while at work read all the books he could lay hands on. For five years from 1828 he worked in a printing-shop, and out of hours studied Latin, Greek, French, German, and Hebrew. In 1833 he landed in New York, expecting to follow his trade, but a chance meeting with Professor (afterward President) John Maclean [q.v.] of Princeton led to his entering the junior class of that college. After his graduation in 1835 he was for two years a private tutor with two students at Yale, and himself studied there. The next two years he spent in Princeton College as tutor in Greek. In 1839 he went to Lafayette College as professor of Latin and Greek, and in 1841 began a service of eleven years as professor of Latin and esthetics at Miami University, Oxford, Ohio. The Presbytery of Oxford licensed him to preach on Jan. 5, 1851, and on Oct. 23 of the same year, ordained him, without his having taken a theological course. His long poem, *Alwyn: A Romance of Study* (1875), which is known to be autobiographical, doubtless interprets his life to this point. It recites the spiritual adventures of the hero, following him through many fields of reading and thought, wide travels in Europe for the sake of study, influences of many forms of art, and experiences with various philosophies. In the end he returns to the Christian faith in which he had been brought up. For a few months in 1852 Moffat taught Greek and Hebrew in a short-lived theological seminary in Cincinnati. Then followed eight years in Princeton College, as professor first of Latin and history and then of Greek. In 1861 he became professor of church history in Princeton Theological Seminary. This place he held for seventeen years. He taught for a year after his resignation, and a year later died in Princeton.

Moffat was not original in mind, and did not impress his students with force of personality, but his nature was refined and cultivated, and sensitive to beauty in nature and art. An industrious student and a copious writer, he was also a lover of the out-door world and a notable walker. While his main intellectual concern was with church history, his interests were varied and enthusiastic. He had poetic aspirations and wrote a good deal of verse, but recognized his own limitations in this faculty. His character was profoundly religious and marked by great simplicity and gentleness. Besides his poem *Alwyn* he published a *Life of Thomas Chalmers*

(1853), in the main an abridgment of William Hanna's biography; *An Introduction to the Study of Aesthetics* (1856); *A Comparative History of Religions* (2 vols., 1871–73); *Outlines of Church History* (1875); *The Church in Scotland* (copr. 1882), a history to the Reformation; *The Story of a Dedicated Life* (1887), a biography of Joseph Owen, missionary at Allahabad; *A Rhyme of the North Country* (1847), and *Song and Scenery: or a Summer Ramble in Scotland* (1874). He was married on Oct. 13, 1840, at Easton, Pa., to Ellen Stewart, who died in 1849, and on Dec. 26, 1850, at Oxford, Ohio, he was married to Mary B. Matthews. Five sons and three daughters survived him.

[*Necrological Report . . . Princeton Theol. Sem.* (1891); *Gen. Cat. Princeton Univ.* (1908); S. J. Coffin, *The Men of Lafayette* (1891); *New York Evangelist,* June 19, 1890; *Presbyt. Banner* (Pittsburgh), June 11, 1890; *Daily True American* (Trenton), June 9, 1890; Moffat's works.]   R. H. N.

MOFFETT, CLEVELAND LANGSTON (Apr. 27, 1863–Oct. 14, 1926), journalist, author, was born in Boonville, N. Y., the son of William H. and Mary (Cleveland) Moffett. After a common schooling in his home town, he entered Yale and was graduated A.B. in 1883. Four years of newspaper reporting followed, and then he was placed on the European staff of the *New York Herald,* where he served from 1887 to 1891. He was on the New York staff of the same newspaper during 1891–92, then joined the *New York Recorder* as foreign editor, 1893–94. At this point he abandoned the newspaper profession and thereafter devoted his time to the writing of books (fiction and non-fiction), plays, and magazine articles, save for one brief period in 1908–09 when he returned to the *New York Herald* as Sunday editor. One of his first literary tasks was the translation of Paul Bourget's *Cosmopolis* from the French in 1893. He was a rapid and versatile writer, usually with a journalistic touch, and in the next few years contributed many articles to magazines and newspapers on almost every imaginable subject, though current topics, often of a semi-scientific nature, were among his favorites. His first original book, *True Detective Stories from the Archives of the Pinkertons,* appeared in 1897; a series of articles, "Careers of Danger and Daring," first ran as a serial in *St. Nicholas* and appeared in book form in 1901; *A King in Rags* was published in 1907, and *Through the Wall,* a mystery story of Paris, where he was then living, in 1909. Other books of fiction from his pen were *The Mysterious Card* (1912), first published in the *Black Cat,* 1896; *The Bishop's Purse* (1913), written in collaboration with

Oliver Herford, and *The Land of Mystery* (1913), first published in *St. Nicholas*.

From the beginning of the World War in 1914 Moffett was much concerned as to America's attitude and was one of the earliest propagandists in favor of preparedness. After some correspondence from the war front, he returned to the United States and wrote in 1916 *The Conquest of America,* in which he pictured a possible invasion by the Germans five years later. When the United States entered the war, he assisted in the organization of the American Defense Society and was made one of its trustees. He made many patriotic addresses, wrote at length on the definition of treason, and was active in the operations of the Vigilantes, an organization formed to combat disloyalty. He was for some time its chairman. In his zealous pursuit of this work he took part in some exciting street incidents when he challenged "soapbox" orators whose utterances he considered seditious; and he appeared as complainant a number of times in court actions against such persons. He continued to write busily during the war, producing, *inter alia,* "How to Live Long —and Love Long" (*McClure's,* September–November 1916); "Glint of Wings," in collaboration with Virginia Hall, issued in book form in 1922; and several "prose poems." A novel, *Possessed,* appeared in 1920. He had written a number of successful plays earlier in his career, all on modern subjects. These included *Money Talks,* produced in 1906; *Playing the Game,* 1907; *The Battle,* a discussion of the antagonism between capital and labor, which had a long run in 1908–09 and caused much discussion; *For Better, For Worse,* produced in 1910; *Greater Than the Law,* 1912. During the last twenty years of his life he made his home for the most part in Paris and died there; though he also spent considerable time in California, adapting some of his books and plays for use in motion pictures and writing original stories for the screen. He was married on Feb. 11, 1899, to Mary E. Lusk who, together with a son and two daughters, survived him.

[*Who's Who in America,* 1926–27; *Yale, 1883: The Book of the Class Comp. after Its Quarter-Centenary Reunion* (1910); *Yale Univ. Obit. Record,* 1927; *Yale Alumni Weekly,* Oct. 29, 1926; *N. Y. Times, N. Y. Herald-Tribune,* and other papers, Oct. 16, 1926; numerous newspaper references during 1917–18; articles by Moffett in newspapers and magazines.]
A.F.H.

MOHR, CHARLES THEODORE (Dec. 28, 1824–July 17, 1901), botanist, was born in Esslingen, Württemberg, the son of Louis M. Mohr. Derived from a family noted for its representatives in chemistry and pharmacology, he entered the polytechnic high school in Stuttgart as a student of chemistry, pharmacy, and mineralogy, having as his instructor in chemistry Hermann von Fehling. Although he had become interested in natural history as a boy, his association at the Polytechnicum with Fehling (who had recently come from Liebig's laboratory at Giessen), with Wilhelm Hochstetter, and with the botanist Johann Hohenacker, decided him to devote himself entirely to natural history. After his graduation in 1845, he accompanied August Kappler to Dutch Guiana as botanical collector. In this work he engaged for a few months, until a protracted illness forced him to return to Germany at the end of 1846.

After the revolution of 1848 he decided, with his brother, to emigrate to the United States, and accordingly came to Cincinnati, then a German community of considerable magnitude, where he took employment as chemist with a chemical manufacturer. During this period he continued his botanical studies and built up a large herbarium, paying particular attention to plants of economic, especially medical, importance. He went to California with the gold rush in 1849, returning the following year with his health permanently impaired. From Cincinnati he removed to Louisville, where he engaged in business as a pharmacist and greatly extended his botanical studies. On Mar. 12, 1852, at Louisville, he married Sophia Roemer, a native of Zweibrücken, Bavaria, who became the mother of three sons and two daughters. In 1857 he moved because of his health to Mobile, Ala., which remained his home until nearly the end of his life.

Here he engaged in pharmacy, and began the extensive studies on the botany of Alabama which constitute his claim to fame. He published nearly a hundred papers on botanical subjects, the most important among them being a report on the forests of Alabama for the Tenth Census (vol. IX, 1884, pp. 525–30); an important memoir on the timber pines of the southern United States (*Bulletin No. 13,* Division of Forestry, United States Department of Agriculture, 1896); and an extensive memoir of over 900 pages on *Plant Life of Alabama* (Contributions from the National Herbarium, vol. VI, United States Department of Agriculture, 1901). The last was reissued, also in 1901, with a biographical sketch and portrait of the author, by the Geological Survey of Alabama. Mohr also made for various organizations important collections of plants and minerals of Alabama; and assembled exhibits for the expositions at Atlanta (1881) and New Orleans (1884).

Of his personality and character, a contemporary said: "Mohr is possessed of a true scientific spirit and great enthusiasm in his botanical work. ... He has not only increased the sum of our knowledge, but has added to our powers of direct usefulness" (Lamson-Scribner, in Mohr's *Plant Life,* Alabama edition, p. xi). Dr. Eugene A. Smith, long his colleague on the Geological Survey of Alabama, writes: "Personally Dr. Mohr was the most lovable and unselfish of men, totally devoid of affectation and pretense . . . inspiring all who knew him with love and respect" (*Ibid.,* p. xii). A year before his death, he moved from Mobile to Asheville, N. C., there to work in the Biltmore Herbarium and finish seeing through the press his *magnum opus,* the *Plant Life of Alabama.* His death, at Asheville, cut short the completion of his projected "Economic Botany of Alabama," which he had planned as the crowning work of his career.

[*Pharmaceutische Rundschau,* Feb., Mar. 1887; *Pharmaceutical Rev.,* Sept. 1901; C. T. Mohr, *Plant Life of Alabama,* Alabama edition (Ala. Geol. Survey, 1901), pp. v–xii; *Who's Who in America,* 1901–02; *Asheville Daily Gazette,* July 18, 1901.]   S. W. G.

MOÏSE, PENINA (Apr. 23, 1797–Sept. 13, 1880), poet, was born in Charleston, S. C., the daughter of Abraham and Sarah Moïse. The death of her father, an Alsatian Jew who had first emigrated to Santo Domingo and had then fled to Charleston during the negro uprising in 1791, compelled her to leave school when she was twelve years old in order to help support the large family. Being very studious, she gave her spare time to study and attained a high degree of scholarship, at the same time cultivating her own literary talents. These early years were filled with self-sacrificing endeavor, for she devoted herself during the early part of her life to her home and community interests, being especially active in religious and welfare work, teaching, nursing, and writing hymns. In the latter years of her life, although handicapped by failing eyesight and finally total blindness, she conducted a small but exceptionally fine school for the young girls of her race. By 1830 she had begun writing poetry voluminously. In 1833 she published *Fancy's Sketch Book* and thereafter contributed many poems to the *Occident and American Jewish Advocate, Godey's Lady's Book,* the *Home Journal,* and the *Boston Daily Times,* the *Washington Union,* and *Heriot's Magazine,* besides many occasional pieces in New Orleans and Charleston papers. Her best-loved and most characteristic work is contained in the volume

of *Hymns Written for the Use of Hebrew Congregations* (1856), especially compiled for the use of the congregation of Beth Elohim, the synagogue of which she was a member. The quality of these poems and hymns is, in the main, not above the average, although some of them are beautiful and stately. The predominant note is reminiscent of eighteenth-century English classicism, but occasionally there is interspersed a hint of romanticism.

[*Secular and Religious Works of Penina Moïse, with a Brief Sketch of her Life* (1911), compiled and published by the Charleston section, Council of Jewish Women; B. A. Elzas, *The Jews of S. C.* (1905); L. C. Harby, "Penina Moïse, Woman and Writer," *The Am. Jewish Year Book,* 1905–06; the *Critic,* Dec. 28, 1889; *News and Courier* (Charleston), Sept. 14, 1880.]
R. D. B.

MOLDEHNKE, EDWARD FREDERICK (Aug. 10, 1836–June 25, 1904), Lutheran clergyman, was born at Insterburg, East Prussia, the son of Franz August and Justine (Kessler) Moldencke. His father, an excise official and amateur inventor, was descended from an officer in the army of Gustavus Adolphus, his mother from one of the exiled Protestants of Salzburg. Her death when he was nine years old made his boyhood and youth dismal and cheerless. He attended the Gymnasium at Lyck, 1845–53, matriculated at the age of seventeen at the University of Königsberg as a student of philosophy and theology, and followed Prof. Justus L. Jacobi in 1855 to the University of Halle, where he remained till 1857. While in Halle he acted as secretary to Friedrich Tholuck, in whose household he lived. He was one of the founders of the anti-dueling students' society, Tuisconia. Having passed his examinations with distinction, he was made head, for a few months, of the parochial school at Eckersberg, East Prussia, and was called in 1859 to a professorship in the Lyck Gymnasium. In that same year he married Elise Harder, a descendant of the baronial house of Mannteufel.

Though eminently happy at Lyck, he was eager for the work of the ministry, and in 1861 agreed to come to the United States for five years of missionary work in the West. He was ordained at Königsberg July 23, 1861, and reached Wisconsin, with his wife and child, in August. For four years he led the hard and at times dangerous life of a traveling missionary among the remote settlements of Germans in Wisconsin and Minnesota. In 1865 he was elected president of the Lutheran Theological Seminary at Watertown, Wis., and became editor of the Wisconsin Synod's *Gemeindeblatt.* The University of Rostock made him an honorary doctor. He returned to Germany in August

1866 to become pastor at Johannisburg, East Prussia. This parish numbered 11,000 German and Polish members, and Moldehnke's post included the oversight of thirty-three schools and several prisons, poorhouses, and hospitals. During his incumbency the district was ravaged by epidemics of cholera and typhus; at one time Moldehnke himself was stricken and pronounced dead by his physician. Illness and overwork, aggravated by dissatisfaction with the Prussian State Church, led him to resign in 1869. Starting his career anew, he came to New York and organized a Lutheran congregation, Zion's, which worshiped temporarily in the Medical College at Twenty-third Street and Fourth Avenue. In 1871, this congregation was merged with St. Peter's, of which he served as pastor until his death thirty-three years later.

He was a man of commanding presence and great personal charm, conversed fluently in German, English, Latin, Polish, French, and Italian, and had few equals as an orator in German. He was a member of the committee that edited the General Council's *Kirchenbuch* (1877) and was president of the Council from 1895 to 1898. He was the author of: *Darstellung der Modernen Deutschen Theologie* (Watertown, Wis., 1865); a life of Luther in verse, *Lutherbüchlein* (Allentown, Pa., 1879); *Das Heilige Vaterunser* (Allentown, 1878); and *Durch Kampf zum Sieg* (New York, 1887), the last being a series of lectures delivered in Cooper Institute. His "Fünf Jahre in Amerika" was published in Hengstenberg's *Evangelische Kirchenzeitung* (Berlin, October 1868–February 1870). He wrote prolifically for various church periodicals in Germany and the United States, was the first editor of the *Lutherisches Kirchenblatt* of Reading, Pa. (1884), and edited *Siloah,* a paper founded in the interest of German home missions, 1882–88. He died at his summer home in Watchung, N. J., while preparing a sermon for the following Sunday. Of his four sons, Charles Edward became a well-known Egyptologist and Richard George Gottlob Moldenke [*q.v.*], a metallurgist.

[This article is based chiefly on material supplied by Moldehnke's son, Dr. Charles Edward Moldenke of Watchung, N. J. See also *Who's Who in America,* 1903–05; J. C. Jensson-Roseland, *Am. Luth. Biogs.* (Milwaukee, 1890); *North Plainfield Review,* July 9, 1904; *N. Y. Times,* June 26, 29, 1904; *New-Yorker Staats-Zeitung,* June 27, 29, 1904. The family name is variously spelled; the forms here adopted are those apparently preferred by the individuals mentioned.]
G. H. G.

MOLDENKE, RICHARD GEORGE GOTTLOB (Nov. 1, 1864–Nov. 17, 1930), metallurgist, was born in Watertown, Wis., the son of the Rev. Edward F. Moldehnke [*q.v.*], a Lutheran clergyman, and Elise (Harder) Moldehnke. Richard changed the spelling of the family name, and rarely used his second and third baptismal names. In 1870 he was taken to New York City, where he attended Columbia Grammar School and later the School of Mines, Columbia University, receiving the degree of E. M. in 1885 and that of Ph.D. in 1887. Late in life, in the course of a public address, he said, "I thank my father because he put me to school when I was three years old, and I have been to school ever since. . . . I shall stay there as long as I live" (*Transactions of the American Foundrymen's Association,* vol. XXXIII, p. xxvii). After two years with the Coast and Geodetic Survey, he organized the mechanical and electrical engineering departments at the Michigan College of Mines and served as professor of mechanical engineering for one year (1889).

With the acceptance in 1890 of a position with McConway & Torley Company, Pittsburgh, Pa., he started on his active career of forty years as a metallurgist. His restless cravings for research led him to originate and follow through some of the most valuable investigations which have been undertaken in the field of foundry science. His cupola study served to revise charging methods and to effect great economies in plant operation. He worked out the action of carbon, silicon, and other basic elements in iron. His study of coke led to a new understanding of that fuel. He was a pioneer in improving practice in the gray-iron industry by substituting science for rule-of-thumb. Because of his great influence in stimulating the scientific study of foundry problems and particularly because of the improvements in the art of producing gray-iron castings which resulted from his investigations and studies, he was awarded in 1925 the Joseph S. Seaman gold medal of the American Foundrymen's Association.

He was an active and influential member of that organization almost from its inception, and was for fourteen years its secretary and treasurer. Through his membership in this and other technical societies in the United States and Europe, his attendance at meetings, and his generous and enthusiastic participation in their proceedings, he not only kept in touch with metallurgical developments but also earned for himself an international reputation as a metallurgist. During the last thirty years of his life he was retained as consultant by a large number of foundries and manufacturing firms both in the United States and abroad. As consultant for the federal government during the World War he supervised the casting of war materials and drafted the specifications for the castings used in the manufacture of Liberty motors.

Moldenke was a prolific writer on foundry and metallurgical subjects, contributing to the technical press, government publications, and the proceedings of technical societies. Two important works, *The Principles of Iron Founding* (1917; 2nd ed., 1930) and *The Production of Malleable Castings* (1910), are outstanding contributions to foundry literature. At Watchung, N. J., he built himself a replica of a German castle and behind it constructed a small foundry in which he performed his experimental work. He was married, Sept. 18, 1891, to Anne, daughter of John D. Heins of New York, who, together with a daughter and two sons, survived him. His death, following an operation, occurred at Plainfield, N. J., Nov. 17, 1930. On Nov. 20 the *Iron Age* remarked: "In his passing the castings industry has lost its great technician and its generous adviser."

[*The Foundry*, Dec. 1, 1930; *Trans. Am. Foundrymen's Asso.*, vol. XXXIII (1926); *Trans. and Bull., Am. Foundrymen's Asso.*, Dec. 1930; *Who's Who in America*, 1930–31; *N. Y. Times*, Nov. 18, 1930.]
B. A. R.

MOLLENHAUER, EMIL (Aug. 4, 1855–Dec. 10, 1927), violinist, conductor, was born in Brooklyn, N. Y., the son of Friedrich and Margaret (Pugh) Mollenhauer. The father was one of three brothers born in Erfurt, Germany, all of whom were excellent musicians. Friedrich and Eduard, who were violinists, came to America as members of the Jullien Orchestra which toured the United States in 1853. They remained as soloists, orchestral players, and teachers. Heinrich, the third brother, a 'cellist, emigrated in 1856 and established a school of music in Brooklyn. Friedrich Mollenhauer was the most brilliant of the three and in addition was an able teacher. Recognizing his son's musical talent, he gave him violin lessons and the boy progressed so rapidly that he made his début with the orchestra in Niblo's Garden before he was quite nine years old. When he was fourteen he became a member of the orchestra of Booth's Theatre and played throughout Joseph Jefferson's run of six months in *Rip Van Winkle*. At the age of seventeen he became one of the first violinists in the Theodore Thomas Orchestra, remaining for about eight years, when he joined the New York Symphony Society founded by Leopold Damrosch. He also became a member of both the New York and the Brooklyn Philharmonic societies.

Meantime he had developed into a well-equipped pianist and was frequently called upon to act as accompanist for soloists appearing on the orchestral programs. In 1884 he settled in Boston, having accepted a position as first violinist in the Boston Symphony Orchestra, but he resigned in 1888 to accept the more responsible position of conductor of the Germania Orchestra, later known as the Boston Festival Orchestra. He was also conductor of the Municipal Concerts until 1903. In 1899 he succeeded Reinhold L. Herman as conductor of the Handel and Haydn Society which was in need of reorganization. He remained head of this organization for twenty-eight years, resigning in May 1927, because of ill health. From 1901 until his death he conducted the Apollo Club of Boston and at various times the oratorio societies of neighboring towns, besides conducting the People's Symphony Orchestra (1920–25) and the Boston Band. For a number of years he toured the country with the Boston Festival Orchestra, visiting especially the cities in the East and Middle West which had excellent choral societies, and supplying the orchestral background for their festivals. In 1904 he conducted the Boston Symphony Orchestra at the St. Louis Exposition and in 1915 at the San Francisco Exposition.

According to Mollenhauer's own statement, Theodore Thomas exerted the greatest influence on his development as a musician, and as he entered the Thomas Orchestra in the most impressionable period of his life, he had ample opportunity to observe and learn from this conductor, whom he adored. He was a versatile musician—an able conductor and an excellent coach in the interpretation of opera, oratorio, and the *Lied*. He was conservative in his taste and extreme innovations did not appeal to him. He was a most serious musician and demanded the same quality of seriousness in those who played or sang under him. On Apr. 1, 1884, he married Mary E. Laverty, a singer of Boston, who survived him. He died suddenly at his home in Boston on the day before he was to have conducted a concert by the People's Symphony Orchestra, in Jordan Hall. At a presentation of the *Messiah* by the Handel and Haydn Society the following week he was to have been presented with a purse as an expression of appreciation of his service.

[*Who's Who in America*, 1926–27; W. F. Bradbury, *Hist. of the Handel and Haydn Soc.*, vol. II, no. 2 (1913); *Internat. Who's Who in Music* (1918); *Music*, Oct. 1892; *Musical America*, Dec. 17, 1927; *Boston Evening Transcript*, Dec. 10, 11, 1927; *N. Y. Times*, Dec. 11, 1927; information from Mollenhauer's friend, Reinhold Faelten.]
F. L. G. C.

MÖLLHAUSEN, HEINRICH BALDUIN (Jan. 27, 1825–May 28, 1905), traveler, author, was born on a small estate near Bonn on the Rhine. His father, Heinrich Möllhausen, began his career as a Prussian artillery officer, but later retired from the army to practise civil engineering. His mother was Elisabeth Baronesse von Falkenstein, who died early, leaving three children to be cared for by her family while the father roamed to the four corners of Europe. Balduin attended the Gymnasium at Bonn until his fourteenth year, when financial difficulties cut short his education. For a time he tried his hand at agriculture in Pomerania and weighed the possibility of becoming an Austrian officer, but after a bit of experience in the Revolution of 1848 his restless blood made its demands on him and in the fall of 1849 he sailed for America. He proceeded to the Middle West, where he "led the roving life of a hunter in the region of the Kaskaskia River in Illinois." On hearing that the Duke Paul William of Württemberg was on the point of setting out on a scientific expedition to the Rocky Mountains, he requested and was granted the privilege of joining the party. The expedition got as far as Fort Laramie, but soon collapsed in the face of repeated Indian attacks. Late in the autumn of 1851 the Duke and Möllhausen retreated alone to the Missouri and from there to Fort Kearny. At some distance from this place the Duke, fallen ill, was picked up by a United States mail coach, leaving Möllhausen alone to battle Indians, famine, snow, and cold for long months. He was ultimately rescued by friendly Indians, and after a considerable lapse of time joined the Duke in New Orleans.

In January 1853 Möllhausen was back in Berlin. Here he came into intimate contact with Alexander von Humboldt, who became his patron and friend. In this cultured home he met and later married (Feb. 6, 1855) Carolina Alexandra Seifert who had been reared as a foster child of the distinguished scientist. After less than four months in Berlin he sailed again for America, provided with letters of recommendation to influential persons in Washington. His arrival, in May 1853, could not have been more opportunely arranged. The United States government was on the point of sending out three different expeditions to chart the best course for a railroad to the Pacific. Möllhausen was assigned as topographer to that commanded by Lieut. A. W. Whipple, while the Smithsonian Institution commissioned him to make physical observations and to act as naturalist on this venture. His unusual ability to sketch played no little part in these appointments. With this expedition he made the trek from Fort Smith to

Pueblo de los Angelos. In August 1854 he was again in Berlin, the house guest of von Humboldt. His renowned patron prevailed upon King Frederick William IV to create for him the position of custodian of the libraries in the royal residences in and about Potsdam, a position which he held until his death. This fortunate turn of affairs gave him the comfort and the leisure necessary for his writing. Once more he heard and followed the call of the American West, accepting an appointment offered him by the United States government as assistant to an expedition to explore and survey the Colorado River (1857–58). The thrills of this adventure he later crystallized into a number of novels. During most of the remaining forty-seven years of his life he stayed at home and developed his art as a voluminous and facile writer of adventure stories. He died in Berlin, in 1905.

Forty-five large works in 157 volumes and eighty novelettes in twenty-one volumes bear emphatic witness to Möllhausen's industry and the fertility of his mind. This voluminous output may be roughly divided into two groups: first, the earlier novels whose action takes place wholly on American soil, such as *Der Halbindianer* (4 vols., 1861) and its sequels, and *Das Mormonenmädchen* (6 vols., 1864); secondly, the later stories, by far the more numerous, which have for their scenes of action both the old and the new country. He must be considered as one of the most prominent exponents of both Indian and emigration fiction. His biographer, P. A. Barba, has summed up his deserts excellently: "Balduin Möllhausen was the most prolific, and at the same time the last great exponent of transatlantic fiction in Germany. He did not write with the passionate pen of Sealsfield [Karl Postl]; he did not give the Indian so prominent a place in his novels as Strubberg did . . . he may lack Gerstäcker's facile style of narrative; but in point of form, and in the skillful motivation of a plot he is the master of all these. . . . In view of his splendid portrayals of Indian and pioneer life, and by virtue of the high character of his sea-novels, there is none who deserves so much the title of 'The German Cooper.'"

[P. A. Barba, *Balduin Möllhausen, The German Cooper* (Americana Germanica, vol. XVII, Pubs. of the Univ. of Pa., 1914), is dedicated to Carolina Alexandra Frau Balduin Möllhausen and opens with a German introduction by the lady; see also a short sketch by Franz Brümmer in *Biographisches Jahrbuch und Deutscher Nekrolog*, X (1907), 123–24; and the obituary article in *Berliner Tageblatt*, May 29, 1905.]

C.F.S.

MOLYNEUX, ROBERT (July 24, 1738–Dec. 9, 1808), Roman Catholic priest and educator, was born near Formby, Lancashire, a scion of a noteworthy North Briton cavalier family which contributed a number of members to the Society of Jesus. Educated by private tutors and reared in the seclusion enforced upon Catholics by the penal laws, he entered the Society of Jesus on Sept. 7, 1757, and studied theology in Belgium, teaching for a time in his community's college at Bruges. Soon after his ordination, he was assigned to the American missions, where a relative, Richard Molyneux, had previously labored as a Jesuit missionary and superior. Arriving in Maryland in 1771, he served two years on the missions and was then appointed to St. Mary's Church, Philadelphia, to succeed Robert Harding [q.v.], who had died in September 1772. Later he became joint pastor of St. Joseph's Church as well. Here after the suppression of his society he continued as a secular priest along with Ferdinand Farmer [q.v.]. During the Revolution he was a moderate patriot, taking the oath of allegiance to Pennsylvania, welcoming the attendance of members of Congress at two funeral masses for foreign envoys, tutoring the Chevalier de la Luzerne in English, burying himself in his library in order to avoid association with the invaders during the British occupation. He opened a parochial school, purchasing its site in 1781, and that same year improved the church. In 1783 he was one of the signers of a petition praying that Congress return to Philadelphia.

A zealous churchman, he urged his intimate friend, John Carroll [q.v.], to accept the appointment as prefect apostolic in order that the church in America might be freed from English jurisdiction. This step accomplished, he advocated the appointment of an American bishop, joining with Carroll and the Rev. John Ashton in a memorial to Rome on this subject. After papal approval had been secured (July 12, 1788), the convention of clergy met at Whitemarsh, Carroll's name was submitted to Rome, and he was forthwith named bishop. Meanwhile, Molyneux left Philadelphia for Bohemia Manor (1788) and later Newtown, Md. As Bishop Carroll's vicar general for the southern district, he took part in the diocesan synod of 1791. Soon afterwards he succeeded Father Robert Plunkett as president of Georgetown College, where he remained until transferred back to Newtown in 1796. Deeply concerned in the negotiations with the Rev. Gabriel Gruber, general of the Society of Jesus in Russia, Molyneux rejoiced in the preliminary restoration of the Society, of which he was named American superior, June 21, 1805. In 1806, upon the res-

ignation of Bishop Leonard Neale [q.v.], he again assumed the rectorship of Georgetown. Two years later, weary and realizing that his end was near, he named Charles Neale as acting superior of the Jesuit priests in America. He left no literary remains save a *Sermon on the Death of Father Farmer* (1786), which, incidentally, was one of the first Catholic publications in the United States.

[J. G. Shea, *Hist. of the Cath. Ch. in the U. S.*, vol. II (1888); Peter Guilday, *The Life and Times of John Carroll* (1922); Thos. Hughes, *Hist. of the Soc. of Jesus in North America* (1910); *Am. Cath. Hist. Researches* (1884–1912), see index volume, and esp. vol. XXIX (1912), pp. 267–78; J. L. J. Kirlin, *Catholicity in Phila.* (1909); *National Intelligencer and Washington Advertiser*, Dec. 26, 1808; *Am. Cath. Quart. Rev.*, Jan. 1886; J. S. Easby-Smith, *Georgetown Univ.* (2 vols., 1907.]
R.J.P.

MOMBERT, JACOB ISIDOR (Nov. 6, 1829–Oct. 7, 1913), Episcopal clergyman, author, was born in Cassel, Germany, the son of Dr. J. L. and Joanna M. Mombert. When twelve years old he went to England. In 1857 he was ordained a deacon of the Anglican church in the Chapel Royal, Whitehall, London, by Dr. Tait, later the Archbishop of Canterbury. Dean Stanley was one of the examiners. The following year he was priested by Bishop Mountain in Quebec, Canada, and served until 1859 as an assistant in Trinity Church, to which he had been called because of his ability to preach in English, French, and German. From 1859 to 1870 he was the rector of St. James Church, Lancaster, Pa., where, on July 5, 1860, he married Emma Elizabeth Muhlenberg, half-sister of Frederick Augustus Muhlenberg [q.v.]. His sermon, "The Open Door," preached before the Congress of Convocation held at Reading, Pa., Feb. 20, 1867 (Paterson *Morning Call*, Dec. 23, 1907), led to the erection of the Central Diocese of Pennsylvania, and his services at Bedford Springs brought about the establishment of a parish. During the Civil War he supported the Union, and jointly with Phillips Brooks ministered to the wounded and performed the last rites for the dead upon the field of Gettysburg. After leaving Lancaster he held the following rectorships: St. John's Dresden, Germany, 1870–76; Christ Church, Jersey City, N. J., 1877–78; St. John's, Passaic, N. J., 1879–82. The last years of his life were devoted to literary labors in Paterson, N. J., where he died, survived by two sons and four daughters.

His published works covered a considerable range. In the Biblical field his *Translation and Commentary on the Book of Psalms* (1858), from the German of Augustus Tholuck, was fraught with peculiar difficulties because Tholuck had taken as a basis Luther's version, for which the English Authorized had to be substituted with inevitable adjustments in the commentary. Mombert's translation of the Catholic Epistles in J. P. Lange's *A Commentary on the Holy Scriptures* (vol. IX, 1867) was enriched by a large number of signed notes. His edition of *William Tyndale's Five Books of Moses* appeared in 1884 (London and New York). His handbook called *English Versions of the Bible* (1883, 1890, 1906) is a learned and yet readable account of all the versions in the English tongue from the Anglo-Saxon to the Anglo-American Revision, with a description of the circumstances of the translation and of the sources employed.

In the field of general and ecclesiastical history, he published *A History of Charles the Great* (1888), intended for the general reader, but based on a thorough and critical use of the sources; *A Short History of the Crusades* (1894), a popular and colorful account; and *Great Lives* (First Series, all that appeared, 1886), a popular "course of history in biographies" from Hercules to Ulysses S. Grant, including Constantine, Charlemagne, and Luther. A volume published in 1882, *Faith Victorious,* is a vindication of Dr. Johann W. Ebel, a Lutheran clergyman of Königsberg, Prussia.

In a class by itself among his writings is *An Authentic History of Lancaster County in the State of Pennsylvania* (1869), a most diverse compilation, its topics ranging all the way from Mennonites to mineralogy and from archeology to agriculture, and presenting for the first time the colonial records, including the names of those from the county who served in the Revolution. His last publication was *Raphael's Sistine Madonna* (1895), an historical account and an artistic appreciation, for which he was fitted not only by his unusual linguistic and historical attainments, but also by an artistic taste which led him at the age of seventy to take up oil painting.

[*Who's Who in America*, 1912–13, slightly inaccurate; *Newark Churchman*, Jan. 1908, Nov. 1913; *N. Y. Times*, Oct. 8, 1913; *Paterson Press*, Dec. 21, 1907, on the occasion of the fiftieth anniversary of his ordination as a deacon; information as to certain facts from Miss Rietta A. Mombert of Paterson, N. J.]

R. H. B.

MONCKTON, ROBERT (June 24, 1726–May 21, 1782), British lieutenant-general, was the second son of John Monckton, created Viscount Galway in 1727, and of his wife Lady Elizabeth Manners, daughter of the second Duke of Rutland. He entered the 3rd Foot Guards in 1741, became captain in the 34th in 1744 and major in 1747. He served at Dettingen and at Fontenoy. In 1751 he became lieutenant-colonel of the 47th, and followed his father as member of Parliament for Pontefract. After joining his regiment in Nova Scotia in 1752, Monckton commanded at Fort Lawrence from August to June 1753, when he was appointed a provincial councilor. In December he quelled an insurrection of German immigrants at Lunenburg by "moderate management and most judicious measures" rather than by force. In June 1755, at the head of 270 regulars and nearly 2,000 New Englanders, he accomplished the only successful British action of the summer, taking Fort Beausejour in an admirably executed two weeks' campaign and destroying the French control of the isthmus. For his "zeal and ability" in this service he was made lieutenant-governor of Nova Scotia. Until November he remained in Chignecto and followed Gov. Charles Lawrence's orders in destroying French villages and in collecting 1,100 French inhabitants for removal southward. In 1756 he was disciplining the 600 new recruits of his regiment in his customary kindly, firm manner, and in December 1757 he was appointed colonel of the 2nd Battalion of the Royal American regiment. In 1758 he acted as governor in Lawrence's absence, commanded in Nova Scotia during Amherst's siege of Louisbourg, and from September to November led an expedition up the River St. John to reduce that section to British obedience. Though Amherst had designed him to succeed Forbes as commander in the south, he was selected by Wolfe in England, and approved by Pitt, as second in command of the Quebec expedition of 1759, with the temporary rank of brigadier-general. He was at the actions of Point Lévis and Montmorency, was wounded through the lungs at the battle of the Plains, and commanded in Canada until ill health forced him south. In October he became colonel of the 17th. In 1760 he received from Amherst the command of the southern district and was at various posts in Pennsylvania and western New York. The following year saw his merits gain full recognition, for he was named governor of New York, major-general and commander-in-chief of an expedition against Martinique. Sailing in November, he effected in conjunction with Admiral Rodney the surrender of the island by Feb. 5, in a sharp, soldierly campaign. In June he returned to assume his government of New York, where his "easy disposition" scarcely fitted him for rigorous administration, and a year later left for England. In 1764 a court-martial triumphantly acquitted him of a trumpery charge brought against him by a cashiered officer, Colin Campbell. In 1765 he became governor of Berwick-on-Tweed; in 1770 lieutenant-general. Three years later he petitioned both King and Parliament for the appointment in India as second in command under Warren Hastings; he was offered instead the chief command in North America, which he refused (Sir John Fortescue, *The Correspondence of King George the Third*, II, 1927, pp. 494–503). The next year he represented Pontefract in Parliament, and in 1778 Portsmouth, having been appointed governor of Portsmouth. There is no record of his marriage, but he left three sons and one daughter.

[D. H. Monckton, *A Geneal. Hist. of the Family of Monckton* (1887); *The Northcliffe Collection* (1926), containing 400 pages of Monckton's papers; *Selections from the Pub. Documents of the Province of Nova Scotia* (1869); E. B. O'Callaghan, *Documents Relative to the Colonial Hist. of the Province of N. Y.*, vols. VII–VIII (1856–57); A. G. Doughty and G. W. Parmelee, *The Siege of Quebec* (6 vols., 1901); Capt. John Knox, *An Hist. Jour. of the Campaigns in North America* (3 vols., 1914–16), ed. by A. G. Doughty; "The Letters and Papers of Cadwallader Colden," vol. VI, which is vol. LV of the *N. Y. Hist. Soc. Colls.* (1923); "Monckton's Report of his Expedition Against the French on the St. John in 1758," *New Brunswick Hist. Soc. Colls.*, No. 5 (1904); "Aspinwall Papers," *Mass. Hist. Soc. Colls.*, 4 ser. IX–X (1871); J. C. Webster, *The Forts of Chignecto* (1930); *Proc. of a General Court-martial . . . for the Trial of a Charge Preferred by C. Campbell* (1764); Public Record Office, W. O. 34, The Amherst Papers.]   S. M. P.

MONCURE, RICHARD CASSIUS LEE (Dec. 11, 1805–Aug. 24, 1882), jurist, was born at "Clermont," his family's ancestral Potomac River plantation, Stafford County, Va., the seventh of nine children of John and Alice Peachy (Gaskins) Moncure. He was descended from the Rev. John Moncure, born in Scotland, who emigrated to Virginia about 1734. Although of distinguished family he was not born to wealth and apparently received little formal schooling, but at the age of twenty he was admitted to the bar. The same year, Dec. 29, 1825, he married Mary Butler Washington Conway. In 1826 he became commonwealth's attorney for Stafford County, a post he long occupied. Although he served in the House of Delegates of 1827–28 he was not attracted by politics, but in the years 1847–49, when the statute law of Virginia was revised, he again represented his native county in the legislature and, as a member of the committee charged with the task of revision, played a prominent part in the promulgation of the code of 1849. The next year, as delegate to the state constitutional convention, he materially aided in framing the constitution of 1851. Already recognized by the bench and bar as a lawyer of the first rank, Moncure now enjoyed a state-wide reputation and in 1851 the legislature appointed him to the supreme court of appeals. When the new constitution, providing for the popular election of judges, went into effect, he was chosen without opposition to continue on the bench, where he remained until the collapse of the Confederacy. After a brief retirement during the confusing days which followed Appomattox he returned to his judicial duties and became president of the court, but with the establishment of military rule during Reconstruction he was removed from office. In 1870, with the return of civil government under a new constitution, the legislature restored him to the bench and he again became president of Virginia's highest court.

The opinions handed down by Moncure during his long judicial career, contained in twenty-nine volumes of the *Virginia Reports* from 7 *Grattan* (47 *Va.*) to 1 *Matthews* (75 *Va.*) are those of an independent and incorruptible judge who was learned in the law and devoted to his task of administering justice. His best decisions, perhaps, are the ones in which he applied the great principles of equity. Plain and unadorned in style, without literary or oratorical pretensions, his opinions generally were clear expositions of the law, although in later years, through his desire to show that no point had been overlooked, they tended to become too detailed and tedious. Moncure labored diligently in his search for truth and justice. He read neither classical nor current literature and cared little for what is usually called pleasure; his happy domestic life, the law, and the "record" completely absorbed him. He seldom perceived a joke unaided, but was genial and could laugh heartily when it was explained to him. Sublime in his unconscious simplicity, free from display, and unoppressed by his heritage and attainments, he had an appropriate conception, however, of the dignity of his office. So thoroughly did he inspire public confidence and affection that when forced into retirement during Reconstruction he was frequently chosen as unofficial arbiter of disputes. He was a vestryman in the Episcopal Church for forty years, devout yet tolerant, basing his belief squarely on the Bible which he deemed the foundation-stone of the law. Strong and fearless in his faith, with a consciousness of life's task completed, he died at his home "Glencairne" in the county that gave him birth.

[H. E. Hayden, *Va. Geneals.* (1891), pp. 437, 443–44; Joseph Christian, "Judge R. C. L. Moncure" in 76 *Va.*, v–xiii; Resolutions by bench and bar on the death of Moncure in 76 *Va.*, xiii–xv; Robert Ould, "Hon. Richard C. L. Moncure," *Va. Law Jour.*, Jan. 1883; J. C. Lamb, "Some Anecdotes of Judge Moncure," *Ibid.*, Aug. 1885; R. W. Moore, address on Moncure in *Va. Law Reg.,* June 1924; S. S. B. Patteson, "The Supreme Court of Appeals of Va.," the *Green Bag,* Aug. 1893; *Daily Dispatch* (Richmond, Va.), Aug. 26, 1882.]   T. S. C.

MONETTE, JOHN WESLEY (Apr. 5, 1803–Mar. 1, 1851), physician, historian, was a native of Virginia, born in the Shenandoah Valley near Staunton, the son of Samuel and Mary (Wayland) Monett. Later he added an "e" to the family name. His father, an ordained Methodist minister and a practising physician, was a descendant of Isaac Monet, a French Huguenot who settled in Maryland sometime before 1707. When John was very young, the family moved to Chillicothe, Ohio, where the lad grew up, receiving at the academy there, under the tutelage of Rev. John McFarland, an excellent education. In 1821 Dr. Monett transferred his residence to the new state of Mississippi, settling at Washington, then the capital. The son, having decided to become a physician, was sent to Transylvania University, Lexington, Ky., where he made an excellent record in scientific studies and graduated with the degree of M.D. in 1825. He then joined his father at Washington, Miss., and thereafter made that place his home. On Dec. 10, 1828, he married Cornelia Jane Newman; four only of their ten children lived to maturity.

Monette gained considerable reputation as a physician from his study of yellow fever epidemics in Mississippi. The results of his observations he incorporated into numerous articles, among which are "An Account of the Epidemic of Yellow Fever that Occurred in Washington, Mississippi, in the Autumn of 1825" (*Western Medical and Physical Journal,* May 1827); *The Epidemic Yellow Fevers of Natchez* (1838); and *Observations on the Epidemic Yellow Fever of Natchez and of the Southwest* (1842). He is credited with being the earliest to suggest the quarantine as a means of preventing the spread of the disease, and the fact that Natchez escaped the epidemic of 1841 has been attributed to the employment of that means. He also recommended the use of oil of turpentine as an irritant, especially in the treatment of typhus fever, publishing "Oil of Turpentine as an External Irritant" (*Western Medical and Physical Journal,* June 1827).

Monette made a number of fortunate investments and accumulated a fortune sufficient to permit him to devote much time to literary and scientific studies. Although a Methodist and a trustee of the local church and college, his studies in physical geography and concerning the origin of man led him toward conclusions similar to those which his English contemporary,

Darwin, later promulgated. His place in the history of science, however, is not a prominent one. He projected but never completed a "Physical History of the Human Race." When about thirty years of age he began collecting material for a work on the physical geography of the Mississippi Valley and in the course of his research he was led to study its history. This portion of his work was the first completed and resulted in his monumental volumes, *History of the Discovery and Settlement of the Valley of the Mississippi by the Three Great European Powers, Spain, France, and Great Britain, and the Subsequent Occupation, Settlement and Extension of Civil Government by the United States until the Year 1846* (2 vols., 1846). The prospectus circular stated that it would be followed by two more volumes on the physical geography of the Valley; but at his death the manuscript was left unfinished and was never published. Monette was one of the first to appreciate the share which the great central valley of the Mississippi River had in the history of the United States.

His work is one of great research and erudition. The style is easy and flowing and less ponderous than that of many histories of his time. He was not always able to refer to original documents and depended upon such authorities as F. X. Martin's *History of Louisiana* and Mann Butler's *History of the Commonwealth of Kentucky,* but the material is well organized and the treatment thorough. Monette was a frequent contributor to various periodicals, among his articles being "Geology of the Mississippi Valley" in *Commercial Review of the South and West* (February, March 1847), "Public Lands Acquired by Treaty," *Ibid.* (January, February 1848), and "Early Spirit of the West," *De Bow's Review* (April, May 1850). Not long before his death he established a home in Madison Parish, La. He is buried at Washington, Miss., however, and always regarded that place as his home. He was mayor and councilman of the town and one of its prominent citizens.

[O. E. Monnette, *Monnet Family Geneal.* (1911); *Miss. Hist. Soc. Pubs.,* vol. V (1902); F. L. Riley, "Life and Literary Services of Dr. John W. Monette," *Ibid.,* vol. IX (1906); H. A. Kelly and W. L. Burrage, *Am. Med. Biogs.* (1920); C. G. Forshey, "John W. Monette, Historian of the Mississippi Valley," in *De Bow's Rev.,* July 1851.]   L. P. K.

MONEY, HERNANDO DE SOTO (Aug. 26, 1839–Sept. 18, 1912), newspaper editor, lawyer, representative and senator from Mississippi, was born on a plantation in Holmes County, Miss., but in early childhood his family moved to Carrollton. His father, Peirson Money,

Money

came from Buncombe County, N. C.; his mother, Tryphena (Vardaman) Money, was a member of a pioneer Mississippi family. A private tutor directed part of his preliminary education. In 1860 he graduated from the law school of the University of Mississippi and began practice at Carrollton. With the beginning of the Civil War he entered the Confederate infantry and served until his defective eyesight caused him to be furloughed. He then joined the cavalry and served to the end of the war. On Nov. 5, 1863, he was married to Claudia Jane Boddie, of Hinds County; six children were born of this union.

After the war Money was for a time a planter in Leflore County. He then edited the *Conservative* at Carrollton and from 1873 to 1875 published the *Advance* at Winona. During the Reconstruction period, and particularly in the exciting times of 1875, he fought valiantly against the Carpet-bag régime, and his election to the lower house of the Forty-fourth Congress was an indication of the return of power to the native white people of the state. He continued to hold this office through five congresses (Mar. 4, 1875–Mar. 3, 1885). Though there was no opposition to his renomination, he retired to private life and practised law at Washington. At the end of eight years he was persuaded to represent his district once more and served through the Fifty-third and the Fifty-fourth congresses (Mar. 4, 1893–Mar. 3, 1897). In January 1896 he was elected by the legislature to fill the senatorial term beginning Mar. 4, 1899. Between these two dates Senator J. Z. George died and Money was first appointed by the governor (Oct. 8, 1897), and soon afterward elected by the legislature, to complete the term begun by George. He was reëlected for a second term and was thus in the Senate from 1897 until 1911, his total congressional career covering almost twenty-eight years. He was never defeated for nomination or election to any office, though he was singularly independent in his political activities, apparently spending little time or thought on his political fences.

His long career in Congress, as well as his ability, brought him a number of important committee appointments. In the House he was a member of the committees on foreign affairs, naval affairs, and for two congresses served as chairman of the committee on post-offices and post-roads, where he displayed strong leadership in the destruction of the "star route" system, in reducing letter postage from three to two cents, and in promulgating the idea that the postal system should not be considered a source of revenue, or even expected to pay its own way.

Monis

He was a member of the Democratic steering committee of the Senate, and was on the finance and foreign relations committees. During his last years he was interested in the cause of peace and believed that it could be best attained by preparedness. He personally favored the Swiss method of military training and was contemplating a book on this subject when his death occurred at his home on the Mississippi coast. He was buried in the family vault at Carrollton.

[Dunbar Rowland, *The Official and Statistical Reg. of the State of Miss.*, 1908, and *Mississippi* (1907), vol. II; F. M. Witty, "Reconstruction in Carroll and Montgomery Counties," *Pubs. Miss. Hist. Soc.*, vol. X (1909); *Cong. Record*, 62 Cong., 3 Sess., pp. 4818–19, and *Ibid.*, App., pp. 129–30, 133–34; *Who's Who in America*, 1912–13; *Daily Democrat* (Natchez), Sept. 19, 20, 1912.]   C. S. S.

MONIS, JUDAH (Feb. 4, 1683–Apr. 25, 1764), Hebrew scholar, theologian, educator, was born in Algiers or Italy and was educated in the Jewish schools of Leghorn and Amsterdam. After a residence in Jamaica he went to New York, where he was made a free citizen on Feb. 28, 1715/16, his occupation being given as that of merchant. In later years, however, he is described as "sometime Rabbi of the Synagogue in *Jamaica,* and afterwards in *New York.*" He appears next in Boston or Cambridge. On June 29, 1720, he submitted to the Corporation of Harvard College the draft of a Hebrew grammar, and, in consequence, at the Commencement of the same year he received the degree of M.A. About two years later (Mar. 27, 1722), he was baptized publicly and with great solemnity in the College Hall at Cambridge. Soon after that (Apr. 30, 1722), he was appointed instructor of Hebrew in Harvard College for one year. This appointment was renewed from year to year until 1760, when he resigned his instructorship and retired to Northborough, Mass. He died there four years later.

Of his life in Cambridge certain pertinent facts are known. In January 1723/24 he married a Christian woman by the name of Abigail Marrett; he owned property, kept a shop even while teaching at Harvard, acted on one occasion as Spanish interpreter to the government, was nominated to be a justice of the peace, and when pressed by straitened circumstances petitioned the legislature for a grant from the public treasury to supplement his meager income. The records of Harvard College contain references to his successive reappointments, to occasional increases in his salary, to regulations regarding attendance at his classes, to a quarrel with one of his colleagues over the use of a class room, to assistance granted to him in connection with the publication of his grammar, and to a promise of support in defense of his privilege of exemption from taxes. His name appears also on the pamphlet issued in 1744 by the Harvard officials against the Rev. George Whitefield. Though there was some misgiving as to the sincerity of his conversion, he was at once allowed by the First Church of Cambridge to partake with its members at the Lord's Supper. Later (Feb. 5, 1736–37), he joined that church as a member. He continued, however, throughout his lifetime to observe the seventh day as the Sabbath. Before his death he professed his firm belief in the Christian religion and left the bulk of his estate as a permanent fund for poor widows of Christian ministers.

Monis is chiefly noted for the circumstance that he was the first in several things—the first Jew to receive a degree from Harvard, the first teacher at Harvard to bear the title of instructor, and the author of the first Hebrew grammar published in America. He is the author of the following works: *Three Discourses . . . The Truth, The Whole Truth, and, Nothing But the Truth: One of Which was Deliver'd by him at his Baptism* (Boston, 1722, printed together with Benjamin Colman's *A Discourse Had in the College-Hall. At Cambridge, Mass., Mar. 27, 1722, Before the Baptism of R. Judah Monis*); *Dickdook Leshon Gnebreet: A Grammar of the Hebrew Tongue* (Cambridge, 1735); "Nomenclatura Hebraica: . . . Short Nomenclator or Vocabular in English and Hebrew," a manuscript in the Harvard College Library.

["Harvard Coll. Records, Part II," in *Colonial Soc. of Mass. Pubs.*, vol. XVI (1925); Hannah Adams, *The Hist. of the Jews* (1812), II, 210–13; Benjamin Peirce, *A Hist. of Harvard Univ.* (1833); Josiah Quincy, *The Hist. of Harvard Univ.* (1840), vol. I; G. A. Kohut, "Judah Monis, M.A., The First Instructor in Hebrew at Harvard Univ.," *Am. Jour. of Semitic Languages and Lits.*, July 1898; L. M. Friedman, "Judah Monis, First Instructor in Hebrew at Harvard Univ.," *Am. Jewish Hist. Soc. Pubs.*, no. 22 (1914); G. F. Moore, "Judah Monis," *Proc. Mass. Hist. Soc.*, vol. LII (1919); F. B. Dexter, *The Lit. Diary of Ezra Stiles* (1901), I, 423. Additional bibliographical data are to be found in Kohut, Friedman, and Moore.]   H. A. W.

MONROE, JAMES (Apr. 28, 1758–July 4, 1831), fifth president of the United States, was born in Westmoreland County, Va. His parents, Spence and Elizabeth (Jones) Monroe, were Virginians of good but not distinguished stock. The paternal line can be traced with considerable probability to Andrew Monroe, who settled in Maryland in 1647, opposed Lord Baltimore, and removed to Westmoreland County, Va. (*William and Mary College Quarterly*, Jan. 1907). James Monroe went to the private school of Parson Archibald Campbell, and at sixteen entered the

College of William and Mary. But the advent of the Revolution soon interrupted his academic career, and at the age of eighteen, after some service as a cadet, he enlisted as a lieutenant in a Virginia regiment of the Continental line. He was present at the battles of Harlem, White Plains, and Trenton; in the last engagement he bore a rather conspicuous part and received a wound in the shoulder. In the campaigns of 1777 and 1778 he served as aide to the Earl of Stirling, with the rank of major, and saw further fighting at the Brandywine, Germantown, and Monmouth. By his promotion, however, he had lost his place in the Continental line, and, although he had aroused the friendly interest of Washington, he found it impossible to secure a suitable military position in the service of his state. Acting in part upon the advice of his uncle, Judge Joseph Jones [*q.v.*], in 1780 he formed a connection as a student of law with Thomas Jefferson, then governor of Virginia, that continued until 1783. The close friendship of the two men endured until the death of the elder in 1826.

In 1782 Monroe was elected to the Virginia legislature and in 1783 to the Congress of the Confederation, where he served until 1786. In the latter body he played a by no means inconspicuous rôle. He had begun to see the necessity of some political mechanism stronger than that set up by the Articles, but his caution, his strong localism, and his fear of centralization, made him espouse a very moderate course. He favored an amendment which would permit the Congress to regulate commerce, but which would leave the imposts to be collected under the authority of the individual states, and to be spent by the state authorities. Even this modest proposal, which he reported to the Congress on Mar. 28, 1785, he did not press vigorously. He made two trips into the western country, in 1784 and 1785, and in the Congress strongly opposed John Jay's negotiations with Gardoqui, which looked to a commercial treaty with Spain and involved the dropping of the claim to the free navigation of the Mississippi. The youthful delegate was not a dominating influence, however, in the great legislation of 1784 and 1785 for the organization of the West. It is difficult to determine his attitude with regard to slavery in these newly organized regions, but he was twice absent from a vote on the question, and in the last of these instances, had he been present, his action might have been decisive in barring slavery from all of Transappalachia. He at least showed no zeal for a policy of restriction.

Monroe was present at the famous Annapolis conference of 1786, but he was not a delegate to the great convention of 1787. His term in the Congress of the Confederation having expired, he returned to the Virginia legislature. He was, however, elected to the state convention called to ratify the Constitution in 1788. He maintained a cautious and neutral policy before his election, but in the convention aligned himself with the opponents of the Constitution. He based his opposition largely upon the tendency towards centralization which he believed to be involved. But the real explanation of his conservative stand seems to have lain in the sentiment of the district he represented, and in his strong sectional feeling. He had been jealous and alarmed all through Jay's negotiations with Gardoqui; and he did not hesitate to assail Jay's policy before the convention and to express his fears lest the federal government, if strengthened, would give up the American claim to the navigation of the Mississippi. That his attitude in this matter was not without influence may be inferred from the fact that of the members of the convention from the Kentucky districts ten out of fourteen voted against ratification (H. B. Grigsby, *The History of the Virginia Federal Convention of 1788*, 2 vols., 1890–91). The final vote was a close one, 79 to 89. Monroe accepted the result, and in the fall of the year he was a candidate against Madison for election to the First Congress. In this election he was badly beaten. In 1790, however, there occurred a vacancy in the Senate of the United States, and the choice fell upon Monroe. His friendship with Jefferson had now become closer than ever; in 1788, indeed, he had moved very near to "Monticello." From the beginning of his service he was severely critical of the Washington administration. He participated little in debate, but opposed the establishment of the Bank of the United States, the selection of Gouverneur Morris as minister to France, and, later, that of John Jay as minister to Great Britain. He was one of the senatorial committee which investigated in 1792 the charges against Alexander Hamilton's handling of the public funds, in the course of which the Secretary of the Treasury was compelled to lay bare his relations with Mrs. Reynolds. Monroe remained in possession of the papers and, before his departure for France, deposited them with a friend, "a respectable character in Virginia," in whose hands they still were in 1797. He disclaimed any agency in or knowledge of their publication that year by the unscrupulous James Thomson Callender [*q.v.*], leading to the publication by Hamilton himself of the famous Reynolds pamphlet (H. C. Lodge, *The Works of Alexander Hamilton*, VI, 1886, pp. 449–535). Monroe was

rather evasive in his comments on the bitterly partisan affair and the full circumstances are still shrouded in considerable mystery; but the fact that the papers saw the light of day, if it does not reflect upon his sense of honor, as Hamilton's defenders have claimed, reflects at least upon his discretion, or that of his unnamed friend.

Monroe's senatorial service was cut short by his appointment as minister to France in June 1794. The task which now confronted him involved great difficulties from the beginning. The French government was naturally suspicious and apprehensive with regard to the Jay mission to England; it was the task of the American minister to quiet these suspicions, if possible, to bring about cordial relationships, and to secure redress for French interference with American commerce and hardships suffered by American citizens. Under the circumstances, perhaps no one could have completely succeeded; but Monroe, in his efforts to command French esteem and secure French cooperation, and moved by his own decided sympathies, pursued a course by no means in accord with the desires of the State Department. On his arrival in France, he sought to be received by the National Convention, and made a speech before that body "the extreme glow" of which later brought him a reproof from Edmund Randolph, the secretary of state (*American State Papers, Foreign Relations*, I, 1832, p. 690). The negotiations with Great Britain seriously embarrassed him, and he was very much displeased with their result. Indeed, he neglected to defend the Jay treaty, finally signed in November 1794, though furnished by the State Department with arguments in partial justification of that document. Though at the outset relatively successful in securing redress for grievances, he soon suffered from what the French considered as the Anglophile policy of the American administration, and during his last year in France he satisfied neither the authorities in Paris nor those at home. He was recalled in 1796 by Randolph's successor, Pickering, and on his return published a vindication of his mission, entitled *A View of the Conduct of the Executive, in the Foreign Affairs of the United States* (1797). In this document wounded pride reveals itself side by side with political ambition and strong partisanship.

Monroe's defeats and discomfitures never shook the confidence of his Virginia supporters. In 1799 he became governor of the state, and held this post until December 1802. Early in 1803 President Jefferson sent him to France to cooperate with Robert R. Livingston [*q.v.*] in the negotiation of a treaty which should secure western interest in the free navigation of the Mississippi. Before the Virginian arrived in Paris, the astonished Livingston had been proffered the whole vast territory ceded to France by Spain and had virtually signified his willingness to negotiate on this basis. In the details of the discussion, however, the new envoy played a part, and from the beginning he was strongly in favor of taking advantage of the French offer. The treaty which resulted contained some ambiguities which were to lead to further negotiations with Spain. In particular, the title to West Florida was left ill-defined. In 1804 Monroe was instructed to proceed to Madrid to negotiate with Charles Pinckney with regard to this matter, and to secure the cession of the eastern portion of the Floridas, either by purchase, or as a setoff against American claims. His treatment by the Spanish government was anything but courteous, and, after months of arduous correspondence and patient waiting, he was compelled to leave Madrid. Once again he had been given an almost impossible task. His diplomatic notes of this period, however, make a favorable impression, revealing his grasp of the subject with which he was instructed to deal.

Monroe's next task, again an extremely difficult one, was to attempt to settle the vexing disputes which had arisen between the United States and Great Britain. In 1805 he proceeded to London. Apparently acting under political pressure, President Jefferson associated with him in this negotiation William Pinkney [q.v.] who commanded to a greater degree the confidence of the Anglophile elements in the United States. The two men carried on long negotiations, and concluded a treaty with the British ministry in December 1806. Monroe had been instructed to secure cessation of the practice of impressments, but he was obliged to content himself with a declaration by the British government that in exercising that "right" the utmost care would be used to avoid injury or molestation of American citizens. In the *Essex* case the British courts had declared that neutral trade between the French and Spanish colonies and their mother countries was prohibited, even when the goods were actually landed in the United States. Monroe secured a concession providing that if such goods paid a small duty in the United States, they might be re-exported. He also secured certain commercial concessions. At the last moment the British ministry made the acceptance of the treaty contingent upon the assurance of the American government that it would not submit to Napoleon's interference with neutral trade. The treaty was deemed so unsatisfactory by Jefferson and Madison that it was never submitted

to the Senate. Indeed, it can hardly be said to have been in any sense superior to the Jay compact of which Monroe had been so severely critical eleven years before.

Whether or not presidential ambitions and the desire to gain Federalist votes motivated Monroe in signing a treaty so favorable to the British (Henry Adams, *History of the United States,* III, 413), he certainly came home in an aggrieved mood, and he permitted his friends to groom him for the presidential race. John Randolph, John Taylor of Caroline, and Littleton Waller Tazewell were among his supporters. In the summer of 1808 Monroe was writing directions for the campaign, and in October still hoped for success. As a matter of fact, he was decisively defeated, receiving in Virginia hardly a fifth of the vote of Madison, and not a single vote in the electoral college. He had not identified himself with the virulent opposition group headed by Randolph, nor had he himself criticized the administration. He continued to pursue this course after Madison's election, arguing that the Republican party must not be split into factions by any act of his. In November 1809, through the good offices of Jefferson, he was offered by Madison the governorship of Upper Louisiana. This post he refused, but he made it clear that he would not be averse to a reconciliation on what he considered proper terms. In the fall of 1810 he was reëlected to the Virginia legislature, and in January 1811 again became governor. In the meantime, factional politics had compelled Madison to remodel his administration. Monroe had political influence in Virginia which was badly needed. In March 1811, therefore, the President offered his former friend and associate the post of secretary of state, and Monroe accepted.

Monroe took office on the theory that he was to have a free hand, and that he would be able to solve the knotty problems raised by American neutrality in the European wars, and particularly to bring about a reconciliation with Great Britain. Just before he entered office, Congress had proclaimed non-intercourse with Great Britain, and the elections of 1810 had been highly unfavorable to any prospect of accord. None the less, he entered into negotiations with Foster, the newly arrived British minister, in July, apparently still hopeful of accommodation. He was doomed to disappointment. The British minister refused to consider the possibility of repealing the Orders in Council, contending, quite correctly, that the United States had not made its views respected by France, and that until it did so, there was little use in asking concessions from the government in London. By December Monroe seems to have been convinced that war must result. Subsequent negotiations, and the British Order in Council of Apr. 12, 1812, only deepened this impression. When, in June, war was actually declared, it apparently was Monroe who prepared the report of the House of Representatives, presented by Calhoun, on which the action was based (W. M. Meigs, *The Life of John Caldwell Calhoun,* 1917, I, 131; *American Historical Review,* Jan. 1908, pp. 303–10).

In this period of his incumbency of the State Department Monroe was in a measure involved in an episode not wholly to his credit. A strong sentiment existed in the South looking to the acquisition of East Florida. Congress indeed authorized taking possession of the province if its possession were threatened by another power. But there were those who were unwilling to wait for any such contingency. General George Mathews [*q.v.*], former governor of Georgia, visited Washington and talked with Madison in the summer of 1811. He also wrote twice to Monroe explaining the situation. The Secretary of State must have understood that what was in the wind was an attempt to revolutionize West Florida. He answered not a word, however, and Mathews went ahead with his plans, and in March 1812, carried out the projected coup. But his band of "patriots" met with considerable resistance, and Monroe was compelled to disavow his activities. The troops who had crossed over into East Florida, however, were withdrawn only after a congressional vote virtually compelled such action in May 1813.

Despite the withdrawal by the British of the obnoxious Orders in Council, Monroe continued to justify the war on other grounds, notably that of impressments. But he stood with Madison in accepting Russian mediation in March 1813, and he deserves part of the credit for the selection of the very able delegation which was sent to negotiate the peace. He had little influence upon the course of negotiations. He was compelled to forego his hope of securing from Great Britain recognition of American claims to Florida, and he was also obliged to abandon the ground which he took at the beginning with regard to impressments. But he accepted apparently without regret the treaty negotiated at Ghent. Throughout the war Monroe had strong presidential ambitions. He sought at various times to secure military command, and was intensely jealous of John Armstrong, who, in 1813, became secretary of war. After the defeat at Bladensburg in August 1814, Madison, at his insistence, dismissed Armstrong, and the Secretary of State became

also secretary of war, a post which he held until Mar. 1. In his discharge of these duties he exercised more energy and resolution than either of his predecessors. The military events of the fall of 1815, the victory at Plattsburg, and the still greater victory at New Orleans, doubtless did much to enhance Monroe's prestige. He was by now definitely in line for the presidency, yet in the congressional caucus of 1816, with the support of the administration behind him, he won by only eleven votes over his rival, William H. Crawford.

Monroe had been in his early years strongly sectional, narrowly partisan, and perhaps a little too ambitious. His diplomatic achievements, taken as a whole, had been anything but brilliant. Yet he had never ceased to command the loyalty of an influential following in Virginia, and after each defeat he had come back stronger than ever, and with his desire for high office unimpaired. He had now reached the summit of his ambition, and in the presidency he was to exhibit a capacity for administration and for the accurate interpretation of the mood of the country which compels respect. In the field of domestic politics few great issues confronted the administration in its eight years of office. On the important question of internal improvements, Monroe began by adopting the conservative course which had been followed by his predecessor. In his first annual message he declared his belief that the Constitution did not empower Congress to establish a system of internal improvements, and recommended an amendment to confer that power. In the course of time his views underwent some modification. In 1822 he vetoed a bill authorizing the erection of tollhouses, gates, and turnpikes on the Cumberland Road, but accompanied his veto message with one of the most formidable state papers on record, "Views on the Subject of Internal Improvements" (*Writings,* VI, 216–84). In this document, while denying to the federal government the right of jurisdiction and construction, he declared that Congress had unlimited power to raise money, "restricted only by the duty to appropriate it to purposes of common defense and of general, not local, national, not State, benefit" (*Ibid.,* VI, 265–66). This middle-of-the-road point of view, entirely characteristic of Monroe, opened the way for an act in 1823 appropriating money for the repair of the Cumberland Road, and for the passage of the first harbor act. In 1824 the President put his signature to the so-called Survey Act, which laid out an elaborate program of internal improvements for the future. He departed again from the strict constructionist point of view when he gave his approval to the tariff bill of the same year.

More important than the question of internal improvement was that of slavery, as it shaped itself in 1819 and 1820 in the struggle over the admission of Missouri. On this issue Monroe's sympathies were naturally with the South, while his conception of his presidential duties led him to abstain from all interference with the struggle over the Missouri bill until it came to him for signature. It is known, however, that he would have refused to sign any bill admitting Missouri "subject to restraint" (*Congressional Globe,* 30 Cong., 2 Sess., Appendix, p. 67). The measure which came to him provided for the admission of Missouri as a slave state, but prohibited slavery north of 36° 30' in the future. He was by no means sure that Congress had the constitutional power to exclude slavery from states formed in the future within this territory, and submitted the question to the cabinet, most of whose members shared his doubts. He finally decided, however, to permit this question to remain unsettled, and signed the measure, no doubt the most momentous of his administration.

At the very outset of his administration Monroe made a journey through the northeastern states. This kind of royal progress naturally came in for some criticism, but it seems to have accomplished useful results, and on the whole enhanced his popularity. A second tour through the South and Southwest followed. Despite the economic depression of 1819, Monroe received in 1820 the tribute of a virtually unanimous reëlection to the presidency. Only one vote was cast against him in the electoral college. He had interpreted with a good deal of accuracy the mood of the country; and he had given evidence that his point of view was no longer sectional, as in his early years. He had gathered about himself a group of excellent advisers. Calhoun was a vigorous and effective secretary of war. Wirt, the attorney-general, was one of the ablest lawyers of his day. Crawford, the secretary of the treasury, was highly regarded in his own time. And above all, the President recognized capacity and rose above sectional predilections in his appointment of John Quincy Adams as secretary of state. No choice for that great office has ever been a happier one, and the large discretion which Monroe left to Adams, while yet maintaining a supervision over foreign affairs, is highly creditable to him.

In the field of foreign politics a considerable number of important issues confronted the Monroe administration. Some of them were matters which had already been under discussion during his term as secretary of state. The great agreement for the limitation of armaments on the Great Lakes had been discussed as early as the summer of 1818. The Newfoundland and Labrador fisheries dispute had also been a subject of consideration for some time when it was liquidated by the convention of 1818. The vexed question of the Northwest was temporarily settled by the principle of joint-occupation. More important was the question of the acquisition of Florida, which Monroe had attempted to broach both at Madrid and at Washington before he became president. Negotiations with Spain, vigorously pursued by Adams, were proceeding favorably when, in April 1818, General Andrew Jackson invaded Florida. Jackson claimed to have written to the President and received encouragement to go ahead. It seems more probable that Monroe, in this as in a former instance, maintained a silence that was somewhat equivocal. At any rate, the incident once having occurred, he was at first inclined to disavow the impetuous military leader, but was dissuaded by Adams. The conversations were resumed, and a treaty was signed on Feb. 22, 1819, and ratified after long delay two years later.

Meanwhile, the former Spanish colonies were clamoring for recognition of their independence, their cause being supported in the House of Representatives by Henry Clay. Monroe had received Mexican agents as early as 1811, and perhaps had even promised them a measure of aid (I. J. Cox, in *Annual Report of the American Historical Association for the Year 1911,* 1913, pp. 199–215); one of his first acts in the presidency was the sending of special agents to Latin-America. He was held in check by Adams, but recognition seemed imminent in the early winter of 1819. The Florida negotiations, however, provided a strong argument for delay and action was not taken until March 1822. Characteristically, even at this late date, Monroe sought to associate Congress with him in this step by the message of Mar. 8, 1822. Out of the recognition of the Spanish colonies grew the events leading up to the famous message of Dec. 2, 1823, enunciating what has come to be known as the Monroe Doctrine. In the fall of 1823, the administration received information from Richard Rush, minister to England, which led to the belief that the Continental powers contemplated the reconquest of Spain's former colonies, and their restitution to the mother country. The language of the Russian minister, Baron Tuyll, encouraged a similar hypothesis. Long cabinet discussions followed, in which the vigorous Adams played an undeniably influential and important part. But it was, almost beyond peradventure, Monroe who thought of dealing with the Spanish colonial question in his forthcoming message to Congress, and who drafted the famous paragraphs dealing with this problem. The clear-cut differentiation between Old World and New World politics may have been due in some measure to the Secretary of State, for the President wished to include a recommendation for the recognition of Greece, and a denunciation of the course of the Allied governments in sanctioning intervention in Spain. But both the initiative and the responsibility for the famous declaration belong to Monroe. On the other hand, the well-known principle that the American continents are no longer subject to European colonization, a principle enunciated in the negotiations with Russia over the northwest coast, was taken over verbatim by Monroe from Adams' report to him, and clearly owes its origin to the Secretary. Thus the Doctrine, considered as a whole, may be said to owe something to both men. It is worth noting that Monroe reiterated his views on Latin-America in the message of 1824. It is also to be observed that his administration carefully avoided making any more definite commitments when invited by the Colombian government to translate the language of the message into a treaty of alliance. Monroe's relations with Adams were cordial; one discerns a genuine respect on the part of the Secretary for his Chief, and an excellent combination of tact and definite-mindedness on the part of the President in dealing with the difficult, prickly New Englander. The caustic *Memoirs* of Adams reflect a remarkably favorable judgment of Monroe.

After the expiration of his presidential term, Monroe returned to Virginia and for a time to private life. His financial affairs were much involved, and in 1826 Congress voted him $30,000 in settlement of certain claims of his against the government. In 1828 he became a visitor of the young University of Virginia. In 1829 he was elected to the Virginia constitutional convention, and became its presiding officer. In this capacity, he was aligned with the conservatives, opposing a broadening of the suffrage, along with Madison, and taking very little interest in any action on the question of slavery. In February 1786 he had married Eliza Kortright, daughter of Lawrence Kortright, a merchant of New York and a descendant of a Dutch emigrant of 1663. In the spring of 1830, after the death of his wife, his private affairs being still involved, he moved to New York City, where he took up his residence with his daughter and her husband. There he died on July 4, 1831, and there he was buried, but in 1858 his remains were removed to Richmond.

Lacking the qualities of high imagination, unpretentious in appearance, far from brilliant in speech, without any genuine graces, Monroe yet attained distinction. "Untiring application and indomitable perseverance" were a part of his character (W. C. Rives, *History of the Life and Times of James Madison,* II, 1866, p. 20). He was undiscouraged by defeat or by failure. He seems never to have lost the loyal support of his friends. The longer grew his term of public service, the wider became the circle of his admirers. Jefferson and Madison, Calhoun, Adams, and Benton, all spoke in praise of him. All alike paid tribute, moreover, to the soundness of his judgment, and while such a tribute, applied to the rising Virginia politician, seems not wholly deserved, it is difficult not to accept it with regard to his years in the presidency. By the Doctrine which bears his name, he is now indissolubly connected with one of the major dogmas of American foreign policy. While in this he promulgated nothing very novel, he consolidated and fortified existing views and gave expression to a growing popular sentiment, in striking form. No colorless personality could have left behind him so favorable a judgment on the part of so many persons of such diverse views and temperaments as did Monroe. Less intellectual than either Jefferson or Madison, he surpassed them both as an administrator. If to this fifth president of the United States can never be assigned a place among the really great men who have held that high office, he must be numbered among the more useful and the more successful.

He was above the medium height, his mouth was rather large, his nose was well-shaped, his forehead was broad, and his eyes were blue-gray. His countenance was rather unexpressive in repose, and his manners were simple.

[Probably the best-known portrait of Monroe, by John Vanderlyn, is in the N. Y. City Hall; a portrait by Rembrandt Peale is owned by J. F. Lewis; one by Sully is at West Point. The most important collection of papers is in the Lib. of Cong., but the N. Y. Pub. Lib. has a considerable collection. Calendars are: Dept. of State, Bureau of Rolls and Library, *Calendar of the Correspondence of James Monroe* (1893); Lib. of Cong., Division of MSS., *Papers of James Monroe* (1904). S. M. Hamilton, *The Writings of James Monroe* (7 vols., 1898–1903), while by no means complete, is of very great value. Some of his letters are in the *Proc. of the Mass. Hist. Soc.,* vol. XLII (1909), and in the *Bulletin of the N. Y. Pub. Lib.,* Feb. 1900, Sept., Nov. 1901, June, July 1902. Much of his diplomatic correspondence, in the files of the Dept. of State, has been published in *Am. State Papers, Foreign Relations,* vol. III (1832).
There is no good general biography. D. C. Gilman, *James Monroe* (1883) is an interesting interpretation, but hardly complete or free from the note of eulogy. George Morgan, *The Life of James Monroe* (1921), is entertainingly written, but cannot be said to furnish a satisfactory picture, or to deal adequately with the more important problems. It is marred, too, by the tendency

to justify Monroe's action at every turn. Among books dealing with particular aspects of his career, mention must be made of B. W. Bond, *The Monroe Mission to France* (Johns Hopkins Studies in Hist. and Pol. Science, ser. 25, nos. 2 and 3, 1907); the remarkable chapters in Henry Adams, *Hist. of the U. S.* (9 vols., 1890–91), invaluable for the Louisiana purchase, and the missions to Spain and Great Britain, though none too sympathetic with Monroe; and S. F. Bemis, ed., *The Am. Secretaries of State and their Diplomacy,* vol. III (1927), which contains a highly discriminating account of Monroe's career as secretary of state by Julius W. Pratt. For the period of the presidency, there is little of value on the side of domestic affairs, viewing the matter from Monroe's personal point of view, but on the side of foreign policy attention is paid to the rôle of the president in the account of John Quincy Adams' secretariat in *The Am. Secretaries of State and their Diplomacy,* vol. IV (1928), by Dexter Perkins; the rôle of the chief executive and of his principal adviser in the enunciation of the Monroe Doctrine has been treated by W. C. Ford in two articles, "John Quincy Adams and The Monroe Doctrine," in the *Am. Hist. Rev.,* July, Oct. 1902, and from a point of view more favorable to Monroe in Dexter Perkins, *The Monroe Doctrine, 1823–26* (1927). Further bibliographical data may be found in Gilman.]   D. P—s.

MONTAGUE, HENRY JAMES (Jan. 20, 1843–Aug. 11, 1878), actor, appears from records that are none too authentic to have been born in a Staffordshire village on the date here given, and to have been the son of an Anglican clergyman. His real name was Mann. His age at the time of his death, the date of which is undisputed, is given on the monument erected to his memory by Lester Wallack in Greenwood Cemetery, Brooklyn, as twenty-seven, but this is obviously inaccurate, since there are reliable records of his appearances in important characters in the London theatres as early as 1863. His first connection with the stage was probably in a secretarial capacity in London with Dion Boucicault, and for about ten years thereafter he was acting continuously at the St. James's, Princess, Vaudeville, Globe and other theatres, in such rôles as Lord Beaufoy in *School,* Charles Courtly in *London Assurance,* Claude Melnotte in *The Lady of Lyons,* and Careless in *The School for Scandal.* He came to the United States in 1874 and appeared here for the first time in Wallack's Theatre, New York, Oct. 6, as Tom Gilroy in *Partners for Life,* becoming an immediate favorite, especially with the feminine portion of theatre audiences, not so much for the quality of his acting, which was of the conventional leading-man type, as for his striking face and figure, his graceful manner, his personal magnetism, and his ability to look the parts assigned to him without the addition or disguise of make-up. He was associated with Lester Wallack in that actor-manager's New York theatre, and on tour, throughout his entire American career, which continued less than four years. His appearance and technical skill confined him mainly to plays

of his own period, although on occasion he played such rôles as Gratiano in *The Merchant of Venice,* for which, says William Winter, he lacked animal spirits and dash, and also Harry Dornton in *The Road to Ruin* and Captain Dudley Smooth in *Money.* Winter sums him up definitely when he says that he "endeared himself by what he was rather than by what he did" (*Brief Chronicles,* p. 218). Among the impersonations by which he was best known in modern plays were Manuel in *The Romance of a Poor Young Man,* Julian Beauclerc in *Diplomacy,* Captain Molyneux in *The Shaughraun,* Captain D'Alroy in *Caste,* Arthur in *False Shame,* and Tom Dexter in *The Overland Route.* His health was failing during his last months on the stage, and going to San Francisco to play an engagement of four weeks at the California Theatre, he died suddenly of hemorrhage of the lungs. Funeral services were held both in San Francisco, and in New York at the Little Church Around the Corner, where a memorial window was later erected to his memory.

[Montague's career in England is well treated in the sketch of him in the *Dict. Nat. Biog.* See also: Wm. Winter, *Brief Chronicles* (1889), and *Vagrant Memories* (1915); Clement Scott and Cecil Howard, *The Life and Reminiscences of E. L. Blanchard* (2 vols., 1891); T. A. Brown, *A Hist. of the N. Y. Stage* (1903), vols. II and III; Lester Wallack, *Memories of Fifty Years* (1889); Marie and Squire Bancroft, *The Bancrofts: Recollections of Sixty Years* (1909); *Mail and Express: Illustrated Saturday Mag.,* Nov. 12, 1898; *Frank Leslie's Illustrated Family Almanac,* 1879; *N. Y. Times,* Aug. 13, 20, 1878. His name is given in some sources as Henry John Montague.]   E.F.E.

MONTEFIORE, JOSHUA (Aug. 7, 1762–June 26, 1843), lawyer, soldier, and author, was born in London, England, the sixth son in a family of seventeen. His father, Moses Haim (or Vita) Montefiore, had emigrated in 1758 from Leghorn, Italy, where his ancestors had been merchants of standing in the Jewish community. There Moses had been married to Ester Hannah Racah, daughter of a Moorish merchant. Most of the children of this union became identified with mercantile enterprises in various quarters of the globe. Joshua's roystering and free-hearted disposition unfitted him for a one track life, and his career, though less prosperous, was much more colorful. At eighteen he began the study of law and in 1784 he was admitted as an attorney and a solicitor in chancery by Sir William Scott. Late in 1791 a group of naval officers and London merchants formed a society for the colonization of the island of Bulama, on the African coast near Sierra Leone. Moses Ximenes, a prominent Jew, was a director in the enterprise, and Montefiore became a subscriber. When in the spring of 1792 the 275 colonists set sail, Montefiore and his wife were members of the party. From the start the expedition was ill-starred. Disease and lack of discipline brought the colonists to their destination in bad humor. A hasty occupation of the island without negotiating with the natives for its purchase led to a raid in which lives were lost and many prisoners captured. Montefiore advocated a policy of negotiation and purchase and took an active part in the defense of the party. Having fallen ill, he was discharged at his own request in June 1792. Thereafter he traveled for a time among the tribes in Sierra Leone, and then returned home.

In 1794 Montefiore published a tract entitled *An Authentic Account of the late Expedition to Bulam, on the Coast of Africa; with a Description of the Present Settlement of Sierra Leone, and the Adjacent Country.* The bulk of his published writings, however, concerned his legal interests. These included a commercial dictionary, compendiums of mercantile and commercial law, and copyright law, and traders' manuals. They gave in convenient form extracts from tariffs and other commercial regulations, notes on judicial opinions, and short articles on commercial law. Since they were principally of contemporary importance, they were in time out-dated and superseded.

From Montefiore's family Bible, which besides being his spiritual guide was also his note book, it appears that "on the 3rd March, 1803, he was, by order of King George III, presented by Lord Boston to His Majesty," and that he was offered and declined the order of knighthood. He did seek a commission in the army, and is said to have been the first of his race to have this mark of favor. The *Army List* shows that he was paymaster of the York Light Infantry Volunteers from about 1807 to Jan. 30, 1812. During this service he was present at the taking of Martinique and Guadeloupe. On resigning from the army he emigrated to America where he practised law and published other volumes on commercial law. One characteristic of the author was his propensity for dedicating his works to various eminent judges. Eventually he settled at St. Albans, Vt. In his seventy-third year he was married a second time, and at his death eight years later left a family of seven children by this marriage. On his death bed he wrote from memory a translation of the Hebrew burial service. This was read as he had wished, and he was buried in his garden at St. Albans.

[*Jewish World,* Supp., Oct. 31, 1884; Philip Beaver, *African Memoranda* (London, 1805); W. H. Smyth, *The Life and Services of Capt. Philip Beaver* (London, 1829); Lucien Wolf, *Sir Moses Montefiore* (1884); Paul Goodman, *Moses Montefiore* (1925), p. 228; the *Vt. Chronicle* (Windsor), July 5, 1843.]
C. F.

MONTGOMERY, DAVID HENRY (Apr. 7, 1837–May 28, 1928), textbook writer, was born at Syracuse, N. Y., the only child of David and Sarah (Prescott) Montgomery. His father was a law partner of the first mayor of the city. Left an orphan at the age of seven, he lived with relatives until he went West and became a ranchman. He was at Brown for three years in the class of 1861, and gained some recognition there as a debater. After completing the course at the Harvard Divinity School (1863) he held Massachusetts pastorates at Leicester and West Bridgewater. He was not fitted by temperament to cope with church administration, and in 1880 he went to England. From unsuccessful business experiences there he returned in 1884 in poverty. John J. May of Boston gave him a desk in his office, and in gratitude Montgomery prepared an elementary history for May's grandchildren. This book, *Leading Facts of English History* (1886), was designed to illustrate, as he said, the great law of national growth in the light thrown upon it by the foremost English historians. On publication by Ginn & Company, it was immediately popular. A life of Franklin, the autobiography supplemented by the story carried on from 1757 to 1790, followed in 1888. *The Leading Facts of French History* (1889) was similar in treatment to the English history, and was likewise well supplemented with maps, chronological tables, and indexes. It has been said that several thousand copies were read by American soldiers in France during the World War. *The Leading Facts of American History* was published in 1890, followed in 1892 by *The Beginner's American History,* of which an edition in Spanish was published in 1901. *The Student's American History* (1897), enlarged from *The Leading Facts of American History* was one of the best textbooks of the period and was widely adopted. It contained maps, as well as illustrations of old letters and documents, and an appendix containing the Constitution and Declaration of Independence, useful tables, and a bibliography. His final work was *An Elementary American History* (1904), designed "to appeal to the eye as well as to the understanding."

Montgomery's works received constant revision. He would spend weeks in study, the only visible result of which would be a change in a shade of meaning. On one occasion, to insure the destruction of the electrotype plates of a superseded edition, he carried a hatchet to the press and demolished the old plates himself. Over nine million copies of his textbooks have been sold. He also published for school use editions of several literary classics. He was fond of travel and spent some fifteen years in England, often quoting Dr. Johnson's words: "He who gets tired of London gets tired of life." As he declined in health he rarely left his residence at 50 Frost Street, Cambridge, where he had surrounded himself with books, pictures, tapestries, statuary, and maps. He married Delia A. Bowman, daughter of Francis Bowman, of Cambridge, on Dec. 10, 1867, a woman of culture and some literary ability. She died in 1908, leaving a son. Harvard College, the Cambridge Hospital, and the Boston Athenæum were remembered generously in Montgomery's will. His copyrights went by gift to the College.

[Sources include: records of Harvard and Brown Universities; Montgomery's letters to C. N. Baxter and Linda F. Wildman at the Boston Athenæum; C. H. Thurber's memoir in *Intramural Stuff*, Ginn & Company leaflet for June 8, 1928; law files of James E. Kelley of Boston; recollections of Mrs. Fanny Knapp Palmer, of Oneida, N. Y., E. K. Robinson, Le Roy Phillips of Boston; librarian's report, Boston Athenæum, for 1930; *Boston Transcript*, May 31, 1928. Reviews of some of Montgomery's works may be found in the *Jour. of Educ.*, May 4, 1886, May 9, 1889; and in the *Am. Hist. Rev.*, Apr. 1898, July 1910.]

C. K. B.

MONTGOMERY, EDMUND DUNCAN (Mar. 19, 1835–Apr. 17, 1911), philosopher, was born in Edinburgh, Scotland, and died at "Liendo," his plantation near Hempstead, Tex. He was the natural son of Isabella Davidson Montgomery and Duncan MacNeill, later Baron Colonsay and Oronsay, an eminent Scottish jurist who rose to the position of lord justice-general in 1852. At the time of Montgomery's birth, his father was solicitor-general for Scotland in Peel's first administration. When but four years old the boy was taken to Paris, remaining there until 1844, when his mother took him to Frankfort. There he lived until 1852, in which year he matriculated as a student of medicine at Heidelberg. From his student notebooks of his Gymnasium days it is evident that he was unusually gifted in languages, science, and mathematics. According to contemporary testimony he was the most popular boy in his school, and it appeared that he would surpass his father, who had obtained the degree of M.D. at St. Andrews and a "first" in mathematics at Edinburgh. In his fourteenth year, however, an event occurred which was destined for many years to cast a shadow on his life. He refused to be confirmed, after having gone through the preliminary training, and was ostracized. Years after

the event Montgomery wrote that at this time he was driven by loneliness and religious perplexity almost to the point of suicide.

In 1848 Montgomery, still a boy, participated in the revolution at Frankfort to the extent of helping to build barricades. In 1850 he frequently saw Schopenhauer. During the years from 1852 to 1858 he studied at various German and Austrian universities (Heidelberg, 1852–54; Berlin, 1855; Bonn, 1856; Würzburg, 1857; and possibly Prague in 1858 and Vienna in 1859). He claimed for himself a degree in medicine, but the records of the universities that he attended yield no evidence to support his assertion. At Heidelberg he was a friend of Moleschott and Kuno Fischer, and at Bonn he was a pupil of Helmholz. He returned to England and became resident physician at the German Hospital (1860–61), Bermondsey Dispensary (1861–62), and demonstrator of morbid anatomy at St. Thomas' Hospital in London (1861–63). For some reason, possibly a tubercular infection, but more probably the discovery of his imposture, he left St. Thomas' and went to Madeira. It was here, Nov. 17, 1863, at the office of the British consul, that he married Elisabet Ney [*q.v.*], whom he had first met and loved while he was a student of medicine at Heidelberg. During the years 1863–69 he practised medicine at Madeira, Mentone, and Rome. In 1869 he retired from medical practice and in 1870 came to America.

The first two years of their residence in America Montgomery and his wife spent in a colony near Thomasville, Ga., devoted to the reclamation of the negro. The colony failed to advance its aims, and in 1872 they removed to Hempstead, Tex. "Liendo" was purchased in 1873. Here, isolated from the world, Montgomery for several years (1873–79) continued intensive researches on the nature of protoplasm which he had begun during his London days (*vide* his *On the Formation of So-Called Cells in Animal Bodies,* London, 1867). The fruits of his biological studies in Texas appeared in a number of papers published in the *Popular Science Monthly* (September, October 1878), *St. Thomas' Hospital Report* (1879), the *Index* (Dec. 25, 1884), *Jenaische Zeitschrift für Naturwissenschaft* (vol. XVIII, 1882), *Archiv für die gesammte Physiologie* (vol. XXV, 1881), and in a final monograph, *The Vitality and Organization of Protoplasm,* an octavo pamphlet of 83 pages, published independently in 1904. In these papers he maintained what may be called a neovitalistic point of view in contrast with the materialism current in his day. At the same time (1878–87), in *Mind, Index,* the *Journal of Spec-*

ulative Philosophy, New Ideal, the *International Journal of Ethics,* the *Monist, New Occasions,* and *Open Court,* he published an imposing series of philosophical articles preliminary to his *magnum opus, Philosophical Problems in the Light of Vital Organization* (1907).

Montgomery in his philosophical position is undoubtedly monistic, but his monism is of a double-aspect type, corresponding to that of Clifford and Hoffding. To him the fundamental philosophical problem was that of the mind-body relation. The principal effort of his thought was "to show, that the two disparate modes of existence, known to us under the name of body and mind, have a common origin in one and the same underlying reality" (*Open Court,* Aug. 21, 1890, p. 2462). He was firmly convinced that this and related problems must be solved by the scientific discovery and demonstration of a unitary substance in the very nature of which inhere the two contradictory attributes of permanence and change. His biological researches convinced him that living protoplasm was such a substance. On this same basis he concluded that nature is wholly teleological. Its highest achievement is human personality (*Index,* Oct. 9, 1884, p. 173), and his ethical theory, which is unique, is based upon this conception. His monism is likewise strikingly similar to that of Bergson, but to him the fundamental reality is not *élan vital,* but living substance. In his concept of the origin and nature of life he anticipated in detail that of the great biochemist, Benjamin Moore (*Problems of Philosophy in the Light of Vital Organization,* 1913, p. 300). He accounted for the appearance of novelties in the evolutionary series by a formulation strikingly anticipatory of the later theory of "emergent evolution."

In intellectual quality and personal appearance Montgomery resembled his father to an unusual degree. His photograph bears a most striking resemblance to Thomas Duncan's portrait of Duncan MacNeill in the National Portrait Gallery in Edinburgh. He was a gracious and outstandingly attractive person. The unfortunate circumstances of his birth, and complications rising out of his marriage with Elisabet Ney combined to make him an aloof figure. Yet he received from his contemporaries a degree of recognition of his ability. (See *Open Court,* Mar. 31, 1887, pp. 103–07, and the papers by Salter and Lane, cited below.) Following close upon the death, in June 1907, of Elisabet Ney, Montgomery sustained an apoplectic attack, and after a period of paralysis lasting over three years, died.

[*Proc. Forty-fourth Ann. Meeting, Free Religious Asso.* (1911); W. M. Salter, "A New Type of Naturalism—Montgomery," *Internat. Jour. Ethics,* Oct. 1908; C. A. Lane, "Edmund Montgomery," *Monist,* Oct. 1909; I. K. Stephens, "Edmund Montgomery, the Hermit Philosopher of Liendo Plantation," *Southwest Rev.,* Jan. 1931; Bride Neill Taylor, *Elisabet Ney, Sculptor* (1916), uncritical and one-sided; Eugen Müller-Münster, *Elisabeth Ney, die seltsamen Lebensschicksale der Elisabeth Ney und des Edmund Montgomery, 1833–1907* (1931); Montgomery's library, with a complete set of his numerous publications in the Library of Southern Methodist University.]
S. W. G.

MONTGOMERY, GEORGE WASHINGTON (1804–June 5, 1841), translator, diplomat, son of John Montgomery, was born in Alicante, Spain, where the father was a well-known American merchant. His mother was probably Spanish. He was educated at Exeter, in England, and returning to Spain, passed his entire life, in that country and in America, in the consular and diplomatic services of the United States. He will be remembered, however, chiefly for his definite and curious services to American literature in connection with Spain and Washington Irving.

He had been before 1826 private secretary in Madrid to the Marquis of Casa Yrujo, a friend of Irving's, but during the two years of Irving's first stay in Madrid, he was attached to the American legation, apparently as official translator. This intimacy with Irving led to his creating and publishing the first version of the writings of this author into Spanish, thus beginning a long list of translations, and laying the foundation for Irving's reputation in Spain. The first was a book, now exceedingly rare, called *Tareas de un Solitario* (1829). It included versions of "The Young Italian," "The Mutability of Literature," and "Rip Van Winkle." Called to account because the last story seemed to the Spanish censor to smack of "libel and treason against the King," Montgomery issued the book anonymously. It was remarkable for its pure and beautiful Spanish, and Longfellow introduced it into Bowdoin College for use in his classes. Its interest lies, however, in its sympathetic interpretation to the Spaniards of Irving's romantic themes. In 1831 Montgomery published his *Crónica de la Conquista de Granada,* an adaptation of Irving's book of similar title, and, in 1832, his *El Bastardo de Castilla,* an historical novel based upon the story of Bernardo del Carpio. "His Spanish works," says Obadiah Rich, the bibliographer, who also knew Montgomery in Madrid, "met with great applause in Spain, for the classical purity of their language, and have been adopted by many Spanish teachers as classbooks" (*post,* II, p. 329).

It is probable that Montgomery planned to

continue his translations of Irving and possibly of other American writers, but in December 1835 he was appointed United States consul at San Juan, Puerto Rico, and three years later he was sent from Washington to Guatemala. Afterward as consul at Tampico he incurred ill health which caused his death, at Washington, in 1841. During these last years he served intermittently in the Department of State as copier and indexer. Two years before his death appeared his *Narrative of a Journey to Guatemala*, a book reëmphasizing by its strong, clear English, Montgomery's odd but remarkable bilingual powers as an obscure man of letters.

[For a full account of Montgomery's writings see S. T. Williams, "The First Version of the Writings of Washington Irving in Spanish," in *Modern Philol.*, Nov. 1930. Briefer accounts of Montgomery occur in S. Austin Allibone, *A Critical Dict. of English Lit. and British and Am. Authors* (1870), and J. DeL. Ferguson, *Am. Lit. in Spain* (1916). Other details have been gleaned from the Ticknor Collection, in the Boston Pub. Lib.; the files of the Dept. of State, Washington; the files of the American embassy, Madrid; Obadiah Rich, *Bibliotheca Americana Nova* (London, 1846); *The Journals of Washington Irving* (1919), vol. III, ed. by W. P. Trent and G. S. Hellman; *Washington Irving Diary, 1828–29* (1926), ed. by C. L. Penny; *Daily Nat. Intelligencer* (Wash., D. C.), June 7, 10, 1841.]

S. T. W.

MONTGOMERY, JAMES (Dec. 22, 1814–Dec. 6, 1871), soldier and jayhawker, was born in Ashtabula County, Ohio, whither his parents had emigrated from New York. He was a great-grandson of James Montgomery, a Scotch Highland chieftain who came to America by way of Ireland. After receiving an academic education in Ohio, he moved to Kentucky in 1837 where he taught school and entered the ministry of the "Campbellite" church. In 1852 he emigrated with his second wife to Missouri, but soon after the passage of the Kansas-Nebraska bill he purchased a claim at Mound City, Linn County, Kan. Pro-slavery settlers were in the majority in the southeastern part of the Territory, and Montgomery soon became the recognized leader of the minority. He organized Free-State men into a "Self-Protective Company" in 1857, which drove pro-slavery advocates from the county and made predatory excursions into Missouri. He made several attempts to destroy Fort Scott, where a pro-slavery district judge pursued a policy of discrimination, and on one occasion he collided with Federal troops. Disturbances in the "infected district," some of which Montgomery created, were eventually quelled by the intervention of Governor Denver. In 1860 Montgomery and eastern associates planned to rescue two of John Brown's men imprisoned at Charles Town, Va. (now W. Va.), but the scheme did not materialize. He was

elected in 1857 to the "state" Senate under the Topeka constitution, but was defeated for the Territorial House of Representatives two years later. He represented Linn County in the Republican state convention of April 1860.

On July 24, 1861, Montgomery was commissioned colonel of the 3rd Kansas Volunteer Infantry which operated as a part of "Lane's brigade" in southeastern Kansas and western Missouri. His regiment soon gained a reputation for jayhawking or plundering. On Apr. 3, 1862, the 3rd was consolidated with other regiments to form the 10th Kansas with Montgomery colonel. Early in 1863 he was authorized to raise a colored regiment in South Carolina. From Hiltonhead he made expeditions into Georgia and Florida, liberated slaves, and destroyed Confederate property. In 1864 he returned to Kansas and was chosen colonel of the 6th Militia Regiment when its commander refused to lead it against Gen. Sterling Price. As a fighter Montgomery excelled in bushwhacker tactics. With limited mental powers, he was daring and fearless, and usually fought without having formed a plan of campaign. At the close of the Civil War he retired to his farm in Linn County, abandoned the "Campbellite" faith, became a First-Day Adventist, and preached that doctrine at various places in Kansas. He died at Mound City.

[A few of Montgomery's letters are preserved in the Kan. State Hist. Lib. at Topeka. Reports of his military activities are scattered through the *Official Records*. Wm. P. Tomlinson, *Kan. in Eighteen Fifty-Eight* (1859), contains a chapter on his early Kansas career. Further sources include: A. T. Andreas, *Hist. of the State of Kan.* (1883); D. W. Wilder, *The Annals of Kan.* (1886); W. E. Connelley, *A Standard Hist. of Kan. and Kansans* (1918), vols. II and III; E. S. W. Drought, "James Montgomery," *Trans. Kan. State Hist. Soc.*, vol. VI (1900); "Col. Montgomery and His Letters," *Kan. State Hist. Soc. Colls.*, vol. XIII (1915); and scattered references in the *Transactions* and *Collections* of the State Hist. Soc.]

W. H. S—n.

MONTGOMERY, JOHN BERRIEN (Nov. 17, 1794–Mar. 25, 1873), naval officer, was born at Allentown, N. J., the son of Dr. Thomas and Mary (Berrien) Montgomery, and a descendant of William Morse Montgomery who was in East Jersey in 1702. He entered the navy as midshipman June 4, 1812, leaving home for war service along with his elder brother Alexander, a surgeon under Porter, and his younger brother Nathaniel Lawrence, who lost an arm in the *President-Belvidera* action and was made lieutenant at sixteen. John Montgomery served in the *Hamilton, Madison,* and *General Pike* on Lake Ontario, then joined Perry on Lake Erie in August 1813 and fought creditably in the *Niagara* at the Battle of Lake Erie, receiving with other officers a sword and thanks from Congress.

In the subsequent Perry-Elliott controversy, Montgomery, like most *Niagara* men, favored his ship-commander Elliott, and he served frequently under him later. In the *Niagara* he took part in the blockade and attack on Mackinac, Aug. 4, 1814. He was in the *Ontario* of Decatur's squadron against Algiers; on the African coast, 1818–20, after promotion to lieutenant; and in the *Erie* on a long Mediterranean cruise, 1821–26. In 1830 he was executive of the *Peacock,* and subsequently commanded the *Erie* on the coast of Mexico. After recruiting duty in Philadelphia and New York, 1833–35, he was executive under Elliott in the *Constitution* when she brought the American minister Livingston from France in 1835. He then returned to receiving-ship and recruiting service, with promotion to commander, 1839. In command of the *Portsmouth* of Sloat's squadron on the West Coast during the Mexican War, he raised the American flag at San Francisco and near-by settlements, July 9, 1846. The name Montgomery Street, San Francisco, commemorates the occupation. The *Portsmouth* also blockaded Mazatlan, March-April 1847, occupied several Lower California ports, and took part in the bombardment of Guaymas, October 1847.

In August 1820 Montgomery had married Mary, daughter of William Henry of New York. They had five sons and four daughters. Two sons were with him on this cruise, one an acting master and the other captain's clerk. Both mysteriously disappeared in November 1846 while in charge of a boat party taking money from the ships off San Francisco to forces ashore, circumstances indicating mutiny and the murder of the two youths. After service in the Washington Navy Yard, 1849–51, Montgomery was made captain, Jan. 6, 1853, and in the *Roanoke* brought back 250 of Walker's filibusters from Aspinwall in 1857. At the outbreak of the Civil War he was commanding the Pacific Squadron, which included four steam and two sailing ships, with the *Lancaster* as flagship. When news of war reached the *Lancaster* at Panama, Montgomery forestalled possible disturbances by requesting all officers to take the oath of allegiance, only one declining. In December 1861 he retired and went home, being promoted to commodore (retired) July 16, 1862. Thereafter he was still actively occupied as commandant of the Charlestown (Massachusetts) Navy Yard, May 1862—December 1863, and then of the Washington yard till October 1865, carrying out efficiently the important services of repair, supply, and training of men. In July 1866 he was made rear admiral (retired), and for two

years subsequently had charge at Sacketts Harbor. He was put on waiting orders, Sept. 1, 1869. His death occurred at Carlisle, Pa., and he was buried in Oak Hill Cemetery, Washington. A destroyer was named for him in 1918. He was of a modest nature, an eminently just man who made the Scriptures his daily study. No quarrels or serious mishaps marred his service career.

[T. H. Montgomery, *A Geneal. Hist. of the Family of Montgomery* (1863); *The Biog. Encyc. of N. J. in the Nineteenth Century* (1877); sketch in *Mag. of Am. Hist.,* July 1878; L. R. Hamersly, *The Records of Living Officers in the U. S. Navy and Marine Corps* (1870); *Army and Navy Jour.,* Apr. 26, 1873; *Evening Star* (Washington), Mar. 28, 1873.] A. W.

MONTGOMERY, RICHARD (Dec. 2, 1738–Dec. 31, 1775), soldier, was the third son of Thomas and Mary (Franklin or Franklyn) Montgomery, and a younger brother of the notorious and cruel Capt. Alexander Montgomery with whom some earlier historians confused him. He was born at Swords, County Dublin, Ireland, and educated at St. Andrews and Trinity College, Dublin. His father was a member of Parliament and he himself chose the army for a career. He was commissioned ensign in the 17th Foot, Sept. 21, 1756, and served with his regiment at the siege of Louisbourg, 1758, and in the Lake Champlain campaign in 1759. After the fall of Montreal he went with his regiment to the West Indies, where he was present at the captures of Martinique and Havana. By May 1762 he attained the rank of captain. When peace was signed in 1763 he was ordered to New York and two years later returned to England. There he became well known among prominent liberal members of Parliament who were friends of the colonies. Foreseeing no chance of military advancement in the peace, he sold out of the army, Apr. 6, 1772. For some reason, never fully determined, he appears to have felt that he had no future in England and that his friends either could not or would not help him. He wrote at this time that he had conceived a violent passion for farming, that he had no friends to advance him, that with little money he could cut no figure among "Peers, Nabobs, etc.," and that therefore he had cast his eye on America where his pride and poverty would be "much more at their ease" (*New York Genealogical and Biographical Record,* July 1871, p. 129). He was, however, by no means penniless and when he arrived in New York, in accordance with his decision to emigrate, he bought a sixty-seven-acre farm at King's Bridge. He became genuinely interested in agriculture and enjoyed rural life. On July 24, 1773, he was married to

Janet, daughter of Robert R. Livingston, 1718–1775 [q.v.], of New York City, and although at that time he bought other property, he spent the short remainder of his life at his wife's estate, "Grassmere," near Rhinebeck.

Montgomery's previous experiences in America, his friendship in England with such men as Burke and Fox, and his own views, all led him to adopt the colonial point of view as troubles thickened with the mother country, and although he had been in New York only three years by 1775 he was elected one of the members of the Provincial Congress. In June of that year he was appointed by the Continental Congress the second in rank of the eight brigadier-generals then designated, and with much honest regret and reluctance he accepted the appointment. It was from a sense of duty only that he left his new home and young wife and took up arms against England. He was made second in command of the expedition which was to proceed under Maj.-Gen. Philip Schuyler against Montreal. As a result of Schuyler's illness the command almost immediately devolved upon Montgomery. His troops, largely New Englanders, were poor military material. They were lacking in discipline, were constantly deserting, and at times practically mutinous. Montgomery deserves the highest praise for working them into shape for the expedition. He captured forts Chambly and St. Johns, and with the latter the first British colors, those of the 7th Fusiliers, taken in the war. Proceeding into Canada, he captured Montreal, and in December joined the forces under Benedict Arnold at Point aux Trembles. The combined forces then laid siege to Quebec. It was obvious that from lack of both morale and supplies, the American army was in no condition to maintain a winter siege. An assault was ordered and made on Dec. 31, and Montgomery was shot and killed. The English recognized his body and it was ordered "decently buried." In 1818 it was moved to St. Paul's Church, New York. Montgomery was a capable commander of high character, wholly unselfish in his adherence to the American cause. He left no children.

[There is a good biography of Montgomery in the *Dict. Nat. Biog.* A longer but less accurate account is John Armstrong's "Life of Richard Montgomery," in Jared Sparks's *Lib. of Am. Biog.*, vol. I (1834). Other sources include: T. H. Montgomery, "Ancestry of Gen. Richard Montgomery," *N. Y. Geneal. and Biog. Record*, July 1871; J. M. Le Moine, "Gen. R. Montgomery and His Detractors," *Ibid.*, Apr. 1891; N. H. E. Faucher de Saint-Maurice, *Notes pour Servir à L'Histoire du Gen. Richard Montgomery* (1893), reprinted from *Proc. and Trans. of the Royal Soc. of Canada*, vol. IX (1892); "Hist. Notes on the Defence of Quebec in 1775," *Trans. of the Lit. and Hist. Soc. of Quebec, . . . 1876–77* (1877); J. H. Smith, *Our Struggle for the Fourteenth Colony* (2 vols., 1907); John Codman, *Arnold's Expedition to Quebec* (1901); Louise L. Hunt, *Biog. Notes Concerning Gen. Richard Montgomery* (1876), reprinted in *Harper's*, Feb. 1885. The date of Montgomery's birth is given in some sources as 1736, in others as 1738. The statement that he was sixteen when he matriculated at Dublin on June 15, 1754, in G. D. Burchtaell and T. U. Sadleir, *Alumni Dublinenses* (1924), substantiates 1738.]   J.T.A.

MONTGOMERY, THOMAS HARRISON (Mar. 5, 1873–Mar. 19, 1912), zoölogist and teacher, was born in New York City, a descendant of Robert Montgomery who emigrated to New Jersey in 1701. His father, Thomas Harrison Montgomery, was president of the Insurance Company of North America for twenty-three years. His mother, Anna, was the daughter of Samuel G. Morton [q.v.], the anthropologist. When Thomas Montgomery, Jr., was nine years of age, his family moved to the country near West Chester, Pa., and soon afterward he became interested in birds, gathered detailed notes on their habits, and made a collection of skins. He was a pupil at Dr. Worrall's School in West Chester and graduated from the Episcopal Academy in Philadelphia at the age of sixteen. He then attended the University of Pennsylvania (1889–91) and transferred from there to the University of Berlin (1891–94) where he attained his doctorate in philosophy with the dissertation: *Stichostemma eilhardi . . . Ein Beitrag zur Kenntnis der Nemertinen* (1894). On his return to Philadelphia in 1895 he continued his morphological research on nemerteans at the Wistar Institute of Anatomy (1895–98), brought out nine additional papers on their structure and phylogeny, and became interested in the hairworms, publishing *The Gordiacea of Certain American Collections, Parts I and II* (1898) and eight subsequent papers. His youthful interest in birds resulted in five papers, written between 1896 and 1906. In 1897 he was appointed lecturer in zoölogy at the University of Pennsylvania. He became instructor the next year and was made assistant professor in 1900. At the same time (1898–1903) he was also professor in biology and director of the museum at the Wagner Free Institute of Science. Most of his summers were spent at the Marine Biological Laboratory, Woods Hole, Mass. In 1901 he married Priscilla Braislin of Crosswicks, N. J.; three sons were born to them.

Montgomery developed two divergent specialties which finally received much of his attention. His brilliant cytological investigations resulted in a rapid succession of papers; in *A Study of the Chromosomes of the Germ Cells of Metazoa* (1901) he was apparently the first to suggest that synapsis might represent a juncture of ma-

Montgomery

ternal and paternal chromosomes. His investigations on the taxonomy and habits of spiders culminated with *The Significance of the Courtship and the Secondary Sexual Characters of Araneads* (1909), in which he presented arguments against Darwin's theory of sexual selection. In 1903 he went as professor in zoölogy to the University of Texas. During this period he published *The Analysis of Racial Descent in Animals* (1906). In 1908 he returned to the University of Pennsylvania as director of the department of zoölogy and there he devoted the last three or four years of his life primarily to the fulfilment of his plans for a new zoölogical laboratory. He was just thirty-nine years of age when pneumonia caused his untimely death. His last paper, "Human Spermatogenesis, Spermatocytes and Spermiogenesis: A Study of Inheritance," appeared after his decease as the leading article in the centennial volume of the Academy of Natural Sciences of Philadelphia (1912). Montgomery was a member of the American Philosophical Society, the American Society of Naturalists, and the American Society of Zoölogists, which he served one term as president.

[Edward G. Conklin, memoir and bibliography in *Science*, Aug. 15, 1913; *Old Penn*, Mar. 23, 1912; T. H. Montgomery, *A Geneal. Hist. of the Family of Montgomery* (1863); *Pub. Ledger* (Phila.), Mar. 20, 1912.]   H. B. B.

MONTGOMERY, WILLIAM BELL (Aug. 21, 1829–Sept. 25, 1904), agriculturist, editor, was born in Fairfield District, S. C. His father, Hugh Montgomery, and his mother, Isabelle (Bell), were of Scotch-Irish descent and members of families that were prominent in colonial days. They moved to Mississippi in 1835 when William was only six years old, and his boyhood was spent in the country. He was educated in the common-schools of Mississippi, in Erskine College, South Carolina, and the College of New Jersey (Princeton), where he was graduated B.A. in 1850. After some years spent in agriculture in Mississippi he became a cotton broker at Mobile, Ala. During the Civil War he was loyal to the South although he had opposed the war and himself took no active part in it. His health impaired by confinement in a broker's office, he returned to Mississippi in 1865, settling in Oktibbeha County, near Starkville, and resumed the practice of agriculture, which afforded him the outdoor life and physical exercise he needed. He introduced new grasses, began to raise fancy Jersey cattle, and soon became a leader in his section of the state, doing much, during a period of more than thirty years, to advance live stock and agricultural interests in Mississippi. In 1875 he founded the *Live Stock*

Montrésor

Journal of which he was editor, publisher, and owner. It was succeeded the next year by the *Southern Live Stock Journal,* published at Starkville and edited by his son. He continued to contribute articles to the new periodical, which for a time ranked as a leading agricultural magazine in the South. In 1870 he founded the Starkville Female Institute, which was operated successfully for a number of years, until the property was purchased by the City of Starkville and rebuilt as a public grammar-school. When the Agricultural and Mechanical College of the state was established in the seventies, he was appointed local trustee and served as such for a period of twenty-six years.

He was married first, in 1852, to Julia Gillespie, daughter of Dr. William and Marjorie Gillespie of Starkville, Miss., and second, in 1865, to Sarah A. Glenn, daughter of William and Elizabeth Glenn. Five children were born to each marriage, and surviving members of the family continue to live in the old homestead.

[*Southern Live Stock Journal*, vol. V (1880); D. B. Montgomery, *Geneal. Hist. of the Montgomerys and Their Descendants* (1903); Dunbar Rowland, *Mississippi* (1907), esp. vol. III; T. B. Carroll, *Hist. Sketch of Oktibbeha County, Miss.* (1931); *Southern Farm Gazette*, Oct. 1, 1904; private papers in the files of the family.]   B. M. W.

MONTRÉSOR, JAMES GABRIEL (Nov. 19, 1702–Jan. 6, 1776), British military engineer, was born at Fort William, Scotland, the son of James Gabriel Le Tresor of Thurland Hall, Nottingham, who, though a native of Caen, Normandy, was a naturalized British subject, a major of the Royal Scots Fusileers, and lieutenant-governor of Fort William. His mother, Nanon de Hauteville, was also of Norman stock. Montrésor began his military career as a matross in the Royal Artillery at Minorca in 1727, and served a year at Gibraltar as bombardier. In 1731 he was commissioned as a practitioner engineer, and for the next twenty-three years, with a single intermission, he lived at Gibraltar, rising finally to be chief engineer there, a subdirector, but with no higher army rank than a lieutenancy in the 14th Foot. His knowledge of fortifications became as profound as his practical, if unimaginative, mind permitted. He improved the defenses of Gibraltar.

In 1754 Montrésor was selected as chief engineer in America, accompanied Braddock's expedition, and was wounded at the Monongahela. The order of 1757 giving army rank to engineers made him a major, and in 1758 he became director and lieutenant-colonel. His services throughout the war were confined to New York, for successive commanders distrusted both his ability to direct a siege and his physical endurance. They left to him the work for which his experience had fitted him, the administration of the corps of engineers and the designing and construction of forts, blockhouses, and such buildings as barracks, hospitals, and storehouses. He was more skilled than his colleagues in adapting European systems of fortification to frontier conditions, and more tactful in working with the provincial troops who performed most of the actual construction work. Montrésor planned and directed considerable building in northern New York, at Albany, along the Mohawk, up the Hudson, especially at Saratoga and Fort Edward, and at Fort William Henry. In 1757 he was with Webb at Fort Edward when Montcalm took Fort William Henry; in 1758 he remained at that post while an engineer of inferior rank directed Abercromby's disastrous attack on the lines before Ticonderoga; in 1759 Amherst left him in charge of the rebuilding of new Fort George at the lower end of Lake George. Following an accident in 1759, leave was given him. He returned to England in 1760 and for two years traveled abroad for his health. During the rest of his life he remained in England, in active service as an engineer, though he resigned his lieutenant's commission in the 14th. He designed and superintended the construction of powder magazines at Purfleet, served as chief engineer at Chatham, and in 1772 received his colonelcy. For his American services he was granted ten thousand acres to the east of Lake Champlain. He died at New Gardens, Teynham, Kent, where he was buried.

Montrésor was married, first, on June 11, 1735, to Mary, daughter of Robert Haswell, who was with him at Gibraltar and accompanied him to New York; second, on Aug. 25, 1766, to Henrietta, daughter of Henry Fielding, the novelist; and third, to Frances, daughter of H. Nicholls, and widow of William Kemp, who brought him New Gardens. John Montrésor [q.v.] was a son of his first marriage.

[Sir Bernard Burke, *A Geneal. and Heraldic Hist. of the Landed Gentry of Great Britain and Ireland* (1898); Whitworth Porter, *Hist. of the Corps of Royal Engineers* (2 vols., 1889); R. H. Vetch, in *Dict. Nat. Biog.*; G. D. Scull, "The Montrésor Jours.," in *N. Y. Hist. Soc. Colls.,* Pub. Fund Ser., vol. XIV (1882); correspondence with the Ordnance Board, including at least one formal journal, and with Amherst, in Public Record Office, London.]   S. M. P.

MONTRÉSOR, JOHN (Apr. 6, 1736–June 26, 1799), British military engineer, the son of James Gabriel Montrésor [q.v.] and his wife Mary (Haswell), was born at Gibraltar. There his father taught him as a youth something of engineering, and in 1754 he took him to America

to join Braddock's army. He became ensign and later lieutenant in 1755, and was appointed by Braddock as an additional engineer, though the ordnance board did not place him on the establishment as a practitioner engineer until 1758. During the Seven Years' War his work consisted principally in leading special scouting expeditions and carrying dispatches. He was wounded at the Monongahela, served along the Mohawk and at Fort Edward in 1756, went to Halifax with Loudoun in 1757, was present at Amherst's capture of Louisbourg and Wolfe's siege of Quebec, and served with Murray in the final campaign of 1760. His extra services included a winter expedition in 1758 to the interior of Cape Breton Island; an arduous overland journey in winter from Quebec to New England, in which his party suffered the extremes of hunger and cold; and the exploration, in 1761, of the Kennebec river route to Canada. For two years he was intermittently engaged upon a survey of the St. Lawrence River. He ended the war as a sub-engineer, with the rank of lieutenant.

In Pontiac's War, 1763, Montrésor carried dispatches from Amherst to the commander at Detroit, Maj. Henry Gladwin [q.v.]. His party was shipwrecked at the east end of Lake Erie, attacked by Indians soon after it came ashore, but succeeded finally in relieving the garrison. The next year he fortified the portage at Niagara, and went with Bradstreet to Detroit, where he improved the defenses. He was a hostile witness of the Stamp Act riots of 1765 in New York and Albany. In 1766 he solicited preferment in England, whence he returned as engineer extraordinary and captain-lieutenant, with a commission as barrackmaster for the ordnance in North America. During the next few years he improved the fortifications or repaired barracks at New York, Boston, Philadelphia, and the Bahamas, and surveyed the boundary line between New York and New Jersey. He purchased Montrésor's (Randall's) Island in New York harbor, where he lived with his wife and family, having married, Mar. 1, 1764, Frances, daughter of Thomas Tucker of Bermuda.

During the Revolution the British made little use of Montrésor's long American experience. He was commissioned as chief engineer in America in 1775, with the rank of engineer in ordinary and captain, was superseded, reappointed, and again superseded. He was present at Lexington, Bunker Hill, and the capture of Long Island; he drew the approaches before Mud Island (Philadelphia), which he himself had built; and acted as chief engineer at the Brandywine. As Howe's aide-de-camp, he brought to the American lines the news and a description of Nathan Hale's execution. In 1778, having incurred Clinton's displeasure, he returned to England, where for twenty years he struggled to pass his accounts at the Treasury. Testifying before a committee of the House of Commons in 1779, he was non-committal, and seemed to know "hardly anything" about the conduct of the war. After retiring from the army, he traveled for a year on the Continent, and spent the remainder of his life at Belmont, Kent, and Portland Place, London. He was a cousin of Susanna Haswell Rowson [q.v.], and is said (Elias Nason, *A Memoir of Mrs. Susanna Rowson*, 1870, p. 46) to have been the model from which the hero of *Charlotte Temple* was drawn.

[Sir Bernard Burke, *A Geneal. and Heraldic Hist. of the Landed Gentry of Great Britain and Ireland* (1898); G. D. Scull, "The Montrésor Jours.," *N. Y. Hist. Soc. Colls.*, Pub. Fund Ser., vol. XIV (1882); "Journal of a March Undertaken in Winter on Snowshoes from Quebec . . . to . . . New England," in *New-Eng. Hist. and Geneal. Reg.*, Jan. 1882; "Arnold's Letters on His Expedition to Canada in 1775," in *Me. Hist. Soc. Colls.*, 1 ser. I (1831); J. C. Webster, *Presidential Address: Life of John Montrésor* (1928), repr. from *Trans. Royal Soc. of Canada*, 3 ser. XXII, section II (1928); A. G. Doughty and G. W. Parmelee, *The Siege of Quebec* (6 vols., 1901); F. H. Severance, "The Achievements of Captain John Montrésor on the Niagara, and the First Construction of Fort Erie," *Buffalo Hist. Soc. Pubs.*, vol. V (1902); F. M. Montrésor, "Capt. John Montrésor in Canada," *Canadian Hist. Rev.*, Dec. 1924; H. P. Johnston, *Nathan Hale* (rev. ed., 1914); *The Detail and Conduct of the American War . . . with a Very Full and Correct State of the Whole of the Evidence as Given before a Committee of the House of Commons* (3rd ed., 1780).] S. M. P.

MOOD, FRANCIS ASBURY (June 23, 1830–Nov. 12, 1884), clergyman of the Methodist Episcopal Church, South, educator, was born at Charleston, S. C., the son of John Mood and Catherine McFarlane. His family name was originally Muth; his paternal ancestor came to Philadelphia from Württemberg about 1750. Mood pursued a classical course at the College of Charleston where he was graduated with honor in 1850. He received the master's degree two years later. During part of his college course he conducted a school in Charleston for the children of free negroes. His parents were warmly interested in the work of the Methodist Episcopal Church, South, and he gladly prepared himself to take up the duties of its ministry as his father had done, and as his two elder brothers were already doing, and, licensed to enter the itinerant ministry, began serving Cypress Circuit in the South Carolina Conference in 1850. He had other circuits in his charge later, and also held pastorates at Columbia, Greenville, and elsewhere. When the Civil War began he supported the Confederacy, and President Davis appointed him in 1863 chaplain to the army hospitals in Charleston.

In December 1865, with a few associates, he began to publish a weekly newspaper, the *Record,* but the unsettled condition of the South made it impossible to continue publication. In the same period he was instrumental in defending his branch of the church: a Northern Methodist clergyman had taken possession of parish property in Charleston and refused to relinquish it, whereupon Mood appealed to President Johnson, who issued an order directing that the property be returned to its rightful owner. While pastor of Trinity Church, Charleston, Mood was offered the presidency of Soule University at Chappell Hill, Tex., and in November 1868 he decided to accept. He had long been interested in educational work, and his address, *A Theory of Education* (Hendersonville, N. C., 1859), shows his firm grasp of principles. He extinguished the debt at Soule and attracted students. Next, drawing plans for the establishment of a college which might count upon the support of the entire body of Texan Methodism, he persuaded the church assemblies to accede to the project, thus fostering one college instead of starving several. Resigning from the presidency of Soule, he became head of Southwestern University, as it is called today, with the title of regent. The new institution opened its doors at Georgetown, Tex., in the autumn of 1873. The Regent worked hard to gain support for Southwestern, but also he found time to teach the courses in philosophy. Resources at his command were but few at first, and he struggled against any relaxation of standards. Surrounded by utilitarianism, he nevertheless continued to encourage students to cultivate the study of the classical languages as the best means of obtaining a liberal education. When he retired from the regency the college was on a firm footing.

Mood wrote one historical work, *Methodism in Charleston, S. C.* (1856), and a considerable number of pamphlets and contributions to the *Charleston Courier* and to the religious press. Some of these articles record impressions of his travels in Europe in 1857 and again in 1865. He went to London in 1881 as a delegate to the Ecumenical Methodist Conference. He was married to Sue Logan in 1858, and when he died, at Waco, Tex., was survived by his wife and nine children.

[C. C. Cody, *The Life and Labors of Francis Asbury Mood* (1886), based upon Mood's unpublished autobiography, now in the keeping of his son, Judge A. M. Mood, Amarillo, Tex.; *A Narrative of the Facts Relating to the Founding and Progress of Southwestern*

University, 1840–1882 (Galveston, n.d.); bibliography of Mood's uncollected writings, on deposit in the Harvard Univ. Lib.; catalogues of the College of Charleston; *Christian Advocate* (Nashville), Nov. 22, 29, 1884.]   F. M—d.

MOODY, DWIGHT LYMAN (Feb. 5, 1837–Dec. 22, 1899), evangelist, was born at Northfield, Mass., son of Edwin Moody, brick-mason, and his wife Betsey (Holton) Moody. He was of Puritan ancestry, a descendant in the sixth generation of John Moody, who emigrated from England in 1633 and was one of the original settlers of Hartford, Conn., in 1635, and of William Holton, who came from England in 1634 and also settled in Hartford. His father died when Dwight was four years old, leaving to his widowed mother the care of nine children, all under thirteen years of age. A healthy lad, full of energy and given to pranks, young Moody attended school until he was thirteen, then went to work in nearby farms or in adjacent towns. Restless and ambitious, he tired of this manner of life, and at seventeen left home to seek his fortune in Boston, finally securing employment in a shoe store conducted by two uncles, brothers of his mother.

With the rest of his family, he had been baptized by the minister of the Unitarian church in Northfield. In Boston he began to attend the Mount Vernon Congregational Church, and here, through the interest of his Sunday-school teacher, Edward Kimball, he experienced what he ever afterward recalled as his conversion. Applying for membership in this church, he was granted a probationary status only, because of his ignorance of its doctrines. Almost a year elapsed before, on May 3, 1856, he was received into full church-membership. Dissatisfied with his situation at Boston, in the fall of 1856 he removed to Chicago, where, first as a retail clerk, then as a traveling salesman for a wholesale firm dealing in shoes, he got started on the road to success in business. At twenty-three he had an income for the year, through salary and commissions, of more than five thousand dollars. Meantime, religion and human welfare began increasingly to claim his time and interest. At Plymouth Church, which he joined, he was soon renting four pews, filling them each Sunday with men whom he invited from hotels, boarding-houses, and street-corners. Volunteering to teach in a mission Sunday school, he gathered a class of youngsters from the slums. In 1858 he organized the North Market Sabbath School, which met in a hall over one of the city markets, and induced John V. Farwell [*q.v.*], prominent merchant, to become its superintendent. In connection with this school he developed a remarkable

program of evangelistic services, prayer-meetings, home-visitation, social recreation, philanthropic relief, and welfare work. In 1860, after a struggle which he later described as the hardest of his life, he decided to give his entire time to this work, and resigned from business to become an independent city missionary, without salary or assured support.

For reasons of conscience, Moody did not enlist as a soldier in the Civil War; but, with John Farwell and B. F. Jacobs, he organized an army and navy committee of the Chicago Young Men's Christian Association, and later made this a branch of the United States Christian Commission. He threw himself actively into its work of promoting the "spiritual good, intellectual improvement, and social and physical comfort" of the soldiers. Nine times he served at the front as a delegate of the Commission. In the intervals between these periods of service with the army, he devoted himself to his missionary work in Chicago. In connection with his Sunday school he organized in 1863 an undenominational church, and erected for it a building. In 1866 he became president of the Chicago Young Men's Christian Association, which he had for some time been serving as a secretary, and erected for it Farwell Hall, the first Association building in the country. He gave considerable time to county, state, and national conventions of Sunday-school workers and of Association leaders, and aided in the national organization of these movements.

Moody visited Great Britain in 1867 and again in 1870, to get acquainted with Christian leaders there and to study their methods. In June 1873, at the invitation of British friends, he embarked for a third visit, this time to conduct evangelistic services. He took with him Ira D. Sankey [*q.v.*], organist and singer, who had been helping him as chorister in the Sunday school and church at Chicago. Beginning quietly at York, the evangelists labored for five months in the north of England, awakening such interest that they were invited to Edinburgh. Here they succeeded in enlisting the cooperation of ministers and university men of both the Church of Scotland and the Free Church in a series of meetings which continued for more than two months. Many professed conversion or a quickening of spiritual life; ecclesiastical party issues sank to a place of relative unimportance; reports of the meetings were given increasing place in the public and religious press; even the traditional Scotch antipathy to the use of instrumental music in the worship of God gave way before Sankey's organ. After Edinburgh, a similar extensive and successful series of meetings was conducted in Glasgow; then four months were devoted to preaching, for shorter periods, in various places throughout Scotland. In September 1874 the evangelists landed in Ireland, where they labored for three months, receiving a warm welcome both at Belfast and at Dublin. The following winter months were devoted to meetings in Manchester, Sheffield, Birmingham, and Liverpool. The work of the evangelists culminated in a four months' mission in London, conducted in the largest buildings available in each of five sections of the city. In the course of this London mission, 285 meetings were held, attended by an estimated total of 2,530,000 people.

Moody and Sankey returned to America in August 1875. Their visit to Great Britain had been prolonged to more than two years, and they had been the instruments in a religious awakening comparable only to that under the preaching of Wesley and Whitefield. They had gone unheralded; they returned in a blaze of public curiosity and interest, which brought them many more invitations than they could accept. Moody went quietly to Northfield, where he henceforth made his home. Here, in this comparatively remote Massachusetts town, he conducted a two weeks' series of meetings; then, with excellent strategy, he selected Brooklyn, Philadelphia, and New York as the cities in which to undertake evangelistic campaigns in the fall and winter of 1875–76. Careful preliminary organization, the ensured cooperation of the churches, judicious advertising and generous publicity, admission by freely distributed tickets, and well-planned methods of handling the throngs that attended the meetings, helped to clear the way for the full persuasive effect of Moody's preaching and Sankey's music. Their success in these American cities was as notable as in Great Britain.

Moody had found his life work. He was experiencing, to use a phrase which was dear to him, "what God can do with a man wholly surrendered to His will." In 1876–77 he successfully met the test of extensive campaigns in Chicago, where he was best known, and in Boston, traditionally conservative and non-revivalistic. He devoted the year 1877–78 to the smaller cities of New England—Burlington and Montpelier, Vt.; Concord and Manchester, N. H.; Providence, R. I.; Springfield, Mass.; Hartford and New Haven, Conn. Changing his plan in the interest of yet closer cooperation with the churches, he spent the winter of 1878–79 at evangelistic work in Baltimore, 1879–80 in St. Louis, and 1880–81 in San Francisco. Meanwhile, his interests were broadening. He believed in the kind

of evangelism that issues in social service; he himself was a doer rather than a preacher merely. In 1879, aroused by the need of the young people in the hills around his home, and heartened by the counsel of Henry F. Durant [q.v.], who had recently founded Wellesley College, he established a school for girls, the Northfield Seminary, intended primarily for those of limited means. In 1881, along somewhat similar lines, he established a school for boys, Mount Hermon School, near Northfield. In the summer of 1880, in the buildings of the Northfield Seminary, he held a general conference of Christian workers, which has been followed by a like conference in each successive summer, except for three years when Moody was abroad.

His second extended evangelistic campaign in Great Britain was undertaken in the autumn of 1881 in response to invitations from Ireland, Scotland, England, and Wales, and culminated in an eight months' mission in London, which closed in June 1884. At one of the London meetings a young doctor, Wilfred T. Grenfell, was attracted by Moody's adroit closure of a clergyman's tedious prayer—"While our brother is finishing his prayer we will sing number 75"—and was inspired by Moody's sermon to give his life to work as a missionary physician in Labrador. In 1891–92 Moody engaged in a final year of work in Great Britain, and in the spring of 1892 visited Palestine.

The seven years between 1884 and 1891 he devoted to evangelistic work, for short periods, in many cities large and small of the United States and Canada. During the first four months of 1887 he conducted an evangelistic campaign in Chicago, which eventuated in his founding the Chicago Bible Institute, formally opened in 1889, primarily for the training of men and women who had not been privileged to receive a college education but felt impelled to enter home or foreign missionary service as lay workers. In connection with this school he organized, in 1894, the Bible Institute Colportage Association for the publication and sale of religious books at prices low enough to secure wide circulation.

In the eighties his mind turned toward college students. In 1876 he had visited Princeton, and in 1878, after conducting an evangelistic campaign in New Haven, he had accepted the invitation of Yale students to give a special series of addresses to them. In both of his extended visits to Great Britain he had interested university men, and many had assisted at his meetings. At his invitation J. E. K. Studd, a young graduate of Cambridge University, who was later to become Lord Mayor of London, visited America in 1885 and told to student audiences the story of the spiritual awakening in British universities. In July 1886 Moody conducted a conference of college students at Mount Hermon, which was attended by two hundred and fifty young men from eighty colleges in twenty-four states. Transferred to Northfield in the following year, the conference was made memorable by the participation of Henry Drummond, who gave an address on "The Greatest Thing in the World," which was later published and became one of the most widely read of his writings. Thereafter, the conference was held annually and a like conference for students in the women's colleges was begun in 1893. These conferences stimulated in the colleges the development of Young Men's Christian Associations and similar voluntary organizations of students devoted to Christian purposes. One of the immediate results of the first gathering was the initiation of the Student Volunteer Movement, an organization of college students pledged to seek appointment to foreign missionary service. With its enthusiastic slogan —"the evangelization of the world in this generation"—the Movement did much in the closing years of the nineteenth century and the opening decades of the twentieth to recruit the foreign missionary forces of the Protestant churches.

After his last visit to Great Britain Moody resumed work in various cities of the United States and Canada. Daring but successful was a six months' campaign of evangelistic services which he conducted in Chicago from May to November 1893, during the progress of the World's Fair. Among other cities in which he labored in this decade were New York, Boston, Philadelphia, Providence, Scranton, Washington, Richmond, Birmingham, St. Louis, Denver, Montreal, Toronto, and Winnipeg. He gave the early months of 1899 to meetings in the Southwest and on the Pacific Coast, and in November of that year he began a campaign in Kansas City. His work here was interrupted by illness and he traveled home to Northfield, where on Dec. 22, he died.

Moody was a layman. He never sought ordination. His work was characteristic of the growing assumption by laymen of responsibility for Christian enterprises, which began about the middle of the nineteenth century, and it powerfully stimulated that movement. A man of large administrative and executive ability, he commanded the confidence of business men, who received him as one of themselves and contributed to the support of his projects because they trusted his judgment as well as his sincerity. Not money-hungry, he refused to accept as personal profit the proceeds of his work, and he and Sankey turned over all royalties accruing from the sale of their hymnbooks to a board of trustees headed by William E. Dodge [q.v.], which devoted these funds chiefly to the endowment of the Northfield schools. Moody's preaching was direct, forceful, intimate. He talked to his audiences as man to man, simply, even colloquially. He used short sentences and the rugged Anglo-Saxon words of common life. His emphasis was upon the gospel of God's fatherly love, rather than the terrors of hell fire. His speech was vivid, moving, but not sensational. Understanding and using the methods of effective publicity, he disdained its cheaper and more personal forms. He believed in personal evangelism and never lost the individual in the mass. His gospel was one of friendship. The "inquiry room" for personal conferences was invariably included in the organization of his campaigns, and he was adept in enlisting and training helpers for this personal service. "Better set ten men to work than do the work of ten men," he often said. With singleness of purpose he combined largeness of spirit and an uncommon degree of common sense. He quite lacked the censoriousness which has marred the work of many itinerant evangelists, or the passion for statistics of the converted which has sometimes distracted them. Kindly and conciliatory, he let no personal quirks or sectarian differences stand in the way of the gospel he preached and lived. He worked effectively with men like Sir George Adam Smith and Henry Drummond, whose positions were in some respects far from his own. He withstood temptation to set up as a faith-healer, and refused to let that cult gain a foothold in his Chicago School. A man of prayer, he was tirelessly and far-sightedly a man of work. "There is no use asking God to do things you can do yourself," he said. A layman, Moody inspired ministers; an evangelist, he understood the importance of Christian education; unschooled, he commanded the admiration and cooperation of University students and teachers; a man of large business ability, he devoted himself unreservedly to what he conceived to be the greatest business in earth or heaven— the saving of souls.

On Aug. 28, 1862, he married Emma C. Revell, daughter of Fleming H. Revell, a Chicago ship builder, and sister of Fleming H. Revell [q.v.], who became a publisher of religious books. She entered into his work with sympathy and good judgment, and her influence on Moody's life was incalculable. She introduced him to certain social graces and increased greatly his charm and effectiveness. They had two sons and one daughter.

[W. R. Moody, *D. L. Moody* (1930), superseding *The Life of Dwight L. Moody* (1900) by the same author, contains an extensive bibliography. See also Lyman Abbott, *Silhouettes of My Contemporaries* (1921); J. V. Farwell, *Early Recollections of Dwight L. Moody* (1907); W. S. Carson and I. D. Sankey in *Boston Daily Globe*, Dec. 23, 1899; Gamaliel Bradford, *D. L. Moody, A Worker in Souls* (1927), with bibliography. Moody published eighteen volumes, chiefly sermons.]

L. A. W.

MOODY, JAMES (1744–Apr. 6, 1809), the most noted spy in British service during the American Revolution, was born in New Jersey. He was living quietly with his wife and three children on his large farm in its northernmost county, Sussex, during the first two years of the war. Like some of his neighbors he rejected the oaths of abjuration and allegiance prescribed by state law, which were tendered by the Council of Safety in 1777. Hence the Whigs molested and even shot at him. In April of that year he fled with seventy-four neighbors and friends to Bergen County and shortly enlisted in the brigade organized by Gen. Cortlandt Skinner, former attorney-general of New Jersey, and soon known as "Skinner's Greens." He served a year as a volunteer without pay, being soon sent back with a hundred men to annoy his former neighborhood. Later he penetrated the country and obtained intelligence about a Whig corps. Early in August 1777 the Council learned that Moody and two others were recruiting in New Jersey and ordered their apprehension. One was caught. In 1778 his property, like that of other Loyalists, was confiscated by the state and, after being cleared of obligations and claims, was sold.

In 1779 Moody was commissioned ensign in the first battalion of Skinner's brigade, and in June in the course of a raid to Tintonfalls, seized four Whig officers and several privates, and drove off three hundred head of live stock. Moody's party plundered a military magazine, and with the prisoners and booty reached their boats at Sandy Hook after repulsing thirty Whigs. He spied on the troops of Washington, Sullivan, and Gates, and in May 1780 undertook to execute the order of the Hessian officer, Lieut.-Gen. Wilhelm von Knyphausen, to bring to New York with their public papers Gov. William Livingston, other officials, and those persons in New Jersey concerned in the execution of three spies. A reward of 2,000 guineas had been offered by General Skinner for the achievement of this feat. The expedition failed, however, because one of Moody's men was apprehended and vaguely revealed its object. In a more successful exploit in July Moody with seven men captured eighteen committeemen and militia officers. For this he was hunted far and wide and taken near Eng-

lishtown by Captain Lawrence of the New York state levies. Falling into the hands of Gen. Anthony Wayne, he was transferred from one prison to another. He was finally lodged in a filthy dungeon at Westpoint and otherwise mistreated until Washington ordered the situation remedied. At length, fearing execution, Moody effected his escape on a stormy night. He received two rewards for waylaying "rebel" mails, and was promoted lieutenant, Aug. 14, 1781. Later in the same year he started for Philadelphia to get the books and papers of the Continental Congress, but learned by chance at the Delaware that the plot had been revealed.

His health was now impaired, and he was urged by Sir Henry Clinton to visit England. There he memorialized several government officials and at mid-June, 1782, was granted £100 a year by the Treasury. In 1783 he published in pamphlet form the *Narrative* of his exertions and sufferings, and in June of the following year testified before the commissioners on Loyalist claims who were so impressed by the nature of his service and the grave risks he had run that they broke their rules by allowing his claim in full for £1,330. They also promised to recommend him to Gov. John Parr of Nova Scotia on his departure for that province, where he expected to obtain a grant of six hundred acres. After a sojourn in Halifax Moody settled at Weymouth, Nova Scotia, in 1786. There he served as colonel of militia. He died in 1809. His younger brother John took part in some of his adventures and was executed in November 1781, at Philadelphia, for attempting to break into the state house there.

[*Lieut. Jas. Moody's Narrative of His Exertions and Sufferings in the Cause of Gov't.* (1782, revised and enlarged, 1783), was edited and republished with notes by C. I. Bushnell under the title: *Narrative of the Exertions and Sufferings of Lieut. Jas. Moody* (1865). See also: *The Royal Commission on the Losses and Services of Am. Loyalists* (1915), ed. by H. E. Egerton; W. S. Stryker, "The N. J. Volunteers" (1887); *Archives of the State of N. J.,* 2 ser. III (1906) and IV (1914); Lorenzo Sabine, *Biog. Sketches of Loyalists of the Am. Revolution* (2 vols., 1864); E. A. Jones, "The Loyalists of N. J.," *N. J. Hist. Soc. Colls.,* vol. X (1927).]

W. H. S—t.

MOODY, PAUL (May 21, 1779–July 8, 1831), inventor, was born in Byfield Parish, Newbury, Mass., the sixth son of Capt. Paul and Mary Moody. His father, a man of influence in Newbury, was a Byfield volunteer at Lexington, March 1776, and commanded a company of sixty-eight Newbury men in the Revolutionary War. At the age of twelve Paul evinced an interest in mechanics and entered a woolen factory at Waltham to learn the art of weaving; he next found employment in a nail-making plant in Byfield; in fact, for several years, he went from one establishment to another where mill machinery was in use, and by close study and handling of machines became a master mechanic. On July 13, 1800, he married Susannah Morrill of Amesbury, and then entered a co-partnership with Ezra Worthen in the operation of a cotton mill of that town. His contacts during the succeeding fourteen years' management of this plant were with those New Englanders who were ambitious to develop domestic manufacture so as to avoid foreign dependence. Accordingly when Francis C. Lowell [q.v.] formed the Boston Manufacturing Company about 1814, to manufacture cotton-mill and other machinery, Moody joined him in establishing the plant at Waltham, Mass. Here he remained for the succeeding eleven years, repairing and manufacturing machinery and inventing a number of improvements. On Mar. 9, 1816, he secured a patent for a new mechanism to wind yarn from bobbins or spools; on Jan. 17, 1818, he perfected soapstone rollers for Horrocks' dressing machine and doubled its efficacy; he improved the "double-speeder" for roping cotton and obtained a patent Apr. 3, 1819; and, finally, on Jan. 19 and February 19, 1821, respectively, he was granted patents for machines to make cotton roping and to rope and spin cotton. Moody's contributions did much to bring to its highest efficiency the Waltham system of cotton manufacture.

In 1823 he went to East Chelmsford, now Lowell, Mass., to superintend the building of new cotton-mills there. A large machine shop, called the Lowell Machine Works, was also established, and after its completion in 1825, Moody, together with a full force of experienced men, was transferred from Waltham to Lowell. Here under his direction the manufacture of cotton machinery was continued and new and improved designs of machinery perfected. In a comparatively short time the shop was manufacturing every item of equipment needed for the operation of a cotton-mill, and its reputation for good designs and workmanship was the highest in the country. Moody, however, enjoyed but little of the reward, for he died suddenly after a three-day illness, when only fifty-two years of age. His special interests outside of business were community welfare and education: he was also a stanch supporter of temperance. His widow and three sons survived him.

[J. L. Ewell, The Story of Byfield, A New England Parish (1904); Vital Records of Newbury, Mass. (1911); Vital Records of Amesbury, Mass. (1913); C. C. P. Moody, Biog. Sketches of the Moody Family (1847); J. D. Van Slyck, Representatives of New Eng. Manufacturers (1879); Alfred Gilman, "Francis Cabot Lowell," in Contributions of the Old Residents' Hist. Asso. (Lowell, Mass.), vol. V, no. 2 (1876); L. B. Lawson, "Lowell and Newburyport," Ibid., no. 3 (1877); Joseph Coffin, A Sketch of the Hist. of Newbury, Newburyport, and West Newbury (1845); H. A. Miles, Lowell As It Was, and As It Is (1845); F. W. Coburn, Hist. of Lowell and Its People (1920), vol. I; Nathan Appleton, Introduction of the Power Loom, and Origin of Lowell (1858); Essex Reg. (Salem, Mass.), July 11, 1831; A List of the Patents Granted by the U. S. from Apr. 10, 1790, to Dec. 31, 1836 (1872).]　　　　　　　　　C. W. M.

MOODY, WILLIAM HENRY (Dec. 23, 1853–July 2, 1917), congressman, cabinet member, jurist, was born in Newbury, Mass. The first William Moody had come to America in 1634 and after a year at Ipswich removed to Newbury where his descendants continued their residence. William Henry Moody was born in the homestead which had been in the family for more than two centuries. His parents were Henry L. and Melissa A. (Emerson) Moody. When he was six years of age the family moved to Danvers where he received his early schooling—later attending Phillips Academy, Andover, from which he graduated in 1872. He then entered Harvard College and received the degree of A.B. cum laude with honors in history in 1876. In September of that year he entered the Harvard Law School but remained only until the following January. He continued his law studies in the office of Richard H. Dana, Jr., author of Two Years Before the Mast, and a prominent member of the Massachusetts bar. Although his period of study was only eighteen months rather than the usual three years he was permitted to present himself for the bar examinations—at that time a process of oral questioning—and was duly admitted to the bar at the April 1878 term of the supreme judicial court before Chief Justice Gray.

He began practice in Haverhill with Edwin N. Hill and later became associated with Joseph K. Jenness. Moody early laid down for himself the rule, "The power of clear statement is the greatest power at the bar" (World's Work, Nov. 1906, p. 8190). Because of his outstanding ability he soon came to be recognized as one of the leading lawyers in Essex County. He served on the Haverhill school board for three years and, 1888–90, was the city solicitor. In 1890 he was chosen district attorney for the Eastern District of Massachusetts. Moody's administration of this office brought him forward as one of the most successful trial lawyers in the Commonwealth; and, although the venue was not in his district, he was engaged specially to take part in the prosecution of the famous Lizzie Borden case in Fall River. The defendant was acquitted but Moody's activities in the case won him wide recognition. At a special election in November 1895, he was elected to succeed William Cogswell in the Fifty-fourth Congress. In this body (1895–1902), as already at the bar, he became a master of fact and detail, and during his second term he was appointed to the important appropriations committee.

His career as a member of the House of Representatives so commanded the notice of President Theodore Roosevelt that on May 1, 1902, he was appointed secretary of the navy. Moody had the obvious qualities of pugnacity and virility, and they appealed strongly to the Roosevelt temperament. A close friendship developed between the two and upon the resignation of Attorney-General Philander C. Knox in 1904 the President selected Moody as his successor. Although perhaps up to that time he had not become known throughout the country as the pre-eminent lawyer, his effective service as the nation's chief law officer soon established him as the leader of the American bar in title and achievement. Roosevelt's anti-trust activities reached their high point while Moody was attorney-general. He personally argued the so-called Beef Trust Case (*Swift & Co.* vs. *U. S.*; 196 *U. S.*, 375), wherein the government contended that a combination of corporations and individuals, after purchasing livestock and converting the same into fresh meat, sold the products in interstate commerce in such manner that competition, both in the purchase of cattle on the hoof and in the sale of meat, was suppressed. The government won the case. Moody also instituted prosecutions alleging restraint of trade against combinations engaged in the paper, fertilizer, salt, tobacco, oil, lumber, and other businesses. Roosevelt said of his work, "his record as Attorney-General can be compared without fear with the record of any other man who ever held that office" (*Outlook,* Nov. 5, 1910, p. 532).

When the retirement of Justice Henry B. Brown was followed by the announcement that the President was to appoint the vigorous Attorney-General to the Supreme Court, it was not met with universal approval. It was feared by some that his administrative attitude toward "big business" would be carried into his judicial functioning and that some of the "radical" ideas of the President with whom he was so friendly would be reflected from the bench. However, on Dec. 12, 1906, the Senate confirmed him and on Dec. 17 he was sworn in as an associate justice. Thus, within five years, Moody had the singular distinction of serving the legislative, executive, and judicial branches of the government.

During his service on the Court, Moody wrote sixty-seven opinions, of which five were dissents,

and he cast dissenting votes in ten cases. His principal dissenting opinion was in the group known as the Employers' Liability Cases (207 *U. S.,* 463), wherein the majority of the Court declared the first Federal Employers' Liability Act to be unconstitutional. Moody supported the proposition that since the Constitution gave Congress the power to regulate interstate commerce, coincidently that body had the right to regulate the relation of master and servant in the matters concerning interstate commerce. The majority opinion, however, declared that the act went beyond this realm and involved the regulation of intrastate commerce also. The burden of Moody's dissent was a contention that the statute could be so interpreted as not to have this effect. An important case having to do with so-called fundamental rights of the individual in which Moody wrote the majority opinion was *Twining* vs. *State of New Jersey* (211 *U. S., 78*), wherein the state trial court had commented unfavorably upon the refusal of the defendants to testify. Unless such refusal was violative of a privilege guaranteed by the federal Constitution, the Supreme Court had no jurisdiction to inquire how it had been dealt with in the courts below. Moody's conclusion that the Constitution embodies no such guarantee either directly or by inference is set out in an opinion marked for its insight, clarity, and thoroughness of consideration.

His rather unusual practical experience in public life and his fundamental soundness as a lawyer promised to make Moody's service on the Court one of much usefulness. His work seemed to promise that he would become one of the great justices of that great body, but ill health beset him and in 1910 Congress by special act (because of his short term of service) granted him the retirement privileges ordinarily extended to federal judges who have served for at least ten years and attained the age of seventy. On Nov. 20, 1910, he resigned. He spent his remaining years in Haverhill, Mass., where on July 2, 1917, he died. He never married.

[*U. S. Supreme Court Reports,* vols. CCIII–CCXVIII; Official Records, Dept. of Justice, Washington, D. C.; 36 *Statutes at Large,* pt. II, 61 Cong., 2 Sess.; ch. ccclxxvii, Act of June 23, 1910; F. B. Wiener, Life and Judicial Career of William Henry Moody, Harvard Law School Thesis, 1930; I. F. Marcosson, in *World's Work,* Nov. 1906; George Whitelock, in *Green Bag,* June 1909; Theodore Roosevelt, in *Outlook,* Nov. 5, 1910; *Who's Who in Am.,* 1916–17; *Proc. at the Meeting of the Essex Bar in the Supreme Judicial Court in Memory of William Henry Moody, Apr. 26, 1919* (n.d.); obituaries in *N. Y. Times, Boston Evening Transcript,* July 2, 1917.]
                                                   C. P. S.

MOODY, WILLIAM VAUGHN (July 8, 1869–Oct. 17, 1910), poet, playwright, educator, was born in Spencer, Ind., the son of Francis Burdette Moody and Henriette Emily (Stoy) Moody. His father, originally from New York, was a steamboat captain, and the boy was brought up in New Albany, Ind. He early manifested a bent for scholarship and the character to achieve it in the face of obstacles. He taught school to earn money to fit himself for college, and he arrived at Harvard in September 1889 with just $25 in his pocket, but he completed what was then almost universally a four-year course in three years, meanwhile supporting himself and partially supporting a sister by typewriting, tutoring, and serving as a proctor. Furthermore, he found time to join in the active literary life of the college, writing both verse and prose, and becoming one of the editors of the *Harvard Monthly*. The group with whom he was associated in college included Daniel Gregory Mason, Robert Herrick, George Santayana, Philip Savage, Norman Hapgood, and other future writers. His senior year (1892–93) he spent in Europe, paying for his trip by accompanying a boy as tutor. Following his graduation he secured the degree of A.M. in 1894 and then served during 1894–95 as an assistant to Lewis E. Gates in the English department at Harvard and Radcliffe. In the autumn of 1895 he became an instructor in English at the University of Chicago. In 1899–1900 he withdrew for a year, living in Boston and East Gloucester, to complete his volume of poems. On his return to the University of Chicago in 1901 he was made an assistant professor, with considerable liberty of movement, and he continued to keep this title till 1907, when he finally resigned completely from teaching and devoted his entire attention to literary production.

Moody's first published book was a drama in verse, *The Masque of Judgment* (1900). This was followed by a volume of *Poems* (1901), and by a second poem in dramatic form, *The Fire-Bringer*, in 1904, originally intended for production by the Chicago Civic Theatre. Feeling the need of a year of leisure he wrote, with Robert Morss Lovett, a textbook, *A First View of English Literature* (1905), which enabled him to make a trip to the West, as well as to Europe, and to devote time to a prose drama which was shaping in his mind. This play, first called *The Sabine Woman*, he brought to Margaret Anglin early in 1906, and she produced it at the Garrick Theatre, Chicago, Apr. 12, 1906. With Henry Miller as Ghent and Miss Anglin as Ruth, and the title changed to *The Great Divide*, it was shown at the Princess Theatre, New York, Oct. 3, 1906, and was at once recognized

as an important contribution to American drama. It was acted in London, Sept. 15, 1909, has often been revived since, and in 1929 was made into a motion picture. Moody's next play, *The Faith Healer*, was acted by Henry Miller at Harvard College in 1909, in Saint Louis, Mar. 15, 1909, and in New York, Jan. 19, 1910. Unlike *The Great Divide*, it was not successful as a popular attraction, but its high merits were recognized, and Moody was looked upon as a leader among American dramatists. In 1908 Moody received the degree of Litt.D. from Yale and was elected to the American Academy of Arts and Letters. In the spring of that year he suffered a severe attack of typhoid fever, at his apartment in Waverley Place, New York, and was nursed by an old friend, Mrs. Harriet Tilden Brainard, of Chicago, whom he married on May 7, 1909. He recovered sufficiently to draft one act of *The Death of Eve*, a poetic drama, but never finished it, as a serious brain disease developed and caused his death at Colorado Springs, Oct. 17, 1910.

Moody was rather small in stature, wore a small, pointed beard, and was taciturn and shy. His college friends used to say, "It took Moody a pipeful to make a remark." At Chicago the students who had to write themes for him called him "The Man in the Iron Mask." But his native taciturn shyness and perhaps a certain academic aloofness developed at Harvard, concealed a man of fine critical as well as creative intellect, and profound feeling. Though outwardly his life was quiet and uneventful, his poetry and plays all came, as Dickinson puts it, "out of moral conviction and mental necessity" (*post*, p. 136). He was constantly striving to come "to grips with the spirit of the age, and expressing his message with force and pure beauty" (*Ibid.*, p. 135)—for beauty was with him a passion. The lyric quality of his verse, exhibited in such a poem as "Gloucester Moors," suggested the *Songs from Vagabondia* by his contemporaries, Carman and Hovey. But in his "Ode in Time of Hesitation" (1900) was visible his spiritual wrestling with problems of the day—here his revolt against "imperialism" in the Philippines. *The Masque of Judgment* is a dramatization of the dignity of the individual, even to rebellion against the Most High. *The Fire Bringer*, a Promethean drama, again stresses "the supreme duty of rebellion." Neither of these verse plays, though the latter was intended for the stage, has been produced (1933). Perhaps they were, in form, not sufficiently in revolt against the academic tradition of poetic drama. As late as 1904 Moody wrote to Percy Mac-

Kaye, "I am heart and soul dedicated to the conviction that modern life can be presented on the stage in the poetic mediums and adequately presented only in that way" (*Letters, post,* p. 148). But shortly thereafter he wrote *The Great Divide* in prose, and at last saw his work reach the stage. In this play of contemporary American life Moody transferred to Stephen Ghent, the rough Westerner, his ideal of personal independence, and to Ruth Jordan, daughter of a long line of Puritans, the inhibitions which choke the growth of the human spirit and may prevent the real conquest of evil, the real achievement of happiness, and the good life. In this play Moody kept his prose dignified and at times poetic, but it was human speech adapted to the ear trained on realistic drama, and therefore he was able to reach large audiences, who realized at once that in Moody the American theatre had found a dramatist who could, in contemporary terms, express philosophic ideas and bring to the theatre new spiritual values. *The Faith Healer* is in the same style and spirit, and shows the struggle between earthly love and consciousness of a "mission." Its failure on the stage was probably due to the extreme difficulty of dramatizing, in contemporary terms, occult religious phenomena. Few dramatists have ever succeeded. But Quinn declares this to be Moody's finest play. *The Death of Eve* was undertaken to complete the trilogy of poetic dramas Moody had planned. Had he lived, he would undoubtedly have contributed more dramas, in the current prose idiom, to the practical theatre, and would have achieved a most important place in the theatrical history of America. *The Great Divide,* alone, coming as it did in the first decade of the twentieth century, when the American theatre was struggling for deeper and more significant expression, marked an important step in the evolution of the drama. But Moody, the lyric poet, also continues to be read and admired, alike for form and content. He was a conscientious artist, and he was also a forward-looking intellect.

[*Some Letters of Wm. Vaughn Moody* (1913), with an Introduction by D. G. Mason; Bliss Perry, memoir in *Proc. Am. Acad. Arts and Letters,* vol. VI (1913), reprinted in the *Commemorative Tributes* (1922) of the Academy; *Selected Poems of Wm. Vaughn Moody* (1931), edited by R. M. Lovett, with biographical sketch; T. H. Dickinson, *Playwrights of the New Am. Theatre* (1925); A. H. Quinn, *A Hist. of the Am. Drama from the Civil War to the Present Day* (1927), vol. II; E. H. Lewis, *Wm. Vaughn Moody* (1914); *Harvard Grads'. Mag.,* Dec. 1910; *Chicago Tribune,* Oct. 19, 1910.] W.P.E.

MOONEY, JAMES (Feb. 10, 1861–Dec. 22, 1921), ethnologist, son of James and Ellin (Devlin) Mooney, was born at Richmond, Ind. He began his education in the common-schools and later taught two terms. He was strongly interested in Indians, reading everything available on the subject, but his interest did not lead to any apparent avenue of support and he entered the office of the *Richmond Palladium,* where he worked both as a compositor and in an editorial capacity. After he had saved a little money he journeyed to Washington with a secret intent of going to Brazil to study the Indians of that country. In Washington he met Maj. J. W. Powell [*q.v.*] in 1885, and through him Mooney found an outlet for his enthusiasm in the Bureau of American Ethnology, where he remained for the rest of his life. His early Indian studies had taken the form of a list of tribes amounting to 3,000 entries, and this came into use as material for the *Handbook of American Indians* (2 vols., 1907–10, ed. by F. W. Hodge), in the preparation of which he took an active part. In North Carolina he studied the language, folk lore, mythology, and material culture of the Cherokees ("Myths of the Cherokees," *Nineteenth Annual Report of the Bureau of American Ethnology,... 1895–96,* 1900). At a fortunate juncture he discovered an ancient Cherokee ritual written in the Cherokee script ("The Sacred Formulas of the Cherokees," *Seventh Annual Report ... 1885–86,* 1891). About 1890 the last ebullition of Indian race-consciousness took place with the outbreak of the Ghost Dance—an endeavor to rehabilitate the Indian to his former status—and this phase of Indian life Mooney studied exhaustively ("The Ghost-dance Religion and the Sioux Outbreak of 1890," *Fourteenth Annual Report ... 1892–93,* 1896). Some of his best years were spent in the investigation of the Kiowa ("Calendar History of the Kiowa Indians," *Seventeenth Annual Report ... 1895–96,* 1898), and at the time of his death he was engrossed with a large work on Kiowa heraldry. He also investigated the seemingly anomalous presence of Siouan language tribes on the borders of the Virginia Algonquians and his research went far to clear up the history of the migrations of this great stock ("The Siouan Tribes of the East," *Bulletin 22 of the Smithsonian Institution, Bureau of Ethnology,* 1894).

Mooney's parents had come from Meath, Ireland, and he was deeply ingrained with Irish lore. One of his first papers was "The Funeral Customs of Ireland" (*Proceedings of the American Philosophical Society, 1888,* vol. XXV, 1888, pp. 1–56). His scientific writing was mostly confined to large, thoroughly prepared monographs. A particularly lucid style characterized his writing. He was active in various scientific organizations and especially in the Anthropological Society of Washington, of which he was president, 1914–15. He threw his whole energy into all matters looking toward the advancement of his science. His own work was never subject to adverse criticism and his faculty of getting along with the Indians whom he studied was phenomenal. Of medium height, with gray eyes and dark hair, he was a true Irish type. In 1897 he married Ione Lee Gaut of Tennessee, who accompanied him on his journeys on the Western frontier.

[*Am. Anthropologist*, Apr. June 1922; *Who's Who in America*, 1920–21; the *Evening Star* (Washington, D. C.), Dec. 23, 1921; personal recollections.]

W. H.

MOONEY, WILLIAM (1756–Nov. 27, 1831), one of the founders of the New York Society of Tammany, was probably born of humble parents in New York City. He is said to have been a soldier in the American army in the Revolution, but his term of service must have been in the early years of the war. In August 1780, three years before the British evacuation, he was engaged in business as an upholsterer and dealer in wall paper in William Street, New York City. He continued in this business at various locations until his retirement in 1821. In the great parade to celebrate the ratification of the Constitution, in 1788, he appeared on a float in the act of upholstering a presidential chair for General Washington.

Mooney and others in 1786 founded the New York Society of Tammany which, like the earlier Tammany societies, seems to have been a social and benevolent organization of the middle class, with strong prejudices against "aristocrats" on the one hand and "foreign adventurers" on the other. When the written constitution of the society was adopted in August 1789, he was chosen the first grand sachem. He was later prominent in all the activities of Tammany over a period of forty years, among others as a director of the museum established for the preservation of historic objects, and as a member of one of the committees for the interment of the remains of eleven thousand American soldiers and sailors who died on board British prison ships in New York harbor. Many charters granted to other Tammany societies bore his signature. When the society became involved in politics he promoted its activity and was eager to share in the spoils of office.

In February 1808, following a Republican victory in the municipal elections, the council made a place for Mooney as superintendent of the almshouse. The position allowed him an expense account and furnished accommodations for his fam-

ily, besides a salary. Within a few months the commissioners of the almshouse complained of Mooney's incompetence and financial irregularities, and in September 1809 the council dismissed him. A committee appointed to investigate his accounts found that he had curtailed the expenditures for necessities for the inmates and had greatly increased the amounts spent for luxuries, especially for rum and other liquors. One heading for entries in his books—"Trifles for Mrs. Mooney"—long continued to be a byword among the opponents of Tammany Hall. Mooney's explanation of his accounts was that there had been an increase in the number of inmates, that the almshouse had been frequently visited by members of the Corporation, and that it had been made the resort of "certain other persons" (*Minutes of the Common Council, post,* V, p. 720). He had probably erred in being too liberal with his party associates. The Tammany Society was apparently satisfied with his explanation, for in 1811 it again chose him grand sachem, and reëlected him at the close of his term.

[E. P. Kilroe, *Saint Tammany and the Origin of the Soc. of Tammany* (1913); *N. Y. Gazette and Weekly Mercury*, Aug. 14, 1780; *An Account of the Interment of the Remains of Am. Patriots* (1865); I. N. P. Stokes, *The Iconography of Manhattan Island*, vol. V (1926); *Minutes of the Common Council of the City of N. Y., 1784–1831* (19 vols., 1917); *Commercial Advertiser* (N. Y.), Nov. 28, 1831.]

E. C. S.

MOORE, ADDISON WEBSTER (July 30, 1866–Aug. 25, 1930), philosopher, was born at Plainfield, Ind., the son of John Sheldon and Adaline (Hockett) Moore. His paternal ancestors came from Virginia by way of Kentucky. His father, an ardent Abolitionist, served throughout the Civil War. On his mother's side he came from a family of Quakers who emigrated from North Carolina to Indiana because of the slavery issue. The son, Addison, attended the Plainfield Academy near his home, then taught school, and at twenty years of age entered the neighboring De Pauw University, from which he received the degree of A.B. in 1890. On Sept. 1, 1891, he was married to Ella E. Adams whom he had known at the University. In 1893 he entered the graduate school of Cornell University as a candidate for the degree of Ph.D. At the end of the academic year 1893–94 he was attracted to the University of Chicago by the philosophy and personality of John Dewey. From that date until his retirement as professor emeritus in 1929, his connection with the Chicago School of Philosophy, as student or teacher, was unbroken and influential. He was granted the degree of Ph.D. in 1898 and in 1901–02 he studied in Berlin. In 1911 the Western Philosophical Association elected him to its presidency and in 1917 he was elected president of the American Philosophical Association. He died in London following a stroke of paralysis; he had just completed an automobile tour of six thousand miles on the continent of Europe.

At Cornell University Moore was methodically trained in the history of philosophical ideas and problems. His interest in historical scholarship was kept fresh during his entire teaching career. It proved to be one of the most valuable parts of his generous equipment for the guidance and instruction of a long line of graduate students. He had little sympathy with the doctrines of absolute idealism which the Cornell School had derived from Kant and the neo-Hegelians, particularly through the mediation of Bosanquet and Bradley. He was temperamentally and by bias of early education interested chiefly in the problems of will and of society, in a philosophy adjustable to the flux of action and purpose. A system of rigid and static reality was, in his opinion, useless for an empirical world of evolution. He rejected, therefore, absolute idealism in all of its forms and allied himself whole-heartedly with the Chicago school of instrumental pragmatism, of which Dewey was the creator and Moore the principal apologete. He believed that truth is identified with ideas that work, that solve our problems, that fit into the purposiveness of empirical processes. In his assumption that both fact and idea have their only being and meaning when they are applied to desiring and willing, to believing and working, that is, to human life, his philosophy was a form of Humanism. This accounts for his indifference to the ordinary problems of epistemology and metaphysics. His contribution to *Studies in Logical Theory*, edited by Dewey and published in 1903, was somewhat tentative and obscure, but in 1910 he published the most complete statement of his views in *Pragmatism and its Critics*. The volume is primarily a work of exposition and defense, although it contains instructive chapters on the historical backgrounds of absolute idealism and pragmatism. The first chapter of this work, "The Issue," rings out a challenge, and as challenger he stood for two decades, lance in hand, in the front rank of pragmatists. Although nearly all of his writings and addresses are controversial in character, few authors have illustrated more happily the amenities of polemical discourse.

His philosophical activity and influence are scarcely to be measured by the number or range of his publications, the chief of which are:

Pragmatism and its Critics (1910); "Bergson and Pragmatism" (*Philosophical Review*, July 1912); "Reformation of Logic," in the volume entitled *Creative Intelligence* (1917), edited by John Dewey; and "The Opportunity of Philosophy" (*Philosophical Review*, March 1918). Perhaps his greatest influence was exerted through the spoken word and the oral dialectic of his graduate seminary.

[*Who's Who in America*, 1930–31; J. M. and Jaques Cattell, *Am. Men of Sci.* (4th ed., 1927); *N. Y. Times, Chicago Daily Tribune*, Aug. 26, 1930; addresses by J. H. Tufts, Mathilde Castro Tufts, and George H. Mead at a memorial service held at the Univ. of Chicago, Nov. 8, 1930.]   W. A. H.

MOORE, ALFRED (May 21, 1755–Oct. 15, 1810), Revolutionary soldier and associate justice of the United States Supreme Court, was born in New Hanover County, N. C. In 1764 his parents, Judge Maurice [*q.v.*] and Anne (Grange) Moore, sent him to Boston for an education. He returned home before the Revolution, studied law under his father, and was licensed to practise in 1775. He married Susanna Elizabeth Eagles of Brunswick County. On Sept. 1, 1775, the Third Provincial Congress elected him a captain in the 1st North Carolina Continental Regiment, and he participated in the Moore's Creek campaign in February 1776 and in the gallant defense of Charlestown (later Charleston), S. C., in June. He resigned his commission, Mar. 8, 1777, and returned to his plantation "Buchoi" in Brunswick County, where until the end of the conflict he was active as a colonel of militia, particularly in harassing the British under Maj. James H. Craig, who occupied Wilmington in 1781. The war left his plantation plundered and his fortune greatly impaired, but by 1790 he was the owner of forty-eight slaves.

In 1782, as representative of Brunswick County in the Senate, Moore opposed the policy of extreme proscription of the Loyalists. On May 3 he was elected attorney-general of North Carolina, and for nearly nine years he executed the duties of the office with unusual distinction. On Jan. 9, 1791, displeased at an act of 1790 which expanded the court system and created the office of solicitor-general with the same powers and remuneration as that of attorney-general, he resigned, stating that no satisfactory division of the work could be arranged without injury to his health or private business. His legal career was brilliant. In his generation he shared the leadership of the North Carolina bar with only William R. Davie [*q.v.*]. His power as an advocate and his knowledge of the criminal law profoundly impressed his contemporaries. With small stature, frail physique, dark, piercing eyes, and clear voice, he was graceful in manner, chaste in style, quick in perception, animated in address, and powerful in analysis. He helped prepare the public mind for the establishment of the state university, contributed to its support, and served as a trustee, 1789–1807.

Moore was designated by the governor as a delegate to the Annapolis Convention in 1786, but no North Carolinian attended. He was a Federalist in politics and in 1788 favored the ratification of the Constitution as drafted. In 1792 he represented Brunswick County in the House of Commons; in 1795 he was defeated by Timothy Bloodworth, Republican, after a stubborn contest in the General Assembly for election to the United States Senate. On Jan. 8, 1798, President Adams nominated him as one of the three commissioners to conclude a treaty with the Cherokee nation of Indians, but he withdrew from the negotiations before the treaty was signed on Oct. 2. He was elected a judge of the superior court by the General Assembly, Dec. 7, 1798. In recognition of his legal eminence, President Adams appointed him an associate justice of the Supreme Court of the United States in December 1799 to succeed James Iredell, deceased. He delivered an opinion in only one case (*Bas* vs. *Tingy, 4 Dallas,* 37) followed *seriatim* by the opinions of the other judges. The court held in this case (1800) that a state of "limited, partial" war existed with France. The opinion was applauded by Federalists but condemned by Republicans. In 1804 Moore resigned on account of ill health, dying on Oct. 15, 1810, at the home of his son-in-law in Bladen County.

[*The Colonial Records of N. C.* (10 vols., 1886–90); *State Records of N. C.* (16 vols., 1895–1905); *Jours. of the Senate and House of Commons,* 1794–95, 1798; Governors' Papers, in N. C. Hist. Commission; S. A. Ashe, "Alfred Moore," in S. A. Ashe, ed., *Biog. Hist. of N. C.,* vol. II (1905); W. H. Hoyt, ed., *The Papers of Archibald D. Murphey* (2 vols., 1914); address of Junius Davis, Apr. 29, 1899, in 124 *N. C. Reports,* 882–92; *Am. State Papers, Indian Affairs,* vol. I (1832); *Raleigh Reg.,* Nov. 1, 1810.]   A. R. N.

MOORE, ANDREW (1752–May 24, 1821), political leader, representative and senator from Virginia, was the son of Mary (Evans) and David Moore, who emigrated from the north of Ireland and settled in the Valley of Virginia. He was born at "Cannicello," about twenty miles south of Staunton, in that part of Augusta County which is now Rockbridge County. After attaining some education at the local log college, Augusta Academy (now Washington and Lee University) he went to Williamsburg, where he studied law under George Wythe. He qualified as an attorney about 1774. When the Revolution

began he asserted his leadership by persuading the neighborhood youths to enlist under him and, as head of a company of the 9th Virginia Regiment of the Continental Line, he had one or more important tours of service. He never advanced beyond a captaincy in the Revolution but, later, as a militia officer reached the rank of major-general. Soon after the Revolution he married Sarah, the daughter of Andrew Reid of Rockbridge County. In his early thirties he had become a political leader of the very important Valley section of Virginia. This leadership was recognized in the state legislature, to which he was consistently elected during the decade before the organization of the federal government in 1789. He became one of Madison's chief lieutenants in the contests against such measures as the emission of paper money, an assessment for religion, and the confiscation of British debts. Likewise he joined with Madison and did service in the movements for religious liberty, the reform in the state court system, and the reorganization of the federal government. While he played a minor part on the floor of the Virginia ratification convention of 1788, he proved his worth to Madison and his colleagues by refusing to be influenced by a nearly successful attempt of the anti-federalists to change the sentiment of his constituents after he had been elected as a federalist. On June 28, 1788, he was elected a member of the privy council, for which he qualified on Nov. 4.

Though one of the younger Valley leaders he was chosen as the representative from his section to the First Congress in 1789 and was reelected for four successive terms. In the House he continued as a Madison lieutenant, opposing drastic amendments to the new Constitution, fighting against the Bank of the United States and, later, the Alien and Sedition Acts. He also joined heartily with Madison and White in the various maneuvers that finally succeeded in bringing the new capital to the banks of the Potomac. His independence, as well as his loyalty to his section, is indicated in his refusal to vote with Madison for the first tariff measures because they contained provisions unfavorable to his frontier section, such as the salt duties and the distillery excise. In 1799, after an absence of ten years, he returned with Madison to the Virginia legislature for the 1799–1800 session and helped to defeat the set of resolutions that proposed to repudiate those of 1798. In the next session, 1800–01, he served in the upper house of the legislature. In 1800 he was a presidential elector on the Republican ticket. The next year he was appointed as one of the commissioners to adjust the boundary line between Tennessee and Virginia, but he was prevented from serving because he accepted the federal appointment to be marshal of the western district of Va. (*Calendar, post,* vol. IX, pp. 205, 276). He was reëlected to Congress but, only after successfully contesting the election with Thomas Lewis, was he able to serve from Mar. 5 to Aug. 11, 1804, when he resigned in order to accept appointment to the United States Senate. He served in the Senate as an administration supporter until March 1809. In the following year he was appointed United States marshal for the state of Virginia and continued in that position until his resignation just before his death (*The Writings of James Monroe,* ed. by S. M. Hamilton, vol. VI, 1902, p. 176). His most important non-political service was in behalf of the academy he had himself attended. He was active in obtaining a charter from the legislature in 1782, served as a trustee from 1782 to 1821, and was largely instrumental in enlisting the sympathy and material aid of Washington for the permanent establishment of the institution which later became Washington and Lee University.

[Sketch by H. B. Grigsby, in *Washington and Lee Hist. Papers,* no. 2 (1890) ; *Biog. Dire. tory Am. Cong.* (1928) ; *Calendar of Va. State Papers,* vols. I, p. 235, III, p. 75, IV, pp. 461, 508, 543, 586, V, pp. 241, 394, VIII, p. 477, IX, pp. 75, 205, 216, 276, 414, 425 ; *Va. Mag. of Hist.,* Oct. 1900, p. 123 ; J. A. Waddell, *Annals of Augusta County, Va.,* 2nd ed. (1902).]   F. H. H.

MOORE, ANNIE AUBERTINE WOODWARD (Sept. 27, 1841–Sept. 22, 1929), musician, author, translator, known also under the pseudonym Auber Forestier, was born in Montgomery County, Pa., the daughter of Joseph Janvier Woodward and Elizabeth Graham (Cox). Educated in private schools in Philadelphia, Pa., and later by private tutors, she specialized in music and the Scandinavian languages, thus preparing herself for the specific line of endeavor which she had in mind and in which she was to make her mark. One of the earliest students of Scandinavian music in America, she began in 1880 to give musical lecture-recitals, being a pioneer in that type of educational entertainment. She continued active on the lecture-stage for some years, giving talks in different cities on music and musicians with illustrative piano playing, and lectures on musical-literary subjects. In 1880 she published *The Spell-bound Fiddler,* a translation from the work of Kristofer N. Janson [*q.v.*]. Subsequently she collaborated with Rasmus Björn Anderson, professor of Scandinavian languages and literature at the University of Wisconsin, in the transla-

tion of Björnstjerne Björnson's *Synnöve Solbakken* (1881) ; *Arne* (1881) ; *A Happy Boy* (1881) ; *The Fisher Maiden* (1882) ; *Captain Mansana and Other Stories* (1882) ; *The Bridal March and Other Stories* (1882) ; *Magnhild* (1883) ; and under the pseudonym of Auber Forestier, in the compilation of *The Norway Music Album* (1881). In 1886 she assisted in translating into English Thuiskon Hauptner's *Voice Culture.* On Dec. 22, 1887, at Madison, Wis., she married Samuel H. Moore.

From 1900 to 1912 she conducted classes in the history and theory of music and musical appreciation and analysis at the Madison Musical College. She was also literary critic for the *Wisconsin State Journal,* from 1900 to 1911, and editor of the department of music in the *Simmons Magazine,* 1910–12. In these later years she published various musical works: *For My Musical Friend* (1900), *For Every Music Lover* (1902), *Faustina, A Venetian Queen of Song* (1918) ; and a collection, *Songs of the North* (1907), also a translation. She died in Madison, Wis.

[*Who's Who in America,* 1916–17; *N. Y. Times,* Sept. 24, 1929; *Capital Times* (Madison, Wis.), Sept. 23, 1929.]   F. H. M.

MOORE, BARTHOLOMEW FIGURES (Jan. 29, 1801–Nov. 27, 1878), lawyer, was born in Halifax County, N. C. He was the son of James Moore, a native of Virginia, and Sally Lowe Lewis of Edgecombe County, N. C. Entering the sophomore class of the University of North Carolina, he was graduated in 1820. He then studied law, was admitted to the bar in 1823, and began practice at Nashville, Nash County, where for twelve years he barely made a living. Employing these lean years in close study, he became, while still a young man, a very learned lawyer, well versed in statute law, and profound in his knowledge of the common law. In 1835 he returned to Halifax County and finally won professional success. Also in a modest way he entered politics. He had been a Crawford Republican, but he disliked intensely Jacksonian Democracy and cast his lot with Clay. In 1836, and again in 1840, 1842, and 1844, he was a member of the House of Commons where he was an active champion of internal improvements, public schools, and the establishment of asylums and hospitals for the unfortunate. From 1848 to 1851 he was attorney-general, resigning upon his selection as one of the commissioners to revise the statute law of the state. The *Revised Code of North Carolina . . . 1854* (1855) is a monument to his legal learning. He achieved his first wide reputation as a lawyer by his brief in *State* vs. *Will* (18 *N. C.*, 121), a case in which the court upheld him in affirming the right of a slave to protect himself by force from unlawful violence, even from his master. This marked a notable lessening of the rigor of the slave code. All of his cases were admirably prepared and forcibly presented, but without a trace of oratory or eloquence. In appearance and manner he was austere, and, utterly frank, he was frequently impetuous and irascible in speech.

As the Civil War approached, Moore found himself out of sympathy with the trend of Southern sentiment. While he believed that the South was justly aggrieved, he denied the right of secession and never changed his opinion. He refused to be a candidate for the secession convention, and his only concession to the Confederate cause was his acceptance of a place on the state board of claims. He refused to take the oath of allegiance to the Confederacy, although he was thereby debarred from practice in the Confederate courts, and, while he took no part in any peace movement, he made no secret of his love for the Union and his wish for its restoration. When the war closed, President Johnson summoned him to Washington for advice on North Carolina affairs, and on May 22, 1865, explained his plan of restoration in detail and showed him the amnesty and North Carolina proclamations which were ready to be issued. Moore vehemently opposed the whole plan, denying its constitutionality, and urged the President to employ the existing legislatures to summon conventions and thus preserve legal continuity. Johnson was friendly but firm, and when he invited Moore to participate in the selection of a provisional governor, the latter declined to have any part in it. He was, however, a member of the convention of 1865 and its outstanding leader. He drew the ordinance declaring the ordinance of secession null and void from the beginning, and favored vacating all offices, but he bitterly resented the President's insistence upon the repudiation of the war debt and voted against the ordinance. He served on the commission to suggest such changes in the laws as were made necessary by emancipation, and wrote the report, later adopted by the legislature, which recognized the citizenship of the freedmen and granted them substantial equality before the law.

In the second session of the convention in 1866 Moore drew up the new constitution, induced the convention to adopt it and submit it to the people, and, in a powerful argument, unsuccessfully urged its ratification. He had little sympathy with the conservatives who were in power in the state from 1866 to 1868, and even less

with the radicals. He opposed congressional reconstruction because he believed it unconstitutional and because he foresaw its evil results, but he saw no hope of immediate relief and took no active part in politics. In 1869, however, when certain justices of the supreme court and other judges took an active part in a political demonstration in behalf of the Republican party, he drew up a solemn protest which was signed by 107 other lawyers and published. The supreme court at its succeeding session ordered the signers disabled from appearing until they could show cause to the contrary, and served the rule upon Moore and two others. Upon their disavowal of intent to bring the court into contempt, the court, which found itself in an awkward position, discharged the rule. Moore continued in active practice, chiefly in the federal courts, until his death. His practice in the United States Supreme Court was large and successful. He was twice married: on Dec. 2, 1828, to Louisa, the daughter of George Boddie, of Nash County, N. C., who died in 1829, and on Apr. 19, 1835, to her sister Lucy.

[S. A. Ashe, ed., *Biog. Hist. of N. C.*, vol. V (1906); J. H. Wheeler, *Reminiscences and Memoirs of N. C.* (1884); J. G. deR. Hamilton, *Reconstruction in N. C.* (1914); E. G. Haywood, address in *Tribute to the Memory of Bartholomew Figures Moore* (1878); *Univ. Mag.* (N. C.), May 1878; the *Observer* (Raleigh, N. C.), Nov. 28, 1878.]   J. G. deR. H.

MOORE, BENJAMIN (Oct. 5, 1748–Feb. 27, 1816), second Protestant Episcopal bishop of New York and president of Columbia College, was a descendant of Rev. John Moore, one of the settlers of Newtown, Long Island. Benjamin was born in Newtown, the son of Samuel Moore, a farmer, and his wife Sarah, daughter of John Fish. He graduated at the head of his class at King's College in 1768, and after studying theology with Rev. Samuel Auchmuty [*q.v.*], went to England, where he received deacon's and priest's orders from the Bishop of London in June 1774 (Dix, *post*, II, 319–20). He became an assistant minister of Trinity Church, New York, in February 1775. After the flight of Myles Cooper [*q.v.*], the Loyalist president of King's College, in May of that year, Moore was made president *pro tempore* and retained the title until 1784. When the college building was taken over by the military officials in the spring of 1776, Moore moved his family and the remaining students to 13 Wall Street, where some instruction was carried on until the British took the city. He remained loyal to the King throughout the war, and acted as deputy chaplain for the hospital in the college building. In November

1783, before the British forces had evacuated New York City, the Loyalist rector of Trinity, Rev. Charles Inglis [q.v.], resigned, and Moore was elected in his place. The election was immediately challenged by the Whig members of the parish, because of Moore's "avowed sympathies with the British cause and his dislike of the new government," and he wisely withdrew (Dix, II, 3). Upon the reorganization of King's College as Columbia in 1784, he was appointed professor of rhetoric and logic, a position he held until 1786, and in December 1800, when the rectorship of Trinity was again offered him, he assumed office without opposition. After the resignation of Bishop Provoost [q.v.] in 1801, Moore was elected his successor, and was consecrated at Trenton, Sept. 11, 1801. In the same year, Rev. Charles Henry Wharton [q.v.] resigned the presidency of Columbia after a few months' service, and on Dec. 31, Moore was elected to that position. He held these three offices until February 1811, when an attack of paralysis incapacitated him for any further public service. An assistant bishop (John Henry Hobart) and an assistant rector (Abraham Beach) were elected to take over his church duties, and on May 6 he resigned the presidency of the college. After suffering repeated paralytic attacks, he died, early in 1816, "at his residence at Greenwich, near New York."

He filled with acceptance, if not distinction, the various offices to which he was called. Both Columbia and Trinity were in financial straits during his terms of office, and he left them unimproved, although it was under his rectorship that Trinity erected St. John's Chapel in Varick Street. As a preacher he commanded attention and respect by his dignity and unaffected solemnity of manner and the skilful management of a naturally feeble voice. In appearance he was slender and graceful, of medium stature, and long-faced. His only publications were sermons, of which a two-volume collection was published posthumously (1824) by his son.

On Apr. 20, 1778, he married Charity, daughter of Maj. Thomas Clarke, deceased, a British officer whose large estate, "Chelsea," in Greenwich Village, Manhattan, was ultimately inherited by the Moores (New York Gazette, May 2, 1778; Collections of the New York Historical Society for the Year 1900, 1901, p. 37). Their only child was Clement Clarke Moore [q.v.], theologian and lexicographer.

[W. B. Sprague, Annals Am. Pulpit, V (1859), 299–304; Morgan Dix, A Hist. of the Parish of Trinity Ch. in the City of N. Y. (4 vols., 1898–1906), John B. Pine, "Benjamin Moore," in Columbia Univ. Quart., June 1900; N. Y. Evening Post, Feb. 28, 1816; J. W. Moore, Rev. John Moore of Newtown, L. I. and Some of His Descendants (1903).]
M. H. T—s.

MOORE, CHARLES HERBERT (Apr. 10, 1840–Feb. 15, 1930), artist, teacher, writer on the fine arts, was born in New York City, the son of Charles and Jane Maria (Benson) Moore. His early education was received in the New York public schools. He did not attend any college, but in 1890 he was given the honorary degree of A.M. by Harvard. In New York he received some training as a landscape painter, but while still a young man he moved to Catskill, where he lived for a number of years.

In 1871 he was called to Harvard as instructor in freehand drawing and water color in the Lawrence Scientific School. Three years later he was invited by Prof. Charles Eliot Norton [q.v.], who had just been appointed lecturer on the history of the fine arts, to offer to undergraduates in Harvard College a course on the principles of design, painting, sculpture, and architecture. This appointment marked the real beginning of his long career as a teacher, and also the beginning of the gradual establishment of fine arts on an equal footing with other subjects included under the general head of liberal education in American colleges and universities. Norton believed that an educated man should know something of the history and principles of the fine arts (the visual arts), and Moore insisted that some actual practice in drawing and painting was necessary as a means of thorough understanding and appreciation of works of art. In developing this rather revolutionary method of teaching fine arts, Moore had the vigorous backing of President Eliot. From this time on Moore was primarily a teacher. He was appointed assistant professor in 1891 and professor in 1896. When the Fogg Art Museum was built in 1895 he was made first curator, and the following year, director, a position which he held until he retired from active service in 1909.

Moore owed much to Ruskin as well as to Norton. The winter of 1876–77 he spent in Europe. He called on Ruskin at Brantwood with a letter of introduction from Norton, and later joined him in Venice. They worked together on Carpaccio's "Vision of St. Ursula," which was put into a separate room for Ruskin's benefit. A small study of the whole picture by Ruskin is in the drawing school at Oxford, and a full-sized copy of the head by Moore is in the Fogg Museum. In a letter to Norton from Venice in October 1876 Ruskin wrote: "I am very much delighted at having Mr. Moore for a companion—we have perfect sympathy in all art matters and are not in dissonance in any others. His voice continually reminds me of yours.—And he's not at all so wicked nor so republican as you, and minds all I say!" (E. T. Cook and Alexander Wedderburn, *The Works of John Ruskin*, 1909, vol. XXXVII, 211). Moore visited Ruskin in Verona and saw him also in Florence; and it must have been at this period that they returned together over the Simplon. The Fogg Museum owns a number of water colors or scenes in and about the Simplon village done by Moore in this and later years. As a painter Moore was perhaps the most accomplished of those who may be thought of as Ruskin's pupils. His handling of body-color and his general point of view place him with the English painter Brabazon, only that he was usually much more precise. A few of his copies—one especially of Botticelli's "Calumny"—have hardly been surpassed. His copies of paintings and most of his studies of natural form were made for use in connection with his teaching, and they are mainly in the collection of the Fogg Museum.

Moore's wide reputation came principally from his study of medieval architecture, to which he devoted much of his time from about 1885. The results of this study are embodied in a series of books, the best known of which is *Development and Character of Gothic Architecture* (1890, revised edition, 1899). He was inspired more especially by Viollet-le-Duc, and he stands close to the latter as a pioneer in the study of the structural side of medieval architecture. Since he found this exemplified notably in the French architecture of the Île de France, he proposed that the term Gothic be employed exclusively in this connection. Such limitation in the use of the term, as well as some of his conclusions in regard to the development and character of English architecture, was objected to, particularly by English writers, but many of them have expressed their great appreciation of the clearness and conviction with which his opinions were stated and the necessity he put upon them of defining their own views with more precision. Perhaps his most extreme statement of the case for expressiveness of function and structure is in *Character of Renaissance Architecture,* published in 1905.

It has been said that the keynote of Moore's character was his hatred of sham, and that in art, as in life, he demanded above all things honesty and simplicity. It was this quality which attracted him to the study of medieval architecture and endeared him to many of his students and to his friends. His former pupils remember him as a picturesque figure, dressed usually in warm-colored tweeds and an English cloth hat. Regular exercise, principally in the sawing of

wood for the fireplaces, kept him in good physical condition, and even when he retired from teaching his cheek showed a round and youthful outline through his full white beard.

On July 19, 1865, he married Mary Jane Tomlinson of Schenectady, N. Y., by whom he had a daughter, Elizabeth, who later assisted him in illustrating with pen-drawings his book on Gothic architecture. After the death of his first wife he married, Dec. 30, 1881, Elizabeth Fisk Hewins. Upon retiring, in 1909, he built a house at Hartfield, Hartley Wintney, Winchfield, Hants, in England, where he lived with his wife and daughter until his death. Here he continued his work on architecture, and in 1912 published *The Mediæval Church Architecture of England.* An interest in Swedenborg increased toward the end of his life and resulted in his publishing in 1918, *Swedenborg: Servant of God.*

[*Who's Who in America*, 1930–31; W. R. Lethaby, "The Late C. H. Moore, A.M.," in *Jour. of the Royal Institute of British Architects*, Mar. 22, 1930; *Times* (London), Feb. 18, 22, 1930; *Harvard Grads. Mag.,* June 1909; *Art News*, Feb. 22, 1930; *Boston Evening Transcript*, Feb. 17, 1930.]   A. P.

MOORE, CLARENCE LEMUEL ELISHA

(May 12, 1876–Dec. 5, 1931), mathematician, the son of George Taylor and Lydia Ann (Bradshaw) Moore, was born in Bainbridge, Ohio. His father was a grain dealer and was descended from the early settlers. After some years of school teaching, Moore entered the Ohio State University, from which he was graduated in 1901. He then pursued graduate study in mathematics at Cornell University, from which he received the degree of M.A. in 1902, and that of Ph.D. in 1904. From this time until his death, he was associated with the Massachusetts Institute of Technology, where he was successively instructor, assistant professor (1909), associate professor (1916), and professor (1920). Shortly after going to the Institute, he spent a year in study abroad, principally at Turin under Segre, and the influence of the Italian geometers profoundly affected his later mathematical work. On June 11, 1913, he married Belle Pease Fuller of Springfield, Mass.

He was outstanding in all three of the fields of activity of an American educator: teaching, administration, and research. He conducted classes in mathematics as applied to aeronautics; for eleven years he was in charge of the course in general science and engineering. In creative mathematical work, he maintained a vigorous interest throughout his entire career, and his accomplishments were large, although he was all his life handicapped by deficient eyesight.

His numerous published papers deal principally with geometry. He began with problems concerning algebraic geometry in Euclidean space of three and higher dimensions, and later proceeded to the differential geometry of Riemannian manifolds. He also (partly with H. B. Phillips) did some work on the applications of vector analysis to geometry. Taken as a whole, his work possesses unusual unity, and gives evidence of a real feeling for vital problems and a keen geometric insight into them. His papers (partly with E. B. Wilson) applying the methods of Ricci to the geometry of hyperspace, a field since made popular by the interest in the theory of relativity, showed him to be one of the first American mathematicians to recognize the importance of these methods. His last few papers (partly with Philip Franklin) dealt with the geometry of Pfaffians. He was a member of various mathematical societies, and a fellow of the American Academy of Arts and Sciences. From 1921 to his death he edited the *Journal of Mathematics and Physics,* which was founded at the Institute of Technology largely through his efforts.

[D. J. Struik, in *Jour. of Math. and Phys.,* vol. XI (1932) gives a complete list of scientific publications; see also D. J. Struik, in *Bull. Am. Math. Soc., Mar.* 1932; Philip Franklin, *Proc. Am. Acad. of Arts and Sciences,* vol. LXVII (1933); *Technology Rev.,* Jan. 1932; *Who's Who in America,* 1930–31; *Boston Transcript,* Dec. 5, 1931.]   P. F.

MOORE, CLEMENT CLARKE (July 15, 1779–July 10, 1863), Hebrew scholar, writer of verse, was born at "Chelsea" in New York, son of the Rev. Benjamin Moore [*q.v.*] and Charity, second daughter of Maj. Thomas Clarke, whose estate fell to Clement Clarke Moore's parents and was inherited by him, their only child. After tutoring the boy at home, his father sent him to Columbia College, where he was graduated in 1798. It was the father's hope that the son would take orders, but he preferred to serve the Church as a layman. If the ascription to him of the anonymous *Observations upon Certain Passages in Mr. Jefferson's Notes on Virginia Which Appear to Have a Tendency to Subvert Religion and Establish a False Philosophy* (1804) be correct, we have an indication of the temper and trend of the young man's thought. He regrets "that more of the well-disposed among his young countrymen do not devote their leisure hours to the attainment of useful learning, rather than to frivolous amusements or political wrangling" (p. 32). His own addiction to "the attainment of useful learning" is shown by his devotion to the study of Hebrew, and led to his publishing in 1809 *A Compendious Lexi-*

con of the Hebrew Language: In Two Volumes. It is a creditable piece of work and doubtless fulfilled his hope that "his young countrymen" would "find it of some service to them, as a sort of pioneer, in breaking down the impediments which present themselves at the entrance of the study of Hebrew" (p. xii). On Nov. 20, 1813, he was married to Catharine Elizabeth Taylor.

After his father's death he took an increasing interest in ecclesiastical affairs. In February 1819 he offered, through Bishop Hobart, sixty lots in New York City (including the present Chelsea Square) on condition that "the buildings of the theological school should be erected thereon." This gift, together with one from a New York layman two years later, made the General Theological Seminary possible. In 1821 he became professor of Biblical learning and interpretation of Scripture in the diocesan seminary at New York, and in 1823, a professor in the General Theological Seminary, into which the diocesan seminary was merged. In 1825 the first permanent seminary building was erected on the ground he had given. He continued to serve the Seminary as professor of Oriental and Greek literature until his resignation in 1850. This same year he published *George Castriot, Surnamed Scanderbeg, King of Albania.* It is based upon an English translation of Jacques Lavardin's work, and the author's task was to "concentrate Lavardin's history by rendering the language more concise" (Preface, p. 6). It is, as are all his serious works, written in a dignified prose based on Johnsonian standards.

Moore is chiefly remembered, however, for his ballad beginning " 'Twas the night before Christmas, when all through the house . . ." According to tradition, he wrote the verses in 1822 as a Christmas gift for his own children; they were transcribed by a guest of the household, and by her given to the press in Troy, N. Y., the following year. First published anonymously in the *Troy Sentinel,* Dec. 23, 1823, the poem was reprinted in school readers and in a collection of the author's verse, *Poems* (1844). It has since been included in many different anthologies, and, losing none of its original freshness, has been loved by American children for more than a hundred years.

[J. W. Moore, *Rev. John Moore of Newtown, Long Island, and Some of His Descendants* (1903); E. A. Hoffman, "Hist. Sketch of the Gen. Theological Sem.," in W. S. Perry, *The Hist. of the Am. Episc. Ch. 1587–1883* (1885), vol. II; W. S. Pelletreau, *The Visit of Saint Nicholas . . . Facsimile of the Original MS. with Life of the Author* (1897); Clarence Cook, "The Author of 'A Visit from St. Nicholas,'" in *Century Mag.,* Dec. 1897; Journals of the N. Y. Diocesan Convention, and minutes of the trustees and faculty of the Gen. Theological Sem.; *N. Y. Times,* July 14, 1863.]

H. E. W. F.

MOORE, CLIFFORD HERSCHEL (Mar. 11, 1866–Aug. 31, 1931), classicist, was born in Sudbury, Mass., where his ancestors had lived since the earliest settlement of the town. His parents were John Herschel and Julia Ann (McCullough) Moore. He studied at the public school in Sudbury and the Framingham High School. Graduating from Harvard College in 1889, he immediately assumed duties as classical master in the Belmont School for Boys, Belmont, Cal. On July 23, 1890, he married Lorena Leadbetter of Charlestown, Mass. In 1892 he succeeded E. G. Coy as professor of Greek at Phillips Academy, Andover, Mass., and later (1902) became a member of its board of trustees. When (July 9, 1892) the National Education Association appointed the Committee of Ten, headed by President Eliot, to examine the state of secondary education in the United States, Moore's ability as a leader and counselor caused him to be chosen as one of the sub-committee which reported on the study of Greek. In 1894 he was appointed instructor in Latin at the University of Chicago, where he was soon promoted to an assistant professorship, which he held until 1898. Receiving leave of absence, he went to the University of Munich, and in 1897 received there the degree of Ph.D.

The following year he accepted President Eliot's invitation to return to Harvard as assistant professor of Greek and Latin. In 1900 he issued a revision of Frederic De Forest Allen's *Medea of Euripides,* in 1902, an edition of *The Odes, Epodes, and Carmen Saeculare of Horace,* and in 1906 *Elements of Latin* (with J. J. Schlicher). He contributed articles to various scientific periodicals and to the *New International Encyclopaedia.* Advanced to the professorship of Latin in 1905, he served that year at the American School of Classical Studies in Rome, Italy. In 1913 he was Harvard Exchange professor with Western colleges. In 1925 he was elected to the Pope Professorship of Latin at Harvard. In this year appeared the first volume of his *Histories of Tacitus* (Loeb Classical Library), followed in 1931 by the second. Combining interest in the more rigorous disciplines of Latin grammar and epigraphy with a wide knowledge of literature and philosophy, he made the religions of Greece and Rome the special field of his research at Harvard and the subject of his course before the Lowell Institute in Boston (1914). The substance of

these lectures is embodied in *The Religious Thought of the Greeks, from Homer to the Triumph of Christianity* (1916, 1925), an admirable discussion of Hellenic ideas concerning the gods and the relations and obligations of men toward them. As president of the American Philological Association (1920), he delivered a notable address on "Prophecy in the Ancient Epic" (*Harvard Studies in Classical Philology,* vol. XXXII, 1921). In 1918 he gave at Harvard the Ingersoll Lecture on the immortality of man. His latest work, completed just before his death, was *Ancient Beliefs in the Immortality of the Soul* (1931).

As an administrative officer he worked with devoted industry, resourcefulness, and tact. During the last years of the World War he took an active part in the difficult task of organizing the Student's Army Training Corps. After the war his executive talents were promptly recognized by his promotion to the deanship of the Graduate School of Arts and Sciences, and later, to that of the Faculty of Arts and Sciences, in which capacity he displayed extraordinary ability as director of the budget and of the curriculum. His wide acquaintance in other colleges at home and abroad, with the hospitable welcome which he and his wife extended to all, made his house in Cambridge the congenial resort of old and young alike. Though he often suffered from ill health, he was fond of outdoor sports. His teaching was lucid and incisive, lighted with humor and apt illustration; his intellectual and moral standards were high. No man did more to improve the relations between secondary schools and the college, and none had greater influence in shaping the new policies of Harvard from 1918 until his death.

[*Class of 1889 Harvard College* (1914); *Report of the President of Harvard College for 1930–31* (1932); *Harvard University Gazette,* Dec. 5, 1931; *Boston Evening Transcript,* Aug. 31, 1931; the *Times* (London), Sept. 8, 1931; *Harvard Alumni Bull.,* Oct. 2, 1931); the *Nation,* Oct. 7, 1931; personal acquaintance.]

C. B. G.

MOORE, EDWARD MOTT (July 15, 1814–Mar. 3, 1902), surgeon, was born in Rahway, N. J., the son of Lindley Murray Moore and Abigail Lydia (Mott). His father was a native of Nova Scotia, the son of Samuel Moore, a New Jersey Quaker who joined the Loyalist emigration after the Revolution; his mother was descended from ancestors who settled about 1644 at Hempstead, L. I. After Edward's birth the family moved successively to New York City, to Westchester, where the father conducted a school, and in 1830 to Rochester, N. Y. Edward commenced his education under his father and began the study of Latin and Greek at the age of four. A robust boy, he was early interested in farming and became one of the prize broadcast sowers of grain in the vicinity. He prepared for college under his father's direction and entered the Rensselaer School at Troy (now Rensselaer Polytechnic Institute) in the class with James Hall [*q.v.*], who was for many years state geologist of New York. He withdrew soon, however, and in 1833 began the study of medicine at Rochester with Dr. Anson Coleman and in 1835 entered the College of Physicians and Surgeons, New York. Later he became a medical student at the University of Pennsylvania, where he was graduated M.D. in 1838. Thereafter he spent one and a half years as interne at Blockley Hospital, where he was associated with Dr. C. W. Pennock. He is given credit for original work on the heart in Pennock's American edition of James Hope's *Treatise on the Diseases of the Heart and Great Vessels* (1842).

Unusually well equipped, he returned to Rochester in 1840 and entered upon the practice of his profession. His ability was immediately recognized and in 1842 he was called to the faculty of the Vermont Medical College, Woodstock, where he taught surgery for eleven years. For a part of that time he also taught surgery at the Berkshire Medical College, Pittsfield, Mass., and in 1852 he became professor of anatomy at Buffalo University. Resigning from these professorships in 1853 or early 1854, he taught surgery at the Starling Medical College, Columbus, Ohio, from 1853 to 1856. In the latter year he severed his Columbus connection and returned to the University of Buffalo, where as professor of surgery he was associated with Dalton, Flint, Hamilton, and others, and continued to teach for twenty-six years.

In 1882 he returned to Rochester. Here he was surgeon-in-chief of St. Mary's Hospital and organized the Infants' Hospital. He was president of the medical associations of Monroe County, Central New York, and New York State, of the American Medical Association, and of the American Surgical Association. In those years such was the lack of knowledge of fractures and dislocations and so great the deformities resulting therefrom that his interest was challenged, and he devoted much attention to the study of their cause and treatment. Before the microscope had come into common use, he examined ground bones microscopically, embodying his conclusions in many lectures and monographs. He contributed "Dislocations" to *A Reference Handbook of Medical Sciences,* ed-

ited by A. H. Buck (vol. II, 1886), and "Gangrene and Gangrenous Diseases" to the *International Encyclopaedia of Surgery,* edited by John Ashhurst (1st ed., vol. II, 1882; 2nd ed., vols. I, 1888, and VII, 1895). His studies of fracture of the collar bone, of the superior end of the humerus, of the elbow joint, and of Colles' Fracture are recognized as pieces of original work, the correctness of which has since been proved by the use of the X-ray. Interested in communicable diseases, he became a member of the Rochester board of health and was first president of the New York state board of health. As an educator, he became a member and president of the board of trustees of the University of Rochester. He early advocated parks and was first president of the Rochester Park Commission. He was a man of robust frame and cultivated manner, kind, helpful, generous, courageous, who freely gave to others all that was in him during a long and useful life. He was married in 1847 to Lucy Richard Prescott of Windsor, Vt. Eight children were born to them, two of whom became successful physicians.

[*Boston Medic. and Surgic. Jour.,* Mar. 13, 1902; *Buffalo Medic. Jour.,* Apr., July 1902; *Jour. Am. Medic. Asso.,* Mar. 15, 1902; *Trans. Medic. Soc. of the State of N. Y.,* 1903; H. A. Kelly and W. L. Burrage, *Am. Medic. Biogs.* (1920); T. C. Cornell, *Adam and Anne Mott: Their Ancestors and Descendants* (1890); *Rochester Democrat and Chronicle,* Mar. 4, 1902; personal acquaintance.]
G. W. G.

MOORE, EDWIN WARD (June 1810–Oct. 5, 1865), naval officer, was born in Alexandria, Va. After attending school at the Alexandria Academy he entered the navy as a midshipman, Jan. 1, 1825, in which rank he served first on board the *Hornet* of the West India Squadron and later on board the *Fairfield* of the Mediterranean Squadron. On reaching the rank of passed midshipman in 1831, he was again attached to the *Fairfield,* at this time stationed in the West Indies. Promoted lieutenant from Mar. 3, 1835, he on July 16, 1839, resigned from the service, as it offered little opportunity for advancement.

On Apr. 21, 1839, he had been offered by the Republic of Texas command of its navy, then consisting of the recently acquired armed steamer *Zavala* and a worthless brig. Between May and December 1839 the navy was increased by the addition of the flagship *Austin,* 20 guns, together with a brig and three schooners. Moore's commission, which was not issued until July 20, 1842, gave him the rank of "post captain commanding." His courtesy title was commodore. Before the last of the new fleet had left Schott & Whitney's Baltimore yard he visited New York, where, in attempting to enlist seamen, he came into conflict with the United States authorities and was compelled to leave the city. In 1840–41 he cruised off the Mexican coast with a fleet of five vessels to expedite the peace negotiations of the Texan diplomat James Treat. When these negotiations collapsed Moore not only swept Mexican commerce from the Gulf but also entered into a *de facto* alliance with Yucatecan rebels and captured the town of Tabasco, upon which he levied a contribution of $25,000. After refitting his ships he surveyed the Texan coast and made a chart of it, which was published in New York and also by the British Admiralty. In the winter of 1841–42 he again cruised with three vessels of his fleet off the coast of Yucatan, thereby saving the federalist Yucatecans from a hasty peace with centralist Santa Anna and continuing an advantageous alliance with the Texans. After capturing several small vessels, he returned to Galveston in May. Thence he proceeded to New Orleans to refit his fleet for the enforcement of a blockade of Mexico, proclaimed by President Sam Houston in retaliation for Mexico's invasion of March 1842. Finances delayed the refitting, by which time a favorable turn in Texan relations with the United States caused Houston to delay further the proposed naval offensive by withholding funds, but without taking Moore or the Yucatecan allies into his confidence. In February 1843 there arrived at New Orleans two commissioners appointed to carry out a secret act of the Texas Congress providing for the sale of the navy. Previous to their arrival Moore had agreed with the authorities of Yucatan, in consideration of the payment of a sum of money sufficient to finish refitting the fleet, to attack the Mexican squadron blockading the Yucatan coast. In accordance with this agreement he attacked the squadron on April 30 and again on May 16, 1843, and in both engagements defeated it. In the second engagement both sides suffered considerable loss and two Mexican ships, *Guadalupe* and *Montezuma,* were badly damaged. On June 1 Moore received a proclamation of Houston declaring that he was guilty of "disobedience, contumacy, and mutiny" and suspending him from his command. He proceeded at once to Galveston and asked for a trial. After a joint committee of the Texas House and Senate had completely vindicated him, he was tried by a court martial and found not guilty on eighteen counts and guilty in respect to matter and form on four counts. The decision, which was a victory for him, was disapproved by Houston. In 1843 he published *To the People of Texas,*

which, in addition to being a personal vindication, is today the best collection of source materials on the Texan navy.

No small part of Moore's later years was spent in prosecuting his claims, in the course of which he published a number of other pamphlets, against the governments of Texas and the United States. From Texas he received more than $20,000 in settlement of claims and payment for relief. A claim in behalf of himself and his fellow officers to incorporation into the federal navy was bitterly opposed by the federal naval officers. Finally, in 1857, Congress voted the Texan officers five years' pay. The last years of Moore's life were passed in New York City, where he was engaged in devising a machine which he believed would revolutionize marine engineering. He died suddenly of apoplexy, leaving, so far as known, no children. In 1849 he was married to Emma M. (Stockton) Cox of Philadelphia. He has been described by those who knew him as a man of science and undoubted gallantry, but having no head for details.

[Record of Officers, Bureau of Navigation, 1825–40; *Tex. State Hist. Asso. Quart.,* Jan. 1904, July, Oct. 1909; *N. Y. Herald,* Oct. 10, 1865; E. W. Moore, *To the People of Texas,* mentioned above; G. P. Garrison, "Diplomatic Correspondence of the Republic of Texas," *Ann. Report Am. Hist. Asso.,* 1907 (1908), vol. II and *1908* (1911), vol. II; Navy registers.]   C.O.P.

MOORE, ELY (July 4, 1798–Jan. 27, 1860), labor leader and congressman, was born near Belvidere, N. J., the son of Moses and Mary (Coryell) Moore and the descendant of John Moore who emigrated from England and settled in Lynn, Mass., before 1641. His education was received partly in the public schools of his birthplace and partly in New York City, where he studied medicine. After a few years of practice he abandoned the profession of medicine to become a printer at a time when great changes were taking place in the printing industry and when technical knowledge on the part of publishers was becoming of less importance than business ability. Men with ambitions and those wishing to promote some special interest, such as politics, agriculture, or labor were crowding into the trade. In 1833 he was elected the first president of the newly formed federation of craft unions of the city of New York, the General Trades' Union (*Address Delivered before the General Trades' Union of the City of New-York,* 1833), and he edited a paper, the *National Trades' Union,* which became its official organ. He was chosen a member of a special commission appointed to investigate the subject of the competition of convict labor from state prisons hired out to contractors. The commission's report approving the continuation of prison labor was not at all satisfactory to the workingmen, who held a public meeting, condemned the report, and demanded his resignation. The demand was not enforced, and the same year he was chosen for a more prominent position in labor politics. In 1834 there was convened in New York a national convention of trades unions with delegates from six eastern cities which took the name of National Trades' Union, electing him its chairman. This position of prominence became a stepping stone to political preferment. The early trade unions had taken a strong stand against political activities, and the politicians, on their side, distrusted the unionists because of their fondness for forming independent parties. However, in New York at this time a working agreement existed with Tammany Hall, and with Tammany support he was elected in 1834 as representative in Congress. Two years later, the workingmen claimed that Tammany had not kept its pledges, deserted, and joined the Equal Rights party. In spite of the fact that he was again a Tammany candidate he received the workingmen's votes and was reëlected to Congress. At the expiration of his second term in 1839 he was appointed surveyor of the port of New York, and in 1845 marshal for the southern district of New York. After a few years he retired to his birthplace in New Jersey where he became the publisher and editor of the *Warren Journal*. About 1850 he emigrated to Kansas and in 1853 became the agent for the Miami and other Indian tribes. Two years later he was appointed register of the United States land office at Lecompton, Kan. In this position he served until his death. He was married twice: first, to Emma Contant who bore him six children and, second, to Mrs. Clara Baker.

[*Biog. Directory Am. Cong.* (1928); J. R. Commons and others, *Hist. of Labor in the U. S.* (1918), vol. I; J. W. Moore, *Rev. John Moore of Newtown, Long Island, and some of his descendants* (1903); *U. S. Mag. and Democratic Rev.*, Oct. 1837, pp. 74–86; *Kan. Natl. Democrat* (Lecompton), Feb. 2, 1860.] P. W. B.

MOORE, FRANK (Dec. 17, 1828–Aug. 10, 1904), author, editor, was baptized Horatio Franklin Moore, but is known only as Frank Moore. He was born in Concord, N. H., the son of Jacob Bailey Moore [*q.v.*] and Mary Adams Hill, and was a brother of George Henry Moore [*q.v.*]. He went to New York City in 1839 with his parents, and attended public school there, moving to Washington, D. C., in 1841 when his father took a position in the post-office in that city. In 1849 he accompanied his father to California. As a secretary to Minister Wash-

burn, he was attached to the American legation at Paris, France, 1869–72, during the Franco-Prussian War, returning to New York in the latter year. He became a member of the New York Historical Society in 1856, and is known for the many books he wrote and edited. Beginning with *Songs and Ballads of the American Revolution* (1856), his works appeared very regularly and included: *American Eloquence: a Collection of Speeches and Addresses* (1857); *Diary of the American Revolution from Newspapers and Original Documents* (2 vols., 1859–60); *Materials for History* (1861); *Heroes and Martyrs: Notable Men of the Time* (1862); *The Rebellion Record* (11 vols. and 1 supp., 1861–68); the Red, White and Blue Series (3 vols., 1864), comprising *Songs of the Soldiers, Personal and Political Ballads of the War,* and *Lyrics of Loyalty*; *Rebel Rhymes and Rhapsodies* (1864); *Speeches of Andrew Johnson* (1865); *Women of the War* (1866); *Anecdotes, Poetry and Incidents of the War* (1866); *Record of the Year* (2 vols., 1876); *Songs and Ballads of the Southern People* (1886); and others. He contributed to the *New York Criterion*, 1855–56, and to other American literary periodicals. His books on the history of the Revolutionary War and the Civil War are considered valuable compilations. He married Laura M. Bailey, daughter of the Hon. John Bailey of Dorchester, Mass., who died in Boston, Nov. 11, 1904. They had no children. Moore died in Waverly, Mass.

[Sources include: manuscript notes made by J. B. Moore and Geo. H. Moore, gathered by Thomas E. V. Smith; manuscript records in the possession of the N. Y. Hist. Soc.; E. S. Stearns, *Geneal. and Family Hist. of the State of N. H.* (1908), II, pp. 491–92; *Boston Transcript*, Aug. 10, 1904. Moore's diary of 36 volumes, covering the years 1877–94, is in the library of the N. H. Hist. Soc.] A. J. W.

MOORE, GABRIEL (1785?–June 9, 1845?), representative and senator in the federal Congress, governor of Alabama, was the son of Matthew and Letitia (Dalton) Moore and the grandson of John and Frances (Jouett) Moore of Albemarle County, Va. He was born in Stokes County, N. C. He removed to Huntsville, Mississippi Territory, about 1810 and entered upon the practice of law. He was soon sent to represent Madison County in the legislature of the territory. After he had served in this capacity for several years the territory was divided in 1817, and Madison County became a part of the new Territory of Alabama. He continued as representative under the new jurisdiction and was at once elected to the speakership of the lower house of the Assembly. When Ala-

Moore

bama became a state he sat in the convention of 1819 that framed her constitution. Immediately thereafter he was elected to the upper house of the new legislature, served in 1819 and 1820, and was chosen speaker in 1820. In 1821 he was sent to Congress and continued to hold this place until 1829, when he was elected without opposition to the governorship of Alabama. Alabama had been a supporter of the Jackson movement from its incipiency, and he was one of the local leaders in the cause. He had an ear for popular favor and was accused of the usual electioneering practices of his partisans. It was said that he made a habit of condemning his opponents as aristocrats and appealing to the reason of his adherents on the hustings through the agency of potent spirits (J. E. Saunders, *Early Settlers of Alabama,* 1899, p. 284). It was as a thoroughgoing Jacksonian that he was elected to the chief magistracy of his state, and his gubernatorial policy was in keeping with his pretensions. He advocated the graduation system for the sale of public lands, deprecated the nullification movement in South Carolina, and proposed that the congressional delegation from Alabama be instructed to vote against the recharter of the Bank of the United States. In local affairs he took an active interest in the beginning of the construction of the canal around Muscle Shoals and in the opening of the state university, both of which events occurred during his administration. He was also much interested in the establishment of a separately organized supreme court for the state, in the revision of the penal code, and in the establishment of a penitentiary (*Journal of the Senate of the State of Alabama,* 1830, pp. 43–47; *Ibid.,* 1831, pp. 7–15; Executive letter book, August 1830).

In 1831 he resigned the governorship in order to take a seat in the Senate of the United States. In this body he voted against the confirmation of Van Buren as minister to the Court of St. James's, and thus broke definitely with the Jackson party (T. H. Benton, *Thirty Years' View,* I, 1854, p. 215). The Alabama legislature requested his resignation, but, in spite of his support of the doctrine of instruction while he was governor, he now refused to comply and continued in his seat until the expiration of his term in 1837 (*Address of Gabriel Moore to the Freemen of Ala. . . . in Reply to Resolutions of the General Assembly Inviting him to Resign his Seat, 1835*). During this year he ran again for the House of Representatives, but the Jackson forces were arrayed against him, and he was defeated. Having thus brought an end to his

political life in Alabama, he removed to Texas in 1843. He is supposed to have died at Caddo in that state two years later, but there is a curious uncertainty in respect to this event (*Southern Advocate,* Huntsville, Ala., Sept. 6, 1844; Addie L. Booker to Marie B. Owen, Nov. 9, 1927. Both are in files of Alabama Department of Archives and History). He was married to a Miss Callier of Washington County, Ala., but an immediate divorce followed. This led to a duel with the bride's brother, who was slightly wounded in the affray. It appears that Moore never married again.

[Material in Ala. Dept. of Archives and Hist. at Montgomery; information from Miss Addie L. Booker, Malta Bend, Mo.; Willis Brewer, *Ala.* (1872); *Biog. Directory Am. Cong.* (1928); Wm. Garrett, *Reminiscences of Public Men in Ala.* (1872), pp. 757–69.]
T. P. A.

MOORE, GEORGE FLEMING (July 17, 1822–Aug. 30, 1883), judge, had the distinction of being twice elevated to the position of chief justice of the supreme court of Texas, with an interval of eleven years between the end of his first and the beginning of his second term of service. His parents, William H. and Mary Garland (Marks) Moore, were members of Virginia families, his mother being the younger half-sister of Meriwether Lewis [*q.v.*]. After their marriage they moved to Elbert County, Ga., where George Fleming Moore was born, the seventh son of a family of ten sons and two daughters. Later the family moved to Alabama. In 1839 he entered the University of Alabama and in 1840 was a law student at the University of Virginia, but, on account of his father's financial reverses, he did not graduate from either institution. He began the study of the law in 1842 and was admitted to the bar in 1844. After two years of practice in Alabama he removed to Texas, residing first in Crockett, then in Austin, and later in Nacogdoches, where he became the senior member of the well-known firm of Moore and Walker. In 1858, his firm was made reporter for the supreme court and brought out volumes 22–24 of the *Texas Reports* (1860–61). During the Civil War he served as colonel of the 17th Regiment of Texas Cavalry but resigned to accept a place on the supreme court of the state, to which he was elected in 1862 to fill the vacancy created by the retirement of Oran M. Roberts. When in 1866 the state, acting under President Johnson's plan of reconstruction, drafted a new constitution and elected a new state government, he was elected chief justice, but in 1867 upon the adoption of the congressional plan of Reconstruction he, with his associates of the supreme court, was removed by the federal military authorities. At the end of the Reconstruction period, when the people of Texas regained control of their government in 1874, he was appointed by Richard Coke as an associate justice of the state supreme court. After the adoption of the Constitution of 1876 he was elected as one of the two associate justices and was appointed chief justice in 1878, when Chief Justice Roberts resigned to become governor. In 1881, because of ill-health and impaired eyesight, he resigned from the court. He died in Washington, D. C. His body was sent to Austin for burial.

One of Moore's successors in the office of chief justice declared him to have been "possibly the greatest equity Judge in the history of the Court" (*Texas Jurisprudence, post*). One of the most important of his opinions may be found in *Ex parte F. H. Coupland* (26 *Texas Reports,* 387), in which he upheld the power of the Confederate Congress to raise an army by conscription. In 1864 he showed the quality of his courage by declaring in contempt of his court the military authorities in Texas who had seized for military punishment five citizens then held in custody by an officer of the supreme court, declaring in his opinion that "there is no officer or tribunal, civil or military, known to the law of the land, that could, without a violation of law and a contempt of this court, forcibly take from under its control, and without its consent, said prisoners, until the final adjudication by the court upon the matter before it" (*The State* vs. *Sparks, 27 Texas Reports,* 632). In the case of *Jacob Kuechler* vs. *Geo. W. Wright* (40 *Texas Reports,* 600) he wrote an exhaustive opinion, establishing the rule, ever since followed in Texas, that all executive officers except the governor are in proper cases subject to control by the writ of mandamus. He was married in Alabama, in 1846, to Susan Spyker, who with six of their seven children survived him.

[Information from Mrs. Mary L. Evans, Denton, Texas; *Texas Jurisprudence*, vol. I (1929), p. xli; J. D. Lynch, *The Bench and Bar of Texas* (1885); *Biog. Encyc. of Texas* (1880); *A Register of the Officers and Students of the Univ. of Ala.*, comp. by T. W. Palmer (1901); *Univ. of Va.* (1904), vol. II; W. T. Lewis, *Geneal. of the Lewis Family* (1893); L. H. A. Minor, *The Meriwethers and Their Connections* (1892), p. 62; *Galveston Daily News,* Aug. 31, Sept. 2, 9, 10, 12, 1883; *Austin Weekly Statesman,* Sept. 13, 1883.]
C. S. P.

MOORE, GEORGE FOOT (Oct. 15, 1851–May 16, 1931), theologian, Orientalist, and historian, was born at West Chester, Pa., the son of William Eves Moore, a Presbyterian minister, and Harriet Francina, daughter of Rev. George Foot, of Connecticut. The Moore stock

was Scotch-Irish, the emigrant ancestor, William, having come from Londonderry, Ireland, early in the eighteenth century, to settle in New Castle, Del. George Foot Moore was prepared for college at the West Chester Academy and by his father. Entering Yale as a junior, he graduated in 1872, second in the class. After four years of teaching and private theological study he entered the senior class of Union Theological Seminary, New York, and graduated in 1877. On Feb. 8, 1878, he was ordained to the Presbyterian ministry at Columbus, Ohio, and on Apr. 25, he married Mary Soper Hanford of Chicago. After a pastorate at Zanesville, Ohio (1878–83), he went to Andover Theological Seminary to be professor of the Old Testament and from 1899 to 1901 served as president of the faculty. In 1902 he became professor of the history of religion at Harvard, where he remained until his retirement from active teaching in 1928.

In Moore's nearly twenty years at Andover his eminence as a critical scholar in the field of Hebrew and the Old Testament became recognized both in the United States and in Europe. He made frequent contributions to the *Andover Review,* of which he was assistant editor (1884–93), and to other journals, and in 1895 published his important *Critical and Exegetical Commentary on Judges.* For the *Encyclopaedia Biblica* (1899–1903) he wrote nearly forty articles, that on "Historical Literature" and the influential article on "Sacrifice" being considerable treatises. At Harvard his personal attractiveness and distinction as a scholar made his position one of great dignity and importance in both the faculties (Arts and Sciences, and Divinity) of which he was a member. His universal knowledge became almost a myth, and he was consulted by all sorts of inquirers on every kind of subject. He was active in administrative matters, as syndic of the Harvard University Press (1913–24), and as editor of the *Harvard Theological Review* (1908–14 and 1921–31); in the establishment and conduct of which he took the leading part. In 1909–10 as Harvard exchange professor he made the second of two visits to Germany, his only earlier stay having been for the greater part of 1885. His contacts with German scholars were always close, as were those with Jewish scholars in the United States and abroad. He was president of the American Academy of Arts and Sciences, the Massachusetts Historical Society, the American Oriental Society, and the Society of Biblical Literature and Exegesis. Yale conferred on him three honorary degrees.

Besides smaller but weighty books on *The*

Moore

Moore

Literature of the Old Testament (1913) and *The Birth and Growth of Religion* (1923), his chief later works were his *History of Religions* (2 vols., 1913–19) and *Judaism in the First Centuries of the Christian Era: the Age of the Tannaim* (3 vols., 1927–30). Important are also the articles in the *Harvard Theological Review* on "Christian Writers on Judaism" (July 1921), "Intermediaries in Jewish Theology" (January 1922), and "The Rise of Normative Judaism" (October 1924, January 1925). As befitted a life-long student of Greek philosophy, Moore's interest lay rather in the philosophical than the anthropological aspects of the history of religions, and he was concerned less with the beginnings of the several religions than with their whole history. It was "the religion of intelligent and religious men" which he chiefly studied and described. His *History of Religions* contains a masterly and very interesting account of the origins and whole history of Christian thought based on his own fresh study of the sources. His greatest work, *Judaism,* was the fruit of a critical knowledge of the rabbinical sources unique among Christian scholars in any age. He held that the Jewish religion of the second century of our era, which he portrayed, was but the culmination of a "normative" system of religious life and thought which had had a development continuous since the sixth century before Christ. From this latter date on, "the salient mark of the following centuries was not the elaboration of the Levitical law, however much of this there was, but the appropriation and assimilation of the religious and moral teachings of the prophets."

Moore was of large frame, disciplined in body as in mind, and tireless in work, but no ascetic. An admirable teacher, a lucid and interesting lecturer, he was also an impressive preacher. His promptness and keenness and power of statement made him formidable in controversy. Somewhat quick of temper, impatient of ignorant presumption, capable of severe judgment, not without his dislikes, he was full of kindness, and ready to do anything at any sacrifice for any one who wanted to learn. He was fond of society, and of music, art, and literature. His generosity, his courage, and his loyalty were the traits of a great soul as well as a great scholar.

[W. W. Fenn, in *Proc. Mass. Hist. Soc.,* vol. LXIV (1932); C. C. Torrey, in *Harvard Grads. Mag.,* June 1931; *Harvard Univ. Gazette,* Feb. 27, 1932; *Yale Univ. Obit. Record,* 1931; J. W. Moore, *Rev. John Moore of Newtown, L. I., and Some of His Descendants* (1903), App., p. 484; *Who's Who in America,* 1928–29; *Boston Transcript,* May 16, 1931.] J. H. R.

MOORE, GEORGE HENRY (Apr. 20, 1823–May 5, 1892), librarian, historian, bibli-ographer, brother of Frank Moore [*q.v.*], was born in Concord, N. H., the son of Jacob Bailey Moore [*q.v.*] and Mary Adams (Hill), and a descendant of Jonathan Moore who emigrated from Scotland to New Hampshire in 1650. His early education was received in Concord and at Holmes's Plymouth Academy. He attended Dartmouth College until the end of the first term of his sophomore year, after which he taught district school in Acworth, N. H., until his removal with his parents to New York City in 1839. There he entered the sophomore class of the University of the City of New York, from which he graduated in 1842.

In 1841, while still a sophomore in college, he entered the employ of the New York Historical Society as assistant librarian to George Folsom, the Society at that time having quarters in the University building. When his father, who was librarian of the Society from 1848 to 1849, resigned, the younger Moore was elected to that position. He had previously (Mar. 7, 1848) been elected secretary of the executive committee, on which he served until 1891. During these fifty years he was the central figure in all the activities of the Society, serving also as secretary to the trustees of the new building, which was completed in 1857. He was recognized as a patient investigator in the field of history, a lover of art and literature, with a wide knowledge of books. His research was confined chiefly to the colonial and revolutionary periods of American history, and among the pamphlets he published, perhaps the one which attracted the most attention, was *"Mr. Lee's Plan—March 29, 1777": The Treason of Charles Lee* (1860). He had addressed the New York Historical Society on this subject on June 22, 1858, and brought to light for the first time the character of that Revolutionary general. His writings also included: *Historical Notes on the Employment of Negroes in the American Army of the Revolution* (1862); *Notes on the History of Slavery in Massachusetts* (1866); *Notes on the History of Witchcraft in Massachusetts* (1883–85); *Washington as an Angler* (1887); *Libels on Washington* (1889); *Typographiae Neo-eboracensis Primitiae: Historical Notes on the Introduction of Printing into New York, 1693* (1888); *The First Folio of the Cambridge Press* (1889); *John Dickinson—The Author of the Declaration on Taking up Arms in 1775* (1890). He was also a frequent contributor to various New York newspapers under the signature of "E. Y. E." In addition to his other duties he acted as secretary of the Mexican Boundary Commission, having been appointed in 1850. He was an excel-

125

lent public speaker and delivered addresses before various societies. In 1876 he was at his own request relieved of his duties at the New York Historical Society to take up the administration of the Lenox Library, of which he had been elected superintendent and trustee on Oct. 3, 1872. He served as secretary of the board from Jan. 6, 1876, until his death. He was a personal friend and adviser of James Lenox [q.v.], the founder of that library, who had rigid ideas as to the public use of it. The formality involved in gaining admittance to it resulted in much hostile public criticism, which was recalled by at least one editor at the time of the death of Moore, on whom he put the blame. The latter, however, was answerable to the board of trustees whose wishes he was obliged to carry out. He is remembered as a man of upright and kindly character. In politics he was originally a Whig and later an ardent Republican. On Oct. 21, 1850, he married, in New York, Mary Howe Givan, widow of Henry S. Richards. They had two children. The sale of his private collection of books and manuscripts in 1893 was one of the noted book auctions of the day.

[E. S. Stearns, *Geneal. and Family Hist., State of N. H.* (1908), vol. II; manuscript notes made by J. B. Moore and G. H. Moore, gathered by T. E. V. Smith; manuscript records in the N. Y. Hist. Soc.; Howard Crosby, in *Hist. Mag.*, Jan. 1870; H. M. Lydenberg, *Hist. of the N. Y. Pub. Lib.* (1923); *Gen. Alumni Cat. of N. Y. Univ.* (1906); *Lib. Jour.*, May 1892; *N. Y. Tribune*, May 6, 1892.]   A. J. W.

MOORE, Sir HENRY (Feb. 7, 1713–Sept. 11, 1769), colonial governor, was born in Vere, Jamaica, the son of Samuel and Elizabeth (Lowe) Moore, and grandson of John Moore, who settled in Barbados in the reign of Charles II and later removed to Jamaica. After receiving his education at Eton and the University of Leyden, he returned to Jamaica, where he married Catharine Maria Long, by whom he had one son. He became successively a member of the Legislative Assembly and of the Council, and secretary of the island. Later he became lieutenant-governor, and upon the departure of Admiral Sir Charles Knowles in June 1756, acting governor, serving in this capacity until 1762, with the exception of a short interval. During his administration he coped successfully with a serious negro insurrection which broke out on Easter Monday, 1760. While in personal command of the pursuing troops, he once narrowly escaped capture, and throughout the campaign displayed a "prudent intrepidity which compensated for the inexperience of his men" (Bridges, *post*, II, p. 97).

On his return to England, the government

created him a baronet, Jan. 26, 1764, and in July of the following year appointed him governor of New York. He arrived at his post November 1765, in the midst of the disturbances due to the Stamp Act, to find the province in the utmost confusion and the acting governor, Cadwallader Colden, confining himself to Fort George and refusing to meet the people. Failing to receive the support of his Council, Moore adopted a policy of watchful waiting, trusting economic pressure to bring the inhabitants to terms. "As I had not the power to do, what my own inclination suggested on this occasion, I contented myself with shewing as much indifference as possible, being fully perswaded, that the distresses which must attend the suspension of the Act will facilitate the carrying it into execution, more than any attempts I could possibly make in its favour" (letter to Lord Dartmouth, Dec. 21, 1765, O'Callaghan, *post*, VII, p. 802). In pursuance of this policy he refused to permit the courts to function and denied vessels permission to sail. In general, he pursued a conciliatory policy, causing Colden to write in June 1766: "He openly caressed the Demagogues—Put on a Homespun Coat, the Badge of the Faction & suffered the Mob to insult the officers of Government without interposing" (Colden Letter Books, II, p. 112).

Moore devoted much effort to the settlement of boundary disputes with neighboring provinces, and in the case of Quebec was successful. Matters of Indian policy also occupied much of his attention, and in this connection he made two trips to the country of the Five Nations. On the second of these, in 1768, he suggested the possibility of improving the navigation of the Mohawk River at Little Falls by a "canal on the side of the Falls with Sluices on the same plan as those built on the great Canal in Languedoc" (O'Callaghan, *post*, vol. VIII, p. 93). His greatest difficulty, other than the Stamp Act disturbances, arose from his controversy with the Assembly over their failure to pass the quartering bill. This led to the prorogation of the Assembly in December 1766, and eventually to the signing by the King of the restraining act the following summer. Upon his death the *New York Gazette* could say with justice (Sept. 18, 1769) that he "conducted himself . . . with such a Degree of Wisdom and Temper, as to gain the Approbation of his Sovereign and the Esteem of the People committed to his Care."

[Sources include: *Dict. Nat. Biog.*; G. E. Cokayne, *Complete Baronetage*, vol. V (1906); G. W. Bridges, *The Annals of Jamaica*, vol. II (1828); E. B. O'Callaghan, *Docs. Relative to the Colonial Hist. of the State of N. Y.*, vols. VII–VIII (1856–57); "The Colden Letter Books," *N. Y. Hist. Soc. Colls.*, Pub. Fund Ser., vols. IX–X (1877–78) and "The Letters and Papers of Cadwallader Colden," *Ibid.*, vols. LV–LVI (1923); "The Montrésor Jours.," *Ibid.*, vol. XIV (1882).]

D. C. H.

MOORE, JACOB BAILEY (Oct. 31, 1797–Sept. 1, 1853), journalist, printer, author, father of George Henry and Frank Moore [qq.v.], was born at Andover, N. H., the son of Jacob Bailey Moore (1772–1813) and Mary Eaton. His father was a physician whose ancestor, Jonathan Moore, of Scotch origin, had settled in Exeter, N. H., by 1650. Young Moore was of studious habits, and though without a college education, he acquired considerable knowledge of the classics and was noted for his love of historical reading, for his musical talents, and for his mechanical ingenuity. In 1813, at the age of sixteen, his father having died, he apprenticed himself to Isaac Hill [q.v.], owner and editor of the *New Hampshire Patriot,* at Concord, N. H. His articles in the newspaper attracted attention, and on Jan. 5, 1819, he became a partner of Hill, whose sister Mary Adams Hill he married Aug. 28, 1820. In 1823 his business partnership was dissolved owing to differences of political opinion, and he carried on printing, bookselling, and publishing, issuing the first three volumes of the *Collections of the New Hampshire Historical Society* (1824–32). Moore was one of the founders of that Society and was elected its first librarian on June 13, 1823, a position he held until 1830, and again from 1837 to 1839. On Sept. 11, 1826, he published at Concord the first issue of the *New Hampshire Journal,* supporting John Quincy Adams for a second term in the presidency, while his brother-in-law, Isaac Hill, supported Andrew Jackson in the *New Hampshire Patriot.* In 1827 Moore helped to prepare by-laws for the Second Congregational (Unitarian) Church in Concord, organized that year. In 1828 he was elected a member of the New Hampshire Assembly but resigned soon after his election. He served as sheriff of Merrimack County, N. H., 1828–33, and as justice of the peace, 1825–35. Moore continued until December 1829 to edit the *New Hampshire Journal,* which attained a very large circulation throughout New England and was a strong political organ. The downfall of the Adams party in New Hampshire, and the bitter differences of political opinion with his brother-in-law, who in 1836 became governor of New Hampshire, caused him to withdraw from public life in his native state, and although he owned three mills, water rights, and considerable land, he was overwhelmed by financial difficulties and was forced into bankruptcy. He moved to New York City in 1839 and edited the *New York Daily Whig* from July 2 of that year to Mar. 18, 1840, in support of William Henry Harrison. In 1841 President Tyler appointed him a chief clerk in the Post-office Department in Washington, D. C., where he served until 1845, being removed by President Polk upon pressure from the New Hampshire Democrats. For a short time he was inspector of the post-office in New Hampshire. On Jan. 4, 1848, he was elected librarian of the New York Historical Society where his son George was acting as assistant librarian. He resigned on June 5, 1849, to accept an appointment of President Taylor to establish the post-office in California, and was made deputy postmaster at San Francisco by President Fillmore in September 1850.

During these many activities his interest in historical writing never ceased, and while in California he sent to his son at the New York Historical Society many of the daily newspapers of the West which form a good collection in the library of that Society. In February 1853 he returned to the East, and died at the home of his brother, John Weeks Moore [q.v.], in Bellows Falls, Vt., where he is buried. He had two daughters and four sons. Among his works may be mentioned: *A Topographical and Historical Sketch of the Town of Andover . . . New Hampshire* (1822); *A Gazetteer of the State of New Hampshire* (1823), in collaboration with John Farmer [q.v.]; *Collections, Historical and Miscellaneous* (3 vols., 1822–24), also in collaboration with Farmer; *Annals of the Town of Concord . . . New Hampshire* (1824); *The Principles and Acts of Mr. Adams' Administration Vindicated* (1828); *Laws of Trade in the United States* (1840); *Memoirs of American Governors* (vol. I, 1846).

[Sources include: manuscript notes made by J. B. Moore and Geo. H. Moore gathered by Thomas E. V. Smith; manuscript records in the possession of the N. Y. Hist. Soc.; J. O. Lyford, *Hist. of Concord, N. H.* (2 vols., 1903); E. S. Stearns, *Geneal. and Family Hist. of the State of N. H.* (1908), II, 490–91; *Memorial Biogs. of the New-Eng. Hist. Geneal. Soc.*, vol. II (1881); *N. H. Patriot and State Gazette* (Concord), Sept. 14, 1853.]

A. J. W.

MOORE, JAMES (d. 1706), colonial governor, is said to have been a descendant of Roger Moore, a leader of the Irish rebellion of 1641. He emigrated to America and located at Charlestown (now Charleston, S. C.) about 1675. There he married Margaret Berringer, the daughter of Lady Yeamans and the step-daughter of Sir John Yeamans [q.v.]. The blood of his rebellious ancestors seemed to evidence itself in Moore's own activities, for he soon identified himself with the discontented elements and was active in movements of protest. In 1684 he was prominent in the opposition to the prerogatives of the proprietors, took part in the overthrow of Governor Colleton in 1690, and was a leading spirit in 1693 and 1694 in the protest against quit rents. He had an important place in colonial politics and served as a member of the councils of Governors Morton, Archdale, and Blake. When Blake died in 1700 he was elected by the council to take his place as governor. He "is said at this time to have been in great debt, and determined if possible to improve his desperate circumstances during his lease of power" (McCrady, *post*, p. 374). In addition to his political activities he had engaged in cattle raising and was a prominent Indian trader. He had had to fight the accusation of enslaving the Indians and in 1692 had been forbidden to leave the colony to engage in trade except with the consent of the governor and council. He had even lost his councilorship when he attempted to reopen the peltry trade, closed by an Indian war. As governor he perhaps saw a way to strengthen his position in the trade, and he had a bill introduced into the Assembly that would have given him a monopoly of the Indian trade. When the bill was defeated he dissolved the Assembly. In the election of a new Assembly charges of illegal voting were raised, and when the Assembly, which was unfavorable to him, attempted to investigate the charges he prorogued it, a course he continued as often as the investigation was taken up. He showed himself a man of adventure, not only in his choice of the hazardous occupation of Indian trader but also in his leadership of expeditions and his aspirations as an explorer. As governor he led a force during Queen Anne's War against Saint Augustine and besieged the city for some weeks but on the appearance of two Spanish frigates burned his own ships and retreated by land. After Nathaniel Johnson arrived in the colony to assume the governorship in 1703 Moore advocated an offensive against the Apalachee Indians for the purpose of counteracting French influence and, possibly, advancing his own interests as a trader. The Assembly refused to support such a move, and he himself gathered an army of whites and Indians at Okmulgee and in 1704 made a successful raid, weakening French power and carrying off many Indians to be slaves. In his activities as a trader he found gold that was assayed in England and reported to be valuable, but he was unsuccessful in interesting the Lords of Trade in his investigations. In 1699 he also tried to obtain support from Edward Randolph in a project to explore the Mississippi, which he declared he could do with a force of fifty whites and a hundred Indians. Nothing

came of his dreams of exploration, however, and a few years later he died of yellow fever in Charlestown.

[Edward McCrady, *The Hist. of S. C. under the Proprietary Gov.* (1897); A. S. Salley, *Narratives of Early Carolina* (1911); Verner W. Crane, *The Southern Frontier* (1928); Mrs. St. Julien Ravenal, *Charleston* (1906); Yates Snowden, *Hist. of S. C.* (1920), vol. I; W. J. Rivers, *A Sketch of the Hist. of S. C.* (1856); Alexander Hewatt, *An Hist. Account of . . . S. C.* (1779), vol. I; B. R. Carroll, *Hist. Colls. of S. C.* (1836), vol. II.]   H. B–C.

MOORE, JAMES (1737–April 1777), Revolutionary soldier, was born in New Hanover County, N. C., the son of Maurice Moore, pioneer settler and a founder of Brunswick, and of his second wife, Mary (Porter) Moore. He was the brother of Maurice Moore [*q.v.*] and of Rebecca who married John Ashe (*c.* 1720–1781, *q.v.*). In the French and Indian War he was a captain and for a year was in command at Fort Johnston at the mouth of the Cape Fear River. He represented New Hanover County in the provincial House of Commons from 1764 to 1771 and in 1773. He was one of the leaders of the Cape Fear mob that marched to Brunswick in February 1766 to prevent the enforcement of the Stamp Act in North Carolina, and he was prominent in the subsequent activities of the Sons of Liberty. Supporting the established government, controlled by the eastern oligarchy of planters and merchants, in its contest with the Regulators, he participated as a colonel of artillery in Governor Tryon's armed expedition of 1768 and in the battle of Alamance on May 16, 1771.

Nevertheless, in the controversy with Great Britain he defied the royal governors. His name was the first signed to the circular letter of the committee that called the first Revolutionary provincial Congress, held at New Bern in August 1774 in defiance of Governor Martin, and he was conspicuous in the activity of the New Hanover Committee of Safety. On Aug. 8, 1775, he was chosen a delegate from New Hanover County to the Third Provincial Congress to be held at Hillsboro on Aug. 20; and on Sept. 1, on account of his military experience and ability, he was selected by this provincial Congress for the position of colonel of the 1st North Carolina Continental Regiment. Although he was absent from the final engagement, he directed the patriot maneuvers in the brief campaign ending on Feb. 27, 1776, in the victory at Moore's Creek Bridge over the Scotch Highlanders who were marching to join the British forces already on their way to Wilmington for the subjugation of the southern colonies. On Mar. 1, 1776, the Continental Congress appointed him brigadier-general in command of the forces in North Carolina. After Moore's Creek he did not accompany the North Carolina troops sent to assist in the defense of Charlestown, S. C., in June but remained relatively inactive at Wilmington, watching a small fleet left in the Cape Fear River when the British departed in May for South Carolina. The Provincial Congress ordered him on Nov. 29 to march at once to Charlestown, where he remained until February 1777. On Feb. 5 the Continental Congress ordered him and his troops to proceed north to join Washington; but, while engaged at Wilmington in preparations for the march that was delayed by lack of money for supplies, he died (Apr. 9, according to Heitman, *post*) from "a fit of Gout in his stomach" (*State Records, post,* XI, p. 454). Regarded as the ablest military leader in North Carolina at the beginning of the Revolution, he was thus denied the opportunity of showing his military ability in a major campaign. He was survived by his wife Ann (Ivie) Moore and their four children.

[Sources include *Biog. Hist. of N. C.,* ed. by S. A. Ashe, vol. II (1905); James Sprunt, *Chronicles of the Cape Fear River* (2nd ed., 1916); *The Colonial Records of N. C.,* esp. vols. I, VI–X (1886–90); *The State Records of N. C.,* esp. vol. XI (1895); *Jour. of the Continental Cong.,* ed. by W. C. Ford, vols. IV–IX (1906–07); *S. C. Gazette* (Charleston), July 5, Aug. 9, 1770. Although Jan. 15 is frequently given as date of death for both James and Maurice Moore, James apparently obeyed a Congressional order of Feb. 5. For his death F. B. Heitman, *Hist. Register of the Officers of the Continental Army* (1893), gives date of Apr. 9, and that he had died very recently is indicated by a letter of Samuel Johnston to Thomas Burke on Apr. 19, 1777 (*State Records, ante,* XI, p. 454).] A. R. N.

MOORE, JAMES (1764–June 22, 1814), pioneer educator and clergyman of the Episcopal Church in Kentucky, came to that state from Virginia some time prior to April 1792. It is recorded that he was a man of engaging manners, superior natural endowments, and considerable learning, though what his ancestral and educational background had been seems to have been forgotten. His ecclesiastical connections were originally Presbyterian, and among his Virginia friends were Archibald Scott, long pastor of the churches in Hebron and Bethel, Augusta County, and John Brown, pastor of the Timber Ridge and New Providence congregations. Soon after his arrival in Kentucky, Moore was received as a candidate by the Transylvania Presbytery, Apr. 27, 1792. The following year he preached a trial sermon on the text, "Except ye repent, ye shall all likewise perish," which did not meet with the approbation of the Presbytery. He refused to be examined again and was dismissed. He then turned to the Episcopal Church and in 1794 was ordained by Bishop Madison of

Virginia (W. S. Perry, *The History of the American Episcopal Church,* 1885, II, 198).

Soon after his arrival in Kentucky Moore had been appointed principal or "director" of Transylvania Seminary, the first public educational institution of that region, which, conducted near Danville, had carried on a precarious existence for several years. He taught the school in his own house and in addition to his salary of twenty-five pounds, later increased to fifty, he was allowed four pounds, thirteen shillings, and fourpence for the portion of his dwelling used for educational purposes. On Apr. 8, 1793, the trustees voted to locate the seminary permanently at Lexington. Moore continued in charge until February 1794 when he was superseded by Harry Toulmin [*q.v.*]. The appointment of the latter, whose theology it was believed was tainted by Socinian errors, was offensive to the Presbyterians, who sought to control the school. Accordingly they established at Pisgah, some eight miles from Lexington, a rival institution, Kentucky Academy. Moore, though an Episcopalian, had the confidence of the Presbyterians, and in April 1796 he became the second principal of the new school. The following September, however, Transylvania Seminary called him back and made him president. In 1798, under a charter from the General Assembly granted Dec. 22, to take effect Jan. 1, 1799, the two schools were united under the name of Transylvania University. Moore was made acting president and professor of logic, metaphysics, moral philosophy, and belles-lettres, in which capacity he served until 1804, when he was succeeded by the Rev. James Blythe.

Throughout these years he had also been engaged in the work of the ministry. In 1796 he began conducting services for a little group of Episcopalians in Lexington, and in 1809 organized them into a church, becoming the first resident rector in Kentucky. He continued to serve them until shortly before his death, at which time he was fifty years old.

[Robert Davidson, *Hist. of the Presbyt. Ch. in the State of Ky.* (1847); G. W. Ranck, *Hist. of Lexington, Ky.* (1872); Lewis and R. H. Collins, *Hist. of Ky.* (1882); Robert and Joanna Peter, *Transylvania Univ.* (1896), being Filson Club. Pubs. No. 11; A. F. Lewis, *Hist. of Higher Educ. in Ky.* (1899).] H. E. S.

MOORE, JAMES EDWARD (Mar. 2, 1852–Nov. 2, 1918), surgeon, was born in Clarksville, Pa., the son of George W. and Margaret (Ziegler) Moore. His father was a Methodist minister who supported himself by his trade and preached on the Sabbath. James attended the public schools of Western Pennsylvania and Poland Union Seminary at Poland, Ohio. His medical studies were begun at the University of Michigan and continued at Bellevue Hospital Medical College from which he received his degree of M.D. in 1873 after the customary two years' course of those days. He went to Ft. Wayne, Ind., to practise, and a year later returned to spend two years in the hospitals of New York City. In 1876 he settled in Emlenton, Pa., where for six years he followed the rather arduous duties of a country practitioner, making most of his calls on horseback and dispensing drugs carried in his saddle-bags. In the summer of 1880 he spent four months as an assistant to Paul F. Munde in the dispensary at Mt. Sinai Hospital, New York. By this time he became restless and felt the urge of ambition for a field in which he could develop a career, for he did not under-estimate his own powers even then. In 1882 he went to Minneapolis, Minn., where he was in general practice until 1885, when he sailed for Europe to study in Berlin, Paris, and London. On his return to Minneapolis in 1887 he confined himself to surgery and orthopedics, and after 1897, gave his entire time to surgery. He claimed for himself the distinction of being the first specialist in surgery west of New York. His book, *Orthopedic Surgery,* one of the first American works on the subject, was published in 1898.

Moore was one of the pioneers in medical education in the state, holding the rank of professor of orthopedics in the old Minneapolis College Hospital, and a connection with the St. Paul Medical School. With the absorption of these two schools into the newly formed medical school of the University of Minnesota in 1888, he continued to hold the chair of professor of orthopedics and in 1894 was appointed professor of orthopedics and adjunct professor of clinical surgery. In 1897 he resigned the chair of orthopedics but continued as clinical professor of surgery. In 1904 he was made professor of surgery and in 1908 professor and director of the department of surgery, a position which he held until his death in 1918. He took an active part in the reorganization of the medical school and was one of the original three about whom the new faculty was formed and with whom the selection of its members largely rested. He was intuitive, clear-minded, forceful, and a born teacher, excelling in clinical subjects. His courtesy, his earnestness, and his personal charm drew his students to him naturally and surely and made a lasting impression upon them. In his will he left the bulk of his estate, after the death of his widow, to the surgical department of the medical school.

In the medical societies Moore was an interested and active member and readily gained a wide circle of friends. He served as first vice-president of the American Surgical Association, 1905; president of the Western Surgical Association, 1902; member of the judicial council of the American Medical Association, and chairman of its surgical section, 1903; fellow of the American College of Surgeons and a member of the board of governors at its founding; president of the Minnesota Academy of Medicine; president of the Hennepin County Medical Society; and delegate from the University of Minnesota to the International Medical Congress at Rome. He was also a frequent visitor to the Southern Surgical and Gynecological Society. As chief of staff of the Northwestern Hospital and chief of the surgical division of the University Hospital, he aided materially in the development of both institutions. His numerous medical writings were mostly articles founded upon his clinical experiences. His original contributions treated mainly surgical technique and bone and joint surgery. In addition to his *Orthopedic Surgery* he wrote a chapter, "General Principles of Surgical Treatment," in *American Practice of Surgery* (J. D. Bryant and A. H. Buck, vol. I, 1906). He was married three times: in 1876 to Bessie Applegate, who died in 1882; in 1883 to Clara Collins, who died in 1884; and in 1887 to Louie (Heckler) Irving, who survived him. As a pioneer in the surgery of the Northwest he rendered a notable service and won a distinction which he well deserved.

[*Trans. Southern Surgic. Asso., 1918,* vol. XXXI (1919); *Minn. Medicine,* Dec. 1918; *Surgery, Gynecology and Obstetrics,* Dec. 1924; H. A. Kelly and W. L. Burrage, *Am. Medic. Biogs.* (1920); *Minneapolis Jour.,* Nov. 3, 1918; records at the Univ. of Minn.; information as to certain facts from Moore's relatives; personal recollections.]   A.T.M.

MOORE, JOHN (*c.* 1659–Dec. 2, 1732), colonial official of South Carolina and Pennsylvania, was born in England. He was of the Moore family of Fawley in Berkshire and was probably a son of Sir Francis Moore. About 1680 he emigrated to South Carolina, where he served as provincial secretary and receiver-general in 1682–83 and as deputy to Sir Peter Colleton, one of the lords proprietors, in 1684. In 1685 he married Rebecca Axtell, a daughter of Daniel Axtell, one of the landgraves of South Carolina. He was a friend and protégé of Robert Quarry, who was for a short time the governor of the province, and it was probably through Quarry's influence that he removed to Philadelphia in 1695 or 1696. The Bishop of London (Henry

Compton) and the English authorities were making an effort at that time to create an Anglican Tory party in Pennsylvania as a balance to the Quakers. As Moore was a devout Churchman and also interested in the spoils of office, he heartily sympathized with this movement. In 1698 he was appointed advocate of the court of vice-admiralty for Pennsylvania, the lower counties (Delaware), and West Jersey. During the next few years he and his friend Quarry, who was the judge of this court, were closely associated in the leadership of the Anglican party and in the efforts to enforce the acts of trade and navigation. They were both vestrymen of Christ Church, Philadelphia, which was the oldest Anglican Church in the province (founded in 1695) and the center of an aggressive movement against the Quakers. They played active parts in the long and complicated struggle with the Quakers over the right of affirmation and also in the effort to improve the administration of the imperial customs system.

In 1700 Moore was appointed the King's attorney-general for Pennsylvania. William Penn confirmed this appointment and also made him register-general of the province. He was disloyal to Penn, however, in the quarrel between Penn and Quarry and, after some legal difficulties, was removed from both of these positions in 1704. He held the post of advocate of the vice-admiralty most of the time until 1704 and then served as deputy judge until about 1713. On July 24, 1704, he wrote to the Bishop of London that John Bewley, the collector of the port of Philadelphia, had recently died and that Quarry had asked him (Moore) to fill the post until a permanent appointment was made by the commissioners of the customs (Board of Trade Manuscripts, Proprieties, vol. VII, 1702–04, M. 46). Owing probably to his Lordship's influence, the appointment was approved and Moore served as collector of the port until 1728 and then as deputy collector until 1732. He was also deputy register-general from 1724 to 1726. He died in Philadelphia and was buried in Christ Church. He was survived by his wife, two daughters, and five sons, one of whom was William Moore, 1699–1783 [q.v.]. In his zeal to enforce the imperial laws, to improve the system of imperial defense, and to advance the cause of the Church of England, Moore came into conflict with both the proprietor and the people of Pennsylvania, and knowledge of his character and his services is largely based upon their complaints. As a historical figure, he belongs in the same class with Edward Randolph, Joseph Dudley, and other early American Tories, who combined a lust for office with a sincere devotion to the cause of imperial unity.

[For genealogical data and material relating to Moore's life in South Carolina, see D. M. Hall, *Six Centuries of the Moores of Fawley, Berkshire, England, and their Descendants* (1904) and *S.-C. Hist. Soc. Colls.*, vol. I (1857). There is a copy of his will, made on Nov. 16, 1731, in the possession of the Hist. Soc. of Pa. For his public career in Pennsylvania, see the Board of Trade Manuscripts, Proprieties, vols. I–VII, the *Minutes of the Provincial Council of Pa.*, vols. I–II (1852), and *Correspondence between Wm. Penn and Jas. Logan* (2 vols., 1870–72), ed. by Edward Armstrong. The best secondary account is given by W. T. Root, *The Relations of Pa. with the British Govt., 1696–1765* (1912).]

W. R. S.

MOORE, JOHN (June 24, 1834–July 30, 1901), Roman Catholic bishop of St. Augustine, was born at Rosmead, County Westmeath, Ireland, of respectable parentage, his mother being an O'Farrell of Scurlockstown. On completion of his elementary schooling, he emigrated in 1848 to Charleston, S. C., where he attended the Collegiate Institute and the Seminary of St. John the Baptist. In 1851, he was sent by Bishop Ignatius Reynolds to the College of Courbrée in France, from which, four years later, he proceeded to the Urban College in Rome. Ordained there by Monsignor Luigi Busso, Apr. 9, 1860, he returned to Charleston where he served as a curate at St. Finbar's Cathedral during the Civil War. Like his ordinary, Bishop P. N. Lynch [q.v.], he was a stout Confederate, and his aggressive Southern sympathies were not abated by the destruction of church properties by Northern forces. He refused to take an oath of allegiance to the Union, and thereafter his mail was censored by the commander of the fleet in Charleston harbor. Despite various inconveniences, however, he managed his parish with the assistance of a single priest and attended the dying and wounded of both sides as confessor and nurse. At the end of the war he commenced a twelve-year rectorship of St. Patrick's Church, during the last few years of which he also served as vicar-general. On the death of Augustine Verot, he was appointed second bishop of St. Augustine and consecrated by Bishop Lynch in St. John's Pro-Cathedral, May 13, 1877.

Simple, studious, diffident, yet approachable, he proved a successful administrator. Without immigration, Catholic growth was slow, yet his tenure was marked by an increase of priests from twelve to thirty-one, of whom a larger proportion were English speaking, by the erection of a number of churches and parochial schools, the founding of a Colored Institute, the establishment of St. Leo's Benedictine College for boys and an orphanage at Jacksonville, and the introduction of the Jesuits into southern Florida. In 1887, the cathedral was burned and the Bishop brought to light old plans for a cathedral drawn by Renwick, the architect of St. Patrick's Cathedral in New York, in harmony with the Spanish tradition of St. Augustine. Seeking financial aid in the North, he obtained generous assistance in rebuilding from Henry M. Flagler [*q.v.*], who was engaged in the development of Florida. In Jacksonville he is especially remembered for his courageous work in the yellow-fever epidemic of 1888. He encouraged immigration to the state and fostered harmonious relations with other denominations. Somewhat liberal in his views, he befriended Fathers Burtsell and McGlynn of New York, actually interceding for McGlynn [*q.v.*] in Rome. He was a member of the Third Plenary Council of Baltimore, 1884, and was named along with Bishop Joseph Dwenger of Fort Wayne to carry its decrees to Rome. There, despite the doubts expressed by Bishops McQuaid of Rochester and Richard Gilmour of Cleveland (who was later also accredited by Cardinal Gibbons), he was largely successful in obtaining papal ratification. As a self-sacrificing bishop of an obscure diocese, however, he naturally had little part in the national affairs of the church.

[J. G. Shea, *The Hierarchy of the Cath. Ch. in the U. S.* (1886); F. J. Zwierlein, *The Life and Letters of Bishop McQuaid* (3 vols., 1925–27); annual Catholic directories; *Florida Times-Union and Citizen* (Jacksonville), July 31, 1901; *Freeman's Jour.* (N. Y.), June 9, 1877; material furnished by an able associate of Moore.]   R. J. P.

MOORE, JOHN TROTWOOD (Aug. 26, 1858–May 10, 1929), Tennessee author and journalist, was born at Marion, Ala., the son of John and Emily Adelia (Billingslea) Moore. His father, a circuit judge in Alabama, came of a family distinguished in early South and North Carolina history, and served as captain in the Confederate army. His mother was of a pioneer Georgia family. After graduation in 1878 from Howard College at Birmingham, Ala., he edited the Marion *Commonwealth* for a year, publishing in it verses that were widely copied. For the next six years he taught school at Monterey and at Pineapple, Ala., establishing Moore's Academy at the latter place. Meanwhile he studied law and passed bar examinations, but never practised. In 1885 he married Florence W. Allen and moved to Maury County, Tenn., where on a farm near Columbia he began to raise blooded stock. Like the Southern gentlemen whose tradition he shared and understood, Moore knew and loved horses but was about equally inclined to literature. The spirit of the Middle Tennessee region into which he had

come stirred him to write, and he became its genial yet passionate interpreter, contributing first to the Columbia *Herald* and more prominently later to the Chicago *Horse Review*. "Trotwood," first chosen from *David Copperfield* as a pen-name, so clung to him that he adopted it as a middle name.

Moore's advocacy of the pacing horse, then coming into favor largely through performances of the Tennessee Hal strain, and his expert knowledge of the breed, got him a regular engagement with the *Review*, which he continued until 1904. In 1897 he published *Songs and Stories from Tennessee,* a collection of sketches and poems that had appeared in the *Review*. It contained his famous race-horse story, "Ole Mistis," and stories of Uncle Wash, a negro creation drawn from life and one of the most authentic representations of the Southern negro in American literature. In 1901 he published his first novel, *A Summer Hymnal,* a romantic story with a Tennessee setting, and began a series of works that won him a devoted following. Although he was a sincere romanticist and hero-worshipper, with a decided turn for the tradition of pathos and gallantry, he offset many of the faults of the sentimental school by his irresistible humor, good use of local detail, and variety of characters. He was himself the epitome of the Southern traits he interpreted—a personality genial and positive, leisurely yet fiery; and his books were not only stories but garnerings of his philosophizing and observations. But with these qualities there appeared in *The Bishop of Cottontown* (1906) a social consciousness in advance of his time; it was perhaps the first important Southern novel to treat industrial forces that were changing Southern life. It was followed in 1910 by *Uncle Wash, His Stories,* and *The Old Cotton Gin,* a poem, and in 1911 by *The Gift of the Grass,* the autobiography of a race-horse, perhaps his best-written novel.

In 1905 Moore had established *Trotwood's Monthly,* into which he poured anecdote, history, story, and verse. In 1906 he moved to Nashville. Changing the title of the monthly to the *Taylor-Trotwood Magazine,* he edited it jointly with Senator Robert Love Taylor of Tennessee until 1911, when it was discontinued. After publishing *Jack Ballington, Forester,* in 1911, he turned his attention largely to Tennessee history. From 1919 until his death he was director of libraries, archives, and history for Tennessee and did extensive and valuable pioneer work in collecting original documents, erecting markers and memorials, and stimulating historical enterprises. In 1923, with Austin P. Foster, he published

Tennessee, the Volunteer State (4 vols.). His devotion to Andrew Jackson, whose career he had long studied, was the basis of his last novel, *Hearts of Hickory* (1926), a spirited historical romance in which he dramatized the episodes of Jackson's early battles. From 1926 until his death he wrote occasional articles on historical subjects, constantly made journeys and filled speaking engagements among the people to whom he had become a familiar and beloved figure, and was at work almost to his last moment on another, unfinished novel. He died of heart failure at his Nashville home, leaving three children. His first wife had died in 1896 and in 1900 he was married to Mary Brown Daniel, who survived him.

[T. M. Owen, *Hist. of Ala. and Dict. of Ala. Biog.* (1921), vol. IV; *Who's Who in America*, 1928–29; the *Horse Rev.*, May 15, 1929; *Nashville Banner*, May 10, 1929; *Nashville Tennessean*, May 11, 12, 19, 1929; family papers supplied by Mrs. John Trotwood Moore.]

D. D.

MOORE, JOHN WEEKS (Apr. 11, 1807–Mar. 23, 1889), editor of musical journals, and musical biographer, was the son of Dr. Jacob Bailey Moore, a physician, and Mary Eaton, and a brother of Jacob Bailey Moore [*q.v.*]. His father settled in Andover, N. H., in 1796; he was a fine singer and a writer of songs. His son was educated in the Concord (N. H.) High School and Plymouth Academy, and while still in his teens was apprenticed to learn the printer's trade in the office of the *New Hampshire Patriot*. In 1827 he began on his own account the publication of the *Androscoggin Free Press*, the first weekly newspaper in the state of Maine, which was printed in Brunswick. On Sept. 17, 1832, he was married to Emily Jane Eastman, of Concord, N. H. Six years later he removed to Bellows Falls, Vt., where for seventeen years he issued the *Bellows Falls Gazette*. In 1840 he began to devote himself more especially to the publication of musical works. He was a good musician and played the piano, violin, and flute. He edited for a time two musical journals, the *World of Music* and the *Musical Library*. His collections included *Sacred Minstrel* (1842?); the *American Collection of Instrumental Music* (1856) and the *Star Collection of Instrumental Music* (1858). At Portsmouth and Manchester he published in eighteen numbers *Puritanism of Music in America*. There followed the five volumes of his *Musical Record* (1867–70), and the *Songs and Song Writers of America* (1859–80), of which two hundred numbers were issued. In 1854 he published his *Complete Encyclopædia of Music, Elementary, Technical, Historical, Biographical,*

Vocal and Instrumental, supplemented in 1875 by an *Appendix,* and in 1876 he brought out *A Dictionary of Musical Information.* These served as source materials in the preparation of definitions of musical terms for general dictionaries. His last work was a product of his many years' experience as a printer: *Moore's Historical, Biographical and Miscellaneous Gatherings . . . Relative to Printers, Printing, Publishing, and Editing . . . from 1420 to 1886* (1886). His chief activity was laid in the period between 1825 and 1860 when musical activity was concentrated in a few metropolitan centers. His contributions to a more general spread of musical knowledge are deserving of respect, for while much of his work is crude, it represents valuable pioneer effort. Moore died in Manchester, N. H., at the age of eighty-two. His brother Henry Eaton Moore, 1803–1841, had a similar but briefer career as a printer and musician.

[E. S. Stearns, *Geneal. and Family Hist. of the State of N. H.* (1908), vol. II; S. P. Cheney, *The Am. Singing Book* (1879); *People and Patriot* (Concord, N. H.), Mar. 28, 1889; musical dictionaries.]

F. H. M.

MOORE, MAURICE (1735–1777), jurist and Revolutionary patriot, the son of Maurice and Mary (Porter) Moore, was born in New Hanover County, N. C., and educated in New England. He was the brother of James Moore and the father of Alfred Moore [*qq.v.*]. He married Anne Grange. He was an influential representative of the borough of Brunswick in the North Carolina House of Commons, serving 1757–60, 1762, 1764–71, and 1773–74. His early "disposition to support his Majesty's Interest" (*Colonial Records, post,* V, 948) elevated him to the governor's council from 1760 to 1761. Appointed to an associate judgeship of the province, he wrote a pamphlet, in 1765 after the passage of the Stamp Act, entitled *The Justice and Policy of Taxing the American Colonies in Great Britain, Considered* (printed in Boyd, *post,* pp. 163–74), maintaining that there could be no rightful taxation of the American colonies by a Parliament in which they had neither actual nor virtual representation, and he was suspended by Governor Tryon for his intemperate zeal and conduct in preventing the enforcement of the Stamp Act. Reinstated in 1768, he held the judgeship until the court ceased to function in 1773 because of a deadlock between the governor and Assembly over the new court law. He was appointed a commissioner to hold the courts established by royal prerogative in 1773, but the Assembly refused to defray their expenses.

He was prominent in the Regulator movement. At first he sympathized with the distressed Regulators and was accused of having encouraged the movement, though he denied the charge. He was a colonel in Governor Tryon's first armed expedition, a judge at the Hillsboro trial of 1768, an advocate of a drastic policy that culminated in the Johnston or Riot Act of 1771, and a judge at the special court in Hillsboro in June 1771 after the battle of Alamance that sentenced twelve Regulators to death on the charge of treason. Bitterly hated by the insurgents, he was attacked in 1770 in a public letter whose reputed author, Hermon Hushands [*q.v.*], was expelled from the House of Commons. Yet after the Hillsboro trial of 1771 he became lenient and sympathetic to the Regulators. The public letter of "Atticus" in 1771, severely criticising Tryon's policy toward the Regulators, was attributed to him (published *Colonial Records, post,* VIII, 718–27); and in 1772 he held in an opinion as judge that there could be no further prosecutions under the Riot Act, which he interpreted liberally, and he actively promoted a policy of leniency toward the leaders. The Third Provincial Congress on Aug. 21, 1775, appointed him on the committee to try to induce the Regulators to support the patriot cause. Representing the borough of Brunswick in this Third Provincial Congress, he served on important committees in the interest of the patriot cause; but he was too conservative to approve actual separation from Great Britain. On Jan. 9, 1776, in a letter to Governor Martin he expressed his belief that North Carolina, if there were opportunity, would renounce every desire of independence and accept reconciliation on the basis of the political conditions of 1763 (*Colonial Records, post,* X, 395–96), but the Moore's Creek campaign made negotiations impossible. Though elected a delegate from Brunswick County he did not attend the Fifth Provincial Congress of November 1776. He died some time before Apr. 20, 1777 (*State Records, post,* XI, 456). Governor Martin characterized him as a man of "considerable influence," but a "visionary in politicks" and "a zealous votary of the bubble popularity," whose political conduct had been fickle and undecided (*Colonial Records, post,* X, 400).

[Printed sources include sketch of life in *Some Eighteenth Century Tracts Concerning N. C.,* ed. by W. K. Boyd (1927); M. DeL. Haywood, *Gov. Wm. Tryon and his Administration in the Province of N. C.* (1903); W. E. Fitch, *Some Neglected Hist. of N. C.* (1905) for unfavorable interpretation with citations; G. J. McRee, *Life and Correspondence of James Iredell,* vol. I (1857), pp. 195, 201; *The Colonial Records of N. C.,* esp. vols. V, VI, VII, VIII, IX, X (1887–90); *The State Records of N. C.,* esp. vol. XI (1895); date of death as Jan. 15 has been rejected because the tradition includes the coincident death of James Moore, which seems impossible. See bibliography to sketch of James Moore.] A. R. N.

MOORE, NATHANIEL FISH (Dec. 25, 1782–Apr. 27, 1872), professor, librarian, and president of Columbia College, was the son of William Moore, M.D., Edinburgh 1780, a distinguished New York physician, and Jane, daughter of Nathaniel Fish. He was born in Newtown, L. I., and graduated from Columbia during the presidency of his uncle, Bishop Benjamin Moore [*q.v.*], in 1802. At Commencement he delivered the Latin salutatory, *De Astronomiae Laudibus.* Choosing the profession of law, he studied under Beverly Robinson and was admitted to the bar in 1805. His practice was never extensive, and in 1817 he accepted the more congenial occupation of adjunct professor of Greek and Latin at Columbia, succeeding Peter Wilson [*q.v.*], as professor in 1820. In 1835 he resigned his professorship and traveled for about two years in Europe. Upon his return he sold his library, a choice collection of about a thousand titles in the classics, philology, and theology of the sixteenth, seventeenth, and eighteenth centuries, to the college for $10,000. In January 1838 he was appointed librarian of the college. He was the first incumbent to devote his entire time to the office, and he classified and arranged the books and made with his own pen a huge catalogue in book form which continued to be used for thirty years. In 1839 he resigned and went abroad again, visiting Egypt, Greece, and Palestine, as well as Germany and England.

On Aug. 1, 1842, Moore was elected president of Columbia, succeeding William Alexander Duer [*q.v.*]. His duties included instruction in the classics to the seniors. During his presidency, the college was situated in one of the quiet, residential sections of the city; the enrolment was slightly over one hundred, the annual income and expenditures were about $23,000, and there was a debt of some $60,000. The duties of the presidency were not particularly congenial to Moore, whose previous life had been spent in scholarly seclusion and reflection among his books, and little more can be said than that the college held its own during his seven-year term. He relinquished his duties in October 1849, to be succeeded by the more worldly and active Charles King [*q.v.*]. While on a visit to London in 1851, Moore was greatly impressed with the specimens of the new art of photography on paper exhibited at Crystal Palace, and on his return he devoted himself assiduously to photography as a hobby. Some of his work is preserved at Columbia. The last sixteen years of his life were spent in retirement, and he died at his brother's home in the Highlands of the Hudson, Apr. 27, 1872 (*Evening Post, New-York Trib-*

une, New York Times, Apr. 29; elsewhere the date is erroneously given as Apr. 25). In *Through the Gates of Old Romance* (1903), W. Jay Mills records the love story of Moore and "the heavenly Ellen Conover, a belle of Chambers Street, New York," whom Moore was forbidden to marry because they were first cousins; perhaps this explains why Moore never married.

Moore's scholarship was in the English tradition rather than the German, and his profound interest in the beauties of the ancient writers inspired his pupils with a deep desire to know more of them and of their works. His publications include: *Remarks on the Pronunciation of the Greek Language, Occasioned by a late Essay . . . by John Pickering* (1819); *Ancient Mineralogy: or, An Inquiry Respecting Mineral Substances Mentioned by the Ancients* (1834), a work little noticed in America but highly appreciated in England; *Lectures on the Greek Language and Literature* (1835); *Addresses . . . at . . . Commencement* (1843); *A Short Introduction to Universal Grammar* (1844); *An Historical Sketch of Columbia College* (1846), an excellent little book, the second work published on this subject; and *An Address to the Alumni of Columbia College* (1848), on the library resources of the United States.

[Benj. I. Haight, *A Memorial Discourse of Nathaniel F. Moore, LL.D.* (N. Y., 1874); J. B. Pine, "Nathaniel F. Moore, LL.D.," *Columbia Univ. Quart.,* Mar. 1903.]   M. H. T—s.

MOORE, NICHOLAS [See More, Nicholas, d. 1689].

MOORE, PHILIP NORTH (July 8, 1849–Jan. 19, 1930), mining engineer, only child of Henry C. and Susan (North) Moore, was a descendant of John North who settled in Connecticut in 1635. Henry Moore was a canal and railroad builder, and Philip was born in Connersville, Ind., where a canal was being constructed. After graduating in 1870 from the classical course at Miami University, he went to the School of Mines, Columbia University, where he was a special student, 1870–72. The next six years he spent in geological work under such distinguished men as T. B. Brooks, Raphael Pumpelly, and N. S. Shaler [*qq.v.*], and then, after six months in Europe, went to Leadville, Colo., in 1878. Here he was superintendent of the first lead smelting works and built the second plant, the La Plata. After a couple of years he ventured into independent development. In 1879 he married Mary Eva Perry (July 24, 1852–Apr. 28,1931), daughter of Seely and Elizabeth (Benedict) Perry of Rockford, Ill., and a descendant of Massachusetts stock. She was a graduate of Vassar College, with a background of European travel and a speaking knowledge of several languages. In 1882 they moved to Kentucky, where at Slate Creek Moore acquired a quarter interest in a smelting works of which he was also manager. In 1889 he moved to St. Louis to obtain better school facilities for his children, but retained charge of the Kentucky enterprise until it was worked out. Meanwhile he had acquired an iron property in Alabama, of which he was president for eighteen years, and during all this time he practised as a consulting mining engineer, sometimes traveling as much as 50,000 miles in twelve months. Among other enterprises he developed the Conrey Placer Mining Company, Montana, an important part of the estate which Gordon McKay left for the benefit of the mining school at Harvard University. During the period of the Great War he developed the Admiralty Zinc Company, Oklahoma. As president of the American Institute of Mining Engineers in 1917 he was an important factor in coördination work on strategic minerals through the War Minerals Committee. In that same year he organized the American Engineering Council, which cooperated with the Council of National Defense in stimulating the production of necessary minerals. In 1919 he was called to Washington to serve as chairman of the War Minerals Relief Commission, created by Congress to indemnify those who undertook mineral production at government solicitation but had not recouped their expenditures by the time of the Armistice. In this capacity he acted until 1921, when he returned to St. Louis. For many years one of the board of managers of the Missouri Geological Survey, he was active in bringing about cooperation between engineers and legislature to promote the best interests of the state and in awakening engineers to a sense of their civic responsibilities. His wife, too, was a leader in civic affairs, being an officer of the General Federation of Women's Clubs, 1894–1912, except for the years 1901–05, when she was president of the Missouri Federation of Women's Clubs; president of the National Council of Women, 1916–25; and vice-president, 1920–30, of the International Council of Women. She was also a trustee of Vassar College and president, 1903–07, of the Association of Collegiate Alumnæ. From April 1917 till it disbanded in 1919 she served as a member of the Women's Committee of the Council of National Defense. She survived her husband only fifteen months, dying Apr. 28, 1931. They left a son and a daughter.

[T. A. Rickard, "Interviews with Mining Engineers," *Mining and Scientific Press* (San Francisco), 1922,

14

pp. 373–86; *Mining and Metallurgy*, Mar. 1930; *Am. Mer. of Sci.* (1927); *Who's Who in America*, 1928–29; *St. Louis Post-Dispatch*, Jan. 20, 1930; Dexter North, *John North of Farmington, Conn., and His Descendants* (1921); information regarding Mary Eva Perry Moore contributed by Miss Katharine Twining Moody; sketch in *Am. Biog.*, vol. XLIX (Am. Hist. Soc. 1931), revised by Mrs. Moore, with additions by her daughter.]   T. T. R.

MOORE, RICHARD BISHOP (May 6, 1871–Jan. 20, 1931), chemist, was the son of William Thomas Moore [*q.v.*], a leading minister of the Disciples of Christ, and Mary A. (Bishop) Moore. He was born at Cincinnati, Ohio, but at the age of seven accompanied his parents to England where they resided till 1895. He attended Argyle College, St. Edmund's College, the Institut Keller in Paris, and University College, London. Here he studied from 1886 to 1890 under William Ramsay and became interested in rare gases and radium. Returning to the United States, he attended the University of Chicago for a year, receiving the degree of B.S. in 1896, and was retained as an assistant in chemistry one year. He then became instructor in chemistry at the University of Missouri, where in addition to his regular duties he did pioneer work in the investigation of radioactive substances. In 1905 he resigned, to accept the professorship of chemistry at Butler College, Indianapolis, Ind. He continued his investigations and during a leave of absence in 1907 worked in Sir William Ramsay's laboratory on the separation and purification of krypton and xenon and the determination of their properties. His work on rare gases became so well known that in 1911 he was called away from teaching by the United States government. Joining at first the staff of the Bureau of Soils, he was transferred the next year to the newly organized Bureau of Mines and as a physical chemist in charge of the chemistry and metallurgy of rare metals established headquarters in Colorado, where he made a survey of radium deposits, devised methods for concentrating the ore, and supervised the preparation of the first radium salts produced in the United States.

In the early years of the World War he and his co-workers devoted much attention to the use of the metals vanadium, tungsten, and molybdenum in making special steels. He was among the first to advocate the use of helium in balloons and airships, and largely through his arguments and insistence steps were taken, first by the Navy Department and later by Congress, to conserve this gas. In 1918 he was given charge of all helium experiments conducted by the Bureau of Mines. The following year he became chief chemist of the bureau, and in this capacity, during the next five years, organized the cryogenic laboratory in Washington, served on the helium board of the army and navy, and directed the work by which the cost of producing helium was reduced to a nominal sum and its use was correspondingly increased.

In 1923 he left the government service to enter commercial work with the Dorr Company, New York, of which he was general manager for two years. The position was not congenial, however, and in 1926 he resigned to become professor of chemistry and dean of the school of science at Purdue University, Lafayette, Ind., where he remained until his death. During his few years of active service at Purdue his work as a teacher, investigator, and executive resulted in permanent contributions to the progress of the University. While in the employ of the Bureau of Mines he published articles, individually or jointly, on helium, radium, and the rare metals uranium, vanadium, tungsten, cerium, thorium, titanium, and zirconium (see, especially, *United States Bureau of Mines Bulletin 70*, 1913, *104*, 1915, *212*, 1923, and *Serial 2363*, 1922). He was the author of several papers on metallurgical subjects published by the American Institute of Mining and Metallurgical Engineers; of a textbook, *A Laboratory Chemistry* (1904); and of a lecture, *The Rare Gases of the Atmosphere* (1927), delivered at Columbia University in 1926. For his work on radium, mesothorium, and helium he was awarded in 1926 the Perkin medal of the American Section of the Society of Chemical Industry. He had previously received the Longstreth and Potts medals of the Franklin Institute. As a public servant he was characterized by unusual ability to grasp the essential factors of large projects, by exceptional capacity to organize varied plans, and by personal power to enlist the cooperation of associates. He married, first, Callie Pemberton of Auxvasse, Mo., on June 11, 1902; and second, June 18, 1924, Georgie E. Dowell of Dallas, Tex.

[*Purdue Alumnus*, Feb. 1931; *Industrial and Engineering Chem.* (News Ed.), Feb. 10, 1931; *Mining and Metallurgy*, Feb. 1931; *Chem. and Met. Engineering*, Feb. 1931; *Who's Who in America*, 1930–31; *Indianapolis Star*, Jan. 21, 1931.]   L. C. N.

MOORE, RICHARD CHANNING (Aug. 21, 1762–Nov. 11, 1841), bishop of the Protestant Episcopal Church, was born in New York City, where his grandfather, John Moore, son of John Moore, c. 1659–1732 [*q.v.*], had attained wealth and eminence, being an alderman, a member of the colonial legislature, and of the King's council for the province. One of his eighteen children was Thomas, who married Elizabeth Channing and had twelve children, among whom was Richard. He received a good classical training under Alexander Leslie, professor of languages in King's College; but the Revolutionary War, which ruined his father's business and caused the removal of the family to West Point, interrupted his education. After a brief trial of sea-faring life, he settled down to the study of medicine under the direction of Dr. Richard Bayley, an eminent New York physician. He practised for a short period in that city, and later in the eastern part of Long Island. At the age of twenty-two he married Christian Jones of New York. About this time his mind became deeply exercised on the subject of religion, and he finally decided to enter the church. After preparation under Bishop Samuel Provoost, he was by him ordained deacon at St. George's Chapel, New York, in July 1787, and was admitted to priest's orders the following September. For about two years he was in charge of Grace Church, Rye, N. Y., and then became rector of St. Andrew's parish, Staten Island. Here for more than twenty years he had a fruitful ministry, eking out his slender salary at the start by continuing to practise medicine, and from 1793 to 1802 by conducting a school. On April 20, 1796, his wife died, leaving him with three children, and on Mar. 23, 1797, he married Sarah Mersereau. He was one of the deputies representing the diocese of New York at the General Convention, held in Baltimore in May 1808, where he was chairman of the committee which selected additional hymns for the use of the churches. In 1809, leaving his son David as his successor at Staten Island, he became rector of St. Stephen's, New York. After five years' service here, marked by notable success, in 1814 he was called to the rectorship of the Monumental Church, Richmond, Va., and to the episcopate of that state. On May 18, at St. James's Church, Philadelphia, he was consecrated bishop.

Owing to the effects of the Revolution, the outgoing of the Methodists, the secularization of the clergy, and a lack of effective leadership, the Episcopal Church in the South was in a prostrate condition. Parishes were impoverished and vacant, priests were few, and apathy and discouragement prevailed. Bishop Moore was ideally adapted to the needs of the situation. He was a man of distinguished ancestry, well-bred, and possessed of social qualities which made him everywhere acceptable. He was a speaker of magnetism and persuasiveness. He could exercise discipline with tact and kindliness. Although loyal to his own church, he was broad-minded, charitable, and disinclined to controversy. More important still, he was a man of deep and sin-

cere piety, zealously devoted to the salvation of souls and the spiritual edification of his people. While warmly attached to the constituted ministry and government of the church and careful to keep enthusiasm within proper bounds, he was strongly evangelical, upholding prayer meetings, lecture-room services, and revivals. He did not escape opposition, but regard for him steadily grew, and under the sway of his wisdom and goodness the diocese began to revive. Discipline was restored, churches were reëstablished, the number of clergy increased, and the Virginia Theological Seminary, at Alexandria, was founded. After 1829 he was assisted by a coadjutor, Bishop William Meade [q.v.]. Together with Bishops John Henry Hobart and Alexander V. Griswold [qq.v.] he is credited with reconstructing the Episcopal Church in the United States, both in spirit and in character. After having directed the affairs of the diocese for twenty-seven years, he died while on a visitation to Lynchburg, and was buried in Richmond.

[J. P. K. Henshaw, *Memoir of the Life of the Rt. Rev. Richard Channing Moore, D.D.* (1842), containing seventeen sermons; W. B. Sprague, *Annals Am. Pulpit*, vol. V (1859); Wm. Meade, *Old Churches, Ministers, and Families of Va.* (1857); F. L. Hawks, *Contributions to the Ecclesiastical Hist. of the U. S.*, vol. I (1836); W. S. Perry, *The Hist. of the Am. Episc. Ch. 1587–1883* (1885); H. G. Batterson, *A Sketch-Book of the Am. Episcopate* (1878); C. C. Tiffany, *A Hist. of the Protestant Episc. Ch. in the U. S. A.* (1895); E. L. Goodwin, *The Colonial Ch. in Va. with Biog. Sketches of the First Six Bishops of the Diocese of Va.* (1927); D. M. Hall, *Six Centuries of the Moores of Fawley* (1904); *Richmond Enquirer*, Nov. 16, 1841.]
H. E. S.

MOORE, SAMUEL PRESTON (1813–May 31, 1889), surgeon general of the Confederate army, was born in Charleston, S. C., the son of Stephen West and Eleanor Screven (Gilbert) Moore. The founder of the Moore family in America was Dr. Mordecai Moore who came to America with Lord Baltimore, as his physician. Samuel graduated from the Medical College of South Carolina on Mar. 8, 1834. One year later he was commissioned assistant surgeon in the United States Army and entered upon a long service in the western posts of Iowa, Kansas, and Missouri. Afterward he went to Florida, where, in 1845, he married Mary Augusta Brown, the daughter of Maj. Jacob Brown. During the Mexican War his entire service was along the Rio Grande, mostly at Camargo, across the Rio Grande from what was later Fort Ringgold. On Apr. 30, 1849, he attained his surgeoncy, with the rank of major, which he held until his resignation in 1861.

The coming of the Civil War was to him, as

to many regular officers, the occasion for much distress of mind. He resigned from the service so as not to fight against his state, and entered the practice of medicine at Little Rock, Ark., apparently hoping that he need not fight against his country. Trained military surgeons were too few in the South, however, for one of so long service to remain unknown. In June 1861 he was made surgeon general of the Confederate army. His task was most difficult. There was a shortage of doctors, as well as of drugs, supplies, and hospitals. Owing to the general practice of organizations electing their own officers, including surgeons, many poorly qualified men were commissioned. Moore established examining boards to weed out the unfit, and introduced, so far as possible, the organization and methods obtaining in the medical department of the United States Army. Probably he succeeded as well as any one could under the circumstances, but when the Union army entered Richmond, the records of his office were almost entirely destroyed by fire, as were most of the books and private papers of his family, so that there is very little documentary evidence of his work. During the war he undertook two methods of keeping medical officers informed as to the progress of their profession. He organized in 1863 and was president of the Association of Army and Navy Surgeons of the Confederate States, and he encouraged the publication of the *Confederate States Medical and Surgical Journal* (January 1864–February 1865). The Association promoted meetings and discussions of medical subjects and, in general, the extension of knowledge, much as does the ordinary medical society. The *Journal* presented interesting articles in the way of case reports, original investigations, and reviews of foreign and Union books and journals. It was a useful publication and its relative value was greatly enhanced by the absence of any other such publication in the Confederacy.

After the war, Moore remained in Richmond, not practising medicine but devoting much time to the furtherance of education and agriculture, incidentally serving as a member of the Richmond school board (1877–89) and of the Virginia Agricultural Society. In the latter capacity he took an important part in the promotion and improvement of the state fairs. He lived quietly and in honor until his death. As surgeon general he was regarded as strict and exacting, and as a severe disciplinarian; yet personally he seems to have been kind, mild, philanthropic, and modest and reserved in manner.

[H. R. McIlwaine, in *Surgery, Gynecology and Obstetrics*, Nov. 1924; S. E. Lewis, in *Southern Practi-*

tioner, Aug. 1901; C. W. Chancellor, *Ibid.*, Nov. 1903; J. E. Pilcher, *The Surgeon Generals of the Army* (1905); *Southern Hist. Soc. Papers*, vol. XXIX (1901); *Va. Medic. Mo.*, June 1889; *Richmond Dispatch*, June 1, 1889.]   P. M. A.

MOORE, THOMAS OVERTON (Apr. 10, 1804–June 25, 1876), governor of Louisiana, was born in Sampson County, N. C., the son of John and Jean (Overton) Moore and the descendant of James Moore (d. 1706, *q.v.*), who emigrated from Ireland in the seventeenth century to what is now South Carolina and became the governor of the Carolinas in 1700. On his mother's side he was descended from William Overton who emigrated from England to Virginia about 1670. He received his education in his native county and remained there until 1829, when he moved to Rapides Parish, La., where his uncle, Walter H. Overton, lived. For some years he managed his uncle's sugar plantation. Later he acquired a plantation of his own in the same parish and soon became one of the important sugar planters of the state. In disposition fiery and inclined to be exacting and uncompromising, he was, nevertheless, a thorough politician and played the political game with great zest and effectiveness. He was active in local politics rather early and for a number of years served as a member of the police jury of his parish. In 1848 he was elected to the state House of Representatives and in 1856 to the Senate. He became the candidate of the regular faction of the Democratic party for governor in 1859. Although he was opposed by Thomas J. Wells of the same parish he was elected in the following November and inaugurated in January 1860.

After the deadlock in the National Democratic Convention at Charleston he supported the Breckinridge-Lane faction and did much towards the success of that ticket in Louisiana in November. With the election of Lincoln as president he issued a call, on Dec. 10, to determine what course Louisiana should pursue. In his message he said: "I do not think it comports with the honor and respect of Louisiana, as a slave holding state, to live under the government of a Black Republican President" (Greer, *post*, p. 622), and on his recommendation the legislature called a state convention to meet on Jan. 23, 1861, in order to decide the matter. Anticipating what the convention would do, he ordered the state troops to take Forts Jackson and St. Philip, which commanded the Mississippi River below New Orleans, and also Fort Pike on the Rigolets and the barracks and arsenal at Baton Rouge, the state capital. Following the adoption of an ordinance of secession by the state convention, he took the lead in making Louisiana a member of the Confederacy, organizing local companies for defense, establishing supply depots on the Red River, and building packing plants to feed the men under arms. He co-operated with the Confederate government in the prosecution of the war. In April 1861 he issued a call for 5,000 troops for the Confederate service in addition to the 3,000 already asked for by President Davis, and he continued to exert his authority to raise troops and supplies for the armies in the field. He had in the meantime requested the banks to suspend specie payments and had instructed them to accept and pay out Confederate treasury notes at par. His administration was disrupted in June 1862 when, after the capture of New Orleans by Benjamin F. Butler, the Federal government appointed George F. Shepley as military governor of Louisiana. Shepley's administration was effective, however, only in the southern part of the state, and Moore continued to act as governor over central and northern Louisiana, still within Confederate lines, until the end of his term early in 1864. He moved the capital from Baton Rouge to Opelousas and later to Shreveport. On reaching Opelousas he issued an address to the people of the state directing what to do under the circumstances. Among other things he forbade their trading with the enemy, entering the Federal lines, bearing Federal passports, or accepting Federal money, and he ordered that steamboats be burned rather than allowed to fall into the hands of the enemy (*Official Records, post,* 1 ser., vol. XV, pp. 504–10). He was greatly handicapped, however, by the loss of New Orleans and the lower river parishes and was therefore unable to carry on an effective administration or to render any great amount of assistance to the Confederate government. When Banks made a raid up the Red River in the spring of 1864, his plantation in Rapides Parish was confiscated and his home and sugar mill destroyed. After the surrender of E. Kirby-Smith in May 1865, Moore, whose arrest had been ordered by the Louisiana state Senate newly organized under the constitution of 1864, fled to Havana, Cuba. Through the intercession of friends he was finally allowed to return home with a full pardon, and he spent the remainder of his days trying to restore his plantation and recover the losses he had sustained in the war. He took no further part in party politics and died on his plantation near Alexandria. He was married on Nov. 30, 1830, to Bethiah Jane Leonard of Rapides Parish, the daughter of Edward Augustus and Sarah (Morris) Leonard. They had five children.

[A few papers in possession of his grand-daughter, Mrs. Shirley Bruce Staples, Alexandria, La., some of which are published in G. P. Whittington, "Thomas O. Moore," and "Concerning the Loyalty of Slaves" in *La. Hist. Quart.,* Jan. 1930, Oct. 1931; see also Alcée Fortier, *A Hist. of La.* (1909), vols. III, IV, and *La.,* vol. II (1909); M. L. McLure, "The Elections of 1860 in La.," *La. Hist. Quart.,* Oct. 1926; J. K. Greer, "La. Politics," *Ibid.,* July, Oct. 1930; *War of the Rebellion: Official Records (Army),* esp. 1 ser., vols. I, VI, XV, 4 ser., vols. I, II; *Jefferson Davis . . . Letters, Papers and Speeches,* ed. by Dunbar Rowland (1923), vols. V, VI.]
         E. M. V.

MOORE, THOMAS PATRICK (1796?–July 21, 1853), Kentucky congressman and minister to Colombia, was born in Charlotte County, Va., but removed in early childhood to Mercer County, Ky. The first record of him in Kentucky history is that of his enlistment during the War of 1812. From August until October 1812 he was a private in the company of Capt. George Trotter of the 1st Regiment of Kentucky Light Dragoons (*Report of the Adjutant General of the State of Kentucky: Soldiers of the War of 1812,* 1891, p. 35). His service in this war is often confused with that of Major T. P. Moore of the Virginia troops. After the war he attended Transylvania University and studied law with Judge John Green. In 1819 and 1820 he served in the state House of Representatives from Mercer County. The *Journal of the House of Representatives . . . of Kentucky* shows that in his first term he was a member of the committee on grievances, and, in his second, of that on courts of justice (1819, p. 7, 1820, p. 7). From March 1823 until March 1829 he was a member of the federal House of Representatives, where his most important committee assignment was that on manufactures which he was holding at the close of his services. It does not appear that he was an active legislator, but as a pronounced partisan of Jackson he achieved considerable prominence. John Quincy Adams recorded his opinion that "his integrity is problematical, and his only public service, the servility of his prostitution to the cause of Jackson's election and the baseness of his slanders upon me," and again that he was "a man generally despised" (*Memoirs of John Quincy Adams,* ed. by C. F. Adams, VIII, 1876, 112, 189). He was named minister plenipotentiary to Colombia on Mar. 13, 1829, to succeed William Henry Harrison [*q.v.*]. He ingratiated himself with Bolivar and in the first few weeks of his ministry obtained important commercial concessions for the United States. After the withdrawal of Ecuador and Venezuela, he remained at Bogotá and exerted himself to bring about a reunion of the three states. When these efforts failed he asked to be recalled in 1832 but at Jackson's request stayed for another year.

In the Black Hawk War, as in the War of 1812, he has been credited with a military record belonging to some one else (F. B. Heitman, *Historical Register and Dictionary of the United States Army,* 1903, vol. I, p. 723). As a matter of fact he did not return from New Granada until June 1833 (*Niles' Weekly Register,* June 8, 1833) and then plunged at once into a campaign for election to Congress against Robert P. Letcher. He was given the certificate of election, but Letcher brought a contest before Congress on the grounds of fraud and that body ordered a new election, in which Moore was defeated (*Ibid.,* Sept. 7, 14, 1833). He remained in private life until the war with Mexico. In March 1847 he was appointed lieutenant-colonel of the 3rd Regiment, United States Infantry, and in April was given the same command in the 3rd Regiment, United States Dragoons. He was honorably mustered out July 31, 1848 (Heitman, *ante*). Returning to Kentucky he was elected a delegate to the constitutional convention of 1849 and served on the committee on miscellaneous provisions. This was his last public service. He died of paralysis at Harrodsburg. He was married three times and was survived by three children.

[H. Levin, *The Lawyers and Lawmakers of Ky.* (1897); Lewis and R. H. Collins, *Hist. of Ky.,* 2 vols. (1874); *Biog. Directory Am. Cong.* (1928); J. D. Richardson, *A Compilation of the Messages and Papers of the Presidents,* vol. II (1896), pp. 467, 595; *House Exec. Doc. 173,* 22 Cong., 1 Sess. (1832); *Louisville Daily Democrat,* July 26, 1853; *Report of the Debates and Proc. of the Convention for the Revision of the Constitution . . . of Ky.* (1849); date of birth from statement of age as 53, in 1849, *Ibid.,* p. 7.]   R. S. C.

MOORE, VERANUS ALVA (Apr. 13, 1859– Feb. 11, 1931), bacteriologist, pathologist, leader in veterinary science, was born at Hounsfield, Jefferson County, N. Y., the son of Alva and Antinette Elizabeth Moore. The physical and mental qualities of a hardy, industrious ancestry characterized his personality and work throughout his life. His early education was obtained in the public schools and at Mexico Academy, Oswego County, N. Y., where he graduated in 1883. He was unfortunate in meeting with an accident in his youth, which necessitated much medical attention and the use of crutches until he was twenty-five years of age. His physical suffering and his frequent contact with physicians aroused his interest in the medical profession, and with a view to entering it, he enrolled at Cornell University in the fall of 1883, graduating with the degree of A.B. in 1887. That same year he accepted a position in the division of animal pathology, United States bureau of animal industry, where he investigated livestock diseases. At night he studied at the Columbian (now George Washington University) Medical School, from which institution he received the degree of M.D. in 1890, and where he was immediately appointed demonstrator, and later, professor of normal histology. In 1895 he succeeded Dr. Theobald Smith as chief of the division of animal pathology, which position he held until 1896, when he resigned to become professor of comparative pathology, bacteriology, and meat inspection at the veterinary college, Cornell University. He served continuously at Cornell until his retirement on June 21, 1929, at the age of seventy. During the last twenty-one years he held the position of dean, and from 1898 to 1910 was also professor of pathology and bacteriology in the Ithaca division of the medical college. The veterinary college developed under his administration until it became an outstanding institution of its kind. It is said that during the thirty-three years he was connected with Cornell he never missed a class on account of personal disability. In the fall following his retirement as dean, he was appointed superintendent of the Ithaca Memorial Hospital, which position he retained until his death.

As a bacteriologist and pathologist Moore had an international reputation. President Theodore Roosevelt appointed him a member of the International Conference on Tuberculosis, and President Hoover made him a member of the Conference on Child Life. He was also one of a commission of scientists appointed by the secretary of agriculture in 1907 to pass judgment upon the federal meat inspection regulations. When the United States entered the World War, Moore was called to Washington to assist in organizing the veterinary corps of the United States Army.

As a research worker he was concerned with tubercle bacilli in milk, bovine tuberculosis, infectious leukemia (now called fowl typhoid), diphtheria in fowls, swine plague, rabies, rabbit septicemia, enterohepatitis, corn-stalk disease, actinomycosis, glanders, and infectious abortion. The incalculable services he rendered to the livestock industry were recognized everywhere and his researches contributed much toward extending the outposts of knowledge in the field of veterinary medicine. Among his principal publications are: *Laboratory Directions for Beginners in Bacteriology* (1898); *The Pathology and Differential Diagnosis of Infectious Diseases of Animals* (1902); *Principles of Mi-*

crobiology (1912); *Bovine Tuberculosis and its Control* (1913); *History of Veterinary Education and Service from 1896 to 1929* (1929). He also delivered many addresses and contributed numerous articles on infectious diseases to government and state publications, and to medical and veterinary journals. On July 12, 1892, he married Mary L. Slawson of Cicero, N. Y., by whom he had three children.

[*Who's Who in America*, 1930–31; J. M. Cattell and D. R. Brimhall, *Am. Men of Sci.* (3rd ed., 1921); *Veterinary Medicine*, Aug. 1929; *Report of the N. Y. State Veterinary Coll., 1928–29* and *1930–31* (1930, 1932); V. A. Moore, *N. Y. State Veterinary Coll., a Special Report to the President of Cornell Univ.* (1908); *N. Y. Times*, Feb. 12, 1931.]   J. R. M.

MOORE, WILLIAM (May 6, 1699–May 30, 1783), Pennsylvania jurist, was born in Philadelphia. He was the son of John Moore [*q.v.*], collector of the port of Philadelphia, and his wife, Rebecca Axtell of South Carolina. According to family tradition, he was educated in England and graduated at Oxford in 1719, but he does not appear in the list of matriculates of the institution. About 1722 he married Williamina Wemyss, a relative of the Earl of Wemyss in the peerage of Scotland. Shortly after his marriage, his father gave him a large tract of land in Chester County, a few miles from Valley Forge, and he lived there for more than fifty years. The stone house that he built on this estate is still called Moore Hall. During the French and Indian War, he was colonel of a Chester County militia regiment. He was a devout churchman and was a vestryman of St. James Church on the Perkiomen and later of the church at Radnor in Delaware County.

He was a member of the Provincial Assembly for Chester County from 1733 until 1740, when he refused to be a candidate for reëlection. He was a justice of the peace from 1741 to 1783 and was the presiding judge of the Chester County court during most of the period from 1750 to 1776. It is believed that he was associated with the Quaker or anti-proprietary party until 1755, when he became involved in a controversy with them over the question of military defense. The frontier settlements of Pennsylvania were ravaged by the Indians, after Braddock's defeat, and on Nov. 5, 1755, a petition was sent to the Assembly from Chester County demanding security and protection. Moore's name heads the list of signatures and he probably wrote the petition itself. This made him obnoxious to the Quaker majority in the Assembly and they organized an attack upon his integrity as a judge. They were helped by Isaac Wayne, the father of Anthony Wayne, who lived near Moore Hall and was one of Moore's personal enemies. Through Wayne's efforts, twenty-eight petitions were presented to the Assembly in 1757 urging Moore's removal as presiding judge on the ground that he had been tyrannical, unjust, and extortionate in the performance of his duties. Moore denied the jurisdiction of the Assembly, but an *ex parte* investigation was conducted and a formal address was sent to Gov. William Denny praying that he should be removed from office. As this document was printed and widely circulated, Moore decided that his answer, in which he referred to the conduct of the Assembly as "virulent and slanderous," should be given equal publicity. On Jan. 6, 1758, he was arrested for libel and for violating the privileges of the Assembly and was imprisoned in the common gaol in Philadelphia. The Rev. William Smith [*q.v.*], the principal of the Academy of Philadelphia, who had opposed the Assembly on the defense issue, was also imprisoned on the charge of assisting Moore in the preparation of his address. The Assembly forbade the courts to issue a writ of *habeas corpus* and both of the prisoners remained in gaol for almost three months, when the house adjourned and they were released by the governor. The governor and council also investigated the judicial charges that had been brought against Moore and he was completely exonerated.

After this episode, Moore returned to his home and his duties as a judge and led an uneventful life until the beginning of the American Revolution. He was too old to take an active part in that movement, but his sympathies were obviously with the Loyalists. When he was visited by a Whig committee in 1775 and asked to recant his views, he signed a curious and somewhat equivocal statement. It is doubtful whether his visitors fully appreciated the sarcasm of the following sentence: "I also further declare that I have of late encouraged and will continue to encourage learning the military art, apprehending that the time is not far distant when there may be occasion for it" (Futhey and Cope, *post*, p. 663). He was always noted for his hospitality, however, and he entertained Col. Clement Biddle and other American officers while Washington's army was encamped at Valley Forge. He died at Moore Hall on May 30, 1783, and was buried in the churchyard at Radnor. He was survived by his wife, who died in 1784; and by five of his twelve children.

[There is a volume of Moore's manuscripts in the possession of the Pa. Hist. Soc., but it contains very little biographical data. The Society also has a manuscript volume entitled *Smith and Moore vs. the Assembly, 1758–59.* For the printed material see D. M. Hall, *Six Centuries of the Moores of Fawley, Berkshire, England, and their Descendants* (1904); H. W. Smith, *Life and Correspondence of the Rev. William Smith, D.D.* (2 vols., 1880); J. S. Futhey and G. Cope, *Hist. of Chester County, Pa.* (1881), containing sketch reprinted in S. W. Pennypacker, *Hist. and Biog. Sketches* (1883); W. R. Riddell, "Libel on the Assembly: A Prerevolutionary Episode," *Pa. Mag. of Hist. and Biog.,* Apr.–Oct. 1928; and the *Pa. Gazette,* June 18, 1783.]

            W. R. S.

MOORE, WILLIAM (*c.* 1735–July 24, 1793), merchant, Revolutionary patriot, jurist, was born in Philadelphia, the son of Robert and Elizabeth Moore. His father, a native of the Isle of Man, was a shopkeeper of some means. Educated for a mercantile career, William became a successful merchant. His marriage to Sarah, daughter of Thomas and Susannah Lloyd, Dec. 13, 1757, allied him with one of the oldest and most influential families of provincial Pennsylvania. Although opposing the Stamp Act and subscribing to the non-importation agreements in 1765, he disapproved of more radical measures in the early revolutionary period, his son of sixteen bringing great distress to his parents by enlisting with the patriot army for the Canadian expedition, 1775–76. Before his return, however, both father and mother had "caught the delusion" of the patriots and from that time on Moore gave liberally of his time and money to the American cause. He supported the state constitution of 1776, not out of thorough agreement with it but from the conviction that the salvation of the state demanded such a course.

 On Dec. 10, 1776, Moore was appointed by the assembly to the council of safety, and on Mar. 13, 1777, by the supreme executive council to the newly organized board of war. Elected to Congress, Feb. 5, 1777, he declined to serve owing to the pressure of business affairs. He was a member of the supreme executive council from October 1779 to October 1782, of which he was vice-president the first two years and president the third. Although a Constitutionalist, he was of a more sober temper than most of his party, and possessed the confidence and warm regard of many in the opposite party, as testified to by his almost unanimous election as president. During his tenure, a period of great financial distress for the state, the Anti-Constitutionalists made further inroads on their steadily weakening opponents. He disagreed with the paper-money views of his own party, accepting the more conservative position of Robert Morris, 1734–1806 [*q.v.*], for whom he entertained a warm friendship. A jealous guardian of executive privilege, he attacked the assembly for withdrawing money from the

treasury without the council's consent. His letters while president reveal a man of character and energy, of broad education, remarkable for his practicality and cool deliberation. On Nov. 14, 1781, by virtue of being president, he was commissioned judge of the Pennsylvania high court of errors and appeals, the council reviewing his commission on Mar. 18, 1783. During and after his presidency he was active in promoting plans to solve Pennsylvania's financial difficulties, and in July 1784 presided at a public meeting in Philadelphia held for that purpose. He was elected to the assembly in 1784, was director of the Bank of Pennsylvania, trustee of the University of the State of Pennsylvania, 1784–89, and a conspicuous member of the St. Tammany Society. In later life he continued to play an important part in Philadelphia's civic affairs. Moore was a man of striking appearance, of dignified bearing, and possessed an agreeable manner. He left three children, his only daughter Elizabeth in 1784 having married François de Barbé Marbois, French chargé d'affaires, who later negotiated the treaty for the sale of Louisiana to the United States.

 [J. P. Parke and Townsend Ward, *Geneal. Notes* (1898); W. C. Armor, *Lives of the Govs. of Pa.* (1872); C. P. Keith, *The Provincial Councillors of Pa.* (1883); *Pa. Archives,* 1 ser. VII–X (1853–54), 2 ser., I (1874), 4 ser. III (1900), 827–54; *Minutes of the Provincial Council of Pa.,* vols. XI–XIII (1852); *Pa. Mag. of Hist. and Biog.,* Oct. 1885, pp. 278–79, Oct. 1902, pp. 341–42; Oct. 1917, p. 435.]

            J. H. P.

MOORE, WILLIAM HENRY (Oct. 25, 1848–Jan. 11, 1923), capitalist and promoter, was born in Utica, N. Y., the son of Nathaniel F. and Rachel (Beckwith) Moore, of colonial descent. His father was a banker and his mother was the daughter of a banker. After attending a seminary at Oneida and then the Cortland Academy at Homer, N. Y., he entered Amherst in 1867 but left in 1870 before graduation because of ill health. He studied law and was admitted to the bar at Eau Claire, Wis., in 1872, but in the same year went to Chicago, where he entered the offices of Edward A. Small, a leading corporation lawyer. After a year and a half as managing clerk he was made partner, under the firm name of Small, Burke, and Moore, and on Oct. 31, 1878, he married Ada W. Small, the daughter of his partner. They had three children. At Small's death in 1882 he took into partnership his younger brother, James Hobart Moore. They continued in active practice until 1887, and in later life Moore was commonly referred to as "Judge." He gained wide repute for his skill in the intricacies of corporation law, but gradually the brothers forsook legal practice for corporate promotion and management. They were among the first to recognize the possibilities of industrial mergers in America, and—next to Morgan—perhaps the most important in developing them.

Their first important venture was the reorganization of the Diamond Match Company with an increase of capitalization to $7,500,000 and later to $11,000,000. Six months later they reorganized a combination of strawboard manufacturers, with a capitalization of $7,000,000. In 1890 they brought several Eastern cracker factories together into the New York Biscuit Company, with a capitalization of $9,000,000. But Moore was playing for higher stakes than promotion returns. With other Chicago financiers to back him, he formed a pool to boost and sustain the price of Diamond Match in the Chicago Exchange. There was talk of technical improvements, and of negotiations with various foreign countries for contracts or the establishment of factories. It is not clear how much of this was genuine expectation on Moore's part, and how much unprincipled conjecture or less. Diamond Match rose from 120 in January 1896 to 248 in May; a similar sympathetic movement took place in New York Biscuit. The plan seems to have been to sustain the prices until some tangible favorable development would enable the holders to "unload" on outsiders at top prices. For six months there was a Diamond Match craze; for weeks almost the entire business of the exchange was in the Moore stocks. But the failure of the mysterious foreign negotiations to eventuate, and the Bryan Populist scare, took the strength out of the boom. Some of the insiders in the pool treacherously began unloading on the Moores. Finally after desperate efforts to bolster their margins—efforts which included the withdrawal of $800,-000 of the match company's funds for that purpose—the Moores gave up, and on the night of Aug. 3 the panicky leaders of the Exchange decided to close it the next morning. The panic was felt a bit on the New York Exchange, and there was even some liquidation in London, while the Chicago Exchange "did not find it convenient" to open for three months. While Moore's losses, which were originally estimated at about eight million, were scaled down to four, they meant a burden of debt and a blow to his prestige.

Moore went about imperturbably retrieving his career. His tall, thick-set, commanding figure, his sure and confident voice, his genial, self-sufficient smile were not those of a shattered man. He was forced out of Diamond Match, but

so successfully did he in his other venture, with the backing of Armour and Pullman, engineer a price war against the American Biscuit and Manufacturing Company that the only possible result was a merger—the National Biscuit Company, formed in February 1898 with a capital of $55,000,000 and a monopoly control of 90 per cent of the cracker-biscuit companies of the country. In its incorporation under the favorable New Jersey laws, in its capitalization not only of tangible assets but also of projected "good-will" and anticipated monopoly profits, and in the large "melon" reserved for promotion, the new company served as a model for subsequent consolidations. It was immediately and immensely successful. Moore's prestige was restored. He was besieged with requests to organize companies "from the marshes of Maine to the Pacific coast" (*Industrial Commission Report, post*, p. 963), of which he selected only a few and on his own terms.

Turning to the steel industry, he organized in rapid succession (December 1898–April 1899) the American Tin Plate Company, the National Steel Company, and the American Steel Hoop Company with a total capitalization of $142,-000,000, of which at least $20,000,000 went for promotion. Despite the fact that the stock of all three companies was plentifully watered and represented anticipated profits rather than actual properties, it was eagerly caught up and oversubscribed. The Moores seemed to have found the secret of successful promotion. Wall Street was probably not far wrong in guessing that it lay in the creation of monopolistic control, the contrivance of devices to avoid the operation of the anti-trust laws, the reorganization of production and marketing to effect economies, and the retention of control in the hands of a small group. This group consisted of the two Moores, Daniel G. Reid, and William B. Leeds, the latter two being accessions from the tin-plate industry. Together they formed the "Moore gang," the "Moore crowd," the "Moore interests," and "the Big Four from the Prairies," as they were variously known on Wall Street, and they continued to work together.

In May 1899 a syndicate headed by Moore agreed to pay $320,000,000 for the combined Carnegie-Frick properties. Carnegie insisted that the dealings should be with his partners Henry Clay Frick and Henry Phipps, Jr. [*qq.v.*], and gave them power of attorney. They joined the syndicate; Moore paid $1,000,000 for a ninety days' option and Frick and Phipps added $170,000. The negotiations seemed to have every chance of success, but the failure of expected financial support to materialize, and the presence on the market of too many "undigested securities" made it impossible for the syndicate to obtain the necessary cash. Carnegie relentlessly refused to extend the option, and kept the option money. The Moores now turned to other consolidations—that of the American Sheet Steel Company in February 1900, and that of the American Can Company in March 1901. Their companies formed one of the four main groups in the steel industry, the other three being the Carnegie, Morgan, and Rockefeller groups, and when Morgan succeeded in buying out Carnegie and launching the new $1,400,000 United States Steel Corporation in 1901, they were included. It was generally believed that the Moore companies, although the most heavily overcapitalized, received the best terms of all. Moore himself was placed on the board of directors of the new corporation, and Reid on the executive committee. But Morgan had no intention of admitting the Moore group to active control: their peculiar type of speculative and predatory activity was too unlike his own conception of business methods. Enormously wealthy now, they turned their money and attention elsewhere.

The West had been partitioned into four railroad empires—those of Hill, Harriman, Gould, and Morgan. But the Chicago, Rock Island, & Pacific Railway, as a comparatively minor road, had been left out of the calculations. Its management was conservative and responsible and paid good dividends, but lacked daring and imagination. These the Moores were ready to supply. After a stock-buying campaign of nine months, during which the stock rose from 80 to 160, Moore forced his way into the control. On June 4, 1901, he and Reid were elected to the board of directors of the Rock Island; on Dec. 12, Leeds was installed in the presidency and James Moore was added to the board of directors; finally on Jan. 30, 1902, the Moore interests placed four of their number on the executive committee of seven, pushing out the Cable interests, and took complete charge of the road. Despite suspicion and hostility on Wall Street, they set out on a brilliant campaign of expansion; technical matters were handled by Reid and matters of financial strategy by Moore himself. In rapid succession they bought up or leased a number of roads, acquiring mileage and terminal facilities that would make of the Rock Island an important transcontinental system. The stock continued to rise, reaching 200 in July 1902. The capitalization, which had remained at fifty million since 1880,

was increased to sixty in July 1901 and to seventy-five in June 1902. Applying to the new field the magnificence of operation that had characterized their steel finance, the Moores announced in August a proposed reorganization of the Rock Island, and a "rearrangement of securities." Wall Street, accustomed as it was to financial manipulation, was bewildered by the intricacies of the new scheme. Three companies were to be created, in a double-holding company arrangement, and each holder of $100 of stock in the original company was to receive $270 in bonds and stock (for details see Poor's Manual of the Railroads of the United States, 1903, pp. 1514–24). Albert W. Atwood, writing in Harper's Weekly, Mar. 28, 1914, called this reorganization "the most astounding piece of stock-watering the world has ever seen." To pay interest and dividends on an increase in capitalization of 270% placed an enormous burden upon properties and revenues, especially since the stock of the railway was replaced by the bonds of the operating company, with the consequent substitution of fixed charges for dividends. The financial world felt doubtful about the whole matter, and in Sunday newspapers, magazines, and financial weeklies the proposed reorganization was met with a burst of disfavor. But the plan was pushed through, and Moore went on with his career of conquest. In the winter of 1902 he added to the Rock Island system the St. Louis & San Francisco Railroad, with a mileage of over 5,000 miles, and B. F. Yoakum of the latter line was added to the inside group of the Rock Island. In 1904, to the great chagrin of Harriman, they captured a stock majority in the Chicago & Alton Railroad Company. Moore became known as the "Sphinx of the Rock Island." He went on his way with a complete indifference to public sentiment, and stood out in the first decade of the new century as the foremost and most daring promoter in American business, just as Morgan was the foremost financier. He had behind him the backing of a dozen banks and trust companies, and was the leader of a group that controlled fifteen thousand miles of railroad.

During the next few years Moore obtained control of the Lehigh Valley Railroad, and with the aid of an English syndicate (Pearson-Farquhar) he began to buy into the Denver & Rio Grande Railroad Company, the Missouri Pacific Railway Company, and the Wabash Railroad Company. But he met with reverses. The St. Louis & San Francisco had turned out to be a distinct loss, and in 1909 it was returned to the original owners with a loss of

$20,000,000. The Chicago & Alton had also been returned at a loss in 1907. The operations of Moore and the English syndicate were hampered by the tightening of the market, and were finally taken over by Kuhn, Loeb & Company. The holding company scheme of the Rock Island drained the road and placed an incubus on all future holdings. In the end the Rock Island went into receivership. The entire period of Moore control was described in periodicals as "the looting of the Rock Island." It was pointed out that the stock had declined from $200 in 1902 to $20 in 1914, although the road's earnings had steadily increased. A stockholders' protective committee was formed under N. L. Amster, with Samuel Untermeyer as counsel, the latter declaring that in comparison with the Moore maneuvers "the manipulators of the old Fisk-Gould days were artless children." In 1916 the Interstate Commerce Commission issued a drastic report, arraigning Moore, Reid, and the other members of the controlling group, and charging them with deliberate misrepresentation and with looting the railroad. The receivership was ended on June 24, 1917, and the Moore group was ousted from control.

Moore now retired from active business interests. He had built up a stable which was regarded as the equal of any in the turf world, and he had the best string of hackneys in the country. He entered his horses in international competitions and had an absorbing interest in the fashionable Madison Square Garden horse shows. His own skill as a four-in-hand driver was internationally known. He died of heart disease at his New York home.

[For Moore's early life and the first stages of his career, see Will Payne, "The Imperturbable Moores," *Everybody's Mag.*, June 1903; the obituaries in the *N. Y. Times* and other papers for Jan. 12, 1923; the accounts in the *N. Y. Times* of the Diamond Match episode on the Chicago Stock Exchange, especially for the week Aug. 3–10, 1896; the National Biscuit Co. house organ, *The N B C*, March 1923, pp. 5–8. For Moore's activities in the steel industry, see his testimony in *Industrial Commission. Preliminary Report on Trusts and Industrial Combinations* (1900), I, 959–67; *Report of the Commissioners of Corporations on the Steel Industry*, pt. I (1911), pp. 1–180, esp. 8–13, 85–91, 133–41, 176–79; the files of the *Commercial and Financial Chronicle*, 1898–1901, containing detailed announcements and comment on stock issues, directors' meetings and corporate reorganizations in the various Moore promotions; for differing versions of the Moore negotiations for buying out Carnegie, see George Harvey, *Henry Clay Frick the Man* (1928), pp. 204–15, and B. J. Hendrick, *The Life of Andrew Carnegie* (1932), II, 76–88, highly illuminating for their contrast; for the Morgan negotiations, see Lewis Corey, *The House of Morgan* (1930), ch. xxiii. For Moore's railroad career, see *Interstate Commerce Commission Reports*, vol. XXXVI (1916), pp. 43–61, the most valuable source; see also the following periodical accounts: C. M. Keys, "The Newest Railroad Power," and "The Overlords of the Railroad Traffic," *World's Work*, June 1905, Jan. 1907; R. W.

Vincent, "The Inside Story of Rock Island—'Frisco Financing,'" *Moody's Mag.*, Jan. 1909; A. Franklin, "Current Railroad Strategy," and "The Big R. R. Deal that Went Wrong," *Bankers Mag.*, July, Sept., 1910; A. W. Atwood, "Upsetting an Inverted Pyramid," *Harper's Weekly*, Mar. 28, 1914; T. Prince, "The Rock Island Situation," and "The Rock Island," *Moody's Mag.*, Mar. 1915, Aug. 1916; T. Gibson, "The Chicago, Rock Island & Pacific Ry. Co.," *Ibid.*, Sept. 1916.]							M. L.

MOORE, WILLIAM THOMAS (Aug. 27, 1832–Sept. 7, 1926), clergyman of the Disciples of Christ, was born in Henry County, Ky. His father, Richard Moore, was of Irish ancestry; his mother, Nancy M. (Jones), of Scotch extraction. They moved from Virginia to Kentucky and thence to Indiana, where Richard Moore died when William Thomas, the eldest son among six children, was nine years old. The family then returned to Kentucky, and William within a few years was its chief support. At eighteen he had received practically no schooling but had read the Bible and a few histories. In 1850 he entered an academy at New Castle, Ky. He then taught and preached, and in 1855 entered Bethany College, Va. (now W. Va.), graduating in 1858.

For six years thereafter he was pastor at Frankfort, Ky. In 1864 he married Mary A. Bishop, daughter of R. M. Bishop of Cincinnati, later governor of Ohio; Richard Bishop Moore [*q.v.*] was one of their children. From January 1865 to February 1866 he was pastor of the Jefferson Avenue Christian Church, Detroit, Mich. Thence he was called to a professorship in Kentucky University and later elected to a pastorate in Cincinnati, Ohio. He accepted the pastorate conditionally, served as professor at Kentucky University for one year, 1866–67, at the same time teaching sacred rhetoric and ecclesiastical history at the College of the Bible, Lexington, and for two years thereafter delivered a brief course of lectures annually at Kentucky University. During his Cincinnati pastorate he made his congregation the largest and most far-reaching in influence of any in his brotherhood.

He was a member of the executive committee of the American Christian Missionary Society and of the committee to revise the church hymnbook (1864). He was chairman of a committee of twenty which drafted a plan of work adopted in 1869 by the national convention of the Society at Louisville, Ky. In 1874, realizing that the "Louisville Plan" was unsatisfactory, he called a meeting and urged the organization of a foreign-missionary society. As a result, during the convention of 1875, the Foreign Christian Missionary Society was formed. Moore was vice-president, 1875–77, secretary, 1876–77, and member of the board of managers, 1883–84.

In July 1878 he entered the service of the Society. After preaching for three years in Southport and Liverpool, England, he was for ten years minister at the West London Tabernacle. While here, in 1881, he began to publish the *Christian Commonwealth,* which he edited actively for sixteen years, and by proxy through his eldest son, Paul, for five years more. His first wife died Apr. 14, 1888, and on Aug. 20, 1890, he married Emma S. Frederick of Carthage, N. Y. In 1896 he became dean of the Bible College of Missouri, a new school established in Columbia, Mo., by the Disciples of Christ, adjacent to the University of Missouri, to train young men for the ministry and to supply to university students such religious studies as a tax-supported institution cannot offer. He remained in Columbia until 1909, serving for part of the time as chaplain and professor in the Christian College there, an institution for women, of which his wife was president. From 1897 to 1900 he edited the *Christian Quarterly,* which he had founded and edited from 1869 to 1877. In 1909 he moved to Florida, where he spent his remaining years. He died at Orlando, at the age of ninety-four.

Moore was the author of a number of books on religious subjects and a contributor to periodicals. His best-known publications include *The Living Pulpit of the Christian Church* (cop. 1867), a series of sermons by representative ministers of the Disciples of Christ, with biographical sketches; a similar series, *The New Living Pulpit of the Christian Church* (1918); and *A Comprehensive History of the Disciples of Christ* (1909). He was more than six feet tall, weighed nearly two hundred pounds, and wore a patriarchal beard reaching to his waist. A man of tremendous vitality (he went swimming in Lake Michigan after he was ninety, and continued to preach until shortly before his death), he was a prominent figure in his denomination for more than half a century.

[F. M. Green, *Christian Missions and Hist. Sketches* (1884); J. T. Brown, *Churches of Christ* (1904); J. W. Monser, *The Literature of the Disciples* (1906); J. H. Garrison, *The Reformation of the Nineteenth Century* (1901) and *The Story of a Century* (1909); Archibald McLean, *The Hist. of the Foreign Christian Missionary Soc.* (1921); A. W. Fortune, *The Disciples in Ky.* (1932); *The Biog. Encyc. of Ky.* (1878); J. F. Brennan, *A Biog. Cyc. . . . of Ohio* (1879); *Who's Who in America,* 1910–11; *Pensacola Jour.,* Sept. 8, 1926; *N. Y. Times,* Sept. 9, 12, 1926; information as to certain facts from friends and relatives.]   G. D. E.

MOORE, ZEPHANIAH SWIFT (Nov. 20, 1770–June 30, 1823), Congregational clergyman, college president, was born in Palmer, Mass., the son of Judah and Mary (Swift)

Moore. He was descended from John Moore who settled at Sudbury, Mass., in 1642. In 1778 the family moved to Wilmington, Vt., where Zephaniah worked for ten years on his father's farm. During this time he evinced a keen intelligence and so strong a desire for a college education that his parents at considerable sacrifice to themselves sent him to Bennington, Vt., for a brief preparatory course and afterwards to Dartmouth College, where he graduated with distinction in 1793. The next year he taught as principal of the academy in Londonderry, N. H. He then took up the study of theology with the Rev. Charles Backus of Somers, Conn., and was licensed to preach in 1796. Having received invitations to various places, he accepted a call in 1797 to the First Congregational Church at Leicester, Mass., where he remained for fourteen years. Throughout this period he served as trustee of Leicester Academy and from July 1806 to October 1807, was principal preceptor. Soon after settling at Leicester he was married, Feb. 21, 1799, to Phebe Drury of Ward (now Auburn), Mass. In 1811 he became professor of learned languages (Latin, Greek, and Hebrew) in Dartmouth College, his alma mater, where he taught with so much success that in 1815 he was elected to the presidency of Williams College. In recognition of this honor Dartmouth conferred on him the degree of doctor of divinity. As chief executive of Williams he proved to be highly efficient. He was, however, one of those who believed that the institution could not continue to prosper in its isolated location and that it should be removed to a more accessible place in the Connecticut Valley. Strong opposition to this plan developed and the controversy was continued until 1820 (Durfee, *post,* p. 157), when the legislature rejected the petition of the trustees for removal of the college to Northampton. Just at this time plans were being formed for the establishment of a college at Amherst, Mass., and Moore was invited to be its first president. He accepted the task in May 1821, and fifteen of the students at Williams accompanied him to Amherst. Under his able leadership, in spite of the meager resources then available in New England for such an enterprise, the institution was successfully launched. He lived, however, to complete barely two years of service in his new position. Weakened by excessive labors he succumbed after a brief illness to an attack of "bilious colic." He left no children, but his widow survived till 1857.

Moore was a large man of even temperament and kindly disposition. He wore the conservative knee-breeches when long trousers were becoming fashionable, and his manners while pleasant and unassuming were marked by a quiet dignity. He readily won the confidence and loyalty of those with whom he worked. He excelled especially as a college officer, governing the undergraduates with great firmness, but so wisely as to win their esteem and even their affection. As a preacher he employed little action or rhetorical embellishment, but by reason of a clear, concise, and logical exposition of the subject and great sincerity and earnestness of delivery he was uniformly impressive. His religious views were strictly orthodox, conforming to those prevalent in New England at that period. As an educationalist he held firmly to the importance of liberal studies as a preparation for professional work, insisting also that religious instruction was quite as essential as intellectual training.

[W. S. Tyler, Hist. of Amherst Coll. (1873); Calvin Durfee, A Hist. of Williams Coll. (1860); L. W. Spring, A Hist. of Williams Coll. (1917); W. B. Sprague, Annals. Am. Pulpit, vol. II (1857); L. B. Richardson, Hist. of Dartmouth Coll. (1932), vol. I; Quarterly Register, Feb. 1833; Emory Washburn, in New-Eng. Hist. and Geneal. Reg., Oct. 1847; Ibid., July 1903, Apr. 1904; Christian Spectator, Sept. 1, 1823; Boston Daily Advertiser, July 4, 1823. A number of Moore's addresses and sermons, some of them in manuscript, are preserved in the Amherst, Dartmouth, and Williams College libraries.]   H. P. G.

MOOREHEAD, WILLIAM GALLOGLY (Mar. 19, 1836–Mar. 1, 1914), United Presbyterian clergyman, Biblical scholar, was born on a farm near Rix Mills, Muskingum County, Ohio. His parents were David and Margaret (Henderson) Moorehead. He graduated at Muskingum College in 1858 and studied theology at the Allegheny and Xenia theological seminaries of the United Presbyterian Church, graduating from the latter in 1862. During his seminary course he was licensed to preach, April 1861, and acted as a stated supply at Urbana, Ohio, until some time in the early part of 1862. On July 1, 1862, he was ordained to the ministry in connection with his appointment by the General Assembly of the United Presbyterian Church as a missionary in Italy under the direction of the American and Foreign Christian Union. About seven years (1862–69) were spent in Italy, the first two being devoted to mastering the language, the last five to missionary work in Florence and Sienna. In 1869 he returned to America and the next year became pastor of the First United Presbyterian Church, Xenia, Ohio, continuing to serve until 1875. While in this pastorate he was elected in 1873 to the chair of New Testament literature and exegesis at Xenia Theological Seminary,

which position he retained until 1908, when he insisted on being relieved. In April 1875 he was called to the Fourth United Presbyterian Church of Allegheny, Pa., where he served until January 1876, without interrupting his classroom work. From 1878 to 1885 he was pastor of the Third Church of Xenia, this charge being an annex to his professorship. When the board of management of the seminary reluctantly consented to his withdrawal, in 1908, from the chair he had occupied since 1873, it induced him to take up the lighter duties of the Newburgh chair of English Bible and Biblical theology. To this work the last years of his life were given so that he completed four decenniums of continuous service as a professor in Xenia Theological Seminary before he died. In 1899 he had become president of the Seminary and he filled that office until his death.

Moorehead had a gracious personality and was an able preacher and teacher. In Bible Schools and at special conferences he was a notably successful lecturer. He was frequently heard at Winona, at Grove City, Pa., in various Chautauquas, at Niagara, and at the Moody Bible Institute, Chicago. He wrote a number of books dealing with the Bible: *Studies in the Mosaic Institutions* (1896), *Outline Studies in the Books of the Old Testament* (1893), *Studies in the Four Gospels* (1900), *Outline Studies in Acts ... Ephesians* (1902), *Outline Studies in the New Testament, Philippians to Hebrews* (1905), *Outline Studies in the New Testament, Catholic Epistles* (1910), and *Studies in the Book of Revelation* (1908). In addition to these publications he contributed to various periodicals articles dealing with subjects in the field of Biblical literature. For some time after 1908 he represented the United Presbyterian Church on the International Sunday School Lesson Committee. In 1892, 1896, and 1904 he was a delegate to the Council of Reformed Churches Throughout the World Holding the Presbyterian System.

He was married three times: first, on Aug. 9, 1864, to Helen King, who died Nov. 13, 1870; second, to Anna L. Beatty, who died Jan. 14, 1874; and third, to Elizabeth Ankeney, who survived him, dying Apr. 22, 1924. Two sons and two daughters survived him.

[United Presbyterian, Mar. 5, 12, 19, Apr. 9, 1914; Christian Union Herald, Nov. 15, 1928; Testimonial and Memorial (1913), issued in connection with the celebration of Dr. Moorehead's fortieth Seminary anniversary; Who's Who in America, 1914–15; Cincinnati Enquirer, Mar. 2, 1914.]   J. M.

MOOREHEAD, JAMES KENNEDY (Sept. 7, 1806–Mar. 6, 1884), Civil War congressman from Pennsylvania, canal builder, and pioneer in commercial telegraphy, was born in Halifax, Dauphin County, Pa. His father, William Moorhead, had emigrated from Ireland and settled in the United States in 1798. In 1814 he was appointed by President James Madison collector of internal revenue for the tenth district of Pennsylvania, but he died in 1817, leaving his wife, Elizabeth (Kennedy) Young Moorhead, a widow with several children to support and no other form of income than that which could be obtained from a farm. Under these circumstances, James's schooling ended when he was eleven years old after he had completed two years in the district school in Harrisburg. At fourteen he had the full responsibility of the farm and Moorhead's ferry. Two years later he served as an apprentice to a tanner, but he never followed the trade. Having gained a fair knowledge of building and a familiarity with water transportation, he offered a low bid and obtained the contract for the construction of the Susquehanna branch of the Pennsylvania Canal—a job which netted him almost four hundred dollars. He then remained as superintendent of the Juniata division and was the first to place a passenger packet on the system. During the ten years he spent in navigating the canal he gained a knowledge of the problems involved in managing canal transportation and in 1839 he began a connection with the Monongahela Navigation Company in Pittsburgh. In 1846 he became president of the company, retaining the position until his death thirty-eight years later. In this capacity he built many dams, locks, and reservoirs in Pennsylvania, Indiana, and Kentucky, and earned for himself the title "Old Slackwater" because of the slackwater dams. In 1840 he established the Union Cotton Factory in what is now the Northside district of Pittsburgh. Nine years later the factory burned along with his house. He rebuilt the latter but it was again destroyed in 1853 by fire. At this time he also owned a part interest in the Novelty Works in Pittsburgh.

Moorhead was one of the first to appreciate the possibilities of commercial telegraphy and it was largely through his efforts and direction, dating from 1853, that lines were established between Pittsburgh and Philadelphia. The operating company, of which he was president, was the Atlantic & Ohio Telegraph Company. He was also the president of the various companies owning lines to Cincinnati and Louisville. Afterward, when these lines were consolidated, they formed the basis of the Western Union System. In politics Moorhead was an active member of the Democratic party of that day and for

a short time held an appointment under President Van Buren as deputy postmaster of Pittsburgh (1840–41). But in the trying years from 1854 to 1858 he left the party and aided in the formation of the Republican party. In 1859 he was its successful candidate for Congress and served continuously in the lower house from 1859 to 1869. During the term of his membership he served on several important committees —commerce, national armories, manufactures, naval affairs, and ways and means—and was chairman of the two first named. In 1868 he served in his last political position, as delegate to the Republican National Convention at Chicago which nominated Ulysses S. Grant.

Moorhead always exhibited a great interest in the affairs of his church, the Presbyterian, in which he was the ruling elder, and in 1884 he went to Belfast, Ireland, as a delegate to the Pan-Presbyterian Council. Shortly afterward, upon his return to Pittsburgh, he died. He had lived to celebrate with his wife, Jane Logan, to whom he was married Dec. 17, 1829, their golden anniversary. Their family consisted of two sons and three daughters. Moorhead's native ability was the deciding factor in his success, overcoming almost total lack of material means. He brought to each task the experience gained from a previous undertaking and thus advanced step by step through his own efforts to a position of responsibility at the head of a large navigation company.

[*Memorial Vol.: Jas. Kennedy Moorhead* (privately printed, 1885); *Biog. Dir. Am. Cong.* (1928); Erasmus Wilson, ed., *Standard Hist. of Pittsburg, Pa.* (1898); the *Pittsburg Dispatch* and *Pittsburgh Post,* Mar. 7, 1884.]   A. I.

MOOSMÜLLER, OSWALD WILLIAM Feb. 26, 1832–Jan. 10, 1901), Roman Catholic priest of the Order of St. Benedict, was born into a wealthy family at Aidling in the Bavarian Alps. He was trained by tutors and in the old Benedictine College of Metten in the diocese of Ratisbon, where he learned of the pressing need for missionary priests among the German immigrants in the United States. He entered the Benedictine order, and at the end of his novitiate, in 1852, was sent to St. Vincent's Abbey at Latrobe, Pa., then under the distinguished Boniface Wimmer [*q.v.*]. Here he completed his theological studies and was ordained to the priesthood in 1856 by Bishop Michael O'Connor [*q.v.*]. After two years as an assistant in Father Gallitzin's old Carrolltown mission and in Holy Trinity Church, Brooklyn, N. Y., under the pioneer German priest, Vicar-General John Raffeiner, he was sent to St. Joseph's Church, Covington, Ky. In 1859, he went to Rio de Janeiro as a missionary to the newly arrived Germans and as a supervisor of the Benedictine program of agricultural and trade schools in Brazil. Although this task proved exceptionally difficult, because of the political anti-clericalism under Pedro II, permanent foundations were laid for subsequent work. After two years, he was transferred to Sandwich, Ont., as superior of a Benedictine monastery whose growth was thwarted by the economic consequences of the American Civil War. In 1863, he commenced a term of three years as prior of St. Mary's in Newark, N. J., a center of German missions for a large area in New York and New Jersey. He was then named procurator of the American congregation and director of St. Elizabeth's Seminary in Rome where, incidentally, he trained Hilary Pfraengle, later abbot of St. Mary's in Newark, and Innocent Wolf, later abbot of St. Benedict's monastery, Atchison, Kan. Upon the seizure of Rome by the Italian armies under King Victor Emmanuel, Dom Oswald returned to America, served as prior and treasurer of St. Vincent's Abbey, 1872–74; as superior of St. Benedict's Abbey in Atchison, 1874–77, where he also acted as an army chaplain and ministered among the Indians; and as superior of a colony of Benedictines who were working among the negroes in Alabama and Georgia. At Skidaway near Savannah he established an agricultural school in which his interest was so intense that he refused to leave it to accept election as first abbot of Belmont Abbey in North Carolina. In 1892, he was selected to organize the monastery of Cluny at Wetaug, Ill., where he labored in the fields and at the desk for the rest of his life. He died on a pallet of straw among the books in his library. Cluny was abandoned in 1903 and its monks were reëstablished at St. Peter's Abbey at Muenster in northern Saskatchewan, whither the remains of its founder were transferred in 1829.

Father Oswald was a gifted man of decided ability as a missionary and as a preacher in several tongues; but he was a visionary and a dreamer, and somewhat impractical. Despite his active, wandering life, he found opportunity to write a number of articles on the school question in *Katholische Volkszeitung* (Baltimore, 1867); sketches of America in the Cincinnati *Wahrheitsfreund*, republished as *Europäer in America vor Columbus* (1879) on the fourteenth centennial of the founding of the Order of St. Benedict; essays in his own historical magazine, *Der Geschichtsfreund* (1882–84); *A Manual of Good Manners* (1874), in English; and two authoritative little books on the Benedic-

tines in Pennsylvania, *St. Vincenz in Pennsylvanien* (1873) and *Bonifaz Wimmer, Erzabt von St. Vincent in Pennsylvanien* (1891). He was offered but did not accept a chair of history in the Catholic University of America at Washington. At Cluny, he published *Legende,* or lives of the saints, in monthly installments (1892–99), but so monumental and impractical was his plan that only the saints commemorated between Jan. 1 and Feb. 7 found place in the seven completed volumes.

[Felix Fellner, in *Records Am. Cath. Hist. Soc.,* Mar. 1923; Fidelis Busam, in *St. Vincent's Journal,* X, 217–30; *Central-Blat and Social Justice,* Feb.–Dec. 1927; annual Catholic directories; E. J. P. Schmitt, *Bibliographia Benedictina* (1893); material from confreres, especially Dr. Fellner.]   R. J. P.

MORAIS, SABATO (Apr. 13, 1823–Nov. 11, 1897), rabbi, was born at Leghorn, Italy, the son of Samuel and Buonina (Wolf) Morais and one of nine children. Descended from a Portuguese family which fled to Italy to escape the persecutions of the Inquisition, he inherited a love of liberty and an interest in republican government which manifested itself throughout his life and led to a friendship with Mazzini. He carried on his Hebrew studies under the rabbis Funaro, Curiat, and Piperno, the latter chief rabbi of Leghorn, acquiring a good knowledge of the Bible, the Talmud, and Jewish literature generally, and an ability to write and speak Hebrew fluently. Secular studies he pursued under Salvatore de Benedetti; in addition to his native Italian, he wrote and spoke French and Spanish with facility. During most of his student life he taught others in order to aid his father in the support of the family.

In 1845 he went to London as a candidate for the position of reader at the Spanish and Portuguese synagogue in Bevis Marks, but the fact that he knew no English prevented his election and he returned to Italy. The following year he was recalled to London to fill the post of Hebrew master of the orphan school of the same congregation. He came to America in March 1851 and the following month was elected minister of the Mikveh Israel Congregation of Philadelphia, which he served until his death. His duties were many; he read the services on Sabbaths and holidays, and preached in English, often using his pulpit for instruction, chiefly in Jewish history. In addition to this work, he visited widely those who were in distress, in his congregation and outside of it, and answered painstakingly all letters asking him for advice or comfort. In the early days he complained of his difficulty with English but as time went on he gained greater command of it, though his style retained a Latin warmth and richness. His most important articles were reprinted in 1926 under the title *Italian Hebrew Literature,* to commemorate the one-hundredth anniversary of his birth.

During the Civil War Morais, who was an ardent abolitionist and a passionate admirer of Abraham Lincoln, had several disagreements with his congregation over the partisan tone of his sermons. At one time a group to whom he refers as "copperheads" prevented his speaking in the pulpit for three months. His attitude won him recognition in another quarter, however, for the Union League Club of Philadelphia elected him an honorary member. Morais was much moved by the persecution of the Jews in Russia in 1881. Through an old schoolmate, Emanuel Felice Veneziani, the aide of Baron Maurice de Hirsch in his varied philanthropies, he was able to get a fund for the settlement of the immigrants from Russia in agricultural colonies in New Jersey. Nor did his interest end with securing the money. He often visited the colonies and burdened himself with countless details of their management.

He was a born teacher and was greatly interested in the local educational organizations. He gave private lessons gratuitously to any one who wanted to learn and collected about him a group of young men who carried on the various interests which he fostered or founded. He was professor of Bible and Biblical literature in the Maimonides College which was established in Philadelphia in 1867, and taught there until it closed in 1873. When the Hebrew Union College was founded in 1875 he hoped that it would serve as a seminary for all the Jews in America desirous of entering the rabbinate, but when he saw that the trend there was away from traditional Judaism, he immediately took steps to start another institution. As a result, the Jewish Theological Seminary was founded in New York in 1886, which from small beginnings has grown to be an important seat of learning. He was president of the faculty and professor of Bible in this institution until his death. He considered the Seminary the most important undertaking of his life and always referred to it as his Benjamin—the child of his old age. The chair of Biblical literature and exegesis there is now named after him.

Morais was a man of genuine humility, tall and spare, and ascetic in his habits. He married Clara Esther Weil in 1855, and they had seven children.

[The principal sources are personal recollections and unpublished letters and documents. Printed sources include biographical sketch by a son, Henry Samuel Morais, in *The Jews of Philadelphia* (1894); "Sabato Morais, a Memoir," also by H. S. Morais, in *Proc. of the Sixth Biennial Conv. of the Jewish Theol. Sem. Asso.* (1898); *Commemoration of the One Hundredth Anniversary of the Birth of the Rev. Dr. Sabato Morais by the Congregation Mikveh Israel, Apr. 18, 1923* (1924); William Rosenau, "Sabato Morais: An Appreciation on the Centenary of His Birth," in *Yearbook of the Central Conf. of Am. Rabbis,* XXXIII (1923), 356–70, and additional material by Marvin Nathan, pp. 370–74; *Jewish Exponent,* Nov. 20, 1897, Apr. 20, 1923; *N. Y. Times,* Apr. 15, 1923; *Pub. Ledger* (Phila.), Nov. 12, 1897.]   C. A.

MORAN, BENJAMIN (Aug. 1, 1820–June 20, 1886), diplomat and author, was born in West Marlboro township, Chester County, Pa. His parents, middle-class English immigrants, settled in the United States in the early nineteenth century, the father, William, first acting as manager of a textile mill in Trenton, N. J., and later setting up as a cloth manufacturer on Doe Run in Pennsylvania. Benjamin received a good public-school education, during which he developed a marked interest in literature. At its close, he entered the employment of a Philadelphia printer to learn his trade. He was there thrown into frequent contact with authors, cultivated their acquaintance and, at thirty-one, determining himself to become a writer, abandoned his craft and sailed for Great Britain. He toured England, Scotland, Wales, and Ireland on foot, and though very short of funds, managed to visit the important literary shrines and other points of interest, and sold to American periodicals a number of short sketches illustrated by drawings. His experiences were subsequently published in book form under the title *The Footpath and Highway: or, Wanderings of an American in Great Britain, in 1851 and '52* (1853), a work of no particular merit.

Moran was strongly attracted to England and, returning in 1853, spent most of the remainder of his life there. He first secured employment as temporary clerk at the American legation, perhaps because James Buchanan, then minister, had known his father through business connections. In 1854 he became Buchanan's private secretary and when his chief retired was appointed permanent clerk on his recommendation. He proved himself an indefatigable worker and gained an exceptional knowledge of the archives. In 1857 he was named assistant secretary of legation, and in 1864, secretary. The latter post he held until the close of 1874. On numerous occasions during this decade he served as chargé d'affaires in the absence of the minister.

His years of service in London coincided with the development of critical relations between the United States and Great Britain arising out of the Civil War, and his voluminous journal, kept with scrupulous care from 1857 to 1874, forms invaluable source material on the subject. As secretary and chargé d'affaires, affording continuity from one minister to another, Moran exercised considerable influence on the diplomatic relations between the two countries. He was stanchly loyal to the Union and, through his popularity in British political circles, played no small part in setting forth the Northern cause and preventing an open rupture. He was held in marked esteem in Great Britain, and the cautious *Times* on one occasion (Dec. 22, 1874) characterized him as a highly trained diplomat and the "ablest and most honest" representative the United States had ever had. In December 1874, in recognition of his services, he was named minister resident to Portugal, the first occasion on which an American secretary of legation had been thus promoted. When that office was discontinued in 1876, he became chargé d'affaires at Lisbon, filling the position until 1882, when he resigned, incapacitated by paralysis. He returned to England, a helpless invalid, and made his home with an intimate friend, Joshua Nunn, former American vice-consul, in Braintree, Essex County. Here he died four years later. The *Times* obituary stated that he had married "an English lady," but failed to give her name.

While closely associated with literary men during his entire official career, Moran made little attempt to carry out his early ambitions and, save for a history of American literature, embodied in *Trübner's Bibliographical Guide to American Literature* (2nd ed., London, 1859), he produced nothing of more than passing value. While at London, he suffered from a grossly exaggerated sense of his own importance which, while hidden from the world at large, becomes painfully apparent in the pages of his diary. He adopts a patronizing air toward legation callers and applies strongly derogatory adjectives to those failing to show him the desired deference; he is filled with scorn and contempt for minor personages in government service, and agonizes over what he considers slights at the hands of his superiors.

[Diary in 43 volumes (1851, 1857–75), "Notes and Queries" (1 vol.), and Moran clippings and drawings, MSS. Div., Lib. of Cong.; "Extracts from the Diary of Benjamin Moran, 1860–68," in *Proc. Mass. Hist. Soc.*, XLVIII (1915), 431 ff.; *Register of the Department of State,* 1874–82; State Dept. Appointments Bureau records; dispatches from London and Lisbon, State Dept.; *Appletons' Ann. Cyc., 1886* (1887); the *Times* (London), Dec. 22, 1874, June 22, 23, 1886; *N. Y. Times,* June 26, 1886; *Evening Telegraph* (Phila.), June 22, 1886.]   L. J. R.

MORAN, EDWARD (Aug. 19, 1829–June 9, 1901), marine painter, born at Bolton, Lancashire, England, was the eldest son of Thomas and Mary (Higson) Moran, and elder brother of Peter and Thomas Moran [*qq.v.*]. His father was a hand-loom weaver, and Edward was put to work at the loom while still a very small child. In 1844 the family emigrated to America and settled in Maryland, where the same occupation was carried on. But Edward, then in his teens, was dissatisfied with the slender wage he was receiving, and dreaming of some more congenial calling, started out on foot one day, without money in his pocket, and walked to Philadelphia in quest of new opportunities. For a while he worked in the shop of a cabinet-maker; then he was in a bronzing establishment, but eventually he was forced to go back to weaving at six dollars a week. While he was so engaged his employer one day found him making a drawing, and realizing that it showed unusual talent, was moved to introduce the youth to Paul Weber, a landscape painter of repute, who accepted him as a pupil. It was evident before long that he had found his vocation. Shortly, Weber passed him on to another painter, James Hamilton, who specialized in marine pictures and illustrations, and, after some hardships, the young man was at last enabled to take a little studio "over a cigar store, with an entrance up a back alley." From this modest start he gradually but steadily progressed in his profession, became an associate of the National Academy, and established himself as one of the earliest of a long line of American marine painters.

In 1862 he went to England and studied for a short time in the school of the Royal Academy, London. In 1871 he exhibited in Philadelphia a collection of seventy-five of his pictures, the entire profits being given in aid of the sufferers from the Franco-Prussian War. In 1872 he moved from Philadelphia to New York, where for some thirty years he was a conspicuous figure in the artistic life of the metropolis. One of his friends and pupils here was Joseph Jefferson, the actor. In 1879–80 he was domiciled in Paris where he sought to perfect himself in the painting of the human figure. He had married, in 1869, Annette Parmentier, a Southern woman of French descent, who was his second wife.

Unquestionably the influence of Turner and of Stanfield can be traced in Moran's sea pieces. His canvases reflect the dramatic element in Turner's work, and his important group of thirteen large paintings, illustrating salient episodes in the history of America, bear resemblance to Stanfield's spirited historical sea compositions.

The ground covered by his historical series extends from the landing of Leif Ericson to the close of the war with Spain in 1898. The subjects comprise such events as the landing of Columbus, the midnight mass for the repose of the soul of De Soto on the Mississippi River, Henry Hudson's little ship entering New York harbor, the embarkation of the Pilgrims, the first salute to the United States flag at sea, the burning of the frigate *Philadelphia,* the engagement between the brig *Armstrong* and the British fleet, the sinking of the *Cumberland* by the *Merrimac,* the farewell salute of the White Squadron to the body of Capt. John Ericsson, and the return of the victorious American squadrons of Dewey, Sampson, and Schley at the end of the Spanish-American War. The series was exhibited at the Metropolitan Museum of Art, New York, in 1904, and was subsequently seen in several other cities, including Washington, where it was installed as a loan in 1907 in the National Gallery of Art, Smithsonian Institution, remaining there for several years. In 1927 it was exhibited at the Ainslie Galleries, New York, and was acquired by Theodore Sutro, who presented it to the Pennsylvania Museum of Art, Philadelphia.

[Theodore Sutro, *Thirteen Chapters of Am. Hist.* (1905); *Am. Art Annual,* 1903–04; Richard Rathbun, *The Nat. Gallery of Art* (1909); Mich. State Lib., *Biog. Sketches of Am. Artists* (1924); G. W. Sheldon, *Am. Painters* (1881); magazine section of the *N. Y. Herald,* Nov. 6, 1904; *N. Y. Times,* June 10, 1901.]
W. H. D—s.

MORAN, PETER (Mar. 4, 1841–Nov. 9, 1914), landscape and animal painter, etcher, born at Bolton, Lancashire, England, was the son of Thomas and Mary (Higson) Moran, and younger brother of Thomas and Edward Moran [qq.v.]. He was brought to the United States by his parents in 1844. When he was sixteen his father apprenticed him to Herline & Hersel of Philadelphia to learn the art of lithographic printing. This specialty, however, failed to appeal to his taste, and after a few months it became so distasteful to him that he picked a quarrel with his employers as a result of which his indenture was canceled. He then made prompt use of his freedom by taking lessons in drawing, painting, and etching from his two elder brothers, who were already established as artists. At this period he was greatly impressed by some landscapes by Émile Lambinet which he had seen in the Philadelphia picture shops. A little later he was enamored of Rosa Bonheur's cattle-pieces and as he matured he came under the influence of Constant Troyon. Animal life chiefly engrossed him as a subject, and he cherished a natural desire to study Landseer's works in Lon-

don, a desire which he was able to gratify in 1863, when he returned to his native land for about a year's sojourn. He took with him a letter of introduction to Landseer, but he never presented it, possibly because of youthful shyness, but also because, when he came to see Landseer's originals in the galleries, he was somewhat disappointed in them.

He returned to Philadelphia in 1864, set up a studio, and passed the rest of his professional life there. On July 7, 1867, he was married to Emily Kelley, of Dublin, Ireland, who was also a painter and etcher. From the sixties on for a half-century he was incessantly at work painting and etching. In the field of animal painting he soon won a reputation not less well deserved than that of his elder brothers in their specialties of landscape and marine work. He made several long trips to the West and Southwest with his brother Thomas, and found in New Mexico a number of picturesque and novel motives in the old Indian pueblos. But it was more especially as a competent and prolific etcher that he made his mark. Few Americans of that period were producing such admirable and thoroughly artistic plates. For his group of etchings of animal subjects shown at the Centennial Exposition, 1876, he was honored by the award of a medal; no less than thirteen of his etchings and dry-points were in the noteworthy exhibition of prints held in the Boston Art Museum in 1881. He became president of the Philadelphia Society of Etchers, a member of several other artistic associations, including the Pennsylvania Academy of the Fine Arts, and received many honors. He died in Philadelphia in his seventy-third year. His second wife was Sarah D. C. Francis, of Philadelphia, whom he married in 1911.

[There is a two-volume grangerized edition of Geo. W. Sheldon's *Am. Painters* (1881) in the Boston Pub. Lib. which contains valuable material on Peter Moran. Other sources include: *Who's Who in America,* 1914–15; *Am. Art Rev.,* Feb. 1880, Aug. 1881; *Century Mag.,* Feb. 1883; *Art Jour.* (London), Feb. 1879; Frank Weitenkampf, *Am. Graphic Art* (1912); Mich. State Lib., *Biog. Sketches of Am. Artists* (1924); *Am. Art Annual,* 1915; *Pub. Ledger* (Phila.), Nov. 11, 1914.]
W. H. D—s.

MORAN, THOMAS (Jan. 12, 1837–Aug. 26, 1926), landscape painter and etcher, was born at Bolton, Lancashire, England, the son of Thomas and Mary (Higson) Moran. Edward and Peter Moran [qq.v.] were his brothers. The story of his early life runs closely parallel to that of his elder brother Edward. In 1844 he emigrated with the family to America; later he found his way to Philadelphia, and, after various vicissitudes, was apprenticed to a wood-engraver with whom he worked for two years. Aided by Edward, he began to paint, at first in water-colors, then, in 1860, in oils; his first picture was an illustration of Shelley's "Alastor." In 1862 he returned to England, and in the National Gallery, London, came at once under the spell of Turner, whose pictures he was copying. This influence remained with him throughout his life, coloring all his subsequent practice, and as it fell out, Turner's method and palette were well adapted to the grandiose motives that Moran most affected, especially in the Far West. In the sixties he made another European tour, this time traveling extensively in France and Italy, remaining abroad for several years and copying many of the works of the old masters. He secured at this time the material for the Venetian series which are among his best-known works.

After his return to America in 1871 he accompanied the United States geological expedition under F. V. Hayden to the Yellowstone region and painted the large panoramic picture entitled "The Grand Canyon of the Yellowstone." Two years later he made a second western exploration to the Grand Canyon of the Colorado, and painted the "Chasm of the Colorado." These two pictures were purchased by Congress for $10,000 each and were hung in the Capitol at Washington. Aside from their artistic aspects these works owed much of their importance and interest to the fact that they were the first adequate pictorial records of the stupendous scenery of still unfamiliar regions. For Louis Prang & Company of Boston, lithographers, he painted a series of water-colors of the Yellowstone country. In 1872 he had made his first visit to California, where he saw the Yosemite Valley. In 1874 he made in Colorado the studies for his celebrated painting of the "Mountain of the Holy Cross," for which he was awarded a medal at the Centennial Exposition of 1876. His name has been perpetuated in Mount Moran, of the Teton Range, in Wyoming, and in Moran Point, Ariz., the former in the Yellowstone and the latter in the Grand Canyon.

Moran was married, in April 1862, to one of his pupils, Mary Nimmo, daughter of Archibald Nimmo, of Strathaven, Scotland; she was also a painter and etcher. A son and daughter were born to them. The family made Philadelphia their home until 1872, when they moved to Newark, N. J., and a little later to New York City. In 1884 Moran was made a member of the National Academy. In the same year he built a summer studio at Easthampton, L. I., where he spent many summers. He traveled far and wide, going to Mexico in 1883, to Italy again in 1886, and to the Pacific Coast several times.

In 1916 he moved to Santa Barbara, Cal., where the last decade of his long life was spent. He worked to the end, and like Corot, lying in bed in his last hours, he saw his still-to-be-painted landscapes on the ceiling and talked of them. He died in his ninetieth year, the senior member of the National Academy of Design, and dean of his profession. If he was among the ablest painters of the great mountains, canyons, waterfalls, and other spectacles of nature in America, it was in large measure because he had assimilated the grand style of his exemplar, Turner, with its daring color, its visible atmosphere, and its spectacular splendor of effect, and knew how to adapt it to his own subject-matter.

In addition to his work in color he was an etcher and illustrator of more than common merit. He began as an engraver; produced many magazine and book illustrations; and was elected a fellow of the British Society of Painter-Etchers. One of his plates, exhibited in London, is said to have been pronounced by John Ruskin one of the best that had come out of America (International Studio, August 1924, p. 361). He also expressed in original lithographs his love of bold scenic effects. Two of his best-known lithographs are "Solitude," a wood interior, one of his set called "Studies and Pictures" (1868), and his "South Shore of Lake Superior" (1869).

[Am. Mag. of Art, Nov., Dec. 1926; Am. Art Rev., Feb. 1880; Internat. Studio, Aug. 1924, Mar. 1927; Brush and Pencil, Oct. 1900; Century Mag., Feb. 1883; Mag. of Art, Jan. 1882; Samuel Isham, Hist. of Am. Painting (1905); Frank Weitenkampf, Am. Graphic Art (1912); Chas. E. Fairman, Art and Artists of the Capitol of the U. S. (1927); Cat. of the Thos. B. Clarke Collection of Am. Pictures (1891); N. Y. Tribune, May 4, 1872; Evening Star (Wash., D. C.), Aug. 27, 1926.]
                                        W. H. D—s.

MORDECAI, ALFRED (Jan. 3, 1804–Oct. 23, 1887), soldier, engineer, was born at Warrenton, N. C., the son of Jacob Mordecai of Warrenton and Rebecca (Myers) of Newport, R. I. His adult life was sharply divided into two periods. Throughout the first he was an officer of the United States Army, with unusual opportunities and responsibilities, which came to him because of his exceptional abilities. Following his resignation from the army at the outbreak of the Civil War, he lived and died a civilian. Although circumstances dictated a complete change in his career, his ability brought him marked success in his later occupations.

He was appointed as a cadet at the United States Military Academy, June 24, 1819. Graduating first in his class, he was commissioned second lieutenant, Corps of Engineers, July 1,

1823. He was detailed as assistant professor at the Military Academy, but was relieved in 1825 to become assistant engineer in the construction of Fortress Monroe, Virginia, and in 1828 he became assistant to the chief of engineers. He was commissioned captain in the ordnance department on its creation in 1832, and from 1833 to 1838 commanded successively the Washington and the Frankford, Pa., arsenals. From 1838 to 1842 he was assistant to the chief of ordnance, becoming in 1839 a member of the ordnance board and retaining membership thereon for many years. During the war with Mexico he was in command of the Washington arsenal and was brevetted major in 1848 for meritorious services on this duty. He was commissioned major in the ordnance department, Dec. 31, 1854. As a member of the ordnance board he studied artillery in Europe, and published the results in *Artillery for the United States Land Service* (1849). In 1853 he visited Mexico in connection with war claims, and from 1855 to 1857 he served on the military commission to the Crimea. His observations made while on the latter duty were published by order of Congress in 1860 (*Senate Executive Document, No. 60*, 36 Cong., 1 Sess.). In addition to the two publications mentioned above, he was the author of numerous technical writings, among which are *A Digest of the Laws Relating to the Military Establishment of the United States* (1833), *The Ordnance Manual for the Use of the Officers of the United States Army* (1841, 1850), *Report of Experiments on Gunpowder* (1845), *Second Report . . .* (1849).

On the outbreak of the Civil War, Mordecai, in common with many other professional army officers of Southern birth, was confronted with the necessity for a momentous personal decision. He was a soldier of unusual ability, who had enjoyed many positions of trust in the service of his country; on the other hand he felt as keen obligations to his state. His decision was that he should fight against neither. His son, also Alfred Mordecai, who was just graduating from West Point, elected differently and fought throughout the war in the service of the Union, dying a brigadier-general of the United States Army. The father resigned from the army, May 5, 1861, and became a teacher of mathematics in Philadelphia. From 1863 to 1866 he was assistant engineer of the Mexico & Pacific Railroad, running from Vera Cruz through the City of Mexico to the Pacific Ocean. From 1867 to 1887 he was treasurer and secretary of canal and coal companies controlled by the Pennsylvania Railroad Company. His wife was Sara Hays of Philadelphia, and they had six children. Mordecai died at Philadelphia.

[Personnel files, War Department, Washington, D. C.; files Army War College, Washington, D. C.; G. W. Cullum, *Biog. Reg. Officers and Grads. U. S. Mil. Acad.* (3rd ed., 1891), vol. I; *Nineteenth Ann. Reunion Asso. Grads. U. S. Mil. Acad. . . . June 11, 1888* (1888); *Army and Navy Jour.*, Oct. 29, 1887; *Public Ledger* (Phila.), Oct. 24, 1887.] J. N. G.

MORDECAI, MOSES COHEN (Feb. 19, 1804–Dec. 30, 1888), ship-owner and merchant, son of David Cohen and Rinah (Cohen) Mordecai, was born in Charleston, S. C., where his grandfather had settled in 1772. This grandfather, Moses Cohen, was a member of the Grenadier Company of Charleston during the Revolution and fought at Fort Moultrie and Yorktown. Mordecai received but little formal education, leaving school when quite young, but he became one of Charleston's most prominent commercial figures and representative citizens in ante-bellum days. On Feb. 20, 1828, he married Isabel Rebecca Lyons of Columbia, S. C. He was the founder of the firm of Mordecai & Company, large ship-owners and extensive importers of Mediterranean fruits, Cuban sugar and tobacco, and Rio coffee. He established a line of steamers between Charleston and Havana and by making Charleston his port of entry, brought a vast amount of business to the city. He was interested in all public enterprises and movements for the improvement of Charleston, and the list of offices of trust he held between 1830 and 1861 is long. He was president of the ancient Synagogue Beth Elohim, then one of the most aristocratic synagogues in America, from 1857 to 1861. In the turbulent politics of his day he played a prominent part. He was a delegate to the Augusta convention in 1838, a representative in the legislature, 1845–46; and state senator, 1855–58. In July 1851, in conjunction with B. C. Pressley and Ker Boyce, he founded the *Southern Standard* (after 1853 the *Charleston Standard*) and in 1852 was joined in this enterprise by five other prominent citizens. The combined wealth of these eight stockholders was estimated at six million dollars, an indication of the wealth of ante-bellum Charleston. Pressley, the editor, was a Union man, and the *Standard* advocated an unpopular cause. It soon emphasized the policy of "no secession without co operation," and in the fall of 1851, succeeded in bringing about a test vote of the people, the result of which was against separate secession. The paper continued to be published till 1858.

In 1860 Mordecai's steamer *Isabel*, named after his wife, was carrying the United States mail between Charleston and Key West. The rescinding of this contract on Jan. 2, 1861, led later to a lawsuit against the United States in the Court of Claims, which was decided against the plaintiff on Dec. 17, 1883 (*Mordecai vs. United States, 19 Court of Claims, 11*). The *Isabel* transferred Anderson and his men to the Federal fleet after the surrender of Fort Sumter and became a famous blockade runner during the Civil War (*Official Records of the Union and Confederate Navies in the War of the Rebellion,* 1 ser. IV, 250, 255, and *passim*). Mordecai was a heavy loser by the war. In 1865, he removed to Baltimore, carrying a goodly competence with him. With his son, he again established the firm of Mordecai & Company and undertook the agency for a line of steamers between Charleston and Baltimore. He never forgot his old home and continued to be a generous contributor to its charities. When the bodies of eighty-four South Carolina soldiers who had fallen at Gettysburg were removed to Charleston in 1870, Mordecai & Company furnished free transportation. For the last eighteen years of his life he was completely blind, but continued to carry on his various activities. A generation after his death he was remembered by old residents of Charleston as a philanthropist and cultured gentleman.

[For history of Mordecai's family, see *Lessee of Levy et al.,* vs. *M'Cartee, 6 Peters,* 101. See also *Lineage Book, Nat. Soc. D. A. R.,* vol. II (1896); obituary notices in *Jewish Exponent* Jan. 4, 1889; *Am. Israelite,* Jan. 3, 1889; *Jewish Messenger,* Jan. 4, 1889; and *News and Courier* (Charleston, S. C.), Jan. 2, 1889; B. A. Elzas, *The Jews of S. C.* (1905); W. L. King, *The Newspaper Press of Charleston, S. C.* (1872); *A Brief Hist. of the Ladies' Memorial Asso. of Charleston, S. C.* (1880); *Sun* (Baltimore), Dec. 31, 1888.]

B.A.E.

MORE, NICHOLAS (d. 1689), first chief justice of Pennsylvania, was born in England. He was educated as a physician, but he did not practise his profession after he went to America. In 1682 he became the president of the Free Society of Traders, a body organized by a group of English merchants to purchase land, establish a manorial settlement, and engage in agriculture, trade, and manufacturing in the province of Pennsylvania. (He is referred to in the charter and other records of the Society as a medical doctor of London.) This Society was not particularly successful, but More's connection with it probably helped him in his political career and made it easier for him to buy land for himself on favorable terms.

He and his family migrated to Pennsylvania with William Penn in 1682 and settled in Philadelphia. There is a tradition that he was the chairman or speaker of the first provincial assembly, which met at Chester in December 1682, but the tradition is not corroborated by the records. He was, however, secretary of the provincial council in 1683, a member of the assembly in 1684-85, and speaker of the assembly in 1684. He was also presiding judge of the county courts of Philadelphia in 1683-84 and, on Aug. 4, 1684, was appointed prior judge or chief justice of the province and the lower counties (Delaware). On Aug. 7 of the same year, he purchased an estate of about 10,000 acres of land in Philadelphia County, which was called the manor of Moreland and is now a part of Moreland township. Shortly after his appointment as chief justice, More became involved in a dispute with the assembly which culminated in the first impeachment trial in American history. Ten charges were brought against him, May 15, 1685, based mainly on complaints from the lower counties. It was alleged that he had held circuit courts at inconvenient times and without consulting the provincial council; that he had summoned juries in an unlawful manner; that he had browbeaten a jury into finding an unjust verdict; and that he had committed various other high crimes and misdemeanors. He was expelled from the assembly and suspended from his judicial position (June 2, 1685) but the council refused to sanction the impeachment proceedings. In 1686 he was appointed a member of the board of five commissioners who were to act as the provincial executive, but his health was failing and he was unable to serve. He died at Moreland, in 1689, survived by his wife, Mary, whom he had married in England, and by four children.

More's troubles were largely due to the defects of his character. He had an ungovernable temper and a fluent vocabulary of abuse. In spite of his temperamental defects, he had some very devoted friends and it was probably owing to their influence that the impeachment proceedings were abandoned. It is also possible that the charges brought against him were exaggerated, because William Penn would hardly have selected as a member of his executive board a man who had been a complete failure as chief justice.

[For the charter and other material relating to the Free Society of Traders, see Samuel Hazard, *Annals of Pa., from the Discovery of the Delaware, 1609-1682* (1850); there are several references to More, including the articles of impeachment, in the *Minutes of the Provincial Council of Pa.,* vol. I (1838); see also the manuscript "Survey by Thomas Fairman, Showing the Division of the Manor of Moreland Between the Children of Nicholas More," in the library of the Hist. Soc. of Pa.; J. H. Martin, *Martin's Bench and Bar of Phila.* (1883); J. C. Martindale, *A Hist. of the Townships of Byberry and Moreland in Phila., Pa.* (1867); T. F. Gordon, *The Hist. of Pa.* (1829); and

Moreau de Saint-Méry

Moreau de Saint-Méry

Lawrence Lewis, Jr., "The Courts of Pa. in the Seventeenth Century," in *Pa. Mag. of Hist. and Biog.*, V (1881), 141–90: this *Magazine*, IV (1880), 445–53, also contains reprint of *A Letter from Dr. More . . . Relating to . . . the Province of Pa.*, which was first printed in London in 1687.] W. R. S.

MOREAU DE SAINT-MÉRY, MÉDÉRIC-LOUIS-ÉLIE (Jan. 13, 1750–Jan. 28, 1819), historian, publisher, the son of Bertrand-Médéric and Marie-Rose (Beeson) Moreau de Saint-Méry, was born at Fort Royal, Martinique, where his ancestors, emigrants from Poitou, had settled in the seventeenth century. Members of his family, ever since that time, had occupied high judicial posts on the island. At nineteen he went to Paris, joined the king's guard, and later was admitted to the bar. He returned to Martinique, but soon left for Cap Français, Santo Domingo, to practise law. Here he made researches with a view to codifying colonial law, and also discovered the tomb of Columbus, which he restored at his own expense. He went back to Paris to arrange for the publication of his books, and the six volumes of his *Loix et Constitutions des Colonies françaises de l'Amérique sous le Vent* appeared there between 1784 and 1790. He helped to found the Museum of Paris and became its president in 1787. It was more of an incubator of revolutionary ideas than a museum, and in 1789 Saint-Méry's connection with it caused him to be appointed president of the Electors of Paris. When the Bastille fell, he received its keys from the hands of the leaders of the mob, and for the next three turbulent days he governed Paris with prudence and courage. It was he who persuaded the Electors to place Lafayette in command of the National Guard.

Having incurred the enmity of Robespierre, he narrowly escaped the guillotine by fleeing with his wife and two children to America, and landed at Norfolk, Va., on Mar. 8, 1794. After working there as a shipping clerk until May, he went to New York and obtained another similar job. In October, however, he moved to Philadelphia and by Dec. 10 had set himself up in business as a bookseller, printer, and stationer. His little shop became the rendezvous of the French *émigrés*. Noailles, Volney, Talon, Démeunier, La Colombe, La Rochefoucauld-Liancourt, de Beaumetz, and many others met there every night, and the Duc d'Orléans, who was later to become King of the French, came often. Saint-Méry's most intimate friend, however, was Talleyrand, and the two men spent hours together drinking Madeira and plotting how to seize Louisiana from the Spanish. In spite of the fact that Saint-Méry followed a humble calling, selling books, maps, music, and even woollen socks, gouty mittens, muffs, drawers, and "gallices," his erudition and intelligence gained for him many friends among the Anglo-Saxon intellectuals of the city. He had been a nonresident member of the American Philosophical Society since 1789, and in January 1795 was made a resident member.

The amount and quality of the printing that he turned out of his little press during the three and one half years it ran is quite amazing. There were numerous pamphlets written by him or by refugee friends, his own exhaustive two-volume *Description topographique et politique de la partie espagnole de l'Isle Saint-Domingue* (1796), and his equally bulky *Description topographique, physique, civile, politique et historique de la partie française de l'Isle Saint-Domingue* (1797–98), together with the translations of both of them by William Cobbett. In addition he printed and published in two volumes A. E. van Braam Houckgeest's handsomely illustrated *Voyage de l'Ambassade de la Compagnie des Indes Orientales Hollandaises, vers l'Empereur de la Chine, en 1794–1795* (1797), and he even did the composition and presswork for a daily newspaper, edited by Gaterau, called *Courrier de la France et des Colonies*. His publications were of such excellence, intellectually as well as typographically, that they entitle him to be classed among the best of the early American printers and publishers.

Since Frenchmen had come to be looked upon with grave suspicions, President Adams included Moreau de Saint-Méry's name in a list of persons to be deported under the Alien Bill. Saint-Méry thought it wise to anticipate any such action and so sailed for France on Aug. 23, 1798. In Paris he obtained a position as historiographer at the Ministry of Marine, became very popular among the intellectuals, and was elected to membership in various learned societies. In 1800 he was made councillor of state, and the following year sent as Resident to the Duke of Parma. Upon the Duke's death in 1802 he became administrator of Parma, Piacenza, and Guastalla, and ruled them until Napoleon recalled him in 1806 because he believed him to have been too lenient in suppressing a mutiny in the militia. The Emperor took him to task very harshly when he arrived in Paris, and it was then that Moreau de Saint-Méry made his famous answer: "Sire, I do not ask you to reward my probity; I only beg that it be tolerated. Do not be afraid, this disease is not catching." Napoleon never quite forgave his temerity, and stopped the payment of his pension and also of

the 40,000 francs already owed him. Saint-Méry
eked out the remainder of his life in penury, assisted by the Empress Josephine, his distant relative, and by scanty and intermittent pensions.
He died in Paris in January 1819, at the age of
sixty-nine.

[M. L. E. Moreau de Saint-Méry, *Voyage aux États-Unis de l'Amérique, 1793–1798* (1913), ed. by S. L. Mims, with a biographical sketch and numerous references to other material; H. W. Kent, "Chez Moreau de Saint-Méry, Philadelphie," in *Bibliographical Essays, A Tribute to Wilberforce Eames* (1924), with bibliography of Saint-Méry's American publications by G. P. Winship; A. F. Silvestre, *Notice Biographique de Moreau de Saint-Méry* (1819); François Fournier-Pescay, *Discours prononcé aux obsèques de Moreau de Saint-Méry le 30 janv. 1819* (1819) and article in *Biographie Universelle*, vol. XXX (1821); Claude Augé, *Nouveau Larousse Illustré*, vol. VI (1903); *Journal de Paris*, Jan. 30, 1819.]   E. L. T.

**MOREAU-LISLET, LOUIS CASIMIR
ELISABETH** (1767–Dec. 3, 1832), Louisiana
jurist and politician, was born in Cap Français,
Santo Domingo, a French dependency. He received in France a solid education both in languages and law, and came to New Orleans in his
thirties, probably driven from his native land by
the negro revolution under Dessalines. He married Anne Philipine de Peters who bore him one
child, a daughter. He adopted the name Lislet
to distinguish himself from an elder brother.
In 1805, with Edward Livingston, Pierre A. C.
B. Derbigny, and Étienne Mazureau [*qq.v.*], he
won a judicial decision insuring the recognition
of the Roman Civil Law in Louisiana. In the
following year he published *Explication des Lois
Criminelles du Territoire d'Orléans* (1806),
and with James Brown was commissioned by
the legislature to prepare a code, which under
the title *Digeste des lois civiles maintenant en
vigueur dans le Territoire d'Orléans* was published in both French and English editions in
1808. He served as a parish judge and worked
on a translation of Spanish laws. In 1817 he
became attorney-general but soon resigned to
accept a state senatorship. Three years later,
with the collaboration of Henry Carleton, he
published *The Laws of Las Siete Partidas
Which Are Still in Force in the State of Louisiana* (2 vols., 1820). He was immediately selected with Derbigny and Livingston to prepare a
revised code, which, as *Civil Code of the State
of Louisiana,* appeared in 1825. In the meantime Moreau continued as the representative of
the second district of New Orleans in the state
legislature. In 1828 he issued *A General Digest
of the Acts of the Legislature of Louisiana,
Passed from the Year 1804 to 1827, Inclusive.*
His last public act was to sign a proclamation,
June 26, 1832, calling a mass meeting to oppose

Nullification. He died less than six months
later at the age of sixty-five.

Moreau-Lislet played a leading rôle in a
troublous time. He fought for the interests of
the French population, but ever in a spirit of
compromise. Governor Claiborne praised his
Digeste of 1808 for allaying jealousies, and as-
suring peace to a people living under three juris-
prudences. In 1820, he was instrumental in the
conciliatory gesture whereby Derbigny withdrew as candidate for governor in favor of
Thomas B. Robertson. The deft hand of Moreau helped much in the work of pacification so
necessary at his time. He possessed an excellent command of his mother tongue, a deep
knowledge of Spanish legal history; and a
trained mind thoroughly versed in the law.

[F. X. Martin, *The Hist. of La.*, vol. II (1829); Charles Gayarré, *Hist. of La.*, vol. IV (1866), and "The New Orleans Bench and Bar in 1823," in *Harper's Mag.*, Nov. 1888; Alcée Fortier, *A Hist. of La.* (1904), vol. III; Carleton Hunt, "Life and Services of Edward Livingston," in *Proc. La. Bar Asso.*, 1903; Henry Favrot, "The First Governor on the First Code," *Report La. Bar Asso.*, 1909; *Official Letter Books of W. C. C. Claiborne* (6 vols., 1917), ed. by Dunbar Rowland; *La. Hist. Quart.*, Jan. 1921; *Courier* (New Orleans), Dec. 6, 13, 1832.]   L. C. D.

MOREHEAD, CHARLES SLAUGHTER
(July 7, 1802–Dec. 21, 1868), Kentucky governor and congressman, was born in Nelson
County, Ky., the son of Charles and Margaret
(Slaughter) Morehead. He was the first cousin of James Turner Morehead and the second
cousin of John Motley Morehead [*qq.v.*]. After
graduating from Transylvania University in
1820, he became a tutor there, studied law, and
received the LL.B. degree in 1822. He practised in Christian County and later in Franklin
County. After serving in the legislature from
1828 to 1829 he was appointed attorney-general,
a position that he filled for almost six years. In
1834 in collaboration with Mason Brown he
published *A Digest of the Statute Laws of Kentucky,* a two-volume work authorized and supported by the legislature. Several times reëlected to the legislature, he served from 1838 to
1845 and again from 1853 to 1854. He was
speaker from 1840 to 1842 and for the session
of 1844–45. He was twice elected as a Whig
to the federal House of Representatives and
served from 1847 to 1851. In 1848, as a member of the committee on ways and means, he opposed the financial plans of the Polk administration (*Speech of Mr. C. S. Morehead of Kentucky on the Loan Bill,* 1848). In 1850, fearing
that President Taylor's policy would disrupt
both the party and the Union, he favored Clay's
compromise measures and a new cabinet with

Webster as secretary of state. When the Whig party declined he joined the American party, primarily, he said, in the hope of saving the Union. In 1855 this party nominated him for governor. In a strenuous contest with the Democratic candidate, Beverly L. Clarke, involving the serious anti-foreign riot at Louisville known as "Bloody Monday," he was elected, and he was inaugurated in September. The only partisan reference in his messages was to the "foreign invasion" and the desirability of a longer naturalization period. He denounced Northern "nullification" of the Fugitive Slave Act, and declared that slaves could be taken into any territory. He also favored the increase of educational facilities, internal improvements by corporations, the limitation of state banks and of the currency, and the encouragement of agriculture. After 1859 he practised in Louisville with his nephew, Charles M. Briggs.

The secession movement brought him back into public life. In February 1861 he was a member of the peace conference, and, with others, had interviews with Lincoln and Seward. In May he was elected to the border states convention at Frankfort. He approved, with the other members, the plea for Kentucky to be neutral, but he refused to sign the address to the people of Kentucky because he did not indorse all the statements therein. Subsequently he accused Seward of inconsistency and publicly criticized cutting off trade with the South. It was doubtless such action that led to his arrest in September 1861 and his imprisonment, by order of the Secretary of War, without trial at Fort Lafayette in New York harbor and later at Fort Warren in Boston harbor. The Kentucky legislature and Louisville Unionists petitioned for his release on parole, which was obtained on Jan. 6, 1862, apparently largely through the influence of his friend, John J. Crittenden. On Mar. 19 he was discharged from the conditions of his parole, but, fearing arrest because of his refusal to take the oath of allegiance, he fled in June to Canada and then to Europe and Mexico. After the war, he resided on one of his plantations near Greenville, Miss., and died there.

[Lewis and R. H. Collins, *Hist. of Ky.* (2 vols., 1874); E. M. Coulter, *The Civil War and Readjustment in Ky.* (1926); H. Levin, *The Lawyers and Lawmakers of Ky.* (1897); W. E. Connelley and E. M. Coulter, *Hist. of Ky.* (1922), vol. II; *War of the Rebellion: Official Records* (Army), 2 ser., vol. II; Mrs. Chapman Coleman, *The Life of John J. Crittenden* (2 vols., 1871); J. M. Morehead, *The Morehead Family* (1921); date of death from copy of inscription on tombstone and from statement of grand-daughter, Mrs. Malcolm Moncreiffe, Bighorn, Wyo., in files of the Congressional Joint Committee on Printing.]
W. C. M.

MOREHEAD, JAMES TURNER (May 24, 1797–Dec. 28, 1854), Kentucky governor and senator, first cousin of Charles Slaughter Morehead and second cousin of John Motley Morehead [*qq.v.*], was born near Shepherdsville, Bullitt County, Ky., his father, Armistead Morehead, having recently migrated from Virginia. The family soon moved to Russellville, where James began his education. After attending Transylvania University, 1813–15, he studied law under Judge H. P. Broadnax and John J. Crittenden. In 1818 he was admitted to the bar and began to practise in Bowling Green, where he became known as an able lawyer. On May 1, 1823, he married Susan A. Roberts of Logan County.

Morehead began his public career in 1816 by writing letters to the newspapers on public affairs. In the twenties he favored the proposed bankruptcy laws, but opposed the new court of appeals established by the Relief party. Elected to the lower house of the legislature, where he served from 1828 to 1831, he became chairman of the committee on internal improvements and in 1831 reported the bill for a state subscription to the Maysville-Lexington Turnpike Company. In that year he was a member of the National Republican Convention at Baltimore which nominated Henry Clay for the presidency, and was nominated by a state convention for the post of lieutenant-governor, to which he was elected, although a Democrat, Breathitt, was elected governor. On the latter's death, Morehead became governor, Feb. 21, 1834, and held the office until September 1836. He strongly urged the legislature to extend the river improvements already begun, and became *ex officio* the first president of the permanent Board of Internal Improvements, of which he was later appointed president by his successor in the governorship (1836–37). During this period, many Kentucky rivers were surveyed and many improvements projected, but the panic of 1837 prevented the execution of most of the plans. As governor, Morehead also favored judicial reform and popular education, and denounced the Abolitionists. He was again a member of the legislature, 1837–38; and in 1839–40 was, with J S Smith, a commissioner to arrange for the return of fugitive slaves from Ohio. In 1841, he was elected to the United States Senate over many competitors, and served from Feb. 20, 1841, to Mar. 3, 1847. He consistently supported the program of his colleague, Henry Clay, being especially prominent in defense of the Bank Bill and the nomination of Everett as minister to London. He opposed the annexation of

Texas, both by treaty and by joint resolution, and the acquisition of territory from Mexico, although, like most of the Whig senators, he felt compelled to vote for waging war on Mexico because it was felt that Mexico had begun the war.

Morehead was also interested in the American Colonization Society, being at one time president of the Kentucky branch. His large library contained many works on early Kentucky history, and in 1840 he published *An Address in Commemoration of the First Settlement of Kentucky,* largely based on earlier writers but containing some original material on the Boonesborough settlement. He was also the author of *Practice in Civil Actions and Proceedings at Law* (1846). During his latter years he practised at Covington, Ky., and there he died.

[Gov. J. T. Morehead's Letters and Papers, 1834–36 (MSS. in the Ky. State Hist. Soc., containing little of interest except on internal improvements); *Journals of the House of Representatives of Ky.,* 1828–38; *Journals of the Senate of Ky.,* 1834–36; W. R. Jillson, "Early Political Papers of Gov. James Turner Morehead," in *Register of the Ky. State Hist. Soc.,* Sept. 1924, Jan. 1925; Lewis and R. H. Collins, *Hist. of Ky.* (2 vols., 1874); J. M. Morehead, *The Morehead Family of N. C. and Va.* (1921), pp. 41–42; *Ky. Statesman* (Lexington), Jan. 2, 1855, reprinting article from *Louisville Courier,* Dec. 30, 1854.] W. C. M.

MOREHEAD, JOHN MOTLEY (July 4, 1796–Aug. 27, 1866), governor of North Carolina and leader in economic and social movements in that state, was born in Pittsylvania County, Va., the son of John Morehead and his wife, Obedience (Motley) Morehead, who were respectively of Scotch and Welsh descent. He was the second cousin of Charles Slaughter Morehead and James Turner Morehead [qq.v.]. The Morehead family had been identified with Virginia affairs since 1630, when Charles Morehead, probably an ancestor, settled in the Northern Neck. John Morehead removed to Rockingham County, N. C., in 1798. His son was sent to the "log college" of David Caldwell [q.v.], then entered at the University of North Carolina in 1815, and was graduated with the class of 1817. He read law with Archibald De Bow Murphey [q.v.] and began the practice of his profession in Wentworth, Rockingham County. On Sept. 6, 1821, he was married to Ann Eliza Lindsay, the daughter of Robert Lindsay of Guilford County, who bore him eight children. In that year he represented his county in the North Carolina House of Commons; removing to Greensboro, he represented Guilford County in the House of Commons in 1826 and 1827. In politics he was identified with the western group that advocated revision of the state constitution, the construction of rail-

ways by state aid, and public education, and he was a member of the constitutional convention of 1835. A Jacksonian Democrat before 1835, in that year he joined the rising Whig forces and in 1840 was elected governor of North Carolina, as he was again in 1842. As executive he advocated state aid to railways, the construction of highways, and the improvement of navigation, but he accomplished little because of a Democratic majority in the legislature. However, he did successfully urge the establishment of a state institution for the deaf, which was opened in Raleigh and to which the blind were admitted sometime later.

His greatest services were not in politics but in the realm of state business. A constant advocate of railroads he became the president of the North Carolina Railroad and was a promoter of the Atlantic & North Carolina Railroad and of the Western North Carolina Railroad, all being lines projected to give North Carolina a complete transportation system from the mountains to the sea. In 1858 he made his last appearance in the legislature for the purpose of obtaining the continuation of the policy of state aid for railway expansion. Distinctly a business man, he was identified with cotton-mills, commission and mercantile houses, and other enterprises. In national economy he believed in a protective tariff and a national banking system. As the crisis of 1860–61 approached he was a conservative, opposed to a dissolution of the Union, and was a delegate from North Carolina to the peace conference held at Washington in February 1861. After secession he represented North Carolina in the provisional Congress of the Confederacy, in which body he was influential in obtaining an extension of the Richmond & Danville Railroad from Richmond, Va., to Greensboro, N. C.

[B. A. Konkle, *John Motley Morehead and the Development of North Carolina* (1922); *Biog. Hist. of N. C.,* ed. by S. A. Ashe, vol. II (1905); R. D. W. Connor, *Antebellum Builders of N. C.* (1914); *In Memoriam Hon. John M. Morehead* (1868); J. M. Morehead, *The Morehead Family* (1921).] W. K. B.

MOREHOUSE, HENRY LYMAN (Oct. 2, 1834–May 5, 1917), Baptist clergyman, was born in Stanfordville, N. Y., the son of Seth S. and Emma (Bentley) Morehouse. On his father's side, he was descended from Thomas Muirhouse, a Scotch Covenanter, who because of the persecutions of King Charles and Archbishop Laud emigrated to Connecticut about 1640; on his mother's side, he was a descendant of William Bentley who came to Massachusetts from Kent, England, in 1635. His Baptist inheritance went back to 1751, when an ancestor participated in the founding of a Baptist church in Stratfield, Conn. Henry Morehouse prepared for college at the Genesee Wesleyan Seminary, Lima, N. Y., and his education was continued at the University of Rochester, from which he graduated in 1858, and at Rochester Theological Seminary. At the university he was under President Martin B. Anderson [q.v.], and at the seminary, under President Ezekiel Gilman Robinson [q.v.], both of whom exerted a strong influence upon him. In 1864 he was ordained at East Saginaw, Mich., and served as pastor there from October 1864 to January 1873. A second pastorate of more than six years followed at the East Avenue Baptist Church in Rochester, N. Y. During part of this period he was trustee of the New York Baptist Union for Ministerial Education as well as its corresponding secretary. For the next thirty-eight years, he was connected with the general work of the Northern Baptist denomination, acting as corresponding secretary of the American Baptist Home Mission Society from 1879 to 1893 and from 1902 to 1917, and as field secretary from 1893 to 1902, during which time he was also corresponding secretary of the American Baptist Education Society. From 1905 he was a member of the American Committee of the Baptist World Alliance. Of commanding stature, free from self-seeking, whole-heartedly devoted to his work, characterized by normal, mental, and spiritual balance, he was easily at the head of the statesmen of the Baptist denomination in the field of home missions during his generation. Except in 1891, when charges were made involving his integrity, but against which he vindicated himself, and his work in such a manner as to receive an enthusiastic reëlection as corresponding secretary, his supremacy as leader was unchallenged.

During the long period that he was connected with the American Baptist Home Mission Society, he succeeded in reorganizing it, expanding it, and making it more dynamic, the annual expenditures increasing from $115,083 to $987,611, and the students in schools for negroes from 1,056 to over 7,000. Always interested in education, he was prominent in organizing the American Baptist Education Society. He was the trusted advisor of Frederick T. Gates and Thomas W. Goodspeed [qq.v.], prominent in the founding of the University of Chicago, and had some influence in persuading William Rainey Harper to become president of that institution. As early as 1892 he suggested extension courses and summer schools for theological students. A believer in Baptist solidarity, he endeavored to lessen the effects of the Baptist schism of 1845

over the question of negro slavery by suggesting the formation of the General Convention of Baptists of North America. Probably his efforts in behalf of the establishment of the Ministers and Missionaries Benefit Board of the Northern Baptist Convention will prove to be his most significant achievement. He was its president from 1911 until his death. His interests extended beyond the limits of his own denomination, and he was one of the promoters of the Federal Council of Churches of Christ in America. He was editor of missionary periodicals and author of numerous missionary pamphlets, of *Baptist Home Missions in America* (1883), and of *History of Seventy-five Years of the First Baptist Church, Brooklyn* (1898). He also wrote a number of poems, among which were the widely circulated "Led About," and "My Song at Seventy." His death occurred in Brooklyn, N. Y. He was unmarried.

[A. H. Newman, *A Century of Bapt. Achievement* (1901); L. A. Crandall, *Henry Lyman Morehouse, a Biog.* (1919); *Jour. and Messenger*, May 17, 1917; *Who's Who in America*, 1916–17; *N. Y. Times*, May 6, 1917.]
C. H. M.

MORELL, GEORGE WEBB (Jan 8, 1815–Feb. 11, 1883), soldier, engineer, lawyer, of French Huguenot descent, was born in Cooperstown, N. Y. His father, Judge George Morell, served through successive grades to that of major-general in the New York militia, and was chief justice of the supreme court of Michigan when he died in 1845. His mother, Maria Webb, was the daughter of Gen. Samuel B. Webb [q.v.] of the Revolutionary army. It was natural, therefore, that George Webb Morell should be inclined toward a career in the army. He entered West Point and graduated in 1835, first in a class of fifty-six cadets. After serving in the Corps of Engineers as assistant engineer in the improvement of the Lake Erie harbors, on the Ohio and Michigan boundary survey, and in the construction of Fort Adams, Newport, R. I., he resigned, June 30, 1837, to become assistant engineer of construction for the Charleston & Cincinnati Railroad. The following year he went to the Michigan Central Railroad, with which he remained until 1840, when he removed to New York City and studied law. In 1842 he was admitted to the bar and practised law until 1861. Upon the outbreak of the Mexican War he was commissioned major (July 23, 1846) of the 4th New York Volunteers, but the regiment was never mustered into the federal service. He became major and division engineer of the New York militia in 1849, and was promoted to colonel in 1852, which rank he held until 1861. He was commissioner of the United States circuit court for the soutnern district of New York from 1854 to 1861.

On Apr. 15, 1861, he was appointed colonel and served as quartermaster and chief of staff to Major-General Sanford, New York Volunteers, in organizing regiments in New York City and sending them to the seat of war. From May 20 to July 7, 1861, he was engaged in the defenses of Washington, D. C. While participating in the operations about Harper's Ferry, Va., July 7 to Aug. 21, 1861, he was promoted (Aug. 9) brigadier-general of United States Volunteers, and assigned to the Army of the Potomac. He was on duty guarding the approaches to Washington from Aug. 21, 1861, to Mar. 10, 1862, and from then until August, in the Virginia Peninsular campaign. During this period he commanded the 1st and later the 2nd Brigade of F. J. Porter's division and from May 1862, the 1st Division of Porter's V Corps. He participated in the following engagements : Howard's Bridge, Apr. 4, 1862 ; siege of Yorktown, Apr. 5 to May 4, 1862 ; capture of Hanover Court House, May 27, 1862 ; Mechanicsville, June 26, 1862 ; Gaines's Mill, June 27, 1862 ; and Malvern Hill, July 1, 1862. On July 4, 1862, he became major-general, United States Volunteers, but since his nomination was never made to the Senate, his recess appointment expired Mar. 4, 1863. He served in the campaign of Northern Virginia and the Maryland campaign, August to October 1862. He was engaged in the second battle of Bull Run (Manassas), Aug. 30, 1862, and Antietam, Sept. 17, 1862. From Oct. 30 to Dec. 16, 1862, he commanded the forces guarding the upper Potomac. He was in Washington awaiting orders until Dec. 15, 1863, when he was placed in command of the draft rendezvous in Indianapolis, Ind. He remained on this duty until Aug. 29, 1864, and was mustered out of the service Dec. 15, 1864.

In 1866 he married Catherine Schermerhorn Creighton, daughter of Rev. William Creighton of Tarrytown, N. Y., and settled in Scarborough, N. Y., where he engaged in farming until his death.

[G. W. Cullum, *Biog. Reg. Officers and Grads. U. S. Mil. Acad.* (1891), vol. I ; War Department records ; F. B. Heitman, *Hist. Reg. and Dict. U. S. Army* (1903), vol. I ; *War of the Rebellion : Official Records (Army)* ; *14th Ann. Reunion, Asso. Grads. U. S. Mil. Acad.* (1883) ; David McAdam and others, *Hist. of the Bench ad Bar of N. Y.,* vol. I (1897) ; *N. Y. Times,* Feb. 13, 1883.]   J. W. L.

MOREY, SAMUEL (Oct. 23, 1762–Apr. 17, 1843), inventor, was born in Hebron, Conn., which was also the birthplace of his parents, Israel and Martha (Palmer) Morey. Before he was four years old the family moved to New

Hampshire and settled in Orford, where Israel Morey became proprietor of a tavern and an influential citizen. During the Revolutionary War he was made a colonel and commanded a body of New Hampshire militia on the frontier. Samuel was educated in the public school of Orford, and during his youth developed considerable mechanical ability and an intense interest in natural philosophy. He became a lumberman with a successful business in Orford but he took part also in the construction of the Connecticut River locks between Windsor, Conn., and Olcott Falls, being engineer in charge at Bellows Falls, Vt. As early as 1780 he began devoting his leisure hours to experimentation with heat and light, and in the course of ten years acquired considerable knowledge of general chemistry and of the properties of steam. His first patent, granted Jan. 29, 1793, was for a steam-operated spit. Two years later, Mar. 25, 1795, he patented a rotary steam-engine. Patents were also issued to him for a windmill, a water-wheel, and a steam pump.

Meanwhile, about 1790, he began his experiments with steamboats, and after three years of work devised a small craft equipped with a steam-engine mounted on the bow, which he operated on the Connecticut River at Orford. In 1794 he is said to have built a stern-wheel steamboat and to have run it from Hartford, Conn., to New York. Preble (*post*) says that this was the sixth steamboat built in the United States. In the hope of securing financial aid, Morey went to Bordentown, N. J., in 1797, and there constructed a side-wheel steamboat, which he demonstrated on the Delaware River ; but this venture failed. When Fulton began his steamboat work in the United States, Morey went to New York with a model of his steamboat and tried to persuade Fulton to adopt it. He was not successful, however, and always claimed that his steamboat ideas were stolen by Fulton. He obtained two patents for steam-engine improvements in 1803 and 1815, respectively, and on Apr. 1, 1826, one of the first American patents for an internal combustion engine. Presumably Morey had been working on this invention for a number of years, for about 1820 he constructed a boat called *Aunt Sally,* and propelled it by a vapor engine on Fairlee Pond, now Lake Morey, at Fairlee, Vt. Morey contributed to Silliman's *American Journal of Science and Arts* a number of articles bearing on his work. He married Hannah Avery in Orford, and at his death in Fairlee, Vt., where he resided during the latter part of his life, he was survived by his widow and a daughter.

[G. H. Preble, *A Chronological Hist. of the Origin and Development of Steam Navigation* (1883); W. A. Mowry, "Who Invented the American Steamboat?," *Colls. N. H. Antiquarian Soc.*, no. I (1874); Gabriel Farrell, Jr., *Capt. Samuel Morey* (1915); *Am. Jour. of Science and Arts*, vol. I (1819), II (1820), XI (1826); *Centennial Celebration of the Town of Orford, N. H., 1865* (n.d.); *A List of Patents Granted by the U. S. from Apr. 10, 1790, to Dec. 31, 1836* (1872).]

C. W. M.

MORFIT, CAMPBELL (Nov. 19, 1820–Dec. 8, 1897), chemist, son of Henry Mason Morfit, a native of Norfolk, Va., and Catherine (Campbell) Morfit, was born at Herculaneum, Mo. His father moved to Baltimore in 1861 and lived there until his death; he was a successful lawyer and held several public offices. Campbell Morfit was one of sixteen children. One brother, Charles, became a physician, and another, Clarence, a chemist. After an interrupted schooling Campbell Morfit enrolled as a student in Columbian College (now George Washington University), Washington, D. C., but before completing his course he went to Philadelphia to enter the private chemical laboratory which had recently been established there by James Curtis Booth [*q.v.*]. Becoming interested in industrial chemistry, he left the Booth laboratory, where the work was largely analytical, entered a laboratory in Philadelphia specializing in the manufacture of industrial chemicals, and in time became its owner. Meanwhile he associated himself with the University of Maryland. Realizing the need of instruction in industrial chemistry, in 1851 he offered to establish at his own expense a school of applied chemistry in connection with the medical department of the University. A plan of the proposed building, which was to be erected on the campus at a cost of $10,000, accompanied the offer. His generous tender was declined, however, because the trustees decided that industrial chemistry did not fall within the field of a medical school, but in appreciation of Morfit's liberality and interest the University gave him the honorary degree of M.D. In 1854 he became professor of applied chemistry in the University and held the post until 1858, when he resigned and went to New York to resume analytical and industrial work.

His researches in industrial chemistry included studies in guano, salt, sugar, coal, gums, and glycerine. Accounts of this varied work were published in the *Journal of the Franklin Institute,* the *American Journal of Science and Arts,* and other scientific periodicals. He was joint author with Booth of three reports (1851–55) to the United States ordnance department on gun metal, published in *Reports of Experiments on the Strength and Other Properties of Metals for Cannon, by the Officers of the Ordnance Department, U. S. Army* (1856); most of the analytical work was done by Morfit in a laboratory established by himself at the Pikesville (Md.) Arsenal. He assisted Booth in preparing *The Encyclopedia of Chemistry* (1850), writing most of the longer and many of the smaller articles on subjects in industrial chemistry, *e.g.* fats, essential oils, dyes, starch, waxes, sugar, and varnish. He also cooperated with Booth in the monograph *On Recent Improvements in the Chemical Arts* (1852). He edited and revised an American edition of H. M. Noad's *Chemical Analysis* (1849). In addition he was the author of several books, the best known being *Chemistry Applied to the Manufacture of Soap and Candles* (1847); 2nd ed., *A Treatise on Chemistry Applied* (1856); *Chemical and Pharmaceutical Manipulations* (1849; 1857), in collaboration first with Alexander Mucklé and then with Clarence Morfit; *A Practical Treatise on the Manufacture of Soap* (1871), and *A Practical Treatise on Pure Fertilizers* (1872). In 1861 he settled permanently in England and thereafter devoted most of his time to the improvement of technical processes, such as the preparation of condensed food rations, the manufacture of paper, soap, and candles, and the refining of oils. His contributions to industrial chemistry were recognized by diplomas and awards from scientific societies and by his election as a Fellow of the Chemical Society of London. He was married, Apr. 13, 1854, to Maria Clapier Chancellor of Germantown, Pa. She died Apr. 26, 1855, leaving a daughter who became a chemist, worked with her father in London, and died there Feb. 21, 1916. Morfit never married again. He died at South Hampstead, a suburb of London, in his seventy-eighth year.

[Private communication from the Medical School of the Univ. of Md., Baltimore, Md.; *Am. Jour. Pharmacy,* Feb. 1898; Royal Soc. of London, *Cat. of Sci. Papers, 1800–1863,* vol. IV (1870); J. C. Poggendorffs *biographisch-literarisches Handwörterbuch . . . 1863–1904* (1926), vol. II; *Chemical News* (London), Dec. 17, 1897; *Times* (London), Dec. 9, 1897.] L. C. N.

MORFORD, HENRY (Mar. 10, 1823–Aug. 4, 1881), journalist and author, was the son of William and Elizabeth (Willett) Morford, who were residents of what is now New Monmouth, N. J., where Henry was born (Ellis, *post,* pp. 568–69). Most of his youth and early manhood were spent in his native town, first as a merchant and later as postmaster of the village, but his leisure during these years was given to writing verses. At sixteen he was already contributing poems to the *New Yorker* and to the Philadelphia *Saturday Evening Post,* and in 1840 he published a

Morford — Morgan

Morford (left column)

thin pamphlet, *Music of the Spheres,* an immature poetical production showing the influence of Bryant. In 1852 he turned his talent for writing to a more lucrative end by establishing at Middletown Point (now Matawan) the *New Jersey Standard,* a weekly newspaper. Besides editing and managing this paper, he contributed to it frequent poems, and a series of supposedly autobiographical "Sketches of a Country Shopkeeper." In 1854 or 1855 he sold the *Standard,* and a year later went to New York, where for some time he served on the editorial staff of a newspaper or magazine. From 1862 to 1868 he acted as a clerk of the court of common pleas (*Manual of the Corporation of the City of New York,* 1862–68). He was for a time on the editorial staff of the New York *Atlas.* During this period he produced several novels having as a background the events of the Civil War, and a volume of humorous sketches, *Sprees and Splashes* (1863). In search of health and of fresh literary materials, he spent the summer of 1865 in England, France, and Scotland, later publishing his observations in *Over-Sea* (1867). Two years later he visited the Paris exposition, which he described in a volume called *Paris in '67* (1867). These short trips abroad suggested to him the possibility of publishing a guidebook to Europe which would benefit the person who had at his disposal but a few months for travel. This idea bore fruit in *Morford's Short-Trip Guide to Europe,* first published in 1868. A similar book, intended for Europeans visiting America, appeared in 1872 under the title *Morford's Short-Trip Guide to America.* In 1878 he again visited Europe, publishing a record of his experiences in *Paris and Half-Europe in '78* (1879). In January 1880 he established and edited the *Brooklyn New Monthly Magazine,* which continued until March 1881. From 1876 to the time of his death he kept a bookstore and travel office at 52 Broadway, where he made a specialty of guidebooks.

His work as an author was uneven. Perhaps the best of his poetical work is *The Rest of Don Juan* (1846), a continuation of Byron's poem, in which he sometimes handles the *ottava rima* as skilfully as the English poet, although the effort as a whole is unevenly sustained. Much weaker are the verses collected in *Rhymes of Twenty Years* (1859) and *Rhymes of an Editor* (1873). Morford undoubtedly possessed the journalist's instinct to turn to literary use the events of the passing moment. Three novels composed during the Civil War were addressed to a war audience—*Shoulder-Straps* (1863), *The Days of Shoddy* (1863), and *The Coward* (1864). With

the coming of the centennial of the Declaration of Independence in 1876, he published another novel, *The Spur of Monmouth,* whose subject was suggested no doubt by the battlefield near which he had lived as a boy. These tales are labored, discursive productions, weak for the most part in characterization, and abounding with trite and improbable incident. Of slightly greater literary value are his books of travel, which, although wholly informal in manner, lack the touch of a descriptive master. A drama, *The Bells of Shandon,* in which he collaborated with John Brougham, was produced at Wallack's Theatre, New York, in 1867, but has never been published (T. A. Brown, *A History of the New York Stage,* 1903, II, 164). Morford is particularly remembered, however, for his guidebooks, whose popularity in his day is evidenced by the many editions through which they passed.

[T. H. Leonard, *From Indian Trail to Electric Rail* (1923), pp. 110–11; Franklin Ellis, *Hist. of Monmouth County, N. J.* (1885); *Trow's New York City Directory,* 1858–82; H. S. Ashbee, "The Rest of Don Juan," *Bibliographer,* July 1883; *N. Y. Times,* Aug. 7, 1881; bound file of the *New Jersey Standard,* Apr. 1, 1852–Apr. 1, 1854, in the N. Y. Hist. Soc.; four letters of Morford in the Hist. Soc. of Pa.]   N. F. A.

MORGAN, ABEL (1673–Dec. 16, 1722), Baptist clergyman and Biblical scholar, was born at Alltgoch in the parish of Llanwenog, Cardiganshire, South Wales. He was the son of Morgan ap Rhydderch ap Dafydd ap Gruffydd, an elder and later a minister of the Rhydwilym Baptist Church, and in accordance with the custom in Wales at a time when family names were almost unknown he took as a surname his father's Christian name. For a number of generations the family had been prominent for its devotion to literature, the best known member of it being Abel's uncle, Sion Rhydderch ("John Roderick"), who, besides being a printer, an antiquary, and something of a poet, compiled the first English-Welsh dictionary, wrote one of the first Welsh grammars, and translated into Welsh a number of religious works.

Abel began to preach before he was eighteen years old, and settled at Llanwenarth in Monmouthshire near Abergavenny. When, about 1696, the Blaenau Gwent branch was established as a separate church independent of Llanwenarth, he was called to preach there and four years later he was ordained its first minister. He soon rose to prominence in the affairs of the Welsh Baptists, but in 1711 he decided to emigrate to Pennsylvania, whither his brother Enoch and other members of the family with many Welsh Baptists had preceded him. He embarked at Bristol on Sept. 28, but the ship was detained by con-

163

trary winds and it was not until Feb. 14, 1712, that he arrived in Philadelphia after a stormy passage. On the voyage his wife, who was Priscilla Powell of Abergavenny, and his infant son died, leaving him with one daughter. Almost immediately upon his arrival he assumed charge of the Pennepek Baptist Church, with its branch in the city of Philadephia, which relationship he retained until his death. He quickly became one of the leaders among the Baptists of Pennsylvania, and also established churches in Delaware and New Jersey. He married in this country Martha Burrows, and, as his third wife, Judith (Griffiths) Gooding (daughter of the Rev. Thomas Griffiths), who, with four children, survived him.

He published nothing during his lifetime but is said to have translated into Welsh the Century Confession, adding to it certain articles embodying his own ideas on the subject of singing hymns and the laying on of hands, and a Catechism similarly modified. Eight years after his death his brother Enoch and his half-brother Benjamin Griffiths published his *Cyd-gordiad Egwyddorawl o'r Scrythurau: neu Daflen Lythyrennol o'r Prif Eiriau Yn y Bibl Sanctaidd. Yn Arwain, dan y Cyfryw eiriau, i fuan ganfod pob rhyw ddymunol ran o'r Scrythurau. A Gyfansoddwyd Drwy Lafurus Boen Abel Morgan, Gwenidog yr Efengyl er lle's y Cymru. Argraphwyd yn Philadelphia, gan Samuel Keimer, a Dafydd Harry. MDCCXXX.* This, the second Welsh book published in America, was the first real concordance to the Welsh Bible, and was long the only one. Of its author a recent writer (David Jones in the *Cambrian*) has said, "To this day his name is a household word in Wales and America among the Welsh People."

[Morgan Edwards, *Materials Towards a Hist. of the Baptists in Pa.* (1770); H. G. Jones, in *Pa. Mag. of Hist. and Biog.,* vol. VI, no. 3 (1882); J. Davis, *Hist. of the Welsh Baptists* (1835); Thomas Rees, *Hist. of Protestant Nonconformity in Wales* (1861); articles in the *Cambrian*, vol. XIII (1893); William Rowlands, *Cambrian Bibliog.* (1869); Charles Ashton, *Hanes Llenyddiaeth Gymreig* (n.d.; 1893?); *Enwogion y Ffydd* (1880).]   J.J.P.

MORGAN, CHARLES (Apr. 21, 1795–May 8, 1878), shipping and railroad owner, was descended from James Morgan, a Welshman who emigrated to Boston about 1636 and later settled in Connecticut. Here on a farm in Killingworth (now Clinton), Conn., Charles was born, the son of Col. George and Elizabeth (Redfield) Morgan. At fourteen he went to New York City, which became his permanent home. Starting as a grocery clerk, he was in business for himself at twenty-one, with a shop on Peck Slip, selling provisions to ships. He next began to import fruit directly from the south. This venture led to a line of sailing vessels to the West Indies. Quick to realize the value of steam, he secured an interest in the *David Brown,* the first steamship on the New York-Charleston run.

In 1835, even before Texas secured its independence, Morgan invaded the Gulf waters which were to be the scene of his greatest activity and success, sending the steamer *Columbia* from New Orleans to Galveston. He soon had a regular line of mail steamers plying between those points. From Galveston, the Morgan service radiated to Indianola, Corpus Christi, and Vera Cruz, while from New Orleans a line ran to Mobile and there was another on Lake Pontchartrain. With Arnold Harris, Morgan established the Texas & New Orleans Mail Line, the Mexican Ocean Mail & Inland Company, and the Southern Mail Steamship Company. Though several of his steamers were lost without, it is said, a cent of insurance, he continued to expand his business. On the eve of the Civil War, Judah P. Benjamin stated to a congressional committee that Morgan's steamers did "all the business on the Gulf."

During the middle fifties came the "war of the three commodores" between Morgan, Cornelius Vanderbilt, and George Law [*qq.v.*]. When Vanderbilt opened the Nicaragua Transit and ran steamships on the Atlantic and Pacific in opposition to the Law-Aspinwall mail subsidy lines, he made Morgan and C. K. Garrison [*q.v.*] his agents in New York and San Francisco respectively, Morgan becoming president when Vanderbilt went to Europe in 1853. During his absence, Morgan and Garrison manipulated stock prices in such a way that they profited while Vanderbilt lost heavily. The latter, on his return, is said to have stormed at them, "I will not sue you, because the law takes too long. I will ruin you." While Morgan and Garrison made use of William Walker [*q.v.*], the filibuster, to get control of the Nicaraguan government and secure the transfer of the Transit concession to themselves, Vanderbilt sent Sylvanus H. Spencer to Nicaragua where, with Costa Rican troops, he definitely closed the Transit. Walker was ruined, but Morgan and Garrison survived.

The Civil War was naturally a crisis for a Northern man with much of his capital tied up in Southern waters. Three of Morgan's steamers were seized at New Orleans for the Confederate service on Apr. 28, 1861, but several others were chartered or sold for Union service, three of them bringing him approximately $650,000, a sum far in excess of their value. In 1850 he had secured control of the T. F. Secor marine engine works in New York, changing the name

Morgan   Morgan

to the Morgan Iron Works, but he turned over the actual control to his son-in-law, G. W. Quintard [*q.v.*], who built more machinery than anyone else for the Union navy. At the close of the war, Morgan picked up several steamers at auction for less than half of what they had cost the government. He started what is still known as the Morgan Line, from New York to New Orleans, and about 1870 was called "the largest shipowner in the United States."

About this time he began to interest himself in railroads. On May 25, 1869, he purchased for $2,050,000 the bankrupt New Orleans, Opelousas & Great Western Railroad, which ran eighty miles westward from New Orleans along the north side of the great swamp region to the foot of Grand Bay at Brashear City. This terminus was renamed Morgan City, while the road became "Morgan's Louisiana & Texas Railroad." With the Morgan Line and his Gulf steamers, it gave him an all-Morgan route from New York to Texas, with a virtual monopoly of transportation in the latter region. Extending his control still further, he acquired two short Texas lines. His master stroke, however, came a year before his death when, for some $4,400,000, he secured control of the 505-mile Houston & Texas Central Railroad. Then he organized "Morgan's Louisiana & Texas Railroad and Steamship Company" as a holding company for all these various lines. He was chairman of the board and his son-in-law Charles A. Whitney, president. In 1883 these lines were purchased from the Morgan heirs for $7,500,000 by the Southern Pacific Railroad, and became part of its system.

Morgan died at his home on Madison Square in New York City. In 1870 he had given $50,000 to establish a school in his native town of Clinton. Like almost everything else with which he was connected it bore the name of Morgan. He is said, however, to have been quiet and unostentatious, and a very kindly master to the thousands in his employ. Although he believed in one-man control, he had the happy faculty of choosing able lieutenants. Three of these, J. C. Harris, Quintard, and Whitney, were his sons-in-law. He was twice married: on Dec. 20, 1817, to Emily Reeves, who bore him five children, and after her death in 1850, to Mary Jane Sexton, June 24, 1852. There were no children by his second marriage.

[N. H. Morgan, *Morgan Geneal.* (1869); L. E. Stanton, *An Account of the Dedication of the Morgan School Building, Clinton, Conn.* (1873); James Parton and others, *Sketches of Men of Progress* (1870–71), pp. 419–23; W. O. Scroggs, *Filibusters and Financiers* (1916); W. V. Wells, *Walker's Expedition to Nicaragua* (1856); W. A. Croffut, *The Vanderbilts and the Story of their Fortune* (1886); *Official Records of the Union and Confed. Navies*, 1 ser. IV, 165; *House Ex. Doc. 29*, 30 Cong., 1 Sess.; *House Ex. Doc. 337*, 40 Cong., 2 Sess., p. 24; H. V. Poor, *Manual of the Railroads of the U. S.*, 1870–71, p. 344, 1877, p. 849, 1878, p. 548; *Commercial & Financial Chronicle* (N. Y.), Feb. 24, 1883; and M. Y. Beach, *The Wealth and Biog. of the Wealthy Citizens of N. Y.* (13th ed., 1855); obituary in *N. Y. Herald*, May 9, 1878; advertisements of Morgan's various lines over a forty-year period.]
R. G. A.

MORGAN, CHARLES HILL (Jan. 8, 1831–Jan. 10, 1911), engineer, inventor, son of Hiram and Clarissa Lucina (Rich) Morgan, was born in Rochester, N. Y., where his father was employed as a mechanic. He was descended from Miles Morgan, one of the founders of Springfield, Mass., who emigrated from Bristol, England, in 1636. Charles Morgan enjoyed but a short schooling, for at the age of twelve he was put to work in a factory and at fifteen entered a machine shop in Clinton, Mass., as apprentice. Here he remained for six years, becoming an expert machinist and, through diligent work in night schools, a draftsman as well. In 1852 he entered the employ of the Clinton Cotton Mills and also served part time as draftsman for the Lawrence Machine Company. From 1855 to 1860 he was draftsman for the inventor and carpet manufacturer, Erastus B. Bigelow [*q.v.*], during which association he devised a system of designing and constructing cam curves for carpet-looms which proved of great value. In 1860 Morgan and his brother established a paper-bag manufacturing plant in Philadelphia, and designed an automatic machine for making bags, the great success of which placed paper-bag making for the first time on a commercial footing. The brothers sold this business to good advantage in 1864 and Morgan then became superintendent of I. Washburn and Moen, later Washburn & Moen Manufacturing Company, Worcester, Mass., makers of wire. Four years later he was made general superintendent and served in this capacity until 1887.

When Morgan joined this organization wire-rolling methods in the United States were far inferior to those in Europe. In 1865 he was sent abroad to study rolling-mill processes. In England, George Bedson had designed and constructed the first type of continuous rolling-mill, and on Morgan's recommendation the Washburn & Moen Company purchased one of Bedson's mills in 1869 and erected it in Worcester, Mass. While this was far superior to anything then existing in the United States, there was room for improvements and Morgan undertook the task of achieving them. After ten years of experimentation the power reel was perfected to handle the product of the mill, replacing the

165

hand-operated reel. Morgan was greatly assisted in this work by Fred H. Daniels [q.v.], and they received patents no. 224,838, no. 224,-840, and no. 224,942, on Feb. 24, 1880. Morgan's second improvement was the perfecting of a continuous train of horizontal rolls, by providing intermediate twist guides which gave the metal the necessary quarter turn as it passed between successive sets of rolls. This was patented jointly with Daniels Oct. 23, 1883, patent no. 287,008 (correspondence with American Steel Wire Company, Worcester, Mass.), and is the only type of continuous mill in use today, being known as the Morgan Mill. His third contribution was that of automatic reels, both of the pouring and the laying type, such as are now in use in wire mills throughout the world. The successful trial of these was made on Mar. 10, 1886. In 1881 Morgan established the Morgan Spring Company in Worcester, and after 1887 he devoted much of his time to his duties as president of this successful enterprise. In 1891 he organized the Morgan Construction Company to manufacture rolling-mill machinery, particularly the pure continuous type of rod mill. This undertaking was likewise successful and today practically all of the continuous wire rod rolling-mills in the world are equipped with this company's products.

Beside attending to his own businesses, Morgan served as a consulting engineer for the American Steel & Wire Company from 1887 until his death. He was very closely identified with the Worcester Polytechnic Institute, being a member of its board of trustees from its founding until his death. He was president of the American Society of Mechanical Engineers in 1899; a member of the International Iron and Steel Institute of Great Britain; and an honorary member of the Société des Ingénieurs Civils de France. He was twice married: first, June 8, 1852, to Harriet C. Plympton of Shrewsbury, Mass., who died July 28, 1862; and second, Aug. 4, 1863, to Rebecca Ann Beagary of Philadelphia. At his death in Worcester he was survived by his widow and five children.

[C. G. Washburn, *Industrial Worcester* (1917); Charles Nutt, *Hist. of Worcester and Its People* (1919), vol. IV; *Trans. Am. Soc. Mech. Engrs.*, vol. XXXIII (1912); *Iron Age*, Jan. 12, 1911; Pat. Office records; *Who's Who in America, 1910–11, Boston Transcript,* Jan. 10, 1911.]   C. W. M.

MORGAN, DANIEL (1736–July 6, 1802), Revolutionary soldier, son of James and Eleanora Morgan, was of Welsh ancestry and born probably in Hunterdon County, N. J., though some authorities say just across the Delaware River in Bucks County, Pa., where his father

was ironmaster at the Durham Iron Works. The meager records of his youth tell us that, after quarreling with his father, he made his way to the Shenandoah Valley in Virginia, where he worked as farm laborer and teamster until he had saved sufficient money to become an independent wagoner, in which capacity he accompanied Braddock's ill-fated expedition. Later, he transported supplies to the frontier posts of Virginia. For striking a British subaltern, the hot-tempered, impulsive youth received five hundred lashes on his bare back, yet freely forgave the officer upon the latter's expression of contrition. He served as lieutenant in Pontiac's War and in 1774 accompanied Lord Dunmore's expedition to western Pennsylvania. Meanwhile, his marriage to Abigail Bailey gradually transformed him from a boisterous, pugnacious youth into a high-spirited man, eager to improve his mind and to acquire a competence.

At the outbreak of the Revolution Congress commissioned him, June 22, 1775, captain of one of the two companies of riflemen to be raised in Virginia. Within ten days he enlisted his company and twenty-one days later reached Boston from Winchester, Va., his company intact. After a short period of comparative inactivity, he volunteered for Arnold's arduous expedition through the Maine wilderness to Quebec, and accompanied Arnold's column in the assault, Dec. 31. When Arnold was wounded, at the insistence of the other officers Morgan assumed command, captured the first barrier, being one of the first over, and penetrated a considerable distance into the lower city; but upon the failure of the other troops to join him he reluctantly surrendered to overwhelming odds. After his release the following autumn, Congress, Nov. 12, 1776, commissioned him colonel of a regiment to be raised in Virginia. Upon rejoining Washington, the following April, he organized, under the latter's order, a corps of five hundred sharpshooters, and participated in various movements in New Jersey until ordered north in August to assist Gates in opposing Burgoyne's advance. Here his troops rendered such signal service at the battles of Freeman's Farm and Bemis Heights that Gates, replying to Washington's request for their return, declared that he could not spare "the corps the army of General Burgoyne are most afraid of" (Sparks, *post*, II, 437). Morgan's indignant refusal to participate in the intrigues against Washington led to an estrangement between him and Gates, though the latter had warmly welcomed him upon his arrival. After Burgoyne's surrender, Washington recalled him to assist in the campaign around

Philadelphia in the fall and winter of 1777. Though not actually engaged at the battle of Monmouth, he effectively pursued the British after that engagement.

Impaired health and dissatisfaction with the course pursued by Congress regarding army promotions led him to resign in July 1779, and retire to Virginia, where he occupied himself in erecting his mansion, "Saratoga." Recalled to active service in 1780, he joined Gates, with whom he had become reconciled, shortly after the latter's disastrous defeat at Camden. When Greene succeeded Gates in command of the southern department, the former placed Morgan, recently created brigadier-general, in command of the troops in western North Carolina which were opposing the advance of the British northward from Charleston. Failing to obtain Greene's consent to his plan of creating a diversion by advancing into Georgia, Morgan gradually retired northward before the advancing British under Tarleton until he reached the Cowpens, a few miles south of the North Carolina boundary. Here, with the Broad River in his rear, he determined to make a stand with his small force of somewhat over eight hundred. On Jan. 17, 1781, largely by the effective work of his cavalry, he won the brilliant victory of Cowpens, one of the decisive victories of the war, for which he received the thanks of Congress and a gold medal. Fearing a union of Tarleton's shattered troops with the main army under Cornwallis and an effort to cut him off, he retreated rapidly northward, effecting a junction early in February with Greene's troops at Guilford Court House. Ill health shortly afterward again forced his retirement from active duty, though he joined Lafayette for a short time in July in the defense of Virginia.

At the conclusion of the war he advanced money, so far as his straitened circumstances permitted, to many of his needy soldiers, taking their scrip as security, subject to redemption. This act led for a time to the charge, which he bitterly resented, even to the point of personal encounter, that he was speculating in his soldiers' necessities. Retiring to "Saratoga," he devoted himself with such success to the restoration of his shattered fortune that by 1796 he owned more than 250,000 acres on the Monongahela and Ohio Rivers (Graham, *post,* p. 413). In 1794, in command of the Virginia militia, he assisted in suppressing the Whiskey Insurrection in western Pennsylvania and, after the withdrawal of the main army, remained in control of the district, where he successfully pursued a policy of conciliation. Defeated for Congress in

1795, he was successful in 1797, serving one term. Indicative of his intense partisanship is his comment in a letter of 1798 regarding the Democrats: "They at this time look like a parsell of Egg sucking Dogs that have been caut Breaking up Hens Nests" (letter to Presley Neville, in New York Public Library). Morgan was stout and active, six feet in height, "exactly fitted for the toils and pomp of war." Wild in his youth, in later years he became a devout member of the Presbyterian Church. His two daughters, Nancy and Betty, became the wives of Presley Neville and James Heard, respectively.

[James Graham, *Life of Daniel Morgan* (1856), and the *Cowpens Papers* (1881) reprint many documents from the Morgan papers in the New York Public Library; see also Henry Lee, *Memoirs of the War in the Southern Department* (2 vols., 1812), esp. I, 386 ff.; J. F. Folsom, in *Proc. N. J. Hist. Soc.,* July 1929; J. H. Brandow, in *Proc. N. Y. Hist. Asso.,* vol. XII (1913); J. H. Smith, *Arnold's March from Cambridge to Quebec* (1903) and *Our Struggle for the Fourteenth Colony* (2 vols., 1907); E. A. Duyckinck, *Nat. Portrait Gallery of Eminent Americans* (1862); Jared Sparks, *Correspondence of the Am. Rev.* (1853); *Virginia Argus* (Richmond), July 21, 1802.]   D. C. H.

MORGAN, EDWIN BARBER (May 2, 1806–Oct. 13, 1881), merchant and philanthropist, was born and lived throughout his life at Aurora, N. Y., on Cayuga Lake. James Morgan, from whom he was descended, emigrated from Wales to Massachusetts about 1636, removed to New London, Conn., about 1650, and later settled at Groton, Conn., where his descendants were substantial farmers. Thence young Christopher Morgan, whose wife was Nancy Barber, went to be clerk of the company building the long bridge across the lower waters of Cayuga. In 1800 he became a merchant at Aurora. Edwin, the eldest of his sons, attended a school there, and when he was thirteen went to work in his father's store. At the age of twenty-one he took over his father's affairs, and soon created a large business in buying and shipping agricultural produce and in boat-building, his brothers becoming his partners. Some of the capital thus acquired he used in developing express companies. In this enterprise he was associated with Henry Wells [*q.v.*], also of Aurora, a pioneer in the express business and the first president of the American Express Company. At the organization, in 1852, of Wells, Fargo & Company's Express, Morgan became its president. He was one of the founders of the United States Express Company in 1854, and a lifelong director of the American. With his brothers he operated extensive gypsum beds at Grand Rapids, Mich., and had important interests in the starch-making industry at Oswego. Through these and other activities he gained a large fortune.

His energies found outlet in politics, also. He was elected representative in Congress in 1852, and twice reëlected, serving from Mar. 4, 1853, to Mar. 3, 1859. During his last term his cousin, Edwin Denison Morgan [q.v.], was chosen governor of the state. In the House Morgan actively expressed his anti-slavery convictions, and was one of the members who rescued Charles Sumner from Brooks's assault. From its formation he was attached to the Republican party. During the Civil War he devoted himself to raising and equipping troops, and the strong representation of central New York in the army was due considerably to his influence and gifts. Every colonel of a regiment from this region received from him a thousand dollars for his command, he also gave regular pay to all volunteers from Aurora and assisted soldiers' families. His work in the war brought him the title of colonel. He rendered an important public service through the *New York Times,* in which he was an original stockholder. In the thick of his fight against Tweed, George Jones [q.v.], the editor, feared that ownership of the paper would pass into unfriendly hands. Accordingly, in 1871, Morgan bought for $375,000 enough stock to assure the continuance of Jones's policy, thus materially contributing to Tweed's downfall.

Morgan's later years were chiefly devoted to education. He long maintained the Cayuga Lake Academy at Aurora, which he had attended, and was a trustee of Cornell University and other institutions in central New York. Soon after the founding of Wells College, at Aurora, by Henry Wells, Morgan became a trustee, and later was the president of the board of the college and its principal benefactor, giving to it much time and more than a quarter of a million dollars. Auburn Theological Seminary, situated near his home, also received from him strong support. Most of the cost of its dormitory was met by him, and he and William E. Dodge [q.v.] made possible its library building.

Morgan died at Aurora, survived by a son and a daughter. His wife, to whom he was married on Sept. 27, 1829, was Charlotte Fidelia Wood of Aurora. Physically and mentally he was quick-moving and incessantly active, even to old age. Extraordinary foresight and sagacity largely explain his commercial success, but in addition he had great self-reliance, determination, perseverance, and courage. Large interests elsewhere never lessened his devotion to his own village. His personal beneficences were innumerable. He helped many young people to get educations and many men to advance in business.

[*Biog. Dir. Am. Cong.* (1928); E. A. Storke, *Hist. of Cayuga County, N. Y.* (1879); E. S. Frisbie, in *Report of Regents of Univ. of State of N. Y.* (1888); W. I. Lowe, *Wells College and Its Founders* (1901); *Wells College Hist. Sketches* (1894); J. Q. Adams, *A Hist. of Auburn Theological Seminary, 1818–1918* (1918); Elmer Davis, *Hist. of the N. Y. Times, 1851–1921* (1921); N. Y. Times, Oct. 14, 1881.]   R. H. N.

MORGAN, EDWIN DENISON (Feb. 8, 1811–Feb. 14, 1883), governor of New York, United States senator, was a descendant of James Morgan, a Welshman, who came to Massachusetts about 1636 and about 1650 settled in New London, where he married Margery Hill. Edwin, the son of Jasper and Catherine (Copp) Avery Morgan and a first cousin of Edwin Barber Morgan [q.v.], was born in Washington, Berkshire County, Mass., but in 1822 removed with his parents to Windsor, Conn. During his boyhood he worked on his father's farm in summer and attended the village school in winter. In 1826 he entered Bacon Academy, Colchester, Conn., but two years later became a clerk in his uncle's grocery store at Hartford, Conn. At twenty, he became his uncle's partner. In 1832 he was elected a member of the Hartford city council. Desiring a wider sphere of activity, he removed to New York in 1836, and here, in partnership with Morris Earle and A. D. Pomeroy, established the wholesale grocery firm of Morgan & Earle. Upon its dissolution at the end of 1837, he began business on his own account. His enterprise and sagacity placed him in a few years among New York's leading merchants. On Jan. 1, 1842, he associated with himself his cousin, George D. Morgan, and the latter's partner, Frederick Avery, who retired one year later, his place being taken by one of Morgan's clerks, J. T. Terry. In 1854 Solon Humphreys joined the firm, and banking and brokerage were added to the wholesale grocery business. Largely through Humphreys, who had spent several years in Missouri, E. D. Morgan & Company in the two years 1858–60 handled over $30,000,000 in securities issued by that state and by the city of St. Louis.

Meanwhile, in 1849 Morgan had been elected a member of the New York City Board of Assistant Aldermen, which acknowledged his ability by electing him its president. His valiant service during a cholera epidemic which swept over the city that year strengthened him in the public eye, and upon the expiration of his term as assistant alderman he was sent to the state Senate. Two years later he was reëlected after a severe contest with the Democratic Locofoco candidate. During both his terms he was president *pro tempore* of the Senate and chairman of its finance committee. He introduced and carried through the legislature the bill establishing Central Park in New York City. When in 1855 he declined to run for a third term he was appointed one of the state commissioners of emigration, a much coveted position which he held until 1858. Although up to 1855 he had been an assiduous Whig, and was an earnest opponent of slavery, he had not identified himself with the abolitionists because he did not believe in the wisdom of their methods. He was vice-president of the conference which made plans for the first Republican National Convention and was chairman of the Republican National Committee which conducted the Frémont campaign. This chairmanship he continued to hold until 1864.

In 1858 he was chosen by Thurlow Weed as Republican candidate for governor of New York. The odds were against him, but his fine personal character, his spotless record, and his reputation as a successful business man, coupled with the energy with which he conducted his campaign, carried him into office in a four-cornered contest by a plurality of over 17,000 votes. Far from being a mere satellite of Weed, he displayed independence and statesmanlike qualities, both in his messages to the legislature and in his use of the veto power. In 1860 he was reëlected by the largest majority which up to that time had ever been given to a gubernatorial candidate in the state. He succeeded during his first administration in improving the state's credit, strengthening its canal system, and making prisons, insurance companies, and charitable organizations more effective. His second administration was devoted to the success of the Union cause in the Civil War. Commissioned major-general of volunteers by Lincoln and placed in command of the military department of New York, he enrolled and equipped 223,000 soldiers. In 1862 he declined renomination for the governorship and upon the expiration of his term was commissioned under a legislative act to put New York harbor in a state of defense. He expended only $6,000 of the $1,000,000 appropriated for this purpose, returning the rest to the state treasury. In 1863 he was chosen United States senator to succeed Preston King. His career in the Senate was not characterized by oratorical display but by hard work both in the committee room and on the floor. In 1865 he declined appointment as secretary of the treasury. He voted with the minority on President Johnson's veto of the Freedman's Bureau Bill and for Johnson's conviction. In 1869 he was defeated for reelection after a bitter contest with Ex-Governor R. E. Fenton [q.v.]. From 1872 to 1876 he was again induced to head the Republican Commit-

tee, and in the latter year his name was mentioned in connection with the presidency. He stood for sound currency and civil service reform. In 1876 he was again nominated for governor, but the machine element of his party headed by Senator Conkling was dissatisfied with him, and he was defeated by Lucius Robinson. When Chester A. Arthur [q.v.], his old and ardent friend, succeeded to the presidency, he nominated Morgan for secretary of the treasury, but although the appointment was unanimously confirmed by the Senate, Morgan for a second time declined. During his last years he retired from all active participation in politics.

Morgan's fortune at the time of his death was estimated to be between eight and ten million dollars. His gifts during his lifetime totaled over a million dollars. Williams College, Union Theological Seminary, and the Women's, Presbyterian, and Eye and Ear hospitals in New York City especially benefited from his generosity. He was a patron of art well known both in America and on the continent of Europe, and a director of many business concerns. He was tall, well-proportioned, dignified, rather aristocratic in bearing. In 1833 he married his first cousin, Eliza Matilda Waterman, daughter of Capt. Henry and Lydia (Morgan) Waterman, of Hartford, Conn. Of their five children only one reached maturity, and he died in 1881, before his parents. The elder Morgan died at his home in New York City and was buried in Cedar Hill Cemetery, Hartford, Conn.

[Jours. of the Senate and the Assembly of . . . N. Y., 1883; N. H. Morgan, Morgan Geneal. (1869); J. A. Morgan, A Hist. of the Family of Morgan (1902); George Wilson, Portrait Gallery of the Chamber of Commerce of the State of N. Y. (1890); C. Z. Lincoln, State of New York, Messages from the Govs. (1909), vol. V; Thurlow Weed Barnes, Memoir of Thurlow Weed (1884); D. S. Alexander, A Pol. Hist. of the State of N. Y., vols. II, III (1906–09); S. D. Brummer, Pol. Hist. of N. Y. State during . . . the Civil War (1911); Frederick Phisterer, N. Y. in the War of the Rebellion (1912), vols. I, V; J. G. Wilson, The Memorial Hist. of N. Y. (1893), vols. III, IV; N. Y. Daily Tribune, Feb. 14, 1883; N. Y. Times, Feb. 15, 1883.]
H. J. C.

MORGAN, GEORGE (Feb. 14, 1743–Mar. 10, 1810), land-speculator and Indian agent, was born in Philadelphia, the brother of John Morgan [q.v.] and the son of Joanna (Biles) and Evan Morgan, a prosperous Philadelphia merchant who had emigrated from Wales probably about 1717. Both his parents were dead before he was six years old. He attended school in Philadelphia and at about thirteen years of age entered the service of Baynton and Wharton, merchants, as an apprentice. In 1763 he entered a new partnership with his employers, which became known as Baynton, Wharton, and

Morgan. On Oct. 21, the next year, he was married to Mary Baynton, the daughter of his partner, John Baynton. They had eleven children. At the end of Pontiac's War the firm, interested in the fur trade, undertook a venture to the Illinois country, recently acquired from the French by England, to profit at the same time from supplying Indian goods to the Crown and provisions to the military posts in the Illinois. He went to the Illinois as the representative of the firm and, though disappointed in his hopes for profits, became well known as a leader in the movement for the establishment of a civil government in the Illinois and as a judge in the civil court established there in 1768. When the trading venture failed the partnership went into a voluntary receivership, counting as the largest of its assets its share in the Indiana grant made by the Six Nations at Fort Stanwix in 1768 to the "suffering traders" whose goods had been destroyed by the Indians in 1763. The grant consisted of some 2,862 square miles of land in what is now West Virginia, just south of the Pennsylvania line. After a period of uncertainty the Indiana Company was reorganized in the spring of 1776 with Morgan as secretary-general and superintendent of the land office, with headquarters at Fort Pitt. The state of Virginia, claiming jurisdiction over this area, opposed the Indiana Company, and there ensued a long struggle in the legislature of Virginia, in the Continental Congress, and in the Supreme Court of the United States. Morgan was prevented from prosecuting his claim by the passage of the Eleventh Amendment to the Constitution in 1798.

During the Revolution he served in the double capacity of Indian agent for the United States in the middle department and deputy commissary-general of purchases for the western district, with the rank of colonel. Having served in these capacities, with headquarters at Fort Pitt, for about three years, he resigned in 1779. He retired to his farm, "Prospect," near Princeton, N. J., where he became a gentleman farmer. He dabbled in science in true eighteenth-century style and wrote several contributions to the proceedings of the two societies of which he was a member, the Philadelphia Society for the Promotion of Agriculture and the American Philosophical Society. His most notable study was an investigation of the life and habits of the Hessian fly, then attacking the eastern wheat fields. He published his results in various contemporary magazines, such as the *American Museum* (June, Sept. 1787).

In 1789, with the financial support of Don

Diego de Gardoqui, Spanish minister to the United States, he founded the colony of New Madrid, in Spanish Louisiana, now Missouri; but Don Estéban Miró, governor of Louisiana, having other plans for the settlement of Americans in Spanish territory, threw obstacles in the way of the project, and Morgan retired again to "Prospect." The last years of his life were spent at "Morganza," his farm near Washington, Pa., whither he removed in 1796. There he continued his scientific farming, devoting special attention to grape culture. The quiet of his life there was broken only once, by the visit of Aaron Burr, who stopped at his house in an attempt to enlist him and his sons in the western scheme. He refused to be drawn into the project and later journeyed to Richmond to testify against Burr at his famous trial.

[Max Savelle, *George Morgan* (1932); C. R. Woodward, *The Development of Agriculture in N. J.* (1927); *Ill. State Hist. Lib. Coll.,* esp. vol. I ed. by H. W. Beckwith (1903); C. W. Alvord and C. E. Carter, "The New Régime" (1916) and "Trade and Politics" (1921); *Papers of Sir William Johnson,* vols. II, IV–VII (1922–31); *Calendar of Va. State Papers,* esp. vol. VI (1886), pp. 1–36; K. M. Rowland, *The Life of George Mason* (2 vols., 1892); Louis Houck, *The Spanish Régime in Mo.* (1909), vol. I.]   M. S.

MORGAN, GEORGE WASHINGTON (Sept. 20, 1820–July 26, 1893), soldier, lawyer, congressman, came of Welsh stock, being descended from George Morgan [q.v.], whose father, Evan, came to America from Wales early in the eighteenth century. The son of Thomas Morgan and his wife Katherine, daughter of William Duane [q.v.], he was born in Washington County, Pa. In his sixteenth year he left Washington College to enlist in a company raised by his brother, Thomas Jefferson Morgan, for service in the war for Texan independence. President Houston appointed him a lieutenant and he soon became a captain. Returning to his home in 1839, he entered the United States Military Academy in 1841 but resigned during his second year. He worked at various tasks, in different places, studying law as opportunity offered. Removing to Mount Vernon, Ohio, in 1843, he studied in the office of his future partner, J. K. Miller. Shortly after his admission to the bar, he became prosecuting attorney for Knox County, but resigned to raise a company for the war with Mexico, in 1846. He was shortly elected colonel of the 2nd Ohio Volunteers, though only twenty-six years old. He acquitted himself creditably under Taylor until Mar. 3, 1847, when he was commissioned colonel of the 15th United States Infantry, and assigned to Pierce's brigade of Scott's army. He was wounded at both Contreras and Churubusco, and in

1848 was brevetted brigadier-general "for gallant and meritorious conduct." From 1848 until 1855 he combined law and farming at Mount Vernon. President Pierce appointed him consul at Marseilles in 1856. Two years later he became minister to Lisbon, which post he resigned at the outbreak of the Civil War.

He was appointed brigadier-general of volunteers in November 1861 and given command of the 7th Division of Buell's Army of the Ohio. With this division he drove the Confederates from Cumberland Gap. In 1863 he was transferred to Sherman's army and commanded a division in the Vicksburg campaign, and the XIII Corps at the capture of Fort Hindman, Ark. There was some disagreement between Morgan and Sherman (see Morgan's account of the fight at Chickasaw Bayou, *Battles and Leaders,* III, 462, and Sherman's comment in his *Memoirs,* I, 320), and within a few months illness and dissatisfaction with the policy of using negro troops caused Morgan's resignation, June 8, 1863. In the National Democratic Convention of the following year he defended General McClellan against the charge of "defeatism." In 1865 Morgan was defeated for governor of Ohio by Gen. J. D. Cox [*q.v.*], Republican. He was elected to Congress in 1866 and served from March 1867 to June 1868, when he was unseated in favor of his Republican fellow townsman, Columbus Delano [*q.v.*]. He was elected to the Forty-first and Forty-second congresses, however, and served 1869–73. He was a member of the committees on military affairs, on foreign affairs, and on reconstruction. In and out of Congress he vigorously opposed the harsh measures of reconstruction favored by the Radical Republicans. Blaine, who defeated him for the speakership, has testified to Morgan's ability. After leaving Congress Morgan resumed his law practice at Mount Vernon, Ohio. He was delegate-at-large to the National Democratic Convention of 1876. On Oct. 7, 1851, he had married Sarah H. Hall of Zanesville, Ohio, who with their two daughters survived him. His death occurred at Fortress Monroe, Va., and he was buried at Mount Vernon, Ohio.

["Extracts from the Reminiscences of Gen. George W. Morgan," with biog. note by J. M. Morgan, *Southwestern Hist. Quart.,* Jan. 1927; *Battles and Leaders of the Civil War,* vol. III (1888); *Appletons' Ann. Cyc., 1893* (1894); *Biog. Dir. Am. Cong.* (1928); Taylor's and Scott's reports in *House Exec. Doc. 60,* 30 Cong., 1 Sess.; *War of the Rebellion: Official Records (Army)*; J. G. Blaine, *Twenty Years of Congress* (2 vols., 1884–86); *The Biog. Encyc. of Ohio of the Nineteenth Century* (1876); *Personal Memoirs of Gen. W. T. Sherman* (3rd ed., 2 vols., 1890); J. H. Smith, *The War with Mexico* (2 vols., 1919); *Evening Star* (Washington, D. C.), July 27, 1893.] M. L. B., Jr.

MORGAN, JAMES DADA (Aug. 1, 1810–Sept. 12, 1896), Union soldier, merchant, and banker, of Welsh-English colonial ancestry, was born at Boston, the son of James Morgan, sea-captain and trader, and Martha (Patch) Morgan. He attended the common-schools in his native city until he was sixteen years of age, when the urge of the sea prompted him to start on a long voyage in a sailing-ship. When it was a month out of Boston, however, a mutiny arose, the vessel was burned, and, after drifting in a small boat for fourteen days, Morgan with certain companions finally reached the shores of South America. He made his way back to Boston, and in the year 1834 went to Quincy, Ill., where, for some twenty-seven years, he engaged in mercantile pursuits. Incidentally, he became interested in local military affairs, and helped organize the Quincy Grays and, later, the Quincy Riflemen. With the latter organization, he saw military service in Hancock County, Ill., during the Mormon difficulties of 1844–45, which ended with the death of the "Prophet," Joseph Smith, and a movement of the Mormon settlers to Utah.

Morgan entered the Mexican War as captain of the 1st Illinois Volunteer Infantry (June 18, 1846), was promoted major for conspicuous gallantry at the battle of Buena Vista, and was mustered out of the volunteer service on June 17, 1847. Returning to Quincy, he reëntered business, in which he continued to engage until the outbreak of the Civil War, when, Apr. 29, 1861, though suffering from a fractured leg, he assumed the duties of lieutenant-colonel of the 10th Illinois Infantry, becoming colonel on July 29 following. With his regiment he was mustered into federal service for three years. He participated in the engagement at Island Number Ten, where he commanded the 1st Brigade, 4th Division of Pope's army. For meritorious services at New Madrid, Mo., and in the capture of Corinth, Miss., where again he commanded a brigade, he was promoted brigadier-general of volunteers, July 17, 1862. He took an active part in the Atlanta campaign and accompanied General Sherman in his march to the sea and through the Carolinas, being brevetted, Mar. 19, 1865, major-general of volunteers for gallantry at Bentonville, N. C., where he contributed largely to saving the left wing of Sherman's army. He also distinguished himself at Buzzard's Roost Gap, Mar. 9, 1864.

He was mustered out of the military service, Aug. 24, 1865, and, returning to Quincy, became identified as a banker with many important corporations and institutions. He served as treasurer of the Illinois Soldiers and Sailors Home from its incorporation in 1887, and as vice-president of the Society of the Army of the Cumberland. He died at his home in Quincy, and there his interment took place. Early in life he was married to Jane Strachan of Boston, by whom he had two sons who survived him. His wife died in 1855, and on June 14, 1869, he married Harriet Evans of Gloucester, Mass.

[*Soc. of the Army of the Cumberland, Twenty-sixth Reunion, Rockford, Ill., 1896* (1897); F. B. Heitman, *Hist. Reg. and Dict. U. S. Army* (1903); *Chicago Tribune,* Sept. 13, 1896; *Portrait and Biog. Record of Adams Co., Ill.,* (1892); *Battles and Leaders of the Civil War,* vol. IV (1888); H. M. Cist, *The Army of the Cumberland,* J. D. Cox, *Atlanta,* and *The March to the Sea,* M. F. Force, *From Fort Henry to Corinth,* all in Campaigns of the Civil War series (1881–82); information as to certain facts from a great-nephew, J. R. Wells, of Quincy, Ill.]   C. D. R.

MORGAN, JAMES MORRIS (Mar. 10, 1845–Apr. 21, 1928), Confederate naval officer, soldier, author, was descended from Evan Morgan, who migrated from Wales to Philadelphia early in the eighteenth century and married Joanna Biles. One of their children was Dr. John Morgan [*q.v.*], Washington's first surgeon-general. Another was Col. George Morgan [*q.v.*], who apprised Jefferson of Burr's suspicious activities. Thomas Gibbes Morgan, grandson of George, removed to Louisiana early in the nineteenth century. His first wife, Eliza McKennan, bore one child, Philip Hicky Morgan [*q.v.*]. James Morris, the eighth child of Sarah Fowler, the second wife, was born in New Orleans. He entered the United States Naval Academy in September 1860, where his class, the first to use "Old Ironsides" as a training-ship, became known as the "brood of the *Constitution.*" The secession of Louisiana ended his career at Annapolis, however, and he became a midshipman in the Confederate navy. Serving first in the sloop *McRae,* on the Mississippi, he was transferred to the James River, then to Charleston. Accompanying Commodore Matthew F. Maury [*q.v.*] to Europe in October 1862, he served on board the cruiser *Georgia* until May 1864, then ran the blockade into Wilmington. Assigned to the schoolship *Patrick Henry,* on the James River (a "realistic war college"), he was soon sent to the naval Battery Semmes, near Dutch Gap. Since he was connected by marriage with Mrs. Jefferson Davis (his brother had married her cousin), he was detailed by the secretary of the navy to accompany her on her flight from Richmond, shortly before its fall. Not yet twenty-one, Morgan married, in October 1865, Helen, daughter of G. A. Trenholm of Charleston, late Confederate secretary of the treasury. She died a year later, leaving an infant daughter. About

this time, through General Sherman, Khedive Ismail Pasha of Egypt engaged ten Union and ten Confederate veterans to drill his army, and Morgan, finding law and agriculture uncongenial, accepted an Egyptian commission. After three busy and exciting years, he returned to the United States in 1872.

He now tried farming and journalism in South Carolina, and participated in the campaign of 1876 which ousted the Carpet-bag rule. His second wife, whom he married in 1873, was Gabriella Burroughs, grand-daughter of Chancellor W. F. DeSaussure of South Carolina. She died in a few years, leaving him another daughter. After serving a while as messenger to a committee of the United States Senate, Morgan tried engineering and prospecting in Mexico. He also helped erect the Statue of Liberty. In 1885 his brother-in-law, F. W. Dawson [*q.v.*], editor of the Charleston *News and Courier,* procured from President Cleveland Morgan's appointment as consul-general to Australasia. He was accompanied to his post by his third wife, Frances, daughter of Judge Charles A. Fincke of New York. One child (another daughter) was born to this marriage. Returning to America in 1888, Morgan tried farming and horse breeding in Maryland until 1898, when he removed to Washington. Besides participating in various financial enterprises, he did some writing and speaking. In 1903, as the representative of a banking house, he was in Panama at the time of the birth of that republic. He contributed numerous articles to magazines, and in 1915, in collaboration with J. P. Marquand, published a small volume of stories, *Prince and Boatswain: Sea Tales from the Recollections of Rear-Admiral Charles E. Clark.* His masterpiece was his autobiography, *Recollections of a Rebel Reefer,* published in 1917. He was stricken with paralysis in January 1928, and died shortly after his eighty-third birthday.

[Besides *Recollections of a Rebel Reefer,* see Sarah Morgan Dawson, *A Confederate Girl's Diary* (1913); *Official Records of the Union and Confederate Navies in the War of the Rebellion,* 1 ser. II, 2 ser. I; M. L. Bonham, Jr., "The Rebel Reefer Furls His Last Sail," in *La. Hist. Quart.,* Oct. 1928; *Evening Star* (Washington, D. C.), Apr. 23, 1928.]   M. L. B., Jr.

MORGAN, JOHN (June 10, 1735–Oct. 15, 1789), physician, founder of the University of Pennsylvania medical school, medical director of the Continental Army, was born in Philadelphia, the son of Evan and Joanna (Biles) Morgan. His father, an emigrant from Wales and a successful merchant, was prominent in Philadelphia civic life. John attended Nottingham School, near Philadelphia, and the College of

Philadelphia (now the University of Pennsylvania), graduating with the first class from the latter institution in 1757. He served six years' apprenticeship under Dr. John Redman [q.v.], having begun his work with him about 1750, and for several years was lieutenant and surgeon with the provincial troops in the French war. In 1760, on the advice of Dr. Redman, he decided to continue his studies abroad. Carrying letters of introduction from Benjamin Franklin, he spent a year in London under William Hewson, John Fothergill, and John and William Hunter, and two years at the University of Edinburgh, where he was granted the degree of M.D. (1763), his thesis, on the formation of pus, winning recognition as a valuable contribution. The following winter he studied anatomy in Paris and subsequently spent several months with Giovanni Morgagni in Italy. A memoir (later published in the *Transactions of the American Philosophical Society,* vol. II, 1786) on the subject of making anatomical preparations by corrosion, an art in which he acquired skill in England, procured his admission to the Académie Royale de Chirurgie de Paris (July 5, 1764). He was also a member of the Royal Society of London and the Belles-Lettres Society of Rome, and a licentiate of the Royal Colleges of Physicians in London and Edinburgh.

While abroad Morgan conceived the idea of establishing a medical school in connection with the College of Philadelphia, and upon his return in 1765 he proposed such a project to the trustees. It was adopted, May 3, 1765, and he was appointed professor of the theory and practice of physic. At the annual Commencement that year he delivered *A Discourse upon the Institution of Medical Schools in America* (1765). This classic is an elaborate exposition of the nature and scope of medical science, its conditions in America, obstacles in the way of medical study, and reasons for the establishment of medical schools. Arguing the need for separating the functions of physician, apothecary, and surgeon, he declared it his intention to confine himself to the practice of internal medicine solely by prescription. His advanced ideas at first met with great opposition, his opponents asserting that they were not adaptable to conditions in America.

At the first sign of trouble with the mother country Morgan hoped for a peaceful settlement of all difficulties and won a gold medal from John Sargent for his paper, published with the work of others in *Four Dissertations on the Reciprocal Advantages of a Perpetual Union between Great Britain and her American Colonies* (1766). At the outbreak of war he cast his lot with the colonies, and on Oct. 17, 1775, Congress elected him director-general of hospitals and physician-in-chief of the American army. He joined the army at Cambridge and later followed it to New York. Drastic reorganization of the medical department followed his appointment, especially with respect to raising the standards of assistants and to the dispensing of medicines. His exacting methods provoked the jealousy and antagonism of his subordinates, who by false charges and political intrigue caused him to be "degraded," Oct. 9, 1776, to director of hospitals east of the Hudson only. Increasing abuses, over which he had no control, brought loud complaints against him from his enemies, and on Jan. 9, 1777, Congress removed him without explanation. The real reason seems to have been the feeling that while there were no particular charges against him, the numerous general complaints made his removal necessary for the good of the service (W. C. Ford, *Journals of the Continental Congress, 1774–1789,* vol. VIII, 1907, p. 626).

Morgan denounced the resolution dismissing him without reason as unfair, and published *A Vindication of His Public Character in the Station of Director-General of the Military Hospitals, and Physician in Chief of the American Army* (1777), in which he charged that "*a mean and invidious* set of men" had plotted his removal, and declared that the intermeddling of Congress had rendered efficiency and honesty impossible in his department. His dismissal was a severe blow to him, and though Washington exonerated him of neglect and wrong-doing and Congress decided that he "hath in the most satisfactory manner vindicated his conduct" and that as director-general he "did conduct himself ably and faithfully in the discharge of the duties of his office" (*Ibid.,* vol. XIV, 1909, p. 724), he considered himself disgraced and withdrew from public life. Thereafter, he confined his efforts to his private practice and to his duties as professor and as physician at the Pennsylvania Hospital.

Morgan was a handsome man, an indefatigable worker, and well versed in Latin and Greek. His writings, in addition to those already mentioned, include *A Recommendation of Inoculation, According to Baron Dimsdale's Method* (1776), and a journal, left in manuscript, which, edited by Julia Morgan Harding, was published in 1907 as *The Journal of Dr. John Morgan of Philadelphia, from the City of Rome to the City of London, 1764.* He possessed a choice medical library, containing many original manuscripts, which was destroyed during the Revolution. He

Morgan

Morgan

was an active member of the American Philosophical Society, while the Philadelphia College of Physicians, organized in 1787, was the outgrowth of his suggestion. His wife, Mary, daughter of Thomas and Mary Hopkinson, whom he married Sept. 4, 1765, died in 1785. There were no children. Morgan's death occurred in Philadelphia.

[Morgan's writings; letters and other MSS. in the Hist. Soc. of Pa., Phila., and in the Papers of the Continental Cong., No. 63, and the Joseph Meredith Toner Papers, Lib. of Cong.; M. I. Wilbert, "John Morgan, the Founder of the First Medical School and the Originator of Pharmacy in America," in *Am. Jour. of Pharmacy,* Jan. 1904; Joseph Carson, *A Hist. of the Medic. Dept. of the Univ. of Pa.* (1869); G. W. Norris, *The Early Hist. of Medicine in Phila.* (1886); and G. B. Wood, *Hist. and Biog. Memoirs* (1872); H. A. Kelly and W. L. Burrage, *Am. Medic. Biogs.* (1920); *Pa. Mag. of Hist. and Biog.,* Apr. 1886, p. 43, Apr. 1894, p. 35, Oct. 1909, pp. 502, 503, July 1924, p. 22; *Phila. Jour. Medic. and Physic. Sci.,* vol. I, no. 2 (1820), pp. 439–42; J. A. Morgan, *A Hist. of the Family of Morgan* (1902).] J. H. P.

MORGAN, JOHN HUNT (June 1, 1825–Sept. 4, 1864), Confederate raider, was born at Huntsville, Ala. His father, Calvin Cogswell Morgan, a merchant, was a Virginian; his mother, Henrietta, was the daughter of John W. Hunt, an influential business man of Lexington, Ky. About 1830 the Morgans moved to a farm in the neighborhood of that city and there John received a good common-school education. He enlisted for the Mexican War in 1846 and saw service at Buena Vista. Shortly after his return, he was married to Rebecca Bruce, who soon became a confirmed invalid and died in July 1861. Morgan prospered in business and, retaining his interest in military affairs, organized, in 1857, the Lexington Rifles.

In September 1861 he joined the Confederate army and immediately became a scout. Elected a captain, he was given a squadron to command, and early in 1862 began his famous raids, during which he harassed the Federals by penetrating their lines, capturing men and trains, and destroying supplies. He became a colonel on Apr. 4, 1862, took part in the Shiloh campaign, and then started a raid, beginning near Iuka, Miss., in which he fought near Columbia, Tenn., on May 1, taking 400 prisoners, but was badly defeated at Lebanon on May 5 by Federal cavalry under General Dumont. Nothing daunted, he rallied his men, and advanced into Kentucky, on May 11 reaching Cave City, where he wrecked the railroad and burned important stores. In June he was placed at the head of a brigade, with which, starting from near Knoxville, Tenn., July 4, 1862, he raided extensively in Kentucky, marching more than 1,000 miles, taking hundreds of prisoners and enormous stocks of supplies, and returning safely to his base. Morgan acted rapidly, he fought hard to secure his objectives, then split his command, striking right and left to confuse his enemies. He withdrew quickly, avoiding fighting wherever possible. During the remainder of 1862, he raided the country between Nashville, Louisville, and Cincinnati. On Dec. 7 he captured a Federal force at Hartsville, Tenn., taking over 1,700 prisoners. For this victory he was appointed brigadier-general and given the command of a cavalry division. On Dec. 14, he was married to the daughter of the Hon. Charles Ready, of Murfreesboro, Tenn. He started a new series of raids in March 1863 and on May 1 the Confederate Congress gave him a vote of thanks for his "varied, heroic and invaluable services."

In June 1863 he secured authority from Gen. Joe Wheeler [*q.v.*] to raid Kentucky with 2,000 men. Nothing was said about going beyond Kentucky, but Morgan had that project in mind. Starting July 2, he crossed the Ohio into Indiana six days later. Pursued by superior forces, he commenced a wild ride through the suburbs of Cincinnati, and east. The ride was so fast, fifty to sixty miles a day, and his column was so harassed by swarms of home guards, that Morgan's men became exhausted, with the result that when their pursuers caught up with them on July 19, near Buffington Island, most of the command surrendered. Morgan himself rode on, but was surrounded near New Lisbon, Ohio, and on July 26 surrendered. This raid destroyed Morgan's division and inflicted only minor losses upon the Federals, but it drew large Federal forces from in front of Bragg's army, and saved East Tennessee to the Confederacy for several months.

Escaping from the Ohio State Penitentiary, Columbus, Ohio, on Nov. 26, Morgan was assigned in April 1864 to command the Department of Southwest Virginia. His forces were poorly equipped and badly disciplined, but he restored order and organized an efficient force, with which he raided Kentucky in June. This raid had some success, but losses were severe, and the troops committed excesses, which led to dissatisfaction on the part of the Confederate government over Morgan's failure to discover and punish the culprits. On Sept. 3, 1864, Morgan decided to attack Federal forces near Knoxville, Tenn., and encamped that evening at Greenville. In the night a Federal force passed unnoticed into his lines. Entering the town early the next morning, Morgan was surprised and killed while endeavoring to join his men. His body was buried at Abington, subsequently interred at Richmond,

174

Va., and finally buried in Lexington, Ky. Gentle and generous, Morgan was bold in thought and action. He was a thorn to his enemies, not because of military genius, but on account of untiring energy and continuous devotion to his cause.

[*War of the Rebellion: Official Records (Army)*; B. W. Duke, *Hist. of Morgan's Cavalry* (1867); A. C. Quisenberry, "Hist. of Morgan's Men," in *Reg. Ky. State Hist. Soc.*, Sept. 1917; S. K. Smith, *Life, Army Record, and Public Services of D. Howard Smith* (1890); *The Biog. Encyc. of Ky. of the Nineteenth Century* (1878); *Biog. Cyc. of the Commonwealth of Ky.* (1896); the *Sentinel* (Richmond), Sept. 10, 1864.]
C. H. L.

MORGAN, JOHN PIERPONT (Apr. 17, 1837–Mar. 31, 1913), banker and foremost leader of American finance, was the son of Junius Spencer Morgan [q.v.], a prominent international banker who did much to open the United States to European capital and left at his death in 1890 an impressively large fortune for his time. On the maternal side his inheritance was equally significant, if different. His mother, Juliet (Pierpont) Morgan, was a daughter of the Rev. John Pierpont [q.v.], poet, impetuous clergyman, and fiery reformer. The Morgan fortune did not begin even with Junius Spencer; it was founded by the latter's father Joseph, who with his wife Sarah Spencer took up a farm near Hartford, Conn., in 1817. Joseph Morgan did not remain a farmer long, but amassed wealth, first in stage coaches, then in hotels, and finally in fire-insurance companies. He purchased a partnership for his son in a local drygoods firm, and shortly thereafter the eldest of Junius' five children, John Pierpont Morgan, known later as J. Pierpont Morgan or as J. P. Morgan, was born. The young Morgans soon moved from a small cottage on Asylum Street to a much larger and more comfortable house, surrounded by farm lands, which Joseph Morgan had built for them on Farmington Avenue. The eldest child entered a local school at the age of six, but when he was fourteen his parents moved to Boston, where his father became partner in one of the leading drygoods houses. There he entered English High, a noted school, from which he graduated in good standing at seventeen. The same year his father accepted a partnership with George Peabody, an American merchant who had become a great London banker. Although Pierpont was large and well built his health was poor for a time, and he was sent to the Azores to recuperate. From there he went to a school at Vevey on Lake Geneva in Switzerland, and then for two years to the University of Göttingen, in Germany, where mathematics was one of his chief studies.

Entering his father's house in London in 1856, he was sent to New York the following year to work in that of Duncan, Sherman & Company, American representatives of George Peabody & Company. From 1860 to 1864, as J. Pierpont Morgan & Company, he acted as agent in New York for his father's firm; in 1864–71 he was a member of the firm of Dabney, Morgan & Company, being associated with Charles H. Dabney, formerly a partner in Duncan, Sherman & Company; and in 1871 with the Drexels of Philadelphia he formed the New York firm of Drexel, Morgan & Company. Anthony J. Drexel, the head of the house, died in 1893, and in 1895 the New York firm became J. P. Morgan & Company. Closely associated with Drexel & Company of Philadelphia, Morgan, Harjes & Company of Paris, and J. S. Morgan & Company (after 1910 Morgan, Grenfell & Company), of London, it became one of the most powerful banking houses of the world, carrying through a long series of operations, of enormous variety and many of great scale. Certain very important ones were in the nature of reorganizations and consolidations, the success of which could generally be ascribed to the ability and leadership of Morgan.

During the trying days of the Civil War, young Morgan, concentrating on business, chiefly foreign exchange, made slow but sure progress. Two incidents of his relatively inconspicuous career during that era of profiteering and speculative orgy do not redound to his credit. To Simon Stevens, who sold to the Federal government obsolete Hall's carbines, he gave financial backing, though he withdrew from the case before Stevens finally brought successful suit for payment in full ("Government Contracts," *House Report No. 2*, 37 Cong., 2 Sess., pp. lxiv–lxxvi, "Case No. 97—J. Pierpont Morgan, New York"; 2 *Court of Claims Reports*, 95–103); and in 1863, with Edward Ketchum, he speculated in gold in a way that was hardly patriotic (*N. Y. Times*, Oct. 11, 16, 21, 1863; *American Gold, 1862–1876*, 1876). More characteristically, in 1869 he engineered a successful contest with Jay Gould and James Fisk [qq.v.], then at the zenith of their powers, over the control of the Albany & Susquehanna Railroad. Essentially an organizer and integrating force, he fought the financial buccaneers of his age with their own weapons, and, triumphing over them, became an influence, though not yet a conspicuous one, for stabilization (Corey, *post*, pp. 90–91). In a sense, his prominence dates from 1873, when by securing a division of a treasury loan between a Morgan syndicate and one organized by Jay Cooke [*q.v.*], he broke the monopoly of that financier in the vast refunding operations of the government. After the failure of Jay Cooke & Company in the panic of that year, the Morgan firm, increasing its already powerful international connections, became dominant in government financing.

Morgan, however, hardly became a large figure in the public eye until he was more than forty. In 1879 he sold a large block of New York Central stock direct to English investors, enabling William H. Vanderbilt to dispose of large holdings without unloading them on the American market and making a great impression on that magnate by his incisive action. The deal, unusual for those days, brought Morgan much prestige and may have influenced him to engage in the work of reorganizing American railroads, with a view to the restoration of faith abroad in American securities. Combatting tendencies toward reckless promotion and construction, unprofitable competition, and general demoralization, and extending centralized financial control, in 1885 he reorganized the New York, West Shore & Buffalo Railroad, causing it to be leased to the New York Central (*Commercial and Financial Chronicle,* Aug. 29, 1885), and forced the Pennsylvania to buy the South Pennsylvania Railroad, a competing line of the same type that was being built by Vanderbilt. In 1886 he reorganized the Philadelphia & Reading, and in 1888 the Chesapeake & Ohio. After the passage of the Interstate Commerce Act in 1887, Morgan, though unsympathetic with governmental regulation, by means of successive conferences (1889, 1890) of generally reluctant railroad presidents, sought to secure the enforcement of the act and agreements for the maintenance of "public, reasonable, uniform and stable rates" (*N. Y. Times,* Jan. 9, 1889). The conferences served at least to establish some community of interest among railroads hitherto engaged in ruthless and wasteful competition, and thus paved the way for the great consolidations of later years (Corey, ch. xvii).

Following the panic of 1893, Morgan was called upon to reorganize a large number of the leading railroad systems of the country, chiefly the Southern Railway, the Erie, the Philadelphia & Reading for a second time, and, with the Deutsche Bank, the Northern Pacific (Daggett, *post*). Moved by a desire to protect the good name of his country abroad, where investors had bought heavily of American securities, as well as the faith and reputation of his own firm, he assumed the greater part of the gigantic task of rehabilitation, after a period of frequently reck-

less and unscrupulous promotion. A characteristic feature of the reorganization effected by him was the creation in a particular road of a "voting trust," whereby the voting power of the stock was vested for a time at least in a small group of trustees selected by him. The device proved extremely useful in securing stability of control during a period of distress, but the immediate result was a vast concentration of power in his hands, much of which was retained by less direct means, such as directorships and fiscal agencies, after the crisis was relieved. By the end of the century, besides the lines under Morgan's unquestioned control which constituted one of the six major railroad "empires," and those controlled by him with James J. Hill, he had great influence in both the Vanderbilt and Pennsylvania systems. Only the Harriman and Gould systems were independent of him.

The power of this imperial financier was made clear to the general public in connection with the crisis of the national Treasury in 1895. Finding that its efforts to maintain by successive bond issues the dangerously depleted gold reserve were being frustrated by the withdrawal from the Treasury itself of gold with which to make the purchases, the Cleveland administration was forced to appeal to international bankers. Morgan formed a syndicate to furnish the government with some $65,000,000 in gold, half of which was obtained abroad, took bonds at 104½ in payment, and by vigorous methods prevented a further outflow of gold for a period of months. As events proved, this bold operation marked the turning point in the financial history of the decade, but both Cleveland and the Morgan-Belmont syndicate received severe criticism at the time because of the terms of the transaction. A disinterested historian has concluded that these were "extremely harsh," and that the financiers "measured with little mercy the emergency of the government" (Noyes, *post,* p. 234). The bonds were disposed of at 112¼ by the syndicate and rose to 119 on the open market. Despite the dangers and uncertainties under which Morgan labored, his profits, which he refused to reveal to a congressional committee, were probably excessive (Allan Nevins, *Grover Cleveland,* 1932, pp. 664–65; *Senate Document No. 187,* 54 Cong., 2 Sess., p. 297). Cleveland himself emphasized the public service that had been rendered, but to the leaders of the swelling popular revolt it appeared that the government itself was at the mercy of private financiers.

With the earlier stages of the consolidation of industry, Morgan, absorbed by his railroad activities, had had little to do. By financing the

Federal Steel Company, however, in 1898, and soon thereafter the National Tube Company and the American Bridge Company, he launched upon a course that led to his organization in 1901 of what was then the largest corporation in the world. With the reaction in the steel market in the middle of 1900, ruinous competition was threatened between the various over-capitalized consolidations that had been recently effected, and between them and Carnegie, the most powerful factor in the industry (Berglund, *post*). Many appeals were made to Morgan to form a combination, and especially to buy out Carnegie, who wanted to sell if he could get his price. The result was the United States Steel Corporation, representing a merger of the Morgan companies with the interests of Carnegie, William H. Moore, John W. Gates [*qq.v.*], and Rockefeller. With characteristic optimism and magnificence of operation, Morgan arranged to buy out the various companies at a very high figure. The new corporation, accordingly, was distinctly over-capitalized, but a Morgan syndicate carried through the colossal task of financing. There was a time when the stock slumped dangerously, but, because of the prosperous years that followed and the general efficacy of centralized financial control, the enterprise, under the direction of Elbert H. Gary [*q.v.*], proved highly successful. Community of interest was recognized in the directors, who in effect were selected by Morgan. About this time he financed the International Harvester Company (1902). He was less happy in organizing the grandiose International Mercantile Marine (1902). Including many but not a majority of the transatlantic lines, which were bought up at huge prices, this over-capitalized combination, after many vicissitudes, ultimately went into the hands of receivers. His prestige was also threatened by the fight with Edward H. Harriman [*q.v.*] over the control of the Northern Pacific Railroad, but, though Morgan was forced to recognize Harriman by giving him a place on the board of directors, his own ally James J. Hill remained in undisputed control after the dissolution of the Northern Securities Company in 1904.

Although Morgan was in his seventy-first year when the panic of 1907 burst upon the nation, the bankers turned instinctively to him for directions. His leadership, indeed, was recognized by the Secretary of the Treasury, who deposited with his house and affiliated banks large sums of government money to be used for purposes of financial relief, subject to the decision of conferences which he dominated (*Commercial and Financial Chronicle*, Oct. 26, 1907). He

had able co-workers in George F. Baker and James Stillman [*q.v.*], but his personal influence was the decisive factor. At one time the only expedient of relief (advocated by Stillman) was the guaranteeing of deposits of certain weak trust companies in New York City by the stronger institutions, a few of which were stubbornly reluctant to join in such a commitment. Probably no one could have rescued the situation but Morgan, who here appeared at the height of his prestige. A final episode has perhaps been unduly emphasized. The brokerage firm of Moore & Schley, about to go bankrupt, were relieved of stock in the Tennessee Coal, Iron & Railroad Company, not readily salable, by the purchase of this by the United States Steel Corporation with its salable bonds (*Hearings before the Committee on Investigation of United States Steel Corporation. House of Representatives*, vol. I, 1911, p. 170). President Theodore Roosevelt approved the transaction, despite the anti-trust laws, because of the emergency; and the Steel Corporation greatly extended its holdings. The action was hardly as important in ending the panic—which was already nearly over—as Roosevelt claimed, but the means employed were none the less effective, as well as profitable.

After the death of Harriman in 1909, Morgan stood without a challenging American rival in the field of finance, and, in the public mind, was the supreme symbol of financial power. Inevitably, during a period of rising economic and political discontent, he became an object of criticism and attack. The investigation of the alleged money trust by the Pujo committee of the House of Representatives in 1912 was aimed directly at him. His own testimony and battle of wits with the committee's counsel, Samuel Untermeyer, marked the high point of the hearings. The elderly banker was treated with deference and, in the prevailing opinion, emerged with unimpaired personal credit and prestige. His replies to questions were polite but generally non-committal; he denied the existence or the possibility of a money trust; he even denied that he himself possessed or desired great financial power. Nothing that was personally discreditable to him was revealed. His statement that the first requisite of credit is character and that he would not lend money to a man that he did not trust in spite "of all the bonds in Christendom," while not surprising to those who knew him, was widely commented upon at the time and afterward; it was strikingly characteristic of the man.

The findings, however, revealed unquestionably that there was vast centralization of financial control (*Money Trust Investigation*, III, pp. 55–106). The undisclosed resources of J. P. Morgan & Company, private bankers, and their deposits of $162,000,000, consisting often of the funds of great corporations for which the firm acted as fiscal agents and on whose boards of directors they were represented, constituted only the nucleus of their far-reaching power. The house controlled or had a powerful voice in banks and trust companies in New York City with resources of $723,000,000, besides the Equitable Life Assurance Society, with half a billion more (*Ibid.,* p. 60). They were closely allied with the powerful First National Bank, and, according to the committee, with the great National City Bank; on Wall Street, however, the general opinion was that their relationship with the latter was more often one of rivalry than of friendliness. In one way or another the company dominated or was intimately connected with a score of railroads, several street-railway systems, the International Mercantile Marine, and, among industrial corporations, United States Steel, International Harvester, General Electric, and American Telephone & Telegraph. Altogether, the eleven Morgan partners held seventy-two directorships in forty-seven of the larger corporations (*Ibid.,* p. 89). A brilliant critic of the "system," writing shortly afterward, said: "Investment bankers, like J. P. Morgan & Co., dealers in bonds, stocks and notes, . . . became the directing power in railroads, public service and industrial companies through which our great business operations are conducted—the makers of bonds and stocks. They became the directing power in the life insurance companies, and other corporate reservoirs of the people's savings—the buyers of bonds and stocks. They became the directing power also in banks and trust companies—the depositaries of the quick capital of the country—the life blood of business, with which they and others carried on their operations. Thus four distinct functions, each essential to business, and each exercised, originally, by a distinct set of men, became united in the investment banker. It is to this union of business functions that the existence of the Money Trust is mainly due" (L. D. Brandeis, *Other People's Money,* 1932, ed., pp. 5–6). In the prepared statement of the Morgan firm, financial concentration was defended on the ground that it was necessary in order that adequate banking facilities might be provided; and power was held to be dangerous only when in evil hands (*N. Y. Times,* Jan. 25, 1913). Nothing in Morgan's available record indicates that he had any doubts of the advantages of continued integration and combination; he said he did not mind a little competition, but he seemed willing to extend his control or influence indefinitely. In his testimony, while denying the possibility of control, in effect he sought to justify it on the grounds of the wisdom, character, and good faith of those that exercised it.

The Pujo committee may have erred in attacking primarily the personal aspects of centralization rather than the system itself, but in seeking to explain the unparalleled position occupied by Morgan in American finance one cannot escape the conclusion that much of his power came from his personality. He had qualities of character that inspired absolute confidence. In his word, and his faith, implicit faith was reposed. His very physique was commanding. He had a large frame with massive shoulders, a big head with piercing eyes, shaggy brows, and a powerful nose. His eyes could be icy and his frown terrifying upon occasion. His manner at times was abrupt and dictatorial. He had a positive way of doing business; he dealt in ultimatums. All who came in contact with him felt the mental vigor, extraordinary ability to concentrate, reserve force, and power of decision of the man. The effect was heightened by long periods of silence and apparent aloofness from those about him. Even at important entertainments given by himself he was known to draw apart from guests, speaking to no one for long periods, or even playing cards alone at a small table. Under an exterior which frightened many there was much kindness, but his strong emotional nature harbored violent dislikes as well as likes. He refused to work with men he disliked, important though they might be. Despite his prejudices he was usually wise in his judgment of men; his knack of picking talented partners became one of the business traditions of America.

In business he was by no means infallible. He long seriously underestimated the abilities of Harriman, whose operations, while not precisely the same as his, had a very similar scope. His great shipping combine was anything but a success. In spite of his usual extraordinary instinct for soundness in finance, at times he lent his aid to the fashioning of instruments of capital inflation, as in the formation of the Northern Securities Company (Noyes, *post,* pp. 349–50). No other chapter of his career has been so criticized as his later connection as director and banker with the New York, New Haven & Hartford Railroad. He had been associated for many years with this company, but toward the end of his life its previous high credit and prosperity suffered a long and grave eclipse, partly because of the extremely costly expansion program of an over-ambitious management. It has been claimed that he bore opprobrium for the errors of others, but President Charles S. Mellen [*q.v.*], testifying before a congressional committee, left little doubt of Morgan's personal interest and dominance ("New York, New Haven and Hartford Railroad Company Evidence," *Senate Document No. 543,* 63 Cong., 2 Sess., 1914, vol. I, pp. 712–13). It would appear that here, as elsewhere, "the Morgan sins, if any, were the sins of magnificence" (Lerner, *post,* p. 313). With his British contacts, Morgan was perhaps the chief instrument by which foreign capital built up his native country. He believed in the phrase attributed to his father, "Never sell a bear on the United States." He was essentially, not the industrial pioneer, but the banker and conservator; while he was the foremost organizer of great corporations in his time, his interest was that of the protector of investors and depositors. In general, he personified legitimate investment throughout a period in which wreckers were typical of financial operations. He did not hesitate in various hearings and lawsuits to describe such men as "dangerous elements," and he emphasized his own moral responsibility to stockholders. As a witness in *Peter Power* vs. *Northern Securities Company,* he said: "I felt bound, since I had reorganized the property and assumed the responsibility for its policy, that I should protect it (*New York Tribune,* Mar. 27, 1902). If he was a somewhat ruthless force making for centralized control of industry and credit, he unquestionably contributed to corporate stability.

Morgan's breadth of view was not equal to changing social outlooks; he was not interested in social reform; Theodore Roosevelt and his anti-trust activities were to him anathema. He was essentially the aristocrat and his inbred attitude was not lessened by close and constant European associations. He cared next to nothing for public opinion, and had the instinctive shrinking from publicity of the man of breeding. Unlike many other great figures of his day he was master rather than slave of his business. IIis outside interests were varied and extensive. An enthusiastic yachtsman, he was four times prominently identified with defense of the *America's* Cup, and was president of the New York Yacht Club, holding the title of commodore. He traveled much, and was the leading art collector of his time.

His activities as a collector are not unworthy of comparison with his financial operations, for, as he was the organizer extraordinary, so was he the super-collector; they may also be regarded as an expression of his richly sensuous nature.

The year before his death he sent to the Metropolitan Museum of Art, of which for a number of years he was president, his collections that had been abroad, planning an exhibition of all his works of art. A preliminary exhibition was placed on view in January 1913, but Morgan died without ever having seen his collection as a unit. All his collections were left unconditionally to his son, J. Pierpont Morgan, Jr., who authorized the loan exhibition of 1914–16; this included enamels, ivories, bronzes, wood-carvings, glass, pottery, tapestries, furniture, miniatures, statuary, and paintings. Subsequently, the greater part of this loan was given outright to the Museum and was, with previous gifts of both Morgans, made permanently available to the public in the Pierpont Morgan Wing. Morgan's literary treasures, including manuscripts, illuminations, incunabula, and other early editions of books, were housed in a beautiful marble library adjoining his residence in New York City. In his lifetime the library was used for his personal pleasure and by a few research scholars. In 1924 it was conveyed by J. Pierpont Morgan, Jr., to six trustees, to be administered as a public reference library for the use of scholars as a memorial to his father. It contained some 25,000 books and manuscripts, besides collections of drawings, etchings, coins, and medals.

Morgan made great gifts during his life, to churches, cathedrals, art museums, and hospitals, but not along the studied, methodical lines followed by Rockefeller and Carnegie. He maintained no special bureaus or organizations for the purpose, but followed personal inclination and associations in his philanthropies. Besides his art collections, valued at *c.* $50,000,000, he left a net estate of more than $68,000,000, but a much larger total might have been expected in view of his influence and the greater accumulations of other men less active in finance than he. The largest single item was his interest in the New York and Philadelphia firms, appraised at $29,875,847. Strangely enough, his estate contained many worthless securities, tokens, no doubt, of friendships, rather than of business misjudgments.

He died at Rome, on Mar. 31, 1913, only a few months after his appearance before the Pujo committee, and was buried in Hartford, Conn. It was generally agreed that he would have no successor. The wording of his lengthy will, his gifts, his art and book collections, his friendships with so many rulers and others among the great of the earth, together with the magnificence of his business operations, have caused the adjective "princely" to be applied to him more often perhaps than to any other American. He was the most prominent and one of the most active lay members of the Protestant Episcopal Church, and in the first article of his will avowed his complete faith in the doctrine of the atonement.

In 1861, in Paris, he was married to Amelia Sturges, daughter of Jonathan Sturges of New York City. She died the next year, and in 1865 he married Frances Louise Tracy, daughter of Charles E. Tracy, a leader of the New York bar and vestryman in St. George's Church, with which Morgan became so closely identified. By his second wife, who survived him, he had four children, a son, John Pierpont Morgan, and three daughters.

[Morgan made practically no speeches, gave the rarest and briefest of interviews, wrote no articles or books. No collection of letters, if such exists, has been made available. Of biographical works, the best is Lewis Corey, *The House of Morgan* (1930); both Carl Hovey, *The Life Story of J. Pierpont Morgan* (1911), and J. K. Winkler, *Morgan the Magnificent*, lack documentation and suffer from the unavailability of source materials, though the latter work is entertaining and in certain respects fairly detailed. An interesting article is Max Lerner, "Jupiter in Wall Street," *American Mercury*, July 1930. The most valuable single source for Morgan's business activities is *Money Trust Investigation. Investigation of Financial and Monetary Conditions in the U. S. . . . before a Subcommittee of the Committee on Banking and Currency* (3 vols., 1913), containing Morgan's testimony, II, 1003–08, 1011–91, and the report, vol. III. For the business background, see works on his contemporaries and the following: B. H. Meyer, *A Hist. of the Northern Securities Case* (1906); Abraham Berglund, *The U. S. Steel Corporation* (1907); Stuart Daggett, *Railroad Reorganization* (1908); A. D. Noyes, *Forty Years of Am. Finance* (1909); John Moody, *The Masters of Capital* (1919). For his collections, see Gardner Teale, "An American Medici. J. Pierpont Morgan and his Various Collections," *Putnam's Mag.*, Nov. 1909; memoir in London *Times*, Apr. 1, 1913; F. J. Mather, Jr., "The Morgan Loan Exhibition," *Art and Progress*, Apr. 1914; "The Pierpont Morgan Library," *Lib. Jour.*, Mar. 1, 1924; Joseph Breck and M. R. Rogers, *The Metropolitan Museum of Art. The Pierpont Morgan Wing* (1929); *The Pierpont Morgan Library . . . 1924 . . . 1929* (1930). For ancestry, see N. H. Morgan, *Morgan Genealogy* (1869); J. A. Morgan, *A Hist. of the Family of Morgan . . .* (1902?). Obituaries appeared in almost all the important papers, Apr. 1, 1913. The above sketch is based in part upon personal information.]   A. W. A.

MORGAN, JOHN TYLER (June 20, 1824– June 11, 1907), senator from Alabama, was the son of George Morgan of New York, who married Frances, the daughter of John Tyler Irby of Virginia, and shortly afterward removed to Athens, Tenn., where their son, John Tyler Morgan, was born. In a pioneer school the boy received a thorough grounding in the Latin and Greek classics. His mother had him memorize long passages from the Bible and from the English classics. Moving in 1833 to Calhoun County, Ala., he was brought up to the pioneer life and, by making friends with the Indians in the neighborhood, obtained a valuable basis for his

important work as chairman of the Senate Indian affairs committee years later. He studied law with William P. Chilton [*q.v.*] of Tuskegee and in 1845 was admitted to the bar. On Feb. 11 of the following year he married Cornelia Willis of Talladega County. They had four children. In 1855 he moved to Selma, where he made his residence till his death. He was elector on the Breckinridge ticket in 1860 and a member of the state secession convention of 1861. At that time thirty-seven years old, he preferred military to political service. Enlisting as a private in the "Cahaba Rifles," he rose to be lieutenant-colonel of the 5th Alabama Regiment, resigned the next year to recruit the 51st Alabama Cavalry, and cooperated with Forrest in the Stone River campaign of 1862–63. For brilliant movements in the Chickamauga and Knoxville campaigns he was made brigadier-general on Nov. 17, 1863, but on Jan. 27 of the next year in eastern Tennessee he was routed and dispersed by the 2nd Indiana Cavalry. With a new command he harassed and scouted in the Atlanta campaign and, as a forlorn hope, he was raising negro troops in Mississippi at the close of the war (*Official Records, post*, 1 ser., XLIX, p. 1276).

After the war he resumed the practice of law, fighting for white supremacy, and in 1876 was elected to the Senate, where he served until his death. An unsuccessful attempt was made at the outset by his Republican colleague to bar his entrance, but despite this his first vote went to confirm the appointment of the negro, Frederick Douglass [*q.v.*], as marshal of the District of Columbia. The old order was changing. In 1879 he defeated the Force Resolutions of Senator Edmunds and fifteen days of filibuster (*Cong. Record*, 45 Cong., 3 Sess., pp. 839–48, 885–93, 960–61, 1003, 1008–27). Using the state-rights argument, he fought effectively from 1886 to 1888 against the Blair education bill for eradicating Southern illiteracy, which cut party lines. Yet with certain environmental limits he was fair and sincere in his approach to the race problem. Ever constructive in aim, his first legislative efforts succeeded in turning over large tracts of national coal and iron land to the University of Alabama and other lands to state normal schools, barring them from exploitation by syndicates. This conception of socializing public resources led him, beginning in 1879, to introduce a series of bills to reclaim from transcontinental railroads unearned land grants which, after a ten-year fight, resulted in a saving of millions of dollars. He planned extensively for improvement of navigation on the important Alabama tributaries of the Mississippi and the Gulf, and one of his earliest speeches was on the deepening of Mobile harbor. This plan was intimately connected with his long fight for an Isthmian Canal, which he envisaged as a means for raising the South from the ashes of the Civil War by opening a gateway for Southern trade to competing Pacific markets (Speech at Democratic Caucus, 1900, Scrap Book No. 1, p. 28, Morgan MSS.). Advocating a policy similar to Blaine's and Frelinghuysen's, he labored ceaselessly, as chairman of the inter-oceanic canals and foreign relations committees, for government control of the privately owned Maritime Canal Company of Nicaragua, reporting the third and fourth bills for this purpose, which passed the Senate but were lost in the House. The Nicaragua route was largely accepted as the American route before 1900 and his fight for it against the tremendous opposition of the railroads and other groups aroused general interest when it might have flagged. This brought him fame and distinction from all America. Rather than defeat the project, he voted for the Spooner amendment to the Hepburn Bill, changing the route to Panama if a treaty could be negotiated. Though shocked at the change, he secretly believed this would fail. He thought that Panama was used as a scheme by Hanna and the railroads to defeat the canal. In the meantime he advocated to Secretary Hay the annexation of Panama as the only solution, but said "Colombia . . . would be likely to be opposed" (W. R. Thayer, *The Life and Letters of John Hay*, 1915, II, 304). Roosevelt's coup d'état was a terrible disappointment, and he condemned it violently. He cooperated in the construction at Panama, but till his death remained a stanch believer in the superior merits of the Nicaragua route.

A strong expansionist, he urged Cuban intervention and then the annexation of Cuba and the Philippines. In order to readjust the balance of power in the Senate to the interest of the South he advocated statehood for Cuba, Puerto Rico, and Hawaii, believing them Southern in politics. In 1898 he was appointed one of three commissioners to draft legislation for Hawaii. Although decrying the show of force against smaller countries, he was very jealous of Great Britain and of other powers, opposing general treaties of arbitration (Letter to John Hay, Apr. 30, 1904, Morgan MSS.). When he served as arbitrator with Justice Harlan in the Bering Sea fisheries dispute to which he was appointed in 1892, he alone voted against Great Britain on every major question. His feelings for the justice of his cause permitted compromise only with great dif-

ficulty. An ardent silver senator during the nineties, he supported Bryan on the sixteen-to-one platform and generally fought for social and anti-trust legislation. Yet he did not mention bimetallism in his proposed Democratic platform in 1901 (Scrapbook, Morgan MSS.), and in 1904 dropped Bryan as leader for what he thought was the good of the party (letter to Alton B. Parker, Jan. 29, Morgan MSS.). His great characteristics were independence and courage. In 1906 his state-rights views made him vote against the Hepburn rate-regulation act contrary to the wishes of his constituents. He defied Cleveland or supported Republican policies with the same equanimity, and, with his extensive learning and subtle logic, he was always a power which it was not safe to disregard. Though an intense Southerner, his national vision made him a national figure to all sections.

[Morgan Coll. in Lib. of Cong.; some important printed speeches and *Letter from Morgan to the Selma Mirror*, Mar. 4, 1900 (1900), filed with Morgan Coll.; *War of the Rebellion: Official Records (Army)*, 1 ser., XVI, pt. 2, XX, pt. 1, XXX, pt. 2, XXXI, pts. 1, 3, XXXII, pt. 1, XXXVIII, pts. 3–5; T. M. Owen, *Hist. of Ala. and Dict. of Ala. Biog.* (1921), vol. IV; *Who's Who in America*, 1906–07; *John Tyler Morgan and Edmund Winston Pettus: Memorial Addresses* (1909); J. A. Morgan, *A Hist. of the Family of Morgan* (1902?); *Evening Star* (Washington), June 12, 1907.]

C. W. G.

MORGAN, JUNIUS SPENCER (Apr. 14, 1813–Apr. 8, 1890), international banker, and one of the chief links in the financial relationship between Great Britain and the United States in the middle portion of the nineteenth century, was in a sense the real founder of the great banking house which his son, John Pierpont Morgan [*q.v.*], later headed. A descendant of Miles Morgan, who settled in Springfield, Mass., in 1636, and the grandson of Joseph Morgan, a soldier in the Revolution, he was born in West Springfield, Mass., but spent most of his childhood, youth, and young manhood in Hartford, Conn. There his father, Joseph Morgan, had acquired a substantial fortune by the time Junius reached man's estate. His mother was Sarah (Spencer) Morgan. For several years the boy attended the academy that later became Norwich University (Vt.), but in his middle teens he became a clerk in a drygoods house. After some experience in New York with A. and M. Ketchum, brokers, he acquired a partnership, first in the Hartford mercantile house of Howe, Mather & Company, and then in one in Boston, J. M. Beebe, Morgan & Company. Levi P. Morton [*q.v.*] was a partner of the latter firm, one of the foremost of its kind in the country.

In 1854 Morgan became a partner in the important London firm of George Peabody & Company, engaged in international banking. Ten years later George Peabody [*q.v.*] retired and the firm name was changed to J. S. Morgan & Company. Morgan headed the firm until his own death in 1890, though his son had come to dominate its affairs by that time, and conducted it on as important a scale as Peabody had done. The firm favored the Union cause in the Civil War, though criticized by some because of its activities in reselling American securities abroad (*New York Times,* Oct. 26, 27, 31, 1866) ; and in 1877 the bankers of New York gave Morgan a dinner in recognition of his services. Gov. Samuel J. Tilden described him as "upholding unsullied the honor of America in the tabernacle of the Old World" (*New York Times,* Nov. 9, 1877). Morgan in his response said that his business aim was never to do anything to cause evil to be spoken of the American name. To him was attributed the injunction, "Never sell a bear on the United States," the term used at that time for selling short.

Possibly the most important event in Morgan's life was his placing of a $50,000,000 loan for France in the fall of 1870, during the war with Prussia. The French were in a distressing plight at the time, part of the government having been removed to Tours, and found it impossible to raise a loan in Paris or from British bankers. Morgan was approached and successfully carried through the loan. Bismarck publicly declared that a loan contracted by the Tours government would not be recognized by the French government with which Germany would make peace, and he even threatened to make non-recognition of the loan one of the conditions of peace. Despite this impressive opposition, the loan, which was at 6%, was successfully placed. For a short time it fell to a slight discount but later advanced and proved a great success. Its effect, besides assisting the French, was at once to place J. S. Morgan & Company in the front rank of issuing houses in London. During this period a large portion of all British investments made in America went through this banking firm, which naturally worked in close conjunction with Drexel, Morgan & Company in New York.

Morgan entertained extensively at "Dover House," Rochampton, where he had some seventy acres. He talked with lucid precision, had definite opinions, and acted upon them. He was a witty man and highly amusing in his conversation. Although he lived more than half his life abroad he always retained his interest in Hartford, Conn. Out of his large fortune he gave in his lifetime $100,000 to establish a free library

at Hartford, a gift which his son and family supplemented with a like amount. He subsequently made a substantial gift to the Hartford Orphan Asylum in memory of his mother. He gave to the Metropolitan Museum of Art in New York a picture by Sir Joshua Reynolds. Other gifts were made to Guy's Hospital in London, to the National Nurses' Pension Fund in England, to Yale University for the establishment of a professorship in the new law department, to Trinity College, and to the Wadsworth Atheneum in Hartford.

Morgan married Juliet, daughter of the Rev. John and Mary Pierpont, of Boston, on May 2, 1836. Of his five children, John Pierpont and three daughters grew to maturity ; one son died in childhood. Morgan died at Monte Carlo from injuries received in leaping from his carriage, when the horses became unmanageable at a point near the village of Èze in the Riviera.

[Published material regarding Junius S. Morgan is of the slightest. The present sketch has been based in part upon personal information. Accounts of the banquet by N. Y. bankers appeared in *N. Y. Times* and *N. Y. Tribune,* Nov. 9, 1877 ; *N. Y. Times* gives an account of his accident and details of his career, Apr. 6, 1890, and an obituary, Apr. 9, 1890 ; *London Times,* Apr. 9, 1890, has an obituary. For further bibliographical details see sketch of John Pierpont Morgan.]

A. W. A.

MORGAN, JUSTIN (1747–Mar. 22, 1798), was an obscure New England teacher who owned and perhaps bred the most remarkable animal in the history of the American horse. Born at or near West Springfield, Mass., he acquired a common-school education there, and being always too frail and sickly for physical labor, supported himself and his family as best he could by giving lessons in singing and penmanship, at which he excelled. In 1774 he married Martha Day (*New-England Historical and Genealogical Register,* January 1875, p. 55). For a time he kept a wayside tavern, and for several years had charge of horses kept for stud service. In 1788 he removed to Randolph, Vt., where he was elected lister and later town clerk. His wife died there in 1791, leaving four small children. Within a short time the family was broken up, the children going to live with neighbors, while the tall, consumptive singing master seems thereafter to have had no home, but to have lived first in one neighborhood and then in another, wherever he could find employment.

According to the recollection of his son Justin, then nine years old, as written to the *Albany Cultivator* forty-seven years afterward, the father in 1795 made a trip to the old home in West Springfield to collect a debt, but instead of the money he received two young horses, one of which, a colt then two years old, he "always while he lived, called a Dutch horse." Though a mere pony in size—he was little more than fourteen hands (fifty-six inches) high—he was thick-set, docile, quick, and intensely energetic, and could outpull some of the largest horses to be found. When Morgan died at the home of William Rice, in Woodstock, Vt., three years later, this horse was apparently his only remaining possession. To compensate Rice for expenses incurred in connection with his last illness, Morgan made the horse over to him.

Long after "the Justin Morgan Horse," as he came to be known, had died of neglect at the age of twenty-nine, it became apparent that he was one of those rare animals having the power to project his own characteristics through succeeding generations to remote descendants. Before the middle of the nineteenth century Morgan horses had become a distinct type or breed, famed throughout the country for their attractive appearance and their endurance, docility, and utility as driving, riding, cavalry, stage, and general-purpose horses. The very popularity of the tribe almost compassed its ruin, through widespread and long-continued use of the best stallions for improving the common horse stock of the new West without perpetuating the original type from mares of their own kind. Representative specimens were fast disappearing when in 1906 the United States Department of Agriculture and the Vermont State Experiment Station began to assemble a small band of Morgan mares at Burlington. In the same year Joseph Battell, historian of the breed, who had collected a stud on his extensive farm near Middlebury, Vt., presented a farm to the United States government, to which the mares were removed in 1907. The establishment, to which Battell added another farm in 1908, became the United States Morgan Horse Farm, operated by the Department of Agriculture for the purpose of reviving and preserving the early Morgan type and distributing surplus stock to foreign and domestic breeders.

[D. C. Linsley, *Morgan Horses* (1857); Joseph Battell, *The Morgan Horse and Register* (2 vols., 1894–1905); "Breeding Morgan Horses," *U. S. Dept. of Agric. Circular 199* (1926); *Wallace's Monthly*, 1875–90; *passim*; W. H. Gocher, *Trotalong* (1928), vol. I; Justin Morgan, Jr., in the *Cultivator* (Albany), June 1842; John Morgan in the same, July 1842; F. J. Metcalf, *Am. Writers and Compilers of Sacred Music* (1925).]　　　　　　　　　G. C. G.

MORGAN, LEWIS HENRY (Nov. 21, 1818–Dec. 17, 1881), ethnologist, was born near Aurora, N. Y., ninth of thirteen children of Jedediah and Harriet (Steele) Morgan. On his father's side he was descended from James Morgan, who came to New England in 1636, settling first at Roxbury, Mass., and in 1650 moved to New London, Conn. Thence Lewis' grandfather, Thomas, migrated to Cayuga County, N. Y., becoming a farmer near Aurora, then surrounded by Iroquois Indians. On his mother's side Lewis was descended from John Steele, who settled in Newtown, now Cambridge, Mass., in 1641.

Morgan entered Union College, Schenectady, and was graduated in 1840. He then read law for four years, occasionally wrote articles for the *Knickerbocker* and other periodicals, was admitted to the bar, moved to Rochester, and there, Aug. 13, 1851, married his cousin, Mary Elizabeth Steele of Albany. In this same year he formed a partnership with George F. Danforth, afterward judge of the court of appeals. During his early residence in Rochester he was a member of "The Club," a select group of professional men, before which papers were read and current affairs discussed. In 1855 Morgan became legal adviser of a railroad in course of construction between Marquette, Mich., and the Lake Superior iron region, in which he also became financially interested and from which he acquired some wealth. Devoting much attention to political affairs, first as a Whig, afterward as a Republican, he served in the New York Assembly from 1861 to 1868 and in the state Senate in 1868–69, but was defeated for renomination in 1870.

It is as a man of science that he is best known, however. While he cannot be regarded as a "born" ethnologist, as some have characterized him, his researches, during a time when anthropology in America had scarcely reached the infant stage, gained for him in later years the title of "Father of American Anthropology." When he returned to Aurora from college, he joined a secret society called the "Gordian Knot," which through the influence and aid of young Ely S. Parker [*q.v.*], the later noted Seneca Indian, was patterned after the Iroquois Confederacy, with chiefs, sachems, and the like, its members wearing Indian garb during their "councils" by firelight in the woods. After making a study of the League of the Iroquois the society became known as "The Grand Order of the Iroquois," with Morgan as its leading spirit, and undertook, as its chief purposes, to study and to perpetuate Indian lore, to educate the Indians, and to reconcile them to the conditions imposed by civilization. Morgan's casual interest in Indian matters thus developed into a serious investigation of Iroquois institutions and customs which led him to further researches among other American tribes and then into the wider field of world anthropology. Sent by the "Grand Order" to Washington to defeat the ratification of a fraudulent treaty by which the Seneca would have parted with their lands in favor of the Ogden Land Company, he succeeded in his purpose and as a result became so popular among the Indians that he was adopted, Oct. 1, 1847, into the Hawk clan of the Seneca, as the son of Jimmy Johnson, nephew of the famous Red Jacket. He was given the name Tayadawahkugh, or "One Lying Across," signifying that he would serve as a bond of union between Indians and whites. This induction admitted him into the innermost councils of the tribe and gave him every facility for pursuing his studies.

The year before his adoption he had read before the New York Historical Society an essay on "The Constitutional Government of the Six Nations of Indians," which was not printed; but he presented before the "Grand Order of the Iroquois" several papers embodying results of his Seneca researches which in amplified form were published in the *American Review* (New York, February-December 1847) in the form of fourteen "Letters on the Iroquois, by Skenandoah." In 1849 the University of the State of New York made an appropriation for the enlargement of its Indian collection and entrusted the execution to Morgan, who added his own collections and submitted illustrated reports of high value to students of Iroquois material culture (*Second Annual Report of the Regents of the University on the Condition of the State Cabinet of Natural History,* 1849; *Third Annual Report,* 1850). Continuing his studies of the subject, he prepared a "Report on the Fabrics, Inventions, Implements and Utensils of the Iroquois," published in the *Fifth Annual Report of the Regents* (1852), while in the following year lists of other objects given by and purchased from him were published. His book, *League of the Ho-dé-no-sau-nee, or Iroquois* (1851), inscribed to his friend and collaborator, Ely S. Parker, and acknowledged as "the fruit of our joint researches," has been distinguished as the first scientific account of an Indian tribe given to the world. Stern (*post*) compares the work with *Notes on the Iroquois* (1847), by H. R. Schoolcraft [*q.v.*], to the disparagement of the latter, a comparison which compels realization of the advance Morgan's study marked in American ethnology; but, he adds, "it fails lamentably to measure up to Morgan's later standard . . . to describe Indian life in terms of itself and not in terms of the culture of the investigator" (*Social Forces,* March 1928, p. 349).

While still engaged in the practice of law,

Morgan read before the American Association for the Advancement of Science in 1857 a paper on "Laws of Descent of the Iroquois" (*Proceedings . . . 1857,* 1858), and in 1859 he published at Rochester a pamphlet under the title: *Laws of Consanguinity and Descent of the Iroquois,* which excited so much interest that he concluded to return actively to ethnological investigations. While in Michigan the previous year (1858) on business connected with his railroad interests, he had learned from some Ojibwa Indians that their kinship system corresponded closely to that of the Iroquois. This discovery led him to pursue similar inquiries among other tribes, for which purpose, in 1859–62, he visited Indians of Kansas and Nebraska and the upper Missouri, and penetrated as far as the Hudson Bay Territory, ultimately recording notes on the kinship systems of upward of seventy tribes and reaching the conclusion that the kinship system of the Iroquois was practically the same as that of the Indians throughout America. With a view to further enlarging his field of observation, he prepared a series of questions which, as *Circular in Reference to the Degrees of Relationship among Different Nations,* was widely distributed by the Smithsonian Institution in 1860. His inquiries were thereby extended to the primitive world in general. The materials thus gathered were classified, a preliminary paper thereon was published by the American Academy of Arts and Sciences under the title "A Conjectural Solution of the Origin of the Classificatory System of Relationship" (*Proceedings,* vol. VII, 1868), and in 1871 the work appeared in its final form in *Smithsonian Contributions to Knowledge* (vol. XVII), with the title: "Systems of Consanguinity and Affinity of the Human Family." It is a quarto of 600 pages which reveals a prodigious amount of labor and forms a valuable addition to the source materials of primitive society; but the fundamental basis of its arrangement has been justifiably questioned.

Morgan's *magnum opus,* his *Ancient Society or Researches in the Lines of Human Progress* (1877; reissued 1878), was the logical outgrowth of "Systems of Consanguinity and Affinity." In it he propounded the doctrine of the common origin and psychic unity of all races of men and asserted that they passed through successive stages of savagery, barbarism, and civilization. His conclusions had a far-reaching influence, but according to Dr. Stern, whose opinion is now that of anthropologists generally, Morgan's evolutionary scheme is extremely tenuous when applied to primitive society, and "the persistence of the application of his methods today is . . .

inexcusable" (*Social Forces*, March 1928, p. 354). Morgan's theory that the family evolved from a state of promiscuity and his interpretation of kinship terms brought forth much acrimonious criticism, particularly on the part of British anthropologists, among whom J. F. McLennan was especially bitter (see his *Studies in Ancient History*, 1886, pp. 249–76) ; yet the influence of Morgan's concept has been acknowledged by many even to the present day.

Believing that the social systems of the Indians exercised a pronounced influence on their customs and arts, and especially on their architecture, Morgan published a paper on "The 'Seven Cities of Cibola'" in the *North American Review*, April 1869, in which he argued that the remains of the great pueblo structures of the Southwest, as well as those of Mexico, rather than being the palaces of princes and potentates, were the communal dwellings of advanced tribes, and that their erection was due to the prevalence of a system of relationships identical with that observed among the tribes of the North. In criticism of H. H. Bancroft's statements of ancient Mexican culture based on accounts by early Spanish chroniclers, Morgan published in the *North American Review*, April 1876, an article entitled "Montezuma's Dinner." It was highly commended, and doubtless tended to disparage Bancroft's valuable work in the public mind. The subject of the migration of the tribes engaging Morgan's attention, he published two articles in the magazine last cited (October 1869, January 1870) in which he advanced the theory that the Columbia Valley had been a cradle of the tribes whence the overflow of population migrated to the north and east—a conjecture which, however, has not been substantiated.

Pursuing his studies of aboriginal American architecture, he wrote the article on that topic in *Johnson's New Universal Cyclopædia* (vol. I, 1875), and another on "Houses of the Mound Builders" in the *North American Review*, July 1876. His attention being directly attracted to the Southwest, in 1878 he studied various ruins and visited some of the existing pueblos, some of the results being embodied in a paper, "On the Ruins of a Stone Pueblo on the Animas River in New Mexico" (*Twelfth Annual Report . . . of the Peabody Museum of American Archæology and Ethnology, Harvard University*, 1880), and "A Study of the Houses of the American Aborigines; with Suggestions for the Exploration of the Ruins in New Mexico, Arizona, the Valley of the San Juan, and in Yucatan and Central America" (*Archæological Institute of America, First Annual Report*, 1880).

His keen interest and scholarly influence led to the appointment of A. F. Bandelier in 1880 to undertake, on the part of the Archæological Institute, a survey of the archaeology and early history of the Pueblo country which continued for several years. Morgan's interest in aboriginal habitations culminated in his last work, *Houses and House-life of the American Aborigines* (1881), published shortly before his death. During his visits to Michigan in the interest of his railroad, he not only pursued his ethnological studies but, following his earlier bent concerning the manifestation of mind by the lower animals, studied the beaver, and in 1868 published *The American Beaver and His Works,* long regarded as a classic on the subject.

Morgan is described as of medium stature and well proportioned; he was energetic and active, alert in manner and cheerful in disposition; an agreeable companion, easily approached, and helpful to those in need of advice. He was an ardent adherent of the Presbyterian faith; "religion was one of his prime interests: it dominated all his researches, and he never emancipated himself from his theological background" (Stern, *Morgan, post*, p. 22). Indeed, his correspondence shows that he entertained a fear lest his ethnological work was "detrimental to the true religion" (*Social Forces*, March 1928, p. 345). He was an enthusiastic advocate of temperance and renounced the use of tobacco late in life, but did not hesitate to engage in a round of poker. He was instrumental in organizing the Section of Anthropology of the American Association for the Advancement of Science in 1875, and was its first chairman. In recognition of his ethnologic researches he was elected a member of the National Academy of Sciences in 1875, and in 1879 became president of the American Association for the Advancement of Science. Although not possessed of great wealth, he bequeathed the better part of his fortune to the University of Rochester, for female education.

[J. W. Powell in *Pop. Sci. Mo.*, Nov. 1880; J. H. McIlvaine, *The Life and Works of Lewis H. Morgan* (1882), and W. H. Holmes, in *Nat. Acad. Sci. Biog. Memoirs*, vol. VI (1909), both repr. in *Rochester Hist. Soc. Pub. Fund Ser.*, vol. II (1923) ; *Proc. Am. Acad. Arts and Sci.*, vol. XVII (1882) ; B. J. Stern, in *Social Forces*, Mar. 1928, in *Am. Anthropologist*, Apr.–July 1930, Jan. 1933, and *Lewis Henry Morgan, Social Evolutionist* (1931) ; N. H. Morgan, *Morgan Geneal.* (1869) ; *The Morgan Centennial Celebration at Wells College, Aurora* (1919) ; *N. Y. Tribune*, Dec. 18, 1881.]
F. W. H.

MORGAN, MATTHEW SOMERVILLE (Apr. 27, 1839–June 2, 1890), cartoonist, painter, was born in Lambeth, London, England. His parents were Matthew Morgan, an actor and music teacher, and Mary Somerville, an actress and singer. They recognized his talent at an early age and permitted him to study art under Telbin, with whom he worked for some years, afterwards painting scenery at the Drury Lane and Princess theatres in London. A natural taste for caricature, however, earned him a connection with the *Illustrated London News* as artist and correspondent. He also found time to study in Paris, Italy, and Spain. In Spain he painted a number of large water colors. In 1858 he traveled to the interior of Africa by way of Algeria, but returned to Europe in 1859 in time to report the Austro-Italian War for the *News*. His next venture was an association with Frank C. Burnand and William S. Gilbert on the staff of a publication called *Fun,* in which Morgan's best-known work, his cartoons of the American Civil War, began to appear in 1862. Some of these were published in book form, with the work of others, as *The American War, Cartoons* (1874). In 1867 he became owner and illustrator of a paper called the *Tomahawk,* which, because of his cartoons ridiculing Queen Victoria and the Prince of Wales and attacking royalty in general, found little favor in England and soon expired. As a side line he occupied the post of scene-painter to the Royal Italian Opera, Covent Garden.

Frank Leslie [*q.v.*], apparently with the intention of pushing Morgan as a rival of Thomas Nast [*q.v.*], induced him to come to America in 1870 and work on *Frank Leslie's Illustrated Newspaper.* In New York also, Morgan did scene-painting on the side for several theatre managers. In 1880 he designed the decorative stone work for the *Ledger* Building in Philadelphia and shortly after the completion of that work went to Cincinnati as manager of the Strobridge Lithographing Company. While here he founded The Matt Morgan Art Pottery Company and the Cincinnati Art Student's League. In 1887 he returned to New York and in 1888 became art editor of the new magazine, *Collier's Once a Week.* Toward the close of his life he seems to have been affected by a desire to do things on a large scale. He painted a number of panoramas of battles of the Civil War, an oil painting thirty by fifteen feet of Christ entering Jerusalem, and a background for Buffalo Bill's Wild West Show in Madison Square Garden, this last work covering 15,000 square yards of canvas. He was married early in life and had nine children by his first wife; shortly before coming to America he was married a second time, and of this union seven children were born

(*New York Tribune,* June 3, 1890). He died in New York City.

[Ralph C. Smith, *Biog. Index of Am. Artists* (1930); C. E. Clement and Laurence Hutton, *Artists of the Nineteenth Century and Their Works* (1907); Frank Weitenkampf, *Am. Graphic Art* (1924); Ulrich Thieme and Felix Becker, *Allgemeines Lexikon der Bildenden Künstler,* vol. XXV (1931); *Art Journal* (N. Y.), Mar. 1875; *N. Y. Times,* June 3, 1890.]   R.H.

MORGAN, MORRIS HICKY (Feb. 8, 1859–Mar. 16, 1910), classicist, was born in Providence, R. I., the son of Morris Barker Morgan and his wife, Isabelle Manton. Of his ancestors, Edward Manton came from England in 1634, Evan Morgan from Wales soon after 1700, Daniel Hicky from Ireland in 1740. Edward Manton was a friend of Roger Williams and followed him to Rhode Island. Evan Morgan's son, George [*q.v.*], ancestor of Morris Hicky Morgan, commanded Fort Pitt during the Revolution. Morgan was educated at St. Mark's School, Southboro, Mass., and at Harvard, where he received the degree of A.B. in 1881 and that of Ph.D. in 1887. From 1881 to 1884 he was a tutor at St. Mark's. He gave instruction in Latin and Greek at Harvard from 1887 to 1896; from 1896 to 1899 he was professor of Latin, and from 1899 to 1910, professor of classical philology. A man of boundless and infectious energy, he was at once an inspiring teacher, a productive scholar, and an effectual administrator in many fields of academic service. His spoken as his written word was charged with a freshness and buoyancy of spirit, a peculiar vivacity and playfulness, that gave adequate expression to his vigorous personality and intellectual ability. Endowed with a fine literary taste, he treated the ancient classics as literature, not as a field for the display of mere learning. Of permanent value is his conception of the study of literature, a study which "must be based upon the understanding of three things: first, the influence of time and surroundings which led the author to write what he has written; secondly, what was the author's message to his contemporaries; thirdly, what ought to be his message to us" (*Addresses and Essays,* 1910, which book has been said to incorporate the Harvard spirit in philology).

Among his publications may be mentioned: *An Illustrated Dictionary to Xenophon's Anabasis* (1892), in conjunction with Prof. J. W. White; two translations, *The Art of Horsemanship by Xenophon* (1893) and *The Phormio of Terence* (1894); an edition of *Eight Orations of Lysias* (1895); "Remarks on the Water Supply of Ancient Rome" (*Transactions and Proceedings of the American Philological Association,* vol. XXXIII, 1902) ; "The First Harvard Doctors of Medicine" (*Harvard Graduates' Magazine,* June 1909) ; "Some Aspects of an Ancient Roman City" (*Harvard Essays on Classical Subjects,* 1912, ed. by H. W. Smyth). He edited and completed George M. Lane's *Latin Grammar for Schools and Colleges* (1898, 1903), and prepared *A School Latin Grammar* (1899) based on the longer work. He published *A Bibliography of Persius* (1909), and presented to the Harvard College Library his private collection of 660 editions and treatises on that poet. His greatest scholarly achievement was a translation of Vitruvius' Architecture (*Vitruvius, the Ten Books on Architecture,* 1914), nearly finished before his death, and completed by Professor A. A. Howard. Morgan was married at Baltimore, June 3, 1896, to Eleanora Semmes Gibson, grand-daughter of Admiral Raphael Semmes [*q.v.*] of the Confederate navy.

[*Harvard Grads.' Mag.,* June 1910 ; B. L. Gildersleeve, in *Am. Jour. of Philol.,* Apr., May, June 1910 ; *Memorial Minute of the Class of 1881* (1910) ; *Harvard College Class of 1881 Fiftieth Anniversary* (1931) ; *Classical Philology,* July 1910 ; *Classical Jour.,* June 1910 ; J. A. Morgan, *A Hist. of the Family of Morgan* (1902?) ; *Boston Transcript,* Mar. 16, 1910.]
H. W. S—h.

MORGAN, PHILIP HICKY (Nov. 9, 1825–Aug. 12, 1900), jurist, diplomat, son of Judge Thomas Gibbes and Eliza (McKennan) Morgan, was born in Baton Rouge, La. On his father's side, he was a descendant in the fourth generation of Evan Morgan who emigrated from Wales to Pennsylvania ; on his mother's side he was a nephew of Thomas M. T. McKennan [*q.v.*] and related to Thomas McKean [*q.v.*], signer of the Declaration of Independence, later chief justice and then governor of Pennsylvania. Thomas Morgan settled in Baton Rouge early in the nineteenth century, and practised law there. Philip was educated in the public schools of that city and at Paris, France, where he laid the foundation for his great knowledge of the civil law. As a very young man he spent some time in Havana, Cuba, and there learned to speak Spanish—one of several modern languages he later commanded with ease and fluency. He returned from his Parisian law studies just in time to enter the Mexican War as first lieutenant of a Louisiana volunteer company. Upon completing this service, he was admitted to the Louisiana bar, and is said to have spent the months immediately following in helping his father annotate the civil code of the state. On May 22, 1852, he married Beatrice Leslie Ford, daughter of Judge James Ford of Baton Rouge, by whom he had five children. Soon after his marriage, he went to practise law in New Orleans, and had not

lived there long before he was elected judge of the second district court of Louisiana, which office he held for four years.

Four of his half-brothers, one of whom was James Morris Morgan [*q.v.*], served the Confederacy, but Morgan was loyal to the Union and devoted his best efforts to its preservation. At a mass meeting on Canal Street, New Orleans, on the eve of the war, he told those assembled that if they would fight the abolitionists within the Union he would fight with them, but warned them that if they fired a shot at the Stars and Stripes their slaves would be their political masters within five years. Just then a large straw man bearing a placard with the words "P. H. Morgan—Traitor" was hoisted on a nearby telegraph pole and set on fire. He is supposed to have spent the Civil War period in England, but, if he did, he returned immediately after the conclusion of hostilities. President Johnson appointed him United States district attorney for Louisiana in December 1866, but the Senate rejected the appointment, Mar. 2, 1867. The following year he was again appointed and this time the appointment was confirmed (Jan. 7, 1869). From 1873 to 1876 he was one of the judges of the state supreme court—the so-called "carpet-bag court." In 1877 he became one of the judges of the recently organized international court in Egypt, for which he was admirably fitted by reason of his linguistic ability and knowledge of foreign codes, and served for one term. While still in Egypt he was appointed envoy extraordinary and minister plenipotentiary to Mexico by President Hayes, which post he occupied from January 1880 until his successor, appointed by President Cleveland, took office early in March 1885. After he returned from Mexico he practised law in New York City until his death there. He was buried in Allegheny Cemetery, Pittsburgh, Pa.

Morgan was a man of large and powerful physique. He had the moral courage to declare his convictions and remain true to them, for which he paid the price in unpopularity. In the end conditions became such that he left the South he loved, never to return, but he accepted his exile uncomplainingly as the fortune of war.

[Information from family records, supplied by Mrs. Miriam Morgan Shepherd of Pittsburgh, Pa., and other relatives. There are numerous references in the volume by his brother, J. M. Morgan, *Recollections of a Rebel Reefer* (1917) ; and in Ella Lonn's *Reconstruction in La. After 1868* (1918), there is an account of his activities during Reconstruction days. See also J. A. Morgan, *A Hist. of the Family of Morgan* (1902?) ; *N. Y. Tribune,* Aug. 14, 1900.]
M. J. W.

MORGAN, THOMAS JEFFERSON (Aug. 17, 1839–July 13, 1902), soldier, Baptist clergyman, educator, and denominational leader, was sixth in descent from Nathan Morgan, the first of his line to emigrate to the New World. The son of Rev. Lewis Morgan and his third wife, Mary C. Causey (or Cansey), he was born in Franklin, Ind. His grandfather had been a slaveholder, but his father was an anti-slavery advocate and a leader in religious, political, and educational matters. Thomas was fitted for college in the preparatory school of Franklin College and received the degree of A.B. from that institution in 1861, though he left in his senior year to enlist in the Union army. After three months' service, he took charge of public education at Atlanta, Ill., but on Aug. 1, 1862, was appointed first lieutenant in the 70th Indiana Volunteer Infantry. His period of military service continued for over three years. Prominent in the enlistment of negro troops and eloquent in their defense, he became lieutenant-colonel of the 14th United States Colored Infantry on Nov. 1, 1863, and colonel on Jan. 1, 1864. He commanded a division at the battle of Nashville and was brevetted brigadier-general, Mar. 13, 1865. Throughout his life he maintained that war is sometimes justifiable, because the Old Testament teaches that it has been a means of accomplishing holy and gracious purposes of God toward mankind; because admittedly good consequences have issued from war; because historians reckon eras from great battles, such as Tours and Waterloo; because it is necessary to repel invasion, protect the innocent, punish national wrong-doing; and because it is right to engage in a struggle for national independence. He defended nationalism even while pleading for internationalism and dedicating his life to the defense of freedom of conscience.

After leaving the army he entered Rochester Theological Seminary, graduating in 1868. He was ordained a Baptist minister, at Rochester, N. Y., in 1869, but held only one brief pastorate—at Brownville, Nebr., 1871–72. From 1872 to 1874 he was president of the Nebraska Normal School at Peru; from 1874 to 1881, he taught homiletics and ecclesiastical history in the Baptist Union Theological Seminary, Chicago, spending several months in Germany in 1879; from 1881 to 1883 he served as principal of the New York State Normal School at Potsdam, and from 1884 to 1889, as principal of the State Normal School at Providence, R. I. In the latter year, he was appointed commissioner of Indian Affairs by President Harrison. For four years he served with zeal, energy, and good judgment, insisting, in spite of much political and ecclesiastical opposition, that the principle of separation of church and state must be recognized in the control of Indian schools, and that they must be placed upon the same basis as public schools.

In 1893 he renewed his denominational activity, accepting the position of corresponding secretary of the American Baptist Home Mission Society, in which position he served until his death almost a decade later. The clarity of his thought and his unswerving loyalty to his convictions, combined with rare ability wisely to choose and judge his coworkers, made him invaluable as an associate of Dr. Henry L. Morehouse [q.v.], field secretary of the society. Under his skilful promotion, schools for thousands of negro men and women were established and equipped. He was editor of the *Baptist Home Mission Monthly,* 1893–1902, and author of *Reminiscences of Service with Colored Troops in the Army of the Cumberland, 1863–65* (1885); *Educational Mosaics* (1887); *Students' Hymnal* (1888); *Studies in Pedagogy* (1889); *Patriotic Citizenship* (1895); *The Praise Hymnary* (1898); *The Negro in America and the Ideal American Republic* (1898). In 1870 he married Caroline Starr. Their only son died before his father.

[*Who's Who in America,* 1901–02; F. B. Heitman, *Hist. Reg. and Dict. U. S. Army* (1903); Comfort Starr, *A Hist. of the Starr Family* (1879); J. A. Morgan, *A Hist. of the Family of Morgan* (1902?); *Examiner,* July 24, 1902; *Bapt. Commonwealth,* July 24, 1902; *N. Y. Times,* July 14, 1902.]   C. H. M.

MORGAN, WILLIAM (Aug. 7, 1774?–1826?), Freemason, was born probably in Culpeper County, Va., served an apprenticeship as a stonemason in Madison County, removed to a western state, possibly Kentucky, returned to Orange County, Va., and then went to Richmond. It has been claimed that he fought with Jackson in the War of 1812. For all these as well as for most of the other statements about his life there seems to be no proof and many of them have been denied in the course of the bitter, long-extended controversy over the circumstances of his death. It is agreed that about 1819 he was married to Lucinda Pendleton, that in 1823 he was in Rochester, N. Y., and that shortly afterward he went to live in the neighboring town of Batavia as a brick-and-stone mason. It has been asserted that at this time he was a respectable though not distinguished member of the community and, on the other hand, that he was a drunken knave. It has been denied that he was ever properly initiated into Freemasonry but there is no doubt that he gained admittance to the order and took an active part in its proceedings and that, on May 31, 1825, at Leroy, N. Y., he became a Royal

Arch Mason. The next year there were rumors that he was writing a book, to be published by David C. Miller of Batavia, in order to expose the secret ritual of the Masonic order. The records of the copyright office show that on Aug. 14, 1826, he made copyright registration of the title of the book, *Illustrations of Masonry.* That summer he was several times sued and imprisoned for small debts. On Sept. 11, arrested on a charge of petty theft, he was taken to Canandaigua to answer the charge. From that place he never returned, and of him there has never appeared any authentic trace. A body found a short time afterward near Oak Orchard, N. Y., was with equal show of probability declared to be that of William Morgan and to be that of one Timothy Munro. For a generation after his disappearance there sprang up various rumors of his existence in many parts of the world, as a merchant in Smyrna, an Indian chief in the Rocky Mountains, a pirate hanged in Havana, a hermit in northern Canada, and a professed Mohammedan on the shores of the Mediterranean.

His disappearance caused great excitement. It was freely charged that the Masons had murdered him in order to prevent the publication of the book he was believed to be writing on Masonic secrets. These charges were uniformly denied by Masons in good standing, and the claim was brought forward that he had disappeared of his own will. Gov. DeWitt Clinton, a high officer in the Masonic organization, offered a reward of $1,000 for his discovery, if alive, and $2,000 for the discovery and conviction of his murderers, if he were dead. Committees were organized by each faction to procure evidence in the matter. Later indictment and trial of several persons failed to reveal the facts. In the autumn of 1826, probably in October, was published the first edition of the *Illustrations of Masonry.* Of this book the Masons said, variously, that it was merely plagiarized from *Jachin and Boaz,* published in London in 1762, that it was actually the work of David C. Miller who corrected and rewrote Morgan's illiterate manuscript, and that it was unimportant since the true secret of Masonry was the development of the spirit rather than the outward form of a ritual. On the other hand, a group of men who had been Masons met to declare solemnly that it was true revelation of Masonic practice. The book was pirated, translated into several European languages, and sold widely. Almost at once the affair assumed a political aspect, furnishing the occasion for the organization of existing objections to all kinds of secret societies and for the rise of the Anti-

Masonic party in which various factors played a part and in which the fate of William Morgan soon lost its importance.

[Of the great number of books and pamphlets on the subject, a collection is in the State Hist. Lib. of Wis.; records of the copyright office are in the Lib. of Cong.; among the partisan accounts are Henry Brown, *A Narrative of the Anti-Masonick Excitement* (1829); Rob Morris, *Wm. Morgan* (1883); P. C. Huntington, *The True Hist. . . . of Wm. Morgan* (1886); S. U. Mock, *The Morgan Episode* (1930); David Bernard, *Light on Free Masonry* (copr. 1858); S. D. Greene, *The Broken Seal* (1870). For bibliography see Charles McCarthy, "The Antimasonic Party," *Am. Hist. Asso. Report . . . 1902,* vol. I (1903), which, however, does not discuss the Morgan episode.]   K. E. C.

MORIARITY, PATRICK EUGENE (July 4, 1804–July 10, 1875), Augustinian superior and preacher, was born, apparently, of well-to-do parents, who resided in Mount Joy Place, Dublin, Ireland. His early instruction was received at the Augustinian convent at Callan, and at Carlow College, where he came under the influence of the Rev. James Warren Doyle, the famous Irish patriot-bishop and publicist ("J. K. L."). At the age of sixteen he joined the order of the Hermits of St. Augustine, and later studied philosophy and theology in the Augustinian colleges at Lucca and Perugia, and finally in Rome, where he was ordained Jan. 28, 1828. For some years he served as a missionary preacher in Ireland, in France at the invitation of Cardinal Cheverus [*q.v.*], from whom he learned of America at first hand, and in Portugal. In 1834 he volunteered for the East Indian missions and was sent as a secretary and vicar-general of Bishop O'Connor of Madras, where he served as chaplain to the British forces and assisted in establishing the *Madras Expositor,* a journal of wide influence. Returning to Rome in 1839, he was awarded a doctorate in divinity by Pope Gregory XVI. Almost immediately he was commissioned by his general to go to America as superior or commissary of the Augustinian missions.

Moriarity had hardly landed in Philadelphia (July 4, 1839), when, as pastor of St. Augustine's Church, he became a temperance reformer and established St. Augustine's Catholic Total Abstinence Society (June 28, 1840), one of the first associations of its kind. Two months later, he instituted the Catholic Temperance Beneficial Society of Philadelphia. A suave gentleman of poise and sturdy physique, a linguist, a cosmopolitan, a raconteur, an eloquent preacher, and a fiery orator, Moriarity became the leading priest of the diocese. He preached everywhere throughout the East for charity-benefits, at ordinations, at temperance meetings, and at corner-stone ceremonies. In 1842 he founded Villa-nova College, just outside of Philadelphia. In 1850 and 1851 he aided in founding manual train-ing schools for orphans at Villanova and at Govanstown, Md. Popular with non-Catholic audiences, he was a frequent lecturer before the Athenian Institute and Mercantile Library Com-pany. Away on a speaking tour in South Caro-lina when his church and library were fired by a nativist mob (1844), Moriarity, on his return, did not hesitate to attack nativism and intoler-ance in a bitter sermon which worried the less bold Bishop F. P. Kenrick [q.v.], who feared that resentment on the part of the natives would prejudice the suit for damages. On behalf of St. Augustine's, he appealed for aid in Lyons, and in Ireland (*Catholic Directory,* Dublin, 1845), where he was stationed for a few years. In 1847 he was assistant-general of the order. Three years later, he was back in the United States as pastor of St. Augustine's, as commissary-gen-eral of the Augustinians (1851–57), and as pro-fessor of sacred eloquence in the seminary at Villanova, of which he became president in 1854. In 1855 he built Our Lady of Consolation Church at Chestnut Hill, where he was officially sta-tioned until his death. He inaugurated the Au-gustinian mission at Lansingburg, N. Y., aided the Sisters of St. Joseph in establishing their mother house in his parish (1858), attended the Councils of Baltimore, compiled a *Life of St. Augustine, Bishop, Confessor, and Doctor of the Church* (1873), and wrote a number of articles for the press, including a series in the *Catholic Record* on the "Marks of the Church" and "Let-ters to a Protestant Friend." As a church-build-er and organizer, he was not a success. In busi-ness, he remained unsophisticated, nor was he a collector of money save for charity. A fervid supporter of the Irish cause, he was not opposed to Fenianism, which Bishop J. E. Wood [q.v.] condemned. Advertised to deliver an address in the Academy of Music (May 23, 1864) on "What Right has England to rule Ireland?", Moriarity gave the lecture despite the inhibition of the bishop. Thousands heard him and many thousand copies of the address were sold for the relief of a parish in the West of Ireland. Wood disciplined Moriarity by withdrawing his facul-ties; these were restored a few months later, however, on his submission of a letter of self-humiliation and an apology from the altar steps to a congregation whose sympathy was with the pastor. His last public appearance was in a se-ries of public lectures in refutation of addresses delivered in Philadelphia by the English his-torian Froude.

[*Sadliers' Cath. Directory,* 1876, p. 57; items in *Am. Cath. Hist. Researches,* Jan. 1891, Apr. 1896, Oct. 1902; *Records of the Am. Cath. Hist. Soc.,* esp. vols. I (1887), 201 f., XII (1901), 139 f., 263 f., 387 f.; *Boston Pilot,* Oct. 24, 1857; F. E. Tourscher, *The Kenrick-Frenaye Correspondence* (1920); T. C. Middleton, *Hist. Sketch of the Augustinian Monastery, College, and Mission of St. Thomas of Villanova* (1893); *Phila. Inquirer,* July 12, 14, 1875; *Cath. Record,* Oct. 1875; *N. Y. Freeman's Jour.,* July 17, 1875.]   R. J. P.

MORINI, AUSTIN JOHN (Mar. 4, 1826–July 29, 1909), Catholic ecclesiastic, son of Paul and Anna (Bartolini) Morini, was born in Flor-ence, Italy. Trained in this cultural, religious center, the boy studied in its art galleries and worshiped at the Annuziata chapel. On June 2, 1844, he entered the Servite Order at its origi-nal novitiate of Monte Senario. Six years later he made his solemn profession and was ordained, May 1, 1850. After necessary training, he took charge of the students in humanities and rhetoric at the Annuziata, where his work won him a doctorate in divinity (1856). From 1864 to 1870, he served in England. Here he established his order, founded churches, and won the con-fidence of Cardinal Manning, who counseled with him on matters of discipline and theology. At the Vatican Council, the Servites were in-vited by Bishop Joseph Melchior of Green Bay, Wis., to establish a foundation in his diocese, and Morini was sent with a group of religious to the United States (July 1870).

He took charge of a congregation at Menasha, Wis., and four years later, on the invitation of Bishop Thomas Foley, established Our Lady of Sorrows Church in Chicago as a mother house. Subsequently, the Servites entered a half dozen dioceses. In the midst of parochial duties, Mo-rini gave missions and retreats and acted as vicar-general of the order. In 1884 he attended the Third Plenary Council of Baltimore, and four years later retired to Rome as one of the general consultors whose chief interest was in the work of the order in England and in the United States. Here he was honored with the privileges of an ex-general until his death at the convent of San-ta Maria in Via. A solid student who gave con-siderable time to researches in ecclesiastical history and doctrine, Morini wrote a number of articles for American and foreign Catholic peri-odicals and published *Poems in Honor of St. Philip Benizi* (1885), *Historical Essays on the Seven Holy Founders and Their Times* (1888), and *The Origin of Devotion to Our Lady of Sor-rows* (1893).

[A. T. Andreas, *Hist. of Chicago,* vol. III (1886); *Golden Jubilee, Our Lady of Sorrows Church, Chicago* (1924); annual Catholic directories; materials in the archives of the Ordo Servorum Beatae Mariae Vir-ginis, through the courtesy of the Am. provincial, Rev. J. Mulherin, O.S.M.]   R. J. P.

MORISON, GEORGE SHATTUCK (Dec. 19, 1842–July 1, 1903), bridge engineer, was born in New Bedford, Mass., the son of the Rev. John Hopkins and Emily (Rogers) Morison and a descendant of John Morison and his son Thomas who settled in Londonderry, N. H., in 1719. He was educated at Phillips Exeter Academy and at Harvard, where he received the degrees of A.B. in 1863 and LL.B. in 1866, was admitted to the New York bar, and became associated with the great law firm of Evarts, Southmayd & Choate. After a year of practice, however, he abandoned the legal career in which he was so well launched to enter the profession of civil engineering, for which he had no special training nor any advantageous connections to assist him. To offset these handicaps he brought to his new profession a mature and disciplined mind, exceptional mathematical talents and training, and a large degree of native constructive genius. His first work was on the construction of a large bridge over the Missouri River at Kansas City, under the direction of Octave Chanute [q.v.], a noted engineer (see Chanute and Morison, *The Kansas City Bridge,* 1870). In 1873, when Chanute became chief engineer of the Erie Railroad, Morison was chosen his principal assistant. In this position he soon acquired a wide experience in railway bridge construction, since the Erie was then replacing many of its old wooden bridges with metal structures.

Leaving the Erie in 1875, he became consulting expert on railway properties to the American agents of Baring Brothers, London. He also organized the firm of Morison, Field & Company, New York, bridge contractors, but in 1880 withdrew from the contracting firm and devoted his attention for the next fourteen years to consulting practice. He built in rapid succession more than a score of great railroad bridges: over the Missouri (at Bismarck, Sioux City, Blair, Omaha, Rulo, Nebraska City, Atchison, Leavenworth, and Bellefontaine Bluffs), over the Mississippi (at Winona, Burlington, Alton, St. Louis, and Memphis), one over the Ohio at Cairo, two over the Snake River and one over the Columbia River in Washington, one over the Willamette at Portland, Ore., one over the St. John's at Jacksonville, Fla., and many smaller bridges in all parts of the United States. Considering the magnitude and difficulty of most of the projects, this record stands unrivaled in the history of bridge construction. The Missouri River was regarded as the most treacherous stream in the country to bridge, and little precedent existed for such work. The perfection of methods for handling the pneumatic founda-

tion work involved in these projects was one of Morison's most notable achievements. This period also marked the transition from wrought iron to steel in bridge construction, and Morison was the great pioneer in the use of the latter metal. The Memphis bridge, the longest truss span in America when completed, practically set the standard for later steel bridge specifications.

During the last decade of his life Morison acted on commissions reporting on the Manhattan Bridge over the East River and the proposed bridge over the Hudson in New York City, as well as on a proposed bridge over the Detroit River—the last two colossal projects not realized until some forty years later. Though primarily a bridge engineer, he was also an expert on railway management and remained a valued consultant to Baring Brothers and other financial houses throughout his career. He was a member of the Isthmian Canal Commission, 1899–1901, and his powerful advocacy of the Panama route, backed as it was by an exhaustive study of the situation, proved an important factor in bringing about the final decision.

At the time of his death he stood at the very pinnacle of the engineering profession. He was regarded as the leading bridge engineer in America, perhaps in the world, and had an international reputation as an expert in railways and waterways. Gifted with a superb physical and intellectual endowment, a prodigious capacity for work, and an indomitable will, he supplemented his exceptional education by life-long habits of scholarship. He amassed a considerable fortune, never married, and was able to indulge to the full his love of travel. He observed keenly, read widely, and thought profoundly. Considering his scholarly bent, his professional publications are few. The most important include: "The River Piers of the Memphis Bridge," which won the Telford Medal of the British Institution of Civil Engineers (*Minutes of Proceedings,* vol. CXIV, 1893); "The Continuous Superstructure of the Memphis Bridge" (*Transactions of the American Society of Civil Engineers,* September 1893); "Suspension Bridges—A Study" (*Ibid.,* December 1896). In June 1895 he delivered the presidential address before the American Society of Civil Engineers. Toward the close of his life he prepared a small volume, published posthumously under the title: *The New Epoch as Developed by the Manufacture of Power* (1903), which presents the essentials of his social and economic philosophy. Though little known, it is a most original and carefully reasoned piece of work.

It was an unfortunate fact that with all his

rare talents, high character, and professional eminence, Morison was intensely unpopular with many of his colleagues. The very abundance of his powers made him somewhat arrogant and intolerant of the opinions of less gifted men; he usually arrived at any conclusion only after an exhaustive study of all the facts, and once his decision was made, he was inclined to enforce it with a tenacity and ruthlessness that bore down all opposition but, even when he was right, did not endear him to those holding different opinions.

[G. S., R. S., and Mary Morison, *John Hopkins Morison: A Memoir* (1897); L. A. Morison, *The Hist. of the Morison or Morrison Family* (1880); *Report of the Secretary of the Class of 1863 of Harvard College,* 1888, 1893, 1903; *Trans. Am. Soc. Civil Engineers,* vol. LIV (1905); *Who's Who in America,* 1901–02; *N. Y. Tribune,* July 3, 1903; recollections of personal acquaintances.]   J.I.P.

MORLEY, EDWARD WILLIAMS (Jan. 29, 1838–Feb. 24, 1923), chemist, physicist, was born in Newark, N. J., the son of Sardis Brewster and Anna Clarissa (Treat) Morley. Both parents were of good New England stock; the father was a Congregational minister and the mother had been a teacher under Catharine E. Beecher [*q.v.*]. The family lived at Hartford, Conn., and Attleboro, Mass., during most of Edward's childhood. Since Edward, though precocious, was very frail, his early education was acquired at home under the tutelage of his father. He could read at three years of age, began the study of Latin at six, and read Greek at eleven. His bent toward science soon became evident, for he found among his father's books a small volume entitled *Conversations in Chemistry* which he read with more interest than the *Arabian Nights.* When fourteen years of age he acquired a copy of Benjamin Silliman's newly published textbook on chemistry, and absorbed its contents so thoroughly that he found nothing new in his first course in chemistry in college. He entered Williams College as a sophomore in 1857 and graduated in 1860. In those days the science of astronomy was much better developed than that of chemistry and besides offered a field for exact measurement, in which young Morley already took an interest. He therefore stayed on at Williams for a year after graduation, working in astronomy under Prof. Albert Hopkins. During this year he mounted a transit instrument, constructed a chronograph, and made the first accurate determination of the latitude of the college observatory, which last achievement was the subject of his first scientific paper, read before the American Association for the Advancement of Science in January 1865 (*Proceedings,* vol. VI, 1866).

In accordance with a strong family tradition, he decided to become a minister and spent the years 1861–64 at Andover Theological Seminary. After graduation his health was so poor that he felt he ought not to enter the active ministry, but instead spent the year 1864–65 in the service of the United States Sanitary Commission in charge of the station at Fortress Monroe. During the next few years he taught in a private school at Marlboro, Mass. About this time, his health having improved, he was offered the pastorate of the church at Twinsburg, Ohio. Before really settling there, however, he accepted the professorship of natural history and chemistry at Western Reserve College, Hudson, Ohio (removed in 1882 to Cleveland as Adelbert College of Western Reserve University). He took up his duties in Hudson in January 1869, and just before moving thither married Isabella Ashley Birdsall of West Winsted, Conn. They had no children.

In 1878 he became interested in studying the variation of the oxygen content of the atmosphere, and in 1880 he determined the proportion of this element in the air on 110 consecutive days, for the purpose of accumulating data bearing on the so-called Loomis-Morley hypothesis. According to this hypothesis, there is a deficiency of oxygen at times of high atmospheric pressure, because downward currents bring air from high altitudes to the surface of the earth; and the results of Morley's measurements showed that this theory agreed fairly well with the facts. From 1883 to 1894 he was engaged on his *magnum opus,* a study of the densities of oxygen and hydrogen and the ratio in which they combine to form water. It was published in 1895 as No. 980 of the *Smithsonian Contributions to Knowledge,* and in shorter form in some of the chemical journals. During this same period Morley was collaborating with A. A. Michelson [*q.v.*] in developing the interferometer, an instrument for measuring lengths in terms of the wave length of light, which device they used in attempting to determine the motion of the earth with reference to the luminiferous ether. These experiments, of fundamental importance to modern physics, were later continued with the cooperation of Prof. Dayton C. Miller. With the latter, Morley also determined the velocity of light in a magnetic field and studied the thermal expansion of air, nitrogen, oxygen, and carbon dioxide. For these last experiments he devised a new form of manometer by which differences of gaseous pressure as small as 1/10,000 millimeter of mercury could be measured. He also was engaged in other researches on the expan-

sion of metallic bars, the conduction of heat
through water vapor, the relative efficiency of
various drying agents, and the vapor tension of
mercury. All of his research work was characterized by great ingenuity in devising and constructing apparatus and by his ability to make
precise and accurate measurements. He received
honorary degrees from many institutions and
was awarded the Sir Humphry Davy Medal by
the Royal Society of London in 1907, the Elliot
Cresson Medal of the Franklin Institute, 1912,
and the Willard Gibbs Medal from the Chicago
Section of the American Chemical Society in
1917. He was president of the American Association for the Advancement of Science in 1895
and of the American Chemical Society in 1899.
He published or read fifty-five scientific papers.
In 1906 he retired from active work, and spent
his declining years in West Hartford, Conn.

[Biographical notes and letters left by Morley and
reports to the secretary of his class, Williams College;
F. W. Clarke, in *Jour. Chem. Soc. of London, Trans.*,
vol. CXXIII, pt. 2 (1923), and Memoirs Nat. Acad.
Sci., vol. XXI (1926), with bibliog.; O. F. Tower in
Science, Apr. 13, 1923, the *Jour. Am. Chem. Soc.*, June
1923, and *Bull. Western Reserve Univ.*, 1923, with
bibliog.; *Hartford Times*, Feb. 24, 1923.]   O.F.T.

MORLEY, MARGARET WARNER (Feb.
17, 1858–Dec. 12, 1923), educator, author,
daughter of Isaac and Sarah Robinson (Warner) Morley, was born in Montrose, Iowa. The
family removed to Brooklyn, N. Y., and there
Margaret attended the public schools, the cur-
ricula of which were supplemented by private
instruction. Her more advanced education was
received at the Oswego, N. Y., Normal School
and the New York City Normal College, from
which she was graduated in 1878. Becoming
interested in biology, she carried on special studies in that subject at Armour Institute, Chicago,
and at the Woods Hole, Mass., marine laboratories. As a teacher she naturally found her way
into normal schools and held positions in the
Oswego and Milwaukee, Wis., State Normal
Schools, as well as in the high school at Leavenworth, Kan. Later she was instructor in biology
at Armour Institute and in the Free Kindergarten Association Training Class of Chicago. She
also lectured on popular nature studies in Boston.

In connection with courses prepared for her
classes, she began to gather material for books
on the life of birds, insects, and small animals
and it is as a writer she did her most important
work. Coming at a time when nature study was
being established as a definite part of grade-
school courses, her books had something of pioneer importance. In addition to their specific information, given in conversational form, they

teach non-pedantic lessons of kindness to animals, tree and flower conservation, and the value
of agriculture to industry and commerce, as well
as in its primary support of all life. Those of her
books written for the purpose of teaching children and young people the facts of sex and birth
shocked many in the nineties but in comparison
with the frankness of later writings on the subject they seem somewhat vague and sentimental.
Her most important books of this type are: *A
Song of Life* (1891); *Life and Love* (1895), a
book for older children; *The Renewal of Life;
How and When to Tell the Story to the Young*
(1906); and *The Spark of Life; the Story of
How Living Things Come into the World, as
Told for Girls and Boys* (1913), which was designed for parents to read to young children. The
last has an occasional religious note and teaches
the importance of heredity and environment.
Some of her most popular nature-study books
are: *Seed Babies* (1896), botany for small children; *Flowers and their Friends* (1897); *The
Honey Makers* (1899); *Little Wanderers*
(1899), descriptions of plants for children; *Down
North and Up Along* (1900), travels in Nova
Scotia and Cape Breton, with good atmosphere
and word pictures of the inhabitants and their
customs; *Wasps and their Ways* (1900); *The
Insect Folk* (1903); *Little Mitchell; the Story
of a Mountain Squirrel* (1904); *Butterflies and
Bees; the Insect Folk*, vol. II (1905); *Donkey
John of the Toy Valley* (1909), the result of a
visit to the Austrian Tyrol; *The Carolina Mountains* (1913), a rhapsody and a super-guide-book
to her much loved North Carolina; *Will-o'-the-
Wasps* (1913); and *The Apple-Tree Sprite*
(1915). Margaret Morley loved out-door life
and spent some months of each year in Tryon,
N. C., where she observed for herself the growth
of plants and the habits of animals. She often
carried a pet squirrel in her pocket, which gave
her the material for *Little Mitchell*. She died
at Garfield Memorial Hospital, Washington, D.
C., following an operation.

[*Who's Who in America*, 1922–23; *Woman's Who's
Who of America*, 1914–15; *New Internat. Year Book*,
1923; Margaret W. Morley, "Nature Study and its
Influence," *Outlook*, July 27, 1901; the *Evening Star*
(Wash., D. C.), Dec. 13, 1923; *N. Y. Times*, Dec. 15,
1923.]   S.G.B.

MORPHY, PAUL CHARLES (June 22,
1837–July 10, 1884), chess player, was born in
New Orleans, the son of Alonzo Morphy, a distinguished member of the Louisiana bar, and his
wife, Thelcide Louise Le Carpentier. The paternal grandfather was a native of Spain, possibly a descendant of an Irish *émigré* named
Murphy. The mother's family was French, hav-

ing come to New Orleans from Santo Domingo. At the age of ten Morphy was taught to play chess by his grandfathers. At the age of twelve he was recognized as the strongest player in New Orleans. In May 1850 he contested three games in New Orleans with the famous Hungarian expert, J. J. Löwenthal, winning two and drawing one. He prepared for college at the Jefferson Academy in New Orleans, entered Spring Hill College, Alabama, in December 1850, and graduated with honor in 1854. He continued there until October 1855, studying chiefly law and mathematics, then attended the law school of the University of Louisiana, graduating in April 1857 and being admitted to practice as soon as he should become of legal age. In early life he acquired a fluent command of French, Spanish, and German.

By urgent solicitation of the Committee of Management he was induced to participate in the first American Chess Congress, meeting at New York City in the fall of 1857. His overwhelming success here and his later games with American experts gave him immediate recognition as the foremost American player. A description of his playing at this time appeared in *Frank Leslie's Illustrated Newspaper* (Oct. 31, 1857): "Mr. Morphy is a most fascinating player for those looking on. . . . His attention is not by any means riveted on the game, and he makes his moves with a speed approaching rapidity. Knights are thrown away and bishops left carelessly *en prise,* but the young general has certain victory in his eye; and when his antagonist perchance thinks he can at last win one game . . . Morphy quietly suggests that mate may be given in five, six, or seven moves." An enthusiastic reception awaited him upon his return to New Orleans at the end of 1857. There he began seriously blindfold play, achieving six games.

In June 1858 he sailed for England, being desirous of testing his strength against Howard Staunton, the foremost English player and writer on chess, who had refused an earlier challenge, and other European experts. As Staunton again declined to play, a match was arranged with J. J. Löwenthal who had recently defeated Staunton in a tournament. Morphy won with nine to three and two drawn games. At a congress in Birmingham, England, he played eight games blindfold against first-rate players, winning six, losing one, and drawing one, a feat which he repeated with great success in Paris and again in England. In Paris, matches were arranged with Harrwitz, Mongredien, and Anderssen, the greatest European expert, all of which Morphy won decisively.

In April 1859 he sailed via England for New York, acclaimed as the recognized champion of the world and as an unparalleled chess genius. Receptions and gifts were showered upon him to his evident embarrassment. His public utterances at this time reveal the natural conflict between his passion for chess and the desire of a well-trained, gifted student for a normal career to satisfy personal and family ambitions. Possibly today Morphy's national prominence would have furthered his personal ambitions in law, but at that time in New Orleans there was no proper opening for him. This conflict, doubtless combined with some personal financial reverses and the general upheaval of the Civil War, proved disastrous to him. Considering chess primarily an amusement and wishing to please his devoted mother, who opposed his playing, Morphy never thought seriously of the game as offering a career, nor accepted compensation for his chess activities. During his stay in New York he formed an editorial connection with the *Chess Monthly.* D. W. Fiske [*q.v.*] has noted (manuscript letters to Seguin, John G. White Collection, Cleveland Public Library) that Morphy annotated hundreds of games and "made frequent suggestions as to the matter of the Chess Monthly which were generally adopted." In 1860, however, he withdrew his name as an editor of the *Chess Monthly* and terminated his connection with the *New York Ledger,* in which he had conducted a column since August 1859.

During 1861 his efforts to launch a legal career in New Orleans failed. During the years 1862 to 1864 he visited Havana and Paris, playing chess privately but, in view of the war, properly avoiding any matches or public performances. Upon his return to New Orleans he became involved in an unfortunate quarrel with the executor of his father's estate. Only occasional games, largely at odds with his friend Charles A. de Maurian, are recorded after 1864, the final recorded game being played in 1869. In 1867 he visited Paris, but apparently played no chess. He continued to live at his home in New Orleans with his mother. He undoubtedly suffered some mental disturbance accounted for by the conflict mentioned above and possibly by a disappointment in love. As late as 1875, however, he apparently gave serious consideration to the invitation to play in the Congress of the Centennial Exhibition at Philadelphia. In 1882, in connection with a projected biographical work on men of Louisiana, he wrote a long letter to the *New Orleans Bee* urging the superior achievements of his father and grandfather as compared with his own achievements in chess. He was short and slight of stature, with dark eyes and hair, careful in dress, and distinguished in appearance and bearing. His speech and his manner marked him as a cultured gentleman. He died, unmarried, at his home in New Orleans. He is universally recognized as the greatest chess genius of history.

[D. W. Fiske, *The Book of the First American Chess Congress* (1859); C. A. Buck, *Paul Morphy* (1902); Regina Morphy-Voitier, *Life of Paul Morphy* (1926); L. A. Morphy, *Poems and Prose Sketches, with a Biog. Memoir of Paul Charles Morphy* (1921); J. J. Löwenthal, *Morphy's Games of Chess* (1860), with a brief preface by Morphy; Max Lange, *Paul Morphy* (3rd ed., Leipzig, 1894); F. M. Edge, *The Exploits and Triumphs, in Europe, of Paul Morphy* (1859); P. W. Sergeant, *Morphy Gleanings* (1932); *Times-Democrat* (New Orleans), July 11, 1884; *Chess Monthly* (N. Y.), 1857–60.]   L. C. K.

MORRELL, BENJAMIN (July 5, 1795–1839), sealing captain and explorer, was born in Rye, N. Y., the son of Benjamin Morrell. His father, a ship-builder, removed his family to Stonington, Conn., when Benjamin was less than one year old. After a childhood of ill health and with only a village-school education, the boy ran away to sea at the age of sixteen (March 1812). Sailing from New York on the ship *Enterprise* under Capt. Alexander Cartwright, with a cargo of contraband provisions for Spain, he reached Cadiz in the midst of a heavy bombardment by the French. On the return voyage the ship was captured by a British sloop and Morrell and the rest of the crew were held in prison at St. John's, Newfoundland, for eight months. After reaching home, he joined the crew of the American privateer, *Joel Barlow*, in May 1813, but it was captured in the following July and Morrell was confined at Dartmoor prison until May 1815. He made a number of deep-sea voyages, always before the mast, since his education did not fit him to be an officer, until he shipped on the *Edward* of New York under Capt. Josiah Macy [*q.v.*], who conceived a deep interest in the young man, taught him navigation and promoted him as rapidly as was fitting, until he became master of his own ship.

Morrell thereupon commenced a series of sealing voyages into the South Seas, in the *Wasp* (1822–24), the *Tartar* (1824–26), and the *Antarctic* (1828–29, 1829–31), and it is upon his written narrative of these voyages that his reputation rests (*A Narrative of Four Voyages to the South Sea*, 1832). The South Seas at this period were little known. According to Morrell's account he was the first American sea-captain to penetrate the Antarctic circle. He reached 70° south which had been surpassed in that period only by Cook (71°) and Weddell (74° 15′). Both of these latter were for ex-

ploration, not commercial ventures. His voyages were made in typical sealers' small topsail schooners, the largest being the *Antarctic* of 175 tons. His voyages were combined with trading and the search for new sealing grounds and it is mainly the variety of his experience with the South Sea natives, many of whom saw white men for the first time with his arrival, that makes his book of interest. Presumably he was on the lookout for pearls. He also describes the building of drying sheds for *bêche-de-mer* and mentions other ventures which show that he was alert for any avenue of profit. His voyages averaged about 6,500 fur-seal skins.

Morrell married first in 1819. Upon his return from his first voyage as master, in June 1824, he found that his wife and two children had died. Before sailing on his second voyage he was married to a cousin barely fifteen years of age, named Abby Jane Wood. His wife accompanied him on his fourth voyage and in 1833 published a *Narrative* of the journey. It would appear that a number of the discoveries Morrell claimed were already known and possibly charted. Nevertheless, he gave a vivid first-hand description of certain parts of the South Seas that was the best obtainable information of his day. Nothing can be said for his literary style; there is much extraneous matter, and many of his conclusions are untenable. Morrell's later journeys included a voyage to the islands of the Pacific on the *Margaret Oakley*, which, according to rumor, he pirated, and which was wrecked at Madagascar. After further wanderings he died of a fever at Mozambique.

[In addition to Morrell's *Narrative of Four Voyages* and his wife's *Narrative of a Voyage . . . 1829, 1830, 1831,* see T. J. Jacobs, *Scenes, Incidents, and Adventures in the Pacific Ocean, . . . under Capt. Benj. Morrell* (1844); the *Am. Quart. Rev.*, June 1833; the *Monthly Rev.* (London), Oct. 1833; and the first census of the United States, 1790.]   C. W. A.

MORRIL, DAVID LAWRENCE (June 10, 1772–Jan. 28, 1849), clergyman, physician, United States senator, and governor of New Hampshire, was born at Epping, N. H., where his father, Samuel Morril, a Harvard graduate and a Congregational minister, had settled and married Anna, daughter of David Lawrence. He studied with his paternal grandfather, Isaac Morril, a Congregational minister at Wilmington, Mass., and went to Exeter Academy. He then studied medicine and began to practise at Epsom, N. H., when only twenty-one. Seven years later, as the result of a religious experience, he commenced to study for the ministry under the Rev. Jesse Remington, of Candia, and in 1802 he became pastor of a church at Goffstown, formed by a union of Presbyterians and Congregationalists. Owing partly to ill-health and partly to difficulties in the church, Morril ended his active ministry in November 1809, and his relations with the parish were formally severed in July 1811. During his years as a minister he had not entirely given up medicine. He had also served as town moderator (1808–14), justice of the peace (1808, and frequently thereafter), and as representative in the state legislature (1808–17). After resigning his pastorate he continued the practice of medicine but became more and more active in politics. In 1816 he was chosen speaker of the state House of Representatives and in the same year was elected for a six-year term in the United States Senate. Here he proved himself a ready speaker, advocating measures for preventing the illegal African slave-trade, opposing the requirement of state enforcement of the federal fugitive-slave laws (though declaring he had "no disposition to deprive slave-holders of that species of property"), and vigorously disapproving the Missouri Compromise. He spoke eloquently, if somewhat sentimentally, in favor of pensions for Revolutionary officers, opposed reimbursing Matthew Lyon for the fine exacted under the Sedition Act, and moved to dismiss from the army and navy, officers who had engaged in dueling.

During his term at Washington Morril and William Hale were both nominated (1820) for governor of New Hampshire against Samuel Bell, but Governor Bell swept the state. When his term as senator expired, however, Morril was immediately elected to the Senate of New Hampshire and was chosen president of that body in June 1823. The next year he was nominated again for governor by the "Adams men," or "old guard" of the Democratic-Republicans, in opposition to the incumbent, Levi Woodbury, who had been elected the preceding year by the "insurgents." Neither candidate received a majority of votes cast, but Morril, having a plurality of more than 3,000, was chosen by the legislature. His reëlection the following year was practically unanimous, 30,167 votes being cast for him out of a total of 30,770. In 1825 he had the honor of receiving Lafayette when the latter visited Concord. The following year he was elected governor for a third time, at the expiration of which tenure he retired to private life. He changed his residence in 1831 from Goffstown to Concord, where during his remaining years he was chiefly engaged in religious activities. He served as a vice-president of the American Bible Society, the Sunday-School

Union, and the Home Missionary Society, and for two years was editor of a religious paper, the *New Hampshire Observer*. Still active within ten days of his death, he died at Concord in his seventy-seventh year.

Morril was an unusual combination of the student and active man of affairs. Medicine, theology, and politics all interested him, and he continued his studies and activities in all three till almost the end of his life. He was strongly Calvinistic in religion, and a stanch, but not violent, anti-Federalist in politics. His intelligence, ability as a speaker, and knowledge of public affairs drew him naturally into political life and made him a popular candidate for office. He seems to have spent his last years in comparative leisure and retirement. He married first, Sept. 25, 1794, Jane Wallace of Epsom, who died Dec. 14, 1823, without children. On Aug. 3, 1824, he married Lydia Poore, of Goffstown, by whom he had four sons, three of whom survived him.

[See Nathaniel Bouton, *Hist. of Concord* (1856); E. S. Stackpole, *Hist. of N. H.* (1916), vol. III; G. P. Hadley, *Hist. of the Town of Goffstown, 1733–1920* (2 vols., 1922–24); and A. M. Smith, *Morrill Kindred in America* (2 vols., 1914–31). Hadley reproduces a portrait of Morrill which is in the State House at Concord. The *New-Eng. Hist. and Geneal. Reg.,* Apr. 1849, gives a sketch of his life based on the best contemporary newspaper account, in the Concord *Democrat and Freeman,* Feb. 1, 1849. There is a brief account of him in the *Biog. Dir. Am. Cong.* (1928) and in N. F. Carter, *The Native Ministry of N. H.* (1906).]

E. V. M.

MORRILL, ANSON PEASLEE (June 10, 1803–July 4, 1887), governor of Maine and congressman, the son of Peaslee and Nancy (Macomber) Morrill and the descendant of John Morrill who was living at Kittery, Me., as early as 1668, was born in Belgrade, Kennebec County, Me. He had the advantages only of a common-school education, working during his spare time in a mill where corn was ground, wood sawed, and wool carded. At one time he taught school at Miramichi, New Brunswick, Canada. In early manhood he became the postmaster at Dearborn in Kennebec County, keeping at the same time a general store. Still a store-keeper, he was later postmaster at North Belgrade, and he lived for some time at Madison. In 1827 he was married to Rowena M. Richardson, who died in 1882. His great business opportunity came in 1844 when he was asked to take charge of a woolen-mill in Readfield, then on the verge of bankruptcy. Here his exceptional talents became evident. Putting the mill on a paying basis, he eventually became the owner of the factory and laid the foundations of a comfortable fortune. His political career began in 1834, when he served a term in the state legislature. He was sheriff of Somerset County in 1839 but lost this office in 1840, when Maine elected the Whig state and national ticket. In 1841 he refused reappointment from the newly elected Democratic governor. From 1850 to 1853 he was land agent of the state.

When the two questions, temperance and slavery, broke the unity of the Democrats in Maine, with considerable courage he led a bolting faction of the Democrats in 1853 on the temperance issue. His supporters were known as "Morrill Democrats," and as an independent candidate for the governorship he ran third. The following year, 1854, the Whigs and the Free-soilers joined the temperance forces to give him a vote of about 44,000 against 28,000 for his opponent, Albion K. Parris. Since, however, there were four candidates he did not have a majority of the votes cast and the legislature chose him when it met the next January. The fusion party that elected him governor took the name Republican for the first time in Maine on Aug. 7, 1854 (see W. F. P. Fogg, *The Republican Party . . . with the History of its Formation in Maine,* 1884). In the election of 1855 he again had a popular plurality, but the same Senate that elected his brother, Lot Myrick Morrill [*q.v.*], its president, appointed his Democratic opponent, Samuel Wells, governor. He was a delegate to the Repubican National Convention of 1856. Elected to Congress in 1860, he served from 1861 to 1863 but declined reelection, preferring to make way for the election of James G. Blaine. With the exception of one more term in the state legislature, 1881–82, this ended his political service. His independence and impetuosity frequently offended many friends. His own acts and words often impeded his political progress. Others, however, were attracted by his ruggedness, honesty, and integrity. His superior business ability was recognized when the railroad interests that had bought largely of the stock of the Maine Central elected him president of the road. During the year he occupied this position he took a special interest in improving the efficiency of operation. From Readfield he moved to Augusta in 1879, where he died after a short illness, leaving two children.

[L. C. Hatch, *Maine* (1919) vol. II; *Reminiscences of Neal Dow* (1898), pp. 482–95, 503–21; A. M. Smith, *Morrill Kindred in America,* vol. II (1931); *Harper's Weekly,* July 16, 1887; *Daily Eastern Argus* (Portland), July 6, 1887.]   R. E. M.

MORRILL, EDMUND NEEDHAM (Feb. 12, 1834–Mar. 14, 1909), congressman from Kansas and governor, the son of Rufus and Mary (Webb) Morrill, was born at Westbrook, Cumberland County, Me., and received his education at Westbrook Seminary. He removed to Brown County, Kan., where he arrived on Mar. 12, 1857, and set up a sawmill, which he operated until 1860. On October 5, 1857, he was elected to the free-state territorial legislature. On Oct. 5, 1861, he enlisted in the 7th Kansas Cavalry and through the influence of Vice-President Hamlin of Maine was appointed, in August 1862, to be commissary of subsistence. He was mustered out with the rank of major, by brevet, in October 1865. On Nov. 27, 1862, he had married Elizabeth A. Brettun, the daughter of William H. Brettun of Leavenworth, Kan., who died in September 1868. On Dec. 25, of the next year, he married Caroline J. Nash of Roxbury, Mass., who bore him three children.

His life after the war was divided between business and politics. Although in political life almost continuously, he was not a professional politician in the usual sense. He was active in promoting the building of two railroads across the county in which he lived. He entered the banking business in 1871 at Hiawatha, later became interested in banks at Leavenworth and Kansas City, as well as in a loan company at Atchison, and acquired extensive land holdings. Toward the end of his life he was rated as one of the wealthiest men in the state. After his retirement from the governorship he developed one of the largest single apple orchards in the state, an orchard of 880 acres. He was active in promoting the educational and cultural interest of his community, established a public library in 1882, and assisted financially in establishing and maintaining the Hiawatha academy. He was a conservative in his general point of view on life and on public questions his attitude was further conditioned to a marked degree by his service as a Union soldier and by his interests as a banker.

From 1866 to 1872 he held county offices. In the latter year he was elected to the state Senate on the Republican ticket and was reelected in 1876. In that body he became chairman of the committee on ways and means and president *pro tempore.* From 1883 to 1891 he was a member of the federal Congress, where he received an assignment on the committee on invalid pensions. The eight years spent in the House of Representatives was devoted almost exclusively to pension legislation. He declined to stand for reelection in 1890. In 1894 he was brought forward against the Populists who then dominated Kansas, and was elected governor in spite of the charge that in his speculations in land with clouded titles he had defrauded large numbers

Morrill

of farmers of their homesteads and thereby built up a large part of his fortune (*Ottawa Journal*, Sept. 20, 27, Oct. 4, 1894, for excellent summary of charges; *Atchison Daily Champion*, Oct. 30, 1894, for defense). His administration was embarrassed in carrying out a program by a Populist Senate. Among the leading problems of his term as governor were those arising from drought and destitution in the western part of the state, from the mortgage laws and rates of interest, and from the prohibition law which he upheld in a conservative although sincere fashion. His conception of his office was that the governor should execute laws and not attempt to make them (Morrill to C. J. Hammonds, Jan. 30, 1895, correspondence of the governors of Kansas, Letter-press Books, vol. III, p. 294). His theory of government was expressed in his statement that "when the government has protected the individual in his life and property . . . he ought to hustle for himself to get bread" (Morrill to William A. Porter, Jan. 19, 1895, correspondence of the governors of Kansas, Letter-press Books, vol. III, p. 23). In 1896 he was renominated and in the bitterly fought campaign the opposing party, a Populist, Democratic, Free Silver combination brought up again the charge of 1894. He was defeated, although he ran ahead of the state ticket and the McKinley electors, and retired to Brown County to devote himself to his varied interests. He died in San Antonio, Texas.

[Private papers in the hands of his family; correspondence as governor **of** Kan. in State Hist. Soc. Lib., Topeka; F. W. Blackmar, *Kansas* (copr. 1912), vol. II; A. T. Andreas, *Hist. of the State of Kan.* (1883); *Kan. State Hist. Soc. Trans.*, vol. X (1908); *Kan. State Hist. Soc. Colls.*, vol. XII (1912); *Who's Who in America*, 1908–09; G. W. Harrington, *Annals of Brown County, Kan.* (1903); D. W. Wilder, *The Annals of Kan.*, new ed. (1886); *World* (Hiawatha, Kan.), esp. Mar. 15–20, 1909.]   J. C. M.

MORRILL, JUSTIN SMITH (Apr. 14, 1810– Dec. 28, 1898), representative and senator from Vermont, was the eldest of the ten children of Nathaniel and Mary (Hunt) Morrill. Of humble, sturdy, English stock, he was the descendant of Abraham Morrill who landed in Boston in 1632 and settled in Salisbury, Mass. The Morrills settled in Strafford, Vt., in 1795, where the boy was born and where his grandfather and father combined farming with the blacksmith's trade. He attended the village school and neighboring academies until the age of fifteen, when he became a clerk in the village store. He was in Portland, Me., from 1828 to 1831 learning merchandising and then returned to Strafford and became a partner of his friend, Jedediah H. Harris, in the village store, which as a center of news and a forum of discussion was an excellent

training-school for politicians. As a merchant he prospered, and in 1848 he was able to retire to a quiet life of reading and farming. On Sept. 17, 1851, he was married to Ruth Barrell Swan of Easton, Mass. They had two sons. As an amateur politician he had served on county and state committees, and in 1852 he was chosen to represent the Whigs at their national convention. The dissension of the Whig party at this convention influenced him throughout his life to labor to preserve harmony in the Republican party, in the Vermont organization of which he had played a prominent part in 1855.

In 1854 he was elected as an Anti-Slavery Whig to the House of Representatives, commencing an unbroken service of twelve years in the House and almost thirty-two years in the Senate, to which he was elected in 1866 and was returned at each election with virtual unanimity. This service in the House and Senate constituted the longest period of continuous service in the United States Congress so far recorded. In the House he became an important member of the committee on ways and means, of which he was chairman from 1865 to 1867; and in the Senate he served effectively as a member of the committee on finance, of which he was chairman from 1877 to 1879, 1881 to 1893, and 1895 to 1898. After an experimental period in the House, in which though a stanch abolitionist he sounded a temperate and conciliatory note on the great question of slavery, he found his real work in problems of tariff and finance. As a member of the committee on ways and means he wrote a bill providing for the payment of outstanding treasury notes, authorizing a loan, and revising the tariff. This act, known as the Morrill Tariff Act, was intended to be a revenue as well as a protective measure, but amendments made it more strongly protectionist than he had desired. Although causing bitter resentment in the South, the bill was passed early in 1861. His tariff views were somewhat colored by a traditional distrust of Great Britain, and he never thoroughly mastered the principles of international trade, but as a conscientious and not uncompromising protectionist he remained throughout his career influential in tariff legislation, especially in the bill of 1883. In the field of finance lay his greatest talents. With an attack upon the legal tender bill, which, however, was passed in 1862, he began a long fight against inconvertible money and financial inflation. During the Civil War he prepared a series of internal revenue bills and became the champion of economy in the House. After the war he was a leader in the financial reconstruction and an inflexible advo-

198

Morrill

cate of a speedy return to specie payments. He was offered a position in the cabinet of President Hayes as secretary of the treasury but declined. In the Cleveland administration he attacked the free-silver heresy.

Perhaps his greatest accomplishment was his Land-Grant College Act, which led to the development of the important system of state educational institutions aided by the federal government. In 1857 he introduced a bill "donating public lands to the several States and Territories which may provide colleges for the benefit of agriculture and the mechanic arts" (*Cong. Globe,* 35 Cong., 1 Sess., p. 32). This was vetoed by Buchanan in 1859, but a similar bill was signed by Lincoln in 1862. In 1890 he introduced in the Senate the so-called Second Morrill Act, under which $25,000 is given annually by the federal government to each of the land-grant colleges. As chairman of the Senate committee on building and grounds he rendered valuable service. He was largely responsible for the plan and execution of the terraces, fountains, and gardens of the Capitol and the completion of the Washington Monument. To his original proposal and persevering legislation is also chiefly due the Library of Congress. His artistic and literary interests found further outlet in his numerous contributions to current periodicals, among them being his book, *Self-Consciousness of Noted Persons* (1882), his *Forum* series of "Notable Letters from my Political Friends" (Oct.–Dec. 1897), and other articles in the *Forum* from time to time (Aug. 1896, Jan., July 1889, Oct. 1898).

As a politician he was noted for sound reasoning, clear apprehension and statement, faithful labor, and temperate, courteous attitude. He was an exceptionally skilful legislator. In appearance he was imposing, being tall and angular and having stern Roman features and side whiskers. As a man he was characterized by urbanity and charm of manner, modesty, culture, and great love of country. He was a genial host at his home on Thomas Circle in Washington, and his birthday parties were among the important social events of the Capitol. In his later days in the Senate his prestige was great, and he was often referred to as "The Nestor of the Senate," "The grand old man of the Republican Party," and "The Gladstone of America." He died in Washington, survived by one of his two sons.

[Papers and letters are in Lib. of Cong.; published material includes W. B. Parker, *The Life and Public Services of Justin Smith Morrill* (1924); G. W. Atherton, *The Legislative Career of Justin Smith Morrill* (1900?); I. M. Tarbell, "The Tariff in Our Times," *Am. Mag.,* Dec. 1906, pp. 116–32; *Memorial Addresses on the Life and Character of Justin Smith Morrill* (1879); *Justin Smith Morrill: Centenary Exercises* (1910); A. M. Smith, *Morrill Kindred in America,* vol. II (1931); *Evening Star* (Washington), Dec. 27, 28, 1898. A discussion of the credit due to Jonathan Baldwin Turner [*q.v.*] for the Land-Grant College Act is in Parker, *ante,* pp. 278–84; the claim is set forth in some detail in E. J. James, "The Origin of the Land Grant Act of 1862," *Univ. of Ill. Studies,* vol. IV, no. 1 (1910); a brief consideration and decision against the Turner claim in I. L. Kandel, "Federal Aid for Vocational Education," *The Carnegie Foundation for the Advancement of Teaching Bulletin,* no. 10 (1917), p. 79.]

C.M.F.
A.R.B.

MORRILL, LOT MYRICK (May 3, 1812–Jan. 10, 1883), governor of Maine, United States senator, secretary of the treasury, one of the fourteen children of Peaslee and Nancy (Macomber) Morrill, was born in Belgrade, Me. After attending the common-school and the local academy he taught in order to obtain money to attend Waterville (now Colby) College, which he entered at the age of eighteen. He remained there but a short time, however. For a year he was principal of a private school in western New York. Returning to Maine, he began the study of law under Judge Fuller of Readfield. Admitted to the bar in 1839, he built up a considerable law practice chiefly among Democratic friends. Being much in demand as a speaker on temperance and political subjects, he won some local fame so that when he moved to the state capital, Augusta, in 1841, he was frequently employed before legislative committees. This was his school of politics. His law partners in Augusta were James W. Bradbury and Richard D. Rice. Becoming chairman of the state Democratic committee in 1849, he held that office until 1856, when he refused to attend the meetings of the state committee, writing, "The candidate [Buchanan] is a good one, but the platform is a flagrant outrage upon the country and an insult to the North" (Talbot, *post,* p. 232). The breach with his party, thus made complete, began in 1855 when he opposed pledging the Democratic party to further concessions to the slave states. The same step had already been taken by his brother, Anson Peaslee Morrill, and his friend, Hannibal Hamlin [*qq.v.*]. He was a member of the state House of Representatives in 1854 and of the Senate in 1856. His immediate election to the presidency of the Senate by the Democratic majority, from whom he had already shown divergence of principles, has been explained on the ground that his ability on the floor was more feared than his prestige as president. His Republicanism became definite in 1856 and, although his nomination to the governorship was opposed by some because of his late conversion, he was elected and twice reëlected governor, serving in 1858, 1859, and 1860. Both in the legislature and as governor he was a strong op-

199

ponent of the repeal of Maine's prohibition law, against which there had been a reaction.

When Hannibal Hamlin resigned from the Senate to accept the vice-presidency under Lincoln, the state legislature, in January 1861, elected Morrill as his successor. Reëlected, he served to March 4, 1869, being succeeded by Hannibal Hamlin, who defeated him by one vote in the Maine Senate. In the so-called peace convention of February 1861 he opposed with conspicuous ability the arguments of Crittenden (L. E. Chittenden, *A Report of the Debates and Proceedings . . . of the Conference Convention,* 1864, pp. 144–50), and he maintained the same position when the Crittenden Resolutions were presented to Congress in March. In March 1862 he spoke in favor of a bill to confiscate the property and to emancipate the slaves of "rebels," seeing clearly that the question was not one of law but one of placing in the hands of the military authorities a weapon to help them win the war (*Speech . . . Delivered in the Senate . . . Mar. 5, 1862,* 1862, also in *Cong. Globe,* 37 Cong., 2 Sess., pp. 1074–78). In April 1862 he led the debate which resulted in the act emancipating slaves in the District of Columbia (*Ibid.,* p. 1516). Later, in June 1866, he was a prominent advocate of the act that conferred suffrage on the colored citizens of the District (*Ibid.,* 39 Cong., 1 Sess., pp. 3432–34). He was a strong adherent of congressional Reconstruction (*Reconstruction. Speech in the Senate . . . Feb. 5, 1868,* 1868; also in *Cong. Globe,* 40 Cong., 2 Sess., app. pp. 110–17), and voted for the impeachment of President Johnson, although his colleague from Maine, William P. Fessenden [*q.v.*], voted for acquittal. On the death of Fessenden in September 1869 he was appointed to fill out the unexpired term. He was reëlected by the state legislature in 1871.

Although he had previously refused to accept appointment as secretary of war, resigning from the Senate on July 7, 1876, he accepted Grant's appointment as secretary of the treasury to succeed Benjamin H. Bristow [*q.v.*]. His studies as chairman of the Senate committee on appropriations had fitted him for the duties of this office and he was a worthy successor to Bristow. When he left the treasury on Mar. 8, 1877, President Hayes offered him the ministry to Great Britain. Enfeebled health, following on a severe illness of 1870 and another attack of 1877, influenced him to accept the lucrative post of collector at Portland rather than a more important and responsible position. He held the collectorship at the time of his death in Portland. His wife, Charlotte Holland Vance, whom he had married in 1845, and four daughters survived him.

[G. F. Talbot, "Lot M. Morrill," *Me. Hist. Soc. Colls.,* 2 ser., vol. V (1894); J. W. North, *The Hist. of Augusta* (1870); *Biog. Encyc. of Me.* (1885); C. E. Hamlin, *The Life and Times of Hannibal Hamlin* (1899); A. M. Smith, *Morrill Kindred in America,* vol. II (1931); *Advertiser* (Portland), Jan. 10, 1883; *Daily Eastern Argus,* Jan. 11, 1883; date of birth from his daughter, Anne Morrill Hamlin.]   R. E. M.

MORRIS, ANTHONY (Aug. 23, 1654–Oct. 23, 1721), Quaker leader of early Pennsylvania, son of Anthony and Elizabeth (Senior) Morris, was born in Old Gravel Lane, Stepney, London. In his youth he joined the Society of Friends "by convincement," and was married to Mary Jones, Mar. 30, 1676, in the Friends' Savoy Meeting House, in the Strand, London. Early in 1683 he removed to Burlington, West Jersey, and about three years later took up residence in Philadelphia, where he served on numerous committees, and held for some time the position of clerk (presiding officer) of the Monthly Meeting. In 1687 he was clerk of Philadelphia Yearly Meeting and as such signed an "Advice" to all Monthly Meetings against the sale of rum to the Indians. In 1688 he sat in the Quarterly Meeting of Philadelphia that considered the famous petition against slavery presented by the German Friends of Germantown, and signed on behalf of the meeting the Minute passing the matter on to the Yearly Meeting. When past middle life he began to speak in meetings for worship. Later he traveled in the ministry to New England and other parts of America, and to Great Britain.

He seems to have prospered financially, judging by the ample properties he owned in Burlington and Philadelphia. His business, in part at least, was brewing, in a day when no odium was attached thereto. He retired from active business, however, when he became engaged in the ministry. His interest in education is indicated by the fact that he signed, in 1697/98, the petition to the governor and council for the charter of a public school (the present William Penn Charter School) and was appointed by the charter as a member of the first board of overseers. As early as 1691 he was serving as a justice of the peace in Philadelphia, and he served in that capacity for some years. In 1693 he became presiding justice of the Court of Common Pleas for the city and county of Philadelphia and held that position for about five years. In August 1694 he was commissioned associate justice of the provincial supreme court, a position which he held, with his other judicial offices, until 1698. In the charter of 1691 incorporating the city of Philadelphia he was named one of six aldermen;

in the city charter of 1701 he was named again to the same office. For one year, 1703–04, he served as mayor of Philadelphia and in that capacity signed an interesting protest to the deputy governor in defense of the rights of the city (*Minutes of the Provincial Council of Pennsylvania,* II, 1852, p. 161). He was twice elected, in 1695 and 1696, a member of the provincial council and was a member of the Assembly from 1698 to 1704. Morris was married four times: in 1689 to his second wife, Agnes, widow of Cornelius Bom, in Philadelphia; in 1693/94 to Mary, widow of Thomas Coddington, at Newport, R. I.; and in 1700 to Elizabeth Watson, in Philadelphia. He had fifteen children.

[Sources include: R. C. Moon, *The Morris Family of Phila.* (5 vols., 1898–1909), esp. vol. I; J. W. Jordan, ed., *Encyc. of Pa. Biog.,* vol. X (1918); G. P. Donehoo, ed., *Pennsylvania: A Hist.* (1926), vol. IX; F. B. Lee, ed., *Geneal. and Memorial Hist. of the State of N. J.* (1910), vol. III; J. H. Martin, *Martin's Bench and Bar of Phila.* (1883); *Bull. of Friends' Hist. Soc. of Phila.,* May 1919; the *Friend,* July 21, 1855; John Smith, "The Lives of the Ministers of the Gospel among the People Called Quakers" (1770), a manuscript in the library of Haverford Coll.; and manuscript records of the Friends preserved at 304 Arch Street, Phila. A few manuscripts written or signed by Anthony Morris are in the library of the Pa. Hist. Soc.]

R. W. K.

MORRIS, ANTHONY (Feb. 10, 1766–Nov. 3, 1860), merchant, was born at Philadelphia, Pa., the son of Samuel and Rebecca (Wistar) Morris and a descendant of Anthony Morris, 1654–1721 [*q.v.*]. His father was a merchant and captain of the 1st Troop, Philadelphia City Cavalry, during the Revolution. He studied with private tutors, then attended the University of Pennsylvania, graduating in 1783. After studying law he was admitted to the Philadelphia bar on July 27, 1787, but he practised little for he was more interested in business and carried on an extensive trade with the East Indies. He was speaker of the Pennsylvania Senate, 1793–94, and from 1800 to 1806 was a director of the Bank of North America. From May 1810, after the American chargé at Madrid, George W. Erving, had been forced to leave the country because of the chaotic conditions of factional and civil war, Morris, together with Thomas L. Brent and Thomas Gough, was an unofficial representative of the United States in Spain. He was accused by his companions of seeking to obtain the appointment as minister to Spain and there is no doubt that he was a party to a rather discreditable intrigue, in which certain Spanish officials were involved, to make himself minister by discrediting Erving with the Spanish government. In 1814 when diplomatic relations were resumed Erving was renamed as minister to Spain and Morris returned to America. During his so-

journ at Madrid he suggested to the United States that East and West Florida could be purchased for a reasonable sum. Though this suggestion received no attention at the time, it was eventually realized in the Treaty of 1819 by which Spain ceded East and West Florida and the adjacent islands to the United States. He seems, however, to have taken no part in the negotiations. About 1830–31 he founded an agricultural school at Bolton Farms in Bristol Township, Bucks County, Pa., but this venture was not successful. He served as a trustee of the University of Pennsylvania from 1806 to 1817. His wife was Mary Pemberton whom he had married on May 13, 1790. They had four children. During the latter part of his life he resided with his daughter at "The Highlands," near Georgetown, D. C., where he died.

[J. L. Chamberlain, ed., *Universities and Their Sons: Univ. of Pa.,* vol. II (1902); R. C. Moon, *The Morris Family of Phila.,* vols. I and II (1898); H. B. Fuller, *The Purchase of Fla.* (1906); J. L. M. Curry, "Diplomatic Services of Geo. Wm. Erving," *Proc. Mass. Hist. Soc.,* 2 ser. V (1890).]

J. H. F.

MORRIS, CADWALADER (Apr. 19, 1741 o.s.–Jan. 25, 1795), merchant, was born in Philadelphia, Pa., the son of Samuel and Hannah (Cadwalader) Morris and a descendant of Anthony Morris, 1654–1721 [*q.v.*]. His father was a prominent lawyer. He attended a private school in Philadelphia and then joined his brother, Samuel C. Morris, in the importing business. He was the firm's representative in the West Indies for several years and lived for some time in Kingston, Jamaica, and elsewhere in the Islands. He was strongly sympathetic toward the cause of the colonists and took a prominent part in the Revolutionary War as a member of the 1st Troop, Philadelphia City Cavalry, commanded by his cousin, Capt. Samuel Morris. He was a signer of the paper bills of credit issued by order of the Pennsylvania Assembly on Mar. 21, 1772, and Apr. 7, 1781. When the Pennsylvania Bank was organized on June 8, 1780, for the purpose of supplying and transporting food to the army, he aided in its establishment by a subscription of £2,500 to its capital and for a time served as one of its inspectors. He was also one of the founders and a director (1781–87) of the Bank of North America. In 1783–84 he was a delegate from Pennsylvania to the Continental Congress and was elected for another term but declined to serve. In 1788 he moved to Birdsboro, Berks County, Pa., where, with some other Philadelphia capitalists, he had purchased two iron forges. In 1790, however, he sold his interests in this venture and returned to Philadelphia where he again engaged in the importing business. He was a member of the Democratic Society of Philadelphia which was organized as an act of good will toward the French Revolution. He died in Philadelphia. He had married, on Apr. 8, 1779, Ann Strettell, by whom he had five children.

[Biog. Dir. Am. Cong. (1928); Hist. of the First Troop, Phila. City Cavalry, 1774–1874 (1874); R. C. Moon, The Morris Family of Phila., vols. I and II (1898); M. L. Montgomery, "Early Furnaces and Forges of Berks County, Pa.," Pa. Mag. of Hist. and Biog., Mar. 1884.]   J. H. F.

MORRIS, CASPAR (May 2, 1805–Mar. 17, 1884), physician, was born in Philadelphia, Pa., the third son of Israel Wistar and Mary (Hollingsworth) Morris, and a descendant of Anthony Morris, 1654–1721 [q.v.]. His father was a prosperous merchant. He attended private schools, the Pine Street Meeting House, David Dulles' school in Church Alley, and the William Penn Charter School. Later he studied medicine at the University of Pennsylvania and was graduated in 1826. While attending the school of medicine he studied also with Dr. Joseph Parrish. After his graduation he traveled to India as surgeon on the Pacific, returning to Philadelphia in 1828. He was appointed physician of the Philadelphia Dispensary soon after his return. The following year, on Nov. 11, 1829, he was married to his cousin, Anne Cheston of Baltimore. In spite of his social position, he chose to live near a poor district. He was one of the founders of the House of Refuge, which he served as physician from 1830 to 1834, and also helped to establish the Pennsylvania Institution for the Instruction of the Blind, serving as its manager and physician from 1833 until his death. In the early fifties he published a brief article emphasizing the need for increased hospital facilities in Philadelphia, the result of which was the movement to establish the Episcopal Hospital, which he served as manager for many years. A list of his writings includes An Appeal on Behalf of the Sick (1851); Lectures on Scarlet Fever (1851); An Essay on the Pathology and Therapeutics of Scarlet Fever (1858); an abridgment (1838) of Robert I. Wilberforce's life of William Wilberforce; and a small volume of poems, privately printed, entitled Heart Voices and Home Songs. In recognition of his experience in America and observation of foreign institutions he was appointed one of five men selected to submit suggestions for the building of the Johns Hopkins Hospital in Baltimore. His contribution, "Hospital Construction and Organization," was published in Hospital Plans: Five Essays Relating to the Construction, Organization and Management of Hospitals (1875).

Morris was a member of the National Academy of Sciences (1829–38) and of the American Philosophical Society (1851–60), and a fellow of the College of Physicians. He aided in founding in 1838 the Philadelphia Medical Institute and was a lecturer there until 1844. Suffering an impairment of his health in 1868, he never fully regained his strength thereafter and died in 1884, having survived his wife by three years.

[J. C. Morris, "Biog. Sketch of Caspar Morris, M.D.," Trans. Coll. of Physicians of Phila., 1888, 3 ser., vol. X (1888); H. A. Kelly and W. L. Burrage, Am. Medic. Biogs. (1920); R. C. Moon, The Morris Family of Phila. (3 vols., 1898); Medic. and Surgic. Reporter, Mar. 29, 1884; Pub. Ledger (Phila.), Mar. 18, 1884.]   R. L. B.

MORRIS, CHARLES (July 26, 1784–Jan. 27, 1856), naval officer, was born at Woodstock, Conn., of early New England ancestry, son of Charles and Miriam (Nichols) Morris. Though a reader and diligent student, he was occupied with farm work and had little regular schooling after his tenth year. Through his father, a naval purser during the American hostilities with France, he secured a midshipman's appointment, July 1, 1799, and made his first cruise in the Congress. By a fall from the mainmast in January 1800, he suffered a broken arm and concussion of the brain, but recovered, and after a winter on the West-Indies station was selected in June 1801 as one of the 159 out of 355 midshipmen retained in the peace establishment. Following nine months in Woodstock Academy he sailed in August 1803 in the Constitution of Preble's squadron against Tripoli. Already marked by professional ambition and enthusiasm, he achieved his first fame when he was selected by Decatur to share in the celebrated exploit of burning the frigate Philadelphia, held by the Tripolitans. Leaping with Decatur, he was first aboard the frigate and figured prominently in her capture and destruction. He took part in subsequent bombardments of Tripoli, and returning home in the President, received his lieutenant's commission (1807) during a second Mediterranean cruise in the Hornet.

After gunboat duty in Maine, and service in the President, 1809–10, Morris was first lieutenant under Hull in the Constitution at the outbreak of the War of 1812. He suggested warping the Constitution ahead with anchors in her extraordinary escape from Broke's squadron, July 17–19, 1812, and was highly praised by Hull for his part in the victory, Aug. 19, following, over the Guerrière, in which he was shot through the body while attempting to lash the ships together. This exploit won him promotion to captain, over the grade of master-commandant, though, owing to protests, his advancement was delayed to avoid his superseding Lawrence and Jacob Jones. Assigned next to command the *John Adams* (26 guns), he escaped from the Chesapeake Jan. 18, 1814, for a cruise on the African and Irish coasts. The *Adams* captured ten prizes, but after grounding on the Maine coast and retreating up the Penobscot, she was attacked, Sept. 3, 1814, by two British vessels with a landing force of over six hundred. Morris had mounted his guns ashore, but upon the flight of his supporting militia, was compelled to burn his ship and retreat. Cleared by a court of inquiry, he was ordered to the *Congress,* which, after the war, in August 1815, joined Decatur's squadron against Algiers. He remained in the *Congress* until 1817, commanding the forces in the Caribbean (1817) while on diplomatic missions to Haiti and Venezuela. His command of the Portsmouth (New Hampshire) station during the next five years was broken by a visit to Georgia (1819) to recover from pneumonia, and a short subsequent cruise to Buenos Aires (1819–20). In 1823 he was appointed to the Board of Navy Commissioners with John Rodgers and Isaac Chauncey. Earlier, in 1815, Rodgers had highly recommended Morris for this important administrative office as "of strong, discriminating mind, of considerable science, and uniting perhaps as much, if not more theoretical knowledge as any man of his age in the service" (C. O. Paullin, *Commodore John Rodgers,* 1910, p. 302). Morris' correspondence in this and later periods shows him constantly occupied with problems of naval construction, signals, regulations; in fact, every phase of naval activity.

Morris held the commissionership until 1827, except for a year, 1825–26, when he commanded the *Brandywine* in which Lafayette returned to France. He afterward visited Lafayette on his estate and made a tour of French and British naval establishments. Following command of the Boston yard, 1827–32, he was again navy commissioner until the board was abolished in 1841. Then, after commanding the Brazil and Mediterranean squadrons, 1841–44, he was head of the bureau of construction, and later the bureau of ordnance, until his death. Of his fifty-six years' service, twenty-two were at sea, and only two unemployed. A strict disciplinarian, Morris was noted for his influence over his men. Farragut called him "the ablest sea officer of his day" (*Autobiography,* note, p. 88). His appellation "Statesman of the American Navy" (*Providence Journal,* Jan. 29, 1856) was justified by the trust placed in his judgment and his

employment in important administrative work throughout his later years. His portrait by Scheffer, a gift from Lafayette, pictures a shrewd, kindly, self-controlled character, and, like his *Autobiography,* bears out contemporary testimony that "he combined in his manners, to a rare degree, unaffected simplicity and manly dignity" (*Ibid.*). He was married, Feb. 1, 1815, to Harriet, daughter of Dr. William Bowen of Providence, R. I., and had six daughters and four sons. The eldest son, Charles, a naval lieutenant, was killed in the Mexican War; another, George, commanded the *Cumberland* at the battle of Hampton Roads.

[The early sketch in Isaac Bailey, *Am. Naval Biog.* (1815), and the later one in Charles Morris, *Heroes of the Navy in America* (1907), are of slight value compared with *The Autobiog. of Commodore Charles Morris, U. S. Navy* (Boston, 1880, and also in *Naval Inst. Proc.,* vol. VI, 1880), covering his life to about 1840. Obituaries in the *Providence Jour.,* Jan. 29, 1856, and *Nat. Intelligencer,* Feb. 1, 1856, are reprinted in J. F. Morris, *A Geneal. and Hist. Reg. of the Descendants of Edward Morris* (1887). Many originals or facsimiles of Morris' letters and papers are in the Navy Dept. Lib.]   A. W.

MORRIS, CLARA (Mar. 17, 1848–Nov. 20, 1925), actress, was born in Toronto, Canada. Her mother, of Scotch-English ancestry, was Sarah Jane Proctor, a servant-maid, who, after being rescued from a mad dog by a French-Canadian cab-driver, Charles La Montagne, married him. The marriage was discovered to be bigamous after three children had been born, the eldest of whom was Clara. The mother assumed her grandmother's maiden name, Morrison, and fled to Cleveland, Ohio, with Clara. The other children were adopted: the daughter by a family in Buffalo; the son, who died at six, by a family in Cleveland. Mrs. Morrison, as she was known, had a struggle for existence, and the two suffered misery and hardship. Clara learned to read and write, however, and in 1862, at fourteen, was engaged by John Ellsler, manager of the Cleveland Academy of Music, as an extra at fifty cents for each public performance. She clipped her name to Clara Morris and began her stage appearances. Owing to a bad fall in childhood, which left her with spinal trouble, her health was permanently impaired and for the rest of her life she suffered ill health.

In 1869 she went to Cincinnati to play at Wood's Theatre and in the spring of 1870 she appeared at the National Theatre, Louisville, Ky., with Joseph Jefferson. By the fall of the year she had reached New York, where she was engaged by Augustin Daly to play in his Fifth Avenue Theatre. The opening play of the season was *Man and Wife.* By chance she was given the leading rôle, Anne Sylvester, which

Morris

she played with sufficient effect to gain an ovation on the opening night, Sept. 13, 1870. She remained with Daly until 1873, when she went to A. M. Palmer of the Union Square Theatre. There, in November 1873, she appeared in *The Wicked World*. Her first season as a star took her to the West Coast, after which she returned to Daly's to appear on Nov. 22, 1875, in *The New Leah*. In November 1876 she appeared at the Union Square Theatre in *Miss Multon*, and a year later she appeared at Wallach's Theatre as Jane Eyre. Thereafter "season followed season until she was known throughout the United States as the most prominent if not the greatest emotional actress on the American stage" (Clapp and Edgett, *post*, p. 266). Her rôles included Camille, Lady Macbeth, Alixe, Blanche de Chelles in *The Sphinx*, Mercy Merrick in *The New Magdalen*, Cora in *L'Article 47*, and Fanny Ten Eyck in *Divorce*. In the nineties, at the height of her career, she was forced by the state of her health to give up regular performances and thereafter she returned to the stage only for occasional appearances and in variety shows.

The reason for Clara Morris' success was baffling even to her critics. It was said of her that she could draw bigger houses on short notice than any other actress, and in certain parts she excited and moved her audiences. Yet her abilities were distinctly limited. William Winter said of her (*Vagrant Memories*, pp. 239-40): "It would not be accurate to designate Clara Morris as either a tragedian or a comedian. She was, intrinsically, an expositor of human nature in self-conflict, of the revolt of humanity against affliction and suffering, of erring virtue tortured in the miserable bonds of fatal circumstance. . . . Her acting was pervaded by a bizarre quality and fraught with hysterical passion and intense tremulous nervous force, but it revealed neither definite intellectual method nor consistent artistic design. The structure of it was perplexed by aimless wanderings across the scene, motiveless posturings, facial contortions, wailing vocalization, extravagant gesture, and spasmodic conduct—as of a haphazard person taking the uncertain chance of somehow coming out right at last." To another critic she was a marvel of cunning. "Nym Crinkle," commenting in the New York *World* after seeing her in *Camille*, wrote: "The wet eyes, the sobs, . . . the hysterical tremor like a little wave of electricity that went through the house. . . . Nothing like it when Bernhardt or Modjeska plays *Camille*. Why? I give it up. Criticism has wrestled with that condition in and out of season—how she can play upon all sensibilities and sweep as with super-

natural fingers the whole gamut of emotions, passes critical knowledge" (*World*, Sept. 25, 1885).

Clara Morris was married on Nov. 30, 1874, to Frederick C. Harriott of New York City. When she left the stage she retired to her home, "The Pines," in Riverdale, N. Y. She was an ardent horsewoman, kept birds and dogs in numbers, and painted and embroidered indefatigably. As her finances waned she took up writing for magazines and papers, and published some separate works. Included among these are: *A Silent Singer* (1899), a volume of short stories; *Life on the Stage* (1901); *A Pasteboard Crown* (1902); and *The Life of a Star* (1906). In 1909 her eyesight failed. After five years of blindness she partially regained her vision. Her husband died in 1914, her mother in 1917, and she herself passed away in 1925 in New Canaan, Conn., and was buried from "The Little Church Around the Corner." Her property, which would have escheated to the state, finally went to her sister, whom Clara Morris had been unable to trace during her own lifetime.

[Clara Morris' diaries, which she kept throughout her life, are in the possession of Mrs. George MacAdam, Scarsdale, N. Y. For printed sources consult: Wm. Winter, *The Wallet of Time* (1913), vol. I, and *Vagrant Memories* (1915); T. A. Brown, *A Hist. of the N. Y. Stage* (1903), vols. II and III; J. B. Clapp and E. F. Edgett, *Players of the Present* (1900); J. R. Towse, *Sixty Years of the Theatre* (1916); Brander Matthews and Lawrence Hutton, *Actors and Actresses of Great Britain and the U. S.* (1886); John Parker, *Who's Who in the Theatre*, 1922; *Theatre Arts Monthly*, Jan. 1926; *N. Y. Times*, Sept. 15, 1870, Nov. 21, 1925, Oct. 28, 1927.]
V. M.

MORRIS, EDMUND (Aug. 28, 1804–May 4, 1874), editor, writer on agriculture and other subjects, was born in Burlington, N. J., a descendant of Anthony Morris, 1654–1721 [*q.v.*]. His father was Richard Hill Morris and his mother was Mary, daughter of Richard S. Smith of Moorestown, N. J. He was married on Dec. 27, 1827, to Mary P. Jenks, daughter of William Jenks of Bridgetown, Bucks County, Pa. They had a son and three daughters. Morris spent his school days in Philadelphia and subsequently learned the printing trade in the office of the *Freeman's Journal*. In 1824, when he was nineteen years of age, he formed a partnership with S. R. Kramer of Philadelphia and bought the *Pennsylvania Correspondent*, published at Doylestown, the name of which was changed to *Bucks County Patriot and Farmers' Advertiser*. The partnership was dissolved in February 1827 and Morris conducted the paper alone until October of the same year, when he sold it. Subsequently he was associated with several Philadelphia publications including the *Ariel*, a

204

literary weekly. He returned to his native town, and in 1846 became the editor of the *Burlington Gazette* with which he remained for two years. In 1854 he assumed the editorship of the *Daily State Gazette,* published at Trenton, N. J., resigning his post in 1856 when he returned to Burlington to remain until his death.

Throughout his life Morris was interested in rural pursuits and wrote on agriculture and other general subjects. He took up farm land in the neighborhood of Burlington and wrote several pamphlets embodying his experience. One of these, *Ten Acres Enough for Intensive Gardening* (1844), had a wide sale and was translated into several languages. This gave him a reputation and brought him into contact with those interested in agriculture and thus led him into the business of selling farms in the vicinity of Burlington. The town of Beverly on the Delaware River below Burlington owes its foundation to his efforts. He also became interested in silk culture and impoverished himself in experimenting with mulberry plants. He was an ardent opponent of slavery and was active with his pen in support of the Union cause. One of his friends was Horace Greeley, for whom he frequently wrote editorials. During and after the Civil War he was a regular contributor to the *New York Tribune,* the *Newark Daily Advertiser,* and the Philadelphia *Press.* He experimented with mechanical inventions, and it is claimed that he was one of the first persons in the United States to print in two colors. His published writings include *How to Get a Farm and Where to Find One* (1864) and *Farming for Boys* (1868). He edited *Derrick and Drill* (1865), a compilation of information regarding the oil fields of Pennsylvania.

[W. E. Schermerhorn, *The Hist. of Burlington, N. J.* (1927); W. W. H. Davis, *Hist. of Doylestown, Old and New* (1903); Mary Morris Ferguson, *The Family of Edmund Morris* (1899); *Report of the State Librarian of Pa., 1900* (1901); *Daily State Gazette* (Trenton), May 6, 1874.]   H. S.

MORRIS, EDWARD DAFYDD (Oct. 31, 1825–Nov. 21, 1915), Presbyterian clergyman, educator, was born at Utica, N. Y. His father, Dafydd Edward Morris, was a native of Wales who came to the United States in his youth; his mother, Anne (Lewis), was of Welsh descent. The father, a man of strong religious principles, was a shoemaker, later conducting a small grocery business. The son enjoyed speaking and preaching in the Welsh language during his public life. He attended private schools in Utica and prepared for college at Whitestown Seminary, N. Y. Entering the sophomore class at Yale in 1846, he ranked high in scholarship while

earning his living. He made political speeches for the Free-Soil party and his writing attracted attention. He graduated at Yale in 1849, a classmate of Timothy Dwight [*q.v.*].

Graduating in 1852 at Auburn Theological Seminary, where he studied theology under Laurens P. Hickok [*q.v.*], Morris was ordained, by the Cayuga Presbytery, pastor of the Second Presbyterian Church of Auburn, N. Y. In 1855 he went to the Second Presbyterian Church of Columbus, Ohio. From this scholarly and productive ministry he was called in 1867 to the professorship of church history in Lane Theological Seminary, Cincinnati, and in 1874 was transferred to the chair of systematic theology, which he held until 1897 when he resigned and was made professor emeritus. Thereafter, he made his home at Columbus, for a time still lecturing at Lane besides speaking in various places and writing for publication. He was in responsible relation to Lane Seminary for thirty-four years, having become one of its trustees in 1863 and serving on the board until he became one of its faculty. He was again elected a trustee in 1870 in order to serve in an emergency as treasurer and superintendent of the Seminary, a task for which his business abilities specially fitted him. During the closing years of his professorship he won the gratitude of the trustees by his strenuous and successful efforts to assist the Seminary through a period of stress and peril.

Morris was moderator of the General Assembly of the Presbyterian Church in 1875. He was a member of the Church's committee on the revision of the creed, to which he gave active service. He was an earnest upholder of the theological standards of his Church, which he interpreted in a liberal spirit that accorded with his training and the temper of his mind. He was a vigorous exponent of the "New School" theology. His students were impressed with the lucidity, catholic range, and deeply evangelical spirit of his instruction, and appreciated his constant personal interest in them. His courtly bearing, brilliant dark eyes, and ruddy complexion gave him an appearance of vigor and distinction, enhanced in his later years by abundant white hair and beard. He was twice married: on July 29, 1852, to Frances Elizabeth, daughter of Dan and Fanny (Rowe) Parmelee of Fair Haven, Conn., who died in 1866; and on Mar. 26, 1867, to Mary Bryan Treat of Tallmadge, Ohio, who died in 1893. Four children were born of the first marriage; two, of the second. He died in Columbus three weeks after his ninetieth birthday, having maintained his mental activity to the end. His published works include: *Outlines of Theol-*

ogy (1880), *Ecclesiology* (1885), *Scripture Readings* (1887), *Is there Salvation after Death?* (1887), *Thirty Years in Lane* (1897), *Theology of the Westminster Symbols* (1900), *The Presbyterian Church, New School* (1905).

[*Ohio State Journal* (Columbus), May 6, 1895, and Nov. 22, 1915; *Herald-Dispatch* (Utica), Nov. 22, 1915; *The Continent* (N. Y.), Aug. 3, 1911, and Dec. 2, 1915; *Herald and Presbyter* (Cincinnati), Nov. 24 and Dec. 1, 1915; *Gen. Biog. Cat. Auburn Theol. Sem.* (1918); *Obit. Record Grads. Yale Univ.*, 1916; personal characteristics described in letters from Rev. Dr. Arthur Judson Brown, New York, and others.]
E. D. E.

MORRIS, EDWARD JOY (July 16, 1815– Dec. 31, 1881), legislator, diplomat, and author, was born in Philadelphia, Pa. He matriculated at the University of Pennsylvania in the class of 1835, left in his freshman year, and was graduated from Harvard College in 1836. He studied law in Philadelphia and was admitted to the bar in 1842, meanwhile being elected to the state Assembly in which he served during the years 1841–43. He was then elected as a Whig representative to the Twenty-eighth Congress for one term, 1843–45. He was an unsuccessful candidate for reëlection. On Jan. 10, 1850, he was appointed chargé d'affaires to the Two Sicilies and was stationed at Naples until Aug. 26, 1853. On his return from Naples he became a member of the board of directors of Girard College, Philadelphia, and was a member of the state House of Representatives in 1856. He took a leading part in the movement for the organization of the Republican party and was elected to the Thirty-fifth, Thirty-sixth and Thirty-seventh congresses and served from Mar. 4, 1857, to June 8, 1861, when he resigned. On the latter date President Lincoln appointed him minister to Turkey, where he served with zeal and fidelity until Oct. 25, 1870. While at Constantinople he negotiated a commercial treaty which was approved by the United States Senate in 1862.

Morris was a fine linguist, speaking French, Italian, and German fluently, was able to converse in Greek, and knew Turkish and Arabic. In manner he was said to be most agreeable and conciliating. He was a frequent contributor to American magazines and newspapers for many years and was also the author of several works. His *Notes of a Tour through Turkey, Greece, Egypt, Arabia Petræa to the Holy Land* (2 vols., 1842) is sometimes referred to as "Morris' Travels." He published in 1854 *The Turkish Empire: Its Historical, Statistical and Religious Condition,* translated from the German of Alfred de Bessé, giving an idea of the "past and present condition of the Ottoman people and empire." In it Morris incorporated ex-cerpts from French writers and a "considerable amount of original matter suggested by his own travels." In 1854 he also published from the original of Theodor Mügge, *Afraja, a Norwegian and Lapland Tale, or Life and Love in Norway,* which Bayard Taylor called "one of the most remarkable romances of the generation." Another translation was his *Corsica, Picturesque, Historical and Social* (1855), from the German of Ferdinand Gregorovius, which contained a sketch of the early life of Napoleon.

Morris left Turkey in 1870 and returned to the United States. He had married, July 15, 1847, Elizabeth Gatliff Ella, daughter of John Ella, of Philadelphia. His wife having died sometime prior to 1870, he married Susan Leighton, in Philadelphia, in October 1876. By his first marriage he had two daughters, one of whom survived him. He died in Philadelphia and was buried in Laurel Hill Cemetery.

[*Biog. Dir. Am. Cong.* (1928); S. A. Allibone, *A Critical Dict. of English Lit. and British and Am. Authors,* vol. II (1870); *Pub. Ledger* (Phila.), Jan. 2, 1882; Probate Court records, Phila.; records of the U. S. Dept. of State.]
A. E. I.

MORRIS, ELIZABETH (*c.* 1753–Apr. 17, 1826), actress, known on the stage as Mrs. Owen Morris, was presumably born in England, but no information is available concerning her before she became the second wife of Owen Morris, comedian in the American Company, and even the date of her marriage remains undisclosed. Her first stage appearance of which there is a definite record was made at the Southwark Theatre, Philadelphia, in the fall of 1772 (G. O. Seilhamer, *History of the American Theatre,* I, 1888, p. 309). In 1773 she performed with the American Company at Charleston, S. C. (Eola Willis, *The Charleston Stage in the XVIII Century,* 1924, p. 67), and the same year made her New York début. During the Revolution the company withdrew to the West Indies, and there Mrs. Morris followed her profession until the troupe returned to the United States in 1785 (Seilhamer, *op. cit.,* II, 1889, pp. 136 ff., 175). In a few years dissension developed within the organization. Thomas Wignell, a prominent comedian, finding his ambitions thwarted by the managers, Lewis Hallam and John Henry, withdrew in 1791 to form a new company, taking with him Mr. and Mrs. Morris, the latter of whom was probably eager to escape the rivalry of Mrs. Henry (J. N. Ireland, *Records of the New York Stage,* I, 1866, p. 83).

While awaiting the completion of the Chestnut Street Theatre at Philadelphia, which was to be the headquarters of Wignell's players, the

Morrises had the distinction of participating, in 1792, in the first theatrical season ever known at Boston, a season conducted in defiance of the law and abruptly terminated after several weeks by the sheriff, who interrupted Mr. and Mrs. Morris as Sir Peter and Lady Teazle in *The School for Scandal* and placed them under arrest (William Dunlap, *A History of the American Theatre,* 1832, pp. 127–28). From the opening of the Chestnut Street Theatre in February 1794, Mrs. Morris was associated mainly with that house until 1810, the year after her husband's death. Two or three years later she apparently acted with an upstart company in Philadelphia, and there is reason to believe that she performed at New York as late as 1815 (G. C. D. Odell, *Annals of the New York Stage,* II, 1927, p. 448). The obituary notice (*Poulson's American Daily Advertiser,* Philadelphia, Apr. 19, 1826), which refers to her as "formerly an eminent actress," indicates that she retired some years before her death.

In her prime, shortly after the Revolution, Mrs. Morris was regarded as the greatest attraction on the American stage. Especially in high comedy rôles, to which her tall and elegant figure and her spirited acting in the grand manner admirably adapted her, she was considered unsurpassed. At least one contemporary, however, held that she was much overrated, that she was extremely defective in education, enunciation, and memory (W. B. Wood, *Personal Recollections of the Stage,* 1855, pp. 26–28). He attributed her appeal to her personal attraction and to a mysterious manner which she affected both on and off the stage. So successfully did she avoid exposure to the common gaze that on the few occasions when she did appear on the street in her extravagantly high heels and her costume of 1775, to which she clung to the end of her life, she never failed to create a sensation. It is doubtful, however, whether Wood's explanation alone can account for her reputation among early American playgoers as "the inimitable Mrs. Morris" (Odell, *op. cit.,* I, 1927, p. 254).

[The principal sources have been mentioned in the body of the article. See also: Thos. C. Pollock, *The Phila. Theatre in the Eighteenth Century* (1933). The date of her death is taken from the burial records of St. Peter's Church, Phila., and verified by the newspaper cited above. The probable year of her birth is arrived at from Wood's statement *op. cit.,* p. 139, that she died at seventy-three.]   O. S. C.

MORRIS, GEORGE POPE (Oct. 10, 1802–July 6, 1864), journalist and poet, was born in Philadelphia, Pa. Early in his youth he removed to New York, where for some years he was employed in a printing office and where he began to contribute verses to various New York newspapers. In 1823 he founded the *New-York Mirror and Ladies' Literary Gazette,* a periodical which he engaged Samuel Woodworth, then well known in literary circles, to edit. After a year's connection with the magazine, Woodworth withdrew, and Morris himself became the sole proprietor and editor of the paper. The importance of the *Mirror* in affording a medium of public expression for the early Knickerbocker school, cannot be overestimated. In a day when literary magazines in New York were few, the *Mirror* encouraged, through its patronage, a local talent then clamoring for expression. A glance over its pages reveals such contributors as William Cullen Bryant, James K. Paulding, Nathaniel P. Willis, and Fitz-Greene Halleck—the leading literary lights of the early New York school. In 1842 the *New-York Mirror* ceased publication, but in the following year the *New Mirror,* edited jointly by Morris and his friend Nathaniel P. Willis, took its place, carrying on the same journalistic tradition. A difficulty over "an interpretation of the postage laws," however, finally led to its discontinuance in 1844. In the same year Morris again associated himself with Willis in the editing of a daily paper called the *Evening Mirror,* which continued for several years. In the meantime (1845) he had started a weekly entitled the *National Press.* After about a year, Willis also became an associate in this enterprise, and the title of the periodical was changed to the *Home Journal.* This weekly, which proved very popular, Morris continued to edit until shortly before his death. In describing his qualifications as a journalist, Evert A. Duyckinck mentions "his editorial tact and judgment; his shrewd sense of the public requirements; and his provision for the more refined and permanently acceptable departments of literature" (*Cyclopædia of American Literature,* 1855, II, 348).

Morris occupies but a minor place in the early Knickerbocker school. His drama, *Brier Cliff,* founded upon incidents of the American Revolution, was produced in 1826 at the Chatham Theatre. It had a long run and is said to have yielded its author the sum of $3,500. The drama has never been published. In his collected works may be found the libretto of an opera in three acts, *The Maid of Saxony,* based "upon historical events in the life of Frederick the Second of Prussia." This opera, for which Charles E. Horn produced the music, had in 1842 a run of about two weeks. As a writer of poetry Morris in his day attained a genuine popularity, and his songs were frequently set to music by distinguished composers in the United States and abroad. Edgar Allan Poe considered "Woodman, Spare that Tree" and "Near the Lake" "compositions of which any poet, living or dead, might justly be proud" (*Southern Literary Messenger,* April 1849, p. 219), and it was said in Morris' day that he could "at any time obtain fifty dollars for a song unread." But his verses were at times sharply censured by contemporary critics. One satirist called *Brier Cliff* a "paltry play," and another spoke of Morris himself as

> A household poet, whose domestic muse
> Is soft as milk, and sage as Mother Goose.

To a later audience his lyrics are uniformly insipid and sentimental. Occasionally, however, he leaves the purely banal for a strain of simple and quiet beauty to which is added a note of genuine pathos. In 1839 he published *The Little Frenchman and his Water Lots,* a volume of prose sketches mostly in a humorous vein.

Of a generous and hearty, though practical, nature, Morris represented well that spirit of *bonhomie* which distinguished New York life of the early nineteenth century. He has been described as "about five feet two or three inches high. . . . Short, crisp, dark curly hair, thinly streaked with silver threads, encircled a high, well-formed forehead, beneath which was a pair of bright, twinkling black eyes. . . . [His] complexion was fresh and florid" (G. W. Bungay, *Off-Hand Takings,* 1854, pp. 44–45). He was usually called "General" Morris—a title derived from his connection with the state militia. For many years he resided at his country estate situated in the Hudson River highlands, near Cold Spring. His personal letters which have survived reveal a domestic life of happiness and comfort, despite occasional financial reverses. His household consisted of his wife, Mary Worthington Hopkins, and several children. A son, William Hopkins Morris [*q.v.*], was a West-Point graduate who served in the Civil War.

[Sources include: "Am. Poetry," *People's and Howitt's Jour.,* vol. X (1850), p. 101; *U. S. Rev.,* June 1855; *North Am. Rev.,* July 1858; *Southern Lit. Messenger,* Oct. 1838; H. B. Wallace, *Lit. Criticisms and Other Papers* (1856); F. L. Mott, *A Hist. of Am. Magazines, 1741–1850* (1930); Timothy Hopkins, *John Hopkins, of Cambridge, Mass., 1634, and Some of His Descendants* (1932); J. G. Wilson, *Bryant and His Friends* (1886); *N. Y. Times,* July 8, 1864. The best collection of Morris' poems is the fourth edition published by Scribner (New York, 1860). The following institutions possess Morris papers and manuscripts: Lib. of Cong., Harvard Coll. Lib., Hist. Soc. of Pa., N. Y. State Lib., and the N. Y. Pub. Lib., which has several manuscript copies of *Brier Cliff.*] N.F.A.

MORRIS, GEORGE SYLVESTER (Nov. 15, 1840–Mar. 23, 1889), educator, philosopher, was born in Norwich, Vt., the son of Sylvester and Susanna (Weston) Morris. The family was of English stock traceable to Nazing, Essex, their original migration to America having occurred in 1636. Morris was educated first in the local district school and then in Kimball Union Academy, Meriden, N. H. In the autumn of 1857 he entered Dartmouth College. He seems to have shown marked ability and was regarded as the best scholar of his class. After graduation he taught for one year. He had planned to enter Auburn Theological Seminary, but the loyalties invoked by the Civil War led to his enlistment in the 16th Vermont Volunteers. Here he was given the detached service of mail carrier for the regiment. There is little doubt that his war experience had its broadening effect upon a boy hitherto too much of a recluse and too much dominated by a family atmosphere of a moralistic and pietistic type. At the end of his enlistment he became a tutor at Dartmouth. While teaching, he continued his studies and secured his master's degree. In September 1864, he entered Union Theological Seminary, New York, where he came in contact with liberal thought in the person of Prof. Henry Boynton Smith. The next important step in his education was a sojourn abroad for two years, spent chiefly in study at Berlin. Here he came under the influence of F. A. Trendelenburg, a noted Aristotelian scholar. This period in Europe brought Morris into touch with a different kind of social life and with art in its various forms. In 1868, at the age of twenty-eight, he returned to America, exceptionally equipped for an academic career.

While waiting for an opening in the college field, he was a tutor in the family of Jesse Seligman, a New York banker. After two years, in 1870, he was appointed to the chair of modern languages and literature in the University of Michigan, an institution with which his life was henceforth to be chiefly associated. His primary interest, however, was in philosophy. He undertook the translation of Friedrich Ueberweg's *History of Philosophy* and carried it through in an extremely creditable fashion, publishing the translation in two volumes, in 1871–73. In 1877 came an invitation to become lecturer on the history of philosophy and ethics in The Johns Hopkins University, a position which required his absence from Michigan for only a short time each year. It is worthy of note that he acted as one of the examiners of Josiah Royce, later the famous idealist philosopher of Harvard. This arrangement at Baltimore did not develop the possibilities which had been hoped from it, but it did lead to his transfer at Michigan to the department of philosophy in 1881. He now entered upon a period of scholarly production. In 1885, he was made head of the department of philosophy and henceforth devoted all his energies to his work at Ann Arbor and to his writing. He was in the full tide of his intellectual powers and much was hoped from him when death came to him suddenly, in March 1889, from the effects of a cold caught in an outing. He was only forty-nine years of age when he died. In June 1876 he had married Victoria Celle, who with a son and a daughter survived him.

Morris was a champion of the idealistic movement initiated by Kant and carried farther by Hegel. His was a point of view which was destined to dominate much of English and American thought during the latter part of the nineteenth century. Thus he can be regarded as a co-worker with W. T. Harris [q.v.] and the St. Louis movement on this side of the Atlantic and with men like T. H. Green and F. H. Bradley in England. This idealism was opposed to traditional empiricism and to Spencerian agnosticism. It was speculative and friendly to moral and religious pieties. It was also marked by a strongly developed historical sense. Aside from the translation already referred to, Morris published many articles dealing with art, education, and religion and wrote four books of some significance: *British Thought and Thinkers* (1880), *Kant's Critique of Pure Reason* (1882), *Philosophy and Christianity* (1883), and *Hegel's Philosophy of the State and of History* (1887). These works show careful scholarship. In appearance, Morris was of average height and rather spare of build. His face was sensitive and somewhat ascetic. A picture of him hangs in a room at the University called, in his honor, the Morris seminary.

[R. M. Wenley, *The Life and Work of George Sylvester Morris* (1917), a labor of love by a fellow idealist, which includes letters from Morris' niece and from various friends and colleagues; John Watson, *A Typical New England Philosopher*, repr. from *Queen's Quart.* (Queen's Univ., Kingston, Ont.), Jan. 1918; Morris' Commonplace book, MS., in Univ. of Mich. Library; *Detroit Free Press*, Mar. 24, 1889.]
                                                            R. W. S.

MORRIS, GOUVERNEUR (Jan. 31, 1752–Nov. 6, 1816), statesman, diplomat, was born in the manor house at Morrisania, N. Y., the son of Lewis Morris, second lord of the manor, by his second wife, Sarah Gouverneur. From his grandfather, Lewis Morris [q.v.], the first lord of the manor, and from his father, both of whom had served on the bench and in the assembly of New York, defending the rights of the colonists against the royal governors, he inherited traditions of public service and political autonomy. His mother was a descendant of a Huguenot family driven from France by the revocation of the Edict of Nantes in 1685; and it was doubtless the French strain in Morris' blood that lent to his conversation and his writings the charming combination of graceful manner, pervasive humor, and cynical philosophical detachment which contrasts so noticeably with the rather ponderous and prosaic rectitude of most of his revolutionary associates.

While he was at school in the Huguenot settlement of New Rochelle where he had frequent opportunity to hear his mother's language spoken, the French power was driven from America and the quarrel between the mother country and the English colonies drew rapidly to its crisis. In the year of the Stamp Act Morris entered King's College, New York, from which he graduated in 1768 at the age of sixteen, just as the British government was dispatching regiments of redcoats to Boston to enforce the provisions of the Townshend legislation. But if the atmosphere of that "provincial Oxford" under its Loyalist president affected the young man with either devotion or repugnance to King George and his friends in Parliament, there is nothing in Morris' record to show it. His bachelor's and master's essays were pretty conceits of rhetoric, the one on "Wit and Beauty" and the other on "Love." After a period of study in the office of William Smith, the historian and later the chief justice of the province, Morris was admitted to the bar at the age of nineteen and soon built up a practice which, had it not been constantly interrupted by his political and diplomatic activities, would have put him in the foremost rank of the lawyers of his day. But family influence, a brilliant intellect, unfailing self-assurance, and a remarkable social aptitude combined to make a political career inevitable for Gouverneur Morris. Before he had reached his majority he arrested the attention of the politicians by a vigorous attack upon a bill proposed by the provincial assembly providing for the emission of paper money to liquidate the debt incurred by the French and Indian War.

Until the clash of arms at Lexington made the breach with Great Britain inevitable, Morris was a conservative. As a member of the landed aristocracy he dreaded the social upheaval which he believed would follow in the train of a "democratic" revolution. "I see, and I see it with fear and trembling," he wrote in 1774, "that if the disputes with Britain continue, we shall be under the worst of all possible dominions . . . the domination of a riotous mob. . . . It is the interest of all men, therefore, to seek for reunion with the parent state" (Sparks, *Life*, I, 25). Yet when the breach came, Morris adhered unreservedly to the American cause, at no small cost to his family and social connections. Though his half-brothers Lewis and Richard [qq.v.], were active patriots, his half-brother Staats Long Morris became a major-general in the British army and married the Duchess of Gordon; and for writing even a filial letter to his Loyalist mother, Gouverneur Morris fell for a time under suspicion.

The last colonial legislature in New York under the royal governor adjourned in April 1775, and on May 22 a provincial congress of some eighty delegates met at New York City to assume the responsibility of governing the colony. Morris took his seat in this revolutionary body as a representative from Westchester County, and from the first took a leading part, holding the balance between the radical agitators who wished to inaugurate a reign of terror against the Loyalists and the strong Loyalist element who hoped that the British warships in the harbor would make short work of the revolutionary congress. Realizing that the colonists must present a united front if they were to win their rights from Great Britain either by remonstrance or by force, Morris was a strong defender of the dignity and power of the Continental Congress at Philadelphia. To that body, he insisted, should be entrusted the whole responsibility of the negotiations for reconciliation with England, as well as the control of the issue of paper money by the colonies. He was a nationalist before the birth of the nation.

When Washington arrived in New York with the Continental Army, after the British evacuation of Boston, the courage of the patriots in the congress and the colony was fortified; and when, three months later, Washington read the Declaration of Independence to his soldiers in Bowling Green, New York was ready to accept the responsibility of an independent state. Morris sat in the constitutional convention which met in July 1776, and with John Jay and Robert R. Livingston drafted the frame of government, adopted the following year, under which the state was to live for nearly half a century. His plea for religious toleration was successful, in spite of Jay's proposal to impose a special oath of loyalty on Roman Catholics, but the combined efforts of Morris and Jay failed to move the convention to abolish slavery in the state. Morris also labored hard for the creation of a strong executive, with powers of suspensive veto and of appointment, subject to the ratification of the legislature. He secured the provision for a single governor instead of an executive board,

but the fear of executive tyranny was still strong enough to hamper the governor by the cumbrous faction-ridden councils of revision and appointment which vexed the politics of the state for more than four decades. When the work of the convention was done Morris was appointed on committees, first to organize the new government, then to act as a council of safety until the new governor, George Clinton [q.v.], and the legislature were elected. As a member of the Council of Safety Morris visited the northern army which was resisting the advance of Burgoyne toward Albany. He was an ardent supporter of General Schuyler [q.v.], and with Jay went to Philadelphia on a belated mission to prevent Schuyler from being superseded by Horatio Gates.

Morris' versatility of talent and soundness of judgment were never more in evidence than during the two years 1778–79, when, as a young man in his middle twenties, he sat in the Continental Congress. Financial, military, and diplomatic matters engaged his chief attention. He was chairman of several leading committees and his facile pen was requisitioned for the draft of many an important document, such as the report on Lord North's conciliation offer of 1778 (reprinted in Morris' Observations on the American Revolution, 1779), a public paper on the significance of the treaty with France (Address of the Congress to the Inhabitants of the United States, 1778), the draft of instructions to Benjamin Franklin, first minister of the United States to the Court of Louis XVI, and a comprehensive letter of instructions for the envoy to be sent to Europe to negotiate a treaty of peace and commerce with Great Britain. These instructions, approved in August 1779, six weeks before John Adams was appointed to carry them out, formed the basis of important provisions in the final treaty of peace four years later. On an official visit of inspection to the army at Valley Forge, early in 1778, Morris came into close contact with Washington, to whom he remained devoted for life, and of whose military policies he became perhaps the most able and ardent defender in Congress. Because he refused to enlist the support of Congress for Governor Clinton and his New Yorkers in their claims to Vermont, Morris was defeated for reelection to the Continental Congress in the autumn of 1779. He thereupon transferred his citizenship to Pennsylvania and resumed the practice of law and the cultivation of polite society in the gay city of Philadelphia. He could not remain long out of public life, however. A series of brilliant articles on the Continental finances which he contributed under the signature "An American" to the *Pennsylvania Packet,* February-April 1780, brought him a year later the invitation from Robert Morris [*q.v.*], newly created superintendent of finance, to serve as his assistant. This position the younger Morris (who was not a relative of the Superintendent) held from 1781 to 1785, his most notable service being a plan for a decimal system of coinage (Sparks, *Diplomatic Correspondence,* XII, 81) which was later simplified and perfected by Jefferson and Hamilton.

Morris was elected to the Pennsylvania delegation to the Constitutional Convention of 1787, and took part in the debates of that body more frequently than any other member on the floor, not even excepting James Madison. He favored a strong, centralized government in the hands of the rich and the well-born. He would have a president elected for life, with power to appoint a Senate of life members. The suffrage for presidential and congressional electors should be limited to freeholders: "Give the votes to the people who have no property," he argued, "and they will sell them to the rich" (Farrand, *post,* II, 203). The federal government should have "compleat and compulsive operation" (*Ibid.,* I, 34) throughout the country. Considering that "State attachments, and State importance" had been the "bane of this Country," Morris was willing to see "all the Charters & Constitutions of the States . . . thrown into the fire" (*Ibid.,* I, 531, 553). He strenuously opposed the equal representation of the states in the Senate, and the concessions to slavery in the three-fifths rule and the extension of the slave trade for twenty years. Yet when he was defeated in this extreme program he loyally accepted the bundle of compromises which compose the Constitution, and used his incomparable skill in putting the document into its final literary form.

None of the framers of the Constitution had better claims to high office under it than Gouverneur Morris. But his frankly cynical contempt for "democracy" was a poor asset for the solicitation of votes, and the large interests which he had acquired in various commercial ventures— some of them in association with Robert Morris —tempted him to forsake public life for business. He had purchased the family mansion at Morrisania from his elder brother and after the Convention he returned to his native state to live, but was hardly settled on the old manor when business took him to France as agent for Robert Morris to press a claim against the Farmers-General rising out of a tobacco contract (Sparks, *Life,* I, 265, 308). Business, diplomatic duties, and recreational travel kept him in Europe for

nearly a decade. He arrived in Paris in February 1789, in time to see the curtain rise on the great drama of the French Revolution. His fame as one of the founders of the American Republic had preceded him. Wealth, affability, family connections, a perfect command of the language, and that sprightly intellectual versatility which is so dear to the heart of the cultured French people opened all doors to him, even the doors of the Court.

After Jefferson's return to the United States at the close of 1789, Morris was the most influential American in Paris. He was engaged in plans for opening the tobacco trade on better terms for Americans, for supplying American wheat to the French market, getting the American debt to France transferred to private hands (his own and those of his associates), and selling American lands. These enterprises brought him often before French ministers and committees to urge the modification of the French customs system for the benefit of American trade. His wide range of friendships brought him into contact with leaders of all shades of political opinion, and his immunity from diplomatic responsibility during the first three years of the Revolution allowed him to dispense criticism and counsel freely. The voluminous diary which he kept during these years, supplemented by a diligent correspondence with Washington, Jay, Hamilton, Livingston, King, and other friends at home, furnishes a mine of information and shrewd comment on the men and measures of the Revolution. "You are constantly making remarkable prophecies which turn out to be true," said the French minister to Great Britain to him in July 1790 (*Diary and Letters,* I, 336). The historian Taine, who drew heavily on Morris in his volumes on the French Revolution, ranked him with Arthur Young, Mallet du Pan, and Mounier in value as a source (*Derniers Essais de Critique et d'Histoire,* 1894; 6th ed., 1923, p. 307). Morris believed in a constitutional monarchy for France; but he had little confidence in the capacity of a people without political training to make a workable constitution, and still less in the capacity of Louis XVI and his courtiers to provide the authority, order, and justice necessary for the maintenance of the monarchy. Nevertheless, if the monarchy were to be saved in France, Louis XVI must be saved: and Morris even went so far as to draft and urge the carrying out of a plan for the rescue of the king from his virtual imprisonment in the Tuileries.

Early in 1792 President Washington named Morris as minister to France. The nomination was bitterly fought in the Senate, partly because

of Morris' aristocratic views and his uncon-
ciliatory manners, partly because of the disappointing results of his special mission to London
in 1790–91, when he attempted to settle the controversies over debts, trading-posts, impressments, and commercial privileges left over from
the peace treaty of 1783 (see S. F. Bemis, *Jay's
Treaty*, 1923). Had the senators known that at
the very moment of their deliberations Morris
was deeply engaged in the plot to get the king
out of Paris, they would certainly not have ratified his nomination—even by the narrow margin
of 16 to 11 votes. Still, no one could have represented the United States at Paris better than
Morris did in the stormy years 1792–94. Morris
was the only foreign minister who refused to
leave Paris when the reign of terror converted
the city into a shambles. He stayed in the face
of repeated insults and perils to vindicate with
dignity and courage the full rights of his countrymen, and to offer the asylum of his house to
many a refugee in danger of the guillotine. He
was recalled at the request of the French government in the late summer of 1794, as a *quid
pro quo* for the dismissal of "Citizen" Genet
[*q.v.*] by President Washington. Morris did
not return to America for another four years,
however; he spent the intervening time traveling
in various countries, from Scotland to Austria,
attending to his manifold business interests,
studying the confused European political scene,
and writing letters to the British Foreign Office
reporting his observations (S. F. Bemis, *The
American Secretaries of State*, vol. II, 1927, p.
21; Sparks, *Life*, I, 424, III, 83–87, 89, 93).

Though he was but forty-two years old when
he quitted his ministerial post at Paris, Morris
was practically done with politics. To be sure,
he had what he called in his diary "the misfor-
tune" to be elected in April 1800 to fill an unexpired term in the United States Senate; but
soon after he took his seat as a pronounced Federalist the Democratic-Republicans, under the
leadership of Aaron Burr, got control of the New
York legislature, and Morris was defeated for
reëlection in the autumn of 1802, despite the fact
that he had supported Jefferson's Louisiana policy.
On the expiration of his term the following March,
he retired to the new mansion which he had
built at Morrisania and spent the remaining thirteen years of his life in cultivating his estate and
his friends. On Christmas day, 1809, he married
Anne Carey Randolph of Virginia, sister of
Thomas Mann Randolph [*q.v.*]. One son was
born of this union.

Morris was active in forwarding the plans for
the Erie Canal, and for many years was chairman of the canal commission. His disgust with
the rule of the Republicans at Washington drove
him to unfortunate extremes in his opposition to
the policies of the national government. He denounced the Embargo, condemned the War of
1812, approved the Hartford Convention, and
even advocated repudiating the national debt incurred by the war. "In his hatred of the opposite
party," says one of his biographers, "he lost all
loyalty to the nation" (Roosevelt, *post*, p. 352).
Perhaps this judgment is too harsh, yet it is distressing to see a man whose faith in the American Republic was so robust in the days of the
Constitutional Convention and the mission to
France writing to Timothy Pickering in 1814
that he would be "glad to meet with some one
who could tell . . . what has become of the union,
in what it consists, and to what useful purpose
it endures" (Sparks, III, 312). He rejoiced in
the restoration of the Bourbons in 1814, but died
two years later with his faith in the future of his
own country unrevived.

[Jared Sparks, *The Life of Gouverneur Morris, with
Selections from his Correspondence* (3 vols., 1832);
Anne Carey Morris (his grand-daughter), *The Diary
and Letters of Gouverneur Morris* (2 vols., 1888);
Theodore Roosevelt, *Gouverneur Morris* (1888), in the
American Statesmen series; H. C. Lodge, "Gouverneur Morris," in the *Atlantic Monthly*, Apr. 1886, repr.
in his *Hist. and Pol. Essays* (1892); Adhémar Esmein,
*Gouverneur Morris, un Témoin américain de la Révo-
lution française* (Paris, 1906); Daniel Walther, *Gouverneur Morris, Témoin de deux Révolutions* (1932),
with extensive bibliography and list of manuscript
sources; Jared Sparks, *The Diplomatic Correspondence
of the Am. Rev.* (12 vols., 1829–30); *Am. State Papers,
For. Rel.*, vol. I (1832); Max Farrand, *The Records of
the Federal Convention* (3 vols.,1911); W.W. Spooner,
Hist. Families of America (copr. 1907); MSS. in
Washington Papers, Jefferson Papers, and William
Short Papers, Lib. of Cong.]   D. S. M.

MORRIS, JOHN GOTTLIEB (Nov. 14,
1803–Oct. 10, 1895), Lutheran clergyman, was
born at York, Pa., the youngest of the seven children of John and Barbara (Myers) Morris. His
father, born in Germany at Rinteln on the
Weser, emigrated to America in 1776, enlisted
immediately in the Revolutionary army, and became a commissioned surgeon in the Marquis de
la Rouerie's regiment. On the advice of friends
who feared that the British might capture and
execute him as a deserter, he changed his name
from Moritz to Morris. After the Revolution he
married and settled as a physician at York. John
Gottlieb attended the York County Academy,
entered the College of New Jersey in 1820, and
transferred after two and a half years to Dickinson College, where he graduated in 1823. Having decided to enter the Lutheran ministry, he
studied with the Rev. Samuel Simon Schmucker
[*q.v.*] at New Market, Va., 1823–24, attended
Princeton Theological Seminary, 1825–26, and

Morris

then returned to Schmucker as a member of the first class in Gettysburg Theological Seminary, 1826–27. He was ordained at Frederick, Md., Oct. 15, 1827, and on Nov. 21 of the same year married Eliza Hay, who bore him several daughters and died in 1875. For the rest of his life he lived in Baltimore, where he was pastor of the First English Lutheran Church, 1827–60, librarian of the Peabody Institute, 1860–65, and pastor of the Third Church, 1864–73.

Even as a young man he was one of the leaders of his church. In 1831 he founded the *Lutheran Observer*, which in 1833 he turned over to Benjamin Kurtz [*q.v.*]. He served repeatedly as president of the Maryland Synod and in 1843 and 1883 of the General Synod. For over sixty years he was a director of Gettysburg Seminary and a trustee of Pennsylvania (now Gettysburg) College. He visited the two institutions annually from 1869 to 1894 to give special courses of lectures. In 1846, with Kurtz and S. S. Schmucker, he went to London to attend the first convention of the Evangelical Alliance. In 1851 he and Kurtz founded Lutherville, a suburb of Baltimore, which thereafter was his summer home. He published a number of books and contributed copiously to church papers, his last article appearing on the day of his death. From the theological dissensions that wracked the General Synod he stood, like his closest friend, Charles Philip Krauth [*q.v.*], apart, trusted and sometimes claimed by all factions, but at heart in sympathy with the moderate conservatives.

Morris was also a diligent student of history, bibliography, and natural science. He and his nephew, Charles Augustus Hay [*q.v.*], founded the Lutheran Historical Society and built up its great collection of books, documents, and other materials. He was a frequent lecturer before the Smithsonian Institution and presided for many years over the entomological section of the American Association for the Advancement of Science. His chief publications are: *Life of John Arndt* (1853); *Synopsis of the Described Lepidoptera of the United States* (1862); *Catalogue of the Described Lepidoptera of North America* (1860); *Bibliotheca Lutherana* (1876); *Fifty Years in the Lutheran Ministry* (1878); *The Stork Family in the Lutheran Church* (1886); and *Life Reminiscences of an Old Lutheran Minister* (1896). He retained into his ninety-second year much of the mental and physical vigor of his prime and enjoyed in the Lutheran Church the honors of a Nestor. His common sense, gruff kindliness, and independence of spirit became proverbial. His one extravagance was an indiscriminate passion for joining historical

and scientific societies. Outside his denomination, he was the best-known Lutheran clergyman in the United States. He died at Lutherville and was buried at York, Pa.

[See Morris' *Life Reminiscences of an Old Lutheran Minister* (1896); P. C. Croll, "Rev. John G. Morris, D.D., LL.D.," *Pa.-German*, Feb. 1907; C. J. Hines, "The Beginnings of English Lutheranism in Baltimore," *Luth. Quarterly*, July 1926; the *Sun* (Baltimore), Oct. 11, 1895; A. R. Wentz, *Hist. Ev. Luth. Synod of Md.* (1920) and *Hist. Gettysburg Theol. Sem.* (1926). The first and last of these contain lists of his publications.]

G. H. G.

MORRIS, LEWIS (Oct. 15, 1671–May 21, 1746), chief justice of New York and governor of New Jersey, was the first lord of the manor of Morrisania in New York. His father, Richard Morris, after service in Cromwell's army had become a merchant in Barbados, where he married Sarah Pole, a lady of substantial fortune. In 1670 Richard and his brother Lewis, also a merchant of Barbados, purchased a tract of five hundred acres, known as Bronck's land, just north of the Harlem River in New York. There Richard and Sarah Morris died in 1672, leaving their infant son, Lewis, as the ward of the uncle for whom he had been named. The elder Lewis Morris, having assumed his responsibilities at Bronck's land in 1675, was greatly disturbed because young Lewis developed into a headstrong boy who resented the discipline of the Society of Friends upon which his uncle insisted and defied his guardian's authority. The youth mended his ways sufficiently to warrant forgiveness, however, and in 1691 inherited not only his uncle's equity in the Bronck's land estate, which had been increased to almost two thousand acres, but also 3,500 acres in Monmouth County, N. J.

The sense of being a man of property seems to have sobered Lewis Morris. On Nov. 3, 1691, he married Isabella, daughter of James Graham, attorney-general of the province of New York, and established a home at "Tintern" (later corrupted to "Tinton"), N. J., named in honor of the ancestral home of the Morrises in Monmouthshire. During the following year he was appointed a judge of the court of common right of East Jersey and was named a member of Gov. Andrew Hamilton's council. He vigorously supported Hamilton [*q.v.*], but in 1698 he opposed the appointment of Gov. Jeremiah Basse [*q.v.*] on the ground that the choice had been made by only ten of the required sixteen proprietors. His obstructive tactics resulted in his dismissal from the governor's council.

Although Governor Fletcher had issued royal letters patent in May 1697 erecting Morris' New York estate into the manor of Morrisania, the new lord was less interested in his manorial

213

grant than in the politics of New Jersey. He went to England in 1702 to promote the transfer of political authority from the Jersey proprietors to the Crown. Ambitious to be the first royal governor of the province, he was keenly disappointed when the ministry named Lord Cornbury [q.v.] to be governor of both New York and New Jersey. As a member of Cornbury's council for New Jersey, Morris became an outspoken opponent of that unscrupulous official. Dismissed from the council, he was elected in 1707 to the assembly, where he collaborated with Samuel Jennings in formulating the protest to Queen Anne against Cornbury's reprehensible conduct, which was largely responsible for the governor's removal from office.

After 1710 Morris supported the admirable administration of his friend Robert Hunter [q.v.]. He spent more time in New York, especially after Hunter appointed him chief justice of the supreme court of that province (1715). He continued, however, to serve upon the governor's council for New Jersey under Burnet and Montgomerie. With the administration of Gov. William Cosby [q.v.] the lord of Morrisania found himself once more at odds with the representative of the Crown. When Cosby sought to establish a court of chancery to hear his suit against Rip Van Dam, chief-justice Morris pronounced the whole proceeding illegal, whereupon the governor removed him and appointed James De Lancey, 1703–1760 [q.v.], in his place (Aug. 21, 1733). Morris was elected to the assembly from the town of Eastchester, and joined James Alexander [q.v.] and William Smith in championing the popular cause against the "court party" led by Cosby and De Lancey. In 1734 he presented the assembly's grievances in London, where he failed to secure the removal of Governor Cosby but won a vindication of his own conduct as chief justice.

When the political connection between New York and New Jersey was severed, he became governor of the latter province (1738). Though he had challenged the royal prerogative as represented by Cornbury and Cosby, he permitted no questioning of his own authority. He frequently lectured the provincial assembly on its duties and complained to the lords of trade in 1740 that the legislators "fancy themselves to have as much power as a British House of commons, and more" ("Papers of Governor Lewis Morris," post, p. 123). His administration was marked by bitter and wordy quarrels with the assembly over taxation, support of the militia, issuance of bills of credit, and validity of land titles.

For many years Lewis Morris was an active churchman, serving from 1697 to 1700 as a vestryman of Trinity Church and encouraging the Society for the Propagation of the Gospel in its missionary enterprises. In 1702 he suggested to the Society that New York, as the center of English America, was a proper place for a college and that Queen Anne might be persuaded to grant her farm in New York toward the project. Morris' public career was never touched by the least suspicion of political jobbery. His enemies accused him of inordinate vanity, and no doubt he was fully conscious of his talents, which were great. The contentious spirit, manifest in his youth, grew stronger with the passing years and involved him in controversy until his death, which occurred at "Kingsbury" near Trenton. He was buried at Morrisania with simple rites in accordance with the terms of his will. The bulk of his estate was divided between his son Lewis, who became second lord of the manor, and his son Robert Hunter Morris [q.v.], who inherited the New Jersey property.

[The Papers of Lewis Morris, Governor of the Province of New Jersey," N. J. Hist. Soc. Colls., vol. IV (1852); Robert Bolton, A Hist. of the County of Westchester (2 vols., 1848); William Smith, The Hist. of the Late Province of N. Y. (1829); Archives of the State of N. J., 1 ser. IV–VII (1882–83); E. B. O'Callaghan, Docs. Rel. to the Col. Hist. of the State of N. Y., vols. IV–VI (1854–55); E. M. W. Lefferts, Descendants of Lewis Morris of Morrisania (1907). A portrait of Morris, done by John Watson in 1715, may be a copy of an earlier portrait.]   J.A.K.

MORRIS, LEWIS (Apr. 8, 1726–Jan. 22, 1798), signer of the Declaration of Independence, the eldest son of Lewis Morris, second lord of the manor of Morrisania, and Tryntje (Staats) Morris, was born at Morrisania, Westchester County, N. Y. His father carefully supervised his early education and with some misgiving allowed him to enter Yale College. He completed the work for the degree of A.B. in 1746, the year that his grandfather, Lewis Morris [q.v.], first royal governor of New Jersey, died, and his father became lord of the manor. After being graduated he returned to Morrisania to assist his father in the management of the family estates. The task proved so congenial that for sixteen years he lived the pleasant life of an aristocratic landholder, satisfied with the quitrents and produce from his own and his father's extensive acres. Lacking the acquisitiveness which had characterized earlier generations of his family, he preferred to use wisely that which had already been accumulated rather than to strive to increase the estate. His marriage, Sept. 24, 1749, however, brought him additional wealth, for Mary Walton, his bride, daughter of Jacob and Maria (Beekman) Walton, was a member of a

New York family famed beyond the borders of the province for its possessions.

At the death of his father in 1762 Morris became the third (and last) lord of the manor of Morrisania. After coming into his inheritance he manifested a spirited interest in politics, probably stimulated by his brother Richard [q.v.] who was inclined to support the Livingstons and the Smiths in their quarrels with the De Lanceys. He served one term in the provincial assembly in 1769, but his growing criticism of British policy and the representatives of imperial authority in the province was not indorsed by all his neighbors in the borough town of Westchester, some of whom attributed his ultimate support of the Revolutionary movement to his resentment that he had not been treated more handsomely in the matter of public offices. Whatever his motives, he represented but a minority in his county when he persuaded certain local politicians from the southeastern towns to issue a call (Mar. 28, 1775) for a meeting at White Plains on Apr. 11 to choose Westchester's deputies to the provincial convention. The Philipses, De Lanceys, and Pells strove to defeat the purpose of the gathering, but Morris and his faction carried the day, securing the appointment of eight deputies to attend the convention scheduled for Apr. 20, 1775, in New York City. Morris was named chairman of the delegation, which was instructed to support a resolution to send representatives of the province to the Second Continental Congress. He was eager to be named on the delegation to represent New York at Philadelphia, an honor which came to him through the action of the provincial convention.

Lewis Morris took his seat in the Continental Congress on May 15, 1775. His service there was concerned with the administration of specific business transactions rather than with the determination of general public policies. He was early placed on the committee charged with the selection of the posts to be defended in the province of New York and somewhat later he was assigned to the committee formed to "supply these colonies with ammunition and military stores." Consequently his time was consumed with correspondence over the purchase of tent cloth, the manufacture of sulphur and saltpetre, and the acquisition of gunpowder. In September 1775 he made a trip to Pittsburgh, acting as commissioner for Indian affairs in the Middle Department, and discussed with representatives of the western tribes the possibility of establishing amicable trading relations. Later he became a member of the permanent committee on Indian affairs.

On June 7, 1776, the third provincial congress of New York made provision for an increase in the militia of Westchester County and appointed Morris brigadier-general in command, naming his son major of brigade. Securing a leave of absence from Congress, Morris assumed his military post promptly, apparently believing that it offered greater opportunity for military service than proved to be the case. He was absent from Philadelphia when the Declaration of Independence was finally adopted, but was present in the fourth provincial congress at White Plains on July 9, 1776, when the action of the Continental Congress was indorsed. Later in the year he returned to Congress and signed the Declaration. He participated in the New York campaign during the autumn of 1776, but thereafter his military duties were constantly interrupted by the responsibilities of civil office. He served as county judge in Westchester from May 8, 1777, until Feb. 17, 1778. From 1777 until 1790 he was intermittently a member of the upper house of the state legislature.

At the close of hostilities he retired with the rank of major-general of militia and set about the task of rehabilitating his estates, which had been burned and plundered by the British. Public duty called him frequently from his private affairs. In 1784 he became a member of the first Board of Regents of the University of the State of New York. Two years later he was named a member of the Council of Appointment. In 1788, at the Poughkeepsie convention, he labored valiantly as a member of the Hamiltonian forces in favor of ratification of the federal Constitution, in the drafting of which his much younger half-brother, Gouverneur Morris [q.v.], had had so prominent a part. His greatest joy, however, was to preside over his establishment at Morrisania, which he proudly insisted had been restored to its pre-war magnificence. Tall, handsome, erect despite his years, he remained a representative of the landed aristocracy until his death in 1798.

[Peter Force, Am. Archives, 4 ser. (6 vols., 1837–46), 5 ser. (3 vols., 1848–53); W. C. Ford, ed., Journals of the Continental Congress, 1774–1789, vols. II–VI (1905–06); "Letters to General Lewis Morris," in N. Y. Hist. Soc. Colls., Pub. Fund Ser., vol. VIII (1876); Robert Bolton, A Hist. of the County of Westchester (2 vols., 1848); J. T. Scharf, Hist. of Westchester County, N. Y. (2 vols., 1886); W. W. Spooner, Hist. Families of America (copr. 1907).] J.A.K.

MORRIS, LEWIS RICHARD (Nov. 2, 1760–Dec. 29, 1825), congressman, Vermont statesman, was born at Scarsdale, N. Y., the son of Richard [q.v.] and Sarah (Ludlow) Morris. His father was a landed proprietor of Westchester County and for a decade, chief justice of New York. Gen. Lewis Morris, signer of the

Declaration of Independence, and Gouverneur Morris [qq.v.] were his uncles. He received a common-school education, and during the Revolution saw military service in New York as aide to General Schuyler and General Clinton. From 1781 to 1783 he was first secretary under Robert R. Livingston, 1746–1813 [q.v.], secretary of the department of foreign affairs.

In 1786 he moved to Springfield, Windsor County, Vt. Here he built a stately residence, acquired extensive lands, engaged in business, furthered plans for bridging the Connecticut River and for locking it at Bellows Falls, and became active in politics. He served as selectman (1788), as town treasurer (1790–94), as clerk of the county court (1789–96), and sat in the Bennington convention of 1791 for ratifying the federal Constitution. He was one of the two commissioners to Congress to arrange for the admission of Vermont to the Union, was secretary of the constitutional convention at Windsor in 1793, and from 1791 to 1801 was the first United States marshal in the Vermont district. After serving as clerk (1790–91), the ubiquitous Morris represented Federalist Springfield in the state assembly in 1795, 1796, 1803, 1805, 1806, and 1808. During his first two years of membership he was speaker. In addition to his other offices, he was elected a brigadier-general of the militia in 1793 and promoted two years later to major-general, a position he held until 1817.

His career in Congress was less distinguished. Elected to the House of Representatives by a close margin in 1796, he sat in the Fifth, Sixth, and Seventh congresses. His six years' service was remarkable only for the part he played in making Jefferson president. When the House was choosing between Jefferson and Burr in the contested election of 1800, Jefferson, until the thirty-sixth ballot, received the votes of only eight of the sixteen states. Morris then absented himself, allowing his Republican colleague to cast the vote of Vermont for Jefferson. This act, combined with a similar procedure in the Maryland delegation and a blank ballot from Delaware, gave Jefferson more than the necessary majority. That Morris was a stanch Federalist was shown in his willingness to have Matthew Lyon [q.v.], his Republican colleague, expelled from the House in February 1798, for using objectionable language (Annals of Congress, 5 Cong., 2 Sess., p. 1008).

Some years before his death he retired from politics and business. He was married, first, in 1786, to Mary, daughter of Timothy and sister of President Timothy Dwight, 1752–1817 [q.v.], of Yale. He left her soon after their marriage.

His second wife was Theodotia, daughter of the Rev. Buckley Olcott of Charlestown, N. H., and his third, Ellen, daughter of Arad Hunt of Vernon, Vt. He died at Springfield, Vt., and was buried at Charlestown, N. H.

[W. H. Crockett, Vt., the Green Mt. State (5 vols., 1921), passim; Biog. Dir. Am. Cong. (1928); W. W. Spooner, Hist. Families of America (1907); E. M. W. Lefferts, Descendants of Lewis Morris of Morrisania (1907); Benj. Dwight, The Hist. of the Descendants of John Dwight (1874), I, 224; H. S. Olcott, The Descendants of Thomas Olcott (1874); E. P. Walton, ed., Records of the Governor and Council of the State of Vt., vols. IV–VI (1876–78); W. H. Crockett, ed., State Papers of Vt., vol. III (in 2 vols., 1928–29); A. P. Lee, "Pioneering with Forty Slaves," in Daughters of the Am. Revolution Mag., July 1926; Brattleboro' Messenger, Jan. 7, 1826.] E. W. S.

MORRIS, LUZON BURRITT (Apr. 16, 1827–Aug. 22, 1895), lawyer, governor of Connecticut, was born in Newtown, Conn., the second child of Eli Gould and Lydia (Bennett) Morris. On both sides of his family his ancestry stretched back through colonial days to England. When his father, a farmer with a small fortune, became an invalid, Morris left school at the age of seventeen and became a mechanic. Four years later he was manager of a tool factory at Seymour and had saved enough money to permit him to continue his education. After two years of college preparation at Suffield he entered Yale with the class of 1854. Here he made a reputation as a debater. By the beginning of his senior year he had decided to study law. To shorten the period of his education and to aid his former employer, who had fallen ill, he left Yale in the autumn of 1853 and resumed the management of the factory at Seymour, meanwhile reading law. He completed his legal training by a year at the Yale Law School, being admitted to the bar in March 1856. In 1858 Yale granted him the degree of A.B. as of the class of 1854.

Morris began practice at Seymour but moved in 1857 to New Haven, where he spent the rest of his life. As judge of probate from 1857 to 1863 he gained a reputation for honesty and fairness as well as learning. Upon retirement from the bench and in the interim between various political offices he devoted himself again to his legal practice, which consisted largely of the administration of estates and of service under the courts as appraiser, referee, and arbitrator. His sound judgment and high sense of honor fitted him admirably for this type of work, while a certain shyness made pleading at the bar distasteful to him.

His political career began soon after he left college. For two terms (1855–56), he represented Seymour in the lower house of the state

Morris

legislature, of which body he was again a member in 1870, 1876, 1880, and 1881. In 1874 he served one term as state senator. Thanks to his wise counsel and genial personality, he soon took high rank among his fellow Democrats of the state. In 1888 they nominated him for governor. Morris stood for a revision of the constitution to permit a secret ballot and the election of officers by a plurality rather than a majority of votes. Population had increased rapidly in Connecticut's industrial centers in previous years but no redistribution of seats had followed. Hence the Democratic strongholds were under-represented. Morris failed to obtain a majority of popular votes, and lost the election when the choice was made by a Republican legislature. After a second campaign, in 1890, he seemed to have won the needed majority vote, but the two houses of the legislature disagreed over the accuracy of the ballot count. A tedious and acrimonious dispute followed. The courts failed to settle it and the legislature was deadlocked when the election of 1892 put an end to the matter by the choice of Morris with a clear majority. He carried out the duties of his office for one term with dignity and success, though he failed to effect the constitutional revision which his party desired. Upon retirement he resumed his professional activity, continuing practice until his death by apoplexy, Aug. 22, 1895.

In 1880 Morris was a member of the commission which settled the ancient dispute over the boundary between Connecticut and New York. In 1884 he presided over a commission which remedied various defects in the probate laws of his state. For many years he was an officer of the Connecticut Savings Bank and for a time director of the New York, New Haven & Hartford Railroad Company. His portrait by Thompson in the governor's room at Hartford shows a strong, kindly face. He married, June 15, 1856, Eugenia L. Tuttle of Seymour, by whom he had three sons and three daughters, one of whom, Helen, married Arthur Twining Hadley [q.v.], later president of Yale University.

[For biographical material see *Obit. Record Grads. Yale Univ.*, 1896; S. E. Baldwin, obituary sketch in 66 *Conn. Reports*, App.; J. E. Johnson, *Newtown's Hist. and Historian* (1917); F. C. Norton, *The Govs. of Conn.* (1905); *New Haven Evening Register*, Aug. 22, 1895. For the election contest see "Connecticut," in *Appletons' Ann. Cyc.*, 1888, 1890, 1891, 1892.] P. D. E.

MORRIS, MARY PHILIPSE (1730–1825). [See MORRIS, ROGER, 1727–1794.]

MORRIS, NELSON (Jan. 21, 1838–Aug. 27, 1907), stock-breeder and meat-packer, was born in Hechingen, province of Hohenzollern, near the Black Forest in the southwest part of Ger-

many. He came to America as a boy and reached Chicago in the fifties, looking for work, having walked most of the way from Buffalo, N. Y. He was first employed at the Myrick Stock Yards, one of a number of small stockyards which preceded the building of the Union Stock Yards. Later, by good fortune, he was given work by John B. Sherman, the founder of the Union Stock Yards. As Sherman's protégé he evolved into a head-hog renderer and after several years left Sherman's employ to become a cattle trader on a small scale. His trading tactics were somewhat unique. He was willing to bid on anything and buy anything at a price, usually named by himself. Frequently staying out of the market until late in the week he found his competitors with full coolers and the holders of stale cattle willing to accept any figure within reason to effect a clearance. These were his harvest periods, when with apparent reluctance, protesting that he could not handle more cattle than he had, he cleared the yards. Within a few years he acquired a leading position in the live-cattle trade, not only from Chicago to the Atlantic seaboard, but also in transatlantic shipments.

Morris was not an innovator, but he was a pioneer in transporting dressed beef from Chicago to the Atlantic seaboard. He early secured contracts to supply the French and other European governments with beef and he was also largely instrumental in supplying the commissariat department of the Union troops with livestock during the Civil War. By 1873 his company was earning more than eleven million dollars a year. In 1874 he entered into partnership with Isaac Waixel and for a while the firm was known as Morris & Waixel. Eventually it became Nelson Morris & Company and later simply Morris & Company. The Morris plant was one of the first packing houses to be opened in Chicago at the Union Stock Yards and finally occupied some thirty acres. Outside of Chicago Morris established packing plants at East St. Louis, Ill., St. Joseph, Mo., and Kansas City, Kan. In addition to these interests he owned large cattle ranches in the Dakotas and in Texas and was one of the first to import Polled-Angus and Galloway cattle. At one time he was the most extensive cattle feeder in the world, turning out approximately seventy-five thousand fat bullocks annually from his feedlots.

A man of many contacts, Morris became a director in various corporations. He was interested in a number of banks and other financial institutions, among which was the First National Bank of Chicago, in which he had always been a heavy stockholder and had taken a prominent part as a member of its board of directors. He also invested heavily in real-estate in Chicago. Throughout his life he kept his original simplicity of character. Although he did not care to have his name associated with many charities, he gave of his means for many worthy causes. He established the Nelson Morris Institute of Pathological Research, for the purpose of study and original research in connection with diseases of all kinds, and contributed generously to public institutions, notably to the Michael Reese Hospital. He was married, in 1863, to Sarah Vogel of Chicago. Of his five children, Edward succeeded him as president of Morris & Company, and Ira Nelson entered the diplomatic service of the United States. He died in Chicago.

[See: *Who's Who in America*, 1906–07; P. T. Gilbert and C. L. Bryson, *Chicago and Its Makers* (1929); R. A. Clemen, *The Am. Livestock and Meat Industry* (1923); the *Nat. Provisioner*, Aug. 31, 1907; *Chicago News*, Aug. 27, 1907; *Chicago Tribune*, Aug. 28, 1907. *Who's Who in America* gives Jan. 21, 1839, for date of birth, but the date given in this sketch is correct according to Morris' family.]   R. A. C.

MORRIS, MRS. OWEN [See Morris, Elizabeth, *c.* 1753–1826].

MORRIS, RICHARD (Aug. 15, 1730–Apr. 11, 1810), jurist, was the third son of Lewis Morris, second lord of the manor of Morrisania, and Tryntje (Staats) Morris, and a brother of Gen. Lewis Morris [*q.v.*], signer of the Declaration of Independence. In temperament he was one of the most aristocratic of the Morrises, though, unlike his brother, Staats Long Morris, he finally supported the movement against British authority. Graduating from Yale in 1748, he followed the family tradition and read law in New York City. He was admitted to the bar in 1752, the year his half-brother, Gouverneur [*q.v.*], was born. He soon attained a reputation for legal learning which placed him among the prominent lawyers of the province. His father, who was judge of the court of vice-admiralty, named him deputy and authorized him to hold court in New Jersey. In 1762, under a royal commission issued in the high court of admiralty at London, he became judge of the vice-admiralty court having jurisdiction over New York, Connecticut, and New Jersey, a position which his father and grandfather had filled before him. He played no part in the rising revolt against British authority, but in the autumn of 1775 he tendered his resignation to Governor Tryon, who urged him to retain his post until the political disturbances of the period should be quieted. His hesitation in embracing the Patriot cause was responsible for his citation in June 1776 (Peter Force, *American Archives*, 4 ser. VI, 1368–69),

to the provincial committee to detect conspiracies, as a person of "equivocal neutrality." Nevertheless, when the provincial congress created a high court of admiralty on July 31, 1776 (*Ibid.*, 5 ser. I, 1461), it urged Richard Morris to become the first judge. He declined on the ground that his Westchester estate had been destroyed by the British and his family needed his assistance.

After the new state government had been established, Morris was named by the assembly in 1778 to serve the unexpired term of a senator from the southern district. He remained an inconspicuous member of the upper house until 1780. Meanwhile, he had been appointed in 1779 to succeed John Jay as chief justice of the supreme court of the state. As a member of the New York county delegation at the Poughkeepsie convention of 1788 he worked vigorously for the ratification of the proposed federal Constitution. On several occasions he ably seconded speeches of Hamilton and Jay, though he offered little that was original in his discussion of the ills which would befall the country if New York failed to indorse the work of the Philadelphia convention. The record indicates that he was absent when the final vote resulted in favor of ratification. The following year his friends urged his claims to the Federalist nomination for governor, but a few party leaders opposed him. Hamilton appreciated his ability and his loyalty to Federalist principles, but felt that the Chief Justice was not the best candidate to placate the more moderate anti-Federalists. Accordingly the nomination went to Robert Yates.

In 1790, Morris, having reached the age of sixty, retired from public life. His residence had originally been at Mount Fordham, not far from Morrisania, where he had established his home when he married Sarah Ludlow, June 13, 1759. Following the Revolutionary War he had purchased several farms in the town of Greenburgh and a delightful country-seat in Scarsdale. At the latter place he spent the last twenty years of his life, content to play the rôle of a gentleman farmer. A dignified though somewhat portly representative of the "tie-wig" aristocracy, he seems to have impressed his generation as a man of integrity and extensive knowledge of jurisprudence, attributes which probably explain his elevation to the post of chief justice. He died in Scarsdale in 1810 and was buried at New York in the family vault in Trinity churchyard. His daughter, Mary, wife of Major William Popham, inherited the Scarsdale seat, while the remainder of the estate was divided between his two sons, Lewis Richard [*q.v.*] and Robert.

Morris

Morris

[M. A. Hamm, *Famous Families of N. Y.* (1901), vol. II; Peter Force, *Am. Archives*, 4 ser. (6 vols., 1837–46), 5 ser. (3 vols., 1848–53); E. B. O'Callaghan, *Calendar of Hist. MSS., 1664–1776*, pt. II (1866); E. A. Werner, *Civil List of . . . N. Y.* (1889); Charles M. Hough, *Reports of Cases in the Vice-Admiralty of the Province of N. Y.* (1925); E. C. Benedict, *The Am. Admiralty* (1850); J. C. Hamilton, *The Works of Alexander Hamilton*, II (1850), 478–79; N. Y. *Evening Post*, Apr. 13, 1810.]

J. A. K.

MORRIS, RICHARD VALENTINE (Mar. 8, 1768–May 13, 1815), naval officer and diplomat, was born at Morrisania, Westchester County, N. Y. He was the youngest son of Lewis Morris, 1726–1798 [*q.v.*], signer of the Declaration of Independence, and Mary (Walton) Morris, member of a prominent shipbuilding family. After the Revolution, during which the family suffered severe hardships and losses, Richard became actively engaged in the maritime enterprises with which his relatives were identified; then, on Jan. 24, 1797, he married his cousin, Anne Walton. On June 8, 1798, he was commissioned captain in the United States Navy, and was placed in command of the U.S.S. *Adams,* then under construction at New York. So satisfactory did his services prove that in 1802 he was given command of a naval squadron which was being sent by the United States to operate against Tripoli. The scope of his authority was subsequently extended by instructions to superintend all negotiations of the United States with Tripoli, Tunis, Algiers, and Morocco.

His first attempt to reach Tripoli failed because of adverse winds, and, although he later blockaded the chief port of the enemy, he was unable to conclude peace on favorable terms (Goldsborough, *post,* pp. 203, 204). Moreover, the Emperor of Morocco demanded certain concessions which Morris quite properly refused to grant; whereupon the Emperor, in June 1803, declared war. The declaration was not followed by the seizure of any American vessels, but throughout the period of his Mediterranean command Morris' concentration upon his chief task was lessened by the hostility of Morocco. Additional difficulties arose when the Algerine government refused to commute, from naval and military stores to cash, certain annual payments which the United States had been accustomed to make to Algiers. The Bey of Tunis was also unfriendly, and constantly made threats against the United States. In order to placate him Morris, in February 1803, landed at Tunis. The Bey thereupon refused him permission to depart until Morris had granted certain concessions.

In June 1803 Morris was ordered to relinquish his command and to return to the United States.

In consequence of the subsequent report of a court of inquiry that he had not displayed "the diligence or activity necessary to execute the important duties of his station," his commission was revoked. There were circumstances other than, or in addition to, lack of diligence on his part which contributed to the squadron's ineffectiveness in 1802–03: the armament was small, and some of the vessels were unseaworthy; means of communication were most unsatisfactory; and all the North African rulers were hostile. These factors Morris emphasized in an elaborate and, on the whole, convincing pamphlet, *A Defence of the Conduct of Commodore Morris During His Command in the Mediterranean* (1804). Since he incorporated in this work many official dispatches relative to the whole field of his Mediterranean activities, it is of considerable importance as a source for the study of relations between the United States and the Barbary Powers.

After thus seeking vindication in the public estimation, he retired with his family to Morrisania, where he busied himself with his estate and other private interests until his death. He was survived by his wife and three children, one son having died in 1798.

[E. M. W. Lefferts, *Descendants of Lewis Morris of Morrisania* (1907); W. W. Spooner, *Hist. Families of America* (copr. 1907); C. W. Goldsborough, *The U. S. Naval Chronicle* (1824); G. W. Allen, *Our Navy and the Barbary Corsairs* (1905); C. O. Paullin, *Diplomatic Negotiations of Am. Naval Officers* (1912); R. W. Irwin, *The Diplomatic Relations of the U. S. with the Barbary Powers* (1931); Dispatches: Algiers, Tunis, and Tripoli, in Archives of Dept. of State, Washington, D. C.; N. Y. *Evening Post*, May 15, 1815.]

R. W. I.

MORRIS, ROBERT (Jan. 31, 1734–May 8, 1806), financier of the American Revolution, was born in or near Liverpool, England. The name of his mother is unknown. At the age of thirteen he appeared in Maryland, where he joined his father, also Robert Morris, who was at the time engaged at Oxford on the Chesapeake in exporting tobacco. He was put to school in Philadelphia, but his time there was brief and his acquisitions were scanty. Soon he was in the service of the Willings, shipping merchants, who held a secure position in the commercial as well as in the social life of Philadelphia. By diligence and industry he won the respect and confidence of his employers to such a degree that in 1754 he was made a member of the firm. To Willing, Morris & Company, and its successors under other names, he gave his interest for thirty-nine years and, for a large part of that period, his active direction. The business of the house involved the importation of British manufactures

219

and colonial produce, and the exportation of American goods for which there was a market abroad. It embraced the ownership of ships and a general exchange and banking business. Prudence, with courage and resolution, led to success and the accumulation of wealth, and Morris individually, as well as the firm, held a leading position in the trade of Philadelphia and of America in general when the first crisis was reached in the controversy with Great Britain on the question of taxation. His first appearance in public affairs occurred during the resistance to the Stamp Act, when he was one of those who signed the non-importation agreement of 1765. In October of that year he served on a committee of citizens appointed to force the collector of the stamp tax in Philadelphia to desist from performing the duties of his office. The following year he was warden of the Port of Philadelphia.

Although, when the first Continental Congress met in Philadelphia in 1774, Morris was not yet committed to the "Patriot" cause, he took his place a few months later among its leading representatives. It is related that the die was cast in his case on St. George's Day (Apr. 23), 1775, when, while he and others were attending a dinner of the Society of the Sons of St. George, a courier brought the news of the battle of Lexington. On June 30, 1775, he was made a member of the Council of Safety by the Assembly, and on Oct. 20 was reappointed on the new Council to serve during the ensuing year. His commercial experience was put to use at once; from the beginning he was a member of the committee charged with procuring munitions, and he frequently acted as its banker. In the absence of Franklin, he presided over the Council. In September, a secret committee of the Continental Congress contracted with Willing & Morris for the importation of arms and ammunition. Morris was elected in October to the last Pennsylvania Assembly held under the colonial charter; he was on the Committee of Correspondence, and in November 1775 was sent by the Assembly as a delegate to the Congress.

Within a fortnight after taking his seat he had been appointed to provide two swift vessels to carry dispatches. On Nov. 29 he succeeded his partner, Willing, on the Secret Committee for the procuring of munitions, and two weeks later, was placed on the committee for providing naval armament. He was appointed, Jan. 30, 1776, to the Committee of Secret Correspondence which during the following month drew up the instructions to Silas Deane [q.v.], envoy to France. In March, he was put on a committee to devise "ways and means" and on another to

consider the fortifying of one or more seaports. Meanwhile he continued, as a member of the firm of Willing & Morris, to import supplies for the army, and from time to time was charged with banking business for the Congress. An able business man, he lost no opportunity to make his profit in a deal, or, when acting as broker, to collect his commission. This fact was recognized by his colleagues, but it in no way lessened their confidence in him. In April John Adams wrote to Horatio Gates: "You ask me what you are to think of Robt. Morris? . . . I think he has a masterly Understanding, an open Temper and an honest Heart. . . . He has vast designs in the mercantile way. And no doubt pursues mercantile ends, which are always gain; but he is an excellent Member of our Body" (Burnett, *post*, I, 433).

Morris voted against the Declaration of Independence in July 1776, thinking it premature (see his letter to Joseph Reed, July 21, 1776, Burnett, *post*, II, 19), but he signed it in August, and thereafter wished the whole attention of the country to be given to the prosecution of the war (Sumner, *Financier, post*, I, 197). He was returned to Congress in July by the Pennsylvania convention, and in August and September was directed by the Secret Committee to purchase tobacco for export in exchange for supplies. In November he was chosen to the first Pennsylvania Assembly under the new constitution, but was unable to give much time to its business, and in the following February another member was elected in his stead.

After the flight of Congress from Philadelphia in December 1776, Morris remained in the city to carry on the work of his committee. He bought supplies and borrowed money in the face of appalling difficulties, providing Washington and the leaders in the field moral support and material assistance without which the army must have been dispersed. In the spring of 1777 the Committee of Secret Correspondence became the Committee of Foreign Affairs, and in July was reconstituted as the Committee of Commerce. Through all these changes Morris remained a member, and frequently served as its banker. There is no doubt that he made large profits in his capacity as middleman, but he likewise took great risks, and he "employed for the public all the knowledge or opportunities which he possessed" (Sumner, I, 205). A contemporary observer, writing in October 1777 said that Congress was ruled by Richard Henry Lee, the Adamses, and Robert Morris; and in the following year, characterized Morris as "active, zealous, . . . Bold and enterprizing—of great mercantile knowledge, fertile in expedients & an able financier. Very popular in & out of the Congress; grown extremely rich. . . . Is much Confided in by all the Cabals" (Paul Wentworth, in B. F. Stevens, *Facsimiles of Manuscripts in European Archives Relating to America, 1773–1780,* 1890, nos. 277, 487).

During the winter of 1777–78 the misbehavior of his younger half-brother, Thomas, for whom he had secured appointment as commercial agent of the United States at Nantes, France, caused a temporary misunderstanding between Morris and the commissioners Deane and Franklin, but the matter was cleared up after the death of the young man early in 1778. In March of that year Morris signed the Articles of Confederation on behalf of Pennsylvania, and in August he was made chairman of the congressional committee on finance, serving until the expiration of his term, Nov. 1, 1778.

Being ineligible to reëlection, under the democratic constitution of Pennsylvania, he retired from Congress, but continued his exertions in the Pennsylvania Assembly, to which he was immediately elected, taking his seat Nov. 6. In swearing allegiance to the new constitution he reserved the right to agitate for its amendment. During the following winter Congress was torn by arguments over the conduct of Silas Deane [*q.v.*]. Morris took no part in the controversy, although his sympathies were with Deane, with whom he had had commercial relations. In January 1779, however, Thomas Paine [*q.v.*], through the press, attacked Morris as well as Deane for conducting private commercial enterprises while holding public office, and in Congress, on Jan. 9, Henry Laurens [*q.v.*] made charges of fraudulent transactions against the firm of Willing & Morris. A congressional committee investigated the charges and at Morris' request examined his books, reporting as their opinion "that the said Robert Morris . . . has acted with fidelity and integrity and an honorable zeal for the happiness of his country" (State Dept. MSS., No. 137, App. 36, quoted by Sumner, I, 226). Nevertheless, this incident and the Deane controversy affected the opinion toward Morris of many of his political opponents who, being poor, resented his great wealth. A mass-meeting in May appointed a committee to investigate his conduct, and although he was vindicated by another mass-meeting in July, his popularity had declined sufficiently to permit his defeat at the polls in November. For a year he held no public office, but in November 1780 was again elected to the Assembly, where he served until June 1781.

In the winter of 1780–81 the outlook for the Continental cause was wholly dark, less for want of military strength and capacity of direction in the field than for the means of making these available. The paper currency was not worth the cost of printing it; on further loans in Europe hope might not confidently rest; the states had been called upon for their quotas, but the Union under the Articles of Confederation was a "rope of sand" and no importunities would avail without power of enforcement. The Treasury was empty, credit was gone. As early as February 1780 Pelatiah Webster had advocated the appointment of a single financier to supplant the committees, and the same proposition had been urged in September by Hamilton, who mentioned Morris for the post (H. C. Lodge, *The Works of Alexander Hamilton,* vol. I, 1885, p. 215). That a financial dictator was needed was recognized by Congress in February 1781, and on the 20th, without a dissenting vote, Morris was chosen superintendent of finance.

Before accepting this unique office, in which he would assume a burden such as had rarely been placed on the shoulders of one man, Morris insisted that Congress recognize his right to retain his private commercial connections, and that he be permitted to control the personnel of his department (Sparks, *post,* XI, 350). Congress at first hesitated to grant him the executive independence his task required, but in view of the desperate need of his services, it finally yielded most of what he asked. In his letter of acceptance, May 14, 1781, he expressed the view of the sound commercial banker, saying that the outstanding debt must be funded so that provision for its payment might be made: "The least breach of faith must ruin us forever. . . . Congress will know that the public credit cannot be restored without method, economy, and punctual performance of contracts. Time is necessary for each" (*Ibid., 363*). The letter also contained the assertion: "The United States may command everything I have, except my integrity, and the loss of that would effectually disable me from serving them more" (*Ibid.,* p. 362). By "integrity" he meant the commercial honor of his signature (Sumner, I, 268, note), which time and again had made it possible for him to borrow money for the public cause. Although he began at once to organize his department, he did not formally assume his new duties for some weeks, but remained in the Pennsylvania Assembly in order to win the support of his own state in the policies he projected.

Morris took office with a definite program which included federal taxes laid in specie, to be used in paying interest on the debt; requisitions from the states, to be used to carry on the war; a possible loan from France; and vigilant economy. To save expense to the government he accepted himself the agency of marine, Sept. 8, and on Sept. 12, 1781, was authorized to fit out and employ the ships of the United States. He assumed the task of buying supplies for the armies, abolishing the wasteful system of regimental commissaries. He made himself unpopular with the medical department by investigating alleged extravagance in hospitals. He used notes which circulated only by reason of his own credit, pressed the states in impassioned phrase for their contributions, which he would have furnished him in cash and not in "specific supplies," called for accounting in reference to financial operations in Europe, and put vigor, as well as order, into civil administration. During all this period, however, he was being driven to greater risks and the use of daring financial sleight-of-hand by the desperate need of money. He has been harshly criticized for possessing the "art or abuse, of dazzling the public eye by the same piece of coin, multiplied by a thousand reflectors" (William Johnson, *Sketches of the Life . . . of Nathanael Greene*, 1822, II, 255), but only the possession of that art enabled him to finance the Yorktown campaign which resulted in the surrender of Cornwallis. A timely loan of $200,000 in specie, brought by the French fleet, made possible the formation of the Bank of North America, which opened its doors in January 1782. Morris was one of the heaviest subscribers, strengthening the bank by his personal credit. "I am . . . determined," he wrote to John Jay, "that the bank shall be well supported, until it can support itself, and then it will support us" (Sparks, VII, 440). From it he was able to borrow heavily on behalf of the Congress.

Despite all his efforts to arouse the states to a sense of their obligations, he failed to secure the revenue upon which he had counted, and in January 1783 there was as little prospect of paying the debts he had contracted since taking office as there had been two years before. In despair and disgust with the states and the impotent Congress, he tendered his resignation, Jan. 24: "To increase our debts, while the prospect of paying them diminishes does not consist with my ideas of integrity. I must therefore quit a situation which becomes utterly insupportable" (Sparks, XII, 326). When the fact became public, he was subjected to violent abuse in the press. In May, because there was no one else to undertake the task, he was prevailed upon to retain office until the army was paid and disbanded. A loan secured

by John Adams in The Netherlands carried him through, and in September 1784 he extricated himself from the affairs of the states with his personal fortune unimpaired and the public credit as high as it could be placed under the circumstances.

The following year (October 1785) he was elected to the General Assembly of Pennsylvania for the special purpose of defending the Bank of North America. He and others hired Thomas Paine to write in favor of the Bank, and Morris is said to have paid Mathew Carey for publishing debates on the bank question. Reëlected the following year, he served on the committee appointed to consider the proposition of Virginia that a convention be held for the purpose of regulating commerce, and was a delegate to that convention (Annapolis, 1786). During this period he gave considerable attention to building up his own business. In 1785 he made a contract with the French Farmers-General which gave him the monopoly of the American tobacco trade with France. This circumstance aroused the antagonism of other American tobacco dealers, and had a marked effect on French politics (Nussbaum, *post*).

Convinced by experience that the Republic could not survive without a firm central government, he took his place naturally among the Federalists. Neither Hamilton, nor Washington, nor John Adams better understood the futility of direct democracy, without "checks and balances," or the danger that the new nation would face, if it were to remain a mere league of states. He sat in the convention at Philadelphia in 1787 which framed the Constitution of the United States, and though he took little part in debates or committee work, lent the weight of his opinion to the *Bundesstaat* rather than the *Staatenbund*. He probably agreed in almost every detail with his business associate and former assistant, Gouverneur Morris [*q.v.*], who was the most frequent speaker on the floor of the Convention. Robert Morris was offered and declined the position of secretary of the treasury in Washington's first cabinet, and was one of the two men whom Pennsylvania sent to the United States Senate immediately upon the organization of the new government, serving 1789–95.

Before his term had come to an end, he was deeply involved in land speculations which, at this period, brought so many to disaster. His belief in the potential value of the undeveloped lands west of the settled areas, together with his audacious confidence in himself by reason of the long-continued and unwavering success of his financial projects, especially his daring maneuvers during the Revolution, led to his downfall. He had not foreseen the Napoleonic wars, the paralysis of Europe, and the distress which at such a time must follow in the wake of a great extension of business founded upon borrowing and credit. He had bought great tracts of land in western New York and elsewhere. With a partner he held a large part of the site of the present city of Washington, a wilderness to which after ten years the capital of the Republic was to be removed. The foundations of a really vast fortune were shaken, and all went down together for want of the opportunity to sell what Morris had so hopefully acquired, and of means to pay the taxes upon it and to meet interest charges upon his loans. On the day of collapse, he had in course of construction a palatial marble house in Philadelphia, designed by L'Enfant [q.v.], architect of the Federal City. To a country estate, "The Hills," on the Schuylkill River, he retreated, and there, in February 1798, a small creditor caused him to be arrested. He was taken to "Prune Street," the debtors' prison in the city, in which, in a good deal of misery, not diminished in summer by devastating epidemics of yellow fever, he remained for three years, six months, and ten days. On Aug. 26, 1801, he was released under the federal bankruptcy law, and thereafter was supported by his wife's annuity, secured for her by Gouverneur Morris. He was by this time broken in body and in spirit and ended his days in a small dwelling house in Philadelphia, a nearly forgotten and much pitied man.

Morris' rise to eminence had been as spectacular as his fall. By sheer personal ability he won and merited the affectionate friendship of the most intelligent and discriminating of the public characters of his time. It has been said that few, if any, in the councils of the young nation so fully commanded the respect and confidence of Washington. Certainly there were none to whom the commander-in-chief owed more. The relationship between the two men was one of frank, open-hearted comradeship, though one was noted for a certain austerity of social manner, while the other was markedly accessible, free and radiant of spirit. Morris was the most generous and lavish of hosts, as many had reason to know who came to Philadelphia while that city was the meeting place of Congress and the capital of the country. At the age of thirty-five, Mar. 2, 1769, he married Mary White, of Maryland, daughter of Col. Thomas White and sister of William White [q.v.], who, as Bishop White, was a venerated figure in the American Episcopal Church for a period of fifty

years. Mrs. Morris adorned her husband's house and increased the reputation of his hospitalities.

Morris' writing was terse and spirited, and few of the men who employed their talents in establishing the republic could put so much common sense, with good humor, into English phrase. Sentences from his letters and "Circulars" while he was superintendent of finance ring with eloquence no less than truth, as he pleaded with the states for money with which to prosecute the war. Though he was not a finished public orator, he could at need speak with directness and force, and draw to him attentive listeners. It was of him that William Pierce, a delegate in the Constitutional Convention from Georgia, wrote, while that body was still in session: "He has an understanding equal to any public object, and possesses an energy of mind that few Men can boast of. Although he is not learned, yet he is as great as those who are. I am told that when he speaks in the Assembly of Pennsylvania he bears down all before him" (Farrand, post, III, 91). Of his five sons and two daughters, two sons died before their father. His wife survived him until 1827. Morris died in his seventy-third year, and was buried in "the family vault of William White and Robert Morris," behind Christ Church, Philadelphia.

[Biographies include E. P. Oberholtzer, *Robert Morris, Patriot and Financier* (1903); W. G. Sumner, *The Financier and Finances of the American Revolution* (2 vols., 1891), condensed and abridged in *Robert Morris* (1892). Noteworthy biographical sketches are by Robert Waln, Jr., in John Sanderson, *Biog. of the Signers to the Declaration of Independence*, vol. V (copr. 1825); E. A. Duyckinck, *Nat. Portrait Gallery of Eminent Americans* (1862), vol. I; Joseph Delaplaine, *Delaplaine's Repository of the Lives and Portraits of Distinguished Americans*, vol. II, pt. 1 (1818); A. N. Hart, "Robert Morris," in *Pa. Mag. of Hist. and Biog.*, I (1877), 333; C. H. Hart, "Mary White—Mrs. Robert Morris," *Ibid.*, II (1878), 157. For the ramifications of Morris' tobacco enterprise, see F. L. Nussbaum, "American Tobacco and French Politics, 1783–89," *Pol. Sci. Quart.*, Dec. 1925. For his land speculations see Orsamus Turner, *Pioneer Hist. of the Holland Purchase* (1849) and *Hist. of the Pioneer Settlement of Phelps and Gorham's Purchase and Morris' Reserve* (1851); P. D. Evans, "The Holland Land Company," *Buffalo Hist. Soc. Pubs.*, vol. XXVIII (1924); A. C. Clark, *Greenleaf and Law in the Federal City* (1901). A thirty-four word obituary notice appeared in Duane's *Aurora* and *Poulson's Am. Daily Advertiser* (both Phila.), May 10, 1806. Published source materials include: "Letters to Robert Morris," in *N. Y. Hist. Soc. Colls., Pub. Fund Ser.*, vol. XI (1879); Jared Sparks, *The Diplomatic Correspondence of the Am. Rev.* (12 vols., 1829–30); E. C. Burnett, *Letters of Members of the Continental Congress* (1921 ff.); and the writings of contemporaries. The most important manuscript sources are the diaries and letter-books of Robert Morris and the Papers of the Continental Congress in the Lib. of Cong.]   E. P. O.

MORRIS, ROBERT (c. 1745–June 2, 1815), federal judge and chief justice of the supreme court of New Jersey, was the natural son of Chief Justice Robert Hunter Morris [q.v.] and the grandson of Lewis Morris, 1671-1746 [q.v.], first lord of the manor of Morrisania, who became royal governor of the province of New Jersey in 1738. He was born at New Brunswick, probably in 1745. His father died suddenly in 1764, but Robert was able to complete his legal studies, in which he manifested that aptitude which had characterized the Morrises for several generations. Admitted to the bar in September 1770, he was licensed as a counselor three years later. Though he had never presided over a court, he was chosen by the joint ballot of the legislature in 1777 as chief justice of the newly created supreme court of the state. The difficult task to which he was called had already been declined by Richard Stockton and John DeHart. Upon Morris, versed only in the theory of judicial procedure, devolved the responsibility of formulating rules for the high court of the state and of organizing county courts and the court of oyer and terminer. Having entered upon his duties in February 1777, he was instructed by the council to hold a term of oyer and terminer in Sussex County in May. With his customary energy he carried out instructions, reporting in vigorous language to Gov. William Livingston the difficulty of holding court with inexperienced officers and with associate judges who were "but reputable farmers, doctors and shopkeepers" (Elmer, post, pp. 267–69). Zealous and fearless in meeting the demands from various parts of the state for the institution of courts, he was angered when the legislature inquired whether he was sufficiently diligent in the performance of his duties. He brusquely replied to his critics: "I accepted my present office to manifest my resolution to serve my country. . . . Whenever the legislature think they can fill it more advantageously the tenor of my commission shall not disappoint them" (Ibid.). The exacting nature of his work, aggravated by the legislators' interference, soon proved irksome to his independent spirit and he tendered his resignation in June 1779. Brief though his term had been, it had demonstrated his competence upon the bench and had marked the translation into reality of the plan for a system of state courts.

For a dozen years Morris practised law in New Brunswick, accumulating in the process a considerable estate in land. He was a member of the Protestant Episcopal Church and served the Christ Church parish almost twenty years as warden. His reputation as a jurist persisted and, being in the good graces of the Federalists of the state, he was recommended for a place on the federal bench. When the United States dis-

trict courts were organized under the Judiciary Act of 1789, President Washington named him judge in the New Jersey district, a position which he filled acceptably for twenty-five years. The docket in his court could not have been heavily burdened, for his prolonged absences, occasioned by serious illness, did not seem to interfere with the administration of justice. He died at New Brunswick on June 2, 1815.

[Archives of the State of N. J., 2 ser. III (1906); L. Q. C. Elmer, "The Constitution and Government of . . . New Jersey," N. J. Hist. Soc. Colls., vol. VII (1872); W. W. Clayton, Hist. of Union and Middlesex Counties, N. J. (1882); E. Q. Keasbey, The Courts and Lawyers of N. J., 1661–1912 (1912), vol. II; W. H. Benedict, New Brunswick in Hist. (1925); Proc. N. J. Hist. Soc., July 1920, Apr. 1921; N. Y. Evening Post, June 5, 1815.]   J.A.K.

MORRIS, ROBERT (Aug. 31, 1818–July 31, 1888), Masonic writer and lecturer, was born near Boston, Mass. His parents were schoolteachers, and he was educated for the same vocation and followed it for a number of years. Shortly after reaching his majority he left New England and settled in Oxford, Miss., where he became principal of Mount Sylvan Academy. On Aug. 26, 1841, he married Charlotte Mendenhall, who resided near Oxford. Three sons and three daughters were born to them. He moved to Lodgeton, Ky., in 1853, to La Grange in 1860, and later lived for some time in Louisville. In 1868 he visited the Holy Land and made extensive researches which are embodied in his work Freemasonry in the Holy Land (1872). For a brief period he was president of the Masonic College at La Grange. In addition to his interest in education, he was an ardent geologist and numismatist and at one time was secretary of the American Association of Numismatists. He was also an honorary member of several archeological societies. His contributions to the scientific and religious press were numerous, and he enriched Sunday-school literature with scores of odes, sketches, addresses, and songs. Many of his poems were composed in stage coaches, railway carriages, steamboats, and on horseback. The most famous of these is "The Level and the Square."

His personality is best expressed by one who referred to him as "lank as a rattlesnake and as swift at a witty stroke; nervous to the last degree; frightfully dyspeptic; extremely fond of nature and an indefatigable collector of shells, arrow-heads and eccentric stones; a glutton for books; fluent as the river and generous as the sea; speaking in all things from the heart, amiable and generous" (quoted by Kenaston, post, p. 73). The fact that a contemporary writer had the same name caused him to shorten his first name to Rob, his reason being that when the other Robert wrote anything which was not well received he got the blame for it.

He was made a Master Mason in Oxford Lodge, No. 33, Oxford, Miss., on July 3, 1846. Owing to changes of residence, his lodge membership was transferred, and in 1860 he is recorded as a Past Master of Fortitude Lodge, No. 47, La Grange, Ky. He was Grand Master of the Grand Lodge of Kentucky, 1858–59, held membership in other rites of Freemasonry, and has been called the founder of the Order of the Eastern Star. In his extensive travels he delivered thousands of lectures, and was crowned "Poet Laureate of Freemasonry" in the Masonic Hall, New York City, Dec. 17, 1884. To the Masonic fraternity he gave a new literature, the result of painstaking research, which has permanent value. Among his publications, besides innumerable articles in magazines, are *The Lights and Shadows of Freemasonry* (1852); *Life in the Triangle* (1854); *A Code of Masonic Law* (1856); *The History of Freemasonry in Kentucky* (1859); *Tales of Masonic Life* (1860); *The Masonic Martyr, the Biography of Eli Bruce* (1861); *Masonic Odes and Poems* (1864); *The Dictionary of Freemasonry* (1867); *Freemasonry in the Holy Land* (1872); *William Morgan; or, Political Anti-Masonry, Its Rise, Growth, and Decadence* (1883); *The Poetry of Freemasonry* (1884). He was the editor of a number of Masonic periodicals and publisher of the Universal Masonic Library in thirty volumes. His death occurred at La Grange, Ky., where he was buried with all honors of Masonry.

[T. R. Austin, *The Well Spent Life, the Masonic Career of Robert Morris* (1878); L. V. Rule, *Pioneering in Masonry, the Life and Times of Rob Morris* (1922); J. M. Kenaston, *Hist. of the Order of the Eastern Star* (1917); *Voice of Masonry and Family Mag.*, Sept. 1888; biographical notice in Morris' *Poetry of Freemasonry* (ed. in 1895); *Courier-Jour.* (Louisville, Ky.), Aug. 1, 1888.]   W. L. B.

MORRIS, ROBERT HUNTER (c. 1700–Jan. 27, 1764), chief justice of New Jersey and governor of Pennsylvania, was born at Morrisania, N. Y., the second son of Lewis Morris, 1671–1746 [q.v.], and Isabella (Graham). He received a "liberal education," as that term was understood in the eighteenth century, and was trained in political affairs by his father, whose argumentative ability he seems to have inherited. When Lewis Morris was appointed governor of New Jersey in 1738, the name of his son, Robert, appeared on the list of councilors. Within the year Governor Morris named Robert as chief justice of the province, his commission to run "during good behavior in same," though the war-

rant of the previous incumbent, Robert L. Hooper, had been phrased "during the royal pleasure." As chief justice, Morris "stuck to punctuality in the forms of the courts, reduced the pleadings to precision and method, and possessed the great qualities of his office, knowledge and integrity in more perfection than had often been known in the colonies" (Smith, *post*, p. 439).

While his father was governor, Morris belligerently defended the royal prerogative, using his influence on the council with telling effect. He became a member of the council of proprietors for East Jersey in 1742 and was soon one of the most active in protecting the interests of the landholders of the province. His great concern after 1745 was for the speedy suppression of the riots occasioned by disputes over land titles and by resentment on the part of tenants against the proprietors. Feeling that Gov. Jonathan Belcher [q.v.] was too lenient with the rioters, Morris secured a power of attorney from the East Jersey proprietors and sailed for England in 1749. Several projects besides the settlement of the land problem were in his mind. During the five years that he remained in England he worked against the plan to reunite the provinces of New York and New Jersey, tried to collect the arrears of salary which the assembly refused to pay his father's estate, and urged his friends to help him secure a suitable executive post in America. In 1754 John and Thomas Penn offered him the governorship of Pennsylvania, which he accepted.

The Pennsylvania interlude was far from happy for Governor Morris. At the outset he clashed with the assembly over his refusal to publish his instructions. The ill feeling thus engendered cropped out in a controversy concerning funds to be devoted to the protection of the frontier against the French and their Indian allies. As the assembly would not vote the money in accordance with the proprietors' instructions, Morris failed to secure adequate support for the militia and was bitterly denounced by the western counties. So ably did Benjamin Franklin present the cause of the legislators that the Governor finally gave up the struggle and resigned in 1756.

Returning to New Jersey, Morris resumed his post as chief justice, for his resignation, presented in 1754, had never been accepted. In 1757, however, he visited England, and during his absence William Aynsley was named chief justice and served until July 1758. When Morris announced his intention of resuming his judicial duties again, he learned that Nathaniel Jones, an unknown London barrister, had been appointed to succeed Aynsley. Jones presented himself in March 1760, but Judge Samuel Nevill of the supreme court ruled that his credentials were not satisfactory, since the commission of Robert Hunter Morris had never been surrendered. Since Jones did not contest the matter, Judge Morris remained on the bench until his death.

Despite his disputatious temperament, Morris was a great favorite socially. Of handsome countenance and imposing presence, he charmed his acquaintances by his facile conversation and compelled their admiration by the wide range of his interests. He was still active in public affairs when he dropped dead at a dance given near his home in Shrewsbury, N. J. Though he had never married, he had at least three natural children, one of whom, Robert Morris, c. 1745–1815 [q.v.], inherited most of his considerable estate.

[R. S. Field, "The Provincial Courts of New Jersey," N. J. Hist. Soc. Colls., vol. III (1849) ; Samuel Smith, The Hist. of the Colony of Nova-Cæsaria or N.J. (1765) ; Benjamin Franklin's autobiography, in A. H. Smyth, The Writings of Benjamin Franklin, vol. I (1905) ; Pa. Archives, 4 ser. II (1900) ; Archives of the State of N. J., 1 ser. V–IX (1882–85), and XXXII (1928), p. 298 ; E. B. O'Callaghan, Docs. Rel. to the Colonial Hist. of the State of N. Y., vol. VI (1855) ; W. W. Spooner, Hist. Families of America (copr. 1907) ; N. J. Hist. Soc. Colls., vol. IX (1916).]   J. A. K.

MORRIS, ROGER (Jan. 28, 1727–Sept. 13, 1794), British soldier and Loyalist, was the third son of Roger Morris of Netherby, Yorkshire, and of his wife Mary, daughter of Sir Peter Jackson. First commissioned in 1745, he accompanied Braddock to Virginia in 1755 as captain in the 48th Regiment and was wounded at the Monongahela. After serving as aide-de-camp to Generals Braddock, Shirley, and Webb successively, he became major of brigade in March 1757, attached to the staff of Webb, his intimate friend, at Fort Edward. Promoted to a belated majority in the 35th in February 1758, he served at Halifax during the summer, accompanied Monckton up the River St. John in September, and remained as commanding officer at Fort Frederic until the following spring. During the next two years in Canada he commanded detachments of grenadiers at the siege of Quebec and at Montreal, took part in the battle of Sillery, 1760, and became lieutenant-colonel of the 47th in May 1760.

In 1764 Morris resigned from the army to assume an entirely different station and mode of life as the husband of one of the wealthiest heiresses in New York, Mary Philipse (July 3, 1730–July 18, 1825), daughter of Frederic Philipse, second lord of Philipse Manor. Charming

"Captain Polly," adored by half the officers in New York, had given her hand to Morris, "a Ladys Man, always something to say," in January 1758, and with it 51,000 acres in Dutchess County, with 156 tenants, a rent-roll worth nearly £1,000 a year. For the next ten years Morris lived in New York, either at the town house on Stone Street, at the impressive Morris Mansion (later the Jumel Mansion) which he built in Harlem, or, for two months in the year only, in a comfortable "loghouse" on Lot Number Five. Though he paid little attention to his estates, he was regular in his attendance at the provincial council, of which he became a member in 1765. After the battle of Lexington he went to England, unwilling to commit himself to either side, and though he returned in December 1777, could not prevent the confiscation of all his property by an act of attainder of the state legislature, in which both he and his wife were named. Even then he took no commission in the British army, serving only as inspector of the claims of refugees with the temporary rank of colonel, and as councilor under Governor Robertson. In 1783 he left America forever with his wife, two sons, and two daughters, and settled in Yorkshire. He or his family subsequently received as compensation from the British government a fourth of the value of their American estates, and his heirs, who by Mary Philipse's marriage settlement had a right to those estates and had not been themselves attainted, sold their claims to John Jacob Astor in 1809 for £20,000. Both Roger Morris and his wife were buried in the churchyard of St. Savioursgate, York.

[See The Northcliffe Collection (Ottawa, 1926) ; W. O. Raymond, The River St. John (1910) ; John Knox, An Hist. Jour. of the Campaigns in North America (3 vols., 1914–16), ed. by A. G. Doughty for the Champlain Soc.; E. H. Hall, Philipse Manor Hall at Yonkers, N. Y. (1912) ; W. H. Shelton, The Jumel Mansion (1916). In the Public Record Office, London, A. O. 12:21, ff. 185 sqq. is the examination of Morris' claim by the Commissioners . . . for enquiring into the Losses and Services of the American Loyalists.]   S. M. P.

MORRIS, THOMAS (Jan. 3, 1776–Dec. 7, 1844), senator from Ohio, was the fifth child in the family of twelve children of a Baptist preacher of Welsh descent, Isaac Morris, and of Ruth (Henton) Morris and his wife. He was the descendant of Thomas Morris who emigrated from England to Massachusetts in 1637. Soon after his birth in Berks County, Pa., his parents settled near Clarksburg, now in West Virginia. With the exception of three months in a common-school he was educated by himself and by his abolitionist mother and father who had a library composed of three Bibles, four New Tes-

taments, a work on elocution, and a few other books. In 1795 he moved to Columbia, now part of Cincinnati, Ohio, where he studied and worked as clerk in a store for the Rev. John Smith, one of the first two United States senators from Ohio. He married Rachael Davis of Welsh descent on Nov. 19, 1797, and moved to Bethel, Ohio, in 1804, where he established his permanent home. He became the father of three daughters and eight sons, one of whom preached at his funeral in the Bethel cemetery and two of whom were elected later to Congress as Democrats. While leading the hard life of a frontier brick-maker he read Blackstone at night by the light of his log-cabin fireplace.

He entered politics after his admission to the bar in 1804 and was elected to the state legislature, where in 1806 he began fifteen terms of service as a state legislator, in the House of Representatives for the fifth, seventh, ninth, tenth, and nineteenth sessions from 1806 to 1821, and in the Senate for the twelfth, thirteenth, twentieth, twenty-first, twenty-fourth to twenty-seventh, thirtieth, and thirty-first sessions from 1813 to 1833. He was chosen judge of the state supreme court in 1809, but later legislation prevented his qualifying. In 1828, with Samuel Medary [*q.v.*], he established the *Ohio Sun* to support Andrew Jackson for president. After his defeat for Congress in 1832 the Ohio legislature elected him United States senator to serve a full term, 1833–39. He was an able speaker in spite of his diffidence. He wielded great power over juries with speeches filled with Biblical quotations. He was a stanch partisan but not of the pro-slavery wing of the Democracy. True Democracy meant to him the supremacy of the Bible in a society wherein men harmonized their lives with the laws of nature. His political doctrines were determined by his legalistic and moralistic temperament. He opposed lotteries, chartered monopolies, and imprisonment for debt, and he advocated temperance, the prohibition of alcohol, freedom of conscience in religion, education at state expense, and the recall of judges. As a Unionist he denounced nullification and secession as revolutionary and destructive of American liberty; as an expansionist and abolitionist he boldly opposed the extension of slavery. He believed slavery was a moral evil, a national calamity, the greatest national sin. At a time when it was political suicide in Ohio to be an aggressive radical he incurred the condemnation of the South and lost the support of tactful politicians in his own state by his introduction of petitions in the United States Senate to abolish slavery in the District of Columbia. Probably his greatest speech was a defense of the abolitionists that he made in the Senate on Feb. 9, 1839, in answer to a severe condemnation of their principles and tactics by Henry Clay (*Congressional Globe,* 25 Cong., 3 Sess., 180–88, app., 167–75). In 1840 he went home ostracized, contemned, and martyred to his cause. The threats of mobs and riotous disturbances did not deter him in his anti-slavery crusade from 1841 to 1844. He was active in the campaign and election of 1844 as the nominee for the vice-presidency of the Liberty party and died of apoplexy soon afterward. His greatest contributions were made as chairman of judiciary committees on which he served for many years and as the abolitionist example and preceptor of the Ohio trio, Salmon P. Chase, Joshua R. Giddings, and Benjamin Wade.

[B. F. Morris, *The Life of Thomas Morris* (1856); C. B. Galbreath, *Hist. of Ohio* (1925), vol. II; *The Biog. Cyc. and Portrait Gallery . . . of the State of Ohio,* vol. I (1883); Henry Howe, *Hist. Colls. of Ohio,* centennial ed., vol. I (1889); J. B. Swing, "Thomas Morris," *Ohio Arch. and Hist. Soc. Quart.,* Jan. 1902; *Ibid.,* July 1922.]

W. E. S—h.

MORRIS, THOMAS ARMSTRONG (Dec. 26, 1811–Mar. 22, 1904), engineer, was born in Nicholas County, Ky. His father, Morris Morris, and his mother, Rachel (Morris) Morris, were cousins, grandchildren respectively of two brothers, James and John Morris, emigrants from Wales to Virginia. Thomas was the third son among their nine children. In 1821 the family moved to Indianapolis, where Morris Morris served on the commission which erected the state house, and as state auditor (1829–44). At the age of twelve, Thomas began work with a printer. Three years afterwards he entered a private school conducted by Ebenezer Sharpe, and finally, July 1, 1830, the United States Military Academy, West Point, N. Y. He graduated four years later, was made a brevet second lieutenant of artillery, and was commissioned second lieutenant, Feb. 25, 1835, but resigned the following year.

Settling in Indianapolis as a civil engineer, he was first given charge of the construction of the Indianapolis section of the Central Canal, which was completed from Broad Ripple into the city. He is also credited with the suggestion and execution of the "state ditch," which saved Indianapolis from recurrent floods and greatly lessened the prevalence of fever incidental to its early settlement. Meanwhile, the state began building the first of the railroads (the Madison & Indianapolis), which ultimately supplanted all the canals within its borders as means of transportation. Morris was chief engineer of

this enterprise from 1841 to 1847, during which time it passed from the state into private hands. He finished its construction from North Vernon to Indianapolis, and conceived and carried through the plan of financing construction by taking subscriptions in land and issuing scrip on this security for payment of construction expenses. From 1847 to 1852 he was chief engineer of the Terre Haute & Richmond Railroad (now part of the Pennsylvania) and of the Indianapolis & Bellefontaine, Ohio (now part of the Big Four). Early in this period he prepared estimates and reports on the Peru & Indianapolis Railroad. He was chief engineer (1852–54) and president (1854–57) of the Indianapolis & Cincinnati (now part of the Big Four); president of the Indianapolis & Bellefontaine (1857–59); chief engineer of the Indianapolis & Cincinnati (1859–61). His services on these different roads suggested to Morris the idea of a union depot at Indianapolis, which he planned and built.

At the outbreak of the Civil War, Gov. Oliver P. Morton [q.v.] appointed him state quartermaster-general. On Apr. 27, 1861, the president commissioned him brigadier-general, and in the last week of May his brigade was ordered into the western part of Virginia by Maj.-Gen. George B. McClellan, who was then in command of the department of the Ohio. Morris insisted upon mustering in volunteer regiments of Western Virginia Unionists (*Official Records*, 1 ser. II, 673), in which move he was supported by McClellan, and the troops did good service. He drove the Confederate forces back from Philippi on June 3, and was well started in the task of driving them out of Western Virginia when McClellan took command in person of the campaign along the Great Kanawha. On July 3, McClellan harshly refused reinforcements which Morris had requested (*Ibid.*, 208–09), and on July 14, in his report, criticized him for not pursuing the Confederates more vigorously at Laurel Hill. A slight pursuit action at Carrick's Ford, July 13, virtually brought Morris' services to an end, since the term of enlistment of his regiments expired in July. He was honorably mustered out July 27. He expected another commission, but none came for more than a year. Believing his services were not really wanted, he declined a commission as brigadier-general in September 1862 and another as junior major-general in October of that year.

As chief engineer of the Indianapolis & Cincinnati Railroad (1862–66), he built the Lawrenceburg-Cincinnati section. From 1866 to 1869 he was president and chief engineer of the Indianapolis & St. Louis, and constructed the road between Terre Haute and Indianapolis. For the three following years he was receiver of the Indianapolis, Cincinnati, & Lafayette Railroad. On Nov. 19, 1840, he married Elizabeth Rachel Irwin, daughter of John Irwin of Madison: they had five children. He accumulated a considerable estate and the twenty-acre tract on which he built his home remained intact for many years after it was entirely surrounded by the growing city. He died at San Diego, Cal., at the age of ninety-three, and was buried at Crown Hill Cemetery, Indianapolis.

[B. R. Sulgrove, *Hist. of Indianapolis and Marion County, Ind.* (1884); *Indianapolis Journal*, Mar. 24, 1904; *Report of the Adjutant General of the State of Ind.*, vol. II (1865); Catherine Merrill, *The Soldier of Ind. in the War for the Union* (1866), vol. I; *War of the Rebellion: Official Records (Army)*, 1 ser. II; F. B. Heitman, *Hist. Reg. and Dict. U. S. Army* (1903), vol. I; G. W. Cullum, *Biog. Reg. Officers and Grads. U. S. Mil. Acad.* (3rd ed., 1891), vol. I; *A Biog. Hist. of Eminent and Self-Made Men of the State of Ind.* (1880), vol. II; *Thirty-Fifth Ann. Reunion Asso. Grads. U. S. Mil. Acad.*, June 14, 1904.]
C. B. C.

MORRIS, WILLIAM HOPKINS (Apr. 22, 1827–Aug. 26, 1900), soldier, author, was born in New York City, the son of George Pope Morris [q.v.] and Mary Worthington Hopkins. After receiving a common-school education he attended West Point, graduating July 1, 1851, and being commissioned a second lieutenant of the 2nd Infantry. His permanent commission as second lieutenant was awarded Dec. 3, 1851. He served on garrison duty at Forts Columbus and Wood, New York, that year, and at Fort Yuma, Cal., in 1852 and 1853. Portions of the next two years he spent on recruiting service, after which he resigned from the service, Feb. 28, 1854, and aided his father in editing the *Home Journal*. In 1859 he invented a repeating carbine for which he and Charles Liston Brown received a patent in 1860. On Aug. 20, 1861, he was appointed staff captain, assistant adjutant-general, on the staff of Gen. J. J. Peck, in the defenses of Washington. He served until the following May, when he was present at the siege of Yorktown and the battle of Williamsburg. At the battle of Fair Oaks (May 31–June 1) he was commended and on Sept. 2, 1862, was elected colonel, 135th New York Infantry, which regiment soon became the 6th New York Heavy Artillery. He was appointed brigadier-general, United States Volunteers, Nov. 29, 1862, and his command was stationed at Maryland Heights, near Harpers Ferry, Va., until the summer. In July 1863, his command joined the Army of the Potomac and was in reserve at the battle of Gettysburg. Following this, he was in small operations in the vicinity, and was later given a brigade in the 3rd Division, III Corps. His brigade took part in the Bristoe, Va., campaign of October and in the advance of the Union forces to the Rappahannock in November.

On Apr. 30, 1864, Morris' brigade was transferred to the VI Corps. It engaged in the campaign from the Rapidan to the James and formed part of the forces operating against Richmond. His work at the battle of the Wilderness was, on the 13th of March, 1865, rewarded by appointment as major-general of volunteers, for "gallant and meritorious services." On May 9, 1864, he was wounded at Spotsylvania Court House and was sent to Washington on sick leave until July, when he served on courts-martial and military commissions until mustered out on Aug. 24, 1864. In the same year he published *Field Tactics for Infantry,* followed some time later by *Tactics for Infantry, Armed with Breechloading or Magazine Rifles* (1882). While neither of these was revolutionary, both were sound attempts at bettering the clumsy infantry tactics of the period and provided one of the steps in the evolution of the squad formation. In 1866 Morris was appointed colonel, division engineer, New York National Guard, and the following year was appointed a brevet major-general of that organization. In 1867 and 1868 he was delegate to the New York state constitutional convention, from Putnam County, and was a member of the military committee. In 1869 he was appointed commissary general of ordnance, New York National Guard, with permanent rank of brigadier-general in addition to his brevet rank. He was married in 1870, to Catharine (Hoffman) Hyatt, daughter of Dr. Adrian Hoffman of Westchester County, N. Y., and widow of Charles C. Hyatt. After his marriage he retired to his estate, "Briarcliff," New York. He died at Long Branch, N. J.

[G. W. Cullum, *Biog. Reg. . . . U. S. Mil. Acad.* (3rd ed., 1891), vol. II; *Ann. Reunion Asso. Grads. U. S. Mil. Acad., June 8, 1901*; F. B. Heitman, *Hist. Reg. and Dict. of the U. S. Army* (1903), vol. I; *Ann. Report of the Adj.-Gen. of the State of N. Y.,* 1866-69, 1896; *War of the Rebellion: Official Records (Army)*; *Documents of the Convention of the State of N. Y., 1867-68* (5 vols., 1868); correspondence with Commandery of the State of N. Y., Military Order of the Loyal Legion.]   D. Y.

MORRISON, JOHN IRWIN (July 25, 1806–July 17, 1882), educator, son of Robert and Ann (Irwin) Morrison, was born near Chambersburg, Franklin County, Pa. Of his boyhood little is known except that he received instruction from local clergymen. In 1824 he moved with his parents to Washington County, Ind., where he soon found employment as a teacher at Wal-nut Ridge. Early in April 1825 he was placed in charge of the Salem Grammar School which he conducted successfully until September 1827, when he resigned to enter Miami University at Oxford, Ohio. With two years' advanced credit, he fulfilled the requirements of the junior and senior years in one year and received the degree of A.B. in 1828. Immediately after graduation he returned to Salem, Ind., to take charge of the first Washington County Seminary, in the fall of 1828. Here, according to contemporary accounts, he achieved a distinguished reputation as a teacher, attracting students from many counties throughout the state. In 1832 he married one of his former pupils, who had just returned from the Friends' School at Westtown, Pa., Catherine Morris, daughter of Benoni and Rebecca (Trueblood) Morris. With her assistance he established in 1835 the Salem Female Institute, which he conducted as a private venture until 1839, when he was elected state representative.

At the end of his term in the House, in 1840, Morrison accepted an appointment as professor of ancient languages at Indiana University, resigning in 1843 to teach again in the Washington County Seminary. From 1847 to 1850 he served as state senator and was appointed senatorial delegate to the constitutional convention of 1850-51. His knowledge of educational matters was recognized at once in his election as chairman of the committee on education, in which position he drafted the article on education. He was also the author of Section 8 of the law which created the office of state superintendent of public instruction, June 14, 1852, and helped to secure the passage of the laws which provided for the establishment of teachers' institutes (1865), and which created the office of county superintendent of schools (1873). He served as trustee of Indiana University, 1846-49, 1850-55, and as president of the board in 1854-55 and from 1875 to 1878. From 1856 to 1860 he was treasurer of Washington County. During these busy years, he found time to engage in various newspaper ventures. In 1847 he purchased the *Washington Republican,* which he renamed the *Washington Democrat* (now the *Salem Democrat*). Three years later he founded, with J. F. Baird, the *Salem Locomotive,* which was short-lived. In May 1861, he became editor of the *Salem Times,* changing its name, in June of that year, to the *Union Advocate.* His editorial career came to an end with his appointment, by President Lincoln, as commissioner of enrolment, in 1863, with an office in Jeffersonville. He was state treasurer, 1865-67, changing his residence to Indianapolis at the beginning of his term. In 1872 he removed to Knightstown, Ind., where he continued his public services as president of the school board, 1874–77, and where he remained until his death.

[R. G. Boone, A Hist. of Educ. in Ind. (1892); Annie Morrison Coffin, "John Irwin Morrison and the Washington County Seminary," Ind. Mag. of Hist., June 1926; Logan Esarey, A Hist. of Ind. (2 vols., 1915); J. H. Smart, ed., The Ind. Schools and the Men who have Worked in Them (1876); T. A. Wylie, ed., Ind. Univ., its Hist. from 1820, when Founded, to 1890 (1890); Indianapolis Jour., July 18, 1882.]
R. F. S.

MORRISON, NATHAN JACKSON (Nov. 25, 1828–Apr. 12, 1907), college president, Congregational clergyman, was born in Sanbornton, now Franklin, N. H., of Scotch-Irish lineage. He was the son of Nathan Smith and Susannah (Chase) Morrison, and a descendant of David Morrison who emigrated to Boston in 1718. Until he was twenty he had only the educational advantages of the district school during four months of the year. He prepared for college at academies in Sanbornton, Meriden, and New Hampton, and graduated from Dartmouth in 1853. He went West to study theology under President Finney of Oberlin, graduating at Oberlin Theological Seminary in 1857. During his seminary course he served as tutor in the classics in the preparatory department of the college. He was ordained, Feb. 11, 1858, pastor of the Congregational church in Rochester, Mich. In 1859 he became professor of Greek and Latin at Olivet College. He married, July 8, 1863, Miranda Capen Dimond, daughter of Isaac Marquand and Sarah Colton (Capen) Dimond of Brooklyn, N. Y.

The school which the founders of the village of Olivet, Mich., had established in the wilderness in 1844 was granted a college charter the year Morrison went there to teach, and a president was elected, who, however, continued in office for only a brief period. The Civil War reduced the struggling institution to a low ebb. It was under these adverse conditions that Morrison was in 1864 unanimously elected to the presidency, an office the duties of which he had already been performing for three and one-half years. He was also transferred to the chair of mental and moral philosophy. His tenacity of purpose and largeness of outlook enabled him to surmount the difficulties of the situation and the college made steady progress throughout his administration, which closed in 1872.

After resigning at Olivet, he became a leading spirit in the organization of Drury College, Springfield, Mo., and was elected its president. From 1873 to 1888 he built up the college, carrying it through the panic of 1873 and the subsequent financial depression, through local and regional misunderstandings of the function and methods of a college, and through the loss sustained by a fire that in December 1882 destroyed the college's finest building. After serving as professor of philosophy in Marietta College, Ohio, from 1888 to 1895, Morrison became interested in the project of raising Fairmount Institute, Wichita, Kan., to the rank of a college. In this enterprise again he was successful, becoming president at the age of sixty-seven and maintaining the struggle for twelve years with unabated enthusiasm through the reverses following the collapse of "boom" conditions in the community, until death closed his career.

Morrison united the ideals and the bearing of the New England educators of his youth with the energy, the ardor, and the optimism of western pioneers. He was nearly six feet in height, of rather slender build, and of dark complexion; in dress and manner he was distinctly the gentleman. His personal interest in his students was keen and of practical helpfulness. As an administrator he was autocratic; but he showed marked ability to secure able men for his faculty and to retain them in spite of meager salaries paid with painful irregularity. The confidence with which he pushed forward his enterprises sometimes appeared to the public and to his fellow workers visionary; but the outcome usually vindicated his judgment and rewarded his courage.

[W. B. Williams, Hist. of Olivet Coll. (1901); A. P. Hall, Hist. Address at the Semi-Centennial of Drury Coll. (1923); M. T. Runnels, Memorial Sketches and Hist. of the Class of 1853 Dartmouth Coll. (1895); The Congreg. Year-Book, 1907 (1908); Congregationalist, May 4, 1907; Topeka State Jour., Apr. 12, 1907.]
E. D. E.

MORRISON, WILLIAM (Mar. 14, 1763–Apr. 19, 1837), pioneer merchant, was born at Doylestown, Bucks County, Pa., the son of John and Rebecca (Bryan) Morrison. His father, the son of Sir John Morrison, of County Cork, Ireland, came to America as a young man. William was probably only a boy when he entered the store of his uncle, Guy Bryan, a noted merchant of Philadelphia. Some time before August 1790, he went to Kaskaskia, Ill., as the western representative of the firm of Bryan & Morrison, and here in later years he was joined by his brothers Robert, James, Jesse, Samuel, and Guy. In this important trading center of pioneer days he rapidly built up a flourishing business, the range of his operations extending from Prairie du Chien, Wis., to New Orleans, and from the Rocky Mountains to Pittsburgh. About 1800 he established a store in Cahokia, Ill. In 1804 he sent Baptiste Lalande with a stock of goods to Santa Fé and was thus the first citizen of the United States to attempt the opening of trade with New Mexico. Though a business competitor and political antagonist of Pierre Menard [q.v.], he joined Menard in backing Manuel Lisa [q.v.] in his trapping venture to the mouth of the Big Horn in 1807, and, two years later, took part with him in organizing the St. Louis Missouri Fur Company. Most of his enterprises prospered, and he acquired great wealth.

In the bitter political contests that marked the early days of the Illinois country he and his brother Robert, with John Edgar, led the faction that opposed Gen. W. H. Harrison, then governor of Indiana Territory. He was also closely allied with the groups and individuals charged by Michael Jones, Harrison's register of the land office and one of the land commissioners at Kaskaskia, with gigantic frauds. He took a prominent part in the movement to oust Jones from office, and on the murder of Rice Jones, the principal attorney for the land speculators, Dec. 7, 1808, sought, with others, to fasten the crime on the register. For this defamation of character he was sued by the register, who had been formally acquitted of the charge, and was mulcted in $200 damages.

Morrison was married three times—to Catherine Thaumur, about 1794; to Euphrosine Huberdeau of Ste. Genevieve, Mo., Nov. 27, 1798; and to Elisa Bissell, of St. Louis, July 20, 1813—and had children by each marriage. About 1801 he built a large and handsome stone residence in Kaskaskia, which became in time perhaps as famous as the home of Menard. He is described by Governor Reynolds (post), who knew him well, as a man of ordinary size, in his later years inclined to corpulency, but of marked dignity and grace of manner. Though he had little schooling, his native intelligence enabled him to pick up a practical education. Reynolds, ignoring his connection with the land frauds, speaks of him as honest and upright, and adds that he was kind and benevolent. He died at his home.

[John Reynolds, *The Pioneer Hist. of Ill.* (1852), pp. 129–33; C. W. Alvord, *The Ill. Country, 1673–1818* (1920); Thomas James, *Three Years among the Indians and Mexicans* (1916), ed. by W. B. Douglas; F. L. Billon, *Annals of St. Louis and Its Territorial Days* (1888), pp. 219–21; Elliott Coues, ed., *The Expeditions of Zebulon Montgomery Pike* (1895), II, 500, 602–03; W. A. B. Jones, "Rice Jones," *Chicago Hist. Soc. Colls.*, IV (1890), 277.]   W. J. G.

MORRISON, WILLIAM McCUTCHAN (Nov. 10, 1867–Mar. 14, 1918), Southern Presbyterian clergyman, missionary to the Congo, was born on a farm near Lexington, Va., the

eldest of the eight children of James Luther Morrison and his wife, Mary Agnes McCutchan. Descended on the paternal side from a line of Scotch-Irish Presbyterians and on his mother's side from a family which had produced many missionaries, he inherited a tradition of religious service which was heightened by the strictly pious atmosphere of his home life. Indeed, almost at his birth his parents had "consecrated William to God." Young Morrison kicked against the pricks, however, and throughout most of his college course at Washington and Lee University he was resolved to become a lawyer. It was only at the death of his father in 1886, the year before his graduation, that he surrendered this ambition for the career to which his parents had destined him. Financial considerations compelled the postponement of his ministerial training. Only after six years of teaching in the South did he enter the Presbyterian Theological seminary in Louisville, Ky., where he graduated in 1896. Soon afterward, having been ordained to the ministry, he set out for Africa as a missionary of the Southern Presbyterian Church (Presbyterian Church in the United States). Six months out of Philadelphia he reached his station at Luebo in the heart of the Congo Free State. Here and in the surrounding country he passed the rest of his life, save for the furloughs which took him back occasionally to America.

Morrison was successful from the beginning. Brought up on a farm, he knew how to use his hands to perform the innumerable practical tasks incident to life in the jungle. Strongly built and of sturdy constitution, he kept his health in spite of incessant labor in the trying climate of the Congo. Knowing from infancy the negro character, he had little difficulty in dealing with the natives; almost instinctively he knew how to win their confidence and affection. Trained as a teacher, he entered immediately into the educational work which is the first step in the civilizing activity of the missionary and a capital one in the training of native evangelists. He early began the study of the native language with the aim of reducing it to writing and of translating the Scriptures. He had a quick ear, a retentive memory, and considerable linguistic training. By dint of great patience and persistent labor, aided by some of the more intelligent natives, he completed in 1906 his *Grammar and Dictionary of the Buluba-Lulua Language as Spoken in the Upper Kasai and Congo Basin,* which was printed in the United States. This work, intended for the use of the missionaries, was followed by translations of Bible paraphrases, of the catechism, of various tracts, and finally of the New Testament. The translation of the last named had proceeded only through Acts when Morrison died. His work was the more useful because the Buluba tongue was a sort of a *lingua franca* over large sections of the Congo. He also edited the *Kasai Herald,* established in 1901 and discontinued sixteen years later.

Morrison's most notable work was his defense of the interests of the natives against the Free State government and its concessionary companies. A man of his humane but aggressive and courageous temper could not remain silent in the face of such outrages as he witnessed in the rubber districts of the Congo. His protests began soon after his arrival at Luebo; they continued until the needed reforms were introduced. At London, in 1903, where the reform movement was already under way, he cooperated with the Congo Reform Association, addressed Parliament on the subject, and wrote several stirring articles for the press. In America he continued the campaign through the press and on the platform. A vigorous and forceful speaker, capable of real eloquence on occasion, he moved his auditors deeply. Calls for American interference in the Congo situation resulted; the government at Washington, not being a signatory to the treaty of Berlin, felt unable to act. Morrison continued his agitation and won the support of numerous American editors and of Mark Twain, whose book, *King Leopold's Soliloquy* (1905), was based in part upon data supplied by Morrison. Undoubtedly his work was effective. He helped to form that public sentiment which, translated into pressure from the British government, caused the appointment by King Leopold of an investigating commission. The resulting revelations, plus the continued campaign in which Morrison had his part, set in train the movement toward reform, effected only after Belgian assumption of sovereignty in the Congo. In 1909 Morrison, with his colleague, W. H. Sheppard, was sued for damages by the Kasai Company on account of an allegedly libelous article written by Sheppard and published by Morrison in the *Kasai Herald.* The missionaries were defended at the trial by Émile Vandervelde, Socialist leader from Brussels, who had long been known as a champion of Congo reform. Thanks to his efforts the missionaries were acquitted. Morrison continued his work at Luebo until March 1918, when he died of tropical dysentery. His wife, Bertha Marion Stebbins, whom he had married in 1906, died in Africa in 1910. They had no children.

[*Who's Who in America,* 1914–15; T. C. Vinson, *William McCutchan Morrison* (1921); S. H. Chester,

Behind the Scenes (1928); *Missionary Review of the World,* June 1918; files of the *Missionary* and the *Missionary Survey,* Nashville, Tenn.]   P.D.E.

MORRISON, WILLIAM RALLS (Sept. 14, 1824?–Sept. 29, 1909), congressman from Illinois and chairman of the Interstate Commerce Commission, was an influential Democratic leader for four decades at the end of the nineteenth century. His parents, John and Ann (Ralls) Morrison, of Anglo-Saxon ancestry, were natives of southern Illinois, where he was born near the present town of Waterloo. His mother died early in the boy's life, and his father left the farm at Prairie du Long, remarried, and took over the management of the inn at Waterloo, Ill. There the boy absorbed politics as he grew, for the tavern was the community center and his father was active in local politics, serving as justice of the peace, sheriff, state assemblyman, and county judge. At twenty-two the son became deputy sheriff but soon left that office to serve as a private in the Mexican War and then went to California in the gold rush. When he returned to Illinois he spent two years in the preparatory department of McKendree College and in 1852 settled down in Waterloo as circuit court clerk. In that year he was married to Mary Jane Drury, who bore him two sons both of whom died young. After her death he was married, in 1857, to her half-sister, Eleanora Horine, who proved an able and industrious assistant in all his political undertakings. They had one child who also died in infancy. From 1854 to 1860 he was a member of the state legislature as a Douglas Democrat and was chosen speaker in his third term. During this period he was admitted to the bar and began the practice of law. At the outbreak of the Civil War he organized a Union regiment, the 49th Illinois Volunteer Infantry, from his border-line region and was elected colonel. He was wounded while leading an attack at Fort Donelson but recuperated sufficiently to take part in the move on Corinth.

Meanwhile his friends at home elected him to the federal House of Representatives as a Democrat. He did not distinguish himself at Washington, 1863–65, and failed of reëlection by seventy-five votes. Except for a season in the state legislature in 1871, he did not appear in politics again until 1872, when, in spite of his tariff-reform campaign, a Republican district sent him to Congress and kept him there from 1873 to 1887. He was chairman of the committee on ways and means, 1875–77 and 1883–87, but throughout his congressional service his influence was greater than committee assignments and speeches indicate. Tariff reduction was his chief concern. In 1876 he stated his principles: "Protection . . . other than that incidental to revenue, is spoliation, because it takes the earnings of the labor of one person or class of persons and gives these earnings to other persons" (*Congressional Record,* 44 Cong., 1 Sess., p. 3313). He achieved a few minor reductions, but his general bills were unsuccessful except as they popularized the idea of reform. His most noted proposal was that of 1884 providing for a general horizontal tariff reduction of 20 per cent., which attached to him the nickname of "Horizontal Bill." Opponents assailed the measure as unscientific, an accusation he himself admitted, but the attacks were impelled by hatred of reduction rather than by abhorrence of unscientific procedure. Although a real reform seems to have been impossible, this attempt failed by only five votes. A strict and active party man, he attended almost all the state and national Democratic conventions and did much committee work. He was a candidate for senator in 1885, when he and John A. Logan fought one of the most spectacular elections in Illinois history. For almost five months the legislature balloted evenly on the two candidates before a well-planned ruse gave Logan the necessary extra vote. Morrison was several times a prominent possibility for the presidential nomination, notably in 1892 and in 1896. Perhaps the decisive obstacle preventing his obtaining this honor was his refusal to barter his bi-metallism principles. Tenacity of ideals was both his strength and his weakness politically.

Defeated in the 1886 election by secret machinations of Pennsylvania manufacturers and the Knights of Labor, he was appointed, in 1887, by Cleveland to the new Interstate Commerce Commission, of which Thomas McIntyre Cooley [*q.v.*] was chairman. As a member of this body and as chairman after Mar. 19, 1892, he labored diligently to guide it through the difficulties of its first period of authority. He conducted a vigorous campaign against railroad privilege, established new rates to displace those declared unjust, and attacked discriminations and rebates that had aroused public feeling. When a series of court decisions, based on defects in the act of 1887, temporarily robbed the commission of real power, he could not have felt disappointed that McKinley refused to reappoint him in 1897. He retired to his home in Waterloo, Ill., and lived quietly until his death.

[Collection of newspaper clippings and some correspondence in the possession of relatives at Waterloo, Ill.; F. D. Scott, "The Political Career of Wm. R. Morrison," *Ill. State Hist. Soc. Trans.*, no. 33 (1926);

J. M. Palmer, *Bench and Bar in Ill.* (1899), vol. II; *Who's Who in America,* 1908–09; *Report of Adjutant-General of . . . Ill.* (1867), vol. II; *Ill. State Register* (Springfield) and *Chicago Daily Tribune,* Sept. 30, 1909; date of birth from McKendree College records.]
             F. D. S.

MORRISSEY, JOHN (Feb. 12, 1831–May 1, 1878), gambler, prizefighter, congressman, and state senator, son of Timothy Morrissey, was born at Templemore, Tipperary, Ireland. There were eight children in the family, seven girls and John. The Morrisseys emigrated to Canada when the boy was a few years old. After three months there the family was destitute and moved to Troy, N. Y., where the father managed to find enough work to keep the children from starving.

It was in Troy that John Morrissey started the career that, like the chapters of a romance, led from rags to riches and from poverty to power. A big boy for his age, he was wild in school and soon began to roam the streets, picking up bad habits and a very definite skill in rough-and-tumble fighting. He worked first in a wall-paper factory and later in the Burden Iron Works, giving up both jobs in disgust. He became something of a local gang leader and a hero for his exploits in street fights. At the age of seventeen he took a job as deckhand on a Hudson River steamer, under Capt. Eli Smith, whose daughter Sarah he later married. By her he had one son, who died at an early age.

Morrissey's first exploit upon arriving in New York City was to invade the Empire Club, a sporting saloon owned by one "Dutch Charley," and challenge all hands to combat. He was worsted in the free-for-all fight that followed but decided that he liked New York City and would remain there. He became a "runner" for a boarding house, his task being to entice to it as many immigrants as possible. The competition in that business led to more fighting and the job just suited the belligerent Irish boy. Soon he began to take up prizefighting in earnest and to hurl challenges at the leading fighters of the day, Tom Hyer, Yankee Sullivan, and others. Lured to California by the gold rush reports and the hope of fighting Hyer, he "bummed" his way across the Continent. He did fight Hyer's trainer, George Thompson, at Mare Island in 1852. While in that area he undertook what practically amounted to a pirate cruise to Queen Charlotte's Island when the rumor arose that the Sitka Indians had discovered gold. The gold was not found and Morrissey returned to the East and prizefighting. He beat Yankee Sullivan at Boston Four Corners (now Boston Corners), N. Y., Oct. 12, 1853, in thirty-seven rounds for $2,000 prize money. This victory gave him something of a claim on the heavy-weight championship. Later he fought a man named Poole on a dock in New York City. Not long after the bout Poole was assassinated, allegedly by Morrissey's friends, and Morrissey was arrested but was soon released. In the next few years he rose rapidly to power as a gambler, saloon-keeper, labor leader, and politician. Challenged by John C. Heenan [q.v.] for the championship, he accepted and announced that the fight would be his last, win or lose. On Oct. 20, 1858, at Long Point, Canada, he defeated Heenan in eleven rounds for $2,500 a side.

He became a huge, flamboyant, and belligerent figure in New York sporting, political, and even financial life. He made Commodore Vanderbilt his friend by presenting him with a fine race horse and is supposed to have profited greatly by financial tips from Vanderbilt in later years. He lost $124,000 in one night to Benjamin Wood at his gambling house. In 1866 he ran for Congress from the fifth district, mainly to annoy the great number of people who said that it was a disgrace to consider him for such an office. He was elected and served for two terms, Mar. 4, 1867, to Mar. 3, 1871. As early as 1862 he had a gambling house in Saratoga, N. Y., his residence in his late years, and in 1870 he opened a "new clubhouse" there. In 1875 he was elected state senator from the fourth district. In 1877 he was elected again, this time from the seventh district. When he died, the following year, he owned three-eighths of the gambling casino at Saratoga, one-third of the racetrack and buildings, and real estate here and there in the town.

He had made and lost several fortunes in Wall Street. Though he was a turbulent character in turbulent times, his fighting exploits, his kind-heartedness, his loyalty to his friends, and other redeeming qualities covered a multitude of his sins. He was buried at Troy, N. Y., with state senators as pall-bearers and 15,000 people following his body to the cemetery in the rain.

[W. E. Harding, *John Morrissey, His Life, Battles, and Wrangles* (1881); *Biog. Dir. Am. Cong.* (1928); A. J. Weise, *Hist. of the City of Troy* (1876); *N. Y. Times, N. Y. Tribune*, May 2, 1878.]   J.K.

MORROW, DWIGHT WHITNEY (Jan. 11, 1873–Oct. 5, 1931), lawyer, banker, diplomat, was born at Huntington, W. Va. His parents James Elmore and Clara (Johnson) Morrow were both of pre-Revolutionary Scotch-Irish stock and both were scholarly. Five surviving children, including Dwight, all taught school. Reared in western Pennsylvania, he won a competitive examination to West Point but was de-

nied the appointment because his elder brother Jay Johnson Morrow, later a brigadier-general, was already at the Military Academy. He therefore decided to go to Amherst College, entering with the Class of 1895, which included Calvin Coolidge. His devotion to Amherst lasted all his life. After graduation with honors, he worked as a clerk for a year. Entering the Columbia Law School in 1896, he paid his expenses by tutoring and graduated in 1899, once more with distinction.

Morrow was first employed by the firm of Reed, Simpson, Thacher and Barnum, of which former Speaker Thomas B. Reed was the newly installed head. His advancement in the law was rapid and by 1905 he had won a partnership in the firm. He continued active in the profession for nine years. His practice was concerned with the larger business affairs of the period, the complicated details of which he could quickly master. Thomas D. Thacher afterward said that he had "an uncanny knack of quickly finding the common ground upon which the conflicting claims of divergent interests could be resolved" (*Bar Association Year Book*, p. 386). This gift was repeatedly shown later in banking and diplomacy. He made his home in New Jersey, at Englewood, and rendered valuable service to the state by drafting, with Col. R. C. Bolling, the workmen's compensation law of 1911. Subsequently he served as chairman of the New Jersey Prison Inquiry Commission (*Report*, 2 vols., 1917), and, as the first president of the State Board of Control (1918–20), carried into effect significant reforms in the administration of penal and corrective institutions. On the eve of the World War (1914) Morrow entered the banking house of J. P. Morgan & Company, and continued there until 1927. In the new occupation he speedily gained the same distinction that he had earned in law. The firm was called upon to finance the purchases of American goods and munitions required by the Allied Powers. In all the financial transactions of the house arising from the war and from the reconstructive efforts following the peace, Morrow participated. When the United States entered the war Morrow's first work was with the National War Savings Committee, as director of New Jersey. His subsequent service as adviser to the Allied Maritime Transport Council was probably his most important in the war itself. He advised General Pershing on his transportation problems and was awarded the Distinguished Service Medal by that officer "for the first intelligent epitomization of the complete Allied tonnage situation and his able presentation of the situation to the Allied countries" (quoted in Howland, *post,* p. 30; McBride, *post,* p. 114). His experiences widened Morrow's acquaintance with the leading men of Europe which in the post-war period developed into friendship and confidence. In 1920 there was an economic and financial collapse in Cuba and Morrow was asked to study the situation and to prepare a plan by which the credit of the government could be restored. After his death there was a recession but his immediate success won the confidence of the government of Cuba.

In 1925 Morrow was chairman of a board appointed by President Coolidge to examine the national interest in aeronautics and its application to national defense. The *Report of the President's Aircraft Board* (1926) led to the separation of control of aircraft for national defense from that of aircraft for commercial purposes, and the adoption of means of encouragement for commercial aviation. Morrow was appointed ambassador to Mexico by President Coolidge in 1927 when relations with that republic were strained. Once more he was changing professions and again success was to attend him. Rare understanding and sympathy marked his mission. Under his intelligent and tactful guidance good relations were reëstablished and a variety of disputes, including those over oil and the agrarian question, were adjusted or put in the way of adjustment. An example of his diplomatic skill was the termination by non-official intervention of the differences between the Mexican government and the Roman Catholic Church, and the return to the country of the expelled clergy of the church. President Hoover named him as one of the delegates to the London Naval Conference in 1930 and so capably did he perform his part that before he died he had been requested by the President to lead the American delegation to the World Disarmament Conference, which was held at Geneva after his death.

Morrow was elected as a Republican to the United States Senate from New Jersey in 1930 with a plurality in the primary of 300,000 and in the election of 200,000. In his campaign he attracted wide attention by his frank advocacy of the repeal of the Eighteenth Amendment and the restoration of the control of the liquor traffic to the states. He served in the Senate only through the short session, from December 1930 to March 1931, and during this time did not make a single speech or offer a single resolution. He revealed to friends that it was his definite plan first to master the rules and procedure of the body, and thoroughly to acquaint himself with its members. In his votes he was entirely regular. His un-

timely death at Englewood, in the midst of an international economic depression, was widely deplored. Sir Arthur Salter, in the London *Times* (Oct. 7, 1931), characterized it as a "world disaster"; and Walter Lippmann in the *New York Herald Tribune* (Oct. 7, 1931) said: "No man of our time has had the complete trust of so many different kinds of people."

Morrow was a trustee of Amherst College, Union Theological Seminary, the Smithsonian Institution, and the Association for the Improvement of the Condition of the Poor in New York, and he held honorary degrees from many institutions of learning. On June 16, 1903, he married Elizabeth Reeve Cutter of Cleveland; with their three daughters and son she survived him.

[M. M. McBride, *The Story of Dwight W. Morrow* (1930), a laudatory account; H. H. Howland, *Dwight Whitney Morrow. A Sketch in Admiration* (1930), of the same type; "Memorial of Dwight Whitney Morrow," in the *Asso. of the Bar of the City of New York Year Book 1932,* pp. 381–405; Carleton Beals, "The Diplomat who won the Mexicans," *N. Y. Times,* Sept. 21, 1930; Edmund Wilson, "Dwight Morrow in New Jersey," in *The American Jitters* (1932), a critical but fair article on the Senate campaign in New Jersey; comments on his career in the Senate, in *N. Y. Times,* editorial, Mar. 5, 1931, and *New Republic,* Mar. 25, 1931; *Who's Who in America,* 1930–31; obituary articles in *N. Y. Times,* Oct. 6, 7, 1931.] M. E—n.

MORROW, JEREMIAH (Oct. 6, 1771–Mar. 22, 1852), first representative from the state of Ohio, senator, and governor, was the grandson of the Scotch-Irish Covenanter, Jeremiah Murray who left Londonderry for the New World about the middle of the eighteenth century and settled near Gettysburg, Pa., in a neighborhood as Scotch and Presbyterian as any parish in Scotland. Jeremiah Murray's son, John, a Federalist farmer (who spelled his name Morrow), had married in 1768 Mary Lockart. Their son Jeremiah was born on the farm near Gettysburg, where he spent his first twenty-three years but managed to obtain a rather good education, particularly in mathematics. This latter attainment he turned to account in 1794, when he went to the Ohio country as a surveyor. He arrived in the Miami Valley in the spring of 1795, surveyed land, grew corn, taught school, and invested in land in Warren County. Four years later, on Feb. 19, 1799, in Pennsylvania, he was married to his cousin, Mary Parkhill, and took her west to share his home on the frontier. He won the esteem of his neighbors, who chose him in October 1800 to represent them in the second territorial legislature. In the legislature he, with the "Chillicothe Junto," opposed the efforts of St. Clair to postpone Ohio's statehood. Two years later he was a delegate to the convention that drew up a constitution for the new state and was a member of the first state Senate in 1803. He was then chosen by the Jeffersonians to represent the state in Congress and took his seat on Oct. 17, 1803. He was regularly reëlected and served in the House of Representatives from 1803 to 1813, when he entered the Senate and served six years. His career in Congress, while not spectacular, was notable for constructive lawmaking. He became expert in matters pertaining to the public lands. He consistently advocated three changes in existing legislation: the sale of land in smaller units, cash payment, and lower price. The act of 1820 that established a minimum cash price of $1.25 an acre for units as small as 80 acres was the result of his advocacy (P. J. Treat, *The National Land System*, 1910, pp. 132, 139). In 1818 he declined reëlection to the Senate.

In 1822 he was elected governor and was reelected in 1824. As governor he inaugurated the canal-building program and was influential in establishing the public-school system. He retired in December 1826, but his interest in politics remained active. He served in the state Senate for the session of 1827–28 in the House of Representatives for the session 1829–30 and 1835–36. He represented Ohio's tariff interests in the Harrisburg convention in 1827; he supported Adams in the election of 1828; he was later a leader of the Whig party in the state; he was a Clay elector in 1832; and he was chairman of the Ohio Whig convention which indorsed Harrison in 1836. In 1840 he was elected to Congress and served from Oct. 13, 1840, to Mar. 3, 1843, but he felt that he belonged to an older generation and declined renomination. He was president of the Little Miami Railroad Company, chartered in 1836, which built the first railroad out of Cincinnati. He seems to have regarded his association with this project more as a piece of constructive statesmanship than as a means of enriching himself. He served without pay and resigned when the road was an assured success. His greatest pleasure was in the management of his flour mill and his large farm. His nature was most unassuming; he lived in "republican simplicity." He died near Lebanon, Ohio. Of a family of six children only his eldest son survived him.

[Manuscripts of Jeremiah Morrow in the Ohio State Lib. and in the Ohio State Arch. and Hist. Soc. Lib., Columbus; W. A. Taylor, *Ohio Statesmen and Hundred Year Book* (1892); biography by Josiah Morrow, his grandson, in *The "Old Northwest" Geneal. Quart.*, Jan., Apr., July 1906; W. H. Smith, "Gov. Jeremiah Morrow; or a Familiar Talk about Monarchists and Jacobins," *Mag. of Western Hist.*, Oct. 1889, and *Ohio Arch. and Hist. Quart.*, June 1888.]   W. T. U.

MORROW, PRINCE ALBERT (Dec. 19, 1846–Mar. 17, 1913), physician, sociologist, was born at Mount Vernon, Christian County, Ky., his parents being Col. William C. Morrow, who at one time represented Christian County in the lower branch of the Kentucky legislature, and Mary (Cox) Morrow. In 1864, he received the degree of A.B. from Princeton College, Kentucky. Soon afterward he began the study of medicine. Through the influence of his uncle, Dr. Thomas V. Morrow [*q.v.*], who was one of the founders of the Eclectic Medical College of Cincinnati, Morrow received his early medical education in an eclectic school. He then studied at the École de Médecine in Paris and later spent about fifteen months in the hospitals of London, Paris, Berlin, and Vienna. In 1874 he graduated in medicine from the University Medical College, New York, and the following year began practising medicine in New York City. The honorary degree of A.M. was conferred upon him by the University of the City of New York in 1883.

Soon after beginning his medical career, Morrow specialized in diseases of the skin, becoming a lecturer in this subject at his medical alma mater in 1882. In the same institution (now New York University and Bellevue Hospital Medical College) he became successively clinical professor of venereal diseases in 1884, professor of genito-urinary diseases in 1886, and emeritus professor in 1890. In the last-mentioned year he was appointed attending physician of the skin and venereal department of the New York Hospital, continuing in this capacity until 1904. From 1884 to 1904, he was attending physician to the City Hospital, and he was also consulting dermatologist to St. Vincent's and to the City Hospital.

Morrow early recognized the importance of the problem of venereal diseases from the social, moral, and economic standpoints. Foreseeing that treatment of these diseases was the least important factor in their control, he purposed to attain their prevention through dissemination of knowledge to the laity. His task was indeed a difficult one. He lived during a period in which there was deep-seated feeling, chiefly the result of tradition, that such a subject should be kept *sub rosa*. His earliest endeavors were met with apathy and indifference. He worked indefatigably, however, and by degrees interested physicians, lawyers, educators, and leaders in all walks of life. Public interest increased and he became a leader in a great social movement. His proposed reforms included the wholesome teaching of sex hygiene to the young, thus appeasing a natural curiosity and encouraging a proper outlook on life. The true nature of venereal diseases was brought to the attention of the public through the medium of press and platform, and Morrow, personally, wrote many pamphlets on the subject. He openly discussed measures for the control of prostitution and advocated the registration of those suffering from venereal diseases as communicable. He was a facile and convincing writer. Among his more important contributions were *Syphilis and Marriage* (1881), translated from the French of Alfred Fournier; *Venereal Memoranda* (1885); *Drug Eruptions* (1887); *An Atlas of Skin and Venereal Diseases* (1888–89); *A System of Genito-Urinary Diseases, Syphilology and Dermatology, by Various Authors* (3 vols., 1893–94), which he edited; *Personal Observations of Leprosy* (1889), written after visits to the Hawaiian Islands, Mexico, and Louisiana; *Social Diseases and Marriage* (1904). He was one of the founders and for sixteen years the editor of the *Journal of Cutaneous Diseases* (now *Archives of Dermatology and Syphilology*). A member of numerous professional societies both American and European, he was president of the American Dermatological Association in 1890–91 and of the American Society of Sanitary and Moral Prophylaxis from its inception in 1905.

He married Lucy B. Slaughter, daughter of Thomas Jefferson and Mary (Henry) Slaughter of New York City, on Apr. 23, 1874. Two sons and a daughter survived him, one of the sons becoming a practising surgeon in New York City. Morrow was a man of strong convictions and a tireless worker. He rarely took a long vacation, but for many years was accustomed to spend weekends at Madison, N. J., where he had a summer home, and here he did much of his early writing. He enjoyed all forms of out-door exercise but especially walking and golf. Though giving little time to it, he was fond of social life and was a prominent figure at the meetings of the Southern Society and the Kentuckians. The last few years of his life were devoted almost solely to social reform and he will probably be remembered more as a pioneer and leader in this field than for his important work in former years in the field of dermatology.

[*Who's Who in America*, 1912–13; *N. Y. Times*, Mar. 18, 1913; E. B. Bronson, in *Jour. of Cutaneous Diseases*, Oct. 1913, p. 775; *Bull. de la Société française de dermatologie et syphiligraphie*, vol. XXIV (1913); *Jour. Am. Medic. Asso.*, Mar. 29, 1913; *Lancet* (London), Apr. 19, 1913; *Social Diseases*, July 1913; H. A. Kelly and W. L. Burrage, *Am. Medic. Biogs.* (1920); personal interview with Morrow's son, Dr. Albert S. Morrow.]   G. M. L.

MORROW, THOMAS VAUGHAN (Apr. 14, 1804–July 16, 1850), pioneer in eclectic medicine, was born at Fairview, Ky. His father, Thomas Morrow, was of Scotch descent, though the occasional appearance of the name as Moreau indicates a French origin. His mother, Elizabeth Vaughan, was of English stock. He attended Transylvania University and then went to New York, where he attended a regular medical school and was later graduated from the Reformed Medical College conducted by Dr. Wooster Beach [*q.v.*], the "founder of eclecticism." After a short period as professor of obstetrics at the latter institution he settled at Hopkinsville, Ky., for practice. In 1830 the Reformed Medical Society of the United States determined to establish a medical school in the Ohio River Valley and accepted the offer of Worthington College to form its medical department. The new school was called the Reformed Medical College of Ohio. Morrow was chosen to head the college as president, dean, and professor of materia medica, obstetrics, and theory and practice of medicine. The *Western Medical Reformer* was established in 1836 in connection with the school. After a stormy career culminating in a mob attack upon the institution it was closed in 1839. Morrow continued practice and private instruction at Worthington until 1842, when he removed to Cincinnati and began at once the organization of a school to succeed the Worthington venture. First named the Reformed Medical School of Cincinnati, Ohio, it was incorporated as the Cincinnati Eclectic Medical Institute in 1845 and as the Eclectic Medical College graduated classes until 1929, when it became extinct. In the Cincinnati school Morrow was appointed dean, treasurer, and professor of physiology, pathology, and theory and practice of medicine, which positions he held until his death. He died from dysentery at the early age of forty-six, and was buried in Wesleyan Cemetery, Cincinnati.

Morrow's claims to remembrance rest upon his championship of the eclectic system of medicine and his part in the foundation of the first schools of that cult in the West. When the National Eclectic Medical Association was inaugurated in Cincinnati in 1848 he was elected its first president. He was a forceful speaker, an able teacher, and a highly successful practitioner both in Worthington and in Cincinnati. His writings include introductory addresses to the classes of the Cincinnati school and many clinical articles and editorials for the pages of the *Western Medical Reformer* and its successor, the *Eclectic Medical Journal*. He was engaged upon the preparation of a "Theory and Practice of

Medicine" at the time of his death. This work was incorporated in *The American Eclectic Practice of Medicine* (2 vols., 1853–54), by I. G. Jones, Morrow's former associate in the Worthington school. Physically Morrow was well over six feet in height, weighing two hundred and fifty pounds. During his stay in Worthington he married Isabel Greer of that place. Prince Albert Morrow [q.v.], noted dermatologist and sociologist, was his nephew.

[*Hist. of the Eclectic Medic. Inst., Cincinnati* (1902); *Eclectic Medic. Jour.* (Cincinnati), Aug. 1850; Alexander Wilder, *Hist. of Medicine* (1901); C. T. Greve, *Centennial Hist. of Cincinnati* (1904), vol. II.]

J. M. P.

MORROW, WILLIAM W. (July 15, 1843–July 24, 1929), jurist, congressman from California, was born near Milton, Wayne County, Ind., of Scotch-Irish parentage, the son of William and Margaret (Hood) Morrow. When he was about three years of age, his parents moved to Adams County, Ill., where he attended the common-schools and heard Lincoln, Douglas, and Trumbull trying cases and speaking upon political issues. In 1859 he moved to Santa Rosa, Cal., where he worked as a harness-maker and taught school. Early in 1862 he rode from Santa Rosa to Oregon and, while lost on the way, discovered rich placers which soon led to the development of Cañon City, Ore. Later in the same year he went east and enlisted in the Union army. He was detailed to California in June 1865 as a special agent of the Treasury Department in charge of $5,000,000 in money, and during the next four years he was employed in a confidential position under the secretary of the treasury. In 1869 he was admitted to the bar and entered upon the practice of law in San Francisco, serving from 1870 to 1874 as assistant United States district attorney. He won some distinction in prosecuting officers of merchant ships for cruelty to sailors and assisted in obtaining important reforms by legislation and shipping regulations in the interest of merchant seamen. In 1872 he assisted in the organization of the San Francisco Bar Association and twice served as its president. Between 1880 and 1885 he was attorney for the state board of harbor commissioners, and special attorney for the United States in connection with the *Alabama* claims and before the French and American claims commission. Interested in politics, he was chairman of the California Republican state central committee from 1879 to 1882 and in 1884 attended the Republican National Convention at Chicago as chairman of the California delegation. That fall he was elected to Congress as

representative from the San Francisco district and served during the Forty-ninth, Fiftieth, and Fifty-first congresses (1885–91). He was active in introducing private or local bills and resolutions but made few extended speeches, although he advocated a more stringent Chinese exclusion law, the free coinage of silver, and a survey of the possibilities of irrigating arid lands in the Far West. He was a member of the committees on commerce, foreign affairs, appropriations, and importation of contract laborers.

In 1891 Morrow entered upon a long judicial career, first as judge of the federal district court for the northern district of California. Three cases which he decided as district judge were especially important: *In re Ezeta* (62 Fed., 964), involving questions of extradition; *United States* vs. *Cassidy et al.* (67 Fed., 698), resulting from the Pullman strike in 1894; and *In re Wong Kim Ark* (71 Fed., 382), in which his dictum that a person born in the United States of Chinese parents is a citizen of the United States, under the Fourteenth Amendment, was afterward sustained by the Supreme Court. His charge to the jury in the second case was said at the time to have been the longest ever delivered in a criminal case in the United States. In 1897 President McKinley advanced Morrow to the federal circuit court. One of the best-known cases coming before him as circuit judge was *In re Noyes* (121 Fed., 209), or the "Nome Case," growing out of the gold discovery in Alaska. The facts in this case formed the basis of Rex Beach's novel, *The Spoilers*. (See Morrow's explanatory article, "The Spoilers," *California Law Review*, January 1916.) He wrote the opinion of the circuit court of appeals in the Salton Sea cases (172 Fed., 792), in the Bisbee deportation cases (1918) involving members of the I. W. W. in Arizona (*United States* vs. *Wheeler et al.*, 254 Fed., 611), in *Fireman's Fund Insurance Company* vs. *Globe Navigation Company et al.* (236 Fed., 618), and in the *Marconi Wireless Telegraph Company of America* vs. *Kilbourne and Clark Manufacturing Company* (265 Fed., 644). Upon his completion of thirty years upon the federal bench in 1921, the bar of San Francisco tendered him a public reception. Two years later he retired from active service. During his judicial career, he is said to have handed down more than 650 decisions.

Morrow was selected by Andrew Carnegie in 1900 to be a trustee of the Carnegie Institution in Washington. In 1905 he became an incorporator of the American National Red Cross, upon its reincorporation by Congress, and received a medal for his relief work in connection

Morse

with the San Francisco fire in 1906. For his services as a member of the American Association for International Conciliation, he was awarded the d'Estournelles de Constant medal by that society in 1925. His wife, Margaret Hulbert, whom he had married at Santa Rosa on June 18, 1865, died in 1926. On Dec. 31, 1927, he was married to Julia E. Neill. She and two children by his first marriage survived him. He died at San Francisco and was buried with Masonic honors in Cypress Lawn Cemetery.

[See: J. G. Jury, "Wm. W. Morrow," *Cal. Law Rev.*, Nov. 1921; *Who's Who in America*, 1928–29; *Biog. Dir. Am. Cong.* (1928); O. T. Shuck, *Sketches of Leading and Representative Men of San Francisco* (1875), pp. 1071–73; *San Francisco Chronicle, San Francisco Examiner*, July 25, 1929. A letter from Morrow in the Lib. of Cong. states that his middle initial does not represent a name.] P. O. R.

MORSE, ANSON DANIEL (Aug. 13, 1846–Mar. 13, 1916), educator and historian, brother of Harmon Northrop Morse [q.v.], was born at Cambridge in one of the most rugged parts of Vermont, the son of Harmon and Elizabeth Murray (Buck) Morse of ancestry reaching back to the earliest years of the settlement of New England. His early training was obtained in the schools of the neighborhood and he was graduated from Amherst College with high honors in the class of 1871. From 1872 to 1875 he taught at Williston Seminary, Easthampton, Mass., then, after a year of study at Heidelberg, he was brought back to teach at his alma mater, to which he was to give more than forty years of most devoted and useful service. In 1876 he was a lecturer on political economy in Amherst College; in the following year he became professor of political economy and instructor in history, in 1879 he was appointed Otis Professor of History and Political Science and in 1885 he was transferred to the Winkley chair. After 1892 this professorship was divided and he became professor of history, which title he held till his retirement in 1907. He had studied again at Heidelberg in 1883. After almost fifty years of residence in Amherst, he died in 1916, a greatly beloved figure.

Morse was a leader in a small group of scholars who in the last quarter of the nineteenth century began to teach that the political party is the most effective organ for expressing and enforcing the popular will. They further pointed out that the United States, through its freedom from deeply rooted antagonistic customs and institutions, offers the most favorable field for the study of the sweep toward democracy, which has characterized the development of civilized government since the eighteenth century. In three

Morse

notable articles: "The Place of Party in the Political System" (*Annals of the American Academy of Political and Social Science*, vol. II, no. 3, 1892); "What is a Party" (*Political Science Quarterly*, March 1896); and "The Natural History of Party" (*Yale Review*, May 1893), Morse presented a philosophical study of the conditions which bring parties into existence, of their nature and organization, their behavior in and out of power, and, finally, the causes and circumstances of their dissolution. These ventures into the realm of political theory were supplemented by a number of purely historical studies of great value, dealing with American parties and political figures. The most important of these studies were collected and published in 1923 in a volume entitled *Parties and Party Leaders*. Thus a relatively few articles and a small book entitled *Civilization and the World War* (1919), published after its author's death, constitute the whole of his published work. Throughout his life he was a most thorough and diligent student of history but he was often reluctant to commit his thought to print. Furthermore his early leaning toward economics and political science led him, in teaching history, to emphasize its bearing upon the present, and his recognition of the rapidly changing character of economic and political experiences may have contributed also to his reluctance. However this may be, his best work was done as a teacher. His method was profoundly suggestive and provocative of discussion; he was never didactic. His presentations were always dignified and quietly persuasive, so much so that he was singularly successful with generations of students, many of whom in public and professional life remained true to his teachings. Morse was married, on Sept. 3, 1878, to Margaret Duncan Ely. She, with six of their seven children, survived him.

[The Introduction to *Parties and Party Leaders* by Dwight W. Morrow and to *Civilization and the World War* by John B. Clark contain biographical information. See also: *Amherst Grads.' Quart.*, May 1916; *Amherst Coll., Biog. Record of the Grads. and Nongrads.* (1927); *Who's Who in America*, 1914–15.] F. L. T.

MORSE, CHARLES WYMAN (Oct. 21, 1856–Jan. 12, 1933), promoter and speculator, was born in Bath, Maine. His parents, Benjamin Wyman and Anna E. J. (Rodbird) Morse were fairly well-to-do, his father having a large part of the control of towing on the Kennebec River. While at Bowdoin College he was already deep in the shipping business and when he graduated in 1877 he had accumulated a considerable capital. He joined forces with his father

239

and a cousin, and as C. W. Morse & Company the firm entered on an extensive ice-shipping and lumber-transporting business. Within a few years Morse outgrew Bath; soon he outgrew even State Street, in Boston; to Wall Street he came in 1897.

Morse first made his fame and fortune in New York in ice. After forming his own Consolidated Ice Company he succeeded, through persuasion or the devious methods of business coercion, in merging it with other companies into the American Ice Company. Formed in 1899 with a capitalization of sixty million, this was one of the earlier and more flagrant instances of corrupt and overcapitalized promotion in the annals of the American trust movement. It gave Morse almost overnight a dubious public prominence as the "Ice King." On May 1, 1900, the trust announced an advance in the price of ice for New York City from twenty-five and thirty to sixty cents per hundred pounds. There was a public outcry, and the *New York Journal and Advertiser* found that disconcertingly large blocks of American Ice stock were held by Mayor Van Wyck, Boss Croker, and other Tammany leaders. Suit was instituted and in the course of the testimony it emerged that Morse had let Van Wyck have the stock at half of par, and had in addition lent him the money with which to buy it; also that the docking commissioners had given Morse's company privileges so favorable as practically to exclude serious competition from independents (32 *Misc. N. Y. Reports*, 1; 55 *Appellate Division Reports*, 245; *Outlook*, June 16, 1900). The Van Wyck administration was turned out at the next election and the price of American Ice stock fell drastically; but not before Morse had formed a holding company, the Ice Securities Corporation, had maneuvered its stock weirdly, and withdrawn with an estimated fortune of twelve million dollars.

He now turned intensively to banking and to shipping. His method in both fields was that of rapid consolidation of individual firms either through peaceful or military penetration; pyramiding of their assets with a bewildering swiftness and complexity; criss-crossing of his two groups of ventures so that the shipping companies bolstered the banks and the banks financed the shipping companies; and the formation of syndicates to take up the flotation of the overcapitalized stock of the consolidated companies. Through a series of brilliant operations he managed to obtain before 1907 something close to a monopoly of the coastwise shipping from Bangor to Galveston and came to be termed "Admiral of the Atlantic Coast." His Consolidated Steamship Company, formed in 1905, combined most of the important lines outside of the New Haven Railroad interests. So close had he come to his monopolistic objective that he frightened not only Wall Street but also President Theodore Roosevelt himself. When the New Haven road was considering in 1907 Morse's offer of twenty million dollars for its Long Island Sound lines, Roosevelt promised President Mellen of the railroad immunity from government interference in his shipping holdings if he would promise not to sell to Morse (*Senate Document No. 543, 63 Cong., 2 Sess.*, vol. I, p. 875). In banking Morse joined forces with F. Augustus Heinze [*q.v.*], a prominent copper speculator, and E. R. Thomas, a young man of considerable inherited fortune. Together they gained a foothold in a dozen New York banks, the principal ones being the Bank of North America and the Mercantile National Bank; but the United Copper pool, which collapsed according to Heinze because of secret unloading of stock by Morse, reacted fatally on their banking ventures. The Heinze-Morse banks became the storm center of the panic of 1907, and on Oct. 20 a "vigilance committee" of fifteen delivered to them an ultimatum to sell out and retire permanently from banking (C. A. Conant, *A History of Modern Banks of Issue,* 1909, p. 713).

An investigation of the Bank of North America by the United States district attorney, Henry L. Stimson, resulted in the indictment and conviction of Morse for false entries in the books of the bank and for criminally misapplying its funds. He was sentenced in November 1908 to a fifteen-year term in the Atlanta penitentiary, and, despite appeals, he had finally to depart for Atlanta on Jan. 2, 1910. "There is no one in Wall Street who is not daily doing as I have done," he said in an interview. "The late administration wanted a victim; the System wanted a scapegoat" (quoted in *Current Literature,* Feb. 1910, p. 153). The kernel of truth in this statement was the continued hostility which the dominant and conservative group of Wall Street bankers felt toward him. This "fat, squatty little man" with the "masterful, inquiring eyes," as he was described by contemporary journalists, had either not played the game or else had played it all too well. Since the ice scandals the white light of publicity had never receded from him. The attempt of his relatives, in 1903, to annul his second marriage, to the divorced wife of a Pullman car conductor, had resulted in unsavory publicity, and one of the lawyers in the case, Abraham H. Hummel [*q.v.*], was sentenced to a year's imprisonment. This episode had embittered Morse and estranged him even further from the reigning Wall Street group.

In little over two years Morse was out of jail. The main outlines of the processes by which his release was accomplished were clarified and documented by Senator Caraway ten years later on the floor of the United States Senate (*New York Times,* May 21, 23, 1922). Every exertion by Morse's friends and relatives to secure a pardon or a commutation of sentence from President Taft had been unavailing. Finally Harry M. Daugherty, later in the Harding cabinet as attorney-general, contracted with Morse, for a retainer of five thousand dollars and the promise of an additional twenty-five thousand in case of success, to secure his release. A commission of doctors was eventually appointed to investigate the report that Morse was a dying man. It reported negatively, but a second commission of army doctors assured the President that Morse had only a few more weeks if he were kept in prison, that he was suffering from a complication of ailments including Bright's disease, and that even if released he could not survive for more than a year. Taft signed his pardon and Morse departed for medical treatment in Wiesbaden. But Daugherty's fee remained unpaid; and the attorney-general's office received information that before his examinations Morse had drunk a combination of soapsuds and chemicals calculated to produce temporarily the effects the army commission noted. President Taft later charged that he had been deluded in the whole matter, and said that the case "shakes one's faith in expert examination" (*New York Times,* Nov. 16, 1913).

On his return from Europe Morse reëntered business with renewed energy, throwing down his gauntlet to the Wall Street group. He reconquered something of his old dominion in the shipping field, until in July 1915 his Hudson Navigation Company was already being sued for unfair competition. On Jan. 11, 1916, he came back to the front pages of the metropolitan newspapers with a grandiose scheme for organizing an American transoceanic shipping combination. This assumed reality in the incorporation of the United States Shipping Company, a holding company for whose stock was exchanged the stock of sixteen separate subsidiary companies, each organized around a steamship. The entrance of the United States into the World War gave Morse an even greater opportunity. He was now given contracts by the Shipping Board for building thirty-six vessels, and he borrowed from the Emergency Fleet Corporation the money with which to do so. Twenty-two of the ships

were eventually completed. But in the investigation of "war frauds" by the Harding administration the findings of a special legal staff attached to the Department of Justice resulted in the charges that Morse had misrepresented his facilities for ship construction, that he had applied much of the money he borrowed to the building of shipyards rather than ships, that he had failed to turn over to the government the profits of the ships it had leased to him, and that he had appropriated some of the equipment for his own purposes (*New York Times,* Apr. 28, 1922). Before an indictment could be found, Morse sailed for Havre. Attorney-General Daugherty sent him a cable to return. Morse, professedly surprised at the whole pother, and insisting that his trip was an innocent attempt to consult with his Italian physician, nevertheless returned to New York. He was arrested and later indicted for conspiracy to defraud the government. Before the case could be brought to trial he was again indicted with twenty-three others of his group, on a charge of using the mails to defraud prospective investors in United States Steamship stock. The long and costly trial on the Shipping Board charges resulted in an acquittal, but a subsequent civil suit in 1925 against Morse's company, the Virginia Shipbuilding Company, on charges growing out of the same transactions, resulted in a judgment for the government of over eleven and a half million dollars. The mail fraud case had a chequered career, but Morse was finally adjudged too ill to stand trial, and after a jury had disagreed the charges against his sons were dismissed. On Sept. 7, 1926, he was placed under guardianship by the probate court of Bath as incompetent to handle his affairs. He suffered several strokes and died in Bath, of pneumonia, on Jan. 12, 1933. He had married Hattie Bishop Hussey of Brooklyn on Apr. 14, 1884. She bore him four children and died probably in 1897. He had no children by his second wife, Clemence (Cowles) Dodge, whom he married in 1901 and who died in 1926.

[For the main outlines of Morse's career until the 1907 panic, see Owen Wilson, "The Admiral of the Atlantic Coast," *World's Work,* April 1907; and C. F. Speare, "Career of a Great Promoter," *Moody's Mag.,* July 1907. For the ice-trust episode, see *N. Y. Times,* Apr. 15, 16, 1899, May 6, 1900; comments in the *Outlook,* May 9, June 9, 16, July 7, 1900, and in the *Independent,* May 31, 1900; and "Water Still Freezes," in *Fortune,* May 1933. For his shipping activities before his imprisonment, see in addition to the above the testimony of Mellen in the investigation of the New Haven Railroad by the Interstate Commerce Commission, reported in *N. Y. Times,* May 22, 1914. For his banking activities, see C. M. Keys, "Regulating Banks by Vigilance Committee," *World's Work,* Dec. 1907, and "The Story of Morse," *Current Literature,* Feb. 1910. For the details of Morse's pardon, see *N. Y. Times,* May

21, 23, 1922; for Daugherty's official statement, *Ibid.*, May 28, 1922. For Morse's later shipping career see especially a feature article, *Ibid.*, July 25, 1926. See also *N. Y. Times*, Jan. 13, 1933; P. M. Reed, *Hist. of Bath and Environs, Sagadahoc County, Me., 1607–1894* (1894).]   M. L.

MORSE, EDWARD SYLVESTER (June 18, 1838–Dec. 20, 1925), zoölogist and museum director, was born at Portland, Me., a son of Jonathan Kimball and Jane Seymour (Beckett) Morse. He began in boyhood to collect and classify shells and minerals. He attended the Bethel (Maine) Academy, then served for a time as mechanical draftsman at the Portland locomotive works. Most important for his development, he registered as a special student of Louis Agassiz at the Lawrence Scientific School, Harvard University, specializing for three years in conchology. His study of the brachiopods led to his undertaking a systematic exploration of the Atlantic Coast from Maine southward, and his publication of this research attracted the attention of Darwin and other European naturalists. After 1866 he made his home at Salem, Mass. He had married, on June 18, 1863, Ellen Elizabeth Owen. He helped to found the *American Naturalist* and in 1869 became a fellow of the American Academy of Arts and Sciences. He was professor of zoölogy and comparative anatomy at Bowdoin College, 1871–74. In 1876 he was elected a vice-president of the American Association for the Advancement of Science, and served in 1886 as president.

The Pacific Ocean brachiopods lured Morse to Japan in 1877. The expedition started the young conchologist in studies which brought him eminence and led to his writing extensively upon archeology, anthropology, architecture, ceramics, ballistics, folk-lore, and astronomy. This versatility was natural, for Morse's mentality was encyclopedic. He was, however, intensely emotional and often prejudiced, as when he allowed his anti-religious bias to cause him to ignore much of the mythological lore and ceremonial life of ancient Japan. Admitted this disqualification, his journals of the Japanese years, carefully kept and illustrated with his expressive and descriptive drawings, are very important documents.

Morse opened a laboratory at Eno Shima and was invited to teach zoölogy at the Imperial University, Tokyo. His tenure of this professorship (1877–80) witnessed the introduction among the Japanese of modern methods of collecting and classifying objects of natural history. From the train between Eno-Shima and the capital Morse's alert eye detected some shell heaps, ignored by the native savants. His excavation of these kitchen-middens with their pre-historic artifacts was an epoch in the annals of anthropology. While visiting Yezo and the Hokkaido Morse first saw the Aino and perceived their probable kinship with the brunette white races. Having found at Omori the earliest of Japanese potteries he set out to form a complete collection of the national ceramics, including the works of living potters. In association with the Boston collectors, William Sturgis Bigelow and Ernest F. Fenollosa [qq.v.], he took part in the preservation of almost countless objects of art at a time when the Japanese were inclined to dispose of them. A friendship formed with Percival Lowell [q.v.], astronomer and author of *The Soul of the Far East* (1888), preceded the astronomical observations and researches to be embodied later in a book on Mars.

Morse's first residence in Japan ended in 1880 when he returned to Salem to take up his life-work as director of the Peabody Museum. He revisited Japan in 1882, extending his journey to China. In 1898 the Japanese Emperor decorated him with the Order of the Rising Sun. He was the first American to be so honored. Beginning with his Lowell Institute lectures on Japanese folkways in 1881, Morse gave to many persons their initial appreciation of the beauty and dignity of the arts and life of *daimyo* and *samurai*. He was an ideal popular lecturer, spontaneous, dramatic, witty, and always well informed. He drew brilliantly, on occasion, with both hands. The Peabody Museum, meantime, became primarily Morse's museum, with his multifarious collections, attractively arranged. His foremost achievement, however, the Morse collection of Japanese potteries, was deposited in 1890 in the Boston Museum of Fine Arts as a loan. It was bought by the museum in 1892 and Morse was made its curator. His great catalogue of the collection, scholarly, discriminating, and readable, was published in 1901. In 1925 the aged author received a copy of the Japanese translation of this work, sponsored by the imperial government. His publications, which concerned, besides the subjects already mentioned, music, archery, numismatics, and other topics, were numerous and yet, apparently, never superficial or casual. He was painstaking if not always patient. A vivid emotionality and an accompanying irritability gave to his writing and conversation a piquant charm, and an obvious limitation. The books, besides the ceramic catalogue mentioned, by which he is best represented are: *First Book of Zoölogy* (1875); *Japanese Homes and their Surroundings* (1886); *Glimpses of China and Chinese Homes* (1902);

Mars and its Mystery (1906) ; *Japan Day by Day* (2 vols., 1917).

[Copious manuscript materials for a life of Morse await a biographer. *Japan Day by Day* is autobiographical. The Boston Museum of Fine Arts possesses the notes on which the *Cat. of the Morse Collection of. Japanese Pottery* (1901) was based. See especially the obituary article by F. S. Kershaw in the *Museum of Fine Arts Bull.*, Feb. 1926, and the obituary, *Boston Herald*, Dec. 21, 1925.]   F. W. C.

MORSE, FREEMAN HARLOW (Feb. 18, 1807–Feb. 6, 1891), carver of figure-heads, congressman from Maine, United States consul at London, the son of William and Eliza (Harlow) Morse, was born in Bath, Me. Until the age of fourteen he attended the public schools. Without serving the usual apprenticeship, he immediately commenced ship-carving in which he attained great skill. Nearly all of his spare time he spent in reading, first on art and poetry, then as his interests changed, on history and politics. A young men's debating society of which he was a member gave him his first training in the preparation and delivery of speeches. His ability attracted the attention of local politicians and as a Whig he represented his district in the state legislature in 1840, 1841, and 1843. Twice he was the Whig candidate for the speaker's office. He was elected to the Twenty-eighth Congress on the Whig ticket in a Democratic district. His first speech before the House was a defense of the Maine commissioners on the Northeastern boundary and of Webster as negotiator of the Treaty of Washington. His last speech before his retirement, Mar. 3, 1845, was in opposition to the annexation of Texas. The Liberty party in Maine so divided the vote in Morse's district that, in spite of the general opposition there to annexation, an annexationist was elected. Morse returned to Bath and resumed ship-carving, entering politics briefly in 1845 only to suffer defeat as the Whig candidate for governor. He was mayor of Bath in 1849, 1850, and 1855, and again served in the state legislature in 1853 and 1856. Becoming a zealous advocate of the principles of the Republican party, he was returned to Congress, serving two terms, Mar. 4, 1857, to Mar. 3, 1861. As a congressman from Maine he attended the so-called Peace Convention of 1861.

On Mar. 22, 1861, Morse accepted appointment from President Lincoln as United States consul at London. As the war proceeded, this office became of increasing importance. Morse was closely associated with Charles Francis Adams in the task of gathering evidence regarding British-built privateers. President Johnson continued Morse in the consulship, while President Grant, in spite of the almost unanimous op-

position of the Maine delegation in Congress, advanced him to consul-general on Apr. 16, 1869. But he was not to hold this post long; Gen. Adam Badeau [*q.v.*] replaced him in July 1870. Unhappy over his retirement, which he ascribed to narrowly partisan politics, Morse refused to return to America. He became a British citizen, continuing, however, to perform many friendly services for Americans in England. He contributed two articles on foreign trade to the *International Review* (January, May 1879) and two articles on civil service to *Harper's New Monthly Magazine* (July 1877, May 1878). His wife, Nancy Leavitt of Bath, whom he had married on Apr. 21, 1834, returned to America with their two daughters and lived for a time in Wellesley Hills, Mass. Morse died of old age in Surbiton, Surrey, England, and is buried in the churchyard of the parish of St. Mary's, Long Ditton.

[Abner Morse, *Memorial of the Morses* (1850), App., p. xc ; H. D. Lord, *Memorial of the Family of Morse* (1896) ; *Souvenir of the 300th Anniversary of Am. Shipbuilding, Bath, Maine*, Aug. 5–9, 1907 ; obituary in Bath (Me.) *Daily Times*.]   R. E. M.

MORSE, HARMON NORTHROP (Oct. 15, 1848–Sept. 8, 1920), professor of chemistry, was born at Cambridge, Vt., where his early years were spent on his father's farm. He was the son of Harmon and Elizabeth Murray (Buck) Morse and a brother of Anson Daniel Morse [*q.v.*]. His first paternal ancestor, John Morse, came to America in 1639 from England and settled at New Haven, Conn. Morse graduated from Amherst in 1873 and after two years in Germany he received the degree of Ph.D. from Göttingen in 1875. After returning to America he taught for one year at Amherst. When The Johns Hopkins University was opened he was made one of the first fellows of that institution but before entering upon the fellowship he was promoted to a position on the staff of the chemistry department of that university and remained connected therewith until his retirement, becoming successively associate professor (1883), professor of analytical chemistry and adjunct director of the laboratory (1892), professor of inorganic and analytical chemistry and director of the chemistry laboratory from 1908 until his retirement in 1916. In 1916 he was awarded the Avogadro Medal offered by the Turin Academy of Sciences. He was also fellow of the American Academy of Arts and Sciences, foreign member of the Utrecht Society of Arts and Sciences, of the American Philosophical Society, and of the National Academy of Sciences. For many years preceding his retirement he was research associate of the Carnegie Institution of Washington, D. C.

Morse's first contributions were in the field of organic chemistry. He made but three contributions in this field, however, when it was necessary for him to give his attention to inorganic and analytical chemistry. His investigations in these fields included many new methods of quantitative analysis both gravimetric and volumetric and a well-known method for the calibration of volumetric apparatus. Besides researches on methods of analysis his work on *The Atomic Weight of Zinc as Determined by the Composition of Its Oxide* (1889), written in collaboration with W. M. Burton, and "A Redetermination of the Atomic Weight of Cadmium" (*American Chemical Journal,* April 1892), in collaboration with H. C. Jones, deserve special mention. Up to this point Morse's work consisted of isolated researches on a variety of analytical problems in which there was frequently exhibited a high order of skill and ingenuity. In 1896 he began his first extended investigation. This was on permanganic acid and its salts and was continued for several years. This work led by accident to what later proved to be his most conspicuous investigation. It was noticed occasionally that the porous clay cell used in the preparation of permanganic acid solutions became filled with finely divided manganese dioxide. From this observation an electrolytic method was developed for depositing semipermeable membranes. The utilization of these membranes in accumulating accurate experimental data on the osmotic pressure of aqueous solutions occupied Morse's whole outstanding accomplishment. In all, Morse published about sixty articles on original researches. All of these except the first three were published in the *American Chemical Journal.* In addition he was the author of *Exercises in Quantitative Chemistry* (1905) and *The Osmotic Pressure of Aqueous Solutions* (1914), monograph No. 198 of the Carnegie Institution of Washington, which is a complete report of the investigations of himself and associates on the subject of osmotic pressure carried out at The Johns Hopkins University under grants from the Carnegie Institution. His death occurred suddenly at his summer home at Chebeague, Cumberland County, Sept. 8, 1920. He had married, Dec. 13, 1876, Caroline Augusta, daughter of John Brooks, a merchant of Montpelier, Vt. In 1887 his wife died leaving four children, and on Dec. 24, 1890, he was married to Elizabeth Dennis Clarke of Portland, Me. There were no children by the second marriage.

[Biographical memoirs in *Memoirs Nat. Acad. Sci.,* vol. XXI (1926), with bibliography; *Who's Who in America,* 1920–21; *Daily Eastern Argus* (Portland, Me.), Sept. 9, 1920.]   J. C. W. F.

MORSE, HENRY DUTTON (Apr. 20, 1826– Jan. 2, 1888), diamond cutter, was born in Boston, Mass., the seventh of the eleven children of Hazen and Lucy (Cary) Morse. Of English descent, he belonged on his father's side to the seventh, and on his mother's to the sixth, generation of native-born New Englanders. His father was a well-known bank-note engraver, in whose office Henry mastered the craft while still a boy in school. From the beginning he had sharp eyes, a cunning hand, and the instinct of workmanship. When eighteen years old he set up for himself as an engraver and designer in gold and silver and a few years later learned jewelry-making in the workshops of Clark & Currier, whom he paid $300 for six months' instruction. For some years he manufactured jewelry; then he became a partner in the retail firm of Crosby, Hunnewell & Morse (later Crosby, Morse & Foss) on Washington Street; on the dissolution of the partnership in 1875 he opened a shop of his own on Tremont, confining himself to a trade in precious stones, and two years later organized the Morse Diamond Cutting Company. He was the first American to learn the technique of diamond-cutting. Although his Dutch workmen took their usual precautions to guard the secrets of their trade, Morse spied them out, experimented until he became expert, imparted his skill to American apprentices, and finally made improvements that revolutionized the whole art of diamond cutting. He invented labor-saving machinery for sawing and polishing the stones and, after studying the application of the laws of optics to the work, boldly sacrificed weight to proportion and so cut the first modern full-fashioned brilliants with their fifty-six facets and dazzling powers of refraction. Absolute precision in cutting was his basic principle. No radical changes have been made in the art since his time. The most famous of Morse's early feats was the cutting in 1859 of the so-called Dewey diamond, an ill-shaped, discolored, badly flawed, but well-advertized "rock," which a laborer turned up in a Manchester, Va., street in 1854. After other cutters had given it over as a bad job, he succeeded in obtaining from it an octahedron, with slightly rounded faces, weighing almost twelve carats. Years later, when his hand, eye, and brain were at their best, he cut the largest diamond ever handled in the United States, the Tiffany No. 2 of 125 carats, which was reduced to 77 carats in the cutting. Morse was married May 22, 1849, to Ann Eliza Hayden, daughter of Ezekiel and Elizabeth (West) Hayden, who with two of their four daughters survived him. Artistic taste, keen eyesight, and manual skill were as evident in his recreations as in his professional work. He was an amateur painter, frequently exhibiting his landscapes and animal pictures at Boston shows, an expert rifle shot, and an ornithologist and bird-stuffer. He died at his home at Jamaica Plain, Mass., of a stroke, after an illness of two days.

[H. D. Lord, *Memorial of the Family of Morse* (1896), pp. 340–42; S. C. Cary, *John Cary, the Plymouth Pilgrim* (1911); *Jeweler's Weekly*, Jan. 5, 12, 1888; G. F. Kunz, *Gems and Precious Stones of North America* (1890), pp. 16–17, 316 17; W. R. Cattelle, *Precious Stones* (1903), pp. 60–61; *Boston Daily Advertiser*, Jan. 3, 1888; *Boston Transcript*, Jan. 3, 5, 1888.]
G. H. G.

MORSE, JEDIDIAH (Aug. 23, 1761–June 9, 1826), Congregational clergyman, "father of American Geography," was born in Woodstock, Conn., the eighth child of Jedidiah and Sarah (Child) Morse. After a rather frail boyhood he entered Yale College with the class of 1783, in which "he had a very fair reputation as a scholar . . . though he scarcely gave promise of the eminence which he finally attained" (Sprague, *Annals, post*, p. 251). As a student, he was a member of the Linonian Society and of Phi Beta Kappa. On the eve of graduation he decided to enter the Christian ministry, and with this end in view remained in New Haven for two more years studying theology and supporting himself by teaching and by writing a school textbook in geography. He was licensed to preach in 1785, and for a time taught school and preached in Norwich, Conn., returning to Yale as tutor in June 1786. Overwork, a desire to further his geographical studies by travel, and the attractions of an evangelical ministry led him, a few months later, to seek ordination (Nov. 9, 1786) and take the vacant pulpit in Midway, Ga., where he remained for five months. The following year he preached as candidate for settlement in the Collegiate Presbyterian Churches of New York and in the First Congregational Church of Charlestown, Mass., finally accepting a call from Charlestown. Following his installation, Apr. 30, 1789, he married, May 14, Elizabeth Ann Breese of Shrewsbury, N. J., the daughter of Judge Samuel Breese and the grand-daughter of Samuel Finley [*q.v.*], president of the College of New Jersey. Over the church in Charlestown Morse remained settled for thirty years. As a preacher he was unusually acceptable and popular. Of his sermons and occasional addresses, some twenty-four were published.

In his theological views Morse was a Calvinist and a stanch supporter of orthodoxy. With growing concern, therefore, he observed the inroads of "Arminianism, blended with Unitarianism" in the Congregational churches of eastern Massachusetts. To combat the progress of these "liberal views" became one of the dominant purposes of his ministry, and it was early his hope to separate the Unitarians from the Orthodox and then draw the Orthodox of different shades into more cordial relations. As the champion of Orthodoxy, Morse stepped to the front following the election of Henry Ware [*q.v.*] as Hollis Professor of Divinity at Harvard in 1805. One of the board of overseers, he vigorously opposed this choice on the ground that Ware's theological views were not the orthodox views of the donor, and that his election was a violation of the terms and spirit of the Hollis bequest. Furthermore, he made public the orthodox position in his *True Reasons on which the Election of a Hollis Professor of Divinity in Harvard College was opposed at the Board of Overseers, 14 February, 1805* (1805), the appearance of which proved decisive in joining the issue between the liberal and the orthodox within the Congregational order in Massachusetts. Determined that the liberal clergy should not wholly carry the day, he launched the *Panoplist* in 1805 to uphold and unify the orthodox cause, and this periodical he edited for five years. Equally important in behalf of orthodoxy were his labors in the organization of the General Association of Massachusetts, and in the establishment of Andover Theological Seminary (1808), of which he was one of the most active founders. In Boston itself, he assisted in founding a bulwark of orthodoxy in the Park Street Church (1809), and finally, in publishing the pamphlet, *American Unitarianism; or a Brief History of "The Progress and Present State of the Unitarian Churches in America"* (1815), extracted from Thomas Belsham's *Memoirs of the Life of the Reverend Theophilus Lindsey* (1812), he did more, perhaps, than any one man to force the Unitarian churches out from the Congregational fold. Morse's own church did not escape division, for a Unitarian defection took place in 1816, and continued friction led to his own request for dismissal in 1819.

Not all Morse's energies went into the Unitarian controversy, however. Quite as important, perhaps, were his efforts to further the progress of evangelical truth. He was among the first in America to see the value of tract distribution, and he helped found the New England Tract Society (1814). Equally active were his efforts in the distribution of the Bible, and in 1816 he aided in establishing the American Bible Society. In 1811 he was elected to the American Board of

Commissioners for Foreign Missions, and served on the prudential committee of that board until 1819. As secretary of the Society for Propagating the Gospel among the Indians and others in North America, he took an active interest in the Indians, as well as in the poor whites on the Isles of Shoals. This interest lasted throughout his ministry, and upon leaving Charlestown in 1819 he was commissioned by the government to study the condition of the Indian nations and to render a report, which he published in 1822 (*A Report to the Secretary of War . . . on Indian Affairs, Comprising a Narrative of a Tour Performed in the Summer of 1820*).

In politics Morse was as conservative as in religion, and quite as outspoken. A strong Federalist, he was startled and dismayed in the 1790's by the rising tide of republicanism and by the prevalence of the "French influence," which seemed to him to threaten "orderly" government and religion in the United States. In 1798 he firmly believed that he had discovered the secret cause of these evils in the spread of Illuminism to this side of the Atlantic, and, giving wide publicity to this rather dubious discovery in three sensational published sermons, he contributed not a little to the wave of popular hysteria which followed the outbreak of the quasi-war with France. So vigorous was his defense of the existing political order that to some of his contemporaries he appeared as a "Pillar of Adamant in the Temple of Federalism." His political convictions led him in 1801 to assist in founding *The Mercury and New England Palladium,* a vigorous Federalist periodical.

Jedidiah Morse is best remembered, however, as the "father of American Geography." It was while teaching school in New Haven that his interest in geography developed. Dissatisfied with the treatment of America in the existing English texts, he prepared a series of geographical lectures, which were published in 1784 as *Geography Made Easy,* the first geography to be published in the United States. During the lifetime of its author this famous little text passed through twenty-five editions. So successful was this first effort that he at once projected a larger work which he published in 1789 as *The American Geography,* and in its later editions as *The American Universal Geography.* This work passed through seven American and almost as many European editions, and firmly established its author's reputation as "the American Geographer." Largely in recognition of his geographical services the University of Edinburgh honored him with its degree of S.T.D. in 1794. In 1795 he published *Elements of Geography,*

for children, followed in 1797 by *The American Gazetteer* and in 1802 by *A New Gazetteer of the Eastern Continent,* prepared in collaboration with Elijah Parish, all of which passed through several editions, as did abridgments of these more basic works. During their author's lifetime the Morse geographies virtually monopolized their field in the United States. He was essentially a compiler, drawing his information from the best American and European sources available, as well as from letters and documents sent him from all parts of the country in response to widely published requests for geographical information. At the request of the publisher Morse wrote the article on America for the American edition of the *Encyclopedia Britannica* (1790), which was also published separately. In collaboration with Elijah Parish he wrote *A Compendious History of New England* (1804), the appearance of which gave rise to a famous literary controversy with Hannah Adams [*q.v.*]. Almost his final literary effort was his *Annals of the American Revolution* (1824).

Following his removal from Charlestown Morse went to New Haven, where he devoted the closing years of his life to Indian affairs, writing, and occasional preaching. In personal appearance he was very prepossessing. "The tall, slender form, the well shaped head, a little bald, but covered thinly with fine silken powdered hair, falling gracefully into curls, gave him, when only middle-aged, a venerable aspect, while the benignant expression of his whole countenance and especially of his bright, speaking eye won for him at first sight respect and love" (S. E. Morse, quoted in Sprague, *Life, post,* p. 281). In dress and manners he was "a gentleman of the old school." Temperamentally he was inclined to be sanguine, impulsive, and rather sensitive, which tendencies made him, perhaps, over controversial at times; but his most marked characteristics were his tremendous industry and intellectual activity. To his friend Timothy Dwight, 1752–1817 [*q.v.*], he was "as full of resources as an egg is of meat" (Prime, *post,* p. 4). Of the eleven children born to him and his wife, three survived infancy: Samuel Finley Breese Morse, Sidney Edwards Morse [*qq.v.*], and Richard Cary Morse.

[The chief source for the life of Morse is a manuscript life by his son, Richard Cary Morse, the property of the late Richard Cary Morse of New York. Published sources include W. B. Sprague, *The Life of Jedidiah Morse* (1874), and *Annals Am. Pulpit,* vol. II (1857); F. B. Dexter, *Biog. Sketches Grads. Yale Coll.,* vol. IV (1907); S. I. Prime, *The Life of Samuel F. B. Morse* (1875); E. L. Morse, *Samuel F. B. Morse; His Letters and Jours.* (2 vols., 1914); *Columbian Register* (New Haven), June 10, 1826. For his part in the

Illuminati episode see V. Stauffer, *New England and the Bavarian Illuminati* (1918).]   W. R. W.

MORSE, SAMUEL FINLEY BREESE (Apr. 27, 1791–Apr. 2, 1872), artist, inventor, was born in Charlestown, Mass., in the Edes House on Main Street, the eldest child of the Rev. Jedidiah Morse [q.v.] and his wife, Elizabeth Ann Breese. He was sixth in descent from Anthony Morse of Marlborough, Wilts, who emigrated to Massachusetts in 1635 and settled in Newbury. Anthony's grandson, Peter, removed before 1698 from Newbury to New Roxbury, which, by a relocation of the colonial boundary, became Woodstock, Conn., in 1749 but remained the seat of the family down to Jedidiah's birth in 1761. Morse's mother was the only child of Samuel Breese by his first wife, Rebecca, daughter of Samuel Finley [q.v.]. Breese, whose father had been a purser in the British navy and later a thriving merchant in New York, lived on his estate at Shrewsbury, N. J., was a district judge, and a colonel in the Continental Army. Mrs. Morse managed her household with shrewd practical sense, held her husband's Calvinist and Federalist convictions without mitigation or dilution, and bore with heroic resignation the death at birth or in infancy of eight of her eleven children. To his surviving brothers, Sidney Edwards Morse [q.v.] and Richard Cary Morse (1795–1868), as to his parents, he was affectionately attached throughout life. The characteristics of the parents descended with little modification to the children; in Finley, as his family called him, the energy and enterprise of the father were fused with the strong will and sense of the mother.

At the age of eight Morse was taken to Phillips Academy, Andover, of which his father was a trustee. He was unhappy under Mark Newman's discipline and twice was so homesick that he fled back to Charlestown. He entered Yale College in 1805, was summoned home, however, during his first year, and did not graduate until 1810. While in residence at Yale he acquired a local reputation for his miniatures on ivory, but his father was reluctant to let him adopt art as a profession.

While he was working as a clerk in a Charlestown bookstore, his pictures of "Marius on the Ruins of Carthage" and "The Landing of the Pilgrims at Plymouth" gained him the approval of Washington Allston and Gilbert Stuart; his parents consented; and on July 13, 1811, he sailed with Allston and his wife for England. Except for two portrait-painting expeditions to Bristol, he spent the next four years in London studying under his master Allston, whom he never ceased

to admire, and at the Royal Academy, where he received courteous attention from Benjamin West. He lived frugally; made a warm friend of his room-mate, Charles Robert Leslie [q.v.]; met a few notables; read Chaucer, Spenser, Dante, and Tasso as part of his education in art; and painted assiduously. He produced three works of distinction: in 1812 a terra-cotta statuette of "Hercules," that won the gold medal of the Society of Arts; in 1813 a large canvas, "The Dying Hercules," which was hung in the spring exhibition that year of the Royal Academy and received much flattering comment; and in 1815 a second painting, "The Judgment of Jupiter," which would probably have won the cash premium of the Royal Academy if Morse had stayed to receive it. That summer, however, he returned to Boston and opened a studio, full of ambition "to be among those who shall revive the splendor of the fifteenth century."

His hopes were soon dashed. He was socially successful, and people visited his studio to admire "The Dying Hercules" and "The Judgment of Jupiter," but no one offered to buy them or gave him commissions for similar work. As a young artist in London he had disdained portrait-painting, but he soon found that portraits were the only works of art that Americans would buy. Since there were not enough commissions to keep him in Boston, he was compelled to lead a rather vagrant existence. The chief centers of his activity, besides Boston, were Concord, N. H., the home of his father-in-law, which he visited for the first time in the summer of 1816; New Haven, the home of his parents in their latter years; Charleston, S. C., where he spent the winters of 1818–21 and achieved his initial successes; and New York, where he made his headquarters after 1823. In four or five years his art reached its maturity. To the vigor and honesty fundamental to his own nature, he added a profound insight into character and a free, delicate technique. He was thus an admirable portrait painter, and though he had to paint many a dull face for the sake of the fee, he seldom failed to respond to a sitter worthy of him. The level excellence of his portraits is high. Perhaps the best known were the two of Lafayette painted in Washington in 1825, the full-length owned by the City of New York and the half-length owned by the New York Public Library. His landscapes and subject-pictures are much fewer in number and are, for the most part, cold and unimaginative. An exception, however, is "The Old House of Representatives" (Corcoran Gallery, Washington), which he painted in 1821–22. With its eighty-six portraits and masterly rendering of the effect of candle-light, it has its own magnificence and has elicited warm admiration. A similar but lesser feat of virtuosity was "The Exhibition Gallery of the Louvre" (College of Fine Arts, Syracuse University), done in 1831–32. Morse painted these pictures in the hope of making money by exhibiting them around the country, but the public was indifferent to them, and both pictures disappeared for some years. He was the leading spirit among the founders of the National Academy of Design and as its first president, 1826–42, made it an active and even aggressive institution. He organized efficient classes for instruction and waged a pamphlet war against the rival American Academy of Fine Arts, which he denounced as exclusive and moribund. His inventive fancy led him to devise ingenious theories about the combination of colors and to make various experiments. For one of his most beautifully executed pictures, a portrait of his wife and their two children, he ground his pigments in milk; for another picture, with results unrecorded, he ground them in beer.

In the intellectual and artistic circles of New York his urbanity, conversational powers, and commanding presence found their appropriate sphere. His income, however, was uncomfortably small and irregular; and the successive deaths of his wife in 1825, his father in 1826, and his mother in 1828 were hard to bear. In 1829 he went to Europe and spent three years in study, travel, and painting. He divided his time chiefly between Italy and Paris, and cultivated close friendships with James Fenimore Cooper and Horatio Greenough. He was too old, unfortunately, to benefit much by the change of environment.

In October 1832 he returned to New York from Havre on the packet Sully. The voyage marked the turning point of his career, but the transition from artist to inventor occupied another five years. In 1832 he was appointed professor of painting and sculpture (later professor of the literature of the arts of design) in the University of the City of New York (now New York University). He retained the title for life, but the position was only nominal; he received no salary, and the fees from his pupils did not pay the rent of his rooms in the University Building on Washington Square. To this period 1832–35 belongs his lapse into anti-Catholic and Native-American agitation. He had come home from Italy with a strong aversion to Catholicism; he fell an easy victim to Maria Monk's imposture, and was inveigled into writing and sponsoring several widely circulated anti-Catholic and Na-

tive-American tracts. In 1836 he ran for mayor of New York on the Native-American ticket, polling about 1500 votes. His example conferred on the movement such respectability as it possessed. In his riper years, he disentangled his facts and his prejudices and grew more tolerant. Several causes contributed to his final withdrawal, about 1837, from painting. The contumelious rejection by a committee of Congress of his application to fill one of the four large vacant panels in the rotunda of the Capitol was probably the deciding factor; but he was weary of the struggle for recognition and even for subsistence; he had reached the limit of his powers as an artist, and a new career was opening before him. But he took the step unwillingly and grieved over it for years (E. L. Morse, post, II, 31).

Morse's preoccupation with the telegraph dates from the voyage on the Sully in October 1832. A fellow passenger, Charles Thomas Jackson [q.v.], led the dinner conversation one day to electricity and exhibited apparatus that he had acquired in Europe. Morse remarked, "If the presence of electricity can be made visible in any part of the circuit, I see no reason why intelligence may not be transmitted instantaneously by electricity." There is evidence that his mind had already toyed with the idea, but the conception of an electro-magnetic recording telegraph came to him now with the power of a revelation, and during the rest of the crossing he lived in a state of intense intellectual excitement, sketching in his note-book a rude but sufficient plan of his invention. His qualifications for the work ahead of him were curiously variegated. Though he had developed little mechanical skill, he had the inventive type of mind. With his brother Sidney he had patented in 1817 a workable, though unremunerative, flexible piston-pump for fire-engines, and five years later he constructed a marble-cutting machine that infringed unluckily on a previous patent. His interest in electrical phenomena had been awakened by the college lectures and demonstrations of Benjamin Silliman and Jeremiah Day. Early in 1827 he attended a course of lectures on electricity delivered before the New York Athenæum by James Freeman Dana [q.v.], who included in his topics a detailed, extremely able exposition of the electro-magnet discovered in 1824 by the Englishman, William Sturgeon. Among Dana's auditors, unknown to each other, were Joseph Henry, Leonard Dunnell Gale (1800–1883), and Morse. Henry went from the lecture room to Albany to embark on his great career; Gale was employed on a geological survey; and Morse continued with his painting. He and Dana became friends, but Dana died Apr. 14, 1827, and the possibilities latent in their association came to an end. What Morse knew about electricity in October 1832 he had learned from Dana; he was ignorant of the progress of the last five years, of Henry's discoveries in electro-magnetism and the several European experiments with an electro-magnetic needle telegraph.

The essential features of his invention, as set down in the 1832 note-book, were: (1) a sending-apparatus to transmit signals by the closing and opening of an electric circuit; (2) a receiving-apparatus, operated by an electro-magnet, to record the signals as dots and spaces on a strip of paper moved by clock-work; (3) a code translating the dots and spaces into numbers and letters. From this original conception Morse wrought his invention through elaboration to eventual simplicity. The sending-apparatus became a "port-rule," through which notched lead types were run to break the circuit automatically in the required sequences of dots and spaces, but this arrangement gave way at last to the simple finger-key. The recording-apparatus went through a similar development before the embossing stylus took the place of clumsier methods of recording. Rather early in the process Morse noticed that the signals could also be read by ear and worked out an efficient sounder. The code went through another series of changes before it became the "Morse code" of American telegraphy. At the outset Morse did not dream of the telegraph as one of the conveniences of daily life; it was to be government-controlled and used only for communications of momentous importance. With this idea in mind, he wasted much time on devising a semi-secret code that required the use of a huge dictionary. He saw from the beginning, however, that another system would be needed for sending proper names. The dash was added to the signals, and dots, dashes, and spaces were translated directly into the letters of the alphabet.

In January 1836 Morse took Gale, now his colleague at the University of the City of New York, into his confidence and showed him his working model. The magnet, however, would not function at a greater distance than forty feet from the battery. Gale's service to the inventor was to bring his knowledge of electro-magnetism up to date. For the one-cup battery and simple Sturgeon magnet he substituted Henry's many-cup battery and intensity magnet, after which they were able to send messages through ten miles of wire wound on reels around Gale's lecture room. Gale also brought Morse into personal contact with Henry, who from time to time gave essential advice and encouragement. At this time, too, Morse worked out a system of electro-magnetic renewers or relays to be placed in the telegraph line at those points where the electric current became too feeble either to print or to project a signal. This was his most brilliant contribution, for it made both possible and practicable the transmission of intelligence from one point on a line through indefinitely great distances, to any number of branch lines, and to an indefinite number of stations, with registration at them all by the manipulation of a single operator at a single station. The general idea was anticipated by Henry and was incorporated in the patents of Morse's contemporaries in England, Wheatstone and Edward Davy, but its practical application, fully described by Morse in his caveat filed in the Patent Office in 1837, would indicate that this was an original discovery. In September 1837 Alfred Vail [q.v.] was also taken into partnership. He provided money for carrying on the work, gave Morse needed moral support, and lent his mechanical skill to the simplifying of the apparatus.

Morse filed his caveat at the Patent Office in September 1837 and went to Europe to secure patents. In England his application was rejected without ceremony; in France he was fêted by scientists and scholars, but the French government was not interested, and he returned empty handed, having been unable to comply with the French patent law. Seven lean years followed, during which Morse preferred poverty and actual hunger to going into debt. Even the Vail family refused him further advances, and Morse's courage almost faltered, but in the confused last minutes of the closing session of 1843, Congress voted $30,000 for an experimental line from Washington to Baltimore. Meanwhile he had been advertising his invention by exhibitions in New York and in 1838 before President Van Buren at Washington, and had been making drastic changes in the apparatus. The Washington-Baltimore line was built by Ezra Cornell [q.v.], and on May 24, 1844, Morse sent the famous salutation, "What hath God wrought!" from the Supreme Court room in the Capitol to Vail in Baltimore. Vail returned the message correctly; and a brief conversation ensued over the wire. The Morse telegraph was in operation.

The telegraph having proved its worth, Morse entered upon the last phase of his career. He and his associates were willing to sell their rights to the government for $100,000, and Morse, satisfied with a competence, would have resumed his painting; but Cave Johnson, the postmaster-general, opined that the invention would not pay its way, Congress adjourned without acting, and the development of the telegraph was left in private hands. The inventor himself had little knowledge of business methods and was sometimes scandalized by what he chanced to discover; though want had taught him to value money, he was too versatile to become engrossed in its acquisition; and he had an artist's repugnance to the necessary routine. It was therefore one of his greatest strokes of luck that he engaged Amos Kendall [q.v.], to manage his business and legal affairs, leaving himself comparatively free. He could not escape, however, from the harassments of almost continuous litigation and detraction. Of all his enemies Francis Ormond Jonathan Smith, a former Congressman from Maine, who had championed Morse in Congress and had become one of his partners, proved the most unscrupulous and implacable, pursuing the inventor even to his death-bed. Morse's rights were upheld in the courts, and in the last analysis the most deplorable feature of his many controversies was the rupture with Joseph Henry. The breach began with an oversight in Vail's book on the telegraph and was rapidly widened by a series of misunderstandings, by the sensitive nature of both men, and by the intrigues of rival entrepreneurs. Morse, usually grateful to his friends and at times magnanimous, was finally goaded into making a headlong, hysterical assault on Henry's integrity. The charges were baseless and have left an unfortunate stain on Morse's reputation. He lived to realize the enormity of his folly and tried awkwardly to make amends, but pride kept him from offering the full confession of guilt that the case demanded.

Otherwise he enjoyed the acclaim, honors, and emoluments of a great inventor and public personage. Yale conferred her LL.D. on him, and European governments, while consistently denying him patents, showered him with medals and decorations until his coat-front, on state occasions, glittered like a lieutenant-general's. In 1858 France, Austria, Belgium, the Netherlands, Piedmont, Russia, the Holy See, Sweden, Tuscany, and Turkey united to give him an honorary gratuity of 400,000 francs, part of which he was compelled to hand over to F. O. J. Smith. His first dividends from the telegraph he gave for church uses. For years his income was slender and uncertain. Kendall's benign efforts to make him rich were constantly thwarted by Morse's open-handed benefactions and the ease with which he could be duped by swindlers, but ultimately both men attained to wealth. In 1854 he ran for Congress on the Democratic ticket and was defeated. In 1857–58 he was electrician for Cyrus W. Field's Company, engaged in laying the transatlantic cable, but resigned when he found himself maneuvered off the board of directors. He distrusted the insulation used on the second cable and, during the few weeks of its operation, predicted its failure. He was one of the founders of Vassar College in 1861 and served again that year as president of the National Academy of Design. In 1864 he made a last effort to paint but found that his skill had departed. His home during these years was a two-hundred-acre estate, "Locust Grove," on the Hudson two miles below Poughkeepsie, which he had bought in 1847. In 1859 he acquired a brownstone house at 5 West 22nd Street, New York City, as a winter residence.

His family life matched his two-fold career as artist and inventor. On Sept. 29, 1818, he married Lucretia Pickering Walker, daughter of Charles and Hannah (Pickering) Walker of Concord, N. H. She died in 1825, and for twenty-three years Morse was a widower. On Aug. 9, 1848, he married Sarah Elizabeth, daughter of Samuel and Catharine (Breese) Griswold of Utica, N. Y., Mrs. Griswold being his first cousin. His second wife was his junior by thirty-one years, but he lived to within a year of their silver wedding. He had four children by each marriage. His youngest son, Edward Lind Morse, graduated from Yale College sixty-eight years after his father.

On June 10, 1871, the telegraph operators of America unveiled a bronze statue of Morse in Central Park, N. Y. It was the work of Byron M. Pickett and was presented to the city by William Cullen Bryant. Morse's last public appearance was on Jan. 17, 1872, when he and Horace Greeley unveiled a statue of Franklin in Printing House Square. His health was now failing. One of his last acts was to take his youngest son downtown to buy him his first gold watch. He died at his city home Apr. 2 and was buried in Greenwood Cemetery.

It was Morse the inventor whose death was commemorated by Congress and at memorial meetings held throughout the nation, the artist having been forgotten. Though his specific inventions have long since been obsolete, even the Morse code giving way to automatic dispatching and printing machines, he remains the greatest figure in the history of the telegraph. Recognition of him as an artist has come slowly, but the exhibition of his paintings at the Metropolitan Museum of Art in 1932 enhanced a reputation that had already begun to grow. The most recent students of American art have been warmest in their appraisal of his successes as a painter and of his influence on the national culture, but his full significance as one of the representative men of his time is revealed only by a study of his whole career and his stalwart, many-sided personality.

[*Samuel F. B. Morse: His Letters and Journals, Edited and Supplemented by his Son, Edward Lind Morse* (2 vols., 1914) is the most authoritative biography but does not wholly supersede the earlier official biography, S. I. Prime, *The Life of Samuel F. B. Morse, LL.D.* (1875). Both were founded on Morse's papers (63 vols., including letter books), now in the Division of Manuscripts, Lib. of Cong. There is other manuscript material in the Yale Univ. Lib. and among the F. O. J. Smith papers in the Me. Hist. Soc. Lib. The U. S. Nat. Museum has the certified copy of the 1832 note-book and various relics of the first Morse telegraph; Cornell Univ. has a few others. Additional biographical material may be found in: *Memorial of Samuel Finley Breese Morse . . . Pub. by Order of Cong.* (1875); Justin Winsor, ed., *The Memorial Hist. of Boston*, III (1881), 552–53; *Personal Reminiscences of the late Mrs. Sarah Breese Walker* (privately printed, 1884); E. G. Porter, "The Morse Tablet at Rome," *Proc. Mass. Hist. Soc.*, 2 ser. XI (1897); J. H. Morse and E. W. Leavitt, *Morse Geneal.* (1903), esp. pp. 216–17; F. B. Dexter, *Biog. Sketches of the Grads. of Yale Coll.*, vol. VI (1912)—the only bibliography of Morse's own writings; *Correspondence of Jas. Fenimore Cooper* (2 vols., 1922); *Diary of Wm. Dunlap, 1776–1839* (3 vols., 1930); T. F. Jones, ed., *N. Y. Univ., 1832–1932* (1933); L. L. Morse, "Samuel F. B. Morse," and H. W. Reynolds, "The Story of Locust Grove," *Year-Book, Dutchess County Hist. Soc.*, vol. XVII (1932). On his work as artist see: *Hist. of the Rise and Progress of the Arts of Design in the U. S.* (1834; rev. ed., 3 vols., 1918, ed. by F. W. Bayley and C. E. Goodspeed); T. S. Cummings, *Hist. Annals of the Nat. Acad. of Design* (1865); E. L. Morse, "Samuel F. B. Morse, the Painter," *Scribner's Mag.*, Mar. 1912; F. J. Mather, Jr., *Estimates in Art, Ser. II* (1931); H. B. Wehle, *Samuel F. B. Morse, Am. Painter* (Met. Museum of Art, 1932)—with finding list of Morse's known paintings and numerous photographic reproductions. On his invention of the telegraph see: *Ann. Report . . . Smithsonian Institution . . . 1857* (1858); E. N. Horsford, *Address at the Morse Memorial Meeting in Faneuil Hall, Apr. 16, 1872* (1872); E. L. Morse, "The Dot-and-Dash Alphabet," *Century Mag.*, Mar. 1912; "The Invention of the Electro-Magnetic Telegraph," *Electrical World*, July 20, 1895–Mar. 28, 1896 —a series of articles by F. W. Jones, F. L. Pope, J. J. Fahie, Rudolf Petsch, A. M. Tanner, E. L. Morse, Jas. D. Reid, Stephen Vail, and Mary A. Henry, together with letters, editorial comment, and other items. For his Native-American activities see: L. D. Scisco, *Pol. Nativism in N. Y. State* (1901) and F. J. Connors, "Samuel Finley Breese Morse and the Anti-Cath. Pol. Movements in the U. S.," *Ill. Cath. Hist. Rev.*, Oct. 1927. The writer is indebted to Carl W. Mitman of the Smithsonian Institution for the passage on the relay.]

G. H. G.

MORSE, SIDNEY EDWARDS (Feb. 7, 1794–Dec. 23, 1871), inventor and author, was born in Charlestown, Mass., the second son of Jedidiah [*q.v.*] and Elizabeth Ann (Breese) Morse. He was graduated A.B. at Yale in 1811, and studied law at Tapping Reeve's law school in Litchfield, Conn. Fresh from college, he set forth his views on the growing preponderance of the South in national affairs in a series of twelve articles signed "Massachusetts," published in the *Columbian Centinel* of Boston, beginning

Dec. 30, 1812. These were reprinted as *The New States, or a Comparison of the . . . Northern and Southern States; with a View to Expose the Injustice of Erecting New States at the South* (1813). The charge of plagiarism brought against his father by Hannah Adams [*q.v.*] caused him to publish *Remarks on the Controversy between Dr. Morse and Miss Adams, together with Some Notice of the Review of Dr. Morse's Appeal*, of which two editions appeared at Boston in 1814.

He definitely cast his lot with the newspaper world when his father and Jeremiah Evarts [*q.v.*], editor of the Boston religious monthly, the *Panoplist*, suggested the establishment of a religious newspaper. On Jan. 3, 1816, the first number of the *Recorder* appeared at Boston, with a prospectus written by Morse setting forth its hopes and ideals. The paper long remained a Boston institution, maintaining its identity until 1867 when it merged with the *Congregationalist*. Morse left it after about a year to enter Andover Theological Seminary, where he studied from 1817 to 1820. In 1823, with his younger brother, Richard Cary Morse, he moved to New York to establish the *New York Observer*, a religious paper of the same type as the Boston *Recorder*, the first number appearing May 17. With Samuel Irenæus Prime [*q.v.*] he made it an influential instrument in Protestant evangelical circles for many years. His obituary notice in the *Observer* (Dec. 28, 1871) records him as "senior editor and proprietor until the year 1858, when he sold his interest to its present senior editor, and retired to private life."

In 1820 he had worked with his father in revising the latter's *Geography*, and father and son joined in editing *A New System of Modern Geography . . . Accompanied by an Atlas*, published at New Haven in 1822. About 1835 (Prefatory note to *The Cerographic Atlas of the United States*, 1842) he began experimenting, with Henry A. Munson, on a new method of printing maps with the letterpress of a book instead of issuing them as plates engraved on metal, wood, or stone. With the *Observer* of June 29, 1839, appeared a map of Connecticut, the first example of what he called "the new art of cerography." He kept the process a secret, but it obviously consisted of engraving on wax and from the wax engraving making a plate to be inserted into the form with the type; the process probably utilized the principles of electrotyping, which had been introduced in 1840. On Oct. 3, 1817, Sidney Morse, with his brother Samuel F. B. Morse [*q.v.*], had been granted a patent for a device for "raising and forcing water and other fluids," usually referred to as "a flexible piston pump." After his cerographic process was established and after he was freed from the daily grind of newspaper work he turned his attention to a "bathometer," for rapid exploration of the depths of the sea, a patent for this "sounding apparatus" being granted him and his son as No. 56,436, July 17, 1866.

A large man of sedentary habits, Morse retained his native strength until he was well along in years. He had a mathematical and statistical mind which found pleasure in the most abstruse, perplexing, and extended calculations. On Apr. 1, 1841, he married Catharine Livingston, daughter of Rev. Gilbert R. Livingston of Philadelphia, and to them were born one son and one daughter. After his death a controversy arose as to whether he or Nathaniel Willis deserved the credit for establishing the *Recorder* as the first religious newspaper (see Frederic Hudson, *Journalism in the United States from 1690 to 1872*, pp. 289–95; also letters in the New York *Evening Post*, Jan. 16, 22, 29, Feb. 15, 22, 1872). Besides the works mentioned above Sidney Edwards Morse was the author of *An Atlas of the United States* (1823); *A Geographical View of Greece, and an Historical Sketch of the Recent Revolution in that Country* (1824); *North American Atlas* (1842); *The Cerographic Atlas of the United States* (1842–45), *The Cerographic Bible Atlas* (1844), and *The Cerographic Missionary Atlas* (1848), the last three being issued as supplements to the *Observer*; *A System of Geography for the Use of Schools* (1844); *A Geographical, Statistical and Ethical View of the American Slaveholders' Rebellion* (1863); *Memorabilia in the Life of Jedidiah Morse* (1867).

[H. D. Lord, *Memorial of the Family of Morse* (1896); obituary notice in the *N. Y. Observer*, Dec. 28, 1871; F. B. Dexter, *Biog. Sketches Grads. Yale Coll.*, vol. VI (1912), with bibliog. of Morse's publications; *Obit. Record Grads. Yale Coll.*, 1872; *N. Y. Times, N. Y. Herald*, and *World* (N. Y.), Dec. 24, 1871; *N. Y. Tribune*, Dec. 25, 1871; biographies of Jedidiah, S. F. B., and Richard Cary Morse.]

H. M. L.

MORTIMER, MARY (Dec. 2, 1816–July 14, 1877), teacher and first principal of Milwaukee College, was a pioneer in the higher education of women in the decades before and after the Civil War. In collaboration with Catharine Esther Beecher [q.v.], she inaugurated in Milwaukee, Wis., in 1851, a college system of instruction for young women. She was a native of Trowbridge, Wiltshire, England, the sixth child of William Mortimer, a blacksmith, and of Mary Pierce Mortimer. When she was five years old her family moved to America, and, after a brief stay of two years in New York City, set-

tled on a farm in western New York in the town of Phelps, and here the transplanted English child grew up. Both of her parents died when she was twelve. At the age of twenty-one (1838), she rounded out her education by two years' study at Geneva Seminary, New York, after which she taught there and in other seminaries near-by; in 1849, she started a school of her own in Ottawa, Ill., only to have it fail on account of an outbreak of cholera. At this juncture she met Catharine Beecher and, as a result, entered upon the task of carrying into practice Miss Beecher's theories for the reform of feminine education, particularly the formation in the West of endowed, nonsectarian schools for young women, organized on the college plan. It was a singularly congenial partnership. In Mary Mortimer, Catharine Beecher found one of the "original, planning minds" for which she and her sister, Harriet Beecher Stowe, had been looking. A private seminary in Milwaukee was selected as the basis for the experiment, with the cooperation of its founder, Mrs. Lucy A. Parsons. Mary Mortimer was made a member of its staff and immediately set in motion such changes embodying the reform ideas that by 1851 there evolved a new institution with a college charter, a board of trustees, and herself as principal; and in the two years following a new building was acquired and also a new name: Milwaukee Female College. In 1852 Catharine Beecher and Mary Mortimer spent June and July at Harriet Beecher Stowe's home in Brunswick, Me., working out a course of study; they also formed the American Woman's Educational Association largely to secure an endowment for the infant college and for similar institutions which it was hoped would spread over the nation in imitation of Milwaukee's example. For two periods: 1850–57, and 1866–74, fifteen years in all, Miss Mortimer served the college, harassed by unceasing financial difficulties. In the interval between she was for a time principal of a seminary in Baraboo, Wis. The last three years of her life she spent at her home, "Willow Glen," Milwaukee, giving lectures, building up a post-graduate course, initiating and organizing the Woman's Club of Wisconsin. Frances E. Willard, a student at the college in 1856, describes Miss Mortimer as a small, plump woman with an astonishingly impressive head. In 1895 Milwaukee Female College merged with Downer College of Fox Lake, and the new institution took the name of Milwaukee-Downer College.

[W. W. Wight, *Annals of Milwaukee Coll., 1848–91* (1891), based on Mary Mortimer's autobiographical sketch and records of the college; Minerva Brace Norton, *A True Teacher: Mary Mortimer* (1894), which contains many private letters; information from a few former students of Milwaukee College.]   A. C. F.

MORTON, CHARLES (*c.* 1627–Apr. 11, 1698), Puritan clergyman and schoolmaster, was born at Pendavy in Cornwall, the home of his mother, Frances (Kestell) Morton, and was baptized Feb. 15, 1626/27. His father was the Rev. Nicholas Morton, chaplain of St. Saviour's, Southwark. Charles was admitted pensioner at Queen's College, Cambridge, in 1646, but transferred to Oxford, became a scholar and fellow of Wadham College, B.A. 1649, M.A. 1652, and was admitted *ad eundem* at Cambridge the next year. In 1655 he was installed rector of Blisland, Cornwall. When the Restoration forced him out of that post, he preached privately at St. Ives, until, in 1666, he set up at Newington Green, near London, what became the most famous of the Dissenters' academies. Here, although chiefly interested in the training of ministers, Morton provided a sound university education for the sons of Nonconformists, then denied admittance to the universities. Among his pupils were Samuel Wesley and Daniel Defoe, both of whom praised his ability. Calamy, historian of the Nonconformists, says of Morton: "He had indeed a Peculiar Talent, of winning Youth to the Love of Virtue and Learning, both by his Pleasant Conversation, and by a Familiar Way he had of making difficult Subjects easily Intelligible" (*Account, post,* II, 145). Nevertheless, constant harassment from the court of the bishop of London, who looked upon such schools as centers of sedition and heresy, finally determined Morton to emigrate to New England, where he expected to become president of Harvard ("The Hutchinson Papers," *Prince Society Publications,* vol. II, 1865, pp. 287, 293). Accompanied by Samuel Penhallow [*q.v.*], he landed in Boston in July 1686.

Unsettled conditions in Massachusetts preventing his being chosen president, he became minister at Charlestown instead. His fame as a teacher attracted pupils to him there, including some rebellious Harvard students; but early in 1687, pressure from the Harvard authorities forced him to give up his teaching, and what might have become a rival college was throttled in infancy (*Collections of the Massachusetts Historical Society,* 4 ser., vol. VIII, 1868, pp. 111 f.). Harvard made use of his ability, however, by electing him fellow in 1692, and vice-president in 1697, Morton being the first to occupy that newly created office. He was an active member of the corporation and an occasional lecturer on scientific subjects. His "Compendium Phys-

icae," a popular work on science, and his "System of Logic" were used in many manuscript copies as textbooks at Harvard far down into the eighteenth century. Treatises by him appeared in the *Philosophical Transactions* of the Royal Society for April 1675, and in *The Harleian Miscellany* (vol. II, 1744). He was the author of about a dozen separate volumes, generally short, on Biblical and religious subjects, including "Two little things in English meeter." His best known work was *The Spirit of Man* . . . (1693).

A leading minister from the time of his arrival, Morton associated himself in matters of polity with the Mathers. Judge Sewall [*q.v.*], a connoisseur of sermons, used often to go over to Charlestown to hear him preach. His popularity was enhanced by an unsuccessful prosecution in 1689 for seditious speaking against the Andros régime. In 1690 he founded an association of twenty-two leading ministers from the vicinity of Boston, who met at Harvard College every six weeks for mutual counsel (Manuscript record book in Harvard University Library; sections reprinted in *Proceedings of the Massachusetts Historical Society,* vol. XVII, 1880, pp. 262–80). He is said to have been the first minister in New England to perform marriages, a right previously reserved to the civil authorities (Budington, *post,* p. 184). He also began what is known among Congregationalists as the ceremony of "installation," when he refused to be reordained by the laying on of hands at his induction into the Charlestown church. His wife, Joan, of whom little is known, died in 1693 and there were no children (T. B. Wyman, *The Genealogies and Estates of Charlestown,* p. 687).

[Sources for Morton's life in England include Edmund Calamy, *An Account of the Ministers . . . Who Were Ejected or Silenced after the Restoration in 1660, by or before the Act of Uniformity,* vol. II (1713), and *A Continuation of the Account of the Ministers, etc.,* vol. I (1727); Joshua Toulmin, *An Hist. View of the State of the Protestant Dissenters in Eng.* (1814); Walter Wilson, *Memoirs of the Life and Times of Daniel De Foe* (1830), vol. I; Luke Tyerman, *The Life and Times of the Rev. Samuel Wesley* (1866); John MacLean, *The Parochial and Family Hist. of the Deanery of Trigg Minor in the County of Cornwall*, vol. I (1873); *Dict. of Nat. Biog.*; Joseph Foster, *Alumni Oxonienses* (1891), vol. III; John and J. A. Venn, *Alumni Cantabrigienses,* pt. I, vol. III (1924). For his life in Mass., besides miscellaneous material printed in the publications of the Mass. Hist. Soc., see: "Harvard College Records," *Pubs. Colonial Soc. of Mass.,* vol. XVI (1925); Josiah Quincy, *The Hist. of Harvard Univ.,* vol. I (1840); "Diary of Samuel Sewall," *Colls. Mass. Hist. Soc.,* 5 ser., vol. V (1878); W. I. Budington, *The Hist. of the First Church, Charlestown* (1845); J. F. Hunnewell, *Records of the First Church in Charlestown, Mass., 1632–1789* (1880); Richard Frothingham, Jr., *The Hist. of Charlestown, Mass.* (1845); W. B. Sprague, *Annals Am. Pulpit,* vol. I (1857); T. B. Wyman, *The Geneals. and Estates of Charlestown* (1879), vol. II. Works of Morton in MS. are to be found in the libraries of Harvard Univ. and Bowdoin Coll.]

W. J. B.

MORTON, GEORGE (1585–June 1624), Pilgrim father, was probably the son and heir of Anthony Morton, a wealthy Catholic gentleman living near Bawtry or Harworth, not far from the little village of Scrooby, in Nottinghamshire, England. When still very young, he was converted by William Brewster [q.v.] to Puritanism. He was a member of the Scrooby congregation before their emigration and either went to Holland with them or followed them after a residence at York. He is one of the three emigrants to America who can be traced to the Scrooby district, the others being Brewster and William Bradford [q.v.]. On July 23, 1612, he was married at Leyden to Juliana Carpenter. Morton was possessed of considerable means, was entered in his marriage record (facsimile in *Mayflower Descendant,* October 1909, p. 193) as a merchant from York, was apparently one of the financial mainstays of the Pilgrims at Leyden, and was certainly closely associated with the leaders. He was one of those who went to London in 1619 to negotiate with the merchants, living probably at Aldgate, where his brother-in-law, Edward Southworth, was already established. Here he changed his name to Mourt, perhaps to escape the displeasure of his Catholic relatives.

While Robert Cushman [q.v.] was absent in America, Morton was probably chief Pilgrim agent in London. He received the writings sent in the *Fortune* from Plymouth in 1622, and published them under the title: *A Relation or Iournall of the beginning and proceedings of the English Plantation setled at Plimoth in New England . . . London, Printed for Iohn Bellamie* (1622), which is still the only contemporary account of the voyage of the *Mayflower* and the first months of the colony. Tradition has assigned to him the authorship, and it has always been known as "Mourt's Relation." It has been conjectured that Bradford and Winslow were the authors and Morton merely the publisher (Alexander Young, *Chronicles of the Pilgrim Fathers,* 1841; Edward Channing, *A History of the United States,* vol. I, 1905, p. 318; W. T. Davis, *Bradford's History of Plymouth Plantation,* 1908, pp. 11–14), but since the narrative Bradford wrote and sent back on the *Fortune* was retained by the captain of the French privateer which captured the *Fortune* on its return voyage (*Calendar of State Papers, Colonial Series, 1574–1660,* 1860, p. 124), it is possible that Morton wrote a narrative from information brought back by those returning on the *Mayflower* and the *Fortune* and published it together with material by Winslow and others not retained by the French captain. The authorship of the book cannot now be definitively established.

Morton was one of the organizers of the voyage of the *Anne* and the *Little James* in 1623 and came himself with his wife and four children, and his wife's sister, Alice Southworth, a widow, who married Governor Bradford the following year. He was assigned an excellent piece of land in 1624, but died in June of that year. His property having by this time been spent in the Pilgrim service, Bradford assumed care of his wife and children. Morton's descendants have been numerous and influential. His eldest son, Nathaniel [q.v.], was secretary of the colony for many years.

[Accounts of Morton's life appear in J. K. Allen, *George Morton of Plymouth Colony and Some of His Descendants* (1908); J. A. Goodwin, *The Pilgrim Republic* (1888); Joseph Hunter, *Colls. Concerning the Church or Congregation of Protestant Separatists Formed at Scrooby . . . The Founders of New Plymouth* (1854); H. M. and M. Dexter, *The England and Holland of the Pilgrims* (1905). The best edition of the *Relation* is *Mourt's Relation or Iournal of the Plantation at Plymouth* (1865), with intro. and notes by H. M. Dexter.]

R. G. U.

MORTON, HENRY (Dec. 11, 1836–May 9, 1902), scientist, first president of Stevens Institute of Technology, was born in New York City, the son of Rev. Henry J. and Helen (MacFarlan) Morton. His father was rector of St. James's Episcopal Church in Philadelphia for more than fifty years. Henry's early education was received at the Episcopal Academy, Philadelphia, and at the age of seventeen he entered the University of Pennsylvania, graduating with the class of 1857. Toward the close of his college course he suggested to some of his classmates that they undertake the translation of the famous Rosetta Stone that had been discovered in Egypt during the occupation of Napoleon, a plaster cast of which had been presented to the Philomathean, a philosophical undergraduate society, of which Morton was a member. Although this stone had been studied by others no complete translations had been made. The inscriptions were in Greek, demotic, and hieroglyphic; Morton undertook the translation of the hieroglyphic inscription while two of his associates worked on the Greek and demotic inscriptions. All of the translations were completed and Morton drew a rich color design for most of the pages of a 160-page book; then, to minimize costs, he drew all the designs on stone for lithographing. Within each page-design was a portion of the translation in Morton's bold,

Morton

clear, characteristic penmanship. The work was published in 1858 (2nd edition, 1859) under the title: *Report of the Committee of the Philomathean Society of the University of Pennsylvania to Translate the Inscription on the Rosetta Stone.*

In 1859 Morton studied law for a short time, but as a result of his success in teaching chemistry and physics at the Episcopal Academy, he soon gave up law to devote himself to science. His lectures were so "novel, . . . entertaining and instructive" that his lecture room had to be enlarged and finally a new wing added to the academy building. The fame of them spread, and in 1863 he became professor of chemistry at the newly organized Philadelphia Dental College and the next year was appointed resident secretary of the Franklin Institute. To upbuild and augment the financial resources of the Institute, he undertook a series of public lectures on light, sound, and cognate topics. His reputation had become such that the Philadelphia Academy of Music, then one of the largest auditoriums in the country, seating 3,500 people, was engaged. Before the first lecture every seat in the house was sold, as was also the case at a repetition of the lecture a few days later. He was made editor of the *Journal of the Franklin Institute* in 1867, serving in this capacity until July 1871. In 1868 he occupied the chair of chemistry and physics at the University of Pennsylvania during the year's leave-of-absence of the regular professor. The following year a separate department of chemistry was created for him. He was employed by the United States Nautical Almanac Office in 1869 to organize and conduct an expedition to Iowa to make photographs of the total eclipse of the sun on Aug. 7. In this connection, he was the first to prove that the bright line on the sun's disk adjacent to the edge of the moon was a photographic phenomenon and not an optical one.

In 1870 he accepted the presidency of Stevens Institute of Technology, then in process of organization, and, together with a strong faculty that he gathered about him, he developed the first curriculum in mechanical engineering in America. He continued his researches and his writings, one of his early laboratory accomplishments at Stevens being the scientific development of plastic materials for filling teeth, work which resulted in widespread changes in dental treatment. He was soon called into consultation in New York by lawyers engaged in patent litigation. From this labor he received sufficient remuneration to leave him a comfortable fortune, even after he had given back to Stevens

Institute a larger total sum for the development of the college than he had received in salary. It is said that his printed testimony given in patent litigation, if collected, would equal in volume a set of Scott's novels (Sellers and Leeds, *post*). He wrote extensively on the subjects of fluorescence, galvanic batteries, pneumatic pyrometer, conservation of energy, gaseous compounds, Roentgen rays, photometry, liquid air, artificial illumination, electric storage, engineering fallacies, and dynamo-electric machines, his articles appearing in various American and European papers, notably in *Engineering* (London). A student of Biblical criticism, he wrote in 1897, at the request of the editor of *Bibliotheca Sacra,* two articles on "The Cosmogony of Genesis and its Reconcilers," published in the April and July issues of that year. He was also a contributor to the *New York Tribune,* the *Churchman,* the *Outlook,* and the *Church Eclectic.* He was interested in archeology and was a member of the committee in charge of the expedition for excavating Ur of the Chaldees and other Babylonian sites, to which enterprises he contributed generously. He had strong artistic instincts and was an art connoisseur throughout his life. "With him," it was said, "poetry was a natural form of expression," but very little of his verse was published. On Aug. 20, 1862, he married Clara Whiting Dodge, and they had two children.

[Coleman Sellers and A. R. Leeds, *Biog. Notice of Prest. Henry Morton* (1892); F. DeR. Furman, *Morton Memorial, A Hist. of the Stevens Inst. of Technology* (1905); *Who's Who in America,* 1901–02; *Science,* May 30, 1902; *Engineering* (London), July 18, 1902; E. L. Nichols, "Biog. Memoir of Henry Morton" (1915), in *Nat. Acad. Sci. Biog. Memoirs,* vol. VIII; name of mother and date of marriage from a grandson.]
F. DeR. F.

MORTON, JAMES ST. CLAIR (Sept. 24, 1829–June 17, 1864), soldier, engineer, and author of works on engineering and fortification, was born in Philadelphia, Pa. He was the son of Dr. Samuel George Morton [*q.v.*] and Rebecca Grellet (Pearsall) Morton. After attending the University of Pennsylvania four years, he entered West Point in 1847 and graduated on July 1, 1851, second in a class of forty-two. He was assigned to the Corps of Engineers as brevet second lieutenant and served as assistant engineer in the construction of the defenses of Charleston harbor, S. C., from 1851 to 1852, and in the building of Fort Delaware, Del., from 1852 to 1855. Promoted second lieutenant, Apr. 1, 1854, he was detailed as assistant professor of engineering at West Point. On July 1, 1856, he was promoted first lieutenant and on June 17 of the following year became assistant engineer in operations preliminary to the construction of

Sandy Hook Fort (Fort Hancock), N. J. Following this assignment, from 1858 to 1859, he was lighthouse engineer of the third district (from Gooseberry Point, Mass., to Squam Inlet, N. J.). Next he was in charge of the Potomac Water Works (1859–60), then engineer in charge of the Chiriqui Expedition to Central America, and from 1860 to 1861 of the Washington Aqueduct.

He was promoted captain of engineers Aug. 6, 1861. Later that year he became superintending engineer of the construction of Fort Jefferson, Dry Tortugas, Fla., and in 1862 was in charge of repairs at Fort Mifflin, Pa. From June 9 to Oct. 27, 1862, he was chief engineer of the Army of the Ohio. He was appointed brigadier-general, United States Volunteers, Nov. 29, 1862. From Oct. 27, 1862, to Aug. 22, 1863, and from Sept. 17 to Nov. 14, 1863, he was chief engineer of the Army of the Cumberland and from Nov. 3 to Nov. 7, 1863, commanded the pioneer brigade attached to the XIV Corps of that army. He participated in the Tennessee campaign and for gallant and meritorious services in the battle of Stone River, Dec. 31, 1862–Jan. 2, 1863, was brevetted lieutenant-colonel of engineers of the Regular Army. Until June 1863 he was engaged in fortifying Nashville and Murfreesboro, Tenn. He was promoted major, corps of engineers, July 3, 1863, and participated in the advance on Tullahoma, June 24 to July 4, and in the crossing of the Cumberland Mountains and the Tennessee River, Aug. 15 to Sept. 4 of that year. He was wounded in the battle of Chickamauga and on Sept. 20, 1863, was brevetted colonel for gallant and meritorious services at that battle. From September to November of the same year he was engaged in fortifying Chattanooga, and on Nov. 7 was mustered out of the volunteer service.

He was superintending engineer of the defenses of Nashville, Murfreesboro, Clarksville, and Fort Donelson, Nov. 14, 1863, to Jan. 30, 1864, when he became assistant to the chief engineer at Washington, D. C. On May 18, 1864, he was appointed chief engineer of the IX Army Corps and participated during the Richmond campaign in the battles of North Anna, May 24, 1864; Totopotomoy, May 28–29, 1864; Bethesda Church, May 30, 1864; and the assault of Petersburg, Va., June 17, 1864, where he was killed while leading the attack. On the same day he was brevetted brigadier-general, United States Army, for gallant and meritorious service. He lies buried in Laurel Hill Cemetery, Philadelphia.

He was the author of a *Memoir on Fortification* (1858); *Memoir on the Dangers and De-fences of New York City* (1858); *Memoir on American Fortification* (1859). These are analytical studies of European fortifications, and of American fortification as it should have been. Written in the days when cannon had a maximum range of less than 5,000 yards, their value today is entirely in their historical interest. His *Memoir of the Life and Services of Captain and Brevet Major John Sanders, of the Corps of Engineers, U. S. Army* (1861) is an appreciation of the work of a great military engineer.

[G. W. Cullum, *Biog. Reg. Officers and Grads. U. S. Mil. Acad.* (1891), vol. II; War Dept. records; F. B. Heitman, *Biog. Reg. and Dict. U. S. Army* (1903), vol. I; Clarence Pearsall, *Hist. and Geneal. of the Pearsall Family in England and America* (1928), vol. II.]

J.W.L.

MORTON, JOHN (*c.* 1724–April 1777), signer of the Declaration of Independence, was born after his father's death in Ridley, Chester (now Delaware) County, Pa., the son of John Morton and Mary Archer. His great-grandfather, Morten Mortenson, had sailed from Gothenburg, Sweden, in 1654, a member of the Tenth Swedish Expedition under Johan Classon Rising, the last governor of New Sweden. Young Morton received only three months of public schooling, but he was efficiently educated at home in all common branches of learning by his foster father, John Sketchley, an Englishman of excellent training and a surveyor by profession, who had married the widowed Mrs. Morton and had taken an affectionate interest in her son. Possessed of an alert, mature mind, great industry, and a fondness for precision, the stepson was soon able to share the work of his teacher, so that his early employment consisted in surveying lands and cultivating his "patrimonial farm." Many tracts on Tinicum Island were surveyed by Morton. In 1754 he married Ann Justice (or Justis), a descendant of the Delaware Swedes, and had by her three sons and five daughters, who survived him. Their descendants are numerous and many have attained distinction.

Morton was early called into public life and served his state and country with unusual faithfulness. Elected a member of the Provincial Assembly from Chester County in 1756, he was reëlected to the same office for ten consecutive years. In February 1767 his position was filled by another—apparently because of political disagreements with the views of Morton—but he was returned to the Assembly in 1769 and served seven more terms, acting after Mar. 15, 1775, as speaker of that body. Beginning in October 1766, he held for three years the position of high sheriff of Chester County. In 1757 he had been chosen justice of the peace for Chester County and in 1770 a judge for the trial of negroes. He also served for a time as president judge of the court of general sessions and common pleas of his county, and became in April 1774 an associate judge of the supreme court of the province. In 1765 he was one of the four Pennsylvania delegates to the Stamp Act Congress and was a delegate to the Continental congresses from 1774 until early in 1777. In the session of July 1776, his vote together with those of Benjamin Franklin and James Wilson placed Pennsylvania on the side of independence by a majority of one. While in Congress Morton served on many important committees and was chairman of the committee of the whole on the adoption of the Articles of Confederation finally ratified after his own death. After the battle of Lexington he had been offered the colonelcy of a volunteer corps in Pennsylvania, but he declined the honor because of his other duties.

Morton was essentially a self-made man, of pleasant social and domestic qualities, sound in judgment, and modest in manner. His character is revealed in his unrelenting stand in favor of colonial freedom, in a state where opinion on the matter was seriously divided. A museum of Swedish-American interests erected in Philadelphia has been named the John Morton Memorial Building.

[Sources include: *Minutes of the Provincial Council of Pa.*, vols. IX and X (1852); *Pa. Archives*, 2 ser. IX (1880); M. A. Leach, "John Morton," *Am. Scandinavian Rev.*, July–Aug. 1915; J. H. Martin, *Chester (and Its Vicinity), Delaware County, in Pa.* (1877); Geo. Smith, *Hist. of Delaware County, Pa.* (1862); H. D. Paxson, *Sketch and Map of a Trip from Phila. to Tinicum Island, Delaware County, Pa.* (1926). There are brief biographies of Morton in the various works on the Signers, though they are for the most part mere eulogies of character. Since there were several contemporaries by the same name, no portrait of Morton, the Signer, is considered authentic. His tombstone in St. Paul's churchyard at Chester, Pa. and the tablet to his memory in the Independence Chamber of the State House in Philadelphia give 1724 as the year of birth, but it may have taken place early in 1725, N.S.]

A.B.B.

MORTON, JULIUS STERLING (Apr. 22, 1832–Apr. 27, 1902), agriculturist, was born at Adams, Jefferson County, N. Y., of New England lineage, the son of Julius Dewey and Emeline (Sterling) Morton. In 1834 Julius Morton followed the tide of emigration into the west, locating first at Monroe, Mich., and later at Detroit, where he became a well-known and prosperous citizen. Young Julius Sterling Morton, who showed signs of mental alertness at an early age, was given excellent educational opportunities. He spent two years at the University of Michigan, but, owing to his independence of the constituted authorities, he was expelled in his senior year. Although he was apparently never in residence at Union College, Schenectady, N. Y., he received the A.B. degree there in 1856. In 1858 the Regents of the University of Michigan voted to confer the A.B. degree as of the class of 1854. On Oct. 30, 1854, he was married to Caroline Joy French, the daughter of Hiram Joy and the adopted daughter of David and Cynthia French of Detroit. The wedding trip was the journey to a new home in Nebraska, then much advertised by reason of the discussion Douglas' Kansas-Nebraska Act had aroused. After a short stay at Bellevue, Neb., he located at Nebraska City, where for a number of years he edited a pioneer newspaper, the *Nebraska City News,* writing, as he was also accustomed to talk, vigorously and with small regard for the consequences.

He early interested himself in territorial politics. As a member of the territorial legislature, the second assembly, 1855–56, and the fourth, 1857–58, he opposed the efforts of Omaha and the North Platte country to dominate the affairs of the territory, and he fought valiantly against the numerous wild-cat banking projects then so generally approved by local speculators. In 1858 his leadership in territorial affairs was recognized when he was appointed by President Buchanan to be secretary of the territory, an office he held until 1861. For several months of that time he also served as acting-governor. He was a Democrat, and as such he was repeatedly a candidate for office. Twice he ran for territorial delegate to Congress, and four times he was his party's nominee for governor. Many times, also, he received the Democratic vote of the legislature for United States senator. In the days when the railroads figured largely in Nebraska politics, he was regarded as the especial friend of the Chicago, Burlington & Quincy Railroad. His highest political honor came in 1893, when he was appointed secretary of agriculture by President Cleveland, a post in which he distinguished himself by his emphasis upon economy. Among other things he eliminated temporarily the free distribution of seeds by congressmen, in his opinion a sheer waste of money.

Cleveland's appointment came to Morton not merely because of his political record and his low-tariff, hard-money views but also because of his standing as an agriculturist. He was a student of agriculture; he owned and lived upon a quarter-section of land adjacent to Nebraska City, and he esteemed it his duty to instruct the people of the state in the subject of farming by precept, perhaps, even more than by example.

Tree-planting was his hobby, and he set out literally hundreds of trees with his own hands. To encourage the same practice on the part of others, he urged that one day each year, to be known as Arbor Day, should be especially dedicated to that purpose, and from 1872 to 1885 some day in April was generally so observed throughout the state (see sketch of Robert W. Furnas). In the latter year the legislature designated his birthday, Apr. 22, as Arbor Day and declared it a legal holiday. From Nebraska the idea spread to many other states and even outside the United States. The success of Arbor Day was to him the crowning achievement of his life. His political and agricultural activities made him a well known figure in Nebraska, as did his editorial and literary activities. Throughout his life he made numerous speeches in Nebraska and elsewhere (*A Speech Delivered at the Nebraska State Fair, 1873; A Commemorative Pamphlet, ... 1876, at Nebraska City, ... Containing ... an Oration, 1876; Addresses ... at Chicago ... 1893,* 1893). In 1897 he undertook the editorship of *The Illustrated History of Nebraska,* planned the volumes, and arranged for some of the contributions before he persuaded another editor to complete the work (edited by J. S. Morton, succeeded by Albert Watkins, 3 vols., 1905–13). The next year, 1898, he began to publish the *Conservative,* a periodical devoted to political and economic discussions, which was suspended soon after his death. His aggressive personality, so well reflected in his sturdy figure, his keen blue-gray eyes, and his prominent features, won admiration even from his enemies. His emergence into national prominence gratified the pride of his fellow citizens, who, before the advent of William Jennings Bryan, were unaccustomed to such honors. While his own fortune was very modest, the extraordinary financial success of his four sons, the second of whom was Paul Morton [*q.v.*], also attracted attention to him. Up to the time of his death, at his son's home in Lake Forest, Ill., he was generally regarded, by friend and foe alike, as one of Nebraska's foremost citizens. Many years after his death his Nebraska City home, "Arbor Lodge," together with the surrounding groves, was given to the state by his heirs as a memorial and a park.

[*Illustrated Hist. of Neb.,* ed. by J. S. Morton succeeded by Albert Watkins, vol. I (1905); A. E. Sheldon, *Nebraska* (1931), vol. I; J. M. Woolworth, *In Memory of Caroline Joy French Morton* (1882); *Univ. of Mich. Regents' Proceedings, 1837–64* (1915); letters from D. Richard Weeks of the Graduate Council of Union College and from Lunette Hadley of the Alumni Catalogue Office of Univ. of Mich.: *Arbor Day,* ed. by R. W. Furnas (1888); *Neb. State Journal* (Lincoln), Apr. 28, 1902.]   J. D. H.

MORTON, LEVI PARSONS (May 16, 1824–May 16, 1920), minister to France, vice-president of the United States, and governor of New York, was primarily a banker whose prominence in New York business extended from the Civil War until after the panic of 1907. He came of old New-England stock, a descendant of George Morton [*q.v.*], and with perhaps no ancestor who arrived in America after 1650. His father, the Rev. Daniel Oliver Morton, was pastor at Shoreham, Vt., when Levi was born. The name, Levi Parsons, was contributed by a missionary brother of his mother, Lucretia (Parsons) Morton. The young man gained much of his early business experience as store-keeper and forwarder at Hanover, N. H., where he lived in the household of a professor at Dartmouth College, but he had neither time nor means for a collegiate career. He met in Hanover his first wife, Lucy Young Kimball, of Long Island, whom he married on Oct. 15, 1856. The channel of wholesale and importing business carried him through Boston, where he was for a time in the same firm with Junius Spencer Morgan, to New York, where on Jan. 1, 1855, he became head of the wholesale house of Morton, Grinnell & Company. He failed, when Southern debts became worthless in 1861, but he reorganized his business and paid his creditors in full, and in 1863 he launched a banking firm in Wall Street. His mastery of the uncertain trends of finance after the Civil War was so complete that, in the operations under the refunding law of 1870 his firm, since 1869 Morton, Bliss & Company, with its London agent, Morton, Rose & Company, found itself, with Drexel, Morgan & Company, on the upward curve, supplanting in some measure the firm of Jay Cooke, that had for ten years been dominant in American finance.

Morton's English partner, Sir John Rose, was go-between in the conversations that preceded the Joint High Commission of 1871, and both Rose and Morton were in frequent communication with President Grant and Secretary Fish during the critical moments of the Geneva arbitration. This concluded, the firm handled the transfer of the Geneva award, and Morton began to see vistas of political preferment. He was nominated for Congress by the Republican party of the eleventh New York district (a residential district on upper Fifth Avenue), in 1876, and was defeated after cutting down the normal Democratic majority. He was successful, however, in the two ensuing elections of 1878 and 1880. He did not sit during the second term to

Morton

which he was elected, having accepted the post of minister to France, after declining the vice-presidential nomination and the post of secretary of the navy. He would have preferred a seat in the Senate, which went to Platt, or the Treasury, but President Garfield would not bestow that office upon a Wall-Street banker. Paris was to his liking, although he preferred not to have the legation offices over a grocer's shop. His first wife having died in 1871, he was married on Feb. 12, 1873, to Anna Livingston Read Street. With abundant wealth, they entertained lavishly and acquired a fondness for European residence. Morton's diplomatic responsibilities were not heavy, involving nothing more than matters of nationality and citizenship, the ceremonies surrounding the gift of the Bartholdi statue of liberty, and interminable correspondence regarding the status of the American hog in France. He came home vainly aspiring to the Senate, in 1885 and again in 1887, but willing to accept the vice-presidency, which he gained in 1889.

Morton had by this time set up a great country estate, "Ellerslie," near Rhinecliff on Hudson, and now as vice-president he bought a house on Scott Circle and established his family in Washington society. As presiding officer over the Senate he was his own master, unyielding to party pressure; yet he was a faithful servant of the Senate rules, showing none of the ambition to command that Reed exhibited in the House and none of the zeal to reform that his next banker-successor, Dawes, displayed in 1925. He was chagrined, but dignified, when accident deprived him of the barren honor of a renomination in 1892. In 1895 he became governor of New York, after twelve years of Democratic rule, succeeding his neighbor Roswell P. Flower who had in 1881 taken his place as congressman. He became governor with the support of Senator Thomas C. Platt, now boss of the state, but he was in no sense a cog in Platt's machine; and in the many moments in which he showed a determination to be a real governor, Platt tried in vain to discipline him by threats of withholding support for the presidential nomination of 1896. He was a firm and moderate advocate of civil-service reform and lent deliberate and constructive aid to the movement for the consolidation of Greater New York. As a banker, he strongly supported the gold standard. He finally received the support of Senator Platt and became a favorite son in 1896, but the support was only for bargaining purposes since before the Republican convention met Hanna and McKinley were already in control of its des-

tiny. Morton supported the party ticket with increasing zeal as the maintenance of the gold standard became the campaign issue, and returned placidly to his banking house after leaving office as governor on Jan. 1, 1897. In 1899 he rearranged his affairs, launching at the age of seventy-five the Morton Trust Company, which increased in wealth and influence until it was amalgamated with the Guaranty Trust Company in 1909. After this amalgamation, he retired from active business to spend much of his time in travel and in contemplation of his various benefactions, among which were generous contributions to the cathedral of St. John the Divine. After the death of his wife in 1918 he lived in almost complete retirement until he followed her on his ninety-sixth birthday, in 1920. Three of his daughters survived him.

[Morton outlived his prominence and received less obituary notice than might have been expected, although there is a good article in the *N. Y. Times,* May 17, 1920. The campaign biography of 1888, by George Alfred Townsend [Gath], was printed in Lew Wallace, *Life of Gen. Ben Harrison* (1888), but is unimportant. There is a somewhat unusual collection of eulogistic speeches by the senators of the Fifty-second Congress in *Testimonial to Vice-President Levi P. Morton* (1893). But all of these are supplanted by the excellent official biography, Robert McElroy, *Levi Parsons Morton: Banker, Diplomat and Statesman* (1930), in which extensive use is made of the Morton papers now deposited in the N. Y. Pub. Lib. For genealogical details, see J. G. Leach, *Memoranda Relating to the Ancestry and Family of Hon. Levi Parsons Morton, Vice-President of the U. S., 1889–93* (1894).]

F. L. P.

MORTON, MARCUS (Feb. 19, 1784–Feb. 6, 1864), jurist, governor of Massachusetts, was born in Freetown, Mass., the son of Nathaniel and Mary (Cary) Morton, and a descendant of George Morton [*q.v.*] who emigrated to America in 1623. His early education was received at home, and when he was fourteen years of age he was placed under the Rev. Calvin Chaddock, at Rochester, Mass., for further instruction. In 1801 he entered Brown University with the sophomore class. Here he began to show much interest in the doctrines of Jefferson with their appeal to reason against custom and precedent and their emphasis on the rights of man. His Commencement oration argued for one of the principles he maintained throughout his life— economy in public affairs, since extravagance leads to privilege and inequality. After graduation in 1804, he studied law for a year in the office of Judge Seth Padelford, at Taunton, and then entered Tapping Reeve's law school at Litchfield, Conn., where he was a schoolmate of John C. Calhoun.

Admitted to the Norfolk bar in 1807, he began to practise in Taunton, and on Dec. 23 of the same year married Charlotte Hodges, daughter of James and Joanna (Tillinghast) Hodges, by whom he had twelve children, among them Marcus Morton [*q.v.*]. Almost at once he became active in politics, and after holding a number of minor offices was from 1817 to 1821 representative in the Fifteenth and Sixteenth congresses. He was lieutenant-governor of Massachusetts, 1824–25, and in the latter year became acting governor on the death of Gov. William Eustis [*q.v.*]. In 1825 Gov. Levi Lincoln [*q.v.*] appointed Morton to the Massachusetts supreme court, a position he held until his resignation in January 1840. His accomplishments as a judge were marked by his ready knowledge of legal principles, his sound judgment in applying them, his patience, courtesy, and strength of character.

Morton's perennial candidacy for governor on the Democratic ticket was one of the most significant features of his life. From 1824 to 1848 the political forces in Massachusetts were fairly definitely aligned. The two major parties were the conservative element, consisting of the wealthy aristocrats, the shipowners, bankers, and manufacturers, largely concentrated in Boston; and the more liberal and progressive element comprising the farmers, workingmen, and recent immigrants. It was at the head of the latter group that Morton placed himself, and for sixteen successive years (1828–43) was its candidate for governor. Only twice during that period was he successful. In 1839 he defeated Edward Everett [*q.v.*] by the majority of a single vote, and in 1842 he was chosen over John Davis by the Senate, neither candidate having received a majority. As governor he advocated and secured retrenchment in public expenditures, reduced the number of supreme court justices from five to three, and abolished the right of appeal from the court of common pleas to the supreme court except on questions of law, this privilege having made the administration of justice slow, expensive, and uncertain.

In 1845 Morton was appointed collector of the port of Boston, which position he held for four years. In 1848 he refused to run for vice-president with Van Buren, for he could not bring himself to bolt his party. Later, however, his life-long opposition to slavery led him to join the Free-Soil party, of which he was delegate to the state constitutional convention in 1853, and by which he was elected to the state legislature in 1858. He was a man of unquestioned probity, whose poise, serenity, and character made him generally admired. In his championship of the lower classes, his distrust of over-large corporations, and his advocacy of shorter hours for the working man he was ahead of his

time, and perhaps partly for this reason a large measure of political success was denied him. He was for thirty-two years an overseer of Harvard. He died at Taunton.

[J. K. Allen, *George Morton of Plymouth Colony and Some of His Descendants* (1908); *A Hist. of Freetown, Mass.* (1902); *Biog. Dir. Am. Cong.* (1928); *U. S. Mag. and Democratic Rev.,* Oct. 1841; *Colls. of the Old Colony Hist. Soc.,* no. 7 (1909); *Law Reporter,* Feb. 1840; A. B. Darling, *Political Changes in Mass., 1824–1848* (1925); "Necrology of Brown Univ., for the Year 1863–4," *Providence Daily Jour.,* Sept. 6, 1864; *Boston Daily Courier,* Feb. 8, 1864; Morton's letter books in possession of the Mass. Hist. Soc; date of birth from *Brown Hist. Cat.:* some sources give Dec. 19.]   S. H. P.

MORTON, MARCUS (Apr. 8, 1819–Feb. 10, 1891), chief justice of the supreme court of Massachusetts, was born in Taunton, Mass., the son of Marcus [*q.v.*] and Charlotte (Hodges) Morton. He attended Bristol County Academy, was graduated from Brown University in 1838, and from the Harvard Law School in 1840. After one year in the Boston office of Judge Peleg Sprague [*q.v.*], he was admitted to the Suffolk bar in 1841 and practised in Boston for seventeen years. His first appearance in a public position was as a member of the constitutional convention of 1853, in which he sat for Andover, Mass., his home from 1850. In 1858 he served in the state House of Representatives, where he was chairman of the committee on elections and rendered reports on important questions regarding election law, which the House has since followed.

His judicial service began with his appointment in 1858 to the superior court of Suffolk County and continued unbroken for over thirty-two years. During these years he was one of the original ten members of the state superior court, organized in 1859; justice of the supreme judicial court of Massachusetts from Apr. 15, 1869; and chief justice from Jan. 16, 1882, to Aug. 27, 1890, at which time he resigned because of ill health. He died of heart failure in Andover, leaving his widow, whom, as Abby B. Hoppin of Providence, R. I., he had married on Oct. 19, 1843, a son, and five daughters.

Morton was by temperament an excellent judge, thorough, strong, and reliable rather than brilliant, rapid in assimilating materials and in dispatching business, forbearing and patient in court, always accessible, of sufficient learning, courageous in deciding according to his convictions, and of unusual practical sagacity and native shrewdness. Possessed of a direct and vigorous sense of justice, he viewed cases comprehensively, aiming at substantial justice rather than "the sharp quillets of the law." His summaries to juries were characterized by their simplicity, intelligibility, accurate sense of proportion, and impartiality. His judgments, of which over twelve hundred are recorded in the *Massachusetts Reports,* are compact, clear, and forcible, and, in the opinion of his associates, contain few dicta which will require overruling or qualifications. As a *nisi prius* judge he is said to have had few equals in the history of the Commonwealth of Massachusetts. In private life he was plain and unassuming and, though of great personal charm and popularity, averse to public display.

[J. K. Allen, *George Morton of Plymouth Colony and Some of His Descendants* (1908); "Brown University Necrology for 1890–91," *Providence Daily Jour.,* June 17, 1891; 153 *Mass. Reports,* 601–08; *Boston Herald, Boston Transcript,* Feb. 11, 1891.]

C. M. F.

MORTON, NATHANIEL (1613–June 29, 1685 o.s.), Pilgrim father, author, was born at Leyden in the Netherlands, the eldest son of George Morton [*q.v.*] and Juliana (Carpenter) of Bath. His mother's sister Agnes married Samuel Fuller, later the Pilgrim doctor, and her sister Alice married at Leyden Edward Southworth and later at Plymouth, Gov. William Bradford [*q.v.*]. Nathaniel came to Plymouth with his father and family on the *Anne* in 1623 and when his father died in 1624 was taken into the family of Governor Bradford, who had just become his uncle by marriage with Alice Southworth. He was educated at Plymouth by Bradford, Brewster, Standish, and Fuller, and well educated, for about 1634 he became his uncle's clerk and amanuensis and apparently his agent in many transactions. His association with Bradford was extremely close until the Governor's death in 1657. From December 1647 to 1685, Nathaniel Morton was secretary of the colony and keeper of the records, and as such was entrusted with most of the routine work of government, which he executed with great fidelity and accuracy. He probably drafted most of the colony's laws, and thus the statute book was largely his work. A part of his duty consisted in making copies of the statutes in longhand for the use of the officers and judges in the other towns, but he seems to have been more than a copyist. He probably resided at Plymouth throughout his life, though he sold land at Duxbury in 1652 and may have lived there for a time (*Mayflower Descendant,* October 1899, p. 214). In the town of Plymouth, he was extremely active as tax collector and assessor, and was constantly member of committees to survey land, determine boundaries, lay out roads, and settle disputes. He was town clerk of Plymouth in

1674 and 1679, and probably in later years. Doubtless as a recompense for his extended and varied services, the colony and the town of Plymouth made him many grants of land at various times, several of sufficient value to be readily sold; and it seems certain that he was one of the wealthier men of the colony during the later half of his life. In 1671 he became member and secretary of the council of war to conduct the campaigns against King Philip, and he remained one of its most active members throughout the war (E. W. Peirce, *Peirce's Colonial Lists,* 1881, p. 93). In the Pilgrim church, he also served for many years as secretary and compiler of the records and was prominent in its management and affairs. Certainly he was one of the most important men at Plymouth from about 1640 until his death in 1685.

On Bradford's death, Morton became custodian of his writings and soon became reputed the best informed man at Plymouth on Pilgrim history. At the request of many, soon reinforced by the requests of the commissioners of the four New England colonies, he prepared *New Englands Memoriall,* printed at Cambridge in 1669. He declared in his preface that it had been prepared from Bradford's papers and from those of Winslow. Until the recovery of Bradford's *History of Plimoth Plantation* in 1855, it was the chief authority for the early history of the colony, but now has little value as far as the earliest period is concerned, although it remains the only authority for the list of the signers of the Compact in 1620, for the name of the *Speedwell,* for many minor biographical details, and for the period after 1646. Criticized at the time for the brevity of his account of the earlier years, Morton prepared a longer account which was completed in 1676; the manuscript was burned in that year, however, and he undertook to rewrite it, finishing the task in 1680. This account, largely from Bradford's papers, was printed in the Congregational Board's edition of the *Memoriall* (*post*), together with a "Dialogue" of Bradford's edited by Morton. He wrote also and included in the *Memoriall* many commemorative verses which deserve notice as some of the earliest verse written in America.

Morton was married twice: in 1635 to Lydia Cooper, who died in 1673, and on Apr. 29, 1674, to Ann (Pritchard), widow of Richard Templar. Most of the later Mortons, however, were descended from Nathaniel's brother, Ephraim.

[J. K. Allen, *George Morton of Plymouth Colony and Some of His Descendants* (1908); J. A. Goodwin, *The Pilgrim Republic* (1888); *Records of the Colony of New Plymouth* (12 vols., 1855–61), ed. by N. B. Shurtleff; *Records of the Town of Plymouth,* vol. I

(1889) ; "Plymouth Church Records," vol. I, being *Col. Soc. Mass. Pubs.*, vol. XXII (1920) ; the best edition of *New Englands Memoriall* is the facsimile edition (1903), with introduction by Arthur Lord; the sixth edition, *New England's Memorial, by Nathaniel Morton* (Congreg. Board of Pub., 1855), contains numerous notes, now somewhat out of date. On the various editions and copies see *Mayflower Descendant*, Apr. 1922, Apr. 1924, and for the alleged London edition of 1669, see Albert Matthews, "A Ghost Book," *Col. Soc. Mass. Pubs.*, vol. XIV (1912).]   R.G.U.

MORTON, OLIVER PERRY (Aug. 4, 1823– Nov. 1, 1877), governor of Indiana and senator, was born in the decaying frontier village of Salisbury, Wayne County, Ind. His full name was Oliver Hazard Perry Throck Morton. Both his parents, James Throck and Sarah (Miller) Morton, were of New Jersey birth, and on the paternal side the ancestral line began with John Throckmorton who emigrated from England with Roger Williams in 1631 and later settled in Providence Plantations. Oliver's father was the first to write his surname as Morton. When the boy was less than three years old his mother died, and he was taken to the farm of his maternal grandparents near Springfield (now Springdale), Ohio, where two of his aunts gave him their solicitous care. Scotch Presbyterianism pervaded their home, and he seems to have received an overdose of it, for he never became a church member, and later he was credited, quite properly, with exceedingly unorthodox views on religion. One of his aunts taught a neighboring school, which he attended, but much of his early education came from a rather indiscriminate reading of all the books he could get. For one year he attended the Wayne County Seminary at Centerville, Ind., to which his father had removed when the village of Salisbury sank into hopeless decline. On his grandfather's death in 1838 he went to work as became a frontier youth of fifteen years, at first as a drug clerk, and later, when he quarreled with his employer and lost his job, as an apprentice to his brother William, who was a hatter. He thoroughly disliked the hatter's trade and obtained his release from service six months before the four years for which he was bound had ended. Financed by a little money from his grandfather's estate, he entered Miami University, where he spent two years in study, excelling in mathematics, learning to write good English, and enjoying himself thoroughly in debate.

In 1845 he left college to read law in a Centerville office, and in spite of his dwindling financial resources he was married on May 15, 1845, to Lucinda M. Burbank, also of Centerville. Five children were born to them, of whom the three sons survived him. Faced with the necessity of maintaining a home of his own, he speedily began the practice of law, gained some advertising through an unsuccessful race for prosecuting attorney in 1848 on the Democratic ticket, and when he was only twenty-nine years old served out the unfinished term of a circuit judge who had died in office. Doubtless his brief judicial career, less than eight months, convinced him that he needed further legal training, for, before resuming his practice at Centerville, he attended one term at the Law School of the Cincinnati College. After this his progress in his profession was rapid, and in a few years he became the leader of the Wayne County bar. Since he was an unusually effective pleader, his services were in great demand, especially by railway corporations, whose fees helped out his income materially. His formal entrance into politics coincided with the beginnings of the Republican party. Earlier he had no particular sentiment on the slavery question and had even opposed the Wilmot proviso as prejudicial to harmony within the Democratic ranks. By 1854, however, his views had changed. He revolted openly against the Kansas-Nebraska Bill, and when the Democratic state convention of that year indorsed the Douglas measure he went over to the People's party, the forerunner of the Republican party in Indiana. He helped with the formation of the new party along national lines, and in 1856 he was its unsuccessful candidate for governor of Indiana. For the next four years he divided his time between politics and his profitable law practice, doubtless expecting to be the Republican candidate again in 1860. But this was not to be. For reasons of expediency the party leaders gave the nomination to Henry S. Lane, who had been a Whig, consoling Morton, who had been a Democrat, with second place on the ticket and the promise that in case the Republicans won the legislature Lane should be speedily transferred to the United States Senate, and Morton should succeed to the governorship.

All fell out as planned, and thus it happened that he became Indiana's war-time governor, according to James Ford Rhodes, "the ablest and most energetic of the war governors of the Western States" (*History of the United States,* vol. IV, p. 182). Believing that war was necessary and inevitable, he visited Washington soon after Lincoln's inauguration to use his influence in favor of a vigorous policy towards the South, and he did what he could to prepare his state for the impending struggle. When at last the president's call for troops came, Indiana responded loyally, offering more than twice the number of men asked. Morton expected the war to be a hard-fought contest, and he was determined that none of those who volunteered should be refused the opportunity to serve. He therefore called the legislature into special session to provide ways and means for accepting into state service such men as the national government could not use at the moment. To this and to other requests of the governor, who believed that the war should be made "instant and terrible" (Foulke, *post*, I, 118), the legislature responded with alacrity. Throughout the struggle he put the full power of his office and of his personality behind every request of the administration for men. Thanks in no small part to his efforts, there were over 150,000 enlistments from Indiana during the four years with only a negligible number of men drafted.

He was at his best in his repeated and notable triumphs over the discouraged and disloyal agitators who tried to weaken the state's effective support of the war. Indiana, like the rest of the Old Northwest, had a large Southern element in its population in which sympathy with the Southern cause and opposition to the war soon became rife. Orders like the Knights of the Golden Circle, the Order of American Knights, or the Sons of Liberty did their best to retard enlistments, encourage desertions, free Confederate prisoners, and even form a new and independent northwestern confederacy. When the election of 1862 was held, Union military reverses and the absence of thousands of voters at the front strengthened the forces of discontent so that the Democratic legislature and state officers elected in Indiana that year were of pacifist views. According to a provision of the Indiana constitution that gave the governor a four-year term, he remained in office, providentially commissioned, he felt, to thwart all "Copperhead" plots. In order to accomplish this end heroic measures were required; for example, a scheme of the majority in the legislature to take his military power from him and to vest it in a board of its own choosing was frustrated only by the withdrawal of the Republican legislators and, ultimately, by the adjournment of the session for want of a quorum. Since the usual appropriation bills had not been passed, he faced the alternative of calling the obnoxious legislature together again or himself raising the money to keep the state government in operation. To the surprise and chagrin of the Democrats, he chose the latter course. He used some profits from the manufacture of munitions in an arsenal he had established, obtained advances from private citizens and from loyal county officials, and borrowed heavily from the government at Washington. The legislature was

not recalled, the state government functioned normally except that the governor reigned as a sort of dictator, and the business of helping win the war went on without relaxation. In 1864 he was reëlected governor, and a Republican legislature was chosen with him, which in the main supported him in what he had done.

The arduous labor of war time told on him physically, and during the summer of 1865 he was visited by a stroke of paralysis that left him a hopeless cripple but did not cloud his brain. A trip to France in search of medical aid was of no avail for that purpose, but he delivered a personal message from President Johnson to Napoleon III, which pointed out the wisdom of the removal of the French troops from Mexico without formal demand from the United States and which was doubtless of some consequence. Returning to the United States he refused, in spite of his infirmity, to retire from politics, and he attacked the Democrats in the campaign of 1866 with a ruthlessness and a ferocity that set the pace for Republican orators for many a year. In an age of extreme partisanship his partisanship was rank. He saw no good in the Democratic party, the war-time record of which he never forgave, and he viewed individual Democrats with grave suspicions. Any Democratic victory seemed to him a dire calamity.

In 1867 he was elected to the United States Senate, where he served until his death. Reconstruction was then the all-absorbing problem, and to it he devoted much thought. Immediately at the close of the war he had favored some such generous terms as were proposed by Lincoln and Johnson, but party necessities drew him irresistibly in the direction of the harsher policies advocated by the congressional leaders, and in the end he became one of the ablest and one of the least compromising of the supporters of "thorough" Reconstruction. Probably he did more than any other man to obtain the ratification of the negro suffrage amendment to the Constitution (Foulke, *post*, II, 117–18). His record on financial matters was as inconsistent as his record on reconstruction. In his earlier senatorial career he was quite free from soft-money heresies. Indeed, he formulated and introduced in 1868 a bill for the resumption of specie payments on Jan. 1, 1872, that differed little from the bill under which later on resumption was actually accomplished, but hard times following the panic of 1873 seem to have changed his opinions on the money question. Familiar with the problems of the western debtors, he saw clearly their point of view, and he came to ridicule as fanaticism the same kind of insistence upon a

Morton

return to specie payments of which, as he freely confessed, he had once been guilty himself. The hard times emergency, he thought, justified further, strictly limited, issues of paper (Foulke, *post*, II, 319–20).

He was a formidable contender for the Republican nomination of 1876, but his physical condition, his soft-money tendencies, and his strict partisanship with its attendant lack of enthusiasm about civil reform, all told against him, while Hayes had no such liabilities. He took an active part in the dispute over the election of that year and was convinced that the Republicans had won. He opposed the plan embodied in the electoral bill for settling the contest because of the chance it gave the Democrats to secure the presidency, but as a member of the electoral commission established when the bill became a law, he had a chance to do his full duty by his party. After the contest was over he went to Oregon to help investigate charges of bribery made against a newly elected senator from that state. He was unsparing of himself on the trip and perhaps on this account suffered, in August 1877, another stroke of paralysis. Returning at once to Indiana, he went first to the residence of his wife's mother in Richmond and later to his own home in Indianapolis, where he died.

He was to a remarkable degree the typical politician of his period. He had, to be sure, a much higher sense of honor than some, and in money matters he was incorruptible. Yet his fanatical devotion to party, his glory in combat, his intolerance of opposition, his heated rhetoric were distinctly of his time. Powerful physically, of commanding voice and presence, he feared no man, nor did the affliction of his later years abate his courage. He was an able lawyer, but he preferred politics, and probably he was not greatly tempted by Grant's offer of the chief-justiceship on the death of Chase. To the end of his life he was a power to be reckoned with in American politics, loved and honored by his friends, cordially hated by his enemies, and almost never ignored. Like many another he coveted the presidency, but his failure to obtain it did not in the least embitter him.

[Wm. D. Foulke, *Life of Oliver P. Morton* (2 vols., 1899); W. M. French, *Life, Speeches, State Papers and Public Services of Gov. Oliver P. Morton* (1864); *Memorial Addresses on . . . Oliver P. Morton . . . in the Senate and House of Representatives* (1878); *Oliver P. Morton . . .* by direction of the Ind. Republican State Central Committee (1876); J. A. Woodburn, "Party Politics in Ind. during the Civil War," *Am. Hist. Asso. Report, 1902*, vol. I (1903); Logan Esary, *A History of Indiana* (1918), vol. II; *Indianapolis Journal*, Nov. 2, 1877.]   J. D. H.

Morton

MORTON, PAUL (May 22, 1857–Jan. 19, 1911), business executive, secretary of the navy for one year after July 1, 1904, was the son of Julius Sterling [*q.v.*] and Caroline (Joy) Morton. His parents, of native stock, were early Nebraska pioneers who resided at Nebraska City, although Paul was born at Detroit, Mich., his mother's home. Impatient of formal education, Paul joined the Burlington Railroad at fifteen and by 1890 had become its general freight agent. He served the Colorado Fuel & Iron Company for the next six years, and the Atchison, Topeka & Santa Fé Railroad for eight years after 1896. A "gold Democrat," like his father, he became a Roosevelt Republican. As second vice-president of the Santa Fé, he handled freight rates on a competitive basis, not caring to deny the illegalities involved when in 1901 the Interstate Commerce Commission questioned him. His "unusual mental poise, energy, and executive ability" (New York *Evening Post,* Jan. 20, 1911) made him a marked figure on the witness stand, developing a tradition that he could "look any man in the eye and tell him to go to hell" (G. B. Clarkson, *Industrial America in the World War,* 1923, p. 44). These traits, perhaps, rather than his record as a rebater, attracted the interest of President Roosevelt, who called him to Washington at the close of the Republican National Convention of 1904; and the next day it was announced that Morton was to become secretary of the navy, vice Moody who was transferred to be attorney-general.

Morton took over the new post July 1, 1904, and shortly declared in Chicago that the United States navy "should be the most formidable in existence" (New York *Evening Post,* July 15, 1904). In his only annual report, in November, he recited the General Board arguments for strengthening the navy, taking pride in the unusual number of fleet additions of the year. But in December 1904, the traffic manager of the Santa Fé admitted the granting of illegal rebates to the Colorado Fuel & Iron Company while Morton was his superior officer, in spite of an injunction against such practices of Mar. 25, 1902, and the Anti-Rebate Law of Feb. 19, 1903, and Morton became "grotesquely out of place in the cabinet of a president who is engaged in declared and open war" against rebates (*Milwaukee Sentinel,* June 3, 1905). The Interstate Commerce Commission handed down the Santa Fé opinion, Feb. 1, 1905 (10 *Interstate Commerce Reports,* 472), forwarding the testimony to the attorney-general who employed Judson Harmon and Frederick N. Judson to inquire into its sufficiency as a basis for prosecution. But the attorney-general, backed by Roosevelt, declined to prosecute Morton, and the special counsel resigned their commission on June 5. Before the resignation was made public, Morton had announced that he would on July 1 leave the cabinet, and early in June he was made chairman of the board of directors of the Equitable Life Assurance Association, the stock of which Thomas Fortune Ryan had bought after the insurance scandals of the spring. On June 21 Roosevelt gave out long letters to Moody and Morton explaining why no personal guilt adhered to the latter in spite of the behavior of his subordinates in the Santa Fé (*New York Tribune,* June 22, 1905). Morton spent the rest of his life in the rehabilitation of the affairs of the Equitable. He was rejected by his own company for a life policy in December 1910, and the rejection was justified when his heart failed him suddenly in January 1911. He was survived by his wife, Charlotte Goodridge of Chicago, whom he married on Oct. 13, 1880, and by two daughters.

[There is a good obituary of Paul Morton in the N. Y. *Evening Post,* Jan. 20, 1911. See also: *Who's Who in America,* 1910–11; Edwin Lefèvre, "Paul Morton—Human Dynamo," *Cosmopolitan Mag.,* Oct. 1905; the *Nation,* June 30, 1904, June 22, 29, 1905.]

F. L. P.

MORTON, SAMUEL GEORGE (Jan. 26, 1799–May 15, 1851), physician and naturalist, son of George and Jane (Cummings) Morton, was born in Philadelphia, Pa., the youngest of nine children. His father, who had emigrated from Ireland in his youth, died when the boy was but six months of age, and his mother then took her family to Westchester, N. Y. His early education was obtained at various boarding schools conducted by the Society of Friends. In 1812, his mother having married Thomas Rogers, the family returned to Philadelphia, and Morton attended the Quaker school in Westtown. His mother died when he was but seventeen. It seems that during her illness the attending physicians became interested in the boy and helped him toward the study of medicine. In 1817 he began his medical education in the office of Dr. Joseph Parrish, and among his associates in this period was the brilliant naturalist, Richard Harlan [*q.v.*], who exerted a marked influence upon him in turning his thoughts toward science. During his period of study under Parrish, Morton attended lectures at the medical department of the University of Pennsylvania and in 1820 was awarded the degree of M.D. It was at this time that he became a member of the Academy of Natural Sciences of Philadelphia, an institution which he served for the period of his life, holding the office of president at the time of his death.

His education was broadened by study in Europe where he attended the medical college of Edinburgh University (M.D., 1823). In 1827 he was married to Rebecca Grellet Pearsall. James St. Clair Morton [*q.v.*] was their son.

Morton's first paper, "An Analysis of Tabular Spar from Bucks County, Pennsylvania" (*Journal of the Academy of Natural Sciences of Philadelphia,* vol. VI, 1829) gives a fair idea of his varied interests, for his researches extended through the fields of medicine, geology, vertebrate paleontology, and zoölogy. In 1834 he published a "Synopsis of the Organic Remains of the Cretaceous Group of the United States," in which were described the fossils brought back by the Lewis and Clark Expedition. This work gave its author a deserved scientific reputation, and according to Marcou, it is the starting point of all paleontological and systematic work on American fossils. In 1830 he published a "Synopsis of the Organic Remains of the Ferruginous Sand Formation of the United States" in the *American Journal of Science and Arts* (vols. XVII and XVIII, 1830). This contribution dealt with many interesting fossil forms including plesiosaurus, crocodiles, horses, elephants, and mastodons found near the Raritan River in New Jersey. His zoölogical papers included his description of a new species of hippopotamus, determined from a skull received from Dr. Goheen of Liberia. In the field of medicine he published an essay, "Observations on Cornine," in 1825 (*Philadelphia Journal of the Medical and Physical Sciences,* vol. XI, 1825). In 1834 appeared his "Illustrations of Pulmonary Consumption" in which he followed Parrish in recommending the open-air treatment of the disease. In 1836 he published in two volumes *Principles of Pathology and Practice of Physics,* an American edition of the work of John Mackintosh. He at first lectured under Parrish and then in 1839 he was elected to the professorship of anatomy in Pennsylvania College, holding this position until his resignation in 1843. In 1849 he published a substantial work, *Human Anatomy,* considered a volume of permanent value and one upon which much of his lasting reputation rests.

Morton's major interests in research consisted of collecting for comparative studies a large series of human skulls. This material is estimated to have cost Morton somewhere between ten and fifteen thousand dollars to assemble, in spite of the fact that most of the specimens were contributed by about one hundred of his friends. Louis Agassiz declared that this collection alone was worth a journey to America. After a careful study of his collection, Morton prepared two technical works, *Crania Americana* (1839) and *Crania Ægyptiaca*. His studies in the field of anthropology led him to conclude that the races of man were of diverse origin. For this conclusion he was bitterly assailed by many persons, including several ministers, who claimed that he was denying the authority of the Scriptures. In 1847 he published an essay on hybridity in the *American Journal of Science and Arts* (January, March 1847). Agassiz accepted in the main Morton's views on this subject. According to Marcou, Morton was second only to Cuvier in his influence upon Agassiz's mind and scientific opinion. Morton died in Philadelphia at the age of fifty-two.

[G. B. Wood, memoir of Morton in *Quart. Summary of the Trans. of the Coll. of Physicians of Phila.*, n.s. vol. I, no. 9 (1853); C. D. Meigs, *A Memoir of Samuel Geo. Morton* (1851); H. S. Patterson, *Memoir of the Life and Scientific Labors of Samuel Geo. Morton, M.D.* (1854); Jules Marcou, *Life, Letters and Works of Louis Agassiz* (1895), II, 28–29; H. A. Kelly and W. L. Burrage, *Am. Medic. Biogs.* (1920); *Pa. Inquirer*, May 16, 1851.]
D. M. F.

MORTON, SARAH WENTWORTH APTHORP (1759–May 14, 1846), considered by her contemporaries the chief American poetess, was baptized at King's Chapel, Boston, Aug. 29, 1759. Her parents, James and Sarah (Wentworth) Apthorp, soon after removed to Braintree, where she was brought up. She was given an unusual education for her day and was reared in the traditions of cultured ancestors, her grandfathers having been wealthy and distinguished merchants of Boston. Her unusual beauty and charm and her poetic talent won the affections of a brilliant young Boston lawyer, Perez Morton, who had gained local fame by his funeral oration over the body of General Warren. After their marriage, Feb. 24, 1781, they occupied the Apthorp family mansion on State Street, where their five children were probably born and where they lived on intimate terms with the families of Governor Bowdoin and Vice-President Adams. In 1789 the newly established *Massachusetts Magazine* enlisted Mrs. Morton's support, and a number of her moralizing or eulogistic lyrics appeared in the issues of the next four years, mostly over her pseudonym "Philenia." Her first published volume, *Ouâbi, or the Virtues of Nature, an Indian Tale* (Boston, 1790), an idealized narrative on the "noble savage" theme, in stilted Popean couplets, was well received in America and in England (*Monthly Review*, September 1793, pp. 72–77), where James Bacon used its plot for his play, *The American Indian* (1795). Her poems continued to appear in the Boston *Columbian Centinel*, the *New York Magazine*, Joseph Dennie's *Tablet*, and other papers; and

"Philenia" became the object of extravagant praise by such contemporary critics as Dennie and Thomas Paine (later Robert Treat Paine, Jr.), who eulogized her as the "American Sappho" and the "American Mrs. Montague."

Many of her verses, like Whittier's favorite, "The African Chief" (*Columbian Centinel*, June 9, 1792), were widely copied. A portion of her most ambitious undertaking, a versified account of the Revolution, was published in 1797 as *Beacon Hill, a Local Poem, Historical and Descriptive*. A second part appeared as *The Virtues of Society* (1799), but the work, if completed, was never published in entirety. In 1797 the family moved to a house of Mrs. Morton's designing in Dorchester, and thence about 1808 to another residence called "the Pavilion," where in later years she and her husband, now attorney-general of Massachusetts, enjoyed the society of many distinguished guests. In 1802 Mrs. Morton visited Washington and Philadelphia, where Stuart painted for her three of his finest portraits, though the third was never finished. These show her to have been a woman of rare personal beauty, which, with her social charm, doubtless enhanced her reputation as a poet. Her verses, called forth by various national and local events and causes, still appeared, some as broadsides, some in the *Port Folio* and the *Monthly Anthology*, and others in the newspapers. Her fame had considerably declined by 1823, however, when she published her miscellany of short didactic prose pieces and fugitive lyrics, with autobiographical notes, under the title *My Mind and Its Thoughts*. Soon after her husband's death, Oct. 14, 1837, she moved to her old Braintree home, by that time in the town of Quincy, where she died, aged eighty-six, having outlived her children and all of her near relatives.

Over thirty years after her death, Mrs. Morton's name was first linked in print with the earliest American novel, *The Power of Sympathy* (by F. S. Drake in *The Town of Roxbury*, 1878, p. 134), which has since usually been attributed to her in bibliographies of American fiction. The sole reason for this attribution appears to be that an episode in the novel was based upon a scandal involving Mrs. Morton's husband and her sister. The real author was probably the Mortons' neighbor, William Hill Brown (1765–1793), a minor novelist, playwright, poet, and essayist.

[See Emily Pendleton and Milton Ellis, *Philenia, the Life and Works of Sarah Wentworth Morton* (1931), University of Maine Studies, 2nd ser., no. 20. The evidence indicating Brown's authorship of *The Power of Sympathy* is summed up in Milton Ellis, "The Authorship of the First American Novel," *Am. Lit.*, Jan. 1933, pp. 359–68. The novel has been twice reprinted: by Walter Littlefield in 1894, with an introduction attributing it to Mrs. Morton; and serially in the *Bostonian*, Oct. 1894–June 1895, accompanied by an article, Dec. 1894, "The Real Author of *The Power of Sympathy*," by A. W. Brayley, in which Brown's authorship was first asserted.] M. E—s.

MORTON, THOMAS (fl. 1622–1647), adventurer, was probably a lawyer and "of Clifford's Inn, Gent" as he designated himself. He seems to have come first with Andrew Weston's party in 1622, remaining at Wessagusset during the summer, and returning to England in the autumn. He was fond of hunting and outdoor life, and later came back to Massachusetts with the Wollaston company, settling within the limits of the present Quincy. His manner of life, which was distinctly licentious and convivial, made him anathema to the Pilgrims of Plymouth, and it was hinted darkly that he had had a horrible past. Wollaston had enough of New England in one winter and went to Virginia, but Morton remained and built his house at Merry Mount, where, in 1627, the Pilgrims came and cut down the Maypole he had erected. He was a fur-trader and enormously increased his business to the danger of the pockets and polls of everyone on the coast by selling guns to the Indians. He forestalled the trading activities of the Plymouth colonists on the Kennebec and, in 1628, was captured by a band under Capt. Standish and was sent to England, with charges. In a year and a half he had returned, brought by Isaac Allerton. By this time the Puritans had arrived at Boston and times had changed. John Endecott [*q.v.*] had visited Merry Mount and the Maypole had again been cut down, and most of Morton's old companions had been scattered. Trouble soon began and in 1630 Morton was once more taken into custody, sentenced to have all his goods confiscated, his house burned, and himself shipped back again to England. After some delay the sentence was carried out. On reaching England, he was confined in Exeter jail but was soon set at liberty, probably through the influence of Gorges. In London he was a useful witness against the Massachusetts colony. He seems to have spent some years in England, ready to the hand of Gorges, who, however, claimed to have set him adrift in 1637. It was in that year that he published his *New English Canaan* in which he somewhat incoherently proclaimed his opinions of New England and gave a description of the country. In 1643 he turned up again in Plymouth. He was ordered to leave and the next spring went to Maine. He was next heard of in Rhode Island but ventured into Massachusetts and was promptly taken and placed in prison. The only charge was that he had complained against the colony to the Privy Council, which as an English citizen he had a legal right to do. He was kept in prison for a year when it was decided he was too expensive for the country to support and was fined and released. By this time he was old and infirm and a winter in Boston jail had not improved his health. He died within two years after. He was himself a worthless rake, in spite of efforts which have been made to rehabilitate his character as a persecuted churchman.

[C. F. Adams, Jr., edited *The New English Canaan of Thos. Morton* with a long biographical introduction, for the Prince Society (1883). Contemporary references in Bradford, Winthrop, and others may be found noted there. A more popular account is given by Adams in his *Three Episodes of Mass. Hist.* (1892), vol. I. Charges against Morton in letters to the Council for New England appear in the *Mass. Hist. Soc. Colls.*, 1 ser. III (1794), 62–64.] J. T. A.

MORTON, WILLIAM JAMES (July 3, 1845–Mar. 26, 1920), neurologist, was born in Boston, Mass., the year before his father, William Thomas Green Morton [*q.v.*], then a young and struggling dentist, began his experiments with ether as an anaesthetic. His mother was Elizabeth (Whitman) Morton. The boy, the only child, attended the Boston Latin School and then Harvard College, graduating in 1867, the year before his father died. After some months of teaching, he entered the Harvard Medical School in 1868, and graduated in 1872. He began practice in Boston that same year, but being restless and venturesome, closed his office in 1873 and went to Vienna. A few months later he became physician to a mining company in Cape Town, South Africa, and a prospector and big game hunter as well (1874–76). Returning to Boston, he contributed to the *Bulletin* of the American Geographical Society an account of his experiences which was reprinted in pamphlet form under the title *South African Diamond Fields, and the Journey to the Mines* (1877). In 1877 he was called to Europe to care for or to decide upon the medico-legal status of a psychotic patient there. This is possibly the event that turned his attention to psychiatry and neurology.

In 1878 he resumed practise in New York City. He became a member of the American Neurological Association the following year, at which time he presented a paper on the toxic effects of tea as seen in tea-tasters (*Journal of Nervous and Mental Disease*, October 1879). In 1880 he was in Paris at the Salpêtrière, that Mecca of all neurologists of the day, attending Charcot's memorable clinics; and in the same year he was appointed professor of mental diseases in the medical department of the University of Vermont, where he gave a series of summer courses, 1880–84. In 1881 he was back in New York, deep in the study of electrical energy. Physics and chemistry had always attracted him and at this time he made some notable experiments in high-frequency currents, inventing what he then called his "static induced current." He read a paper, "On Statical Electro-Therapeutics," before the New York Academy of Medicine, Mar. 3, 1881, which was published in the *Medical Record* of Apr. 2 and 9. His practice as a neurologist grew rapidly, for his personality was attractive and his originality and verve quite sweeping. In 1882, with C. L. Dana, he published a description of the brain of Guiteau, assassin of President Garfield (*Medical Record,* July 5, 1882), and in the same year became editor and publisher of the *Journal of Nervous and Mental Disease,* then the leading neuropsychiatric publication in the United States. He continued as editor until 1885 when he was joined by Dr. B. Sachs, to whom in 1886 he turned over the entire work. He was president of the New York Neurological Society in 1883. Before the American Neurological Association he read a number of papers: *A Contribution to the Subject of Nerve Stretching* (1882), *Neuritis following Dislocation* (1883), *An Apparatus for Scrivener's Palsy* (1883), and *Treatment of Migraine* (1883). These early papers were full of promise, but his attention became more and more engrossed in his electrotherapeutic work and an ingenious and original mind was in large measure lost to neurology. From 1890 to 1909, however, he was professor of diseases of the mind and nervous system and of electrotherapeutics at the New York Post Graduate Medical School and Hospital, and for some time was neurologist to the Metropolitan Throat Hospital and the New York Infant Asylum.

Working incessantly at his electrotherapeutics, Morton hoped great things from his many experiments. In 1890, before the New York Neurological Society, he read a paper on "The Franklinic Interrupted Current; or My New System of Therapeutic Administration of Static Electricity" (*Medical Record,* Jan. 24, 1891). He was very enthusiastic in his experiments on cataphoresis, hoping to perfect a means of driving metallic and other remedies into the body by other than the hypodermic method now so much in vogue (*"Cataphoresis," or Electric Medicamental Diffusion as Applied in Medicine, Surgery and Dentistry,* 1898); and his various publications on this subject contributed definitely to the development of the therapeutic method later

known as ionization. He was also one of the first physicians in America to use the X-ray in the treatment of skin disorders and cancerous growths, publishing in the years 1902–07 several papers based on his experiments.

Morton's manner was courteous and pleasing, although to some of his colleagues he seemed shut in and reserved, as if the bitterness of his father's disappointment had left its effect upon him. His later years, like those of his father, were not happy. His adventurous and daring spirit led him to speculate in certain Canadian mining properties, which despite his lack of experience he endeavored to develop, in association with some friends and one Albert Freeman, a promoter. In November 1912, with his associates, he was indicted, and in March 1913 convicted of using the mails to defraud, in promoting the sale of stock. Morton and one of his friends were sentenced to a year and a day in the Atlanta penitentiary, while Freeman received a sentence of five years (*New York Times,* Mar. 15, 1913). In October, however, Morton and his friend were released on parole (*Ibid.,* Oct. 16, 1913), and in December were pardoned by President Wilson (*Ibid.,* Dec. 17, 1913). In the following June Morton was restored to his status as a medical practitioner by the State Board of Regents at the request of prominent physicians and other citizens (*Ibid.,* June 26, 1914). Six years later he died of heart disease at Miami, Fla. He had married Elizabeth Campbell Lee, May 20, 1880. There were no children.

[I. A. Watson, *Physicians and Surgeons of America* (1896); classbooks, Class of 1867, Harvard College; C. L. Dana, in *Jour. Nervous and Mental Disease,* Mar. 1921; *N. Y. Medic. Jour.,* May 1, 1920; *Boston Medic. and Surgic. Jour.,* Apr. 15, 1920; *Semicentennial Vol. of the Am. Neurological Asso., 1875–1924* (1924); C. H. Farnam, *Hist. of the Descendants of John Whitman* (1889); *N. Y. Times,* Apr. 4, 1920.]
S. E. J.

MORTON, WILLIAM THOMAS GREEN (Aug. 9, 1819–July 15, 1868), dentist, anaesthetist, was born at Charlton, a village in Worcester County, Mass. He was the son of James Morton, a farmer of that town, by his wife, Rebecca, daughter of William Needham of Charlton. Morton's ancestor, Robert Morton, had emigrated from Scotland early in the seventeenth century and settled in Salem, Mass. After receiving a New England common school education at Northfield and Leicester Academies, William, at the age of seventeen, went to Boston, where he became clerk and salesman in various business houses, but finding these occupations distasteful he betook himself to Baltimore in 1840 and there began the study of dentistry at the College of Dental Surgery. Two years later he settled at Farmington, Conn., and acquired a moderate dental practice. In 1842 he met Horace Wells [q.v.] of Hartford, Conn., who later (1844) employed nitrous oxide for the extraction of teeth. During the winter of 1842–43 these two dentists practised together at 19 Tremont St., Boston, but since the partnership proved unremunerative it was amicably dissolved in the autumn of 1843, Wells returning to Hartford and Morton remaining in Boston. In March 1844 Morton, conscious of his inadequate medical training, matriculated at Harvard Medical School, but, having married in that same year, he was compelled by financial difficulties to practise dentistry; consequently he never received a medical degree from Harvard.

During 1844 he lived with Prof. Charles T. Jackson [q.v.] and in July, at Jackson's recommendation, he used ether in drops as a local anaesthetic during the filling of a tooth (Hodges, post, p. 11). Morton at this time had become especially interested in the manufacture of artificial teeth and in order to render his work effective found it necessary to remove the roots of all old teeth remaining in the jaw. Few patients would submit to this painful procedure, and he had tried intoxicants, opium, mesmerism, and other questionable methods to deaden pain, but none were effective. Jackson had demonstrated before his chemical classes that inhalation of sulphuric ether causes loss of consciousness. Morton accordingly tried ether upon himself, but before using it on patients he tested it further, during July and August 1846, by anaesthetizing a goldfish, a hen, and his pet spaniel; as they all recovered without obvious impairment of faculties he decided to use ether upon human beings. On Sept. 30, 1846, he had a conference with Jackson during which, for some unaccountable reason, he professed complete ignorance of the effects of ether inhalation (Hodges). That afternoon, however, a patient named Frost came to Morton in agony with a toothache. Morton let him breathe the fumes of the ether which he had borrowed that morning from Jackson, and within less than five minutes the tooth was painlessly extracted. Public notice of this incident, which appeared in the Boston Daily Journal of Oct. 1, 1846, read as follows: "Last evening, as we were informed by a gentleman who witnessed the operation, an ulcerated tooth was extracted from the mouth of an individual without giving him the slightest pain. He was put into a kind of sleep, by inhaling a preparation, the effects of which lasted for about three-quarters of a minute, just long enough to extract the tooth." Other successful

extractions followed. This announcement attracted the attention of Henry Jacob Bigelow [q.v.], a young surgeon of Boston, who called upon Morton to obtain further details. Through Bigelow the news reached the ears of John Collins Warren [q.v.], who made arrangements with Morton to try his new discovery at the Massachusetts General Hospital. The day set was Oct. 16, 1846, and Warren was to remove a vascular tumor from the left side of the neck of a young man named Gilbert Abbott. The growth was excised in five minutes and the patient showed no evidence of pain, though toward the end of the operation he moved slightly, owing to incomplete etherization. Again under Morton's supervision a second operation was carried out on the following day by Dr. George Hayward [q.v.] with equal success. During the next two weeks a disagreement arose as to the advisability of continuing the procedure, since Morton was not a medical man and refused to tell the composition of the anaesthetic agent. The difficulties were finally overcome and the discovery was first announced by H. J. Bigelow on Nov. 18, 1846, in the Boston Medical and Surgical Journal.

Morton at once sought to secure profit from his discovery and applied for a patent to protect his rights. He did not reveal that the anaesthetic agent was sulphuric ether, but designated it by the mysterious name of "letheon." On Oct. 27, 1846, he applied (with Jackson, whom he had been forced to include by legal advisers) for letters patent, which were issued Nov. 12, 1846 (patent no. 4848) for a period of fourteen years. On Nov. 26, 1846, Morton stated publicly that he was prepared to grant licenses for use of his apparatus and discovery, but on Bigelow's advice agreed to repay the fee should the United States government adopt his invention (Circular—Morton's Letheon). On Nov. 28 he stated that certain charitable hospitals might use "letheon" free of charge (Warren Papers, post, vol. xxiii). A few months later the Monthyon prize of 5,000 francs was awarded by the French Academy of Medicine to Jackson and Morton jointly, but Morton refused to take his share, saying that the discovery was entirely his. In 1847 a memorial was sent to Congress by the surgeons and physicians of the Massachusetts General Hospital, praying that adequate compensation be given to the discoverer of the anaesthetic uses of ether. In 1849, however, when his patent and the memorial to Congress had brought him nothing, Morton solicited Congress himself for financial reward. As a result of this and other pressure which was brought to bear, two bills appropriating $100,-000 for the discovery of practical anaesthesia were introduced into Congress at three separate sessions of that body, but, owing to the activities of the supporters of Jackson, Wells, and Crawford W. Long [*q.v.*], the appropriations were never carried. The deliberations of committees and sub-committees were drawn out for nearly two decades. Valuable reports and hearings were published (*Statements Supported by Evidence of Wm. T. G. Morton, Submitted to the . . . Committee Appointed by the Senate of the United States, Jan. 21, 1853,* 1853), but when the Civil War came the cause was lost in a maze of unfinished business. Several plans were instituted to give Morton financial support, but these brought him honor without riches. The last twenty years of his life were spent in the perpetual torment of bitter controversy and litigation, as a result of which he was reduced to dire poverty. He died from apoplexy which came on while driving in Central Park, New York. The seizure was thought to have been induced by reading a publication just then issued in behalf of Jackson in order to prejudice another testimonial subscription which was being raised for Morton.

Personally Morton was tall, dark-haired, quick of thought and movement, methodical in his habits, neat in personal appearance, and of agreeable manners. In the heat of controversy he often exerted remarkable forbearance and he is said never to have attempted to retaliate upon his enemies. His education was faulty, however, and the fact that he sought personal benefit from his discovery will, perhaps rightly, always be held against him. He married Elizabeth Whitman of Connecticut in May 1844, and they had one son, William James Morton [*q.v.*], a pioneer in the use of the X-ray in the United States.

In the discovery of surgical anaesthesia Crawford W. Long, Horace Wells, and Charles T. Jackson all shared, yet Morton acted independently and conducted experiments with ether on his own initiative. Moreover, he took entire responsibility for the outcome of his first public demonstrations upon human beings, and in so doing he, before any one else, convinced the surgical world of the value of the discovery; for this contribution alone one may allow him credit as the discoverer, and this, indeed, was the opinion of those of his contemporaries most competent to judge (Welch, *post,* p. 11). The fact that the demonstration was a triumph of the experimental method makes Morton's position even more secure. The regrettable features

of his conduct may lessen but cannot rob him of the honor which is his due.

His published works relating to ether are rare and little known. Beginning on Nov. 26, 1846, he issued, usually weekly and at his own expense, a little publication entitled *Circular—Morton's Letheon,* in which he communicated the results of his experiments on anaesthetization and cautioned others concerning the use of the new agent (see back page, *Boston Medical and Surgical Journal,* Dec. 9, 1846). These sheets soon became a receptacle of newspaper articles and correspondence from all parts of the world reporting the success of surgical anaesthesia, and were then issued in pamphlet form (Rice, *post,* p. 115), under the same title. Of this brochure five editions appeared under Morton's direction. (The Surgeon General's Library has a 14-page edition of the pamphlet, evidently issued in 1846, which is probably the first edition.) In 1847 he published his most important work, *Remarks on the Proper Mode of Administering Sulphuric Ether by Inhalation,* a small duodecimo of forty-four pages, dedicated "To the surgeons of the Mass. Gen. [*sic*] Hospital . . . as an evidence that their early and continued interest in the administration of sulphuric ether is gratefully appreciated." It contains detailed direction concerning the use of ether in dentistry, general surgery, and obstetrics, and gives a list of "the symptoms indicating danger" during its administration. A 60-page pamphlet, *Mémoire sur la découverte du nouvel emploi de l'éther sulfurique, suivi des pièces justificatives,* containing a carefully documented statement of Morton's claims to priority in the introduction of anaesthesia, was issued in Paris in 1847. A brochure, *On the Physiological Effects of Sulphuric Ether, and Its Superiority to Chloroform,* was published in Boston in 1850, called forth largely by the claims of Simpson in Edinburgh as to the virtues of chloroform. In addition to controversial matter and a history of the discovery of ether, it contains a clear description of the two stages of etherization (p. 10), and a discussion of the sequence of action of ether upon various parts of the central nervous system. There is also an appendix containing six pages of testimonials. The foregoing works are all that Morton published on ether, except for a small 48-page booklet bearing the title, *Remarks on the Comparative Value of Ether and Chloroform, with Hints upon Natural and Artificial Teeth* (1850), on the back cover of which appeared a print of a building labeled "Morton's tooth factory." A paper written in 1864, "On the First Use of Ether as an

Anesthetic [*sic*] at the Battle of the Wilderness in the Civil War," was published by his son in the *Journal of the American Medical Association,* Apr. 23, 1904. Morton wrote also several pamphlets on dentistry, such as *On the Loss of the Teeth and the Modern Way of Restoring Them* (1848).

[Of the many accounts of Morton's career the most reliable are the following: N. P. Rice, *Trials of a Public Benefactor, as Illustrated in the Discovery of Etherization* (1859); B. P. Poore, *Hist. Materials for the Biog. of W. T. G. Morton, M.D.* (1856); H. J. Bigelow, "A History of the Discovery of Modern Anaesthesia," in *A Century of Am. Medicine* (1876); R. M. Hodges, *A Narrative of Events Connected with the Introduction of Sulphuric Ether into Surgical Use* (1891); W. H. Welch, *A Consideration of the Introduction of Surgical Anaesthesia* (n.d.), Ether Day address, Mass. Gen. Hosp., Oct. 1908; William Osler, "The First Printed Documents Relating to Modern Surgical Anaesthesia," *Proc. Roy. Soc. Med.,* Sect. Hist. Med. (London, 1918), XI, 65–69, and in *Annals Medic. Hist.* (N. Y.), Dec. 1917. See also G. B. Roth, " 'Original Morton Inhaler' for Ether," *Annals Medic. Hist.,* July 1932; and a useful account by W. J. Morton, "Memoranda Relating to the Discovery of Surgical Anaesthesia and Dr. William T. G. Morton's Relation to This Event," *Post-Graduate,* Apr. 1905. The *Bibliotheca Osleriana* (1928) contains a *catalogue raisonné* of the most extensive collection of documents relating to the history of anaesthesia which has yet been assembled, and is invaluable on all points of reference. A volume of Morton's letters and MSS. relating to the introduction of ether, deposited by Mrs. Morton, Nov. 13, 1869, is available at the Mass. Hist. Soc., Boston, where the Warren Papers are also to be found. Notices of Morton's death appeared in *Evening Post* (N. Y.), July 16, and *Boston Transcript,* July 17, 1868.]

J.F.F.

MORWITZ, EDWARD (June 11, 1815–Dec. 13, 1893), physician and publisher, the son of a wealthy merchant, was born in Danzig, Prussia. After receiving his Jewish education in his native city, he was sent to Halle, where he studied Semitic languages, Oriental literature, and theology. Deciding upon a career as a physician he began the study of medicine in the college at Danzig and continued at Leipzig University and finally at the University of Berlin, receiving the degree of M.D. from the latter institution in 1841. After his graduation he was appointed first assistant of the Hufeland clinic in Berlin, remaining for two years. In 1843 he settled in Konitz, where he began to practise his profession, specializing in the treatment of nervous and mental disorders. His success was gratifying, and he opened a hospital for the sick poor, supporting it himself. While thus engaged in this small town he began to write his *Geschichte der Medicin* (2 vols., 1848–49) which was published in Leipzig. As the work was coming from the press, the Revolutionary movement in Central Europe and France began to assume an ominous phase, and Morwitz, who was strongly inclined to democratic principles,

threw in his lot with the Revolutionists. His views became well known and he found himself an object of political hatred. On one occasion, the carriage in which he was riding was overturned by the royalists, and he was severely injured. Upon his recovery he was obliged to emigrate.

He had invented a breech-loading mechanism for field guns, and as he could not offer it to Germany he went to England to seek a purchaser. Failing there in his efforts he decided in 1850 to go to the United States, where at first he fared no better, but his love for democracy influenced him in determining to remain. He made a visit to Europe to settle his affairs and then returned in 1852, taking up his residence in Philadelphia, Pa. In that city he once more engaged in the practice of his profession and in time established a German dispensary for the poor. He took an active interest in the affairs of the city and began to contribute articles to the *Philadelphia Demokrat,* a daily printed there in the German language. About 1853 he bought a controlling interest in the paper from John S. Hoffmann. Morwitz formulated many plans for the improvement of Philadelphia and through the *Demokrat* strongly supported the consolidation of the city. In 1855 he began the publication of a political weekly, *Die Vereinigte Staaten Zeitung,* and was active in securing the election of Richard Vaux as mayor of the city in 1856. In the same year he started a Sunday literary paper, *Die Neue Welt,* which was virtually the Sunday edition of his daily. As a Democrat, he advocated the election of James Buchanan for president, and for campaign purposes purchased a newspaper called the *Pennsylvanian,* but sold it in 1860 when Stephen A. Douglas and John C. Breckinridge were separately nominated for the presidency. Confining his efforts to the *Demokrat,* he tried to use his influence in preventing the Civil War, but when the die was cast he remained loyal to the Union and assisted in raising regiments to send into the field of operations. In 1866 he issued the *Abendpost,* which he continued to publish for some years.

He took a prominent part in the organization of the German Press Association of Pennsylvania and in 1870 called a meeting to raise funds to assist German soldiers in the Franco-Prussian War, which resulted in the collection of $600,000 for the purpose. In 1874 he purchased the *Age,* a Philadelphia daily, but the following year sold it. He published German newspapers in several sections of Pennsylvania. It is said that at one time three hundred newspapers in both the German and English languages were printed by the Newspaper Union, which he organized. This was "the most extensive German establishment of its kind in the United States" (Scharf and Westcott, *post,* III, p. 2012). It was in his establishment that the so-called "patent-inside" was adopted. By this method miscellaneous matter and advertisements were printed on the second and third pages, then the papers were shipped to the country newspaper offices where the local news, editorials, and local advertisements were printed on the other pages. In 1873 Morwitz began the publication of *Uncle Sam's Almanac,* a cheap annual which had a large sale, and in 1875 he started the *Jewish Record,* which he carried on for eleven years. With others he compiled the *New American Pocket Dictionary of the English and German Languages* (in 2 parts, 1883), the forty-seventh edition of which was published in Milwaukee in 1911. Morwitz died in Philadelphia, leaving one son, Joseph, who carried on his publishing business.

[J. T. Scharf and Thompson Westcott, *Hist. of Phila.* (1884), vol. III; H. S. Morais, *The Jews of Phila.* (1894); the *Jewish Encyc.*; the *North American* (Phila.), *Phila. Inquirer,* and *Pub. Ledger,* Dec. 14, 1893.]   J. J.

MOSBY, JOHN SINGLETON (Dec. 6, 1833–May 30, 1916), Confederate ranger, was born at Edgemont, Powhatan County, Va., the eldest child of Alfred D. Mosby of Amherst County, and of Virginia, daughter of the Rev. Dr. McLaurine, of Edgemont. In 1838 the family moved from Nelson County to a farm near Charlottesville. In 1849 Mosby entered the University of Virginia, where he showed special aptitude in his studies. While an undergraduate, he was sentenced to six months in jail and fined $1,000 for shooting and wounding a fellow student in an altercation. The sentence was annulled by the legislature. In 1855 he was admitted to the bar at Bristol, Va., and in 1857 married Pauline, daughter of Judge Beverly L. Clarke, of Kentucky. With the outbreak of the Civil War in 1861, he enlisted in the cavalry, participating in the Bull Run campaign. In February 1862 he became adjutant of his regiment, and commenced to work as a scout. Failing of reëlection to the adjutancy in April, he was attached to Gen. J. E. B. Stuart's staff, and served with him during the campaigns in the Peninsula, at Manassas, and at Antietam, except for about a month's absence while he was a prisoner of war.

On Jan. 2, 1863, Mosby commenced independent operations as a ranger, in Loudoun County, Va., with only nine men. He acted under the partisan ranger law, which permitted the division of captured property among the captors. Mosby attacked isolated pickets and men with success from the first, and was commissioned a lieutenant in February. His rangers never had camps. Within limits, they boarded where they chose. Each man furnished his own food, horse, arms, and uniforms. After an engagement the command scattered, to meet at a future date and place as agreed upon. Besides dividing captured public property, the men freely took personal belongings, and were soon regarded as robbers by the Federals. Mosby, personally, however, never received anything. There were no drills; revolvers were the principal weapons, carbines were few; sabers were not used. The life with its booty and adventures, free from camp drudgery, fascinated many, and the rangers were constantly increasing in numbers through the recruiting of bold riders and fearless fighters. Mosby's first great success was on Mar. 9, 1863, when silently and unseen he crept within the Federal lines in the small hours of the morning, and entering Fairfax Court House, seized General Stoughton, about 100 others, and mounts for all. For this achievement he was appointed a captain, and for a raid on Chantilly in April, a major. Directed to organize a regular company, he declined, stating that he wanted rangers, not regulars. His request was granted, and on June 10, his men became Company A, 43rd Battalion Partisan Rangers. Additional companies were organized later.

In June, operations were extended across the Potomac into Maryland. Mosby performed valuable scouting at the commencement of the Gettysburg campaign, but he was unable to accompany Lee's army North. In the autumn, the rangers were the only disciplined force in northern Virginia. By common consent, Mosby acted as judge and administrator and maintained order. He was well liked, and in turn the people helped him in his military expeditions, the country becoming popularly known as "Mosby's Confederacy." In February 1864, he was promoted lieutenant-colonel. He was mercilessly hunted by the Federals, but since his forces dispersed when danger threatened, he was never caught. Two famous raids occurred this year: one, July 4, on Point of Rocks, Md., obtained much plunder; the other, Oct. 14, the "greenback raid," seized some $168,000, which was divided among the men and used to buy new uniforms and equipments. In this year, Mosby operated extensively in the Shenandoah Valley.

In November he hung seven prisoners, selected by lot, as a reprisal for the execution by the Federals of seven of his men, charged with being outlaws. (*Official Records*, 1 ser. XLIII, pt. 2, p. 920). Mosby informed General Sheridan of what he had done, and why, adding that he hoped it would not be necessary so to act again. It never was. In December he was promoted colonel and in the same month was severely wounded. His last engagement was on Apr. 10, 1865. The rangers had now grown to eight companies, and were never more efficient, better equipped, or better mounted. When Lee surrendered, Mosby realized that the war was over, and on Apr. 21, he reviewed his men at Salem, Va., and disbanded them. He himself surrendered at the end of June.

Settling at Warrenton, Va., he practised law, and later joined the Republican party. Because of this affiliation he was subjected to severe criticism, and his popularity with Southerners suffered. He was a great admirer of General Grant, however, and was willing to make personal sacrifices on this account. In 1878 he was appointed consul at Hong Kong, serving until 1885. Soon after, he became a land agent in Colorado, and from 1904 to 1910 was an assistant attorney for the Department of Justice. In 1887 he published *Mosby's War Reminiscences, and Stuart's Cavalry Campaigns*; and in 1908, *Stuart's Cavalry in the Gettysburg Campaign*. He was also the author of some minor publications. He died at Washington, D. C., survived by three daughters and a son, and was buried at Warrenton, Va. Mosby was of medium height, slender, with deep eyes and large features; he was smooth-shaven except during the war, when he wore a full beard. Genial and energetic, he was more of a thinker than a talker.

[*War of the Rebellion; Official Records (Army)*; J. J. Williamson, *Mosby's Rangers: A Record of the Operations of the Forty-third Battalion Va. Cavalry* (1896); *The Memoirs of Col. John S. Mosby* (1917), ed. by C. W. Russell; *Richmond Times-Dispatch*, May 31, 1916.]   C. H. L.

MOSCOSO DE ALVARADO, LUIS de (fl. 1530–1543), *maestre de campo* or second in command under Hernando de Soto [*q.v.*] during the "conquest" of Florida by the latter, was born in Zafra, Spain, a son of the Comendador Alonso Hernández de Diosdado and Isabel de Alvarado, two brothers being Juan de Alvarado and Christóbal de Mosquero. After serving under Pedro de Alvarado in Guatemala and Quito, 1530–35, Moscoso sailed from San Lucar with Soto in April 1538, in command of the galleon *La Concepción*. His two brothers accompanied the army. That Moscoso enjoyed the confidence

and trust of his superior is shown by the fact that he lodged with him, for instance at the house of the chief of Ucita in Florida, that he was trusted with separate commands, as at Cale, and was sent in advance from Tallise to Tascaluça to announce to the chief the coming of his commander. His cautious spirit made him advise against entry of Mauvila, fearing a trap; had his advice been heeded, the defeat there might have been avoided. But when it appeared that Moscoso was partially to blame for the disaster at the Chicaça winter camp in 1541, he was replaced by Baltazar Gallegos. There is no record of complaint at this discipline, and Soto dying made him his successor.

The new governor then, "longing to be again where he could get his full measure of sleep" rather than search mythical kingdoms, undertook to reach New Spain. From Guachoya (near Arkansas City) on June 5 the army struggled to do so overland. Probably Moscoso moved west through broken timber country to Naguatex, held by a northern branch of the Natchitoches Indians, in the bend of the Red River; thence he turned southeast through villages of Caddoans to Guasco, then southwest some two hundred miles to the Daycao (probably the Brazos) River, not crossing nor entering the buffalo plains. There, despairing, he returned to the Mississippi to essay the journey by the Gulf. Seven brigantines were built by June 1543. The voyage, begun on July 2, was marked by hard Indian fighting for several of the seventeen days to the Gulf; fifty-two more days by hazards ensued before Pánuco was reached. There an army of 311 survivors out of six to nine hundred enlistments was royally received by the surprised settlers, for they had been counted lost. Food and clothing were lavished upon them; they sold their armor for horses, or walked, traversing sixty leagues to Mexico city. They were welcomed by the viceroy, Antonio de Mendoza, and replenished at royal expense. Moscoso delivered to him a copy of the narrative of the expedition written by Luis Hernández de Biedma, and it was sent to Charles V.

[Moscoso's route from Guachoya was studied by T. H. Lewis in *Spanish Explorers in the Southern United States* (1907). The direction is turned southwestward from that of Lewis by H. E. Bolton, in an unpublished study. This correlates the Soto sources with the topography and ethnography of the La Salle episode and the La Salle literature and that of the Spanish expeditions sent to expel the French after 1685. See: J. E. Kelly, *Pedro de Alvarado, Conquistador* (1932); Antonio del Solar y Taboada and José de Rújula y de Ochotorena, *El Adelantado Hernando de Soto* (1929); and the bibliography following the sketch of Hernando de Soto.]   H. I. P.

MOSELEY, EDWARD AUGUSTUS (Mar. 23, 1846–Apr. 18, 1911), lawyer, public official, was born in Newburyport, Mass., the eldest child of Edward Strong and Charlotte Augusta (Chapman) Moseley. He was a descendant in the seventh generation from John Maudesley or Moseley, an English Puritan, who emigrated to America in the seventeenth century. His maternal grandfather was George T. Chapman, an Episcopal clergyman, who was born in Devonshire, England. His father early in life was a prominent and successful shipowner but as the trade between New England and the East declined, he turned to banking and for the forty years preceding his death was president of two banks of Newburyport. The son first attended private schools, and later the public high school, though he did not graduate. At the age of sixteen he shipped to Africa and India as a sailor before the mast on one of his father's vessels. The voyage was a miserable experience and he returned at the end of a year, wasted and racked by Asiatic dysentery. After his recovery, he turned to business and eventually at the age of twenty-six formed the lumber firm of Moseley & Wheelwright. Business interests took him to the Gulf states, Central and South America, the West Indies, and Europe. He served two successive terms as city alderman and in 1885 and 1886 was elected to the state legislature. On Apr. 13, 1869, he married Kate Montague Prescott, the daughter of Joseph Newmarch and Sarah (Bridges) Prescott.

After the enactment of the Interstate Commerce Act, Moseley applied for an appointment as one of the commissioners. Cleveland had determined to appoint the commissioners in accordance with a geographical plan which did not admit of the appointment of a Democrat from the New England States, but he suggested Moseley's appointment to the secretaryship. The commissioners elected him at their first meeting on Apr. 19, 1887. The chairman of the Commission, Thomas M. Cooley, was not at first cordial to Moseley, but as the routine of the office settled the two men became fast friends, and it was at Cooley's suggestion and with his aid that Moseley studied law and became a member of the bar in 1889. Moseley's work as secretary, aside from the routine of the office, was devoted to one great cause—the protection of railroad employees and travelers from the dangers of trains operated without proper safety appliances. His work took him into the courts, before congressional committees, into conferences with politicians, railroad executives, labor unions, and lawyers. He also wrote numerous articles and pamphlets setting forth detailed arguments in support of his position. After some twenty years the railroads were required by law to equip their trains with the automatic coupler, the air brake, the block signal, and similar devices to insure safety to trainmen.

In 1902, at the request of Gen. Leonard Wood, then military governor of Cuba, Moseley went to Havana to assist in the revision of the island's railway laws. In the actual drafting of the laws, he performed services of great value and many measures were introduced to safeguard the public and employees. In the same year, President Roosevelt appointed him an assistant recorder of the Anthracite Coal Strike Commission; upon his assuming office, he was made disbursing officer. The only unpleasant incident that marred Moseley's long tenure of office occurred in 1904 when charges of misconduct in office were made against him. At once he laid aside his duties and absented himself for six months, giving the investigators free access to all private and official records. He was completely exonerated. He died in 1911, while working in Washington, and was buried in Newburyport. One of his three children survived him.

[Sources include: Jas. Morgan, *The Life Work of Edward A. Moseley in the Service of Humanity* (1913); manuscript autobiography of Moseley deposited in the library of the Interstate Commerce Commission, Wash., D. C.; *Ann. Reports of the Interstate Commerce Commission*, 1887–1911; the *Evening Star* (Wash., D. C.), Apr. 18, 1911; information as to certain facts from F. S. Moseley.]   H. Ca—s.

MOSES, BERNARD (Aug. 27, 1846–Mar. 4, 1930), political scientist and historian, was born in Burlington, Conn., the son of Richard and Rachel (Norton) Moses and a descendant of John Moses who was in Windsor, Conn., in 1647. He was educated at the University of Michigan, where he took his bachelor's degree in 1870, and at Heidelberg, Germany, where he received the degree of Ph.D. in 1873. After a year as professor of history at Albion College in Michigan, he accepted an appointment to the faculty of the University of California in 1876, continuing in service at that university, either actively or as professor emeritus, until his death in 1930. During the first quarter-century of his work there, he built up a reputation as a scholar in the fields of his activities. Gradually, however, he became drawn more and more to a hitherto neglected phase of history, at least by Anglo-American students, the colonial era of Spanish America. Most of his research efforts were henceforth directed to that subject, and with such enthusiasm that even when past eighty years of age he was still engaged in productive work. His best-known books were the following: *The Establishment of Spanish Rule in America* (1898); *South America on the Eve of Emancipation* (1908); *The Spanish Dependencies in South America* (2 vols., 1914); *Spain's Declining Power in South America, 1730–1806* (1919); *Spanish Colonial Literature in South America* (1922); *The Intellectual Background of the Revolution in South America, 1810–1814* (1926); and *Spain Overseas* (1929). A pioneer in this work, he had to write his own monographs. In consequence his books had a somewhat novel style. The story he told was not necessarily a continuous and united whole, but more often a series of essays which bore a relation to the general title. Often some rare or little-known work in a foreign tongue would be digested to serve as the basis for a single chapter, with other volumes being used in like manner as the foundation of other chapters. Always his investigations were painstaking and scholarly.

Moses is to be remembered especially for the impulse that he gave to the study of Hispanic-American history in the United States. He established a course in 1894–95 and at the beginning of the twentieth century he was perhaps the only professor in the United States devoting his full time to Hispanic-American subject matter. As a teacher he inspired others to follow in his footsteps until universities generally in the United States offered such courses. He became widely known as a specialist in his field and was often invited to be a member of various commissions upon which his knowledge of Hispanic institutions would be valuable. Most noteworthy in this connection was his service as a member of the United States Philippine Commission in the important years from 1900 to 1902, when American policies in the recently acquired Philippine group were in the early stages of formulation. He was also a member of various Pan-American congresses in the United States and Hispanic America and in 1910 was one of the United States ministers plenipotentiary to Chile on the occasion of the one-hundredth anniversary of the beginning of the Chilean war of independence. On June 15, 1880, he was married to Mary Edith Briggs, by whom he had one daughter. During the last twenty years of his life he was rarely in active service at the University of California. Much of his time he spent abroad, especially in Paris, pursuing his researches. When in California he resided at his Walnut Creek ranch, a few miles from the University.

Moses was tall and distinguished in appearance. His extreme dignity gave him an outward austerity of manner, but he was most genial and kindly to those who were in the inner circle of his acquaintance. Although his studies in his special field were his most important contributions to scholarship, his other works deserve mention. They include: *Politics* (1884), with W. W. Crane; *The Federal Government in Switzerland* (1889); *Democracy and Social Growth in America* (1898); *The Railway Revolution in Mexico* (1895); *The Establishment of Municipal Government in San Francisco* (1889); and *The Government of the United States* (1906).

[This article is based largely on records on file at the University of California, on personal acquaintance, and on information from others who were personal friends of Moses. For printed sources see: *Who's Who in America*, 1928–29; Zebina Moses, *Hist. Sketches of John Moses, of Plymouth. . . . John Moses, of Windsor and Simsbury. . . . Also a Geneal. Record of Some of Their Descendants* (2 vols., 1890–1907); *San Francisco Chronicle, San Francisco Examiner*, Mar. 6, 1930.]   C. E. C.

MOSES, FRANKLIN J. (1838–Dec. 11, 1906), governor of South Carolina, had a career that fulfilled in most details the conventional Southern conception of a scalawag. He was born in 1838 in Sumter District, S. C., the son of Franklin J. and Jane (McLelland) Moses. His original name was Franklin Israel Moses, but for reasons unknown he and his father, for whom he was named, both dropped Israel entirely and substituted the initial J. His father belonged to a Jewish family that had served the state with distinction, and was, himself, an able and successful lawyer, a member of the state Senate from 1842 to 1862, commissioner of South Carolina before the North Carolina secession convention, a circuit judge in 1865, and, after the accession of the Republicans to power in 1868, chief justice of the state, in which position he served with great distinction until his death in 1877. The younger Moses was a freshman in South Carolina College in 1855 but withdrew without finishing the course. On Dec. 20, 1859, he married Emma Buford Richardson, the daughter of James S. G. Richardson, a distinguished lawyer. He began his public career in December 1860, as private secretary to Gov. Francis W. Pickens, and he became an influence in politics. He raised the Confederate flag over Fort Sumter when the Federals surrendered that stronghold. He was made an enrolling officer with the rank of colonel under the Confederate conscription act. On Nov. 28, 1866, he was admitted to the bar, and the following April he was elected a vestryman of the Sumter Episcopal Church. During 1866 and 1867, as editor of

Moses

the *Sumter News,* he favored President Johnson's Reconstruction plans and in 1866 was a delegate to a state convention called to indorse the president.

In 1867 he suddenly became a renegade to all his previous code of conduct. His writings became so radical that he was dismissed from his editorship, and it was discovered that he was closely affiliated with the Union League. Blessed with great gifts of personality and eloquence and cursed with underlying moral weakness, he yielded to the temptation to seize the opportunity of leading the black majority that was gaining the political mastery of the state. Elected a delegate from Sumter District to the constitutional convention of 1868, he became chairman of an important committee and in his speeches advocated those measures calculated to please the negroes. In the new government he served, simultaneously, as speaker of the House of Representatives, as adjutant and inspector-general of the armed forces of the state, and as trustee of the state university. In 1872 he was elected governor by an overwhelming majority over the candidate of the reform faction of the Republican party, and he served for two years. In his public service he was thoroughly unscrupulous; while he was speaker he issued fraudulent pay certificates and accepted bribes for influencing legislation; as adjutant-general he misappropriated funds for the purchase of arms for the militia; as governor he accepted bribes for his approval of legislation, for pardons, and for official appointments. In his private life his extravagance and immorality caused public scandal.

When he finished his term as governor he was a ruined man. His ill-gotten gain passed from him as easily as it had come; in May 1874 it became known that he was a hopeless bankrupt. His associates deserted him; there was no thought of nominating him for reëlection in 1874. When Gov. Daniel Chamberlain [*q.v.*] refused to commission him as a circuit judge in 1875 after the legislature had elected him to that position, the action of the governor won universal applause. To save himself from prison Moses testified against his former associates. In 1878 his wife divorced him, and the knowledge of his career was hidden from his children. Some of the members of his family, feeling the disgrace of his career, changed their name to Harby. From 1878 until his death he was a hopeless wanderer, a victim of poverty and of the drug habit. His sole asset was his ingratiating manner. For a time he was moderator of the town meeting of Winthrop, Mass.,

Mosessohn

and editor of a local newspaper. Several times he was convicted of petty frauds and thefts and served short terms in various prisons. He died at Winthrop, a victim of accidental asphyxiation.

[F. B. Simkins and R. H. Woody, *S. C. during Reconstruction* (1932); R. H. Woody, "Franklin J. Moses, jr.," *N. C. Hist. Rev.,* Apr. 1933; J. S. Reynolds, *Reconstruction in S. C.* (1905); B. A. Elzas, *The Jews of S. C.* (1903); *Report of the Joint Investigating Committee on Public Frauds and Election of Hon. J. J. Patterson to the United States Senate Made to the General Assembly of S. C.* (1878); *Sumter News,* Dec. 6, 1866, Apr. 25, 1867; (Columbia) *State* and (Charleston) *News and Courier,* Dec. 12, 1906; *Charleston Mercury,* Jan. 15, 1868; register of the Church of the Holy Comforter at Sumter; a few details of personal history from members of the Moses family of Sumter.]
F. B. S.
R. H. W.

MOSESSOHN, DAVID NEHEMIAH (Jan. 1, 1883–Dec. 16, 1930), lawyer, editor, business executive and arbiter, was born at Ekaterinoslav, Russia, the son of Dr. Nehemiah and Theresa (Nissenson) Mosessohn. The home of his father, at one time chief rabbi of Odessa, was characterized by religion, scholarship, and ideals of public service. In 1888, when David was five years old, the family emigrated to the United States, and after brief sojourns in Philadelphia and Dallas, finally settled in Portland, Ore. After graduating from the Portland high school in 1900, he studied law at the University of Oregon and received the degree of LL.B. in 1902. That same year he was admitted to the bar and began practising law in Portland in partnership with his brother Moses Dayyan. From 1908 to 1910 he was deputy district attorney for Multnomah County. He served as president of the district grand lodge of the Independent Order B'nai B'rith in 1917, and took an active part in civic and Jewish communal affairs in the Northwest. On July 9, 1905, at Alameda, Cal., he married Manya Lerner, who with one son survived him.

In 1918 he moved to New York and devoted himself to war activities, in the course of which he met J. J. Goldman, a leader in the garment trade. At that time, although New York was the center of America's dress industry, and the annual business done, the capital invested, and the human, social, and economic factors involved were all on a colossal scale, the industry was in a chaotic condition. Uncontrolled individualism and cutthroat competition were weakening its whole structure. Goldman invited Mosessohn to examine the situation and report how it could be improved. Within thirty days, he presented a plan which resulted in the organization, in 1918, of the Associated Dress Industries of America. He was appointed its executive director, and from 1923 was its executive chairman and supreme arbiter, with wellnigh dictatorial powers. Through his high gifts of organization, he made the Associated Dress Industries a clearing house for ideas and methods pertaining to manufacture and distribution, the expansion of markets, the prevention of overproduction, and the handling of credit problems. Perhaps his greatest personal achievement was that of educating the industry in the advantage of arbitration over litigation. His eminent fairness gained for him implicit confidence, and he achieved widespread distinction as an impartial arbitrator. In recognition of his position in the dress trade, President Hoover, in December 1929, named him a member of the National Business Survey Conference.

Mosessohn was also an able publicist. While still in his teens he gained newspaper experience with the *Oregon State Journal*. In 1903 he and his brother began publishing in Portland a weekly magazine, the *Jewish Tribune*, with his father as editor, a publication which they transferred to New York on coming East. After his father's death in 1926, David Mosessohn assumed the editorship. Manifesting in this capacity the impartiality which characterized his business activities, he conducted the periodical as a non-partisan organ of Jewish enlightenment, defense, and good will, dedicated to the promotion of unity and harmony in Israel. In his communal activities in New York, he showed special interest in educational work among the Jewish youth. He was a leader in the Jewish Education Association, and in the Avukah Organization of the Zionist student youth, and was a founder of the council on American Jewish student affairs. To the United Synagogue of America, of which he was a director, to Zionism, and to charitable and philanthropic campaigns, he gave both active personal service and generous space in the *Jewish Tribune*. He was a thirty-second degree Mason, a past grand master of the Odd Fellows, and past chancellor of the Knights of Pythias. In addition he found time for participation in numerous business, social, and civic organizations. His intellectual interests were wide, and he was a member of several legal, historical, and other learned societies. His outstanding characteristics were executive ability, a keen mind, an energetic personality, a tender heart, and a touching loyalty to the inspiration of his father's life.

[Annual reports of the Associated Dress Industries of America; *Who's Who in America*, 1930–31; *Who's Who in American Jewry* (1928); *Popular Finance*, Sept. 1923; *Jewish Tribune*, Dec. 19, 26, 1930; *N. Y. Times*, Dec. 17, editorial Dec. 18, 1930.] D. deS. P.

MOSHER, ELIZA MARIA (Oct. 2, 1846–Oct. 16, 1928), physician, educator, civic worker, daughter of Augustus and Maria (Sutton) Mosher, was born in Cayuga County, N. Y., of conservative Quaker ancestry. She overcame the objections interposed by family and friends and at the age of twenty entered the New England Hospital for Women and Children as the first step in the medical career to which she was determined to devote herself. On Oct. 3, 1871, she matriculated in the medical course of the University of Michigan which had only the year before opened its doors to women. She received her degree of M.D. in 1875, and with a classmate, Dr. Elizabeth Hait Gerow, opened her office for private practice in Poughkeepsie, N. Y. In 1877 she was made resident physician at the Massachusetts State Reformatory Prison for Women at Sherborn, Mass. Resigning in 1879 in order to study in Europe, she returned in 1881 as superintendent of the institution. An injury to her knee forced her to abandon this position, but while she was still on crutches her friend and former associate at the University of Michigan, Alice E. Freeman, then president of Wellesley College, induced her to lecture for two semesters in that young institution. With Dr. Lucy Hall, with whom she had been associated at Sherborn, she opened an office in 1883 for private practice in Brooklyn, N. Y., but was almost immediately called to Vassar College as resident physician and professor of physiology and hygiene. Here she instituted the systematic physical examination of students. In 1886 she resumed her practice in Brooklyn. Ten years later President James B. Angell asked her to the University of Michigan to become the first dean of women, and first professor of hygiene, sanitation, and household economics, positions which she held until 1902, when she again returned to her Brooklyn practice. Here she continued to work until in March 1928 she suffered an accident which caused her death a few months later.

Eliza Mosher made important studies in posture, designed the seats in several types of rapid-transit streetcars, and invented a kindergarten-chair. She was the author of a book, *Health and Happiness, a Message to Girls* (1912), and for more than twenty years was senior editor of the *Medical Woman's Journal*. At a dinner given in her honor on Mar. 25, 1925, at the Hotel Roosevelt in New York City, five hundred persons from all parts of the country gathered to do her honor, and to celebrate the fiftieth anniversary of her medical service. Testimony was forthcoming as to her services to the colleges she had served; to the Union Missionary Training Institute where she had established a medical training department and herself taught the course in anatomy; to the Chautauqua Summer School which she had served twenty years as a member of the board of directors; to the American Posture League, of which she was a founder; to the American Women's Hospitals, of which she was a founder and a member of the board of governors for eleven years; to the Medical Women's National Association, of which she was honorary president; to Plymouth Congregational Church; to the medical societies; and to the city of Brooklyn. At the University of Michigan she shaped with dignity, understanding, and great humanity, the position of dean of women. She was the first woman physician in the university and organized the women's department of physical education. She also instituted physical examinations for women and was chiefly instrumental in securing the Barbour Gymnasium for women at the university. In June 1927, nearly fifty-four years after her matriculation, she turned the first sod for the construction of the Women's League Building of the University of Michigan in which "The Eliza M. Mosher Hostess Room" is dedicated to her.

[See *Mich. Alumnus*, Oct. 27, 1928, May 16, 1925; *Woman's Who's Who of America*, 1914–15; B. A. Hinsdale, *A Hist. of the Univ. of Mich.* (1906); the *Medic. Woman's Jour.*, July 1924, May 1925—the latter devoted to Dr. Mosher; *Jour. Am. Medic. Asso.*, Oct. 27, 1928; *N. Y. Times*, Oct. 17, 1928; information from friends and associates of the subject of the sketch.]   L. K. M. R.

MOSHER, THOMAS BIRD (Sept. 11, 1852–Aug. 31, 1923), publisher, was born in Biddeford, Me., the son of Benjamin and Mary Elizabeth (Merrill) Mosher. His forebears were mainly seafaring people but his parents were familiar with good literature. He attended the grammar-school and was to go to a private school in Boston, but his father, then in Hamburg, sent for his young son to accompany him on a sea voyage in the winter of 1866–67. "Thus," said Mosher, "I escaped college." On a trip to the Rhine the indulgent parent bought his son, for reading on shipboard, a set of Bell's *British Theatre* (1792) in thirty-four volumes. This set young Mosher devoured from Milton's *Comus* to Wycherley's plays, declaring that "with it I unlocked the gate and entered the enchanted garden of literature." The voyage did not end until the winter of 1870. In 1871 he began his career in the book world as a clerk in a publishing house on Exchange Street, Portland, Me., above which his office was afterward situated, and in 1882 he became one of the firm of

McLellan, Mosher & Company. He had in mind the production of beautiful books at low cost, which should introduce to the American public little-known masterpieces of literature. Uninfluenced by the revival of printing in heavy types and sumptuous forms led by William Morris in England in 1890, Mosher followed classical models and made his books not only beautiful in type and paper, but in small and inexpensive format. He selected for their contents, with rare discrimination, the best literature of all times and all countries. In 1891 he produced the first of the "Mosher Books"—George Meredith's *Modern Love and Other Poems*—then all but unknown. Some of the works of English authors who had failed to secure American copyright, Mosher appropriated for his books. His reprint of Andrew Lang's *Aucassin and Nicolette* (1896) so aroused Lang's ire as an act of piracy that he never forgave him. On the other hand, many authors, like William Sharp, were glad to have their works reprinted in the United States, and in many cases Mosher paid substantial honorariums to authors unprotected by American copyright.

Though not a practical printer, Mosher followed very definite ideas and ideals in the more than five hundred works which he designed and published. In January 1895 he brought out the first number of *The Bibelot*, "a reprint of poetry and prose from scarce editions and sources not generally known." Produced in monthly parts of some twenty-four pages each, he continued it for twenty years, the series ending in 1915 with an index volume. Everything that he published bore the mark of his good taste. Two volumes of *Amphora* (1912–26) contain selections made by him from opuscula printed in his catalogues. The second, issued after his death by Flora Macdonald Lamb, holds tributes to his memory by noted authors. He was better known as a publisher in London literary circles than in Portland, and he was internationally known as a collector. He formed a large library of his favorite authors, though he was not primarily a collector of first editions. He was a genial person. Of medium height, rather thick-set and somewhat portly in later life, with his twinkling blue eyes and quizzical smile, he was in appearance far from the ascetic scholar. He was a member of the Bibliographical Society of London, the Grolier Club of New York, and the Authors', Omar Khayyam, and City clubs of Boston. He died in Portland. He had married, on July 2, 1892, Anna M. Littlefield of Saco, Me.

[A. E. Newton, "The Decay of the Bookshop," *Atlantic Monthly*, Jan. 1920, and *This Book-Collecting Game* (1928); "Thos. Bird Mosher — Publisher," *Pub-*

lisher's Weekly, Sept. 15, 1923; F. A. Pottle, "Aldi Discipulus Americanus," Lit. Rev. of the N. Y. Evening Post, Dec. 29, 1923; H. L. Koopman, "Modern Am. Painting," Am. Mercury, May 1924; Richard Le Gallienne, "In Praise of a Literary 'Pirate,'" Lit. Digest Internat. Book Rev., Oct. 1924; Christopher Morley, "A Golden String," Saturday Rev. of Lit., July 11, 1925; Maine Lib. Bull. (Augusta), Jan. 1921; Sun-Up (Portland), June 1927; Will Ransom, Private Presses and Their Books (1929), containing a bibliography of Mosher's publications; Alice F. Lord, article in the magazine section of the Lewiston Jour., July 7, 1928; Portland Press Herald, Sept. 1, 1923; original papers and letters.]   G. H. S.

MOSLER, HENRY (June 6, 1841–Apr. 21, 1920), genre painter, was the son of Gustav and Sophie (Wiener) Mosler, Germans living in New York City. His father was a lithographer. The family moved to Cincinnati, Ohio, in 1851; thence to Nashville, Tenn., in 1854, but after a year there returned to Cincinnati in 1855. Young Mosler was precocious; he acquired some knowledge of wood-engraving and painting without much assistance, and while still a youth made drawings for the *Omnibus,* a humorous weekly published in Cincinnati. His first serious instruction came from James H. Beard, who was his teacher from 1859 to 1861. In 1862–63 he was attached to the staff of Gen. R. W. Johnson as special war artist for *Harper's Weekly* with the Army of the West. Then, at the instance of Buchanan Read, the poet, he went to Düsseldorf, in the spring of 1863, entered the Royal Academy, and studied drawing and painting under H. K. A. Mücke and A. Kindler for some two years and a half. From Düsseldorf he proceeded to Paris in 1865, and for a half-year worked in the atelier of A. A. E. Hébert. In 1866 he returned to Cincinnati, and three years later he was married to Sarah Cahn. He remained in Cincinnati until 1874, when, with his wife and son, he went to Munich and passed three years there, studying under Ferdinand Wagner and Karl von Piloty. In 1877 he moved to Paris, where he lived for seventeen years, with two or three trips to America and many summer vacations in Brittany. He began to send his works to the Salon in 1878 and continued to exhibit there fairly regularly until he left Paris in 1894.

Mosler's first painting to gain notable recognition was "Le Retour," 1879, which was bought by the French government for the Luxembourg Museum, being the first picture by an American thus honored. On his return to America in 1894 he established his studio in New York. His "Wedding Feast in Brittany," 1892, a large composition with nearly a score of figures, quite typical, was bought by the Metropolitan Museum of Art, New York. Standing behind a

long table set with the marriage feast, surrounded by his family and friends, the bridegroom is proposing a toast, while brimming glasses are raised in response. In 1896 an important exhibition of his paintings was held at Avery's Galleries in New York. Among his works in public collections, besides those in Paris and New York, may be mentioned his "Saying Grace" in the Corcoran Gallery, Washington; "The Rainy Day" in the Pennsylvania Academy, Philadelphia; "Return of the Shrimp Fishers" and "Head of a Monk" in the Cincinnati Museum; "The Biskarin Minstrel" in the Toledo Museum; "The Village Tinker" in the Springfield (Mass.) Museum; and other examples in the museums of Sydney, N. S. W., Grenoble, France, and Louisville, Ky. The artist's death occurred in New York in his seventy-ninth year. Muther sums up in a few words the verdict on Mosler's pictures when he says they "are good genre pictures"; they tell their stories well, with obvious pathos or humor.

[Catalogue of the Mosler exhibition, Avery Gallery, N. Y. (1896), with appreciation by J. S. Covington; W. A. Cooper, article in Godey's Mag., June 1895; Am. Art Ann. 1915; L. M. Bryant, Am. Pictures and their Painters (1917); Illustrated Cat.: Paintings in the Metropolitan Museum of Art (1905); Richard Muther, The Hist. of Modern Painting (1896), vol. III; Mich. State Lib., Biog. Sketches of Am. Artists (1924); Am. Art News, Apr. 24, 1920; N. Y. Times, Apr. 22, 1920.]   W. H. D—s.

MOSS, FRANK (Mar. 16, 1860–June 5, 1920), reformer, was born in Coldspring, Putnam County, N. Y. His father, John R. Moss, had emigrated from England in 1850. Eliza (Wood) Moss, his mother, was of English and Dutch parentage. He was educated in the public schools and studied for some time at the College of the City of New York. He also took courses in science and literature in the Chautauqua University. Meanwhile he was reading law and at the age of twenty-one was admitted to the New York bar. New York City in 1881 offered many opportunities to a young lawyer with ability and a crusading spirit. Tammany Hall, defeated after the exposure of the "Tweed ring" ten years before, had come back into power. A small group of unscrupulous politicians, manipulating masses of ignorant, foreign-born voters, controlled the city government. Gamblers and prostitutes plied their trades openly under police protection. Moss first came into public notice when, in 1887 as counsel for the Society for the Prevention of Crime, he successfully prosecuted the keepers of disorderly houses in the "Tenderloin" and the police captain who had protected them. The president of the society, Howard Crosby [q.v.], wrote that he had "established a reputation for wisdom, boldness, and energy, which any lawyer might covet . . ." (Parkhurst, *post*, p. 144). He continued to act as counsel for the society and in 1892 became a member of its executive board. In 1891 Charles H. Parkhurst [*q.v.*] was chosen president of the society and, inaugurating a radical change in policy, he made the society the instrument of a vigorous attack on the police administration and on Tammany. In the two-year battle that ensued the famous preacher aroused public opinion by his dramatic denunciations of the mayor and his subordinates, but it was Moss and his associate, Thaddeus D. Kenneson, who accumulated evidence, examined witnesses, and prepared cases. This service, to which a large part of their time and energy was devoted, was performed entirely without compensation. At a critical point in the struggle, the New York Senate appointed the Lexow investigating committee, which selected Moss as one of its counsel (see sketch of Clarence Lexow). In this position he added to his reputation as a persistent prosecutor and investigator. The elections of November 1894 resulted in the defeat of Tammany, and the reformers' candidate, Mayor William L. Strong, came into office. When after two years of strenuous service Theodore Roosevelt, the president of the board of police commissioners, resigned, Moss was chosen to succeed him. Two years later, in 1899, when the municipal administration was again under legislative scrutiny he was chosen as leading counsel for the Mazet investigating committee. For a number of years thereafter he devoted himself to private law practice. Although nominally a Republican in politics he was too independent to be a favorite with the machine. He reëntered political life, however, in 1909 as first assistant to District Attorney Whitman. In this capacity he served until 1914, conducting the successful prosecution of the four gunmen who murdered the gambler Rosenthal, and participating actively in the trial of Police Lieutenant Becker.

It was not merely a zealot's hatred of wrongdoing which inspired his work; he was moved also by genuine love and pride for his city. These sentiments inspired him to write *The American Metropolis* (3 vols., 1897), which does not conform to the standard type of local history but is "a reminiscent, observant, reflective journey on historical lines" (Author's Preface, p. xiii). The reader is conducted on a tour of lower Manhattan, and as the successive landmarks are reached he is taught their history. The description of life on the East Side incorporates many incidents that the author must

have witnessed. Crime and criminals occupy a large part of the third volume. In 1919 he published *America's Mission to Serve Humanity,* which he wrote to show that President Wilson's foreign policy was consistent with that of American statesmen since the days of Washington. He was married on Jan. 24, 1883, to Eva Estelle Bruce, who with their two children survived him.

[C. H. Parkhurst, *Our Fight with Tammany* (1895), esp. pp. 142–44, 204–07, 251; *Who's Who in America,* 1920–21; *N. Y. Times,* June 6, 1920; *Sun and the. N. Y. Herald,* June 6, 1920.]   P. W. B.

MOSS, JOHN CALVIN (Jan. 5, 1838–Apr. 8, 1892), pioneer photoengraver, was born near Bentleyville, Washington County, Pa., the son of Alexander J. and Mary (Calvin) Moss. His mother intended him for the ministry, but the youth learned the printer's trade instead. The daguerreotype was then a sensation, and Moss learned something about making portraits in that manner. On learning of William Robert Grove's attempts to turn a daguerreotype into a printing plate, Moss made a Grove battery and began to experiment in that direction. This probably started him toward what later became his life work. In 1856 he married Mary A. Bryant, who became as ardent as himself in the search for a method of engraving through the aid of photography. In 1859 he became publisher of the *Colleague,* at Washington, Pa., but in 1860 he was again working at his trade as a printer in Philadelphia. Here he haunted the libraries, studying optics, chemistry, photography, acquiring knowledge that would help him toward a realization of his ambition to engrave by the aid of the camera. After the Civil War he got work at his trade in New York, and turned his home in Jersey City, N. J., into a laboratory. His wife carried out experiments in the daylight while he was setting type to earn a living for them both. He became so confident that he had solved the problem that he induced a friend to invest some money and they founded in January 1871 the Actinic Engraving Company, 113 Liberty Street, New York. Printers would not accept his engravings so the enterprise failed. Obtaining more capital (Moss established the Photoengraving Company, May 2, 1872, which he moved later to 67 Park Place, New York. Here he was successful. He depended upon secrecy to protect himself from competition, but his workmen would leave him and begin business for themselves in a small way. Finally he decided to go into business on a large scale, employ hundreds of men, and retain his leadership.

In 1881 he accordingly sold out his business

and established the Moss Engraving Company at 535 Pearl Street, New York. Here the dreams of nearly a quarter century came true; he became the best-known photoengraver in the world. In attempting to supplant the wood-cut he found that he must train pen-and-ink draftsmen to imitate the line of the wood engraver in the treatment of portraits, figures, architecture, and landscapes, in order to sell his photoengravings. So successful was he in counterfeiting the work of the wood-engraver that the public could not distinguish the new from the old methods of engraving. He trained a new school of draftsmen from which many famous illustrators graduated. Moss's printing blocks were stereotypes, so shallow that it required a large staff of trained wood-engravers to deepen them between the lines. When printers complained that they could not get results from his engravings Moss established his own printery to prove that the fault was with the printer. In the meantime other experimenters had devised methods of photoengraving that were improvements upon his and more artistic in quality. Moss was obliged to adopt these newer methods and died in 1892 a disappointed man. From his plant went forth photoengravers who carried the knowledge gained under his tutorage into other places and cities and in many instances became more successful financially than their master. To him, however, remains the credit of being the first to establish photoengraving in the United States as a commercial business.

[["John Calvin Moss," *Photo-Engravers' Bull.* (Chicago), Feb. 1926; *Appletons' Ann. Cyc.*, 1892; *N. Y. Times*, Apr. 9, 1892; *Ann. Reports of the Commissioner of Patents*, 1877–78; personal acquaintance.]
S. H. H.

MOSS, LEMUEL (Dec. 27, 1829–July 12, 1904), Baptist clergyman, editor, educator, was born in Boone County, Ky., the son of Rev. Demas and Esther (Lewis) Moss, pioneer Baptists of southern Indiana. On Dec. 24, 1851, he married Harriet Bingham of Cincinnati. After following the printer's trade for nine years, he entered the University of Rochester in 1853 as a special student. President Martin B. Anderson [q.v.] soon persuaded him to pursue the full course, and he graduated from the University with high honors in 1858 and from the Rochester Theological Seminary in 1860.

Ordained at Worcester, Mass., he served as pastor of the First Baptist Church there from 1860 to 1864, when he accepted the secretaryship of the United States Christian Commission. He was the author of the only published account of the work of that body—*Annals of the*

United States Christian Commission (1868). His educational work began at Bucknell University, where from 1865 to 1868 he held the professorship of systematic theology. For the next four years the editorship of the *National Baptist* interrupted his teaching career, but in 1872 he was installed as professor of New Testament interpretation at Crozer Theological Seminary. Two years later, he assumed the presidency of the old, moribund Chicago University, and from 1875 to 1884 he was president of Indiana State University. After a few years without charge, he became in 1889 editor of the *Ensign* of Minneapolis, Minn., which position he occupied until 1893. Returning to the pastorate for a brief period, he was minister of the First Baptist Church, Woodbury, N. J., 1894–96. In 1897 he was editor of the *Baptist Commonwealth*, Philadelphia. During the last eight years of his life, he promoted the work of the American Baptist Historical Society, acting as president from 1895 to 1900 and as vice-president, 1900 to 1904; from 1898 to 1904 he also lectured on social science at Bucknell University.

In 1902 he averted a serious crisis at the National Baptist Anniversaries at St. Paul. For many years the Baptists of the North had conducted their national and international work through three societies, the Missionary Union, the Home Mission Society, and the Publication Society. Criticisms of inefficiency, overlapping, and waste had been repeatedly made. Considerable feeling was developing, and at the St. Paul meeting Moss offered resolutions, enthusiastically adopted, providing for the appointment of a committee of fifteen charged with the function of promoting harmony and consolidation. By serving upon this commission, he paved the way for larger endeavor and more harmonious cooperation among these societies. Truly democratic in his attitude toward their consolidation, he insisted that the Baptist constituency decide upon the type of national Baptist organization. The ultimate result was the provisional organization in 1907 of the Northern Baptist Convention. Liberal in his intellectual attitude, he occasionally appeared upon the platform of the Baptist Congress and by apt suggestion and comparison stimulated the movement toward a broader interpretation of Christianity. Among his publications were *The Baptists and the National Centenary: A Record of Christian Work* (1876) and *A Day with Paul* (1894). Loyal to Baptist principles but not sectarian in his religious attitude, by nature fearless and courteous, given to ceaseless mental toil although long a sufferer from bodily ills, he used his pen to promote the best interests of his denomination. He died in New York City, survived by his wife and three children.

[*Rochester Theological Sem., Gen. Cat.* (1910); *Am. Baptist Year Book,* 1868–1904; *Who's Who in America,* 1901–02; *Watchman,* July 21, 1904; *Examiner,* July 21, 1904; *N. Y. Times,* July 13, 1904.]
                                        C. H. M.

MOST, JOHANN JOSEPH (Feb. 5, 1846–Mar. 17, 1906), anarchist, was born in Augsburg, Germany, the son of Josef Most, a lawyer's copyist who was unable because of poverty to secure a marriage license until two years after the son was born. His mother was educated and a liberal but died when he was ten. His childhood embittered by a five years' illness (following exposure when intoxicated at seven years), an operation which left his face disfigured for life, a cruel stepmother, and a brutal employer, he started forth at seventeen equipped with the trade of bookbinder, a meager general education, a love of reading, extreme sensitiveness because of his deformity, and a thwarted ambition to become an actor. After wandering for five years through Germany, Austria, Italy, and Switzerland, encountering difficulty in getting work and making friends, he joined the International Workingmen's Association in Zurich and threw his feverish energy into the Socialist movement. Between 1868 and 1878 he edited Socialist papers in Vienna, Chemnitz, and Berlin, spent two years in prison in Austria and three in Germany, was elected twice to the Reichstag, lectured frequently, wrote many pamphlets and labor songs, and was expelled first from Austria and finally from Germany. In 1878 he established in London a weekly organ, *Die Freiheit.* Gradually his ideas became more extreme, he became an anarchist, and in 1880 was expelled from the German Socialist party. An article glorifying the assassination of Alexander II, in March 1881, led to the suppression of his paper and to a sentence of sixteen months' imprisonment. Upon his release he transferred himself and *Freiheit* to New York, where he landed on Dec. 12, 1882, and was welcomed as a martyr by a mass meeting of social revolutionists—a man slightly above medium height, with a large head, bushy hair and beard, and mild blue eyes. Later he made a series of tours advocating violence against rulers and capitalists and inspiring terror among the timid.

A magnetic speaker with a sinister power of hatred and invective, and a brilliant writer full of biting wit and sarcasm, Most became leader of the extreme faction of American anarchists, most of them German-speaking, and dictated the declaration of principles adopted by the Pittsburgh convention of 1883 which became the Bible of communist anarchism in America. Just before the Chicago Haymarket tragedy of May 1886, he was sent to Blackwell's Island for a year for inciting to violence, and after his release was almost immediately returned there because of his pamphlet on "the scientific art of revolutionary warfare" which described how to use bombs and other methods of destruction. By the end of this second year's sentence Most had begun to doubt the efficacy of direct individual action and when, in 1892, he repudiated the act of Alexander Berkman in attempting the life of Frick he lost his influence among the younger anarchists. Nevertheless, after the assassination of McKinley in 1901 he served a third term on Blackwell's Island. In his later years, with only a small following and slight power to attract attention, he took to drink but continued *Freiheit* and was on a lecture tour when he died at Cincinnati. Early in life he married in Germany but this connection is lost in as much obscurity as his frequent later emotional experiences. Though not one of the constructive theorists of anarchism he is widely known as the apostle of "propaganda by deed." Yet his many imprisonments were all for what he said and not for what he did. Except for his influence over others he might be considered primarily as an example of twisted psychological development.

[The most recent and extensive biography is Rudolf Rocker, *Johann Most, Das Leben eines Rebellen* (1924). Most wrote an autobiography, entitled *Memorien, Erlebtes, Erforschtes und Erdachtes,* which was published in four parts, beginning in 1903. In addition, his numerous pamphlets and files of the papers he edited, practically all in German, furnish biographical material. A list of his writings and speeches, as well as a brief biography, is contained in Ernst Drahn, *Johann Most: Eine Bio-Bibliographie* (1925), in the *Bio-Bibliographishe Beiträge zur Geschichte der Rechts- und Staatswissenschaften.* This study also contains a list of the principal German works relating to his place in the socialist and anarchist movements. With reference to his career in the United States, consult John R. Commons and associates, *Hist. of Labour in the U. S.* (1918), vol. II; Morris Hillquit, *Hist. of Socialism in the U. S.* (1903); Richard T. Ely, *The Labor Movement in America* (1886) and *French and German Socialism* (1883); Robert Hunter, *Violence and the Labor Movement* (1914). A biographical sketch by Emma Goldman is contained in the *Am. Mercury* for June 1926, and an article by Karl Kautsky reviewing Rocker's biography is contained in *Die Gesellschaft* (Berlin), vol. I, 1924, pp. 545–64.]
                                        H. S. W.

MOTLEY, JOHN LOTHROP (Apr. 15, 1814–May 29, 1877), historian, diplomat, was born in Dorchester, a suburb of Boston, Mass. He was descended from a long New England ancestry, mostly merchants on his father's side, clergymen on his mother's. His father, Thomas

Motley, and his father's brother, Edward Motley, were well-to-do Boston merchants; his mother, Anna Lothrop, was a daughter of the minister of the Old North Church. From his parents John Lothrop Motley inherited the handsome face and fine presence which were marked characteristics and he was surrounded from his birth by ease and typical Boston culture. Through life he was a member of an enviable group of friends: in America, Holmes, Prescott, Longfellow, Emerson, Hawthorne, Lowell, Agassiz, Dana, Sumner, Amory, and others; in England, the Russells, Bright, Dickens, Hughes, and other cultured and prominent members of the nobility, gentry, and learned and literary groups; on the Continent, the royal, court, and diplomatic personages with whom his position as United States minister and his repute as an historian brought him in contact. He was naturally intelligent, a ready speaker and writer. His early years were spent at private schools; at Round Hill, Northampton, one of his teachers was George Bancroft, the future historian. Much attention was paid at these schools to languages and Motley learned languages easily; at eleven he wrote a letter to his brother in French as an exercise, and in the same year he was studying Greek, Latin, and Spanish. He was a great reader, reading Hume's *History of England* before he was twelve and Scott's and Cooper's novels as they appeared. He entered Harvard in 1827 and graduated in 1831, at the age of seventeen. College life made little impression upon him, apparently, except as it gave him opportunity for reading, a little writing, and social enjoyments. He was elected to Phi Beta Kappa, although at the bottom of the list. Two years' study in Germany, first in Göttingen, then in Berlin, followed. Such studying as he did, apart from steady drill in the German language, as part of which he translated Goethe's *Faust* into English, was in Roman and international law; but he made interesting observations and acquaintances, among the latter, Bismarck, whose affectionate remembrances of their young men's life together were renewed at several intervals when the great statesman had reached his later eminence.

After a trip through Austria, Italy, France, and Great Britain in 1834 and 1835, Motley returned to Boston, living with his parents, nominally studying law, actually trying his hand at literature. On Mar. 2, 1837, he married Mary Benjamin, sister of Park Benjamin [*q.v.*], the writer, who lived for a time with his sisters in Boston. They were a refined and attractive family and Motley's marriage was a particularly

happy one. His long and vivacious letters to his mother, his wife, and his three daughters (his one son had died young), whenever they were separated, and those to his friends, vie in bulk and interest with the written remains of his historical and diplomatic life. After his marriage he lived in a house built for him by his father on his estate at Riverdale near Boston.

Motley's principal adventures in literature were two novels, *Morton's Hope,* published in 1839, and *Merrymount,* written near the same time but not published till 1849. Neither of them was of great significance or reached appreciable recognition. Nor did a term in the Massachusetts House of Representatives in 1849 give promise of success in local political life. On the other hand it was during this decade, between 1840 and 1850, that the two lines of his future life work were indicated, diplomatic service abroad and the writing of history. He wrote to his wife that he would prefer the profession of diplomacy to any other and considered himself especially well fitted for it. It was to be his fortune to find each of his three experiences in it unsatisfactory. The first was brief and uneventful. In the fall of 1841 he was appointed secretary of legation at St. Petersburg, but he found the climate there unpleasant, his duties uninteresting, and living expensive. As he had left his wife and children in the United States he soon resigned and returned to Boston. His first piece of historical writing may have been suggested by his Russian experience. It was an essay on Peter the Great, published in the *North American Review* (October 1845) in the form of a review of two recent works on Peter, one French, the other English. It has little importance from the historical point of view, indicating no knowledge of the subject beyond what was drawn from the works reviewed and no special powers of criticism or interpretation. On the other hand it showed, as did his other two essays of the same period, "The Novels of Balzac" (*Ibid.,* July 1847) and "Polity of the Puritans" (*Ibid.,* October 1849), a clear and picturesque style, the flow of humor and the eloquence which characterized his later historical writings.

It was apparently in the year 1847 that he settled on the field of history that was to be his interest for the rest of his life, the attainment of independence by the Netherlands and the struggles of their early years. Just why he chose that subject does not appear, though he told a Dutch scholar long afterward that he was struck with the analogies between the United Provinces and the United States and between William of Orange and Washington. He said at one time, "I had not first made up my mind to write a history and then cast about to take up a subject. My subject had taken me up, drawn me on, and absorbed me into itself" (Holmes, *post*, p. 63). Hearing that Prescott, already famous, was planning to follow the *Conquest of Mexico* with a life of Philip II, Motley called on him to offer to give up his own newly formed plan, but the older scholar encouraged him to proceed, offered him any help he could give, and called attention to Motley's forthcoming work in the preface of his next volume.

Motley wrote his first large work practically three times, once in the United States, a second time in Germany, a third time in Holland. Without training as an historian and with little conception of the requirements of original historical work, he labored for some time with such materials as he could find in Boston. Then realizing the necessity for better access to at least the printed sources, in 1851 he took his family with him to Europe and settled for two years in Dresden, working steadily in the excellent collections of the Saxon royal library, which possessed almost half a million volumes. He wrote that he was "working as hard as a wood sawyer," and was digging "raw material out of subterranean depths of black-letter folios in half a dozen different languages" (*Correspondence*, I, 145–46). He was occupied "ten hours a day, with folks who lived three centuries ago" (*Ibid.*, I, 142). By the early part of 1853 he had worked through that portentous list of sixteenth-century chronicles and other contemporary materials that he gives in the preface of his first volume and refers to in his footnotes, writing as he collected his material, and had brought to seeming completion the three volumes he had planned as the first part of his work, covering the period down to the death of William of Orange. Going next to The Hague and then to Brussels for the purpose of subjecting his work to some revision, in the archives there he found so much new and unexpected matter, mostly in manuscript, that he confesses to have been almost in despair, but set to work emending, reorganizing, and rewriting. He wrote to Holmes, "Whatever may be the result of my labors, nobody can say that I have not worked hard like a brute beast; but I do not care for the result. The labor is in itself its own reward and all I want" (*Ibid.*, I, 163), almost the same words that another great American historian, Henry C. Lea, used privately, though neither of them was by any means uninterested in the subsequent reception by the public of his writing. As a

matter of fact, Motley was supremely happy in his work, and after some eight months in the Netherlands, by the middle of 1854 had his book in satisfactory shape and set out with the manuscript for London to find a publisher. Murray, to whom he had letters of introduction, kept the manuscript for some weeks but finally declined it on account of its considerable length and unfamiliar subject. After some further negotiations Chapman agreed to publish it in England simultaneously with Harper & Brothers in America, at the author's expense. Motley's father and uncle joined him in defraying the cost. *The Rise of the Dutch Republic* appeared in London and New York early in 1856. Both by scholars and the public it was received with praise from which there were but few dissenting voices. Instead of the sales of less than a hundred which Motley had feared and the unremunerative response the publishers had apprehended, some 17,000 copies were sold in little more than a year in England alone, and almost as many more in the United States. A second edition was immediately required.

The reasons for this acclaim and the lasting repute of the work are obvious. It is a picturesque, dramatic narrative of a striking series of events, gathering around a group of clearly marked personalities, and is suffused with a warm glow of love of political and religious liberty. "If ten people in the world hate despotism a little more and love civil and religious liberty a little better in consequence of what I have written, I shall be satisfied," he wrote to a friend (Mildmay, *post*, p. 42). The faithful investigation Motley had made of the sources gave him sureness of touch, his eager spirit provided the illumination, and his literary gifts gave him the ability to draw a series of pictures almost unrivaled in their brilliancy in historical literature. His view of history is of a series of episodes, interesting in themselves, and illustrative of his general conception of the time and its lessons. On the other hand his warm partisan admiration for William and hatred of Philip II, his personal addiction to liberty, as he considered it to exist in America and England and among the patriot party in the Netherlands, and his dislike of Catholicism undoubtedly lessened the value of the work as true history. It shows more learning than insight and more enthusiasm than sobriety. It is almost purely political and religious, paying scarcely any attention to economic or social matters. It can never be considered a definitive history of its period. It will always remain a brilliant personal interpretation of it. Later editions and translations into

Dutch, French, German, and Russian appeared within the next few years and there were several abbreviated and unauthorized publications founded upon it.

In the intervals of a short visit to America, European travel with his family, and his next diplomatic appointment, Motley continued his work. It was now more largely drawn from manuscript sources. He worked with the assistance of copyists in the British Museum and state paper office in London, in the archives at The Hague and Brussels, and among the copies from the Simancas Archives in Paris. He wrote from The Hague, "I work every morning at home two hours before breakfast, then to the Archives till three, after which, in the course of the day and evening I get a few hours more" (*Correspondence*, I, 307). The *History of the United Netherlands* was published almost simultaneously in England and America, the first two volumes in 1860 in London (New York, 1861), the second two in 1867 (New York, 1868). This work covers the period from the death of William to the truce of 1609 only, though he had originally intended to extend it to the entrance of the Netherlands into the Thirty Years' War. His remaining work, *The Life and Death of John of Barneveld, Advocate of Holland; with a View of the Primary Causes and Movements of the Thirty Years War* (2 vols., 1874), filled in this interval. The *United Netherlands* is occupied more with the general affairs of Europe, especially with Dutch relations with England and France, than his earlier work; it has not its dramatic interest, though it has still its devotion to personal and picturesque occurrences and to what he called "fruitful examples of the dangers which come from superstition and despotism, and the blessings which flow from the maintenance of religious and political freedom." In *John of Barneveld*, Motley's analysis of the tortuous and troubled interplay of religious and political dissension and his inevitable sympathy with the Arminian side subjected him to more criticism in the Netherlands than did his earlier works (see Groen van Prinsterer, *Guillaume Maurice et Barneveldt. Étude Historique*, Utrecht, 1875). On the other hand he was already deeply entrenched in the national admiration and affections of the Dutch; for some time he lived in a house set apart for him at The Hague by the queen, with whom he and his family were on friendly terms, and later in the old de Witt mansion. The history of the Thirty Years' War, bringing the work down to 1648, which he had planned from the first, and which led him to visit Bohemia in

search of local color in 1871, was never written. With ill health, beginning with a slight stroke of paralysis in 1873, with the death of his wife on the last day of 1874, and with the disappointments of his later diplomatic career, he lost energy and spirit for further study or writing.

The long interval between the appearance of the first and the second two volumes of the *United Netherlands*, 1860 and 1867, was due partly to Motley's absorption in the occurrences of the Civil War, partly to his duties as minister to Austria. He was appointed to that post by President Lincoln while he was on a visit to America, on the strong urgency of Senator Sumner, Aug. 12, 1861. There was some opposition on the ground of too many appointments having been made from Massachusetts. He went to Vienna by way of England and France, conversing informally while in England with Lord John Russell, whom he visited at his summer home in Scotland and by whom he was taken to visit the Queen and Prince Consort at Balmoral. These and other interviews in 1860 and 1861, two long letters he wrote to the London *Times* (May 23, 24, 1861) which were immediately republished in England and America, and his reports on what he knew of English opinion given to Lincoln, Seward, and others while in Washington before his appointment, although not a part of his formal diplomatic service, were of the greatest value in the increase of good understanding between Great Britain and the United States. He remained in Vienna from November 1861 to July 1867. Early in 1862 Secretary Seward, at the suggestion of Gustavus Körner, who had been appointed minister to Spain, offered Motley the opportunity to exchange Vienna for Madrid, on the ground that he might be able better to prosecute there his studies of the Dutch revolt from Spain. Motley declined, partly from his belief that Körner, being by birth a German, would not be welcome at Vienna, partly because he had already secured all the material needed for his present work, whereas for the history of the Thirty Years' War which he hoped to write next, Vienna was the fountain head of knowledge. Of the two hundred and thirty-six official dispatches sent home during the six years of his ministry a large part consisted of reports of European reactions to the Civil War, of his negotiations concerning the election of Maximilian to the throne of Mexico, and of his observations on Austrian and general European society. The Austrian government responded in a friendly spirit to American protests against their attitude on Mexican affairs, although in 1866 Motley informed the foreign minister that he had received orders to withdraw from Vienna if the rumored plan for sending Austrian troops to Mexico were carried out, and later American efforts to prevent the execution of Maximilian were acknowledged gratefully. Motley's dispatches at this period are almost as full, intimate, and interesting as are his family letters, and Seward repeatedly expressed his appreciation and gratitude for them.

These pleasant relations were suddenly broken by a dispatch from the Department of State, dated Nov. 21, 1866, in which Seward informed him that a "citizen of the United States," whose name Motley afterward learned was George W. McCrackin, but whom he did not know, had written from Paris to President Johnson, saying that he had observed during his recent travels in Europe that the ministers and consuls of the United States were for the most part bitterly hostile to the President and his administration and expressed their hostility openly. More especially he charged Motley with expressing his "disgust" for the President's conduct, with saying that Seward was "hopelessly degraded," and with showing general contempt for American democracy. Seward asked Motley, as he did the other American ministers named in the letter, to deny or confirm the charges. Immediately on the receipt of this dispatch, Dec. 11, 1866, Motley wrote with his own hand a long statement of his views on Reconstruction, which certainly differed somewhat from those of President Johnson, but explained that he had carefully avoided any public expression of his views and characterized as a "vile calumny" the assertion that he had spoken disrespectfully of the President or Secretary or of American democracy. Resenting being questioned on such charges he closed his letter by resigning his position as minister. In acknowledging this dispatch, Jan. 5, 1867, Seward said that the President did not find Motley's answer to be unsatisfactory, and since there seemed no consideration of public policy requiring his resignation it lay within his own choice whether this should be considered absolute or not. Johnson, however, insisted on the recall of Seward's dispatch, and Motley had no reply to his letter of Dec. 11 until he received a brusque dispatch dated at Washington, Apr. 18, 1867, accepting his resignation and instructing him to present his recall to the Emperor and to hand over the embassy to the chargé d'affaires, which he did early in June 1867. This controversy, which was evidently part of the political struggle in which President Johnson was engaged, became a matter of wide

discussion, and much sympathy was expressed for Motley. (Senate Executive Document No. 8, 39 Cong., 2 Sess.; No. 9, Ibid.; No. 1, 40 Cong., 2 Sess.; John Bigelow, "Mr. Seward and Mr. Motley," International Review, July–August, 1878.)

During 1868, while Motley was again in America, he delivered two addresses which were printed, and in London he published a pamphlet in 1869, Democracy the Climax of Political Progress. In March 1869, again on the urgency of Sumner, President Grant appointed Motley minister to Great Britain. It was a time of strained relations between the two countries. A number of subjects were in dispute, the most serious being the Alabama claims. Before Motley left America he went through the official correspondence, drew up a general account of these disputes, and submitted a memorial on them to Hamilton Fish, secretary of state. This was however laid aside, and instructions were handed him the day he sailed. With the most sincere intention of following out his instructions, either because of their indefiniteness or because of his long-settled opinions, he did not succeed in representing in his early conversations with the British foreign secretary the President's exact intentions, and although other negotiations were left in his hands he was instructed to ask that the Alabama claims should in future be discussed in Washington, not in London. This was apparently an indication of dissatisfaction of Grant and Fish with his mission, but Motley was quite unaware of this and believed he still had their entire confidence. In June 1869 Fish told him he had stated American claims well and forcibly, and as late as May 27, 1870, congratulated him warmly on his success in negotiating the naturalization treaty. Even when in June 1870 it was stated in the English newspapers that he was to be recalled, he could not believe he was to be so discourteously treated and supposed the report mere gossip. On June 30, 1870, however, he received a dispatch from Washington stating that the President wanted to make a change in the mission to Great Britain and offering him the opportunity to resign. Secretary Fish, on July 13, wired him for a reply and Motley telegraphed back his refusal, explaining at length in a letter written the same day his unwillingness to admit by such resignation that he had failed in any way in his duty to his country. For the next four months official relations were kept up, though on somewhat strained terms, until a dispatch, dated Nov. 10, 1870, reached Motley, enclosing a letter to the queen announcing his recall, and ordering him to commit the property of the embassy to the secretary of legation. On Dec. 7 Motley sent a long letter of protest, which was answered by a still longer and certainly a much exaggerated letter of complaint from Secretary Fish, addressed not to him but to the secretary of the embassy. It is hard to believe that Motley's dismissal was not influenced by the anger of Grant against Sumner, Motley's friend, who had opposed Grant in his Santo Dominican policy. The matter was discussed in the Senate and the whole correspondence called for and published (*Senate Executive Document No. 11,* 41 Cong., 3 Sess.; *New York Herald,* Jan. 4, 1878). Motley should have made an ideal ambassador. He was traveled, polished, rich, attractive, conciliatory, intensely patriotic, yet not unwilling to follow official instructions; his ill-success was part of the political misfortunes of that time.

He died at the house of one of his married daughters in England, from a stroke of apoplexy, May 29, 1877, and was buried with his wife in Kensal Green Cemetery, just outside of London, Dean Stanley reading the service to a notable gathering, including John Bright, the Duke of Argyll, Froude, Thomas Hughes, Lord Houghton, Lecky, the ministers of the Netherlands and Belgium, and others. His daughters all married and remained in England.

[*John Lothrop Motley. A Memoir* (1879), by his friend O. W. Holmes, an excellent memoir based on personal knowledge and his correspondence; *The Correspondence of John Lothrop Motley* (2 vols., 1889), ed. by G. W. Curtis; *John Lothrop Motley and His Family. Further Letters and Records* (1910), ed. by his daughter Susan St John Mildmay and Herbert St John; Ruth Putnam, "Prescott and Motley," *Cambridge Hist. of Am. Literature*, II (1918), pp. 131–47; bibliography of his works, *Ibid.*, pp. 501–03; a study of his last diplomatic mission in Beckles Wilson, *America's Ambassadors to England, 1785–1929* (1929); letters to the secretary of state in Dept. of State, Washington; obituary in *Boston Evening Transcript*, May 30, 31, 1877; memorials in *Proc. Mass. Hist. Soc.*, XV (1878); *The Writings of John Lothrop Motley* (17 vols., 1900).] E. P. C.

MOTT, GERSHOM (Apr. 7, 1822–Nov. 29, 1884), Union soldier, was born at Lamberton, now part of Trenton, N. J., the youngest of five children of Gershom and Phoebe Rose (Scudder) Mott. He received schooling at Trenton Academy until he was fourteen years old, when he became a clerk in a drygoods store in New York. On Apr. 23, 1847, he received appointment as second lieutenant, 10th United States Infantry, and was presented a sword by citizens of Trenton. He served throughout the Mexican War without distinguishing incident. On Aug. 8, 1849, he married Elizabeth, daughter of John E. Smith of Trenton, by whom he had one child.

Following his discharge from the army, he served as collector of the port, Lamberton, N. J., until his appointment in 1850 to a position with the Bordentown, Delaware & Raritan Canal Company. In 1855 he became teller of the Bordentown Banking Company, continuing in that position until the outbreak of the Civil War.

His military career was one of promotions earned by distinguished service. In August 1861 he was appointed lieutenant-colonel of the 5th New Jersey Volunteers, and remained with that regiment until his promotion to colonel of the 6th New Jersey Volunteers, May 7, 1862, for achievement at the battle of Williamsburg. His active service was with the Army of the Potomac. His regiment was in support during the Seven Days' battles, but saw action at the second battle of Bull Run, where Mott was wounded. He was promoted brigadier-general of volunteers Sept. 7, 1862, and assigned to command a brigade of Hooker's Center Grand Division, which operated against Lee. He was wounded again at the battle of Chancellorsville in May 1863. His brigade took part in the operations of the summer and fall of 1863 against Lee, being present during the Mine Run Campaign in Meade's attempt to surprise Lee on the Rapidan, and operated from the Rapidan to the James in the winter and spring of 1864. During the battles of the Wilderness and at Spotsylvania Court House in May and June 1864, he earned special recognition. At the latter, he was particularly selected to command the 4th Division and restore its fighting efficiency after casualties and hardships had so lowered its morale that its officers could not control the men. In this task he succeeded admirably. As a division commander on July 30, 1864, he personally led his 3rd Division in making important gains at the crater of Petersburg. Appointed brevet major-general of volunteers on Aug. 1, for distinguished services, he continued with his division through the Richmond campaign until its completion. In May 1865, he was appointed major-general of volunteers and ordered to Washington for duty, serving there until discharged on Feb. 20, 1866.

Although appointed colonel of the 33rd United States Infantry in 1868, he declined the appointment, wishing to reënter civil life. His civilian pursuits included appointments as paymaster of the Camden & Amboy Railroad in 1866; treasurer of the state of New Jersey, 1875; keeper of the state prison, 1876–81; member of the Riparian Commission of New Jersey from 1882 until his death. He was a member of the iron-foundry firm of Thompson & Mott,

1873–76, and was a director of the Bordentown Banking Company. From 1873 until his death he was major-general, commanding the New Jersey National Guard. His memory was publicly honored at Trenton, N. J., in 1896, when the Mott School was named after him.

[*Colls. N. J. Hist. Soc.*, vol. IX (1916); E. M. Woodward and J. F. Hageman, *Hist. of Burlington and Mercer Counties, N. J.* (1883); *Record of Officers and Men of N. J. in the Civil War* (2 vols., 1876); F. B. Heitman, *Hist. Reg. and Dict. U. S. Army* (1903); *The Soc. of the Cincinnati in the State of N. J.* (1898); *Report of the Adj. Gen. of the State of N. J., 1906* (1907); *Boyd's N. J. State Directory*, 1874; *War of the Rebellion: Official Records (Army)*; *N. Y. Geneal. and Biog. Record*, Apr. 1894; *N. Y. Times*, Nov. 30, 1884.]
D. Y.

MOTT, JAMES (June 20, 1788–Jan. 26, 1868), reformer, abolitionist, was born in North Hempstead, Long Island, N. Y., the son of Adam and Anne (Mott) Mott, through both of whom he inherited the blood of a seventeenth-century English emigrant, Adam Mott, and of a long line of Quaker ancestors. His father was a farmer and miller. Both parents were worthy people, moderately strict in following the principles of their religion, but they appear to have influenced the intellectual and moral development of their son less than did his mother's father, also named James Mott, a man of unusual intelligence and culture, interested in the advancement of education and in the movements for temperance and abolition. The boy received his education chiefly in the Friends' boarding school at Nine Partners, about fifteen miles from Poughkeepsie, N. Y., where he was a student for ten years and assistant and teacher for two years. There he met Lucretia Coffin and on Apr. 10, 1811, the two were married. In the spring of 1810 he had gone to Philadelphia, where he became a partner of Lucretia's father in the manufacture and sale of cut nails. When the hard times following the War of 1812 brought reverses he tried various business positions in an effort to make an adequate living for his family but met with little success. About 1822 he went into the commission business in Philadelphia, dealing especially in cotton.

He prospered in this enterprise but eight years later gave it up, for he had reached the decision that it was wrong to have even such an indirect part in slavery, since cotton was produced by slave labor. Though the step meant a serious financial loss at first, he was able to turn to the wool commission business, from which he retired in 1852 with a fair competence. In deciding that indirect participation in slavery was wrong he was influenced by the teachings of Elias Hicks, the leader of the liberal movement

in the Society of Friends, with whose theological views he also sympathized. After the separation in the Society in 1827 the Motts aligned themselves with the Hicksite group of Friends. During these years of spiritual and moral upheaval they became very active against slavery, at the time defended by many Quakers, and for these activities as well as for their religious heterodoxy were the objects of bitter attack. In 1833 both were present at the Philadelphia convention that founded the American Anti-Slavery Society, and James Mott was a member. Both he and his wife were delegates to the world anti-slavery convention held in London in 1840, and on his return he published his experiences in a little book called *Three Months in Great Britain* (1841). After the passage of the fugitive-slave law of 1850, the Mott home in Philadelphia became a refuge for runaway negro bondmen.

He took an advanced attitude, rare for the period, toward the position of women and early spoke in favor of giving them additional recognition in the Society of Friends. Fully appreciating his wife's superior abilities as a public speaker, he accompanied her on extensive preaching and lecturing tours, thus saving her from the criticism to which, as a woman, she would have been liable at that time. When, under the lead of Lucretia Mott, Elizabeth Cady Stanton, and a few other women, the first woman's rights convention was held at Seneca Falls, N. Y., in 1848, he presided over some of the sessions. His ability to express ideas in writing, his sympathy, and his judgment were potent factors in the development of his wife's reputation and usefulness. In 1857 the Motts gave up their large house in Philadelphia and moved to a little farm, called "Roadside," eight miles out of town on the old York road, but he continued his activity in the anti-slavery cause until emancipation was achieved. During the last few years of his life he worked insistently in the interest of better educational facilities for young people of the Society of Friends, and partly as a result of his efforts Swarthmore College was founded in 1864. Four years later, while visiting a daughter in Brooklyn, N. Y., he died from an attack of pneumonia.

[*James and Lucretia Mott: Life and Letters*, ed. by A. D. Hallowell (1884); *Three Months in Great Britain*, ante; T. C. Cornell, *Adam and Anne Mott* (1890); *N. Y. Tribune*, Jan. 27, 1868.]
M. W. W.

MOTT, LUCRETIA COFFIN (Jan. 3, 1793–Nov. 11, 1880), reformer and preacher of the Society of Friends, was born on the island of Nantucket, the descendant of Tristram Coffin who emigrated from Devonshire, England, and became one of the original purchasers of the island. She was the second cousin of Isaac and John Coffin [qq.v.]. Her parents were Quakers, as were most of her forebears for some generations. Her mother, Anna Folger, a descendant of Peter Folger [q.v.], was an energetic, capable, conservative woman whose family had stood firmly on the British side during the Revolution. Thomas Coffin, her father, appears to have been of a milder, more democratic bent. During her early childhood he was a ship's captain who voyaged to China, but about 1803 he gave up the sea and took his wife and six children to Boston, where he engaged in business. This journey, when Lucretia was eleven years old, was her first trip to the "continent," as the islanders called the mainland. In Boston she was sent to the public school for a time because her father thought his children ought to acquire democratic sympathies, but at the age of thirteen she entered the Friends' boarding school at Nine Partners near Poughkeepsie, N. Y. There she spent almost two years in study and two more as assistant and teacher in the girls' section before she returned to her father's home, now removed to Philadelphia. Shortly afterward a fellow pupil and teacher at Nine Partners, James Mott [q.v.], joined her father in business and on Apr. 10, 1811, she was married to him. They had six children, of whom five lived to adult life.

The death of an infant son in 1817 gave her thoughts a decidedly religious turn. The next year she began to speak in meeting and soon showed such marked gifts that she was made an "acknowledged minister" of the Society. But her views were so liberal as, before long, to excite some criticism. She sympathized with Elias Hicks, whose teachings brought about a controversy in the Society of Friends early in the 1820's, and after the separation and reorganization in the Society she, like her husband, aligned herself with the liberal or Hicksite group and remained thereafter a member of it. She became known as one of the most eloquent preachers in Philadelphia and traveled extensively to speak at Quaker meetings in different parts of the country. With William Penn she felt that "men are to be judged by their likeness to Christ, rather than by their notions of Christ" (Hallowell, post, p. 92) and consequently in her religious discourses she emphasized righteousness and ignored technical theology. Many of her sermons and addresses were concerned directly with reform subjects, especially temperance, peace, woman's rights, and antislavery.

Her most notable work was connected with the question of woman's rights and antislavery. Her interest in woman's wrongs and woman's rights began at Nine Partners school, where, merely because of her sex, she was paid but half as much salary as were the men doing the same work. In the years that followed she occasionally spoke in public on the unjust status of women. Her interest in the subject was further roused by the refusal of the world anti-slavery convention held in London in 1840 officially to recognize herself and a number of other women who were delegates from the United States. One result of this rebuff was the first woman's rights convention, held on July 19 and 20, 1848, in the Wesleyan Methodist Church at Seneca Falls, N. Y., at which was formally launched the woman's rights movement in the United States. The chief promoters of the gathering were herself and Elizabeth Cady Stanton [q.v.]. Her greatest interest, however, was the abolition of slavery, to the importance of which Elias Hicks first roused her. When she first began to speak against it, slavery was defended by many Friends, and, consequently, her activities led to persistent but futile efforts to depose her from the ministry and to drop her from the Society. She attended the convention that met in Philadelphia in 1833 and organized the American Anti-Slavery Society. Immediately afterward she helped form the Philadelphia female anti-slavery society, of which she was president during most of its existence. At the anti-slavery gathering of 1840 in London she made her influence felt, in spite of her failure to be recognized as a delegate, and she was referred to as the lioness of the convention. Following the passage of the new fugitive-slave law, she and her husband gave much attention to the protection of runaway bondmen, to whom the Mott home was an asylum.

In 1857 the family moved from Philadelphia to a quiet farm place called "Roadside" near the city, but she kept up her interest in preaching and in various reform movements, especially in activities for improving the condition of the negro. Her last public address was made in May 1880 at the Philadelphia yearly meeting of the Society of Friends. She was sprightly, impulsive, cheerful, and energetic, and, though very fond of approbation, showed firmness and courage in what she believed to be right. In her busy life she found time to be a good cook, was a careful housekeeper equal to the many emergencies incident to a growing family, and was able to manage a large and hospitable household with a grace to be envied by many women of lesser attainment in the world of affairs.

[*James and Lucretia Mott: Life and Letters,* ed. by A. D. Hallowell (1884); *Hist. of Woman Suffrage,* ed. by E. C. Stanton (6 vols., 1881–1922), esp. sketch in vol. I; T. C. Cornell, *Adam and Anne Mott* (1890); *N. Y. Tribune,* Nov. 12, 1880.]   M. W. W.

MOTT, VALENTINE (Aug. 20, 1785–Apr. 26, 1865), surgeon, was born in Glen Cove, Long Island, the son of Henry and Jane (Way) Mott and a descendant of Adam Mott, an English Quaker who emigrated to America about the middle of the seventeenth century. Henry Mott was a physician, and at the age of nineteen his son entered the office of a kinsman, Dr. Valentine Seaman, a surgeon to the New York Hospital, to study medicine. Here he remained until 1807, meanwhile obtaining his medical degree in 1806 from the Medical Department of Columbia College. During these undergraduate years he became a devoted pupil of Dr. Wright Post, the professor of surgery and New York's ranking surgeon. In 1807 he went to London for post-graduate instruction. He was a pupil of Astley Cooper in surgery and surgical anatomy and assisted him in numerous operations, but studied also under other London surgeons and later in Edinburgh.

Returning to New York in 1809, he opened an office and within a few months began to give a private course of lectures and demonstrations on surgery in the anatomical rooms of Columbia College. He was appointed professor of surgery here in 1811 and retained his chair when, in 1813, the Columbia medical school merged with the College of Physicians and Surgeons. Here he continued until 1826, when with other members of the faculty he resigned to found the short-lived Rutgers Medical College, under the leadership of David Hosack and S. L. Mitchill [*qq.v.*]. This institution closed in 1830, and Mott resumed his old chair in the College of Physicians and Surgeons, but resigned it again in 1835 because of ill health. He spent the next six years abroad, visiting not only Europe but Asia and Africa as well, and on his return assisted in founding the medical department of the University of the City of New York, where he became professor of surgery and surgical anatomy. Resigning this post in 1850 he again visited Europe, and upon his return rejoined the faculty of the College of Physicians and Surgeons. Although his nominal status was that of professor emeritus, he was active in teaching up to the time of his death.

Very early in his career Mott became known as a bold and original surgeon, and a few daring operations gave him a world-wide reputation. In 1818 he was the first to tie the innominate artery with the object of preventing death from a subclavian aneurism. This operation was a technical success, the patient living for three weeks, but his death at the end of the period was charged up to an error in placing the ligature. Mott at once reported the case in a series of medical and surgical reports which appeared during the years 1818–20. In 1827 he successfully tied the common iliac artery for an aneurism of the external iliac, and the patient survived (*American Journal of the Medical Sciences,* vol. XIV, 1827). He was one of the first to perform a successful amputation at the hip joint, and to excise the jaw for necrosis, and was a pioneer in surgery of the veins, which he resected and sutured, chiefly in the course of major operations. During his career he performed nearly a thousand amputations, operated 150 times for stone in the bladder, and ligated forty large arteries. According to his former teacher, Sir Astley Cooper, he performed more major operations than any surgeon in history, up to his time. So great was his reputation that when living in Europe he was summoned to operate on the Sultan of Turkey. After the introduction of surgical anaesthesia (1846), he soon became an authority on the subject, and during the Civil War prepared by request of the Sanitary Commission a report entitled *Pain and Anaesthetics* (1862). Like many of the pre-anesthetic surgeons he was an extremely rapid and skilful operator and was ambidextrous.

He wrote no major work, and it is stated that he had a repugnance to authorship, although he published some twenty-five medical papers, including eulogies on his friends Wright Post, John Revere, and John W. Francis, and supervised the publication of *New Elements of Operative Surgery* (3 vols., 1847), translated by P. S. Townsend from the French of A. A. L. M. Velpeau, which he augmented with notes and observations. On his return from his six-year sojourn in the Old World, he published *Travels in Europe and the East* (1842). He was co-editor of the *Medical Magazine,* 1814–15, and of the *Medical and Surgical Reporter,* 1818–20, but after that period showed little interest in medical journalism. He assembled a library which he bequeathed to the medical profession, and also a surgical and a pathological museum which were ultimately merged with larger units. During his entire active life and for many years after his death his reputation was of the highest as a surgeon, a progressive member of the medical profession, a citizen, and a man. He was brilliant, free from any erratic quality, and without any of the reactionary element so often encountered in men who have become famous. In 1819 he married Louisa Dunmore Mums, by whom he had nine children. After his death, she erected a building to house the Mott Memorial Library. He died in New York City after a very brief illness, having retained his surgical deftness and much of his physical vigor until within a few days of the end.

[S. D. Gross, *Memoir of Valentine Mott* (1868); A. C. Post, *Eulogy on the Late Valentine Mott* (1866); S. W. Francis, *Memoir of Valentine Mott* (1865); G. S. Bedford, in *Trans. Medic. Soc. of the State of N. Y.*, 1866; *Boston Medic. and Surgic. Jour.*, Dec. 11, 1850; *Medic. and Surgic. Reporter*, May 21, 28, 1864; *Lancet* (London), May 20, 1865; *Pacific Medic. and Surgic. Jour.*, Oct. 1865; *Annali universali di medicina* (Milano), Feb. 1868; *Bull. N. Y. Acad. of Medicine*, Aug. 1925.]
                                                    E. P.

MOULTON, ELLEN LOUISE CHANDLER (Apr. 10, 1835–Aug. 10, 1908), writer of verse and juvenile stories, daughter of Lucius Lemuel and Louisa Rebecca (Clark) Chandler, was born in Pomfret, Conn. She attended the school of the Rev. Roswell Park there and then went for a year to Emma Willard's Female Seminary at Troy, N. Y. Her parents were rigid Calvinists and her upbringing, from which all frivolity was excluded, may have been responsible for the strain of melancholy in her mature personality. One of her Pomfret schoolmates was James McNeill Whistler, who gave her one of his juvenile paintings, which she always preserved. She later knew him well in London. When she was only fifteen, her writing began to find a magazine market and her first volume, *This, That, and the Other*, a miscellaneous collection, was published in 1854. On Aug. 27, 1855, a few weeks after leaving school, she was married to William U. Moulton, a Boston journalist and publisher, who died Feb. 19, 1898. After her marriage she resided in Boston, where her Friday salon was frequented by artists, musicians, and writers, among them Lowell, Whittier, Longfellow, and Holmes. From 1876 on, she spent summers and autumns in Europe and came to be quite at home in London, where she numbered among her friends Monckton Milnes (Lord Houghton), Browning, Carlyle, Holman Hunt, Madox Brown, Burne-Jones, the Rossettis, William Morris, Swinburne, Watts-Dunton, Pater, the Meynells, Hardy, and Meredith.

Though devoted to her only child, a daughter, she was not domestic in her tastes and found her happiness in her writing and in friends whose pursuits were similar to her own. She wrote for many newspapers and magazines. From 1870 to 1876 she was Boston literary correspondent for the *New York Tribune*, and from 1886 to 1892 contributed a weekly letter on books to the *Boston Sunday Herald*. Her published volumes include several books of bed-time stories for children and some travel reminiscences, of which the best known, perhaps, is *Lazy Tours in Spain and Elsewhere* (1896). In *The Poems and Sonnets of Louise Chandler Moulton* (1909), published in the year after her death, are collected many of her verses which had appeared in earlier publications. She edited, with biographies, *A Last Harvest* (1891) and *The Collected Poems of Philip Bourke Marston* (1893), by the blind poet Marston, and *Arthur O'Shaughnessy, His Life and His Work, with Selections from His Poems* (1894). For *Recent English Dramatists* (1901) she wrote the life of Stephen Phillips.

Her place in American literature she achieved through her poetry, which is intensely personal. Lady Wilde, mother of Oscar Wilde, once said to her: "I have read your poems, but they deal with the sorrows and emotions of one individual; they have naught in them of the passion of the world" (Rittenhouse, *post*, p. 606). Though there is truth in the statement, some of her poetry escapes this judgment. It is subjective, often melancholy, and burdened with a sense of the fleeting quality of all happiness. It reveals an unfulfilled longing for the ideal in life and love, and a reaching out for religious belief in the midst of doubts. It is essentially the expression of a woman's feeling, and in form, it has beauty, fancy, and melody. Her sonnets are her best work and have been highly praised. She died in Boston, after a long illness from Bright's disease. During the last year of her life she carried on a correspondence with Clara Louise Burnham, through whose instrumentality she endeavored to find help in the teachings of Christian Science.

[See: Harriet Prescott Spofford, biographical introduction to *The Poems and Sonnets of Louise Chandler Moulton* (1909); Lilian Whiting, *Louise Chandler Moulton, Poet and Friend* (1910); *Who's Who in America*, 1908–09; Frances E. Willard and Mary A. Livermore, *Am. Women* (1897), vol. II; A. F. Johnson, "The Poetry of Louise Chandler Moulton," *Poet-Lore*, winter 1908; Jessie B. Rittenhouse, "Louise Chandler Moulton and her London Friendships," *Bookman*, Feb. 1909; obituaries in the *Boston Herald*, Aug. 11, 1908, and *Boston Evening Transcript*, Aug. 10, 1908, and an appreciation by T. W. Higginson in the *Transcript* for Aug. 12, 1908. Mrs. Moulton's library was presented to the Boston Pub. Lib.; the bulk of her correspondence, classified by Arlo Bates, went to the Lib. of Cong., and a considerable collection of letters and original manuscripts of her poetry and fiction was given to the American Antiquarian Soc., Worcester, Mass.]
                                                    S. G. B.

MOULTON, RICHARD GREEN (May 5, 1849–Aug. 15, 1924), college professor, lecturer, and author, was born in Preston, England, the sixth child of Rev. James Egan Moulton, a Wesleyan Methodist minister, and Catherine

Moulton

(Fiddian) Moulton. When he was six years old his mother died, and he was brought up by a step-mother, a woman of Huguenot descent who had been reared in France, and to whom, he felt later, he owed much. He attended schools at Northampton and Bath, and in 1869 received the degree of A.B. from London University, and in 1874, from Christ College, Cambridge. Just at this time the university extension movement was developing, and Cambridge was a center of its influence. Soon after his graduation young Moulton became one of its most enthusiastic representatives, giving hundreds of lectures. In 1890 he visited America, where he also had immediate success as a lecturer and shared in the organization of the American Society for the Extension of University Teaching. In 1892 he became the professor of literature (in English) at the newly organized University of Chicago, at first dividing his time between university lectures and university extension work. In 1901 his title was changed to professor of literary theory and interpretation, and he became the head of the department of general literature. On Aug. 13, 1896, he married Alice Maud Cole. Retired from his professorship in July 1919 because of having reached the age limit, he returned to England, where he lived until his death, five years later, at Hallauleigh, Tunbridge Wells.

Moulton was an evangelist in the field of literature. By lecture and by published volume he sought to interest all classes of persons in understanding literature as an interpretation of life and as a source of spiritual culture. He felt that an understanding of the forms of different literatures would disclose a universal philosophy of life. His own interest lay chiefly in Shakespeare, ancient classical drama, and the Bible. The unity which he found in these various fields, each the object of technical study on the part of others, was a group of principles which governed a "world literature."

His personality was forcible and unique. He was gifted as a musician; had a memory which enabled him to recite all of the masterpieces which he expounded; and was capable of a dramatic delivery which few if any lecturers of his time could equal. To him form was an important element in the interpretation of literature, but literature to him was much more than form. His early writings dealt with Shakespeare and the classical drama, but throughout his life he emphasized the literary study of the Bible. Probably his most significant work was *The Modern Reader's Bible* (21 vols., 1896–98; one-volume edition, 1907). With a stimulating ingenuity, he so analyzed and printed the text as to enable the

Moultrie

reader, even though unacquainted with the original languages, to appreciate the dramatic quality of the Biblical material. Technical Biblical scholarship has not altogether accepted his ideas or methods, but the wide circulation of this work shows that, as in his lectures and university work, he popularized literature as an aid to culture, and stimulated interest in an intelligent reading of the Bible as an instrument of culture rather than as a quarry for systems of theology. Among his other publications were *Shakespeare as a Dramatic Artist* (1885); *Shakespeare as a Dramatic Thinker* (1907); *The Ancient Classical Drama* (1890); *The Literary Study of the Bible* (1895); *World Literature and Its Place in General Culture* (1911); *The Modern Study of Literature* (copr. 1915).

[W. F. Moulton, *Richard Green Moulton* (1926); *Biog. Reg. of Christ's Coll.*, vol. II (1913); *Who's Who in America*, 1918–19; *Univ. Record* (Univ. of Chicago), Oct. 1924; *Times* (London), Aug. 16, 1924.]

S. M—s.

MOULTRIE, JOHN (Jan. 18, 1729–Mar. 19, 1798), physician, lieutenant-governor of East Florida, Loyalist, was the eldest of six sons of Dr. John Moultrie, an eminent physician of Charlestown (Charleston), S. C., and descendant of an ancient Scotch family whose seat was Seafield Tower on the Firth of Forth, County Fife. The father was educated at Edinburgh and emigrated to Charlestown about 1728, where on Apr. 22 of that year he married Lucretia Cooper. The son also went to Edinburgh and was graduated M.D. in 1749, his thesis being *De Febre Maligna Biliosa Americæ*. He returned to Charlestown and on Apr. 30, 1753, was married to Dorothy Dry, widow of John Morton, by whom he had a daughter. After her death he was married on Jan. 5, 1762, to Eleanor Austin, daughter of George Austin, by whom he had four sons and two daughters. Meantime, he acquired several plantations and many slaves and became a major in the militia. In 1761 he accompanied Lieut.-Col. James Grant's expedition against the Cherokees. When Grant formed the government of East Florida in the autumn of 1764 he appointed Moultrie and his brother James, then acting attorney-general of South Carolina, members of his council. The latter was also made chief justice, but died on Aug. 6, 1765. For James's children John Moultrie took up grants of land totaling some three thousand acres and for himself others amounting to more than fourteen thousand. Among the latter was his residential plantation, "Bella Vista," four miles south of St. Augustine, where his artificers erected a large stone mansion and numerous other buildings, laid out a park and garden, and

292

planted a great number of fruit trees of various kinds.

Grant was in poor health and sailed for England on leave early in May 1771, having recommended Moultrie, the president of the council, for lieutenant-governor. A few days later thirty inhabitants presented an address congratulating Moultrie, complaining of the decline of population in the province, and calling for a legislative assembly. Inaugurated in August, he sold his plantations near Charlestown, and brought eighty more slaves to Florida. Soon differences arose between Moultrie and two members of his council, Chief Justice William Drayton and Dr. Andrew Turnbull [qq.v.]. The two members resigned their seats but Drayton was soon restored by the King, only to be suspended by Moultrie for "obstructing public business." Both antagonists sent their complaints to Lord Dartmouth, who in a few weeks communicated notice of the appointment of Col. Patrick Tonyn as governor. Otherwise Moultrie was occupied with locating new roads, building a state house, completing St. Peter's church, and remodeling the Spanish bishop's house for public offices. Retaining his post after Tonyn's arrival, Mar. 1, 1774, he prejudiced his successor against the Drayton-Turnbull faction and obtained from him many grants of land. With the outbreak of the Revolution, which cut off supplies from the neighboring colonies, Moultrie induced his fellow-planters to raise more provisions. At the end of the war he shipped his slaves to the Bahamas, sold his live stock and effects, and in July 1784, sailed with his family for England, where they became dependent upon his wife's life annuity of £500. In 1787 he was awarded £4,479 11s. of his claim of £9,432 for losses. He seems to have passed his closing years obscurely in Oxfordshire and in Shropshire, where, in St. Andrews Parish, in Shifnal, he was buried. Three of his brothers, Alexander, Thomas, and William [q.v.], fought in the Continental Army.

[W. H. Siebert, *Loyalists in East Fla., 1774 to 1785* (1929), vol. II; *S. C. Hist. and Geneal. Mag.*, Oct. 1904, Apr. 1924; Colonial Office Papers, 5/540, 5/545, 5/552, 5/553, 5/562, 5/563; *S. C. Gazette*, June 5, 1755, April 1, 1761, Aug. 25–Oct. 1, 1764, Aug. 3–10, 1765, Apr. 7, May 9, 23, 30, Oct. 24, 31, 1771; manuscript Minutes of the Council of East Fla., Aug. 7, 1771, to July 6, 1772, July 20, Aug. 2, 20, 1773; Carita Doggett, *Dr. Andrew Turnbull and the New Smyrna Colony of Fla.* (1919); *Gentleman's Mag.*, Mar. 1798.]
W. H. S—t.

MOULTRIE, WILLIAM (Nov. 23/Dec. 4, 1730–Sept. 27, 1805), Revolutionary general, governor of South Carolina, was born in Charlestown (Charleston), S. C., the son of Dr. John and Lucretia (Cooper) Moultrie, and the brother of John Moultrie [q.v.]. He was married on

Dec. 10, 1749, to Elizabeth Damaris de St. Julien. On Oct. 10, 1779, he was married to Hannah (Motte) Lynch, the daughter of Jacob Motte and widow of Thomas Lynch. By his first marriage and by purchase he acquired a large estate in St. John's Berkeley, and he made his home there. It was perhaps the weight of his property that sent him, a month after he became of age, to the House of Commons where for eight years he played an inconspicuous part. But as a captain in the provincial regiment during the Cherokee War he found his rôle, and during ten more years of almost continuous service in the Assembly, he became a recognized leader in the military affairs of the province. From 1775 to 1780 he was member, successively, of the two provincial congresses, and of the legislative council and Senate, but these duties were incidental, for the first Congress had elected him colonel of the 2nd Regiment. The fort on Sullivan's Island, which guarded one of the entrances to the harbor, was a sixteen-foot wall of sand held in place by palmetto logs. Here on June 28, 1776, with four hundred men and thirty-one guns, Moultrie received the attack of the British fleet. His courage and judgment were vindicated, though his preparations for the battle offered some ground for the criticism that he was too easy-going and neglected his opportunities, a criticism that followed later incidents in his career. The next September his regiment was taken over by Congress, and Moultrie shortly afterward was promoted to brigadier-general in the Continental service. On the fall of Savannah, in December 1778, he was sent to the southwest part of the state, and though subject to Lincoln's orders, was on detached command. In February he defeated a force of the enemy at Beaufort. In May, when the British commander took advantage of Lincoln's invasion of Georgia to march on Charlestown, Moultrie saved the city by a rapid and skilful retreat, and by a determined stand against surrender. In May 1780 he was captured with the garrison of Charlestown and was quartered for nearly two years with other Continental officers who were held as prisoners on parole at Haddrell's Point, opposite the town. His own moderation and his Loyalist connections were responsible for an attempt of the British to win him over to their cause. His reply was courteous but resolute. In February 1782 he was exchanged and served to the end of the war, being made major-general in October 1782.

In 1783 Moultrie sat in the state House of Representatives, the next year was elected lieutenant-governor, and in February 1785 was made governor. The violent political divisions in the state made the military hero an ideal choice, and his good sense and experience enabled him to serve successfully. He urged the reëstablishment of the state's credit, the better organization of the militia, and the improvement of internal navigation. At the end of his term in 1787 he was elected from his parish to the Senate, and also represented the same district in the convention which ratified the Federal Constitution. In 1791 he resigned from the Senate but a year later was again elected for a two-year term as governor. After this he retired to private life. He suffered heavy losses during the Revolution, and his fortune further declined afterward. He continued, however, high in public esteem, and was president of the state Society of the Cincinnati from its organization to his death.

[Moultrie's *Memoirs of the Am. Revolution* (2 vols., 1802), composed largely of his own correspondence, is the chief source for his campaigns and is of great value for the history of the Revolution in South Carolina and Georgia. His political career must be traced from the manuscript journals of the legislative bodies of the state. Other sources include: *S. C. Hist. and Geneal. Mag.*, Oct. 1904, Apr. 1928; *Reg. of St. Philip's Parish, . . . 1754–1810* (1927), ed. by D. E. Huger Smith and A. S. Salley, Jr.; Edward McCrady, *The Hist. of S. C. in the Revolution* (2 vols., 1901–02); Wm. Hollinshed, *A Discourse Commemorative of the Late Maj.-Gen. Wm. Moultrie* (1805); S. C. Soc. of the Cincinnati, *Remarks of Wilmot G. De Saussure, . . . 4th July, 1884* (n.d.).]   R. L. M.

MOUNT, WILLIAM SIDNEY (Nov. 26, 1807–Nov. 19, 1868), painter, was born at Setauket, Long Island, N. Y., one of the five children of Thomas Shepard and Julia (Hawkins) Mount. His father, a farmer, died when William was seven years old, and the family removed to the Hawkins homestead at Stony Brook, near Setauket. "To the age of 17," Mount later told William Dunlap, "I was a hard working farmer's boy" (*post*, vol. III, p. 263). An elder brother, Henry S. Mount, had established himself as a sign-painter in New York, and in 1824 William became his apprentice. At about the same time another brother, Shepard A. Mount, also became an apprentice and all three brothers were ambitious to qualify as artist painters, and all eventually attained membership in the National Academy of Design. William, while still painting signs, "eagerly sought and examined pictures" (Dunlap, III, 263). He greatly admired Benjamin West, whose "Madness of Lear" and "Ophelia" he studied attentively. In 1826 he entered the Academy as a student and a year later, his health affected by overwork, he returned to Setauket. Here he painted three canvases that were exhibited: a self-portrait and two large compositions—"Christ Raising the Daughter of Jairus" and "Saul and the Witch of Endor."

In 1829 he was again in New York, eager to paint portraits. An amusing legend of the studios had it that Luman Reed, a wealthy art collector whose paintings afterward went to the New York Historical Society, bought Mount's first exhibited work for $1,000, and that the young painter, who hardly knew that so much money existed, planned to live on it for the rest of his life at Stony Brook. T. S. Cummings, however, the Academy's annalist, discredits this story by insisting that Mount was "by no means so ridiculous a person as these statements would make him appear to be" (*post*, p. 141). His first Academy picture was bought, Cummings contends, by a Mr. Kemble and not by Luman Reed. Mount acquired associate membership in the Academy in 1832; full membership a year later. His full-length portrait of Bishop Onderdonk in the 1833 exhibition "elicited a universal burst of applause" (Dunlap, III, 263). Throughout his career he was popular, "endeared," as said a minute of the Academy's council, passed Nov. 30, 1868, "by his frank, cheerful and manly character, by the wit and humor that brightened his social hours."

Love of the country led Mount to spend much of his time at Setauket where he made the studies for his popular genre pictures, such as "Raffling for the Goose," now in the Metropolitan Museum of Art, New York; "The Long Story," at the Corcoran Gallery of Art, Washington; "Coming to the Point," New York Public Library; and "The Truant Gamblers," "The Fortune Teller," and "Bargaining for a Horse," New York Historical Society. Among his many portraits were those of Gen. Jeremiah Johnson, mayor, at the Brooklyn City Hall; Daniel Webster; the Rev. Zachariah Green; Selah B. Strong; Robert Schenck; and Benjamin F. Thompson, historian of Long Island. His likeness of the last named, a former neighbor at Setauket, is reproduced as a frontispiece in Thompson's *History of Long Island*. About 1859 Mount constructed a portable studio, on wheels, which greatly interested his fellow artists. In his last ten years he painted but little as his health steadily declined. He never married. He can hardly be said to have attained great distinction but his portraits and figure pieces have a sturdy honesty and constructive solidity that entitle them to respect. He was represented in 1925 at the National Academy's centennial exhibition by his "Power of Music," lent by the Century Association.

[Wm. Dunlap, *A Hist. of the Rise and Progress of the Arts of Design in the U. S.* (1918), vol. III; T. S. Cummings, *Hist. Annals of the Nat. Acad. of Design* (1865); B. F. Thompson, *Hist. of Long Island* (1918), vol. I, p. xxviii, vol. IV, pp. 290, 293; *N. Y. Times*, Nov. 21, 1868; manuscript memorandum prepared for the author of this article by Clara Brewster Mount, Setauket, N. Y., great-niece of the artist.] F. W. C.

MOURT, GEORGE [See MORTON, GEORGE, 1585–1624].

MOUTON, ALEXANDER (Nov. 19, 1804–Feb. 12, 1885), governor of Louisiana and senator, was born on the Bayou Carencro, in Attakapas County, now Lafayette Parish, La., the son of Jean and Marie Marthe (Bordat) Mouton and the descendant of Acadian exiles on both sides of his family. He received his elementary education in the district schools of his county and later attended Georgetown College in the District of Columbia. He spoke French as his native tongue and received his instruction in the district schools altogether in that language, but during his youth he acquired a good knowledge of English, which he spoke fluently and effectively. He studied law in the offices first of Charles Antoine and later of Edward Simon of St. Martinville, La., in 1825 was admitted to the bar, and began to practise in Lafayette Parish. He soon gave up practice, however, to manage a plantation given him by his father near Vermilionville, the present town of Lafayette, La., where he became one of the more prosperous sugar planters of the state. In 1826 he was married to Zelia Rousseau, a grand-daughter of Jacques Dupre, one of the wealthiest cattle raisers in the Opelousas country and later acting-governor of Louisiana. They had four children. In the same year he was elected from Lafayette Parish to the lower house of the state legislature and served from 1829 to 1832. He was speaker in 1831 and 1832. He was named presidential elector on the Democratic ticket in the elections of 1828, 1832, and 1836. In 1836 he was again elected to the state legislature, which, in 1837, chose him to the United States Senate to fill out the unexpired term of Alexander Porter, who had resigned. At the end of that term he was re-elected and served from Jan. 12, 1837, to Mar. 1, 1842, when he resigned to campaign for the governorship of Louisiana on the Democratic ticket. While he was senator he was married in 1842, to his second wife, Emma K. Gardner, the daughter of Charles K. Gardner [q.v.]. They had six children.

He was inaugurated governor in January 1843 for a term of four years but, under the new constitution of 1845 which made some rearrangements in the terms of the state officers, he retired in February 1846. At the beginning of his administration the state was deeply in debt, but by its close most of the indebtedness had been liquidated and provision had been made for the

payment of the rest by 1872. He was very active in the presidential campaign of 1844 in behalf of Polk and Dallas and contributed effectively toward carrying the state in their behalf. He was interested in the development of railroads in Louisiana and was president of the southwestern railroad convention held at New Orleans in January 1852. He was also made president in 1858 of the vigilance committee of the Attakapas country, which was organized for the purpose of ridding that part of the state of bandits and marauders. In 1856 and in 1860 he was a delegate from Louisiana to the Democratic conventions in Cincinnati and Charleston respectively. In 1861 he was a delegate to the Louisiana secession convention, served as president of that body, and voted for secession. He was subsequently a candidate for the senate of the Southern Confederacy but was defeated. During the Civil War he sustained heavy losses both in his family and in his fortune. To the end of his life he remained a picturesque type. He is said to have been the original for George W. Cable's brief description, in "Carancro" (*Century Magazine,* Jan. 1887, p. 355), of "the Acadian of the Acadians," the grandson of the Acadian widow who took refuge in Louisiana, whom the people of Louisiana made "Senator, Governor and President of the Convention."

[Alcée Fortier, *Louisiana* (1909), vol. II and *A Hist. of La.* (4 vols., 1904); W. H. Perrin, *Southwest La.,* 1891; *Biog. and Hist. Memoirs of La.,* 1892, vol. II; *Biog. Dir. Am. Cong.* (1928); *Times-Democrat* (New Orleans), Feb. 14, 1885; the spelling of the Christian name follows that printed on the form of the official certificate of appointment in the Lib. of Cong.]
E. M. V.

MOWATT, ANNA CORA OGDEN (Mar. 5, 1819–July 21, 1870), writer, actress, was the daughter of Samuel Gouverneur and Eliza (Lewis) Ogden. Her father, a New York merchant, was the son of the Rev. Uzal Ogden [q.v.]; her mother was the grand-daughter of Francis Lewis [q.v.], a signer of the Declaration of Independence. Anna Cora Ogden was born at Bordeaux, France, near which place she lived until her seventh year, when her family returned to New York. She attended private schools, but got her education mainly by extensive reading at home in French and English authors, especially Shakespeare. As a child she wrote verse, and frequently wrote, acted, and directed dramatic pieces with her brothers and sisters, taking part also in school plays. On Oct. 6, 1834, at the age of fifteen, she married James Mowatt, a well-to-do New York lawyer, and lived happily with him at Flatbush, Long Island, continuing her studies and literary efforts. Her first published work, signed "Isabel," was *Pelayo; or, The*

Cavern of Covadonga (1836)—an imitative historical verse romance in six cantos, which was followed by a sharp verse satire in its defense, *Reviewers Reviewed* (1837). Advised to take a sea voyage, because of a serious breakdown from tuberculosis, she spent fifteen months abroad, visiting London (where she saw and admired Madame Vestris at her theatre), Hamburg, Bremen, and other cities. In Paris she was greatly impressed by the impassioned acting of Rachel in her famous rôles. Here she began a short blank-verse play in five acts, finishing it after she returned to America in restored health; this was *Gulzara; or, The Persian Slave,* acted at her home, and published in the *New World,* Apr. 24, 1841.

Since her husband had lost his fortune, she determined to earn money by giving public readings of poetry and made her first appearance Oct. 28, 1841, before an enthusiastic audience at the Masonic Temple in Boston. Later she appeared in New York, but in 1842 was obliged to give up this work because of a recurrence of illness. During her convalescence, which she attributed to mesmerism, she wrote under the name of "Helen Berkley" for *Godey's Lady's Book, Graham's,* and other magazines; compiled books on etiquette, cooking, and miscellaneous subjects, and in 1842 was awarded a prize of $100 by the *New World* for a novel, "The Fortune Hunter; or, The Adventures of a Man about Town," with realistic hits at contemporary New York Society. She also published, in 1844, a life of Goethe under the pseudonym Henry C. Browning, and an abridged edition of the *Memoirs of Madame d'Arblay,* and wrote, under Frederika Bremer's influence, a two-volume domestic tale, *Evelyn,* which appeared in 1845.

Her most important imaginative work was a play entitled *Fashion; or, Life in New York,* first published in February 1850. Undertaken at the suggestion of Epes Sargent and rapidly written, it was produced at the Park Theatre in New York on Mar. 24, 1845, running for three weeks. Immediately afterward it was produced in Philadelphia, and later in other leading American cities, everywhere with notable success, and in January 1850, ran for two weeks at the Olympic Theatre, London. In 1924 it was revived at the Provincetown Playhouse, New York, in a burlesqued version arranged by Brian Hooker and Deems Taylor, with songs of the Victorian period inserted. A five-act farcical comedy, *Fashion* deals with members of a new-rich New York family and their circle who ape French manners and are unfavorably contrasted with a true-hearted prosperous farmer and his grand-daughter. Though it has touches of lively humor and characterization and is well adapted to the stage, its effects are generally exaggerated, and its plot is conventional. The author's enthusiasm for democratic institutions appears also in *Armand, The Child of the People,* a five-act romantic pseudo-historical play of the reign of Louis XV, in prose and blank verse, first produced Sept. 27, 1847, at the Park Theatre, New York. It met with favor here, in other American cities, and also in London when Mrs. Mowatt acted in it there in January 1849. It was first published as *Armand; or, The Peer and the Peasant* (1849).

Following the production of *Fashion,* Mrs. Mowatt received flattering invitations from managers to go on the stage. She made a highly successful début as Pauline in *The Lady of Lyons* at the Park Theatre, June 13, 1845, and during the next eight years acted in most of the important American cities, with E. L. Davenport [*q.v.*], after her first season, as her leading man. Among her rôles were Juliet, Beatrice, Rosalind, Desdemona, Ariadne, Blanche in *Armand,* and Gertrude in *Fashion.* Poe, who was a severe critic of *Fashion,* joined in the general commendation of her qualities as an actress, praising her "brilliant and expressive" eyes, her "radiantly beautiful smile," her charming grace and naturalness of manner, and her singularly rich voice. She was slight in figure, with light auburn hair and prominent, distinguished features. From December 1847 to July 1851 she played with E. L. Davenport in England and was warmly received in London and other large English cities, as well as in Dublin. During this period she worked under grave difficulties owing to her husband's ill health, a serious attack of brain fever which disabled her for some months in 1850, and fresh financial reverses. In 1851 James Mowatt died in London.

Returning to America in August of that year, she appeared at Niblo's Garden, New York, and then undertook a new American tour. Again disabled by ill health, she devoted some months in 1853 to writing her *Autobiography of an Actress; or, Eight Years on the Stage* (1854), which had a large sale. It is facile and vivacious in style, idealistic in tone, and gives vivid glimpses into the life and theatre of the day. On June 3, 1854, in New York, she made her final appearance on the stage, and on June 6, married William Foushee Ritchie, editor of the *Richmond Enquirer.*

After her retirement, she published *Mimic Life; or, Before and Behind the Curtain* (1856), three romantic narratives of stage life with some realistic pages based on her own experiences; and in the same vein, *Twin Roses* (1857). Soon afterward she became active in the movement for the purchase and preservation of Mount Vernon, was secretary of the state committee organized in Richmond, and from 1858 to 1866 was vice-regent (representing Virginia) of the Mount Vernon Ladies' Association of the Union. After 1861 she lived abroad (apart from her husband, with whom, it is said, she differed over Civil War issues), mainly in Florence, writing romantic novels: *Fairy Fingers* (1865), *The Mute Singer* (1866), and *The Clergyman's Wife and Other Sketches* (1867); and occasional articles on events in Florence which appeared after her death in a volume with historical sketches entitled *Italian Life and Legends* (1870). She died in Twickenham, England.

[Autobiography and other writings mentioned above; *New World* (ed. by Park Benjamin), Jan. 22, 1842; E. A. Poe, notices in *Broadway Journal*, of Mar. 29, Apr. 5, July 19, 29, 1845, and article in *Godey's Lady's Book*, June 1846, repr. in *The Complete Works of Edgar Allan Poe*, Virginia Edition (1902), ed. by J. A. Harrison, vols. XII, XV; *Howitt's Journal*, Mar. 4, 11, 18, 1848; W. J. Clapp, Jr., *A Record of the Boston Stage* (1853); Laurence Hutton, *Curiosities of the American Stage* (1891); Laurence Hutton and Brander Matthews, *Actors and Actresses of Great Britain and the United States* (1886), vol. IV; A. H. Quinn, *A Hist. of the Am. Drama from the Beginning to the Civil War* (1923); M. J. Moses, *Representative Plays by Am. Dramatists*, 2 ser., 1815–58 (1925); R. S. Hammer, *A Daughter of Firenze* (1924); Grace King, *Mount Vernon on the Potomac* (1929); T. A. Brown, *A Hist. of the N. Y. Stage* (3 vols., 1903); W. O. Wheeler, *The Ogden Family in America* (1907); J. N. Ireland, *Records of the N. Y. Stage*, vol. II (1867); *N. Y. Times*, June 7, 1854, July 30, 1870; *N. Y. Tribune*, July 30, 1870; G. C. D. Odell, *Annals of the N. Y. Stage*, vols. V, VI (1931); information as to certain facts from Archives Municipales, Bordeaux, France; Register of Deaths, District of Brentford, England, and relatives and acquaintances; memoirs of actors of the period.]
H. M.

MOWBRAY, GEORGE MORDEY (May 5, 1814–June 21, 1891), pioneer oil refiner, inventor of explosives, was born in Brighton, England. As a youth he studied chemistry in England, France, and Germany, becoming a manufacturer of drugs in his native land. Later he joined a firm of wholesale druggists. In 1854 his health became impaired and he took a long sea voyage around South America. Landing in California, he there filled an important need as doctor, surgeon, and chemist in the gold fields. In 1858 he moved to New York and became associated with Schieffelin Brothers & Company, wholesale druggists. In the following year, however, when at Titusville, Pa., Edwin L. Drake [*q.v.*] drilled the first successful oil well and thus initiated a new industry, Mowbray was among the first to remove to the oil field. He produced the first refined oil there, and was the

first to use nitroglycerin (or tri-nitro-glycerin as he preferred to call it) in the shooting of dormant wells. He obtained several patents for devices and methods relating to the production of oil.

Depression following the speculation of the period 1859–65 forced him to close his refinery in 1866, but he remained in Titusville and turned his attention to the manufacture of nitroglycerin. His advertisements in the *Scientific American*, which show him to be the only manufacturer in America offering nitroglycerin in quantity, won the interest of the Massachusetts commissioners who were building the Hoosac Tunnel and they invited him to North Adams to furnish the explosives for the work. He arrived on Oct. 29, 1868, and the next day began to build his plant on a site provided by the state. By the end of the year the plant was completed. Up to this time most of the nitric acid used in the United States was imported from abroad, but Mowbray began to make his own. He also manufactured the insulation (guttapercha) and fuses needed for the work. His manufacturing method, which was very simple, is described in full in his *Tri-nitro-glycerin* (1872), which went through three editions and was the first treatise on this subject in America. The Hoosac Tunnel, considered one of the great engineering feats of the time, was the first to show the possibilities of high explosives in tunneling.

Mowbray manufactured over a million pounds of nitroglycerin, with such care and success that he dominated the explosives market in the northeastern and central parts of the United States long after the modern type of dynamite was introduced. He supplied, without accident, the one hundred thousand pounds required for the building of the Canadian Pacific Railway in lots of twenty thousand pounds, fifty pounds to a can. For shipment by rail, cars divided into compartments were used, each can being placed in a separate compartment, padded with thick hair felt and provided with ice to keep the product in frozen condition. When the train reached Fargo, N. Dak., the cans were carried to a Red River steamboat by Indians, the only help available. Unloaded from the steamer, they were placed on two-wheeled ox-carts and hauled 110 miles to the Lake of the Woods, thence across the lake by boat, and finally carried on men's backs to the construction camps. Finding that an explosive of less shattering power would be better for some work, Mowbray developed a method of diluting nitroglycerin with finely divided scales of mica. Although all his improvements were the results of his own research, some of them were declared to infringe the Nobel patents held in the United States by the Atlantic Giant Powder Company, and, following an injunction, Mowbray gave up the manufacture of nitroglycerin.

His interest continued along related lines, however, and he did valuable work in the developing of zylonite (celluloid), serving as technical manager for the American Zylonite Company from 1881 until his death. In 1886 he turned his attention to research in ammunition and contracted with Sir Hiram Stevens Maxim [*q.v.*] of the Maxim-Nordenfeldt Guns and Ammunition Company of England to turn over to that concern all patents for smokeless powder that might result from his experiments. He received patents for a long series of improvements in explosives, the earliest being No. 76,499 (Apr. 7, 1868) and the last, No. 443,105 (Dec. 23, 1890). During the last year of his life he directed his experiments from his bed, one of his assistants being Hudson Maxim [*q.v.*]. He died in North Adams at the age of seventy-seven.

Mowbray and his wife, Annie Fade, had no children of their own, but adopted Mrs. Mowbray's five-year old orphaned nephew, who as Henry Siddons Mowbray [*q.v.*] became a distinguished painter. He is quoted as saying (Mowbray, *post*, p. 11) : "There was never, to my mind, a man quite like my foster father. Strong and masterful to the world, to me he showed a surprising tenderness and affection, and never . . . do I recollect an unkind word or action on his part. We became close comrades. He had a wonderful way of smoothing out youthful trouble, clearing away the unessentials, and setting forth the thing so simply that all the clouds disappeared."

[A. P. Van Gelder and Hugo Schlatter, *Hist. of the Explosives Industry in America* (1927), with portrait; Florence Millard Mowbray, *H. Siddons Mowbray* (privately printed, 1928) ; *Atlantic Giant Powder Co., Complainant, v. George M. Mowbray et al., Defendant; Pleading and Evidence* (1876) ; *Boston Transcript,* June 23, 1891.]   A. I.

MOWBRAY, HENRY SIDDONS (Aug. 5, 1858–Jan. 13, 1928), figure and mural painter, was born at Alexandria, Egypt, of English parents, John Henry and Eliza (Fade) Siddons. His father had gone from England to Egypt as the representative of an English banking house and died in 1859. The widow returned to England with her infant son and shortly determined to come to the United States. Not long after their arrival she was burned to death in Brooklyn, and the boy was adopted by his uncle and aunt, George [*q.v.*] and Annie (Fade) Mowbray who were then living at Titusville, Pa.

They moved from Titusville to North Adams, Mass., when the boy was about eleven years old. He was sent to the Drury Academy at North Adams from 1869 to 1878, with a brief interregnum. An appointment had been obtained for him to the United States Military Academy at West Point, but he stayed there only a short time. He returned to North Adams and then at the age of twenty went to Paris and entered the atelier of Léon Bonnat. A year after his arrival in Paris his "Young Bacchus" was hung in the Salon. In the spring of this year (1879), in company with Henry Walker, he went to Spain, spent a month in Madrid, copying the Velasquez pictures, and, after visiting Toledo, Seville, and Granada, returned to Paris, where he sold his first picture. In 1883 he exhibited at the Salon "The Etchers" and "Le Récit," both of which were sold. He remained in France eight years, spending several summers at Rablay, in Anjou. "In those impressionable years," he wrote, "I acquired an affection for France and its people that has always remained" (*H. Siddons Mowbray, post,* p. 24). Returning to the United States in 1886, he settled in New York, became an academician, a member of the Society of American Artists, and took charge of the men's life classes at the Art Students' League. One of his first patrons was Thomas B. Clarke, who bought four of his pictures, "Scheherazade," "Aladdin," "The Evening Breeze," and "The Last Favorite." On June 7, 1888, he married Helen Amelia Millard, daughter of Henry S. Millard, of North Adams, Mass. A son was born to them. His wife died on Aug. 5, 1912, and three years later he married her sister, Florence Gertrude Millard, by whom he had a son and a daughter. In 1890 he had bought a house in West Eleventh Street and converted the upper floor into a studio. There he lived until 1907 when he moved to Washington, Conn., where he passed the rest of his life.

In an undated note Mowbray wrote : "A fondness for the Italian art of the Renaissance came over me. I wanted above all things to do mural work" (*H. Siddons Mowbray,* p. 56). His first small commission came from Thomas B. Clarke in 1889. It was for an over-mantel panel for the reception room of an athletic club. In 1892 a more important opportunity was offered him : this was a series of twenty-one lunettes in the main hall of Collis P. Huntington's New York mansion, a commission which kept him busy for two years. From this time until the end of his life his desire to do mural work was fully gratified. In 1896 he painted "The Transmission of the Law," a frieze in the Appellate Court

Mower

House, New York. In 1897 he decorated the ceiling of the drawing-room in the F. W. Vanderbilt mansion at Hyde Park, N. Y. The oval central panel, ten by eighteen feet in dimensions, represents a scene from the legend of Ceres and Proserpine—Mercury bringing back the daughter for whom her mother has mourned. The color scheme is opalescent, with a play of rose pinks, blue-greens, violets, mauves, and reds. From 1900 to 1927 he was kept busy with mural painting. He collaborated with E. H. Blashfield in the work in the board-room of the Prudential Life Insurance Company at Newark, N. J. He decorated the J. P. Morgan library; Larz Anderson's house in Washington; the United States court room in the Federal Building at Cleveland, Ohio; the ceiling of the Gunn Memorial Library, Washington, Conn.; a gallery in the home of Breckenridge Long, St. Louis, Mo.; the chancel of St. John's Church, Washington, Conn.; the chancel of St. Michael's Church, Litchfield, Conn.; a triptych in a private chapel; and the pediment of the Madison Square Presbyterian Church, New York. But his most important and most brilliant work was the decoration of the library of the University Club, New York. For the purpose of studying Pinturicchio's wall paintings of the Borgia apartments in the Vatican, upon the general style of which he had decided to base this work, he went to Rome in 1902, and while there he was appointed director of the American Academy in Rome, an office which he filled acceptably through 1903–04. In 1921 President Wilson appointed him a member of the National Commission of Fine Arts. He held this office for seven years, or until his death, which occurred at his home in Washington, Conn., in 1928. After his death a very complete and impressive memorial exhibition, held by the Century Association, New York, May 6 to 29, 1928, served to confirm the most favorable estimate of his work.

[A full account of the life and work of Mowbray is given in *H. Siddons Mowbray, Mural Painter, 1858–1928* (1928), the privately printed volume issued by his wife and edited by H. F. Sherwood. Other sources are: Royal Cortissoz, article in *Scribner's Mag.*, May 1928; Pauline King, *Am. Mural Painting* (1902); Mich. State Lib., *Biog. Sketches of Am. Artists* (1924); *Am. Art Annual*, 1923–24; *N. Y. Times*, Jan. 14, 1928; *Hartford Daily Times*, Jan. 16, 1928; Mobray's first name often appears as Henry.]

W. H. D—s.

MOWER, JOSEPH ANTHONY (Aug. 22, 1827–Jan. 6, 1870), soldier, was born at Woodstock, Vt., the youngest of the five children of Nathaniel and Sophia (Holmes) Mower. When he was six years old the family moved to Lowell, Mass., where Joseph received a common-school education. A distinguishing trait of his early years was a love of reading military and naval history. In 1843 he matriculated at Norwich (Vt.) University and was a student there two years. Upon leaving he became a carpenter. When the Mexican War broke out he enlisted as a private of engineers, serving throughout the war, and being discharged July 25, 1848. On June 18, 1855, he was commissioned second lieutenant in the regular army, advancing to the grade of first lieutenant, Mar. 13, 1857, and to that of captain, Sept. 9, 1861.

Mower's combat record during the Civil War was one rarely equaled in the American army, and it is a fair deduction that had the war not ended in 1865 he would probably have attained command of an army. Within a period of two years commencing in March 1862 he was commended by his superiors in orders or official letters no less than twelve times, most of these stressing his conspicuous personal bravery, though, with the exception of Vicksburg and the final campaigns of the war under Sherman, he was not in particularly conspicuous theatres of action. His brevet commissions in the regular army were additional to more rapid promotions in the volunteer forces. These brevet commissions were: major, May 9, 1862, for gallant and meritorious service at Farmington, Miss.; lieutenant-colonel, Sept. 19, 1862, battle of Iuka, Miss., where, though forced back, his regiment camped on the field and found no enemy in the morning; colonel, May 14, 1863, for gallant and meritorious service at the capture of Jackson, Miss.; brigadier-general, Mar. 13, 1865, for gallant and meritorious conduct at the capture of Fort de Russy, La., a year previously, when he rode in on horseback ahead of his troops; major-general, Mar. 13, 1865, for gallant and meritorious conduct at the passage of the Salkehatchie, Georgia.

The above-mentioned events appear as high spots in a military career which properly commenced its period of command at his election as colonel of the 11th Missouri Volunteers, May 3, 1862, after his successful capture of New Madrid, Mo., in March. At the capture of Corinth, Mo., he discovered the dispositions of the Confederate General Lovell, and was wounded, captured, and recaptured in the course of the battle. During May 1863, his regiment planted itself on the ramparts of Vicksburg and stayed until relieved by Sherman in person. Following Vicksburg, Mower was a man marked for distinction, and was given many minor independent commands in Mississippi and northern Louisiana in preparation for his projected employment by

Sherman against Forrest. In spite of repeated efforts of Sherman, however, he was not made a major-general until Aug. 12, 1864, by which time Forrest's raids had ceased to be a danger. Ordered to join Sherman in the Nashville campaign, Mower first obeyed prior orders to accompany the expedition into Missouri against Price, where the rapid marches and maneuvering of his division were noteworthy. Upon joining Sherman in the Atlanta campaign, November 1864, he was given a division, commanding it through the march to the sea, and subsequently serving in the Carolinas, where he was given command of the XX Corps.

Mustered out as a brevet major-general in February 1866, he was reappointed in the regular army as colonel, 39th Infantry, July 28, serving as such until his transfer, as colonel, to the 25th Infantry in March 1869. At the time of his death in New Orleans he was in command of the department of Louisiana. On June 6, 1851, he married Betsey A. Bailey.

[Data on Mower's early life are in the Norman Williams Public Library, Woodstock, Vt. See also, W. L. Mower, *Mower Family Hist., A Geneal. Record of the Me. Branch* (1923); G. M. Dodge and W. A. Ellis, *Norwich Univ. 1819–1911* (1911), vol. II; F. B. Heitman, *Hist. Reg. and Dict. U. S. Army* (1903); *War of the Rebellion: Official Records (Army)*; *Am. Ann. Cyc. and Reg. of Important Events of the Year 1870* (1871); *Army and Navy Jour.*, Jan. 15, 22, Mar. 26, 1870; tribute by Gen. Sherman in *Vermont Standard* (Woodstock), Jan. 20, 1870.]   D. Y.

MOWRY, WILLIAM AUGUSTUS (Aug. 13, 1829–May 22, 1917), educator and author, was born in Uxbridge, Mass., the only son of Jonathan and Hannah (Brayton) Mowry and the descendant of Nathaniel Mowry who in 1672 was made a freeman of Providence. His parents were both members of the Society of Friends, but he became a member of the Congregational Church. Left fatherless at the age of three, he shared the life of his grandfather's farm and from the age of four attended the district school. After his thirteenth year he was self-supporting, working on farms and in mills, selling books, and teaching school. His early youth was a constant, although apparently joyous, struggle with grim necessity. Among his chief characteristics were tireless industry, cheerful common sense, originality, keen insight, and a never wanting buoyancy of spirit. Terms of district school taught in Rhode Island and in Massachusetts alternated with attendance at Uxbridge Academy and at the Phillips Academy at Andover, which he entered in 1851. At the age of twenty-five he entered Brown University in the class with John Hay and worked his way through the junior year, when he broke

down in health and withdrew from college, but in 1866 he received an honorary degree of A.M., and was elected to the Phi Beta Kappa society. He received an honorary Ph.D. degree from Bates College in 1882.

His comprehension of the needs of school children and teachers was gained from ample experience. After teaching boys for four years in the Providence High School and serving a period as captain in the 11th Rhode Island Volunteers during the Civil War, he opened in Providence the English and Classical School for boys, popularly known as Mowry and Goff's, and served as its principal for over twenty years. This notable school was a demonstration of the most enlightened ideas of school hygiene, equipment, methods of teaching, and discipline. There he had that contact with school problems which made him a national authority on many phases of practical pedagogy. In the teachers' institutes, which were the main source of assistance for the entire mass of public school teachers, he was a leader for over half a century, during which time he gave more than 1800 lectures to teachers in twenty-six states. For nineteen years he was executive head of the pioneer summer school for teachers, the famous Martha's Vineyard Summer Institute, which was established in 1878 and was a forerunner of the now almost universal summer schools of pedagogy. During his long career he served on Providence and Boston school boards, was superintendent of schools in Cranston, R. I., and in Salem, Mass., edited educational journals in Rhode Island and in Massachusetts, and was the author of many books. His various elementary books of history and civil government, widely used as texts, have influenced the ideas concerning citizenship of school children for several generations. He compiled several books of genealogy such as *The Descendants of Nathaniel Mowry* (1878) concerning his own ancestral line and *The Descendants of John Mowry* (1909), of a collateral line. He also published *The Uxbridge Academy* (1897), partly devoted to his own schooldays, and *Talks with my Boys* (1885), which went through several editions. His *Recollections of a New England Educator* (1908) was a review of school conditions in New England from 1838 to 1908. On Nov. 15, 1849, he married Rufina M. E. Weaver, of Slatersville, R. I., who died four months later. On Apr. 29, 1858, he married Caroline E. Aldrich of Woonsocket, R. I., who died in January 1897. They had three children.

[Biog. material in own books, *ante*; *Memories and Appreciations of Wm. Augustus Mowry*, ed. by R. M.

Moxham

Brown (1918); *Hist. Cat. of Brown Univ.* (1914); Whitman College *Pioneer,* May 1902; *Providence Daily Journal,* May 23, 1917.]   J.L.A.

MOXHAM, ARTHUR JAMES (Sept. 19, 1854–May 16, 1931), steel manufacturer, was born at Neath, Glamorganshire, South Wales, the son of Egbert and Katherine (Morgan) Moxham. His father was an architect of some prominence who died when the boy was quite young, and he was educated in the Clapton Orphan Asylum near London, from which he graduated in 1869 and came to America. He settled first in Louisville, Ky., and was employed in an iron foundry, where he learned the business and at the same time educated himself along general and engineering lines.

In 1878 he went to Birmingham, Ala., and organized the Birmingham Rolling-Mill Company, planning and building the Birmingham Rolling Mills, which he operated for several years. About 1883 he moved to Johnstown, Pa., where, in partnership with Tom L. Johnson [*q.v.*], inventor of an iron girder rail, he formed the Johnson Company. At the start the rails were made by the Cambria Steel Company, but the business grew rapidly and in a few years the Johnson Company had its own plant at Woodvale, just above Johnstown. This plant was wiped out by the Johnstown Flood in 1889, but was rebuilt in another suburb named Moxham. The business expanded to such an extent that the company at length controlled over ninety per cent. of the girder-rail business of the United States, which at that time was of very considerable volume due to the development of street railways throughout the country. This increase in business was largely due to Moxham's ingenuity in organization and production. The Johnson Company subsequently moved to Lorain, Ohio, and became the Lorain Steel Company. In 1899 Moxham was instrumental in the formation of the Illinois Steel Company through the merging of the Lorain Steel Company and the Minnesota Iron Company. It was later absorbed by the United States Steel Company. Soon afterward Moxham retired from active business for a year and took a trip around the world in his yacht. Later, he formed a partnership with H. M. Whitney of Boston, Mass., and went to Sydney, Nova Scotia, where he built the Dominion Iron & Steel Company. He left there in 1902 and became associated with T. C. du Pont in forming the E. I. du Pont de Nemours Powder Company, of which he was a vice-president, director, and member of the executive committee until 1914, when he resigned to become president of the Ætna Explosives Com-

Moxom

pany, which he organized and which, under his direction, operated on a large scale to meet the demands occasioned by the World War.

Resigning from this position in 1917, he spent much of the later part of his life in the study of special processes for the enhancement of ore values. He was regarded as one of the foremost steel experts both in the United States and abroad. At the time of the Johnstown Flood, he was named, by common acclaim of the citizens, chairman of the relief committee, and as such acted as virtual dictator over the stricken community until the authorities appointed by the governor of Pennsylvania took charge. On July 3, 1876, he married Helen Jilson Coleman of Louisville, Ky., and they had three children. He died at Great Neck, Long Island, N. Y.

[A. P. Van Gelder and Hugo Schlatter, *Hist. of the Explosives Industry in America* (1927); D. J. Beale, *Through the Johnstown Flood* (1890); *N. Y. Times* and *N. Y. Herald Tribune,* May 17, 1931; information as to certain facts furnished by a son, Egbert Moxham of New York City.]   J.H.F.

MOXOM, PHILIP STAFFORD (Aug. 10, 1848–Aug. 13, 1923), clergyman, was born in Markham, Ontario, Canada. His father, Job Hibbard Moxom, a grenadier in the British army, came to Canada as a member of a regiment sent out to suppress the famous Papineau rebellion among the French-Canadians. After peace had been restored, the elder Moxom left the army to study for the ministry, and became pastor first of a Methodist, and later of a Baptist church. With his wife, Anne Turner, who had been brought to Canada from England by her parents when three years of age, he emigrated in 1857 to the United States, settling first at Dement, and then at DeKalb, Ill. At the outbreak of the Civil War, the father offered his services to the government and was promptly commissioned a second lieutenant. Philip, only thirteen years old, but man-grown, was also eager to enlist. Though rejected on account of his youth, he was permitted to go to the front as a "captain's boy," and saw active service at Fort Donelson. Two years later, after a period of illness at home, he was accepted as a member of Company C, 17th Illinois Cavalry, and served with this regiment until the end of the conflict.

The young man now decided to become a lawyer. Supporting himself by teaching school, he spent two years at Kalamazoo College (1866–68), and two years more at Shurtleff College, Alton, Ill., where he was graduated in 1870. He then began reading law in a Kalamazoo office, but the next year received a most unusual "call" to the ministry. His father, pastor of a Baptist

301

church in Bellevue, Mich., had announced his resignation and the date of a farewell sermon. Prevented from being present on this date, he directed his son to take his place. The young man so pleased his surprised audience that they asked him to come again, and then to be their regular pastor. This experience marked the turning-point of his career. He was ordained at Bellevue on Sept. 19, 1871, and the following year he went to a Baptist church at Albion, Mich., where he remained three years. In 1875, feeling the need of a proper education, he entered the Rochester Theological Seminary, at the same time preaching each Sunday at a Baptist church in Mount Morris, N. Y. After receiving his theological degree in 1878, he entered Rochester University, and a year later was granted a bachelor's degree.

It was in his thirty-first year (1879) that Moxom began his brilliant career in the Christian ministry. A superb specimen of manhood, six feet four inches tall, graceful, forceful, eloquent, devoted, he was called to the First Baptist Church in Cleveland, Ohio. Six years later (1885), he went to the First Baptist Church in Boston, where he remained for eight years. It was during this period that he became generally known and admired as one of the most progressive and fearless preachers in the orthodox pulpit. It was at this time, also, that he found certain restrictions of the Baptist church irksome —its rigorous practice of immersion, and its exclusion of the unbaptized from the communion table. Unable to conform or be silent, he suddenly in December 1893 resigned his Boston pulpit, "not knowing where he would go." In quick succession, however, he received invitations from five different churches—a Baptist, a Presbyterian, a Congregational, a Universalist, and a Unitarian. Accepting a call to the South Congregational Church, Springfield, Mass., in March 1894, he was installed on Apr. 3, and entered upon a distinguished pastorate of twenty-one years.

He was of an ardent, enthusiastic, often impulsive temperament. In his opinions he was "strong-bitted," as he put it, and free, sometimes blunt, in their expression. In personal relations he was warm-hearted, expansive, companionable, yet frank and independent. In public, whether alone in the pulpit or mingled with others in a hall or on the street, he was a notable figure. He held his own with such contemporaries as Phillips Brooks, Minot J. Savage, George A. Gordon, Edward Everett Hale, as one of the most popular and influential preachers of his day. He was always welcome at the

colleges, and for three years (1894–97) served as university preacher at Harvard. His greatest hour, perhaps, came in 1893, at the World Parliament of Religions in Chicago, where he was selected to present to that remarkable assembly the Christian argument for immortality. His theological attitude was liberal; from the orthodox point of view, radical. He sought always the essentials of belief, and was impatient of petty refinements of doctrine or practice. An ardent patriot and active civic leader, he insisted upon identifying the church with public affairs, and was a pioneer in the idea of social centers and institutional features of church life. He attacked unflinchingly the social evils of his time, identified himself with progressive political causes, and was conspicuous for years as a worker for world peace. He visited Europe seventeen times, frequently to attend international peace conferences and church councils. His scholarship was wide and deep. No parish minister of his time was more familiar with the literature of theology. In addition, he mastered philosophy, history, and literature in various languages. Among his manuscripts were found after his death an unfinished translation of Rousseau's "Confessions" and a study of the Hebrew vocabulary of the Psalms. He published the following books: *The Aim of Life* (1894), *From Jerusalem to Nicaea: the Church in the First Three Centuries* (Lowell Institute Lectures, 1895), *The Religion of Hope* (1896), *Two Masters: Browning and Turgenief* (1912).

He was twice married: first, on Sept. 6, 1871, to Isabel Elliott (died in May 1919), by whom he had three sons and one daughter, and second, in June 1920, to Mrs. Jessie Braman Daggett, of Indiana. He resigned his Springfield pulpit June 30, 1917, owing to age and serious impairment of health, but maintained his connection with the South Church as pastor emeritus.

[*Rochester Theolog. Sem. Gen. Cat.* (1910); *The Congregational Year-Book,* 1923; *Congregationalist,* Aug. 23, 1923; *Springfield Republican,* Aug. 14, 1923; *Who's Who in America,* 1922–23; collection of clippings from *Springfield Republican* for entire time of Moxom's stay in Springfield and now preserved in the public library of that city.]   J. H. H.

MOYLAN, STEPHEN (1737–Apr. 13, 1811), Revolutionary soldier, was born in Cork, Ireland, son of John Moylan, a merchant of substance. The family was Catholic and as a result of the severe penal laws Stephen was educated in Paris. He engaged in the shipping business in Lisbon for three years before coming to Philadelphia in 1768, where he gained wealth and social prestige. In 1771 he became the first president of the Friendly Sons of St.

Patrick. At the outbreak of the Revolution his friend John Dickinson [q.v.] commended him to Washington as a zealous patriot; Moylan joined the army at Cambridge and became muster-master general, Aug. 11, 1775. In this position he fitted out several privateers which in the early months of the war considerably damaged British shipping. From January 1776 he actively agitated for the complete independence of the colonies; at the same time he entertained the vain hope of being appointed American ambassador to Spain. He became secretary to Washington in March; in June Congress elected him quartermaster-general of the army to succeed Thomas Mifflin [q.v.]. Moylan attempted, with little success, to block the progress of Lord Howe up the Hudson River; he also attempted to reorganize the army. Under the circumstances this latter task was impossible and a congressional committee of investigation could only recommend a change of quartermaster-general. Moylan promptly resigned and wrote a lengthy letter of vindication to Washington. Refusing several minor appointments, he remained with the army as a volunteer; a bitter snowstorm kept him out of the victory over the British at Trenton, but at the battle of Princeton he served with distinction: "I know I never felt so much like one of Homer's Deities before. We trod on air—it was a glorious day!" (Griffin, post, p. 48).

In December 1776 Washington requested him to organize and command a regiment of cavalry or light dragoons. The regiment was prepared for active service the following April and became a part of the American cavalry commanded by Casimir Pulaski [q.v.]. Moylan quarreled with Pulaski and Zielinski, another Polish officer, so that in October 1777 he was tried by a court martial for his unseemly conduct. He was acquitted, but in December Zielinski had the satisfaction of "unhorsing" Moylan in a tilt. When in March 1778 Pulaski resigned his command of the cavalry to form an independent corps of dragoons, Moylan was appointed, in spite of Pulaski's protests, to the command. The cavalry, though poor in numbers and equipment, became more efficient and useful. In May 1781 Moylan and his cavalry were sent to join Lafayette in Virginia; after the surrender of Cornwallis at Yorktown ill health forced Moylan to return to Philadelphia. At the end of the war the military establishment was reduced and his services were no longer needed. Congress, on Nov. 3, 1783, made him a brevet brigadier-general.

In the midst of the distresses of war he had

become engaged to Mary Ricketts Van Horn of Phil's Hill, N. J. She was the daughter of a retired merchant, whose five daughters all found husbands during the war. She was captivated by Moylan's jovial nature and by his very remarkable uniform, consisting of a red waistcoat, buckskin breeches, bright green coat and bearskin hat. On Sept. 12, 1778, Moylan married her, "a lady possessed of every accomplishment to render the married state happy." An interesting glimpse of the Moylans and Van Horns is given by the Marquis de Chastellux (post, I, 141–73), who dined with them and who "conceived a great friendship" for Moylan. Washington appointed him commissioner of loans in Philadelphia in 1793; and in 1796 he was again elected the president of the Friendly Sons of St. Patrick.

[Marquis de Chastellux, *Travels in North America* (2 vols., London, 1787); M. J. Griffin, *Stephen Moylan* (1909); Frank Monaghan, "Stephen Moylan in the American Revolution," in *Studies: an Irish Quart. Rev.* (Dublin), Sept. 1930; *Poulson's Am. Daily Advertiser*, Apr. 16, 1811.]   F. M—n.

MOZIER, JOSEPH (Aug. 22, 1812–Oct. 3, 1870), sculptor, was born in Burlington, Vt. Although he entered business in New York City, he is said to have spent much of his early manhood in Mount Vernon, Ohio, and to have married there. In the forties he was reported as a successful Broad Street merchant in New York, pursuing art only as a recreation. Like the sculptors Gould and MacDonald, he gave up business to devote himself wholly to sculpture. He went to Italy and made some preliminary studies in Florence. In 1845 he established himself in Rome, where he spent the rest of his life, aside from at least one visit made to his native land to show his works in the Tenth Street Studio, New York. In his day, the theme in a work of art was regarded as particularly important. Most of Mozier's themes had a strong literary or historic or anecdotic appeal, and both critics and clients appraised his output first of all from the point of view of the subject. One of his best works is in New Haven, Conn. It is the "Wept of Wish-ton-Wish," a life-size marble figure representing in nondescript Indian costume the heroine of Cooper's novel of that name. His "White Lady of Avenel" issues from the pages of Scott, and his "Indian Girl" illustrates a stanza from Bryant. Of his "Il Penseroso," Miltonic in derivation, a life-size draped female figure in marble, one copy is in the National Gallery of Art, Washington, D. C., and one is in Horticultural Hall, Fairmount Park, Philadelphia. His "Peri," representing another poetic theme, is in Mt. Olivet Cemetery, Nashville, Tenn.

Mozier's Old Testament figures include "Queen Esther," of which at least two copies were sold in the sixties, "Jephthah's Daughter," "Rebecca at the Well," "Rizpah," now in seclusion at the Metropolitan Museum, New York, and the marble group of the "Prodigal Son," owned by the Pennsylvania Academy of the Fine Arts. Of all his works, this group is the most ambitious and impressive. The emotion of the moment of meeting is well rendered in the action of both figures; the laborious carving of the details of the father's costume does not materially impair the effect of the whole. Samuel Osgood, writing in 1870, commented: "Mozier deals chiefly with subjects of feeling. . . . He designs somewhat in the tone of Thompson's 'Seasons.' . . . He studies faithfully, and is content with completing one statue each year" (post, p. 422). In 1878, Clark enthusiastically included the "Prodigal Son" in Great American Sculptures. Few of Mozier's critics were as severe as Nathaniel Hawthorne, who, friendly enough toward Powers and Harriet Hosmer, was not attracted by the art of "Mr. ——," as he cautiously designated Mozier; admitting meanwhile that "Mr. —— is sensible, shrewd, keen, clever . . . nor did I hear a single idea from him that struck me as otherwise than sensible." Probably present-day criticism would in general find Hawthorne correct in most of his estimates of the various works he saw in Mozier's studio, although even he approved of two genre pieces, "Boy Whittling," and "Girl with Cat and Dog." Two well-known works were the companion pieces, "Truth" and "Silence," formerly seen in the Lenox Library, New York City, and the oft-repeated "Pocahontas." Unlike most of his confrères, Mozier dealt little with the portrait bust, choosing as his province the draped ideal or genre figure. After twenty-five years of honorable activity in Rome, he died at Faido, Switzerland. His "Undine," which won the grand prize in Rome in 1867, was acquired by the University of Dayton in 1930 (Dayton News, Mar. 16, 1930).

[Rodman J. Sheirr has an article on Mozier, with eight illustrations, in Potter's Am. Monthly, Jan. 1876. Nathaniel Hawthorne, in his Italian Note-Books (1858), vol. I, pp. 154–56, gives a penetrating contemporary description of Mozier's productions and personal characteristics. From another point of view, Samuel H. Osgood, in "Am. Artists in Italy," Harper's Magazine, Aug. 1870, writes a friendly notice of this sculptor's studio work and social position in Rome. H. T. Tuckerman, in his Book of the Artists (1867), and Wm. J. Clark, Jr., in Great Am. Sculptures (1878), give additional data. C. E. Fairman's Art and Artists of the Capitol of the U. S. (1927) has a note, p. 317, on "Il Penseroso." Lorado Taft, The Hist. of

Am. Sculpture (1930), has the best general summary, with special descriptions and one full-page illustration. The Art Jour. (London), Apr. 1, 1859, has a comment on the "Prodigal Son" and on Jan. 1, 1871, an obituary. For other obituaries see the Cincinnati Commercial, Oct. 24, 1870, and the N. Y. Times, Oct. 30, 1870.]
A. A.

MUDD, SAMUEL A. [See BOOTH, JOHN WILKES, 1838–1865].

MUDGE, ENOCH (June 28, 1776–Apr. 2, 1850), Methodist Episcopal clergyman, the son of Enoch and Lydia (Ingalls) Mudge, was born in Lynn, Mass. Both his parents were of old New England ancestry, his father being a descendant of Thomas Mudge, born in 1624, and in 1657 a resident of Malden, Mass. In 1791 Jesse Lee [q.v.] of Virginia, the pioneer Methodist evangelist of New England, preached his first sermon in Lynn. He made a deep impression on several persons who had been members of the local Congregational church, which was then rent with internal strife. Among these were Enoch and Lydia Mudge, who joined the Methodist class which Lee organized, the first in Massachusetts, of which Mudge became the leader. The younger Enoch, a lad of fifteen, was stirred by what went on in the meetings and by the religious conversation he heard in his home, and with the help of John Lee, another Methodist itinerant, he, too, reached the satisfying experience of conversion. From the first he was an evangelist, winning his companions, and as a youthful exhorter making addresses in the neighboring towns. In 1793, at the age of seventeen, he was received into the New England Conference on trial as a Methodist preacher and appointed to the Greenwich circuit, which covered the state of Rhode Island and parts of Massachusetts. Thus he was the first native of New England to enter the ministry of this aggressive sect that was getting a hearing for the first time in territory long monopolized by the Puritan churches. The next year he was junior preacher on the New London, Conn., circuit, and in 1795 he was appointed to Readfield in the District of Maine. In 1796, though still a minor, he was ordained elder, and appointed to Bath, from which he pushed on farther east to Penobscot, pioneering new territory. Here, with his young companion, Timothy Merritt, one of his own Connecticut recruits who became a leader of New England Methodism, he formed numerous societies in rural hamlets and fishing villages.

On Nov. 29, 1797 (Alfred Mudge, post), he married Mrs. Jerusha Hinckley, daughter of John Holbrook, and settled on a farm at Orrington, Me., ceasing to travel as a member of the

Conference, though he continued to exercise the functions of a minister. On this account he was prosecuted for solemnizing a marriage, though the court dismissed the case as "malicious persecution." On another occasion, when he publicly denounced some young people for a "frolic," he was prosecuted for defamation. In 1811–12 and in 1815–16 he represented Orrington in the Massachusetts legislature, where he aided in the passage of the "religious freedom bill," which relieved the younger churches from the disabilities imposed upon them by the old laws giving special privileges to original Puritan churches. In 1817 Mudge reëntered the traveling ministry, serving as pastor in Boston (1817–18), Lynn (1819–21), Portsmouth (1821–22), Providence (1823–24), Newport (1825–26), and other city churches. While stationed at Lynn he was a delegate to the constitutional convention of Massachusetts (1819). From 1831 to 1844, when his health failed, he was port chaplain at New Bedford, where his kindliness, sympathy, and good cheer greatly commended him to the seamen of that flourishing whaling port. The last seven years of his life were spent in his native town of Lynn. He was a short, thickset man, of ruddy countenance, ready of speech and quick of wit. Common sense, a simple practical mind and a marked ability to command the confidence and support of other men were among his distinguishing traits. He made no pretensions to scholarship, but had a plain, direct style of discourse. He was an incorporator of Wilbraham Academy (1824), and served on the committee in the same year to establish a Methodist weekly in Boston. His publications include sermons, lectures to young people, a system of Biblical instruction, *Camp-Meeting Hymn Book* (1818), *The Parables* (1832), and "History of the Missions of the Methodist Episcopal Church," in *History of American Missions to the Heathen from Their Commencement to the Present Time* (1840).

[W. B. Sprague, *Annals Am. Pulpit*, vol. VII (1873); *Vital Records of Lynn, Mass.* (1905), vol. I, births; Alfred Mudge, *Memorials: Being a Geneal., Biog., and Hist. Account of the Name of Mudge in America* (1868); Stephen Allen and W. H. Pillsbury, *Hist. of Methodism in Me.* (1887); *Minutes of the Ann. Conferences of the M. E. Ch.,* 1850; Abel Stevens, *Memorials of the Early Progress of Methodism in the Eastern States* (1852); James Mudge, *Hist. of the New Eng. Conference of the M. E. Ch.* (1910); *Zion's Herald,* May 8, 1850; *Boston Journal,* Apr. 5, 1850.]
J.R.J.

MUDGE, JAMES (Apr. 5, 1844–May 7, 1918), Methodist clergyman and missionary, was born at West Springfield, Mass., the son of the Rev. James and Harriet Wilde (Goodridge) Mudge, and a descendant of Thomas Mudge, who was a resident of Malden, Mass., as early as 1657. James attended the public schools of South Harwich and Lynn, and at the age of seventeen entered Wesleyan University, Middletown, Conn., from which he received in 1865 the degree of A.B. He spent the two succeeding years as a teacher of Greek and Latin in the seminary at Pennington, N. J., and then entered the newly opened Boston University School of Theology, from which he received the degree of S.T.B. in 1870. He was ordained on Mar. 30, 1868, at a session of the New England Conference of the Methodist Episcopal Church, and was assigned shortly afterwards to the North Avenue Church, Cambridge, Mass. Upon the completion of his theological course, he took charge for three years of a church at Wilbraham, Mass., to which he had been appointed in Apr. 29, 1870, by the Springfield Conference. He married, on Apr. 29, 1873, Martha Maria Wiswell of New Haven, Conn., whom he had met while she was a teacher in Wilbraham Academy.

Shortly before his marriage, Mudge's mind was turned toward missionary service in India by a specific request from J. M. Thoburn [*q.v.*], of Lucknow, for a "first class, scholarly young man of literary turn" to act as editor of books and periodicals. He received appointment by the mission board of his Church and on July 1, 1873, sailed with his bride for India by way of Europe. Upon their arrival in Lucknow, Oct. 25, 1873, he assumed charge at once of the *Lucknow Witness,* a religious periodical published in English. During his ten years in India he carried on editorial work, issued various pamphlets, contributed numerous articles to American papers, compiled, mostly from materials which had appeared in the *Witness,* three volumes of *Good Stories and Best Poems,* prepared a Methodist catechism (in Hindustani), and published a history of Methodism. He had charge for a time of a vernacular Sunday school in Lucknow, and from 1878 to 1882 was pastor of the English-speaking Methodist congregation of that city. During 1882–83 he was stationed at Shahjahanpore as a general missionary in charge of vernacular work, a change of mission policy having ordained that missionary service should be devoted to native rather than to English constituencies. In 1883, with his wife and three children (a fourth, the eldest, having died in Lucknow), he returned to America, deeming himself ill-fitted for a general missionary career.

He resumed pastoral service under the auspices of the New England Conference, and for the next twenty-five years served churches in eastern Massachusetts. From 1888 to 1913 he was secretary and treasurer of the missionary society of the New England Conference; from 1888 until 1904, lecturer on missions at the Boston University School of Theology; and from 1889 until 1918, secretary of the New England Conference. He was also book editor of *Zion's Herald* (1908–12). He compiled *Poems with Power to Strengthen the Soul* (1907, 1909) and *The Best of Browning* (1898), edited *Sunday School Missionary Speaker* (1905), thirty volumes of Conference minutes, and *Hymns of Trust* (1912), and was the author of the following books: *Faber* (1885), *In Memoriam, or a Portraiture of the Rev. Zachariah Atwell Mudge* (1890), *Pastors' Missionary Manual* (1891), *Growth in Holiness* (1895), *Honey from Many Hives* (1899), *China* (1900), *The Life of Love* (1902), *The Land of Faith* (1903), *The Saintly Calling* (1905), *The Life Ecstatic* (1906), *Fenelon the Mystic* (1906), *The Riches of His Grace* (1909), *History of the New England Conference of the Methodist Episcopal Church* (1910), *The Perfect Life* (1911), *Religious Experience* (1913), and *Heart Religion as Described by John Wesley* (1913). He died in Malden, Mass., and was buried in the lot with his father in Pine Grove Cemetery, Lynn. Enoch Mudge [*q.v.*] was his great-uncle.

[Alfred Mudge, *Memorials: Being a Geneal., Biog., and Hist. Account of the Name Mudge in America 1638 to 1868* (1868); *Minutes of the New Eng. Conference of the M. E. Ch.*, 1919; *Who's Who in America*, 1918–19; *Zion's Herald*, May 15, 1918; *Boston Transcript*, May 7, 1918.]   J. C. A—h—r.

MUHLENBERG, FREDERICK AUGUSTUS (Aug. 25, 1818–Mar. 21, 1901), Lutheran clergyman, teacher, college president, grandson of Gotthilf Henry Ernest Mühlenberg and great-grandson of Henry Melchior Mühlenberg [*qq.v.*], was born at Lancaster, Pa., the second of the five children of Frederick Augustus Hall Muhlenberg (1795–1867) by his first wife, Elizabeth Schaum. His father, a physician, banker, and prominent citizen of Lancaster, had been a pupil of Benjamin Rush and was a graduate in arts and medicine of the University of Pennsylvania; his mother was a granddaughter of John Helfrich Schaum, who was sent from Halle to Philadelphia in 1745 to work as a catechist under H. M. Mühlenberg. Frederick Augustus entered Pennsylvania (now Gettysburg) College in 1833, only a few months after its opening, but transferred later to Jefferson (now Washington and Jefferson) College at Canonsburg, where he graduated in 1836. While at Jefferson he was much influenced by its

president, Matthew Brown, a Calvinist of deepest dye, whose character was more genial than his doctrine. After a year's breathing spell at home, studying anatomy and physiology with his father, he spent the year 1837–38 at Princeton Theological Seminary and entered on his long career as an educator. In generous measure he possessed the vigor of mind and body, the executive capacity, and the strong sense of duty that were recurrent traits in his family. Though he wrote little, he was a notable scholar, especially in Greek, and an excellent teacher, inculcating, at least in his apter pupils, an accurate, appreciative knowledge of the Greek classics and efficient habits of study and thought. As professor or president he contributed richly to the life of five colleges of his native state. He was a member, 1840–50, of the faculty of Franklin College at Lancaster, of which his grandfather had been the first president, and in 1849 proposed the union of Franklin, Marshall, and Pennsylvania colleges. This motion led to the transfer to Pennsylvania College in 1850 of the Lutheran interest in Franklin College and to the organization in 1852–53 of Franklin and Marshall College as an institution of the German Reformed Church.

Muhlenberg was the first incumbent, 1850–67, of the Franklin professorship of ancient languages in Pennsylvania College, his tenure corresponding almost exactly with the presidency of Henry Louis Baugher [*q.v.*]. He was licensed in 1854 and ordained in 1855 by the Ministerium of Pennsylvania, preached regularly in Christ Church, and was librarian of the college. During the Gettysburg campaign his house was pierced by a shell and pillaged by marauding soldiers. In 1867 he removed to Allentown to become the first president of Muhlenberg College. For nine years, besides teaching Greek, the mental and moral sciences, and the evidences of Christianity, he bore the burdensome responsibility of organizing and administering a college that was crippled from the start by financial difficulties. With the able cooperation of two of the professors, Matthias Henry Richards and Theodore Lorenzo Seip [*q.v.*], he kept the college alive, and when he resigned in 1876 its continuance and usefulness seemed assured. For the next twelve years he was professor of the Greek language and literature in the University of Pennsylvania. For the first time since his graduation from college he recrossed the Alleghanies in 1891 to assume the presidency of Thiel College at Greenville, which was in dire need of his firm, orderly control. Having reorganized the institution, he retired in 1893 at the age of seventy-five. Muhlenberg was married on Aug. 8, 1848, to Catharine Anna (1827–94), daughter of Maj. Peter Muhlenberg, U. S. A., and grand-daughter of John Peter Gabriel Muhlenberg [q.v.]. Four of their six sons outlived him. He spent his last years in Reading, where he died and was buried in the Charles Evans Cemetery.

[H. M. M. Richards, "Descendants of H. M. Mühlenberg," *Proc. and Addresses Pa.-Ger. Soc.*, vol. X (1900); biog. sketch by H. E. Jacobs in S. E. Ochsenford, *Muhlenberg Coll.* (1892); *Biog. and Hist. Cat. Washington and Jefferson Coll.* (1902); J. H. Dubbs, *Hist. of Franklin and Marshall Coll.* (1903); *Necrological Report, Princeton Theol. Sem.*, 1901; sketch of F. A. H. Muhlenberg in J. L. Chamberlain, *Univ. of Pa.*, vol. II (1902); *Press* (Phila.), Mar. 22, 1901.]
G. H. G.

MUHLENBERG, FREDERICK AUGUSTUS CONRAD (Jan. 1, 1750–June 4, 1801), Lutheran clergyman, politician, first speaker of the federal House of Representatives, was born at Trappe, Montgomery County, Pa., the third child and second son of Henry Melchior Mühlenberg [q.v.] by his wife, Anna Maria Weiser, daughter of the younger John Conrad Weiser [q.v.]. He was sent to Halle in 1763 with his brothers, John Peter Gabriel and Gotthilf Henry Ernest [qq.v.], attended the schools of the Francke Stiftungen and the University, returned to Philadelphia in 1770 with Gotthilf and their future brother-in-law, John Christopher Kunze [q.v.], and was ordained at Reading, Oct. 25, 1770, by the Ministerium of Pennsylvania. On Oct. 15, 1771, he married Catharine (1750–1835), daughter of Frederick Schaefer, a Philadelphia sugar refiner, by whom he had three sons and four daughters. His ministerial career extended until the summer of 1779. After his ordination he acted as assistant to his brother-in-law, Christian Emanuel Schulze, preaching and performing other ministerial duties at Tulpehocken, Schaeferstown, Lebanon, and other points in that region. In 1771 he made two arduous trips to Sunbury. In November 1773 he went to New York as pastor of Christ Church ("The Old Swamp Church") at Frankford and William Streets. In 1775 he wrote to his brother Peter rebuking him for mixing revolutionary and martial activities with the ministry of the Word, but he himself was known to be in sympathy with the Revolution. As a measure of precaution he sent his wife and two children to Philadelphia in February 1776 and late in June, when Howe's fleet appeared in the offing, he followed them. A month later he removed to Trappe with his family and relieved his father of the charge at New Hanover. He also preached regularly at Oley Hills and New Goshenhoppen and occasionally at Reading.

The turning-point of his life was his election Mar. 2, 1779, to fill the unexpired term of Edward Biddle in the Continental Congress. He had been an honest, faithful, laborious clergyman, but his choice of that profession had been dictated by circumstance rather than by his own volition, and to the political career now opening ahead of him he turned with renewed hope and energies. He was reëlected to the Continental Congress Nov. 12, 1779, his term expiring Oct. 28, 1780, when he became ineligible for three years. Meanwhile he had been elected to the General Assembly, of which he was speaker 1780–83. He was president of the Council of Censors 1783–84, and one of the party striving for a revision of the state constitution. He was commissioned justice of the peace Mar. 9, 1784; and on the organization of Montgomery County that autumn he was made registrar of wills and recorder of deeds. He wrote occasionally for the press, both in German and English, and his private letters are enlivened with racy comments on the politics and politicians of the day. In 1787 he presided over the convention called to ratify the Federal Constitution, and the next year he was elected to the First Congress as a Federalist from the Philadelphia district. Financial necessity compelled him, meanwhile, to engage in business: he was a partner in the firm of Muhlenberg & Wegmann, importers, and in that of Muhlenberg & Lawersweiler, sugar refiners, in Philadelphia, and owned a house and fifty acres of land at Trappe, with which a store of some kind was connected. When Congress assembled at New York, Muhlenberg came to it with the reputation of an experienced, urbane, impartial presiding officer and was elected speaker, the choice being undoubtedly influenced by the consideration that, since the President came from the South and the Vice-President from New England, it was desirable to select the speaker from the most powerful of the middle states. He was reëlected to the Second, Third, and Fourth congresses as a Federalist, but was displaced as speaker in the Second Congress by Jonathan Trumbull, the change being motivated probably by the fact that Muhlenberg's Federalism had been growing lukewarm. When the Third Congress was organized he was elected speaker again, this time by the help of Republican votes. During the ensuing years he steered a political course that must have been as puzzling sometimes to himself as it has since been to historians. As the Federalist candidate for governor of Pennsylvania, he was badly beaten by Thomas McKean [q.v.] in 1793 and overwhelmingly in 1796, while in Congress he worked harmoniously with Jefferson's supporters. In 1796, as chairman of the House acting as a committee of the whole, he cast the deciding vote to refer again to the House the bill appropriating money for the ratification of Jay's Treaty. It was a courageous, statesmanlike act, and cost him his popularity in Pennsylvania. About two years before his death he abandoned the Federalist party and threw his support to the Republicans. John Adams attributed the Federalist loss of Pennsylvania in the national elections to the influence of Frederick Muhlenberg and his brother Peter. On Jan. 8, 1800, Gov. Thomas Mifflin [q.v.] appointed him receiver-general of the Pennsylvania Land Office, and he moved to Lancaster, then the seat of the government. He was extremely corpulent, and his death in 1801 resulted from an apoplectic stroke. He was buried in the Lutheran churchyard at Lancaster.

[H. M. M. Richards, "Descendants of H. M. Mühlenberg," *Proc. and Addresses Pa.-Ger. Soc.*, vol. X (1900); D. M. Gregg, "Three Pennsylvania Statesmen of the Olden Time" (unpublished, written 1932); letter to Gen. Peter Muhlenberg, and MSS. in the Gregg Collection (vol. I), Lib. of Cong.; B. M. Schmucker, "The Luth. Ch. in the City of N. Y., II," *Luth. Ch. Rev.*, Apr. 1885; Oswald Seidensticker, "Friedrich August Conrad Mühlenberg," *Deutsch-Amerikanische Geschichtsblätter*, Jan. 1909; W. J. Mann, *Life and Times of H. M. Mühlenberg* (1887); *Doc. Hist. Ev. Luth. Min. of Pa. 1748–1821* (1898); M. P. Follett, *The Speaker of the House of Representatives* (1896); *The Journal of William Maclay* (1927); *Aurora and Gen. Advertiser* (Phila.), June 22, 1801.]   G. H. G.

MÜHLENBERG, GOTTHILF HENRY ERNEST (Nov. 17, 1753–May 23, 1815), Lutheran clergyman, botanist, was born at Trappe, Montgomery County, Pa., the fifth child and third son of Henry Melchior [q.v.] and Anna Maria (Weiser) Mühlenberg. Accompanied by his brothers, John Peter Gabriel and Frederick Augustus Conrad Muhlenberg [qq.v.], he was sent to Germany in April 1763 to be educated at Halle. There he spent six years in the Waisenhaus, mastering Greek, Latin, Hebrew, and French, and exhibiting at times a spirit as fiery as that of his brother Peter. In September 1769 he matriculated at the University, and a year later, with Frederick and their future brother-in-law, John Christopher Kunze [q.v.], he returned to Philadelphia. Though he was still a stripling, the members of the Lutheran Ministerium of Pennsylvania were so impressed by his scholarship and had such faith in the Mühlenberg name that they ordained him at Reading, Oct. 25, 1770, with but slight misgiving. For the next few years he was his father's assistant at Philadelphia and in the Raritan Valley in New Jersey, and in April 1774 he was elected third pastor at Philadelphia. On July 26 of that year he married Mary Catharine Hall (Dec. 26, 1756–May 1, 1841) of Philadelphia, who bore him four sons and four daughters. As the British forces approached Philadelphia, he sent his family to his father's house at New Providence (Trappe), and on Sept. 22, 1777, four days before the occupation, he himself retired thither. After the British withdrawal in June 1778 he returned. In April 1779, as the upshot of a misunderstanding with Kunze, he resigned abruptly. The next year he succeeded J. H. C. Helmuth [q.v.] as pastor of Holy Trinity, Lancaster, where he remained till his death thirty-five years later. He was secretary of the Ministerium of Pennsylvania for six terms and president for eleven. He was the first president (1787) of Franklin College.

He began the study of botany in the spring of 1778 during his enforced rustication and was an accomplished botanist when Johann David Schöpf [q.v.] visited him in 1783. Schöpf gave him confidence in the soundness and value of his work and brought him into correspondence with various European botanists. Thereafter Mühlenberg exchanged letters and specimens with scientists in England, France, Switzerland, Germany, and Sweden, and was elected to honorary membership in several learned societies. In his own country he was even better known. He did as much field work as his arduous professional duties would permit, kept a calendar of the flowering plants of his neighborhood, and by 1791 had listed more than 1,100 plants growing within three miles of Lancaster. In the precision and accuracy of his descriptions, his scrupulous regard for correct nomenclature, his aversion to splitting species into numerous varieties on the basis of minute variations, and his recognition of the necessity for collaborative effort in compiling a complete flora of North America, he was a true forerunner of Torrey and Gray. He also gave much attention to the economic and medicinal uses of plants. His total contribution to descriptive botany—some hundred species and varieties—is the more remarkable because of the restricted area that he explored personally.

His publications include: *Eine Rede, gehalten den 6ten Juny 1787, bey der Einweihung von der Deutschen Hohen Schule oder Franklin Collegium in Lancäster* (Lancaster, 1788); "Index Florae Lancastriensis" and "Supplementum Indicis," *Transactions of the American Philosophical Society*, vols. III (1793) and IV (1799); *Observations on the Genera Juglans, Fraxinus, and Quercus, in the Neighbourhood of Lancaster, in North America* (copr. 1801); *English-German and German-English Dictionary* (2 vols., Lancaster, 1812), in collaboration with Benedict J. Schipper; *Catalogus Plantarum Americae Septentrionalis Huc Usque Cognitarum Indigenarum et Cicurum: Or, A Catalogue of the Hitherto Known Native and Naturalized Plants of North America, Arranged According to the Sexual System of Linnæus* (Lancaster, 1813); and *Descriptio Uberior Graminum et Plantarum Calamariarum Americae Septentrionalis Indigenarum et Cicurum* (Philadelphia, 1817). He also left much work unpublished.

A representative both of the later phase of German Pietism and of the Enlightenment, Mühlenberg was a man of exemplary character and great personal charm. In his prime he had a strong body and enjoyed traveling on foot between Lancaster and Philadelphia, a distance of more than sixty miles. In later life he suffered repeated apoplectic attacks, to which he finally succumbed. He was buried in his churchyard at Lancaster.

[Muhlenberg papers are in the archives of the Am. Phil. Soc., the Ev. Luth. Min. of Pa., and the Hist. Soc. of Pa. Printed materials include: "Kurze Nachricht von dem Leben und Tode des Hochwürdigen Hrn. Doctor Mühlenbergs," *Evangelisches Magazin*, 1816, pp. 13–16 (probably by J. H. C. Helmuth); G. F. Krotel, *Memorial Vol. of the Ev. Luth. Ch. of the Holy Trinity* (Lancaster, 1861); *Doc. Hist. Ev. Luth. Min. of Pa. 1748–1821* (1898); J. H. Dubbs, *Hist. Franklin and Marshall Coll.* (1903); *Reliquiae Baldwinianae: Selections from the Correspondence of the Late William Baldwin, M.D.* (1843); Wm. Darlington, *Memorials of John Bartram and Humphry Marshall* (1849); "The Muhlenberg Herbarium," *Bull. Torrey Botanical Club*, July 1881, pp. 80–81; J. M. Maisch, "G. H. E. Mühlenberg als Botaniker," *Pharmaceutische Rundschau* (New York), June 1886; *Life, Journals and Correspondence of Rev. Manasseh Cutler, LL.D.* (1888); W. J. Youmans, *Pioneers of Science in America* (1896); *Poulson's Am. Daily Advertiser* (Phila.), May 26, 1815.]   G. H. G.

MUHLENBERG, HENRY AUGUSTUS PHILIP (May 13, 1782–Aug. 11, 1844), Lutheran clergyman, politician, diplomat, was born at Lancaster, Pa., the third of the eight children of Gotthilf Henry Ernest Mühlenberg [*q.v.*] and Mary Catharine Hall. He received a thorough classical training from his father, studied theology with his uncle, John Christopher Kunze [*q.v.*], and, having been licensed by the Ministerium of Pennsylvania, became pastor in April 1803 of Trinity Church, Reading, Pa. He was ordained at Easton in 1804. The next year he married Mary Elizabeth, daughter of Joseph Hiester [*q.v.*]. She died in childbed in 1806, and in 1808 Muhlenberg married her sister Rebecca. His official call to Reading stip-

ulated that he should receive, in addition to his salary and perquisites, "all love and friendship which a faithful and conscientious pastor should have, so that he may fulfill his office among us with joy and not with grief" (Fry, *post,* p. 134), and this proved to be more than a pious wish, for under him the congregation enjoyed a quarter-century of peace, good will, and prosperity. During these years he maintained an extensive correspondence with other Lutheran clergymen and served as secretary and as president of the Ministerium. His only known published sermon is *Busstags-Predigt Gehalten Donnerstags den 20sten August 1812* (Reading, 1812). In 1828, because of indifferent health, he resigned his charge and removed to a farm on the outskirts of the town, but he continued to preach to his congregation until his successor, Jacob Miller, was installed in March 1829.

Meanwhile, taking advantage of his prestige among the Pennsylvania Germans, the Democrats of Berks County nominated him for Congress. He was readily elected, took his seat Mar. 4, 1829, in the Twenty-first Congress, and served continuously until his resignation, Feb. 9, 1838. Muhlenberg took to politics as a duck to water. In Berks County he had a large personal following that gave its vote to the entire Democratic ticket, and the county became known —in the words of campaign orators—as "the tenth legion of the Democracy." In Congress he served continuously as chairman of the House committee on Revolutionary claims, gave loyal, intelligent support to President Jackson's measures, and made a good friend of Martin Van Buren. Meanwhile in state politics he was less fortunate. As a result of internal dissensions, the Democrats put two candidates for governor into the field in 1835, George Wolf, who was running to succeed himself for the second time, and Muhlenberg. The ensuing defeat engendered bitterness that lasted for years, and finally it became obvious that in the interests of party harmony Muhlenberg would have to be removed, at least temporarily, from Pennsylvania politics. Van Buren offered him the secretaryship of the navy and the ministry to Russia, but Muhlenberg felt that he could not afford to accept them. Then it was decided to send a legation to Austria, and on Feb. 8, 1838, he was made the first American minister to Austria. John Randolph Clay, later minister to Peru, was his secretary of legation. Muhlenberg did something to promote the use of American cotton in Austria, enjoyed the society of Prince Metternich, and traveled in Germany, Switzerland, and Italy; but the legation was a severe

Mühlenberg

drain on his resources, and on Sept. 18, 1840, he was recalled at his own request. In 1844 he was again nominated for governor of Pennsylvania, and with the united support of his party his election was assured, but he died, in the midst of the campaign, of a stroke of apoplexy. He was buried in the Charles Evans Cemetery.

[H. M. M. Richards, "Descendants of H. M. Mühlenberg," *Proc. and Addresses Pa.-Ger. Soc.*, vol. X (1900); Jacob Fry, *The Hist. of Trinity Luth. Ch., Reading, Pa.* (1894); *Doc. Hist. Ev. Luth. Min. of Pa. 1748–1821* (1898); "Biog. Memoir of the Late Henry A. Muhlenberg," *U. S. Mag. and Dem. Rev.*, Jan. 1845; the *Pennsyvanian* (Phila.), Aug. 13, 15, 1844; W. U. Hensel, "Sidelights on an Early Political Campaign," *Lancaster County Hist. Soc. Papers*, Apr. 1914; Van Buren Papers, MSS. Div., Lib. of Cong.]
G. H. G.

MÜHLENBERG, HENRY MELCHIOR (Sept. 6, 1711–Oct. 7, 1787), Lutheran clergyman, was born at Einbeck, Hanover, the seventh of the nine children of Nicolaus Melchior and Anna Maria (Kleinschmid) Mühlenberg. His father was an hereditary member of the Brewers' Company, a master-shoemaker by trade, and an officer of St. Mary's Church. His mother was the daughter of a retired army officer. The father's death in 1723 left the family in narrow circumstances, so that for three years Mühlenberg had to forgo his studies and work for an elder brother. He learned meanwhile to play the organ and completed his preliminary education later in classical schools at Einbeck and Zellersfeld. The close connection between the University of Göttingen and American cultural life begins with Mühlenberg, who was one of its first matriculants in March 1735. While a student at the University he lived in the household of a Dr. Oporin, a member of the theological faculty, opened a school, which still exists, for the elementary instruction of poor children, and gained the friendship of several men of influence, among them Count Reuss of Koestritz and Count Henkel of Poeltzig. Having completed the theological course in 1738, he made a short visit to the University of Jena and then was appointed teacher in the famous Waisenhaus at Halle. The year under G. A. Francke at Halle was decisive. He thought of going to the East Indies as a missionary, but since no opening occurred, he became in 1739 co-pastor and inspector of an orphanage at Grosshennersdorf in Upper Lusatia, where the Baroness von Gersdorf, an aunt of Count von Zinzendorf, was his patroness. His ordination took place at Leipzig Aug. 24, 1739. While Mühlenberg was visiting in Halle on his birthday, Sept. 6, 1741, Francke, acting for himself and for F. M. Ziegenhagen, German court-preacher in London,

Mühlenberg

laid before him a call to the United Congregations (Philadelphia, New Providence, New Hanover), in Pennsylvania. This call had been unfinished business with him and Ziegenhagen for eight years, but rumors of Zinzendorf's efforts at church union among the Germans of the colony had at last galvanized them into action. Mühlenberg took six weeks to consider the proposal and on Oct. 18 accepted by letter. After a pleasant farewell journey through Saxony and Hanover he reached London Apr. 17, 1742, and spent nine weeks with Ziegenhagen, familiarizing himself with conditions in America and practising his English, the rudiments of which he had acquired in his student days at Göttingen. A harrowing voyage of twelve weeks brought him to Charleston, S. C., whence he proceeded to Ebenezer, Ga., for a week's conference with Johann Martin Boltzius [*q.v.*]. On Nov. 25, 1742, after a two weeks' sail from Charleston, he landed at Philadelphia.

Since no one expected him, no one welcomed him. The Philadelphia congregation was split between Zinzendorf and a clerical vagabond, Valentine Kraft. His rural congregations were known in the vernacular by the sinister names of "Die Trappe" and "Der Schwamm." When he found out where they were and reached them, over miles of wretched road and through unbridged streams, he was received with skepticism. He soon made a friend, however, in the Swedish pastor, Peter Tranberg, the more intelligent members of the congregations came to his support, and he was duly installed. The conflict with Zinzendorf, deplorable but inevitable, was fortunately brief; a month later the Count abandoned his great dream and departed for Europe. Dismal as was Mühlenberg's reception in Pennsylvania, it began an epoch in the history of his denomination. He saw his task, almost from the beginning, not as the serving of three isolated congregations but as the planting of a Church, and to that great enterprise he brought talents of the highest order. Though of but medium stature and hardly an athlete, he grew strong and active of body, capable of enduring long days in the saddle, exposure to every inclemency, and an unending round of duties. His intellect was clear, vigorous, alert, not original, but able to assimilate whatever nutriment it required. He had been a good scholar in Germany, and in Pennsylvania he did not forget what he had learned. His Biblical and theological scholarship was sound, and his personal religious life was warmed and mellowed by a mild type of Pietism. He was a good linguist: his German was pure and idiomatic, un-

310

Mühlenberg

Muhlenberg

corrupted by the fashionable barbarities and complexities of the time; he spoke Latin with ease and learned, with amazing rapidity, to preach in English and Dutch. Among his minor assets were a well-trained tenor voice, some familiarity with legal principles, and a rather greater knowledge of medicine and hygiene. He was dignified in manner, urbane and affable, and wholly devoid of any desire for self-aggrandizement. To his fundamental pastoral and missionary zeal he added a genius for organization.

Nominally, he remained pastor of the United Congregations till almost the close of his life, but he soon made them the nucleus of an organization that spread rapidly wherever German Lutherans had settled in the middle colonies. In January 1745 his first helpers—Peter Brunnholtz, John Nicolas Kurtz, John Helfrich Schaum—arrived from Halle. On Apr. 22, of that year, he married Anna Maria, daughter of the younger John Conrad Weiser [q.v.], who bore him six sons and five daughters and outlived him by many years. Her mother was long believed to have been an Indian woman; she was, however, Anna Eve, daughter of Peter Feg (Feck), an immigrant from the Palatinate. As new congregations were formed or old ones allied themselves with Mühlenberg, the need of closer organization became apparent, and on Aug. 26, 1748, the first convention of the Evangelical Lutheran Ministerium of Pennsylvania was held at Philadelphia. By that date he had already made trips to the Raritan Valley in New Jersey, to Frederick, Md., and to various points in eastern Pennsylvania. Until the outbreak of the Revolution he continued to visit Lutheran congregations scattered all the way from the Hudson River to the Potomac. During parts of 1751 and 1752 he resided in New York, ministering temporarily to the churches there and at Hackensack; in 1758 and 1759 he made similar stays in the Raritan Valley. In 1774-75 he made a notable journey to the Salzburgers at Ebenezer, Ga. Until 1761 his home was at New Providence; from 1761 to 1776 he lived in Philadelphia; but with the oncoming of the Revolution he found it safest to return to his rural retreat at New Providence. With the addition to his forces of such men as J. H. C. Helmuth, John Christopher Kunze [qq.v.], and Christian Emanuel Schulze—the two latter became his sons-in-law—he was the leader of a highly intelligent, constantly expanding society. He remained its revered leader even after the infirmities of age compelled him to restrict his activities.

In 1779 he formally resigned as rector of St. Michael's and Zion's in Philadelphia; two years

later he made his last appearance at a meeting of the Ministerium. In 1784 the University of Pennsylvania made him a doctor of divinity. He did most of the editorial work on the *Gesangbuch* published by the Ministerium in 1786. Though his mind was still clear and active, he was confined more and more to New Providence and finally to his own house, where he died Oct. 7, 1787, of a complication of diseases. He is buried beside the Augustus Church at New Providence (Trappe). At the time of his death his significance as the virtual founder of the Lutheran church in America was recognized on all sides, and his fame has grown with the church. Thanks to the remarkably full records of his life, he is still one of the molding forces of his denomination.

[The chief repositories of Mühlenberg's papers are the Ostindische Bibliothek of the Franckesche Stiftungen at Halle and the Archives of the Ministerium of Pa. in the Theological Seminary at Mount Airy, Phila. The Francke Nachlass in the Preussiche Staatsbibliothek in Berlin and the Lutheran Hist. Soc. Library at Gettysburg contain some additional matter. The Library of Congress has photostats of the material at Halle and Berlin, and the Ministerium Archives eventually will have copies of all papers not in its possession; see C. H. Kraeling, "In Quest of Muhlenbergiana," *Luth. Ch. Quarterly*, Apr. 1929. Printed materials comprise *Nachrichten von den vereinigten Deutschen Evangelisch-Lutherischen Gemeinen in Nord America, absonderlich in Pensylvanien* (2 vols., Halle, 1787; new ed., by W. J. Mann and B. M. Schmucker, the first volume richly annotated, Allentown, Pa., 1886-95); *Heinrich Melchior Mühlenberg—Selbstbiographie, 1711-43*, ed. by Wm. Germann (Allentown, 1881); "The Autobiog. of H. M. Muhlenberg," tr. by J. W. Early, *Luth. Ch. Rev.*, Oct. 1914; "Jour. of a Voyage from Phila. to Ebenezer, Ga., in the Years 1774-75," tr. by J. W. Richards, *Evangelical Rev.*, Jan. 1850-Oct. 1852; "Account of the march of the Paxton Boys against Phila. in the Year 1764" and "Extracts from the Rev. Dr. Muhlenberg's Jours. of 1776 and 1777 relating to Military events about that period," tr. by H. H. Muhlenberg, *Colls. Hist. Soc. of Pa.*, Nov. 1851, May 1852; "Abstract of a letter . . . on the Constitutional Convention of Pa., 1776," *Pa. Mag. of Hist. and Biog.*, Notes and Queries, Apr. 1898, pp. 129-31. The first biog. accounts were two memorial sermons: J. H. C. Helmuth, *Denkmal der Liebe und Achtung, Welches seiner Hochwürden dem Herrn D. Heinrich Melchior Mühlenberg . . . ist Gesetzet Worden* (1788) and J. C. Kunze, *Elisas Betränter Nachruf bei der Hinwegnahme seines Gottesmannes Elias* (1788). M. L. Stoever, *Memoir of the Life and Times of Henry Melchior Muhlenberg* (1856) was several times reprinted. W. J. Mann, *Life and Times of Henry Melchior Mühlenberg* (1887; German ed., 1891), reviewed by H. E. Jacobs, *Luth. Ch. Rev.*, July 1887, is the standard biog. and a masterpiece of scholarship and understanding. See also his "Conservatism of Henry Melchior Mühlenberg," *Luth. Ch. Rev.*, Jan. 1888, and "Lutherans in America before Mühlenberg," *Ibid.*, Apr. 1887. For family data consult: H. M. M. Richards, "Descendants of H. M. Mühlenberg," *Proc. and Addresses Pa.-Ger. Soc.*, vol. X (1900) and "The Weiser Family," *Ibid.*, vol. XXXII (1924); H. M. Oakley and J. C. Schwab, *Muhlenberg Album* (privately printed, 1910); J. C. Schwab, *The Descendants of H. M. Muhlenberg* (privately printed, 1912), a chart.]
G. H. G.

MÜHLENBERG, JOHN PETER GABRIEL (Oct. 1, 1746–Oct. 1, 1807), Lutheran

Muhlenberg

Muhlenberg

clergyman, Revolutionary soldier, politician, was born at Trappe, Montgomery County, Pa., the eldest of the eleven children of Henry Melchior Mühlenberg [q.v.] and his wife, Anna Maria Weiser. As a boy he displayed frontiersman-like traits, natural enough in a grandson of John Conrad Weiser [q.v.] but perturbing to his father. After learning a little Latin at the Philadelphia Academy, he was sent to Halle in 1763, with his brothers Frederick and Gotthilf [qq.v.], to be educated at the Waisenhaus or, at the discretion of its director, Gotthilf August Francke, to be apprenticed to a merchant. Francke ill-advisedly bound the high-spirited, quick-witted youth for a term of six years to a petty Lübeck grocer. When Peter could endure his situation no longer, he absconded, joined the 60th (Royal American) Regiment of Foot, and as secretary to one of the officers, a friend of his father, returned to Philadelphia and was discharged early in 1767. He then prepared for the ministry with Carl Magnus von Wrangel, provost of the Swedish churches on the Delaware, preached in various pulpits with more than ordinary approval, and in February 1769 took charge, as his father's assistant, of the Lutheran churches at Bedminster and New Germantown, N. J. On Nov. 6, 1770, he married Anna Barbara Meyer of Philadelphia, who bore him four sons and two daughters and died a year before him. In 1771 he accepted a call to the German Lutheran congregation at Woodstock, Va., and, in order to secure the privileges of a clergyman of the Established Church, went to England and was ordained priest, Apr. 23, 1772, by the bishop of London. William White [q.v.] was ordained at the same time. Apparently Muhlenberg never received Lutheran ordination, and his status as a Luthero-Episcopalian is of considerable interest. His grandnephew, William Augustus Muhlenberg [q.v.], may well have had this precedent in mind when he proposed in 1853 that Episcopal ordination, under certain circumstances, be conferred on ministers of other denominations. Muhlenberg began work at Woodstock in the late summer or early autumn of 1772, and was soon the leader of the community. He was elected to the House of Burgesses in 1774, associated with the leaders of the Revolutionary party, and was made chairman of the committee on public safety for Dunmore County. In January 1776 he preached his farewell sermon, with Ecclesiastes, iii, 1, for his text, and at the close of the service cast off his clerical gown, revealing beneath it the uniform of a militia officer.

He raised and commanded the 8th Virginia Regiment, composed largely of Germans from the Shenandoah Valley, and gave a good account of himself at the battle of Sullivan's Island in June 1776. On Feb. 21, 1777, he was commissioned brigadier-general in the Continental Army and ordered north to Morristown, N. J. On Sept. 11 his brigade and Weedon's bore the brunt of the fighting at Brandywine, and on Oct. 8 he distinguished himself again at Germantown. He was stationed at Valley Forge that winter; was in charge of the second line of the right wing under Greene at Monmouth Court House, July 28, 1778; was with Putnam's division on the North River later in the year; and during the winter, while Putnam was detailed for other duties, commanded the division. He was in winter quarters at Middlebrook, N. J., 1778–79, and the next summer supported Anthony Wayne in the assault on Stony Point. In December 1779 Washington sent him to Virginia to take chief command in that state, but heavy snowfalls and impassable roads prevented him from reaching Richmond until March. In December Major-General Von Steuben succeeded to his position, and Muhlenberg became Steuben's second-in-command. He was engaged in most of the numerous but indecisive actions at this stage of the war, was in charge of the troops on the south bank of the James when Cornwallis was bottled up at Yorktown, and on Oct. 14, 1781, he commanded the American brigade that stormed one of the two British redoubts. In this action Alexander Hamilton, as senior colonel of the brigade, led the advance force. At the close of the war, on Sept. 30, 1783, Muhlenberg was brevetted major-general. He had proved himself a courageous, level-headed officer, strict in discipline, but vigilant for the welfare and comfort of his men, and possessed of marked executive ability.

After settling his affairs at Woodstock, he removed in 1783 to Philadelphia and made two journeys to Ohio and Kentucky to attend to the military bounty lands assigned to him and several of his friends, among them Von Steuben. His health had been permanently impaired by the war, and he was uneasy about his finances. A political career, however, was opening to him, for among the Germans of his native state he was a hero second only to Washington. He was elected to the Supreme Executive Council of the state in 1784, was vice-president of Pennsylvania, Franklin being president, 1785–88, and was influential in securing the early adoption of the Federal Constitution. Up to this time his inclinations had been toward the Federalists, but in 1788 the Republicans nominated him and his brother Frederick for congressmen-at-large, and they were triumphantly elected. Peter was thus a representative at large in the First Congress, 1789–91, and a representative for Montgomery County in the Third and Sixth congresses, 1793–95 and 1799–1801. In 1790 he was a member of the state constitutional convention. As a presidential elector he voted for Jefferson in 1796 and again as a member of the House of Representatives in 1801. He was president of the German Society of Pennsylvania in 1788 and 1801–07. On Feb. 18, 1801, he was elected to the United States Senate but resigned a month later in order to accept the appointment as supervisor of revenue for Philadelphia. From 1802 until his death he was collector of customs for Philadelphia.

In his political views he was a thorough Jeffersonian, but Jeffersonianism in him, as in its author, was not incompatible with a fundamentally aristocratic temper. In person he was tall, active of body, strikingly handsome, and courtly in manners. He died at his suburban home at Gray's Ferry on the Schuylkill (now part of Philadelphia) and was buried beside his father at the Augustus Church at Trappe. Patriotic historians and poets have commemorated his virtues and his deeds, and statues of him stand in City Hall Plaza, Philadelphia, and in Statuary Hall in the national Capitol.

[H. A. Muhlenberg, *The Life of Major-Gen. Peter Muhlenberg* (1849); H. M. M. Richards, "Descendants of H. M. Mühlenberg," *Proc. and Addresses Pa.-German Soc.*, vol. X (1900); William (Wilhelm) Germann, "The Crisis in the Early Life of General Peter Mühlenberg," *Pa. Mag. of Hist. and Biog.*, July, Oct., 1913, translated, without acknowledgment, from H. A. Rattermann's *Deutsch-Amerikanisches Magazin*, Oct. 1886, Jan., Apr., 1887; J. C. Honeyman, "Zion, St. Paul, and Other Early Luth. Churches in Central N. J.," *Proc. N. J. Hist. Soc.*, Apr., July 1928; C. W. Cassell, W. J. Finck, E. O. Henkel, *Hist. of the Luth. Church in Va. and East Tenn.* (Strasburg, Va., 1930); "Orderly Book of Gen. John Peter Gabriel Muhlenberg, Mar. 26–Dec. 20, 1777," *Pa. Mag. of Hist. and Biog.*, July, Oct. 1909, Jan.–Oct. 1910, Jan.–July 1911; Gaillard Hunt, *Calendar of Applications and Recommendations for Office during the Presidency of George Washington* (1901); "Letter to Col. Richard C. Anderson," *Mag. of Am. Hist.*, Nov. 1887, p. 440; *The Works of John Adams*, X (1856), p. 121; *The Journal of William Maclay* (1927); Washington and Jefferson Papers, Lib. of Cong.; Allan Nevins, *The Am. States During and After the Revolution, 1775–89* (1924); *Doc. Hist. Ev. Luth. Min. of Pa.*, 1748–1821 (1898); "Journal of Rev. Peter Muhlenberg in London, 1772," *Luth. Ch. Rev.*, Oct. 1885; *Aurora and General Advertiser* (Phila.), Oct. 2, 1807.]   G. H. G.

MUHLENBERG, WILLIAM AUGUSTUS Sept. 16, 1796–Apr. 8, 1877), Episcopal clergyman, was born in Philadelphia, the eldest of the three children of Henry William and Mary (Sheaff) Muhlenberg, and a grandson of Frederick Augustus Conrad Muhlenberg [*q.v.*]. He was baptized in the Lutheran Church by J. H. C. Helmuth and attended the Lutheran services for a few years of childhood, although he understood no German; but when his widowed mother sold a lot to St. James' Episcopal Church, the vestry gave her a pew, which she was too thrifty to leave unoccupied, and Muhlenberg accordingly grew up an Episcopalian. Even as a boy he displayed the delicate sensibilities and profound religious feeling that characterized him as a man. After graduating in 1815 from the University of Pennsylvania, he studied with Bishop White and Jackson Kemper, his assistant, was ordained deacon in 1817 and priest in 1820, and, having assisted White for three years, went to Lancaster in December 1820 as co-rector with Joseph Clarkson of St. James' and two filials. He remained at Lancaster until July 1826 and for the next two years was rector of St. George's, Flushing, L. I. These early years of his ministry were a period of preparation, busy but not altogether happy, for the half century of achievement still before him. His life was to be a series of experiments in broadening and enriching the work of the church.

For seventeen years his primary interest was in education. He was the founder, chief stockholder, and headmaster of Flushing Institute, a boys' school, which opened to receive pupils in the spring of 1828. Having purchased the tract of land on Long Island Sound known as College Point, he established St. Paul's College in 1838. Muhlenberg is traditionally regarded as one of the great schoolmasters of recent times: although the two institutions had but a short life, they proved what could be done in the way of education under Christian auspices, and they provided a model for many subsequent enterprises. The death of his beloved brother, Frederick Augustus, who had been closely associated with him in the work, the panic of 1837, the refusal of the New York legislature to grant degree-conferring privileges to a denominational school, and perhaps, too, his own restless imagination, made Muhlenberg lose interest in St. Paul's, and in 1843, after a visit to England and the Continent, he turned to a new enterprise.

This was the Church of the Holy Communion, which was erected at the corner of Sixth Avenue and 20th Street, New York, by his sister, Mrs. Mary A. Rogers, and of which he became rector in 1846. It was the first important free church of his denomination in the United States and became the seat of a highly developed and, at that time, unique parish life. One episode in the development of the parish was the founding in 1852 of the Sisterhood of the Holy Communion,

Muhlenberg

with Anne Ayres [q.v.] as the first member of the order. In this, as in several other innovations, Muhlenberg seems to have been inspired by Lutheran example. The best known of his many philanthropies, St. Luke's Hospital, originally built at Fifth Avenue and 34th Street, was also an outgrowth of the Church of the Holy Communion. Meanwhile, Muhlenberg became the leader of what was later known as the Memorial Movement and drafted the Memorial presented in 1853 to the House of Bishops. Among other things, the signers of the Memorial asked for certain reforms of the liturgy and for the episcopal ordination, under definite safeguards, of clergymen of other denominations. The Memorial, a noble, carefully reasoned statement of Muhlenberg's conception of the church, had little effect at the time, but it has been a subterranean influence on the thought of the Episcopal Church ever since. St. Luke's Hospital was incorporated in 1850, and after its opening in 1858 Muhlenberg resigned from the Church of the Holy Communion in order to give all his time to the Hospital, in which he made his home till his death. Like his other enterprises it was highly successful and has been frequently imitated. The last of his foundations was St. Johnsland, incorporated in 1870, an experiment in Christian communal life. It consisted of a small industrial community on the north side of Long Island, with schools, a church, an orphanage, and a home for old people. Less successful than his earlier experiments, it was in some ways the most characteristic, and was the darling of his old age.

He also influenced strongly the development of hymnody in the Episcopal Church. Of his own compositions, the sentimental "I would not live alway" (written 1824) was the best known. In later years its author became ashamed of it and tried to rewrite it in conformity with his maturer thought, but without effect. Much more representative of his religious verse is the fine baptismal hymn, "Saviour, Who Thy flock art feeding" (1826). He made visits to Europe in 1855 and again in 1872. In 1874 an attack of malarial fever left him permanently weak, and thereafter body and mind declined slowly together. Reverenced as one of the prophets of his church, he died in his hospital on Apr. 8, 1877, and was buried at St. Johnsland.

[Anne Ayres, *The Life and Work of William Augustus Muhlenberg* (1880; 4th ed., 1889); W. W. Newton, *Dr. Muhlenberg* (1890); H. E. Jacobs, "'A Common-Place Lutheran,'" *Luth. Ch. Rev.*, Apr. 1890; Alonzo Potter, *The Memorial* (1857); Hall Harrison, *Life of the Right Rev. John Barrett Kerfoot* (2 vols., 1886); N. O. Halsted, "Dr. Muhlenberg and Saint Johnland," *Pa.-Ger.*, Apr. 1905; Robert Abbe, "A New View of the Boyhood of the Rev. Dr. Muhlenberg," *Medic. Jour. and Record*, Nov. 17, 1926; *N. Y. Tribune*, Apr. 9, 1877; *Eve. Post* (N. Y.), Apr. 6, 9, 1877; John Julian, *A Dict. of Hymnology* (rev. ed., London, 1907). C. C. Tiffany, *A Hist. of the Protestant Episcopal Church in the U. S. A.* (1895); E. Harwood and G. D. Wildes, *In Memory of William Augustus Muhlenberg, D.D., LL.D.* (1877); E. A. Washburn, *Sermons in Memorial of William Augustus Muhlenberg, D.D.* (1877); *Churchman* (Hartford, Conn.), Apr. 14, 21, 1877; E. A. Washburn, "Dr. Muhlenberg," *Ibid.*, May 5, 1877.]
G. H. G.

Muir

MUIR, JOHN (Apr. 21, 1838–Dec. 24, 1914), naturalist and explorer, was born at Dunbar, Scotland. His ancestry was Scotch both on his father's and on his mother's side. Daniel Muir married Anne Gilrye of Dunbar in 1833. John Muir was the eldest son and the third in a succession of five daughters and three sons. His early education, to the age of eleven, was secured in the schools of Dunbar. The ordinary subjects of instruction included also Latin and French, and in addition to the school tasks his father imposed the daily memorizing of a certain number of verses in the King James version of the Bible. This extra task was exacted by his father with military precision and enforced with much corporal punishment. Though grievous at the time, this memory work undoubtedly contributed much to the formation of his engaging English style. In 1849 Daniel Muir emigrated to America, taking along with him three of the older children, Sarah, David, and John. The remainder of the family followed after a homestead had been established in the wilds of Wisconsin, not far from Portage. Muir's autobiographical volume, *The Story of My Boyhood and Youth* (1913), furnishes a vivid account of his experiences on the Wisconsin farm. With relentless severity his father exacted from him all kinds of adult labor when he was a mere boy. Such farm labor included rail-splitting, fencing, plowing, hoeing maize, mowing with the scythe, and cutting grain with the cradle. He was no doubt right in thinking that the long hours and severe labor of the farm so far exceeded his strength that it checked his growth. John had a consuming desire for knowledge and read every book he could buy, exchange, or borrow for miles around. His father would not let him read in the evening, but said he might rise as early as he liked. Fearing to lose precious morning hours, and being "an ingenious whittler," he made a wooden clock, pivoted his bed on a crossbar, and hitched the clock to it by a special contrivance which he called "an early-rising machine" and which could be depended upon to set him on his feet at any desired time in the morning. By this heroic means he managed to acquire a sufficient general education to enable him

314

to enter the University of Wisconsin when he came of age. A variety of astonishingly ingenious mechanical inventions, exhibited in 1860 at the Wisconsin State Fair in Madison, brought him to the favorable notice of the university authorities.

Muir took no degree when he left his university in 1863, because he preferred to choose his studies rather than conform to a prescribed curriculum. Chemistry and geology were his major interests. At the close of his college career botany became an absorbing passion which sent him on extensive foot-tours through Wisconsin, Iowa, Illinois, Indiana, and into Canada. In 1867, while employed in a wagon factory in Indianapolis, he suffered an accidental injury to one of his eyes. This occurrence decided him to "bid adieu to mechanical inventions" and devote the rest of his life "to the study of the inventions of God." Under the urge of this determination he started off at once on foot from Indiana to the Gulf of Mexico. He kept a journal in which he entered day by day his observations on the flora, the forests, physiography of the country, and experiences with the inhabitants. He also confided to it his personal reflections on man's attitude toward nature, the animal world, and the processes of life and death. The journal is important for an understanding of Muir at this stage of his career. It was edited by the writer after Muir's death under the title of *A Thousand-Mile Walk to the Gulf* (1916). He arrived in California in 1868 and immediately went to Yosemite Valley which remained the center of his studies and explorations for about six years. Then Nevada, Utah, the Northwest, and Alaska attracted him. On all his excursions he kept a journal in which he noted his observations, interspersed with abundant pencil sketches. These notebooks, of which seventy or more survive, formed the raw materials of his books and articles.

On Apr. 14, 1880, Muir married Louie Wanda Strentzel, the only surviving child of Dr. John Strentzel, an expatriate Pole who sought refuge in America after the unsuccessful Polish revolution of 1830. After some years of pioneering in Texas, where he had married Louisiana Erwin, a native of Tennessee, Strentzel had joined the Clarksville train of emigrants to California in 1849. Settling in the Alhambra Valley near Martinez, he soon became one of the most noted of the early horticulturists of the state. After his marriage Muir first rented and later bought from his father-in-law a part of the Strentzel fruit ranch, and then proceeded with great thoroughness to master the art of horticulture, for which

he possessed natural aptitude. During the decade from 1881 to 1891 he wrote and traveled little, devoting his attention wholly to the winning of a competence. This he did so successfully that at the end of this period he had, by his own testimony, enough money to provide permanently for his wife, his two daughters, and his own needs. He then sold a part of the ranch and leased the rest, in order to be able to devote the remainder of his life to travel and study.

As a naturalist Muir was interested in all the life and phenomena of the natural world. But he gave the most enthusiastic and continuous study to glaciers and forests. He was the first to demonstrate the origin of Yosemite Valley by glacial erosion (Badè, *Life and Letters of John Muir,* vol. I, ch. ix), opposing the views of Whitney and other scientists of the time. The generic use of the word "yosemite" was originated by him, for he saw clearly that it was only a type of valley similarly formed. After his discovery of residual glaciers in the Sierra Nevada, he extended his explorations into Alaska, discovering and describing many great glaciers, among them the one which now bears his name. The study of trees, particularly the sequoias and the pines, was another great passion of his life, and he made special journeys to Australia, Africa, and South America, in order to see the most impressive forest trees of these countries. On some of his expeditions to study trees in Alaska and in the Alleghanies he was accompanied by Charles S. Sargent [q.v.], director of the Arnold Arboretum, who dedicated to him the eleventh volume of his *Silva,* devoted to the *Coniferæ.*

In 1889 John Muir took Robert Underwood Johnson, then one of the editors of the *Century Magazine,* on a camping tour in the region of Yosemite Valley and the adjacent Tuolumne watershed, and showed him the devastation wrought by uncountable hordes of sheep. At Johnson's suggestion, they jointly determined to initiate a campaign for the establishment of what is now the Yosemite National Park. During the preceding decade Muir had written for *Scribner's Monthly* and the *Century* a series of brilliant articles on Western forests and scenery, which had a profound educative effect upon the public mind. One result was that public-spirited men all over the country rallied to the support of the Muir-Johnson movement; and one of the great conservation eras of our country began with the passage of the Yosemite National Park bill by Congress in October 1890. In the following year Congress passed an act empowering the president to create forest reserves. As early as 1876 Muir had proposed the appointment of a national commission to inquire into the fearful wastage of forests, to make a survey of existing forest lands in public ownership, and to recommend measures for their conservation. When at last such a commission was appointed in 1896, Charles S. Sargent, its chairman, invited John Muir to accompany the party on its tour of investigation. The Forestry Commission reported in 1897 and on the basis of its recommendations President Cleveland created thirteen forest reservations comprising more than twenty-one million acres. Predatory interests immediately sought to nullify the reserves by congressional action, and through their tools in Congress, succeeded in restoring to the public domain until Mar. 1, 1898, all forest reservations created by Cleveland, except those of California.

In the battle which now was joined, in Muir's phrase, "between landscape righteousness and the devil," he found his greatest opportunity for public service. Two brilliant articles, one in *Harper's Weekly* (June 5, 1897), entitled "Forest Reservations and National Parks," the other written at the request of Walter Hines Page for the *Atlantic Monthly* (August 1897) on "The American Forests," turned the tide of public sentiment. In both these articles Muir's style rose to the impassioned oratory of a Hebrew prophet arraigning wickedness in high places and preaching the sacred duty of so using the country we live in that we may not leave it ravished by greed and ignorance, but may pass it on to future generations undiminished in richness and beauty. Muir's invective caught the public ear and became effective in Congress, for when in 1898 enemies of the reservation policy again started a move to annul the reservations it failed. John F. Lacey, then chairman of the public lands committee of the House, insisted that Muir's judgment was probably better than that of any of his opponents. Muir had now become the acknowledged leader of the forest conservation movement in the United States. In the spring of 1903 he went on a brief camping trip in and about Yosemite with Theodore Roosevelt, then in his first term as president. Muir used the opportunity to expound to a willing and sympathetic listener his views on the urgent need of more forest reserves and national parks. The following six years of Roosevelt's presidency were distinguished by the setting aside of 148,000,000 acres of additional forest reserves, the establishment of sixteen national monuments, and the doubling of the number of national parks. In the accomplishment of this result Muir's informed enthusiasm played an imponderable but influential part. The last six years of Muir's life were saddened by the unsuccessful struggle to preserve the beautiful Hetch-Hetchy Valley in the Yosemite National Park from conversion into a reservoir. Although a Board of Army Engineers had reported that "several sources of water supply could be obtained and used by the city of San Francisco," political intrigue, misrepresentation, and commercial considerations prevailed, to quote Muir, "over the best aroused sentiment of the entire country." One result of his leadership of the opposition was the consolidation of public sentiment against any possible repetition of such a raid.

Muir was a man of medium height, lithe, spare of frame, and during his prime was possessed of extraordinary powers of physical endurance. He was auburn-haired, had inquiring blue eyes, and an engaging personality. "The impression of his personality," wrote David Starr Jordan, "was so strong on those who knew him, that all words seem cheap beside it." His conversation was easy, vivid, and interspersed with flashes of delicious humor. In a conversational argument Muir was a formidable opponent, for he was quick at repartee and had an instinctive gift for seizing the essence of an issue and condensing it into a pungent phrase, like his description of sheep in forests as "hoofed locusts." According to the unanimous testimony of friends who knew him during the seventies and eighties he was an absorbingly fascinating talker, and it was the effect produced upon them by his conversation and letters that led them persistently to urge him to write for publication (*Life and Letters,* vol. II, pp. 6–7), a task which he always found more or less irksome. In his nature philosophy he was a theist with strong leanings toward Emerson and Thoreau, yet quite unlike either of them. With the mechanistic tendencies of his friend and contemporary John Burroughs he found himself at variance. He was a fellow of the American Association for the Advancement of Science, a member of the American Academy of Arts and Sciences, and he was the recipient of honorary degrees from the universities of Harvard, Wisconsin, Yale, and California, in the order mentioned. He died in Los Angeles and his remains were laid to rest beside those of his wife on his ranch near Martinez. Muir's books published during his lifetime, in addition to *The Story of My Boyhood and Youth,* include: *The Mountains of California* (1894); *Our National Parks* (1901); *Stickeen* (1909); *My First Summer in the Sierra* (1911); and *The Yosemite* (1912). Published posthumously were: *Travels in Alaska* (1915); *A Thousand-Mile Walk to the*

Gulf (1916) ; *The Cruise of the Corwin* (1917) ; and *Steep Trails* (1918).

[See: W. F. Badè, ed., *The Life and Letters of John Muir* (2 vols., 1923–24) ; S. Hall Young, *Alaska Days with John Muir* (1915) ; H. F. Osborn, *Impressions of Great Naturalists* (1924) ; R. U. Johnson, *Remembered Yesterdays* (1923) and "John Muir," in *Proc. Am. Acad. Arts and Letters*, vol. IX (1916) ; *Who's Who in America*, 1912–13 ; *Los Angeles Daily Times*, Dec. 25, 1914.]

W. F. B.

MULFORD, ELISHA (Nov. 19, 1833–Dec. 9, 1885), Protestant Episcopal clergyman, teacher, and author, was born in Montrose, Pa., the son of Silvanus Sandford Mulford. He prepared for college in the academy at Homer, N. Y., and entered the sophomore class at Yale, from which institution he graduated in 1855. Deciding to enter the ministry, he studied at Union Seminary, New York City, and at Andover Seminary, Andover, Mass. Later, he traveled abroad, studying at Berlin, Heidelberg, and Halle. He then became a clergyman in the Episcopal Church, being ordained deacon by Bishop Williams at Middletown, Conn., Apr. 20, 1861, and priest, by Bishop Odenheimer, at South Orange, N. J., Mar. 19, 1862. On Sept. 17 of the latter year he was married to Rachel Price Carmalt of Lakeside, Pa. After serving as rector in South Orange, he retired from the active ministry in 1864 (because of deafness) and moved to Lakeside, Pa., where he devoted himself to study and writing. In 1870 he published *The Nation,* and ten years later, *The Republic of God* (1880). Removing to Cambridge, Mass., in 1880, he became a lecturer in theology and apologetics in the Episcopal Theological School (1881 to 1885). He died at Cambridge and was buried in Sleepy Hollow Cemetery, Concord, Mass.

Mulford was preëminently a student, scholar, and writer. He was especially influenced in his philosophical and religious thinking by Hegel, Stahl, Trendelenburg, and Bluntschli, and, among English theologians, by Frederick Denison Maurice, whom he personally knew. He read largely in science, economics, social philosophy, art, and literature. His book *The Nation* is a well ordered and serious effort to define the substance and purpose of the state, reviewing the theories of its origin and development from Plato's ideas to those of Rousseau and modern philosophical writers. In it he attempts to show that the doctrines which regard the nation as an historical accident, or as a jural society or an economic society, are vague and partly untrue. The nation is an organism, a personality responding in its total life to ethical ideals, and cannot perform its proper function of progress and helpfulness without an everliving ethical conscious-

ness, fulfilling a divine purpose. The nation and its history is God in history working to a purposeful end. The later work, *The Republic of God,* was more distinctly a theological book, written with a background of historical religious scholarship and a new and modern spiritual outlook. The central theme of theism and Christianity is illustrated by skilful arguments drawn from literature, science, and art, as well as from philosophy. The antithesis between the kingdom of God and the republic of God brings out the dignity and responsibility of the individual who in human society becomes a kingly citizen to benefit the whole. As a teacher in the theological school, Mulford was inspiring and reverent, always connecting religion with life as well as with thought.

[*Obit. Records of Grads. of Yale Coll.,* 1886 ; C. D. Warner, *Lib. of the World's Best Literature,* vol. XVIII (1897) ; T. T. Munger, in *Independent,* Jan. 7, 1886, and *Century,* Apr. 1888 ; *Boston Transcript,* Dec. 10, 1885 ; appreciation by A. V. G. Allen (MS.) in Wright Memorial Lib., Cambridge, Mass. ; information as to certain facts from members of the family.]

D. D. A.

MULFORD, PRENTICE (Apr. 5, 1834–*c.* May 27, 1891), journalist, philosopher, was born to Ezekiel and Julia (Prentice) Mulford at Sag Harbor, Long Island. Named for his maternal grandfather, Amos Prentice, he seems never to have used the first name. He grew up in Sag Harbor, at sixteen was working in his father's hotel, spent a few months at the state normal school but soon abandoned the idea of becoming a teacher, held a job as clerk in New York City for a year, then one in Illinois, and, having returned to Sag Harbor, at twenty-one shipped on board the clipper *Wizard,* bound for San Francisco. Upon reaching that port late in 1856, he was told by the captain that he was "not cut out for a sailor," and discharged from the crew. After a few months in San Francisco, he shipped with the schooner *Henry* down the California coast. Lured by the gold fields, he went in 1858 to Hawkins' Bar on the Tuolumne River, but prospecting proved unprofitable and accordingly, he taught school for two years in a mining camp in Tuolumne County. During the copper fever of 1862–63, he became, he says, "a copper expert," sinking unsuccessful shafts on his gold claim near Swett's Bar. Next came the silver excitement, but by this time he was finding more remuneration in other fields. In March 1865 he tramped to Sonora, Cal., to begin his career as a comic lecturer, and about the same time began to contribute poems and essays to the Sonora *Union Democrat* under the pen name, "Dogberry." In the political campaign of 1866–67 he was a candidate for the state assembly, but failed of election.

Through his "Dogberry" articles in the *Union Democrat,* he had, he says, "gained a small county but cashless reputation" (*Prentice Mulford's Story,* ed. of 1913, p. 260) and in 1866 Joseph Lawrence of the *Golden Era,* then the leading literary weekly west of the Mississippi, numbering among its contributors Bret Harte and Mark Twain, called him to San Francisco. During the next five years he wrote for several papers, including the *Dramatic Chronicle,* forerunner of the *San Francisco Chronicle,* and for a few months in 1868 edited the Stockton *Gazette,* a Democratic campaign paper. In 1872 he sailed for Europe, "to advance by writing and talking the good and glory of California" (*Ibid.,* p. 296), the mission being financed by San Francisco business men. He remained for a time in London, recording his impressions in letters to the San Francisco *Bulletin,* for which he also reported the Vienna world's fair. When he returned to New York in 1873 with but nine dollars in cash, he brought a young English girl as his bride. According to all accounts she was charming and exceedingly attractive, but the marriage was not successful and after a few years there was an amicable separation. In New York Mulford lectured for a time, but in the middle seventies joined the *Daily Graphic,* then under David G. Croly [*q.v.*], creating the column of condensed local news called "The History of a Day." Sick, after six years, of the sordid routine of this work, he gave up his job and retired alone to a small cabin which he built himself in the New Jersey woods near Passaic. In *The Swamp Angel,* published in 1888, he humorously described some of his experiences. The following year he published *Prentice Mulford's Story,* an account of his life up to the time of his leaving California.

While in the New Jersey wilderness, Mulford began to write the philosophical essays known as the White Cross Library. He published the first of these in Boston in May 1886, and for several years thereafter issued one a month, in pamphlet form. They were later collected in six volumes under the title, *Your Forces and How to Use Them.* In these essays and in the lectures he gave during the same period he expounded many of the ideas comprehended in the system of popular philosophy which came to be known as "New Thought." He maintained that the individual, by controlling his thought, directing it toward worthy objects, and cultivating a serene and confident attitude of mind, can achieve health and success. He believed in the evolu-

tion of man through a series of reincarnations leading toward the final perfection of the spirit and the loss of the "material parts that decay." Though his literary style lacked grace and was often actually crude, it was characterized by a directness and force which gained him an increasing number of readers, who found encouragement in his teachings. The quality of his thought brought a tribute from Whittier, who in the little poem, "Mulford," speaks of him as "a sage and seer." On May 24, 1891, having been troubled and depressed for some time (*National Magazine,* September 1906, p. 568), he set out in a dory for a solitary cruise along the south shore of Long Island, seeking quiet and a chance to order his thoughts. On May 30 he was found dead in his boat, which had been anchored in Sheepshead Bay since the morning of the 27th. His body, identified the next day by an intimate friend, was placed on June 2 in the family vault at Sag Harbor.

[*About Prentice Mulford* (1891), White Cross Library, no. 64; C. W. Stoddard, in *Nat. Mag.,* Apr. 1905; Sept. 1906; *Prentice Mulford's Story* (London, 1913); E. M. Martin, *Prentice Mulford, "New Thought" Pioneer* (1921); *Occult Review,* Mar. 1910, Jan. 1916; *A Hist. of Tuolumne County, Cal.* (1882); E. S. C. Mighels, *The Story of the Files* (1893); C. J. F. Binney, *The Hist. and Geneal. of the Prentice or Prentiss Family* (1883); *N. Y. Times,* June 1, 1891; information as to first name from H. D. Sleight, Sag Harbor, L. I.]　　　　　　　I. V–F.

MULHOLLAND, ST. CLAIR AUGUSTIN (Apr. 1, 1839–Feb. 17, 1910), Union soldier, was a native of Ireland, being born in Lisburn, County Antrim, the son of Henry and Georgina (St. Clair) Mulholland. When he was but a boy, his parents emigrated to the United States and settled in Philadelphia, where young Mulholland received his early education. He became active in local militia organizations, and as a first lieutenant, assisted in organizing the 116th Pennsylvania Volunteers for Civil War service. He was appointed lieutenant-colonel of the regiment, June 26, 1862, and received his first wound in the charge of the Irish Brigade up Marye's Heights, Fredericksburg, Va., Dec. 13, 1862. His regiment being subsequently consolidated into a battalion, Mulholland was mustered out Feb. 24, 1863, and three days later, recommissioned major. At the battle of Chancellorsville, May 3–4, 1863, he distinguished himself by recapturing the guns of the 5th Maine Battery, and brilliantly commanded the picket-line covering the withdrawal of the Army of the Potomac across the Rappahannock River. The latter hazardous duty won for him the official commendation of Maj.-Gen. John Hancock, and the award, years later (Mar. 26, 1895), of the Congressional Medal of Honor. At Gettysburg, July

Mullan   Mullan

1–3, 1863, his own regiment having been seriously disorganized in the first day's battle, Mulholland led the 140th Pennsylvania Volunteers into action; and upon the reorganization of the 116th Pennsylvania Volunteers, was commissioned its colonel, May 3, 1864. In the Wilderness, May 5, 1864, he received his second wound, and for gallantry in action was subsequently brevetted (Mar. 13, 1865) brigadier-general of volunteers. At Po River (May 10, 1864), he was again wounded, but after a short convalescence returned to his command and on May 31 was dangerously wounded at Tolopotomy Creek. On Oct. 15, 1864, he assumed command of the 4th Brigade, 1st Division, II Army Corps, and participated in all the operations around Petersburg, Va. For gallantry at Boydton Plank Road, Oct. 27, 1864, in charging and capturing Confederate fortifications, he received, Mar. 13, 1865, the brevet of major-general of volunteers. He was honorably mustered out of the military service, June 3, 1865, and returned to his home in Philadelphia, where he served efficiently (1868–71) as the city's chief of police. President Cleveland appointed him United States pension agent at Philadelphia, which office he held for twelve years, through the administrations of Presidents McKinley and Roosevelt. In his spare hours, Mulholland devoted much time to art studies, and to the preparation of articles and lectures on the Civil War. He was also regarded as an authority on the subject of penology. In the year 1864 he was married to Mary Dooner, by whom he had three daughters and a son; and subsequently, to Mary Josephine Leeman, by whom he had two daughters.

[See Mulholland's *The Story of the 116th Regiment, Pa. Infantry* (1899) and *Mil. Order: Cong. Medal of Honor Legion of the U. S.* (1905); F. B. Heitman, *Hist. Reg. and Dict. of the U. S. Army* (1903), vol. I; D. P. Conyngham, *The Irish Brigade and Its Campaigns* (1867); *Who's Who in Pa.* (2nd ed., 1908); *The Cath. Encyc.*; *Cath. Standard and Times* (Phila.), Feb. 26, 1910; the *Press* (Phila.), Feb. 18, 1910. The spelling of Mulholland's middle name follows *Who's Who in Pa.* Heitman gives Agustin; the *Cath. Encyc.*, Augustine.]   C.D.R.

MULLAN, JOHN (July 31, 1830–Dec. 28, 1909), explorer, pioneer road-builder, was the son of John Mullan, a native of Ireland, and of Mary (Bright) Mullan, an American. He was born at Norfolk, Va., the first of ten children, but when he was three years old the family moved to Annapolis, Md. His parents, though poor, determined to give him an education. At nine he entered the grammar school of St. John's College, where he was graduated A.B. in 1847. In 1848, finding himself without a job or a profession, he sought admission to the United States Military Academy, interviewing President Polk, who soon afterward gave him an appointment. In 1852 he graduated, fifteenth in his class, and was assigned first to the topographical engineers and then to the artillery.

In 1853 he joined Gen. I. I. Stevens [q.v.] in exploring a route for a railroad from St. Paul to the Pacific. Stevens sent him on a mission of friendship to the Flatheads who were reported in camp on the Mussel-shell River, and Mullan followed the Indians, who were moving about, and brought them to a conference. He was then sent, during the winter, to the Bitterroot to examine the mountain passes. He explored the Rocky Mountains southward to Fort Hall on the Snake River and north to Canada, discovering Mullan Pass. According to General Stevens, he "made remarkable contributions to existing knowledge, both of the snows and the geography of the country, at a season of the year and under circumstances when most men would have done nothing" ("Narrative," *post,* p. 182).

Promoted first lieutenant in 1855, Mullan was recalled to active military duty and spent two years in the South fighting the Seminoles. Meanwhile Congress authorized the construction of a military road from Fort Benton to Walla Walla to connect navigation on the Missouri with that on the Columbia. Mullan's fine record of exploration won for him the position of chief of construction. While he was on his way to begin work the Indians became hostile and he found that his first task was to fight them. He distinguished himself in the battle of the Four Lakes, Sept. 1, 1858, and in other encounters. When the Indian war was over he found his resources exhausted and went to Washington to secure a new appropriation. He was aided by Stevens, then delegate to Congress, and in March 1859 that body appropriated $100,000 to begin construction. Mullan's surveys of 1853 and 1854 made selection of a route easy; work was begun in the summer of 1859, and continued till the spring of 1863 (John Mullan, *Report on the Construction of a Military Road from Fort Walla Walla to Fort Benton,* 1863). In 1860, while the road was under construction, Maj. Blake with 400 troops conducted the first wagon train over it and for the next twenty years it was a highway for immigrants to the Northwest. In 1862 Mullan urged the building of a new road from Deer Lodge Valley to the Yellowstone, then south to the Platte, anticipating the Bozeman road, but the government was too busy with war to pay attention to this recommendation.

On Apr. 28, 1863, Mullan and Rebecca Williamson were married. To them five children

319

were born, three of whom survived their father. Soon after his marriage he resigned from the army and started a huge ranch near Walla Walla which failed the next year. He then obtained a four-year contract to carry the mail from Chico, California to Ruby City, Idaho, a distance of 600 miles, at the rate of $75,000 a year, and attempted to establish an express business, but within a year was forced out of business by a competitor and gave up his contract. Settling in San Francisco, he began the practice of law and was quite successful. In 1865 he published *Miners' and Travelers' Guide to Oregon, Washington, Idaho, Montana, Wyoming, and Colorado via the Missouri and Columbia Rivers.* He moved to Washington, D. C., in 1878, and there continued his legal work until failing health forced his retirement. He died in Washington.

[I. I. Stevens, "Narrative and Final Report of Explorations for a Route for a Pacific Railroad ... from St. Paul to Puget Sound," in *Explorations and Surveys ... for a Railroad Route from the Mississippi River to the Pacific Ocean,* vol. XII (1855); Lawrence Kip, *Army Life on the Pacific* (1859); G. W. Cullum, *Biog. Reg. Officers and Grads. U. S. Mil. Acad.* (3rd ed., 1891); *Army and Navy Jour.,* Jan. 1, 1910; *Evening Star* (Washington), Dec. 29, 1909; Mullan's journal from Fort Dalles to Fort Walla Walla, July 1858, ed. by Pal Clark, in *The Frontier* (Missoula, Mont.), May 1932; *Contribs. to the Hist. Soc. of Mont.,* VIII (1917), 162–69; D. A. Willey, "Building the M. R.," in *Sunset,* June 1910; clippings and memoir by Rebecca W. Mullan in the possession of a daughter, Mrs. Henry H. Flather, Tulip Hill, Md., and Washington, D. C.]
P. C. P.

MULLANY, JAMES ROBERT MADISON (Oct. 26, 1818–Sept. 17, 1887), naval officer, was born in New York, the son of Col. James R. Mullany, quartermaster-general of the army, and Maria (Burger) Mullany. Appointed midshipman from New Jersey on Jan. 7, 1832, he served for three years on the *Constellation,* and, after an intermission, for two years on the *United States,* both of the Mediterranean Squadron. His first assignments to sea duty, after being warranted passed midshipman in 1838, were to the *Dolphin* of the Brazil Squadron in 1839 and to the *Missouri* of the home squadron in 1841. After serving as acting master of the *Somers,* he was in July 1844, a few months after obtaining his lieutenancy, ordered to the Coast Survey where he remained for four years. In the years 1848–50 he served on the *St. Louis* and the *Brandywine* of the Brazil Squadron; and from 1852 to 1855 on board the *Columbia* of the home squadron. After a term of four years at the New York navy yard on ordnance duty, he in 1859 again joined the home squadron and was serving therein on the *Sabine* at the outbreak of the Civil War.

During April and May, 1861, Mullany commanded, successively, the *Wyandotte* and *Supply*

at Pensacola and aided in the defense of Fort Pickens. Promoted commander from Oct. 18, 1861, he was in the spring of the following year placed in command of the *Bienville,* a position that he held for more than three years, with the exception of a few days in August 1864, at the time of the battle of Mobile Bay. As the *Bienville* was not fit to engage the Confederate forts defending Mobile, he volunteered for service on some other vessel and was assigned the *Oneida* by Admiral Farragut. This ship held a position at the rear end of the line of battle and suffered considerable damage while passing the forts. In her engagement with the ram *Tennessee* Mullany received several wounds, one of which necessitated the amputation of his left arm. For his brave conduct he was commended by Admiral Farragut. During the war he was elsewhere several times under fire. In 1862 he captured off the South Carolina coast several blockade runners and in 1863 he commanded a division of the West Gulf blockading squadron operating off the coast of Texas.

Mullany was promoted captain in 1866, commodore in 1870, and rear admiral in 1874. In the years 1868–70 he commanded the *Richmond* of the European fleet; in 1870–71, the Mediterranean Squadron; and from 1874 to 1876, the North Atlantic station. At the time of his retirement on Oct. 26, 1879, he was governor of the naval asylum at Philadelphia, in which city he made his home. Mullany was twice married. He was a communicant of the Roman Catholic Church. The torpedo boat destroyer *Mullany* was named for him.

[Record of Officers, Bureau of Navigation, 1832–93; *War of the Rebellion: Official Records* (Navy), 1 ser. IV, XII, XIII, XX–XXII; *Army and Navy Jour.,* Sept. 24, 1887; *N. Y. Tribune,* Sept. 18, 1887.]
C. O. P.

MULLANY, PATRICK FRANCIS [See AZARIAS, BROTHER, 1847–1893].

MÜLLER, WILHELM MAX (May 15, 1862–July 12, 1919), Orientalist, was born at Gliessenberg, Bavaria, the son of Frederic and Pauline (Barthel) Müller. He was reared in a devoutly religious home and, when prepared for university studies, went to Erlangen, then a center of Lutheran theological learning. Later he attended the universities of Berlin, Munich, and Leipzig, receiving from the last-mentioned the degree of Ph.D. He was an able linguist. It is said that he could speak both Greek and Hebrew, but his fame as a scholar rests upon his contributions to the science of Egyptology. He was well grounded in Egyptian, having been at Berlin a pupil of Adolf Erman, and, while working in the Museum at Munich, made his first important contribution to the subject. In 1888 he came to the United States, and on Apr. 13, 1889, he was married to Bettie Caspar of New York. In 1890 he was made professor of ancient languages and Old and New Testament exegesis in the Theological Seminary of the Reformed Episcopal Church in Philadelphia, a position which he held until his death. He was an excellent teacher and his accurate scholarship and simple piety made a deep impression upon his students. Here for almost thirty years he taught Hebrew and Greek, although nearly all of his publications were in the field of Egyptology. His Egyptological researches were carried on in his spare hours.

His earliest book, *Asien und Europa nach altägyptischen Denkmälern* (1893), at once took its place as the chief authority on the subject. His next book, *Die Liebpoesie der alten Ägypter* (1899), which contained Egyptian poems in hieroglyphic and demotic, together with translations into German, placed within the reach of students of the Bible Egyptian expressions of the tender passion, comparable in many ways to the Song of Songs. Like his earlier book, it gave evidence of competent scholarship. Through the good offices of Dr. S. Weir Mitchell [*q.v.*], Müller was sent to Egypt by the Carnegie Institution in the summer of 1904 to prosecute researches there. Although summer is the worst time to visit Egypt, it was the only time that his duties as a teacher would permit him to go. His work was so successful that he was sent back in 1906 and again in 1910. This last visit proved so great a strain upon his health that he did not go again. The fruit of these expeditions he published in *Egyptological Researches,* Volumes I and II (1906–10). A third volume, nearly ready for publication at the time of his death, was edited by H. F. Lutz and published in 1920. His other principal work was "Egyptian Mythology" in Volume XII of Louis H. Gray's *Mythology of all Races* (1918). In addition to these books, he was a contributor to the *Encyclopædia Biblica,* the *Jewish Encyclopedia,* to various revisions of Gesenius' Hebrew dictionary, and to Oriental journals.

During the last few years of his life he became assistant professor of Egyptology in the University of Pennsylvania in connection with his professorship in the Theological Seminary. He was never fully understood by some persons and possessed in his adopted country a narrower circle of friends than many scholars. Foreign scholars, however, appreciated his work, and, when passing through Philadelphia, many of

them sought him out. During the trying years of the World War he was thoroughly loyal to the United States. He borrowed money with which to buy a "liberty bond" and paid it back in instalments at considerable sacrifice. He was drowned at Wildwood, N. J., while swimming alone.

[*Jour. Am. Oriental Soc.,* Oct. 1919; *Who's Who in America,* 1918–19; *Pub. Ledger* (Phila.), July 13, 1919; *N. Y. Times,* July 13, 1919; personal information.]   G. A. B.

MULLIGAN, CHARLES J. (Sept. 28, 1866–Mar. 25, 1916), sculptor, was born in Riverdale, County Tyrone, Ireland, in humble circumstances, and came to this country at the age of seventeen. A vigorous boy, with a passion for work, he found employment as a stone-cutter in Pullman, near Chicago, Ill. Here he was discovered by the sculptor Lorado Taft, who was trying to forward artistic craftsmanship by means of a small vocational school in Pullman. Soon Taft received him as pupil-assistant in his own studio in Chicago and first called upon the apprentice to help in the carving of a marble bust. The master noted that this young Irishman of twenty had not only a skilful hand and an active imagination, but also a radiant personality which kindled the enthusiasm of the students in the evening classes of the Art Institute of Chicago, where "Charley," not content with hard work all day long, spent three evenings a week in modeling. Perhaps his greatest service to art was the inspiration he gave to others. In addition to his Art Institute training, he had a brief period of study in Paris, under Alexandre Falguière. In 1891 he was chosen by Taft to be the foreman of his Exposition workshop. Though cleverer artists than the new director were busy there, the manliness and tact of Mulligan minimized friction and brought about an atmosphere of harmony. His earliest attempts in creative work revealed his aspiration to become "the prophet of hopeful, cheerful labor." At the Buffalo Exposition, 1901, his statue "The Digger" attracted attention by its lively sincerity, while his four architectural figures of workingmen for the Illinois building stood forth as unusually good examples in this field. Later, his "Miner and Child," or "Home," an interesting pyramidal group in marble, showed his advance in technical competence, and in the expression of profound feeling. It is now in Humboldt Park, Chicago. Garfield Park, of the same city, has his statues of "Lincoln as Railsplitter," and of John F. Finerty; his "President McKinley" is in McKinley Park.

Mulligan never turned over his plaster models to be carved and finished in stone or marble by a practitioner, as is often the case. His ideal was to do his carving himself, and as he did not despise valuable mechanical aids, he had a pneumatic tool outfit in his studio. He was popular among his artist companions in Chicago and was instrumental in forming the nucleus of the artist colony, "Eagle's Nest," later established in Oregon, Ill. He was one of the founders of the Palette and Chisel Club; a member of the Society of Western Artists, Society of Chicago Artists, Beaux Arts Club, the Cliff Dwellers, and the Irish Fellowship Club. After Taft's resignation as head of the department of sculpture at the Art Institute, Mulligan was chosen to this position, in which he remained until his death. Among his many works in the West and South are "Justice and Power," with "Law and Knowledge," a pair of entrance groups for the State House, Springfield, Ill.; an impressive statue of Gen. George Rogers Clark, Quincy, Ill.; the soldiers' monument at Decatur, Ind.; and the Illinois monument, depicting Lincoln, the president, Grant, the warrior, and Yates, the governor, at Vicksburg, Miss. There was a tragic side to his career. "Much work he did," wrote Taft, "but never sufficiently recompensed to permit of adequate study" (*History of American Sculpture*, 1924, p. 540). In 1889, Mulligan married Margaret Ely, of Chicago. He died in St. Luke's Hospital, Chicago, from the effects of an operation, leaving a widow and three sons.

[The *Monumental News,* May 1916, published a sketch of Mulligan's life, with complete list of works, and Taft's tribute. Taft's *Hist. of Am. Sculpture* (1924, 1930) has brief references and one illustration. Other illustrations are found in *Harper's Weekly,* Nov. 27, 1909, p. 11, and in the *Art Interchange,* June 1904, p. 150. See also: *Bull. of the Art Inst. of Chicago,* Apr. 1916; *Art and Archæology,* Sept.–Oct. 1921; *Am. Art News,* Apr. 1, 1916; *Chicago Tribune,* Mar. 26, 27, 1916.]   A. A.

MULLINS, EDGAR YOUNG (Jan. 5, 1860–Nov. 23, 1928), Baptist clergyman, educator, and author, was born in Franklin County, Miss., the son of Seth Granberry and Cornelia Blair (Tillman) Mullins. His father and paternal grandfather were Baptist ministers and successful planters; while his maternal grandfather, Stephen Tillman, was a planter and politician, being for some years a member of the Mississippi legislature. When Edgar was eight years old the family moved to Corsicana, Tex., where the father became pastor and also established a school. Here Edgar grew to manhood and prepared for college. Because the family was large and the income very moderate, it was necessary for him to go to work early. He was at intervals printer's devil, newsboy, typesetter, printer, messenger boy, and telegrapher. Proving dependable

and efficient, he was put in charge of a telegraph office on full pay at fifteen years of age. This business experience was excellent preparation for the management of the greater interests which were later entrusted to his care. His father was a graduate of Mississippi College, a Baptist institution, but Edgar chose to enter Texas Agricultural and Mechanical College, where he graduated in 1879.

He then began the study of law, but was converted in 1880 and decided to follow his father's profession. Entering the Southern Baptist Theological Seminary, Louisville, Ky., in 1881, he spent four years in theological preparation. Upon graduation in 1885, he was ordained and became pastor of a town-country church at Harrodsburg, Ky., where he remained until 1888. His other pastorates were those of Lee Street Baptist Church, in downtown Baltimore from 1888 to 1895, and the wealthy, cultured suburban church at Newton Centre, Mass., from 1896 to 1899. For a few months in 1895–96 he was assistant secretary of the Foreign Mission Board. While in Baltimore he continued his studies in The Johns Hopkins University and also served as correspondent for the *Examiner.* During his three pastorates, which gave him experience in three different types of churches, he developed into an exceedingly effective preacher. His sermons were distinguished by universal appeal, freshness and vigor of thought, lucidity of language, and aptness in illustration.

When, in 1899, the presidency of the Southern Baptist Theological Seminary became vacant, he was elected to the position, which he held until his death. Here, as president and professor of theology, he did his greatest work. He was an able administrator, a clear and vigorous theological thinker, a stimulating teacher, and a prolific author. His more important works included: *Why Is Christianity True?* (1905); *The Axioms of Religion* (1908); *Baptist Beliefs* (1912); *Freedom and Authority in Religion* (1913); *Studies in Ephesians and Colossians* (1913); *The Life in Christ* (1917); *The Christian Religion in Its Doctrinal Expression* (1917); *Spiritualism a Delusion* (1920); *Christianity at the Cross Roads* (1924). In addition to the above, he wrote many tracts and pamphlets on religious subjects and was a frequent contributor to the religious press. As a theologian, he was a moderate Calvinist. His theological position was based on a careful interpretation of the scriptures and was little affected by current scientific thought. He was conservative as to position and progressive as to method. He was thoroughly evangelical, holding the generally recognized views of the great body of Protestant scholars, but reaching them in an independent way. His later writing was devoted largely to the problems arising from the impact of the natural sciences upon Christianity, and had a considerable influence upon the thought of Southern Baptists with regard to these questions. He was president of the Southern Baptist Convention from 1921 to 1924, and of the Baptist World Alliance from 1923 to 1928. In these positions he exercised a powerful influence in the promotion of unity, harmony, and progress among the Baptists of the world, seeking to avoid extremes and to hold the discordant elements of his people together in harmonious fraternal cooperation.

On June 2, 1886, he was married to Isla May Hawley of Alabama, a charming and cultured woman who made a worthy companion to her husband. To this union were born two children, neither of whom lived beyond childhood. He died in Louisville, Ky., at the age of sixty-eight; his wife survived him.

[Isla May Mullins, *Edgar Young Mullins* (1929); B. J. W. Graham, *Bapt. Biog.*, vol. I (copr. 1917); Isla May Mullins, *Captain Pluck* (1923); *Who's Who in Louisville*, 1926; *Who's Who in America*, 1928–29; *Hist. of Ky.* (1928), vol. IV; *Review and Expositor*, Apr., July, Oct. 1929; *Baptist*, Dec. 8, 1928; *Watchman-Examiner*, Nov. 29, 1928; *Courier-Journal* (Louisville), Nov. 24, 1928.]   W. J. M.

MULRY, THOMAS MAURICE (Feb. 13, 1855–Mar. 10, 1916), Vincentian, son of Thomas and Parthenia (Crolius) Mulry, was born in Greenwich Village, New York, the second child in a family of fourteen, of whom one became a Sister of Charity and four, members of the Society of Jesus. The father, one of five brothers who came from Roscommon, Ireland, about 1837, had developed into a successful building contractor. Thomas' schooling at St. Joseph's parochial school and the De La Salle Academy was broken by two temporary removals of the family to a farm at Pleasant Prairie, Wis., but after returning to New York, while working with his father, to whose business he succeeded, he attended night classes at the Cooper Institute. On Oct. 6, 1880, he married Mary E. Gallagher, a school-teacher, and set up housekeeping in Greenwich Village, where he reared a large family. Three of his sons became Jesuits and a daughter, a Sister of Charity. Deeply religious in a practical way, Mulry so sympathized with the poor inhabitants of the cellars and tenements of the congested Village and with the impoverished immigrants landing at Castle Garden that he gave all his spare time to charity and poor relief. This work, he believed, could be best accomplished through the Society of St. Vincent de Paul, with which he became affiliated in

1872. He was scrupulously honest and dependable, and his business prospered until he became recognized as one of the solid men of the city: a trustee of the Emigrant Industrial Savings Bank (1901), of which he was elected president in 1906, and a director in a number of real-estate corporations and trust companies. After the insurance scandal, he served on a committee under former President Cleveland which sought to rehabilitate the Mutual Life Insurance Company. No politician, he held no official positions, although he refused offers of Democratic nominations for controller and mayor (1905) when such nominations would have virtually insured election. Apparently he knew the temptations of office too well. A delegate to the state constitutional convention in 1915, he defended private charitable institutions against the onslaught of professional philanthropists.

It is as a Vincentian that Mulry was nationally known. A member of the Superior Council of New York in 1885, he became its secretary in 1887 and was its president from 1905 to 1915. For some time he had an editorial interest in the *St. Vincent de Paul Quarterly*. In 1915, he aided in the reorganization of the society on provincial, diocesan, and parochial lines, with a Superior Council in the United States responsible to the Council-General at Paris. He was elected national president in recognition of his character as an "American Ozanam." A founder of the National Conference of Catholic Charities (1910), he won the support of the Vincentians for its program of cooperative effort and scientific means of relief and reformation. A frequent speaker and reader of papers at the conventions of the National Conference of Charities and Corrections, at meetings of the New York State Charity Conference (of which he was president in 1903), and at the meetings of the City Conference of Charities and Corrections (over which he presided in 1912), he was so direct, earnest, and informative that he won recognition in the field as a sane counselor with solid business acumen. Hence he was named to positions on a number of boards: member of the State Board of Charities; president of the board of managers of Manhattan Hospital for the Insane; chairman of the committee on children of the National Conference of Charities, of which he was president at the Minneapolis meeting in 1907; and vice-president of the White House Conference on the Standards of Child Welfare (1909), which President Roosevelt declared was successful largely because of Mulry's cooperation. In the field of Catholic charities, he was a patron of the Marquette League for Indian Welfare, a trustee of the Catholic Summer School, founder and president of the Catholic Home Bureau for Dependent Children, and founder of St. Elizabeth's Home for Children, the St. Vincent de Paul Summer Home for Children, St. Elizabeth's Home for Convalescent Women and Girls. He was also a patron of the Ozanam Association for promotion of boys' clubs, a manager of the New York Foundling Asylum, and vice-president of the Friendly Sons of St. Patrick. For his services, he was not without honors: the knighthood of the Pontifical Order of St. Gregory was conferred upon him by Pope Pius X; the honorary degree of LL.D. by the Catholic University of America (1915); and the Laetare Medal, annually awarded to an outstanding Catholic layman, by Notre Dame University (1912). His last public appearance was in defense of the State Board of Charities before the Strong Commission of Investigation (1915). He died the following year, and with services in St. Patrick's Cathedral presided over by Cardinal Farley and Bishops Hayes and Shahan, was buried in Calvary Cemetery.

[T. F. Meehan, *Thomas Maurice Mulry* (1917); Patrick Mulry, *A Memoir of George Mulry, S. I.* (1891); *St. Vincent de Paul Quart.*, May 1916, memorial number, containing tributes by leaders in Church and State; an appreciation by W. J. Kerby, in *Cath. World*, July 1916; *America*, Mar. 18, 1916; *N. Y. Herald*, Mar. 11, 1916; *Truth*, Oct. 1933.]   R. J. P.

MUMFORD, JAMES GREGORY (Dec. 2, 1863–Oct. 18, 1914), surgeon and author, was born in Rochester, N. Y., the son of George Elihu and Julia Emma (Hills) Mumford and a descendant of Thomas Mumford who settled in Rhode Island in 1655. He prepared for college at St. Paul's School, an institution of which he was eventually a trustee, and was graduated by Harvard College in 1885 and the Harvard Medical School in 1890. After an internship at the Massachusetts General Hospital he settled in practice in Boston as a surgeon. He became a fairly successful surgeon, although he could not be considered an unusual one. For many years he was on the staff of the Massachusetts General Hospital, where he did excellent work. He never held more than a minor teaching position at the Harvard Medical School. He wrote eight books, as well as fifty or sixty papers, the great majority of them on surgical subjects. In 1903 appeared his *Clinical Talks on Minor Surgery*, in 1905 *Surgical Aspects of Digestive Disorders*, written in collaboration with A. K. Stone, in 1908 *Some End Results of Surgery*, and, in 1910, a textbook on *The Practice of Surgery*, a second edition of which appeared in 1914. In 1911 came a minor book entitled *One Hundred Surgical*

Problems; the Experiences of Daily Practice Dissected and Explained. All these books were sound contributions to American surgery. Early in his career he also showed a marked interest in the history of medicine and one of his first books, in 1903, was *A Narrative of Medicine in America.* Two years later he edited *The Harvard Medical School* (3 vols.), written by Thomas Francis Harrington [*q.v.*]. In 1908 he published *Surgical Memoirs and Other Essays* and in 1912 one of the most delightful of his short works, *A Doctor's Table Talk.* These latter publications were written in a charming, winsome style.

He was somewhat of a medical reformer, although not of the aggressive, disagreeable type. He became interested in the relations between religion and medicine and identified himself with the Emmanuel Movement, led by the Rev. Elwood Worcester of Boston. He foresaw the establishment of great medical centers, including hospitals and medical schools, and with full-time teachers upon the staff. He was also interested in providing good medical care for persons of moderate means and in 1910 he planned such a hospital; but the scheme got no farther than its prospectus. The idea was partly realized, however, at the Clifton Springs Sanitarium, New York, where he spent the last two years of his life. He was a member of many medical societies and social clubs and he took an active interest in bodies for civic uplift, such as the Economic Club and the Reform Club. His health was never good in the last dozen years of his life, for he suffered from a severe cardiac disease, of which he finally died. Greatly beloved by many of his contemporaries, he characterized himself, in a letter written in 1910, at the time of the twenty-fifth anniversary of his graduation by Harvard College, as follows: "I like teaching; students pass me out the usual compliments due to credulous senility. I like practising surgery; patients toss me roses mingled with thorns. I like writing about people and things, for the reviewers deal me comments which chasten the soul. Altogether, life continues a pleasant experience." His writings were characteristic of the man, for they exhibit sound judgment, keen perception, and a clarity of statement which is seldom found in scientific or lay literature. Mumford married, in 1892, Helen Sherwood Ford of Troy, N. Y.; there were no children.

[*Trans. Am. Surgic. Asso.*, vol. XXXIV (1916); *Boston Medic. and Surgic. Jour.*, Apr. 1, 1915, Feb. 6, 1919; *Class of 1885, Harvard Coll., Secretary's Report No. 7* (1910); *Johns Hopkins Hospital Bull.*, vol. XXVI (1915); J. G. Mumford, *Mumford Memories, Being the Story of the New Eng. Mumfords from the*

Year 1655 to the Present Time (1900); *Boston Transcript*, Oct. 19, 1914.]   H. R. V.

MUNDÉ, PAUL FORTUNATUS (Sept. 7, 1846–Feb. 7, 1902), physician, was born in Dresden, Germany. His mother, Bertha, was the daughter of Baron von Hornemann, a councilor of the King of Saxony. His father, Dr. Charles Mundé, a man of intense democratic ideals, participated actively in the Revolution of 1848, was proscribed, and as a political exile fled with wife and child to America. The family settled in Florence, Mass., where Dr. Charles Mundé conducted a sanatorium until his return to Germany. The son inherited intrepidity and a sturdy physical constitution from his father. His studious nature was early exhibited; he entered the Boston Latin School, and at the age of seventeen years was prepared to start the study of medicine at Yale. The Civil War interrupted his studies, but the spirit of adventure which seems to have been one of his essential characteristics was not satisfied by service in the garrison at Boston, and after six months he returned to the study of medicine at Harvard. He graduated with high honors in 1866 and spent the next seven years in Germany.

He arrived just in time to take part in the War of 1866 as an assistant surgeon in the Bavarian army. Upon his release from service in 1867 he went to Würzburg, where the famous gynecologist and obstetrician, Scanzoni, was in charge of the Maternity Hospital. Mundé was resident physician for three years and here obtained the training which determined his future work and gave him the ideals of German scientific medicine. Again a war interrupted his studies. He joined the Bavarian army at the outbreak of the Franco-Prussian conflict, and at the siege of Paris had charge of a hospital which was destroyed by the enemy's fire. During the conflagration he rescued the wounded personally and received the Iron Cross for this deed. It is characteristic of Mundé that the honors which he won in both these foreign wars were unknown to most of his friends until after he had died. At the close of the war he traveled throughout Europe and visited the centers where medical thought was particularly active—Heidelberg, Berlin, Vienna, London, Edinburgh, and Paris.

After this extraordinary preparation he returned to America in 1873 and entered practice in New York City. In November of that year he married Eleanor Claire Hughes of New Haven, Conn. His subsequent life was one of devotion to scientific medicine. The time was propitious for the development of the specialties. New York City was the scene of labors of J. M.

Sims, T. A. Emmett, and Abraham Jacobi [*qq.v.*], but there was great need for such well-trained men as Mundé. His assiduity marked him as fitted for positions which require painstaking energy and these he filled with such skill that only the physical incapacities of later years relieved him of his labors. In 1874 he became chief editor of the *American Journal of Obstetrics* and he retained that position until 1892. In this time the *Journal* rose to a position of pre-eminence in its field. He was secretary and (1886–88) president of the New York Obstetrical Society and treasurer (1876–83), vice-president (1884), and president (1898) of the American Gynecological Society. He became gynecologist to Mount Sinai Hospital in 1881, and its Gynecological Outpatient Department was his creation. As professor of gynecology he taught in the New York Polyclinic and at Dartmouth College.

His publications include over one hundred scientific articles and three textbooks: *Minor Surgical Gynecology* (1880), *Diagnosis and Treatment of Obstetrical Cases by External Examination and Manipulation* (1880), and *A Practical Treatise on the Diseases of Women* (1891), rewritten and reëdited from the original of Theodore Gaillard Thomas. Mundé exerted a powerful influence on the course of the gynecological specialty in America, not because of any important scientific discovery but because he brought excellent training, a passion for scientific truth, and weighed judgment to a country which still lacked workers of quality. In this activity of transferring European ideals to American soil he was aided by a charming personality which was energetic and resourceful but not combative or zealous. He died in New York City in his fifty-sixth year.

[*Mount Sinai Hosp. Reports, 1901–02*, vol. III (1903); H. A. Kelly and W. L. Burrage, *Am. Medic. Biogs.* (1920); *Trans. Am. Gynecol. Soc.*, vol. XXVII (1902); *Am. Jour. Obstet.*, Apr. 1902; *Boston Medic. and Surgic. Jour.*, Feb. 13, 1902; *Medic. News* (N. Y.), Feb. 15, 1902; *N. Y. Times*, Feb. 8, 1902.]   H. S. R.

MUNFORD, ROBERT (d. 1784), Revolutionary soldier and dramatist, was born at "Whitehall," Prince George County, Va., of aristocratic stock, son of Robert Munford (2nd) and his wife Anna Bland. He was educated at Wakefield, Yorkshire, England, along with other sons of the Virginia gentry, and while quite a young man was a soldier in the French-Indian wars, serving as captain in the 2nd Virginia Regiment, under William Byrd III, in the campaign of 1758. There are extant several letters written by him from Fort Cumberland to his uncle Theodorick Bland, Sr., which give interesting details of his military experience as well as his estimate of Colonel Washington. When Mecklenburg County was formed in 1765 he was made county-lieutenant and continued in that office until his death, the while representing the district in the House of Burgesses, 1765–75, and in the General Assembly, 1779 and 1780–81. In the pre-Revolutionary period he followed a temperate but courageous part in resisting British aggressions, and he was among those who signed the Williamsburg Association, a non-importation agreement, on June 22, 1770. During the war he saw much service of different kinds, his efforts in recruiting soldiers for the American army being especially beneficial, and rose to the rank of major. He married his first cousin, Anne, daughter of William Beverley of "Blandfield," Essex County.

A fine type of the cultured colonial gentleman and planter, Munford found diversion in literature from his professional activities. His reputation as a writer depends, save for occasional letters, upon his single posthumous volume, *A Collection of Plays and Poems* (1798), published, with a preface, by his son William [*q.v.*]; but this miscellany suffices to demonstrate, besides an aim to combine instruction with entertainment, his grace and vigor of expression, shrewd observation of men and events, broad humor, and turn for trenchant satire. Save for a spirited "Patriotic Song" and an amusing narrative, "The Ram," ridiculing feminine vanity, the half-score original poems lack distinction. More should be said, however, for the two prose plays and for the rhymed translation of Book I of Ovid's *Metamorphoses*—his death prevented the completion of this task—which is both scholarly and pleasing. *The Candidates,* written apparently several years before the Revolution, is a three-act satire upon country election practices which spares neither the heedless voter nor the unscrupulous aspirant; in spite of certain limitations, it mixes sound sense and passable farce with its gibes, and "it introduces in Ralpho probably the first negro character in the American drama" (A. H. Quinn, *A History of the American Drama from the Beginning to the Civil War,* 1923, p. 55). *The Patriots* (first published in Philadelphia, 1776, although seemingly never acted) is a much more significant piece, not only in structure, characters, dialogue, and particularly in plot, but also in its general temper. Avowedly a contrast between real and pretended patriotism, this early purpose drama from the pen of a man whose devotion and services to his country were above question is of added interest for its undertone of almost pacifistic hatred of war and its impatience with extremes of conduct and precept, whether Whig or Tory.

[See: Philip Slaughter, *A Hist. of Bristol Parish, Va.* (2nd ed., 1879); *Tyler's Quart. Hist. and Geneal. Mag.,* Jan. 1922; *Va. Mag. of Hist. and Biog.,* Jan., Apr. 1928; *Va. Hist. Reg.,* Jan. 1850, pp. 17–24; B. B. Munford, *Random Recollections* (1905); and Chas. Campbell, ed., *The Bland Papers* (2 vols., 1840–43). Detailed data concerning Munford are relatively scarce, partly no doubt owing to the destruction by fire of "Richlands," his Mecklenburg plantation, in the early nineteenth century.]   A. C. G., Jr.

MUNFORD, WILLIAM (Aug. 15, 1775–June 21, 1825), legislator, court reporter, poet, and classicist, was born in Mecklenburg County, Va., the eldest child and only son of Col. Robert [*q.v.*] and Anne (Beverley) Munford. He was educated in the grammar school connected with the College of William and Mary and later at the college itself. His early training might have terminated with his father's death and the resulting straitened circumstances had not Chancellor Wythe, then professor of law at Williamsburg, enabled him to continue. From Wythe, Munford gained a deep insight into the law and learned to love the classics. Completing his legal education at the age of twenty-one he almost immediately entered politics. During the session of 1797–98 he represented his native county in the House of Delegates, to which he was returned from 1800 to 1802 when he was elected to the state Senate. In that year, 1802, he was married to Sally Radford, daughter of William Radford of Richmond. After four years in the upper house he was placed on the privy council or council of state and thereafter made his home in Richmond. In 1811 he was appointed clerk of the House of Delegates, holding this office until his death. From 1808 to 1811, in conjunction with William W. Hening, he reported the decisions of the Virginia supreme court of appeals for the years 1806–10, the four volumes (11–14 *Va.*) bearing both names. After Hening's death Munford continued as reporter until 1821, publishing the decisions for the years 1810–21 in *Munford's Reports* (15–20 *Va.*). Under the direction of Benjamin Watkins Leigh he materially assisted in preparing the Code of 1819. He was an Episcopalian and from 1815 to 1824 served as secretary and treasurer of the Convention of the Diocese of Virginia.

The son of one of Virginia's early poets and dramatists, Munford was to achieve his greatest distinction, perhaps, in the field of letters rather than in public service or the law. In 1798 he published *Poems and Compositions in Prose on Several Occasions,* comprising poems on various themes, translations from Horace and Ossian, and a five-act tragedy, *Almoran and Hamet,* a dramatized story of the East. Designed to benefit his readers, enhance his reputation, and afford economic return, it was, however, a rather juvenile adventure into the realms of literature. But Munford's love for the classics was to produce one noteworthy contribution to literature, his translation into blank verse of the *Iliad.* Not content with existing translations, he undertook one of his own. For many years he labored painstakingly at his cherished work and completed it just before his death. Published in 1846, twenty-one years later, it received warm contemporary praise and was hailed as one of the greatest accomplishments in the history of classical scholarship in Virginia. Although it lacked, perhaps, Homer's poetic fire, it succeeded to a considerable degree in reproducing the beauty and magnificence of the original. It still stands as a significant milestone in the progress of American letters—an honorable and fitting close to a busy professional life.

[G. D. Fisher, *Hist. and Reminiscences of the Monumental Church* (1880); G. W. Munford, *The Two Parsons* (1884); F. V. N. Painter, *Poets of Va.* (1907); Preface to *The Revised Code of the Laws of Va.* (2 vols., 1819); *The Hist. of the Coll. of Wm. and Mary* (1874); *Wm. and Mary Coll. Quart.,* Jan. 1900, Oct. 1909; *Tyler's Quart. Hist. and Geneal. Mag.,* Jan. 1922; E. G. Swem and J. W. Williams, *A Reg. of the Gen. Assembly of Va., 1776–1918* (1918); *North Am. Rev.,* July 1846; the *Am. Rev.: A Whig Jour.,* Oct. 1846; *Christian Examiner,* Sept. 1846; family data supplied by Mrs. W. S. Robertson, Richmond, Va., Munford's grand-daughter.]   T. S. C.

MUNGER, ROBERT SYLVESTER (July 24, 1854–Apr. 20, 1923), inventor, manufacturer, was born in Rutersville, Fayette County, Texas, the son of Henry Martin and Jane C. (McNutt) Munger and a descendant of Nicholas Munger who emigrated from England to Connecticut in the seventeenth century. His father was a successful merchant and farmer and, in addition, was engaged in a small way in the manufacture of cotton-gins. When Robert was sixteen years old the family moved to Mexia, Tex. He had attended the public schools at Rutersville and he now entered the preparatory department of Trinity University, soon after its establishment at the old town of Tehuacana. After three years there, but before graduating, he returned to his home and took charge of his father's ginning plant, where he quickly developed a keen interest in the machinery, and soon manifested a considerable inventive talent. He conceived the idea of a pneumatic system for handling seed cotton and conveying it from the wagon to the gin, but a number of years elapsed before he devised a practical system. Meanwhile he patented several machines essential to cotton

ginning, including three saw cleaners, patented Apr. 23, 1878, May 20, 1879, and July 22, 1879, respectively, and a saw-sharpening tool, patented Oct. 10, 1882. In 1885 he attempted to get manufacturing companies interested in exploiting his patents but was unsuccesful, and accordingly established a manufacturing plant of his own at Dallas, which he operated for three years. Then, in 1888, he organized the Munger Improved Cotton Machine Company of Dallas and assumed the office of president. He resigned this position the following year and shortly thereafter moved to Birmingham, Ala., where he organized the Northington-Munger-Pratt Company in 1892 for the manufacture of cotton-gin machinery. During this time he had made progress in the perfection of his idea for pneumatic handling, and on July 12, 1892, obtained patent No. 478,-883 for a machine "for handling, cleaning and distributing seed cotton." The Munger system, as it came to be known, was a revolutionary improvement over the old system used at cotton-gins and was quickly adopted throughout the cotton-states and the world generally. Although serving as vice-president and director of both Dallas and Birmingham companies, Munger found time to continue with his inventive work and patented a duplex cotton-press (Oct. 4, 1892); an improvement in his pneumatic system (Nov. 28, 1893); a baling machine and a cotton elevator, cleaner and feeder (both Aug. 6, 1901); and an additional improvement on his cotton cleaner (Aug. 5, 1919). He is recognized as the pioneer of most of the improved ginning machinery used in the United States today. He retired from active management of his companies in 1902, following their purchase by the Continental Gin Company of Dallas, and thereafter devoted his attention mainly to real-estate interests. He was an active philanthropist and much interested in educational enterprises throughout the South. He married Mary Collett of Austin, Tex., May 2, 1878, and at the time of his death in Birmingham was survived by eight children.

[T. M. Owen, *Hist. of Ala. and Dict. of Ala. Biog.* (1921), vol. IV; L. B. Hill, *A Hist. of Greater Dallas and Vicinity* (1909), vol. II; J. B. Munger, *The Munger Book* (1915); Patent Office records; *Birmingham Age-Herald,* Apr. 20, 21, 1923; *Dallas Morning News,* Apr. 21, 1923.]   C. W. M.

MUNGER, THEODORE THORNTON (Mar. 5, 1830–Jan. 11, 1910), Congregational clergyman, was born in Bainbridge, N. Y., the fifth child of Dr. Ebenezer and Cynthia (Selden) Munger, and a descendant of Nicholas Munger who emigrated from England to New Haven probably about 1639. On his father's side he

Munger

was of the sixth generation from John Eliot [*q.v.*], apostle to the Indians, and by his mother he was in direct descent from Thomas Selden who came to Hartford, Conn., with Thomas Hooker in 1636. When he was six years of age the family removed to Homer, N. Y. Entering Yale in 1847, he gave himself more to general reading than to the prescribed course of studies. He graduated in 1851, and from the Yale Divinity School in 1855. After spending a term in Andover Theological Seminary, he accepted a call to the village church (Congregational) of Dorchester, Mass., in which he was ordained Feb. 6, 1856. He served successively churches in Haverhill, Mass., Providence, R. I., Lawrence, Mass., San José, Cal., East Hartford, Conn., and North Adams, Mass. In 1885 he became minister of the United Church, New Haven, Conn., continuing until, having reached the age of seventy, he resigned and was made pastor emeritus. He was married to Elizabeth Kinsman Duncan of Haverhill, Mass., Oct. 12, 1864, and to Harriet King Osgood of Salem, Mass., Mar. 5, 1889.

An unassertive man, his rise to general recognition was slow. He studied seriously and made himself a master of prose style; from time to time he wrote articles for the religious press. He was fifty, however, before his first book was published—a series of sermons to young people entitled *On the Threshold* (1880), of which more than 25,000 had been sold when the publishers reissued it as one of the Cambridge Classics. *Lamps and Paths,* a companion volume for younger readers, appeared in 1883, and the next year, a second edition, enlarged by four chapters. His most characteristic thought found expression in *The Freedom of Faith* (1883), which Whittier welcomed as being "refreshing and tonic as the north wind." It attracted wide attention, for, coming at a time of great religious unsettlement, it shed light on fundamental spiritual problems, and also revealed the essential vitality of the newer ways of thinking. With his eager, intuitional mind and his ardent faith in an ever-increasing revelation of truth, Munger was constitutionally sympathetic with the New Theology. Instinctively he had been drawn to Horace Bushnell; he was also greatly inspired by F. D. Maurice; but it was Frederick Robertson who molded his manner of thinking. Robertson's six principles of thought, he affirmed in his last years, told him "how to know under what principles of thought to express myself." The first three, especially, go far to explain his ideals and methods—"the establishment of positive truth, instead of the negative destruction of error;

Munn

truth is made up of two opposite propositions; spiritual truth is discerned by the spirit, instead of intellectually in propositions, and therefore should be taught suggestively, not dogmatically." These principles, early adopted, guided him through life. In the heated debate between the champions of the old and the new ways of religious thinking, Munger was a recognized leader. Under his touch theology became literature. In a volume of sermons and essays called *The Appeal to Life* (1887) he characteristically interpreted truth through human experience. In 1897 appeared a book of sermons bearing the title *Character Through Inspiration*. Next to *The Freedom of Faith* his most important book was *Horace Bushnell, Preacher and Theologian* (1899), a masterly interpretation of a spiritual predecessor to whom he was much indebted. If Munger's talent was slow in maturing, it continued fruitful in old age, for after his retirement he wrote frequently for current periodicals and published an important book, *Essays for the Day* (1904), in his seventy-fourth year.

A devoted pastor, his chief distinction was as a preacher and writer. Though lacking the peculiar gifts which make one popular with the masses, he was effective in reaching select minds of every class and condition. In his sermons there was an intensity of conviction, a swiftness of movement, a penetration and rich suggestiveness of thought, a stimulating terseness of expression, which brought light and power to his hearers. Thoughtful students in the university sought his counsel because of a certain mental flexibility which enabled him to think out their problems with them. Memorial tablets in his honor have been placed in Woolsey Hall, Yale University, and in the United Church, New Haven.

[J. B. Munger, *The Munger Book* (1915); *Obit. Record Grads. Yale Univ.,* 1910; *The Congregational Year-Book,* 1911; *Who's Who in America,* 1908–09; B. W. Bacon, *Theodore Thornton Munger* (1913); J. W. Buckham, *Progressive Religious Thought in America* (1919); *Congregational and Christian World,* Jan. 22, 1910; *New Haven Evening Register,* Jan. 12, 1910.]

C. A. D.

MUNN, ORSON DESAIX (June 11, 1824–Feb. 28, 1907), editor, publisher, was the youngest son of Rice and Lavinia (Shaw) Munn and was born in Monson, Mass., where his father was engaged in business. His first direct American ancestor was Benjamin Munn who in 1649 removed from Hartford, Conn., and settled in Springfield, Mass. Orson was educated at Monson Academy, and, having decided upon a commercial career, began work at the age of nineteen as a clerk in a bookstore in Springfield,

328

Munn

Mass. After two years he became a clerk in a general store in Monson and was so engaged when, in 1846, he was asked by his friend and schoolmate, Alfred E. Beach [*q.v.*], to join him in the purchase of a publication called the *Scientific American,* which had been founded Aug. 28, 1845, by Rufus Porter [*q.v.*]. Munn accepted, the firm of Munn & Company, consisting of Beach, Munn, and Salem H. Wales, was established, and office space was secured in New York in the building occupied by the New York *Sun,* a paper then owned by Beach's father.

The first issue of the *Scientific American* under the new firm appeared July 23, 1846, and from that time until his death, sixty-one years later, Munn gave his whole attention to its interests. Inasmuch as it was the first American periodical devoted purely to science and mechanics, the partners were constantly brought into contact with inventors seeking information and advice regarding patents. Consequently, they established a patent department, which, coming at a time when patent attorneys were practically unknown, met with immediate response. Under the directorship of Judge Charles Mason [*q.v.*], a former commissioner of patents, the business grew at a rapid rate, necessitating the opening of an office in Washington, D. C., and at the time of Munn's death over 100,000 patents had been secured by the department for clients. Properly to describe and illustrate the interesting exhibits at the Centennial Exhibition of 1876, the partners began in that year the publication of the *Scientific American Supplement.* Its success led them to continue it as a weekly review of current scientific literature and to add also articles too long or too technical for the ordinary reader. About 1890 they began still another publication, *La América científica e industrial,* designed for the Spanish-speaking peoples of South America. One of the features of the *Scientific American* was its information bureau; and in view of the many requests for data on home building and furnishing, Munn began in 1885 the publication of a monthly magazine devoted to this subject. It appeared for a time as the Building Edition of the *Scientific American,* but in 1905 it was remodeled and issued under the name *American Homes and Gardens.* Aside from his business, Munn's chief interest centered in his farm near Orange, N. J., and in his prize stock of Dutch belted cattle. He married Julia Augusta Allen of Monson, Mass., in 1849, and at the time of his death was survived by a son.

[*Sci. Am.,* Mar. 9, 1907; *Who's Who in America,* 1906–07; *N. Y. Times,* Mar. 2, 1907.]   C. W. M.

Muñoz-Rivera

MUÑOZ-RIVERA, LUIS (July 17, 1859–Nov. 15, 1916), resident commissioner of Puerto Rico at Washington, poet, editor, political leader, was born in Barranquitas, a small town in Puerto Rico, eldest son of Luis Ramón Muñoz-Barrios and Monserrate Rivera-Vásquez. He largely educated himself, aside from instruction received in the elementary schools of his native town, by diligent reading in Spanish and French literature. As a young man he began writing poetry, designed particularly to inspire his people with a spirit of nationalism and with patriotic ideals, which was published in various papers from 1882; later he became more interested in editorial writing directed to the same ends. In 1887 he was a member of the assembly of protest at Ponce which demanded from Spain for Puerto Rico autonomy, decentralization of administration, and the right to vote upon the island's budget. Moving to Ponce he launched *La Democracia* (July 1, 1890) as an organ for expounding its program. His editorials aroused opposition from the Spanish administration and led to many lawsuits, but they evoked the enthusiastic support of many liberals, and soon he became a leader of the Autonomist party. A small extreme group, which desired independence obtained by insurrection, organized a Puerto Rican branch of the Cuban Revolutionary party, but he persuaded his party to send a commission to Spain (1896), of which he was a member, where an agreement was made with Sagasta and the Liberals that, when that party should again return to power, they would grant autonomy to Puerto Rico. Those who accepted this pact became the Insular Liberal party (1897), with *El Liberal* which he founded in San Juan as its organ; those who rejected it were known as *"Puros."*

The assassination of the Conservative leader, Cánovas, led to the return to power of the Liberals and a royal decree of Nov. 25, 1897, granted autonomy to Cuba and Puerto Rico. In the first Autonomist cabinet (Feb. 12, 1898), consisting of three Liberals and three *Puros,* Muñoz-Rivera was secretary of grace, justice, and government, but later he became president. War between Spain and the United States interrupted these plans and resulted in the transfer of sovereignty to the latter (Oct. 18, 1898). The resignation of the Autonomist cabinet was not accepted by General Brooks, the first military governor, and its members continued to serve until he was succeeded by Gen. Guy V. Henry, who sought to abridge the powers they were exercising, accepted their resignation, and reorganized the cabinet in another form (1899). Muñoz-Rivera

329

then went to Washington to secure free trade with the United States on behalf of the agriculturists of the island. Opposing the Foraker Act, which initiated civil government, as inadequate and unsatisfactory, he organized the Federal party and launched *El Diario de Puerto Rico* as its organ (1900). His party being in the minority—and he claimed harshly treated—he went to New York in 1901 and launched the *Puerto Rico Herald*. In 1902 a fusion of the Federals with dissatisfied Republicans became the Unionist party. He returned to the island, campaigned for it, and was elected to the Puerto Rican House of Delegates (1906–10). The Unionists then elected him resident commissioner for Puerto Rico to the United States. While in Washington he continued his articles for *La Democracia* as a means of informing the people of Puerto Rico of conditions in the United States and gained a speaking knowledge of English after he was fifty so that he could present his country's needs to Congress.

His last and most important speech in Congress (*Congressional Record,* 64 Cong., 1 Sess., pp. 7470–73) was in favor of the Jones Bill, which became Puerto Rico's organic act, although he did not live to see its passage. After securing the postponement of the general elections until this should be in force, he returned to San Juan to receive a great welcome from his people (Sept. 20). But the following day he fell ill and died at Santurce, a suburb of San Juan, on Nov. 15, 1916. Accompanied by thousands his body was carried to his birthplace and buried at Barranquitas. He had married, on Jan. 3, 1893, Amalia Marín. Among his own people he is famed as a poet, as an editor, as an orator, and as a statesman; his birthday is celebrated each year, and his character held up for imitation to the young people of the island. It has been said, "in politics, he harmonized the promptings of idealism with the needs of reality, as he cooperated more than any one else to form governing parties of the Island's liberal elements, thus facilitating the fulfilment of Porto Rico's desires and the solution of its problems" (*El Libro de Puerto Rico, post,* p. 1037).

[Muñoz-Rivera's writings, *Obras Completas de Luis Muñoz Rivera* (Madrid, 4 vols., 1925), edited by his son, Luis Muñoz-Marín, include his important editorials and contributions to newspapers and the poems published in 1902 under the title *Tropicales.* See also: José Gonzáles Ginorio, *Luis Muñoz Rivera, a la Luz de sus Obras y de su Vida* (1919); Eugenio Fernández García, *El Libro de Puerto Rico* (1923); *Boletín Histórico de Puerto Rico,* 1914–27; *Puerto Rico Illustrado,* Nov. 18, 25, Dec. 7, 1916.]   C. R. W—s.

MUNRO, DANA CARLETON (June 7, 1866–Jan. 13, 1933), historian, was born in Bristol, R. I., where his ancestors had lived for five generations. His father was John B., his mother Abby Howland (Batt) Munro. He graduated from Brown University in 1887, and was given the degree of A.M. by the same university in 1890. He studied at Strassburg in the autumn and winter of 1889 and at Freiburg in Breisgau in the spring of 1890. Here he came under the influence of Professor Paul Scheffer-Boichorst and began the interest in the Crusades which remained his throughout life. In 1890 he returned to America and taught for two years in a grammar school in Haverford, Pa. During this time he continued his post-graduate study at the University of Pennsylvania where in 1893 he became instructor and later assistant professor of medieval history. It was at this time that along with Professor J. H. Robinson and E. P. Cheyney he established and prepared eight numbers of the series of *Translations and Reprints from the Original Sources of European History,* published 1895–99, the pioneer effort in America to take students back to the sources. It was during this period also that he became intimate with the historian Henry C. Lea [*q.v.*], in whose library he read, and whose methods of work he has interpreted in various articles.

From the beginning Munro insisted on the most rigorous scientific method. He laid down a rigorous rule that no statement must be made in historical writing for which a satisfactory reference to a contemporary source cannot be given. His influence has thus been marked on a long series of younger scholars. This practice also was probably responsible, at least in part, for the slow progress of what was to be his *magnum opus,* a detailed and scholarly history of the Crusades, based on an exhaustive and critical use of the contemporary sources and vivified by a careful study on the ground of the regions traversed and occupied by the Crusaders. For the latter purpose he made two visits to the Near East. The work was still incomplete at his death. The Crusades were in the meantime the subject of many special studies, seminar and lecture courses, and detached papers and of a series of Lowell lectures delivered in Boston in 1924. Several of these studies were published.

In 1902 Munro was called as professor of European history to the University of Wisconsin, where he remained thirteen years. While there he acted as director of the Summer School and fulfiled other administrative duties. Although these interfered with the progress of his larger work, as a member of the active teaching group in that university he published textbooks and other material for teaching and started several younger scholars on their career. He was an active member of the Wisconsin State Historical Society, and president of the Wisconsin Academy from 1912 to 1915. In 1915 he went to Princeton University as professor of medieval history and remained there during the succeeding eighteen years of his life. American entrance into the World War in 1917 brought him into government service, first, as one of the principal research assistants to the Committee on Public Information, then as chairman of the National Board of Historical Service. In this capacity he prepared two pamphlets, *German War Practices* (1917) and *German Treatment of Conquered Territory* (1918). He was responsible for preserving in many government publications a tone of moderation in criticism of German actions and policy, though he was convinced of the rightfulness of the allied cause and confident of future restriction of war's barbarities. He contributed also to the collection of material for the "Inquiry," to be used by the American representatives at the Paris peace conference. He was chairman of the New Jersey State War History Commission from 1919 onward. He was president of the American Historical Association in the years 1925–26, and served as managing editor of the *American Historical Review* for 1928–29. He became chairman of the advisory board of the American Council of Learned Societies in 1928, when it was formed, and served in that capacity till his death. He was active in the affairs of the American Philosophical Society. In 1930 he became president of the Medieval Academy.

The published historical work of Munro is a slight though not unworthy measure of his accomplishments. *The Middle Ages,* first published in 1902, and subsequently revised and enlarged, is more than a textbook; it is an original contribution to knowledge drawn directly from medieval documents. His edition of L. J. Paetow's *A Guide to the Study of Medieval History* (1931), the preparation of which occupied much of his time in his later years, required a breadth of scholarship and an industry which might well have produced independent work. The volume, edited by L. J. Paetow, *The Crusades and Other Historical Essays* (1928), presented to him in manuscript by his former students when he retired from the presidency of the American Historical Association in 1926, gives testimony to much work on his part vicariously performed. There are some historians, like Lord Acton in England, whose contribution to the writing of history is to be sought in the incentive to production they have given to others, the standards they have set by their own work, scanty as it may be

in bulk, and their preparation of materials for later work. The writing of history in modern times is largely a cooperative task, and in this general activity of workers probably no other American historian of his time was better known, more valued, or more useful than Munro. He was married on July 16, 1891, to Alice Gardner Beecher and left two sons and three daughters. He died in New York from a sudden attack of pneumonia, Jan. 13, 1933.

[*Who's Who in America,* 1932–33; *N. Y. Times,* Jan. 14, 1933; E. P. Cheyney, in *Am. Hist. Review,* April 1933, pp. 618–20; personal acquaintance and private information.]   E. P. C.

MUNRO, GEORGE (Nov. 12, 1825–Apr. 23, 1896), publisher, was born at West River, Pictou County, Nova Scotia. He was a member of a large family and was dependent upon his own efforts for anything more than an elementary education. He learned printing in the office of the Pictou *Observer,* attended Pictou Academy three years, and, after teaching three years at New Glasgow, became instructor of mathematics and headmaster of the Free Church Academy in Halifax. He was winning a reputation as a teacher, when, in 1856 with several hundred dollars saved up, he suddenly departed for New York City. There he worked at various jobs; he was for a time in the employ of the American News Company, and, about 1863, he became a clerk in the firm of Beadle & Adams, dime-novel publishers. Beadle, in speaking one day to Edward S. Ellis, according to a story told by the latter, nodded toward an outer room where Munro, then forty years old, was tying up bundles and remarked, "That man has worked for us nearly two years. I pay him sixteen dollars a week; he is perfectly content with that; he will never wish to change his situation or try to improve it" (Pearson, *post,* p. 84). Scarcely a year later Munro began his own publishing house, and a decade later he was Beadle's most formidable rival. "Munro's Ten Cent Novels" were patterned after Beadle's original dime novels, and the series soon numbered several hundred titles. He began the publication, in 1867, of the *Fireside Companion,* a cheap family paper of entertainment and amusement that reached a phenomenal circulation figure. In 1872 he published *Old Sleuth the Dectective* by Harlan P. Halsey, the first of the famous Old Sleuth Series by that author, which eventually totaled over one hundred titles. This was followed by the scarcely less popular Old Cap Collier Series. However, his most successful venture was the "Seaside Library," a series of reprints of English works in paper-covered, octavo pamphlets, which could be forwarded in the mails at newspaper rates. The works of Scott, Dickens, Charlotte Brontë, George Eliot, Charles Reade, and other standard British writers were printed in this manner with no thought of compensation to the authors. Through the medium of the American News Company the nearly 2,000 titles that eventually were included in the series were scattered broadcast through the country and sold for ten cents each. Though the margin of profit was small, he rapidly became rich. On Vandewater and Rose streets he erected in 1883 a nine-story building with the most up-to-date equipment then known to care for his tremendous output. Though his reprints undoubtedly brought to the masses cheap and, at the same time, good reading material, they also hastened the passage of the international copyright law, when the more dignified publishers at last arrayed themselves in favor of the copyright side.

His interest in education led him to give liberally for education purposes. He was of great assistance to Dalhousie University at Halifax, when for a time its very existence was at stake, and endowed it with professorships of English literature, history, physics, metaphysics, and constitutional and international law. He also established tutorships in the classics and mathematics and an endowment for competitive scholarships. His total benefactions to this school amounted to about half a million dollars. He was also a benefactor and long a member of the council of the University of the City of New York. In build he was sturdy of frame and slightly below the average height. He was simple and frank in character, eminently practical, and possessed a high capacity for application to his business. He was married to Catherine, the daughter of Alexander Forrest of Halifax, who, together with their two sons and two daughters, survived him. His sons assumed control of the publishing business shortly before their father's death and continued to carry it on into the present century.

[E. L. Pearson, *Dime Novels* (1929); *Encyc. of Contemporary Biog. of N. Y.*, vol. IV (1885); J. P. MacPhie, *Pictonians at Home and Abroad* (1914); *New York University*, ed. by T. F. Jones (1933); *One Hundred Years of Dalhousie* (1919), pp. 24–30; *Publishers' Weekly*, May 2, 1896; *N. Y. Times*, Apr. 25, 1896.]   O. W. H.

MUNRO, HENRY (1730–May 30, 1801), clergyman, army chaplain, Loyalist, or Harry Munro, as he signed his name, was born in Scotland, the son of Robert Munro of Dingwall, near Inverness, and Anne (Munro) Munro, both connected with the landed gentry. He attended the University of St. Andrews, where he took the degrees of bachelor and master of arts, after which he studied divinity at the University of Edinburgh. In 1757 he took orders in the Church of Scotland and purchased the chaplaincy of the 77th Regiment of Highlanders, which proceeded in the same year to America. He served in this capacity for a period of six years, seeing much active service. He accompanied the regiment on the expedition against Fort Duquesne in 1758, was present at the taking of Ticonderoga and Crown Point in 1759, and at the capture of Montreal in 1760. He later served in the West Indies with the forces which took Dominica and Martinique. His health being undermined by yellow fever, he obtained leave to return to New York, where he arrived about the close of the year 1762.

With the coming of peace and the reduction of his regiment, he left the military service and for a while made his residence at Princeton, N. J. During this period his religious views appear to have undergone a change and he decided to become a member of the Church of England. He proceeded to England toward the end of 1764 and was ordained on Feb. 10, 1765. Returning to America in the same year, he became missionary at Philipsburgh (now Yonkers), to which position he had been appointed by the Society for the Propagation of the Gospel in Foreign Parts. Early in 1768 he removed to Albany, where he became rector of St. Peter's Church and also missionary of the Society for the Propagation of the Gospel. He was appointed chaplain to the military garrison at Albany in July 1770. From 1768 until the Revolution, he was active in that portion of the New York frontier extending from Albany to Fort Stanwix. He preached in the frontier settlements and exercised considerable influence among the Indians, particularly the Mohawks. He seems to have worked in close understanding with Sir William Johnson, with whom he occasionally corresponded. As a veteran of the French war, he was granted a considerable tract of land between the Hudson and Lake Champlain, which he was endeavoring to settle on the eve of the Revolution. Being a Loyalist in his sympathies, Munro was seized and imprisoned at Albany late in 1776 or early in 1777. He succeeded in escaping in October 1777 and joined the British forces in Canada, with which he again served for a time as chaplain. He returned to England in 1778 and in 1783 went to Scotland, where he resided until his death, which occurred in Edinburgh in 1801. He received a grant from the British government by way of compensation for the loss of his property in America.

Munro enjoyed a considerable reputation as a

scholar. In 1773 he had been awarded the honorary degree of master of arts at King's College, New York, and in 1782 the University of St. Andrews conferred upon him the degree of doctor of divinity. He was married three times. The name of his first wife is unknown; his second was a Miss Stockton of Princeton; while his third, whom he married Mar. 31, 1766, was Eve Jay of New York, sister of Chief Justice John Jay [q.v.]. By her he had a son, Peter Jay Munro, who attained some distinction later in the state of New York.

[The best sketch available is E. F. DeLancey's "Memoir of the Rev. Dr. Harry Munro, the Last Rector of St. Peter's Church, Albany, under the English Crown," in *N. Y. Geneal. and Biog. Record*, July 1873; this treatment is based in large part upon Munro's personal papers, the present repository of which is unknown. See also "American Loyalists: Transcript of the Manuscript Books and Papers of the Commission of Enquiry into the Losses and Services of the American Loyalists . . .," vol. XLV, bk. 5, in N. Y. Pub. Lib., and E. A. Jones, "The Loyalists of N. J.," in *Colls. N. J. Hist. Soc.*, vol. X (1927), pp. 150-51. A few letters are contained in E. B. O'Callaghan, *Documentary Hist. of the State of N. Y.*, vol. IV (1851); biog. note on p. 410 should be used with caution.]   W. E. S—s.

MUNSELL, JOEL (Apr. 14, 1808–Jan. 15, 1880), printer and antiquarian, was born at Northfield, Mass., the son of Joel and Cynthia (Paine) Munsell. In the public schools of Northfield he received his early education, which was continued by private study throughout the succeeding years. Beginning with the trade of wheelwright, young Munsell soon turned his attention to the printer's trade, obtaining his first lessons at the case in Greenfield, Mass. Going to Albany, N. Y., in 1827, he was not long in finding employment in a printing shop. Albany even at that day was a center of political contention and newspaper activity. Thurlow Weed was soon to exhibit his powers of editorial leadership, and the "Albany regency" was in the ascendant, with Edwin Croswell giving expression to its policies in the *Albany Argus*. Munsell never wholly surrendered to the emotions which were absorbing much of the journalistic ability of the country. After a brief period of adjustment to the new environment, he entered upon a career as a printer that is singular for the variety of its interests and a certain degree of detachment from the main currents of public activity. This is illustrated by a list of newspapers and periodicals that issued from his presses. The *Albany Minerva*, a semi-monthly of which only eight numbers saw the light, heads a series comprising the following publications, some of which he edited: The *New York State Mechanic*, the *Mechanics' Journal*, the *Lady's Magazine*, the *American Literary Magazine*, the *Northern Star and Freeman's Advocate*, the *Albany Religious Spectator*, the *Gavel*, an Odd Fellows' journal, the *Daily Unionist*, the *State Register*, a daily, the *New York Teacher*, a monthly, the *Albany Morning Express*, the *Albany Daily Statesman*, *Webster's Calendar, or the Albany Almanac*, and for three years, 1862–64, the *New-England Historical and Genealogical Register*.

In addition to these, Munsell produced various compilations. They include: *Outline of the History of Printing* (1839); *Annals of Albany* (10 vols., 1850–59); *The Every Day Book of History and Chronology* (1843); *A Chronology of Paper and Paper Making* (1856); *Collections on the History of Albany* (4 vols., 1865–71); and *The Typographical Miscellany* (1850), a limited edition. He also published books of reference relating to the early wars and settlements of America, a service which has given him a secure place among the pioneer workers who, by their labors in source material, have opened to others more inviting fields of historic production. A catalogue of the works which had issued from his press appeared in 1872 under the title *Bibliotheca Munselliana*. His general library was rich in *Americana* and comprised many writings connected with the early life of Albany. On Apr. 18, 1876, he read before the Albany Institute a paper thus introduced: "I now propose to take you on a tour about the streets within the purlieus of these quaint old walls for the purpose of pointing out . . . some interesting localities as they existed two-hundred years ago, and to revive a memory of men and things long since departed" (*Men and Things in Albany Two Centuries Ago*, 1876, p. 5). The purpose of that talk was an animating principle of Munsell's activities in the transmission of local annals, knowledge that is as perishable as it is important. Interested in the history and practical adaptations of the printing art, he gathered a large collection of works on printing which was purchased in part by the New York State Library. His collection of newspapers, comprising 10,000 specimens, is a notable instance of his interest in the progress of journalism. He was one of the founders of the Albany Institute, which is now a corporate part of the Institute of History and Art. Munsell was married on June 17, 1834, to Jane C. Bigelow; and after her death was married, on Sept. 11, 1856, to Mary Anne Reid.

[Sources include: Publications in the N. Y. State Lib., including newspaper files; in the same library Munsell's scrapbooks, one of which contains a personal narrative essentially autobiographical; G. R. Howell and Jonathan Tenney, *Hist. of the County of Albany* (1886); J. H. Temple and Geo. Sheldon, *Hist. of the Town of Northfield, Mass.* (1875); G. R. Howell, "Biog. Sketch of Joel Munsell," *New-Eng. Hist. and*

Geneal. Reg., July 1880; J. J. Latting, sketch in the
N. Y. Geneal. and Biog. Record, Apr. 1880; Albany
Evening Jour., Jan. 18, 1880.]   R. E. D.

MUNSEY, FRANK ANDREW (Aug. 21,
1854–Dec. 22, 1925), publisher, the son of Andrew Chauncey Munsey, a Maine farmer and
builder, and Mary Jane Merritt Hopkins, his
wife, was born at Mercer, Me. His father, who
served his country for three years during the
Civil War, was known in the various places in
which he lived as a hard worker of severely rigid
opinions. His mother, according to a genealogist
employed by her son, was the lawful descendant
of four passengers on the *Mayflower*; hers was
therefore "the better family." Despite his father's industry, there was but a small income to
maintain his large family, as a member of which
Frank Munsey enjoyed little schooling and suffered much from illness. At fifteen his ambition
made him hire himself out to the local postmaster
for $100 a year. From this he graduated into
the service of the Western Union Telegraph
Company in Portland, first as night and Sunday
operator, in due course becoming manager of the
Augusta, Me., office. It was here, in a boarding
house, that he met a successful mail-order publisher and became inspired by him to enter the
publishing field himself. With only forty dollars
of his own and two hundred and sixty dollars of
borrowed money, but without training, experience, tradition, or backing, he arrived in New
York on Sept. 23, 1882, to begin a career which
was carried to success by extraordinary pluck
and determination and by his ability to devote
himself entirely to his work. He was at first his
own office-boy, bookkeeper, clerk, advertising
solicitor, manager, editor, and serial-story writer
—as he himself set forth in his latter years in a
booklet covering the first twenty-five years of
his publishing career.

His first venture was the *Golden Argosy*, established in 1882, a magazine for boys and girls.
It is said that he had twenty salesmen on the
road east of the Mississippi before he engaged a
stenographer or bookkeeper (Duffus, *post*, p.
299). The first ten years were financially fruitless; but from 1894 to 1907 inclusive his magazines earned him $8,780,905.70 in net profits.
Throughout his career he never took a partner,
nor created else than a dummy board of directors, nor yielded any of his authority to a powerful legal advisor. Nor did he marry. He
never held staff conferences, seldom took suggestions, and supervised all details himself. The
Munsey Publishing House was Frank A. Munsey, and his life was so ordered that he could live
for his business and for success alone. He was

not a reformer, nor an idealist, nor was he deeply interested in any causes. His passion was to
found or purchase magazines and, later, newspapers. If one of his magazines failed to earn
well he killed it and began another; if public
taste passed from one of his productions he
dropped it to develop another. As he progressed
from cheap, inconsequential magazines to more
important ones and then to daily newspapers, so
he turned later to the stock market, became owner of the chain of Mohican grocery stores and
at least one hotel (The Mohican) in New London, Conn., in search of wider fields to conquer.

So quick was he to destroy not only the cre-
ations of his own imagination but various newspapers which he bought to suppress in order to
increase the power and influence of others he
possessed that the phrase "Let Munsey kill it"
became current newspaper slang whenever a
daily was reported in distress. Thus he destroyed,
merged, or renamed among magazines the *Scrap
Book*, the *Quaker*, the *Puritan*, the historic
Godey's Magazine (eagerly sought by collectors), *Peterson's Magazine*, the *Live Wire*,
Junior Munsey, *Woman*, the *Cavalier*, the *Railroad Man's Magazine*, and the *All-Story Magazine*. He failed in his effort to create a successful tabloid daily only to see the New York *Daily
News* succeed. In the newspaper field he similarly merged or destroyed the New York morning
Sun, the *New York Press*, the *Daily Continent*,
the *Globe*, the *Mail and Express*, the *Herald* (by
sale to the *Tribune*), the Baltimore *Star*, and the
Philadelphia *Times*. After owning them for a
time he also sold the *Boston Morning Journal*,
the Washington *Times*, the *Baltimore American*
and the *Baltimore News*, thus meriting the description of him as "a dealer in dailies." At his
death there survived him as his possessions the
New York evening *Sun*, one of the three most
successful New York dailies, and the *Evening
Telegram*. Of the magazines there were left only
the *Argosy All-Story Weekly*, *Munsey's Magazine*, and *Flynn's Weekly Detective Fiction*; yet
Munsey was able to boast in 1907 that *Munsey's*
was then the leading magazine in the world in
circulation and earning power. Although in the
daily field he more often failed than succeeded,
he was able to carry on by the millions made in
the Mohican stores, through the Munsey Trust
Company of Washington, D. C., and by successful speculation in Wall Street; he indignantly
and specifically denied on Aug. 28, 1922, published charges that he was a war-profiteer in
munitions-making, declaring, "I made no money
whatever, directly or indirectly, out of the war
or anything associated with the war" (*New York*

Herald, Aug. 28, 1922). After his death his estate was appraised at $19,747,687, the bulk of which went to the Metropolitan Museum of Art in New York.

A lifelong adherent of the Republican party, Munsey bolted with Theodore Roosevelt in 1912 and with his dailies espoused the Progressive cause because of his admiration for the former president rather than for any belief in his platform. This was the only time that his journals took a liberal position; for the rest they were usually conventional and conservative under his management, though opposed to what he called (in the *New York Herald*) "damn fool protectionism," ship subsidies, and the soldier bonus. There was in them no editorial illumination, or passion, or power. He stood with the great capitalists, of whom he was one, and his dailies safeguarded their interests. But they were also clean and respectable (as well as dull) both in their news and advertising columns. No salacious stories crept into them. It is to his credit that he never stooped to the gutter to succeed; he preferred to kill or sell a daily rather than to degrade it. In other words, his newspapers reflected the viewpoint of the average prosperous American concerned with his own affairs and his own success. None the less he once declared that America "has cut loose from the conservatism of our fathers and penetrated deep into the wilderness of radicalism" (*An Address by Frank A. Munsey before the American Bankers' Association,* 1922, p. 14). While there was much feeling against him in journalistic circles, because of his killing of historic dailies and turning their employees into the street, it came to be recognized that he was merely illustrating dramatically a trend toward consolidation and combination and decreasing competition, which became the most striking phase of the newspaper business. While in his early days Munsey wrote fiction and sport news, and in later years numerous editorials for his dailies, he was without distinction as a writer. He died in New York City following an operation for appendicitis.

[Of Munsey's writings, see especially *The Founding of the Munsey Publishing House* (1907); *The Daily Newspaper; Its Relation to the Public* (1910); *Getting on in Journalism* (1898); and *Militant Am. Journalism* (1922), a pamphlet consisting of editorials reprinted from the *N. Y. Herald.* Other sources include: O. G. Villard, *Some Newspapers and Newspaper-Men* (2nd ed., 1926); E. J. Ridgway, *Frank A. Munsey: An Appreciation* (1926); R. L. Duffus, "Mr. Munsey," *Am. Mercury,* July 1924; Allan Nevins, *McNaught's Monthly,* Mar. 1926; R. H. Titherington, "In Memoriam: Frank A. Munsey," *Munsey's Mag.,* Mar. 1926; D. O. S. Lowell, *A Munsey-Hopkins Geneal., Being the Ancestry of Andrew Chauncey Munsey and Mary Jane Merritt Hopkins* (1920); the *N. Y. Times,* Dec. 23, 1925; Jan. 10, 1926; the *Sun* (N. Y.), Dec. 22, 1925.]   O. G. V.

MUNSON, THOMAS VOLNEY (Sept. 26, 1843–Jan. 21, 1913), viticulturist, horticulturist, son of William and Maria (Linley) Munson, was born near Astoria, Fulton County, Ill., and died at Denison, Tex. His father was of New Hampshire stock, and his mother was from Kentucky. After an elementary education in the country schools, he taught in Illinois (1861–64) to earn money for his course at the University of Kentucky, which he attended with his brother, William B. Munson, receiving the degree of B.S. in 1870. On June 27, 1870, he married Ellen Scott Bell, daughter of Charles Stuart Bell, a horticulturist and nurseryman of Lexington, Ky. They had two sons and five daughters. During the years 1870–71 he was professor of science in the University of Kentucky, and from 1871 to 1873 he was engaged in the nursery business with his wife's father in Lexington. He established himself in Lincoln, Nebr., in 1873, and three years later, at the solicitation of his brother William, removed his business to Denison, Tex., his home until his death.

It was here that all of his scientific and horticultural work was done. He developed a vineyard and experimental grounds, while at the same time he became one of the most prominent general horticulturists of the South. In 1883 he published his "Forests and Forest Trees of Texas" (*American Journal of Forestry,* July 1883) for which the Agricultural and Mechanical College of Kentucky conferred on him the degree of M.Sc. In the eighties, at the instance of the French government, he sought for and experimented with American species of wild grape resistant to the phylloxera pest of the French grape, and received, in recognition of his work, membership in the Legion of Honor, election as foreign corresponding member of the Société Nationale d'Agriculture de France (1898), and honorary membership in the Société des Viticulteurs de France. His admirable work on the grape appears in his "Classification and Generic Synopsis of the Wild Grapes of North America" (*United States Department of Agriculture, Division of Pomology, Bulletin No. 3,* 1890); in *Texas Agricultural Experiment Station, Bulletin No. 56,* 1900; in articles in L. H. Bailey, *Cyclopedia of American Horticulture,* vol. II (1900); and in his own *Foundations of American Grape Culture* (1909). He was a prominent member of numerous scientific and horticultural societies in America, lecturer for years in the farmers' institutes of Texas, a member of the Texas World's Fair Commission (1903–04), and one of the international jury of awards at the St. Louis Exposition (1904). His death, which occurred in his seventieth year, was due to influenza, followed by pneumonia.

Munson was gifted with a singular ability to see the possibilities of horticultural stocks. By his hybridization and selection experiments, he was able to give hundreds of new horticultural varieties to the world. His work on the grape is almost without a parallel. What is said to be the most complete botanical display of the whole grape genus ever made was prepared by him for the Chicago World's Fair (1893) and is now in the United States Department of Agriculture. His work on the culture of the American grape is a monumental achievement. With all his abilities and accomplishments, he was a man of singularly modest disposition, and was widely loved. "Probably no man ever lived in Texas whose character attracted greater admiration, or whose removal caused more general regret . . . he loved his kind and was lavish in his benefactions to those, who, helpless, appealed to his sympathy" (Johnson and Barker, *post*, IV, 1722).

[F. W. Johnson and E. C. Barker, *A Hist. of Texas and Texans* (1914), vol. IV; *Dallas Morning News*, Jan. 23, 1913; family papers.]   S. W. G.

MUNSON, WALTER DAVID (Feb. 18, 1843–Apr. 24, 1908), ship-owner, developer of the Munson Line, was descended from Thomas Munson, an Englishman who had settled at Hartford by 1637. He was born on a farm in Cheshire, Conn., fifth of the six children of Barnabas Daniel and Delia (Canfield) Munson. He was only three when his father died. His mother later married David W. Wood, a widower whose daughter Emily M. Wood became Munson's wife on Dec. 31, 1863. He was brought up on the farm, with a fair schooling. At eighteen he enlisted as a private in Company E of the 8th Connecticut Volunteers and fought through the Civil War. He became second lieutenant, first lieutenant, and finally captain in the 2nd United States Cavalry and served as assistant adjutant-general of the 3rd Division of the XVIII Army Corps. Remaining in the army for a year after the war, he was with Sheridan's force which was sent to the Rio Grande in protest against the French occupation of Mexico. Finally mustered out early in 1866 in Texas, he settled in Brownsville for two years. In 1868 he moved to Havana and from that time until his death he was intimately connected with Cuba. He became interested in the refining of petroleum there and eventually that led to shipping, which became his most important field of activity.

The nucleus of the future Munson Line was a schooner with which he began regular freight service between New York and Havana in 1873. By 1882, when he moved to New York, he had five sailing vessels regularly engaged in trade between the two ports. Three of his five children were born by that time and Munson took a very keen interest in their upbringing. It is said that the principal reason for his leaving Cuba was the desire to give them better surroundings and educational opportunities. For the remainder of his life he made his home in Brooklyn and conducted his business from New York. He continued to develop the line of ships between New York and Cuba, adding steamships to the sailing vessels. The line specialized in freight, but he later put some excellent passenger ships on the New York-Havana run. The Munson freighters connected New York not only with Havana but also with Matanzas, Santiago, and many other ports on the island. He extended his service to Mexico and developed a regular service between Havana and Mobile and other Gulf ports. In 1894 he was also serving as agent for the Prince Steamship Company which connected Haiti, Jamaica, Central America, and Colombia. This shipping business was at first Munson's private venture, but in 1899 it was incorporated as the Munson Steamship Line, remaining a fairly close corporation. Munson himself was president and a director.

Munson also extended his shipping line northward to Nova Scotia and the Maritime Provinces where pulpwood and other bulky commodities offered good freight. He was president of the Cameron Steamship Company, vice-president of the Atlantic & Mexican Gulf Steamship Company, and secretary-treasurer of the International Coal Company. He was a director of the Compania Maritima Cubana and of the Cuban & Pan-American Express Company. The Munson Line itself, however, was his chief interest. By the time of his death, it had expanded in thirty-five years from a single schooner to sixty steamships. In size and volume of trade, it was the largest freighting organization in the American coastal trade and was a powerful influence in Caribbean commerce. His sons Carlos W. and Frank C. Munson became respectively president and vice-president-treasurer of the line after his death. Munson himself was a large and kindly man, bald and with a drooping moustache. He was liberal in his views, being non-sectarian in religion and non-partisan in politics. Devoted to business and his family, he took almost no part in public life.

[The principal source is M. A. Munson, *The Munson Record* (1895), vol. I. See also the *Munson Line Bull.* (later the *Cuba Bull.*, *Cuba Rev. and Bull.*, and finally the *Cuba Rev.*) ; *Directory of Directors in the City of N. Y.*, and the *N. Y. Herald*, Apr. 25, 1908.]

R. G. A.

MÜNSTERBERG, HUGO (June 1, 1863–Dec. 16, 1916), psychologist, was born in Danzig, Germany. His father, Moritz Münsterberg, was a lumber merchant who bought lumber in Russia and sold it in England. The business took his father frequently abroad and he always returned with glowing accounts of foreign countries, which undoubtedly stimulated the young son's imagination. His mother, Anna Münsterberg, was an artist and although she took devoted care of her four sons, and supervised her household in true German thoroughness, she had sufficient time to continue her painting and pen-and-ink drawings. The boys were encouraged in their love of good books, and Hugo and his brother Otto also devoted much time to music, the former playing the 'cello and the latter the violin. It was in this atmosphere of broad and intelligent thinking and reverence for the arts that Münsterberg spent a happy, care-free childhood. The influence of his early environment was a strong factor in his future development. It is true that he became primarily a scholar, rather than an artist, but the love of beauty remained always with him. He wrote his first poem at the age of seven. At fourteen he wrote a ballad, and some years later published a volume of poems under the *nom de plume* of Hugo Terberg. He also retained his passion for music throughout his life. It is necessary to realize the two sides of his nature in order to understand the man and his works, for the artistic had a profound influence upon the structure and the expression of his thought.

Münsterberg's education began with kindergarten. After a few years at a private school, he entered the Gymnasium of Danzig at the age of nine. His mother died when he was twelve, and this first and great sorrow changed him from a child into a thoughtful and serious youth. During his school years he engaged in many intellectual pursuits outside of the regular curriculum. When he was only fifteen he diverted himself by compiling a dictionary of foreign words used in German. He also amused himself with the study of Arabic and Sanskrit, and dipped into archeology. He was by no means a grind, however, for he had ample time to engage in outdoor sports, and he was also fond of dancing with his numerous girl companions. In 1882 he passed the final examination of the Gymnasium with credit, and as he desired to see more of the world, he spent a semester at the University of Geneva, where he improved his knowledge of the French language and literature. In September of the same year he began his serious studies at the University of Leipzig. He started with social psychology but soon changed to medicine. In 1883 he attended lectures by Wilhelm Wundt and was so deeply impressed by the great teacher of psychology that he determined to devote himself to that subject, and entered the psychological laboratory at Leipzig, which has been the training ground of many American psychologists. He continued his study of medicine, however, along with psychology and passed the preliminary examination in the former subject in 1884. In July 1885, he received his Ph.D. degree in psychology, his dissertation being upon the doctrine of natural adaptation. He then went to Heidelberg to continue his medical studies, and in the summer of 1887 he received his medical degree and also passed an examination which permitted him to lecture as "privatdocent" at Freiburg. On Aug. 7, 1887, he was married to Selma Oppler of Strassburg.

During this period he lectured principally in philosophy. There was no psychological laboratory in the university, so he equipped rooms in his own house with apparatus, and attracted many students from Germany and foreign countries. In 1891 he was promoted to an assistant professorship. In 1889 he had attended the First International Congress of Psychology at Paris, and here it was that he first met William James. They corresponded frequently for the next few years, and James was so impressed by the young man's genius that in 1892 he invited him to come to Harvard for three years to take charge of the psychological laboratory, which was then in old Dane Hall. Münsterberg accepted, after obtaining leave of absence from Freiburg. He was highly successful as a teacher and an administrator and was offered a permanent professorship at the end of his three years' appointment, but he preferred to postpone the decision to settle in America and returned to Freiburg for two years. Harvard, however, sent him urgent invitations to return, and in 1897 he yielded to the persuasive letters of President Eliot and William James. The decision was, as it turned out, a crucial one in his career, for he remained at Harvard until his death, and devoted himself without reserve to the furtherance of American psychology and to the education of the American youth. His ability was early recognized beyond the Harvard Yard. In 1898 he was elected president of the American Psychological Association. He also soon began to give public lectures in various cities throughout the country, an activity that occupied much of his time in later years.

The department of philosophy was sorely in need of a building of its own, and Münsterberg was one of the most active members in arousing interest in this project, and in raising funds for the purpose. On Monday, May 25, 1903, the hundredth anniversary of the birth of Ralph Waldo Emerson, the cornerstone of Emerson Hall was laid, and soon thereafter Münsterberg saw his dream come true of a laboratory especially equipped for experimental psychology. In the same year he took a prominent part in insuring the success of the Congress of Arts and Science at the St. Louis Exposition. Besides his scientific and literary work, he gave numerous lectures throughout the country on both psychological and cultural subjects. He carried on an extensive correspondence with the leading men of Europe and America and also found time to test his belief in the application of psychological methods to practical affairs, one of his first ventures being in the detection of crime. He also paved the way for the more extensive use of psychology in industry, medicine, arts, and education, and may justly be called one of the pioneers in the field of applied psychology. In the laboratory he directed the research of a large group of students, and occasionally he gave psychotherapeutic treatment to patients whose cases seemed likely to yield data of scientific value. He was interested in psychic research, and although firmly convinced from his experience and his theory of mind that there was no such thing as mental telepathy or spiritism, he took part in a few scientific investigations of such alleged phenomena. In 1910 he was appointed exchange professor from Harvard to the University of Berlin. Inspired by the belief that harmony among nations could be brought about only by fostering the cultural ties between them, he devoted much of his time while in Berlin to the creation of the America Institute.

On his return to Harvard, he became more engrossed than ever in applied psychology and devised many ingenious tests which he and his students tried out on the personnel of a number of large industrial plants. With characteristic impulsiveness, he made a hurried trip to Berlin in April 1912, to attend the meeting of German experimental psychologists. His last visit to his fatherland was in the summer of the same year, and although he was needing a vacation, the inner drive for creative work kept him busy on a book on applied psychology for part of the time. The last years of his life were full of stress and sorrow. He was devoted to America,

but he always remained loyal to his own country, and so from the first days of war until his death, he continued to write books and numerous newspaper and magazine articles in defense of Germany's action and in explanation of her motives and ideals. He was violently criticized and attacked from many quarters, and lost numerous friendships of long standing. He faced the storm courageously, but he felt the situation keenly, and the strain undoubtedly undermined his strength. On Dec. 16, 1916, he had to walk to his lecture at Radcliffe against a stiff, cold wind. He was exhausted on his arrival and died on the lecture platform before he had finished his opening sentence.

He was a large man of dignified appearance. He always maintained a certain reserve, so characteristic of the German professor, especially towards his students. He was never familiar, yet always gracious and genial. He had a keen sense of humor, generosity of spirit, and warmth of heart, and delighted in the companionship of his friends. He was firm in his own opinion, and aggressive in debate, yet tolerant of the views of others. He took little physical exercise, but he had great energy and his mind was never idle. He was an unusually logical and clear thinker. He had a great love of beauty in every form, and his esthetic nature showed itself in the balance and smoothness of his literary style, and the well-developed pattern of his lecture. He had the constructive imagination of the genius, and also that other characteristic so often possessed by men accustomed to think in the abstract, a certain childlike simplicity and naïveté. As a lecturer he was fluent and convincing, and never failed to hold his audience. He seldom, if ever, used notes, and his extemporaneous speeches seemed as finished as his well-prepared lectures. In philosophy, he was an idealist of the type of Fichte. In psychology he had two principles. He believed that the causal law held for mental phenomena in so far as they were correlated with physiological processes. Here he was a determinist. When, however, he considered the mental from the viewpoint of values, he believed in freedom. His chief contribution to theoretical psychology was probably his "action theory" which defined attention in terms of the openness of the nerve paths to the muscles of adjustment. His insistence upon the motor response as an essential factor of consciousness makes him a forerunner of modern behaviorism.

He composed rapidly and usually by dictation. Some of his books were produced in less than a month. His first comprehensive publication was

Die Willenshandlung (1888) in which he placed emphasis upon the motor process. His *Beiträge zur experimentellen Psychologie* (1889–92), in two volumes, contains an account of the experiments he performed before coming to Harvard, and it was followed by the *Grundzüge der Psychologie* (1900), which was one of his most profound treatises. In it he set forth his views upon the philosophical presuppositions of psychology, views which formed the structure for much of his future thinking. While at Harvard he edited four volumes of *Harvard Psychological Studies* (1903–15), which presented the work of the students of the laboratory. In *The Principles of Art Education* (1905) he described his views, both philosophical and psychological, upon esthetics, and elaborated them in *The Eternal Values* (1909). This latter book was based upon his idealistic principles in the fields of philosophy, morals, and beauty. In *American Traits from the Point of View of a German* (1901) he endeavored to interpret and explain the life of the American people and their political institutions. He wrote a number of semi-popular books on applied psychology: *On the Witness Stand* (1908); *Psychology and the Teacher* (1909); *Psychotherapy* (1909); *Psychology and Industrial Efficiency* (1913); and *Psychology and Social Sanity* (1914). His *Grundzüge der Psychotechnik* (1914) was an ambitious attempt to explain the use of psychological methods in industry and was influential in furthering the cause of industrial psychology both in America and Germany. His only textbook was *Psychology, General and Applied* (1914). During the stress of war, he wrote his last book, *Tomorrow* (1916), which looked toward peace and the restoration of international relations.

[The sketch is based mainly upon *Hugo Münsterberg: His Life and Work* (1922), by Margaret Münsterberg, and upon the writer's impressions during a long acquaintance with Münsterberg. Other sources include: Wm. Stern, "Hugo Münsterberg: In Memoriam," *Jour. of Applied Psychol.*, June 1917; H. E. Burtt, "Prof. Münsterberg's Vocational Tests," *Ibid.*, Sept. 1917; J. W. Baird, "Hugo Münsterberg: 1863–1916," *Jour. of Philos., Psychol. and Sci. Methods*, Feb. 15, 1917; R. M. Yerkes, "Hugo Münsterberg," *Philos. Rev.*, July 1917; *Science*, Jan. 26, 1917; *Boston Transcript*, Dec. 16, 1916.]   H.S.L.

MURAT, ACHILLE (Jan. 21, 1801–Apr. 15, 1847), author, christened Charles Louis Napoléon Achille, was born in Paris, France, the elder son of Joachim Murat and Caroline (Maria Annunciata Carolina Buonaparte) Murat. When Joachim was created Grand Duke of Berg and Cleves (1806), Achille became heir apparent to the duchies; and when in 1808 his father was made King of Naples, Achille became the crown prince. His education was suitable to his rank.

After Joachim's defeat by the Austrians at Tolentino, May 3, 1815, Caroline and her children took refuge at Trieste, where the mother lived as the Countess Lipona (Napoli). After the father's death, the widow and her children removed to Schloss Hamburg, thence in 1817 to Frohsdorf near Vienna. The Neapolitan Revolution (1820) naturally threw suspicion upon them, and to avoid persecution Achille determined to emigrate to the United States. After three months in Hamburg, where he spent almost half his fortune, he arrived in New York on May 19, 1823. According to the story he later related to Hortense Bonaparte, after visiting Joseph Bonaparte in New Jersey, he sailed for Spain to join the Constitutionalist party, but after spending 40,000 francs fruitlessly, returned to the United States. At Washington in 1824 he met Richard Keith Call, territorial representative of Florida in Congress, who advised him to settle in that region. Murat went to Tallahassee, near which he bought and developed the plantation known as "Lipona." Here he married, July 12, 1826, Catherine Daingerfield (Willis) Gray, daughter of Byrd C. Willis of Virginia and a great-grandniece of Washington. The next year Murat and his wife made a northern tour; on the vessel from St. Augustine to Charleston he met Emerson, with whom he conversed on philosophical and political subjects, and with whom he later corresponded. At Point Breeze they visited Joseph Bonaparte whom Murat later served as agent in Europe.

In Florida Murat took an active part in the life of the rising community about Tallahassee. He was admitted to the bar in 1828; he was active in promoting the Florida Institute of Agriculture, and in developing the resources of the country; and he held various minor offices, including a postmastership. At this period he regarded himself as an American; his *Lettres sur les États-Unis . . . à un de ses amis d'Europe* (1830) addressed to Count Thibeaudeau and originally printed in the *Revue Trimestrielle* (1828), are a republican manifesto to Europe. From these later developed his important *Esquisse morale et politique des États-Unis de l'Amérique du Nord* (1832), a philosophic account of American institutions.

The Revolution of July took Murat to Europe, and though, on leaving Florida, he informed his fellow citizens that it was his duty as a Frenchman to support the present government of France, he did not expect the July monarchy to endure and hoped to advance the fortunes of the Bonapartes, with whose Parisian agents he was in correspondence. His arrival in London in 1830 alarmed Metternich, and he was unable to penetrate the Continent farther than Belgium, where he was compelled to give up the command of a regiment which had been given him. The Murats spent some time in London (1831), where they were socially popular, and then returned to Florida to resume their life there. His *Exposition des principes du gouvernement républicain, tel qu'il a été perfectionné en Amérique* (Paris, 1833), widely distributed on the Continent, was regarded by the reactionaries as a dangerous work. He served in the Seminole War as aide-de-camp to General Call and was later commissioned colonel and appointed to the command of the frontier. He died in 1847 and was buried with Masonic ceremony in the Episcopal cemetery at Tallahassee. An editorial in the *Floridian* (Apr. 17, 1847) justly speaks of him as "a man of great eccentricity of character," but "gifted with a high order of mind, which was enriched by solid literary acquirements, ... withal a most interesting and agreeable companion." In person he is said to have resembled Napoleon. His three books on the United States are those of a candid observer; if they are not as philosophic as de Tocqueville, they are often more graphic. In the year after his death his wife was made a princess of the Second Empire by Louis Napoleon and provided with an annuity.

[On the earlier life of Murat see especially *Lettres et documents pour servir à l'histoire de Joachim Murat, 1767–1815, publiés par S. A. le Prince Murat* (8 vols., 1908–14), ed. by Paul le Brethon, and the *Diario Napoletano, 1798–1825* (1906), of Carlo de Nicola. For his American career see Emerson's *Journals*, vol. II (1909); Georges Bertin, *Jos. Bonaparte en Amérique* (1893); "Personal Reminiscences of Madame Murat. By a Friend and Relative," *Potter's Am. Monthly*, Feb. 1882. In his relation to Bonapartist politics see Valérie Masuyer, "La Reine Hortense et le Prince Louis en Angleterre (Mai–Juin 1831)," *Revue des Deux Mondes*, Mar. 1, 1915; and Richard de Metternich, ed., *Mémoires, documents, et écrits divers laissés par le Prince de Metternich*, vol. V (1882). For general accounts see "The Murats of Fla.," the *Galaxy*, June 1875; J. F. Bouchelle, "An Am. Prince and Princess," *Gulf States Hist. Mag.*, Sept. 1903; M. L. McConnell, "The Prince and Princess Achille Murat in Fla.," *Century Mag.*, Aug. 1893; Caroline M. Brevard, *A Hist. of Fla. from the Treaty of 1763 to Our Own Times*, vol. I (1924); and B. C. and R. H. Willis, *A Sketch of the Willis Family of Va.* (1898). Murat's *Esquisse morale et politique* was translated twice: as *A Moral and Political Sketch of the U. S. of North America*, etc. (London, 1833), and as *America and the Americans* (New York, 1849). The translations differ in important respects.]   H. M. J.

MURDOCH, FRANK HITCHCOCK (Mar. 11, 1843–Nov. 13, 1872), actor, playwright, was born at Chelsea, Mass., the eldest of the six children of George Frank and Mary (Murdoch) Hitchcock, and the eighth in descent from Luke Hitchcock, a shoemaker, who took the freeman's oath at New Haven in 1644 and died in Wethers-field, Conn., in 1659. In 1861, through the interest of his uncle, James Edward Murdoch [*q.v.*], whose name he adopted, he secured employment at the Arch Street Theatre, Philadelphia, of which Louisa Lane Drew [*q.v.*] had just become manager. He remained with her company, playing juvenile and light comedy parts, until his death. A half-century later her son still remembered him as "a fine actor" (John Drew, *My Years on the Stage*, 1922, p. 32). He was a modest, agreeable young man with a good sense of his vocation and ambition for honors as a dramatist. Four plays are ascribed to him. Of *The Keepers of Lighthouse Cliff* the time and place of production are unknown; David Belasco, however, told William Winter that James A. Herne [*q.v.*] had acted in it and had lifted from it the climax of *Shore Acres* (*The Life of David Belasco*, 1918, vol. I, p. 200). *Only a Jew* was produced by John T. Raymond, Feb. 24, 1873, at the Globe Theatre, Boston, three months after Murdoch's death. A flimsy, impossible little comedy of parted lovers and a stolen will, it was rendered entertaining and even charming by the novel scenes in a pawnshop and by the sweet amiableness of Nathan Rosenthal, the *deus ex machina* of the piece (*Boston Evening Transcript*, Feb. 25, 1873; *Boston Daily Advertiser*, Feb. 26, 1873). As Murdoch was acting in Philadelphia at the time, he did not see the production of his *Davy Crockett*, which he wrote for Frank Mayo [*q.v.*], at the Opera House, Rochester, N. Y., Sept. 23, 1872 (*Rochester Democrat and Chronicle*, Sept. 23, 1872). It was received somewhat tepidly, but Mayo believed in the piece, wrote encouragingly to its author, continued to tinker the script, and from time to time tried it out on audiences. After a few years it gained favor and for two decades it was immensely popular. To the actual Davy Crockett the play owed only its name, but to Scott's ballad of young Lochinvar and to the youthful Natty Bumpo of the *Deerslayer* it owed almost everything. An idyl of the backwoods, its famous scenes showed Davy barring the door with his arm while wolves gnawed their way almost through the floor and wall of the log-cabin, and later confessing bashfully to his cultured sweetheart that he could not read or write. Hamlin Garland has testified to the relief felt by the spectators when the girl offered to teach Davy his letters (Introduction to *The Autobiography of David Crockett*, 1923, p. 3). Critics pining for an autochthonous drama beheld great virtues in what was essentially a piece of claptrap (Brander Matthews, "The American on the Stage," *Scribner's Monthly*, July 1879, pp. 327–28; Laurence Hutton, *Curi-*

osities of the American Stage, 1891, pp. 30–35). Murdoch himself took the part of Bob Tangent, a "sensation writer," in his fourth play, *Bohemia, or The Lottery of Art,* which was put on for the usual week's run at the Arch Street Theatre Oct. 28, 1872, and which was ascribed on the program to a "young gentleman of Philadelphia." Intended for a satire on the venality and unscrupulousness of dramatic critics, and motivated perhaps by newspaper treatment of his wife, Jennie Workman, a member of the Arch Street company, Murdoch mixed too much indignation with his humor, and the result was a flat failure. The critics, impenitent and unabashed, made the most of the situation. Although they attributed the play to Barton Hill, Mrs. Drew's leading man, and praised Murdoch's own acting warmly, the young author was deeply grieved. He was still brooding over his fiasco when he was stricken twelve days later with meningitis and died after a brief illness.

[Mrs. Edward Hitchcock, Sr. (M. L. J. Hitchcock), *The Geneal. of the Hitchcock Family* (1894) ; *Phila. Inquirer* and *Public Ledger,* Nov. 14, 1872; *Press* (Phila.), Oct. 29, Nov. 15, 1872; A. H. Quinn, *A Hist. of the Am. Drama from the Civil War to the Present Day* (1927), vol. I.]   G. H. G.

MURDOCH, JAMES EDWARD (Jan. 25, 1811–May 19, 1893), actor, lecturer, teacher of elocution, was the eldest of four sons of Thomas and Elizabeth Murdoch of Philadelphia, Pa. His father, although a book-binder and paper ruler by trade, was also interested in local politics and acted as a volunteer fireman. James Murdoch, after a few years of common-school education, became an apprentice in his father's shop. His interest in the stage first manifested itself when he joined a local group of amateur Thespians and in his spare time devoted himself under the instruction of two teachers to studies of elocution. His father, although disappointed at the boy's unwillingness to pursue further the family trade, started him on his career as an actor by engaging for him the Philadelphia Arch Street Theatre and its company for the night of Oct. 13, 1829. Murdoch chose for his début the rôle of Frederick in Kotzebue's *Lovers' Vows,* and during the remainder of the season he was assigned a few other rôles, although without pay. With the hope of securing a more lucrative opening Murdoch went in the following year to Halifax, Nova Scotia, but when the troupe of actors shortly afterward found itself without funds, he was forced again to seek financial aid from his father. A barnstorming tour in South Carolina and Georgia under the management of Vincent De Camp was equally unsuccessful. While play-

ing minor rôles at the Arch Street Theatre in 1832 he seriously impaired his health by taking a dose of arsenic which he had mistaken for medicine. Throughout his career as an actor he was forced at all times to husband carefully his strength.

Leaving the Arch Street shortly after this accident he played as leading juvenile at the Chestnut Street Theatre opposite Frances Ann (Fanny) Kemble [*q.v.*], but was soon forced by reason of his health to go to New Orleans to recuperate. During the next ten years he appeared intermittently in many theatres : at the St. Charles in New Orleans; at the Emmanuel Street in Mobile; in Pittsburgh and Philadelphia under the management of Francis Courtney Wemyss; at the Park Theatre, New York, supporting Ellen Tree; and at the Tremont and National Theatres in Boston. In 1842 he retired temporarily from the stage and gave a series of lectures on "The Uses and Abuses of the Stage" and on Shakespearian characters. He also gave lessons in elocution to students of law and theology and collaborated on a book called *Orthophony, or Vocal Culture in Elocution* (1845). His most important period as an actor was from 1845 to 1860, during which time he established a national reputation both as tragedian and comedian. Noah Miller Ludlow praised his Hamlet as "the best representation of the Danish prince that I have ever seen." Sol Smith declared that Murdoch had very few if any equals as a light comedian—a tribute corroborated by the sound judgment of Wemyss. In 1853, after many successful engagements throughout the East and the Middle West, Murdoch went for a short season to California where he achieved great popularity. Three years later he visited England, playing one hundred and ten nights at the London Haymarket, and later appearing for a short engagement in Liverpool. On his return to the United States he engaged in intermittent starring tours, after which he would retire for long periods of rest to a farm which he had bought near Cincinnati. During the Civil War he visited the Federal camps and aroused the fervor of the soldiers by eloquent recitals of patriotic poems. After the war he returned to his Ohio farm. His wife, Eliza Middlecott, whom he married in 1831, was English by birth.

[Consult: Biographical sketch by J. Bunting prefacing J. E. Murdoch, *The Stage, or Recollections of Actors and Acting* (1880) ; J. N. Ireland, *Records of the N. Y. Stage,* vol. II (1867) ; G. C. D. Odell, *Annals of the N. Y. Stage,* vols. V and VII (1931) ; N. M. Ludlow, *Dramatic Life as I Found It* (1880) ; Sol Smith, *Theatrical Management in the West and South for Thirty Years* (1868) ; O. S. Coad and Edwin Mims, Jr., *The Am. Stage* (1929) ; C. T. Greve, *Centennial Hist. of Cin-*

cinnati and Representative Citizens (1904), vol. II;
Cincinnati Commercial Gazette, May 20, 1893.]
E. M., Jr.

MURDOCK, JAMES (Feb. 16, 1776–Aug. 10, 1856), Congregational clergyman, author, was born at Westbrook, Conn., of Protestant Scotch-Irish ancestry, being a descendant of Peter Murdock who emigrated to Long Island in 1700. His father, Abraham, a farmer, died in his twenty-sixth year (1777), leaving James, then fourteen months old, another child, and a widow, Hannah (Lay) Murdock, who married again. The son picked up his early education in the midst of severe manual labor, yet was able to enter Yale at seventeen and to graduate in 1797, second in a class of distinguished men, among whom was Lyman Beecher. The next few years were spent in theological study, pastoral supply, and teaching. During this period, Oct. 8, 1799, he married Rebecca Lydia, daughter of Jeremiah Atwater of New Haven; they had ten children. In January 1801 he was licensed to preach by the Oneida Association of Congregational Ministers and on June 23, 1802, he was ordained as pastor of the church in Princeton, Worcester County, Mass., at a salary of $366. His ministry produced a revival in 1810. In 1815 he became professor of the learned languages in the University of Vermont, and also of mathematics and natural philosophy. In 1818 he was elected to, but declined, the professorship of languages in Dartmouth College. He was appointed Brown Professor of Sacred Rhetoric and Ecclesiastical History in the Theological Seminary at Andover in 1819, but in 1828 was dismissed because of his unwillingness to see ecclesiastical history crowded out of the curriculum in favor of sacred rhetoric. Settling in New Haven in 1829, he devoted the remainder of his life to Christian scholarship. He was a member of a committee of the Connecticut Academy of Arts and Sciences which in 1842 reported that the customary suppers following the meetings were "a bad example to be exhibited in the vicinity of the college." The suppers ended and the Academy declined. In 1844 Murdock gathered the like-minded into the Philological Society of Connecticut. In 1848 he became a member of the American Oriental Society. He died at the home of his son in Columbus, Miss., and was buried in New Haven.

Among his original works may be noted a sermon, *Nature of the Atonement* (1823), in which he developed the governmental theory of Grotius, and thereby gave occasion for "some imputations against his orthodoxy" (Richardson, *post,* p. 10). The rôle was reversed when he tilted against Hegel's "pantheism," "this species of

Atheism" (*Church Review,* July 1851, p. 257). Murdock's chief original work was called *Sketches of Modern Philosophy, Especially Among the Germans* (1842, 1844). One chapter was devoted to France and two to the influence of German philosophy through Coleridge on America. Almost an original production was *Institutes of Ecclesiastical History* (3 vols., 1832), a translation of the work of J. L. von Mosheim, with notes so copious as to constitute nearly an independent treatment. In 1852 he edited the translation of the first and translated the eleventh volume of Mosheim's *Historical Commentaries on the State of Christianity.* When seventy years old he resumed the study of Syriac and brought out a translation of the Peshito version of the New Testament (1851), being led on by "the pleasing thought that the words were, probably, in great part, the very terms which the Saviour and his Apostles actually uttered in their discourses and conversations."

[F. B. Dexter, *Biog. Sketches Grads. Yale Coll.,* vol. V (1911); N. S. Richardson, *Biog. Sketch of Rev. James Murdock* (1856), reprinted in *Church Rev.,* Jan. 1857; *Trans. Conn. Acad. Arts and Sciences,* vol. II, pt. II (1901–02); J. B. Murdock, *Murdock Geneal.* (1925); Francis Atwater, *Atwater Hist. and Geneal.* (1901); *Am. Congreg. Year-Book,* 1857; C. T. Russell, *The Hist. of Princeton, Worcester County, Mass.* (1838); *A Memorial of the Semi-Centennial Celebration of the Founding of the Theol. Sem. at Andover* (1859); *The Independent,* Aug. 28, 1856; *Columbian Weekly Reg.* (New Haven), Aug. 23, 1856.]
R. H. B.

MURDOCK, JOSEPH BALLARD (Feb. 13, 1851–Mar. 20, 1931), naval officer, was born at Hartford, Conn., son of Rev. John Nelson and Martha (Ballard) Murdock, and descendant of Robert Murdock, a Scotchman who came to Massachusetts sometime before 1692. Appointed to the Naval Academy in 1866, he spent five years after graduation in the Atlantic and Caribbean, four years in the coast survey, and three as instructor in physics at the Naval Academy, 1880–83. Here began the specialization in science, particularly in electricity, which gave added distinction to his professional career. Subsequently, during a year's leave, he was assistant in physics at the University of Pennsylvania, and thereafter engaged in tests of incandescent lights and dynamos under the Franklin Institute, in recognition of which work he was made honorary member of the Institute.

Following a year in the *Dolphin,* the first ship of the new steel navy, he spent two years developing electrical equipment at the Newport Torpedo Station; then served on Admiral Belknap's staff in the Orient, 1888–91; and, after returning through Europe to inspect electrical equipment in foreign navies, carried on electrical work at the New York Navy Yard, 1891–94. In 1886 he was elected to membership in the American Philosophical Society. From December 1894 to March 1897 he was in the Mediterranean as navigator of the *Minneapolis,* which rendered effective service in checking Turkish massacres in the Near East. The Spanish-American War called him from the War College, Newport, where he was an instructor then and twice thereafter, to be executive of the transport *Panther,* which landed a marine battalion at Guantanamo, June 10–14, 1898, and assisted in its occupation and defense. Made lieutenant commander (1899), and commander (1901), he was executive of Sampson's flagship *New York,* 1899–1901, commander of the *Alliance* and later the *Denver,* and commander of the battleship *Rhode Island,* 1907–09, during the world cruise of the American fleet. Upon promotion to rear admiral (November 1909), he commanded a division of the Atlantic Fleet, May 1910–April 1911, and subsequently the Asiatic Fleet, May 1911–July 1912, during the revolution which set up a Chinese republic. In this troubled period he stood firmly for protection of American interests, on one occasion insisting effectively—alone among foreign officers —on the right of foreign shipping to occupy the international anchorage near Shanghai (*Army and Navy Journal,* Feb. 15, 1913).

Retired for age Feb. 13, 1913, after brief duty on the General Board, he was again in active service during the World War, May 1918–May 1919, as president of general courts martial, Portsmouth Navy Yard. He was married June 26, 1879, to Anne, daughter of Dr. Simeon Dillingham of Philadelphia, but had no children. After retirement he spent the summers in Hill, N. H., and the winters usually in travel. He took active interest in public affairs, was twice elected to the New Hampshire House of Representatives (in 1921 and 1923), served on the state forestry commission and as trustee of the state historical society, and made a special study of genealogy and American history. He was author of *Notes on Electricity and Magnetism* (1884), *Murdock Genealogy* (1925), and articles on electricity and professional subjects, notably "The Naval Use of the Dynamo Machine and Electric Light," *Proceedings of the United States Naval Institute,* April 1882, and "Torpedo Tubes on Battleships," *Ibid.,* September 1903.

[*Who's Who in America,* 1930–31; J. B. Murdock, *Murdock Geneal.* (1925); L. R. Hamersly, *Records of Living Officers of the U. S. Navy and Marine Corps* (6th ed., 1898); *Manchester Union* (Manchester, N. H.), Mar. 21, 1931; *N. Y. Times,* Mar. 21, 1931; brief autobiographical service record and other data supplied by Harold Murdock, Chestnut Hill, Mass.]   A. W.

MUREL, JOHN A. [See MURRELL, JOHN A., fl. 1804–1844].

MURFEE, JAMES THOMAS (Sept. 13, 1833–Apr. 23, 1912), educator, was born in Southampton County, Va. His parents, James Wilson and Anne (Parker) Murfee, were of the Tidewater gentry of Virginia. His preparatory education was done under his father and private tutors and in Stone's popular academy at Stony Mount. At the age of twenty he was graduated from the Virginia Military Institute with highest honors in civil engineering, and immediately after graduation he began the profession of teaching which he pursued for fifty years. In 1854 he became professor of natural sciences in Madison College, Pa., and the following year he served as professor of mathematics and commandant of cadets at Lynchburg College, Va. The next two years he gave to preparing his younger brothers for college. In 1860 the University of Alabama adopted the Virginia Military Institute system of discipline and appointed Maj. Caleb Huse commandant. Murfee, who was familiar with the system, was made professor of mathematics. In 1862 he was appointed commandant of cadets at the university. He was commissioned lieutenant-colonel by the Confederate government and was in charge of the university cadets when Gen. Croxton invaded Tuscaloosa and burned the university. At the end of the war Murfee was employed to design and erect new buildings for the University.

In 1871 he was elected president of Howard College, a Baptist institution then situated at Marion, Ala., and remained in this position for sixteen years. He nurtured the college through the troublous days of Reconstruction, expunged its debt, and established it upon a firm basis. When it was moved to Birmingham he declined to go with it. In the old college buildings he set up, in 1887, the Marion Military Institute of which he was superintendent until 1906. Here his academy, founded upon the old Virginia Military Institute plan, was a boon to the young men of Alabama when educational opportunities were pitifully meager. It became well known, and from various states and sections candidates for admission to West Point and Annapolis came to Marion to make their preparations. Murfee's work led President Harrison to appoint him a member of the Board of Visitors to the West Point Military Academy. He retired from active service upon an award of annuity given by the Carnegie Foundation because of "long and distinguished service" to the cause of education in Alabama. Murfee was married in July 1861 to Laura Owen of Tuscaloosa, Ala. A historian of Alabama has written of him: "There are hundreds of men adorning the different vocations in this state and in others,—who gratefully trace the inception of their success to this great teacher of youth" (Riley, *post*, p. 318).

[T. M. Owen, *Hist. of Ala. and Dict. of Ala. Biog.* (1921), vol. IV; B. F. Riley, *Makers and Romance of Ala. Hist.* (n.d.); M. B. Garrett, "Sixty Years of Howard College," *Howard Coll. Bull.*, Oct. 1927; the *Montgomery Advertiser*, Apr. 25, 1912; information as to certain facts from members of Murfee's family.]

A. B. M—e.

MURFREE, MARY NOAILLES (Jan. 24, 1850–July 31, 1922), novelist and short-story writer, better known under her pen-name, Charles Egbert Craddock, was born near Murfreesboro, Tenn., at "Grantlands." Her mother, Priscilla Dickinson, inherited this estate from her father, David Dickinson, owner of extensive plantations in both Tennessee and Mississippi. Her father, William Law Murfree, a prominent lawyer, was the grandson of Lieut.-Col. Hardy Murfree, an officer of distinguished North Carolina ancestry in the Continental Army who, settling in Tennessee in 1807, became a large landholder and gave his name to Murfreesboro. Both families were of English descent, though there was also a strain of Huguenot blood in Mary Murfree, which came through the Maney and Noailles families. Her early childhood was passed happily at "Grantlands" until a fever left her partially paralyzed and somewhat lame for the remainder of her life. When she was six, her family moved to Nashville where she made rapid progress in school, always leading her classes. A governess taught her to speak French, and after the war she attended a boarding school in Philadelphia. As a pianist she acquired a technique unusual for an amateur. Early becoming an omnivorous reader, she read extensively in history, in English, French, Italian, and Latin literature, and in law under the direction of her father. For many years her summers were spent in the Cumberland Mountains where she became thoroughly familiar with both scenery and mountaineers, and was inspired to portray them in fiction.

Her literary career began with the publication of some short stories in *Lippincott's Magazine* (May 1874, July 1875) under the name R. Emmet Dembry. In May 1878 her "Dancin' Party at Harrison's Cove" appeared in the *Atlantic* under the pen-name Charles Egbert Craddock. This story with seven others from the *Atlantic* appeared in 1884 in a collection of her stories entitled *In the Tennessee Mountains,* which created a literary sensation and contributed to that year's being called "the climactic year in the

history of the short story" (F. L. Pattee, in *Cambridge History of American Literature,* II, 388). Her masculine pseudonym, taken from the name of the hero in one of her earliest stories, suited her virile, robust, forthright style as well as her bold, heavily shaded handwriting, which caused Aldrich to write, "I wonder if Craddock has laid in his winter's ink yet, so that I can get a serial out of him" (Baskervill, *post,* p. 372). The editor of the *Atlantic,* completely deceived, was astonished, on meeting "Mr. Craddock" the following year, to find the person to be a little lady, slightly a cripple, who quietly remarked that she was Charles Egbert Craddock. Other stories of the mountains followed: namely, *Down the Ravine* (1885); *The Prophet of the Great Smoky Mountains* (1885); *In the Clouds* (1887); *The Story of Keedon Bluffs* (1888); *The Despot of Broomsedge Cove* (1889); *In the "Stranger Peoples'" Country* (1891); *His Vanished Star* (1894); *The Phantoms of the Footbridge and Other Stories* (1895); *The Mystery of Witch-Face Mountain and Other Stories* (1895); *The Juggler* (1897), and *The Young Mountaineers* (1897).

With simplicity and originality she revealed in these stories in a singularly rhythmical prose the pathos of the lonely, frustrated lives of the mountaineers and the solemn poetic beauty of their surroundings. The dialect is faithfully reproduced, with its dry caustic wit and drawling intonations. Her style is marred by too many landscape pictures, and grandiloquent phrases and unusual and pedantic words. Her dénouements are sometimes weak, and the characters of her heroes are not always sustained with the promise of her opening chapters. Yet her talent for graphic description and her charm as a storyteller carry the reader forward with interest. The best work of the latter half of her literary career belongs to historical fiction, after the manner of her first novel, *Where the Battle Was Fought* (completed in 1876 but not published until 1884), a picture of the devastation wrought by the Civil War. *The Story of Old Fort Loudon* (1899), *A Spectre of Power* (1903), *The Frontiersmen* (1904), and *The Amulet* (1906) are based upon the colonial history of the Old Southwest. *The Storm Centre* (1905) has the Civil War for its background; while *The Bushwhackers and Other Stories* (1899) and *The Raid of the Guerilla and Other Stories* (1912) interweave mountain characters in the incidents of the Civil War. Of her remaining stories, *The Champion* (1902) is a juvenile, *The Windfall* (1907) and *The Ordeal* (1912) have their setting partially in the mountains, while *The Fair Mississippian*

(1908) and *The Story of Duciehurst* (1914) portray the region with which Mary Murfree had become familiar in her youth. Her later works are free from some of the stylistic imperfections of her earlier stories, but they do not have the unstudied naïveté and charming spontaneity of her romances of the Tennessee mountains. As an author, she had a passion for accuracy and exactness, often quoting Scott's saying, "I love to be particular." She had a well-poised "judicial mind," was devoted to nature, and was sincerely religious. A vivacious and interesting conversationalist, she drew friends to her through her generosity and hearty responsiveness. In appearance, she had a "blond complexion and lightbrown, almost golden hair, bright, rather sharp face, with all the features quite prominent—forehead square and projecting, eyes gray, deep-set, and keen, nose Grecian, chin projecting, and mouth large" (Baskervill, *post*, p. 373). Failing eyesight prevented her from doing much literary work during her last years. Her death occurred at Murfreesboro in 1922. She was never married. Another novel of Mississippi River life, entitled "The Erskine Honeymoon," was left nearly completed at the time of her death and appeared as a serial in 1930 in the *Nashville Banner*.

[Sources include: W. M. Baskervil, *Southern Writers* (1897), vol. I; F. L. Pattee, *A Hist. of Am. Lit. Since 1870* (1915); *The Cambridge Hist. of Am. Lit.* (1918), vol. II; H. A. Toulmin, Jr., *Social Historians* (1911); Mildred L. Rutherford, *The South in Hist. and Lit.* (1907); *Lib. of Southern Lit.*, vol. VIII (1907); H. S. Fiske, *Provincial Types in Am. Fiction* (1903); *Nashville Banner*, Aug. 1, 1922; memoranda and manuscript material supplied by Miss Murfree's sister, Fanny N. D. Murfree, Murfreesboro, Tenn.]

C. L. L.

MURIETTA (MURIETA), JOAQUIN [See MURRIETA, JOAQUIN, *c.* 1832–1853].

MURPHEY, ARCHIBALD DE BOW (1777?–Feb. 1, 1832), jurist, pioneer in social and economic reforms in North Carolina, was born in Caswell County, N. C., the son of Archibald and Jane (De Bow) Murphey. After preparatory training at the log college of David Caldwell [*q.v.*] near Greensboro, he entered the University of North Carolina and graduated in 1799. There he was retained as tutor and professor of ancient languages for two years. On Nov. 5, 1801, he was married to Jane Armistead Scott. They had four sons and one daughter. In 1802 he qualified for the bar and began the practice of law in Hillsboro. He soon won distinction as an equity pleader and in the handling of testimony. From 1818 to 1820 he was superior-court judge and frequently acted as special justice of the supreme court when cases were

heard in which one of the three regular justices had been of counsel or on the lower bench during the litigation leading to appeal. He also edited three volumes of reports consisting of the cases heard from 1804 to 1819 by the supreme court and its antecedent, the court of conference (*Reports of Cases in the Supreme Court . . . 1804 to 1819*, 3 vols., 1821–26).

His prime interests were not in the law but in the improvement of economic and social conditions in North Carolina. From 1812 to 1818, inclusive, he was a member of the state Senate from Orange County and assumed a distinct leadership in many public causes. Believing that the chief factor that retarded prosperity in North Carolina was its lack of adequate transportation facilities, he advocated a system of internal improvements with aid from the state, proposing a comprehensive program that included the improvement of harbors, the dredging of rivers, the construction of canals and turnpikes, and the drainage of swamp lands. A number of navigation companies had been chartered before 1815, and the policy of state aid had been recommended without results, but after proposals in that year by a committee on internal navigation, of which he was chairman, appropriations were made by the state to various enterprises. In 1819 he set forth a comprehensive survey of the transportation problem in his *Memoir on the Internal Improvements*. In the same year the state established a fund for internal improvements, its income to be used to finance transportation enterprises. Unfortunately most of the enterprises were too expensive for the financial resources available, and not until the advent of railroads was transportation adequately improved in North Carolina. Along with internal improvements he urged public education. Of this he was by no means the first advocate, but a *Report on Education . . . to the General Assembly of North Carolina* (1817), written by him, offered the first definite plan for public education submitted in North Carolina. That plan was not unlike one proposed by Thomas Jefferson for Virginia; primary schools and academies should be established and larger support given the university, but free education was to be confined to poor children. Nothing was accomplished in his lifetime, except the establishment of a literary fund in 1826; not until 1838 was a public-school law enacted. In other reforms, also, he was interested, notably the revision of the state constitution, the colonization of the free negroes, humanizing the criminal law, and the abolition of imprisonment for debt. He was instrumental in obtaining the passage of a statute in 1820 abolishing the imprisonment of debtors, but the law was repealed the following year; and in 1829 he was compelled to spend some time in jail as part of the procedure by which his property was turned over to his creditors. Another of his projects was the writing of a history of North Carolina. To this end he collected materials and memorialized the legislature for appropriations with which to copy documents in the British archives. He was granted permission to float a lottery which, however, was not successful. Only the introductory chapter of his history was ever completed. He was preëminently a scholar and idealist in politics with social concepts too advanced for his day and time; but in later years he came to be regarded as the prophet of a new era.

[*The Papers of Archibald D. Murphey*, ed. by W. H. Hoyt (2 vols., 1914); W. A. Graham, "Memoir of Hon. Archibald D. Murphey," *N. C. Univ. Mag.*, Aug. 1860; *Index to the . . . Records of N. C.*, vol. IV (1914), pp. 15–29; W. H. Hoyt, "Archibald D. Murphey," *Biog. Hist. of N. C.*, ed. by S. A. Ashe, vol. IV (1906); K. P. Battle, *Hist. of the Univ. of N. C.* (2 vols., 1907–12); C. L. Coon, *The Beginnings of Public Education in N. C.* (2 vols., 1908).]   W. K. B.

MURPHY, CHARLES FRANCIS (June 20, 1858–Apr. 25, 1924), political boss, was the son of John and Mary (Prendergrass) Murphy, Irish immigrants. Born in New York City, he and seven brothers and sisters were reared in an East Side neighborhood. His formal education, like the family means, was limited; he worked at one time or another in a wire factory, as caulker in a shipyard, and as a horse-car driver. He had become a leader of the youths of the neighborhood and organized a highly successful baseball team before he opened in 1878 a small saloon, which prospered and became the headquarters of his gang. Murphy soon established himself as the friend and counselor of dockyard men, gas-house workers, clerks, and politicians who lived in the neighborhood. He later opened a couple of other saloons and a hotel. He identified himself with Tammany and was so successful in politics that in 1892 he was elected leader of the eighteenth assembly district. Six years later he was rewarded for his services by Mayor Van Wyck, who appointed him dock commissioner. This was the only salaried political office he ever held. It subsequently appeared that his board leased piers and granted contracts to members of the organization without public bidding (Report of the Mazet committee, *New York Tribune*, June 17, 1903).

Murphy's great opportunity came with the forced retirement of Richard Croker [*q.v.*] from the leadership of Tammany Hall in 1901. After the unsuccessful attempt of Lewis Nixon, Croker's political heir, to assume his power, a tri-umvirate consisting of Murphy, McMahon, and Haffen was appointed in May 1902. In September, by vote of the executive committee, the leadership was vested in Murphy alone, though the general expectation was that he would not long retain it. His rule, which continued until his death nearly twenty-two years later, was longer than that of any other of Tammany's absolute bosses. During that period, he may be said to have elected three mayors, George B. McClellan in 1903 and again in 1905, William J. Gaynor [*q.v.*] in 1909, and John F. Hylan in 1917 and 1921. In his second term, however, McClellan turned against Murphy and tried unsuccessfully to overthrow him, while Gaynor proved far from pliable. Like Tweed, Murphy conjoined with the control of Tammany the Democratic leadership of New York state. He procured the election of John A. Dix as governor in 1910, and of William Sulzer in 1912, but the latter proved a disappointment to him in matters of patronage, was impeached at his instance, and removed from office. In the next municipal election, the Tammany candidate was defeated by John Purroy Mitchel [*q.v.*], and in 1914 the state was carried by the Republicans. There was considerable agitation at this time for the removal of Murphy, who was distinctly out of favor with the Wilson administration and seemed at the lowest point of his leadership. In 1917, however, he recovered the city and in 1918, under Alfred E. Smith, a Tammany man, the Democrats swept the state. At the time of Murphy's death, Tammany was at the highest point of its prestige and power.

Much of his success may be attributed to his mastery of a taciturn diplomacy. He substituted for Croker's assertiveness the quiet purpose of an umpire. Silent, unspectacular, and extraordinarily tactful, he held together the warring elements in his organization, even at the lowest point of his political fortunes. He was gifted with great political intuition. In his first municipal campaign, when Tammany was being denounced by the reform element as nothing but a graft ring, he took the wind out of the opposition's sails by nominating on the Democratic ticket two of the most important Fusion candidates. In 1909, in effect, he repeated this coup by nominating Gaynor, a man above reproach, to oppose William Randolph Hearst, who advocated civic reform. Many unusual persons who later held high office were discovered and nurtured by Murphy. The so-called "New Tammany" took its name because of these protégés of his. There was something hopeful and stimulating about the relationship of Murphy with his young men during the later years of his life. He sat with them and

Murphy

Murphy

challenged their arguments, and when they convinced him backed them up. He found, it was said, a demonstration of independence a sure mark of the fundamental courage necessary for the welfare of his own organization. Murphy's insistence that the police must be kept out of politics was as much the expression of profound political wisdom as of stern opposition to the exploitation of commercialized vice. He knew that though the public might philosophically accept "honest" graft, the discovery of police corruption would have an inflammatory effect. The Becker-Rosenthal débâcle, in the middle of his leadership, brought him bitter confirmation of this axiom. Tammany figured in no scandals of this sort during the latter half of his period of rule. The schools and the judiciary were also kept rigorously out of politics.

There is no doubt that Murphy was a clever business man and that his wide acquaintance inevitably opened the way to profits. His real-estate investments enabled him to live comfortably. But it is greatly to his credit that his fortune was no larger when he died than when he became leader of Tammany Hall. He married Mrs. Margaret Graham, a widow, when he was over forty. The year he became leader of Tammany, newspapers described him as resembling an Irish clergyman. As he grew older he became stouter and ruddier, but he by no means created the impression of joviality. His cold gray eyes and austere silence preserved his air of detachment and dignity. Although he received any one who came to Tammany Hall, he remained a shadowy figure in the public mind, for he never made speeches, never gave interviews, and, with the one exception noted above, never held or sought public office. If he had any theory or philosophy of government, if he had political views on any subject, he never expressed them publicly. His life was a masterpiece of reticence.

[J. J. Hoey, in *Jour. of the Am. Irish Hist. Soc.,* XXIII (1924), pp. 231–40, also reprinted in *The Soc. of the Friendly Sons of St. Patrick . . . One Hundred and Forty-Second Anniversary Dinner, Mar. 17, 1926;* Isabel Paterson, "Murphy," *Am. Mercury,* July 1928; M. R. Werner, *Tammany Hall* (1928); Harold Zink, *City Bosses in the U. S.* (1930); *N. Y. Times,* and *N. Y. World,* Apr. 26–28, 1924; *Outlook,* May 7, 1924; *Literary Digest,* May 17, 1924; *Nation,* May 21, 1924. The press comments after his death were rather favorable to the man, but wholly condemnatory of the system he represented. The above sketch is based in part on information supplied by Judge James Foley and others in personal interviews.]　　　　R. M.

MURPHY, DOMINIC IGNATIUS (May 31, 1847–Apr. 13, 1930), pension commissioner, consular officer, was born in Philadelphia, Pa., the son of Dominic J. Murphy, a cotton manufacturer. He was educated in the private and public schools of that city, graduating from the Central High School with the degree of A.B. in 1865. He entered the Pension Office in Washington as a clerk on Mar. 22, 1871, and made an especially good record there, rising grade by grade to be chief of division, supervising special examiner, and chief clerk of the office. In 1893 he became deputy commissioner, and in 1896 President Cleveland appointed him commissioner of pensions, in which office he served with unusual efficiency for a year. From 1902 to 1904 he engaged in private practice as a patent attorney in Washington, and also, from 1903 to 1905, he edited and published a weekly journal entitled the *New Century,* devoted to the interests of the Catholic Church. He was prominent in Catholic societies and was a trustee of the St. Vincent Orphan Asylum.

On Apr. 30, 1904, he was appointed secretary of the Isthmian Canal Commission and served until May 23, 1905, when President Roosevelt appointed him consul at Bordeaux, France. While at that post he acted also, in 1907, as honorary commissioner to the International Maritime Exposition at Bordeaux. His next post was at St. Gall, Switzerland, where he served from 1909 to Feb. 7, 1914, when he was transferred to Amsterdam. On Feb. 22, 1915, he was promoted to consul general and assigned to Sofia, Bulgaria. He was temporarily detailed to the American consulate-general at London, England, from May 20 to Oct. 15, 1915, for special duty in the war claims department in charge of claims against the British government. He then returned to Sofia, where during the World War his services were particularly important and valuable, both to his own country and to Bulgaria; they were subsequently recognized by the naming of a hospital and a street in Sofia after him, and in various other ways. He is credited with having induced the Bulgarian government to ask the Allies for an armistice. After the war General Ludendorff wrote with feeling of Murphy's influence (*Ludendorff's Own Story,* 1920, II, 162, 367). While at Sofia he was also in charge of British interests in Bulgaria, and was presented by the British government with a silver bowl for "very special services" there to British prisoners of war and interned subjects. On July 8, 1919, he was transferred to Stockholm, where he remained until July 1, 1924, when he retired. During his term at Stockholm, he contributed efficiently to the development of the commercial and cultural relations between Sweden and the United States. After his retirement he continued to reside there until his death. He married, Oct. 24, 1904, Mrs. Bessie (Throckmorton) Atkinson, of

Washington, D. C., who with two sons survived him.

[Information from U. S. Pension Office; records of the Dept. of State; *Who's Who in America,* 1924–25; *N. Y. Times,* Apr. 14, 1930.]   A. E. I.

MURPHY, EDGAR GARDNER (Aug. 31, 1869–June 23, 1913), Episcopal clergyman, publicist, the son of Samuel W. and Janie (Gardner) Murphy, was born at Fort Smith, Ark. He was educated in the schools of San Antonio, Tex., at the University of the South, Sewanee, Tenn., and the General Theological Seminary, New York City, but took no degree. On Aug. 31, 1891, he married Maud King of Concord, Mass. Two sons were born to them. Ordained deacon (1890) and priest (1893) in the Protestant Episcopal Church, for more than a decade he served with distinction as rector of churches in San Antonio and Laredo, Tex., Chillicothe, Ohio, Kingston, N. Y., and Montgomery, Ala. The intensity of his devotion to the Kingdom of God as represented by his church is revealed in his books, *Words for the Church* (1897) and *The Larger Life* (1897). In Montgomery, he was instrumental in the founding of an Episcopal church for negroes. The erection and equipment of the Young Men's and Young Women's Christian Association buildings, in the city were largely due to his initiative, and Andrew Carnegie's gift to Montgomery of the first public-library building in Alabama was made in response to Murphy's efforts.

While in Montgomery he became vitally interested in the social problems of the new industrial era then rapidly opening in the South, and from this period the subjects of child-labor and popular education, and the race problem, largely dominated his life. With the assistance of a strong local committee he organized a conference for the free discussion of the race problem and conditions in the South. This was held in Montgomery in 1900, with Hilary A. Herbert [*q.v.*] as the presiding officer and Murphy as secretary. While the conference was under the direction of Southern men, the speakers were representative of both races and of all sections of the country. Its spirit was one of notable fairness and candor, and the published proceedings aroused wide interest in both America and Europe. Keenly sensitive to conditions in the textile industry, Murphy was responsible for the organization of the Alabama child-labor committee. Investigation disclosed that a number of Alabama cotton-mills were owned and controlled by Northern capitalists, whose influence had been effective in securing the repeal of laws enacted for the protection of women and chil-

dren working in factories (Murphy, *Problems of the Present South,* 1904, pp. 309–29). Murphy thus realized that child-labor was not a local problem, and became the leading spirit in the organization of the National Child Labor Committee. Convinced, however, of the need for an aroused and sustained public opinion, expressing itself in local rather than national legislation, he opposed the efforts of the committee to secure congressional action regulating child-labor. His open letter on national child-labor legislation to Senator Albert J. Beveridge (New York *Evening Post,* Mar. 9, 1907) was a brilliant defense of constitutional principles, later sustained by the Supreme Court of the United States. On account of differences on this issue between him and the majority of the National Child Labor Committee Murphy later resigned from it, but his interest in its work never abated. After his death, the statement was made that it was he "who pricked the conscience of the country alive to the existence of child labor as a shame and a curse to America" (*Child Labor Bulletin,* November 1913, p. 9).

A more intimate acquaintance with industrial, social, and racial problems showed him the necessity for a broader support, and more effective policies of public education. Realizing that his best work could be done outside the official ministry of the church he withdrew from that ministry (1903), and became executive secretary of the Southern Education Board (1903–08). The sincerity of his purposes, the clarity of his vision, and the statesmanlike quality of his thinking drew to him the leaders of the educational revival in his section and won for him an honored place among them. Besides editing the reports of several conferences on race problems and education in the South, and contributing to the *Outlook,* the *North American Review,* the *Century Magazine,* and other periodicals, he presented the results of his constructive thinking in two influential books, *Problems of the Present South* (1904) and *The Basis of Ascendancy* (1909). In the *Outlook* (July 5, 1913), he was described as "a leader not merely of Southern liberalism, but of national progress in social welfare," and the statement was made that "no man in this generation has succeeded so well in interpreting the South to the rest of the country."

He was compelled to give up active public work in 1908, but his physical sufferings in no way diminished the vigor of his intellect. Lying on his cot on the roof of his New York apartment he gave himself to the study of the heavens, and in 1912, under the pseudonym Kelvin Mc-

Kready, published *A Beginner's Star Book* (quarto), which won favorable notices in scientific journals. He was engaged in preparing an unfinished volume on the subjects to which he had devoted his life, at the time of his death, June 23, 1913.

[T. M. Owen, *Hist. of Ala. and Dict. of Ala. Biography* (1921), vol. IV; *Annals of the Am. Academy of Pol. and Social Science*, May 1905, Mar. 1906; *Who's Who in America*, 1912–13; obituaries in *Montgomery Advertiser*, June 24, 1913, and *Living Church*, June 28, 1913; letter of O. R. Lovejoy in N. Y. *Evening Post*, July 2, 1913.]   N. L. A.

MURPHY, FRANCIS (Apr. 24, 1836–June 30, 1907), temperance reformer, was born at Tagoat, County Wexford, Ireland. He was the younger of two sons of a poor tenant farmer, who died three months before Francis' birth. His schooling, not over four years in all, was received in a parish school conducted by a priest who apparently treated him unkindly, so that the boy was glad to be put to service at an early age in the household of his mother's landlord. For some years he contributed to the support of his widowed mother, who was a devout Catholic.

At the age of sixteen he emigrated to the United States. Landing in New York, he fell in with a group of convivial companions and lost all his money in a week of dissipation. Without a trade, he drifted from job to job and eventually into the country, where he worked on an upstate farm. He fell in love with his employer's daughter, Elizabeth Jane Ginn, and, overcoming strong parental objections, on Apr. 10, 1856, he married her. They had seven children, six of whom lived to maturity. His first wife died in 1870, and in 1890 he married Mrs. Rebecca Johnstone Fisher, of Council Bluffs, Iowa, who had been prominent in the work of the Woman's Christian Temperance Union and who became his faithful co-worker in temperance activities.

At the outbreak of the Civil War, Murphy enlisted as a private in the 92nd Regiment, New York Infantry, and served a three-year term in the army. In 1865, with the financial assistance of his brother James, who had also come to America, he became proprietor of the Bradley Hotel, Portland, Me. The habit of drinking formed in his youth fastened itself upon him here, and he sank rapidly in the social scale. In 1870 he was sentenced to jail for a drunken assault in his tavern. While in prison he was visited by Cyrus Sturdevant, a pious sea captain, whose appeals led, Apr. 3, 1870, to his conversion and the signing of a total-abstinence pledge.

After his release he was induced by friends to testify in meetings and found, to his surprise, that his endeavors provoked an enthusiastic response. He became president of a state reform club, and his evangelistic work soon extended to adjoining states and the Middle West. He adopted the blue ribbon as the badge of his crusade for "gospel temperance," and framed the Murphy pledge. In 1876 he was invited to conduct meetings in Pittsburgh and for a decade he made his headquarters there. During his first campaign of ten weeks he induced 40,000 men to sign his pledge, some $15,000 was raised by business men to support his work for sobriety among their employees, and 500 saloons in Allegheny and adjoining counties are said to have closed for lack of trade. During the Centennial Exhibition in Philadelphia he held meetings promoted by John Wanamaker. Assisted by his sons, he made a memorable tour through England, Scotland, and Ireland, during which he was received by Queen Victoria. He later conducted campaigns in Canada, Hawaii, and Australia. During his entire career he is said to have secured over 12,000,000 signatures to his pledge, and to have addressed more than 25,000 meetings.

He served in the Spanish-American War as chaplain of the 5th Pennsylvania Volunteers. In 1901 he moved from Pittsburgh to Los Angeles to spend his declining years, though he continued active until his last illness.

Murphy's power lay almost entirely in the charm of his personality. He was a man of fine physique and bearing, with heavy mustache, bushy eyebrows, and a shock of white hair. His manner was simple, earnest, and transparently honest, his smile constant, and his handclasp magnetic. His oratory was unstudied and extemporaneous, making large use of his personal experience, practical argument, and emotional appeal. From the standpoint of organization, however, his work was weak and the results not of real permanence. Religiously he was orthodox and evangelical, having become a Protestant after his conversion, but he never accepted ordination, though it was offered him in the Methodist Church. He had the broadest tolerance for the views of others and was eagerly supported by religious leaders of every faith. He never joined in the drive for legislative prohibition through the Prohibition Party or the Anti-Saloon League, believing that the public could not be permanently influenced by institutional or coercive methods.

[*Memories of Francis Murphy* (n.d.), by his wife; *Talks by Francis Murphy* (1907); E. H. Cherrington, *Standard Encyc. of the Alcohol Problem*, vol. IV (1928); A. F. Fehlandt, *A Century of Drink Reform in the U. S.* (1904); H. M. Chalfant, *Father Penn and John Barleycorn* (1920); J. S. Vandersloot, *The True*

Path; or, Gospel Temperance, Being the Life, Work, and Speeches of Francis Murphy, Dr. Henry A. Reynolds, and Their Co-laborers (1878); *Pittsburgh Gazette,* Nov. 29, 1876, and ff.; *Los Angeles Times,* July 1, 1907.]   K. M. G.

MURPHY, FRANKLIN (Jan. 3, 1846–Feb. 24, 1920), manufacturer, governor of New Jersey, was born in Jersey City, N. J., the son of William Hayes and Abby Elizabeth (Hagar) Murphy. He came of colonial stock, being a descendant of Robert Murphy, who settled in Connecticut in 1756, and whose son moved to New Jersey in 1766, and later fought in the Revolutionary War. Through his grandmother, Sarah (Lyon) Murphy, he was descended from another soldier in the Revolution—Benjamin Lyon, who was a private in the Essex New Jersey Light Horse. When Franklin was ten years old, his parents moved from Jersey City to Newark. The boy attended the Newark Academy until he was sixteen. Leaving school in July 1862, he enlisted as a private in the 13th Regiment, New Jersey Volunteers. During nearly three years of active service, he took part in nineteen battles, including Antietam, Chancellorsville, Gettysburg, Missionary Ridge, and Lookout Mountain. He was mustered out as a first lieutenant in June 1865. Immediately upon returning to civil life, though only nineteen years of age, he organized in Newark the firm of Murphy & Company, varnish manufacturers. This concern grew steadily until in 1891 it was incorporated as the Murphy Varnish Company, with its founder as president. Under his direction a system of profit-sharing for all employees was introduced, and also a pension system. In 1915 he resigned as president, to be succeeded by his son, Franklin Murphy, Jr., but he remained chairman of the board of directors until his death.

After securely establishing himself in business, Murphy entered politics as a Republican. He became a member of the Newark common council in 1883, and served until 1886, in the last year as president. In 1885 he was elected to the state Assembly. The range of his public interests is shown by his work as a trustee of the state reform school at Jamesburg, 1886–89; as the commissioner who planned Essex County's system of parks, 1895–1902; as one of the American commissioners to the Paris Universal Exposition in 1900; as a member of the board of managers of the National Home for Disabled Volunteer Soldiers, 1905–12; and as president-general of the national society of the Sons of the American Revolution, 1898–1900. In 1897 he declined the ambassadorship to Russia. He was for many years chairman of the Republican

state committee, and from 1900 to 1918 was a member of the Republican National Committee. In 1908 he was a candidate for the Republican nomination for vice-president, receiving seventy-seven votes at the national convention in Chicago, and in 1916 was defeated by Joseph S. Frelinghuysen as a candidate for the nomination for United States senator. He was a delegate to five national conventions (1900–16). The most valuable public service which he rendered, however, was during his three years as governor of New Jersey. Elected in 1901, he entered office at the beginning of 1902, and immediately applied the methods of the successful business man to the affairs of state. The result was that during his administration New Jersey enacted its first primary-election law, child-labor law, workshop-ventilation law, and tenement-house-commission law. Moreover, he introduced a complete audit system of state expenditures, and compelled banks to pay interest on state deposits. He abolished the fee systems in state and county offices. Largely through his efforts the state sanitarium for tuberculous patients was established at Glen Gardner, and an appropriation was made for the industrial school for colored children at Bordentown. Even after he retired from the governorship, he exerted considerable influence on the politics of the state.

In private life he was well liked for his courtesy and good humor. He was a man of culture, interested in American history and particularly in patriotic societies. He was married, June 24, 1868, to Janet Colwell of Newark. She died in 1904, leaving two children who survived him. His death occurred at Palm Beach, Fla.

[*Lyon Memorial,* vol. II (1907); *Manual of the Legislature of N. J.,* 1904; *Who's Who in America,* 1918–19; *N. Y. Times, N. Y. Tribune,* Feb. 25, 1920; *Newark Evening News,* Feb. 24, 1920.]   J. E. F.

MURPHY, HENRY CRUSE (July 5, 1810–Dec. 1, 1882), lawyer, political leader, scholar, was born in Brooklyn, N. Y. His paternal grandfather, Timothy Murphy, an Irish physician, emigrated to New Jersey before the Revolution. John G. Murphy, his father, a skilled mechanic and millwright, married Clarissa Runyon of an old Dutch family of Princeton, N. J., and about 1808 established himself in Brooklyn. Henry, the eldest son, graduated with honors from Columbia in 1830, studied law with the Hon. Peter W. Radcliffe, and, after admission to the bar, began to practise in Brooklyn. In 1834 he became city attorney, and the following year he joined John A. Lott, then the ablest lawyer in Brooklyn, in partnership. Shortly afterwards John Vanderbilt was admitted, and the firm entered upon a long and prosperous career.

All of its members were able politicians, and so completely did they control the local affairs of the Democratic party that in the words of Stiles, the Brooklyn historian, to write a history of the firm "would be to write the political history of Brooklyn from 1835 to 1857" (*post*, p. 10). Murphy, at the age of thirty-one (1842) was elected mayor of Brooklyn. Before his term was completed he was sent to Congress, where he served from 1843 to 1845, and again from 1847 to 1849. At the state constitutional convention of 1846 he contended vainly for a notably advanced program of city charters, taxation, and government, and repeated his efforts, without effect, at the constitutional convention of 1867–68. In 1852, when the Virginia delegation introduced the name of Franklin Pierce into the deadlocked National Democratic Convention, with the result that he was nominated and subsequently elected, it was only after Pierce had won the delegation's preference over Murphy by one vote. In 1857 he was appointed minister to the Netherlands by Buchanan, and served until recalled by Lincoln. The period was a quiet one in the relations of the two countries until the secession crisis, when Murphy communicated to the Dutch government a notably able statement of the Federal viewpoint (*Papers Relating to Foreign Affairs*, 1861, I, 327 ff.). Upon his return he was elected without much effort on his part for six successive terms in the state Senate, 1861–73. He urged support of the war by the Democratic party in speeches at the state convention, and before the Tammany Society. At the National Democratic Convention of 1868, as chairman of the committee on resolutions, he battled vainly against the Greenbackers and their Ohio program. The same year he lost a bitterly fought battle at the Democratic state convention for nomination for governor, being supported by the opponents of John T. Hoffman [q.v.], the Tammany candidate. He was the party's unsuccessful nominee for the United States Senate in 1867 and 1869, and his hopes for the same office in 1875 were dashed when Governor Seymour supported his henchman, Francis Kernan [q.v.]. During the entire period after his return from The Hague Murphy's political career was handicapped by the fact that he belonged to a minority faction of a minority party.

In the meantime he had been turning more and more to business and scholarly pursuits. He aided in securing many local improvements for the city. His interest in the development of Coney Island led him to accept the presidency of the Flatbush & Coney Island Railroad and to build Brighton Beach Hotel at its terminus. He drafted and secured the passage of the legislation necessary for the building of Brooklyn Bridge, and was president of the private company which, in the beginning, conducted the enterprise, and also of the corporation which succeeded it. He relentlessly fought all opposition, and worked against both natural and legal obstacles, remaining at his post "when almost any other man would have retired in disgust" (editorial, New York *Sun*, Dec. 2, 1882).

While studying law he had served as the chief editorial writer of the *Brooklyn Advocate* and as a rising party leader he contributed political articles to the *United States Magazine and Democratic Review* and to the *North American Review*. Having persuaded a few friends of the desirability of establishing a Democratic newspaper in Brooklyn, he issued in October 1841, the first number of the *Brooklyn Eagle*, of which he remained proprietor and associate editor for almost a year, placing the paper upon a firm foundation. His increasing interest in early American history led him to collect, with rare discrimination, a library of Americana, which at his death was rivaled by only two or three collections in the country. His chief contributions to American history were his translations of works relating to New Netherland, especially *The Representation of New Netherland* (1849), from the Dutch of Adriaen van der Donck, *Voyages from Holland to America* (1853), from the Dutch of D. P. deVries, and the valuable journal of Jasper Dankers and Peter Sluyter, which he discovered in manuscript in an Amsterdam bookstore, purchased, and translated for the first volume (1867) of the *Memoirs* of the Long Island Historical Society. A unique piece of work was his *Anthology of New Netherland; or Translations from the Early Dutch Poets of New York* (Bradford Club Series, no. 4, 1865). His *Henry Hudson in Holland* (1859) is still valuable, having been reprinted with notes, documents, and bibliography by Wouter Nijhoff in 1909. In his *Voyage of Verrazzano* (1875), however, he unfortunately took the view that Verrazzano's claims of discovery were unfounded.

Murphy married, July 29, 1833, his cousin, Amelia, daughter of Richard Greenwood of Haverstraw, N. Y., who survived him; to them were born two sons.

[H. R. Stiles, in *N. Y. Geneal. and Biog. Record*, Jan. 1883; Frederick Greenwood, *Greenwood Geneals.* (1914); D. S. Alexander, *A Political Hist. of the State of N. Y.*, vol. III (1909); *Proc. at the Dinner . . . to the Hon. Henry C. Murphy* (1857); *Cat. of the Magnificent Lib. of the Late Henry C. Murphy* (1884);

U. S. Mag. and Democratic Rev., July 1847; Brooklyn Eagle, N. Y. Times, N. Y. Tribune, Dec. 2, 1882.]
                             O. W. H.

MURPHY, ISAAC (Oct. 16, 1802–Sept. 8, 1882), governor of Arkansas, was born near Pittsburgh, Pa., the son of Hugh and Jane Murphy. In 1830 he settled in Tennessee, where he taught school. In 1834 he moved to Arkansas and taught in Fayetteville and the surrounding country. The next year he was admitted to the bar and for several years taught, practised law, and surveyed public lands. He was elected to the legislature in 1848 but went to California in 1849 and remained until 1854. On returning to Arkansas he moved to Huntsville, where he and two of his daughters conducted the Huntsville Female Seminary. His impress upon the educational system of northwest Arkansas was good. In 1856 he was elected to the state Senate to fill a vacancy, and thereafter he devoted himself to the law and politics. In 1861 he was elected a delegate from Madison County to the state convention which had been called to consider secession. A majority of the delegates, including Murphy, opposed secession, but they allowed the secessionists to put through a resolution submitting "secession" or "cooperation" to the people to be voted upon in August. After the bombardment of Fort Sumter the convention was called together again and voted secession with only five negative votes (May 6). Four of the five members were won over by the secessionists but Murphy remained impervious to all appeals for unanimity (*Journal, post*, pp. 123–24). He remained in the convention, however, until it adjourned in June. He then returned to his home, but the situation became unbearable and after the battle of Pea Ridge he fled (April 1862) to the Union army commanded by Gen. Samuel R. Curtis, leaving his family at Huntsville. There his wife and daughters suffered many hardships at the hands of Confederate sympathizers.

Murphy was made a member of General Curtis' staff and remained with the Union army until the capture of Little Rock, Sept. 10, 1863. He then became active in forming a loyal state government. President Lincoln issued an order on Jan. 20, 1864, for an election to be held on Mar. 28, but the loyalists had already anticipated him and a convention, assembled at Little Rock on Jan. 8, elected Murphy provisional governor. Lincoln then directed the military authorities to cooperate in the establishment of a government. In March the revised constitution was adopted by popular vote, mainly in the counties north of the Arkansas River, and Murphy was elected governor. His program included cooperation with the Federal authorities to crush the Confederates, the abolition of slavery, the education of the masses, and the rebuilding of the state by encouraging the immigration of people with capital. Confederate sympathizers gave him much trouble and he appealed to Lincoln several times. He reported that loyalists were dying of starvation, but he could not help them. There was no money in the treasury when he was elected, but he conducted the government economically, paid expenses, and had $167,221.27 in greenbacks and bonds in the treasury when the Carpet-bag convention met in 1868. In 1866 former Confederates captured the legislature and passed numerous laws and resolutions distasteful to him, but he was never swept into the camp of the Radical Republicans and thereby regained to a large extent the confidence and respect of his opponents. When displaced by the new government he returned to his home in Madison County and remained there until his death, passing his last days in obscurity. He had married, on July 31, 1830, Angelina A. Lockhart in Tennessee. Six daughters were born of this marriage. He was not a forceful leader, but he was honest and straightforward and held tenaciously to his opinions.

[Fay Hempstead, *A Pictorial Hist. of Ark.* (1890); T. S. Staples, *Reconstruction in Ark., 1862–74* (1923); C. H. McCarthy, *Lincoln's Plan of Reconstruction* (1901); M. W. Downes, *The Murphy Family* (1900); journals of the House and Senate of Arkansas, 1864–65; *Jour. of Both Sessions of the Convention of the State of Ark., Little Rock* (1861); *Daily Ark. Gazette*, Sept. 12, 1882.]
             D. Y. T.

MURPHY, JOHN (Mar. 12, 1812–May 27, 1880), book-publisher, son of Bernard and Mary (McCullough) Murphy, was born in Omagh, Tyrone, Ireland, and was brought by his parents to New Castle, Del., in 1822. Here he attended the New Castle Academy and worked in a store until he was sixteen years of age, when he went to Philadelphia to learn the printing trade. Becoming a skilled craftsman, with an artistic touch, and possessing business acumen, he was soon superintendent of a thriving concern. About 1835 he established a printing and stationery house in Baltimore, where the trade was less crowded, and two years later he added the publication of books. In 1852, he married Margaret E. O'Donnoghue of Georgetown, D. C., who died in 1869, leaving two sons and four daughters.

As a publishing house of high standards and laudable ideals, Murphy & Company did a substantial general business, although its specialty was Catholic books. Catholic writers, some of whom became prelates, owed Murphy a debt of gratitude, for he courageously undertook ponderous theological works for which there was a restricted market, and assumed losses which were met by the profits from commercial printing and the sale of textbooks. Furthermore, he was available when secular publishing houses practically refused manuscripts by Catholic writers. He also brought out Bibles, hymnals, prayerbooks in various languages, and devotional guides, putting them on the market at a commendably low price; through translations issued by him foreign Catholic writings were made known to the American public. He printed *The Religious Cabinet,* the first number of which appeared in January 1842. A year later he became proprietor of the periodical, and the name of it was changed to the *United States Catholic Magazine,* under which title he published it until December 1848. He also published *The Metropolitan; A Monthly Magazine* (1853–59), a monthly devoted to religion, education, literature, and general information; the *Metropolitan Catholic Almanac and Laity's Directory;* the *Catholic Youth's Magazine* (1857–61); *The Works of the Right Reverend John England* (5 vols., 1849); theological writings of the Kenricks and the Spaldings; Peter Fredet's popular histories, Gibbons' *Faith of Our Fathers,* which proved a best seller; and numerous works of lesser clergymen. The foreign books brought out by him included Butler's *Lives of the Saints,* Faber's writings, Thomas Moore's *Travels of an Irish Gentleman in Search of a Religion, Rituale Romanum Pauli V,* John Lingard's *Abridgment of the History of England,* J. M. V. Audin's *Life of Luther,* Cardinal Wiseman's works, Hendrik Conscience's Belgian novels, Châteaubriand's *Genius of Christianity,* and Balmes's *Protestantism and Catholicity Compared.* For the publication of the *Definition of the Dogma of the Immaculate Conception,* Murphy was awarded a papal medal of merit (1855); for his *Acts and Decrees of the Second Plenary Council of Baltimore,* he was honored with the title of "typographer to the Apostolic See" (1866). Among his secular publications were James McSherry's *History of Maryland* (1850), the new constitution of Maryland of 1851 and also those of 1864 and 1867, and *The Maryland Code, Public General Laws* (2 vols., 1860), with later supplements, which won the encomium of his friend, Chief Justice Taney. It was said justly that Murphy elevated the standard of law publications and uplifted the publishing business to a higher ethical basis. A man of integrity, he lived quietly through the trying Civil War years and paid off all liabilities when many businessmen took refuge in bankruptcy. On his sudden death from paralysis, he was buried from the cathedral in Baltimore, attended by an unusual concourse of friends of various ranks, who bore witness to his character and numerous charities.

[*Gazette* (Baltimore), May 28, 1880; *Sun* (Baltimore), May 28, 31, 1880; *Stationer* (N. Y.), June 3, 1880; *N. Y. Freeman's Journal,* June 5, 1880; *Catholic Review* (Baltimore), June 5, 1880; information from Murphy's son and successor, Frank K. Murphy.]

R. J. P.

MURPHY, JOHN BENJAMIN (Dec. 21, 1857–Aug. 11, 1916), surgeon, was born of Irish parents, Michael and Ann (Grimes) Murphy, on a farm near Appleton, Wis. After a preliminary education in the public schools and some medical studies under Dr. John R. Reilly of Appleton, he entered Rush Medical College, Chicago, where he was graduated in 1879. Following an internship in the Cook County Hospital, he spent two years in graduate study in Vienna. Returning to Chicago, he associated himself in practice with Dr. Edward W. Lee. In 1884 he became lecturer in surgery at Rush Medical College. His later teaching positions were as follows: professor of clinical surgery in the College of Physicians and Surgeons, Chicago, 1892–1901; professor of surgery, Northwestern University Medical School, 1901–05; professor of surgery, Rush Medical College, 1905–08; and again professor of surgery, Northwestern University Medical School, 1908–16. He became chief of the surgical staff of Mercy Hospital in 1895, which position he held until his death. For much of his career he was an attending surgeon at Cook County Hospital.

Murphy began his professional career at a time when bacteriological investigation and antiseptic methods were greatly increasing the possibilities of abdominal surgery. It was to this field that he turned his early efforts. He was one of the first to investigate the cause and treatment of peritonitis following appendicitis. Being of an inventive turn of mind, he produced in 1892 the Murphy button, a mechanical device for making rapid and accurate intestinal and gastro-intestinal anastomosis. This device revolutionized the gastro-intestinal surgery of the time and made possible life-saving operations that never would have been attempted without its help. Though the Murphy button will be remembered as his outstanding contribution to surgery, he advanced the surgical knowledge of every region of the abdomen. Later, he devoted himself to the principles underlying the surgery of the lungs and of the nervous system, and his later years were largely devoted to the surgery of bones and joints, particularly to deformities due to infections. He was a rapid operator with mechanical skill of the highest order. He was also the first of the master-surgeons of Chicago to whom surgical asepsis was a matter of intuition. It was as a teacher of surgery, however, that he was preëminent. Despite a high shrill voice, he had an eloquence and a force of personality that made him one of the greatest interpreters of surgery that America has produced. His presentation was dramatic. Dr. William J. Mayo has said that as a teacher of clinical surgery he was "without a peer," characterizing him as "the surgical genius of our generation" (Kelly and Burrage, *post*, p. 839).

Murphy was the recipient of many honorary degrees, from both American and foreign universities. He was awarded the Laetare medal by Notre Dame University in 1902 and in 1916 the Pope made him Knight-Commander of the order of Saint Gregory the Great. He held membership in the principal surgical societies of America and Europe and was president of the American Medical Association, 1910–11, and of the Clinical Congress of Surgeons, 1914–15. His writings were largely confined to contributions upon clinical surgery to journals. He wrote the article entitled "Surgery of the Appendix Vermiformis" in W. W. Keen's *Surgery, Its Principles and Practice* (1908), and published *General Surgery* in 1911. His other most noteworthy work is *The Surgical Clinics of John B. Murphy, M.D., at Mercy Hospital, Chicago* (5 vols., 1912–16).

Physically he was tall and powerfully built, with a florid complexion, thin hair, a red beard, carefully parted, and a red moustache. He had extraordinary energy, which showed in his quick movements and terse decisive speech. He was invariably kind and courteous, deeply religious, and scrupulous in his religious obligations. The stress of his work brought on attacks of angina pectoris, from which he was invalided for several months before his death, which took place at Mackinac Island, Mich. He was married on Nov. 25, 1885, to Jeannette C. Plamondon of Chicago, who survived him; they had five children, one son and four daughters. In 1926 the American College of Surgeons inaugurated in Chicago the John B. Murphy Memorial, a monumental building to house the headquarters of the college. His name is also borne by the Murphy Hospital opened in 1921 on Belmont Avenue.

[*Surgery, Gynecology and Obstetrics*, Aug. 1916; *Ibid.*, Dec. 1920; *Bull. Am. Coll. of Surgeons*, July 1926; *Trans. Am. Surgic. Asso.*, vol. XXXVI (1918); H. A. Kelly and W. L. Burrage, *Am. Medic. Biogs.* (1920); *Chicago Daily Tribune*, Aug. 12, 1916.]

J. M. P.

MURPHY, JOHN FRANCIS (Dec. 11, 1853–Jan. 30, 1921), landscape painter, was born at Oswego, N. Y. He attended the public schools of Oswego but took slight interest in any line of study save that of painting. In his art he was wholly self-taught. At the age of seventeen he went to Chicago and found employment as a painter of advertising signboards, but he soon lost this job because of laziness. Returning to the East, he spent several years in New Jersey, not far from Orange, where he sketched and during the summer months taught a group of girl students, one of whom, Adah Clifford, later became his wife. In 1875 he opened a studio in New York, and a year later he exhibited his first picture at the National Academy. His early years in New York were a period of severe struggle for a living. He was elected a member of the Salmagundi Club in 1878 and thereafter for nearly a half-century was closely identified with that organization. He struck his gait in the early eighties and began to experience the satisfactions of relative prosperity. He was awarded the second Hallgarten prize at the National Academy in 1885 and became an academician in 1887. At the same time he built a summer home and studio at Arkville, N. Y., a hamlet at the western edge of the Catskill region. There, from that time to the end of his life, he spent many happy summers and autumns in leisurely contemplation; he never painted out-of-doors, and his pictures were never literal portraits of places, but he made pencil notes and was constantly observing.

In time numerous honors as well as higher prices for his pictures told the story of his popularity. The list of prizes lengthened; the museums were eager to acquire his works; and at the time of his death in the winter of 1921, he was at the acme of his renown. He was given a funeral at the Fine Arts building, and he was buried at Arkville. Five exhibitions of his work were opened soon after his death. The Lotos Club opened a memorial exhibition of seventy-five of his landscapes; the Salmagundi Club exhibited a somewhat smaller collection of his works; there was an exhibition at the Macbeth Gallery; the Kansas City Art Institute displayed a group of nineteen pictures; and in Boston the Vose Gallery placed on view a collection of landscapes. Examples of his art are to be seen in the leading museums of the United States. The chief merit of his landscapes, to which, perhaps, there is a certain sameness, is their poetic sentiment. The designs are simple and good; the quiet phases of nature are pictured with harmony of tone. Of all his work, some of his small early canvases are among his best productions.

[Eliot Clark, *J. Francis Murphy* (1926), containing bibliography; F. F. Sherman, *Am. Painters of Yesterday and Today* (1919); Elliott Daingerfield, article in *Scribner's Mag.*, Jan. 1917; Royal Cortissoz, in *N. Y. Herald-Tribune*, Feb. 6, 1921; C. L. Buchanan, in *Internat. Studio*, July 1914 and Mar. 1921; *Am. Art News*, Feb. 5, Dec. 3, 10, 1921; Handbook of loan exhibition, Macbeth Gallery, 1921; H. T. Lawrence, article in *Brush and Pencil*, July 1902; Mich. State Lib., *Biog. Sketches of Am. Artists* (1924); S. G. W. Benjamin, article in *Am. Art Review*, Mar. 1881; catalogues of the memorial exhibitions at the Lotos Club, Salmagundi Club, and Vose Gallery; Sadakichi Hartmann, *A Hist. of Am. Art* (1932), vol. I; the *Arts*, Feb.-Mar. 1921; *N. Y. Times*, Jan. 31, 1921.]
W. H. D—s.

MURPHY, JOHN W. (Jan. 20, 1828–Sept. 27, 1874), bridge engineer, was born at New Scotland, N. Y. When he entered Rensselaer Polytechnic Institute, he was already a practical surveyor, seasoned by a sound apprenticeship; and after he was graduated, in 1847, he obtained a position of some responsibility on the Erie Canal. During the next twenty-five years he explored many fields of engineering: in 1851–52 he erected the levees on the Alabama River; in 1860–61 he served as chief engineer of Montgomery, Ala.; in 1864 he constructed the Union Hall, in Philadelphia, which was taken over by the Pennsylvania Railroad; in 1869 he built the aqueduct over the valley of the Wissahickon; but he is remembered primarily as a pioneer in the design, construction, and manufacture of bridges.

On the Erie Canal he became assistant to Squire Whipple [*q.v.*], who, in 1840, had built an iron bridge with wrought-iron tension and cast-iron compression members. Under Whipple's influence he advanced rapidly in his profession. While engaged on the construction of a wooden bridge at Easton, Pa., he substituted a temporary bridge for the falsework usually employed; and this method he developed more fully in the erection of the aqueduct at Germantown. Another of his more notable innovations was a testing machine for determining the elasticity of construction materials. His chief contribution to the art of bridge-building sprang, however, from his association with Whipple, who, in 1848, introduced the type of truss bridge which bears his name. As modified by Murphy, it soon came to be known as the Murphy-Whipple bridge. In its final form, which was in wide use throughout the United States until 1885, the struts were vertical and the ties intersected twice. As early as 1859, in a bridge on the Lehigh Valley Railroad, Murphy initiated the use of pin connections, long a characteristic feature of American metal bridge construction. In this instance

the pins were turned and the eyes formed by bending the bars around the pins and welding the ends. In 1863, he designed for the Lehigh Valley Railroad a pin-connected bridge in which all the members were of wrought iron. This was the first bridge of its kind in the United States. His chief monument is the Broad Street Bridge. in Philadelphia, in the erection of which he had to overcome unprecedented difficulties. In 1855 he entered into partnership, at Trenton, N. J., with his classmate, George Washington Plympton, who was associated with him in the development of his testing machine. In 1859, with several of his fellow alumni of Rensselaer, including George Brooke Roberts [*q.v.*] and Percival Roberts, he organized a company which constructed many important bridges of the Murphy-Whipple type during the era of railroad expansion.

Murphy, who was twice married, was popular in social and musical circles. He was a pleasant companion, an entertaining anecdotist, an effective speaker, and a composer of some ability. By his first marriage he had a son and a daughter. He died in Philadelphia.

[Zerah Colburn, "American Iron Bridges," *Minutes of Proc. of the Inst. of Civil Engineers* (London), XXII (1863), 540–75; W. C. Unwin, *Wrought Iron Bridges and Roofs* (1869); J. A. L. Waddell, *Bridge Engineering* (2 vols., 1916); R. P. Baker, *A Chapter in Am. Educ.* (1924); H. B. Nason, *Biog. Record Officers and Grads. Rensselaer Polytechnic Inst.* (1887); the *Press* (Phila.), Sept. 29, 1874.]
R. P. B.

MURPHY, MICHAEL CHARLES (Feb. 28, 1861–June 4, 1913), coach, pioneer of athletic training in the United States, was born at Westboro, Mass. As a boy, he was frail and slim. Early in life he took up physical exercise in the form of athletic competition, hoping to improve his physique. Ambitious to become an athlete, he soon excelled in running and in baseball. He even tried long-distance running and walking, but it was as a sprinter that his talent was best displayed. Possessing an unusually keen and active mind, he studied closely the methods of every professional athlete with whom he came in contact and adapted the hints thus obtained to his own use with marked success. In the middle eighties he established a training camp for athletes near his home in Westboro, and put his ideas into practice. His success in improving the performance of his pupils brought him in 1887 to the attention of A. B. Coxe, who induced him to become athletic trainer at Yale. After two years there, he went to the Detroit Athletic Club, where he stayed three years. He returned to Yale in the summer of 1892 as coach of the track team and trainer of the football team, remaining until the summer of 1896, when the University of Pennsylvania secured his services. After a four-year period of tremendous success at Pennsylvania, he returned to Yale in the fall of 1900, remaining in New Haven until 1905, when he again returned to the University of Pennsylvania. In this connection he continued until his death. During most of his summer vacations he coached the track team of the New York Athletic Club. He was elected without question to coach the American Olympic teams of 1908 at London and of 1912 at Stockholm, both of his teams winning overwhelming victories. He was again chosen coach for the American team of 1916, an appointment canceled by his death in 1913. The Olympic Games themselves were canceled by the World War.

Murphy had an alert mind and an inquiring spirit, and was quick to catch the meaning of any innovation or suggestion that his athletes had to offer. The nervousness of Charles H. Sherrill on the starting line of the sprint was turned by Murphy from a handicap to an advantage when he introduced the crouching start, the greatest contribution to the art of sprinting in modern times. He continually studied and remembered the little tricks and devices that went to improve the technique of jumping, pole vaulting, hurdling, and weight throwing, until he had a knowledge of these feats which was unique. He was a keen judge of character and had an astonishing ability to get the best out of his athletes by persuasion, flattery, or the lash of sarcasm, each used to suit the case. He had supreme confidence in himself and was fearless in upholding his views; above all, he had the evangelist's ability to work himself up to a state of fervor that communicated itself to his athletes and inspired them to superhuman efforts. A list of the victories of his teams at Yale and Pennsylvania would be a history of the intercollegiate championships of his time. In his later years, Pennsylvania became the place to which coaches from all over America and abroad came for advice and counsel, which was always freely given. His trainer's lore and his theories were written down by E. R. Bushnell and published after his death in a book entitled *Athletic Training, by Michael C. Murphy* (1914). Apart from this work, he was author of little except some small handbooks in the Spalding Athletic Library and ephemeral newspaper articles. He died in Philadelphia. His wife was Nora B. Long.

[*Old Penn* (Univ. of Pa.), June 14, 1913; *Phila. Record*, June 5, 1913; *North American* (Phila.), June 5, 1913; intro. by E. R. Bushnell to *Athletic Training, by Michael C. Murphy* (1914); F. A. M. Webster, *Athletics of Today* (1929); C. H. Mapes, *The Man Who One Day a Year Would go "Eelin'"* (1915); certain facts and dates from E. R. Bushnell.]   R. T. M.

MURPHY, WILLIAM SUMTER (1796?–July 13, 1844), chargé d'affaires in Texas, was born in South Carolina and removed to Chillicothe, Ohio, in 1818. He married Lucinda Sterret in 1821. He was a practising lawyer with a taste for politics and military affairs, a taste so strong that his place in the history of the Ohio bar is not an important one. His oratorical powers, however, were considerable, and it is said that he was in demand as counsel for the defense in criminal cases and that his friends liked to refer to him as "the Patrick Henry of the West." His only public service in Ohio was as one of the commissioners who in 1835, after the "Toledo War," remarked the disputed portion of the Ohio-Michigan boundary (*Special Message of Governor Lucas . . . in regard to the Northern Boundary Line . . . Dec. 8, 1835*, 1835, p. 8). A brigadier-general in the militia, he was always known as General Murphy. The story is told that, at first a Democrat, he became soured by his failure to obtain a nomination for Congress in 1832. At any rate, he was a supporter of Harrison in 1836 and 1840 and after that a supporter of Tyler.

In 1843 Tyler, by a recess appointment, made him minister extraordinary to Central America and chargé d'affaires to Texas. The Central-American mission amounted to little, but for a year he was the representative of the United States in Texas. He was not, however, entrusted with much responsibility, though serving as a useful instrument in the promotion of the annexation plans of Tyler and his secretaries of state. Neither the Washington nor the Texan government kept him informed as to what was going on, so that he, an ardent annexationist, believed that Great Britain's power over President Houston was complete. In fact the burden of his dispatches was the dark machinations of the British, and in this way they were equally acceptable at Washington and at the capital of Texas. In January 1844 negotiations for annexation were promising after Secretary Upshur had assured Houston, through Murphy, that a clear two-thirds of the Senate was in favor of a treaty. Houston at once obtained from the eager Murphy a promise of military protection by the United States pending the conclusion of the affair, and Murphy went so far as to order an American vessel to Vera Cruz to warn other naval units that they would soon be needed to repel a Mexican invasion of Texas. This was a little too much, and Washington informed the chargé

that he had pledged the president to action unwarranted by the Constitution. However, by
the time this dispatch reached Texas, on Apr.
11, 1844, the treaty of annexation was signed.
Soon the treaty came before the Senate and was
rejected, while the confirmation of Murphy's
appointment was refused at the same time. "The
tail went with the hide," he pleasantly remarked
in reporting the rejection and his recall to the
Texan government (Reeves, *post,* p. 160).
Within a few weeks he died of yellow fever at
Galveston.

[*Hist. of Ross and Highland Counties, Ohio* (1880),
p. 77; L. S. Evans, *A Standard Hist. of Ross County,
Ohio* (1917), vol. I; J. S. Reeves, *Am. Diplomacy under Tyler and Polk* (1907); J. H. Smith, *The Annexation of Texas* (1911); G. P. Garrison, "Diplomatic
Correspondence of the Republic of Texas," *Am. Hist.
Assoc. Report . . . 1908,* vol. II, pts. 1, 2 (1911); "Calhoun Correspondence," *Ibid. . . . 1899,* vol. II (1900);
L. G. Tyler, *The Letters and Times of the Tylers,* vol.
II (1885); *Sen. Doc., 341, 349, 28 Cong., 1 Sess.*
(1844); *Southwestern Hist. Quart.,* Jan. 1913, July
1915; *Niles' National Register,* June 15, 1844, Aug. 17,
1844.]   H. D. J.

MURPHY, WILLIAM WALTON (Apr. 3,
1816–June 8, 1886), United States consul-general, was born at Ernestown, Canada, but was
brought to Ovid, Seneca County, N. Y., at an
early age. As a youth of nineteen he joined the
pioneer emigration from New York State to
Michigan and entered the United States land
office at Monroe as a clerk in 1835, when the
speculation in land was at its height. He remained in the land office for two years and studied
law in his leisure hours. In 1837 he removed to
the pioneer community of Jonesville and with
William T. Howell opened the first law office in
Hillsdale County, continuing in practice until
1861, the firm from 1848 being that of Murphy
& Baxter. In addition to practising law, he conducted a land agency, founded a newspaper, the
Jonesville Telegraph, and was a partner in the
banking firm of E. O. Grosvenor & Company.
He served one term as prosecutor of Hillsdale
County and in 1844 was elected representative in
the Michigan legislature. For many years he
was an ardent Democrat, but his strong anti-
slavery views impelled him to join the Free-Soil
party in 1848. After the passage of the Kansas-
Nebraska bill in May 1854, he supported Isaac
P. Christiancy in his efforts to have the Free-
Soil party withdraw its state nominations during the coming campaign and call a mass convention of all anti-slavery elements, which
resulted in the convention at Jackson, July 6,
1854, the first Republican state convention ever
held, at which Murphy was one of the vice-presidents. He was a member of the Michigan delegation which supported Seward at the Repub-

lican National Convention held at Chicago in
May 1860. In July 1861 he was appointed by
President Lincoln consul-general for the free city
of Frankfort-on-the-Main, Germany.

On his arrival at Frankfort in November 1861,
Murphy found that his predecessor, Samuel
Ricker, was aiding the Confederate cause, and
was remaining in Frankfort with the hope of establishing a consulateship there for the Confederate states. Murphy frustrated this hope by
persuading Frankfort's Senate to permit him to
place the flag of the United States on the consular premises, thus recognizing him as consul-
general for the entire Union rather than for the
Northern states alone. When Ricker negotiated
with a banking firm to take up a Confederate
cotton-loan, Murphy obtained a statement from
the head of the banking house of M. A. von Roths-
child, which influenced the more conservative
houses against participating in the loan. Murphy
also had published in the *Neue Frankfurter
Zeitung* and other journals the latest annual reports of the Confederate secretary of the treasury, and Jefferson Davis' defense of repudiation
of the bonds of the South. Gaining the friendship of the editor of *L'Europe,* he was permitted
to use its columns for articles written by himself
and his friends in aid of the Union cause. Thus,
when the English and French exchanges were
closed to the sale of United States bonds issued
to prosecute the War they found a ready market
in Germany, and large sales were made in Frankfort. Murphy remained consul-general at Frankfort until 1869, after which he settled in Heidelberg as the financial agent of several American
railway companies. He died on June 8, 1886. He
had married, in 1849, Ellen Beaumont.

[*Hist. of Hillsdale County, Mich.* (1879); S. D. Bing-
ham, *Mich. Biogs.* (2 vols., 1924); *Hist. Colls. . . .
Mich. Pioneer and Hist. Soc.,* vol. XI (1888); H. M.
Utley and B. M. Cutcheon, *Mich. as a Province, Terri-
tory, and State* (1906), vol. III; *100 Years of the Am.
Consulate Gen. at Frankfort on the Main, 1829–1929*
(1929); *Autobiog. of Andrew Dickson White* (1905),
I, 97–99.]   J. L. R.

MURRAY, ALEXANDER (July 12, 1754 or
1755–Oct. 6, 1821), naval officer, was born at
Chestertown, Md., one of eight children of Dr.
William Murray and Ann (Smith) Murray. Of
Highland-Scotch descent, the Murrays emigrated
to America after a residence in Barbados. Alexander was regularly bred to the sea and at the
age of nineteen commanded a vessel trading with
Europe. On the outbreak of the Revolution he
obtained a lieutenant in the 1st Maryland Regiment and rose to the rank of captain, taking part
in Washington's campaign of 1776–77 in New
York and New Jersey. As he was a mariner by

profession, he applied for a lieutenancy in the navy and was promised one by John Hancock and other members of Congress. While awaiting his appointment he entered the privateer service and commanded successively the *General Mercer, Saratoga, Columbus,* and *Revenge.* He captured several British merchantmen and privateers and was himself twice captured, losing the *Saratoga* and the *Revenge.* On July 20, 1781, he finally obtained a naval lieutenancy and a few days later went to sea on board the frigate *Trumbull.* He was wounded when that ship was captured by the frigate *Iris,* after a severe engagement. On being exchanged he went to Richmond, Va., took command of the privateer *Prosperity,* and sailed for the West Indies with a cargo of tobacco. On this voyage he displayed skill and courage in a fight with a privateer of superior force. In 1782 he took part in a joint Spanish-American expedition that effected the capture of New Providence. Returning to the Continental Navy as a lieutenant in the *Alliance,* he remained in the service until 1785, one of the last officers to leave it.

After the Revolution Murray established himself in Philadelphia as a merchant, a calling that he followed with much success. In 1794 when the navy under the Constitution was organized he offered his services to President Washington and early in the war with France was appointed captain, taking rank from July 1, 1798. Ordered to the *Montezuma,* he cruised for nine months in the West Indies, capturing one small prize and convoying many merchantmen. He contracted yellow fever and was compelled to give up his ship. He next went to sea as the commander of the *Insurgente,* with a roving commission, and made an extended cruise, visiting, among other places, the Azores, Lisbon, Cayenne, Jamaica, and Havana. In the last year of the war he cruised in the West Indies as commander of the *Constellation,* and for a time served as commander of the Santo Domingo station.

Retained under the peace establishment of 1801 and ranking sixth in the list of captains, Murray in 1802–03 commanded the *Constellation* of the Mediterranean Squadron, and for some two months blockaded Tripoli. On one occasion he attacked the Tripolitan gunboats, doing them considerable damage. In the latter part of 1805 he commanded the *Adams* and cruised off the Carolina coast for the protection of American commerce. This was his last sea duty. After serving as president of the *Chesapeake* and *Leopard* court of inquiry, he in 1808 was made commanding naval officer at Philadelphia, an office that he held until his death, which occurred

at his country residence near that city. He had been the ranking officer of the navy since 1811. On June 18, 1782, he was married to Mary Miller of Philadelphia. A son, Alexander M. Murray, died when a midshipman in the navy; and a grandson, Alexander Murray, entered the navy and rose to the rank of rear admiral.

[The earliest sketch of Murray's life, not entirely to be relied on, is found in the *Port Folio,* May 1814. See also S. P. Waldo, *Biog. Sketches of Distinguished Am. Naval Heroes in the War of the Revolution* (1823); G. A. Hanson, *Old Kent: The Eastern Shore of Md.* (1876); G. W. Allen, *Our Naval War with France* (1909) and *Our Navy and the Barbary Corsairs* (1905); *Poulson's Am. Daily Advertiser* (Phila.), Oct. 8, 10, 1821. The *Port Folio* and Waldo give year of birth as 1755, while Hanson gives 1754.] C.O.P.

MURRAY, DAVID (Oct. 15, 1830–Mar. 6, 1905), educator, author, the son of William and Jean (Black) Murray, both of Scotch extraction, was born at Bovina, Delaware County, N. Y. After obtaining his early education at Delaware Academy, Delhi, and Fergusonville Academy, he entered the sophomore class of Union College. He was a graduate of Union College (1852), and from 1852 to 1863 was connected with Albany Academy (New York) as teacher and principal. He then went to Rutgers College as professor of mathematics and astronomy for a decade (1863–73). During that period, according to the testimony of a pupil, he was able to make his courses seem so valuable that several students elected to study calculus "because we wished to study under our favorite professor." In 1873 he was invited by the Japanese government to become superintendent of educational affairs and adviser to the minister of education. For six years (1873–79), he rendered good services in the establishment of a universal educational system, largely along American lines. Particularly valuable was his work in laying the foundations for women's education. During this engagement, Murray was appointed a commissioner to the Centennial Exhibition at Philadelphia; he also assisted in the collection of materials for a Tokio educational museum. His *Outline History of Japanese Education* (1876) was the first official presentation abroad of that subject. He devoted himself also to arousing public sentiment in favor of returning to Japan America's share ($750,000) of the Shimonoseki Indemnity Fund, and he lived to see the fruition of his efforts (1883).

Soon after his return to America Murray became secretary of the board of regents of the University of the State of New York and served from 1880 to 1889 in this capacity, displaying marked administrative ability. He was also author of a history of the board of regents. In

1889, on account of ill health, he retired to private life in New Brunswick, N. J., and engaged chiefly in literary labors, of which a *History of Education in New Jersey* (United States Bureau of Education, 1899), and the volume on *Japan* in the Story of the Nations Series (*1894*; revised edition, 1906), were notable results. When the centenary of the establishment of Delaware County was celebrated in 1897, he was the editor and one of the authors of *Delaware County, New York: History of the Century, 1797–1897* (1898), and he prepared a paper, "The Antirent Episode in the State of New York," which was published in the American Historical Association *Annual Report for 1896* (vol. I, 1897). In his later years he was a trustee of Rutgers College and secretary of the board, and was officially connected with New Brunswick Theological Seminary and Wells Memorial Hospital. In 1867 he had married Martha Neilson who survived him. He died in New Brunswick.

[The best sketch of Murray is W. I. Chamberlin, *In Memoriam, David Murray* (1915), containing a list of unpublished manuscripts by Murray in the Lib. of Cong. See also: the *New Brunswick Weekly Fredonian*, July 26, 1866; the *New Brunswick Times*, May 3, 1873; the *Christian Intelligencer* (N. Y.), June 3, 1908; and the *Sunday Times* (New Brunswick), Jan. 16, 1927, and Feb. 5, 1928.]   E. W. C.

MURRAY, JAMES ORMSBEE (Nov. 27, 1827–Mar. 27, 1899), clergyman, first dean of Princeton University, was born at Camden, S. C. His grandfather, John Murray, whose parents came from Scotland, was a merchant in Philadelphia. John Murray's wife, Elizabeth, was a daughter of Philip Syng [*q.v.*], an original member of the American Philosophical Society and friend of Benjamin Franklin. Their son, James Syng Murray, removed to Camden, S. C., where he was engaged in business. He married Aurelia Pearce, of English descent, grand-daughter of William Blanding and Lydia Ormsbee, New Englanders. James Ormsbee Murray, son of James and Aurelia, was eight years old when his father, being opposed to slavery, emancipated some of his slaves, provided for the emancipation of the others, and removed with his family to Springfield, Ohio. Here the boy was prepared for college. He entered Brown University with the class of 1848, but was obliged by ill health to drop back two years, graduating as valedictorian in 1850. He spent the next year as instructor in Greek at Brown, then entered Andover Theological Seminary, where he graduated in 1854. From 1854 to 1861 he was pastor of the Congregational church at South Danvers, now Peabody, Mass.; from 1861 to 1865 pastor of the Prospect Street church in Cambridgeport, Mass.; and then became associate pastor with

Dr. Gardiner Spring [*q.v.*] of the Brick Church (Presbyterian) in New York City. From 1873 to 1875 he was sole pastor of this church. During these years in the ministry he wrote many articles on literary subjects and gained a reputation for his wide acquaintance with English letters. In 1875 he was elected to the Holmes Professorship of Belles Lettres and English Language and Literature in the College of New Jersey (Princeton). His lectures at Princeton dealt principally with writers of the sixteenth and eighteenth centuries and were of a broad and human, rather than a narrowly scholastic kind. In the latter years of the administration of President James McCosh [*q.v.*] matters of internal administration fell more and more into Professor Murray's hands, and in 1883 he was appointed dean of the faculty. The office was at first a difficult one, for it included discipline and the enforcement of standards of scholarship; but Dean Murray soon obtained general good will without sacrificing just severity. He had an enthusiastic, impulsive, and affectionate disposition. In his teaching and his administrative methods he formed a link between the men of an older generation whose equipment consisted chiefly of general culture and the later generation of trained specialists. He was retained in the deanship by President Patton and died in office at the dean's house, Mar. 27, 1899. On Oct. 22, 1856, at Brookline, Mass., he had married Julia Richards Haughton, who with four sons and a daughter survived him.

In collaboration with other editors, Murray compiled a hymnbook, *The Sacrifice of Praise* (1869). He edited *Orations and Essays with Selected Parish Sermons by J. L. Diman* (1882) and *Selections from the Poetical Works of William Cowper* (1898); and was the author of *George Ide Chace: A Memorial* (1886), *William Gammell: A Biographical Sketch* (1890), *Francis Wayland* (1891).

[John DeWitt, *James Ormsbee Murray: a Memorial Sermon* (1899); *Princeton Bull.*, May 1899; *Hist. Cat. Brown Univ.* (1905); *Daily True American* (Trenton), Mar. 28, 1899; communications from Murray's daughter, Mrs. A. C. Armstrong, Middletown, Conn.; personal acquaintance.]   G. M. H.

MURRAY, JOHN (1737–Oct. 11, 1808), Quaker merchant, was born on Swatara Creek, near Lancaster, Pa., the son of John Murray who emigrated from Scotland in 1732, and a younger brother of Robert Murray [*q.v.*]. In 1753 the two brothers removed to New York City, and entered into a mercantile partnership, importing on a large scale and becoming the chief ship-owners in the colonies. They also obtained valuable landholdings on Manhattan Island, in a locality which was to become one of the fashionable centers of the city. In the political contests which agitated the city before the outbreak of the Revolution they took no part. John, however, was involved with Robert in the difficulties with the Committee of Sixty occasioned by landing a part of the cargo of the ship *Beulah,* February 1775, in violation of the non-importation agreement. During the War of Independence they remained in their homes, preserving the attitude enjoined by the Quakers' conscientious repugnance to the appeal to arms. Both were distinguished by acts of kindness to American prisoners. As members of the Chamber of Commerce, which, from July 1779 to the end of the struggle, directed largely the internal affairs of the city, they shared responsibilities for which the military command had little fitness, thus easing the rigor of the military control.

After the war, the Chamber of Commerce received a new charter from the legislature, and on Feb. 13, 1787, John Murray, with thirteen others belonging to the old colonial body, was admitted to membership. From 1798 to 1806 Murray was its president. He was also elected in 1789 a director of the Bank of New York established in 1784, and was director of an insurance association. He took a leading part in the philanthropic activities of the city. With Thomas Eddy [*q.v.*] and others he was appointed on a commission to build one of the state prisons in New York City (1796). In 1805, with Eddy, he issued a call for a meeting, at his house in Pearl Street, to provide means for the education of neglected children. From this invitation came the "Act to incorporate the Society instituted in the City of New York, for the Establishment of a Free School for the Education of Poor Children who do not belong to, or are not provided for by, any religious society." DeWitt Clinton was the first president, and Murray the first vice-president. Murray was also associated with Eddy in efforts for improvement of the Oneida and other central New York Indians. He was a director of the Humane Society, organized for the relief of distressed prisoners at a time when insolvent debtors were subject to peculiar hardships. It is related (Scoville, *post,* I, 294) that Murray was once perilously near bankruptcy, but at the last moment was rescued by a turn of fortune through a ticket purchased in an English lottery. Although the importation of English goods, in which the transactions of the Murrays largely consisted, was seriously affected before the Revolution by the cessation of American demands and during the war by the activity of privateers, John, at death, owned valuable property on Murray Hill, and his entire estate was estimated to be worth half a million dollars. In December 1766 he was married to Hannah Lindley, daughter of James and Susanna (Lownes) Lindley and a niece of his brother Robert's wife.

[J. M. Lindly, *The Hist. of the Lindley, Lindsley-Linsley Families in America, 1639–1924,* vol. II (1924); I. N. P. Stokes, *The Iconography of Manhattan Island, 1498–1909* (6 vols., 1915–28); J. G. Wilson, *The Memorial Hist. of the City of N. Y.* (4 vols., 1892–93); J. A. Scoville, *The Old Merchants of New York City,* 1 and 2 series (1863); A. M. Schlesinger, *The Colonial Merchants and the Am. Revolution, 1763–1776* (1917); J. A. Stevens, *Colonial Records of the N. Y. Chamber of Commerce, 1768–1784, with Hist. and Biog. Sketches* (1867); *American Citizen* (N. Y.), Oct. 12, 1808.]
R.E.D.

MURRAY, JOHN (Dec. 10, 1741–Sept. 3, 1815), founder of Universalism in America, was born in Alton, Hampshire, England, into a family comfortably circumstanced but subject to stern religious discipline. The paternal grandmother, a Frenchwoman converted to the Church of England, sacrificed an inheritance for her new faith, and in her son this firmness became an extreme rigor of Calvinist conviction. The boy John, merry by nature but schooled to the belief that he was predestined to eternal misery, became excessively emotional. When in 1751 the family removed to Cork, Ireland, the father intensified the family discipline to a morbid absorption in worship and chastisements, refused an offer of school and university education for his son, and being himself now incapacitated by pulmonary disease placed the boy in an occupation.

Happier days began for the son, however, when—though still an unrelenting Calvinist—the father joined the Wesleyan group and won the friendship of John Wesley. Appointed by Wesley as leader of a boys' class, John soon became facile in singing, in public prayer, in examining the soul experiences of his mates. Now admired and praised, he had emotional ecstasies that assured him of eternal joy. A welcome visitor in the home of a Mr. Little, a man of means who had been converted to Methodism, he had access, without his father's knowledge, to the novels, plays, and poems current in that age of luxurious sentiment, and fell in love with a lady ten years his senior. The spell was broken when his letter offering eternal devotion was returned by her to her irate father. Then the death of one of his friends, Mr. Little's son, his own illness, and the death of his father brought him back to intensities of religious concern. His widowed mother consenting, he joined the Little family to replace the lost son, but the lure of London soon made him part with home and friends.

Before leaving Ireland he had a transport of enthusiasm for the Calvinist Methodism of Whitefield, whom he heard in Cork. In London his susceptible temperament yielded to the fascination of music, dancing, theatre going, and convivial parties until embarrassing debts and Whitefield's preaching at the Tabernacle brought him again to sober seriousness. Employment in a broadcloth factory paid his debts and a romantic courtship of Eliza Neale, a devotee of the Tabernacle, led to a marriage blest with "as much of happiness as ever fell to the lot of humanity" (*The Life of the Rev. John Murray*, ed. of 1869, p. 144). But after some years of this felicity, a crisis developed. Evangelical circles in London were now disturbed by James Relly's preaching of universal redemption finally effective for each and every man, and the hatred which Murray felt for such a "destroyer of souls" was embittered by defeat in argument with one of Relly's adherents. With fear and trembling he read Relly's *Union* (1759), then with his wife visited Relly's meeting and agreed with his wife that the sermon had unadulterated truth. The result was attendance on Relly's preaching, searching study of Scripture in the light of the new doctrine, excommunication from the Tabernacle, the loss of all friends, and serious financial distress. Then came the death of his child, soon followed by the death of his wife and his own arrest for debt. Though rescued by his wife's brother, he was now in emotional collapse. Conceiving America as a vast wilderness where he might bury a ruined life, he embarked in July 1770, at Gravesend, on the brig *Hand-in-hand*.

What happened on his arrival in America was ever after viewed by him as a supernatural calling to an independent apostolate. The brig grounded on a shoal in Cranberry Inlet, New Jersey, and much of the cargo was transferred to a sloop of which Murray was put in charge. Going ashore for provisions, he found a farmstead and a meeting-house which the farmer, Thomas Potter, had built in hope that heaven would send a preacher in whose belief all men were equally dear to God. An inward voice assured the farmer that the approaching stranger was the divinely sent preacher. Before sailing Murray reluctantly discoursed to the neighbors, and he soon returned to Potter's farm at "Good Luck," proposing to help in the farm labor and to preach without monetary reward. Unordained, untrained in theology, shrinking from conflicts that his doctrine would excite, he was nevertheless led on by popular response to his warm emotional speech into two years of itinerant evan-

gelism with "Good Luck" as a center. Though he was later accused of concealing his faith in universal redemption, the purport of his preaching was seen from the outset. When, for this departure from orthodoxy and his presumption in preaching without church authorization, pulpits were closed to him, the hearing given him in homes, court houses, or in the open fields assured him that like St. Paul he had an apostolate conferred not by ecclesiastical officers but by the Spirit active in his heart.

In 1772 invitations led him to New England, where he won admiration from laymen of high repute and hostility from clergy of the Standing Order. Reaching Newport he was engaged by prominent parishioners of the Rev. Ezra Stiles [q.v.], who was absent, to preach on Sunday, Sept. 27, and on several weekdays thereafter. When Stiles returned, Oct. 10, he forbade further preaching from a wanderer without credentials. Abundant entries in Stiles's diary record that clergyman's credulous acceptance of slanderous rumors concerning Murray in contrast to the marked respect shown him by the laymen. A year later, October 1773, Murray, again in Newport, was invited by the Governor to preach in the State House and was offered a new church if he would remain. The itinerant went on. Arriving in Boston, Oct. 26, he became the guest of the noted Thomas Handasyde Peck, preached in Manufacturing House, in a private home, and on return from pulpits in Newburyport and Portsmouth, in Andrew Croswell's church and Faneuil Hall. In the autumn of 1774, in spite of Croswell's bitter opposition, he was again invited to preach by action of the proprietors. On one occasion stones were hurled at him through the church window and he needed the escort of a body of friends to reach his dwelling.

In the midst of these disturbances, Winthrop Sargent, a prosperous ship-master, representing a group in Gloucester who had studied Relly's *Union*, secured his service in the place of the Gloucester pastor, Rev. Samuel Chandler, who was ill. When Murray explained his heretical view, Chandler refused him further permission to preach and in the *Salem Gazette*, Feb. 14, 1775, printed a warning against the dangerous doctrine. Murray, however, remained in Gloucester, preaching in Sargent's mansion and in neighboring towns, refusing all compensation beyond his simple necessities. In the following May his friendly admirers, Varnum, Greene, and Hitchcock, commanding the Rhode Island regiments camped near Boston, made him their chaplain, and when other chaplains protested against him, Washington in General Orders, Sept. 17,

1775, announced that "The Rev. Mr. John Murray is appointed Chaplain to the Rhode Island Regiments, and is to be respected as such" (Eddy, *post,* p. 14, quoting Order Book). Illness cut short his chaplaincy but did not prevent arduous winter journeys to raise money for Gloucester families made destitute by the war. In May 1776 a pamphlet by the Rev. John Cleaveland of Ipswich, one of the protesting chaplains, attacked the heresy of "a certain stranger who calls himself John Murray" (*An Attempt to Nip in the Bud the Unscriptural Doctrine of Universal Salvation . . .*). The gift of a bit of land to make Murray a freeholder foiled an attempt to expel him as a vagrant, but letters like that of Ezra Stiles (Dec. 24, 1777; see Eddy, pp. 162-65) which called him a Romanist in disguise and an enemy to the American cause led the town authorities to order him to leave. These accusations against his character and patriotism were brought to an end by a letter from Major-General Greene, May 27, 1777.

In January 1779, sixty-one persons, including some fifteen suspended members of Gloucester First Church, united to form the Independent Church of Christ, with Murray as its minister. When on their refusal to pay taxes for the First Church their goods were sold at auction, the members brought suit under the bill of rights of the new constitution of Massachusetts. Repeated trials ended with a decision in their favor, June 1786. Fined for performing a marriage ceremony without an ordination recognized as sufficiently public, Murray with the support of his congregation, petitioned the legislature for relief, which was granted in 1788. While the petition was pending Murray visited old scenes in England (January–July 1788). In October 1788 he married Judith (Sargent) Stevens, widowed daughter of Winthrop Sargent [see Judith Sargent Stevens Murray], and on Christmas Day was re-ordained in more formal and public manner. On Oct. 23, 1793, he was installed as pastor of a Universalist society in Boston, and, being now responsible for a family, at last accepted a modest salary. His pastoral activity and preaching tours were ended by a stroke of paralysis, Oct. 19, 1809, though he lived nearly six years longer. He was buried first in the Granary Burying Ground, but in 1837 his remains were moved to Mount Auburn Cemetery, where a monument was erected over his grave by the many churches which owe their existence chiefly to him.

Murray's departure from the Old Calvinists lay in the belief "that *every individual* shall in due time be separated from sin, and rendered fit to associate with the denizens of heaven" (*Letters and Sketches of Sermons,* I, 144). This faith was based on texts that show Christ as dying for the redemption of all men. Murray prided himself on his ability to make all texts consistent with this belief, but the consistency required some arbitrary efforts at allegorical interpretation.

[The main sources are *Records of the Life of the Rev. John Murray, Preacher of Universal Redemption, Written by Himself, with a Continuation by Mrs. Judith Sargent Murray* (1816, and many later editions); John Murray, *Letters and Sketches of Sermons* (3 vols., 1812-13); documentary materials in Richard Eddy, *Universalism in Gloucester, Mass.* (1892). See also F. B. Dexter, *The Lit. Diary of Ezra Stiles* (3 vols., 1901); *The Diary of William Bentley* (4 vols., 1905-14); F. A. Bisbee, *1770-1920, From Good Luck to Gloucester* (1920); *Columbian Centinel,* Sept. 6, 1815.]   F. A. C.

MURRAY, JOHN GARDNER (Aug. 31, 1857–Oct. 3, 1929), first elected presiding bishop of the Protestant Episcopal Church, was born at Lonaconing, Md., the only son among the four children of James and Anne (Kirkwood) Murray. He grew up at Lonaconing and passed through its public schools, and in 1876 entered the Wyoming Seminary, near Wilkes-Barre, Pa. The following year the family moved to Osage City, Kan., where his father became a coal dealer. Having decided to enter the ministry of the Methodist Episcopal Church, in which he had been brought up, Murray became a student at Drew Theological Seminary, Madison, N. J., in the fall of 1879, expecting to spend four years there. Before he had finished the course, however, his father died, and to help support the family Murray abandoned his preparation for the ministry and entered upon a business career. He became the trusted agent and confidential clerk of Col. T. J. Peter, principal owner of the Carbon Coal Company of Osage City, whose business interests were later extended to central Alabama. In 1882 Murray was transferred to Brierfield, Ala., and made secretary and treasurer of the Brierfield Iron Company. Seven years later, Dec. 4, 1889, he married Clara Alice Hunsicker of Osage City, and established a home at Selma, Ala., where he became a wholesale grocer and a dealer in real estate, in both of which ventures he was successful.

While at Brierfield he had transferred his church connection from the Methodist Episcopal Church to the Protestant Episcopal Church, being confirmed July 4, 1886. Throughout his business career his desire to become a minister persisted and he held religious services as he had opportunity. In 1891 he was licensed to act as lay reader in the Episcopal Church; in 1893 he was made deacon by Coadjutor Bishop Henry

M. Jackson, and in 1894 was ordained priest by Bishop Richard Hooker Wilmer. He was now thirty-six years old. For two years he served as diocesan missionary and had charge of the Alabama River Mission, consisting of eight small stations which he reached on horseback. So signal was his success that in 1896 he was elected rector of the Church of the Advent, Birmingham, the largest parish in the Diocese of Alabama, and here soon took a leading place in the city as well as the Church. He remained there nearly seven years. When Bishop Wilmer died in 1900, Murray came within a few votes of being elected his successor.

In January 1903 he was chosen rector of the largest parish in the Diocese of Maryland, the Church of St. Michael and All Angels, Baltimore, and at once gained prominence because of his great popularity, especially among men. He continued as rector of this church for six years. The Diocese of Kentucky and the Diocese of Mississippi each elected him to be its bishop; but he declined both offices. In May 1909 he was elected almost unanimously to be bishop coadjutor of Maryland, and was consecrated in his own church on Sept. 29 by Bishops Paret, Adams, Randolph, Nelson, and DuMoulin of Canada. Upon the death of Bishop Paret, Jan. 18, 1911, Murray succeeded at once to the office of bishop of Maryland. Owing to his exceptional business ability and his personal popularity the diocese made great progress during his episcopate of twenty years.

At the General Convention of the Protestant Episcopal Church held at New Orleans, La., in October 1925, Bishop Murray was elected presiding bishop of the Church. Previously the senior bishop had automatically succeeded to that office; Murray was the first to hold it through the choice of his brother bishops. To share his labors as bishop of Maryland he was granted a coadjutor the following year. His most distinctive services to the Church as a whole were executive and administrative; he succeeded in eliminating the deficit and raising funds to balance a generous budget. In addition, however, as a leader possessing spiritual depth and power as well as the gift of inspiring oratory, he was responsible for an awakening felt throughout the Church. He gave himself so unreservedly to the discharge of his duties that he overtaxed his strength. Death came to him suddenly while he was presiding over a special session of the House of Bishops held in the Church of Our Saviour at Atlantic City, N. J. Being greatly beloved, he was greatly mourned. His funeral took place in the Church of St. Michael and All Angels, Baltimore, and he was interred in the Druid Ridge Cemetery. His wife and five children survived him.

[M. P. Andrews, *Tercentenary Hist. of Md.* (1925), vol. II; *Who's Who in America*, 1928–29; *The Living Church Annual*, 1931; *Living Church*, Oct. 12, 1929; *Sun* (Baltimore), Oct. 4, 1929; information as to certain facts from Mrs. Murray; personal acquaintance.]
A. C. P.

MURRAY, JOSEPH (*c.* 1694–Apr. 28, 1757), lawyer, was born in Queen's County, Ireland, the son of Thomas Murray, and emigrated to New York early in life, appearing at the New York bar in 1718 (*Mayor's Court Minutes,* 1718–20, fol. 28). He interrupted his legal practice in New York to attend the Middle Temple, where he was admitted in 1725. Returning to New York, where he was voted the freedom of the city in 1728, he quickly gained recognition as an erudite lawyer. He appeared in the Mayor's Court in most of the principal cases in his generation, and his arguments reveal a thorough grounding in the civil as well as the common law. His form books are models of eighteenth-century pleading. He was associated as counsel or arbiter in some of the most important real-estate litigation in New York and New Jersey. He appeared for the proprietors of the Oblong or Equivalent Lands (Colden Papers, *post,* II, pp. 203, 232); again, with James Alexander, for the plaintiffs in 1752 in the suit of the Earl of Stair and other proprietors of East New Jersey against Bond and others; and for the city of New York in its boundary dispute with the town of Harlem (*Minutes of the Common Council, post,* V, p. 345), and in its protracted litigation with Brooklyn over ferry rights (*Ibid.,* pp. 110–11). He was a New York commissioner in the boundary dispute with Massachusetts in 1754 and in the same year rendered an extensive report to the counsel with regard to the boundary dispute with New Jersey.

Murray appears to have had a principal share in amending and completing a draft of the Montgomerie Charter, in which task, according to the official resolution of thanks, he was said to have given "a lasting Instance of his great Learning Ability and Integrity in his Profession as well as for his Regard to this Corporation" (*Minutes of the Common Council, post,* IV, p. 43). Through his marriage in 1738 with Grace (Cosby) Freeman, widow of Thomas Freeman and a daughter of Governor Cosby, Murray was brought into close alliance with the governor and undertook a defense of the prerogative against the attacks of William Smith [*q.v.*], arguing before the Assembly in 1734 the legality of the court of exchequer. Murray's

"Opinion Relating to the Courts of Justice in the Colony of New York" (appended to Smith's *Opinion,* 1734), his only published work, is one of the few really important contributions to legal history penned in the American colonies. The author enlisted the full weight of common-law precedent against the assertion that courts of law could be established only by statute, and set forth convincingly the view that "Fundamental Courts" are a part of the constitution of England. He appears on less solid ground, however, in claiming that the authority of the colonial legislatures and courts is derived, not from the King's commission, but from the common law to which the colonies are entitled. He concluded his argument by citing colonial precedents of 1702 and 1729, when the New York Supreme Court of Judicature sat as a court of exchequer. The substance of his arguments was embodied by Governor Cosby in an aggressive opinion in defense of the Court of Chancery the following year (*Rex* vs. *Birdsall et al.,* Chancery Minutes, 1720–48, pp. 67–68). Once again Murray and Smith clashed. In the election dispute between Garret Van Horne and Adolph Philipse in 1737, when the question was raised whether Jews were qualified to vote, Murray argued in the affirmative, because the law mentioned all freeholders of competent estate.

A member of the executive council under George Clinton [*q.v.*], Murray was soon prominently identified with the opposition faction headed by Chief Justice James De Lancey, ultimately breaking with Clinton and Colden and effectually tying up the governor's military program. The joy of De Lancey and Murray when Sir Danvers Osborne succeeded Clinton in the governorship was soon tempered when that official, while a guest of Murray, committed suicide as a result of private grief. With De Lancey in the saddle, Murray was made one of the New York delegates at the Albany Congress of 1754. In addition, he was a member of the first board of trustees of the New York Society Library and a governor of that institution. A strict Episcopalian, he was active in the affairs of Trinity Church and was named one of the governors of King's College in the charter of 1754. Murray devised to King's College his residuary estate, including a fine library, the origin of the Columbia collection. Unfortunately the greater part of this collection was destroyed or scattered during the occupation of the British or the fire of 1776.

[Obituary notices are found in the *N.-Y. Mercury,* and the *N.-Y. Gazette, or the Weekly Post-Boy* for May 2, 1757. See also: *N. Y. Hist. Soc., Colls.,* Pub. Fund Series, vol. XXVIII (1896), p. 454, and vol. XXIX (1897), pp. 165–66; "The Letters and Papers of Cadwallader Colden," *Ibid.,* vols. LI–LII (1910–20); *Minutes of the Common Council of the City of N. Y., 1675–1776* (8 vols., 1905); E. B. O'Callaghan, *Docs. Relative to the Colonial Hist. . . . of N. Y.,* vol. VI (1855); Thos. Jones, *Hist. of N. Y. during the Revolutionary War* (1879), I, 136–37; E. A. Jones, *Am. Members of the Inns of Court* (1924). Murray's pleadings and other legal papers are available in part in the Office of the Commissioner of Records, New York City; a Form Book is in the Columbia Law Lib., and miscellaneous correspondence may be found in Alexander MSS. V, N. Y. Hist. Soc.]　　　　　R. B. M.

MURRAY, JUDITH SARGENT STEVENS (May 1, 1751–July 6, 1820), author, was the daughter of Capt. Winthrop Sargent, a prominent citizen and merchant of Gloucester, Mass., and his wife, Judith Saunders, descendant of an active seafaring family. She was given an unusual education, sharing the studies of her brother Winthrop [*q.v.*], in his preparation for Harvard. She early began writing verses and essays, some of which were printed in the *Gentleman's and Lady's Town and Country Magazine* at Boston in 1784, over her pen-name, "Constantia." She married first, Oct. 3, 1769, Capt. John Stevens of Gloucester, who, after financial difficulties, sailed in 1786 for the West Indies, where he died on the island of St. Eustatius shortly afterward. In the meantime the Gloucester Sargents had been converted to Universalism by the Rev. John Murray, 1741–1815 [*q.v.*], who had begun his ministration in the town in 1774. A warm friendship and mutual admiration between Murray and Mrs. Stevens culminated in their marriage, Oct. 6, 1788. She was devoted to him and his religious interests and shared his preaching tours, notably a visit to Philadelphia in 1790, of which she wrote an interesting account in her letters (*Universalist Quarterly,* April 1881, April 1882).

In 1789 she began actively contributing poetry to the *Massachusetts Magazine,* the first contribution appearing in the issue for January 1790. Her most important work, however, was a series of essays called "The Gleaner," begun in that magazine in February 1792 and continued with few interruptions to August 1794. When the managers of the newly established theatre in Boston called for original dramas by American writers, she was apparently the first to respond (see G. O. Seilhamer, *History of the American Theatre,* vol. III, 1891, p. 248, which wrongly attributes her play to Royall Tyler) with a comedy, *The Medium, or A Happy Tea-Party* (called for publication, *The Medium, or Virtue Triumphant*), produced at the Federal Street Theatre, Mar. 2, 1795. Neither this play nor its successor, *The Traveller Returned,* was a success, though the latter survived two performances, the first on Mar. 9, 1796. It was caustically criticized by Robert Treat Paine, Jr. (quoted in J. T. Buckingham, *Specimens of Newspaper Literature,* 1850, II, 243), who supposed John Murray to be the author. These two plays, with her essays and other short prose pieces and her poems, were collected in three volumes and published by subscription at Boston in February 1798 under the general title, *The Gleaner.* Mrs. Murray's later work, except for seven poems in the *Boston Weekly Magazine* (Oct. 30, 1802–Mar. 19, 1803), and one in the *Boston Magazine* (Dec. 14, 1805), was of an editorial nature. During her husband's decline she prepared for publication his *Letters, and Sketches of Sermons* (3 vols., 1812–13); and after his death in 1815, she added the three concluding chapters to his autobiography. The value of both works she lessened by conscientiously suppressing material of a personal application, deleting dates and names of persons and places. She died at the home of her daughter, Julia Maria (Murray) Bingaman, near Natchez, Miss. Her work as a poet and dramatist is negligible; but her essays rival in firmness of texture and in interest those of Joseph Dennie, Freneau, and Noah Webster, her best contemporaries.

[The authoritative biography is Vena B. Field, *Constantia, A Study of the Life and Works of Judith Sargent Murray* (1931), in Univ. of Maine Studies, 2 ser. See also E. W. and C. S. Sargent, *Epes Sargent of Gloucester and His Descendants* (1925); *Boston Commercial Gazette,* Aug. 7, 1820. The extensive family MSS. stored on the Bingaman plantation near Natchez, have become illegible. Two fine portraits of Mrs. Murray, by Copley and Stuart, are displayed in the Sargent-Murray-Gilman House at Gloucester, which was her residence as wife to John Stevens and John Murray.]

M. E—s.

MURRAY, LINDLEY (June 7, 1745–Jan. 16, 1826), grammarian, was born on Swatara Creek in what is now Dauphin County, Pa., the eldest, and the last to survive, of the twelve children of Robert [*q.v.*] and Mary (Lindley) Murray. His father, who had emigrated from Scotland in 1732, was at the time of his son's birth a miller. Later he embarked in the West Indies trade, tried his luck for a few years in North Carolina, and in 1753 settled as a merchant in New York, where he rose to affluence. Brought up in the Westminster Confession, he joined the Quakers but lived with a sumptuousness that scandalized poorer members of the sect. He sternly denied his son's desire for a literary education until finally the boy ran away from home and enrolled in a school at Burlington, N. J. A compromise was then effected and Lindley studied law in the office of Benjamin Kissam, with John Jay for a fellow pupil. He was called to the bar and acquired a lucrative practice among the Quakers. On June 22, 1767, he married Hannah Dobson, who died Sept. 25, 1834. They had no children.

With the outbreak of the Revolution he retired to Islip, Long Island, on Great South Bay, hunted and fished, and experimented with the making of salt, but in 1779 he returned to New York and, with capital supplied by his father, set up as a merchant. Having amassed a comfortable fortune, he retired in 1783 to his estate, "Bellevue," the site of which is now occupied by Bellevue Hospital. In the hope of restoring his failing health he made a leisurely tour through New Jersey and eastern Pennsylvania and in 1784 went to England, which he had already visited in 1770–71. He bought a small estate at Holgate, just outside York, and made his home there until his death forty-two years later. In these years of retirement he cultivated a garden which was said to rival those at Kew, and gave considerable time to writing. He moved about as little as possible, seldom ventured further than the Friends' Meeting House in York, and for many years before his death never left the house.

He produced a number of schoolbooks, including an *English Grammar* (1795); *English Exercises* (1797); *A Key to the Exercises* (1797); *The English Reader* (1799); *Sequel to the English Reader* (1800); *Introduction to the English Reader* (1801); *Lecteur François* (1802); *Introduction au Lecteur François* (1807); *An English Spelling-Book* (1804); and *An English Grammar* (1818), this last a complete revision and elaboration of his first publication. These books were widely circulated in England and the United States; for a time the grammars virtually monopolized the field. According to R. L. Lyman (*post,* p. 80), "A very conservative estimate of the total number of Murray's grammars, including his own and his followers' before 1850, is 200 editions, totaling between 1,500,000 and 2,000,000 copies." They were eclectic in principle and well arranged for pedagogical purposes; but rival grammarians, often with much heat, pointed to numerous shortcomings, and Murray was frequently charged with forgetting his own rules; for half a century, nevertheless, he was to grammar what Hoyle was to whist. Goold Brown [*q.v.*] and Samuel Kirkham ultimately displaced him.

Of Murray's religious tracts the most popular was *The Power of Religion on the Mind in Retirement, Sickness, and Death* (1787), the first edition of which was printed privately for presentation to his friends. His other publications include: *The Sentiments of Pious and Emi-*

nent Men, on the Pernicious Tendency of Dramatic Entertainments and Other Vain Amusements (c. 1789); *Some Account of the Life and Religious Labours of Sarah Grubb* (1792); *A Selection from Bishop Horne's Commentary on the Psalms* (1812); *A Biographical Sketch of Henry Tuke* (1815); *A Compendium of Religious Faith and Practice* (1815); and *The Duty and Benefit of a Daily Perusal of the Holy Scripture in Families* (1817). "A purified edition of the British Poets" was another project dear to his heart, but was never completed. In sentiment and deportment Murray was an almost perfect Sir Charles Grandison; decorum, virtue, propriety were his watchwords. By his own generation he was admired unreservedly; visitors thronged to Holgate to see the famous garden, to meet its proprietor, and to be edified by his conversation. For eleven years he was a recorded minister of the Society of Friends. His many years of confining illness he bore cheerfully. He died at York and was buried there.

[The major source is *Memoirs of the Life and Writings of Lindley Murray: In a Series of Letters, Written by Himself, with a Preface, and a Continuation of the Memoirs by Elizabeth Frank* (1826). See also Joseph Smith, *A Descriptive Catalogue of Friends' Books* (2 vols., 1867) and *Supplement* (1893); C. F. Smith, article in *Dict. Nat. Biog.*, vol. XXXIX (1894); W. H. Egle, *Pa. Geneals.* (1886); J. M. Lindly, *The Hist. of the Lindley Lindsley-Linsley Families in America*, vol. II (1924); *Biog. Cat. . . . of the . . . London Friends' Inst.* (1888); W. C. Abbott, *N. Y. in the Am. Rev.* (1929), p. 198; R. L. Lyman, *English Grammar in Am. Schools before 1850* (1922); S. A. Leonard, *The Doctrine of Correctness in English Usage 1700–1800* (Madison, Wis., 1929); *Gentleman's Mag.* (London), Feb. 1826; letters (MS.) Oct. 6, 1799, and Mar. 26, 1804, MSS. Div., Lib. of Cong. Some authorities give Apr. 22 as day of birth, but June 7, 1745, is given by Lindly (*ante*, p. 330) as from the family Bible, and appears also in the *Memoirs*, p. 189).   G. H. G.

MURRAY, LOUISE SHIPMAN WELLES (Jan. 2, 1854–Apr. 22, 1931), archaeologist and local historian, daughter of Charles Fisher and Elizabeth (Laporte) Welles, was born at Athens, Pa. Descended on the paternal side from Thomas Welles, a colonial governor of Connecticut, and on the maternal side from Bartholomew Laporte, one of the French *emigrés* who founded Asylum, Pa., she had by inheritance a particular interest in the history of the two principal elements of population that settled the region about Athens. She attended the Athens Academy, the Moravian Seminary at Bethlehem, Pa., and Brown's School at Auburn, N. Y. In 1870 she entered Wells College, Aurora, N. Y., where she was graduated in 1872. She married Millard P. Murray, June 27, 1876, and to them were born three daughters.

Excavations for their home in Athens in 1882 revealed an unusual Indian burial plot containing portrait pottery and skeletal remains of great size. For nearly fifty years thereafter Mrs. Murray followed up the theory that the Andastes or Susquehannocks of Captain John Smith's account were the Indians who left these remains; her last publication, on which she was at work at the time of her death and which was published posthumously, was concerned with this theory. Stimulated by these archaeological discoveries, she founded the Tioga Point Historical Society, which opened and maintained the Tioga Point Museum. In 1898 this institution was installed in the Spalding Memorial Building, a model museum structure secured through her efforts. As director and archaeologist of this museum, she spent more than three decades of indefatigable labor endeavoring to correlate museum activity with school and community aims. With this end in view, she made a study of museums in Buffalo, Cleveland, Ann Arbor, Chicago, and Milwaukee. Her bulletins and pamphlets, her scheduled lectures for school children, and her methods of exhibition reveal a body of progressive museum criteria not often found in small-town institutions.

Meanwhile, in addition to her educational work with the museum, she carried on independent researches in local history and for this purpose accumulated at the museum valuable manuscript and other primary sources. In 1903 she published her first study, *The Story of Some French Refugees and their "Azilum," 1793–1800*; in 1908 appeared her most important work, *A History of Old Tioga Point and Early Athens, Pennsylvania*. Both of these studies reveal an aptitude for research in original sources, are well documented, and remain the standard authority for the subjects they treat. In 1921 she contributed articles to the *American Anthropologist* on the aboriginal sites in and near "Teaoga" (Athens). In 1929 she published *Notes . . . on the Sullivan Expedition of 1799*, a series of documents drawn from the Tioga Point Museum and other archives. In 1931 the Society for Pennsylvania Archæology, of which she was a charter member and second vice-president, issued as its first publication her *Selected Manuscripts of General John S. Clark Relating to the Aboriginal History of the Susquehanna*. She was a founder of the Athens Library Club and was active in patriotic and historical societies. Possessed of the instincts of a genuine scholar, she was also adept and persevering in the recruiting of finances with which to execute her archaeological and historical projects. Her personality and her achievements are best appreciated when it is recognized that, over a period of several decades, neither lack of finances, domestic cares, lack of formal training in research, nor the apathy of a small town were sufficient to thwart her.

[*Elmira Star-Gazette*, Apr. 24, 1931; *Sayre Times*, Apr. 23, 1931; bulletins of the Tioga Point Museum.]
J. P. B.

MURRAY, ROBERT (1721–July 22, 1786), Quaker merchant, was born in Scotland, and emigrated to America with his father, John, in 1732. At Swatara Creek, now in Dauphin County, Pa., a region noted for its thriving agriculture, the younger Murray in early life operated a small flour mill, in which he shared an interest with other members of his family. Later he undertook trading voyages to the West Indies, and from 1750 to 1753 he lived in North Carolina. In 1753 he engaged in general trade in New York with a younger brother, John [*q.v.*], as a partner. The import and export trade of the brothers with England and her colonies, carried on in their own ships, gradually advanced the Murrays to the foremost rank of American merchants. From 1767 to 1775 Robert was on business in England.

When the interests of commerce were required to yield to a patriotic consideration, and New York merchants agreed, in opposition to the tea duty, to exclude British goods from the domestic market, Murray acquiesced in the policy of non-importation. In February 1775, however, the ship *Beulah* arrived from London and, failing to get past the boat of the Committee of Sixty, went to Sandy Hook, where a part of its cargo was taken off by a boat from Elizabethtown. Robert and John Murray confessed to the Committee that they were principals in the affair and promised to reship the goods in seven days' time. In May 1775 they petitioned Congress for restoration of former commercial privileges (Schlesinger, *post*, pp. 491, 565). That Murray's sympathies were with the British may be inferred from the fact that in 1779 Gen. Alexander McDougall, describing in a letter to Governor Clinton a plot to get supplies to the King's troops, said this of the Quaker merchant: "Robert Murray is on Long Island, with a store of goods, which makes one link of the chain" (*Public Papers of George Clinton*, vol. IV, 1900, p. 511). There is little doubt that Murray's ocean trade was brisk, and profits approached the normal magnitude, when British warships were able to keep the lanes of commerce open. It is significant that Murray's house "on the Heights of Inklenberg" (Murray Hill) was exempted from seizure by the British during their occupation (Stokes, *post*, I, 325).

Murray was an original member of the New York Chamber of Commerce, formed Apr. 5, 1768, and served on a committee of the chamber to consider the condition of the coinage and the embarrassments springing from variations in colonial standards. In 1768 he invested money in the whale fishery. His country house on Murray Hill was famous for its elegance and its hospitality. Murray's wife, whom he married in 1744, was Mary Lindley; their son, Lindley [*q.v.*], the grammarian, was the eldest of twelve children. Mary Lindley Murray is remembered because on Sept. 15, 1776, when the British, with a view to capturing Manhattan, landed at Kip's Bay, she invited the officers to avail themselves of the hospitality of her home on what is now Murray Hill. They accepted and thereby, intentionally or unintentionally, she delayed the British force, while General Putnam and his men were quietly leaving Manhattan to join the main army on Harlem Heights.

[W. H. Egle, *Pa. Geneals.* (1886); J. M. Lindly, *The Hist. of the Lindley Lindsley-Linsley Families in America 1639–1924*, vol. II (1924); I. N. P. Stokes, *The Iconography of Manhattan Island, 1498–1909* (6 vols., 1915–28); J. G. Wilson, *The Memorial Hist. of the City of N. Y.* (4 vols., 1892–93); *Memoirs of the Life and Writings of Lindley Murray* (1826); J. A. Scoville, *The Old Merchants of N. Y. City*, 1 and 2 ser. (1863); C. H. Haswell, *Reminiscences of an Octogenarian* (1896); A. M. Schlesinger, *The Colonial Merchants and the Am. Revolution, 1763–1776* (1917).]
R. E. D.

MURRAY, THOMAS EDWARD (Oct. 21, 1860–July 21, 1929), consulting engineer, inventor, was the son of John and Anastatia (McGrath) Murray and was born in Albany, N. Y., where his parents also were born and where his father was employed as a carpenter. He attended the public schools until he was nine years old, when, owing to the death of his father, he was compelled to go to work. Thereafter, he attended night school and for two years worked in the drafting rooms of local architects and engineers. He then served his machinist apprenticeship for four years in various shops in Albany, and in 1881 became an operating engineer at the pumping plant of the Albany Waterworks.

In 1887 Anthony N. Brady [*q.v.*] employed Murray to take charge of the power station of the Municipal Gas Company at Albany, and in that company his rise was rapid. He was soon in complete charge of the company's activities and was called into consultation in connection with other Brady properties, including the Troy City Railway Company, the Troy Electric Light Company, the Kings County Electric Light and Power Company, and the Albany Railway Company. He also had a part in consolidating Brady electric companies in Brooklyn and the formation of the Edison Electric Illuminating Company, later known as the Brooklyn Edison Company. During this period, too, his inventive genius, which was to secure for him over eleven hundred patents, began to assert itself. In 1895, having been intrusted by Brady with the task of consolidating the electric properties in Manhattan, Murray moved with his family to New York, and when, five years later, this consolidation was effected through the organization of the New York Edison Company, he was made second vice-president and general manager. In 1913, he became vice-president, in 1924 senior vice-president, and finally, after the merging of the New York Edison Company and the Brooklyn Edison Company in 1928, vice-chairman of the board of directors. Under Murray's general direction many of the great electric power stations which supply the various boroughs of New York City were built. Among these are Waterside No. 1 and No. 2, Sherman Creek, Hell Gate, Gold Street, Hudson Avenue, and East River stations, and the Williamsburg power house. He was also the designer of steam-power plants in Albany, Utica, and Rochester, N. Y., as well as in Dayton, Ohio; and of hydro-electric-power plants, in Chattanooga, Tenn., and in Trenton Falls and Cohoes, N. Y. It is believed that the total capacity of these plants is greater than that of those designed by any other man in the electrical industry.

Murray also organized and maintained supervision over several corporations of his own— Thomas E. Murray, Inc., the Metropolitan Device Corporation, the Metropolitan Engineering Company, and the Murray Radiator Company. Although most of his earlier engineering and inventive work was in the electrical and gas-appliance fields, the influence of his activities has been felt in almost every phase of industry. His inventions were exceeded in number only by those of Thomas A. Edison and included water wall furnaces for steam boilers, electrical protection devices, copper radiators, cinder catchers, pulverized fuel equipment, and automatic welding. His method of welding shells was found to be the only one that could be used for the production of the 240 mm. mortar shell, and because of it he received high commendation from the War Department. For the numerous safety appliances he invented he received in 1913 the gold medal of the American Museum of Safety, New York. He served as president of the Association of Edison Illuminating Companies; he was an active member of the American Society of Mechanical Engineers for thirty-five years; and he was a fellow of the American Institute of Electrical Engineers. Among his publications were several technical works which include *Electric Power Plants* (1910), *Power Stations* (1922), and *Applied Engineering* (1928). He was active in charitable and religious work, taking a prominent part in the affairs of the Roman Catholic Church, for which service membership in the orders of the Knights of St. Gregory and in the Knights of Malta was conferred on him. In 1887 he married Catherine Bradley of Brooklyn, N. Y., and at the time of his death, at his summer home, "Wickapogue," Southampton, L. I., he was survived by eight children.

[*Jour. Am. Inst. Electrical Engineers*, Aug. 1929; *Electrical World*, July 27, 1929; *N. Y. Herald Tribune, N. Y. Times, World* (N. Y.), July 22, 1929; *Jour. of Commerce* (N. Y.), July 23, 1929; information from Edison Pioneers, Asso. of Edison Illuminating Companies, and Thomas E. Murray, Inc.; Patent Office records.]
　　　　　　　　　　　　　　　　　C. W. M.

MURRAY, WILLIAM VANS (Feb. 9, 1760–Dec. 11, 1803), diplomatist, was born in Cambridge, Md., the son of Dr. Henry Murray, a prominent physician and influential citizen of Dorchester County. His mother was Rebeckah Orrick, the daughter of John Orrick of Anne Arundel County and Baltimore. William Vans Murray received his early education in Maryland and later went to London, where he entered upon the study of law at the Middle Temple, Apr. 28, 1784. While in England he married Charlotte Hughins. Here also he became interested in politics and diplomacy and wrote *Political Sketches* (1787), inscribed to John Adams, minister plenipotentiary from the United States to Great Britain. He returned to Cambridge at the close of the summer in 1787, was admitted to the bar, and began the practice of law. He was chosen to represent Dorchester County in the Maryland legislature but resigned to serve in Congress, where he continued from Mar. 4, 1791, to Mar. 3, 1797. A loyal Federalist, he was frequently consulted by Washington upon matters of patronage, and the appointments of James McHenry as secretary of war and Samuel Chase to the federal bench were made after his advice was taken. His longest and most important speech in the House of Representatives was delivered Mar. 23, 1796, against the resolution calling upon the President to produce the correspondence and documents relating to Jay's treaty with Great Britain.

In the campaign of 1796, Murray warmly advocated the election of Adams to the presidency and wrote numerous "pieces for the press" in his behalf. When his friends suggested early in 1797 that he be given a diplomatic post, Washington had already determined to appoint him minister to the Netherlands. The nomination was sent to the Senate on Feb. 27 and was confirmed Mar. 2. Murray was eager to enter upon the mission and, accompanied by his wife and secretary, sailed on the ship *Friend* and landed at the Helder June 7, 1797. He arrived at The Hague during a very critical period. The misunderstandings and disputes between the United States and France were already beyond mending. Within a year the envoys sent by President Adams had returned to report their shameful reception at the hands of Talleyrand's agents, X, Y and Z. Diplomatic relations were severed, and Adams, supported by the people of the United States, insisted that a renewal of friendly intercourse awaited advances on the part of the French government. The first overtures came through conversations between M. Pichon, secretary of the French legation at The Hague, and Murray. Although Pichon displayed a letter from Talleyrand, the suggestions therein contained were so indefinite that Murray thought them of little value. But Talleyrand continued to pursue negotiations for a reconciliation through the channel opened up at The Hague, and in September 1798 assured Murray that "whatever plenipotentiary the government of the United States might send to France, in order to terminate the existing differences between the two countries, would undoubtedly be received with the respect due to the representative of a free, independent, and powerful nation" (*American State Papers, Foreign Relations,* vol. II, 1832, p. 239). When this declaration was communicated to President Adams, he nominated Murray as minister plenipotentiary. A few days later he decided to send a commission and added the names of Oliver Ellsworth [*q.v.*] and Patrick Henry. Henry was unable to serve and Gov. W. R. Davie [*q.v.*] of North Carolina was chosen in his stead.

When Murray met the other commissioners in France in February 1800, they found that the Directory had been overthrown and the Consulate set up, with Napoleon Bonaparte at its head. It was to Napoleon that they presented their credentials on Mar. 8, in the hall of the ambassadors in the Tuileries. The French commissioners were Joseph Bonaparte, M. Fleurieu, formerly minister of marine, and M. Roederer, counselor of state. The negotiation continued throughout the summer until, "at ½ past 3 in the morning" of Oct. 1, the convention between France and the United States, though not entirely satisfactory, was signed. Murray returned to his post at The Hague to remain until Sept. 2, 1801, when he resigned. The remaining days of his life he spent on his farm near Cambridge.

"He had," said John Quincy Adams (*post,* p. 5), "a strong and genuine relish for the fine arts, a refined and delicate taste for literature, and a persevering and patient fondness for the pursuits of science." Because Murray was pleasing in his manners and also amusing and instructive in his conversation, he was able to carry through to a successful conclusion negotiations which, in the hands of a duller man, would likely have failed.

[The materials for the life of William Vans Murray are nearly all in manuscript. The Murray MSS. in the Lib. of Cong. contain his diary written at The Hague and "Some Remarks on the Stages of Our Negotiations at Paris, 1800." His commonplace book, begun at London and Chelsea, 1786, and renewed at Cambridge, 1795, is in the Princeton Univ. Lib. Numerous letters from Murray to John Quincy Adams are printed in the *Ann. Report Am. Hist. Asso.,* 1912 (1914). See also extracts from his diary, in *Proc. Am. Antiq. Soc.,* n.s. XII (1899), 245–55; J. Q. Adams, in *Port Folio,* Jan. 7, 1804; B. C. Steiner, *The Life and Corresp. of James McHenry* (1907); C. F. Adams, *The Works of John Adams* (10 vols., 1850–56); E. A. Jones, *Am. Members of the Inns of Court* (1924); *Biog. Dir. Am. Cong.* (1928); G. N. Mackenzie, *Colonial Families of the U. S. A.,* vol. II (1911); *Poulson's Am. Daily Advertiser* (Phila.), Dec. 17, 1803.]   W. S. C.

MURRELL, JOHN A. (fl. 1804–1844), outlaw, was the leader of a clan purporting to number more than a thousand members, whose activities touched eight states of the Old Southwest. Apart from a few court records and dates from documentary sources there is little contemporary information about Murrell himself (whose name is also spelled Murrel and Murel), except the narrative written by his captor, Virgil A. Stewart, who wormed his way into the desperado's confidence, took the oath of allegiance to the clan, and thus secured the leader's story. According to Murrell's statement, as retailed by Stewart (*post*), he was born in Middle Tennessee in 1804. His parents (unnamed and unknown) were poor, his father, "an honest man, I expect," but his mother a woman who "learnt me and all her children to steal so soon as we could walk." His name first appears in the court records of Williamson County in 1823 when he was fined for "riot." In 1825 he was before the court for gaming, and in 1826 he was twice tried for horse stealing, being sentenced the second time to twelve months in prison. As he told Stewart, he "began to see the value of having friends in this business," and with an older hand, Daniel Crenshaw (whom tradition sometimes makes the real leader of the clan), he set off on a round of highway robberies which took him from Georgia to New Orleans and back to Tennessee. Valuable connections were made with local groups of bandits and the framework of his organization was created. Channels of exchange were organized whereby the spoils—money, horses, or negroes—were traded from one part of the country to another to be disposed of. Negro-stealing became Murrell's specialty. By promises of freedom he would entice a negro from his owner, sell him several counties distant, steal him again, and repeat the process until the negro became so well known by the posting of repeated rewards that he could no longer be sold. He was then murdered and his body disposed of so that no tales were told.

Captured by Stewart in 1834 after a reign of some eight years, Murrell was brought to trial before the circuit court in Jackson, Tenn., in July of that year. He was convicted of negro-stealing and sentenced to a ten-year term in the state penitentiary. The most sensational part of Stewart's testimony against him, however, was the assertion that for some time Murrell and his agents had been planning a great negro rebellion in the Southwest. So strongly did this allegation affect the imaginations of the people that when in the summer of 1835 several outbreaks did occur and some of the instigators confessed to belonging to Murrell's gang, more than a score were hanged before the excitement was allayed. Murrell was discharged from the Nashville penitentiary Apr. 3, 1844 (*Journal of the House of Representatives of the State of Tennessee, October 1845*, 1846, App., p. 317), and lived but a few years longer, dying of consumption at Pikesville, Tenn.

[A. Q. Walton (pseud.), *Hist. of the Detection, Conviction, Life, and Designs of John A. Murel* (Athens, Tenn., 1835) is the first edition of the Stewart narrative, while *The Hist. of Virgil A. Stewart* (New York, 1836), compiled by H. R. Howard, is an expanded version. The stilted dialogue, the melodramatic style, and the dime-novel fashion in which events occur in the Stewart narratives lessen one's confidence in them. See also "Uses and Abuses of Lynch Law," *Am. Whig Rev.*, Nov. 1850, Mar. 1851; Park Marshall, "John A. Murrell and Daniel Crenshaw," *Tenn. Hist. Mag.*, Apr. 1920; James Phelan, *Hist. of Tenn.* (1888), ch. xxxii; Douglas Anderson, "A Famous Outlaw of the Early Southwest," *Nashville Banner*, Mar. 20, 1921; S. C. Williams, *Beginnings of West Tenn.* (1930); R. M. Coates, *The Outlaw Years* (1930). The Murrell gang receives fictional treatment in W. G. Simms, *Richard Hurdis* (1838) and *Border Beagles* (1840), and in Vaughan Kester, *The Prodigal Judge* (1911).]   O.W.H.

MURRIETA, JOAQUIN (c. 1832–July 25, 1853), brigand, was the most noted of the California bandits of the gold discovery days. Herrera (*post*) says that he was born in Santiago, Chile, in 1830; but the weight of evidence makes him a native of Sonora, Mexico, and gives him a later birthyear. His surname may have been Carrillo. He arrived in California probably in 1849, when prejudice against Latin-Americans in the mines was beginning to express itself in numerous outrages. He is said to have been driven from a claim on Stanislaus River, in the early spring of 1850, by men who abused his wife or mistress, and later to have been driven from the placers on Calaveras River. At Murphy's Diggings, Calaveras County, where he worked for a time as a monte dealer, he is said to have been flogged and his half-brother hanged for the alleged theft of a horse.

Accounts of his life are contradictory, and few of the details given can be fully authenticated. By Latin-American writers and by Bancroft he has been invested with a considerable degree of romantic glamor, but the probability is that he was a ruffian, brutal, avaricious, and lawless. The account by Hittell (*post*), drawn largely from a rare book by F. L. Ridge, is perhaps the safest guide to his character and career. Because of some grievance, real or imagined, Murrieta vowed vengeance against the Americans, and for more than two years, at the head of a band of desperadoes, he ranged over a large part of the state and committed an appalling number of robberies and murders. In 1852, in Mariposa County, he narrowly escaped capture at the hands of Capt. Harry S. Love, deputy sheriff of Los Angeles County, who on his own initiative had tracked the bandit to one of his hiding places. A fresh series of robberies and murders in the spring of 1853 caused the legislature to pass an act authorizing Love to organize a company of mounted rangers to pursue him. Love, with his company, soon took the field, and on a morning in July surprised a part of Murrieta's band at a point west of Tulare Lake. In a running fight the bandit chief and three others were killed and two captured, while two or three escaped. For purposes of identification Murrieta's head was cut off and preserved in alcohol, and was later exhibited in various parts of the state.

[T. H. Hittell, *Hist. of Cal.*, III (1897), 712–25; H. H. Bancroft, *Hist. of Cal.*, VII (1890), 203, and *Cal. Pastoral* (1888), p. 645; Ireneo Paz, *Life and Adventures of the Celebrated Bandit, Joaquin Murrieta* (1925), translated by Frances P. Belle; Ignacio Herrera, *Joaquin Murrieta, El Bandido Chileno en Cal.* (1926), a pamphlet; Jos. Gollomb, *Master Highwaymen* (1927); Horace Bell, *Reminiscences of a Ranger* (1881), reprinted in 1927 with an introduction by A. M. Ellis; J. L. Cossley-Batt, *The Last of the Cal. Rangers* (1928); W. N. Burns, *The Robin Hood of El Dorado* (1932); *Joaquin Murieta, the Brigand Chief of Cal.* (1859), reprinted in 1932 with notes by F. P. Farquhar; J. R. Ridge, *The Life and Adventures of Joaquin Murieta* (1854, and later editions).] W.J.G.

MURROW, JOSEPH SAMUEL (June 7, 1835–Sept. 8, 1929), missionary to the Indians, son of John and Mary Amelia (Badger) Murrow, was born in Jefferson County, Ga. His paternal grandfather had been a member of Marion's band of revolutionary heroes in South Carolina, and his maternal great-grandfather is said to have held a patent to Sullivan's Island. Young Murrow was early converted and united with the Green Fork Baptist Church, Burke County, Ga., in 1854, was licensed to preach in 1855, and entered Mercer University, Macon, Ga., as a sophomore in January 1856. He did not complete his studies there, but was ordained in September 1857 to go as a missionary to the Indians in the West. He was appointed by the Domestic and Indian Mission Board of the Southern Baptist Convention but was supported by the Rehoboth Association of Georgia.

Setting out for his future field of labor at once, he married on the way Mannie Elizabeth Tatom, and arrived at old North Fork Town, Indian Territory, now Eufaula, Okla., Nov. 13, 1857. Rev. H. F. Buckner, then the only white missionary in the Creek nation, who had been on the field since 1845, welcomed his new colleague and assisted him in many ways. They worked a good deal together among the Creeks, Seminoles, and Choctaws, Murrow riding a pony over wide areas and preaching through interpreters. He lost his young wife within ten months, and in 1859 married Clara, daughter of Rev. Willis Burns, who had come to the territory as a missionary the year before. Soon after his second marriage, he moved into the Seminole nation and established a mission there, organizing in 1861 the first church in that tribe. When the Civil War broke out the United States government withdrew its soldiers from the various forts in the territory, leaving the Indians to the care and control of the Confederate government. Murrow was selected by the Seminole council as agent in dealings with this government, a position which he held throughout the war, acting after 1863 as subsistence commissary in providing food for the Seminole, Comanche, Osage, and Wichita refugees along the Red River. While attending to these temporal matters, he was carrying on as far as possible his missionary work. Near the end of the war he was forced to remove to Texas for the safety of his family, where, at Linden, he engaged in teaching.

On his return from Texas in 1867 he settled at Atoka in the Choctaw nation, which became the center of his operations thereafter. For some years he spent considerable time in reëstablishing and reviving among the Choctaws, Creeks, and Seminoles the mission work which had been disrupted by the war. At his call representatives of sixteen churches met at Atoka in July 1872 and organized the Choctaw and Chickasaw Baptist Association, a body which has done much for the spread of Christianity among the Indians.

He was also largely instrumental in beginning mission work among the wild or blanket Indians through the native Indian preacher, John McIntosh. In 1876 he began a movement for the organization of all the Indian associations into a general body which could promote a larger fellowship and more vigorous work. As a result the Baptist Missionary and Educational Convention was organized in 1881, of which he was president for seventeen years. The founding at Bacone of Indian University, or Bacone College, was also due to his activities. In 1885 the American Baptist Home Mission Society appointed him superintendent of its Indian mission work and he severed his connection with the Southern Baptist Convention. Two years later, the Atoka Baptist Academy was founded; it was operated for some eighteen years and then merged into the Murrow Indian Orphans' Home, which was Murrow's last important contribution to the welfare of the Indians. For seventy years he lived among them, building many churches, a college, and an orphanage, preaching the gospel and serving their interests in all possible ways. He was greatly loved by the Indians of the entire territory, being known everywhere as "Father Murrow."

[Narrative (MS.) by A. J. Holt in archives of Home Mission Board, Atlanta, Ga.; "Fifty Beautiful Years" (MS.), narrative by Murrow's daughter, Clara A. McBride; minutes of Southern Baptist Convention; minutes of Baptist Home Mission Soc.; *Hist. of the Bapt. Denomination in Ga.* (1881); the *Baptist*, Sept. 28, 1929; *Muskogee Daily Phoenix*, Sept. 10, 1929.]

W. J. M.

MUSIN, OVIDE (Sept. 22, 1854–Nov. 24, 1929), violinist and composer, was the son of Jaques Musin, a civil engineer, and Louise de Milles, of Nandrin near Liège, Belgium, where he was born. He was admitted to the Liège Conservatory at the age of nine, and in 1867 he shared with Eugène Ysaye the second prize of the Conservatory. When Henri Léonard was appointed professor of violin at the Conservatory in 1870, Musin became his pupil and followed the Belgian master to the Paris Conservatory, where he won the gold medal for solo and quartet-playing. He began his professional career at fifteen as solo violinist of the Théâtre Royale in Spa. His first concert tours (1873–74) were made, on the recommendations of Léonard and Vieuxtemps, to fill concert engagements they could not undertake, and until 1882 Musin toured Europe triumphantly as a virtuoso violinist, appearing with leading orchestras in London, Vienna, and Paris, under various conductors: Hans Richter, Edvard Grieg, Edouard Colonne, Charles Lamoureux. In 1875 he organized in Paris a stringed quartet to popularize newer ensemble works and was the first to acquaint Parisians with Brahms's chamber music. In 1876 the King of Holland appointed him court violinist, but the following year he went to London. He remained in Great Britain for five years, touring England, Scotland, and Ireland, playing at Sir Julius Benedict's *soirées,* and in the homes of the nobility. He made his first appearance in America in the eighties with the New York Symphony Society, under Leopold Damrosch, and with the New York Philharmonic Society under Theodore Thomas, playing the Godard violin concerto for the first time in the United States.

He made various tours in the United States and Canada with a concert troupe of his own. In 1892 he visited Australia, New Zealand, and Mexico, and in the late nineties he appeared in Japan, China, the Philippines, and Hawaii. From 1898 to 1908 he was head of the advanced class for violin at the Liège Conservatory, but he spent half of his time in New York. In 1908 he resigned his position and established a violin school of his own in New York. Here he was prominent as a teacher for some twenty-one years, until he died in his home in Brooklyn. On Oct. 7, 1891, he had married Annie Louise Hodges-Tanner of New York.

Musin wrote a number of works for the violin and orchestra and for violin and piano. They include the "Valse de Concert," "Mazurka de Concert," "Extase," "Valse Lente," "Berceuse et Prière," and "Mazurka Élégante." His compositions for the most part were brilliant virtuoso pieces after the manner of Vieuxtemps and Wieniawski; he also arranged a number of transcriptions. His chief contributions to the teaching literature of the violin were his *System of Daily Practise* (1899) and *The Belgian School of the Violin* (1916), four volumes of studies which represent a combination of Léonard's methods and his own. *My Memories* (1920) is his record of a half-century as a globe-trotting violin virtuoso. He was the recipient of many orders and decorations, including the Order of Leopold (Belgium) and the Order of Bolivar (Venezuela).

[In addition to *My Memories* see: *Who's Who in America,* 1924–25; *Le Monde Musical,* Jan. 31, 1930; *Musical America,* Dec. 19, 1929; *Musical Observer,* Nov. 1907; *N. Y. Times, N. Y. Herald-Tribune,* Nov. 25, 1929.]
                                                    F. H. M.

MUSSEY, REUBEN DIMOND (June 23, 1780–June 21, 1866), surgeon, was born in Pelham, Rockingham County, N. H., the son of a country doctor, John Mussey, and his wife, Beulah Butler. He obtained his early education in Pelham, and later attended the district school

of Amherst, N. H., and Dartmouth College, where he was graduated A.B. in 1803. He began the study of medicine under Nathan Smith and Luke Howe, and devoted a portion of each winter, during the period 1803–05, to teaching school in Peterborough, N. H., in order to secure money to finish his medical education. The degree of bachelor of medicine was conferred upon him by the Medical Department of Dartmouth College in 1805, and that of doctor of medicine by the University of Pennsylvania in 1809.

Following his graduation from the University of Pennsylvania, he opened an office in Salem, Mass., and for five years enjoyed a large practice in association with Dr. Daniel Oliver. Besides practising general medicine, he gave courses of lectures on chemistry. He left Salem in 1814 to teach the theory and practice of medicine, materia medica, and obstetrics at Dartmouth, becoming professor of anatomy and surgery there in 1822. He spent ten months in Paris and London during the year 1830. In addition to his work at Dartmouth, he lectured on anatomy and surgery at Bowdoin College, 1831–35, and on surgery at the College of Physicians and Surgeons, Fairfield, Herkimer County, N. Y., 1836–38. In 1838 he resigned his professorship at Dartmouth to become professor of surgery in the Medical College of Ohio. This post he held until 1852, when the Miami Medical College was organized in Cincinnati, and he accepted the chair of surgery in the new institution. He continued in this capacity until 1857, then went to live with his daughter and son-in-law, Mary and Lyman Mason, in Boston, where he died.

Aside from six pamphlets which are in the library of the Cincinnati General Hospital, Mussey published a book: *Health, Its Friends and Foes* (1862), largely devoted to matters of hygiene and sanitation, and *Essay on Ardent Spirits and Its Substitutes as a Means of Invigorating Health* (1835), reissued the same year together with an essay by Dr. Harvey Lindsly, in a volume entitled: *Temperance Prize Essays.* His earliest research was undertaken to prove that the skin possesses powers of absorption, the idea being in direct conflict with the teaching of the eminent physician Benjamin Rush. Mussey proved his contention by making experiments upon himself (*Philadelphia Medical and Physical Journal,* 3rd supplement, May 1809). The cataphoric action of galvanism was demonstrated by him in 1821, while still a student at the University of Pennsylvania. In 1830, while in London, he discussed with Sir Astley Cooper the possibility of bony union after fracture of the neck of the femur, having taken with him specimens to prove his contention that such union is possible. These specimens are now in the Museum of the Cincinnati General Hospital. Mussey began very early to use chloroform and ether as anesthetics, reporting his experiences in a letter to Dr. Isaac Parrish, published in the *Transactions of the American Medical Association,* vol. I (1848). He was president of the American Medical Association in 1850, being the fourth to hold that office. He was a total abstainer from the use of both tobacco and alcohol, and seems to have written more upon this subject than any other. He was a vegetarian, very religious, and quite musical. He was married twice; his first wife, Mary Sewall, died May 31, 1807, and in 1813 he married his second wife, Mehitable Osgood, daughter of Dr. Joseph Osgood, an army surgeon. They had two daughters and seven sons, two of whom, William H. Mussey and Francis B. Mussey, became physicians.

[Otto Juettner, *Daniel Drake and His Followers* (1909); H. A. Kelly and W. L. Burrage, *Am. Medic. Biogs.* (1920); Minutes of Faculty Meetings of the Medical College of Ohio, 1838–52 (MSS.); J. B. Hamilton, "Life and Times of Dr. Reuben D. Mussey," *Jour. Am. Medic. Asso.,* Apr. 4, 1896; A. B. Crosby, *An Address Commemorative of Reuben Dimond Mussey* (1869), repr. from *Trans. N. H. Medic. Soc.;* H. S. Webster, *Thomas Sewall; Some of His Ancestors and All of His Descendants* (1904); *New-Eng. Hist. and Geneal. Reg.,* Jan. 1849, p. 73; *Autobiog. of Samuel D. Gross, M.D.* (1887), vol. II; *Boston Transcript,* June 25, 1866; pamphlets, reprints, and books by Mussey in the Library of the Cincinnati General Hospital; correspondence with a grand-daughter, Miss Theodora Mussey of Denver, Colo.]   J. C. O.

MUYBRIDGE, EADWEARD (Apr. 9, 1830– May 8, 1904), a pioneer in motion photography, was born at Kingston-on-Thames, England, the son of John Muggeridge, a grain dealer, and his wife Susannah. His name was originally Edward James Muggeridge, but at an early age he changed it to Eadweard Muybridge. After receiving a common-school education in England, he emigrated to the United States. Engaged at first in mercantile pursuits, he shortly became interested in photography, and in the course of time his skill in the art led to his employment as a photographer in the United States Coast and Geodetic Survey, for photographic survey work on the Pacific Coast. While so engaged, in May 1872 his services were secured by Leland Stanford [*q.v.*] of Palo Alto, Cal., to prove by photography whether a running horse at any period of his stride has all his feet entirely off the ground. Using one camera and a string stretched across the path of the horse to operate the·shutter, Muybridge secured a series of photographs in silhouette which proved that at certain times all four feet of a running horse are off the ground.

This investigation projected him into a most interesting field of experiment, namely, animal locomotion, which occupied his attent.on for the remainder of his life. With the financial aid of Stanford, he made a series of elaborate experiments, covering a period of six years, at the former's stud farm in Palo Alto. A course similar to a running path was built, one side being bounded by a white background, and opposite it, twelve to twenty-four cameras were set up in a line and arranged to obtain photographs from three different points of view. The best of the results of these experiments were published in book form by Muybridge in 1878, under the title *The Horse in Motion.* The book excited world-wide interest, and particularly that of Dr. E. J. Marey of Paris, the renowned physiologist. Between 1878 and 1881 Muybridge continued his experiments in California, photographing athletes, oxen, dogs, and birds. He also developed in 1879 an apparatus which he called the zoopraxiscope, by the aid of which he successfully reproduced the moving figures in large size on a screen. In this machine, photographs of the successive phases of the analyzed motion were reproduced around the rim of a large glass disk. This was placed on a shaft connected to a projection lantern, and when the disk was rapidly revolved the enlarged images were projected upon the screen, giving the impression of the original motion. In 1881 and 1882 Muybridge spent most of his time in Europe working with Dr. Marey and lecturing on the subject of animal motion both in Paris and in London.

After returning to the United States in 1883 he continued his lectures for a time and in 1884 began a series of new experiments in Philadelphia under the auspices of the University of Pennsylvania. For these he developed a timing mechanism and an electro-magnetic latch to release the camera shutters. The work continued for two years, and the results were published in eleven volumes containing 100,000 photographic plates, under the title, *Animal Locomotion; An Electro-photographic Investigation of Consecutive Phases of Animal Movements, 1872–1885* (1887). Upon the completion of this work Muybridge returned to England and, except for a few brief visits to the United States, resided henceforth at his birthplace. During the World's Columbian Exposition in Chicago in 1893, he gave illustrated lectures to pay audiences in a specially erected building called "Zoopraxographical Hall." He also published *Descriptive Zoopraxography* (1893) and *The Human Figure in Motion* (1901). He never married. He died in England and his remains were cremated at Woking. His pioneer work in motion photography was commemorated by an inscribed tablet bearing his portrait which was placed in the Public Library at Kingston-on-Thames, England, July 17, 1931. In this institution is preserved his original zoopraxiscope.

[Waldemer Kaempffert, *A Pop. Hist. of Am. Invention* (2 vols., 1924); L. F. Rondinella, "Muybridge's Motion Pictures," *Jour. Franklin Inst.*, Sept. 1929; Merritt Crawford, "Men in the Movie Vanguard," *Cinema*, June 1930; *Gen. Mag. and Hist. Chron.* (Univ. of Pa., Alumni Soc.), Apr. 1928; *Notices of the Proc. at the Meetings of the Members of the Royal Inst. of Great Britain*, vol. X (1884); *Dict. Nat. Biog.*, second supplement; *Times* (London), May 10, 1904; *Illustrated London News*, July 18, 1931.]   C. W. M.

MYER, ALBERT JAMES (Sept. 20, 1829–Aug. 24, 1880), soldier, signal officer, founder of the Weather Bureau, was born in Newburgh, N. Y., the son of Henry Beekman Myer and Eleanor Pope (McLannan) Myer. While he was still a child his mother died, and he was brought up by an aunt, with whom, about 1836, he moved to Buffalo. He graduated from Hobart College (A.B.) in 1847 and from Buffalo Medical College (M.D) in 1851. On Sept. 18, 1854, he entered the army as an assistant surgeon. From the close of his college days he had known how to operate a telegraph instrument, and while serving on the Texas plains where the clearness of the air made it possible to see objects at a great distance, he became enthusiastic over the possibilities of visual signaling. In 1856 he drafted a memorandum on his signal devices, and in 1858 succeeded in having a military board authorized to consider them. Two more years of effort on his part resulted in an act of Congress adding to the staff of the army one signal officer with the rank and pay of major, and on June 27, 1860, Myer was appointed to the post. He had as yet, however, no organization to carry on his work, and almost immediately was ordered to the West, where until March 1861 he took part in General Canby's expedition against the Navajos in New Mexico. He carried his enthusiasm with him, and his visual signaling, with a code of three elements, was successfully used in that campaign. On the outbreak of the Civil War he called attention to the need for a signal service, and in June 1861 was ordered to Washington to organize and command the Signal Corps of the army. He also furnished plans for naval signaling at the request of the secretary of the navy. Although still handicapped by lack of personnel, he succeeded in having signal schools organized, and himself conducted signal communications in the Army of the Potomac. He was on the staffs of Generals Butler, McDowell, and McClellan, serving from the first battle of Bull Run through much of the fighting in Northern Virginia. He was brevetted lieutenant-colonel, May 27, 1862, for gallant services in the battle of Hanover Court House, and colonel, July 2, 1862, for similar services at Malvern Hill.

In the meantime he was busy in Washington extending the scope of his activities. He succeeded finally in securing the establishment of the Signal Corps through the enactment of the Sundry Civil Act, Mar. 3, 1863. This gave him the position of colonel and chief signal officer. He held the appointment as colonel until it expired and was revoked July 21, 1864. The expansion of his activities—he supervised the building of some five thousand miles of telegraph lines to frontier posts—kept him in conflict with the United States Military Telegraph, which was under the direct supervision of an assistant secretary of war, and at length, owing to the friction between the two services, he was relieved as chief signal officer (November 1863) and ordered to a reconnaissance of the Mississippi River. From May 1864 to the end of the war he was signal officer of the Division of West Mississippi, and participated in operations along the river. He published *A Manual of Signals: For the Use of Signal Officers in the Field* (1864). On May 13, 1865, he was brevetted brigadier-general for his services as chief signal officer and for special service Oct. 5, 1864, when the post of Allatoona was saved by relief secured through signal communication.

On July 28, 1866, an act of Congress reorganized the Signal Corps and gave Myer the permanent rank of colonel as chief signal officer. He assumed charge Aug. 21, 1867. For some years prior to the Civil War the Smithsonian Institution had issued weather predictions and storm warnings based on telegraphic weather reports; but this work was interrupted by the war, and its resumption afterward delayed by a fire at the Smithsonian. In his report of 1869 Myer proposed that the peacetime activities of the Signal Corps be extended to include the sending out of storm warnings. His arguments, in conjunction with those of certain others interested in the matter, led Congress, in February 1870, to authorize the establishment of the United States Weather Bureau under the direction of the Signal Corps. During the first ten years of its existence Myer supervised the new bureau, which was soon rendering an extremely valuable service to commerce. He represented the United States at meteorological congresses in Vienna (1873) and Rome (1879), and by his perseverance and tact succeeded in bringing about the establishment of a uniform international system of simultaneous meteorological observations. On June 16, 1880, he was promoted brigadier-general in conformity with legislation giving the chief signal officer that rank. He died at Buffalo, N. Y., two months later, while still in active service.

Myer was married early in his military career to Catherine, daughter of Judge Ebenezer Walden, who with two sons and four daughters survived him. Fort Myer, Virginia, is named for him.

[Personnel files, War Dept., Washington, D. C.; files of Army War College, Washington, D. C.; *The Army of the United States* (1896); *War of the Rebellion: Official Records* (*Army*), 1 and 2 ser.; F. B. Heitman, *Hist. Reg. and Dict. U. S. Army* (1903); Cleveland Abbe [*q.v.*], in *Am. Jour. Sci.*, Aug. 1871; G. M. Kober, "General Albert J. Myer and the United States Weather Bureau," *Mil. Surgeon*, July 1929; *Frank Leslie's Pop. Mo.*, Sept. 1878; *Pop. Sci. Mo.*, Jan. 1880; *Harper's Mag.*, May 1866, Aug. 1871, Dec. 1873; obituaries in *Army and Navy Jour.*, Aug. 28, 1880; *Buffalo Commercial Advertiser*, Aug. 24, 1880; *Buffalo Express*, Aug. 25, 1880; year of birth and spellings of family names from a daughter, Miss Gertrude W. Myer, Washington, D. C.]   J. N. G.

MYERS, ABRAHAM CHARLES (May? 1811–June 20, 1889), first quartermaster-general of the Confederate Army, the son of Abraham Myers, a lawyer, and the descendant of Moses Cohen, the first rabbi of Charleston, was born in Georgetown, S. C. He entered the United States Military Academy from South Carolina on July 1, 1828, but because of deficiency in his studies was turned back to the next class at the end of his first year. He was graduated on July 1, 1833, was appointed brevet second lieutenant, and was stationed at Baton Rouge. He served in the Indian wars in Florida in 1836–38 and again in 1841–42. In November 1839 he became a captain in the quartermaster department. He served under Gen. Zachary Taylor in Texas and northern Mexico and was brevetted major for gallant and meritorious conduct in the battles of Palo Alto and Resaca de la Palma. Transferred to Scott's army, he was brevetted colonel for gallant conduct at Churubusco and was chief quartermaster of the Army of Mexico from April to June 1848. During the next thirteen years, still in the quartermaster service, he was stationed at various posts in the southern states. In the meantime he married Marion Twiggs, the daughter of Gen. David E. Twiggs, the commander of the Department of Texas.

At the beginning of 1861 he was stationed at New Orleans, where on Jan. 28, on demand of the state officials, he surrendered the quartermaster and commissary stores in his possession. On the same date he resigned his position in the United States Army. On Mar. 16, 1861, he was

appointed lieutenant-colonel in the quartermaster-general's department of the Confederate States Army. On Mar. 25 he was announced as acting quartermaster-general. He became quartermaster-general in December and was raised to the rank of colonel on Feb. 15, 1862. During the first months of the war he procured supplies by purchase in the open market; but when this source approached exhaustion in the fall of 1861 he made contracts throughout the country with local manufacturers for cotton and woolen cloth and with tanners for leather, and he established government shops for making clothing, shoes, tents, wagons, and other equipage. He purchased horses and mules at market prices as long as possible; but by the spring of 1862, much against his inclination, he was forced to resort to impressment. He was constantly hampered by the inability of the treasury to furnish him sufficient funds, by the rapid deterioration of the currency, and by poor railway transportation. By the middle of 1863 he had built up an extensive organization of purchasing agents, post quartermasters, shops, and supply depots; but he was never able to provide adequately for the armies, especially in the essentials of clothing and shoes. His bureau therefore became the target of severe criticism. A careful survey of the records and correspondence of Myers's office indicates that he was very efficient as an accountant, but that he was unable to rise above the routine he had learned in the old army or to overcome the laxity, carelessness, and inefficiency of remote subordinates.

On Aug. 7, 1863, by order of Jefferson Davis, he was superseded as quartermaster-general by Brig.-Gen. Alexander R. Lawton. The only reason ever given for the change was that it was in the interest of efficiency (*Journal, post,* III, 627). Myers and his friends resented his removal, and the senate on Jan. 26, 1864, resolved that, since Lawton had not been nominated to that body, Myers and not Lawton was legally quartermaster-general. Davis then submitted Lawton's nomination, and on Feb. 17 it was confirmed. Myers refused to serve under Lawton and presently found himself, on a technicality, "out of the army" (*Official Records, post,* ser. 4, vol. 3, pp. 318–20; letters from Myers to General Bragg, June 13, Aug. 9, 1864, in Bragg Papers, Western Reserve Historical Society, Cleveland, Ohio). He lived during the rest of the war in Georgia, "almost in want, on the charity of friends" (*Ibid.*). He was never reconciled with Davis. Of his life after the war, little is known. He is said to have traveled in Europe from 1866 to 1877. He seems to have made his home at

Lake Roland, Md., and then in Washington, D. C., where he died.

[G. W. Cullum, *Biog. Register of the Officers and Grads. of the U. S. Military Acad. at West Point*, vols. I, III supplement (1868–79) ; *War of the Rebellion: Official Records (Army)*, for dates esp. 4 ser., vols. I–III, 2 ser., vols. III–V, 3 ser., vol. I ; *Jour. of the Cong. of the Confederate States of America*, vols. I–V (1904–05) ; *Jefferson Davis*, ed. by Dunbar Rowland (1923), vol. VII ; *Times-Democrat* (New Orleans), June 21, 1889 ; information supplied by Mabel L. Webber, Librarian of the S. C. Hist. Soc.]   C.W.R.

MYLES, JOHN (*c.* 1621–Feb. 3, 1683), pioneer Baptist minister, whose name also appears as Miles, was probably the John Myles, son of Walter Myles of Newton, Herefordshire, who matriculated at the University of Oxford from Brasenose College on Mar. 18, 1635/36, at the age of fifteen (Joseph Foster, *Alumni Oxonienses*, 1891, III, 1012). But the first certain glimpse of John Myles comes on Oct. 1, 1649, when he and Thomas Proud, after a visit to the Baptist society at the Glasshouse in Broadstreet, London, formed one of the earliest Baptist churches in Wales, at Ilston, near Swansea. Myles became pastor of the church and an active leader among the Welsh Baptists. The act of Parliament of Feb. 22, 1650, "for the better Propagation and Preaching of the Gospel in Wales" names him as one of the twenty-five Welsh ministers who should recommend "godly and painful men" as worthy to preach and teach in Wales (C. S. Firth and R. S. Rait, *Acts and Ordinances of the Interregnum, 1642–1660*, 1911, II, 345). He helped to form an association of Welsh Baptist churches, which in 1651 sent him as delegate to a meeting of Baptist ministers in London. At the Restoration he was ejected from his parish, and, after the passage of the Act of Uniformity (Aug. 24, 1662), decided to leave the country (Edmund Calamy, *A Continuation of the Account of the Ministers . . . Eject . . . after the Restoration*, 1727, II, 747). Taking the records of the church at Ilston, he and several friends emigrated to New England.

At Rehoboth in Plymouth Colony in 1663 he helped to organize one of the earliest Baptist churches in America, and became its pastor. It is evident that he no longer advocated strict communion as he had in Wales, for his church at Rehoboth was unusually liberal in admitting paedobaptists to the Lord's Supper (Bicknell, *post*, p. 226). On July 2, 1667, Myles and another member were fined £5 each by the General Court of Plymouth Colony "for theire breach of order in seting up of a publicke meeting without the knowlidge and approbation of the Court," and were ordered to leave Rehoboth within the month (*Records of the Colony of New Plymouth,*

vol. IV, 1855, p. 162). Accordingly, the Baptists migrated a short distance into Wannamoisett and erected a meeting house there. On Oct. 30 of the same year the Court meeting at Plymouth granted the land at Wannamoisett to "Capt Willett and Mr Myles, and others theire naighbours" (*Ibid.*, IV, 169). On this land they built the town of Swansea. Myles became the minister of the settlement and master of the first school. When the members of his congregation were scattered by King Philip's War, he went to Boston and became acting pastor of the First Baptist Church there. Although he was invited to remain, he later resumed his pastorate at Swansea, and held it until his death. Cotton Mather, in his *Magnalia Christi Americana* (1702), characterized Myles as one "of those Persons, whose Names deserve to live in our *Book* for their *Piety*," and added that he had "a respectful Character in the Churches of this Wilderness" (Bk. III, p. 7). Thomas Hutchinson, in his *History of the Colony of Massachusets-Bay* (1764), testified to Myles's catholic spirit (I, 228). Myles married Ann, daughter of John Humphreys and widow of William Palmes, or Palmer. Their son Samuel Myles (*c.* 1664–1728) graduated from Harvard, was incorporated M.A. at the University of Oxford on July 15, 1693 (Foster, *op. cit.*, III, 1012), and became the second rector of King's Chapel, Boston.

[The old record book of the church at Ilston which Myles brought with him in 1663 is still in the possession of the First Baptist Church, Swansea, Mass. It was used by Isaac Backus in writing *A Hist. of New-England, with Particular Reference to the Denomination of Christians Called Baptists* (2 vols., 1777), and was the source of his information about Myles. See also Joshua Thomas, *A Hist. of the Bapt. Asso. in Wales* (1795) ; A. H. Mason, *Book A. Records of the Town of Swansea* (1900) ; Francis Baylies, *An Hist. Memoir of the Colony of New Plymouth* (1830) ; Leonard Bliss, *The Hist. of Rehoboth* (1836) ; T. W. Bicknell, "John Myles: Religious Toleration in Massachusetts," *Mag. of New England Hist.*, Oct. 1892 ; David Benedict, *A Gen. Hist. of the Bapt. Denomination* (1848) ; H. M. King, *Rev. John Myles and the Founding of the First Bapt. Ch. in Mass.* (1905) ; for Samuel Myles, H. W. Foote, *Annals of King's Chapel* (2 vols., 1882–96).]   D.M.D.

MYRICK, HERBERT (Aug. 20, 1860–July 6, 1927), agricultural editor, publisher, publicist, was born at Arlington, Mass., the son of Henry L. and Lucy Caroline (Whittemore) Myrick. He was educated at Massachusetts Agricultural College and Boston University, being graduated B.S. in 1882. He earned much of his own way, and while setting type in a printing shop, saw a copy of the *New England Homestead*, of Springfield, Mass., which decided him to become an agricultural editor. He found work with this journal during vacation, at two dollars a month and commissions on what subscriptions he could get. After leaving college he bought for $1449.57 a one-twelfth interest in the Phelps Publishing Company, which issued the paper, raising $49.57 in cash and giving his note for the rest. He lived on $4.50 a week until the note was paid.

Myrick's tremendous energy and peppery editorship increased circulation rapidly; the company prospered and began taking over other publications. It issued *Farm and Home* at Springfield and Chicago for more than forty years. The *Orange Judd Farmer* of Chicago was taken over in 1889 together with the *American Agriculturist* of New York, and *Southern Farming* of Atlanta in 1913. Although these periodicals were theoretically edited in various cities, Myrick, who for many years was president of the company, was editor in chief of them all. He likewise headed the company publishing the *Dakota Farmer;* and from 1905 until his death, the American Educational Press, which for some years issued the little paper, *Current Events.* In 1900 his Phelps Company purchased a small magazine called *Good Housekeeping,* which in a short time he developed into one of the most popular of women's publications. In connection with it he founded the Good Housekeeping Institute, where articles offered for advertisement in the magazine were tested before acceptance. This magazine was sold to the Hearst interests in 1911.

Myrick was always a crusader, and usually a fiery one. In 1883 he organized the United States Postal Improvement Association, which helped to enlist public opinion in behalf of rural free delivery and later induced Congress to grant lower mail rates on bulbs, seeds, and plants. In the same year he was instrumental in organizing the New England Tobacco Growers' Association and later, the Nurserymen's Protective Association. He was one of the first advocates of cooperative dairying and cooperative buying and selling by farmers, and was from the first in favor of the farmer's taking a more active part in politics. In 1901 he organized the Farmers' Political League, which did much to influence legislation in New England, New York, and Pennsylvania, and was the germ of the so-called Farm Bloc which in later years wielded much power in Congress. He aided in the passage of the Massachusetts credit union law, which was copied by several other states, also the Massachusetts farmland bank act. He spent much time and money in promoting the Hatch Act of 1887 which established a federal system of agricultural experiment stations. In behalf of the beet-sugar industry he campaigned for more than a quarter of a century. In 1900 he helped organize the League of Domestic Producers (of

sugar, tobacco, cotton, wool, fruit, and nuts) which exerted an influence on tariff legislation. In 1916 he toured the United States, lecturing on the new Federal Farm Loan System, published a book upon the subject (*The Federal Farm Loan System,* 1916), aided in locating twelve banks and their districts, and became a director of the Springfield bank. He advocated an international institute of agriculture until such an organization was established at Rome by the King of Italy.

In addition to his other activities, he developed a device for drawing the fiber of cotton, and to manufacture it organized the Metallic Drawing Roll Company in 1891, of which he was president until 1923. He was long prominent in civic affairs in Springfield, and donated to the city an extensive right of way for a new street, Broadway. He wrote a number of books, including *Cooperative Finance* (1912) and *Rural Credits System for the United States* (1922). In 1926 he published *Ode to the Organ and Other Poems by Mother and Son,* a collection of verses by his mother and himself. He died in Bad Nauheim, Germany, whither he had gone for medical treatment, and was survived by his wife, Elvira Lawrence (Kenson) Myrick, together with a son and two daughters.

[*Who's Who in America,* 1926–27; obituary notices in *Springfield Republican, N. Y. Times,* July 7, 1927, and in the *New England Homestead,* July 16, 1927; J. E. Tower, *Springfield, Present and Prospective* (1905); information from Myrick's associates in the Phelps Publishing Company.]   A. F. H.

NACK, JAMES M. (Jan. 4, 1809–Sept. 23, 1879), "deaf and dumb poet," was born and reared in New York City. Cut off from educational advantages through financial reverses which came to his father, he was taught by a sister in her spare time, and was able to read at four and to write verses before he was nine. As a small boy he imitated preachers he heard at church and made up couplets in the style of hymns. In his eighth year, while carrying a playmate, he fell on a stairway and dragged a heavy fire screen down upon his head. When he recovered consciousness, after some weeks, his hearing was gone. Through his inability to hear his own voice, gradually his power of speech decayed also, though he could make himself understood to those who were closest to him. From August 1818 to December 1823 he was an inmate of the New York Deaf and Dumb Asylum, where he showed ability in grammar and arithmetic. His passion for poetic composition never waned, however, and it became the means by which he rose above the poverty and misery of his lonely life. He wrote a tragedy at twelve and another at fifteen, "on his knees," in a cold garret, without a table, with the stump of a pen; both of which productions, like many other early ones, he destroyed. But a poem of his, "The Blue-Eyed Maid," attracted the notice of Abraham Asten, clerk of the city and county of New York. Asten first secured the boy employment with a lawyer, a man of taste possessing a fine library, but eventually took him into his own office as an assistant, and introduced him to the *literati* of the city.

With the publication of his first volume, *The Legend of the Rocks and Other Poems* (1827), Nack became the literary sensation of the day. The New York *Critic* praised the music of a mind cut off from all sounds; another periodical hailed him as an intellectual wonder and a second Byron; Samuel Knapp pronounced him the most promising young writer he had ever met, and became his friend. In 1833, he published his *Ode on the Proclamation of President Jackson*; in 1839, *Earl Rupert and Other Tales and Poems,* including some prose selections and dedicated to Washington Irving; in 1850, *The Immortal, a Dramatic Romance,* with dedicatory verses to Dickens, reprinted under the title, *Poems,* in 1852; and *The Romance of the Ring and Other Poems,* with a portrait and facsimile signature, in 1859. Many of the early poems reappeared in subsequent volumes. He married Martha W. Simon, whom he had known from childhood, in 1838, and his married life was one of great felicity. Throughout his career he saw his poems quoted and reprinted; but he died regretting he had not done more as a poet.

The best that can be said of Nack is that his achievement in becoming a poet in spite of physical handicaps was a greater one than his poetry itself. Haunted by the material of Scott and the landscape of Byron, and stirred by a passion for adventure that he must satisfy second-hand, he never rose to the level of the poets he imitated. He wrote for a period, and his poems have been buried with the obvious sentimentality of that day.

[S. L. Knapp, *Sketches of Public Characters* (1830); memoir by J. Hancock, in *An Ode on the Proclamation of President Jackson* (1833); memoir by Prosper M. Wetmore, in *Earl Rupert and Other Tales and Poems* (1839); memoir by G. P. Morris, in *The Immortal* (1850); E. A. and G. L. Duyckinck, *Cyc. of Am. Lit.* (1875), vol. II; records of the N. Y. Institution . . . for the Deaf and Dumb; *N. Y. Tribune,* Sept. 25, 1879.]
R. P. T. C.

NADAL, EHRMAN SYME (Feb. 13, 1843–July 26, 1922), author, was born in Greenbrier County, Virginia (now West Virginia), the son of Bernard Harrison and Jane (Mays) Nadal. His father, then minister of the Metho-dist church in Lewisburg, Va., later served parishes in Maryland and Pennsylvania, became professor of English in Indiana Asbury, now De Pauw, University in 1854, and at the time of his death was acting president at Drew Theological Seminary. Because his father's place of employment was so frequently changed, Nadal attended a variety of elementary and secondary schools. In 1860 he entered Columbia College, transferring in 1862 to Yale, from which he was graduated in 1864. The next year he was an instructor in Dickinson Seminary, Williamsport, Pa., and from 1865 to 1867 he taught in schools in Dansville, N. Y., and Leavenworth, Kan. From 1867 to 1870 he was employed by the federal government, first in the Philadelphia mint and afterwards in the dead-letter office, Washington. He was a secretary of legation in London, from Jan. 28, 1870, to May 12, 1871, and was in England for eighteen months. During the next five years he wrote for various periodicals, including the *Nation,* and for some time was employed by the New York *Evening Post.* On June 8, 1877, he was commissioned second secretary to the London legation, and held that office until Nov. 26, 1883. After his return to the United States, he served for some time as secretary to the three civil-service boards of examiners in New York City, contributed to magazines, wrote for the *Evening Post,* and, in 1892–93, was lecturer on English composition at Columbia. From 1900 until his death, at Princeton, N. J., though he continued to engage in literary work, his principal occupation was dealing in horses, chiefly saddle horses. He never married.

Nadal's interest in writing was stimulated by his father, who contributed to various denominational periodicals. His own first literary venture was an editorial on civil-service reform, written while he was a government employee. It was printed by the New York *Evening Post,* and Nadal's connection with that journal was thus established. During his first residence in London, he began to write essays on various aspects of English life that interested him, and these were collected in 1875 under the title *Impressions of London Social Life.* A rather shrewd observer, he made some illuminating comments on British customs, and the essays still have value as reflections of the life of that time. A second collection, containing some critical articles, followed in 1882—*Essays at Home and Elsewhere.* In 1895 appeared *Notes of a Professional Exile,* a slight volume made up of impressionistic comments on English and Americans at a German resort. He contributed an essay on Milton to *The Warner Classics: Poets* (1899). In 1917 he published *A Virginian Village,* which reprinted a number of essays that he had written for periodicals during the preceding two decades. One of Nadal's last essays was a rather valuable account of Henry James ("Personal Recollections of Henry James," *Scribner's Magazine,* July 1920). He belongs to the group of informal essayists that enjoyed some popularity in the later decades of the nineteenth century. He wrote with no great distinction, and literature was with him only an avocation, but he was able to impart to his work enough charm to win at least a small circle of readers. Though he wrote more or less on literary subjects, and though his judgment was independent and at times keen, he was too little disciplined to become a first-rate critic, and his best essays are descriptions of social customs. In tone his work is invariably personal.

["Autobiog. Notes," in *A Virginian Village* (1917); *Decennial Record of the Class of 1864, Yale Coll.* (1875); *Hist. of the Class of 1864, Yale Coll.* (1895); *Yale Univ. Obit. Record,* 1923; *Who's Who in America,* 1922–23; *N. Y. Times,* July 28, 1922.]   G.H.

NAIRNE, THOMAS (d. April 1715), South Carolina assemblyman and Indian agent, was probably born in Scotland, though it is possible that he was born of Scottish descent in one of the plantations. He was first mentioned in the Carolina records in 1698 as a landowner on St. Helena Island. Sometime before this he had married Elizabeth Quintine, by whom he had one son. As a large planter on the extreme southern border of the English settlements he acquired an influence over the Indians that made him the most remarkable frontier figure of the South in the period of Queen Anne's War. He was captain of a company in Gov. James Moore's unsuccessful attack upon St. Augustine in 1702, and a partizan leader in the later destructive raids into Florida. In 1702 he was employed by the Assembly to regulate the traders among his neighbors, the Yamasee. He was also active in efforts to procure missionaries to the Indians through the agency of the Society for the Propagation of the Gospel. As a representative of the Colleton County dissenters he first clashed with the governor, Sir Nathaniel Johnson, over the conformity and church acts; and in the assembly of 1707 he became the aggressive leader of the country party in the successful struggle to wrest administrative powers from the governor. The issues were the appointment of the public receiver and the regulation of Indian affairs under control of the Commons. His Indian act of 1707 laid the basis of the southern regulative system. Under it he served as the first provincial Indian agent with a jurisdiction as "itinerary justice" and diplomatic agent as far westward as the Mis-

sissippi. In this office he launched an ambitious scheme for extending British influence among the western tribes and driving the French from Louisiana. He himself at great risk made peace with the Choctaw, the bulwark of the French colony. His memorial of July 10, 1708, to the secretary of state, elaborating his project, was a remarkable statement of the expansionist aims of the Carolinians. Yet his activities in regulating the traders had brought him again into conflict with the governor, and in June 1708 he had been thrown into prison on an obviously manufactured charge of high treason. He was later denied his seat in the Assembly and discharged as agent. Apparently he was never tried; and by a journey to England in 1710 he won the favor of the Lords Proprietors, on whose nomination to the Admiralty he was appointed judge advocate of South Carolina. In England he was energetic in stimulating the settlement of the Port Royal region, and was probably the author of the promotion tract, *A Letter from South Carolina* (1710).

Restored to his Indian agency in 1712, he was engaged in parleys with the discontented Yamasee at Pocotaligo Town, when, on Apr. 15, 1715, the great southern Indian war broke out, a revolt against the abuses of a trade to whose reform he had directed his efforts. He died at the stake after tortures prolonged, a contemporary reported, for several days.

[This sketch is based upon materials cited in V. W. Crane, *The Southern Frontier, 1670–1732* (1928), which contains a fuller account of Nairne's activities. A manuscript note, apparently contemporary, in the British Museum copy of *A Letter from South Carolina* (1710), says by "Capt. Tho. Nairn a North Britain"; this ascription is supported by internal evidence.]   V.W.C.

NANCRÈDE, CHARLES BEYLARD GUÉRARD de (Dec. 30, 1847–Apr. 12, 1921), surgeon, was born in Philadelphia, Pa., the son of Thomas Dixey and Mary Elizabeth (Bull) Nancrède. His father, a wholesale importer, was the son of Paul Joseph Guérard de Nancrède [q.v.] who came to America with the French army of Count Rochambeau and served at the battle of Yorktown. Nancrède's premedical education was obtained in private schools of Philadelphia and at the University of Pennsylvania, from which institution he obtained his degree of M.D. in 1869. In 1883 he obtained a similar degree from Jefferson Medical College. Following an internship in the Protestant Episcopal Hospital he began practice in Philadelphia, where, during the following twenty years, he developed into one of the foremost surgeons of the city. From the beginning of his medical career he kept in the forefront of professional progress, particularly in the art of surgery. He early joined the following of Lord Lister in the advocacy, first of antiseptic, later of aseptic, surgery. Together with Doctors W. W. Keen and J. E. Mears, he was instrumental in establishing these procedures in Philadelphia surgical practice. He is credited with being the first surgeon in Philadelphia to operate for bullet wounds of the stomach and intestines and to have participated in the first operation for appendicitis in that city. He made a specialty of the diagnosis and surgical treatment of brain abscess and tumors and of cortical epilepsy. He was at various times on the surgical staffs of the Protestant Episcopal, Jefferson, and St. Christopher's hospitals.

Nancrède began his teaching career as an instructor in physiology while still a medical student at the University of Pennsylvania. Later he became successively demonstrator in anatomy and lecturer on regional anatomy. In 1882 he was appointed professor of general and orthopedic surgery at the Philadelphia Polyclinic. After this active and varied experience he was called to the chair of surgery and clinical surgery at the University of Michigan at Ann Arbor in 1889, which position he held for the remainder of his life. This appointment also made him chief of the surgical service of the university hospital and clinic. He had been appointed lecturer on surgery at Dartmouth Medical College in 1887, and in 1900 he was promoted to professor, which post he held until his retirement in 1913. His courses at Dartmouth were held during the summer months. His teaching was marked by enthusiasm, with a genial sympathy and understanding of his students. He was keen and critical in analysis and positive from a broad knowledge of his subject. His two text-books, *Essentials of Anatomy* (1888) and *Lectures upon the Principles of Surgery* (1899), went through several editions. He contributed articles on injuries to the bursae and injuries to the head to Ashhurst's *International Encyclopædia of Surgery;* a section on "Symptoms, Diagnosis, and Treatment of Inflammation, Abscess, Ulcer, and Gangrene" to *System of Surgery* (vol. I, 1895), edited by F. S. Dennis and J. S. Billings; and "The Surgical Treatment of Croup and Diphtheria" to C. H. Burnett's *System of Diseases of the Ear, Nose, and Throat* (1893, vol. II). He discussed "Hæmorrhoids" and "Hæmorrhage" in Wood's *Reference Handbook of the Medical Sciences* and contributed articles for Park's *Treatise on Surgery,* Bryant and Buck's *American Practice of Surgery,* and *An American Text-Book of Surgery,* edited by W. W. Keen and J. W. White. In his early years he took an active

part in the meetings of the Philadelphia Pathological Society, presenting papers and specimens and acting as editor of the society's proceedings.

An inherited martial spirit led Nancrède into the Spanish-American War at its outbreak in 1898. He was commissioned a major in the volunteer army and went to Cuba as chief surgeon of the 3rd Division, II Army Corps, in which capacity he participated in the battle of Santiago. He continued his military connection as a reserve medical officer and member of the Association of Military Surgeons, but his age precluded active service in the World War. Though known primarily as a surgeon, he kept up his knowledge and interest in internal medicine and described himself as a medical man who operated. He had marked artistic ability, was fond of sketching and drawing, and was a member of the Philadelphia Sketching Club. He was also a member of the Philadelphia Choral Society. In addition to the organization already mentioned he was a member of the International Society of Surgery, the Philadelphia Academy of Natural Sciences, and the American Surgical Association of which he was elected president in 1908. He was also a corresponding member of the Royal Academy of Medicine of Rome. He was married on June 3, 1872, to Alice, daughter of Francis P. Dunnington of Baltimore, Md. He died at his home in Ann Arbor.

[*Jour. Mich. State Medic. Soc.,* Jan. 1922; *Trans. Am. Surgic. Asso.,* vol. XXXIX (1921); *Jour. Am. Medic. Asso.,* Apr. 30, 1921; *Who's Who in America,* 1918–19; *Detroit Free Press,* Apr. 14, 1921.]

            J. M. P.

NANCRÈDE, PAUL JOSEPH GUÉRARD de (Mar. 16, 1761–Dec. 15, 1841), soldier, instructor, bookseller, editor, and printer, was born at Héricy, near Fontainebleau, France, the son of Jean Joseph and Louise Françoise (Gautier) Guérard. On Aug. 19, 1779, he enlisted in the French army under the name of Joseph Guérard. As a private in the regiment of the Soissonnais, company of Jean-Baptiste Marin, which embarked at Brest, Apr. 6, 1780, he participated in all the important operations of the army of Rochambeau including Yorktown, returning to France, upon the close of the war, some time in March 1783. Two years later he came back to America, going to Boston, where he married Hannah Dixey, Nov. 11, 1788. From 1787 to 1797–98, he was instructor of the French language and literature at Harvard College. In a letter to the gentlemen of the Corporation of Harvard, signing his name as Joseph de Nancrède, he complains of the difficulties that confront him in his teaching on account of the lack of suitable French texts: "With a view to supply this deficiency, I have been engaged, for upwards of twelve months, in collecting pieces, in several different styles, from our best authors" (Nancrède correspondence, Harvard Library).

This collection, which was published in 1792 under the title of *L'Abeille Françoise,* is undoubtedly the first French school text composed especially for use in American colleges. It is filled with the philosophical sentiments of Rousseau and Helvétius. He had previously attempted to supply suitable class-room material in the publication of a French newspaper which was to serve also as an organ of intelligence to the French inhabitants of Boston. Through the personal influence of Brissot de Warville he was inspired to publish this French paper, the *Courier de Boston,* a political and literary journal, appearing weekly from Apr. 23 to Oct. 15, 1789, which was intended to disseminate the theories of Brissot in America. It was through this journalistic enterprise that he became associated with Samuel Hall, the printer of his newspaper. This relationship opened up a new field of endeavor to him, that of printing, which he successfully pursued in addition to his duties at the University until 1804. For a time, Hall and Nancrède were partners in the printing and book-selling business. In 1796, however, Nancrède went into business for himself, opening up a shop at 49 Marlborough Street, Boston. From the nature of the French and English works that issued from his press one sees further exemplified the ideas which pervaded *L'Abeille Françoise:* "l'humanitarianisme sentimental." And from the number, which is considerable, of the editions of French authors published by him one cannot help realizing how zealously he worked to introduce in America the Rousseauistic *genre* of French literature. In 1804, with eight of his nine children he went to France, where he remained until 1812, when he returned to the United States, this time to transfer his business from Boston to Philadelphia. Practically nothing is known about this period of his life. Some time later he made his last trip to Paris, where he died, Dec. 15, 1841. One of his sons was Joseph Guerard Nancrède, who became a well-known Philadelphia physician.

Two strikingly different estimates of Nancrède have been made by his contemporaries. In the diary of the Rev. W. A. Bentley there is the following entry: "This week Nancrede has a very valuable sale of Books. . . . His domestic affairs & his general manners have not contributed to the public confidence" (*post,* III, p. 73). De Sales La Terrière, on the other hand, says of him: "I came to have a close friendship with him, as he was a most estimable person. He rendered me great services and wherever I or any of my sons may be let us be mindful of them. He was married to a very pretty woman" (translated by David Heald in the *Boston Medical and Surgical Journal,* Apr. 21, 1910).

[Important dates were obtained from copies of original documents in the possession of Mrs. De Nancrède Pond, great-grand-daughter of Nancrède. Printed sources include: Alexandre Belisle, *Histoire de la Presse Franco-Americaine* (1911); G. P. Winship, "Two or Three Boston Papers," *The Papers of the Bibliog. Soc. of America,* vol. XIV, pt. 2 (1920); Albert Schinz, "Un 'Rousseauiste' en Amérique," *Modern Language Notes,* Jan. 1920; Fernand Baldensperger, "Le Premier 'instructeur' de Français à Harvard Coll.: Jos. Nancrède," *Harvard Advocate,* Dec. 5, 1913; *The Diary of Wm. Bentley, D.D.,* vols. II and III (1907–11).]

A. J. B—d.

NANUNTENOO [See CANONCHET, d. 1676].

NAPTON, WILLIAM BARCLAY (Mar. 23, 1808–Jan. 8, 1883), jurist, the son of John and Susan (Hight) Napton, was born near Princeton, N. J. He attended the grammar school at Lawrenceville, and in 1826 was graduated from the College of New Jersey. For three years thereafter he served as tutor in the family of William Fitzhugh Gordon [*q.v.*] near Charlottesville, Va. His spare time he devoted to the study of law under John Tayloe Lomax at the University of Virginia and in 1830 he was graduated from the department of law of the university with high honors. During his five or six years of residence in a "strict-construction" atmosphere he naturally imbibed much that tended to make him a lifelong advocate of state rights. In 1832 he moved to Fayette, Mo., where he took up the practice of law, and at the same time for a few years edited the *Boone's Lick Democrat.* Governor Boggs appointed him attorney-general in 1836, an office which he held for three years. In 1838 he married Malinda Williams, the daughter of Judge Thomas L. Williams, who was for several years chancellor of eastern Tennessee and also a judge of the supreme court of Tennessee. Nine of their ten children lived to maturity.

In 1839 Napton was appointed a judge of the supreme court of Missouri and held the office until his defeat in the election of 1851. He was the chief if not the sole author of the famous Jackson Resolutions (instructions to Senator Thomas H. Benton to uphold the extreme pro-slavery program in Congress) passed by the state legislature in 1847. He first admitted and then, to save the face of their legislative sponsor, Claiborne F. Jackson, denied that he formulated the resolutions. When the trouble over slavery arose in Kansas, Napton, whose home was in Saline County—a strong pro-slavery section of western Missouri—aligned himself against the abolitionists. While this struggle was growing more acute a pro-slavery convention of considerable proportions was held (July 1855) at Lexington, then the largest town in western Missouri. Napton was the chairman of the resolutions committee, prime mover and general mouthpiece of this convention. It took, practically unanimously, a belligerent stand against the abolition movement and condemned the "diabolical" activities of the Emigrant Aid Society in Kansas.

Napton was elected to the state supreme bench in 1857 but was automatically retired from the position when he refused to take the specially devised oath of office in 1861. Apparently he took no active part in the Civil War. For a decade after 1863 he was a successful lawyer in St. Louis, and then (1873) was again chosen to the supreme court. He was generally considered the leading member of the bench until his voluntary retirement on Dec. 31, 1880. He takes unusually high rank among Missouri jurists. His judicial decisions bear the earmarks of painstaking research and were always clothed in beautiful and clear diction. In the jurisprudence of commercial law, land titles, and equity, the principles and conclusions which he set forth are counted as valuable and lasting contributions. Except perhaps where his favored doctrine of state rights was involved he was forward-looking in the adjustment of legal principles to new social and economic conditions. In this respect he helped to create precedents and through them to shape the course of legal development.

[*The Bench and Bar of Mo.* (1899); W. B. Napton, *Past and Present of Saline County, Mo.* (ed. 1910); *76 Mo. Reports,* i–xiii; *The Bench and Bar of St. Louis . . . and other Mo. Cities* (1884); L. C. Krauthoff, *The Supreme Court of Mo.* (1891); *Address to the People of the U. S., Together with the Proc. and Resolutions of the Pro-Slavery Convention of Mo., Held at Lexington, July 1855* (1855); J. F. Philips, *Reminiscences of Some Deceased Lawyers of Central Mo.* (1914); Wm. Hyde and H. L. Conard, *Encyc. of the Hist. of St. Louis* (1899), vol. III; W. B. Davis and D. S. Durrie, *An Illustrated Hist. of Mo.* (1876); A. J. D. Stewart, *The Hist. of the Bench and Bar of Mo.* (1898); *Jefferson Inquirer,* Aug. 18, 1849, June 4, 1853; *Mo. Republican,* Jan. 10, 1883.]   H. E. N.

NARVÁEZ, PÁNFILO de (c. 1478–1528), Spanish conquistador, was born in Valladolid, about 1478. Entering upon the profession of arms at an early age, he had already acquired considerable reputation as a soldier when he went to the Indies during the early years of the sixteenth century. He served at first in Jamaica, but when Diego Velázquez was sent to Cuba (then called Fernandina), Narváez, by special request, as he and Velázquez were old friends, was transferred thither, together with his thirty

specially trained archers. As chief captain of Velázquez, he took an active and ruthless part in pacifying and settling Cuba. In recompense, he was granted several Indian towns and amassed considerable wealth. In Cuba he married a widow, María de Valenzuela, who possessed other Indian towns. He acted in a civil capacity as accountant and special agent (*procurador*), and in the latter capacity, together with Antonio Velázquez, presented many petitions for the betterment of Cuba (1515–18), one being for better roads. In 1520, Velázquez commissioned Narváez to seize or kill Cortés who was charged with disobedience and disloyalty in the conquest he had undertaken. Accordingly, on Mar. 11, with title as captain-general of the Mexican conquest, thus superseding Cortés, he left Cuba with eighteen or nineteen vessels and a force numbering at least nine hundred Spaniards and some Indians—all well equipped. On May 23, however, he was defeated by Cortés, losing an eye in the encounter, besides being captured with all his men, most of whom were added to those of his rival. He was held prisoner until 1521, when he was freed by direct order of the council of the Indies.

In 1526, he obtained concessions granting titles of grand constable, governor, captain general, and *adelantado* to himself and his heirs and successors forever, with the right to make an expedition of conquest and settlement to Florida, the usual obligations, privileges, and exemptions being annexed. He left San Lúcar, Spain, on June 17, 1527, with five vessels and six hundred soldiers, colonists, and friars, with Alvar Núñez Cabeza de Vaca as treasurer. One hundred and forty men deserted during the forty-five days he spent at Santo Domingo. Two vessels, sixty men, and twenty horses were lost in a hurricane along the Cuban coast. After wintering in Cuba, the expedition (now four hundred men and eighty horses) set sail on Feb. 20, 1528, for Havana, but could not make that port, being held for a fortnight on a reef and then driven northward to Florida, reaching land on Apr. 14, near Clement's Point on the small peninsula west of Tampa Bay and about five leagues from the mouth of the bay which they had missed. On Apr. 16, possession of Florida was taken for the King, Narváez causing to be read aloud the long, absurd proclamation usual in such cases. A few explorations and forays among the sullen and hostile Indians netted little, except the crossing of the small peninsula and the discovery of the inner waters of Tampa Bay.

Understanding that great riches abounded in the town of Apalache, Narváez, after dispatching his ships along the coast toward Mexico (against the advice of Cabeza de Vaca), on May 1, 1528, led a shore party of three hundred men northward. They never saw their ships again. Crossing the Withlacoochie and Suwanee rivers, they turned west and after great suffering reached Apalache (in the neighborhood of the present Tallahassee), only to find it a wretched village of forty huts, whose Indians were hostile. Twenty-five days later they turned south and in a nine days' march through swamps, lakes, and dense forests, ever pursued by the Indians, they reached the town of Auté, at about the present St. Marks. This marked the end of the expedition. Narváez and others fell sick. Their only hope now was to reach Mexico. With but one carpenter and without tools or materials, they contrived to build five crazy boats on one of the many bays of South Florida. The horses were killed and eaten and from their hides were fashioned bellows, water bottles, and other necessities. From their weapons, stirrups, and other appliances, they made tools and nails. On Sept. 22, the two hundred and forty men left were divided among the boats and they set out along the coast, no person among them having a knowledge of navigation. The water bottles rotted and the men were assailed by thirst, hunger, storms, and sickness and death. For over a month they wandered about the gulf, finding but little comfort among the few Indians they saw. Three of the boats were wrecked or foundered at sea. Finally at a place probably near Matagorda Bay, toward the end of October or during the first few days in November 1528, Narváez was swept out to sea by a sudden storm that came up during the night. He had remained alone on his boat with the coxswain and a boy, all the others having gone ashore. He was never heard of again.

[*Colección de Documentos Inéditos . . . de las antiguas Posesiones Españolas*, 1 ser. (42 vols., 1864–84), esp. vols. X, XI, XII, XIV, XVI, XXII, XXIV, XXV, XXXV, 2 ser. (21 vols., 1885–1928), esp. vols. I and IV; Bartolomé de las Casas, *Historia de las Indias*, vol. IV (1876); Gonzalo Fernández de Oviedo y Valdéz, *Historia General y Natural de las Indias* (4 vols., 1851–55), vol. III; Alvar Núñez Cabeza de Vaca, *La Relacion* (1542, 1555), pub. in English translation by Buckingham Smith under the title, *The Narrative of Alvar Núñez Cabeça de Vaca* (1871); translation of Narváez's proclamation in B. F. French, *Hist. Colls. of La. and Fla.*, 2 ser. (1875), pp. 153–58; Morris Bishop, *The Odyssey of Cabeza de Vaca* (1933); A. P. Maudslay, *The True Hist. of the Conquest of New Spain* (5 vols., 1908–16), translated from the Spanish of Bernal Díaz del Castillo; Francisco López de Gómara, *La Historia General de las Indias* (1553); Antonio de Herrera y Tordesillas, *Historia General* (4 vols., 1601–15), pub. in English translation by John Stevens under the title, *The Gen. Hist. of the Vast Continent and Islands of America* (6 vols., 1725–26); Juan de Torquemada, *Segunda Parte de . . . Monarchia Indiana* (1723).]
                                                           J. A. R.

NASBY, PETROLEUM V. [See Locke, David Ross, 1833–1888].

NASH, ABNER (*c.* 1740–Dec. 2, 1786), governor of North Carolina and delegate to the Continental Congress, was born at "Templeton Manor," his father's plantation in Amelia County, later Prince Edward County, Va. He was the third son of Ann (Owen) Nash, the daughter of Hugh Owen of Tenby, Pembrokeshire, Wales, and John Nash who had emigrated from Wales to Virginia about 1730, and was the brother of Francis Nash and the father of Frederick Nash [*qq.v.*]. In 1761 and 1762 he represented Prince Edward County in the Virginia House of Burgesses. Removing to North Carolina in 1762, he settled at Halifax, where he rose quickly to prominence in local politics and in the practice of law, as he did also at New Bern to which he removed in the early 1770's. Twice he was married advantageously: first, to Justina (Davis) Dobbs, the widow of Gov. Arthur Dobbs [*q.v.*], through whom he was involved in the famous Dobbs land suit, and, second, in 1774 to Mary Whiting Jones. His representation of Halifax town in 1764 and 1765 and Halifax County from 1770 to 1771 in the House of Commons, his connection with the Dobbs land suit, and his rôle in the Regulator and Revolutionary movements brought him considerable reputation. In the Regulator disturbance he supported the conservative eastern interests and the established government under Gov. William Tryon, who appointed him a major of brigade in 1768. From the beginning of the contest with the mother country he was a zealous and active patriot. He was a leader in the local events that induced Gov. Josiah Martin to flee from New Bern in May 1775, was the choice of the borough of New Bern as delegate to each of the five Revolutionary provincial congresses from 1774 to 1776, was a member of several prominent committees in the congresses, notably those that drafted the Halifax resolution of Apr. 12, 1776, and the constitution of 1776, was a member of the Provincial Council in 1775 and 1776, and was an agent of the Council in 1776 to confer with the South Carolina authorities at Charleston in regard to defense. His conspicuous revolutionary activity led Governor Martin, who admitted he was "an eminent lawyer," to brand him as "a most unprincipled character," one of four persons in the province "foremost among the patrons of revolt and anarchy" whose "unremitted labours to promote sedition and rebellion" had marked them as proper objects of proscription (*Colonial Records, post*, IX, 1155, X, 98).

Under the new government he was speaker of the first House of Commons and was the second governor. He represented New Bern for 1777 and Craven County for 1778 in the House of Commons, and Jones County in the Senate for 1779, when he was also chosen speaker. His greatest responsibility, however, was as governor during the military crisis of 1780 and 1781. Elected in the spring of 1780, he displayed energy in preparing for British invasion from the south; but, embarrassed by the constitutional weakness of his office, he requested the General Assembly to create a board of war to share responsibility while the Assembly was not in session. The board of war, as created by the radical Assembly in the fall of 1780, was given and exercised the constitutional powers of the governor and was independent in its attitude toward him. Already piqued in the spring by the Assembly's unconstitutional action of selecting Richard Caswell to command the militia, he resented the usurpation of the board of war, refused to fill a vacancy, and wrote that the executive power was so divided that "men not knowing who to obey, obey nobody" (*State Records, post,* XVII, 882). He expressed to the Assembly in January 1781 his determination to resign the "useless and contemptible" office unless it was restored to a condition of respectability (*State Records, post,* XV, 228–29). The board of war was merely replaced by the council extraordinary which likewise was given unconstitutional powers. On June 24, 1781, learning that he had been nominated for reëlection, he requested the withdrawal of his name on account of "excessive Fatigues of late and want of Health" (*State Records, post,* XVII, 802).

However, he soon reëntered public life as representative from Jones County in 1782, 1784, and 1785, and was an unsuccessful candidate for governor in 1784. In the House he was a leader in opposition to the restoration to the Loyalists of such of their confiscated property as had not been sold and to the repeal of all laws inconsistent with the treaty of 1783. He declined election to the Continental Congress in 1778, but accepted election in 1782, 1783, and 1785. In Congress he soon recognized the necessity of a stronger federal government. He was appointed delegate to the Annapolis Convention in 1786 but did not attend. In his personal life he was genial, suave, luxurious in habit and taste, improvident, convivial, and gracious in hospitality. He died while in New York to attend Congress and was buried with elaborate ceremony in St. Paul's Churchyard. Later his remains were removed to "Pembroke," his home near New Bern.

[Governors' papers and letter books in the Lib. of the N. C. Hist. Commission, Raleigh; *The Colonial Records of N. C.,* vols. II, VI–X (1888–90); *The State Records of N. C.,* vols. XI–XXIV (1895–1905); *Jours. of the House of Burgesses of Va., 1761–65,* ed. by J. P. Kennedy (1907); *Jours. of the Continental Cong.,* vols. XXII–XXV (1914–22); G. J. McRee, *Life and Correspondence of James Iredell,* vol. I, pp. 396–97, vol. II, pp. 35–36 (1857–58); *Presentation of Portrait of Governor Abner Nash, Address of J. G. deR. Hamilton* (1909); *Biog. Hist. of N. C.,* ed. by S. A. Ashe, vol. I (1905); A. R. House, *The Reads and their Relatives* (1930).]   A. R. N.

NASH, ARTHUR (June 26, 1870–Oct. 30, 1927), originator of the "Golden Rule Nash" plan of copartnership with workers, was born in a log cabin in Tipton County, Ind., the eldest of nine children of Evermont Nash and Rachel Mitchel. Both his parents were zealous Seventh Day Adventists, and after attending high school at Greentown, Ind., he went to the Adventist Theological Seminary at Battle Creek, Mich. Ordained in 1894 he became instructor in a school for Adventist missionaries at Detroit, but within a few months he was dismissed because he refused to affirm that a humanitarian woman who had not been an Adventist, had gone to hell. There ensued a period of painful religious readjustment during which he fed his mind on atheistic literature while wandering about the Middle West as a box-car hobo, carrying a hod, plastering, making brooms, and working on bridge construction. In 1898 he returned to Detroit and organized a laundry and other measures for the relief of the unemployed. He met there a Y.W.C.A. worker, Maud Lena Southwell, whom he married at Cleveland, Ohio, on Apr. 9, 1899, and who turned him back to religion. In 1900 he entered the ministry of the Disciples of Christ and took a pastorate at Bluffton, Ohio, only to be asked to resign some two years later because in a memorial sermon he had eulogized the virtues of a kind-hearted but professedly unreligious man. He then began selling clothing for a Chicago house and was so successful that in 1909 he established himself as a manufacturer of men's clothing in Columbus, Ohio. In 1913 he moved to Cincinnati and there organized in June 1916 the A. Nash Company which produced clothing by cutting the garments in its own establishment and "farming out" their making to a contractor. Early in 1917 he accepted an invitation to preach a sermon on the theme, "What is the matter with Christianity?" After two months of reading and hard thinking he became convinced that the way to establish on earth the Kingdom of Heaven was to apply literally the Golden Rule.

Late in 1918, on taking over the business of the contractor who had been making his clothing, he discovered that the wage scale paid by a sweatshop did not square with the Golden Rule and, though his balance sheet for 1918 showed a loss, at once raised wages throughout the shop. At the same time he prepared to liquidate his business. But two months later he found that his employees were voluntarily working far more rapidly and efficiently than before and that his business was growing by leaps and bounds. From that time until his death Nash spent a large part of his time preaching with fiery oratory and sincere fervor the Golden Rule to business men's and social-welfare organizations throughout the country. By 1925 the Nash Company had grown to the largest establishment producing direct maker-to-consumer clothing in the United States. Meanwhile Nash lowered prices, stabilized employment, inaugurated a five-day week with eight hours a day, increased wages repeatedly, and paid his workers cash dividends based on time worked. In 1920 he began issuing stock dividends to employees and in May 1924 distributed among them his own share of a stock dividend, giving them, at the expiration of the five years, control over the business. In December 1925 he called together his employees, the majority of whom were anti-union, and, after a dramatic struggle which attracted nation-wide attention, persuaded them to consent to the unionization of the entire plant by the Amalgamated Clothing Workers of America. This struggle he called the supreme hour of his life. A shrewd business man, with a *flair* for leadership and a full understanding of the value of the publicity secured by his speeches, Nash was by nature and training a sincere and aggressive evangelist. To him the "Golden Rule in Business" was a religion and not merely a successful advertising slogan. Shortly after having placed a representative of the union on his board of management Nash died of heart disease in Cincinnati. In addition to several magazine articles he told the story of his life and his experiment in *The Golden Rule in Business* (1923, rev. ed., 1930). Nash also founded and endowed a movement called the "Brotherhood of Man," an organization intended to aid young Turks in Turkey and promote amity between them and their Christian neighbors.

[In addition to *The Golden Rule in Business*, see Nash's articles: "A Bible Text that Worked a Business Miracle," *Am. Mag.*, Oct. 1921, and "Bigger Dividends —No More Labor Troubles," *Collier's*, Aug. 22, 1925; and *Who's Who in America*, 1926–27. For several years there was much newspaper and magazine discussion of his ideas, including articles in the *N. Y. Times*, June 1, 1924; *Collier's Weekly*, July 28, 1923; *Lit. Digest*, July 12, 1924; *Nation*, Jan. 6, 1926; *New Republic*, Mar. 10, 1926; *Century Mag.*, Oct. 1926, and *Survey*, Jan. 1, 1926, May 1, 1927. Obituaries were published in the *N. Y. Times* and the *Cincinnati En-*

quirer; Oct. 31, 1927, *Survey*, Dec. 15, 1927, and other periodicals. Additional information was secured from Nash's daughter Mrs. Erwin Strachley, Jr., of Cincinnati.]
H. S. W.

NASH, CHARLES SUMNER (Feb. 18, 1856–Nov. 22, 1926), Congregational clergyman, educator, was born in Granby, Hampshire County, Mass., the son of Lorenzo Smith and Nancie Swinington (Knight) Nash. He graduated from Amherst College in the class of 1877, and was at once appointed instructor in Robert College, Constantinople, Turkey, where he taught for three years. Returning to America in 1880, he entered Hartford Theological Seminary, Hartford, Conn., and after receiving the degree of B.D. in 1883, pursued graduate study for another year. He was ordained to the Congregational ministry on Oct. 22, 1884, and served the First Congregational Church of East Hartford as pastor from 1884 until 1890. On May 15, 1889, he married Marie Louise Henry of Hartford. Their only children were a boy who did not survive infancy, and a girl who died at the age of ten.

In 1890 he was appointed instructor in Biblical theology and elocution in Hartford Seminary. The following year he resigned to become professor of homiletics and pastoral theology in Pacific Theological Seminary, then located in Oakland, Cal., but in 1901 removed to Berkeley. To this school, still in its pioneer stage when he came to it, he thenceforth devoted all his energies, serving as professor from 1891, as dean from 1906 to 1911, and as president from 1911 until his resignation in 1920. Thereafter as president emeritus and professor of church polity he continued in active association with the school until his death.

Nash was a man of earnest religious convictions and constantly enlarging vision, as is well illustrated in his little book entitled *Our Widening Thought of God* (1914). His outreaching personality and influence filled a large place in the religious life of the Pacific Coast. As teacher and administrator his career was noteworthy. Under his leadership Pacific Theological Seminary—up to that time a Congregational school— became in 1912 an undenominational institution, and at its fiftieth anniversary in 1916 changed its name to Pacific School of Religion. During his administration new departments were added and the funds of the school greatly enlarged.

He was a member of the Commission of Nineteen which formulated the plan adopted in 1913 for the reorganization of the National Congregational Council and a member of the Commission on Polity of the Council of 1921. In 1908–09 he delivered the Carew Lectures at Hartford

Nash   Nash

Seminary, published under the title *Congregational Administration* (1909). He was an earnest advocate of church unity and was one of the framers of an overture adopted by the National Congregational Council inviting the union of the Universalist with the Congregational churches. Although thoroughly attached to his profession and convinced of its large responsibilities and opportunities, he was not narrowly professional. He was one of the founders of the Outlook Club of Oakland, a well-known social and discussion group, and kept in close touch with world affairs. Fond of outdoor life he found the Berkeley Hills an unfailing source of health and recreation. He was a member of the Sierra Club, and an ardent lover of the High Sierra.

[*Pacific School of Religion Bull.*, Dec. 1926; C. S. Nash and J. W. Buckham, *Religious Progress on the Pacific Slope* (copr. 1917); *Congregationalist*, Dec. 9, 1926; *Who's Who in America*, 1924–25; *San Francisco Chronicle*, Nov. 23, 1926.]   J.W.B.

NASH, DANIEL (May 28, 1763–June 4, 1836), Protestant Episcopal clergyman, frontier missionary in New York State, was born not far from the western border of Massachusetts in what is now Great Barrington, a descendant of Thomas Nash, who signed the Fundamental Agreement of New Haven in 1639. Daniel's father, Jonathan, son of Daniel and Experience (Clark) Nash, had married Anna Maria Spoor of Taghkanick, Columbia County, N. Y., and Daniel was the youngest of their nine children. He prepared for college and entered Yale, graduating in the class of 1785. President Ezra Stiles records in his diary under date of July 6, 1783, that after the forenoon sermon Daniel Nash, sophomore, among others, was admitted to the College Church (F. B. Dexter, *The Literary Diary of Ezra Stiles*, 1901, III, 78). For some years after his graduation he engaged in teaching, first at Pittsgrove, N. J., and later at Swedesboro. During this period changes in his ecclesiastical views led him to leave the Congregational for the Episcopal Church, and at Swedesboro he studied theology under Rev. John Croes, principal of the academy where Nash was teaching, and rector of the local church. In 1794 he became head of an academy in New Lebanon Springs, N. Y., and served as a lay reader for the Episcopalians of that town. In January 1796 he married Olive Lusk of Richmond, Mass.

Under the influence of Rev. Daniel Burhans who had been instrumental in establishing the church at New Lebanon Springs, Nash became imbued with intense missionary zeal. He was ordained deacon by Bishop Samuel Provoost on Feb. 8, 1797, and at once began work on the west-

ern frontier, making his first home at Exeter, Otsego County. For nearly forty years thereafter, indifferent to discomfort and hardship, abounding in labors and fervent in spirit, he devoted himself to extending the teachings and worship of what he had come ardently to believe was the Apostolically established church. Because he felt that Bishop Provoost did not display a proper missionary ardor, he did not wish to be ordained priest by him, and waited until Oct. 11, 1801, when the recently consecrated Bishop Benjamin Moore ordained him. His field was a difficult one, not only because it was frontier territory, but also because the settlers had Presbyterian traditions behind them; but Nash had great success. He lived in log-cabins, was content with few possessions, traveled on horseback, often with his wife holding a child behind him. Her help in the music and responses, he testified, was invaluable. He was not a great preacher, nor especially keen mentally, but he was diligent in season and out of season, entering the homes of the people, baptizing and catechizing the children, and conducting private and public worship. He came to be affectionately known everywhere as "Father Nash." In the annual Conventions he was styled "Rector of the Episcopal Churches in Otsego County." Others built on his foundations, but he established practically all the Episcopal churches of that county and extended his labors to some eight other counties, going as far north as Ogdensburg. Whatever his peculiarities and limitations, he was admirably fitted physically for his work, being "of rugged health, six feet in height, full in figure, over two hundred pounds in weight" (Ralph Birdsall, *The Story of Cooperstown*, 1917, p. 155). On Jan. 1, 1811, due to his activities, Christ Church, Cooperstown, was formally organized, and he was chosen rector. This position he informally held until his death, still continuing his missionary labors. He is supposed to have been the original of Rev. Mr. Grant in J. Fenimore Cooper's *The Pioneers*. He died in the home of a daughter in Burlington, N. Y., and was buried in the churchyard of Christ Church, Cooperstown, under a pine tree, a spot which he had chosen.

[F. B. Dexter, *Biog. Sketches Grads. Yale Coll.*, vol. IV (1907); W. B. Sprague, *Annals Am. Pulpit*, vol. V (1859); F. W. Halsey, *The Old N. Y. Frontier* (1901); G. P. Reese, *Hist. Records of Christ Ch., Cooperstown, N. Y.* (n.d.); J. N. Norton, *Pioneer Missionaries; or the Lives of Phelps and Nash* (1859); Philander Chase, *Reminiscences* (1844); Sylvester Nash, *The Nash Family* (1853).]   H.E.S.

NASH, FRANCIS (c. 1742–Oct. 7, 1777), Revolutionary soldier, the fourth son of John

and Ann (Owen) Nash and the brother of Abner Nash [q.v.], was born at "Templeton Manor" in Amelia, later Prince Edward County, Va. In early manhood he settled at Childsburg, later Hillsboro, in the frontier North Carolina county of Orange. Of superior training, handsome in person, affable, and industrious, he rose quickly to local prominence as merchant and attorney and, in 1763, to position as justice of the peace and clerk of the court of pleas and quarter sessions. He was representative to the House of Commons for Orange County in 1764, 1765, and 1771, and for the borough of Hillsboro from 1773 to 1775. He married Sarah, the daughter of Maurice Moore and the niece of James Moore [qq.v.]. Two of their children survived him. Holding the most lucrative county office, he was obnoxious to the Regulators and was charged by them with taking excessive fees. Station, temperament, and position fixed his sympathies with the established government, and he served as captain in Governor Tryon's army that crushed the Regulators in the battle of Alamance on May 16, 1771. In 1774 and 1775 he was judge of the court of oyer and terminer in Hillsboro district.

In the contest with Great Britain he supported the patriot cause, representing Orange County in the second revolutionary Provincial Congress of April 1775 and the town of Halifax in the third Congress of August 1775. However, it was in the field of military affairs that he excelled. Brave and high-spirited, he had risen to the rank of colonel of militia; and at Alamance he acquired experience and a reputation for courage and ability. On Sept. 1, 1775, the Provincial Congress elected him lieutenant-colonel of the 1st North Carolina Regiment of Continental troops and promoted him to colonel seven months later, on Apr. 10. He was with the expedition commanded by James Moore to aid Charleston in the winter of 1776–77. The Continental Congress elected him brigadier-general on Feb. 5, 1777, and ordered him to recruit soldiers in western North Carolina and to proceed northward in March with Moore and his Continental regiments. At Moore's death he succeeded to command and after some delay led the North Carolina brigade northward to join Washington's army. Placed in the reserves commanded by Lord Stirling at Germantown on Oct. 4, the brigade became involved in the confusion and disorder of that fog-obscured battlefield; and he, while leading his men bravely but ineffectually, was mortally wounded. Three days later he died and was buried at Kulpsville, Pa. He was regarded by Washington as a brave man and a valuable officer and by Gov. Richard Caswell as

the ablest North Carolina officer in the field at the time of his death. Nash County, N. C., and Nashville, Tenn., were named in his honor, and, at the Guilford Battleground, a monument was erected to his memory by congressional appropriation.

[The Colonial Records of N. C., vols. VI–X (1888–90); The State Records of N. C., vols. XI–XV, XVII, XXII, XXIV (1895–1905); Journals of the Continental Cong., vols. IV, VII–IX (1906–07); Biog. Hist. of N. C., ed. by S. A. Ashe, vol. III (1905); A. M. Waddell, "Gen. Francis Nash," The N. C. Booklet, Oct. 1914; A. R. Rouse, The Reads and their Relatives (1930).]
A. R. N.

NASH, FREDERICK (Feb. 19, 1781–Dec. 4, 1858), jurist, was born in Tryon's Palace at New Bern, N. C., during the governorship of his father, Abner Nash [q.v.], whose death in 1786 left the cares of the family to the mother, Mary (Jones) Nash. Prominent family connections, a devout mother, religious training, the experience of exhortation from President Washington in 1791, and responsibility as the eldest of the children operated to make him from youth manly, serious, sensitive to duty, and lacking in humor. He was educated by the Rev. Henry Patillo at Williamsboro, at the academy of the Rev. Thomas P. Irving in New Bern, and at the College of New Jersey (Princeton), from which he was graduated with high rank in 1799. After studying law in the office of Edward Harris, he commenced practice in New Bern in 1801. On Sept. 1, 1803, he was married to Mary G. Kollock of Elizabethtown, N. J. His public career began as a representative from New Bern in the House of Commons, in 1804 and 1805; but his later career was associated chiefly with Hillsboro, to which he moved in 1807. In an extensive law practice and in the House of Commons, as representative of Orange County in 1814, 1815, 1816, 1817, and of Hillsboro in 1828 and 1829, he achieved reputation as an able advocate, a man of sturdy character and sound judgment, and an orator of pleasing voice, fine diction, lucid reasoning, and persuasive power. Intensely religious and devoted to the Presbyterian Church, he was, to a degree marked even in his generation, motivated by a sense of personal accountability to an ever-present God. He was particularly interested in judicial reforms, banking, and humanitarian legislation. He introduced bills in 1815 to prevent dueling and in 1817 to erect a state penitentiary, and he vigorously opposed the popular anti-bank movement in the session of 1828–29. He was speaker in 1814.

However, he attained chief distinction as a jurist. A notable career as superior court judge from 1818 to 1826 and again from 1836 to 1844 brought about his appointment in 1844, upon the death of William Gaston, to the supreme court, of which he remained a judge until his death, and in 1852 he was chosen by his associates as chief justice, succeeding Thomas Ruffin. Though not so brilliant as Gaston, or so powerful in logic as Ruffin, he was a worthy successor and a sound and able judge, whose learning, industry, evenness of temper, character, courtesy, and respect for truth and justice brought distinction to him and greater popular respect to the court. His opinions are characterized by clearness of legal conception, terseness of style, and cogency of reasoning (54–56 *N. C. Reports*).

In his political career he was a nominal Republican, though he voted against legislative resolutions praising the national administration in 1804 and 1815. He indorsed Jackson's nullification proclamation in 1832, but his opposition to the anti-bank policy of the administration and to what he considered a pronounced trend from republicanism toward pure democracy, led him into the Whig party. However, during his judicial career, he scrupulously refrained from public interest or activity in politics.

[Francis Nash Collection in possession of the N. C. Hist. Commission; Willie P. Mangum Papers in Lib. of Cong.; *The Papers of Thomas Ruffin*, ed. by J. G. deR. Hamilton, vols. I–III (1918–20); *The Papers of Archibald D. Murphey*, ed. by W. H. Hoyt (2 vols. 1914); *Biog. Hist. of N. C.*, ed. by S. A. Ashe, vol. I (1905); K. P. Battle, "An Address on the Hist. of the Supreme Court," 103 *N. C. Reports*, pp. 500–01; John H. Bryan "Memoir," *N. C. Univ. Mag.*, Dec. 1859.]

A. R. N.

NASH, HENRY SYLVESTER (Dec. 23, 1854–Nov. 6, 1912), Episcopal clergyman, teacher, and author, was born in Newark, Ohio, the son of Francis and Elizabeth (Burdett) Nash. He graduated at Harvard in the class of 1878, and at the Episcopal Theological School, Cambridge, Mass., in the class of 1881. He was ordained to the priesthood by Bishop Benjamin H. Paddock of Massachusetts, June 1, 1882, and at once became instructor in Biblical study and church polity in the Episcopal Theological School, being appointed later professor of literature and interpretation of the New Testament. Believing that a student should have practical experience in parochial work, he served for a time as assistant at Christ Church, Waltham, and on June 26, 1883, married Bessie Kiefler Curtis of that town. From 1889 to 1902, he was in charge of the Church of the Redeemer, Chestnut Hill, Newton, Mass. He was a preacher of rare power and originality and all his life was in frequent demand as a special preacher and lecturer, particularly in Massachusetts, Rhode Island, and New York.

On a generation of students for the ministry, he left the impression of a brave, versatile, original, and spiritual scholar, lifting them above the details of the lesson, opening up to them a wide vision, and forming within them a will to serve. In addition to his teaching and preaching, he found time for much writing. The first of his published works was *Genesis of the Social Conscience* (1897), originally prepared and delivered as the Lowell Lectures, Boston. This was followed by *Ethics and Revelation* (1899), *The History of the Higher Criticism of the New Testament* (1900), *The Belief in Democracy and Justification by Faith* (1903–04), and *The Atoning Life* (1908). His articles include "The Exegesis of the School of Antioch" (*Journal of Biblical Literature*, vol. XI, 1892), "The Nature and Definition of Religion" (*Harvard Theological Review*, January 1913). His *Genesis of the Social Conscience* was a book of much significance in its generalization and originality of statement, and discloses an intense interest in humanity. The supreme need, as he saw it, was "to get the world personalized." He was "a glad participant in the struggle for a truer democracy. . . . His own superb faith was a bridge for many who could not find their way alone" (New York *Evening Post*, Nov. 23, 1912). He was a brilliant conversationalist, and was fond of making extreme statements to emphasize his point. His spiritual nature expressed itself in beautiful devotional utterances which are preserved in *Prayers and Meditations* (1915).

[E. S. Drown, *Henry Sylvester Nash* (1913); *Official Bull. of the Episc. Theol. School*, Nov. 1912; *Who's Who in America*, 1912–13; *Harvard Coll., Class of 1878, Fiftieth Anniversary Report* (1928); *Harvard Grads. Mag.*, Mar. 1913; *Am. Ch. Almanac*, 1913; *Boston Transcript*, Nov. 6, 1912.]

D. D. A.

NASH, SIMEON (Sept. 21, 1804–Jan. 17, 1879), judge and author, the son of Simeon and Amy (White) Nash, was born at South Hadley, Mass. Both his mother and father were of English origin and of early colonial ancestry, his paternal ancestor, Thomas Nash, having been one of the signers of the Fundamental Agreement of New Haven in 1639. Prepared for college in the schools of South Hadley and in Hopkins Academy at Hadley, in spite of paternal opposition he entered Amherst College in 1825, where he was graduated in 1829. He began the study of law with Edward Hooker of South Hadley, while teaching Greek and mathematics in Woodbridge High School for boys there. On Dec. 16, 1831, he married Cynthia Smith of Granby, Mass. They had seven children. He left South Hadley to go to Gallipolis, Ohio, where he continued the study of law in the office of Samuel F. Vinton who represented his district for some time in Congress. In 1833 he was admitted to the bar of Ohio and settled in Gallipolis, which continued to be his home for the remainder of his life. He soon acquired an extensive legal practice. Elected to the Senate of Ohio, he sat in that body from 1839 to 1843. Refusing a third term he returned to the practice of law. In 1845 he was a member of a commission created by the legislature to inquire into the manner of spending the $14,000,000 which had been used in public works. The committee spent two years in its investigation and it is said that he traveled over 10,000 miles along the lines of public work and about the state gathering evidence. At the end of two years the committee made a report revealing much corruption and fraud. In 1850 he was elected a member of the convention called to draft a new constitution of that state. He was one of the most active and distinguished members of the body and as much as any one was responsible for the results accomplished. In 1851 he was elected a judge of the court of common pleas of Ohio, in which position he served with distinction for the following ten years. After leaving the bench he returned again to the practice of law in the city of Gallipolis, Ohio, for the remainder of his life.

Distinguished as he was as a lawyer and as a judge and in public office, it is probably as an author that he was best known. He was the author of *A Digest of Decisions of the Supreme Court of Ohio* (1853), devoted to the cases in the *Ohio Reports* from 1821 to 1851. By far the most important of his books was that on the civil code. Although raised under the common law pleadings and bitterly opposed to the adoption in 1851 of the civil code, after it was adopted he felt the need of a book upon the subject for the use of the lawyers of the state who were unfamiliar with anything but the common law pleadings. He, therefore, set himself to the task of writing such a work and his *Pleadings and Practice under the Civil Code* (1856) was of invaluable service to the bar. In fact, so useful was this book that it ran into five editions, the latest edition being published in two volumes in 1906-07, under the editorship of Hiram L. Sibley. He also wrote two books of less purely professional interest, *Morality and the State* (1859), a philosophical attempt to analyze man's moral and spiritual nature, and *Crime and the Family* (1876) which expressed some early ideas that later were embodied in the juvenile-court movement.

[*The Biog. Encyc. of Ohio* (1876); *Amherst College Biog. Record of the Grads.* (1927); Henry Howe, *Hist. Colls. of Ohio* centennial ed., vol. I (1889); *The*

Nash Family; or Records of the Descendants of Thomas Nash (1853), collected by Sylvester Nash.]
A. H. T.

NASON, ELIAS (Apr. 21, 1811–June 17, 1887), schoolmaster, writer, lecturer, and Congregational clergyman, was born at Wrentham, Mass., the son of Levi and Sarah (Newton) Nason, and a descendant of Willoughby Nason who came to Massachusetts before 1691. His father was a farmer at Wrentham, Hopkinton, Medway, and Ashland successively, and Elias attended schools in all these towns. In 1826 he entered the paper-mill of David Bigelow & Company at Framingham, and for five years divided his time between making paper and attending school. In 1831, after a year's study under Chauncey Colton and Justin Perkins at Amherst, he entered Brown University, where he supported himself by teaching school during the winters. He graduated in 1835, and for five months was principal of the Cambridge Latin Grammar School. He then sailed for Charleston with John E. Holbrook [*q.v.*], the naturalist, and lived for four years in Georgia, where he edited a newspaper, was principal of an academy at Waynesboro, and lectured on botanical subjects. His active sympathy for the negroes more than once endangered his life. On Nov. 28, 1836, he married Myra Anne Bigelow, of Framingham, Mass., by whom he had six children.

Moving to Newburyport, Mass., in 1840, he opened a school for young ladies, and in 1844 became principal of the high school, and later of the Latin School. He also kept a book store in partnership with his brother, contributed to magazines, gave popular lectures on a variety of subjects, and is said to have edited a periodical called the *Watch Tower*. In the year 1849 he was licensed to preach, and became principal of the high school at Milford. After missing by two votes election as master of the Boston Latin School, he was in May 1852 ordained minister of the Congregational church in Natick. In 1858 he took charge of the Mystic Church, Medford, and from 1861 to 1865 was pastor of a church at Exeter, N. H. During the Civil War he served on the Christian Commission, visited the seat of war, and was an ardent advocate of the Union. In 1865 he bought a farm at North Billerica, which remained his home until his death. In 1866 and 1867 he edited the *New-England Historical and Genealogical Register*. From 1876 to 1884 he served as pastor of a church in Lowell (variously known as the Pawtucket Church and as the Centre Church of Dracut). He traveled widely as a popular lecturer, and contributed often to Congregationalist periodicals.

Nason knew something of every branch of

science, could read twelve languages, and was a skilled musician. As a lecturer he was distinguished by his pleasing address, his fervor of manner, and the apt and homely illustrations which he derived from conversations with mechanics and laborers. He published some thirty-nine books and pamphlets, of which the most important were *Congregational Hymn Book* (1857); *Sir Charles Henry Frankland, Baronet: or Boston in the Colonial Times* (1865); *A Memoir of Mrs. Susannah Rowson* (1870); *The Life and Public Services of Hon. Henry Wilson* (1872), in collaboration with Thomas Russell; *The Life and Times of Charles Sumner* (1874); *The American Evangelists, Dwight L. Moody and Ira D. Sankey* (copr. 1877); *A Gazetteer of the State of Massachusetts* (1874); *A History of Dunstable, Mass.* (1877), and *A Literary History of the Bible* (1881).

[W. B. Trask, in *New-Eng. Hist. and Geneal. Reg.*, Jan. 1889; *Hist. Cat. Brown Univ.* (1914); *Congregationalist*, June 23, 1887; A. C. Varnum, *Hist. of Pawtucket Church and Society* (1888); J. J. Currier, *Hist. of Newburyport, 1864–1905*, vol. I (1906); *Boston Post*, June 18, 1887.]   H. B. P.

NASON, HENRY BRADFORD (June 22, 1831–Jan. 18, 1895), educator, was born at Foxboro, Mass., the son of Elias and Susanna (Keith) Nason. His father and Levi, the father of Elias Nason [*q.v.*], were half-brothers. Henry was graduated from Williston Seminary, Easthampton, Mass., in 1851, and from Amherst College in 1855, then studied at Göttingen (1855–57), where he obtained his doctor's degree, at Heidelberg, and at Freiberg. Returning to the United States, he taught for a year at the Raymond Collegiate Institute, Carmel, N. Y., and in 1858 became professor of natural history in Rensselaer Polytechnic Institute. Until 1866, when he was appointed professor of chemistry and natural science at Rensselaer, he also taught natural history at Beloit College, Beloit, Wis., dividing his time between the two institutions. He retained his professorship at Rensselaer until his death. In Troy he married, Sept. 7, 1864, Frances Kellogg Townsend, by whom he had a son and a daughter.

As adviser to the Standard Oil Company, 1880–90, he introduced a number of improvements in the process of treating crude oil. In 1881 he was appointed inspector under the New York State Board of Health to eliminate nuisances due to the use of petroleum. He was later delegated by the United States, which he had represented at the Paris Exposition of 1878, to attend the International Congress called to consider the same subject. In connection with his studies in geology and mineralogy, to which, be-

cause of traditions at Rensselaer Polytechnic Institute, he was increasingly attracted, he also visited most countries in Europe and all the principal mining areas of the United States. Except, however, for advancements in technique, particularly in the analytical procedures applicable to the problems of geology and mineralogy, he appears to have done little original work in chemistry. Even his *Table of Reactions for Qualitative Analysis* (1865) and his *Table for Qualitative Analysis in Colors* (1870) are largely compilations based to a considerable extent upon results obtained in the laboratories of the Institute. His most useful service was that of translator, editor, and organizer of scientific activities. At Rensselaer he not only continued the scholarly traditions established by his predecessors, William Elderhorst and Charles Anthony Goessman [*q.v.*], both of whom were educated in Germany, but he also published *Handbook of Mineral Analysis* (1871), translated, with some revision, from the German of Friedrich Wöhler, and with Charles F. Chandler [*q.v.*] edited *Elderhorst's Manual of Qualitative Blowpipe Analysis, and Determinative Mineralogy* (6th ed., 1873, and subsequent editions).

Gifted with an easy address and an affable manner, he was prominent in the organization of the Geological Society of America and the American Chemical Society, of which he was president in 1889–90, and participated actively in the affairs of the General Alumni Association of Rensselaer Polytechnic Institute, which he served as secretary, 1872–86. In this capacity he prepared the *Proceedings of the Semi-Centennial Celebration of the Rensselaer Polytechnic Institute, Troy, N. Y., with a Catalogue of Officers and Students, 1824–74* (1875) and the more important *Biographical Record of the Officers and Graduates of the Rensselaer Polytechnic Institute, 1824–86* (1887), which throws considerable light upon the development of science and engineering in the United States.

[*Proc. of the Semi-Centennial Celebration of the Rensselaer Poly. Inst.* (1875); H. B. Nason, *Biog. Record Officers and Grads. Rensselaer Poly. Inst.* (1887); P. C. Ricketts, *Hist. of Rensselaer Poly. Inst.* (1914); W. P. Mason, in *Jour. Am. Chem. Soc.*, May 1895; *New-Eng. Hist. and Geneal. Reg.*, Jan. 1889; files of the *Polytechnic*, esp. issue for Jan. 26, 1895; *N. Y. Tribune*, Jan. 19, 1895.]   R. P. B.

NASSAU, ROBERT HAMILL (Oct. 11, 1835–May 6, 1921), missionary in Africa, the son of Charles William and Hannah McClintock (Hamill) Nassau, was born at Montgomery Square, near Norristown, Pa. He pursued the studies of the freshman year at Lafayette College, where his father was for some time a professor. The next year he spent in the high school at Lawrenceville, N. J., conducted by his mother's brothers. He then entered the College of New Jersey, from which he graduated in 1854. After teaching in Lawrenceville, he studied three years in Princeton Theological Seminary (1856–59). In 1859 he asked the Presbyterian Board of Foreign Missions to send him to its most difficult and dangerous post. He was appointed to the Corisco or West Africa mission, on the west coast, a degree north of the equator. To prepare himself further, he studied medicine at the University of Pennsylvania, receiving his degree in 1861. On July 2 of that year he was ordained to the Presbyterian ministry; September saw him at Corisco.

In this region, a French protectorate inhabited by Bantu tribes, there had been American missionaries since 1842. On Corisco Island, the headquarters of the Presbyterian mission, Nassau taught and preached for four years, working also over a wide stretch of mainland coast. He was married on Sept. 17, 1862, to Mary Cloyd Latta, a missionary in his station, who died in 1870. After he had mastered the Benga language, his pioneering instinct moved him to take charge of the mission's first station on the mainland, at Benito, fifty miles north of Corisco. Here he worked for six years, going out to preach along a hundred miles of coast, and penetrating as far up the Benito River. During a furlough in the United States in 1872–73, he was instructed to found a missionary station in the interior, a project which native opposition had thus far prevented. In 1874 he ascended the Ogowai (Ogowe) River, which enters the Atlantic seventy miles south of the equator, and there served for seventeen years. He learned well the Mpongwe and Fang dialects and the characters of the peoples. He established two stations—the furthest two hundred miles up the Ogowai—which proved permanent missionary centers, and organized four churches. On a furlough in 1881 he was married at Lakewood, N. J., Oct. 10, to Mary Brunette Foster, who died in 1884. Relieved in 1891, he spent two years in the United States, and then had three more terms in Africa, in 1893–98, 1900–03, and 1904–06. In these years he worked at Libreville and at Batanga, on the coast a hundred and twenty-five miles north of Corisco. There his duties were so arranged as to allow him to write his *Fetichism in West Africa* (1904). In 1906 he retired, after forty-five years of service. During 1907–08 he had charge of churches in Florida. His last eleven years, in which he wrote several books, were passed in Ambler, Pa.

To make Nassau an effective missionary there combined rare linguistic ability, intimate knowledge of African thought and customs, shrewd judgment of the character of the natives and skill in managing them, a resourceful, original mind, and never-flagging zeal. Somewhat conventional in his piety, he was anything but this in his methods. He was ahead of his time in using industrial training for missionary purposes. His cherished Winchester rifle figures largely in his journals of missionary labors. He was selfless in surrender to his task, yet amusingly egotistical. Along with consuming missionary devotion he carried other interests. He did valuable work in recording African folkstories, published in *Where Animals Talk* (1912), *In an Elephant Corral* (1912), and *Batanga Tales* (1915). His *Fetichism in West Africa* is a treasury of knowledge of African religion, and contains also a sketch of Bantu sociology. He sent home zoölogical and entomological specimens. With associates he translated the Old Testament and part of the New into Benga. These versions were published in original and revised forms between 1863 and 1881. His missionary activity was described, often minutely and vividly, in books of which the most important are *Tales Out of School* (1911), *Corisco Days: the First Thirty Years of the West African Mission* (1910), and *My Ogowe* (1914). During his furloughs he made many missionary speeches and became a well-known and striking figure in ecclesiastical meetings. By his first wife he had three sons, and by his second, a daughter.

[Annual reports of the Board of Foreign Missions of the Presbyterian Church in the U. S. A.; personal information and autobiog. sketch (MS.) in library of this board; *Biog. Cat. Princeton Theol. Sem.* (1933); *Princeton Theol. Sem. Bull., Necrological Report*, Aug. 1921; *Presbyterian* (Phila.), May 26, 1921; *Who's Who in America*, 1920–21; *Public Ledger* (Phila.), May 8, 1921.]   R. H. N.

NAST, THOMAS (Sept. 27, 1840–Dec. 7, 1902), cartoonist, was born in Landau, Germany, where his father was a musician in the 9th Bavarian Regiment. In 1846 his mother took him to New York, where four years later his father, who had left Germany for political reasons and had enlisted in the French navy, joined them. The elder Nast, whose name is given in the city directory as Thomas, became a member of the Philharmonic Society and of various theatrical orchestras, while the boy attended the public schools. A gift of crayons by a neighbor led young Nast to develop a passion for drawing. After attending a class taught by the artist Theodore Kaufmann, he entered the

Academy of Design, receiving also much personal instruction from Alfred Fredericks. At fifteen he showed some of his sketches to the publisher Frank Leslie, received a trial commission to draw the Sunday-morning crowd at Christopher Street Ferry, and was promptly engaged by *Frank Leslie's Illustrated Newspaper* at four dollars a week. The office, frequented by some of the best illustrators of the period, was an excellent practical school. Sol Eytinge of the staff gave him invaluable technical training, while Nast carefully studied the methods of the English illustrators, Leech, Gilbert, and Tenniel. When in 1857 *Harper's Weekly* began its career he resolved to contribute, and his first important drawing, a page savagely satirizing a current police scandal in New York, appeared in it on Mar. 19, 1859. When later that same year the *New York Illustrated News* was established he left *Leslie's*, and covered important assignments for the new periodical, including the funeral of John Brown. The great Heenan-Sayers fight in 1860 drew him to England, and Garibaldi's revolt of that year led him to extend his tour to Italy, whence he sent pictures of the fighting to both London and New York periodicals. He returned to America on Feb. 1, 1861, with a dollar and a half in his pocket, and on Sept. 26, 1861, the day before his twenty-first birthday, he was married to Sarah Edwards. It was characteristic both of his self-confidence and love of music that his first purchase was a $350 piano on credit.

Following the outbreak of the Civil War, Nast quickly found his true rôle. He hurried to Baltimore and Washington, publishing his drawings at first in the tottering *New York Illustrated News*, then briefly renewing his connection with *Leslie's*, and finally contributing sketches to *Harper's Weekly*. In the summer of 1862 he became a staff artist for the last-named journal. Fletcher Harper, who was in charge of the *Weekly*, perceived his talent, and encouraged him to follow his own bent, making pictures with ideas rather than illustrations of events. By 1863 he was recognized as one of the pillars of the journal. His spirited drawing, "After the Battle," on Oct. 25, 1862, aimed at those who opposed vigorous prosecution of the war, his touching double-page Christmas picture of that year, his pictorial arraignments of guerrilla warfare in the border states, and his "Emancipation" of Jan. 24, 1863, depicting negro life of the past and the future, all produced a powerful impression. Several pictures of 1864, notably his spirited "On to Richmond" on June 18, and his sardonic sketch, "Compromise with the South"

on Sept. 3, just after the Democratic Convention (showing a triumphant Southerner clasping hands with a crippled Northern soldier over the grave of Union heroes), were circulated in tremendous numbers. Lincoln declared near the close of the war: "Thomas Nast has been our best recruiting sergeant" (Harper, *post*, p. 188). The Reconstruction cartoons expressed a bitterness which often became intemperate, notably in the portrayal of Andrew Johnson as a bully and dictator, and of Southerners as engaged in outrages upon the defenseless negroes; but they marked an advance in the art of political caricature. In 1866 he began his very effective use of Shakespearian situations as vehicles for his ideas. Ablest of all were the fierce attacks he maintained in the years 1869–72 upon the "Tweed ring," to the overthrow of which he contributed as much as any single man. Caricature has seldom if ever been more eloquent and impressive than in his drawings, "The Tammany Tiger Let Loose" (Nov. 11, 1871), "Who Stole the People's Money?" (Aug. 19, 1871), and "A Group of Vultures Waiting for the Storm to 'Blow Over'" (Sept. 23, 1871). His final triumph was the apprehension of Tweed in Spain through a cartoon which made him recognizable even in that country.

Throughout the 'seventies and until 1886 Nast remained one of the greatest influences in American journalism. While the policies of *Harper's Weekly* were dictated by G. W. Curtis and Fletcher Harper, Nast's pen was the most distinctive element in the journal. He made Greeley ludicrous in the campaign of 1872, mercilessly ridiculed the political hobgoblin of Grant's "Caesarism," defended Hayes against Tilden, and forsook the Republican party only when Blaine was nominated. The Tammany tiger, which he had popularized, was borrowed from the Americus Club emblem, but the Democratic donkey and Republican elephant were his own inventions, both becoming fixed in his pictures in 1874. Following his own inclination as well as that of the editors of *Harper's Weekly*, he stanchly upheld sound money and currency reform and was a devoted adherent of Grover Cleveland. In 1885 and 1886 his contributions to the *Weekly* grew fewer, he chafed under restrictions which he felt robbed his pen of its old slashing vigor, and his Christmas picture of 1886 was his last. For a time he contributed to other journals and in 1892–93 briefly managed a sheet called *Nast's Weekly*, but his great days were over. He had lost most of his savings, amassed in lecturing as well as journalism, by the Grant & Ward failure. In May 1902, Theodore Roosevelt appointed him consul at Guayaquil, Ecuador, where he succumbed to the climate.

[A. B. Paine, *Th. Nast: His Period and His Pictures* (1904), is an exceptionally interesting biography, fully illustrated, but sometimes lacking in definite facts. A few details are supplied by J. Henry Harper in *The House of Harper* (1912). A son, Cyril Nast, published "Thomas Nast as I Knew Him," in the *Am. Art Student,* Feb. 1927. A three-volume scrapbook collection of Nast's pictures is available in the N. Y. Pub. Lib. He illustrated a number of books, but the indispensable repository of his work is the files of *Harper's Weekly.* Obituaries appeared in *N. Y. Times,* Dec. 8, 1902; *Harper's Weekly,* Dec. 29, 1902.]   A. N.

NAST, WILLIAM (June 15, 1807–May 16, 1899), Methodist Episcopal clergyman and editor, founder of the first German Methodist church in the United States, was born in Stuttgart, Württemberg. His father, Johann Wilhelm, was a government official; his mother, Elisabetha Magdalena Ludovika (Böhm), the daughter of an Austrian officer. Both parents died in Nast's early childhood and his rearing was left in the hands of an elder sister, Frau Dr. Süsskind. He attended school at Stuttgart and at Vaihingen-an-der-Enz, and after his confirmation (1821) he entered the theological seminary at Blaubeuren. Earlier, he had attended meetings of the Pietists, and had read Arndt, Spener, Francke, and Thomas à Kempis. At the seminary Nast had as his roommate David Friedrich Strauss, later the well-known disciple of Ferdinand Christian Baur, and though for a time young Nast fought against the current rationalistic intellectual tendencies, he finally gave way to the *Zeitgeist,* and at the age of eighteen entered the University of Tübingen. After two years of study he left the university in a whirl of doubt, and after wandering about, visiting Vienna, Munich, and Dresden, he finally took the advice of his brother-in-law, Dr. Süsskind, and came to America.

Arriving in 1828, he secured a position as tutor in a Methodist family on Duncan's Island, near Harrisburg, Pa., where he had a pleasant home, gained his first impressions of Methodism, and became acquainted with several Methodist ministers. In 1832 he went to West Point as librarian and instructor in German, and here amidst the "godless atmosphere of the military academy" he felt again the call to the ministry. Another period of confusion of mind now followed. Wandering more or less aimlessly about, he finally came to the communistic community of Württembergers at Economy, Pa., where he remained for a time, working in the fields. Through Bishop McIlvaine of the Protestant Episcopal Church he secured a position as teacher of Greek and Hebrew at Kenyon College, Gambier, Ohio. Here he became acquainted with

a pious Methodist shoemaker, who took him to a nearby Methodist quarterly meeting. Finally, he made the definite decision to enter the Methodist ministry, and was admitted on trial to the Ohio Conference.

Just at this time T. A. Morris, editor of the *Western Christian Advocate,* the Methodist journal at Cincinnati, was urging that work be begun among the rapidly increasing German population, and in 1835 Nast was appointed German missionary to Cincinnati. Among his early converts was John Swahlen, who became the co-founder with Nast of German Methodism. Nast was soon traveling over Ohio and adjoining states, averaging some three hundred miles per month, visiting German communities. In 1838 he was able to organize the first German Methodist church in the city of Cincinnati. In September of the same year a German church-paper, *Der Christliche Apologete,* was founded (first issue January 1839), with Nast as the editor, a position which he held for some fifty-three years. Besides editing this paper, he busied himself with extensive writing and translating and was the founder of German Methodist Christian literature in America. Among his most important publications were *Das Leben und Wirken des Johannes Wesley und Seiner Haupt-mitarbeiter* (1852); *Die Aufgabe der Christlichen Kirche im neunzehnten Jahrhundert* (1857); a commentary in German on the gospels of Matthew and Mark (c. 1862), with an English edition in 1864; *Das Christentum und seine Gegensätze* (1883).

Nast made several journeys to Europe in the interest of his work; in 1844 he was permitted by the General Conference to visit Germany; in 1857 he attended the meeting of the Evangelical Alliance at Berlin, where he delivered an address on Methodism; and in 1877 he again visited Germany and Switzerland. He was one of the founders of German Wallace College at Berea, Ohio, originally a department of Baldwin University, and a separate institution from 1863 to 1913, when it was merged with Baldwin to form Baldwin-Wallace College. For many years he was nominally its president. On Aug. 1, 1836, he married Margaret Eliza McDowell, of a Scotch Presbyterian family of Cincinnati. Of the five children born to them, three were living at the time of Nast's death.

[The best source is C. Golder, J. H. Horst, and J. B. Schall, *Geschichte der Zentral Deutschen Konferenz Einschliesslich der Anfangsgeschichte des deutschen Methodismus* (Cincinnati, n.d.); see also Adam Miller, *Experience of German Methodist Preachers* (1859); files of *Der Christliche Apologete*; Rudolf Krauss, in *Biographisches Jahrbuch und Deutscher Nekrolog.,* vol. IV (1900); *Western Christian Advocate,* Feb. 10, 1837; *Cincinnati Enquirer,* May 17, 1899.]   W. W. S.

NATION, CARRY AMELIA MOORE (Nov. 25, 1846–June 9, 1911), temperance agitator, was born in Garrard County, Ky., the daughter of George Moore, a prosperous stock-dealer and planter who was the descendant of a pioneer Irish settler in the region, and of Mary Campbell who was descended by way of Virginia from the Scotch clan of Campbell and related to Alexander Campbell, the religious leader. The name "Carry" is correctly so spelled because her unlettered father wrote it thus in the family Bible at her birth. Her mother developed a psychosis, probably of a manic-depressive type with grandiose delusions that she was Queen Victoria, and her appetite for extravagant dress and equipage was humored by her family. Mrs. Moore spent the last three years of her life in the Missouri State Hospital for the Insane, and her mother, brother, and sister were also insane. The Moores and Campbells were slave-holders, and Carry's childhood was strongly influenced by the superstitious lore and religious excitements of the negroes. At ten she underwent a spectacular conversion in a "protracted meeting." Moore had a *Wanderlust,* and before Carry was sixteen the family had lived in a dozen counties of Kentucky, Missouri, and Texas. Her schooling was brief and sporadic. She attended for a time boarding schools in Missouri and the State Normal School at Warrensburg, where she received a teaching certificate. Throughout this period she was a semi-invalid from digestive troubles.

Moore's fortunes were broken by the Civil War. Stripped of his property and slaves after a disastrous venture in Texas, he returned in 1865 to Belton, Mo. There Carry met and married (Nov. 21, 1867) her first and only love, Dr. Charles Gloyd, a young physician and Union veteran from Ohio. Gloyd was addicted to liquor, and all his bride's reform efforts were wasted. He was a Mason and spent much time roistering at the lodge, which incited in her a permanent hatred of fraternal orders. After a few wretchedly unhappy months she was persuaded by her parents to abandon Gloyd, who died of alcoholism six months later, leaving her with an infant daughter, Charlien, her only child, who lived to a weak and insane maturity. For the next four years she taught in a primary school at Holden, Mo., supporting her child and her mother-in-law. In 1877 she married David Nation, a lawyer, minister, and editor nineteen years older than herself. They had little in common and were constantly bickering. Nation assisted her in some of her public activities but he disapproved of her extremism in religion and reform. The Nations spent ten futile years in small towns of Texas, where Carry, with the most arduous labor, supported the family by running hotels. At this period she had many mystic experiences. In 1889 Nation removed to Medicine Lodge, Kan., near the Oklahoma border, to become pastor of the Christian Church, but shortly resigned to practise law. He divorced her for desertion in 1901.

Kansas was one of the original prohibition states, a constitutional amendment having been voted in 1880. Despite stringent enforcement laws, there were numerous "joints" where liquor was sold more or less openly. In 1890 the United States Supreme Court held that liquor shipped into Kansas and sold from the "original package" was subject only to the interstate commerce laws. The "wets," financed by distilleries which flooded the state with liquor, almost secured the resubmission of the amendment. Carry Nation was soon deeply involved in this struggle. She organized a branch of the Woman's Christian Temperance Union and with a few militant women began a campaign to expel the "jointists" from Medicine Lodge. So far as she had a definite theory of action, it was that since the saloon was illegal in Kansas, it was permissible for any citizen to force his way in and destroy not only liquor but furniture and fixtures. Saloon property, she avowed, "has no rights that anybody is bound to respect."

In the spring of 1900, always supported by "visions" of her divinely infallible mission, her activities spread rapidly and with increasing violence to neighboring towns and counties. In Wichita she wrecked the Hotel Carey and other expensive saloons, smashing mirrors, windows, bars, panelling, pornographic paintings, and liquor stocks valued at thousands of dollars. It was here that she first used the hatchet which became her distinctive weapon, and was confined in the Sedgwick County jail for seven weeks, when she was released on a writ of *habeas corpus.* In her subsequent career through Enterprise, Danville, Winfield, and Leavenworth, to Topeka, the capital, where she invaded the governor's chambers, and later in New York, Washington, Pittsburgh, Rochester, San Francisco, and other large cities, she was arrested some thirty times, usually on such charges as "disturbing the peace." Her numerous fines she paid from her earnings by the sale of souvenir hatchets, lecture tours, and stage appearances. She never became wealthy, but for half a dozen years she sometimes earned as much as $300 a week. At one time she was under the managership of the Furlong Lyceum Bureau, and later employed her own manager, Harry C. Turner. She had little business sense and was excessively generous, giving large sums to the poor and to temperance projects, and was easy prey for swindlers. She built a home for drunkards' wives at Kansas City, Kan. Among other propaganda methods she carried on several short-lived publishing ventures, such as *The Smasher's Mail, The Hatchet, The Home Defender,* and published her autobiography. She was often in physical danger of reprisal from her enemies and was frequently clubbed, cut, shot at, or otherwise attacked.

Her later years were marked by numerous melodramatic experiences, for her notoriety was now international. She visited several American universities, including Harvard and Yale, which she denounced as "hellholes"; the students greeted her with wild burlesque. In 1908 she toured the British Isles but was antagonistically received. Increasing feebleness compelled her retirement to a farm in the Ozark Mountains of Arkansas. Her last five months were spent in a Leavenworth hospital with a clouded and apathetic mind. She was buried in the family plot at Belton, Mo., where friends later erected a monument inscribed, "She hath done what she could."

Carry Nation was a woman of commanding presence, nearly six feet tall, weighing 175 pounds, with extremely muscular arms. She dressed in a sort of black-and-white deaconess uniform. Her fierceness and garrulity when aroused were proverbial. Her invective was amazingly vigorous, couched in a King James version of billingsgate. An ignorant, unbalanced, and contentious woman of vast energies, afflicted with an hereditary paranoia, she was subjected to early hardships and mystic seizures which fused all her powers into a flaming enmity to intoxicating liquor and its corrupt purveyors. During her crusading years the temperance advocates were sharply divided on the righteousness of her tactics, and although many indorsed her work, she never received the whole-hearted support of any national body. The tangible results of her activities in her own lifetime were slight beyond the closure and intimidation of many saloons and the probable prevention of a "backward step" by the Kansas legislature. In a very real sense, however, she was the spearhead as well as the goad of an aroused public opinion against the saloon. When in 1920 the long drive for constitutional prohibition reached its goal, Carry Nation had been largely forgotten, but a just appraisal of the social and psychological forces contributing to that end must certainly give her a large, if unpremeditated, place in

the furthering of the program for forcible prohibition.

[Her autobiography, *The Use and Need of the Life of Carry A. Nation* (1904), of which 56,000 copies were sold in five years; Herbert Asbury, *Carry Nation* (1929), a definitive life, on the whole sympathetic and impartial, by a sophisticated modern; J. L. Dwyer, "The Lady with the Hatchet," *American Mercury,* March 1926; *American Monthly Review of Reviews,* March 1901; *Current Literature,* March, April 1901; *Outlook,* Feb. 9, 1901; *Literary Digest,* Feb. 15, 1919; obituaries in *N. Y. Times, Leavenworth* (Kan.) *Times,* June 10, 1911.]   K. M. G.

NAVARRE, PIERRE (Mar. 28, 1790?–Mar. 20, 1874), fur-trader and scout in the War of 1812, was born in Detroit. His grandfather was a well-known settler, Robert Navarre; his father, François *dit* Hutro (or Utreau) Navarre. His mother, through her mother, was a member of the Campau family, probably Marie Louise Godet, though Pierre at one time gave her name as Marie Louise Panat Campau. He was also inconsistent in giving his age and was generally considered to be eighty-nine at the time of his death, although he was probably five years younger. The family moved to the River Raisin country when Pierre was still young, but it was not until about 1807 that he and his elder brother, Robert, built the cabin near the mouth of the Maumee which was to be Pierre's permanent home. The boy, inured to the woods and skilled in Indian ways, became a fur-trader, and is said to have traded with the Miamis at Fort Wayne, where he made the friendship of Chief Little Turtle [*q.v.*].

When the War of 1812 disrupted the border trade, Navarre and three of his brothers joined the army of Gen. William Hull. They were included in the surrender of Detroit, but, released on parole, went to the River Raisin, where they served as scouts to Gen. James Winchester. They managed to escape from the massacre in January 1813, and a little later, Navarre became a scout in William Henry Harrison's army. Many tales were told in later years of his daring adventures: of his great speed in carrying messages over the wilderness trails; of his courageous escape after capture by the British; of his racing the British to carry the news of their approach to Fort Stephenson. He was present at the battle of the Thames, where his services were valuable because of the respect that the Indians in the British service had for his abilities. Navarre himself said that he witnessed the death of Tecumseh and that he was one of the soldiers detailed to bury that chief.

After the war, he devoted himself again to the fur trade, and was probably the Pierre Navarre who was employed as a trader in the St. Joseph's and Kankakee Outfit of the American Fur Company in 1820. After a disagreement with his superior, Navarre was discharged, only to be hired by William H. Wallace, another Company trader, to trade near Terre Haute, Ind. He was again discharged. Later Navarre left the fur trade and spent the rest of his life on his farm near Toledo. In 1864 a special bill was introduced into Congress to grant him a pension of eight dollars a month. The bill was reported adversely by the Senate committee, but the pension was later granted and helped to swell his scanty income in the last years of his life. As an old settler and a veteran of the War of 1812, he was held in some respect at Toledo. He served for a time as president of the Maumee Valley Pioneer Association. He was twice married: in 1825 to Geneveva Robert, who died in 1827, and some time later, to Catherine Bourdeau. He was survived by several children, two of his sons having served in the Civil War.

[Clark Waggoner, *Hist. of the City of Toledo and Lucas County, Ohio* (1888); H. L. Hosmer, *Early Hist. of the Maumee Valley* (1858); *Pioneer Colls., Report of the Pioneer Soc. . . . of Mich.*, esp. vol. V (1884); *Cong. Globe*, 38 Cong., 1 Sess., pp. 1531, 2272, 2274, 2279; Christian Denissen, *Navarre, or Researches after the Descendants of Robert Navarre* (1879); *Toledo Times*, Feb. 2, 1931; Am. Fur Company Letterbooks (photostats), in Burton Hist. Coll., Detroit.]
W. B—r.

NEAGLE, JOHN (Nov. 4, 1796–Sept. 17, 1865), portrait painter, was born in Boston, his parents, Philadelphians, being in that city on a visit at the time of his birth. His father was a native of Doneraile, County Cork, Ireland; his mother, *née* Taylor, was the daughter of a New Jersey farmer. His father died when John was four years old and his mother married again. Her second husband, a grocer, was "no friend to John or to the arts." From Edward F. Petticolas, afterwards a well-known portrait painter and miniaturist in Richmond, Va., the boy received his first elementary instruction in drawing. After leaving the grammar school he was sent to a drawing school conducted by Pietro Ancora. For a short time he worked in his stepfather's grocery store; then, at his own suggestion, he was apprenticed to one Thomas Wilson, "coach and ornamental painter." This man had artistic aspirations, and was taking painting lessons of Bass Otis [*q.v.*], the portrait painter. Like master, like man: young Neagle, brought into casual contact with Otis, began to form plans to make an artist of himself. Out of his regular working hours he gave much time and energy to independent drawing and painting.

During his apprenticeship, which lasted more than five years, his employer allowed him to take painting lessons from Otis for about two months,

and Otis took him to call on Thomas Sully [*q.v.*] in his studio. He had already made his first essays in portraiture and his work had won the praise of Otis, Sully, and C. W. Peale. From the first he had a remarkable faculty for getting a good likeness. When his apprenticeship came to its end in 1818, he undertook what was then an arduous journey, traveling over the mountains all the way to Lexington, Ky., with the intention of settling there as a portrait painter; but to his surprise he found Matthew Harris Jouett [*q.v.*], an accomplished painter, was already well established in that part of the country, and it seemed useless to attempt to compete with him. Accordingly, Neagle determined to try New Orleans, but there he was wholly unknown and had no success in getting sitters. He returned, therefore, by sea to Philadelphia, deeply discouraged. William Dunlap [*q.v.*] gives a picturesque account of this episode (*post*, III, 167–68), which must have been given him by Neagle himself, with full details as to the precarious methods of financing his travels. After his return to Philadelphia the artist had little difficulty in securing all the sitters he could conveniently attend to. Beginning by charging only fifteen dollars for a head, he gradually increased his stipend as he became better known, until he could ask and get $100, which was then a handsome figure.

In May 1826 he married Mary Chester Sully, niece and step-daughter of Thomas Sully. In that year his picture, "Pat Lyon the Blacksmith," a full-length portrait commission, had a most enthusiastic reception and added greatly to his reputation. It was exhibited in Philadelphia and New York, and, owing partly to its intrinsic merit as a picture, but probably still more to certain interesting stories about Pat Lyon, had an amazing success. Lyon was a picturesque local figure. A master locksmith, he had been unjustly convicted of complicity in a bank robbery in Philadelphia and sentenced to a term in prison. When the real culprits were discovered, he was set free and awarded damages. The background of Neagle's picture is a glimpse of the city prison, seen through an open door or window. One can in imagination hear the brawny smith telling with relish of his adventures as he poses in his shirtsleeves and grimy leather apron to Neagle.

Neagle was fond of a good story. He went to Boston to see Gilbert Stuart, and there painted the best existing likeness of Stuart, now in the Boston Museum of Fine Arts. His notes of his studio intercourse with Stuart, which he placed at Dunlap's disposal, are of great value; he could not resist the temptation to record also the preposterous yarn told him by Stuart apropos of the pernicious habit of taking snuff. Neagle had his full share of eminent sitters, most of them Philadelphians. His portrait of Washington hangs in Independence Hall; that of Henry Clay is in the possession of the Union League Club. A replica of "Pat Lyon the Blacksmith" is in the Boston Athenæum. The Corcoran Gallery, Washington, owns his portrait of Col. Richard M. Johnson [q.v.], vice-president of the United States, 1837–41. In the Thomas B. Clarke collection of early American portraits there are eight by Neagle, including those of John Davis, governor of Massachusetts and United States senator, William Rush, the Philadelphia sculptor, and several other men of mark. For some years before his death Neagle was paralyzed. He died in Philadelphia in 1865.

[Wm. Dunlap, *A Hist. of the Rise and Progress of the Arts of Design in the U. S.* (2 vols., 1834; rev. ed., 3 vols., 1918); H. T. Tuckerman, *Book of the Artists* (1867); Samuel Isham, *The Hist. of Am. Painting* (1905); F. F. Sherman, *Early Am. Painting* (1932); Cat. of Gallery of Nat. Portraiture, Penn. Acad., 1905; Cat. of Thos. B. Clarke Coll. of portraits by early Am. artists, 1928; H. W. Henderson, *The Pa. Acad. of the Fine Arts* (1911); Virgil Barker, "John Neagle," *The Arts*, July 1925; *Art in America*, Aug. 1916, Aug. 1918; dates of birth and marriage from C. H. Hart, *A Reg. of Portraits Printed by Thos. Sully* (1909), which contains information from the Sully family Bible, *Press* (Phila.), Sept. 20, 1865.]   W. H. D—s.

NEAL, ALICE BRADLEY [See HAVEN, EMILY BRADLEY, 1827–1863].

NEAL, DAVID DALHOFF (Oct. 20, 1838–May 2, 1915), historical and portrait painter, born at Lowell, Mass., the son of Stephen B. and Mary (Dalhoff) Neal, was of Dutch descent. His early education was received in the Lowell grammar schools, the Lawrence high school, and a private academy at Andover, N. H. Before coming of age he went to New Orleans, and thence via the Isthmus of Panama to San Francisco, where he found employment in making drawings on wood and painting an occasional portrait, though his artistic training had been of a very elementary character. In 1861 a rich Californian, S. P. Dewey, convinced that Neal had unusual talent and needed only the right sort of training to achieve fame as an artist, offered to supply him with sufficient money to take him to Europe and support him there for several years. He forthwith went to Munich and entered the Bavarian Royal Academy, where he worked in the antique classes for two years, and then became a pupil of Max Emanuel Ainmiller, best known as a painter on glass, whose daughter Marie he had married on Dec. 9, 1862. She died Sept. 29, 1897.

In 1869 Neal entered the atelier of Karl von Piloty, the historical painter, with whom he remained until 1876. He now began to devote himself wholly to figure painting. His first historical painting of importance was completed in 1876, and for it he was awarded the great medal of the Bavarian Royal Academy. The subject was "The First Meeting of Mary Stuart and Rizzio." Bought by D. O. Mills of San Francisco, it was exhibited in all the chief cities of the United States and was also extensively reproduced. The leading critics of the time were enthusiastic. Dr. Foerster wrote in the *Wartburg* of Munich that the scene was excellently conceived and represented in a most masterly manner; the critic of the *Zeitschrift für bildende Kunst* (1878) was equally emphatic in his praise.

Neal lived many years in Munich. Before coming under the influence of Piloty he had painted several interiors, including the "Chapel of the Kings, Westminster Abbey," and a "St. Mark's, Venice," both of which were exhibited at the Munich international exposition of 1869 and later at the National Academy in New York. Following the success of the "Mary Stuart and Rizzio" he produced his important picture of "Oliver Cromwell of Ely Visiting Mr. John Milton," which was shown in Munich, Vienna, Boston, and many other cities. It shows Cromwell when he was but a simple farmer and Milton in the full vigor of his youth, and has undeniable human interest. In execution it is typical of the Munich school of the nineteenth century, with bravura in the brushwork, and a heavy color scheme. Another large historical canvas, "James Watt," which was exhibited at the Royal Academy, London, became the property of Sir Benjamin S. Phillips, a former lord mayor of the City of London. In 1884 an exhibition of Neal's pictures was held at the galleries of Noyes & Blakeslee in Boston. The later years of the artist's life were for the most part devoted to portrait painting. Among his subjects were Whitelaw Reid, Mark Hopkins, D. O. Mills, William Henry Green, Adolph Sutro, and Judge Ogden Hoffman of California. He now divided his time between Europe and America, but Munich continued to be his home and he died there in 1915. Neal is one of the Americans trained in Munich of whom Isham remarks that they mastered the Munich technique and assimilated the Munich ideals so thoroughly that they reveal no trace of anything distinctly American.

[*Boston Transcript*, Mar. 19, 1884; Catalogue of Boston exhibit, Mar. 7–15, 1884; *Wartburg* (Munich), no. 9, 1876; *Chicago Tribune*, Mar. 24, 1878; E. Ransoni in *Neue Feie Presse* (Vienna), 1882; Samuel Isham, *The Hist. of Am. Painting* (1905); J. R. Tait, "David Neal," in *Mag. of Art*, Jan. 1886; Ulrich

Thieme and Felix Becker, *Allgemeines Lexikon der Bildenden Künstler,* vol. XXV (1931) ; *Who's Who in America,* 1914–15 ; *Am. Art News,* June 12, 1915 ; *Münchner Neeste Nachrichten,* May 4, 1915.]

W. H. D—s.

NEAL, JOHN (Aug. 25, 1793–June 20, 1876), author, editor, man of affairs, was the son of a Quaker schoolmaster of the same name, who died in September 1793, at Falmouth, now Portland, Me., leaving to his wife, Rachel (Hall) Neal, the rearing of their month-old twins, John and Rachel. The boy proved strong, active, and self-reliant, and after brief schooling was soon supporting himself as clerk in a succession of shops and then as itinerant teacher of penmanship and drawing in the Kennebec River towns. At twenty-two he found himself stranded in Baltimore, after the failure of a business venture in partnership with John Pierpont [*q.v.*]. He then turned to the study of law, meanwhile writing for a living. During the next eight years he worked prodigiously, studying history, languages, and literature, besides the law, editing for brief periods the *Baltimore Telegraph* and the *Portico,* a magazine projected by the Delphians, a club of which he and Pierpont were members ; compiling a considerable portion of *A History of the American Revolution* (2 vols., 1819) credited to Paul Allen [*q.v.*] ; and writing actively for the *Portico* and other publications. His own works during this period include two spirited narrative poems published together as *Battle of Niagara, a Poem, without Notes; and Goldau, or, the Maniac Harper* (1818), under the pseudonym "Jehu O'Cataract"; a tragedy in verse, *Otho* (1819) ; and five novels: *Keep Cool* (1817) ; *Logan, a Family History* (1822), a highly romantic fictionizing of the celebrated Indian chieftain; *Errata, or the Works of Will Adams* (2 vols., 1823) ; *Seventy-Six* (1823), a historical romance, probably his best work; and *Randolph* (1823). Neal boasted (*Blackwood's,* February 1825, p. 197) that the novels were written in odd hours at breakneck speed—*Logan* in six or eight weeks, *Randolph* in thirty-six days, and *Seventy-Six* in twenty-nine—but this is doubtful. Aspersions in *Randolph* on the deceased William Pinkney brought a challenge from the latter's high-spirited son, Edward Coote Pinkney [*q.v.*], which Neal, who in *Keep Cool* had ridiculed the practice of dueling, rather ostentatiously ignored. At this time, according to his own account, he was dismissed from the Society of Friends "for knocking a man who insulted him head over heels; for paying a militia fine; for making a tragedy; and for desiring to be turned out, whether or no" (*Ibid.,* p. 190). His novels had a considerable sale, *Logan* and *Seventy-Six*

achieving English reprints, and he was the closest American rival of Cooper in fiction.

In December 1823, desirous of extending his literary reputation, he sailed for England. There he won access to the pages of *Blackwood's Magazine* in May 1824, with an astute survey of the candidates and issues in the current American presidential campaign. Then followed, in the chief British periodicals, some two dozen or more other long articles, written partly from the assumed viewpoint of an Englishman familiar with the United States, and with the design of creating better understanding and respect for America in England. Most notable was "American Writers" (*Blackwood's,* September 1824–February 1825), critical estimates of 135 different American authors, based solely upon memory and ranging in length from a single curt sentence to ten pages for Irving, eight for himself, four for Charles Brockden Brown, and a half page for his rival, Cooper. His own poems he characterized as "abounding throughout in absurdity, intemperance, affectation, extravagance —with continual, but involuntary imitation : yet, nevertheless, containing, altogether, more sincere poetry, more exalted, *original,* pure, bold poetry, than *all* the works, of *all* the other authors that have ever appeared in America" (issue of February 1825, p. 194). Blackwood published in July 1825 Neal's novel, *Brother Jonathan,* containing some good scenes from New England life. The later months of his stay abroad were spent in the household of the aged utilitarian, Jeremy Bentham, for whom Neal later became an enthusiastic spokesman in America, publishing in 1830 a translation of Bentham's *Principles of Legislation* from Dumont's French rendition, with a memoir of the author.

In the summer of 1827, Neal landed in New York, intending to practise law there. On a visit to his home, however, hearing of threats against him, based upon supposed reflections on local characters in his novels, he changed his plans and settled in Portland for life. Within ten years he had overcome prejudice against him; received the honorary degree of M.A. from Bowdoin (1836) ; published three more novels: *Rachel Dyer* (1828), *Authorship* (1830), and *The Down-Easters* (1833) ; done valuable pioneer work in organizing gymnasium classes; won some note as a public speaker, and established a fortune by prudent investments in Maine granite quarries. On Oct. 12, 1828, he married Eleanor Hall, his cousin, by whom he had five children. From January 1828 to the end of 1829 he edited a literary periodical, the *Yankee,* published first at Portland, later at Portland and

Boston in fusion with the *Boston Literary Gazette*. As writer of most of the articles he voiced his opinions on temperance, phrenology, utilitarianism, and other hobbies, and encouraged young contributors, among them Whittier and Poe. The latter remarked that Neal gave him "the very first words of encouragement I ever remember to have heard" (the *Yankee*, December 1829). Later Neal edited for short periods the *New England Galaxy*, at Boston, and a Portland newspaper. Stories and poems of his were published in the annuals, the *Atlantic Souvenir* and the *Token;* in Lowell's magazine, the *Pioneer;* and later in *Godey's, Graham's,* and several other periodicals.

After 1840 Neal devoted less attention to the law (*Wandering Recollections,* p. 182) and more to real-estate promotion and civic interests. His activities in the latter field brought him occasionally into bitter conflict with his cousin, "mischief-making, meddlesome Neal Dow" [*q.v.*]. In January and February 1843, at the New York Tabernacle, he delivered a series of addresses in behalf of woman's rights, culminating in a debate with Park Benjamin and Col. William L. Stone (Daggett, *post,* pp. 30–51). Later in that year, from May to December, he succeeded N. P. Willis [*q.v.*] as editor of the weekly *Brother Jonathan,* at New York, in which his novel "Ruth Elder" appeared as a serial. After 1850 he continued writing actively for periodicals, with contributions to the *North American Review, Harper's Magazine,* the *Northern Monthly* (Portland), the *Atlantic Monthly,* and numerous others. His later books included *One Word More* (1854), a religious treatise; another novel, *True Womanhood* (1859); three dime novels for Beadle, *The White Faced Pacer* (1863), *The Moose Hunter* (1864), and *Little Moccasin, or, Along the Madawaska* (1866); and *Great Mysteries and Little Plagues* (1870), a book "for and about children." The great fire of 1866 in Portland destroyed much of his property, but he threw himself whole-heartedly into the task of rebuilding the city. His pride in it is shown in *Portland Illustrated* (1874) and in frequent passages in his autobiography. This work, published as *Wandering Recollections of a Somewhat Busy Life,* was suggested to him by his lifelong friend, Longfellow, in 1859, but though thrice rewritten, it did not appear until 1869. Garrulous, ill-proportioned, and not wholly reliable, it is invaluable as self-portraiture. Neal died at Portland after a brief illness, in his eighty-third year.

His appearance was striking: his frame was not large but he was finely built and his physical strength and agility were remarkable. At seven-ty-nine, he threw into the street a hoodlum who persisted in smoking in a horsecar. He was fearless, energetic, easily angered by injustice or insult, but was ordinarily kindly and courteous, sympathetic to children, and chivalrous toward women. He was always enthusiastic about something—a characteristic which proved both a strength and a weakness in his writing. He wrote too hastily and voluminously. Poe in the *Southern Literary Messenger* (February 1836) and Lowell in *A Fable for Critics* (1848) attest his strength and genius but lament his wastefulness and lack of restraint.

[The major sources are Neal's *Wandering Recollections,* his sketch of himself in *Blackwood's,* Feb. 1825, and several hundred letters to his friends Pierpont, Longfellow, and others. An admirably full and authoritative biography, with an inclusive bibliography of other sources and of Neal's works, has recently been compiled by Irving T. Richards, but is as yet (1933) unpublished. An extensive collection of Neal's letters is also being edited by Professor Richards. Certain phases of his life are discussed in Windsor P. Daggett's preliminary sketch, *A Down East Yankee from the District of Maine* (1920). See also Hervey Allen, *Israfel* (2 vols., 1926); F. L. Mott, *A Hist. of Am. Mags., 1741–1850* (1930); W. B. Cairns, *A Hist. of Am. Lit.* (1912), pp. 208–09; *Daily Eastern Argus* (Portland), June 21, 1876.]

M. E—s.

NEAL, JOSEPH CLAY (Feb. 3, 1807–July 17, 1847), journalist and humorist, was born in Greenland, N. H., the only son of the Rev. James A. Neal and Christina (Palmer) Neal. The father had been principal of a school for girls in Philadelphia, but was compelled by failing health to live in the country, where he served as a Congregational minister. Upon his death in 1809 his widow returned to Philadelphia, and there her son grew to manhood. After the discovery of the anthracite coal fields near Pottsville, he spent some time in that vicinity, but returned to Philadelphia in 1831 to engage in newspaper work. The *Pennsylvanian,* a Democratic daily newspaper established in 1832, attracted him, and he soon became its editor. In 1836, with Morton McMichael and Louis A. Godey [*qq.v.*], he established the *Saturday News and Literary Gazette,* later *Neal's Saturday Gazette and Lady's Literary Museum,* of which he was editor until his death. In 1841–42 he visited Europe and Africa in the interest of his health. Six months before his sudden death, he married, in December 1846, Emily Bradley of Hudson, N. Y., who under the pen name of Alice G. Lee had sent many contributions to the *Saturday Gazette* [see Haven, Emily Bradley Neal].

As a political writer at a time when violent partisanship gave rise to vituperation and abuse, Neal was distinguished for his mild, urbane, and courteous attitude towards his political opponents. He met them with argument, or turned aside their shafts with pleasant irony and grotesque humor. But it was not as a political writer that he was best known. He is memorable chiefly as one of the most popular humorists of his day. His first humorous sketches, published under the title of "City Worthies," appeared in the *Pennsylvanian*. The "worthies" that he depicted were the idlers, the spendthrifts, the pretenders to fashion, and generally those who were the victims of the minor follies and difficulties of city life. These sketches at once became extremely popular and were reprinted and praised in many newspapers. In 1838 Neal published eighteen of them in *Charcoal Sketches: or Scenes in a Metropolis,* with illustrations by David Claypoole Johnston [*q.v.*]. They passed through six editions in four years and were reprinted in the second volume of *The Pic Nic Papers* (3 vols., London, 1841), edited by Charles Dickens. Another collection, *In Town and About,* followed in 1843, and *Peter Ploddy, and Other Oddities* came in 1844. After Neal's death his widow published *Charcoal Sketches: Second Series* (1848). Another posthumous volume, *The Misfortunes of Peter Faber, and Other Sketches,* appeared in 1856, and as late as 1865 forty-six of his sketches were reprinted in *Charcoal Sketches: Three Books Complete in One.*

An abundant geniality is the pervading quality in his mildly satirical portraits. Their similarity to the early work of Dickens is obvious, but unlike Dickens, Neal coined no memorable phrases and created no memorable characters. His humor lacked substance and originality. His popularity, considerable in his day, waned as the Civil War approached, and in the generation that followed him—the generation of Artemus Ward, Josh Billings, Petroleum V. Nasby, and Mark Twain—his fame was eclipsed by a more vigorous and original humor, American in background and spirit.

[Registers of the Second Presbyterian Church of Phila.; *Pennsylvanian* (Phila.) and *Public Ledger* (Phila.), July 19, 1847; *North American* (Phila.), July 20, 1847; R. W. Griswold, *The Prose Writers of America* (1847); Henry Simpson, *The Lives of Eminent Philadelphians Now Deceased* (1859); A. H. Smyth, *The Phila. Mags. and Their Contributors* (1892); F. L. Mott, *A Hist. of Am. Mags., 1741–1850* (1930).]
N. E. M.

NEALE, LEONARD (Oct. 15, 1746–June 18, 1817), Roman Catholic prelate, a direct descendant of Capt. James Neale, a favorite of Charles I who settled in Lord Baltimore's colony before 1642, was born on the family manor near Port Tobacco, Md. His father, William, died early in life, leaving seven sons and three daughters to the care of his widow, Anne (Brooke) Neale, who also came of substantial old Maryland stock.

Leonard obtained his first schooling from the Jesuits at Bohemia Manor, but the penal laws made it necessary to send him to an English Catholic refugee college on the Continent for his further education. In 1758, accordingly, he entered the Jesuit College of St. Omer in Flanders and later went to Bruges. Following the family tradition, he entered the Society of Jesus at Ghent, on Sept. 7, 1767, as did four of his brothers, including Charles, who founded the Carmelite Order in the United States, and Francis, who was at one time president of Georgetown College. Later he completed the course in theology at Liège and was ordained. On the suppression of the Society he went to England where he labored as a missionary until 1779, when he volunteered for service in Demerara, British Guiana. Here he labored among the pagans and vicious settlers until 1783, then petitioned for removal to the United States. He was captured en route by a British cruiser but apparently freed, for in April 1783 he arrived in Maryland and was welcomed by his family and the group of former Jesuit priests.

While stationed at St. Thomas Manor, he took part in the Whitemarsh meeting which led to a reorganization of the church and to the appointment of John Carroll [*q.v.*] as prefect apostolic. Although Neale was not in favor of the foundation of a college or the establishment of an American bishopric lest it be prejudicial to Jesuit property interests if the Society were revived, he thoroughly approved of Carroll's promotion and was an active participant in the first diocesan synod (1791). Two years later he was sent to Philadelphia during the yellow-fever plague, as pastor of St. Mary's Church and Carroll's vicar-general. As priest and nurse, he was exposed to the fever, but without harm, though in the later epidemic of 1797–98 he fell ill and narrowly escaped death. In 1799, he was selected president of Georgetown College by Carroll. During his régime, ending in 1806, he transformed the school from an academy into a *bona fide* college which soon won a reputation for classical scholarship. When Father Graessl [*q.v.*] died, Carroll with the consent of his clergy urged that Neale be named bishop coadjutor with the right of succession. The bulls of appointment were issued by Pius VI on Apr. 17, 1795, but did not reach Baltimore until 1800. On Dec. 7 of that year Neale was consecrated by Carroll as coadjutor, with the title of bishop of Gortyna.

While nursing the victims of yellow fever in Philadelphia, Neale had been aided by three devoted women, led by Alice Lalor, later Mother Theresa [*q.v.*], who wished to become nuns.

Needham

Upon his removal to Georgetown in 1799 he invited them to establish an academy there. Following him, they lived for a time in a small convent of Poor Clares, of which community Neale's sister, Anne, was a member at Aire in Artois. When the Poor Clares returned to France, Neale purchased their house for his society (1805), which, on the restoration of Pius VII to his freedom and prerogatives in 1816, was finally affiliated with the Visitation Order. The establishment of this community was one of Neale's principal achievements, for the Visitation nuns have since developed into a large body with a number of academies and schools throughout the United States.

As a coadjutor, Neale was not especially active, but apparently Carroll was satisfied with the assurance that the Church's organization would continue under a bishop who would automatically succeed him. Among contemporaries, at least John Thayer, a convert priest, thought Neale a man of no great ability; and James Barry wrote that "there is no danger of Neale setting the Potomac on fire" (Guilday, post, II, 577). When upon the death of Carroll he did succeed to the archbishopric of Baltimore, Dec. 3, 1815, he was too feeble to enjoy his opportunities for distinguished service. He soon petitioned for a coadjutor, and Ambrose Maréchal [q.v.] was appointed, but before the papal briefs arrived, Neale died from a stroke of apoplexy. His remains were interred in the crypt of the Visitation chapel at Georgetown.

[J. G. Shea, *Hist. of the Cath. Ch. in the U. S.* (1888–90), vols. II, III; Peter Guilday, *The Life and Times of John Carroll* (2 vols., 1922); *Cath. Encyc.*, X, (1911), 728; R. H. Clarke, *Lives of the Deceased Bishops of the Cath. Ch. in the U. S.*, vol. I (1888); Mary Paulina Finn (M.S. Pine), *A Glory of Maryland* (1917); Thomas Hughes, *Hist. of the Society of Jesus in North America*, vol. I, pt. I (1908), pt. II (1910); *Messenger* (Georgetown, D. C.), June 23, 1817; manuscript life in the files of the Visitation Academy of Georgetown.]   R.J.P.

NEEDHAM, JAMES (d. September 1673), explorer, a young Englishman, arrived in the southern Carolina settlement from Barbados in September 1670. Possibly he was the son of George Needham, Esq., of Little Wymondley, Hertfordshire, and his wife Barbara Fitch; it is evident that he belonged to a family of some social rank and was a man of education. He soon had a seat on the Ashley River. When Dr. Henry Woodward was sent by Sir John Yeamans in July 1671 to make discoveries in Virginia, Needham may have been one of the company. And when in August of 1672 Woodward was sent by the colonial council to arrest and overtake a traitor who was attempting to escape through the wilderness from Carolina to St. Augustine

in the Spanish Dominions, Needham was named to accompany him. Again when Col. Abraham Wood residing on his plantation at Fort Henry, the present site of Petersburg on the James River, fitted out an expedition to trade with the Indians and discover a passage by water to the southwest, James Needham was selected to head the party. His companion was Gabriel Arthur, an uneducated but very intelligent lad, who was probably an indentured servant of Wood. The party also included eight Indians. The journey was begun from Wood's post on Apr. 10, 1673. Proceeding westward they were turned back by hostile Occaneeches who were encamped on the Roanoke River near the present site of Clarksville. The party reformed and again left Fort Henry in May 1673. They met some friendly Cherokees and safely passed the Occaneechi stronghold and pushed on to the west, crossing nine eastward-flowing streams. Beyond the Yadkin the party struck due west over the North Carolina Blue Ridge Mountains. About two weeks later, after traversing the northwest-flowing headwaters of the New River, they came down into the valley where the water flowed to the southwest and were soon at the main Cherokee village which stood on a high bluff on the headwaters tributary of the Tennessee River, in what is now the state of Tennessee. While Needham was viewing the Valley of the Tennessee as he crossed the Alleghanies, Marquette and Joliet first saw the Tennessee country on their trip down the Mississippi.

While returning from his travels Needham readily effected a treaty with the Cherokees, and leaving Arthur to learn the language of the Indians, returned to Fort Henry accompanied by a band of Cherokees. Wood welcomed him and refitted him for a return trip, which was begun in September 1673. Everything went well until the party passed the Occaneechi village, when on the Yadkin "Indian John," who had been hired as a guide by Wood, fell upon Needham and murdered him in cold blood. So far as is known Needham was the first Englishman to penetrate the domain of the over-hill Cherokees. Of him Wood wrote: "Soe died this heroyick English man whose fame shall never die if my penn were able to eternize it, which had adventured where never any English man had dared to atempt before" (Alvord and Bidgood, post, p. 217).

[There is no available primary source material for information on James Needham. It was through the researches of C. W. Alvord and Lee Bidgood and the subsequent publishing of their findings in a volume entitled *The First Explorations of the Trans-Allegheny Region, . . . 1650–1674* (1912) that Needham's work became known. The account of Needham's travels was found in a letter by Abraham Wood to his friend John Richards, treasurer of the Lords Propri-

401

etors of Carolina in London, dated Aug. 22, 1674. The letter was found with the Shaftsbury Papers, section ix, bundle 48, no. 94, and first appeared in the above-mentioned publication. There is also evidence that Needham left a journal of his expedition but it has been lost for a century. Further printed sources include: S. C. Williams, *Early Travels in the Tenn. Country, 1540–1800* (1928); W. R. Jillson, "The Discovery of Ky.," in *Ky. State Hist. Reg.,* May 1922; *Va. Mag. of Hist. and Biog.,* July 1903; Oct. 1912; Sir Henry Chauncy, *The Hist. Antiquities of Hertfordshire* (1826), II, 111.]   F. W. S.

NEEF, FRANCIS JOSEPH NICHOLAS

(Dec. 6, 1770–Apr. 6, 1854), educator, was born at Soultz, Alsace, the son of Francis Joseph and Anastasia (Ackerman) Neef. His father, a miller who had built up a substantial, thriving business, had hopes of seeing his son in holy orders, but at twenty-one Joseph, as he preferred to style himself, decided that nature had not intended him for the life of the priesthood, and enlisted in the French army under Napoleon. Within a few years, various promotions came to him in recognition of his courage and efficiency. He distinguished himself especially during the Italian campaign. Severely wounded in the battle of Arcole, Nov. 15–19, 1796, he resigned his commission and left the army. After a brief period of wandering, he was engaged by Pestalozzi, in 1799, as a teacher of languages and gymnastics in the famous institution at Burgdorf, in the canton of Berne, Switzerland. Here, July 5, 1803, he married one of his students, Eloisa Buss, sister of the drawing and music master at the school. Later in the same year, when Pestalozzi was asked by a group of French philanthropists to send a teacher to Paris to conduct a school there according to his own ideas, he honored Neef by selecting him for the task. Neef's success at Paris justified his choice. Two years later a similar honor was conferred upon him: during a sojourn in Switzerland in the summer of 1805, William Maclure [q.v.], a wealthy Philadelphian, visited Pestalozzi's school at Yverdun and became so enthusiastic over the methods employed in the classroom that he at once asked Pestalozzi to suggest some one qualified to establish and conduct a similar school in Philadelphia. Following Pestalozzi's recommendation, Maclure called on Neef in Paris, and persuaded him to come to the United States, allowing him two years in which to learn the English language.

Neef came to Philadelphia in 1806, and was so successful in his efforts to master the language that he was able to publish, in 1808, a book entitled *Sketch of a Plan and Method of Education, Founded on an Analysis of the Human Faculties and Natural Reason, Suitable for the Offspring of a Free People and for All Ra-*

tional Beings, frequently called "the first strictly pedagogical work published in the English language in this country" (Carman, *post*). The essence of his master's teaching is clearly and briefly stated: "All possible knowledge, which we shall in any way be able to derive from our senses and immediate sensations, shall be exclusively derived from them. . . . Books, therefore, shall be the last fountain from which we shall endeavor to draw our knowledge." This treatise was followed by *The Logic of Condillac. Tr. by Joseph Neef, as an Illustration of the Plan of Education Established at His School near Philadelphia* (1809). About 1808 or 1809, he established at the Falls of the Schuylkill, some five miles from Philadelphia, the first Pestalozzian school in the United States. During this period, he acquired a small reputation as a naturalist: on June 4, 1812, he was elected a corresponding member of the Academy of Natural Sciences of Philadelphia. In 1813 he removed his school to Village Green, Delaware County, Pa., where he completed his *Method of Instructing Children Rationally in the Arts of Writing and Reading,* published in that year. Among his pupils there was David Glasgow Farragut [q.v.], later admiral in the United States Navy. Financially unsuccessful in Village Green, Neef moved in 1814 to Louisville, Ky., where he maintained a school until 1826. Then, at the invitation of Robert Owen, of New Lanark, Scotland, Neef and his wife took charge of the educational program in the recently founded experimental community at New Harmony, Ind. They taught here until the failure of the venture, two years later. From New Harmony, Neef went to Cincinnati, and then to his last school at Steubenville, Ohio. After a brief period of retirement on a farm in Jeffersonville, Ind., he returned, in 1834, to New Harmony to spend the remainder of his life.

[R. G. Boone, *A Hist. of Educ. in Ind.* (1892); N. A. Calkins, "The History of Object Teaching," *Am. Jour. Educ.,* Dec. 1862; Paul Monroe, *A Cyc. of Educ.* (1912), IV, 404; C. D. Gardette, "Pestalozzi in America," *Galaxy,* Aug. 1867; C. H. Wood, "The First Disciple of Pestalozzi in America," *Indiana School Jour.,* Nov. 1892; W. S. Monroe, *Hist. of the Pestalozzian Movement in the U. S.* (1907), and "Joseph Neef and Pestalozzianism in America," *Education,* Apr. 1894; Ada Carman, "Joseph Neef: A Pestalozzian Pioneer," *Pop. Sci. Mo.,* July 1894; Caroline Dale Snedeker, *The Town of the Fearless* (1931), reminiscences and family traditions recorded by Neef's great-grand-daughter; copy of baptismal certificate, and date of death, from another great-grand-daughter, Mrs. Aline Owen Neal, New Harmony, Ind.; G. B. Lockwood, *The New Harmony Movement* (1905); Robert Dale Owen, *Threading My Way* (1874).]   R. F. S.

NEELY, THOMAS BENJAMIN (June 12, 1841–Sept. 4, 1925), Methodist Episcopal bishop and writer, was born in Philadelphia, Pa., the

son of Thomas and Frances (Armstrong) Neely. He studied at Dickinson Seminary and at Dickinson College, receiving from the latter institution the honorary degree of A.M. in 1875. He was admitted to the Philadelphia Conference of the Methodist Episcopal Church in 1865, and rose rapidly to a position of leadership in that body. He held thirteen pastorates, chiefly in Philadelphia and vicinity, and from 1889 to 1894 was presiding elder. In March 1882 he married Elizabeth Cheney Hickman of Philadelphia.

His talents were most conspicuous in the deliberative assemblies of the Church. In 1884, at the age of forty-two, he was elected to the General Conference, where he seized upon the first opportunity that offered to break lances with the veteran champions of that tilting-ground. A member of the five succeeding quadrennial sessions, also, he came to be recognized as one of the most influential members of that body. Years of indefatigable study of the history, laws, and constitution of the denomination, and of the broad principles which underlie all law, were the foundations of his power. Intense application to the study of special questions equipped him with a reserve fund of information which few of his opponents could match. His mind worked with order and precision in the presentation of his argument. Moreover, his self-control seldom relaxed in the heat of forensic strife, and he was ever ready to thrust the thin blade of fact and logic between the joints of his adversary's armor. The attitude of his mind was conservative. An expression in his maiden speech in the General Conference, "Radical changes should be approached with great caution," was the keynote of his public life, and his habitual caution heightened with the years.

As early as 1888 he began to receive votes for the episcopacy. In 1900, when he failed of election, he was chosen secretary of the Sunday School Union and the Tract Society. In this capacity he traveled widely among the churches, and showed himself to be an intelligent, industrious, and vigorous executive. Numerous improvements were introduced into the educational material of which he was editor. In 1904 he was elected bishop and assigned to Buenos Aires, Argentina. He had been the champion of the party which resisted the High Church theory that the Methodist episcopacy was a distinct order in the ministry. He held that it was but an office to which an ordained elder was commissioned for a special service. His own period of service was a troubled one. He was no longer young, and his field, the South American continent, subjected him to hardships of travel, alti-

tude, and climate. His assertion of authority was not always acceptable among a people unaccustomed to the close supervision of one who conscientiously tried to be "every inch a bishop." In 1908 he was transferred to New Orleans, La., a residence which did not please him and the climate of which perhaps hastened the death of his wife in 1912. His uncompromising assertion of episcopal prerogative in the use of the appointing power in certain annual conferences in the North, where he held temporary assignments, added to the growing feeling of dissatisfaction with him as bishop. At the General Conference of 1912 he was retired by a vote of 496 to 297, no reasons being formally stated. He believed himself to be the victim of injustice, and protested bitterly, though he acquiesced in the decision.

Returning to Philadelphia, he devoted himself to studies which resulted in several learned treatises on Methodist polity and doctrine. He spoke and wrote against Methodist unification, against the idea of granting a degree of autonomy to the churches in mission lands, against uniting with other denominations in the joint support of missionary institutions, and against the ambitious, and, as he believed, disastrous, plans of missionary expansion known as the Centenary Movement (1919) and the Interchurch World Movement. He fired his heaviest guns against the League of Nations. He lacked traits which make for the widest popularity, but his place is assured among American churchmen, as a productive legislator, an acute parliamentarian, an erudite historian, and a worthy expounder and defender of Methodist doctrine and polity. In his long list of published works, the most important are: *Parliamentary Practice* (1883); *The Evolution of Episcopacy and Organic Methodism* (1888); *A History of the Origin and Development of the Governing Conference in Methodism* (1892); *The Bishops and the Supervisional System of the Methodist Episcopal Church* (1912); *The Minister in the Itinerant System* (1914); *American Methodism, Its Divisions and Unification* (1915); *Doctrinal Standards of Methodism* (1918); *The League—the Nation's Danger* (1919); *Present Perils of Methodism* (1920); *The Only Condition* (1920); *The Methodist Episcopal Church and Its Foreign Missions* (1923).

[R. C. Wells, in *Jour. of the General Conference of the M. E. Ch.*, 1928; *Christian Advocate* (N. Y.), Sept. 17, 1925; *Who's Who in America*, 1924–25; *Public Ledger* (Phila.), Sept. 6, 1925.]   J.R.J.

NEF, JOHN ULRIC (June 14, 1862–Aug. 13, 1915), chemist, the eldest son of Johann Ulric Nef and Katherine (Mock) Nef, was born in

Herisau, Switzerland. In 1864, his father came to the United States and was employed as superintendent of a textile factory in Housatonic, Mass. Four years later the family joined him and they settled on a farm near Housatonic. John attended school at Great Barrington, four miles from his home, walking each way daily. He had one year in a high school in New York City. Funds were meager, and during the summers he worked diligently on the farm. In 1880 he entered Harvard with the intention of studying medicine but soon became fascinated with chemistry and proved to be so brilliant a student that in 1884 he was awarded the Kirkland Traveling Fellowship. After his graduation he went to Munich and began studying at once under Adolph von Baeyer, receiving the degree of doctor of philosophy in 1886. His thesis, entitled *Ueber Benzochinoncarbonsäuren,* treated of the compounds related to succinosuccinic-ethyl-ester.

In 1887 he returned to the United States as professor of chemistry at Purdue University. Two years later he went to Clark University as assistant professor of chemistry and was made acting head of the department shortly afterward, following the resignation of Professor Michael. Here he remained until 1892, when he responded to the invitation of President Harper to organize and head the department of chemistry at the University of Chicago. This position he held until his death. It was at Chicago that he met Louise Bates Comstock who became one of his students, and his wife on May 17, 1898. She died Mar. 20, 1909. To them one son was born.

Nef was small of stature, with a massive brow and bright, penetrating eyes. He had an all-consuming and contagious love for his science. The rapidity of his thought so outdistanced the speed of his words that his students could take only sketchy notes which they would later piece out and amplify in order to get the full value of his lectures. His restless enthusiasm for the problems in which he was engrossed developed in him an appearance of brusqueness which amounted almost to impatience when the research did not progress smoothly. Back of this intellectual eagerness, however, dwelt kindly human qualities. He was by temperament intense and found his relaxation in long walks which he pursued at an uncompanionable speed. He loved music and was a weekly attendant during the season of the concerts of the Chicago Symphony Orchestra. He died of heart disease at Carmel, Cal., while traveling with his son.

Nef's pioneer work on bivalent carbon, on the fulminates, on the sugars, on the mechanism of organic reactions, and on many other subjects contributed greatly to the advance of chemical knowledge. It was his signal research at Purdue University on the structure of quinone which led to his call to Clark University. This work forms a very important part of the chemistry of dyes and is universally accepted. As a result of his research in organic chemistry, he published thirty-seven independent articles, most of which were written in German. Thirty-six others represent work carried on under him, twenty-eight of which were the theses of those taking the doctorate of philosophy with him. He may be said to have stood for an individual school of thought in organic chemistry, a fact recognized by its separate treatment in advanced texts in this field, but he never assembled his theories of organic chemistry in a single volume, nor wrote a textbook. His scientific papers may be found scattered through *Justus Liebig's Annalen der Chemie* from vol. CCLXX (Apr. 27, 1892) to vol. CCCCIII (Sept. 28, 1913) and *Berichte der Deutschen Chemischen Gesellschaft.* His students Hedenburg and Glattfeld assembled after his death the remaining unpublished results of his researches, and published them in the *Journal of the American Chemical Society,* August 1917. Articles prepared in collaboration with his students appeared in the *American Chemical Journal* and the *Journal of the American Chemical Society* during the period of his active work.

[The chief sources for the above sketch are a memorial by Prof. L. W. Jones in the *Proc. Am. Chem. Soc.,* 1917 (incorporated in *Jour. Am. Chem. Soc.,* Feb. 1917), and personal acquaintance. See also Julius Stieglitz, "John Ulric Nef," in *Univ. of Chi. Mag.,* Nov. 1915; *San Francisco Chronicle,* Aug. 14, 1915. A biography by Prof. Stieglitz for the *Memoirs of the National Academy of Sciences* is in course of preparation.]
W.L.L.

NEGLEY, JAMES SCOTT (Dec. 22, 1826–Aug. 7, 1901), Union soldier, congressman, and railway executive, was born in East Liberty, Allegheny County, Pa., the son of Jacob and Mary Ann (Scott) Negley. On his paternal side he was descended from Swiss-German ancestors who spelled the name Nägeli. From the public schools he went to the Western University of Pennsylvania, the institution later known as the University of Pittsburgh. On the outbreak of war with Mexico, as a member of the Duquesne Grays, he entered the 1st Pennsylvania Regiment. Mustered into service, Dec. 16, 1846, he served throughout the remainder of the war, rose to the rank of sergeant, and was honorably discharged, July 25, 1848. On his return to civilian life, he engaged for a time in business, but soon took up the pursuit of horticulture in which he became well known. Meanwhile, maintaining his connection with the local militia, he was elected brigadier-general of the 18th Division, Pennsylvania Militia. At the beginning of the hostilities of the Civil War in April 1861 he was placed in command of military affairs in Pittsburgh, where the vigor with which he organized and equipped forces gave great satisfaction.

In the summer of 1861 he served under Maj.-Gen. Robert Patterson in Pennsylvania, Maryland, and Virginia, and on the disbandment of his three months' volunteer troops, returned to Pittsburgh where he raised a new brigade which in October was sent to Kentucky. Under General Buell he played an important part in the movements in central Tennessee and northern Alabama in the summer of 1862, at one time threatening the capture of Chattanooga. But on the dramatic Confederate advance across Tennessee into Kentucky late in the summer, he was drawn back by Buell and left in command of Nashville, where he ably held his position until the return of the Union forces. In the midwinter battle of Stone River, he commanded the Union center and by conspicuous skill and gallantry won promotion to the rank of major-general. He again figured prominently in the advance of General Rosecrans against Chattanooga in the autumn of 1863, but in the battle of Chickamauga, along with other commanders on the right wing of the Union line, he was swept back from the battlefield. Criticized by Generals John M. Brannan and Thomas J. Wood, he was relieved from command by General Rosecrans. Appeals to the latter's successors were in vain and, though a court of inquiry cleared him of the charges of cowardice and desertion (*Official Records*, 1 ser. XXX, pt. 1, pp. 1004–53), he failed to secure reassignment to command. He resigned from the army Jan. 19, 1865. He always bore resentment for the way he had been treated and said it was due to jealousy between West Pointers and "civilian soldiers." (See *Congressional Globe*, 41 Cong., 2 Sess., p. 1850.)

Returning to Pittsburgh, Negley again entered business. He was elected to Congress in 1868 on the Republican ticket and was reëlected in 1870, 1872, and 1884. In Congress he was an ardent Republican and a faithful representative of his constituency. He presented many petitions in favor of tariff protection and supported this policy in votes and speeches. His chief interest, however, was inland waterways, and he several times introduced bills for the improvement of navigation of the Ohio, Monongahela, and Allegheny rivers. He also introduced a bill "to complete a water highway from tidewater

on the James river to the Ohio river at the mouth of the Kanawha" (*Congressional Globe,* 42 Cong., 3 Sess., p. 83).

In the interval between the Forty-third and Forty-ninth congresses, Negley resided in Pittsburgh. In local administration he was made gas inspector, while in business he was vice-president of the Pittsburg, New Castle, & Lake Erie Railroad in 1879, and president of the New York, Pittsburgh & Chicago Railway in 1884–85. During his final term in Congress, while maintaining his earlier activities, he displayed particular interest in the National Home for Disabled Volunteer Soldiers (*Congressional Record,* 49 Cong., 2 Sess., p. 611), of which he later became one of the managers. Defeated for the Republican nomination in 1886, by John Dalzell, he removed to New York, where he organized the Railroad Supply Company with which he was still connected at the time of his death at his home in Plainfield, N. J., Aug. 7, 1901. He was twice married. By his first wife, Kate de Losey, whom he married in 1848, he had three sons who predeceased him. By his second wife, Grace Ashton, he left three daughters. He was a man of large physique and fine appearance, affable and urbane, but of an independent spirit.

[J. W. Jordan, *Encyc. of Pa. Biog.*, vol. V (1915); *Biog. Dir. Am. Cong.* (1928); *Who's Who in America,* 1901–02; A. P. James, "Gen. Jas. Scott Negley," *Western Pa. Hist. Mag.*, Apr. 1931; memoriam obituary in the *Year Book of the Pa. Soc. of N. Y.*, 1902; *War of the Rebellion: Official Records (Army)*; Pittsburgh directories, 1856–87; the Pittsburgh *Post*, the title of which varies, for Dec. 18, 1846, July 18, 26, 1848, Apr. 15–25, 1861, Aug. 8, 1901; inscription on tombstone, Allegheny Cemetery, Pittsburgh.]

A.P.J.

NEHRLING, HENRY (May 9, 1853–Nov. 22, 1929), ornithologist, horticulturist, was born in the town of Herman, near Howard's Grove, Sheboygan County, Wis., the son of Carl and Elizabeth (Ruge) Nehrling. His family on both sides was of German descent. His early education was received from his mother and grandfather and he was later sent to a Lutheran parochial school situated several miles from his home. His daily walks to and from school through what was then primeval forest familiarized him with every aspect of nature and helped to develop the passionate love for the outdoors—especially for birds and flowers—that was to characterize his entire life. From 1869 to 1873 he attended the State Normal School at Addison, Ill., and upon graduation taught in various towns in Illinois, Missouri, and Texas. In 1887 he accepted an appointment as deputy collector and inspector of customs at the port of Milwaukee, a

Nehrling

position which he held until 1890 when he became secretary and custodian of the Public Museum of Milwaukee, a post much more to his liking. During his connection with the museum he made many important additions to the collections and laid the foundations for the future usefulness of the institution. Owing to politics, a factor with which he was unable to cope, he lost his position in 1903 after several years of service.

As early as 1884 Nehrling had bought a tract of land at Gotha, Fla., not far from Orlando. Thither he now repaired after a short association with the Philadelphia Commercial Museum. Always a lover of flowers, he had become somewhat of a horticulturist and during his residence in Milwaukee had built a greenhouse and had interested himself in growing various tropical plants, an interest greatly stimulated by the horticultural exhibits at the Columbian Exposition at Chicago. He now set about more seriously and developed a notable botanic garden, devoting himself particularly to the breeding of the amaryllis and caladium of which he developed many new forms while he maintained a correspondence with horticulturists in all parts of the world. In view of his outstanding knowledge of the subject he was appointed a collaborator of the Bureau of Plant Industry of the United States Department of Agriculture in 1906 and at the convention of garden clubs in Miami in 1929 was awarded the Meyer Medal for distinguished service in his field. Unfortunately, like many another gifted scientist, he lacked business sense, and was constantly in financial difficulties, losing, in the end, his gardens and practically all of his other worldly possessions. Worry over his losses brought on the breakdown that resulted in his death.

Nehrling was married on July 20, 1874, to Sophia Schoff of Oak Park, Ill., and had a family of seven children. After the death of his wife (1911), he married, June 7, 1916, Mrs. Betty B. Mitchell. His outstanding publication was his *Die Nordamerikanische Vogelwelt*, published in Germany. An English edition appeared simultaneously in America under the title: *North American Birds* (1889–93), later changed to *Our Native Birds of Song and Beauty* (2 vols., 1893–97), illustrated with colored plates by German and American artists. This work was designed to fill the gap between the very expensive and the merely technical ornithological books. He also published many popular articles on North American birds in various journals and newspapers in Germany and America and an account of the birds of various parts of Texas, in the *Bulletin of the Nuttall Ornithological Club* (January,

Neidhard

July, October 1882), an important volume entitled *Die Amaryllis* (1908). He was not primarily a scientist but rather a man of high literary attainments with a broad knowledge of birds and plants, an intense lover of the beautiful in nature with an ambition to impart that interest to others regardless of the cost to himself. In personality he was of a lovable and kindly disposition but with a child-like lack of business acumen.

[J. M. and Jaques Cattell, *Am. Men of Science* (1927); *Who's Who in America*, 1928–29; the *Auk*, Jan. 1930; letters from Nehrling's friends, and a brief personal acquaintance.]

W. S.

NEIDHARD, CHARLES (Apr. 19, 1809–Apr. 17, 1895), pioneer homeopathist and physician, was born at Bremen, Germany, the son of Friedrich Neidhard and his wife, the daughter of Prof. David Christoph Seybold. He came of an old and distinguished patrician family of Ulm, in the Cathedral of which town is the Neidhard Chapel more than five hundred years old. His grandfather was a Lutheran bishop of eminence; in the Austrian branch of the family was Cardinal Nithard, who later became prime minister of Spain. His father died when Charles was six years old. His mother then married Professor Georg Friedrich List [q.v.] of Württemberg, a distinguished political economist. The boy's early education was obtained at the Buxweiler College, in Alsace, and at the Gymnasium at Stuttgart. His career at the latter institution was interrupted summarily at the end of the first year, that is in 1825, because List had incurred the displeasure of the government and was banished, whereupon he soon removed to America. Neidhard accompanied his step-father and shortly after his arrival in America began the study of medicine in the office of a physician at Reading, Pa. He took two courses in the Philadelphia Medical Institute, two years of clinical lectures at the Pennsylvania Hospital, Philadelphia, and three and one-half courses at the University of Pennsylvania. Through his arduous studies he became broken in health. Regular treatment proving unavailing he consulted Dr. William Wesselhoeft, of Bath, Pa. The result was good and Neidhard became a convert to homeopathy. In 1834 he accompanied his step-father to Leipzig, Saxony, to which city the latter had been appointed United States consul. While there he continued his studies and joined the Leipzig Medical Society in 1835 and later graduated at Jena. He returned to America in 1836 and took up the practice of homeopathy, which he continued up to the time of his death.

In 1837 Neidhard was graduated from the Al-

406

lentown Homœopathic Medical College. In 1839, associated with Dr. Constantine Hering and Dr. Walter Williamson, he organized and incorporated the Hahnemann Medical College of Pennsylvania. For the first three years of the institution's existence he held the chair of clinical medicine. He then resigned from the faculty because facilities for clinical instruction had been afforded in the hospital. In 1862 he received the honorary degree of M.D. from the Hahnemann Medical College of Chicago. He was one of the charter members of the American Institute of Homeopathy and for many years was very active in the work of various scientific committees. He was by nature a studious man and possessed strong literary tastes. He was an associate editor of the *American Journal of Homeopathy* in 1838 and a co-editor of the *North American Journal of Homeopathy* from 1862 to 1868. He was a voluminous contributor to various homeopathic medical journals. He published provings of realgar, calcarea phosphorica, cinnabaris, oxalic acid, oleum jecoris asseli, antimonium sulphuratum auratum, cannabis indica, formic acid, mephitis putorius, rhus tox., sanguinaria, phytolacca decandra, tarentula, balsam of Peru, and calcarea arsenica. His most notable contributions to literature were *Neidhard on Diptheria, as it Prevailed in the United States from 1860 to 1866* (1867), and *On the Efficacy of Crotalus Horridus in Yellow Fever* (1860, 1868), both of which were leading authorities of their day.

Neidhard was ordinary and corresponding member of the medical societies of Leipzig, Paris, Munich, Brazil, and of the state societies of Massachusetts and Rhode Island. He built up a large practice in Philadelphia. As a physician he exhibited a kind personality, was ever observant of phenomena of illness. He died of heart disease, suddenly, on Apr. 17, 1895. He had married Isabella Taylor, the daughter of Richard Taylor, an English geologist. They had five daughters. His sole interests in life were his patients and the promotion of the organization of homeopathy as a healing art. Though an intense believer in his school of medicine, he was always tolerant of the views of others.

[T. L. Bradford, *Homœopathic Bibliog. of the U. S.* (1892), *Hist. of the Homœopathic Medic. Coll. of Phila.* (1898), and "Biogs. of Homœopathic Physicians," vol. XXIII, in the library of the Hahnemann Medic. Coll. of Phila.; *Trans. Fifty-first Session Am. Inst. of Homœopathy*, 1895; T. L. Montgomery, *Encyc. of Pa. Biog.*, vol. XIV (1923); *Pub. Ledger* (Phila.), Apr. 18, 1895; personal acquaintance.] C. B—t.

NEIGHBORS, ROBERT SIMPSON (Nov. 3, 1815–Sept. 14, 1859), Texas pioneer, Indian agent, was a native of Virginia. He went from Louisiana to Texas, either in 1833 or in 1837; but as there is evidence that he was in the Texas army at San Jacinto the earlier date seems more probably correct. He was a man of imposing personality, tall, and notable for his courage, energy, and strength of character. In January 1840 he was commissioned a lieutenant in the Texas army and in December 1841 was made a captain. He was one of the prisoners taken by the Mexican General Woll in the raid upon San Antonio in 1842 and was confined in Castle Perote, Mexico, for two years. In February 1845 he was appointed sub-agent of the Republic of Texas for the Lipan and Tonkawa Indians. In May 1846 he was a state commissioner to a great council on the upper Brazos at which the United States commissioners, P. M. Butler and M. G. Lewis, made a treaty with the Comanche and other wild tribes. After this he conducted a delegation of Indian chiefs to Washington to visit President Polk. In 1847 he was commissioned special agent of the United States for the Texas Indians with instructions to go out among the tribes, keep them friendly but away from the settlements, prevent the sale of intoxicating liquors to them, and keep the whites from intruding into the Indian country. This extremely difficult task he performed well, but entire success was impossible since the United States did not extend its Indian intercourse laws over Texas, the state owned the public lands and granted them to settlers who constantly encroached upon the Indian country, and the loose authority of the chiefs could not restrain the warriors from depredations. He made long visits to the Indians, studied them carefully, and sent in reports that constitute the most reliable information extant of the tribes in Texas, especially of the Comanche, for that period.

He was removed from office by the Whig administration in 1849, and in the spring of that year he led an expedition to locate a route from Austin to El Paso. Early in 1850 Governor Bell sent him to organize new counties in the El Paso-Santa Fé region; but because of the attitude of the federal authorities, who disputed the jurisdiction of Texas, he could accomplish nothing. His report to the governor caused great excitement in Texas and almost brought about a conflict of arms. In 1851 he was a member of the Texas legislature from San Antonio, and the next year he was a Democratic presidential elector. In 1853 he returned to his former post as general United States agent for the Texas Indians. His advocacy of reservations for the Indians resulted in an agreement between the state and federal governments for two reservations on the upper Brazos; and, with the aid of Capt. Randolph Barnes Marcy, he selected the sites and induced the smaller tribes to settle on one and a portion of the Comanche on the other. However, the experiment proved an unhappy one, for the white settlements soon spread to the neighborhood and the wild prairie tribes continued their depredations. The incensed settlers came to believe the reservation Indians guilty of the raids and, under a group of reckless leaders, threatened to attack them. After trying in vain to settle the difficulty, he recommended that the Indians be removed from Texas into the Indian Territory, and in the summer of 1859 he led the more peaceful tribes to their new homes. The Comanche on the upper reserve returned to the prairies and to the war-path. On his return to Fort Belknap in Texas to wind up the affairs of his agency, he was assassinated by an outlaw. He left a wife and two small children.

[Photostats from files of the Office of Indian Affairs, Neighbors Papers, Maverick Papers, and manuscript Memoirs of John S. Ford in Univ. of Texas Lib.; Texas Indian Papers in Texas State Lib., Austin; *Texas Almanac,* 1859, p. 130; R. B. Marcy, *Thirty Years of Army Life* (1866), pp. 170–223; W. B. Parker, *Notes Taken ... through Unexplored Texas* (1856), esp. pp. 116, 130–31, 139, 152, 168, 237–38; R. N. Richardson, *The Comanche Barrier* (1933); W. C. Binkley, *The Expansionist Movement in Texas* (1925); *Southwestern Hist. Quart.,* Apr., Oct. 1925, Oct. 1927; *State Gazette* (Austin, Tex.), esp. Sept. 24, 1859; information from Mrs. Alice Atkinson Neighbors, grand-daughter-in-law.]   C. W. R.

NEILL, EDWARD DUFFIELD (Aug. 9, 1823–Sept. 26, 1893), clergyman, educator, historian, a brother of John and Thomas Hewson Neill [*qq.v.*], was born in Philadelphia, Pa., the son of Dr. Henry and Martha R. (Duffield) Neill. After two years at the University of Pennsylvania, he went to Amherst College in 1839 and was graduated in 1842. He then spent a year in Andover Theological Seminary and completed his theological studies in Philadelphia. In 1847 he was licensed by the presbytery of Galena, Ill., to preach among the lead-miners of the vicinity. In the same year, on Oct. 4, he was married to Nancy, daughter of Richard Hall. On Apr. 26, 1848, he was ordained, and a year later he went to St. Paul, Minnesota Territory, where he established the First Presbyterian Church, of which he was pastor, 1849–54. From 1851 to 1863 he was secretary of the Minnesota Historical Society and contributed numerous articles to its *Collections.* From 1855 to 1860 he was pastor of the House of Hope Presbyterian Church, which he had organized. He promoted education as well as religion: he helped establish public schools in St. Paul, was the first

superintendent of instruction for Minnesota Territory, 1851–53, founded and became president of the Baldwin School and the College of St. Paul, both abortive institutions, was chancellor of the state university, 1858–61—at this time a university without students—and state superintendent of public instruction, 1860–61. In 1858 he published the first edition of his *History of Minnesota.*

In the next decade Neill's activities lay outside of Minnesota. He was chaplain of the First Minnesota Infantry, 1861–62, and United States Army hospital chaplain in Philadelphia, 1862–64. From February 1864 to 1869 he served as assistant secretary to Presidents Lincoln and Johnson, after which he was consul in Dublin for two years. These various services gave him opportunity for historical research which resulted in his most important works, *Terra Mariæ; or, Threads of Maryland Colonial History* (1867), *History of the Virginia Company of London* (1869), and *The English Colonization of America during the 17th Century* (1871). Returning home, Neill flung himself again into educational projects. In 1872 he opened in Minneapolis "Jesus College," a religious but nonsectarian institution, with himself as provost. This being unsuccessful, he persuaded Charles Macalester of Philadelphia to give a building, contingent upon the raising of an endowment fund, for a Christian but nonsectarian college. The fund was raised, and in 1874 Macalester College was started with Neill as president. In the same year he deserted the Presbyterians to become "presbyter in charge" of Calvary Reformed Episcopal Church. In 1880 Macalester College was transferred to the control of the Presbyterian synod, in 1883 it was removed to St. Paul, and in 1884 Neill resigned as president. From 1885 until his death he occupied the chair of history, English literature, and political economy, and for some years he was also librarian. He published two volumes of *Macalester College Contributions* (series 1 and 2, 1890–92), containing papers on historical subjects.

Neill's works are lacking in organization and interpretation and have been largely superseded, but he made valuable contributions to historical knowledge by bringing to light important documentary material. In education he was rather the promoter than the successful administrator, with more versatility than tenacity of purpose. In an era of beginnings in Minnesota this versatility was not to his disadvantage. It enabled him to turn from one venture to the next with undiminished enthusiasm and faith in his own abilities. He is noteworthy as a prophet of the

Neill

mind and spirit at a time when most of his associates were preoccupied with material things.

[W. W. Folwell, *A Hist. of Minn.*, vol. IV (1930); Warren Upham, memoir in *Minn. Hist. Colls.*, vol. VIII (1898); H. D. Funk, *A Hist. of Macalester Coll.* (1910); E. D. Neill, *John Neill of Lewes, Del., 1739, and His Descendants* (1875); *Obit. Record of Grads. of Amherst Coll., for the Academical Year Ending June 27, 1894* (1894). The Neill papers of the Minn. Hist. Soc. are described in *Minn. Hist. Bull.*, Aug. 1916.] S. J. B.

NEILL, JOHN (July 9, 1819–Feb. 11, 1880), surgeon, brother of Edward Duffield and Thomas Hewson Neill [*qq.v.*], was born in Philadelphia, Pa., the son of Dr. Henry and Martha R. (Duffield) Neill, and a grandson of Dr. Benjamin Duffield, one of the founders of the College of Physicians of Philadelphia. He was descended from John Neill who probably emigrated from Tyrone, County Ulster, Ireland, to America about 1739. He was graduated from the University of Pennsylvania in 1837, with the degree of A.B., and in 1840 received the degree of M.D. He then made a voyage to the West Indies, in charge of a patient, and in 1842 returned to his native city to begin practice. In the autumn of the same year he was made an assistant demonstrator, and in 1845 he became demonstrator of anatomy, in the medical department of the University of Pennsylvania. In 1849, during the epidemic of cholera in Philadelphia, he contracted the disease, probably while making postmortem examinations of patients in the Southeast Cholera Hospital. In 1852 he was elected surgeon to the Pennsylvania Hospital, but he resigned this position in 1859. From 1854 to 1859 he was professor of surgery in the medical department of Pennsylvania College; he was also for some years surgeon to the Philadelphia Hospital at Blockley.

During the Civil War Neill's enterprise and activity were much in evidence. On the day of the announcement of the fall of Fort Sumter, he drove about the city in search of public buildings adaptable to hospital purposes. He found such a place on Christian Street above Ninth and obtained permission from the mayor of the city to take possession of it. Later, with authority obtained from the surgeon-general of the army, he established there the first United States Military Hospital in Philadelphia. About the same time, upon the organization of the home guard, Neill was appointed medical director of that body. In 1863, upon the invasion of Pennsylvania by Lee's army, he was appointed medical director of the forces from the state, and, under Gen. William F. Smith, he established military hospitals at Carlisle and Pine Grove, Pa., and at Hagerstown, Md. In 1862

he had been given rank as surgeon of volunteers, and in 1863, for meritorious services in the Gettysburg campaign, he was brevetted lieutenant-colonel.

In 1874 Neill was elected to the chair of clinical surgery in the University of Pennsylvania, but it appears that he was not entirely in sympathy with the removal of the University to West Philadelphia, and he resigned his chair the next year. About this time he lost his eyesight and remained totally blind until his death. Early in life he acquired a certain popularity with medical students, not only by his "quiz" classes, but by the publication of three little books with colored figures, on the arteries, the veins, and the nerves, and by the compilation, in conjunction with Dr. Francis Gurney Smith, of *An Analytical Compendium of the Various Branches of Medical Science* (1848). It is said that in later life he frequently expressed regret that "he had ever been connected with a publication, however successful, which contributed so largely to make medical education superficial" (Shippen, *post*, p. cliv). He published in 1852 *The Principles and Practice of Surgery*, an American edition of the work of William Pirrie, and just before his last illness is said to have projected an original work on the principles of surgery. He is remembered more for his work during the war than for his activities in civil life. He left a reputation of not getting along well with his colleagues, and of being always dissatisfied with the positions he held. He invented an apparatus for the treatment of fractures of the leg and modified Desault's splint for fractures of the femur. He died in Philadelphia in his sixty-first year. He had married, Sept. 24, 1844, Anna Maria Wharton Hollingsworth, daughter of Samuel Hollingsworth.

[Edward Shippen, "Memoir of John Neill, M.D.," *Trans. Coll. of Physicians of Phila.*, 3 ser. V (1881); T. G. Morton and Frank Woodbury, *The Hist. of the Pa. Hospital* (1895); H. A. Kelly and W. L. Burrage, *Am. Medic. Biogs.* (1920); E. D. Neill, *John Neill of Lewes, Del., 1739, and His Descendants* (1875); *Proc. Am. Phil. Soc.*, vol. XIX (1882); *Phila. Medic. Times*, Feb. 28, 1880; the *Press* (Phila.), Feb. 12, 1880.] A. P. C. A.

NEILL, THOMAS HEWSON (Apr. 9, 1826–Mar. 12, 1885), soldier, was born in Philadelphia, Pa., a brother of John and Edward Duffield Neill [*qq.v.*] and the son of Dr. Henry and Martha R. (Duffield) Neill. After an elementary education in the public schools of his native city, he entered the University of Pennsylvania, but left that institution at the close of his sophomore year. On July 1, 1843, he was appointed a cadet at the United States Military Academy. Commissioned brevet second lieutenant of infantry,

July 1, 1847, he was regularly promoted through the intermediate grades and made captain on Apr. 1, 1857. During the Mexican War he served in garrison, and on the frontier until 1853 when he became assistant professor of drawing at the Military Academy, continuing in this capacity till 1857. He was with the Utah expedition in 1858 and remained in the West until 1861, when he was made mustering officer at Philadelphia.

Throughout the Civil War he rendered notable service, which received appropriate recognition. During Patterson's campaign on the upper Potomac in the summer of 1861 he was on General Cadwalader's staff. Commissioned colonel of volunteers on Feb. 17, 1862, he assumed command of the 23rd Pennsylvania Infantry and served with his regiment in McClellan's Peninsular campaign (March to August 1862). For gallantry in the battle of Malvern Hill he was brevetted, July 1, major, regular army. He took part in the Antietam campaign, but his regiment did not participate in the battle of Antietam. Made a brigadier-general of volunteers on Nov. 29, 1862, he assumed command at Fredericksburg, after its previous commander had been wounded, of the 3rd Brigade, 2nd Division, VI Army Corps. At Chancellorsville he took part in the operations of Sedgwick's VI Corps. With his brigade he participated in the assault on Marye's Heights, May 3, 1863, and on the following day defended the rear of Sedgwick's position at Salem Church, for which service he was brevetted lieutenant-colonel in the regular army. After a forced march of over thirty miles, his brigade reached Gettysburg on the afternoon of July 2, 1863, and supported elements of the I and XII corps on Cemetery Hill. The following day he held the extreme right of the Union line. During the pursuit of Lee, he commanded a division made up of his own brigade and McIntosh's cavalry brigade. On May 7, 1864, at the battle of the Wilderness, after General Getty was wounded, he took command of the 2nd Division, VI Corps. He was brevetted colonel, regular army, for gallantry at Spotsylvania and participated in the Cold Harbor and Petersburg campaigns. On June 21, 1864, he was transferred to the staff of the XVIII Army Corps, where he served until Sept. 12; then joining Sheridan's army in the Shenandoah Valley, he commanded the base at Martinsburg and served as an inspector. Later he was on duty in Washington, D. C., and in command of Fort Independence. On Mar. 13, 1865, he was brevetted brigadier-general, regular army, and major-general of volunteers for gallant and meri-

torious service during the Civil War. He reverted, Aug. 24, 1865, to the rank of major, 11th Infantry, to which he had been promoted Aug. 26, 1863.

After the war he served in various capacities until Feb. 22, 1869, when he was promoted to lieutenant-colonel. The following year, Dec. 15, he was transferred to the 6th Cavalry and went to the frontier to take part in the Indian campaigns. From 1875 to 1879 he was commandant at West Point, and on Apr. 2 of the latter year was made colonel of the 6th Cavalry. He retired from active service, Apr. 2, 1883, for disability contracted in line of duty, and died in Philadelphia almost two years later. His wife, whom he married, Nov. 20, 1873, was Eva D. Looney, and he was survived by one of their three children.

[War Department records; *War of the Rebellion: Official Records (Army)*; F. B. Heitman, *Hist. Reg. and Dict. U. S. Army* (1903); G. W. Cullum, *Biog. Reg. Officers and Grads. U. S. Mil. Acad.* (3rd ed., 1891), vol. II; *Sixteenth Ann. Reunion Asso. Grads. U. S. Mil. Acad.* (1885); S. P. Bates, *Martial Deeds of Pa.* (1875); G. J. Fiebeger, *Campaigns of the Am. Civil War* (1914); *Press* (Phila.), Mar. 13, 14, 1885; E. D. Neill, *Hist. Notes on the Ancestry and Descendants of Henry Neill, M.D.* (1886).]   H. O. S.

NEILL, WILLIAM (d. Aug. 8, 1860), Presbyterian clergyman and educator, was born near McKeesport, Pa., in 1778 or 1779, his family later fixing Apr. 25 as the probable day. His father, also William Neill, who was of Irish descent and had removed with his family from Lancaster County about 1775, was killed by Indians on his farm during William's infancy. The mother, Jane (Snodgrass) Neill, of Scottish ancestry, rapidly failed in health, and died when the boy was not more than four years old. After a boyhood in the homes of relatives, and several years' attendance at country schools, he became clerk of a country store in Canonsburg. Without early religious training, as an adolescent he was influenced by the pioneer minister, Rev. John McMillan, was deeply affected by a two months' illness, and later was led to attend prayer meetings at Canonsburg Academy by some of the students. In 1797 he entered the academy, determined to become a minister, and in 1800 enrolled in the College of New Jersey, from which he graduated in 1803. Thereafter for two years he was tutor in the college and studied theology under Dr. Henry Kollock, pastor of the church at Princeton.

Licensed by the Presbytery of New Brunswick in 1805, he immediately took charge of the Presbyterian church at Cooperstown, N. Y. There he was tutor of Samuel and James Feni-

Neill

more, sons of Judge William Cooper. From Cooperstown, in 1809, Neill went to Albany to succeed Dr. John B. Romeyn as pastor of the church attended by the governor and several state judges. Both at Albany and at Philadelphia, where he took charge of the Sixth Church in 1816, he was notably successful in Bible-class work. The Albany class was one of the first formed in the United States. He believed that he influenced more people to join the church by his teaching in these classes than by his preaching. He succeeded John M. Mason [q.v.] as president of Dickinson College in 1824, serving for about five years. Like his predecessor he encountered serious difficulties, due largely to the partial control over the institution exercised by the state legislature. During his administration, however, the attendance and faculty were doubled. From 1829 to 1831 he performed laborious pioneer work as secretary of the board of education of the Presbyterian Church, and from 1831 to 1842 was stated supply of the church at Germantown.

Returning to Philadelphia, he was a volunteer city missionary, supplying vacant pulpits and ministering to the Widows' Asylum, a Magdalen Asylum, and other charitable institutions. During this period he published his *Lectures on Biblical History* (1846) and his *Practical Exposition of the Epistle to the Ephesians* (1850). He issued also some occasional discourses and other small publications. He married, Oct. 5, 1805, Elizabeth Van Dyke of Princeton, who died in 1809; on Feb. 25, 1811, Frances, daughter of Gen. Joshua King of Connecticut, who died in 1832; and on Apr. 15, 1835, Sarah, daughter of Dr. Ebenezer Elmer of Bridgeton, N. J. There were two children by the first marriage, three by the second, and two by the third. He was moderator of the Presbyterian General Assembly in 1815, helped organize the American Bible Society, and was a director of Princeton Theological Seminary from its founding. Ranking among the more distinguished clergymen of his time, he was known as a man of unselfish and beneficent disposition, unusually attractive manner, and direct, methodical, and persuasive preaching.

[J. H. Jones, *Autobiog. of William Neill, D.D., with a Selection from His Sermons* (1861), including a sermon on Neill's life and character; Neill's *Discourse Reviewing a Ministry of Fifty Years* (1857); W. B. Sprague, *Presbyterian Reunion: A Memorial Vol.* (1870); E. H. Gillett, *Hist. of the Presbyterian Church in the U. S. A.* (2 vols., 1864); Alfred Nevin, *Encyc. of the Presbyterian Church in the U. S. A.* (1884); J. M. Wilson, *The Presbyterian Hist. Almanac,* 1861; *The Centennial Memorial of the Presbytery of Carlisle* (2 vols., 1889); *Phila. Daily News,* Aug. 11, 1860.] P. P. F.

Neilson

NEILSON, JOHN (Mar. 11, 1745–Mar. 3, 1833), officer in the Revolution and member of the Continental Congress, was born at Raritan Landing, near New Brunswick, N. J., the only son of Dr. John Neilson, who came to America from Belfast, Ireland, and Joanna Coejeman, of the Albany family of that name. Losing his father when he was but eight days old, he was adopted by his uncle, James Neilson, a shipping merchant in New Brunswick. He was brought up in the business and later succeeded to it. On Dec. 31, 1768, he married Catherine, daughter of John and Catherine (Schuyler) Voorhees, of the same city. On the outbreak of the Revolutionary War, "bitterly resenting the attempt of a venal Parliament, bought by an oppressive ministry, to tax his country," he raised a company of militia, was appointed its captain, and was called into service at the east end of Long Island under General Heard, to disarm the Loyalists. On Aug. 31, 1775, he was appointed by the Provincial Congress colonel of a battalion of Minute Men of Middlesex County. Early the next year he was urged to take a seat in the Continental Congress but declined, believing he could be more useful in the military service of the state. He read in public the Declaration of Independence when it first appeared and then began recruiting for the army. In August 1776 he was appointed colonel of the 2nd Regiment, Middlesex militia, and served with it in Essex and Bergen counties, where the Loyalists were prominent. In December he retired with the army under Washington to the west bank of the Delaware, but in a few days (Dec. 31), Washington directed him to return to New Jersey to call out more of the state militia. On Feb. 18, 1777, with a detachment of his regiment, he surprised and captured an outpost of Loyalist refugees on the Island Farm, near New Brunswick. In acknowledgment of this service he was appointed, on Feb. 21, brigadier-general of militia, but he acted so little in that capacity that the name "Colonel Neilson" always followed him. While the British were at New Brunswick that winter Lord Howe made Neilson's house his headquarters.

Neilson served the rest of 1777 with the militia of Middlesex and Somerset counties, and in 1778 in Monmouth County, part of the time under General Dickerson, but otherwise holding a separate command. During this year he was again chosen to be a delegate to the Continental Congress but again declined. In 1779 he commanded the militia at Elizabethtown and Newark, aiding in the attempts to ward off the British raids from New York. The same year he intercepted the Simcoe raid, which was doing so much damage in Somerset County. On Sept. 20, 1780, he was appointed deputy quartermaster-general for New Jersey, in which position he continued until January 1783. In the meantime, on June 18, 1782, he was appointed a commissioner to settle, in terms of a depreciated currency, the pay of the New Jersey Line. He enjoyed the confidence of Washington, as published letters from the latter show, and their friendship continued after the war. Lafayette, on his visit to America in 1824, presented Neilson with his sword. The war over, Neilson returned to his business and carried on an extensive trade with Lisbon, Madeira, London, Dublin, and the West Indies. He also held various public offices. He was a member of the state convention which adopted the Constitution of the United States; from 1795 to 1798 he was judge of the court of common pleas; in 1800 and 1801 he was a member of the state Assembly, and from April 1796 to February 1821 he was successively register and recorder of New Brunswick, N. J. He was an elder and trustee in the First Presbyterian Church of New Brunswick, and a trustee of Rutgers College from 1782 until his death. His wife died Aug. 2, 1816. They had eleven children, the best known being James, who served with the rank of captain in the War of 1812 and was later a colonel of militia, and who succeeded his father as trustee of Rutgers College.

[W. W. Clayton, ed., *Hist. of Union and Middlesex Counties, N. J.* (1882); W. H. Benedict, *New Brunswick in Hist.* (1925); F. B. Lee, *Geneal. and Memorial Hist. of the State of N. J.* (1910), vol. IV; E. W. Van Voorhis, *A Geneal. of the Van Voorhees Family in America* (1888); *Newark Daily Advertiser,* Mar. 6, 1833.]　　　　　　　A. V–D. H.

NEILSON, WILLIAM GEORGE (Aug. 12, 1842–Dec. 29, 1906), mining engineer, the son of William Smith Neilson of Philadelphia and Esther (LaCoste) of Trinidad, who was of French descent, was born in Philadelphia and died in that city. He graduated from the Polytechnic College of the State of Pennsylvania in 1862, and shortly after became an instructor in mathematics there. Later he was connected with Booth & Garrett, a prominent firm of analytical chemists in Philadelphia.

In 1867 he was associated with the interests of Jay Cooke [*q.v.*] in the Adirondacks, spending three years in those mountains operating forges at Elizabethtown, Essex County, N. Y. He was next, for a short time, with the Pennsylvania Steel Company. During 1871, when the Logan Iron & Steel Company of Burnham, Pa., failed, Neilson was appointed its receiver

and upon subsequent reorganization of the company was made its general manager. In the meantime he became interested in the Freedom Forge of the same place, and with William Burnham of Philadelphia laid the foundations for what later became the Standard Steel Works, an affiliated interest of what was then called Burnham, Parry, Williams & Company, and is now known as the Baldwin Locomotive Works. He was manager of the Standard Steel Works for thirteen years (1877–90), and in 1878 was given charge of the first consignment of American-made locomotives to Russia. He was accompanied by a picked crew of men from Baldwin's for the purpose of placing these engines in service at Eydtkuhnen, an important railroad point on the border of East Prussia (now Lithuania). In 1890 he resigned from the Standard Steel Works to accept a position with the Chester Rolling Mills, later becoming vice-president of the Wellman Iron & Steel Company (1890–92). From 1893 to 1895 he was general manager of the Taylor Iron & Steel Company of Highbridge, N. J., and subsequently, for a period of eight years, treasurer of the Keystone Drop Forge Works at Chester, Pa.

With William Burnham and Edward Nichols, who subsequently became the president of the Brooks Locomotive Works, Tarrytown, N. Y., now a part of the American Locomotive Works system, Neilson, in 1882, purchased the Ridge Valley Iron Company, makers of charcoal pig-iron, in Floyd County, Ga.; and in that year formed the Republic Mining & Manufacturing Company for purchasing and operating mineral properties in the South. Bauxite, the ore from which aluminum metal is derived, was first discovered in the United States the following year at Hermitage, about one mile from the Ridge Valley Furnace. Neilson became a pioneer in the bauxite industry and was closely associated with its remarkable development. He was president of the Republic Mining & Manufacturing Company from 1892 until his death.

In 1888, with a few friends, he purchased land which was about to be sold for its timber and established the Adirondack Mountain Reserve, one of the largest and most attractive forest reserves in New York State. Its area, which includes Mount Marcy and the Ausable lakes, still retains its original wildness and beauty and has served as a game refuge to the present time. Neilson served as president of the controlling organization from its formation until 1903. He was also for many years a member of the Pennsylvania Forestry Association.

His religious interests covered a broad field,

his activities centering chiefly in the Protestant Episcopal Church of the Epiphany, Philadelphia, of which he was long a vestryman, and in the Philadelphia Branch of the Young Men's Christian Association, which he served as director and for three years as president. He was secretary of the centennial committee of the American Institute of Mining Engineers and his tact and the charm of his personality are attested by the successful manner in which he carried out the work of this office at the Centennial Exhibition at Philadelphia in 1876. For his services he received distinguished recognition from foreign governments. In 1872 he married Mary Louise Cunningham, of Philadelphia. He was survived by two sons and four daughters.

[*Trans. Am. Institute of Mining Engineers,* vol. XXXVIII (1908); *Who's Who in America,* 1906–07; *North American* (Phila.), *Public Ledger* (Phila.), Dec. 30, 1906; information from a son, Winthrop C. Nelson.]   F. L. G.

NELL, WILLIAM COOPER (Dec. 20, 1816–May 25, 1874), negro writer, was born in Boston. He was the son of William G. and Louisa M. Nell, the latter a native of Brookline, Mass., and the former of Charleston, S. C. The father, a tailor by trade, was steward on the ship *General Gadsden* when she escaped from the British brig *Recruit* in July 1812, and became a member of the General Colored Association of Massachusetts in 1826. Young Nell attended one of the separate primary schools, which had been established for negro children in Boston in 1820, and subsequently graduated with honors from the Smith School, of grammar grade, opened in 1835. He looked on while the white children were given prizes which he, although of equal scholarship, was debarred from receiving on account of his color.

This incident made a deep impression on him and henceforth he worked unceasingly for equal school rights to all children irrespective of the color of their skins. He read law for a time in the office of William I. Bowditch but, on the advice of Wendell Phillips, refrained from applying for admission to the bar, an act that would have entailed the taking of an oath to support the Constitution of the United States, which, in Phillips' opinion, compromised with the slave power. Nell then became affiliated with the antislavery movement as an organizer of meetings, at some of which he spoke acceptably. He also made himself useful by carefully preserving data and documents that would be helpful to the cause. In 1840 his name headed the list of signers of the first petition presented to the Massachusetts legislature asking for the opening of the public schools to negro children. For many years

thereafter he was to agitate this reform, since it was not until Apr. 28, 1855, that a law was passed abolishing the separate schools for colored children.

In the meantime he had developed into a journalist and author. During 1851 he assisted Frederick Douglass [*q.v.*] in the publication at Rochester, N. Y., of the *North Star*. In May of the same year he issued a pamphlet entitled *Services of Colored Americans in the Wars of 1776 and 1812.* This was followed in 1855 by a larger volume, *The Colored Patriots of the American Revolution,* to which Harriet Beecher Stowe wrote an introduction. In this book Nell paid a tribute to Crispus Attucks [*q.v.*], the first martyr of the Revolution, for whom, on Mar. 5, 1851, he had unsuccessfully petitioned the Massachusetts legislature to erect a monument. In it he also dwelt on the injustice of making only free white persons eligible for positions in the federal service. When, however, John G. Palfrey was named postmaster of Boston in 1861 he ignored this restriction and appointed Nell one of his clerks; thus he became the first colored man to hold a post under the federal government. This position he filled until the time of his death. A wife survived him.

[*William Lloyd Garrison, 1805–1879: the Story of His Life, Told by His Children* (4 vols., 1885–89); S. J. May, *Some Recollections of Our Anti-Slavery Conflict* (1869); W. W. Brown, *The Rising Sun* (1874); John Daniels, *In Freedom's Birthplace* (1914); Vernon Loggins, *The Negro Author: His Development in America* (1931); *Liberator,* Dec. 18, 1846, Feb. 11, 1848; C. G. Woodson, *The Mind of the Negro as Reflected in Letters Written During the Crisis 1800–1860* (1926); *Boston Daily Globe,* May 26, 1874; *Boston Transcript,* May 26, 29, 1874.]   H. G. V.

NELSON, CHARLES ALEXANDER (Apr. 14, 1839–Jan. 13, 1933), librarian, bibliographer, and expert indexer, was born in Calais, Me., the son of Israel Potter and Jane (Capen) Nelson, both members of old New England families. His early education was obtained at private schools in Fredericton and St. John, New Brunswick, and in Eastport, Me. In the fall of 1854 he entered the Male Academy at Gorham, Me., but a year later, December 1855, his family having moved to Cambridge, Mass., he joined the college class of the Cambridge High School. Entering Harvard College in 1857, he graduated in 1860. For one year he was tutor in Latin and Greek in the Albany Male Academy, then spent a year in the Lawrence Scientific School, and for more than a year was in business in Boston. In the fall of 1863 he became sub-master and professor of mathematics in the Collegiate School of Boston and resumed his studies at Harvard College, receiving the degree of master of arts in 1863.

From April 1864 to March 1865, he served as civil engineer and draftsman in the quartermaster's department of the United States Army at New Bern, N. C. After the war he remained in New Bern until 1873, serving as superintendent of schools and justice of the peace, and holding various other civil positions. In the spring of 1865 he was acting superintendent of white refugees, and in 1867 had charge of registration work in Craven County, under the reconstruction acts. From 1865 to 1871 he was also interested in the furniture business in New Bern, and from 1866 to 1873 was cashier of the Freedman's Savings & Trust Company. He returned to Boston in 1874 and was engaged in the book business and literary work until 1879, when he became professor of Greek and librarian at Drury College, Springfield, Mo., but returned to Boston one year later. For two years he was manager of the Old South Bookstore and editor of the firm's publications.

For the remainder of his life Nelson was engaged in library and bibliographical work at various institutions, holding numerous offices in professional organizations, contributing constantly to professional library journals, and publishing many bibliographical works of significance. His interest in library work began when as a boy of sixteen he served as librarian of the Male Academy, Gorham, Me. While a student in Harvard he worked as assistant in the college library under the tutelage of John Langdon Sibley and Ezra Abbot [qq.v.], whose work aroused his interest in cataloguing. In 1881 Nelson went to the Astor Library, New York, as catalogue librarian, to prepare a continuation of the catalogue made by Joseph G. Cogswell [q.v.]. This supplement was published in four volumes (1886–88), and gained for Nelson the diploma of honorable mention at the Pan-American Exposition in Buffalo in 1901, and at the exposition held in Charleston, S. C., in the same year. He left the Astor Library in 1888 to become the first librarian of the Howard Memorial Library at New Orleans, which was intended by its donors to excel in size and value all other libraries of the South. Having established a reputation as an expert cataloguer through his work on the catalogue of the Astor Library, he was called to the Newberry Library, Chicago, in 1891, to prepare a dictionary catalogue, but in 1893, before the work was completed, he accepted an appointment as deputy librarian of Columbia University, where he remained until he was retired on a pension from the Carnegie Foundation in 1909. In November 1913 he joined the staff of the Merchants' Association of New York, where he organized and maintained an index-digest of the activities of the Association until his final retirement in July 1926.

The most important of Nelson's published works, in addition to the catalogue of the Astor Library, were: *Waltham, Past and Present* (1879); *Catalogue of the Avery Architectural Library* (1895); *Books on Education in the Libraries of Columbia University* (1901); *Catalogue raisonnée; Works on Bookbinding, Practical and Historical . . . from the Collection of Samuel Putnam Avery . . .* (1903); *Analytical Index to Volumes 1–25 of the Educational Review* (1903); Index to *Minutes of the Common Council of the City of New York, 1675–1776* (8 vols., 1905–06). In 1872, at New Bern, N. C., Nelson married Emma Norris of Slaterville Springs, N. Y., who died Apr. 6, 1926. Two daughters survived him.

[*Who's Who in America*, 1932–33; H. M. Lydenberg, *Hist. of the N. Y. Pub. Lib.* (1923); *Lib. Jour.*, Feb. 1, 1933; *Bull. of the Am. Lib. Asso.*, Feb. 27, 1933; *N. Y. Times*, Jan. 14, 1933; autobiographical material supplied by a daughter, Mrs. R. A. Wetzel, Mount Vernon, N. Y.]
C. C. W.

NELSON, DAVID (Sept. 24, 1793–Oct. 17, 1844), Presbyterian clergyman, educator, abolitionist, was born near Jonesboro, Tenn., one of a family of Presbyterian ministers. His parents, Henry and Anna (Kelsey) Nelson, of English and Scotch extraction respectively, had migrated to East Tennessee from Rockbridge County, Va. David studied under the Rev. Samuel Doak [q.v.] at Washington College, two miles from his home. Upon his graduation at the age of sixteen he determined to become a physician, and after an apprenticeship to Dr. Ephraim McDowell [q.v.] at Danville, Ky., he went to Philadelphia for further study. He began his active practice as surgeon in the War of 1812 with an expeditionary force that invaded Canada, and later served with Andrew Jackson's army in Alabama and Florida. After peace was declared he returned to Jonesboro, and during the ensuing decade built up a lucrative practice in his profession.

While studying medicine, Nelson had been captured by the naturalistic doctrines then rife among members of his profession, and had become "an honest, unreflecting deist." He was big, fun loving, and attractive; he drank and played cards to an extent distressing to his family, and after settling in Jonesboro, he eloped at the age of twenty-two with the charming young daughter of David Deaderick, a prominent merchant. She appears to have been sincerely religious, however, and her influence, together with several years of reflection upon his deistical principles, brought him back to the Presbyterian Church. His return from deism to Calvinism he later recorded in a powerful tract, *The Cause and Cure of Infidelity,* written in 1836, of which more than a hundred thousand copies were distributed by the American Tract Society, and many thousands more by tract societies in England. With time his convictions deepened; in April 1825 he was licensed to preach by the Abingdon Presbytery, and six months later he gave up his medical practice and was ordained as an evangelist. From 1827 to 1829 he was one of the editors of the *Calvinistic Magazine* and in 1828 he succeeded his brother, Samuel Kelsey Nelson, as pastor of the Presbyterian church at Danville, Ky. Though careless in dress and eccentric in manner, he was a pulpit orator of great ability (R. J. Breckinridge, in Sprague, *post,* p. 687) and became one of the notable preachers of his day in his denomination.

In 1831 he founded and became president of Marion College, near Palmyra, Mo., "for the training of pious young men," converts of the Great Revival of 1830. The next year the "modern abolition" movement invaded the Presbyterian Church in the West. At Western Reserve College, Theodore D. Weld, abolition revivalist extraordinary, started among the faculty an anti-slavery discussion whose repercussions were heard throughout the Western Reserve. The next year among the students at Lane Theological Seminary in Cincinnati he inspired a debate on slavery that converted the student body and disrupted the school. At St. Louis, Mo., Elijah P. Lovejoy [*q.v.*] echoed the perilous agitation in the columns of the *St. Louis Observer,* the Presbyterian paper for the Far West. Nelson's convictions had led him, before he went to Missouri, to free his own slaves, and now, surrounded as he was by the agitation, he could not remain unmoved: at the Presbyterian General Assembly of 1835, in Pittsburgh, Theodore Weld found him ready for the abolition gospel. Together with more than one-fourth of his fellow delegates, he "pledged himself openly to the Cause" (*Emancipator,* Boston, June 16, 1835).

Nelson was no faint-hearted reformer. A month after his return to Marion College he accepted a regular agency from the American Anti-Slavery Society, and in 1836, from the pulpit of his Presbyterian church in Palmyra, he called upon the slave-holders of his congregation to repent their sins and free their slaves. He was straightway expelled from Marion College and from Missouri, not escaping mob violence on the way, and the faculty of Marion College published a manifesto, nervously asseverating

their loyalty to the institutions of the community. At Quincy, Ill., he now founded a new college, a "manual labour institution," where students were to support themselves by building their own dwellings and raising food for their sustenance on the college farm. The school did not survive its first year, and Nelson again took up agency work for the American Anti-Slavery Society. As anti-slavery lecturer in western Illinois, he was only moderately successful, partly on account of increasing disability from epilepsy. Intermittently he labored for the slave until 1840, when his health gave way completely. He died at Oakland, Ill., four years later.

[A short biography of Nelson is in the second American edition (n.d.) of his *Cause and Cure of Infidelity;* and a biographical sketch, with reminiscences of several colleagues, appears in W. B. Sprague, *Annals Am. Pulpit,* vol. IV (1858). Contemporary events are recorded in the *Calvinistic Mag.,* 1827–28; *St. Louis Observer,* 1835–36; *Alton Observer,* 1837; *Philanthropist,* 1836–40; and Minutes of the Agency Committee, Am. Anti-Slavery Soc., 1835–40. An obituary appears in *Presbyterian of the West* (Springfield, Ohio), Nov. 21, 1844. D. L. Leonard, *The Story of Oberlin* (1898).]

G. H. B.

NELSON, HENRY LOOMIS (Jan. 5, 1846–Feb. 29, 1908), author, editor, and teacher, was born in New York City, the son of Theophilus and Catherine (Lyons) Nelson. He was graduated from Williams College in the class of 1867, and among its members he was known as an original thinker, a picturesque speaker, and a friendly and delightful companion. From Williams College he went to the law school of Columbia University, received the degree of LL.B. in 1869, was admitted to the New York bar, and began the practice of law. On Oct. 14, 1874, he married Ida Frances Wyman of Brooklyn. Business called him to Kalamazoo, Mich., in the year of his marriage; during his two years of residence in that city his interest in public questions prompted him to send frequent letters to the newspapers, and ultimately resulted in shifting his attention from law to journalism. In 1876 he moved to Greenfield, Mass., where he became owner and editor of the *Franklin County Times.* From the concerns of a small New England city he was soon attracted to the national capital. He was Washington correspondent of the *Boston Post* from 1878 to 1885. His shrewd common sense, political sagacity, and lively style not only commended him to his Boston readers but also brought him to the notice of men prominent in public life. Eventually, while continuing to act as correspondent for the *Post,* he became private secretary to John G. Carlisle, then speaker of the House of Representatives. In 1885 he was called from Washington to become editor of the newspaper that he had been representing. A year

Nelson

later a change in the ownership of the *Post* set him adrift. He returned to New York and for eight years he engaged in editorial work, first for the *Star,* then for the *Mail and Express,* then for the *World.* From 1894 to 1898, during the turbulent final years of the Cleveland administration, the free-silver campaign of 1896, and the tumult of the Spanish-American War, he was editor of *Harper's Weekly.* A supporter of Cleveland, an opponent of Bryan, and a sceptical and suspicious observer of the rising star of Theodore Roosevelt, he made his periodical a powerful factor in the thought of the time.

The succeeding years he gave to free-lance writing, until in 1902 Williams College called him to the newly created David A. Wells Professorship of Political Science. He was markedly successful as a teacher, bringing to his new work a vigorous mind and a sense of realities. During his professorial life he continued to write on political problems and personalities for the leading magazines and kept in touch with men and affairs. He died suddenly in 1908 from an attack of angina pectoris while on a visit to New York. Aside from the editorials in *Harper's Weekly,* numerous essays in periodicals, and unidentifiable contributions to newspapers, his chief works are *John Rantoul,* a novel, published in 1885, and two small books, *Our Unjust Tariff Laws* (1884), and *The Money We Need* (1895). A man of strong convictions, a good hater and a loyal friend, he was typical of the best of that group of Americans who were proud to call themselves Cleveland Democrats. He was a fighter for civil-service reform, a free-trader, a believer in the gold standard, an anti-imperialist. Politically he typified a party and an era. As an educator he was eloquent in support of the humanities, upheld the intellectual life against the excesses of organized athletics, employed the project method years before the term was known to college men, and in the classroom stirred his students by his piquant speech and his faculty of revealing the simple principles underlying complicated governmental problems. His positive, dynamic personality made itself felt in all of his undertakings.

[*Who's Who in America,* 1907–08; sketch by H. W. Mabie, in *Obit. Record of the Soc. of Alumni, Williams Coll.,* May 1908; *Thirty-fifth Anniversary Papers of the Class of Sixty-Seven, Williams Coll.;* sketch by E. S. Martin, in *Harper's Weekly,* Mar. 14, 1908; L. W. Spring, *A Hist. of Williams Coll.* (1917); *N. Y. Daily Tribune,* Dec. 20, 1894; *N. Y. Times,* Mar. 1, 1908; *Springfield* (Mass.) *Republican,* Mar. 1, 1908; personal recollections.]   G. B. D.

NELSON, HUGH (Sept. 30, 1768–Mar. 18, 1836), politician, jurist, diplomat, was of the third generation of the Nelson family born on the soil of York County, Virginia, in the then thriving Yorktown, to play a conspicuous rôle in the public affairs of the Old Dominion. He was the fifth child of Thomas Nelson [*q.v.*], Revolutionary governor of Virginia, and his wife Lucy, daughter of Philip and Mary Randolph Grymes of Middlesex. He was of the vintage of Revolutionary Virginia sons who were not sent like their fathers to old England but were given their education at the College of William and Mary at Williamsburg, where he was graduated in 1790. Soon after reaching manhood he moved to Albemarle County. On Apr. 28, 1799, he was married to Eliza, only child of Francis Kinloch and Mildred Walker, granddaughter of Jefferson's guardian, Dr. Thomas Walker. Through his wife the estate of "Belvoir" came into his possession and he lived there among the Albemarle hills for many years with an ever increasing family to add liveliness to rural seclusion. There were nine children of this union who reached maturity.

Nelson practised law in Albemarle and began his official career as delegate from the county in the Virginia Assembly from 1805 to 1809. In the interval between his service in the Virginia legislature and his congressional services he was judge of the General Court of Virginia. In 1811 he was sent to Congress from his district and was returned continuously to that body until he resigned in 1823 to accept appointment by his former neighbor, President Monroe, as minister plenipotentiary to the Court of Spain. During the years of his congressional office he kept in close touch with Jefferson, reporting to him from the inside such critical issues as the Missouri question. Monroe constantly esteemed him as a loyal, dependable friend. On his request he was relieved of his Spanish post in 1825, just before Monroe left the presidency, and returned to Albemarle. There he spent the declining years of his life with a brief interruption when he again represented that county in the Virginia House of Delegates of 1828–29. Through his father he had had intimate knowledge of the Revolutionary leaders in Virginia and was frequently consulted in his later years for information on figures even then becoming legendary. It is on his authority that Patrick Henry has enjoyed the reputation for having read Livy every year. Church affairs had his keen interest and hearty support. He served as a vestryman in the Episcopal Church in his Albemarle parish, was often a member of the annual diocesan convention, and on several occasions represented the church in Virginia in the General Convention

416

of the Protestant Episcopal Church in the United States.

[Material on the career of Hugh Nelson is fragmentary and scattered. The best brief sketch is to be found in R. C. M. Page, *Geneal. of the Page Family in Va.* (2nd ed., 1893). See also: C. F. Adams, ed., *Memoirs of John Quincy Adams*, vols. IV–VI (1874–75); S. M. Hamilton, *The Writings of Jas. Monroe* (7 vols., 1898–1903); E. C. Mead, *Hist. Homes of the South-west Mountains, Va.* (1899), pp. 163–64; and *Southern Churchman*, Apr. 1, 1836. There are some forty of Nelson's letters, written for the most part between 1808 and 1818, in the Division of Manuscripts of the Lib. of Cong.] M. H. W.

NELSON, JOHN (1654–Nov. 15, 1734), New England trader, statesman, was the son of Robert Nelson, a member of Gray's Inn, and of Mary (Temple) Nelson, the daughter of Sir John Temple of Stanton Bury, Buckinghamshire, and the sister of Sir Thomas Temple, proprietor and governor of Nova Scotia, 1656–70. Probably shortly after 1670 when Sir Thomas settled in Boston Nelson came from his home in England to join him. When Sir Thomas died in 1674 the nephew inherited his uncle's pretensions to land and trade in Nova Scotia. As early as 1677 Nelson was engaged in the fur trade in the Kennebec country. In the interest of this trade he went to Canada in 1682 where he became acquainted with prominent French officials. In Boston he married Elizabeth, the daughter of William Tailer and the niece of William Stoughton. To them were born two sons and four daughters. He was an outspoken opponent of Randolph and Andros, and when news of the overthrow of James II reached Boston in 1689 he joined in demanding the surrender of Andros and led the militia that captured him. Nelson was ignored in the reorganization of the colony. Hutchinson explained that it was because he was an Anglican and "of a gay free temper" (*post*, I, p. 378). Probably a bitter personal and political rivalry existing between himself and William Phips also prevented his receiving recognition. In 1691, however, the colony sent him on an expedition to Nova Scotia. He was captured by the French and held prisoner in Quebec for a year. The French treated him kindly but feared him, and when his captors learned that he had sent military information to Boston they sent him to France where he was confined in a dungeon of the castle of Angoulême for two years. In 1694 his importance was sufficiently recognized to secure his transfer to the Bastille. There French officials entered into discussions with him regarding a project for gaining the neutrality of America during the war and Nelson wrote to Blathwayt regarding the proposition. The French king finally offered him a parole to go to London to discuss the matter.

In London Nelson was reprimanded by the Privy Council for entering into negotiations with the French, but the Board of Trade listened to his views. He informed the latter of French designs to establish a colony on the Mississippi and to develop there the fur trade, upon which their power in America depended. He urged that the English encourage the "bush-lopers" to extend their trade, and that plans be formed to unite the colonies under one head to resist the French. Then the conquest of Canada could be accomplished. Blathwayt and apparently the whole Board of Trade were impressed with his arguments and his memorial was discussed by the Board years afterward. England was not then in position to demand the cession of Canada but Nelson's arguments apparently were conclusive in establishing the southern boundary of Acadia at the St. George River instead of at the Kennebec as claimed by the French. After the Peace of Ryswick Nelson was released from parole and returned to Boston. During the War of the Spanish Succession he continued to address arguments to Blathwayt for the expulsion of the French from America, and especially from the country south of the St. Lawrence. It was due in no small measure to his propaganda that Nova Scotia and Newfoundland were ceded to England at the Peace of Utrecht. After the peace Nelson continued his efforts to have the boundaries of New France restricted by the boundary commission. After his return to Boston he was appointed a commissioner to treat with the Indians. Although still an Anglican he supported Benjamin Colman in his efforts to liberalize the New England church. He opposed the intrigues to supplant Governor Dudley by Sir Charles Hobby. He resumed his fur trade with the Indians of the northeast and he succeeded in regaining some of the lands his uncle had held in Nova Scotia. He was a capable business man and died wealthy.

[Temple Prime, *Descent of John Nelson and of his Children* (1886, 4th ed., *Some Account of the Temple Family*, 1899); Timothy Cutler, *The Final Peace.... A Sermon Deliver'd at Christ-Church in Boston Nov. 28, 1734, on the Occasion of the Death of John Nelson, Esq.* (1735); Thos. Hutchinson, *The Hist. of the Colony of Mass. Bay*, vol. I (1764); A. H. Buffington, "John Nelson's Voyage to Quebec in 1682," *Col. Soc. Mass. Pubs.*, vol. XXVI (1927); "Papers of the Lloyd Family of ... Lloyd's Neck," *N. Y. Hist. Soc. Colls.*, Pub. Fund Series, vols. LIX–LX (1927); *Mass. Hist. Soc. Colls.*, 3 ser. I (1825), 4 ser. VIII (1868), 5 ser. VIII (1882); *Proc. Mass. Hist. Soc.*, 1 ser. VII (1864); *Me. Hist. Soc. Colls.*, 2 ser., "Doc. Hist.," X (1907); E. B. O'Callaghan, *Docs. Rel. to the Col. Hist. ... of N. Y.*, vol. IV (1854), vol. IX (1855); W. T. Morgan, "A Crisis in the Hist. of the Hudson's Bay Company," *N. Dak. Hist. Quart.*, July 1931; *Calendar of State Papers, Colonial Ser., America and West Indies ... 1696 ... 1697* (1904); *Jour. of the Commissioners for Trade and Plantations ... 1704 ... 1709*

(1925) and *1718 . . . 1722* (1925) ; J. B. Brebner, *New England's Outpost, Acadia, Before the Conquest of Canada* (1927) ; *Collection de Manuscrits . . . Relatifs à la Nouvelle-France* (4 vols., 1883–85).]   P. C. P.

NELSON, JULIUS (Mar. 6, 1858–Feb. 15, 1916), biologist and specialist in oyster culture, was born in Copenhagen, Denmark, the son of Christian and Julia (Jörgensen) Nelson. In 1863 his family came to America and settled near Waupaca, Wis. The young man prepared for college in the Waupaca High School and entered the University of Wisconsin, graduating with the degree of B.S. in 1881. For a time he served as principal of the high school at Rio, Wis., but he continued his studies and received the degree of M.S. from the University of Wisconsin in 1884. He enrolled for further graduate study at Johns Hopkins University where subsequently he was appointed to a fellowship. Shortly after finishing his studies there with the doctor's degree in 1888, he was appointed biologist of the New Jersey Agricultural Experiment Station and professor of biology at Rutgers College, positions he held until the time of his death.

During his first ten years at the New Jersey Station he conducted extensive investigations of cattle diseases and their relation to public health. To the knowledge of bovine tuberculosis, then in a primitive stage, his studies yielded valuable results. His investigations also embraced contagious abortion and garget in cattle, poultry diseases, egg production by virgin fowls, dairy bacteriology, sewage disposal, and home sanitation. His greatest contributions, however, were made subsequent to 1900 in the field of oyster culture. Aided by special state appropriations and with the cooperation of progressive oystermen, he established laboratories on the New Jersey coast where through successive summers he studied the life history and habits of the oyster. His findings were put into practical application by the oyster industry of New Jersey. As a result of his studies, Nelson came to be recognized as the outstanding American authority on oyster culture and was frequently called upon for expert testimony before such bodies as the National Board of Food and Drug Inspectors and the United States Fish Commission. In 1915 he was engaged by the Biological Board of Canada to make a survey of oyster-producing resources in Canadian waters. His sudden death in 1916, resulting from an attack of pneumonia, cut short a scientific career that had just begun to enjoy the full fruition of pioneering and painstaking labor. Nelson had married, on Aug. 9, 1888, Nellie Cynthia Chase of Madison, Wis. They reared a family of three sons and three daughters.

Nelson's writings include a long list of studies, most of which were published in the annual reports and bulletins of the New Jersey Agricultural Experiment Station. In addition he was the author of "Heredity and Sex" (*American Journal of Psychology,* January 1890), and a *Descriptive Catalogue of the Vertebrates of New Jersey* (New Jersey Geological Survey, 1890). He was also a contributor to Bailey's *Cyclopedia of American Agriculture.* He was a member of the Nature Study Society of America, of the National Association of Shell Fish Commissioners, of the New Jersey Tuberculosis Commission, and of the New Jersey State Science Teachers' Association, and served as president of the New Jersey State Microscopical Society, 1896–97. He was also vice-president and consulting advisor of the Lederle Laboratories, New York.

[See the annual reports and bulletins of the N. J. Agric. Experiment Station, 1888–1916; the *Targum,* Rutgers College, Feb. 23, Mar. 8, 1916; *Rutgers Alumni Quart.,* Apr. 1916; and the *Daily State Gazette* (Trenton), Feb. 17, 1916. Nelson's oyster investigations are summarized in the *Thirty-Seventh Ann. Report of the N. J. State Agric. Experiment Station* (1917); they are treated in further detail in Carl R. Woodward and Ingrid N. Waller, *New Jersey's Agric. Experiment Station, 1880–1930* (1932).]
C. R. W—d.

NELSON, KNUTE (Feb. 2, 1843–Apr. 28, 1923), governor of Minnesota, United States senator, was born at Evanger in the district of Voss, Norway. His mother, Ingeborg Kvilekval, brought him to the United States when he was six years old, and, after a brief period of much hardship in Chicago, the two went to La Grange, Wis. There the mother was married to Nels Nelson, an immigrant from Norway, and the boy assumed his name. In 1853 the family settled on a farm in the town of Deerfield, about twenty miles east of Madison. After attending local schools the youth at fifteen entered Albion Academy, a school conducted by Seventh-Day Adventists and chosen by Nelson because it was only fourteen miles from his home. He worked for the principal of the academy to pay for his tuition and a room, and he fetched supplies of fuel and food from his home. In the winter of 1860–61 he taught a district school; and in May 1861 he enlisted in the 4th Wisconsin Infantry, a regiment which, after 1863, was mounted and designated as the 4th Wisconsin Cavalry. He participated in Butler's expedition against New Orleans and Sherman's first expedition against Vicksburg. He was wounded during the siege of Port Hudson and was held prisoner within the city for a month until its capitulation. After recovering from his wound he served with his regiment until the expiration of his enlistment, July 1864. In 1863 he had become a corporal. Returning to Wisconsin, he reëntered Albion Academy in the fall of 1864, completed his course, and was graduated with the degree of Ph.B.

Having already determined upon a career in politics, Nelson read law with William F. Vilas of Madison and was admitted to the bar in 1867. In that year also he married Nicholina Jacobson, and was elected to the Wisconsin Assembly, in which he served two terms. After living a short time at Cambridge, Wis., he removed to Alexandria, Minn., at that time (1871) a frontier county seat. He took up government land and combined homesteading with law practice, managing, as he said, "to get on one side or the other of about every case of importance in the six or seven counties in my part of the country" (*Minnesota History Bulletin,* February 1924, p. 350). His first public office in Minnesota was that of county attorney for Douglas County (1872–74); he was thereafter state senator, 1874–78. In 1882 he was elected to Congress as a Republican, after a bitter fight for the nomination had resulted in a split in the party in his district. He served three terms in Congress and then refused a fourth nomination and returned to his law practice. In 1892 the Republicans in Minnesota, alarmed by the tendency of the Scandinavian settlers to join the Populists, selected Nelson as their candidate for governor. He was elected, and was reëlected in 1894 but resigned the office in 1895 upon being chosen by the legislature as United States senator.

The office of senator Nelson held by successive reëlections until his death. During these years he was member of the committees on Indian affairs and public lands, and member and chairman of the judiciary committee. He was interested in legislation relating to Chippewa Indian lands in Minnesota and to the development of Alaska. Among the more notable measures ascribed to him are the Nelson bankruptcy act (1898) and the act creating the Department of Commerce and Labor (1902). His Republican conservatism was modified by low tariff leanings. He advocated a federal income tax and the constitutional amendment necessary to secure it, supported the prohibition amendment and the Volstead Act, was active in establishing the Interstate Commerce Commission, fought amendments designed to weaken the Sherman Anti-trust law, was violently opposed to the Adamson law, and arrayed himself against his party in advocating the entrance of the United States into the League of Nations. In appearance he was short and broad of stature, blue-eyed, with black hair and chin whiskers which turned gray soon enough to win him the sobriquet of "the grand old man of Minnesota." His habits were simple and frugal; he died possessed of a modest competence. He was politically astute, especially in his earlier years when astuteness was necessary to his political survival. The first Norwegian-born American citizen to serve as congressman, as a state senator, or as United States senator, he had the vote of his countrymen behind him in his early career, though later agrarian unrest and the increasing liberalism of his compatriots alienated many. A statue of Nelson, erected by popular subscription, stands before the state capitol of Minnesota.

[See M. W. Odland, *The Life of Knute Nelson* (1926); J. A. O. Preus, "Knute Nelson," in *Minn. Hist. Bull.,* Feb. 1924, followed by two autobiographical letters; E. E. Adams, "Nelson-Kindred Campaign of 1882," in *Ibid.,* May 1923; *St. Paul Sunday Pioneer Press,* Apr. 29, 30, 1923. Nelson's papers are in the possession of the Minn. Hist. Soc.]

S. J. B.

NELSON, NELSON OLSEN (Sept. 11, 1844–Oct. 5, 1922), manufacturer and promoter of profit-sharing, was born in Lillesand, Norway, the son of Anders and Gertrude Nelson. His father emigrated to the United States in 1847 and settled in Buchanan County, Mo. Nelson's boyhood years were divided between work on a farm in summer and attendance at rural school in winter. At the outbreak of the Civil War he enlisted in the Union army and served throughout its duration. Upon reëntering civil life he settled in St. Louis and took employment with a wholesale grocery firm. A year later he started a business of his own in St. Joseph, Mo. In April 1868 he was married to Almeria Posegate. From 1870 to 1872 he was established in Hiawatha, Kan., but in the latter year he again went to St. Louis and in 1877 he founded the N. O. Nelson Manufacturing Company, makers of building and plumbing supplies, which became one of the largest concerns of its kind in the world.

The problems of labor had for a long time attracted Nelson's interest, and in 1886, because of the reputation for wisdom and justice he had established among business and labor elements, he served as conciliator and arbitrator of a strike on parts of the Gould system of railroads. He then began to study the basic causes of industrial disharmony and acquainted himself with several plans of profit-sharing, especially with those of the Maison Leclaire in Paris, and Godin in Guise, France. He became convinced that the essentials of such a system possessed all the attributes necessary to the maintenance of a just and practicable relationship between capital and labor. Capitalism, notwithstanding its shortcomings, was preferable, so he held, to any alternative order, and he believed that a major reason for the practicability of profit-sharing was that it rested "automatically upon conditions already in effect." The plan of profit-sharing in his plant Nelson put into operation in 1886. After allowance had been made for "customary salaries, wages, expenses, and interest," the remainder of the firm's income for the year was to be divided pro rata upon the total amount of wages paid and capital employed. The dividends were payable in cash or in stock in the firm. In 1890 a tract of land near Edwardsville, Ill., was purchased, and upon it Nelson founded the village of Leclaire, in which were built factories and employees' dwellings and which was laid out as a model community. For many years it was the worthy boast of its residents that it had no policemen, no pauperism, and an extraordinarily low rate for death and infant mortality. In 1905 Nelson extended the provisions of the profit-sharing plan to the customers of the firm.

In his effort to minimize economic waste and to increase in all feasible ways the incomes of his employees, Nelson started in 1902 a cooperative store in Leclaire based upon the Rochdale plan. By 1916 it had about 150 members. The success of this project heightened Nelson's belief in the practicability of cooperation in merchandizing. In 1911, during a visit to New Orleans, he was affected by the evidence of want on the part of the inhabitants of the poorer districts, and he established at his own expense a grocery-store in which commodities were sold at the lowest possible margin of profit. He developed the enterprise into a chain and in 1915 organized a cooperative association. The business grew to consist of sixty-three stores, a bakery, a creamery, a condiment factory, and the stock and equipment on a farm. Notwithstanding early prospects of success, the enterprise as expanded, experienced a succession of losses culminating in 1918 in its failure, and Nelson filed a personal petition for bankruptcy on the New Orleans undertaking.

For many years Nelson had been strongly interested in numerous matters of civic, social, and philanthropic import. In 1887 and 1890 he was a member of the St. Louis City Council. In 1895 he was a delegate to the meeting in London of the Profit-Sharing and Co-operative Associations of the World. He organized the Fresh Air Mission for children in the downtown districts of St. Louis, free-steamboat excursions for poor children and mothers, and built free swimming-pools. He aided in founding work-ingmen's self-culture clubs and lecture courses; he started traveling libraries for country-school districts. In politics he was for many years a Republican but with the passage of the McKinley tariff, which he strongly opposed, he allied himself with the Democratic party. He favored free trade, and believed in "free silver" and the single tax. In religion he was until middle life a Lutheran, but in later years he became a Unitarian. His character, personality, and intellect, combined with his energy and superior business sense, were the basis for his accomplishments. But it seems fair to say that he at no time appreciated the deeper implications of a system of profit-sharing or recognized the limitations operating against its widespread and permanent adoption. He failed to understand that the success accomplished in his own plant was more personal than institutional. The collapse of his venture in New Orleans hastened his loss of interest, already considerably diminished, in the major business in St. Louis. For three years preceding his death he lived in California.

[Nelson wrote occasional articles treating of his business experiments. For the best of these see the *Independent*, Feb. 21, 1901, May 25, 1905, Feb. 13, 1913, Jan. 19, 1914; the *North Am. Rev.*, Apr. 1887; and *System*, Oct. 1915. For biographical details see *Who's Who in America*, 1914–15; H. L. Conard, *Encyc. of the Hist. of Mo.* (1901), vol. IV; Wm. Hyde and H. L. Conard, *Encyc. of the Hist. of St. Louis* (1899); *St. Louis Globe Democrat*, Oct. 7, 1922. Nelson's correspondence was made available to the writer of this sketch by his private secretary.]   G. W. S.

NELSON, RENSSELAER RUSSELL (May 12, 1826–Oct. 15, 1904), Minnesota jurist, was born at Cooperstown, N. Y., the son of Catherine Ann (Russell) and Samuel Nelson [*q.v.*]. He was of mixed New England and Irish ancestry, with a dash of Dutch and Scotch. The boy was prepared for college at a military academy at Cooperstown and at Haerwick Seminary. He was graduated from Yale in 1846, read law in the offices of James R. Whiting of New York and George A. Starkweather of Cooperstown, and was admitted to the bar in 1849. After practising a short time in Buffalo, he went to Minnesota Territory in 1850 and opened a law office in St. Paul, although informed by the landlord of his hotel that the population of the town (about a thousand) included "fifty lawyers, mostly starving." Soon thereafter he joined with five other St. Paul men in a land speculation, which in August 1853 took them as settlers to Superior, Wis. Having helped to organize Douglas County, with Superior as the county seat, Nelson was appointed county attorney by the governor, and at the first election, in November 1854, he was elected to the same office. But the vision of Superior as a great inland port was not to be realized at so early a day, and he returned to St. Paul in 1855.

In 1857 Nelson was appointed by President Buchanan associate justice of the supreme court of Minnesota Territory. In the same year he rendered an important decision, refusing a writ of mandamus to compel the territorial officers to remove the capital from St. Paul to St. Peter. A bill for this removal had passed both houses of the legislature but had been sequestered by the chairman of the committee on engrossed bills until the legislature had adjourned. Nelson ruled that, the power to fix the location of the territorial capital having been granted to and exercised by the first territorial legislature, no subsequent legislature had the power to change that location; he further ruled that the bill substituted for the missing bill and signed by the governor was not the bill passed by the legislature and that hence no act had been passed.

In May 1858, when Minnesota became a state, Nelson was appointed a United States district judge for Minnesota. A Democrat in a normally Republican state, he had no temptation to forsake the bench for politics and did not retire until 1896. He was married on Nov. 3, 1858, to Emma F. Wright (née Beebe) of New York. From 1862 to 1864 he was vice-president of the St. Paul & Pacific Railroad Company. He was reputed to be an unprejudiced and liberal-minded judge whose decisions were seldom reversed; he had "a serene composure which seemed natural to the man, becoming to a judge," and "the courteous gentility of the old school of which he was one of the best examples."

[W. H. C. Folsom, *Fifty Years in the Northwest* (1888); H. F. Stevens, *Hist. of the Bench and Bar of Minn.* (2 vols., 1904); J. F. Williams, *A Hist. of the City of St. Paul* (1876); "Proceedings in Memory of the Honorable Rensselaer R. Nelson," in 93 *Minnesota*, xxi–xxxvi; *Bull. of Yale Univ., First Ser., No. 5, July 1905: Obit. Record of Grads.*; obituaries in St. Paul and Minneapolis newspapers, Oct. 15, 16, 1904.]
S. J. B.

NELSON, REUBEN (Dec. 16, 1818–Feb. 20, 1879), Methodist Episcopal clergyman, educator, and administrator, was born in New York City, one of the twelve children of Abraham and Huldah Nelson. In his early youth he lost his right arm below the elbow while working in a woolen mill. When a lad of fifteen he joined the church, and within a year he was licensed as an exhorter; at the end of another year, in spite of his youth, he was licensed to preach. He early saw his need of education and was keen to avail himself of every opportunity for intellectual and cultural development. For a period he studied at Hartwick Seminary, Otsego County, N. Y. On Aug.

19, 1840, he was admitted on trial to the Oneida Conference of the Methodist Episcopal Church and was appointed as third preacher on the Otsego circuit; the next year he held a similar appointment on the Westford circuit. He was ordained deacon Aug. 10, 1842, and in that year married Jane Scott Eddy, daughter of Col. Asa Eddy of Milford, N. Y. In addition to his work as a preacher, he performed the duties of principal of Otsego Academy at Cooperstown, N. Y. When, in 1844, the Oneida Conference founded Wyoming Seminary at Kingston, Pa., he was chosen its first principal. His ordination as elder occurred July 22, 1846. For twenty-seven years he served as principal at Wyoming Seminary, and placed it in the forefront of institutions of its class.

Having risen to a place of leadership of his church, he was elected, in 1872, a publishing agent of the Methodist Book Concern at New York. Although this great publishing house at that time was passing through the most critical period of its long existence, Nelson proved remarkably well fitted for his new position with its many complicated and difficult problems. He was held in high regard by his associates in the ministry, and represented his Conference five times as a delegate to the General Conference, holding at each of these sessions committee positions of commanding importance and responsibility. In addition to his service as publishing agent, he was, from 1872 to the time of his death, treasurer of the Missionary Society of the Methodist Episcopal Church, an office involving the most careful scrutiny of contributions, investments, and expenditures of world-wide range. He died in New York City, and was buried in the Cemetery at Forty Fort, Pa.

[*Hist. of Wyoming Conference* (1904); *Jour. of the General Conference of the M. E. Ch.* (1880); *Methodist Quart. Rev.*, Oct. 1879; the *Christian Advocate*, Feb. 27, 1879; H. C. Jennings, *The Methodist Book Concern* (1924); J. W. Jordan, *Encyc. of Pa. Biog.*, vol. VII (1916); *N. Y. Times*, Feb. 20, 21, 1879.]
S. J. H.

NELSON, ROGER (1759–June 7, 1815), Revolutionary soldier, congressman, jurist, youngest son of Dr. Arthur and Lucy (Waters) Nelson, was born at their homestead near Point of Rocks, Frederick County, Md. After completing his preparatory work, he studied at the College of William and Mary. Commissioned a lieutenant in the 5th Regiment of the Maryland Line July 15, 1780, he was sent south immediately to the army commanded by General Gates. At the battle of Camden the following month he fought with courage but fell wounded in the retreat. Surrounded by a band of British, and further wounded, he was left on the field for dead but was later discovered, only to be carried off a prisoner to Charleston. After several months of hardship on British prison-ships he was exchanged, whereupon he was transferred to the regiment of cavalry commanded by Col. William Washington. At the battle of Guilford Court House, Mar. 15, 1781, he took part in the charge against the British guards led by Colonel Washington. He engaged in the battle of Eutaw Springs, September 1781, and was present at the surrender at Yorktown. In 1793 he engaged in the suppression of the Whiskey Rebellion by organizing and leading a troop of cavalry. He closed his military career as brigadier-general of militia.

Meanwhile he had embarked upon his career of civilian service. After his return from the Revolutionary War he studied law and was admitted to the bar about 1785. After a brief residence at Taneytown, Md., he moved to Frederick where he soon gained a large practice. After serving in the Maryland House of Delegates, he was elected without opposition to fill a vacancy in the federal House of Representatives caused by the death of Daniel Heister [q.v.]. Reëlected for three successive terms, he served from November 1804 until his resignation in May 1810. He was named by the House one of the managers for the impeachment proceedings against Associate Justice Chase but refused to serve because of the latter's Revolutionary record. Although he supported Jefferson in an embargo policy which bore heavily upon the rural districts in depressed agricultural prices, he weathered the political storm in the election of 1808 which swept out many fellow Democrats—an evidence of his great personal popularity. He thus maintained a record of never having been defeated in an election. His final public service was as associate judge of the sixth judicial circuit of Maryland, which post he filled from 1810 to his death in 1815. He married Mary Brooke Sim in 1787. Though not regarded as a learned or profound lawyer, it was said of him that his persuasiveness was irresistible with a Frederick County jury. As a political speaker he was eloquent and dramatic and was a force in Congress. For many years he was the recognized Democratic leader in his county. He died at Frederick.

[There is an account of Nelson in T. J. C. Williams, *Hist. of Frederick County, Md.* (1910), vol. I. See also: *Ancestral Records and Portraits* (1910), vol. II; J. T. Scharf, *Hist. of Western Md.* (1882), vol. I; *Archives of Md.*, vols. XVIII (1900) and XLVIII (1931); *Biog. Dir. Am. Cong.* (1928); *Army and Navy Chronicle*, Mar. 14, 1839; *Md. Republican*, June 17, 24, 1815, *Baltimore Patriot and Evening Advertiser*, June 9, 1815.]   E. L.

NELSON, SAMUEL (Nov. 10, 1792–Dec. 13, 1873), jurist, was born in Hebron, Washington County, N. Y. His parents, John Rogers and Jean McArthur (Jane McCarter according to some accounts) Nelson were Scotch-Irish who came to America about 1760. He spent his boyhood on a farm and attended the district school where his aptness as a pupil led to plans for his entrance into the ministry. At fifteen he went for two years to the Washington Academy at Salem, N. Y., and for one year to Granville Academy. He entered Middlebury College as a sophomore and graduated in 1813. To the disappointment of his parents he entered the law office of Savage & Woods in Salem as a clerk. After two years he moved with Judge Woods to Madison County and remained with him for two more years. Upon admission to the bar in 1817 he opened an office in Cortland, N. Y., where he developed a remunerative practice.

Nelson's entrance into public life occurred in 1820 when he served as a presidential elector for James Monroe and was also appointed to the postmastership of Cortland, which he held for three years. In 1821 he was a delegate to the New York constitutional convention where he strongly advocated the abolition of property qualifications upon the suffrage. In 1823 he was appointed as judge of the sixth circuit under the new arrangements set up by the constitution of 1821. He held this post until 1831 when he was appointed associate justice of the supreme court of New York. In 1837 he became chief justice and held that position for eight years. In 1845 he received the support of a substantial group of Democrats in the New York legislature for the United States Senate but failed of election. He was a member of the state constitutional convention of 1846 but took no active part in its proceedings.

In February 1845 President Tyler nominated Nelson, unexpectedly to him and to his friends, to the associate justiceship on the Supreme Court of the United States left vacant by the death of Smith Thompson. In spite of the Senate's bitter hostility to Tyler the nomination was confirmed without delay and Nelson took his seat on the Court on Mar. 5, 1845. He became one of the most useful and hard-working members of the Court and a recognized authority in the fields of admiralty and maritime law, international law, patent law, and conflict of laws. As a result of his attention to these more technical problems his interest in questions of constitutional law was correspondingly less, or perhaps it may be said that his training as a common-law lawyer and judge made him somewhat less willing than some of his colleagues to blaze new trails in the politico-judicial realm of judicial review and constitutional interpretation. Ten years elapsed after he entered the Court before he delivered a majority opinion upon a constitutional question (*Pennsylvania* vs. *Wheeling & Belmont Bridge Company*, 18 *Howard*, 421). During his twenty-eight years on the Court he wrote but twenty-two majority opinions in constitutional cases as against three hundred and seven in other cases. He wrote four concurring and seventeen dissenting opinions. His opinions delivered on the circuit bench for the second circuit were of importance in the fields in which he was expert and his decisions were seldom appealed from. There was little about him or his work as a judge which was spectacular or scintillating, but his opinions could be relied upon for logic, lucidity, brevity, and freedom from *obiter dicta* and academic digressions.

Nelson's unwillingness to play politics under the guise of constitutional interpretation is well illustrated by his attitude in the case of Dred Scott [*q.v.*]. The issue presented in this case (19 *Howard*, 393) was the citizenship in Missouri of Scott, such citizenship being requisite to the jurisdiction of any federal court. By its own earlier decision in the case of *Strader* vs. *Graham* (10 *Howard*, 82) the Court had supposedly settled this matter by holding that the status of a negro slave taken by his master into free territory and then back into a slave state was determined by the law of the latter state. The Court's original intention was to dispose of the Dred Scott case in this manner, dismissing it for want of jurisdiction, and to Nelson was assigned the writing of the opinion. On the grounds just outlined he held Scott to be not a citizen of Missouri, the Missouri courts having so held, and consequently incapable of bringing suit as a citizen in a federal court; and he omitted as irrelevant all consideration of the validity of the Missouri Compromise Act of 1820. Stirred by the information that Justices Curtis and McLean were preparing elaborate opinions upholding the citizenship of Scott and the power of Congress to exclude slavery from the territories, the majority of the Court decided to deal with these larger problems and withdrew its support from the narrower and sounder position which Nelson had assumed. Taney's famous opinion and those of his concurring colleagues were the result. But Nelson stood his ground and his opinion remains today as the only one in the case free alike from *obiter dictum* and evidences of political bias.

Nelson's attitude during the Civil War was that of the conservative but loyal Northern Democrat. He doubted the constitutionality of coercing the Southern states and acted with Justice John A. Campbell as an intermediary early in 1861 between the Southern commissioners and Secretary Seward. He strongly urged a policy of conciliation and when Lincoln refused to support Seward to this end he withdrew from the negotiations and left Washington. He looked askance upon what seemed to him to be unwarranted accretions of power to the executive and military branches of the government. He dissented from the majority decision in the Prize Cases and joined with the majority in the Milligan decision. He was one of the original majority in the Legal Tender Cases denying the validity of the Legal Tender Acts and dissented both against the Court's decision to rehear the case and its final judgment of reversal. The Legal Tender Cases were the last in which he participated.

In 1871 Nelson was named by President Grant as a member of the Joint High Commission to negotiate the settlement of the *Alabama* claims, a task for which his knowledge of international law, his tact, and his firmness made him eminently fit. This arduous work extending over several months withdrew him from the bench temporarily. It also hastened his death. A protracted conference in an unheated room induced an illness from which he never fully recovered. He resigned from the Court on Nov. 28, 1872, retiring upon full pay under the Act of 1869. Had he delayed his resignation for a few months, he would have rounded out a full fifty years of service on the state and federal bench. In 1819 Nelson had married Pamela Woods, the daughter of his partner. She died in 1822, leaving one son. In 1825 he moved to Cooperstown, N. Y., where he married Catherine Ann Russell, by whom he had two daughters and a son, Rensselaer Russell Nelson [*q.v.*]. He always maintained a home in Cooperstown and became an intimate friend of James Fenimore Cooper. He died there of apoplexy on Dec. 13, 1873.

[See Alden Chester, *Courts and Lawyers of N. Y.* (1925), vol. III; Edwin Countryman, "Samuel Nelson," *Green Bag*, June 1907; Charles Warren, *The Supreme Court in U. S. Hist.* (1922), vols. II and III; H. L. Carson, *The Supreme Court of the U. S.* (1891); E. J. Wiley, *Cat. of the Officers and Students of Middlebury Coll.* (1917); E. S. Corwin, "The Dred Scott Decision, in the Light of Contemporary Legal Doctrines," *Am. Hist. Rev.*, Oct. 1911; tributes at the time of retirement from the bench in 14 *Wallace*, vii–x; *N.-Y. Tribune*, Dec. 15, 1873. Nelson's Supreme Court decisions are to be found in 4 *Howard* to 12 *Wallace*, inclusive. His circuit court reports are in 1–10 *Blatchford's Circuit Court Reports* (2nd circuit).]

R. E. C.

NELSON, THOMAS (Dec. 26, 1738–Jan. 4, 1789), merchant, signer of the Declaration of Independence, soldier, governor, was the eldest son of William Nelson [q.v.] of Yorktown, Va., and his wife Elizabeth Burwell. He was sent to England to be educated and after attending a private school at Hackney, he entered Christ's College, Cambridge, in May 1758, to stay until Ladyday in 1761. In the year after his return from England, on July 29, 1762, he was married to Lucy, daughter of Philip and Mary (Randolph) Grymes, who bore him eleven children, among them Hugh Nelson [q.v.]. While yet on board the vessel returning from England he had been chosen by the voters of York County to represent them in the House of Burgesses, but he soon took his place among his fellow planters in His Majesty's Council of Virginia in 1764. As the first stages of the Revolution passed in Virginia he was an articulate member of the conventions and supported ardently the preparation for war, especially Patrick Henry's motion to arm Virginia in March 1775. He went to the Continental Congress in 1775, resigning as colonel of the 2nd Virginia Regiment. The none too kindly pen of John Adams described Nelson, when they met in Philadelphia, as "a fat man, like the late Colonel Lee of Marblehead. He is a speaker, and alert and lively for his weight" (C. F. Adams, *The Works of John Adams,* II, 1850, p. 422). In the Virginia convention of 1776 he introduced the resolutions drafted by Edmund Pendleton and advocated by Patrick Henry calling upon Congress to declare the colonies free and independent. These resolutions passed the Virginia convention on May 15 and were taken by Nelson to the Congress in Philadelphia. Thus Thomas Nelson, the embodiment of wealth and established position in Virginia, stood shoulder to shoulder with the then impecunious frontiersman Henry as they swung their followings into the path of independence.

When the Declaration of Independence was adopted Nelson was one of the Virginia signers. Ill health, however, forced him to give up service in the Congress and he returned to Virginia in the spring of 1777. Although he was an ardent revolutionist, he was in no sense a radical and he keenly opposed the Virginia Act of Sequestration of British property in 1777 and is said to have declared that he would pay his debts like an honest man. Appointed by the governor and council of Virginia brigadier-general and commander-in-chief of the forces in the commonwealth, he raised a company with large personal expenditure and marched to Philadelphia in 1778, but these troops were disbanded when

Congress felt unable to support them. In 1779 Nelson returned to Congress but was ill again after several months of service and returned to Virginia to serve for the remainder of the conflict in the rôle of financier, governor, and commander of the militia of his state. In 1781 he was elected in succession to Jefferson governor of Virginia, the first conservative to hold that office. His powers were strengthened by the legislature to meet the military crisis, but he even exceeded these grants of authority in his virtual position as military dictator. In September with over three thousand Virginia militia he joined Washington in the siege of Yorktown. His aid brought expressions of gratitude from Washington and his selfless patriotism in offering his own mansion in the town as a target for the bullets of his fellow countrymen has become one of the lasting tales of the Revolution in Virginia. Again the burden of office proved too great a strain for his constitution and he was forced to resign from the governorship before the end of 1781.

With the victory of the American cause Nelson reaped the ruin of his personal fortune. He sacrificed his private means to pay his public debts, accumulated in security for Virginia's loan of 1780 and in fitting out and provisioning troops. This course with the other hazards of the Revolution left him a poor man with a wife and eleven children. He moved to a small estate, "Offley," in Hanover County, and there spent in simple surroundings the last years of his life. Asthma, the foe he had fought so long, brought his death early in 1789. He was buried in the old churchyard at Yorktown.

[Family Bible of Thos. Nelson in the possession of the Va. Hist. Soc.; "Letters of Thos. Nelson, Jr.," *Va. Hist. Soc. Pubs.,* n.s., no. 1 (1874); *Official Letters of the Govs. . . . of Va.,* vol. III (1929); R. C. M. Page, *Geneal. of the Page Family in Va.* (2nd ed., 1893); Wm. Meade, *Old Churches, Ministers and Families of Va.* (1857); M. V. Smith, *Virginia, 1492–1892, . . . A Hist. of the Executives of the Colony and of the Commonwealth* (1893).] M. H. W.

NELSON, THOMAS HENRY (c. 1823–Mar. 14, 1896), lawyer, diplomat, was born near Maysville, Ky., an elder brother of William Nelson [q.v.], and the son of Dr. Thomas W. Nelson and Frances (Doniphan) Nelson of Mason County, Ky., in whose home the Clays, the Crittendens, and other members of the old Kentucky aristocracy were familiar guests. After completing his studies in the Maysville schools, he went in 1844 to Rockville, Ind., where he studied and practised law for six years, and then moved to Terre Haute, which became his permanent home. In 1855 he formed a law partnership with Abram Adams Hammond, who afterward became governor of Indiana, and in 1856 a partnership with Isaac N. Pierce. In his active law practice in western Indiana and eastern Illinois he met as a legal opponent, and presently as a friend, Abraham Lincoln. He became a leader of the Whig party, and was one of the founders of the Republican party in the Middle West. Several times he was a delegate to state and national conventions. Only once, however, was he a candidate for a public office: in 1860 he made a joint canvass with Daniel W. Voorhees in a campaign for Congress, and his rival won the election. On June 1, 1861, Nelson was appointed minister to Chile by his old friend Lincoln.

Tall and soldierly in bearing, distinguished in appearance, vigorous in action, a brilliant and compelling orator, skilful in public affairs, gifted with a contagious friendliness, he exerted his best efforts to win the friendship of Chile for the United States, and was notably successful, even while he was bringing American claims outstanding against Chile to a speedy and satisfactory settlement. Perhaps the high point of Chilean enthusiasm for Nelson was reached after the terrible fire in the Church of Campañia in Santiago on Dec. 8, 1863, in which about 2,000 persons perished. On this occasion Nelson, with other Americans, showed great heroism in rescuing several individuals. The people of Santiago devoted the following Fourth of July to a celebration to do him honor. In 1865, when hostilities broke out between Chile and Spain, Chile believed that the United States would become her ally. Nelson labored tirelessly to bring about a peaceful settlement between the two warring countries, but was not authorized to involve the United States as a belligerent. The people of Chile were much disappointed, even resentful, but the Minister's policy of neutrality was subsequently indorsed by the State Department.

Returning to the United States in 1866, he campaigned vigorously in favor of the Fourteenth Amendment to the Constitution. In 1869 he was appointed minister to Mexico, and served there ably and faithfully until 1873, although no outstanding incident marked this period of service. The death of his wife, Elizabeth (Key) Nelson, in Mexico city in 1872 was a severe blow to him. The daughter of Col. Marshall Key, a Kentucky political leader, she was possessed of great charm, intelligence, and many accomplishments, and since her marriage in 1844 had taken an important part in her husband's career. (See the article on Mrs. Nelson written by William Cullen Bryant, in the *Annual Cyclopedia* for 1872.) After his resignation from the diplomatic service, Nelson returned to Terre Haute, where he

again practised law and took a prominent part in politics. He died there in 1896, survived by two of his six children.

[*A Biog. Hist. of Eminent and Self-Made Men of the State of Ind.* (1880), vol. II; H. C. Bradsby, *Hist. of Vigo County, Ind., with Biog. Selections* (1891); Osgood Hardy, "When the Monroe Doctrine Was Forgotten," in *Chile* (N. Y.), Mar. 1930; C. C. Oakey, *Greater Terre Haute and Vigo County* (1908), vol. I; U. S. Dept. of State, Diplomatic Correspondence, Chile, vols. XVIII–XXIII, Mexico, vols. XXXVI–XLVIII; *Papers Relating to the Foreign Relations of the U. S.*, 1863 (pt. 2), 1864 (pt. 4), 1866 (pt. 2), 1870, 1871, 1872 (pt. 1), 1873 (pt. 1); Thomas H. Nelson, Official Letter Books, 1861–65 (MSS.), MSS. Div., Lib. of Cong.; "Report and Accompanying Documents . . . on the Relations of the United States with Mexico," *House Report No. 701*, 45 Cong., 2 Sess.; F. F. Hamilton, *Ancestral Lines of the Doniphan, Frazee, and Hamilton Families* (1928); *Sunday Journal* (Indianapolis), Mar. 15, 1896. Date of birth, given in secondary accounts as Aug. 12, 1824, is incompatible with date of Sept. 27, 1824, given for birth of his brother William.]   I. L. T.

NELSON, WILLIAM (1711–Nov. 19, 1772), merchant, planter, councilor, was born in the region of Yorktown, a notable member of the first generation of the Nelson family who bore so vital a part in eighteenth-century Virginia. He was the son of Margaret Reade and Thomas Nelson, "Scotch Tom," as he was called, who emigrated to Virginia at the close of the seventeenth century from Penrith, on the English side of the Scotch border, where the Nelsons were numerous and were occupied in various trades and callings. Scotch Tom settled about 1700 at Yorktown, where he became a successful merchant and landholder. As early as 1738 William Nelson was made sheriff of York and represented that county in the House of Burgesses from 1742 to 1744. He became a member of the Virginia council in 1744 and retained membership until his death in 1772. He served as president of the council and hence was generally known as President Nelson. On the death of Governor Botetourt he was *ex officio* acting governor from October 1770 to August 1771. He was a member of the Committee of Correspondence of the Virginia Assembly, established in 1759, and took a leading part in opposing the taxation policy of England in the decades before the Revolution. In 1770 he declared that the colonists were learning to make many things for themselves and boasted that he wore a "good suit of cloth of my son's wool, manufactured as well as my shirts, in Albemarle, my shoes, hose, Buckles, Wigg & hat, etc., of our own country, and in these we improve every year in Quantity as well as Quality" (*William and Mary College Quarterly*, July 1898, p. 26).

Interested in sports as well as politics, he was keenly concerned in the horse racing of his generation and is credited with having promoted distance racing at the earliest subscription meets. He was a zealous communicant of the Anglican church and stanchly sought to train his children in that faith and with something of austerity he censored their social habits. He patented lands widely scattered over Virginia, thus adding to the considerable patrimony inherited from his father. He cooperated in the forming of the Dismal Swamp Company of 1763 to take up and drain the vast domain of the Dismal Swamp. As a merchant in the thriving town of York, building on the trade inherited from his father, he became the leading merchant of that region and one of the best known in the colonies. For many years he served on the board of visitors of the College of William and Mary. In his marriage he allied himself to two of the most prominent families of the Virginia aristocracy. In 1738 he married Elizabeth, only daughter of Nathaniel Burwell, of Gloucester County, and Elizabeth Carter, second daughter of "King Carter" and his wife Judith Armistead. There were of this union six children who reached maturity, among them Thomas Nelson [q.v.], signer of the Declaration of Independence and Revolutionary governor of Virginia. On his death in 1772 Nelson was buried in the churchyard at Yorktown. In his will he left bequests for the relief of patients in the Public Hospital and to the poor of the parish of York-Hampton.

[Nelson's letter book is preserved at the Episcopal Seminary in Alexandria, Va. Extracts from his letter book appear in the *Wm. and Mary Coll. Quart.*, July 1898, and his will is reprinted in R. C. M. Page, *Geneal. of the Page Family in Va.* (2nd ed., 1893). See also: Wm. Meade, *Old Churches, Ministers, and Families of Va.* (1857), vol. I; and the *Va. Mag. of Hist. and Biog.*, Apr. 1902, Apr. 1903, Apr. 1909, Apr. 1925 (reprint of will), Oct. 1927 (article by Fairfax Harrison), Jan. 1929.]　　　　M. H. W.

NELSON, WILLIAM (Sept. 27, 1824–Sept. 29, 1862), naval officer, Union soldier, was born near Maysville, Ky., youngest son of Dr. Thomas W. Nelson and Frances (Doniphan) Nelson. His elder brothers were Anderson Doniphan Nelson, who became an army officer, and Thomas Henry Nelson [q.v.]. William was appointed midshipman in the United States Navy, Jan. 28, 1840, and became passed midshipman July 11, 1846. He served with the fleet which supported Scott's invasion of Mexico and commanded a battery during the siege of Vera Cruz, Mar. 9–29, 1847. Later he served with the Mediterranean Squadron and on board the *Niagara* when that ship was used to return to Africa the slaves taken from the slaver *Echo*. He was promoted master in September 1854 and lieutenant, Apr. 18, 1855.

During the spring of 1861, Nelson, who was devoted to the Union, made several visits to his native state to study conditions there, reporting his observations to the President, who in April sent him into Kentucky to arm the loyalists and to organize regiments for the Union Army. Some five thousand stand of arms were distributed to the Kentucky Home Guard, the Unionist military organization of the state. Early in August, Nelson established Camp Dick Robinson in Garrard County and began to organize troops for an expedition into East Tennessee. He was commissioned brigadier-general of volunteers, Sept. 16, 1861, and later in the fall was sent into Eastern Kentucky to supervise recruiting camps. During November he expelled a small Confederate column which had invaded the state. Later he joined Buell's Army of the Ohio before Louisville and was given command of the 4th Division. He marched with Buell's command to Pittsburg Landing. Nelson's division was the first element of the Army of the Ohio to arrive on the field of Shiloh. He reached the battlefield with his leading brigades about 5:00 P.M., Apr. 6, 1862, and checked the victorious Confederate advance near the river bank. He bore an important part in the Union counterattack on Apr. 7 and participated in the occupation of Corinth, Miss. After Corinth, he participated in the advance against Chattanooga. On July 17, 1862, he was commissioned major-general of volunteers.

In that month he was ordered, with his division, to Nashville to protect Buell's communications against raid by Forrest's Confederate cavalry. When the Confederate armies of Bragg and E. Kirby-Smith [qq.v.] invaded Kentucky, Nelson was sent thither to organize troops. On Aug. 30, he was wounded at Richmond, Ky., while attempting to rally two of his brigades which had been severely defeated. Later he was placed in command at Louisville to organize its defense. While thus engaged, he had occasion to reprimand Brig.-Gen. Jefferson C. Davis [q.v.] for alleged negligence. A few days later, Sept. 29, 1862, Davis, in company with Gov. O. P. Morton of Indiana, encountered Nelson in the lobby of the Galt House in Louisville. During the altercation which ensued, Davis shot Nelson, who died in about half an hour. Nelson was a strong and dominating character, of great energy, a strict disciplinarian, and intolerant of neglect of duty. His untimely death lost a valuable officer to the Union cause.

[*War of the Rebellion: Official Records (Army)*; F. B. Heitman, *Hist. Reg. and Dict. U. S. Army* (1903); *Battles and Leaders of the Civil War* (4 vols., 1887–88); Thomas Speed, *The Union Cause in Ky.* (1907); W. C. Goodloe, *Kentucky Unionists of 1861* (1884); C. A. Evans, *Confed. Mil. Hist.* (1899), vol. IX; E. M.

Coulter, *The Civil War and Readjustment in Ky.* (1926); G. J. Fiebeger, *Campaigns of the Am. Civil War* (1914); A. M. Ellis, "Major General William Nelson," *Reg. Ky. State Hist. Soc.,* May 1906; J. B. Fry, *Military Miscellanies* (1889); *Cincinnati Daily Commercial,* Sept. 30, Oct. 1, 1862; date of birth from Ellis and Fry.]   H. O. S.

NELSON, WILLIAM (Feb. 10, 1847–Aug. 10, 1914), lawyer, historian, was born in Newark, N. J., the son of William and Susan (Cherry) Nelson. He attended the Newark public schools, graduating from the high school in 1862. The next year, when only sixteen, he became reporter for the *Newark Daily Advertiser,* and the following two years he taught English in German schools in Newark and South Orange, and general subjects in a district school at Connecticut Farms (now Union), N. J. Deciding to devote more time to journalism he took up his residence in Paterson in June 1865, and for ten years was a reporter for the *Paterson Daily Press.* In April 1868 he was elected a member of the Paterson board of education. In May 1871 he was appointed clerk of the Passaic County Board of Chosen Freeholders, serving as such until May 1894, a period of twenty-three years. In the meantime, for ten years (1877–87), he was clerk of the Paterson district court. As a young man he had begun to study law in a desultory way. In his late twenties he entered the office of Hon. John Hopper in Paterson and at the June Term, 1878, was admitted as attorney at the New Jersey bar. In February 1900 he became counselor-at-law and also a master and special examiner in Chancery and from 1902 until his death he served as United States commissioner. From the time of his admission to the bar he practised in Paterson. He amassed the most valuable private law library in the state, consisting of about 10,000 volumes.

In 1872 Nelson read a paper upon the discovery and early history of New Jersey before the Passaic County Historical Society. From that period onward, during the forty-two years of his remaining life, while in a measure active in law practice, he gave most of his time to historical, ethnological, and antiquarian subjects. In 1880 he became recording secretary of the New Jersey Historical Society, in 1890 its corresponding secretary, and this position he retained until his death. While so serving he edited the *Proceedings* of the Society, some dozen volumes, and was brought into wide correspondence with other historians and societies. In 1897, by appointment of the legislature, he was made chairman of the Public Records Commission of New Jersey. While in politics a Republican, he did not care to hold party offices, although he was frequently a delegate to local and national conventions. He

was active in religious and social groups, serving as elder and clerk of the session in the First Presbyterian Church of Paterson, on the advisory board of the Paterson General Hospital, and as trustee of the Pennington Seminary. He held membership in many of the leading scientific, historical, and genealogical societies throughout the country. A bibliography of his books and pamphlets, including a few magazine articles reproduced in pamphlet form, comprises about one hundred and thirty titles. His chief contributions to New Jersey history are in the *Archives of the State of New Jersey,* six volumes of which he edited jointly, and fourteen of which he alone edited, with copious notes, and in a few cases with lengthy historical preliminary monographs. Some other important works were: *The Indians of New Jersey* (1894); *Genealogy of the Doremus Family in America* (1897); *Personal Names of Indians of New Jersey* (1904); *The Law and Practice of New Jersey . . . Concerning the Probate of Wills* (1909); and *Nelson's Biographical Cyclopedia of New Jersey* (2 vols., 1913). He also wrote a three-volume *History of Paterson and Its Environs* (1920), published after his death, and he left various other uncompleted manuscripts, all on historical topics. A nearly complete list of his publications may be found in the *Proceedings of the New Jersey Historical Society* (April 1918). He died at Matamoras, Pa., where he had gone to regain his health in the early summer, but was buried in Cedar Lawn Cemetery, Paterson. He was twice married, in 1872 to Martha Buckley, daughter of Mayor Benjamin Buckley of Paterson, who died in 1885, and, on July 25, 1889, to Salome Williams Doremus, daughter of Henry C. and Ann Eliza (Banta) Doremus, who survived him. He left no children.

[E. Q. Keasbey, *The Courts and Lawyers of N. J.* (1912), vol. III; J. F. Folsom, "Wm. Nelson," *Proc. N. J. Hist. Soc.,* July, Oct. 1914; M. D. Ogden, *Memorial Cyc. of N. J.,* vol. II (1915); *N. J. Law Jour.,* Sept. 1914; *N. Y. Times,* Aug. 11, 1914.] A. V–D. H.

NELSON, WILLIAM ROCKHILL (Mar. 7, 1841–Apr. 13, 1915), journalist, son of Isaac DeGroff Nelson, who emigrated in 1836 from New York state to Indiana, and Elizabeth Rockhill Nelson, whose father had removed in 1819 from New Jersey, was born in Fort Wayne, where he spent a rough-and-tumble boyhood. He was put down as "unruly" and his father, though a vestryman in the Episcopal church, sent him "for discipline" to Notre Dame College, a Catholic institution, from which, at the end of his second year, he carried home a note saying he should not return. Studying law, he was admitted to the bar and entered practice, but not for long. Immediately after the Civil War—his absence from the front is ascribed to parental opposition—he forsook the law and with a companion sought a fortune growing cotton in the southland. This venture ended disastrously. Re-established in his native town, he became a contractor, built roads and bridges, and introduced wooden-block pavement into numerous midwestern cities. His incessant energy had accumulated for him, at thirty-three, the then amazing sum of $200,000 which was swept away in the collapse of his former partner whose notes he had indorsed too freely.

Meanwhile, Nelson had become an enthusiastic Democrat and figured as manager of the Tilden campaign in Indiana. This experience led him, in 1878, to acquire part ownership in the *Fort Wayne Sentinel,* the local Democratic organ, and to take on its active conduct. Two years convinced him his true calling lay in journalism. Desiring a larger field, he chose Kansas City, and with Samuel E. Morss, previously associated with him on the *Sentinel* but soon retired by ill health, he launched the *Kansas City Evening Star,* Sept. 18, 1880. From that time until his death, Nelson had sole control of the publication and every copy irradiated his personal characteristics and aims. At the very outset the editor announced his newspaper ideals. He wanted a paper made particularly for the reader, presenting all the day's happenings concisely without distortion, attractively printed and easily legible, combined with useful information and entertaining reading matter—a family journal in the best sense. He rated the reporter as most important in producing a newspaper.

The paper avowed its independence politically : it was to be "independent but never neutral." The corollary that it had "no fixed policy" was reflected later in strangely contradictory turns and alliances. Disgusted when Tilden was not renominated, Nelson had renounced all party ties but found a successor to worship as his political idol in Cleveland, whom he supported steadfastly, and again in Roosevelt, whose name the *Star* listed as a contributing editor for a time. The chronic inconsistency of the paper convinced its readers of Nelson's complete freedom from "the bosses" and stimulated confidence in his integrity of purpose. The *Star* attacked election frauds, crusaded against vice and gambling and corrupt protection of lawlessness, and forced the construction of cable and electric street-railways. It urged unceasingly, well-paved streets, winding boulevards, and beautiful parks. Its constant tugging "pulled Kansas City out of the mud" and set it on the way to primacy among Missouri Valley cities. Nelson's warranted boast that his papers were read in every home in Kansas City rested upon his policy of recouping the entire cost of production from the advertisers. Originally the *Star* was a six-day, four-page, two-cent sheet, sold to subscribers for ten cents a week. It was successively enlarged, a Sunday issue was added in 1894, and then, on the purchase of the *Kansas City Times* in 1901, a morning paper, giving thirteen copies of a metropolitan daily for ten cents, barely the press-room and delivery expense. The *Star* was to be cheap in price but not in quality. Willing or unwilling, the advertisers had to pay the bill and handsome profits as well. Recalcitrants begged his forgiveness after boycotts or alternative measures taught them that they could not get along in Kansas City without using its columns. Similarly a weekly issue of the paper circulated widely in rural districts of the Southwest at twenty-five cents a year.

Nelson did almost no writing but vigilantly directed the preparation or selection of all that he published. He withstood the lure of office, stressing the superior opportunities for public service of the faithful journalist. Easily accessible to both coworkers and public, he kept aloof from outside enterprises except the Associated Press, of which he was a director, and a paper-mill, erected in Kansas City as a stroke of independence, which, like his cotton-growing, proved a failure. He is to be credited, however, for his fruitful efforts to promote home-building and to develop the city's residential suburbs. A big man physically, the picture of tenacity and pugnacity, his face conveyed at the same time an impression of "massive dignity." By familiars he was called "Colonel," though at no time in military ranks. On Nov. 29, 1881, he was married to Ida Houston of Champaign, Ill. To her, jointly with their daughter, Laura, wife of Irwin R. Kirkwood, he bequeathed his newspapers in trust, to be sold on the death of the survivor to provide an art foundation and museum for Kansas City.

[See *Wm. Rockhill Nelson* (1915), a memorial volume published by members of the staff of the *Kansas City Star*; *Who's Who in America*, 1914–15; W. G. Bleyer, *Main Currents in the Hist. of Am. Journalism* (1927); O. G. Villard, *Some Newspapers and Newspaper-men* (1923); W. B. Stevens, *Centennial Hist. of Mo.* (1921), vol. III, and "The New Journalism in Mo.," *Mo. Hist. Rev.*, Jan. 1925; W. A. White, "The Man Who Made the 'Star'," *Collier's*, June 26, 1915; *Kan. City Star*, Apr. 13, 14, 15, 1915.]   V. R.

NERINCKX, CHARLES (Oct. 2, 1761–Aug. 12, 1824), Roman Catholic missionary, was born in Herffelingen, Belgium, the eldest son of Dr. Sebastian and Petronilla (Langendries) Nerinckx, one of fourteen children. Educated at the preparatory schools of Enghien and Gheel and at Louvain University, Charles followed the traditions of a religious family, when, at the seminary of Mechlin, he began preparation for the priesthood. His uncle was a priest and two aunts were nuns; three of his sisters became nuns; his brother, Peter, was a Brother of Charity; and another brother, John, became a priest on the English missions; three of his cousins also became nuns, while a nephew, F. X. Decoen, S. J., labored in America. After his ordination (1785), Father Nerinckx was a curate at St. Rumoldus, Mechlin, where he interested himself in the welfare of the laboring class. In 1794, he became pastor of Everberg-Meerbeke. His uncompromising manner so aroused the hatred of Revolutionists that the French Directory ordered his arrest. He eluded the police by living in studious seclusion in Dendermonde, where he acted secretly as substitute for the chaplain of the Hospital of St. Blase, who had been sentenced to penal servitude on the Isle of Rhé. Of his writings there remain a treatise on missionaries and an exposition of the reign of Satan, both in Latin (edited by A. F. Vandewyer, Mechlin, 1844). By stealth he visited his abandoned parish, but refused a reappointment in 1801, because he could not accept the Concordat. He was considering service at the Cape of Good Hope or in England, when he learned of opportunities in America. Since his archbishop was in prison, he sought aid from Princess Gallitzin, mother of Demetrius Gallitzin [q.v.], who wrote to Bishop John Carroll [q.v.]. In sore need of priests, the bishop welcomed Nerinckx, who arrived in Baltimore, Nov. 14, 1804. After a few months at Georgetown College, he set out for Kentucky and joined Father Stephen T. Badin [q.v.] in July 1805.

Nerinckx and Badin became warm friends, but neither relished the coming of the Dominicans (1806), who took over their parish on Cartwright's Creek. Indeed, the relations between the rival missionaries were long strained and far from edifying. In Nerinckx's view, the Dominicans were too lax in parish rule; while the religious regarded him as tainted with Jansenist rigorism and as too fearful of republicanism. Carroll refused to take sides, and time healed their petty differences. Nerinckx won the people, even frontiersmen of no faith, who appreciated his self-discipline and courageous acceptance of danger, whether from Indians or the swollen rivers which he was accustomed to swim on his missionary tours. Of powerful physique, he lifted logs heavy enough to tax the strength of two or three men as he built his log chapels at Rolling Fork, Lexington, Hardin's Creek (1806), on Long Lick (1812), and Casey's Creek (1812), and at stations in the wilderness. Nor did he hesitate to carry the hod when erecting a brick church at Danville (1807). He refused a titular bishopric with administrative control over Louisiana (1809), probably realizing that his conscience would render him unfitted for episcopal responsibilities. During a number of journeys to Europe, he obtained financial aid, secured art treasures and paintings, which are now cherished by the Louisville diocese, and brought over novices for his convent, as well as a number of missionaries and Jesuit recruits. He is said to have brought the first organ and the first stoves into Kentucky. In 1812 he founded the Sisters of Loretto at the Foot of the Cross, with Mothers Ann and Mary Rhodes as first superiors. He not only served as spiritual director and author of their strict rule, but aided materially in building their mother house at Loretto, where he lived in a log cabin. Bishop Flaget [q.v.] described this community as "the most valuable legacy which good Mr. Nerinckx had left to his diocese"; it has come to comprise more than 900 nuns, who have the care of two colleges, thirty-one high schools, seventy-one parochial schools, a negro school, two Indian schools, and a branch in Han Yang, China.

In trouble with Rev. Guy I. Chabrat who regarded him as too rigorous and who wished to modify the rules of the Lorettines, Nerinckx left Loretto for The Barrens, Mo., in 1824, although Bishop Flaget made no decision regarding Chabrat's complaints. Accepting his cross, he asked Bishop Rosati for an assignment to his most needy mission, but death came to him while he was visiting at Ste. Geneviève. His remains were interred at The Barrens, and later removed to the sisters' cemetery at Loretto.

[C. P. Maes, The Life of Rev. Charles Nerinckx (1880); W. J. Howlett, Life of Charles Nerinckx (1915); Cath. Encyc., X (1911), 752; Cath. Miscellany and Monthly Repository (London), Apr. 1825; Cath. Hist. Rev., Apr. 1920; M. J. Spalding, Sketches of the Early Cath. Missions of Ky. (1844); Metropolitan Cath. Almanac (1854); Am. Cath. Quart. Rev., July 1880; B. J. Webb, The Centenary of Catholicity in Ky. (1884); Loretto Centennial Discourses (1912); A. C. Minogue, Loretto, Annals of the Century (1912); V. F. O'Daniel, The Rt. Rev. Edward Dominic Fenwick (1920); W. J. Howlett, A Review of Father O'Daniel's Estimate of the Early Secular Missionaries of Ky. (n.d.); John Rothensteiner, Hist. of the Archdiocese of St. Louis (1928).]   R. J. P.

NESBITT, JOHN MAXWELL (c. 1730–Jan. 22, 1802), merchant, was born in Loughbrickland, County Down, Ireland, the son of Jonathan Nesbitt and his wife, whose maiden name was Lang. He emigrated to Philadelphia in 1747 and was apprenticed by his uncle, Alexander Lang, to Redmond Conyngham, a distant relative, to learn the shipping trade. In 1756 he was admitted to partnership by his employer and the firm became Conyngham & Nesbitt. The company was one of the most prosperous and highly regarded mercantile organizations in the city of Philadelphia. Nesbitt took a prominent part among the citizens of Philadelphia during the Revolution. He was appointed a member of the Committee of Correspondence, May 20, 1774, paymaster of the state navy, Sept. 14, 1775; treasurer of the Council of Safety, July 27, 1776, by virtue of which he was treasurer of the state navy board, and treasurer of the state board of war for land service. When the Pennsylvania Bank was organized in 1780 to supply the Continental Army with provisions his firm subscribed five thousand pounds sterling to its funds and he acted as one of the first five inspectors for the bank. He was one of those who cooperated most generously with Robert Morris in the latter's efforts to sustain the public credit and provide for the continuance of the Revolution.

In March 1776 Nesbitt was elected a member of the First Troop, Philadelphia City Cavalry, and remained an active member of this organization during the Revolution, serving principally in its New Jersey campaign. On his resignation he was made an honorary member of the troop, Sept. 10, 1787. When the Bank of North America was organized in November 1781 he was made one of the directors and continued in that capacity until Jan. 9, 1792. He served on the organization committee of the Insurance Company of North America, and upon completion of its organization, Dec. 10, 1792, was chosen as its first president, a position he held until Jan. 13, 1796. He served as one of the wardens for the Port of Philadelphia in 1788 and as an alderman in 1790. In 1793 he was a member of the committee of merchants which collected information regarding the capture or detention of vessels belonging to citizens of the United States by cruisers of European nations then at war. He wrote the report of this committee and was one of those who laid it before the president of the United States. He was one of the original members of the Friendly Sons of St. Patrick, serving first as vice-president of the society (1771–73) and later as president (1773–74, 1782–96). He was never married and died in Philadelphia.

[J. T. Scharf and Thompson Westcott, Hist. of Phila. (1884), vol. I; J. H. Campbell, Hist. of the Friendly Sons of St. Patrick and of the Hibernian Soc. (1892); B. T. Hartman, A Geneal. of the Nesbit, Ross, Porter, Taggart Families of Pa. (1929); T. H. Montgomery, A Hist. of the Insurance Company of North America (1885); H. E. Hayden, ed., The Reminiscences of David Hayfield Conyngham (1904); Reg. of Pa.,
July 10, 1830; Hist. of the First Troop, Phila. City Cavalry (1874); Poulson's Am. Daily Advertiser, Jan. 27, 1802.]   J. H. F.

NESMITH, JAMES WILLIS (July 23, 1820– June 17, 1885), pioneer, lawyer, soldier, legislator, was born in New Brunswick, Canada, while his parents were visiting there. Descended from James Nesmith, a Scotch-Irish founder of Londonderry, N. H., he was the son of William Morrison Nesmith, of Washington County, Me., and Harriet Willis, who died before he was a year old. His father's extensive holdings in New Brunswick were destroyed in 1825 by a forest fire from which the family barely escaped, the step-mother dying from resulting exposure. James then lived with various relatives in New England, learning at a tender age to earn his own living. Winters he attended common-schools desultorily, and as a strapping boy worked near Cincinnati for some years where he had his last chance at schooling. But he loved books, mastered their contents almost without effort, and retained what he had learned, an aspiring spirit in a superb body. At seventeen or eighteen he drifted to Missouri, then to western Iowa, and spent the season of 1842 working as a carpenter at Fort Scott, Kan. From there he joined the Great Emigration of 1843 which established the Oregon colony. He was a natural leader of men, for he was handsome, rugged, democratic, and fun-loving. He was elected orderly sergeant of the Emigrating Company. In Oregon he read some law, was elected supreme judge under the provisional constitution in 1845, was a member of the legislature later, was commissioned captain of volunteers in the Cayuse War in 1848 and in the Rogue River War of 1853, and colonel in the Yakima War of 1855–56. In the years 1857–59 he was superintendent of Indian affairs.

In 1860, as a Douglas Democrat, he gained one of two United States senatorships owing to a combination of Republicans and Douglas men in the legislature against the Lane followers, Edward Dickinson Baker, Republican, winning the other. Powerful in debate, whole-hearted in defense of the Union, Nesmith was a tower of strength to the Lincoln cause. He took an independent stand as a Democrat to vote for the Thirteenth Amendment and he came to the administration's rescue in several critical situations. But fallible judgment betrayed him into supporting McClellan for the presidency in 1864, and this mistake, together with his ardent friendship for Andrew Johnson, virtually terminated his political course. In 1873, as a purely personal triumph, he was elected to Congress, and in 1876 he had the votes to be chosen senator but lost the prize. He had married in 1846 Pauline Goff and settled on a farm at Rickreall, Ore., which was thereafter his home, and there he was buried. Though most men loved him, others hated or feared him. Few were indifferent. He nourished bitter animosities, and George H. Williams, for preventing Nesmith's confirmation as minister to Austria, later found himself checkmated by Nesmith when Grant wished to make him chief justice of the Supreme Court. But he was essentially genial, humorous, and kindly.

[There are important Nesmith letters in the Deady Collection, Ore. Hist. Soc. An intimate sketch by Harriet K. McArthur, his daughter, is in the *Trans.* . . . *Ore. Pioneer Asso.*, 1886. See also: Nesmith's address, *Ibid.*, 1875, "A Reminiscence of the Indian War, 1853," *Quart. Ore. Hist. Soc.*, June 1906, and his reports as superintendent of Indian affairs. Other sources include: G. H. Williams and W. D. Fenton, "Pol. Hist. of Ore. from 1853 to 1865," *Quart. Ore. Hist. Soc.*, Mar., Dec. 1901; W. C. Woodward, "Rise and Early Hist. of Pol. Parties in Ore.," *Quart. Ore. Hist. Soc.*, Mar. 1912; R. C. Clark, *Hist. of the Willamette Valley, Ore.* (1927), vol. I; C. H. Carey, *Hist. of Ore.* (1922).]   J. S.

NESMITH, JOHN (Aug. 3, 1793–Oct. 15, 1869), merchant, manufacturer, inventor, was born in the part of Londonderry, N. H., that is now Windham, son of John and Lucy (Martin) Nesmith. The father, a successful farmer, was a grandson of Deacon James Nesmith, one of the Irish Presbyterians who settled Londonderry. John, after scanty schooling, was apprenticed at fourteen to John Dow, a merchant of Haverhill, Mass. Having learned the business, he returned to Windham where with his brother Thomas (1788–1870) he opened a general store. The two also worked up a profitable trade in buying and selling linen thread, then manufactured in the neighborhood by the Irish descendants. In 1822 they opened a second store, in Derry. They might have continued to be country merchants but in the thirties, attracted by the opportunities developing at Lowell, Mass., they sold their New Hampshire interests and bought the estate on which Judge Edward St. Loe Livermore had lived in the confluence of the Merrimack and Concord rivers, and to which he had given the name "Belvidere." There the Nesmiths laid out streets and house lots on which were built many of the most pretentious residences of a fast-growing community. Their own houses were large, solidly constructed, and in good taste. Of the brothers, John Nesmith, positive, aggressive, and yet public-spirited, became the more prominent in business and politics. Educating himself broadly, he studied the sciences and made himself an expert mechanic. He operated woolen-mills at Lowell, Dracut, and Chelmsford, Mass., and at Hookset, N. H.; he invented machines for shawl

fringing and for weaving wire fence; and he inaugurated a system of using several New Hampshire lakes as storage basins to regulate the flow of the Merrimack River. As a member of the Essex Company he was one of the founders of the city of Lawrence.

As a young man he served a term in the New Hampshire legislature. His interest in the anti-slavery and temperance movements made him later in life an active member of the newly formed Republican party, and as a presidential elector he voted twice for Abraham Lincoln. In 1862 he was elected lieutenant-governor of Massachusetts. Declining a renomination in 1863 he was appointed collector of internal revenue for his district, an office which he held until just before his death. His enthusiasm for the temperance cause was intense and practical. He gave liberally to the local charities. He was interested in the arts of design, a generous patron of the portrait painter Thomas B. Lawson, for several years resident at Lowell. His death was said to be due to his suddenly wearing out after a life of unusual physical and mental activity. Resolutions of the Massachusetts State Temperance Society, of which he was a vice-president, stated: "We tenderly remember his benignant countenance and gentle manly bearing, his form somewhat bowed with the weight of age but his heart aglow with the sensibilities of youth." He had married three times: in June 1825, Mary Ann, daughter of Samuel Bell [q.v.], of Chester, N. H.; in 1831, Eliza Thom, daughter of John Bell, of Chester; in October 1840, Harriet Rebecca, daughter of Aaron Mansur, of Lowell. He had nine children.

[See: L. A. Morrison, *The Hist. of Windham* (1883); C. C. Chase's "Lowell," in D. H. Hurd, *Hist. of Middlesex County, Mass.* (1890), vol. II; *Illustrated Hist. of Lowell and Vicinity* (1897), published by the Courier-Citizen Company; F. W. Coburn, *Hist. of Lowell and Its People* (1920), vol. II; J. C. Chase, *Hist. of Chester, N. H.* (1926); obituaries and editorials in the *Lowell Daily Citizen* and *Lowell Courier*, Oct. 15, 1869. The author of this sketch was given access to letters and other manuscript material in the possession of the family.]   F. W. C.

NETTLETON, ALVRED BAYARD (Nov. 14, 1838–Aug. 10, 1911), soldier, journalist, financier and associate of Jay Cooke in his Northern Pacific operations, was born in Berlin township, Delaware County, Ohio, the son of Hiram and Lavina (Janes) Nettleton. After the customary earlier schooling of his day he entered Oberlin College with the class of 1863, but his college days were cut short when he enlisted as a private in the 2nd Regiment of the Ohio Volunteer Cavalry, September 1861. His rise from the ranks was rapid and spectacular, for when he was mustered out in June 1865, he was brevet brigadier-general. He had seen service in nearly every part of the country to which the military operations of the Civil War extended, from Kentucky and Missouri, where his regiment was first sent, to the campaigns in North Carolina and about Richmond when he was in Sheridan's cavalry corps. In all he participated in more than seventy battles and minor engagements.

While Nettleton left Oberlin at the close of his sophomore year and did not reënter college after the war, his degree, as of the class of 1863, was subsequently bestowed upon him. He read law and was admitted to the bar, but for many years his real interest lay in the field of journalism and finance. During his stay at Oberlin he had worked on the *Oberlin News*. In 1866 he became editor of the *Sandusky Register* and two years later was financial editor of the Chicago *Advance*. It was while at Sandusky that he became acquainted with Jay Cooke who was accustomed to spend much time in the summer at "Gibraltar," his island home in Lake Erie, and, through Nettleton, Cooke got into print his views on the national banking system and on the resumption of specie payments. It was apparent that the financial magnate was impressed by the abilities of the young journalist, for when he took over the moribund Northern Pacific one of the first things he did was to engage him to take charge of the publicity work which was involved in marketing the securities of the railroad. In preparation for this task Nettleton traversed the whole of the proposed route of the road in Minnesota and Dakota Territory. He then made his home at Chelten Hills, Philadelphia, near Cooke's "Ogontz," while his office was at Cooke's bank in town. When the Northern Pacific proved too heavy a burden even for the famous banking concern of Jay Cooke & Company, Nettleton was out of his publicity job, but he was retained for some time to work out a plan of reorganization satisfactory to the bondholders of the railroad.

The brief connection with this type of high finance ended, Nettleton turned again to journalism. After a connection with the *Philadelphia Inquirer,* in 1885 he bought a half interest in the *Daily Minnesota Tribune,* published in Minneapolis, which he made over into a morning daily. Five years later he sold his interest and for the next five years was the Minneapolis representative of various eastern banks and capitalists, placing mortgage loans and dealing in investments generally. In July 1890 he was appointed by President Harrison assistant secretary of the treasury, a position which made him director of the United States Immigration Bureau, and in that capacity he supervised the enlarging and

rebuilding of the facilities at Ellis Island. For a brief interim after the death of Secretary Windom and before the appointment of Charles Foster, he served as acting secretary of the treasury. A subsequent appointment to the World's Columbian Exposition Commission and diverse other interests kept him in Washington for a few more years.

In 1899 Nettleton removed to Chicago where he resided until his death. Those twelve years found him occupied with various business enterprises and with occasional journalistic and magazine work. His interest in Oberlin was always strong and for twenty-two years (1870–92) he was a trustee of that institution. On Jan. 8, 1863, he had married Melissa R. Tenney; she, with three children, survived him when he died in 1911.

[*Annual Reports of the President and the Treasurer of Oberlin Coll.,* 1910–11; E. P. Oberholtzer, *Jay Cooke, Financier of the Civil War* (1907), vol. II; G. E. Warner and C. M. Foote, *Hist. of Hennepin County and the City of Minneapolis* (1881); Military Order of the Loyal Legion of the U. S., Minn. Commandery, *In Memoriam, Companion Bvt. Brig. Gen. A. B. Nettleton* (Circular No. 12, 1912, whole no. 444); Frederick Janes, *The Janes Family* (1868); *Who's Who in America,* 1910–11; *Minneapolis Morning Tribune,* Aug. 12, 1911.]   L.B.S.

NETTLETON, ASAHEL (Apr. 21, 1783– May 16, 1844), Congregational evangelist, was born in what is now the town of Killingworth, Conn., second child of Samuel and Anne (Kelsey) Nettleton. He grew up on his father's farm with only the ordinary advantages of a country boy. His parents were Half-Way Covenant members of the Congregational Church, and he received a good grounding in religious and moral principles. After a period of painful conflict and uncertainty, when he was eighteen years old he became conscious of a change of heart. As the eldest son, the death of his father, shortly afterwards, brought added responsibilities to him. While he went about his duties on the farm, however, the desire to be a means of saving souls possessed him with increasing force, and the reading of missionary literature made him resolve to go to non-Christian lands. With some assistance from the local pastor, Rev. Josiah B. Andrews, he prepared himself for college, and entered Yale in 1805. Here his thoughts were much occupied with religion, and he took but ordinary rank as a student. Graduating in 1809, he served as college butler for a year, studying theology in the meantime, and later, under Rev. Bezaleel Pinneo of Milford, Conn. The Western Association of New Haven County licensed him to preach on May 28, 1811.

Since opportunity to enter the foreign missionary field did not then open, he engaged in evangelistic work in eastern Connecticut, where the excesses and strife engendered by the revival of 1740 were most conspicuous, and many of the churches were without pastors. A study of the causes which had produced these disorders did much to determine the sane and effective spirit and methods which he himself came to employ. The success that accompanied his early labors, together with the solicitation of his brethren, led him to postpone his entrance upon a missionary career, and he was ordained as an evangelist by the Consociation of Litchfield County, Conn., on Apr. 9, 1817. Ill health, following an attack of typhus fever in 1822, finally forced him reluctantly to abandon the missionary project.

Nettleton is said to have been instrumental in the conversion of thousands. He never had a settled pastorate, never married, never asked remuneration for his services, but with single-minded zeal devoted himself to the awakening of souls. He was strictly Calvinistic in his theological views; of no exceptional intellectual power or oratorical ability; simple, searching, practical, and energetic in his preaching. There was nothing fanatical about him or sensational in his methods. To effective address from the pulpit, he added house-to-house visitation, personal conference, and inquiry meetings for instruction. Converts were always thoroughly schooled in the fundamentals of the Christian faith. During the first ten or eleven years of his ministry his labors were chiefly in Connecticut with excursions into neighboring states. After his health broke in 1820 his activities were curtailed. While recuperating he prepared *Village Hymns for Social Worship, Selected and Original* (1824). This same year there also appeared *Zion's Harp; or, a New Collection of Music, Intended as a Companion to "Village Hymns for Social Worship."* Gradually, so far as his strength permitted, he resumed his former manner of life. He spent three winters (1827–29) in Virginia, and a little more than a year (1831–32) in England. The revival methods of Charles Grandison Finney [q.v.] he strongly opposed (see *Letters of the Rev. Dr. Beecher and Rev. Mr. Nettleton on the "New Measures" in Conducting Revivals of Religion,* pamphlet, 1828). Sympathizing with those who were averse to the "New Haven Theology," he joined with them in forming the Connecticut Pastoral Union, which in 1834 founded the Theological Institute of Connecticut at East Windsor Hill, Conn., later transferred to Hartford and named Hartford Theological Seminary. He declined a professorship, but made his home in East Windsor until his death, occasionally lecturing at the Institute,

and preaching in various places as he was able. After his death appeared *Remains of the Late Rev. Asahel Nettleton, D.D., Consisting of Sermons, Outlines and Plans of Sermons, Brief Observations on Texts of Scripture, and Miscellaneous Remarks* (1845), compiled by Bennet Tyler.

[Bennet Tyler, *Nettleton and His Labours, Being the Memoir of Dr. Nettleton . . . Remodelled in Some Parts* (1854); F. B. Dexter, *Biog. Sketches Grads. Yale Coll.,* vol. VI (1912); W. B. Sprague, *Annals Am. Pulpit,* vol. II (1857); *Christian Review,* June 1845; *The New Englander,* Jan. 1845; F. G. Beardsley, *A Hist. of Am. Revivals* (1904); F. J. Metcalf, *Am. Writers and Compilers of Sacred Music* (1925).]   H. E. S.

NETTLETON, EDWIN S. (Oct. 22, 1831–Apr. 22, 1901), civil and irrigation engineer, was born on a farm near Medina, Ohio, the son of Lewis Baldwin and Julia (Baldwin) Nettleton, both of whom were natives of Washington, Conn. He had no middle name but adopted the initial "S" when he started business for himself. Although his formal education was cut short after a period at Oberlin College (1853–54), by reason of lack of funds, he never ceased to be a student of engineering subjects.

Upon leaving college, he went into the lumber business with his cousin, Frank Broadwell, at Kalamazoo, Mich. Removing to Pleasantville, Pa., early in 1865, he took an interest in some oil wells and served as county surveyor. In the spring of 1870, he started West. At Council Bluffs he met and joined the Union or Greeley Colony, organized by Nathan C. Meeker [q.v.], agricultural editor of the *New York Tribune,* then on its way to Colorado. As engineer of the colony, he surveyed the town site of Greeley and laid out its irrigation ditches, which aggregated forty-six miles in length. This system was built out of a common fund and the rights transferred to the water-using farmers, probably the first instance where the use of water for irrigation was put on a truly practical and cooperative basis. Later, Nettleton built the Larimer and Weld Canal for the Colorado Mortgage & Investment Company, commonly known as the English Company. This irrigation system was the largest in Colorado up to that time, covering, in 1881, 60,000 acres of land between Greeley and Fort Collins. He also built the High Line Canal, known as the English Ditch because it was under the financial control of the English Company. A weir invented by Nettleton was first built for the English Company. He surveyed the town sites of Colorado Springs in 1871, Manitou in 1872, and South Pueblo, now a part of Pueblo, in 1873. For a few years he was president of a flour-milling company in Pueblo. From 1883 to 1887 he served as state engineer of Colorado, during which time he inaugurated the work of gauging the streams and ditches. To him more than to anyone else is due the excellent system of stream control and water distribution in irrigation which Colorado now possesses. Following this period, he engaged in consulting work, laying out for construction a number of irrigation works in Wyoming and Idaho. He was chief engineer in diverting the Yaqui River in Mexico for irrigation purposes.

When the first investigation of irrigation was made by the United States government, Nettleton was appointed consulting engineer, acting in that capacity from 1889 to 1893. He was sent to Spain in 1889 and to Spain and Italy in 1892, to investigate irrigation systems, the manner of reforesting denuded tracts, and methods of preventing destruction of forests. The results of his investigation are included in *A Report on Irrigation and the Cultivation of the Soil Thereby* (1893), Part II, published by the United States Department of Agriculture. His last two years were spent as irrigation expert, under Dr. Elwood Mead of the United States Department of Agriculture. In this capacity he made a number of studies in Idaho, Wyoming, and Colorado, and was concerned in devising instruments for the better measurement of water. Shortly before his death, the Department of Agriculture published a bulletin by him, entitled *The Reservoir System of the Cache La Poudre Valley* (1901).

He was one of the founders and one of the first trustees of Colorado College, at Colorado Springs. He established the weather bureau on Pike's Peak, taking the levels up twice, the second time simply to verify the first. An owner of real estate in the suburbs of Denver when the boom began in 1898, he became wealthy, but lost much of his fortune in the failure of one of the Denver banks. On Oct. 17, 1861, he married Lucy F. Grosvenor, of Medina, Ohio; they had four children. Nettleton died in Denver and was buried in Forest Hill Cemetery, Kansas City, Mo.

[*Science*, May 3, 1901; *Denver Republican*, Apr. 23, 24, 1901; David Boyd, *A Hist.: Greeley and the Union Colony of Col.* (1890); J. F. Willard, *The Union Colony at Greeley, Colo., 1869–71* (1918); A. T. Steinel, *Hist. of Agriculture in Colo.* (1926); C. C. Baldwin *The Baldwin Geneal.* (1881); letter from a daughter, Mrs. Willis N. Pickhard, and information from Dr. Elwood Mead, a former associate.]   B. A. R.

NEUENDORFF, ADOLPH HEINRICH ANTON MAGNUS (June 13, 1843–Dec. 4, 1897), musician, conductor, impresario, was born in Hamburg, Germany. In 1854 he accompanied his parents to New York, where he studied violin with George Matzka and Joseph Wein-

lich, and piano with Gustav Schilling. He made his début as a concert-pianist at Dodworth Hall in 1859. The record of his subsequent years is one of practically uninterrupted activity as a solo player, conductor, operatic manager, and composer. After serving for a year as concertmaster of the orchestra at the old Stadt Theatre in New York in 1860, he toured South America from 1861 to 1863 as a violinist. Upon his return he took over the musical directorship of the German Theatre in Milwaukee (1864–65). He then went to New York as chorus master for Karl Anchütz at the new Stadt Theatre, succeeding the latter as director in 1867. At his theatre *Lohengrin* was performed for the first time in America on Apr. 3, 1871. In the same year he brought to America the famous German tenor, Theodor Wachtel, to sing in concert and opera. In 1872 he conducted at the Academy of Music in New York, and from 1872 to 1874 was manager of the Germania Theatre. In 1875 he gave a season of German opera in New York with Wachtel and Eugenie Pappenheim, and two years later he acted as director and conductor of the Wagner Festival in New York at which *Die Walküre* was given for the first time in this country, Apr. 2, 1877. Gustav Kobbé, in *The Complete Opera Book* (1919), calls this première, at the Academy of Music, "an incomplete and inadequate performance with Pappenheim as Brünnhilde" (p. 163).

In 1876 Neuendorff had attended the first performance of the *Nibelungen Ring* at Beyreuth as the correspondent of the *New Yorker Staats-Zeitung*. During 1878–79 he conducted the New York Philharmonic Society, succeeding Theodore Thomas. In the year 1881 he transferred the Germania Theatre to the building vacated by Lester Wallack and there lost a fortune in two years' time. He was subsequently active as conductor of the Promenade Concerts in Boston (1884–89); as conductor of the Emma Juch Opera Company (1889–91); and of English grand opera in New York (1892). From 1893 to 1895 he conducted at the Vienna *Hofoper*, where his wife, Georgine von Januschowsky, was one of the *prime donne*. He returned to New York in 1896 and became director of music in the Temple Emanu-El, the following year succeeding Anton Seidl as conductor of the permanent orchestra of the Metropolitan Opera House. His last appearance in public was as conductor of this organization at the Madison Square Roof Garden concerts during the summer of 1897. He died in New York City later in the same year. He had conducted opera and choral societies in practically all of the larger cities of the United States and produced some forty operas while at the Stadt Theatre in New York. In spite of his uninterrupted activity as a practical musician he was a prolific composer. His comic operas include *The Rat-Charmer of Hamelin* (1880), *Don Quixote* (1882), *Prince Waldmeister* (1887), and *The Minstrel* (1892); he also composed two symphonies and several overtures, cantatas, and a number of songs. He probably did more to bring German drama to a high state of development in New York than any other one man.

[See: the *Musical Courier*, Dec. 8, 1897; *Musical Record*, Jan. 1, 1898; *Grove's Dict. of Music and Musicians, Am. Supp.* (1920); *Appletons' Ann. Cyc.* 1897; *N. Y. Times*, Apr. 4, 1871; *N. Y. Tribune*, Dec. 5, 1897.]   F. H. M.

NEUMANN, JOHN NEPOMUCENE (Mar. 28, 1811–Jan. 5, 1860), Roman Catholic prelate, son of Philip and Agnes (Lebisch) Neumann, was born in Prachatitz, Bohemia, where his father operated a stocking factory and his uncle ruled as mayor. Reared by devout parents, two of whose six children became Sisters of St. Charles, John evidenced remarkable religious fervor in the elementary school which he attended and in the Cistercian college at Budweis. Despite paternal urging to study medicine, he managed to enter the seminary at Budweis although only a fourth of the candidates could be admitted. A laborious student, he gained a deep knowledge of canon law, scriptures, and Hebrew, and also found opportunity to study English at the University of Prague, with the intention of going on the American missions, in which a crusading interest had been aroused by the publications of the Leopoldine Society. In vain he sought adoption by the dioceses of Vincennes and Philadelphia. Undaunted, he set forth for New York, where he was received by Bishop Dubois, who ordained him in old St. Patrick's (June 25, 1836). Assigned to Williamsville, N. Y., Father Neumann attended a number of missions, journeying on foot as often as by wagon as he ministered to scattered and impoverished immigrant congregations. His self-sacrifice and zealous acceptance of privations attracted the attention of the Redemptorist Fathers who were establishing a monastery at Pittsburgh. He in turn, appreciating the value of their rigorous rule, joined the congregation on Oct. 13, 1840. After a period of probation he took the full vows in St. James's Church, Baltimore, Jan. 16, 1842.

As a Redemptorist, Neumann's life and work were changed but little. He continued to preach on missions in the German centers of New York, Pennsylvania, Virginia, Maryland, and Ohio, until he was appointed superior of the community at Pittsburgh (1844). Here he carrried a heavy burden, building the elaborate St. Philomena's Church and winning the gratitude of Bishop O'Connor [*q.v.*] for his effective work among the Germans. In 1847 he was chosen vice-provincial with headquarters at Baltimore. During his tenure, he established a number of parishes and schools and stimulated vocations. Interested in their work among the negroes, he saved the Colored Oblate Sisters from dissolution. As a confessional priest who courted seclusion and shunned worldly applause and influence, he rejoiced when, in 1851, he was permitted to become pastor of the unfinished church of St. Alphonsus, Baltimore. This interim of comparative ease was brief, however, for Neumann was named successor to Francis P. Kenrick [*q.v.*] as bishop of Philadelphia, to the intense satisfaction of the German element who were under-represented in the hierarchy. Neumann sought relief from episcopal honors, but under the rule of obedience accepted and was consecrated in his parish church by Archbishop Kenrick on Mar. 28, 1852. He was a determined promoter of parochial education. His diocese built about a hundred elementary schools, which were assigned to the various teaching sisterhoods, among which were the Sisters of Notre Dame of Munich, whom he aided in coming to America; the Sisters of the Holy Cross, whom he introduced from France; and the sisters of St. Francis, whose Philadelphia branch he founded. To the Christian Brothers, he assigned boys' schools. Meanwhile, he compiled such doctrinal aids for children as the *Kleiner Katechismus* (1853), and *Katholischer Katechismus* (1855), which appeared in later German and English editions. In an effort to encourage priestly vocations, he established a model preparatory seminary and improved the standards at the major seminary of St. Charles Borromeo. Yet it was not as a builder primarily that Neumann was notable, but as a writer of spiritual pastorals, a retreat master, an exact ritualist, a promoter of devotional practices, a lover of children, and a friend of the poor and the unfortunate. Even the bitterest Know-Nothings found little to condemn in a man who could accept affronts with forgiving humility. Together with his brother he assigned his patrimony for the endowment of a hospital in his native village, where he received every possible honor when he visited the town in connection with his journey to Rome for the promulgation of the doctrine of the Immaculate Conception (1854).

The tradition of Neumann's sanctity strengthened when miracles were said to have occurred at his tomb in St. Peter's Church. A commission was instituted to inquire into his life and furnish testimony to Rome with the view of his ultimate beatification (1886). Ten years later (Dec. 15), he was declared venerable and his cause is still under advisement before the Sacred Congregation of Rites.

[There are several lives: one by J. A. Berger (a nephew), translated from the German by Eugene Grimm (1884); one by J. Magnier (1897); and, in Dutch, another by J. L. Jansen (Amsterdam, 1899); see also *Funeral Obsequies of Rt. Rev. John Nepomucene Neumann* (1860); U. S. Cath. Hist. Soc., *Records and Studies*, Oct. 1900; R. H. Clarke, *Lives of the Deceased Bishops of the Cath. Church in the U. S.*, II (1888), 431–67; G. F. Houck, *The Church in Northern Ohio* (1887); Neumann's notebook in *Records Am. Cath. Hist. Soc.* (1930); *Cath. Encyc.*, X, 773; J. G. Shea, *Hist. of the Cath. Church in the U. S.*, IV (1892); *Ave Maria*, Feb. 1890; *Cath. World*, Dec. 1892; *Morning Pennsylvanian*, Jan. 6, 10, 1860; *Philadelphia Daily News*, Jan. 10, 1860; *Cath. Herald* (Phila.), Jan. 14, 1860; *Ecclesiastical Rev.*, June 1930.]

R. J. P.

NEUMARK, DAVID (Aug. 3, 1866–Dec. 15, 1924), Jewish philosopher, was born in Szczerzec, Galicia, the son of Solomon and Schifrah Schuetz Neumark. His father was a private scholar who devoted himself altogether to study, while the maintenance of the family devolved upon the mother, a woman of energy and resourcefulness. Her great ambition was to have her only son, David, the youngest of three children, study for the rabbinate. He was a child of exceptional gifts. His schooling began in the *cheder*, the communal Jewish school, when he was but two and one half years old; at the age of six he began the study of the Talmud under his father's tutelage. Upon the death of the father a year later, the mother at great personal sacrifice decided that the child must continue his studies. He attended the Beth ha-Midrash (Hebrew Academy) and also studied privately. After a time he frustrated his mother's hope that he would prepare for an active rabbinical position by deciding to enter a university. Leaving home in 1887 without her consent, he proceeded to the Galician metropolis, Lemberg, where, after studying for three and one half years, he took the entrance examinations for the Obergymnasium. Here he specialized in philosophy, devoting particular attention to Kant, and graduated in 1892.

In November of that year he proceeded to Berlin where he matriculated at the University and entered also the liberal rabbinical seminary known as the Hochschule für die Wissenschaft des Judenthums. Here he again specialized in philosophy and also studied intensively Semitic languages and literature. At this time he wrote the essay which was awarded the Mendelssohn

prize in 1894—"Die Verschollenheit des Ehegatten im rabbinischen Rechte." This was soon followed by a study of Nietzsche's philosophy which was published in the Hebrew periodical *Mimizrach umimaarab*, Vienna. He received the degree of doctor of philosophy from the University of Berlin on Mar. 26, 1896. Professor Hans Vaihinger of the University of Halle, president of the Kant Society, thought so highly of Neumark's thesis that he recommended it to a well-known publishing firm, and it appeared under the title *Die Freiheitslehre bei Kant und Schopenhauer* (1896). A year later Neumark was graduated from the rabbinical seminary. His thesis here was an outline of the history of dogmas in Judaism, which sketch he elaborated and published in Hebrew in two volumes some years later (Odessa, vol. I, 1913; vol. II, 1919).

He obtained his first and only rabbinical post in Rakonitz, Bohemia, where he served from March 1897 to February 1904. While here he married, June 7, 1898, Dora Turnheim of Przemysl. In 1903 he was considered for the position of chief rabbi of Rome, but about that time he accepted the position of editor in chief for the sections of Jewish Philosophy and Talmud in the new Hebrew encyclopedia, launched by the Achiasaf, a Hebrew publishing society of Warsaw. It established a branch bureau for him in Berlin, to which city he removed in February 1904. While in the German metropolis he taught for a while in the Lehrerinnen-Seminar of the central Jewish congregation (Haupt Gemeinde). In 1907 he was elected to succeed the noted scholar Dr. Moritz Steinschneider as professor of Jewish philosophy in the Veitel-Heine-Ephraimische Anstalt. He had scarcely been named for this position when the invitation came from Cincinnati, Ohio, to occupy the chair of Jewish philosophy at the Hebrew Union College. He finally determined to go to the United States, where he arrived with his family on Nov. 28, 1907. A week later he reached Cincinnati and entered at once upon his work, continuing therein for the remainder of his life.

At the time of his death Neumark was generally conceded to be the leading student of Jewish philosophy. He made the entire field of Hebrew learning his own and was a daring and original thinker. His philosophical studies comprised "Jehudah Hallevi's Philosophy in its Principles," his first publication in English, which appeared in the *Catalogue* of Hebrew Union College in May 1908; "Crescas and Spinoza," which was published in the *Year Book of the Central Conference of American Rabbis* (vol. XVIII, 1909); and "Steinthal and Lazarus" and "Historical and Systematic Relations of Judaism to Kant," the latter in commemoration of the two-hundredth anniversary of the birth of Kant, both of which appeared in the *Year Book* (vol. XXXIV, copr. 1925). He published also a work entitled *The Philosophy of the Bible* (1918). His *magnum opus,* however, was to be a history of medieval Jewish philosophy, which he planned on a comprehensive scale, but did not live to complete. Two volumes only, the second in two parts, were published under the title *Geschichte der Jüdischen Philosophie des Mittelalters* (1907–28). A Hebrew edition was also issued (1921–29). At the time of his death he had done the preliminary work for the remaining volumes, but had asked that his notes should not be given to anyone else to use, though he hoped that someone would be inspired by his work to continue a history of Jewish philosophy. Neumark contributed extensively in the form of essays and reviews to Hebrew, German, and English periodicals. A glance at the titles of these articles makes clear how broad was his outlook and how encyclopedic his learning. In order to make the most important of these studies more accessible to scholars the Central Conference of American Rabbis published a volume in 1929 entitled *Essays in Jewish Philosophy by David Neumark.* To this volume is appended a full bibliography of his writings.

In 1919 he founded a quarterly review under the title *Journal of Jewish Lore and Philosophy.* After four numbers had appeared, he suggested that the authorities of the Hebrew Union College take it over and publish it as an official organ of the institution. This suggestion was adopted in 1921, but in place of a quarterly it was issued as an annual publication under the title *Hebrew Union College Annual.* Neumark was a member of the board of editors until his death.

[*Hebrew Union Coll. Mo.*, Jan., Feb. 1924; *Hebrew Union Coll. Ann.*, vol. II (1925); *Year Book Central Conf. of Am. Rabbis*, vol. XXXV (1925); *Jewish Exponent*, Dec. 19, 1924; *Cincinnati Enquirer*, Dec. 16, 1924; *Jewish Tribune*, Dec. 26, 1924; *Who's Who in America*, 1924–25.]   D. P—n.

NEVILLE, JOHN (July 26, 1731–July 29, 1803), Revolutionary soldier, was the son of George and Ann (Burroughs) Neville. George Neville apparently came to the colonies in his early youth (family tradition recorded in *Potter's American Monthly*, February 1876), settled on the headwaters of the Occoquan River in Virginia, and acquired a large estate, which appears on Pownall's, Fry's, and Jefferson's maps and on the map accompanying the 1787 edition of Jefferson's *Notes on the State of Virginia.* There John Neville was born and reared. On Aug. 24,

1754, he married Winifred Oldham. He served under Washington in Braddock's expedition (1755) and then settled near Winchester, Va., where he was elected sheriff. He later made large purchases of land on Chartier's Creek, near Pittsburgh, and for his services in the Dunmore War (1774) received, with Valentine Crawford, a joint patent for 1,000 acres. This region was in dispute between Pennsylvania and Virginia and the inhabitants elected Neville a delegate to the Virginia convention of 1774, but he was too ill to attend. In August 1775 the Virginia Committee of Safety ordered him to proceed to Pennsylvania with the militia company which he commanded and occupy Fort Pitt. This accomplished, he was appointed justice of "Yohogania County," the new county organized by Virginia for the government of the disputed area. Neville declined to take any further part in the boundary dispute and remained commandant at Fort Pitt during the first two years of the Revolution. With George Morgan, Indian agent, he tried to keep the tribes friendly, but only the Delawares responded. On Nov. 12, 1776, Neville was promoted lieutenant-colonel and later was ordered to join Washington's army, to which he was attached for the remainder of the war. He was promoted colonel in 1777 and brevetted brigadier-general in 1783. After the Revolution he was elected to the Supreme Executive Council of Pennsylvania, to the Pennsylvania convention which ratified the federal Constitution, and to the Pennsylvania constitutional convention of 1789–90. As "inspector of survey" for the collection of the whiskey tax in western Pennsylvania (1792–95) he was a central figure in the Whiskey Rebellion of 1794. His house was repeatedly threatened and finally destroyed by the volatile citizenry (*Olden Time*, Pittsburgh, October 1846, December 1847). Neville escaped and with other "exiles" returned with the army sent to put down the rebellion. In 1796 he served as federal agent for the sale of public lands northwest of the Ohio. During his later years he lived at his estate on Montour's Island, near Pittsburgh, where he entertained visitors of note, including Louis Philippe, the duc d'Orléans (King of the French, 1830–48), and his two brothers, the duc de Montpensier and the comte de Beaujolais (1797). Neville died on the island in 1803. His descendants, bearing the surnames Neville and Craig, were of considerable importance in Pittsburgh and Cincinnati for the next fifty years. His son, Col. Presley Neville, married Nancy, daughter of Gen. Daniel Morgan [*q.v.*].

[R. G. Thwaites and L. P. Kellogg, *The Revolution on the Upper Ohio, 1775–77* (1908); Morgan Neville,

"Reminiscence of Pittsburgh," *Cincinnati Chronicle and Lit. Gazette*, Jan. 8, 1831, reprinted in *Western Pa. Hist. Mag.*, Oct. 1922; Samuel Wilkeson, "Early Recollections of the West," *Am. Pioneer* (Cincinnati), May 1843; W. H. Egle, *Pa. Geneals.* (2nd ed., 1896); Neville B. Craig, *The Hist. of Pittsburgh* (1851, new ed. with index, 1917); Boyd Crumrine, *Hist. of Washington County, Pa.* (1882); H. M. Brackenridge, *Recollections of Persons and Places in the West* (1834) and *Hist. of the Western Insurrection in Western Pa.* (1859).]
F. E. R.

NEVILLE, WENDELL CUSHING (May 12, 1870–July 8, 1930), commandant of the United States Marine Corps, was born at Portsmouth, Va., the son of Willis H. and Mary Elizabeth (Cushing) Neville. He was educated at Galt's Academy, Norfolk, Va., and entered the United States Naval Academy Sept. 13, 1886. Completing the four years' academic course in June 1890, he served two years at sea as a naval cadet on board the *Kearsarge* and the *Newark*. He was commissioned a second lieutenant in the United States Marine Corps July 1, 1892, his first station being the marine barracks, Washington, D. C., where he spent two years. This was followed by service on various vessels. On Jan. 4, 1898, he was married to Frances Adelphia Howell of Washington, D. C. While on duty with the marine battalion of the North Atlantic Squadron in 1898 he participated in the battle of Guantanamo Bay, Cuba, and was appointed captain by brevet for conspicuous service in this battle. Upon the outbreak of the Philippine Insurrection, he became a member of the 4th Battalion organized for duty in the Philippines. This battalion, however, was diverted to China, thus giving Neville the opportunity to participate in the Boxer Campaign from Aug. 5 to Oct. 9, 1900. This service was followed by a tour of duty in the Philippine Islands where he commanded the barracks of Isabela de Basilan in the Moro country of the southern islands. His return in March 1903 was followed by various assignments and duties in the United States; by this time he had reached the grade of major.

When the United States intervened in Cuba, he served as a battalion commander in the initial phase of the occupation of the island during the month of October 1906. This was followed during the next few years largely by sea duty, but it also included service in Nicaragua. Early in 1914 he embarked at Pensacola in command of the 2nd Regiment and in April participated in the engagement which resulted in the occupation of Vera Cruz, Mexico. For this service he received the Naval Medal of Honor with commendation for conspicuous courage, coolness, and skill in the conduct of the fighting. From December 1915 to October 1917 he commanded the marine detachment of the American legation at Peking, China. Upon his return to the United States late in 1917, he was immediately ordered to France. He arrived there Dec. 28, 1917, assumed command of the 5th Regiment of Marines, and at the end of the month received his commission as colonel. His long and varied service had qualified him for the training of a regiment for the great conflict and the command of it on the battlefields of France. His regiment, together with the 6th Marines, constituted the 4th Brigade of the 2nd Division. While in command of the 5th Regiment he participated in the Aisne-Marne defensive, at Château-Thierry and in the battle of Belleau Woods. As commander of the 4th Brigade he participated in the battle of Soissons, the St. Mihiel offensive, the offensive in the Champagne (Blanc Mont), and in the Meuse-Argonne offensive. He was promoted brigadier-general on Aug. 28, 1918. The award of the Distinguished Service Medal cites these actions in which he participated and states most simply: "In all of these he proved himself to be a leader of great skill and ability." An American military officer could hardly ask greater distinction than to have exercised command in the 2nd Division in these actions.

After the signing of the armistice Neville served with the Army of Occupation in Germany and returned to the United States in the summer of 1919. He was promoted to the grade of major-general with rank from Dec. 10, 1923. He occupied important positions including that of assistant to the major-general; commandant; commander of the Department of the Pacific; commanding general of the Marine Corps Expeditionary Force, United States fleet; commanding general of Quantico; and finally commandant of the United States Marine Corps, to which position he was appointed Feb. 7, 1929, by President Coolidge, succeeding Gen. John A. Lejeune. He died on July 8, 1930, survived by a daughter, and was buried in the Arlington National Cemetery. He was the recipient of numerous decorations.

[*Who's Who in America*, 1930–31; *Army and Navy Reg.*, July 12, 1930; *Outlook*, Mar. 20, 1929; *Washington Post*, July 9, 1930; *N. Y. Times*, July 9, 10, 1930; official records of the U. S. Navy Dept.]
M. E. S.

NEVIN, ALFRED (Mar. 14, 1816–Sept. 2, 1890), Presbyterian clergyman, editor, and author, was a native of Shippensburg, Pa., the second son of Maj. David and Mary (Peirce) Nevin, a younger brother of Edwin H. Nevin [q.v.], and first cousin of John Williamson Nevin [q.v.]. He was educated at Jefferson College and at Judge Reed's law school, which was the law department of Dickinson College, receiving his degree in 1837. That same year he was admitted to the bar, but appears not to have practised the profession, for he at once entered Western Theological Seminary at Allegheny, graduating and being licensed to preach by the Presbytery of Carlisle in 1840. For twenty years he served in the pastorate, acquiring an experience of life and a wide acquaintance with other ministers which was invaluable in his later career as a writer, editor, and publisher in the religious field. His pastorates were at Cedar Grove, Pa., 1840–45; Chambersburg, where he served the German Lutheran Church, 1845–52; Second Presbyterian Church, Lancaster, 1852–57; and in Philadelphia, where, in 1857, he organized the Alexander Presbyterian Church, named in honor of Dr. Archibald Alexander [q.v.], first professor of Princeton Theological Seminary, and was its pastor four years.

He resigned from the Alexander Church in order to edit and publish a weekly religious periodical, the *Standard,* at a period when such denominational papers were issued in large numbers throughout the country, and when many of them were financially profitable. In 1866 ill health compelled him to relinquish control of the *Standard* and it was merged with the *Northwestern Presbyterian.* After a time he published the *Presbyterian Weekly,* which in a few years became the *Baltimore Presbyterian,* and for a number of years, until 1880, he was editor-in-chief of the *Presbyterian Journal,* Philadelphia. Each of these papers has since passed through one or more changes in name and ownership, the *Standard* and the *Journal* now being represented by the *Presbyterian Advance,* published at Nashville, Tenn. From the early years of his ministry Nevin was the author of books, *Churches of the Valley* (1852), being his first volume of note. Among the others, which totaled more than twenty, were *The Age Question* (1868); *Notes on Exodus* (1874); *Centennial Biography: Men of Mark of the Cumberland Valley, Pa., 1776–1876* (1876); *Parables of Jesus* (1881); *Letters Addressed to Col. Robert G. Ingersoll; or Infidelity Rebuked and Truth Victorious* (1882); and *Encyclopædia of the Presbyterian Church in the United States of America* (1884). In editing the last work he was assisted by his youngest brother, David Robert Bruce Nevin.

During Nevin's editorship of the *Standard* he was also an army chaplain, serving at Satterlee General Hospital, Philadelphia, from November 1863 to July 1865. He was a member of the first board of trustees of the Presbyterian Historical Society, of the state historical societies of Pennsylvania and Wisconsin, and of the Presbyterian

Board of Education. While he was located at Lancaster he was elected moderator of the Synod of Pennsylvania, and he attended several of the annual sessions of the General Assembly as an elected commissioner. In 1841 he married Sara, daughter of Robert Jenkins, of Lancaster.

[See Nevin's *Encyc.* and his *Hist. of the Presbytery of Phila.* (1888); also, F. B. Heitman, *Hist. Reg. and Dict. U. S. Army* (1903); *Biog. and Hist. Cat. of Washington and Jefferson Coll.* (1902); *The Western Theol. Sem. Gen. Biog. Cat.* (1927); *Presbyterian Banner,* Sept. 10, 1890; *Presbyterian,* Sept. 10, 1890; *Phila. Inquirer,* Sept. 3, 1890.]   P. P. F.

NEVIN, EDWIN HENRY (May 9, 1814–June 2, 1889), clergyman, educator, and author, was born at Shippensburg, Cumberland County, Pa., son of Maj. David and Mary (Peirce) Nevin, a brother of Alfred Nevin [q.v.], and a cousin of John Williamson Nevin [q.v.]. His father served in the defense of Baltimore during the War of 1812, and was a member of the convention which revised Pennsylvania's state constitution (1837–38). He was a successful merchant, and was known for his enterprise and philanthropies. Edwin Nevin was graduated from Jefferson College in 1833, and from Princeton Theological Seminary in 1836, after having taken his first year of theology in Western Seminary at Allegheny, Pa. Following his licensure by the First Presbytery of Philadelphia in 1836, he served the church at Portsmouth, Ohio, and from 1839 to 1841 was pastor at Poland in the same state.

When only twenty-six years old he was elected president of Franklin College, New Athens, Ohio, where he was received as "a young man of ardent temperament, with a well cultured mind, and . . . an attractive pulpit orator" (*Franklin College,* 1908). Under his administration the college gained wide repute, considerable funds were raised, and a new building was erected. He was instrumental in having a bell for this building cast in exact facsimile of the bell on Independence Hall, Philadelphia, even to the inscription: "Proclaim liberty throughout the land, and to all the inhabitants thereof." He resigned in 1844 to accept a pastorate in Cleveland. Though ill health hampered his activities during much of his later life, he served the Presbyterian church at Mount Vernon, Ohio, several Congregational churches in New England, St. Paul's Reformed Church at Lancaster, Pa., and the First Reformed Church of Philadelphia. In 1875 he retired from the active ministry.

In addition to his pastoral work he wrote many articles for the religious press, numerous hymns and poems, and books on religious subjects. Among the last-named were *Mode of Baptism*

(1847); *Warning Against Popery* (1851); *Faith in God, the Foundation of Individual and National Greatness* (1852); *The Man of Faith* (1856); *The City of God* (1868). He had a wide reputation in his day as an impressive preacher, a ready debater—particularly in opposition to slavery—a man of comprehensive literary knowledge, and a warm advocate of conservative religious belief. Late in life he was elected a member of the Victoria Philosophical Society of Great Britain. His wife was Ruth C. Little, whom he married in 1837.

[Alfred Nevin, *Encyc. of the Presbyterian Ch. in the U. S. A.* (1884), and *Centennial Biog.: Men of Mark of the Cumberland Valley, 1776–1876* (1876); *Princeton Theol. Sem. Biog. Cat.* (1909); *The Western Theol. Sem. Gen. Biog. Cat.* (1927); *Presbyterian Banner,* June 12, 1889; *Presbyterian,* June 8, 1889; *Public Ledger* (Phila.), June 3, 1889.]   P. P. F.

NEVIN, ETHELBERT WOODBRIDGE (Nov. 25, 1862–Feb. 17, 1901), composer, was among the first native-born American composers to display strongly individual qualities of style. He was born at Edgeworth, near Pittsburgh, Pa., the fifth in a family of eight children. His ancestors, of Scottish origin on both sides, had been in America since the early eighteenth century. His father was Robert Peebles Nevin [q.v.]. His mother, Elizabeth Duncan (Oliphant) Nevin, of Uniontown, Pa., was descended from Duncan Oliphant, who had come to America from Gash, Scotland, in 1721. She was a trained musician of wide culture, and the first grand piano to be carted over the Alleghany Mountains into Western Pennsylvania was for her girlhood home. Her love of music made a powerful impression upon Ethelbert. At the age of three he learned to sing the stirring songs of the times and at five he played his own accompaniments at the piano while he sang. At ten he took his first formal piano lessons from Von der Heide and a little later from William Guenther, both of Pittsburgh, and at eleven he played in a public concert in Pittsburgh. In 1877–78 his parents took him abroad for a year's travel and study and placed him for a time for piano instruction under Franz Böhme in Dresden. On his return to Edgeworth he entered the Western University of Pennsylvania but remained only till the end of his freshman year in 1879, when he decided to enter the path of the professional musician.

He overcame his father's opposition to such a career, and in the early fall of 1881 he went to Boston and for two years studied piano with Benjamin Johnson Lang and harmony and composition with Stephen A. Emery. Ambitious to perfect himself as a concert pianist, he went to

Berlin in August 1884 and spent two years with Karl Klindworth (piano) and Carl Bial (theory), also a short period with Hans Von Bülow (piano) and Otto Tiersch (composition). A few weeks after his return to America he made a successful début as a pianist in Pittsburgh, Dec. 10, 1886, then settled in Boston, where he remained for nearly five years, teaching, concertizing, and composing. The rapidly growing popularity of his earlier compositions (notably the *Sketch Book*) made him turn more and more to composition as his life-work. Feeling the need for further study, he sailed for Europe in May 1891, spending a year in Paris composing and teaching and eight months in Berlin given wholly to study and composition. In December 1892 he was in America again, but he was overworked and ill, and to recuperate he made a brief trip to Algiers in the early months of 1894. Midsummer found him at "Vineacre," the old home at Edgeworth, preparing for the most successful concert tour of his career—and the last. Abandoning concert-life, he again went abroad early in 1895 to find there a more serene and inspiring atmosphere for composition. The stay in Europe included sojourns in Florence, Montepulsiano in the Tuscan Apennines, Venice, and then Paris. He returned to America in October 1897 and established himself in New York. In the late autumn of 1900 he moved to New Haven, Conn., where he lived quietly and in increasing ill health till his death. The funeral service was held in the Presbyterian Church at Sewickley, Pa., and he was buried in the cemetery close by. He was married on Jan. 5, 1888, to Anne Paul of Pittsburgh, who with two children survived him.

Nevin was slender and rather frail in figure, never robust nor fond of any sport. Though struggling much with ill health, he possessed a happy, buoyant, lovable nature and rare social gifts. As a pianist of ample technical equipment he was happiest in the interpretation of his own compositions, which always evoked enthusiasm. His total published compositions number about one hundred and thirty (seventy songs, forty-two for piano, three for violin, sixteen for chorus). His genius was essentially lyrical. Aside from the fine early song "Herbstgefühl" (1889), there are but few dramatic passages in all his music. Recognizing this, he had the wisdom to confine himself to the smaller instrumental and vocal forms, of which he was a complete master. The exceptional popularity of many of his compositions is due to their unaffected simplicity, spontaneity, grace, and melodic charm. His music reflects his instinctive love for light rather than shadow, for joy rather than sorrow. His love for nature finds full expression in such groups as *Water Scenes* (*opus* 13, 1891), *In Arcady* (*opus* 16, 1892), *May in Tuscany* (*opus* 21, 1896), and *A Day in Venice* (*opus* 25, 1898). He was fortunate in gaining early recognition for his talent. The *Sketch Book* (*opus* 2, 1888), a versatile collection of thirteen songs and piano pieces, had a remarkable sale and contained several of his finest compositions—"Im wunderschönen Monat Mai," "Lehn' deine Wang," and "Oh! that We Two Were Maying." "One Spring Morning" (from *opus* 3, 1888) and "'Twas April" (from *opus* 4, 1889) also made wide appeal. He attained international fame when he published *Water Scenes,* owing largely to one of the group, "Narcissus," which soon became a world favorite. The same measure of popularity has also been accorded to "The Rosary" (1898), which was the most famous song written by an American after the melodies of Foster, who was an intimate friend of Nevin's father. This song was first publicly sung by Francis Rogers accompanied by the composer, Feb. 15, 1898, in Madison Square Garden Concert Hall, New York. His most pretentious work is *The Quest* (1902), a cantata on which he was working when he died. The orchestration was completed by Horatio Parker.

[Vance Thompson, *The Life of Ethelbert Nevin* (1913), based upon Nevin's letters and his wife's memories; Francis Rogers, "Some Memories of Ethelbert Nevin," *Musical Quart.*, July 1917; J. T. Howard, *Our Am. Music* (1931); Rupert Hughes, *Contempory Am. Composers* (1900); L. C. Elson, *The Hist. of Am. Music* (1904); Louis Tipton-Campbell, *Music*, Apr. 1901; Willa Cather, "The Man Who Wrote 'Narcissus,'" *Ladies' Home Jour.*, Nov. 1900; the *Musician*, Mar. 1901; *Pittsburg Dispatch*, Dec. 11, 1886; *N. Y. Times*, Feb. 18, 1901.]   R. G. C—e.

NEVIN, GEORGE BALCH (Mar. 15, 1859–Apr. 17, 1933), composer, was born in Shippensburg, Pa., a descendant of Daniel Nevin who settled in the Cumberland Valley in the eighteenth century. His father, Samuel Williamson Nevin, was a prosperous farmer who married Harriet Macomb Balch. George Nevin passed his boyhood on his father's farm. He rode the saddle horses, learned to fish and hunt, and had for his hobby a completely equipped carpenter shop, from which one of his proudest products was a banjo made with his own hands. He was educated at the Cumberland Valley State Normal School, and for one year at Lafayette College as a member of the class of 1883. In later years Lafayette awarded him two honorary degrees. At the normal school Nevin specialized in chemistry and in drawing, but at the same time he spent part of his time for three years studying singing with Julia E. Crane, who helped him develop a baritone voice that enabled him to sing regularly in church choirs for twenty-five years. On leaving Lafayette College he went to Philadelphia, where he had a position for a few years with the firm of John Wanamaker. In Philadelphia he was a member of the choir of Holy Trinity, where David Bispham was soloist. During these years he was also a member of the Philadelphia Cecilian Society. About 1884 he returned to the town in which he had attended college—Easton, Pa.—where he opened a wholesale paper business at 320 Ferry Street. He conducted this enterprise until 1919.

Simultaneously with the conduct of his business Nevin continued his activities as a singer, becoming a member of various church choirs and of the Orpheus Glee Club. He also became interested in composing music, particularly for the church, and in this field he achieved a distinction that won him a national reputation. Sitting at his desk in his paper store, he would work on the anthem or song, "while overhead a battery of six or more printing presses was pounding out that many conflicting rhythms" (*Diapason,* Dec. 1, 1929, p. 10). In 1918, during the World War, Nevin organized the Victory Drummers, with a membership of forty men who averaged sixty years in age. This group was much in demand for patriotic rallies. During his later years he spent much of his time lecturing for women's clubs, with programs of his own compositions. He was physically and mentally active until two weeks before his death, when he was stricken with paralysis at his home in Easton. He had married, Apr. 25, 1888, Lillias Clara Dean of San Francisco, who became the mother of his three children, two of whom survived him. His wife wrote the texts of many of his anthems, songs, and cantatas.

As a composer Nevin was termed "a wellschooled musician, abundantly supplied with a pleasing melodic flow." He published a quantity of music, principally for the church. Among his larger works were the cantatas: *The Adoration, The Crown of Life, The Crucified, The Incarnation, The Gift of God,* and *The Angel of the Dawn.* It is said that *The Adoration* achieved a sale of sixty thousand copies. He also wrote many shorter anthems, among them "At the Sepulchre"; "The Walk to Emmaus"; a setting of "Crossing the Bar"; "Let this Mind Be in You"; "Hail, Gladdening Light"; "The Gift of God"; "Beloved, Let Us Love One Another"; "There Were Shepherds," and more than fifty others. Among his songs, sacred and secular, was a setting of Sidney Lanier's "Into the Woods my Master Went," and his part-songs numbered, among many others, "My Bonnie Lass, She Smileth"; "It Was a Lover and his Lass"; "O Mistress Mine"; "Smile Again, my Bonnie Lassie"; and "O, Little Mother of Mine." During the World War he published "When the Flag Goes By," a song which had wide use.

[See *Who's Who in America,* 1932–33; Gordon B. Nevin, "George Balch Nevin as Biographically Viewed by his Son," the *Diapason,* Dec. 1, 1929; "George B. Nevin," *Etude,* Sept. 1910; *Easton Express,* Apr. 17, 1933; *N. Y. Times, New York Herald Tribune,* Apr. 18, 1933.]   J.T.H.

NEVIN, JOHN WILLIAMSON (Feb. 20, 1803–June 6, 1886), theologian, educator, came of Scotch-Irish ancestry. His grandfather, Daniel Nevin, settled as a young man in the Cumberland Valley of Pennsylvania, where he took up land and married Margaret Williamson. John, the elder of his two sons, married Martha Mc-Cracken, became a prosperous farmer, and reared a family of nine children of whom John Williamson was the eldest. The family were devout Presbyterians; the father had graduated from Dickinson College (1795) when that institution was under Presbyterian control, and the son was sent, at fourteen years of age, to Union College, Schenectady, N. Y., where he graduated in 1821, the youngest member of his class. Poor health caused him to remain two years on his father's farm after graduation, and in 1823, when he entered Princeton Theological Seminary, he had not yet definitely chosen his life work.

Upon completing his course at Princeton in 1826, he was appointed to fill temporarily the place of Dr. Charles Hodge [q.v.], while the latter spent two years in foreign study. During this period Nevin prepared *A Summary of Biblical Antiquities* (2 vols., 1828), which for many years had wide use. On the completion of his instructorship at Princeton he was offered the professorship of Biblical literature in a new Presbyterian institution, Western Theological Seminary, then being organized at Allegheny, Pa. He began his work here in 1830 and remained for ten years, gaining a reputation as a scholar and a thoughtful preacher. He became a mild abolitionist and although he took no part in the doctrinal controversy which in 1837–38 divided the Presbyterian Church, he came gradually to a position out of harmony with Old-School Calvinistic orthodoxy. Commencing the study of German, he began to read the works of contemporary German theologians and church historians. He was especially influenced by Neander, and began to emphasize, more and more, the churchly and sacramental side of Christianity. In 1840, entirely without his knowledge, he

was unanimously elected by the General Synod of the Reformed Church to a professorship in their seminary at Mercersburg, Pa., and was finally persuaded to accept the call. Transferring his ecclesiastical relationship from the Presbyterian to the Reformed Church, he was soon exercising a large influence within that body, especially through his writings. His teachings came to be the cause of controversy within the denomination. In 1843 he published a pamphlet called *The Anxious Bench—A Tract for the Times,* in which he opposed the revivalistic methods which were gaining considerable acceptance among all the Protestant churches. At once the pamphlet caused a flood of replies from writers in several denominations.

The coming of Dr. Philip Schaff [q.v.] to Mercersburg Seminary from Berlin in 1844 greatly influenced Nevin's career. He and Schaff were in full sympathy in their points of view. Schaff's inaugural address, "The Principle of Protestantism as Related to the Present State of the Church," delivered in German, was translated into English by Nevin and published, together with a sermon of Nevin's on "Catholic Unity" (*The Principle, etc.,* 1845). At once bitter attacks were made upon the publication, and especially upon Nevin for the position he had taken in regard to the Catholic Church. Nevin now set forth in numerous articles, pamphlets, and books his position in regard to tradition, the sacraments, mystical union, and the church question, which came to be known as the "Mercersburg theology." His most important work was *The Mystical Presence: A Vindication of the Reformed or Calvinistic Doctrine of the Holy Eucharist* (1846) and *History and Genius of the Heidelberg Catechism* (1847). At this period Schaff was beginning the publication of the first volumes of his monumental *History of the Christian Church,* though he took little part in the controversy. The year 1849 was marked by the establishment of the quarterly *Mercersburg Review,* of which Nevin was editor and chief contributor until 1853. Altogether about a hundred of his articles appeared in the *Review,* filling nearly three thousand pages.

During the years 1841 to 1853 he was not only a professor in the Seminary but was acting president of Marshall College, also located at Mercersburg. In the latter year an agreement was reached with Franklin College at Lancaster to unite the two institutions, and when this had been accomplished, Nevin, whose health had failed, retired to private life. Some years later, after his removal to a small farm near Lancaster, he again became connected with the college as

Nevin

lecturer, holding this position from 1861 to 1866, when the institution was reorganized and at the request of the trustees he assumed the presidency. He was at the head of Franklin and Marshall College thenceforward until advancing age caused his final resignation in 1876. For the next ten years he lived in retirement at his country home near Lancaster, where he died in 1886 of old age.

Nevin was a quiet man, of grave countenance, with a strong, deep voice, which, added to his great earnestness and logical presentation, gave to his pulpit ministration and public address singular impressiveness. He was married in 1835 to Martha Jenkins, second daughter of Robert Jenkins, a wealthy iron-master of Lancaster County. They had seven children, but three of the five sons died in infancy. Nevin's brother, Robert Peebles Nevin [q.v.], father of the composer Ethelbert Nevin [q.v.], was a well-known journalist and man of affairs, while two first cousins, Alfred and Edwin H. Nevin [qq.v.], were Presbyterian ministers of some note.

[Theodore Appel, *The Life and Work of John Williamson Nevin* (1889); A. R. Kremer, *A Biog. Sketch of John Williamson Nevin* (1890); *Centennial Biog.: Men of Mark of the Cumberland Valley, Pa., 1776–1876* (1876); *Princeton Theol. Sem. Biog. Cat.* (1909); *Phila. Inquirer*, June 7, 1886.]   W. W. S.

NEVIN, ROBERT PEEBLES (July 31, 1820–June 28, 1908), journalist, pioneer oil-refiner, was born in Shippensburg, Pa., the son of John and Martha (McCracken) Nevin and a brother of John Williamson Nevin [q.v.]. While an infant he was taken by his parents to a farm in Cumberland County where the father died in Robert's ninth year. At the age of twelve the boy went to Chillicothe, Ohio, and subsequently lived at various times in Niles, Mich., and Pittsburgh. He received his elementary schooling partly at Chillicothe Academy, later attended Sewickley Academy, of which his brother, William M. Nevin, was in charge, and at length entered Jefferson College, Canonsburg, Pa. (now Washington and Jefferson, Washington, Pa.), from which he was graduated in 1842.

He then entered into partnership with a brother as a dealer in drugs and white lead, at Pittsburgh, and was engaged in this business until 1870. He had begun to write verse at the age of twelve, and he now devoted his leisure to writing poems and sketches for newspapers and magazines. He also became a correspondent of the *Washington Reporter* and during the presidential campaign of 1844 was one of the most popular writers of campaign songs, his "Our Nominee" being widely reprinted. Later he contributed several noteworthy articles to magazines,

Nevin

among them being "Stephen C. Foster and Negro Minstrelsy" (*Atlantic Monthly*, November 1867), and "Tom, the Tinker" (*Lippincott's Magazine*, October 1868), dealing with a romantic character of the Whiskey Rebellion. He also wrote *Black-Robes, or Sketches of Missions and Ministers in the Wilderness and on the Border* (1872), taking up in order the Jesuit, Moravian, Methodist, and Presbyterian missionaries and ministers. In 1888 he published *Les Trois Rois*, in which he likened William Thaw (transportation), Andrew Carnegie (steel), and George Westinghouse, Jr. (natural gas), to the three magi of the early legend. During 1887–88 he published "Tracks of a Traveller" as a serial in the Pittsburgh *Leader*. In 1899 he made a collection of his poems, including verses written at the age of twelve, his campaign song, "Our Nominee," and "Tracks of a Traveller," which he published in a volume entitled *The "Beautiful River" and Other Poems* (1899). These verses are not remarkable in any sense; for the most part they were written for specific, local occasions and they have no universal appeal.

Retiring from the drug business in 1870, Nevin purchased an interest in the *Weekly Leader*, a Sunday paper, and as part owner and editor made it over into a daily newspaper. In 1880 he founded the *Pittsburg Times*, which he sold four years later. In the field of oil refining, far removed from literary interests, he took a leading part, being among the first, if not the first Pittsburgher to become interested in petroleum. In 1855, more than three years before Edwin L. Drake [q.v.] sank the first oil well at Titusville, Pa., Nevin bought the crude oil which came to the surface of the salt wells at Tarentum, Pa., and refined it for illuminating purposes, producing three barrels a week. After Drake's discovery, Nevin with associates drilled a well near Titusville, but lost most of their product by a fire, and sold out the same year.

Nevin died at his home, "Vineacre," near Pittsburgh, just before reaching the age of eighty-eight, after two years' illness. His wife, Elizabeth Duncan Oliphant, whom he married Jan. 9, 1851, had died in 1898. The daughter of Gen. F. H. Oliphant, prominent in the iron trade, she was an accomplished musician, and one of her eight children (of whom four survived their father) was Ethelbert Woodbridge Nevin [q.v.] the composer.

[*Who's Who in America*, 1906–07; Vance Thompson, *The Life of Ethelbert Nevin* (1913); *Biog. and Hist. Cat. of Washington and Jefferson Coll.* (1902); Erasmus Wilson, *Standard Hist. of Pittsburg, Pa.* (1898); *Pittsburg Dispatch, Pittsburgh Post*, June 29, 1908.]   A. I.

443

NEVIUS, JOHN LIVINGSTON

NEVIUS, JOHN LIVINGSTON (Mar. 4, 1829–Oct. 19, 1893), missionary in China, was of the seventh generation after the Joannes Nevius who became *schepen* of New Amsterdam in 1654. About 1818 John P. Nevius, then the head of the family, had moved from New Jersey to a farm in the township of Ovid, Seneca County, among the "Finger Lakes" of western New York. His son, Benjamin Hageman Nevius, in 1826 married Mary Denton, of English descent; and on the day when Andrew Jackson was first entering office as president, their son, John Livingston Nevius, was born. During his early years on the farm the boy developed a sturdy physique and some acquaintance with the mysteries of farming. With his brother Reuben he attended Ovid Academy and then entered Union College. Upon graduating in 1848, he yielded to the lure of new country and went south to Georgia. There he taught school for a year with a considerable measure of success. The year's greatest significance to him, however, was that it dated his conversion. From his intimate letters to his brother Reuben it is evident that the conversion was the result not of sudden influences from without but of months of inner questioning. Returning north, he entered Princeton Theological Seminary; and by the time of his graduation in 1853 he had received appointment from the Presbyterian Board as missionary to China. He was ordained by the Presbytery of New Brunswick on May 23; in June he married Helen Sanford Coan, a school friend of Ovid Academy days; and in September they sailed, by way of the Cape of Good Hope, for China.

Their first years in China were full of uncertainties. The climate of Ningpo, to which they had been assigned, is notoriously difficult. Mrs. Nevius' health failed, and in 1857 she had to return to the United States for a period. Nevius became pastor of a church at Ningpo and started evangelistic work in San-Poh, an inland district "north of the hills." He and his wife were pioneers in a mission station in Hangchow in 1859, but had to withdraw because of political unrest. They then spent several months in Japan, and on their return to China proceeded north to aid in the establishment of a mission in Shantung province.

There Nevius toiled with characteristic energy for more than thirty years. His evangelistic zeal prepared the way for many local churches, the work in each locality being delegated as far as possible to native residents. He kept up a steady output of written material both in Chinese and in English. This included at least sixteen tracts or books or translations in Chinese, and several works in English: *San-Poh* (1869); *China and the Chinese* (1869); *Methods of Mission Work* (1886); and *Demon Possession and Allied Themes* (1894), which was published after his death. A lasting benefit to China's material well-being resulted from his experiments in acclimatizing Western fruits and vegetables. The statesmanship of his contribution to the missionary program was recognized in China by his appointment as American chairman of the Second Missionary Conference in Shanghai, 1890; and in America by the prominence accorded to his counsels and addresses. Study of the "Nevius method" became a part of the preparation of missionary candidates. The commanding presence and the powers of concentration which this record suggests were characteristic of Nevius, but equally characteristic were qualities of geniality and sympathy and good comradeship. His life continued active and full to the last day; and it ended peacefully at his desk after daily prayers in "San-lou," the house which he had himself erected on a hill overlooking the Chinese city of Chefoo.

[The chief source of information is *The Life of John Livingston Nevius* (1895), by his wife, Helen S. C. Nevius. See also A. Van Doren Honeyman, *Joannes Nevius ... and His Descendants ... 1627–1900* (1900); H. P. Beach, *Princely Men in the Heavenly Kingdom* (1903); F. F. Ellinwood, "Rev. John L. Nevius, D.D.," in *Church at Home and Abroad*, Feb. 1894; Gilbert Reid, "The Rev. John L. Nevius, D.D.," in *Missionary Review of the World*, May 1894; C. A. Clark, *The Korean Church and the Nevius Methods* (1930); *Necrological Report ... Princeton Theol. Sem.*, 1894; records of the Board of Foreign Missions, Presbyt. Ch. in the U. S. A.]
H. Cl—s.

NEWBERRY, JOHN STOUGHTON

NEWBERRY, JOHN STOUGHTON (Nov. 18, 1826–Jan. 2, 1887), lawyer, manufacturer, congressman, was born at Sangerfield, Oneida County, N. Y., the son of Elihu and Rhoda (Phelps) Newberry. He was a descendant of Thomas Newberry who emigrated from Devonshire, England, to Dorchester, Mass., in 1634. Oliver and Walter Loomis Newberry [*qq.v.*] were John's uncles. Elihu moved from Oneida County westward, finally settling at Romeo, Mich., where John prepared for college. Later he entered the University of Michigan, took high rank as a student, and graduated in 1847.

Having acquired a practical knowledge of civil engineering, he spent two years with the Michigan Central Railroad. Then, after a year of travel, he entered a law office in Detroit, and was admitted to the bar in 1853. He was soon recognized as an expert in admiralty cases and in 1857 published *Reports of Admiralty Cases in the Several District Courts of the United States*. In 1855 he married Harriet Newell Robinson, who died in 1856 leaving one son; on Oct. 6, 1859, he married Helen Parmelee Handy and to this union were born two sons. From his majority he had supported and voted the Whig ticket, but upon the formation of the Republican party he joined forces with it and thereafter remained a stanch supporter. President Lincoln appointed him provost-marshal of Michigan in 1862, with the rank of captain of cavalry, an office which he held until 1864, during which time he organized two drafts. Familiar with the needs of the army, he was one of a company of Detroit capitalists who established in 1862 or 1863 the Michigan Car Company to build freight cars for the Union forces; of this company he became president, continuing as such until 1880. Although this venture led him to abandon the practice of law, it developed into a highly profitable enterprise and formed the basis of his large personal fortune, estimated at his death to be from three to four million dollars. The firm soon had branches in London, Ontario, and St. Louis, and employed some five thousand men. In 1878, with James McMillan [q.v.], who was associated with the Michigan Car Company, he formed the firm of Newberry & McMillan, capitalists. As the car-building enterprise prospered, so did his other ever-widening business ventures. He helped organize a corporation to build the Detroit, Mackinac & Marquette Railroad. He also established the Vulcan Furnace Company at Newberry, Mich. As investor he held large interests in banks, factories, and centrally located Detroit real estate. So wide and varied were these holdings that at his death he was a director in almost every local industry.

With the exception of his term as provost-marshal, he held public office but twice. In 1862 he was elected to the Detroit board of education, and in 1878 he won the Republican nomination for representative to Congress from the First District, and was elected. He served on several important committees and was chairman of the committee on commerce. After one term he retired, feeling that his business interests demanded his full attention. A Congregationalist in his youth, he later joined the Jefferson Avenue Presbyterian Church, where he was noted for regular attendance and his stanch support of church activities. He was interested in philanthropic projects and one of his last undertakings was the establishment, together with James McMillan, of the Grace Homeopathic Hospital, to which Newberry gave $100,000. His will contained bequests of $650,000 to institutions and charities.

[J. G. Bartlett, *Newberry Geneal.* (1914); *Cyc. of Mich.* (1890); Charles Moore, *Hist. of Michigan*

(1915); Henry Hall, *America's Successful Men of Affairs*, vol. II (1896); *Biog. Dir. Am. Cong.* (1928); *Detroit Free Press*, Jan. 3, 1887; *Evening News* (Detroit), Jan. 3, 1887.]   J.J.S.

NEWBERRY, JOHN STRONG (Dec. 22, 1822–Dec. 7, 1892), geologist and paleontologist, son of Henry and Elizabeth (Strong) Newberry and a descendant of Thomas Newberry who came from Devonshire, England, to Dorchester, Mass., about 1634, was born in the town of Windsor, Conn. When he was but two years of age his father moved the family to Ohio, where he founded the town of Cuyahoga Falls in the Western Reserve. Engaging in various enterprises including coal mining, then an entirely new industry, he prospered and was able to bring up his family of nine children in reasonable comfort and amid agreeable surroundings. John received his early education in the local schools and a special school in the adjoining town of Hudson, then entered Western Reserve College, where he graduated in 1846 at the age of twenty-four. During his last two years in college he also studied medicine, and in 1848 graduated from the Cleveland Medical School. In the autumn of 1849 he went abroad to study in the medical schools of Paris, where he also attended geological lectures by distinguished scientists.

Returning to America in 1851, he settled down to the practice of medicine in Cleveland, Ohio, and is said to have been very successful. While thus engaged, he received an appointment as assistant surgeon on an expedition under command of Lieut. R. S. Wilkinson, organized for the purpose of exploring the country along the line of the projected Pacific Railroad from San Francisco Bay to the Columbia River. In January 1856, the work completed, he accompanied the rest of the party to Washington, where they spent the remainder of the year in the preparation of the report. While here Newberry became associated with the Smithsonian Institution and also received appointment as professor of geology in Columbian (now George Washington) University. In 1857 he was appointed physician and naturalist to the expedition under Lieut. J. C. Ives [q.v.], sent out to make a military exploration of the Colorado River. After ascending that stream from its mouth to a point called Fortification Rock, north of the 40th Parallel, the explorers returned to Washington in the early summer of 1858. The following year Newberry was again in the field, this time as member of a topographic surveying party under Capt. J. N. Macomb, exploring the region northwest of Santa Fé as far as the Colorado and Green rivers. With the outbreak of the Civil War, he entered upon duty with the United States Sanitary Commission (June 1861), remaining in this service until the close of the war.

In 1866, after a short association with the Smithsonian Institution, he was chosen professor of geology and paleontology in the School of Mines of Columbia University, New York, a position which he held for the rest of his life. As a teacher he was eminently successful. His relations with his students were always kindly; he was never too busy to receive a caller; never trivial, flippant, or superficial. He is to be credited with an influential part in the organization of the School of Mines. In addition to his academic responsibilities, he was state geologist of Ohio, 1869–74. In this capacity he met with the usual obstacles of an unappreciative legislature, aggravated perhaps by the fact that he postponed publication of the economic results of the survey until the last, thereby giving cause for the complaint that too much attention was being devoted to the academic subject of paleontology.

As a scientist Newberry was of the old school, a general naturalist rather than a specialist. He had been attracted in boyhood by the abundant plant remains in the coal mines near Cuyahoga Falls and had made large collections. Fossil plants and fishes remained always his favorites; he rarely touched upon the broader tectonic problems. His first scientific paper, "Description of the Quarries Yielding Fossil Fishes, Monte Bolca, Italy," was published in the *Family Visitor* in 1851, while he was abroad. His best-known works and those upon which his reputation largely rests were his two volumes on the paleontology of the Ohio Survey (*Report of the Geological Survey of Ohio,* vol. I, pt. 2, 1873, and vol. II, pt. 2, 1875); *Fossil Fishes and Fossil Plants of the Triassic Rocks of New Jersey and the Connecticut Valley* (1888); and *The Paleozoic Fishes of North America* (1889), the last two published as Monographs XIV and XVI of the United States Geological Survey. He received many scientific honors, including membership in the National Academy of Sciences, the presidency of the American Association for the Advancement of Science in 1867, the vice-presidency of the Geological Society of America in 1889, and the presidency of the International Geological Congress in 1891. In 1888, he was awarded the Murchison Medal of the Geological Society of London.

Personally, Newberry is represented by those who knew him best as of a cheerful and buoyant temperament, fond of companionship, but with a sensitive and delicate spirit that sometimes sub-jected him to periods of depression. He was fond of music and played the violin. In 1848 he married Sarah Brownell Gaylord of Cleveland, Ohio. They had five sons and one daughter. Though his domestic ties were strong, he was separated from his family in his early days by his western explorations and army service; and later, with his family in Cleveland or in New Haven, where they settled at the close of his Ohio work, he lived a lonely life in his rooms at Columbia. He died at his home in New Haven in 1892 from a stroke of apoplexy sustained some two years earlier.

[C. A. White, in *Nat. Acad. Sci. Biog. Memoirs,* vol. VI (1909); J. F. Kemp, in *School of Mines Quart.,* Jan. 1893; memoir by H. L. Fairchild and bibliography by J. F. Kemp, in *Trans. N. Y. Acad. Sci.,* vol. XII (1893); *Proc. Second Joint Meeting of the Scientific Alliance of N. Y. Mar. 27, 1893, in Memory of Prof. John Strong Newberry* (1893); bibliography of Newberry's writings, purporting to be complete, in each of the foregoing publications; J. G. Bartlett, *Newberry Geneal.* (1914); *New Haven Reg.,* Dec. 8, 1892.]

G. P. M.

NEWBERRY, OLIVER (Nov. 17, 1789–July 30, 1860), merchant, ship-builder, known as the "Admiral of the Lakes," was born in East (now South) Windsor, Conn., the son of Amasa and Ruth (Warner) Newberry. His father, a soldier of the Revolution, moved to Oneida County, N. Y., in 1805. In 1808 Oliver left for the Ohio country, where he worked until the opening of the War of 1812. Enlisting in the army, he marched to Sacketts Harbor. At the close of the war he opened a store in Buffalo and was later joined by his brother Walter [*q.v.*]. A visit to Detroit so impressed him with the prospects there that he sold the Buffalo store and in 1826 moved to Detroit. Here he opened a store that carried everything from oxbows to hairpins. He soon became agent for the American Fur Company and entered the commission and forwarding business, took government contracts, and began to build sailing vessels at Newport, Mich. (now Marine City). He was one of the first to foresee the future of Chicago and opened a branch office there. This office dealt in salt meats, which were shipped to Detroit, and helped to build up the large business of Newberry's ever-growing fleet of ships. By 1832 he was the owner of eight vessels. In 1833 he built the steamship *Michigan,* then the largest on the Great Lakes, and two years later he established regular steamship service between Detroit and Chicago. This service aided him in taking care of his ever increasing shipping business. It is said his boats carried the first bituminous coal sent to Chicago by water. During this period he was sutler for Fort Dearborn and made money on the contract. About this time, however, he refused to "profiteer" in flour, thus winning popular support. He built the first lightship at the Strait of Mackinac and was instrumental in opening the Chicago River to large ships by dredging.

In Detroit his interests were many and varied. He was a large holder of real estate; he bought and sold everything; his warehouse was the largest on the lakes. He was the "ready money man" of the city, one of the stockholders in the Detroit & St. Joseph Railroad, and a director in the company. He is often credited with coining the term "wild cat" money, and his adventures in stopping cutthroat competition between the Milwaukee banks and the Bank of Michigan show his ability to meet situations quickly.

In 1859 Newberry made his last complete inspection of his branch offices and shipping interests. The panics of 1837 and 1857 had reduced his wealth, but at the time of his death he was a man of comparatively large means. He left few records of his activities, for he handled his papers carelessly, depositing those needed for each day's business in his hat. He was never married. John Stoughton Newberry [q.v.] was his nephew.

[J. G. Bartlett, *Newberry Geneal.* (1914); G. B. Catlin, *The Story of Detroit* (1926); A. T. Andreas, *Hist. of Chicago*, vols. I, II (1884–85); *Detroit Free Press*, July 31, 1860; Woodbridge Papers, Burton Collection, Detroit Pub. Lib.]   J. J. S.

NEWBERRY, WALTER LOOMIS (Sept. 18, 1804–Nov. 6, 1868), merchant, banker, philanthropist, son of Amasa and Ruth (Warner) Newberry, and a descendant of Thomas Newberry who emigrated from Devonshire in 1634, was born in East (now South) Windsor, Conn. Save through heritage, however, New England influenced him but little, for when he was only a year old the family moved to Sangerfield, Oneida County, N. Y. His father saw active service in the Revolution, and later was a captain in the Connecticut militia. Walter Newberry's limited schooling was obtained at an academy in the neighboring town of Clinton, and in 1820 he received an appointment to West Point, but failed to pass the physical examination. Leaving school, he went to Buffalo and entered the employ of his brother Oliver [q.v.]. In 1826 his brother moved to Detroit and Walter accompanied him, established a drygoods business, and prospered. He took an active interest in public affairs, serving as adjutant-general of the Territory of Michigan from 1829 to 1831, and as alderman of the little frontier city of Detroit in 1832.

Newberry's first extensive land investments, from which he afterwards gained a fortune, were made in 1833, when, in company with his brother Oliver, W. B. Astor, and Lewis Cass [qq.v.], he bought large tracts of land in Wisconsin, northern Michigan, and in the newly established town of Chicago. The raw little colony at the southern end of Lake Michigan attracted him from his first visit; he had the imagination to see its future importance, and determined to grasp the business opportunities it presented. Closing up his affairs in Detroit, he removed to Chicago in 1833 and made that city his home for the rest of his life, seeing it grow, during his thirty-five years' residence, from a straggling board-shack settlement of less than four thousand to a city of nearly three hundred thousand inhabitants. Engaging in the commission business and later in banking, and prospering in both, he invested his profits for years in Chicago real estate. What he bought by the acre he sold later by the front foot, and the increase in value provided him a fortune ample for that period. As the city developed he was active in large business enterprises. He was head of the banking house of Newberry & Burch; founder (1857) and director for years of the Merchants Loan & Trust Company; and a director (from 1857) and president (1859) of the Galena & Chicago Union Railroad Company, which in 1864 became a part of the Chicago & North Western system. He held many positions of trust and honor, a fact indicative both of the esteem of his contemporaries and of his interest in civic affairs. He was a member (1843) of the Chicago board of health, city comptroller (1851), and for a time acting mayor. He was a founder and the first president (1841) of the Young Men's Library Association, the modest institution which more than any other was the forerunner of the Chicago public library. His interest in its affairs very probably influenced him in providing in his will for the Newberry Library. From 1859 to 1863 he was a member of the board of education and in the latter year its president. In 1857 he became a member of the newly organized Chicago Historical Society, was its vice-president from 1858 to 1860, and its president from 1860 until his death eight years later. He gave land to several religious congregations, on which churches were built, and his gifts of money to various enterprises were doubtless greater than is now known. He married, Nov. 22, 1842, Julia Butler Clapp, daughter of James and Julia (Butler) Clapp, of Oxford, N. Y., by whom he had four children, two sons who died in infancy, and two daughters who died unmarried. Newberry's death occurred at sea while he was on his way to join his family in Paris. His body was brought back to Chicago and buried in Graceland Cemetery.

As a result of a contingent provision in Newberry's will, one half of his estate, or about $2,-100,000, went in 1887 to the founding of the independent free public reference library in Chicago that bears his name. Much of the property bequeathed was in undeveloped real estate, which in later years greatly increased in value. Under a cooperative agreement with other reference libraries of the city, the Newberry Library has specialized almost exclusively in the fields of literature, history, philology, and music. Within these limits, its collection of about 500,-000 books and manuscripts has given the institution an international reputation.

[Will of Walter Loomis Newberry, probated 1868; J. G. Bartlett, *Newberry Geneal.* (1914); H. R. Stiles, *The Hist. and Geneals. of Ancient Windsor, Conn.*, vol. II (1892); Silas Farmer, *The Hist. of Detroit and Mich.* (1884); A. T. Andreas, *Hist. of Chicago*, vols. I, II (1884–85); Joseph and Caroline Kirkland, *The Story of Chicago* (2 vols., 1892–94); H. J. Galpin, *Annals of Oxford, N. Y.* (1906); E. O. Gale, *Reminiscences of Early Chicago* (1902); *Chicago Tribune*, Nov. 20, 1868.]   G. B. U.

NEWBOLD, WILLIAM ROMAINE (Nov. 20, 1865–Sept. 26, 1926), philosopher, psychologist, Orientalist, was of English lineage, in the eighth generation from Michael Newbould who settled in Burlington County, N. J., before 1681. He was born at Wilmington, Del., the eldest child of William Allibone Newbold by his second marriage, to Martha Smith Baily, and one of seven children. Marked by special devotion to books and to languages, as a boy he taught himself Hebrew and on entering the University of Pennsylvania as a sophomore in 1884 he organized a group of fellow students to whom he taught that language. He induced M. W. Easton, professor of English, to offer Sanskrit, and pursued the subject for two years. In college he won all the prizes for which he competed, against classmates of later distinction who freely admitted his preëminent qualities.

Receiving the bachelor's degree in 1887, he taught Latin two years in the Cheltenham Military Academy, and then became instructor in Latin and lecturer in philosophy at the University of Pennsylvania. His graduate studies, begun in 1887, brought him the doctorate of philosophy in 1891, and he then studied abroad for one year, chiefly in Berlin. On returning, he resumed teaching at his alma mater, with which he was connected for the rest of his life: as lecturer in philosophy, 1892–94; assistant professor, 1894–1903; professor, 1903–07; and Adam Seybert Professor of Intellectual and Moral Philosophy from 1907 until his death. As dean of the Graduate School, 1896–1904, he rendered important service in raising the standards of graduate work.

His interests were many, his knowledge encyclopedic. At first particularly interested in psychology and in the work of the Society for Psychical Research, he next turned to philosophy, and became a master in expounding Plato and Aristotle. By these studies he was led from a state of religious unrest to a firm Christian orthodoxy; he gave a course at the University on the development of early Christian thought and twice (1923–25) gave a similar course at the General Theological Seminary of the Protestant Episcopal Church in New York. He was even invited, though a layman, to assume the chair of ecclesiastical history in this seminary, but declined it.

Between 1892 and 1902 he published a number of brief papers and reviews on psychological and philosophical subjects. His more important published writings include: "Bardaisan and the Odes of Solomon" (*Journal of Biblical Literature*, vol. XXX, pt. 2, 1911); "The Descent of Christ in the Odes of Solomon" (*Ibid.*, vol. XXXI, pt. 4, 1912); "A Syriac Valentinian Hymn" (*Journal of the American Oriental Society*, February 1918); "The Syriac Dialogue 'Socrates'" (*Proceedings of the American Philosophical Society*, vol. LVII, 1918); "The Great Chalice of Antioch" (*Ladies' Home Journal*, November 1924); "The Eagle and the Basket on the Chalice of Antioch" (*American Journal of Archaeology*, October–December 1925); "Five Transliterated Aramaic Inscriptions" (*Ibid.*, July–September 1926). His lectures on the Valentinian Gnosis, delivered in 1920 at Philadelphia on the Bohlen Foundation, were left in manuscript. Perhaps his best-known achievement was the partial decipherment of the Roger Bacon Manuscript owned by the late W. M. Voynich of New York, which had previously defied all efforts of cipher experts. His studies of the manuscript were begun in 1919, but were left incomplete by his sudden death; the material found among his papers was edited by a colleague and published under the title, *The Cipher of Roger Bacon*, in 1928.

Newbold was a short, slight man, with a pointed beard trimmed close on the cheeks; he habitually read and studied until well after midnight, despite his lack of robust health, but was fond of outdoor life during his vacations, and was expert with a sailboat. His black hair never became thin nor touched with gray; his keen brown eyes revealed his unusual intellectual and spiritual gifts. Of his inclusive human sympathy he gave freely to all who came to him; in colleagues and in students alike, he inspired a love that approached worship. His course on Greek philosophy was regularly elected by about a hundred students, who gave a tribute of applause at the hour's end (a rarity at his University) ; in his last year the course was taken by over a hundred and fifty. He was married on Apr. 9, 1896, to Ethel Kent Sprague Packard of Boston, who survived him; they had no children. He died in Philadelphia in his sixty-first year.

[*Newbold Memorial Meeting* (Univ. of Pa., 1927), ed. by R. G. Kent, containing portrait and bibliography; *Gen. Mag. and Hist. Chronicle* (Univ. of Pa.), Jan. 1927; *Public Ledger* (Phila.), Sept. 27, 1926; *Am. Jour. Archaeology*, Jan.–Mar. 1927; *Jour. Am. Oriental Soc.*, Dec. 1927; *Who's Who in America*, 1926–27: F. A. Virkus, *The Abridged Compendium of Am. Geneal.*, I (1925), 946; H. V. Cubberly, *Bloomsdale: Sketches of the Old-time Home of the John Newbold Family and Geneal. Notes* (1930); Foreword to *The Cipher of Roger Bacon* (1928), ed. by R. G. Kent.]

R. G. K.

NEWBROUGH, JOHN BALLOU (June 5, 1828–Apr. 22, 1891), founder of Shalam religious community, was born near Springfield, Ohio, the son of Jacob and Mary Newbrough. He left home at the age of sixteen and worked for a dentist, Dr. Slauson, in Cleveland. In 1849 he graduated from a Cincinnati dental college. Within a few months, however, he joined the gold rush for California and in 1851 went to the goldfields of Australia. After six years of travel he returned to Cincinnati, where he practised medicine and dentistry. In 1860 he was married in Scotland to Rachel Turnbull, and returned with his bride to Philadelphia, where he practised dentistry until 1862, when he moved to New York. In 1865 he published *A Catechism on Human Teeth,* in which he speaks of his experience abroad. He continued to practise his profession until 1884 and is credited with the invention of a rubber plate.

During these years he became increasingly interested in spiritualism and finally discovered that he had an unusual gift for automatic writing. In order to facilitate his communication with angels, he undertook a systematic discipline of "purification," avoiding meat and stimulants. In 1881, according to his own account, "one morning the light struck both my hands on the back and they went for the typewriter, for some fifteen minutes, very vigorously. I was told not to read what was printed. . . . For fifty weeks this continued . . . and then it ceased, and I was told to read and publish Oahspe" (preface to 1932 edition of *Oahspe.*)

Oahspe: A New Bible (first edition, 1882) was written in Biblical idiom for "faithists." It outlines in elaborate detail the history and structure of the universe and announces the dawn of the "Kosmon Age," beginning in 1848, during which "Jehovih's [*sic*] Kingdom on Earth" is to be established. The revelations of *Oahspe* induced Newbrough to collect a large number of orphans and foundlings at Pearl River, N. Y., and, with the help of a faithful band of followers, to organize the communistic society of Shalam, N. Mex. This community controlled about 1,000 acres of irrigated land near Doña Ana in Mesilla Valley. It was planned to build another community for adults, named Levitica, nearby, but the limited resources of the group made this venture impossible. The children were legally adopted by Shalam Community and were given a systematic, practical education, which was intended to make them competent to do the work of the community and to despise the "filth and luxury" of "the land of UZ" (the cities of the world). A "Faithist's Infants' Home" was established in New Orleans for castaways, foundlings, and orphans: "said babes are to be taken to a place in the country, distant from vice, such as drunkenness, using tobacco, flesh-eating and so on" (*The Castaway, post,* p. 101). Newbrough labored in and with this community until his death, and the work was continued for about ten years longer under the direction of A. M. Howland of Boston, who had provided most of the funds for the venture. Divorced from his wife because she refused to follow him to New Mexico, he married Frances Van de Water. He had a son by his first marriage, and a daughter by his second. He was a 33rd degree Mason and his grave is in the Masonic Burial Grounds at Las Cruces, N. Mex.

[W. A. Hinds, *Am. Communities* (1902); L. H. Gray, "Oahspe," in James Hastings, *Encyc. of Religion and Ethics,* vol. IX (1917); *Vohu Esfoma* (London, 1927); *The Castaway* (New Orleans, 1889); preface to 1932 ed. of *Oahspe* and other publications of the Kosmon Press, London, and the Oahspe Publishing Asso., Los Angeles; obituary in *Santa Fé Daily New Mexican,* Apr. 25, 1891.]

H. W. S—d—r.

NEWCOMB, CHARLES LEONARD (Aug. 7, 1854–Mar. 13, 1930), mechanical engineer, inventor, was born at West Willington, Conn., the son of Charles Leonard and Martha Jane (Hudson) Newcomb, and a descendant of Andrew Newcomb who was in New England as early as 1666. After obtaining a common-school education and while still in his teens, Charles, having a natural interest in the metal trades, went to work in an iron foundry. After several years of experience in this field, he began a machinist apprenticeship, upon the completion of which he spent upwards of ten years practising his trade in various places in Connecticut. He was millwright and stationary engineer for the Florence Mills; millwright and machinist of the

Rock Manufacturing Company at Rockville; master mechanic for the Pratt & Whitney Company at Hartford; and a machinist for the American Clutch Company at Middletown. Feeling the need of a technical education, he entered the Worcester Free Institute (later the Worcester Polytechnic Institute), Worcester, Mass., from which he was graduated with the degrees B.S. and M.E. in 1880.

Following his graduation, he was made superintendent of the American Electric Lighting Company, New Britain, Conn., and established there the first municipal electric lighting plant in the United States. In 1881 he moved to Holyoke, Mass., to accept the position of superintendent of the Deane Steam Pump Company, makers of pumping machinery. Until his retirement in 1927 he was directly connected with this establishment, and through his engineering and executive ability developed it into one of the most important manufacturing enterprises of New England. When in 1899 the International Steam Pump Company obtained control of the Deane Works, Newcomb was elected president and general manager of the reorganized concern. Later he was influential in bringing the Worthington Pump & Machinery Corporation to Holyoke, and when that corporation gained control of the Deane Works in 1914, Newcomb became general manager, continuing in that capacity until his retirement. From 1907 to 1911 he also served as general manager of the Blake-Knowles Works of the International Steam Pump Company at East Cambridge, Mass. Newcomb not only managed the affairs of these organizations but also employed his mechanical training and ingenuity in effecting the remarkable improvements in pumping machinery that took place between 1880 and 1930. Nationally recognized as an authority on mechanics and hydraulics, he acted in a consulting capacity as an expert in various lines of engineering.

In addition to his business and engineering work, Newcomb was active in the human relations side of industry. As an executive of the Silver Bay Industrial Conference Board he took part in its annual conferences and became well known throughout the world for the ideas he projected looking toward improved working conditions in manufacturing plants. He was vitally interested in national affairs affecting the metal trades. He helped to found the National Foundry Association in 1898 and was its first vice-president; he was instrumental in forming in 1899 the National Metal Trades Association; and he was an active member of the American Society of Mechanical Engineers from 1883 until his

death, a manager from 1919 to 1921, and vice-president in 1926–28 under the leadership of Charles M. Schwab. He was also the organizer in 1919, and the first president of the Engineering Society of Western Massachusetts; a member of the American Society of Naval Architects and Marine Engineers; and a member of the executive committee of the Associated Industries of Massachusetts. From the very beginning of his residence in Holyoke, he took an active part in municipal affairs. He served two terms as councilman (1886–87) and one as alderman (1888). When, in 1893, the newly created fire commission was established he was named chairman, a position which he occupied for seventeen years. While on this commission he devised the rotary deluge nozzle, for which he received patent No. 616,200 on Dec. 20, 1898. By the use of this nozzle in connection with the aerial fire ladder, the latter was converted into a water tower. He did much research work looking toward the improvement of fire hydrants, and the standards developed by him were adopted by the National Board of Fire Underwriters and by the American Water Works Association. During the whole of his extremely busy life he wrote prolifically for the technical press. At the time of his death he was president of the Holyoke Cooperative Bank; a director of the Holyoke Valve and Hydrant Company; and a member of the board of trustees of the Worcester Polytechnic Institute. On Jan. 20, 1874, he married Inez Louise Kendall of Rockville, Conn.; he was survived by his widow and six children.

[B. M. Newcomb, *Andrew Newcomb 1618–1686 and His Descendants* (1923); *Who's Who in America,* 1928–29; *Mechanical Engineering,* June 1930; *Power,* Apr. 1, 1930; *Springfield Republican,* Mar. 15, 16, 1930; *Holyoke Daily Transcript,* Mar. 13, 14, 1930; *N. Y. Times,* Mar. 14, 1930; Pat. Off. records.]

C. W. M.

NEWCOMB, HARVEY (Sept. 2, 1803–Aug. 30, 1863), Congregational clergyman, editor, and author, a descendant of Capt. Andrew Newcomb who was in America as early as 1666, was born in Thetford, Vt., the son of Simon and Hannah (Curtis) Newcomb. In 1818 the family moved to Alfred, N. Y., where Harvey taught school for eight years. Turning his attention to journalism, he became the owner and editor of the *Western Star* of Westfield, N. Y. (1826–28), editor of the Buffalo *Patriot,* an anti-Masonic paper (1828–30), and of the Pittsburgh *Christian Herald,* a paper for children (1830–31). The following ten years were devoted to writing books for children and young people.

Without a college or seminary training, but with the preparation afforded by his years of teaching and writing, Newcomb turned toward the ministry. He was licensed in 1840 and supplied the Congregational church in West Roxbury, Mass., during the two following years. On Oct. 6, 1842, he was ordained pastor of the church in West Needham, now Wellesley, Mass., where he remained till July 1, 1846, when with twenty-six of his parishoners he withdrew and founded the church at Grantville, now Wellesley Hills. Returning to journalism in 1849 he was assistant editor of the *Boston Traveller* for a year and of the *New York Observer* for two years. He then settled in Brooklyn, where he conducted a private school for young ladies and engaged in authorship and in Sunday-school and mission work. In 1859 he became pastor of a church in Hancock, Pa., and remained as such till ill health forced his retirement to Brooklyn, in which city he died.

Newcomb had a genius for assimilating and imparting information and his literary output is estimated at as high as 178 volumes, some of which were published anonymously. He had an intelligent conception of Bible study and in some respects anticipated the historical criticism of a later generation. He probably, also, came as near as any author of his day to adapting his writings to the mental capacity of children and young people. His series of nineteen Sunday-school question books had a circulation of 300,000 copies, and his fourteen volumes of church history had wide popularity. His *How to be a Man* (1847) and *How to be a Lady* (1846; 8th ed., 1850) had a circulation of 34,000 copies each. A series on the Indians of North America and missionary work among them was abandoned at the end of the second volume for lack of popular interest in the subject. His most important work was his *Cyclopaedia of Missions* (1854), in which the enterprises of all denominations and the fields occupied were fully described, together with the histories of individual missions and missionaries. His writings are characterized by taste, judgment, wide and accurate information, and an intense desire to benefit humanity. He was an ardent and zealous worker, but in his contact with people his zeal sometimes outran his tact, a factor which tended to make his pastorates of short duration. He was deeply interested in city mission work and has been called the father of the mission Sunday school. He wrote constantly for the press and was a frequent contributor to such papers as the *Boston Recorder,* the *Puritan Recorder,* and the *New York Evangelist.* His contributions to the *Youth's Companion* cover a period of many years. He left in manuscript an interesting autobiography.

On May 19, 1830, he was married to Alithea A. Wells by whom he had two sons and two daughters.

[J. B. Newcomb, *Geneal. Memoir of the Newcomb Family* (1874); B. M. Newcomb, *Andrew Newcomb and His Descendants* (1923); *Congregational Quart.,* Oct. 1863; E. H. Chandler, *Hist. of the Wellesley Congregational Ch.* (1898); G. K. Clarke, *Hist. of Needham, Mass., 1711–1911* (1912); *N. Y. Observer,* Sept. 3, 1863.]   F. T. P.

NEWCOMB, JOSEPHINE LOUISE LE MONNIER (Oct. 31, 1816–Apr. 7, 1901), philanthropist, was born in Baltimore, Md., the youngest daughter of Alexander Louis and Mary Sophia (Waters) LeMonnier. Her mother was of English extraction and her father had emigrated to America from France. She lost her mother when very young and, being almost penniless, went to New Orleans to live with a married sister. There she received a large part if not all of her education, and there she met her future husband, Warren Newcomb, a man of New England ancestry then on a visit to New Orleans from Louisville, Ky., where he was a member of the firm of H. D. Newcomb & Brother, merchants. After their marriage they lived for a time in New York City, where they had a son, who died in infancy, and a daughter, Harriott Sophie, who was born on July 29, 1855. In 1866 Newcomb died, leaving his fortune to his widow and to their daughter, with whom she continued to live in New York until the child died on Dec. 16, 1870. Already saddened by the death of her husband and her son and harassed by the efforts of her husband's relatives to set aside his will, this death of the last member of her immediate family was an unusually severe blow. She lived in retirement for a number of years, and then vainly sought relief in travel.

Finally she decided to give her money to found a woman's college in memory of her beloved daughter, and she returned to New Orleans to make the necessary arrangements. The H. Sophie Newcomb Memorial College, in the Tulane University of Louisiana, for the higher education of white girls and young women, came into existence with her initial gift of $100,000 to the Tulane educational fund on Oct. 11, 1886. From that time until her death the welfare of the institution was her greatest personal interest. She made other gifts to it during her lifetime, and by her will, dated May 12, 1898, she made the university her residuary legatee, a bequest amounting to about $2,700,000. She was small in stature, modest, and retiring, and would not allow her philanthropies to be extolled in her presence. She had a clear idea of the value and administration of wealth and under her care the fortune of about half a million dollars left by her husband grew to important proportions and provided abundant means for the charities of her long life. Her gifts were by no means confined to Newcomb College; wherever she saw that money was needed she gave freely. During her lifetime she built a memorial chapel to Robert E. Lee at Lexington, Ky.; she made gifts to the Confederate orphans' home at Charleston, S. C., and to a deaf mutes' school in New York City; and in the Eye, Ear, Nose, and Throat Hospital of New Orleans she established a bed and named it after her daughter. She died on Easter Sunday 1901 in New York City and was buried in Greenwood Cemetery, N. Y.

[Records of the Tulane University; *Bulletin of the Tulane University of La.*, 31 ser., no. 4 (1930); *Newcomb College, Pictures and Practical Information,* May 1930; B. V. B. Dixon, *A Brief Hist. of H. Sophie Newcomb Coll.* (1928); B. M. Newcomb, *Andrew Newcomb . . . and His Descendants* (1923); *Daily Picayune* (New Orleans), Apr. 9–11, 14, 1901; date of birth from certificate of registra of St. Paul's parish, Baltimore, Md.; spelling of daughter's name from *In Memoriam* (n.d.), a booklet placed in archives of Newcomb Coll. by Mrs. Newcomb, through courtesy of Alice M. Labouisse, Newcomb Coll.]   M. J. W.

NEWCOMB, SIMON (Mar. 12, 1835–July 11, 1909), astronomer, was born in humble circumstances at Wallace, Nova Scotia. His father, John Burton Newcomb, was an itinerant school teacher of New England and Pennsylvania Scotch-Irish ancestry, his mother, Emily (Prince) Newcomb, a village girl of good mind, descended from a family of New England country preachers. Although showing precocity in school, at sixteen years of age Simon was apprenticed to a herbalist doctor, whom he soon discovered to be no more than a quack. At the age of eighteen, he ran away empty-handed, to make his career. After walking nearly a hundred miles, he reached St. John, New Brunswick. Finding no means of support there, he pressed on in great distress till he reached Calais, Me. Thence a kindly ship-captain allowed him to work his passage to Salem, Mass., for he hoped that opportunities for intellectual occupation might be found in the United States.

Drifting to Maryland, he taught country school for several years. Sometimes he traveled in high leather boots over the muddy or dusty road the long way to Washington. On one occasion he introduced himself to Joseph Henry [*q.v.*], first secretary of the Smithsonian Institution, and then the most influential man of science in America. Seeing promise in the boy, Henry recommended him to J. E. Hilgard [*q.v.*], then in charge of the Coast Survey. By the loan and recommendation of books, and in other ways, they both encouraged the hard-working, en-

thusiastic youth. Newcomb even undertook to read Newton's *Principia* and Bowditch's translation of Laplace's *Mécanique céleste,* but with the meager mathematical knowledge he then possessed found it impossible to master these abstruse works. Through the recommendations of Henry and Hilgard, Newcomb was appointed a computer in the Nautical Almanac Office, then located at Harvard University. He says in his *Reminiscences of an Astronomer* (p. 1), "I date my birth into the world of sweetness and light on one frosty morning in January, 1857, when I took my seat between two well-known mathematicians, before a blazing fire in the office of the 'Nautical Almanac.'" At Cambridge, he availed himself of the opportunity to attend the Lawrence Scientific School of Harvard University, from which he was graduated (B.Sc.) July 2, 1858. In 1860 he published his first important research, done while still a computer at the Nautical Almanac Office. The astronomer Olbers had suggested that the minor planets of the solar system had originated in the disruption of a larger planet. Newcomb was able to show that the orbits of these bodies had never intersected, so that this origin is impossible (*Proceedings of the American Association for the Advancement of Science,* vol. XIII, 1860; *Memoirs of the American Academy of Arts and Sciences,* n.s. VIII, pt. 1, 1861). In 1860 he and William Ferrel [*q.v.*] were sent to the wilderness of Saskatchewan north of Lake Winnipeg to observe a total eclipse of the sun. Upon reaching their station after many adventures, they found it inundated. They set up their instruments in puddles of water and slept in their canoe, but the eclipse was entirely hidden by thick clouds. On Sept. 21, 1861, Newcomb was commissioned professor of mathematics in the United States Navy. In this service he continued at the Naval Observatory and the Nautical Almanac Office until his retirement for age with the naval rank of captain in 1897. He was promoted to be rear-admiral (retired) in 1906.

Although he was assigned to the new 8-inch transit circle in 1862, and made many observations during his connection with the Naval Observatory, he was primarily a mathematical rather than an observational astronomer. In 1866 and in 1873 he published in the *Smithsonian Contributions to Knowledge* (vols. XV, XIX) fundamental investigations and tables of the orbits of Neptune and of Uranus. In recognition of these investigations he was awarded the gold medal of the Royal Astronomical Society of London in 1874. Having arranged his observing with a view to determining errors in the catalogue positions of the stars, he published a memoir on the right ascensions of the equatorial fundamental stars, and on the corrections required to reduce existing observations of star positions in right ascension to a homogeneous system (*Astronomical and Meteorological Observations Made during the Year 1870, at the United States Naval Observatory,* generally cited as *Washington Observations,* App. 3, 1873).

About 1868 he began his celebrated studies of the motion of the moon, to which he gave much of his attention up to the very end of his life. They first led him to search the early European records for occultations of stars. He carried on this search at the Paris Observatory during the reign of the Commune in 1871, while the city was besieged by the National forces. He had such success as to push back a fairly exact knowledge of lunar positions from the year 1750 to about 1645, and in this way disclosed an unsuspected inadequacy of Hansen's tables of the moon's motion, which till then had been regarded as definitive. About this time, he became deeply concerned with the question of the sun's parallax. All approaches to it interested him. He took part in observing the total solar eclipses of 1869 and 1870, as well as in the preparations and observations relating to the transits of Venus in 1874 and 1882. While in Vienna in 1883, he was able to rescue from discredit the records made by Father Maximilian Hell, S.J., of the transit of Venus as observed at Wardhus in Norway in 1769, which were regarded as of great importance if trustworthy (*Monthly Notices of the Royal Astronomical Society,* May 1883; *Reminiscences of an Astronomer,* pp. 154–60). With the assistance of A. A. Michelson [*q.v.*] he redetermined the velocity of light by the revolving-mirror method. Gravitational approaches through the lunar and planetary inequalities of motion were also investigated by him. His revision of the value of the solar parallax published in *Washington Observations, 1865* (1867) remained standard for many years, but was itself superseded by his own new revision of 1895 (published in *The Elements of the Four Inner Planets, and the Fundamental Constants of Astronomy,* 1895, which was issued as a supplement to the *American Ephemeris . . . for 1897*). This second revision since then has been slightly improved in its turn by later results depending on the discovery of the minor planet Eros.

With his achievements so widely recognized that already he had been elected to the principal academies and societies of the world, and had received their most honorable decorations and medals, he was appointed, Sept. 15, 1877, to be superintendent of the American Ephemeris and Nautical Almanac. When he assumed charge, the Nautical Almanac Office was cramped into a dilapidated old dwelling-house in Cambridge, and much of the computing was done as piecework at high prices by distant college professors. Newcomb found this piecework method well suited to economical administration after he had, little by little, brought in the work to less expensive computers in Washington. He removed the offices to more commodious quarters, where they remained until the completion of the present Naval Observatory. Inefficient personnel, which had received appointment by influence in those days antedating civil-service reform, he succeeded in removing. Thus the office was reorganized to do its great work.

Immediately after assuming his new responsibilities, Newcomb conceived the astonishing program of critically reforming the entire basis of fundamental data involved in the computation of the Ephemeris. The fundamental star places, the mass and distance of the sun, the motion of the moon, and the masses and orbits of the planets and their satellites, all were to be redetermined and new tables computed to suit the revised theory. Surprising to relate, he was able to accomplish all of this during his own lifetime excepting new tables of the moon's motion, which have since his death been computed by Prof. Ernest W. Brown of Yale University. Newcomb's program involved the discussion of all the worthwhile observations of the positions of the sun, moon, and planets, as well as those of many of the fixed stars, which had been made at the principal observatories of the world since 1750. These observations numbered several hundred thousands. The work also involved investigating the mathematical theory of the perturbations caused by the several planets upon the motions of each other. In this highest type of practical mathematical research, he was fortunate in enlisting the services of George William Hill [*q.v.*], to whom was assigned the theory and tables of motion of Jupiter and Saturn. Newcomb himself discussed the orbits of Neptune, Uranus, and the four inner planets, Mercury, Venus, Earth, and Mars, and computed tables of their motions. He also expended enormous labor on lunar theory. As Hill remarked: "He seems to be determined that no inequality of sensible magnitude should escape him" (Hill, *post,* p. 356). In 1896 he took a leading part at the Paris Conference on a common international catalogue of fundamental stars. Different portions of the required research being assigned to different astronomers, Newcomb worked up for international use the best value of the constant of precession (*Astronomical Papers,* vol. VIII, pt. 1, 1897), and following this he published a catalogue of about fifteen hundred fundamental star positions (*Ibid.,* pt. 2, 1898).

To the *Astronomical Papers Prepared for the Use of the American Ephemeris and Nautical Almanac,* of which he was the founder, he contributed a great number of classic memoirs. In the opinion of his colleague Hill, some ten of these, in addition to the two just mentioned, were of outstanding importance. His "Discussion and Results of Observations on Transits of Mercury, from 1677 to 1881" (*Astronomical Papers,* vol. I, pt. 6, 1882) corroborated Leverrier's assertion that a secular motion of the perihelion of the planet amounting to 40″ is unaccounted for by gravitational theory. This is the peculiarity of Mercury's orbit that in recent years has become celebrated as evidence of the soundness of Einstein's theory of relativity (see "Einstein's Appreciation of Simon Newcomb," *Science,* Mar. 1, 1929). A memoir on the velocity of light (*Astronomical Papers,* vol. II, pt. 3, 1885), the work in which he collaborated with Michelson, gave an account of the investigation by Foucault's method made at Washington in the years 1880–82. An exhaustive discussion of the observations of the transit of Venus in 1761 and 1769 and their bearing on the solar parallax and the position of the node of Venus appeared in 1890 (vol. II, pt. 5) and a memoir on the constant of nutation as determined by observations with the transit circles of Greenwich and Washington, in 1891 (vol. II, pt. 6).

Deeming "that improvements could be made in the mode of deriving the periodic expressions needed in the subject of planetary perturbations" (Hill, p. 355), he elaborated his method of treatment in "A Method of Developing the Perturbative Function of Planetary Motion" (*American Journal of Mathematics,* September 1880), and, more extensively, in "Development of the Perturbative Function and Its Derivatives in Sines and Cosines of Multiples of the Eccentric Anomaly and in Powers of the Eccentricities and Inclinations" (*Astronomical Papers,* vol. III, pt. 1, 1884). Finally, he applied this method to the four interior planets in "Periodic Perturbation of the Longitudes and Radii Vectors of the Four Inner Planets of the First Order as to the Masses" (*Ibid.,* vol. III, pt. 5, 1891). "For certain long-period inequalities in these planets," says Hill (*loc. cit.*), "it was found convenient to employ expressions involving time-arguments; this led to the composition of two memoirs in Volume V of the same collection" (*Astronomical Papers,*

pts. 1, 2, 1894). "The secular variations of the elements of these planets are derived and the mass of Jupiter determined from observations of Polyhymnia in parts 4 and 5 of the same volume" (1894–95). In 1884 (vol. III, pt. 3) appeared a memoir on the retrograde motion of the line of Jupiter's satellite Hyperion, which he ascribed to the disturbing influence of Titan; while a highly important memoir on the elements of the four inner planets and certain fundamental constants of astronomy was published (1895) as a supplement to the *American Ephemeris* for the year 1897. Following this were issued the actual tables of motion of these planets (*Astronomical Papers,* vol. VI, pts. 1–4, 1895–98). In 1899, Newcomb's revision of the motions of six planets was completed by publication of the tables of motion of Uranus and Neptune (*Ibid.,* vol. VII, 1899). Other work laid out by him but finished by his colleagues appeared in later volumes.

After his retirement in 1897, some slight provision was made by Congress for several years to employ his great powers for the benefit of the Nautical Almanac Office. The Carnegie Institution, however, almost immediately after its establishment, made grants which enabled him to go on with his work till the end of his life. Among his later investigations, besides those of a purely astronomical type, were some relating to meteorology and the influence of sunspots on terrestrial climate. He took a prominent part in procuring the 26-inch telescope of the United States Naval Observatory, in the foundation of the Lick Observatory, and in other important steps in astronomical progress both in America and abroad. As a presiding officer, he was a most extraordinary and impressive figure. Not unconscious of the high worth implied by the numerous honors, doctorates, and decorations heaped upon him from all parts of the world (see *Who's Who in America,* 1908–09), he conducted himself with great dignity, heightened by the massive leonine head with its crown of iron-gray hair and the strong mouth framed by beard and mustache. To see him presiding at a meeting of astronomers was indeed a serious sight, well calculated to inspire awe of the profession in a youthful mind. Besides the classic memoirs of the *American Ephemeris* which issued under his direction, and a long memoir on the lunar theory, *Investigation of Inequalities in the Motion of the Moon, Produced by the Action of the Planets* (Carnegie Institution of Washington, 1907), Newcomb published numerous articles in astronomical journals both in America and abroad. These treated in masterly fashion almost every conceivable subject in astronomy. In addition, he published a number of mathematical textbooks and several outstanding astronomical books for the general reader, including *Popular Astronomy* (1878), *The Stars* (1901), *Astronomy for Everybody* (1902), and *Reminiscences of an Astronomer* (1903). The author's good sense of humor is often betrayed in these writings. He did not at all confine his thoughts to astronomy, but wrote a romance, *His Wisdom, the Defender* (1900); *The A B C of Finance* (1877), consisting in large part of articles that had first appeared in *Harper's Weekly, 1875–76*; *Principles of Political Economy* (1886); and *A Plain Man's Talk on the Labor Question* (1886). He used to say that while astronomy was his vocation, political economy was his avocation. He was also the first president of the American Society for Psychical Research.

Throughout most of his career he was closely associated with collegiate work. In 1879–80, he delivered four lectures in a course on political economy at Harvard University. For two years, 1884–86, he was nominally professor of astronomy at Columbian College (now George Washington University). In October 1884, he was appointed professor of mathematics and astronomy at The Johns Hopkins University, and lectured there twice a week till 1894, and again 1898–1900. In 1885, he was invited to assume the presidency of the University of California, but declined.

He married, Aug. 4, 1863, Mary Caroline Hassler, daughter of Dr. C. A. Hassler, United States Navy, and grand-daughter of Ferdinand Rudolph Hassler [*q.v.*], first superintendent of the United States Coast Survey. Three daughters were born of this marriage. His death occurred at Washington in his seventy-fifth year.

[Newcomb's notebooks, MSS., and letters are in the MSS. Div., Lib. of Cong. For biography, in addition to his *Reminiscences of an Astronomer* (1903), see W. W. Campbell, "Simon Newcomb," with bibliography by R. C. Archibald of Newcomb's writings and articles about him, in *Memoirs Nat. Acad. Sci.*, vol. XVII (1924); Orville Stone, in *Ann. Report ... Smithsonian Inst., 1909* (1910); *Proc. Am. Phil. Soc.*, vol. XLIX (1910); R. C. Archibald, "Simon Newcomb," a collection of facts and dates, in *Science*, Dec. 22, 1916; G. W. Hill, "Professor Simon Newcomb as an Astronomer," *Science*, Sept. 17, 1909; Irving Fisher, in *Economic Jour.* (London), Dec. 1909. For genealogy, see B. M. Newcomb, *Andrew Newcomb, 1618–1686, and His Descendants* (1923).] C. G. A.

NEWCOMER, CHRISTIAN (Jan. 21, 1749–o.s.–Mar. 12, 1830), one of the founders of the Church of the United Brethren in Christ, was born in Lancaster County, Pa. His father, Wolfgang Newcomer, emigrated with his parents from Switzerland to America some time between 1719 and 1729. He married a Miss Baer—who died about a year later—and as his second wife,

Elizabeth Weller. Christian was one of their eight children. The family was identified with the Mennonite faith.

At the age of seventeen Christian experienced a religious conversion. At this time there was a small but growing body in the ministry and laity of different churches, which gave special emphasis to the inner experiential elements of religion. The movement which it furthered contributed, among English-speaking people, to the development of American Methodism, and among the Germans to the organization, in 1800, of the Church of the United Brethren in Christ, under the leadership of Philip William Otterbein [*q.v.*], a minister of the German Reformed Church. Newcomer, some time subsequent to his conversion and partly as a result of a critical illness which led to a more serious consideration of spiritual matters, became inwardly convinced that he was divinely called to preach the Gospel, but through natural timidity he remained in a state of indecision for a number of years. He had been married, Mar. 31, 1770, to Elizabeth Baer, and in 1775, during this period of vacillation, he moved to Frederick County, Md., his residence later being included, by change of boundary, in Washington County. Finding no peace of mind as a fugitive from duty, as he regarded himself, he finally yielded to his convictions, entering upon the work of the ministry in 1777. Withdrawing from the Mennonite communion, he became identified with the movement headed by Otterbein, which, though lacking in compact organization, was assuming considerable proportions and wielding a growing influence. He took a leading part in the founding of the Church of the United Brethren in Christ and became a most ardent promoter of its activities. In his zeal for extending the work he made excursions into western Pennsylvania, Kentucky, Ohio and Indiana, and did much to establish his Church west of the Alleghany mountains. He early perceived the necessity of effective organization, and wherever conditions permitted he formed local congregations, at the same time urging and developing a more complete plan for missionary enterprise. He was among the first to attempt to formulate a discipline for the government of the general body, and to promote organic unity of the congregations east and west of the Alleghanies. In his itineraries, he made at least nineteen trips through the mountains, invariably on horseback. Later historians are much indebted for information regarding the early history of the Church to the diary, known as "Newcomer's Journal," which records, though incompletely, his labors from 1795 to 1830. This journal, translated and edited by John Hildt, was published in 1834, under the title, *The Life and Journal of the Rev'd. Christian Newcomer, Late Bishop of the Church of the United Brethren in Christ*. He was elected bishop in 1813, being the third to occupy that office, and was successively reëlected to that position in 1814, 1817, 1821, 1825, and 1829. His strength as a preacher was more in his intense earnestness and spiritual zeal than in any marked oratorical ability, though he was recognized as possessing a high degree of persuasive power and ability to expound the Scripture.

[In addition to *The Life and Journal,* see Daniel Berger, *Hist. of the Ch. of the United Brethren in Christ* (1897); H. A. Thompson, *Our Bishops* (1889); A. W. Drury, *Hist. of the Ch. of the United Brethren in Christ* (1924).]   W. E. S—r.

NEWEL, STANFORD (June 7, 1839–Apr. 6, 1907), lawyer, diplomat, was the son of Stanford and Abby Lee (Penniman) Newel. He was born in Providence, R. I., but at the age of fifteen went with his parents to St. Anthony Falls (now Minneapolis), Minn. He graduated from Yale College in 1861 and in 1864 he completed the course in Harvard Law School. Returning to Minnesota he was admitted to the bar and began the practice of law in St. Paul. On June 24, 1880, he was married to Helen F. Fiedler, daughter of Ernest and Helen F. Fiedler of New York. With a private income which made it unnecessary to depend upon his profession for support, he took less and less interest as time went on in litigation, and made it his aim to keep his clients out of lawsuits whenever possible. Nevertheless he was known as one of the outstanding lawyers of the Northwest. A large part of his practice was devoted to giving counsel to those who could not afford to pay regular fees. For many years he was a member of the St. Paul park board and was active in other civic affairs. He was the principal founder and many times president of the Minnesota Club of St. Paul. He took great interest in state and local politics, and while he never ran for public office, his advice on Republican policies and candidates had great influence; he was said to have been the confidential friend and adviser of nearly every prominent man in Minnesota politics between 1880 and 1896. He was chairman of the state Republican central committee for six years and was twice delegate to national Republican conventions. Several times he drafted the party platforms of the Minnesota Republicans.

It was not merely as a reward for his political services, however, that Newel received the appointment of United States minister to the Netherlands from President McKinley in 1897.

His background of culture, learning, and experience, his record of quiet and unpretentious but effective public service, his capacity for making and keeping friends, combined with a keen mind, quick perceptions, and a gift for turning a happy and meaningful phrase, made him most valuable as a diplomatic representative abroad. He soon became popular with the diplomatic corps at The Hague and with the people of the Netherlands, and won respect as an able representative of American national interests. He arrived at The Hague in July 1897. A year later, on Sept. 6, 1898, he attended the coronation of the youthful Queen Wilhelmina as the specially accredited representative of the United States, and on Feb. 7, 1901, attended her marriage to Duke Hendrik of Mecklenburg-Schwerin. His most important work at The Hague was as a member of the American delegation to the first Hague Peace Conference in 1899. He was a member of the Second Committee, which had reference to the extension of the Red Cross rules of 1864 and 1868 to maritime warfare, and the revision of the declaration of 1874 concerning the laws and customs of war. With the other members of the delegation he signed the Hague Agreements at the end of the Conference for the United States. He subsequently shared in the organization of the Hague Permanent Court of Arbitration. Newel was the first accredited diplomatic representative of the United States to Luxemburg, to which he was appointed minister on June 5, 1903, in combination with his duties as minister to the Netherlands. In 1905 he resigned from the diplomatic service and returned to St. Paul, where he died a little less than two years later.

[Newel's diplomatic dispatches are preserved in the archives of the State Department; a portion are published in *Papers Relating to the Foreign Relations of the U. S., 1898–1905.* Biographical articles are found in *Minn. Hist. Soc. Colls.,* vol. XII (1908); Warren Upham and Rose B. Dunlap, "Minn. Biogs.," *Ibid.,* vol. XIV (1912); *Obit. Record of Grads. of Yale Univ., 1907; Sunday Pioneer Press* (St. Paul), Apr. 7, 1907; *Am. Rev. of Revs.,* May 1899; *Who's Who in America,* 1906–07.]   I. L. T.

NEWELL, FREDERICK HAYNES (Mar. 5, 1862–July 5, 1932), civil engineer, was born in Bradford, Pa., the son of Augustus William and Annie Maria (Haynes) Newell. He lost his mother when he was a child and was reared in Newton, Mass., by his maiden aunts, graduating from the high school of that city in 1881. In 1885 he received the degree of B.Sc. in mining engineering from the Massachusetts Institute of Technology. He was then engaged for three years in various surveys in Pennsylvania, Colorado, and other states, and was appointed, Oct. 2, 1888, as assistant hydraulic engineer in the United States Geological Survey under **Maj. John Wesley Powell** [*q.v.*]. For nearly fourteen years he was engaged in irrigation surveys as hydrographer in charge of stream measurements, selection and survey of reservoir sites, and irrigation projects in the arid West.

On the passage of the Reclamation Act in 1902, in the preparation of which he had been prominently concerned, he was made chief engineer of the Reclamation Service under Charles D. Walcott, director of the Geological Survey. In 1907, he was made director of the Reclamation Service, which then became an independent bureau of the Department of the Interior. In this position he continued until 1914, when he was succeeded by Arthur P. Davis, and became consulting engineer for the same service. During his incumbency of these positions the Reclamation Service surveyed and began construction of twenty-five irrigation projects in eighteen different states, involving an investment of nearly $100,000,000 in dams, reservoirs, tunnels, canals, and power and pumping plants. These and auxiliary minor works served about 1,500,000 acres of arid land.

A good speaker, of pleasing personality, he delivered many lectures on irrigation before schools and scientific and civic organizations in various parts of the country. In 1915, he became head of the department of civil engineering of the University of Illinois, but resigned from this position in 1920 and returned to his former home in Washington, D. C. He was associated with others in the organization of the American Association of Engineers, of which he became president in 1919. In 1924, with A. B. McDaniel, he founded the Research Service, in Washington, D. C., an organization of engineering consultants, of which he became president. He was at various times a member of the United States Land Commission, Inland Waterways Commission, Advisory Board on Fuels and Structural Materials, and Illinois State Board of Examiners of Structural Materials. During his career he wrote *Hydrography of the Arid Regions* (1891); *Report on Agriculture by Irrigation in the Western Part of the United States* (1894), published by the 11th Census; *The Public Lands of the United States and Their Water Supply* (1895); *Irrigation in the United States* (1902); *Hawaii, Its Natural Resources and Opportunities for Home-Making* (1909); *Principles of Irrigation Engineering* (1913), with D. W. Murphy; *Irrigation Management* (1916); *Water Resources, Present and Future Uses* (1920). He was joint editor of *Engineering as a Career* (1916), a series of papers by distinguished members of the profes-

sion; and editor of *Planning and Building the City of Washington* (1932). In 1918, he was awarded the Cullum Gold Medal by the American Geographical Society for his achievements in irrigation. He died suddenly in Washington, D. C., of heart failure. On Apr. 3, 1890, he married Effie Josephine Mackintosh of Milton, Mass., who with one son and two daughters survived him.

[*Who's Who in America*, 1932–33; memoir prepared by Allen B. McDaniel for *Trans. Am. Soc. Civil Engineers*; *The Semi-Centennial Alumni Record of the Univ. of Ill.* (1918); F. H. Newell, "Descendants of Walter Haynes and Peter Noyes of Sudbury, Mass.," *New-Eng. Hist. and Geneal. Reg.*, Jan. 1893; *Evening Star* (Washington, D. C.), July 6, 1932; reminiscences of A. B. McDaniel and Mrs. F. H. Newell; personal acquaintance.]　　　　　　　　　　　　　　**A. P. D.**

NEWELL, PETER SHEAF HERSEY (Mar. 5, 1862–Jan. 15, 1924), cartoonist and illustrator, son of George Frederick and Louisa N. Newell, was born near Bushnell, MacDonough County, Ill. In spite of an early predilection for sketching and caricaturing, at the age of sixteen he attempted to work in a cigar factory. This experiment lasted three months and was followed by an apprenticeship to a maker of crayon portraits in Jacksonville, Ill. He made enlargements, thereby gaining his first knowledge of drawing, and though he later studied in an art school he may be said to have been largely self-taught, for his work was free from the prevailing influences in illustration and he evolved a definitely original technique. At about this time he sent a humorous drawing to *Harper's Bazar* with a note asking the editor whether it showed talent. The reply came back: "No talent indicated," but a check was enclosed. Successful contributions to the New York *Graphic* and various periodicals took him to New York in 1882, where he studied at the Art Students' League. He tolerated academic training only three months, believing that the value of his work —its originality—would be sacrificed by adapting it to accepted methods. In 1893, using negro subjects in his new flat-tone technique, he achieved success with *Harper's Magazine* (August 1893) and sudden popularity by an amusing bit of naïveté: "Wild Flowers."

He contributed full-page illustrations to holiday numbers of *Harper's Weekly* and *Harper's Bazar*, continued to do comics with captions of his own invention, and then turned this knack to making children's books, starting with *Topsys and Turvys* (1893). This reversible little volume resulted from the distressing occasion upon which he discovered one of his children scrutinizing a picture-book upside down. He determined to produce a book which could be looked at from any angle. Thereafter he illustrated contemporary fiction, notably: John Kendrick Bangs's *A House-Boat on the Styx* (1896) and *The Pursuit of the House-Boat* (1897), and in 1901 tried his hand at *Alice in Wonderland*. The appearance of substitutes for Sir John Tenniel's inimitable illustrations was attended by considerable controversy. Newell defended the new edition in an article in *Harper's Monthly Magazine* (October 1901), in which he asserted that any distinctly personal reaction to character justifies a new version of interpretation.

Considered by his contemporaries to be an illustrator of ability and conspicuous originality, Newell has survived by reason of his good humor rather than on grounds of artistic merit. Whenever his work lacks the animation of wit its execution appears unimpressive. The flat decorative use of wash does not conceal an inadequacy of drawing and composition. His strength lay in whimsical interpretation of nonsense set forth in simple and direct terms. He was inventive rather than imaginative, giving a certain zest to his own cartoons which is not felt in his illustrations of the ideas of others. Newell was married, Feb. 5, 1884, to Leona Dow Ashcraft. They had two daughters. He died in his sixty-second year at Little Neck, L. I.

[*Peter Newell's Pictures and Rhymes* (1899) contains a biographical sketch by John Kendrick Bangs. See also: C. B. Loomis, "Interesting People—Peter Newell," *Am. Mag.*, May 1911; Albert Lee, "Book Illustrators—Peter Newell," *Book Buyer*, July 1896; Louise M. Sill, "Mr. Newell's Latest Drawings," *Harper's Bazar*, Sept. 1902; Mich. State Lib., *Biog. Sketches of Am. Artists* (1924); Regina Armstrong, "The New Leaders in Am. Illustration," *Bookman*, June 1900; P. L. Allen, "Illustrations of Alice in Wonderland," *Ibid.*, Feb. 1908; Peter Newell, "Alice's Adventures in Wonderland from an Artist's Standpoint," *Harper's Monthly*, Oct. 1901; *N. Y. Times*, Jan. 16, 1924.]
F. B.

NEWELL, ROBERT (Mar. 30, 1807–November 1869), trapper, Oregon pioneer, was born in Muskingum County, Ohio. The names of his parents are not known. After meager schooling he became a saddler's apprentice in Cincinnati. On Mar. 17, 1829, he left St. Louis with a trapping party for the mountains, forming on the way a lasting friendship with a youth of nineteen, afterward well known, Joseph L. Meek [*q.v.*]. He remained a trapper for eleven years. In 1833 he married a Nez Percé woman, and at some time he acquired the nickname of "Doc" (or "Doctor"), which ever afterward he bore. In 1840 he and Meek, with their Indian families, accompanied by two white men, started from Fort Hall for Oregon, taking with them three wagons, and thus brought the first wheels to the Columbia. Newell and Meek settled near the

present Hillsboro, in the Willamette Valley. Newell from the first actively interested himself in the affairs of the settlements and soon became a leader. In the meeting of May 2, 1843, which took the first effective steps toward the formation of a government, he was chosen a member of the legislative committee which drew up the constitution ratified on July 5. Throughout the life of the Provisional Government he was a member of the House of Representatives, and for two sessions the speaker.

In 1844 he removed to a place near Champoeg. About this time he built two keelboats, probably the first on the upper Willamette, and engaged in transportation. His Indian wife died in December 1845 and in 1846 he married Rebecca Newman. In the winter of 1848–49 he joined the gold rush to California but returned in the fall of 1850, when he engaged in merchandizing. He commanded a company of scouts in the Indian troubles of 1855–56, and in 1860 he was elected to the state legislature. The floods of December 1861 destroyed most of his property except his residence. He moved to Lapwai, Idaho, where for six years he served as an interpreter and a special commissioner at the army post and the Indian agency. His second wife died in May 1867. He became agent on Oct. 1, 1868. In June 1869 he married a Mrs. Ward, and in July he was replaced as agent. He then moved to Lewiston, where, four months later, he died of heart disease. His wife and several children of his second marriage survived him.

Newell was an Episcopalian and a Mason. He holds a place of unique importance in the early history of Oregon. With the death of Ewing Young he assumed a leadership in the affairs of the colony which was maintained for some years. Like Meek he was a jester; but unlike Meek he was sober, studious, prudent, and dependable. The early chroniclers, with but one outstanding exception, pay tribute to his high character and recount his notable services to the community.

[T. C. Elliott, "'Doctor' Robt. Newell: Pioneer," *Quart. Ore. Hist. Soc.*, June 1908; H. W. Scott, *Hist. of the Ore. Country* (6 vols., 1924); C. H. Carey, *Hist. of Ore.* (1922); Mrs. F. F. Victor, *The River of the West* (1870).]
W. J. G.

NEWELL, ROBERT HENRY (Dec. 13, 1836–July 1901), American journalist, poet, and humorist, who wrote under the pen-name Orpheus C. Kerr, was born in New York, the son of Robert and Ann Lawrence Newell. His father was a manufacturer and inventor, the designer of a patent lock and a sewing machine, whose work received the award of a gold medal at the "Great Exhibition" in London, 1851. Robert Henry Newell attended a private academy but the death of his father left the family in straitened circumstances and he was denied a college education. He began to write fugitive pieces for the New York press in which work he achieved immediate recognition and employment. He became an assistant editor of the New York *Sunday Mercury* in 1858, for which during the next two years he contributed a variety of verse and current comment all of which has proved as ephemeral as it was successful. The outbreak of the Civil War gave him the opportunity and the occasion to write the Orpheus C. Kerr papers, originally initiated in the form of Washington correspondence to the *Mercury,* continued for other journals, and published later in three volumes (1862–65). The name was a supposedly laughable transposition of "office seeker." The flood of applicants for office, when President Buchanan went out and Lincoln came in, was an outstanding political feature of the moment and the "office seeker" became a stock character of political lampoonery.

The Orpheus C. Kerr papers possess now only a historical interest as a sort of comic commentary on the history of the Civil War. They contain a mixture of what is meant to be funny dialogue, imaginary episodes and war incidents, interspersed with various verses and poems intended to be pathetic but rarely more than sentimental. One chapter of the papers (Letter no. VIII of the First Series) deserves perhaps a permanent place in the history of American burlesque writing, containing parodies of the best-known authors of the day in their supposed attempts to compose a new national anthem. The style of the papers represents a mixture of the mock heroic style adopted and popularized by Dickens, written in correct orthography and grammatical language, but with a false elevation of tone, and the loose, comic humor of gargantuan exaggeration, gross misspelling, and wilful irreverence for solemnity which had been already initiated in the West (Artemus Ward, Mark Twain). On Sept. 24, 1862, Newell married Adah Isaacs Menken [*q.v.*], an actress, who divorced him in 1865. His connection with the *Mercury* (1858–62) was followed by his occupancy of various literary editorships in New York. He was a war correspondent for the *New York Herald,* an editor of the New York *World* (1869–74), editor of the *Daily Graphic,* and later of a weekly journal called *Hearth and Home,* his last position as a journalist.

A painful nervous affliction which rendered writing physically difficult and impaired his sight removed Newell in 1876 from active employment and the last quarter-century of his

life was spent in the shadow. Apart from *The Orpheus C. Kerr Papers* by which his name is chiefly remembered, Newell collected and published two volumes of his verse, *The Palace Beautiful and Other Poems* (1865) and *Versatilities* (1871). While still active as a journalist he had written *Avery Glibun, or Between Two Fires* (1867). After his retirement he wrote a romance, *There was once a Man* (1884), a story intended to satirize the still novel and still wicked Darwinian theory of the descent of man. He also wrote a book called *The Cloven Foot,* one of the many attempts to interpret and complete (1870) Charles Dickens' unfinished *Mystery of Edwin Drood.* Newell introduced a novel feature in transferring the setting of the story to American conditions, but his work appears to have passed without recognition in the voluminous Edwin Drood controversies. He also published a novel of New York life in 1872 under the title of *The Walking Doll, or the Asters and Disasters of Society.* He died in Brooklyn early in July 1901. His writings are marked with the conventional merits and defects of his time and show nothing to elevate him above the crowd. His pathos is based upon genuine feeling but runs easily to sentiment, his tears flow kindly but easily run to drivel, his humor demands an uproarious reader. His work is interesting nowadays only as illustrating, for those who care to know it, the current way of writing, joking, and weeping, which has been replaced by our own.

[Jennette Tandy, *Crackerbox Philosophers in Am. Humor and Satire* (1925); W. P. Trent, "A Retrospect of Am. Humor," *Century Mag.,* Nov. 1901; Robt. Ford, *Am. Humorists* (1897); *Who's Who in America,* 1901–02; *Appletons' Ann. Cyc.,* 1901; *N. Y. Daily Tribune,* July 13, 14, 1901; *Brooklyn Daily Eagle,* July 12, 13, 28, 1901.]   S. L.

NEWELL, WILLIAM AUGUSTUS (Sept. 5, 1817–Aug. 8, 1901), congressman and governor of New Jersey, was born in Franklin, Ohio, the son of James Hugh and Eliza D. (Hankinson) Newell of Freehold, N. J. His parents had temporarily moved to Ohio but returned to New Jersey when he was three years of age. He attended school at New Brunswick, N. J., and was graduated from Rutgers College in 1836. He received the M.D. degree from the medical department of the University of Pennsylvania in 1839 and began the practice of medicine with his uncle at Manahawkin, Ocean County, N. J. He went to Imlaystown and about 1844 settled at Allentown, N. J., where he built up a large and lucrative practice. The same year he began practice his attention was called to a shipwreck off the coast near his home, and, appalled at the loss of life when thirteen bodies were brought ashore, he began to experiment with lines and with a mortar to reach a wrecked vessel in the hope of preventing future accidents. He was so far successful that, eight years later when serving in Congress, he had plans for a life-saving service, which gave impetus to the establishment of a federal life-saving service that was adapted for the entire sea and lake coasts (*Remarks of William A. Newell . . . Aug. 3, 1848,* 1848; *Letter from William A. Newell . . . to Hon. William J. Sewell,* 1898, with useful citations). He served two terms in Congress as a Whig, from 1847 to 1851, and then resumed practice in Allentown.

In 1856 he had identified himself with the American party and was elected governor of New Jersey; he served two terms from 1857 to 1861. In these critical years he led in the unification of the interests of the American and Republican parties in the state. By 1860 he had become a Republican and was a delegate to the Republican convention at Chicago. Under Lincoln's administration he was appointed superintendent of the life-saving service in New Jersey. He was for a period examining surgeon of drafted soldiers in his state. In 1865 he returned to Congress for one term. He was defeated for reëlection as he was in several later efforts to be elected to the House and to the Senate as well as to the governorship. Nevertheless he continued to keep a firm hold on party patronage in the state. In 1875 he became president of the New Jersey state board of agriculture, and his efforts were important in the establishment of the federal agricultural bureau. In 1880 President Hayes appointed him governor of Washington Territory, in which office he served four years. Then he was appointed Indian inspector for the same territory. He practised a year in Olympia and was resident surgeon in the soldiers' and sailors' home there. He returned to Allentown, N. J., in 1889, where he continued to practise until the time of his death. He was married in early life to Joanna Van Deursen of New Brunswick, N. J., who died while he was governor of Washington Territory. They had three children.

[Information from Mrs. Wm. S. Meek, Elizabeth, N. J.; *The Biog. Encyc. of N. J.* (1877); *The New Jersey Coast* (3 vols., 1902); *Biog. Dir. Am. Cong.* (1928); *Who's Who in America,* 1901–02; C. M. Knapp, *N. J. Politics during the Period of the Civil War* (1924); C. A. Snowden, *Hist. of Wash.* (1909), vol. IV; *Newark Evening News,* Aug. 8, 11, 1901.]

A. V–D. H.

NEWELL, WILLIAM WELLS (Jan. 24, 1839–Jan. 21, 1907), scholar, folklorist, and editor, was born in Cambridge, Mass., the son of the Rev. William Newell, minister of the First Parish Church, Cambridge, and Frances Boott (Wells) Newell. He came by his studious tastes naturally, as both his father and William Wells, his mother's father, were well-known classical scholars. His early education was in the Cambridge schools, from which he entered Harvard College, graduating with the class of 1859. He then studied for the ministry, taking his degree from the Harvard Divinity School in 1863. At first he served as assistant to the Rev. Edward Everett Hale at the South Congregational Church, Boston, but after a short time left to join the Sanitary Service of the War Department in Washington. Returning to ministerial work again at the close of the war, he was settled for a time at the Unitarian Church in Germantown, Pa., but later, feeling that he had mistaken his vocation, he gave up the ministry and turned to teaching. From 1868 to 1870 he was tutor in philosophy at Harvard College, leaving to open a school in New York City. In this he was very successful, but wishing to have more leisure for scholarly pursuits, he gave up teaching in the early eighties and after a year or two of travel and study in Europe, settled down in Cambridge to the pleasant life of the private scholar. His major interests had long lain in the fields of literature and the fine arts, and already his attention had been turned in the direction of folklore, of which he had acquired a wide and accurate knowledge.

His more purely literary work comprised *King Œdipus: The Œdipus Tyrannus of Sophocles Rendered into English Verse* (1881), and *Sonnets and Madrigals of Michelangelo Buonarroti* (1900). In 1895 he published a small volume of original poems, entitled *Words for Music,* later (1904) reprinted at a small private press which he had set up at Wayland. His interest in the fine arts had always been keen, and during his residence in New York he was closely in touch with artistic circles there. An able and discerning student of painting, he discovered and acquired during his stay abroad a number of canvases of real distinction, which later found their way into the Metropolitan Museum in New York and other public and private collections.

Newell is best known, however, for his work in folklore and related subjects. It was largely through his efforts and enthusiasm that the American Folk-Lore Society was founded in 1888, and he served as the permanent secretary of the organization and editor of the *Journal of American Folk-Lore* and the *Memoirs* of the American Folk-Lore Society until his death in

1907. Although his best-known studies lay large-ly in the European field, his interests were wide, and one of his earliest publications was *Games and Songs of American Children* (1883). Cur-rent superstitions, negro practices and beliefs, and those of the American Indians all strongly attracted his attention, and his enthusiasm en-listed the services of many students and collec-tors in gathering data. He contributed many papers on diverse topics to the *Journal of Amer-ican Folk-Lore* and to the *Publications* of the Modern Language Association, but his major interest for many years was concerned with the Arthurian romances and kindred literary mate-rials of the medieval period. In 1897 he pub-lished *King Arthur and the Table Round* and in 1902 issued *The Legend of the Holy Grail and the Perceval of Crestien of Troyes,* a collec-tion of papers originally appearing in the *Jour-nal.* A third study on which he was engaged at the time of his death, *Isolt's Return* (1907) was printed posthumously at his Wayland press.

Newell was a fine example of the private scholar. He made no parade of his learning, gave freely of his time and energy to aid and advise other students both young and old, and inspired with his enthusiasm all with whom he came into contact. His influence in the develop-ment of folklore studies in America was great, and in the related field of anthropology he did much to inculcate the value of the historical method of approach. He had much charm of per-sonality, and his wit and vivacity made him a delightful companion.

[*Jour. of Am. Folk-Lore,* Jan.-Mar. 1907; *Harvard Grads.' Mag.,* Mar. 1907; *Who's Who in America,* 1906–07; *Boston Evening Transcript,* Jan. 23, 1907.]
R. B. D.

NEWHOUSE, SAMUEL (Oct. 14, 1853–Sept. 22, 1930), mine owner and operator, finan-cier, the son of Isaac and Babetta Newhouse, was born in New York City. His father was a pioneer merchant in the anthracite coal region of Pennsylvania. After graduating from the Central High School, Philadelphia, Pa., Samuel read law in Scranton until 1873, when he was appointed clerk of the court in Luzerne County. He served in this capacity until 1879, and then went West, arriving in Leadville, Colo., at the height of the mining boom. He soon engaged in freighting, which proved so profitable, espe-cially before the railroad reached Leadville, that he accumulated sufficient capital to invest in mining prospects. The Leadville and San Juan districts, the Prussian tunnel in Boulder County, and the region around Idaho Springs, all in Colorado, were fields for his mining ventures. In 1891 he originated and in 1894 became presi-dent of the Denver, Lakewood & Golden Rail-road. During this period he projected the Argo (more commonly called the Newhouse) tunnel, with portal at Idaho Springs, perhaps the most celebrated mining tunnel in the world. Begun in January 1894 and completed in November 1910, it is over five miles long, with nearly twenty miles of workings. The mines under which it passes are estimated to have produced gold, sil-ver, lead, and copper to the value of about $75,-000,000. The tunnel provided cheaper drainage, ventilation, and transportation facilities than would otherwise have been possible, permitted mining at greater depths and the profitable ex-traction of comparatively low-grade ore. In the driving of this tunnel and in other enterprises Newhouse secured the interest of English capi-talists.

From 1888 to 1896 he made his headquarters in Denver, but in the latter year removed to Salt Lake City, since his Utah holdings were becom-ing more important than those in Colorado. In Utah, he opened the Highland Boy mine at Bing-ham and through its sale made his first large fortune. He then became head of the Boston Consolidated Mining Company at Bingham Canyon, which in 1910 was merged into the Utah Copper Company. In working the property of this concern he used the first steam-shovel ever operated on a copper mine. Upon his pioneer work with this style of mining was subsequently based the success of the great Utah copper mine. He also organized and operated the Newhouse Mines & Smelters, at Newhouse, Beaver Coun-ty, Utah. In 1907 he introduced modern steel skyscraper construction into Salt Lake City: the Newhouse and Boston buildings and the Newhouse Hotel still stand (1933) as monu-ments to his memory. He did much to improve and beautify his other property holdings in this city, and was one of the organizers of the Na-tional Copper Bank. At one time his interests were so widespread that in addition to his head-quarters at Salt Lake City he had offices in New York and London. He was married, Jan. 1, 1883, to Ida H. Stingley, daughter of Hiram Stingley of Virginia. He retired from business about 1925 because of failing health, and spent the last years of his life in Europe, dying at his château at Marnes La Coquette, Seine et Oise, seven miles from Paris.

[*Who's Who in America,* 1899–1929; *Engineering & Mining Journal,* Oct. 9, 1930; *Deseret News* (Salt Lake City), Sept. 24, 1930; Arthur Lakes, "The New-house Tunnel," *Engineering Mag.,* Oct. 1895; *Mines Handbook* (1926), p. 570; letter from Lafayette Han-chett of Salt Lake City, long-time friend of Samuel Newhouse and manager of his mining operations.]
B. A. R.

Newlands

NEWLANDS, FRANCIS GRIFFITH
(Aug. 28, 1848–Dec. 24, 1917), representative
and senator from Nevada, was born in Natchez,
Miss., the son of Scottish parents, James Bir-
ney and Jessie (Barland) Newlands. His father, a physician, went to Troy, N. Y., but soon
removed to the South. He might have been content to remain there in the congenial society of
the cotton-planters, but his wife, an accomplished
musician, desired better opportunities for the
education of her children, and so they went to
Quincy, Ill. When Francis was but three years
old, the father died leaving his wife with four
sons and a daughter. They were in reduced circumstances, for the income that professional
skill had won easily had been liberally spent in
living. The marriage of the mother, however,
to Eben Moore, a banker and mayor of Quincy,
so lightened the family burden that Francis could
go from the schools of Quincy and Payson to
high school in Chicago and have private tutoring in Washington, D. C., to prepare for
Yale College. He entered at the age of sixteen
with the class of 1867, in which he quickly
gained distinction, but, even though friends
wished to provide funds in order that he might
stay, he decided to withdraw from college in
the middle of his junior year. He knew that his
step-father had lost heavily in the panic of 1857;
his mother's small fortune, too, was gone; moreover, he had long thought of becoming a lawyer
and seeking a public career. He returned to
Washington, obtained a position in the service
of the government, attended the evening sessions
of the law school of Columbian College (George
Washington University), and gained admission
to the bar in 1869.

As the death of his step-father threw more of
the family responsibility upon him, he decided
to begin his practice of law in a newer community. He, therefore, accepted a loan from a
classmate, James Allen, and went to San Francisco in 1870. At first he was dependent upon
the court for his cases; but his ability quickly
attracted the attention of persons prominent in
business; and he turned from criminal to corporation law. By 1873 he had become well established. On Nov. 19, 1874, he was married to
the daughter of William Sharon, Clara Adelaide Sharon, who bore him three daughters and
died in February 1882, on the day following
the birth and death of their son. Newlands gave
himself over intensively to business and politics
for the next six years. He became trustee of the
Sharon estate in 1885 and continued in that
capacity through difficult litigation. While in
England, he was married, on Sept. 4, 1888, to

Edith McAllister, the daughter of Hall McAllister [q.v.]. Both their sons died in infancy.
The Civil War and the reconstruction of the
South had deeply affected him, and he had gone
to California with inclinations toward the Democratic party. Before an infuriated audience in
the Democratic state convention of June 1884,
he indorsed for president Stephen J. Field [q.v.]
of the United States Supreme Court, who had
aroused bitter feeling by his decisions concerning the rights of those who had supported the
Confederacy, of the railroads, and, particularly,
of the Chinese in California. Newlands himself
was actually in danger of violence; but his self-
possession and his determination won a hearing,
and he gained recognition as a man of political
promise.

The fulfilment of his political ambitions came
soon after his removal to Nevada, in the winter
of 1888. Beyond his hope for the future of that
state and personal concerns there in connection
with the Sharon properties, he saw the possibility of a national program. To him the silver issue involved not only the interest of Nevada's
mines but the advancement of all those productive areas where men needed to be able to borrow money easily. He thought it a matter of
justice that the quantity of money should be increased to aid those who, under previous conditions of artificially inflated prices, had incurred
financial obligations in endeavoring to develop
the country. Definitely turned from the law
to politics, therefore, he proceeded from his
work for the National Silver Committee in
Washington to seek a place in Congress as the
representative of Nevada. In 1892 as the candidate of the Silver party, with the indorsement
of the Republican organization in the state, he
won election to the House of Representatives
and was reëlected, but, when the national Democratic party took over the cause of silver in
1896, he returned to the party of his youth. He
became a member of the Senate in 1903.

He had a significant rôle in the councils of his
party; there was hardly an economic plank in
any of its platforms that was not shaped by his
thinking. In the House of Representatives he
was an active member of the committee on foreign relations, but he was far more interested in
his work on the committee on ways and means
and in domestic problems. The reclamation act
in 1902, the act in 1913 for mediation and conciliation of labor disputes, the law of 1914
establishing the federal trade commission, his
successive proposals for a waterways commission finally enacted in the river and harbor legislation of 1917, his support of the movement

for a federal bureau of fine arts, and his persistent demand that the problem of the tariff should be placed in charge of a board of experts, all bore witness to his conception of democratic government by scientific services and administrative boards with delegated authority from Congress. He was among the ablest critics of Republican financial policy and of the program of Nelson W. Aldrich [q.v.] for reorganizing the banking system. His plan for national incorporation of the railroads, long opposed, came finally to impressive indorsement in its practical acceptance by railroad executives. His years of activity in the important committee of the Senate on interstate commerce culminated during the Wilson administration in the chairmanship of the commission of inquiry which sat in 1916–17 to make an entire reappraisal of the problems of transportation. In the midst of this undertaking, as President Wilson was about to take control of the railroads in the war with Germany, Newlands died. In framing the transportation act of 1920, however, fellow members of the commission drew heavily upon the fund of knowledge that had been gathered under his guidance. Kindliness in debate, a serene persistence in introducing defeated measures again and again, skill in applying theory to detail, and astuteness in business undertakings marked his public life; intimate friends remembered his appreciation of the beautiful, his considerateness for men of all kinds and classes, and his joyous love of children.

[The Newlands Collection, deposited in Yale Univ. Lib.; other papers in the possession of the family; *The Public Papers of Francis G. Newlands*, ed. by A. B. Darling (2 vols., 1932); H. H. Bancroft, *Chronicles of the Builders of the Commonwealth*, vol. IV (1892); *Senator Francis G. Newlands; his Work*, comp. by M. F. Hudson (1914); *Francis Griffith Newlands . . . Memorial Addresses . . . in the Senate* (1920); *Supplementary Record of the Class of 1867 in Yale College* (1914); *Evening Star* (Washington, D. C.), Dec. 25, 1917.]   A. B. D.

NEWMAN, HENRY (Nov. 20, 1670–June 26, 1743), philanthropist, the son of the Rev. Noah and Joanna (Flynt) Newman, was born in Rehoboth, Mass., the town founded by his grandfather, the Rev. Samuel Newman. Brought up by his maternal grandmother after the death of both parents in his early youth, he prepared for college in the grammar schools at Dorchester, Roxbury, and Braintree. He graduated from Harvard with the degree of A.B. in 1687, and was awarded the degree of A.M. in 1690. His preference for other things, notably mathematics, and his Anglican leanings, which soon carried him over to the Church of England, led him to abandon his original intention of entering the

Congregational ministry. Instead, after graduating he engaged for the time being in a variety of occupations, ranging from librarian at Harvard to merchant at St. John's, Newfoundland.

About 1703 he moved to London, where he was to spend the rest of his life. Early contact with the Rev. Thomas Bray [q.v.] and members of his philanthropic circle shaped the main outlines of Newman's career. For some years he was the secretary of Bray's Trustees for Erecting Parochial Librarys: and Promoting Other Charitable Designs. He was also one of the Commissioners for the Relief of Poor Proselytes, a body formed to administer relief to needy converts from the Roman Church among the French Protestant population in England. Most important, however, was his connection with the Society for Promoting Christian Knowledge, the earlier of Bray's two great religious-philanthropic organizations. Elected a corresponding member in 1703, he was chosen its secretary in 1708, remaining in that position until his death. No branch of the society's multifarious activities escaped his careful and efficient attention, but among them the charity schools, the missions in India, and the transporting of persecuted Protestant Salzburgers to the newly founded colony of Georgia clearly appealed most strongly to him.

A New Englander with his qualifications and connections, resident in London, was a likely man for a colonial agent. Hence it was that, sponsored at the outset by Governor Dudley, he was occasionally employed in that capacity by New Hampshire from 1709 to 1720 and permanently from the latter date until the Belcher administration. He always considered himself a loyal New Englander, though he was an ardent prerogative man, and his interest in affairs at home was further fostered by his work as agent for Harvard College, the more formal side of which he supplemented by zealous endeavors to procure money and books for his alma mater. His early liking for mathematics and astronomy had led him to prepare and publish two almanacs, *Harvard's Ephemeris* (1690) and *News from the Stars* (1691). Throughout his life this field remained something of an avocation for him. Because of this fact his services were frequently sought by friends at home, whether to get communications from New Englanders like Cotton Mather before the Royal Society, with many of the members of which he had an acquaintance, or to select astronomical apparatus for Yale College.

It is in his work for the Society for Promoting Christian Knowledge, however, that the man himself is most clearly revealed, his deep but unobtrusive piety, his broad tolerance, and his joy in giving himself for the welfare of others. All of these qualities made him deeply sympathetic with that movement of reform which, slowly gaining momentum in the later seventeenth century, branched out into a wide variety of humanitarian endeavor during the years of his London life. He was never married.

[A sketch of Newman is in J. L. Sibley's *Biog. Sketches of Grads. of Harvard Univ.*, III (1885), 389-94, but the bulk of the source material is in the archives of the Society for Promoting Christian Knowledge, London, including, besides the official Minutes, etc., many volumes of Newman's letter-books, which contain both personal and official correspondence.]

A. B. F.

NEWMAN, HENRY RODERICK (*c.* 1843-1918), painter of architectural subjects and flower pieces, was born at Easton, N. Y. His father, Roderick Newman, a physician and surgeon, worked so incessantly that he undermined his health. He thereupon sold his home and his practice in Easton and moved to New York City. His son, at that time eleven years old, was a delicate boy, and his studies were often interrupted by sickness, but in spite of this handicap he always kept his place at the head of his class. Dr. Newman hoped that Henry would become a physician, but his artistic bent was strong and his mother encouraged his ambition in this direction. When Henry was eighteen years of age his father died. Soon afterward the youth left his New York home and went to Stockbridge, Mass., where he spent six months making studies and sketches from nature. His work was received with so much favor on his return to New York that his purpose of becoming a painter was confirmed. He then went to the Green Mountain region of Vermont and passed another year in field work. Again returning to New York, he taught an art class in the Cooper Institute until he fell ill from overwork, but shortly he was able to go to Stockbridge for a second time, taking his mother with him. In 1868 she died. He spent the winter of 1868-69 in Florida and then determined to go to France for the purpose of continuing his studies.

After a few weeks in Fontainebleau, he found himself in Paris at the moment of the outbreak of the Franco-Prussian War. He pursued his studies in Gérôme's class for about three weeks, but the German armies were then advancing toward Paris, and he betook himself to Chartres, where he spent two months making careful and elaborate studies of the cathedral. After this he went to Switzerland and to Italy, arriving in Florence late in the summer of 1870. His work soon came to the attention of John Ruskin, who

was extremely enthusiastic about his draftsmanship, and expressed himself so strongly on the subject that Newman's drawings began to find many eager buyers in Italy, England, and America. His personal relations with Ruskin became more and more intimate, during the decade from 1870 to 1880, and more than once he was a guest at Coniston. Ruskin bought his watercolors and persuaded his friends to do likewise; the two men rambled about the old Italian cities together, making sketches; and they jointly assembled the materials for the illustrations for the *Stones of Venice*. Newman's motives included such historic architectural monuments as the Duomo, the Bigallo, Or San Michele, the Palazzo Vecchio, the Mercato Vecchio, and Santa Maria Novella. His flower pieces were also in high favor among amateurs. After his marriage to a cultured English woman in 1884, his home and studio in the Piazza dei Rossi, Florence, became an interesting and attractive social center, more especially for the British and American colony. Such personages as the Brownings, the De Morgans, Henry James, and Nathaniel Hawthorne were among the friends who foregathered there. The Newmans traveled widely. They spent several winters in Egypt, where the artist made a series of pictures of the temples and royal tombs along the valley of the Nile. He died at Florence in 1918 and was survived by his widow. His view of the Church of St. Martin of Lucca is in the Birmingham (England) Museum.

[H. B. Forman, "An Am. Studio in Florence," *Manhattan*, June 1884; *Continental Times* (Geneva), Dec. 31, 1881; E. T. Cook and A. Wedderburn, eds., *The Works of John Ruskin* (1907), vol. XXX; *Cat. of Paintings, Museum of Fine Arts, Boston* (1921); *Am. Art News*, Feb. 9, 1918; *N. Y. Times*, Jan. 31, 1918.]

W. H. D—s.

NEWMAN, JOHN PHILIP (Sept. 1, 1826-July 5, 1899), Methodist Episcopal bishop, was born in New York City. His father, Philip Newman, was a thoughtful, studious man of German descent, who died when John was eight years old, leaving seven children and his wife, Mary D'Orfey Allen, a vivacious and richly intelligent woman of Huguenot ancestry. At sixteen the lad underwent a spiritual experience which gave him an ambition and directed him to the Methodist ministry. After a few terms in Cazenovia (N. Y.) Seminary, he began to preach with crude eloquence in country churches, and in 1847 was admitted to the Oneida Conference. At Fort Plain, N. Y., a blunt schoolmaster punctured his self-esteem by telling him that his pronunciation and grammar were abominable. Immediately Newman began to toil with passionate diligence to remedy these and other defects. His wife, Angeline Ensign, whom he married in 1855, was an inspiring companion. He wrote out and memorized his sermons, sparing no pains to have every word correct. Imagination, a noble presence, and a rich and musical voice were his natural gifts. Soon he was stationed in Albany with the governor listening in admiration to his preaching; then, in New York City, where he crowded the largest churches (Bedford Street, 1859; Washington Square, 1862–64). Meantime, a year abroad expanded his horizons and enabled him to write a respectable volume on Palestine. From 1864 to 1869 he was at New Orleans, charged with reëstablishing the Methodist Episcopal Church in the Southwest, which was then in control of Union troops. Here he "blew both the Federal and Gospel trumpets," founded schools, a paper, and several Conferences.

In 1869 he was appointed to the new Metropolitan Church in Washington, D. C. President Grant, Vice-President Colfax, Chief Justice Chase, Major-General Logan, and other notables, were members of his great congregation. His rôle was almost that of "court preacher." From 1869 to 1874 he was also chaplain of the Senate. When his three years' term as pastor expired, his friend at the White House created him "Inspector of United States Consulates," and with his accomplished wife as secretary he made a leisurely trip around the world. Although the appointment evoked criticism, Newman took his commission seriously and his report yielded valuable suggestions. Returning to the Metropolitan Church for a second term (1876–79), he found the presidential pew vacant, but all others filled. His next pastorate (1879–82) was in Central Church, New York City, of which his faithful friend, Grant, became a trustee. When the operation of the three-year limit again moved him, he yielded to the invitation of a Congregational society (Church of the Disciples), taking the status of "acting pastor" and Methodist local preacher, to the scandal of the stricter Methodists, and of some Congregationalists. He soon sought readmission to the Methodist Conference and was reappointed to his former church in Washington.

In 1868, 1872, and 1880 he was a delegate to the General Conference. As early as 1872 his influential lay friends had been proposing his name for office, and in that year he received 100 votes for bishop. In 1880 he had 121 votes for missionary secretary. In 1888, with the active help of the Grant family and Grand Army friends, he was elected bishop on the fourteenth ballot, over determined opposition. His official resi-

dences were Omaha (1888–96) and San Francisco (1896–99); he also made visitations to Japan, South America, and Mexico. As an administrator he was not distinguished. He was accused of pomposity and self-esteem, but his fine spirit, which mellowed with the years, and his broad sympathy, redeemed some of these faults. His rather grandiose style, with rehearsed gesture and pose, and a wealth of allusion and illustration from literature and foreign travel, delighted the prevailing taste. His sermons and lectures were laboriously prepared to the last detail. Doubtless his commanding and ingratiating countenance, his stalwart figure, his distinguished bearing, and his musical and sonorous voice, made his audience uncritical of his thought, which was not analytical or profound. In the public mind he was "Grant's pastor." That famous friendship never waned. Newman watched by his hero's bedside at Mount McGregor, administered the rite of baptism, and pronounced the official eulogy. Childless himself, he had a deep interest in ambitious youth, and joined with Mrs. Newman in educating scores of young men who met his specifications of "piety, poverty, pluck and brains." He died at Saratoga, N. Y., where he had long maintained a summer residence. His estate was divided between Drew Theological Seminary and a school in Jerusalem. He has been described as "one of the most superbly ornamental figures that ever took its stately walk through Methodism" (Kelley, post, p. 616). Among his published writings are From Dan to Beersheba (1864); The Bible and Polygamy (1874), a debate with Orson Pratt, Salt Lake City; Sermons (1876); Thrones and Palaces of Babylon and Nineveh (1876); Christianity Triumphant (copr. 1883); Supremacy of Law (1890); Conversations with Christ (1900).

[J. M. Buckley, in Christian Advocate (N. Y.), July 13, 1899; J. E. King, in Christian Advocate (N. Y.), May 4, 1911; L. C. Matlack, The Antislavery Struggle and Triumph in the M. E. Ch. (1881); W. W. Sweet, The M. E. Ch. in the Civil War (1912); W. V. Kelley, in the Meth. Rev., July 1900; Official Journal . . . N. Y. Conf. M. E. Ch., 1900; N. Y. Tribune, July 6, 1899; manuscript records and journals in possession of Mrs. Emma Manson, Saratoga Springs, N. Y.]   J. R. J.

NEWMAN, ROBERT LOFTIN (Nov. 10, 1827–Mar. 31, 1912), figure painter, was born at Richmond, Va. The family moved to Louisa Court House, Va., then when Robert was eleven years old, to Clarksville, Tenn. As a boy he read much about art and artists, and at the age of seventeen he had already begun to experiment for himself with paints and brushes. Six years later he was enabled to go to France to take up

Newman

the serious study of painting. He entered the atelier of Thomas Couture in Paris but remained there only a few months and never received any subsequent academic instruction. After a year's absence from home he returned to Tennessee in 1851. During a second journey to France in 1854 he formed the acquaintance of William Morris Hunt [q.v.], another pupil of Couture, who took him to Barbizon and introduced him to Jean François Millet. Newman at once bought "Le Vanneur" and other paintings by Millet, but in later years he was obliged to part with them. He returned to the United States in 1855. Upon the outbreak of the Civil War in 1861 he was employed by the Confederate government at Richmond as a draftsman, and in 1864 he was conscripted and served in the 16th Virginia Regiment. After the war was over he pursued his art in obscurity, for a time in Baltimore, where he worked in a sign-painter's loft, and afterward in New York, where he had a studio in West Tenth Street.

In 1882 and twice thereafter he found his way back to Barbizon. Altogether he spent a year and a half there. He was deeply in sympathy with the tendencies of the Barbizon painters, and had much in common with them in his ideals and sentiment. After making New York his home he exhibited rarely, and those artists and collectors who knew him and appreciated his work were obliged to seek him out in his studio. Nevertheless, in the course of a few years, such men as Wyatt Eaton, William M. Chase, Richard Watson Gilder, Thomas B. Clarke, Stanford White, Francis Lathrop, John Gellatly, R. U. Johnson, and Sir William Van Horne not only bought his pictures but tried to bring him into popular favor. It was not until 1894 that an adequate loan exhibition of his work was opened at Knoedler's Gallery, New York, when a collection of oil paintings was shown. After the close of this New York exhibition the same collection was shown at the Museum of Fine Arts in Boston. The foreword in the catalogue alluded very justly to his delicate and beautiful sense of color, his poetic feeling, and the suggestiveness of his work. An article in the *Critic* (Mar. 10, 1894) gave him credit for "that rare and delightful characteristic which we call quality"; and other New York and Boston critics were greatly impressed. "That Newman was a great colorist in the best sense," wrote F. F. Sherman, "is evident in all of his finished work. . . . In all his pictures it is the poetry of color and of life rather than the prose that one finds" (*post,* pp. 16–17). Nevertheless, Newman's name was all but unknown, and he was never financially successful. At the sale of the studio effects of Francis Lathrop after that artist's death a number of Newman's pictures were sold for insignificant prices. He died in his eighty-fifth year. His death, which may have been accidental, was caused by asphyxiation.

[F. F. Sherman, *Landscape and Figure Painters of America* (1917); Nelson Sanborn, "Robt. Loftin Newman," *Brooklyn Museum Quart.*, Oct. 1921; Sadakichi Hartmann, *A Hist. of Am. Art* (1932), vol. I; catalogue of the loan exhibition, Boston Art Museum, 1894; *Metropolitan Museum of Art Cat. of Paintings* (1921); *Critic*, Mar. 24, 1894; *Am. Art News*, Apr. 6, 1912; *N. Y. Tribune*, Apr. 1, 1912.]   W. H. D—s.

NEWMAN, SAMUEL PHILLIPS (June 6, 1797–Feb. 10, 1842), preacher, author, teacher, was born in Andover, Mass., the son of Rev. Mark Newman, third principal of Phillips Academy (1795–1810) and Sarah Phillips Newman, daughter of William Phillips, a merchant of Boston. As a boy he attended Phillips Academy and in 1816 he was graduated with honors from Harvard College. For a year after his graduation he was a private instructor in a family in Lexington, Ky.; he then studied for one year at Andover Theological Seminary. In 1818 he went to Bowdoin College as a tutor, with the privilege of continuing his theological studies under President Appleton. The next year he was elected professor of Greek and Latin, and upon the establishment of the professorship of rhetoric and oratory in 1824, he was transferred to that chair. Although his time was chiefly devoted to the teaching of English, he was also, from 1824 to 1839, lecturer on civil polity and political economy. His versatility is also shown by the fact that in 1820 he was licensed to preach as a Congregationalist (although in those searching times he was somewhat suspected of Unitarian leanings) and for nearly three years, 1830–33, during the absence of President Allen, was the acting-president of the college. He had a decided bent not only for the art of teaching but also for the conduct of business, the administration of affairs, and the leadership of men. A Bowdoin historian writes of him: "During the whole period of his professorship at Brunswick he was probably the most influential member of the college government" (Cleaveland and Packard, *post,* p. 131). On May 31, 1821, he married Caroline, daughter of Col. William A. and Charlotte (Mellen) Kent of Concord, N. H., and before he left Brunswick in 1839 he had a family of five daughters.

In 1827 Newman published a textbook, *A Practical System of Rhetoric or the Principles and Rules of Style,* which for a score of years was widely used in the schools and colleges of

466

Newman

the country. It went through more than sixty editions in the United States and was republished in England. Although the terms used are a bit different from those in modern rhetorics, and the philosophical principles and abstract qualities of style more heavily stressed, it is clearly and pleasantly written. Both in this book and also in an important address, "A Practical Method of Teaching Rhetoric," delivered before the American Institute of Instruction in Boston in 1830, he advocated principles and suggested methods, such as teaching by illustrative examples, by translation of other languages, by "talking lectures," and by individual conferences, for many years regarded as good devices. In 1835 he published *Elements of Political Economy*. Largely based upon the writings of Adam Smith, the book could not lay much claim to originality, but it did expound in clear language the principles of the then rapidly rising subject and in the opinion of Professor Amasa Walker of Harvard was "the best work of its kind in the United States" (Hatch, *post*, p. 49). In 1839, after twenty-one years of efficient service at Bowdoin, he "yielded to an application of the Massachusetts Board of Education" and became head of the newly established State Normal School at Barre. But after two years his health broke and he returned to his birthplace, dying there at the age of forty-four. Those closest to him at Bowdoin regarded him not only as an understanding and sagacious teacher and an able administrator, but as a lovable and loyal friend.

[Nehemiah Cleaveland and A. S. Packard, *Hist. of Bowdoin Coll. with Biog. Sketches of its Grads.* (1882); L. C. Hatch, *The Hist. of Bowdoin Coll.* (1927); W. W. Lockwood, "An Early Bowdoin Economist," *Bowdoin Alumnus*, June 1931; *Zion's Herald and Wesleyan Jour.*, Sept. 21, 1864; *Portland Evening Advertiser*, Mar. 7, 1842.]   W. B. M.

NEWMAN, WILLIAM TRUSLOW (June 23, 1843–Feb. 14, 1920), federal judge, was born near Knoxville, Tenn., the son of Henry Baker and Martha (Truslow) Newman. At the outbreak of the Civil War he volunteered as a private soldier in the 2nd Tennessee Cavalry. After some months of service he was promoted to the rank of lieutenant. In 1863 he was wounded and captured by Federal skirmishers in Kentucky. Exchanged, he was again wounded the next year near Jonesboro, Ga., and lost his right arm. At the close of the war he went to live in Atlanta, Ga., read law with Judge John L. Hopkins, was admitted to the bar in 1866, began practice. From 1871 to 1883 he was city attorney. During these years he built up a substantial private practice and became prominent in the life of the community. On Sept. 20, 1871, he was married to Frances Percy Alexander of Knoxville, Tenn.

In August 1888 he was appointed by President Cleveland to be federal judge of the northern district of Georgia, in which position he continued to serve until his death. He discouraged litigation and brought to bear all the weight of his influence to obtain settlements out of court. His rulings in bankruptcy cases and in cases involving public regulation of utilities became important in determining practice in his district. Yet it was for more unusual qualities that his judicial career made a profound impression on the people among whom he administered federal justice for nearly two generations. Without any claim to erudition his decisions never lacked the essential quality that was recognized as justice by both parties, and his rendering of justice was always tempered with mercy. He made it his custom to parole rural prisoners until they had gathered their crops and, in spite of rumors of some official disapproval, continued to exercise his prerogative of paroling prisoners whenever he thought the situation warranted and to enjoy the kind of respect that brought the paroled men back to prison without violation of trust.

Of his six children one daughter, Frances Newman (Sept. 13, 1883–Oct. 22, 1928, from records of West View Cemetery Assoc., Atlanta) attained distinction as a magazine writer and novelist of the radical sentiment of a changing South. Perhaps *The Hard Boiled Virgin* (1926) is the best-known of her writings, but her book reviews and *Frances Newman's Letters*, ed. by Hansell Baugh (1929) show a curious combination of her father's independence of mind and the spirit of revolt typical of another generation.

[Information from his son, Henry A. Newman and Judge Blanton Fortson; *Report of the Thirty-seventh Ann. Session of the Ga. Bar. Asso. . . . 1920* (1920); *Who's Who in America*, 1918–19; *Atlantic Journal*, Feb. 14, 15, 1920; *Ibid.*, Nov. 18, 1928, and Emily Clark, *Innocence Abroad* (1931) for material on daughter.]   J. H. T. M.

NEWPORT, CHRISTOPHER (d. August 1617), mariner, began his sea-faring career during the reign of Queen Elizabeth. He served with Drake's Cadiz expedition of 1587 (Corbett, *post*, pp. 160, 163) and in 1592 commanded a successful privateering expedition of the West Indies, taking nineteen Spanish vessels and plundering three small towns in Hispaniola and one on the mainland of Honduras. Upon his return, he assisted Sir John Burgh off the Azores in the capture of the "great carrack," the *Madre de Dios* (Aug. 3, 1592), and brought the prize into Dartmouth. He doubtless made other voyages to America in subsequent years (early in

1603 an unfounded rumor spread that he had taken an entire plate fleet), and in September 1605 he presented King James I with "two young Crocodiles and a wild Bore" brought alive from the West Indies (Howes, *post,* p. 871). The next year he entered the service of the newly chartered Virginia Company and was given charge of its early voyages. The first expedition, consisting of three vessels (the *Susan Constant,* the *Godspeed,* and the *Discovery*) and about 120 settlers, left London Dec. 20, 1606, went by way of the southern route and the West Indies, and entered Chesapeake Bay Apr. 26, 1607. The site of Jamestown was selected May 13. Between May 21 and 27, Newport, in accordance with his instructions, ascended the James as far as the falls, near the present Richmond. On June 22, after a fruitless endeavor to persuade the members of the council to maintain harmony during his absence, he sailed for England, leaving provisions expected to last thirteen and a half weeks, and promising to return in twenty.

Arriving at Plymouth on July 29, he raised high the hopes of the Council for Virginia by his announcement of gold, remained sanguine even after the goldsmiths had reported, and continued the vain quest on subsequent voyages. On Oct. 8 he was off with the "first supply" of two ships and 120 emigrants, of whom about a hundred survived the voyage. He arrived at Jamestown six weeks behind his schedule, on Jan. 2, 1608, to find only some forty alive of the 104 he had left, the president of the council, E. M. Wingfield [*q.v.*], imprisoned, and Capt. John Smith [*q.v.*] about to be hanged. Newport effected the liberation of Smith and Wingfield and restored a measure of harmony, but renewed exertions were paralyzed by the fire which destroyed the settlement on Jan. 7. Toward the close of February Newport and Smith visited Powhatan at Werowocomoco on the York River and returned well supplied with corn. On Apr. 9 Newport returned to England, carrying back Wingfield and the troublesome Archer.

On his third voyage (August 1608–January 1609) he brought out one ship and some seventy settlers, including the first skilled craftsmen the Company had attempted to send the colony. He brought gifts and a crown for Powhatan, and performed the somewhat ridiculous ceremony of his coronation at Werowocomoco. Later he conducted an expedition several days' march beyond the falls of the James, and may have reached the mouth of the Rivanna. Before his fourth voyage the Company was reorganized. In 1609 Newport, with the title of vice-admiral, brought out Sir Thomas Gates [*q.v.*] and Sir George Somers.

Attempting the northern route, he was wrecked with them on the Bermudas (Sept. 28), and reached Virginia in May 1610, using pinnaces built on the island. On July 15, he embarked on the return voyage with Gates. The next year, in March, he brought out Sir Thomas Dale [*q.v.*] with three vessels and about three hundred colonists. On their arrival in Virginia in May Sir Thomas pulled Newport's beard and threatened to hang him, apparently for having indorsed Sir Thomas Smyth's too optimistic account of the state of the colony ("A Briefe Declaration of the Plantation of Virginia," *Colonial Records of Virginia,* 1874, p. 79).

Newport returned to England in mid-December 1611, taking home Gates's daughters, and shortly afterward left the service of the Virginia Company for that of the East India Company. Howes's statement is credible, that he took this step "seeing the necessary yeerely supplies for this plantation not to proceed as was requisite for so honourable an action" (Howes, p. 1018). He made three voyages to the East Indies. On the first (Jan. 7, 1613–July 10, 1614), he carried back Sir Robert Sherley, the Persianized Englishman and Shah's ambassador, and established a new record for speed. On the second (Jan. 24, 1615–*c.* September 1616), Newport, second in command to Keeling, carried out Sir Thomas Roe on his famous embassy to the Mogul emperor of Hindustan. The third (November 1616) was his last. He died at Bantam in the last days of August 1617.

Newport was thrice married: Oct. 19, 1584, to Katharine Procter; Jan. 29, 1590, to Ellen Ade; and Oct. 1, 1595, to Elizabeth Glanfield, who survived him (G. W. Hill and W. H. Frere, *Memorials of Stepney Parish,* 1890–91, pp. 25–26, note 6). He left two daughters and two sons, one of whom, John, lived to acquire land in Virginia in return for his father's investment of £400. Newport is generally well spoken of by his contemporaries, with the exception of Smith, who speaks well of no one but himself. He seems to have taken a very genuine concern in the Virginia enterprise, and to have served it to the best of his considerable abilities. His position as intermediary between colonists and Company in the early days was not an easy one.

[A narrative of the voyage of 1592 appears in Richard Hakluyt's *The Principal Navigations, Voyages, Traffiques & Discoveries of the English Nation* (see MacLehose ed., 1904, vols. VII, XII), and narratives of the voyages of 1607, 1609, and 1613 in Samuel Purchas, *Hakluytus Posthumus, or Purchas His Pilgrimes,* vols. III, IV, XVI, XVIII, XIX (ed. of 1905–06). See also J. S. Corbett, *Papers Relating to the Navy during the Spanish War, 1585–87* (1898), being Pubs. Navy Records Soc., vol. XI; Alexander Brown, *The Genesis of the U. S.* (2 vols., 1890) and *The First*

Republic in America (1898); *Travels and Works of Captain John Smith* (2 vols., 1910), ed. by Edward Arber and A. G. Bradley; *Calendar of State Papers, Domestic* and *Colonial Ser.*; Edmund Howes, *Annales, or, A Generall Chronicle of England, Begun by John Stow: Continued and Augmented* (1616; ed. used, that of 1631); William Strachey, *The Historie of Travaile into Virginia Britannia* (Hakluyt Society, 1849); Newport's and his son's wills, summarized in *New-Eng. Hist. and Geneal. Reg.*, Apr. 1894.]   D. H. M.

NEWSAM, ALBERT (May 20, 1809–Nov. 20, 1864), lithographer, was born in Steubenville, Ohio. He was a deaf mute from birth. His father, William, an Ohio River boatman, was accidentally drowned while the boy was a small child, and nothing is known of his mother. The afflicted boy was brought up by Thomas Hamilton, an Irishman, who kept a small hotel in the village. Without any advantages, and with only the inspiration born of the sight of a few prints in the very few books within his reach, he early displayed a considerable talent for drawing. When he was about ten years of age, a deaf-mute impostor, who called himself William P. Davis, came to Steubenville and lodged at Hamilton's hotel. Detecting the talent of the boy, he proposed to the inn-keeper that he take Albert and provide for him, which was assented to. The pair were not long on the road from Steubenville before it became evident that the boy was being used to display his talents for the purpose of exciting the interest of the charitable. He revolted, but the man appeased him with the argument that he was taking him to Philadelphia for the purpose of having him educated. To all who questioned him Davis told the same story, and always referred to Albert as his brother.

When they arrived in Philadelphia in May 1820, they took lodgings in a small hotel and then ventured to the marketplace to see the town. At the corner of Fifth and Market streets there was a watchman's box on the side of which Newsam began to sketch the busy scene before him. A group assembled around the young artist, and later it was joined by the aged Bishop William White, who was then president of the recently organized Asylum for the Deaf and Dumb. The Bishop heard with interest the tale told him by Davis, and the upshot of the meeting was that the managers of the asylum gave an outfit of clothing to both of the strangers; gave Davis a sum of money to take him South, ostensibly to seek relatives; and admitted Newsam to the institution as a state pupil, first protégé of the legislature of Pennsylvania. The boy learned rapidly, spending six years (1820–26) in the institution, and after his graduation remaining as monitor for a year. His talents brought him into contact with Sully, Inman, Rembrandt Peale, Neagle,

and J. R. Lambdin. The last-named sought to teach him to paint portraits, but found he was not likely to succeed because he could not animate his model by conversation. In 1827 he attracted the attention of Col. Cephas G. Childs [*q.v.*], whose engraving establishment in Philadelphia was widely known. He was apprenticed to Childs, and remained with him for four years. During this period lithography in the United States was slowly advancing as a commercial enterprise. Newsam was taught the new process by Duval, whom Colonel Childs had brought from Paris, and thus became a lithographer instead of an engraver. During his apprenticeship he attended the classes in the Pennsylvania Academy of the Fine Arts, and improved himself in his art by remarkable industry. His beautiful and accurate drawings of portraits soon became noted and he remained at the head of American lithographic artists until illness forced his retirement. In 1853 he designed the monument to Thomas H. Gallaudet [*q.v.*] in Hartford, Conn. In 1857 he became partly blind, and in 1859, partly paralyzed. After a year spent in the Pennsylvania Hospital, his funds were exhausted, and he was removed to the city almshouse, where he remained for two years. Then some of his old friends collected a fund and had him placed in the Living Home, near Wilmington, Del., where he died in November 1864. His remains were interred in Laurel Hill Cemetery, Phila. Newsam was married Mar. 26, 1834, to Rosanna Edgar, a Philadelphia woman who was not a mute, but the pair separated a week after the ceremony.

[The Hist. Soc. of Pa. has a large collection of lithographs by Newsam, principally proofs once owned by the artist himself. J. O. Pyatt, *Memoir of Albert Newsam* (1868) is the chief authority for his career; see also sketch by D. M. Stauffer, in *Pa. Mag. of Hist. and Biog.*, Oct. 1900, and lists of Newsam's lithographs, *Ibid.*, Jan., Apr. 1901, Oct. 1902; D. M. Stauffer, *Am. Engravers Upon Copper and Steel* (1907), vol. I; J. T. Scharf and T. Westcott, *Hist. of Phila.* (1884), vol. II; *Pennsylvanian* (Phila.), Mar. 31, 1834 (note of marriage); *Phila. Inquirer*, Nov. 22, 1864.]   J. J.

NEWTON, HENRY JOTHAM (Feb. 9, 1823–Dec. 23, 1895), manufacturer and inventor, was born at Hartleton, Pa., the younger son of Dr. Jotham and Harriet (Wood) Newton, both originally of Connecticut. When the father, a young physician of promise, died within a year of his son's birth, the mother returned to her father's home in Somers, Conn. Henry was sent to school there and afterwards finished at the Literary Institute of Suffield. He was then apprenticed for four years to Whittlesey Brothers, piano-makers of Salem, Conn. His progress was so rapid that in three years he became a member of the firm. Five years later (1849) he went to New York City, where he associated himself with Ferdinand Lighte in the piano business. In 1853 William B. Bradbury [q.v.] and his brother Edward G. Bradbury also became partners, and the firm Lighte, Newton & Bradbury soon won a leading place in the trade. In 1858 Newton retired with a competency, which he invested so judiciously in New York City real estate that he died a millionaire. Except for the attention which his real-estate holdings required and for his presidency after 1884 of the Henry-Bonnard Bronze Company, a successful business run chiefly by his son and son-in-law, he was free for the rest of his life to devote himself to his various hobbies.

The chief of these was photography. His early steps in the art were taken under the guidance of Charles A. Seely, publisher of the *American Journal of Photography*. The top floor of Newton's home at 128 West 43rd St. soon became an amateur's photographic laboratory as he experimented with different kinds of emulsions, developing solutions, washes, and sensitized papers, in different processes and under varying conditions. The history of photography in this period is confused, and there were so many workers in the field that his exact contributions are difficult to determine. He made a number of improvements in the dry-plate process, however, and so popularized it that he came to be known as "the father of the dry-plate process in America." He experimented with the use of various alkalis in developing dry plates. He was also a pioneer in the preparation of ready-sensitized paper, and is credited with working out the paraffin paper process. His findings were usually presented orally at the meetings of the American Photographical Society, and are merely referred to, or summarized, in the reports in the *American Journal of Photography* of that society's meetings. He was long treasurer of the organization, which in 1867 became the Photographical Section of the American Institute of the City of New York, and after 1873 served as its chairman.

A scientific interest in spirit photography led Newton to study the subject of Spiritualism, and he spent much time and money in the investigation of various mediums. He exposed a number of them, including the famous Etta Roberts, by apparatus and tests which he originated. Despite such fakes, he became a convert to Spiritualism, and his faith was unshaken to the last. He was trustee and, for the last twenty years of his life, president of the First Society of Spir-

itualists in New York, the society benefiting greatly from his scientific support and from his generous donations. He was also a founder of the Theosophical Society (1875), and its treasurer during the first few years. He always claimed that the society was organized for the scientific study of occultism, and after the publication by Madame Blavatsky [q.v.] of her *Isis Unveiled* (1877), which became the Bible of a new religion with teachings hostile to Spiritualism, he resigned in much bitterness. He was instrumental in effecting the first scientific cremation of a human body in America, Dec. 6, 1876, at the crematory in Washington, Pa., erected by F. J. Le Moyne [q.v.], when, as an executor of the Baron de Palm's will, he carried out the Baron's last wishes in regard to the disposition of his body. The event was viewed by a number of scientists and received nation-wide newspaper publicity.

It is significant that at Newton's death newspaper obituaries emphasized his Spiritualist and Theosophic connections, his more tangible contributions having been almost forgotten. In later years his gray hair and long gray beard gave him somewhat the appearance of a self-appointed prophet. His wife, Mary A. Gates of Wethersfield, Conn., whom he married in 1850, was an accomplished musician, a woman of culture and social charm, who encouraged her husband's unorthodox interests. They entertained frequently, and were members of many organizations. Newton was run down by a street car during an evening rush hour as he was crossing Broadway between 22nd and 23rd Streets, then "the most dangerous spot in New York." Besides his wife, a son and two daughters survived him.

[*Sun* (N. Y.) and *N. Y. Herald*, Dec. 24, 1895; *Photographic Times*, Feb. 1896; files of the photographical magazines for the 60's and 70's; proceedings of Photographical Section, in *Ann. Reports* of the Am. Inst. of the City of N. Y.; H. S. Olcott, *Old Diary Leaves* (1895); for father's family, E. N. Leonard, *Newton Geneal.* (1915), p. 189.]   O. W. H.

NEWTON, HUBERT ANSON (Mar. 19, 1830–Aug. 12, 1896), mathematician, was the fifth son of a family of seven sons and four daughters, children of William and Lois (Butler) Newton, of Sherburne, N. Y. He was of good New England stock, his ancestors on both sides being among the first settlers in Massachusetts and Connecticut. Prepared for college in the local schools of Sherburne, he entered Yale at the age of sixteen, graduating with the class of 1850. For the next three years he pursued mathematical studies at his home and in New

Haven. He was only twenty-three when, on the death of Prof. Anthony Dumond Stanley (1810–53), he was called upon to take control of the department of mathematics in his alma mater. Upon receiving the rank of professor two years later, he was given a leave of absence for a year, and spent his time studying at Paris under the eminent French geometer, Michel Chasles (1793–1880). Upon his return to Yale, he cultivated an interest in astronomy, paying considerable attention to the subject of meteors. The results of his investigations were published in the *American Journal of Science*, 1860–62, and in an elaborate paper, "On Shooting Stars," which was read before the National Academy of Sciences in 1864 and appeared in the first volume (1866) of its *Memoirs*.

According to a colleague (Gibbs, *post*, p. 118), the most important side of his life was that identified with the organic life of the University. His scientific studies, which he loved, were almost "the recreations . . . of one whose serious occupation has been that of an instructor." Despite his preference for a quiet, scholarly existence, he was for one term an alderman of New Haven. His influence upon mathematics and astronomy was rather due to his expository articles and his connection with learned societies than to original investigations. He was a member of many scientific organizations, including the National Academy of Sciences and the American Philosophical Society, and was president of the American Association for the Advancement of Science in 1885, and for several years president of the Connecticut Academy of Arts and Sciences. He was an ardent advocate of the metric system of weights and measures, and one of the founders of the American Metrological Society. He realized, however, that the practice of generations could be successfully altered only after a period of education, and therefore labored to interest the makers of scales and rulers and to secure the inclusion of metric tables in school arithmetics. Perhaps his most important single contribution to the cause was a set of tables, *The Metric System of Weights and Measures* (1868), reprinted with corrections from the *Report* for 1865 of the Smithsonian Institution. Among his most notable publications in addition to those already mentioned were "Explanation of the Motion of the Gyroscope" (*American Journal of Science*, September 1857); "On the Origin of Comets" (*Ibid.*, September 1878); "The Story of Biela's Comet" and "The Biela Meteors of Nov. 27th, 1885" (*Ibid.*, February and June 1886); "On the Transcendental Curves $\sin y \sin my = a \sin x \sin nx + b$," in collabora-

tion with A. W. Phillips (*Transactions of the Connecticut Academy of Arts and Sciences,* vol. III, 1874–78, p. 97). He also contributed articles on meteors to *Johnson's Universal Cyclopedia* (1877) and the *Encyclopædia Britannica* (1883), and mathematical and astronomical definitions to *Webster's International Dictionary* (1890). On Apr. 14, 1859, he married Anna C. Stiles. He died in New Haven.

[J. W. Gibbs, in *Nat. Acad. Sci. Biog. Memoirs,* vol. IV (1902); M. Faye, in *Comptes rendus . . . de l'Académie des Sciences,* vol. LXIV (1867); *Obit. Record Grads. Yale Univ.,* 1897; *New Haven Evening Register,* Aug. 13, 1896.]   D. E. S.

NEWTON, ISAAC (Jan. 10, 1794–Nov. 23, 1858), steamboat designer and proprietor, was born in Schodack, Rensselaer County, N. Y., the son of Abner and Alice (Baker) Newton. Little is known of his youth; but that his attention was early drawn to steamboats is shown by his vivid recollections in later years of witnessing at the age of thirteen the *Clermont's* first trip up the Hudson. In 1826 he was associated with several others in establishing the first line of tow boats on the Hudson. In 1839 he brought out the *Balloon,* a small passenger steamer which attracted attention because of its speed. He then associated himself with Daniel Drew [*q.v.*] in the promotion of the People's Line and became president and manager, while Drew became treasurer. For this line he designed the *North America* and *South America,* built in 1840 and 1841, which set the style for river boats of the day. On these two vessels he introduced the burning of anthracite coal, the first instance of practical success with a fuel that was both cheaper and more economical of stowage space than wood, and which was to permit rapid advances in the size and speed of boats. He designed and added to the line the *Hendrick Hudson* (1845), the *Isaac Newton* (1846), and the *New World* (1847), each in its turn the largest steamer on the Hudson. They were also fast boats, participating in many races which made exciting river history. The People's Line Association was incorporated in 1854 as the New Jersey Steamboat Company. In 1855 the *Isaac Newton* and the *New World* were renovated and lengthened and put on night service. They were the first inland river steamers to have a double tier of staterooms above the main deck, and in them Newton introduced the grand saloon extending through both decks and surrounded by galleries leading to the staterooms, a feature of river steamers which has become standard in America. The ornate saloon decorations, the gas-lighting fixtures, the rich cabin furnishings, made the boats the most popular on the river and established the success and fame of the line. Newton was also interested in a railroad connection to the Great Lakes, and was for a time president of the Mohawk & Hudson, resigning in 1846. He extended his steamboat interests to the Great Lakes, and in 1854 the *Western World* and *Plymouth Rock* were built after his design by John Englis & Son of New York who sent their crew to a Buffalo yard to do the work. These were for a time the finest steamers on the lakes. Altogether Newton is said to have designed and supervised the construction of more than ninety barges, river boats, and ocean steamers. He lived most of his adult life in New York City and was a member and long a Sunday-school teacher in the old Oliver Street Baptist Church. He married Hannah Humphreys Cauldwell who survived him many years, and had ten children. Of these Henry Newton won some fame as a geologist and Isaac Newton became an engineer of note.

[D. L. Buckman, *Old Steamboat Days on the Hudson River* (1907); F. E. Dayton, *Steamboat Days* (1925); Joel Munsell, *The Annals of Albany*, vols. VIII (1857), X (1859); S. W. Stanton, *Am. Steam Vessels* (1895); J. H. Morrison, *Hist. of Am. Steam Navigation* (1903); *Hist. Mag.* (N. Y.), Jan. 1859; *Evening Post* (N. Y.), Nov. 23, 1858; *N. Y. Daily Tribune*, Nov. 24, 1858; will in the Hall of Records, New York City.]

O. W. H.

NEWTON, ISAAC (Mar. 31, 1800–June 19, 1867), first United States commissioner of agriculture, was born in Burlington County, N. J., the son of Isaac and Mary (Newton) Newton, of English ancestry and orthodox Quaker stock. His father, a farmer, died young, and his mother, left a widow at eighteen when Isaac was only a few months old, continued to live in the home of her father-in-law, a prosperous farmer of Burlington County. Isaac's education was gained mostly in the county and state schools of New Jersey and Pennsylvania, and he was thoroughly taught the principles of farming on his grandfather's farm. He was married Oct. 18, 1821, to Dorothy Burdsall of Philadelphia. A few years later he was asked to take charge of two adjoining farms in Springfield, Delaware County, Pa., which under his care became celebrated for their neatness, order, and productiveness. To make use of the surplus of milk and cream from his farm he opened an ice-cream and confectionery shop in Philadelphia. He was one of the early and active members of the Pennsylvania State Agricultural Society and the United States Agricultural Society and for years was prominent in urging upon Congress the policy of establishing a department of agriculture. About 1854, acting on the advice of a friend, he purchased a

thousand-acre tract of farm land in Prince William County, Va., but this venture later proved unsuccessful, partly because of the outbreak of the Civil War.

Early in 1861 Newton, who was personally acquainted with Lincoln, was appointed by him superintendent of the agricultural division of the Patent Office, the small bureau which at that time had charge of national agricultural interests. This was enlarged the following year by the Act of May 15, 1862, establishing a department of agriculture with a commissioner at its head. To this post Newton was appointed by President Lincoln and was thus the first incumbent of the office. Within the first few months, a skilled horticulturist, William Saunders [q.v.] of Pennsylvania, was appointed botanist and superintendent of the propagating garden, and C. M. Wetherill [q.v.], department chemist. Other early appointments were those of Lewis Bollman to be statistician, and Townend Glover [q.v.] to be entomologist. These appointments were the beginnings of the present large bureaus of plant industry, chemistry, agricultural economics, and entomology. In his first and second annual reports Newton dwelt upon the vital importance in agriculture of the weather and climate. In his third report, that for 1864, he advocated (p. 10) that daily weather reports be communicated by telegraph over the whole country under the supervision of the government. His recommendations were among the factors that contributed to the organization of the government meteorological service, or Weather Bureau, first established in the office of the chief signal officer of the army [see Myer, Albert James], and in July 1891 transferred to the Department of Agriculture. Newton obtained land in Washington on the Mall, between 12th and 14th Streets, for an experimental farm, and he secured from Congress the appropriation for a new building to house the Department.

In July 1866, while on the Department experimental field, he suffered a sunstroke, and though he partially recovered, he died from its effects within a year. Despite his limited education, the evidence indicates that he was a man of good sense and vision and earnestly devoted to the interests of agriculture. The foundations of the Department which he laid were solid and not unworthy of the superstructure of later years. The important records of his efforts are contained in the annual *Report of the Commissioner of Agriculture* for the years 1862–66. His *Circular on the Present Agricultural, Mineral, and Manufacturing Condition and Resources of the United States*, issued in 1862, was his initial plea to the "farmers and friends of agriculture" for co-operation with the new Department in carrying into effect "the beneficent and important ends contemplated by its organization."

[J. W. Stokes, "Death of Hon. Isaac Newton," in *Monthly Report of the Agric. Dept.*, May–June 1867; C. H. Greathouse, *Hist. Sketch of the U. S. Dept. of Agric.* (1898); J. M. Swank, *The Dept. of Agric. Its Hist. and Objects* (1872); "Isaac Newton, first United States Commissioner of Agriculture," by Amanda A. Newton, a grand-daughter (typewritten; copy in the U. S. Dept. of Agric. Lib.); *Evening Star* (Washington, D. C.), June 20, 1867.]　　　　C. R. B.

NEWTON, JOHN (Aug. 24, 1823–May 1, 1895), soldier, engineer, was born in Norfolk, Va., the son of Thomas Newton, 1768–1847 [q.v.], and his second wife, Margaret (Jordan) Pool. His father was a representative in Congress for twenty-nine years. John Newton was graduated second in his class at the United States Military Academy, July 1, 1842, and was commissioned second lieutenant of engineers. Prior to the Civil War, he served as assistant to the Board of Engineers, as instructor at West Point, and on fortification, lighthouse, and river and harbor work. His name is identified with the construction of Fort Warren, Mass., Fort Trumbull, Conn., Forts Porter, Niagara, and Ontario, New York, Fort Wayne, Mich., and Forts Pulaski and Jackson, Ga. He became first lieutenant, Oct. 16, 1852, and captain, July 1, 1856. He was chief engineer of the Utah Expedition of 1858. In 1848 he was married to Anna M. Starr, daughter of Jonathan Starr, a leading banker of New London, Conn. They had five sons and one daughter.

The outbreak of the Civil War found him engaged in fortification work on Delaware Bay. He was successively chief engineer of the Departments of Pennsylvania and of the Shenandoah, was in action at Falling Waters, Va., June 30, 1861, and did much field reconnaissance. Promoted to major Aug. 6, 1861, and made brigadier-general of volunteers Sept. 23, he was on duty as engineer in constructing the defenses of Washington from Aug. 28 of that year to March 1862. He constructed Fort Lyon, one of the larger works of the Washington defenses. Subsequently he commanded a brigade at West Point, Va., May 7, 1862, and at Gaines's Mill, Glendale, South Mountain, and Antietam. He selected the Union position at West Point, and showed good judgment and skill in handling troops. At South Mountain he ordered his men to advance with the bayonet, without firing, until the enemy should begin to retreat. He accompanied them and carried the enemy's position with a rush. His corps commander recommended him for promotion to major-general for conspicuous gallantry and important services at Antietam. He commanded a division at Fredericksburg, Chancellorsville, and Gettysburg. In the Chancellorsville campaign, he was ordered to attack Marye's Heights, which had defied attack in the memorable battle of Fredericksburg. He carried the position with the bayonet in three minutes, with the loss of 1,000 out of 3,500. On the first day at Gettysburg, General Meade selected him to command the I Corps, upon the death of Gen. John F. Reynolds.

When the I Corps was broken up in March 1864, he was ordered to report to General Sherman and was assigned to the 2nd Division, IV Corps, Sheridan's old division. At the beginning of the Atlanta campaign, he carried Rocky-face Ridge. He was in the operations around Dalton and Adairsville, and the battles of Dallas, Kenesaw Mountain, Peach Tree Creek, Jonesborough, and Lovejoy's Station. Never did his soldiership show to better advantage than at Peach Tree Creek. His division prevented the penetration of Sherman's forces. "The blow was sudden and somewhat unexpected," said Sherman in his report, "but General Newton had hastily covered his front by a line of rail piles, which enabled him to meet and repulse the attack on him" (*Official Records*, 1 ser. XXXVIII, pt. 1, p. 71). After the fall of Atlanta, he commanded the District of West Florida, where he showed great activity. He was brevetted lieutenant-colonel, colonel, brigadier-general, major-general of volunteers, and major-general, United States Army, and held the rank of major-general of volunteers from Mar. 30, 1863, to Apr. 18, 1864.

After the close of the war, he became lieutenant-colonel of engineers, Dec. 28, 1865, was mustered out of the volunteer service, Jan. 15, 1866, and returned to fortification and river and harbor work. His most notable achievements were the removal of obstructions in the East River, New York. He blasted away Pot Rock, a large, submerged stone that had caused many wrecks and had baffled previous efforts to remove it. He mined a reef, three acres in area, projecting at Hallet's Point into Hell Gate, and placed in it 50,000 pounds of high explosives. To allay public excitement, he let it be known that he and his family would be at the electric batteries, near the shaft, and that his daughter Mary, two years old, would touch the electric button. The mines were exploded Sept. 24, 1876, with complete success. He blew up, with 200,000 pounds of dynamite, Flood Rock, or Middle Reef, nine acres in area, in Hell Gate, Oct. 10, 1885. Earth tremors were recorded 183 miles away. He had been promoted to the rank of colonel,

June 30, 1879, and on Mar. 6, 1884, he became brigadier-general and chief of engineers, but he retained personal charge of the Hell Gate operations until Dec. 31, 1885. He was retired at his own request, Aug. 27, 1886, and on the following day accepted the office of commissioner of public works of New York City. He declined a reappointment two years later and accepted the presidency of the Panama Railroad Company, a position which he held until his death in New York City, May 1, 1895. He was buried in Post Cemetery, New York. Newton was a handsome man of commanding presence and pleasing personality. From early manhood he was a devout member of the Roman Catholic Church. He was awarded the degree of LL.D. by St. Francis Xavier College in 1886, and was a member of the National Academy of Sciences and an honorary member of the American Society of Civil Engineers.

[G. W. Cullum, *Biog. Reg. Officers and Grads. U. S. Mil. Acad.* (3rd ed., 1891), vol. II; *Professional Memoirs, Corps of Engineers, U. S. Army,* Mar.–Apr. 1912; *Twenty-sixth Ann. Reunion Asso. Grads. U. S. Mil. Acad.* (1895); *Ann. Report of the Chief of Engineers, U. S. Army,* 1843–62, 1867–87; *War of the Rebellion: Official Records* (Army), 1, 2, 3 ser. (see Index vol.); *Nat. Acad. Sci. Biog. Memoirs,* vol. IV (1902); *N. Y. Times,* May 2, 1895.]   S.C.V.

NEWTON, RICHARD (July 26, 1812–May 25, 1887), Protestant Episcopal clergyman, was born in Liverpool, England. His parents, Richard and Elizabeth (Cluett) Newton, with their family of six children, settled in Philadelphia in August 1824. After a little schooling in that city, Richard left home rather than work in his father's store on Sunday, and earned his board and tuition at a manual-training school in Wilmington, Del. He entered the University of Pennsylvania, was graduated in 1836, and spent three years in study at the General Theological Seminary, New York. On July 4, 1839, he was made deacon by the Rt. Rev. H. U. Onderdonk, and on July 26, 1840, was ordained priest by the same bishop. On July 31, 1839, he married Lydia, daughter of Lawrence Greatorex of Wilmington. He became rector of Holy Trinity Church, West Chester, Pa., immediately upon his ordination, but shortly afterward accepted a call to St. Paul's Church, Philadelphia, of which he was rector until 1862. This was the most fruitful period of his ministry. He became a stanch evangelical, and one of the leaders of that party in his church. Notable features of his parish work were his sermons to children and his missionary services. A very large per cent of young men confirmed under him became clergymen. In many ways he anticipated modern methods in church administration. During the Civil War he was a firm supporter of the Union. In 1862 he accepted a call to the Church of the Epiphany, Philadelphia. During the disputes of the early seventies over ritualism, which led to the secession of the Reformed Episcopal Church, it was expected that Newton, as a pronounced "Low Churchman," would follow Bishop George David Cummins [*q.v.*], but he refused to leave his Church and retained his rectorship until 1881 when his health broke down and he resigned. After a year's rest, however, he felt fit for duty again, and accepted the rectorship of the less burdensome Church of the Covenant, where he remained until his death.

Newton was a man of deep evangelical piety and the most evident sincerity. Although extremely dignified in manner, he was famous for his success with children. His sermons for them fill no less than eighteen volumes, of which more than a hundred thousand copies have been sold. Translations of these discourses appeared in eighteen different languages, including Siamese, Japanese, Arabic, and even Zulu, and they were very largely used in missionary work. He was also the author of a number of books, including *The King's Highway* (1861); *The Jewish Tabernacle and Its Furnishings* (1864); *Bible Jewels* (1867); *Illustrated Rambles in Bible Lands* (1875); *The Life of Jesus Christ for the Young* (1876). Like most works of the sort their usefulness declined with changes of taste and religious outlook.

Though small of stature, Newton was strongly built. He was always plainly but carefully dressed. He died in Philadelphia in his seventy-fifth year, leaving two sons, Richard Heber Newton and William Wilberforce Newton [*qq.v.*], both clergymen. His wife predeceased him by a few weeks.

[Bibliography of Newton's writings in *The New Schaff-Herzog Encyc. of Religious Knowledge,* vol. VIII (1910); memoir by W. W. Newton prefixed to *The Heath in the Wilderness, or Sermons to the People, by the Late Rev. Richard Newton, D.D.* (1888); N. S. Barratt, *Outline of the Hist. of Old St. Paul's Ch.,* Phila. (1917); *Churchman,* June 4, 1887; *Public Ledger* (Phila.), May 26, 1887; personal acquaintance.]
                                    J.C.Ay—r.

NEWTON, RICHARD HEBER (Oct. 31, 1840–Dec. 19, 1914), Protestant Episcopal clergyman, generally known as Heber Newton, was born in Philadelphia. He was the son of the Rev. Richard [*q.v.*] and Lydia (Greatorex) Newton and the elder brother of William Wilberforce Newton [*q.v.*]. He was educated in Philadelphia, spending the years 1857–59 at the University of Pennsylvania. Forced to leave college on account of his health, he was later awarded the degree of A.B. as of the class of 1861. In

1863 he graduated from the Divinity School of the Protestant Episcopal Church in Philadelphia. Ordered deacon, Jan. 19, 1862, by the Rt. Rev. Alonzo Potter, he was ordained priest by the same prelate in 1866. He was successively assistant minister at St. Paul's Church, Philadelphia, 1862–63, minister-in-charge of Trinity Church, Sharon Springs, N. Y., 1864–66; and rector of St. Paul's Church, Philadelphia, 1864–69. On Apr. 14, 1864, he married Mary Elizabeth Lewis, daughter of Charles S. Lewis, by whom he had four children. In 1869 he accepted a call to All Souls' Church (Anthon Memorial) in New York City. Here he found his real career and remained for more than thirty years, establishing a reputation as the foremost liberal preacher in his denomination. Resigning this charge in 1902, he removed to California and became resident preacher at the Leland Stanford, Jr., University, where he enjoyed great popularity with the students because of his clear and fearless handling of current theological and moral questions. His last years were spent in retirement at East Hampton, L. I., where he died.

Heber Newton had a keen and powerful mind and a wide range of interests. As a theologian he was especially interested in the modern critical and historical study of the Bible, a matter which was just beginning to attract attention in the early years of his ministry. Although not an original student or investigator, he endeavored to make the results of the "Higher Criticism" common property. In this field his best and most popular work was *The Right and Wrong Uses of the Bible* (1883), of which in the first edition 25,000 copies were sold in a year. Two attempts were made to bring him to trial, the failure of which strengthened the position of the liberals who held that there was a place in the Church for such critical views.

Since he belonged to a transition age when the new type of theology was establishing itself, Newton's work was almost wholly for his own generation. As yet there were few who were interested in the subjects in which he was absorbed and fewer still who had the fearlessness or the opportunity to discuss them in public. He added nothing to the substance of theological learning, but accomplished much in its dissemination; his more spiritual message, however, did not find embodiment in works of permanent value. Personally he was interested in the teaching of F. D. Maurice and F. W. Robertson, but himself lacked the mystic appeal of the former or the religious fervor of the latter. His appeal was preëminently intellectual and ethical. He gave much attention to evolutionary science, was one of the first serious American students of psychic research and the phenomena of spiritualism, and was deeply interested in civic and labor questions. The scope of his interests is suggested by the list of his publications, among which were, in addition to that already mentioned, *The Children's Church* (1872), a Sunday-school service book; *The Morals of Trade* (1876); *Studies of Jesus* (1880); *Womanhood* (1881); *Book of the Beginnings* (1884); *Philistinism* (1885); *Social Studies* (1887); *Church and Creed* (1891); *Christian Science* (1898); *Parsifal* (1904); and *The Mysticism of Music* (1915), published posthumously. His appearance was intellectual and forceful, his voice was rich and carefully modulated. No rhetorician, he had a sense of humor, was at times epigrammatic, and was always incisive.

[*Churchman,* Jan. 23, 1915; *A Service to Honor the Memory of the Rev. R. Heber Newton, D.D.* (1915); N. S. Barratt, *Outline of the Hist. of Old St. Paul's Ch., Phila.* (1917); *N. Y. Times,* Dec. 20, 1914; personal acquaintance.]   J. C. Ay—r.

NEWTON, ROBERT SAFFORD (Dec. 12, 1818–Oct. 9, 1881), eclectic physician and editor, was born on a farm near Gallipolis, Ohio. His father, John Newton, and his mother, a daughter of Robert Safford, were early Ohio pioneers of Massachusetts Puritan stock. After the log schoolhouse of his home district, he attended academies at Lewisburg, Va., and Gallipolis. While engaged in farming and schoolteaching he studied medicine with a pharmacist-physician in Gallipolis, and later attended the Medical College of Ohio at Cincinnati and the Louisville Medical College, where he was graduated in 1841. He settled in Gallipolis for practice, and on Sept. 14, 1843, married Mary M. Hoy of that town. His choice of cancer for a specialty brought him the questionable title of "cancer doctor" and some disrepute with his fellow practitioners. This name and fame followed him to Cincinnati, whither he moved in 1845, and soon led him to become an eclectic practitioner. In 1849 he went to Memphis, Tenn., to accept the chair of surgery in the Memphis Institute. Following the death of Dr. T. V. Morrow [*q.v.*], founder of the Eclectic Medical Institute of Cincinnati, he was invited in 1851 to the chair of surgery in that institution, thus made vacant. In 1853 he transferred to the chair of medical practice and pathology, continuing an active member of the faculty until 1862. During this period he also conducted Newton's Clinical Institute, a hospital and school, assisted by Dr. Zoheth Freeman.

These were years of storm and strife in the

Newton

Eclectic Medical Institute, and Newton was in the midst of every controversy. His early professional troubles caused him to take up writing on medical reform, and in 1852 he founded the *Eclectic Medical Journal,* which he edited for the next ten years. During this period and later he wrote *The Eclectic Treatise on the Practice of Medicine, Embracing the Pathology of Inflammation and Fevers* (1861); aided Dr. John King [*q.v.*] in preparing the *American Dispensatory (Eclectic),* first published in 1852; and collaborated with Dr. W. B. Powell in writing *The Eclectic Practice of Medicine* (1854), and *The Eclectic Practice of Medicine (Diseases of Children)* (1858). He edited an American edition of James Syme's *Principles and Practice of Surgery* (1865) and several other works. At various times he was editor or co-editor of the *Western Medical News* of Cincinnati (1851–59); the *American Eclectic Medical Review,* New York (1866–72); the *American Eclectic Register,* New York (1868); the *Medical Eclectic,* after 1878 the *New York Medical Eclectic* (1873–81); and the *New York Quarterly Journal* (1875).

As a surgeon his chief interest was the pathology and treatment of cancer. He is credited with having originated the circular incision for removal of the breast. With the outbreak of the Civil War he interested himself in the recruitment of men for the Union Army. Later he was a severe and constant critic of the treatment of patients in the military hospitals and of the sanitation of army camps. He instituted a movement for the recognition of eclectic practitioners in the army, in which he was successful. He was appointed surgeon to a brigade of Cincinnati home guards. In 1863 he moved to New York City, where he secured a charter for and organized the Eclectic Medical Society of the State of New York, of which he was president for the three following years. In 1865 he participated in the founding of the Eclectic Medical College of the City of New York. He held the chair of surgery in this institution and continued one of the most conspicuous figures in American Eclectic medicine for the rest of his life. He died at this home in New York, from apoplexy. A son, Robert Safford, Jr., became a prominent member of the faculty of the New York school.

[*Medical Truth* (N. Y.), Apr. 1883; H. W. Felter, *Hist. of the Eclectic Medical Inst., Cincinnati, Ohio* (1902); H. A. Kelly and W. L. Burrage, *Am. Medic. Biogs.* (1920); *N. Y. Tribune,* Oct. 11, 1881.]

J. M. P.

NEWTON, THOMAS (June 10, 1660–May 28, 1721), New England colonial official, was born and educated in England. His profession was the law and he doubtless received his training in England, although his name does not appear in the list of those called to the bar during his early years in any of the Inns of Court. He arrived in Boston during the régime of Edmund Andros [*q.v.*], was sworn as an attorney June 7, 1688, and found early and important employment of an official character. In 1691 he was in New York as attorney for the Crown in the trial of Jacob Leisler [*q.v.*], Milborne, and others for high treason. In 1692 he was secretary of New Hampshire; and he was still a member of the council of that province in 1698. In 1702 he was appointed deputy judge of the court of Admiralty for Massachusetts Bay, Rhode Island, and New Hampshire. In 1707 he became comptroller of the customs in Massachusetts, and in 1720, attorney-general.

Meanwhile his private practice of the law flourished. Conditions of life in Boston were becoming less simple and judges and attorneys began to have more frequent recourse to the principles and precedents of the English common law than theretofore. Newton quickly became a leading member of the bar in Massachusetts, and is given credit for having "a greater influence in molding the early jurisprudence" of the province, "than any of his contemporaries" (Goodell, *post,* p. 371). In particular, he appears to have been the first to use the title "barrister" in the courts of Massachusetts (Alger, *post,* p. 206), a title that did not receive an official sanction and rating until 1761. In 1701–02 he appeared as counsel for a slave seeking to establish his freedom under an act of manumission granted by his master. His law library, advertised for sale after his death, was estimated by his contemporaries to be the largest and best collection of law books to be found in America.

When in May 1692 a special commission of oyer and terminer was appointed for the trial of the supposed witches at Salem, of the ten commissioners only Newton was a trained lawyer. Accordingly he was appointed attorney for the Crown and served in that capacity from May 27 to July 26, 1692, when he was superseded by Anthony Checkley, the attorney general. It is clear, from a letter written by Newton from Salem a few days after taking up his work there, that he was as completely obsessed by the prevailing delusion as his fellows who were not trained in the law (C. W. Upham, *Salem Witchcraft,* 1867, II, 255). Spectre evidence was admitted, confessions were extorted, and menaces used against those who denied their guilt while he was attorney for the Crown as well as later. In

476

fact, it was only after Newton had been super-seded that the Salem juries began to acquit. His connection with the "judicial murder" of Leisler, Milborne, and others in New York has been noted. In 1705, when some twenty men were placed on trial in Boston for alleged piracy, he was the principal attorney for the Crown. The evidence admitted and the procedure used in this trial were indefensible even according to the common-law precedents then prevalent. His conduct of these trials seems to have been "not only greatly to his discredit but morally crim-inal" (Goodell, p. 397).

As a citizen of Boston, he bore his fair share of the duties of government and frequently placed his legal talents at the disposal of the town. He became a member of the Ancient and Honorable Artillery Company in 1702. He was a communicant of King's Chapel, the first Epis-copal church in Massachusetts, and a leading member in its early and difficult days, serving as vestryman and churchwarden on numerous occasions. He married an English woman, Christian Phillips (?), and by her had four chil-dren, Hibbert, Elizabeth, Christian, and Han-nah. His son Hibbert was appointed collector of customs in Nova Scotia in 1711, and had a worthy if not distinguished career in that prov-ince and in Boston.

[Boston records; A. C. Goodell, *The Acts and Re-solves of the Province of Mass. Bay*, vol. VIII (1895); Nathaniel Bouton, *Provincial Papers: Docs. and Rec-ords Relating to the Province of N. H.*, vol. II (1868); E. B. O'Callaghan, *Docs. Rel. to the Col. Hist. of the State of N. Y.*, vols. III, IV (1853–54); *Pubs. Col. Soc. of Mass.*, I (1895), 93–99; *Mass. Hist. Soc. Colls.*, 5 ser. V–VI (1868–72); *Proc. Mass. Hist. Soc.*, vols. XX, XXI (1884–85); *Proc. Am. Antiq. Soc.*, n.s. II (1883), 170–71; O. A. Roberts, *Hist. of the Military Company of the Massachusetts*, I (1895), 344–45; E. N. Leonard, *Newton Geneal.* (1915), p. 799; H. W. Foote, *Annals of King's Chapel* (2 vols., 1882–96); A. M. Alger, in *New-Eng. Hist. and Geneal. Reg.*, Apr. 1877; obituary from *Boston News-Letter*, May 29–June 5, 1725, repr. in *New-Eng. Hist. and Geneal. Reg.*, Apr. 1893; see also *Ibid.*, Jan. 1914, p. 102.]   W. O. A.

NEWTON, THOMAS (Nov. 21, 1768–1847), congressman from Virginia, was the son of Thomas and Martha (Tucker) Newton and the descendant of George Newton who was living in lower Norfolk County as early as 1670. His great-grandfather was educated in England and was the first mayor of Norfolk chosen by the council under the charter, and his father was a colonel of militia and a member of the House of Burgesses and of the committee of safety. The boy was educated at the College of William and Mary and studied law privately in Norfolk. From 1796 to 1799 he served in the Virginia House of Delegates. He was elected to Congress as a Republican. Taking his seat on Dec. 7, 1801,

he was placed on the committee of commerce and manufactures. During the impeachment trial of John Pickering, federal judge for the district of New Hampshire, in 1804 he was one of the managers chosen by the House of Representa-tives. In Congress he acted in the interests of the seacoast commercial classes. The commer-cial dispute with Great Britain, brought to a head by the Chesapeake affair, caused him to take a bellicose stand. He advocated arming the militia, building a navy, and going to war with Great Britain. In speeches and resolutions in Congress and in letters to the governor he urged adequate defenses for Norfolk. The best defense, he said, would be a large navy rather than coastal forts. Such measures as the Embargo would have lasting effect, since it would force Europe to recognize the value of American commerce and would place a premium on American friend-ship. In 1818 he was made chairman of the committee on commerce and manufactures and his activity on the floor of Congress ceased. The few speeches he made were on technical subjects. He presented his credentials to the Twenty-first Congress, but the election was con-tested, and after serving one year of the term he relinquished the seat to George Loyall on Mar. 9, 1830. In the next election he was clearly the victor. At the expiration of this term he re-tired.

He returned to Norfolk, resumed his law prac-tice, and acted as recorder of the hustings court. He was twice married. His first wife was Mrs. Myers, a widow of Barbados, who bore him one daughter. His second wife was Margaret (Jordan) Pool, the widow of Howard Pool. They had nine children, among them John New-ton [q.v.]. A quiet, kind, and unostentatious person, he was regarded as Norfolk's leading citizen. His speeches were short and were adorned with statistics and Latin quotations. Always ready to protect and advance the eco-nomic interests of his city, he clothed his utter-ances with a fine patriotic sentiment. He at-tributed to Great Britain the cause of the com-mercial distress of the East and characterized her as an "insidious foe, who never gave notice when ... about to strike a blow" (*Annals of Con-gress*, 10 Cong., 1 Sess., 1852, col. 1029). In state politics he was active as member of the committee to frame a Republican ticket and to choose electors. Both he and his father were in constant correspondence with the various gov-ernors of Virginia on such needs of the Tide-water district as new docks for Norfolk harbor and the draining of the Dismal Swamp. The date of his death is given variously. The probate of his will, on Oct. 27, 1847, is recorded in Norfolk.

[W. S. Forrest, *Hist. and Descriptive Sketches of Norfolk and Vicinity* (1853); T. J. Wertenbaker, *Norfolk* (1931); *Memoirs of J. Q. Adams*, ed. by C. F. Adams, vols. IV–VII (1875); *William and Mary College Quart.*, Jan. 1912; *Va. Mag. of Hist.*, Oct. 1921, Jan., July 1922; *Cal. of Va. State Papers*, vols. IX, X (1890–92).]   F. T. W.

NEWTON, WILLIAM WILBERFORCE (Nov. 4, 1843–June 25, 1914), Protestant Episcopal clergyman, was born in Philadelphia, the son of the Rev. Richard Newton [*q.v.*] and his wife, Lydia Greatorex, and younger brother of Richard Heber Newton [*q.v.*]. He was educated in Philadelphia, graduating at the University of Pennsylvania in 1865 and at the Divinity School of the Protestant Episcopal Church in Philadelphia in 1868. Ordered deacon, June 19, 1868, by the Rt. Rev. W. B. Stevens, he was ordained priest Feb. 19, 1869, by the same bishop. On Nov. 16, 1870, he married Emily Stevenson Cooke of Philadelphia, by whom he had one son. After serving one year at the Church of the Epiphany as assistant to his father, he became successively rector of St. Paul's Church, Brookline, Mass., 1870–75; Trinity Church, Newark, N. J., 1875–77; St. Paul's, Boston, 1877–78; and St. Stephen's, Pittsfield, Mass., 1881–1900. On account of a severe affection of the throat, which rendered public speaking almost impossible, he gave up the pastoral ministry in 1900.

Like his father, he was markedly successful in preaching to children. He published the Pilgrim Series of sermons for children in six volumes (1877–90), *The Gate of the Temple, or Prayers for Children* (1876), and edited the *American Church Sunday School Magazine* from 1885 to 1906. His best works for adults were his *Essays of To-day: Religious and Theological* (1879), and an excellent life of the Rev. W. A. Muhlenberg, *Dr. Muhlenberg* (1890), in the series of American Religious Leaders. He wrote several novels including *The Priest and the Man; or, Abelard and Heloisa* (1883) and *Philip MacGregor* (1895). Other works were *The Voice of St. John* (1881, and later editions), poems; *The Vine out of Egypt* (1887), sermons; *A Run through Russia* (1894), travels, including an account of a visit to Tolstoy; *The Child and the Bishop* (1894); *The Abiding Value of First Principles* (n.d.). In the years of his retirement he contributed many articles and stories to periodicals. His writings were of merit but not such as to secure any permanent place in literature. In theology he was a Broad Churchman and sympathized with the liberalizing tendencies in his Church. He organized the American Congress of Churches, a short-lived attempt at bringing about greater comity among churches, which met at Hartford, Conn., in 1885, and at Cleveland, Ohio, in 1886. He was tall and spare in build; his complexion was florid, his manner hearty and affable. He had a delicate sense of humor, and before his throat affection developed, a ringing voice, which, with his pleasing personality and appearance, made him an effective speaker.

[Biographical sketch revised by Newton himself in *The New Schaff-Herzog Encyc. of Religious Knowledge*, vol. VIII (1910); journals of the diocese of Pa.; *Boston Transcript*, June 26, 1914; personal acquaintance.]   J. C. Ay—r.

NEY, ELISABET (Jan. 26, 1833–June 29, 1907), sculptor, daughter of Johann Adam and Elisabeth (Wernze) Ney, was born in Münster, Westphalia, and was christened Franzisca Bernardina Wilhelmina Elisabeth. At an early age she was seized with a desire to become a sculptor and worked in the atelier of her father, a well-known sculptor of ecclesiastical works. After attending the schools of her native town, she determined, as a seventeen-year-old girl, to go to Berlin to study sculpture under the great master, Christian Daniel Rauch. For two years her parents steadfastly opposed her purpose but finally compromised in permitting her to attend the Academy of Fine Arts at Munich. While there she met, as a medical student, her future husband, Edmund Duncan Montgomery [*q.v.*], who was destined to exert a very great influence upon her development. After two years in the academy at Munich, during which time her brilliant work made her a marked student, she transferred in 1855 to Berlin, where Rauch accepted her as a student. With him she continued until his death two years later. Her extraordinary gifts, her unusual beauty, and her indomitable will carried her to heights of popularity. In 1856 she exhibited her work at the Berlin Exposition and gained warm praise. After the death of Rauch she took over some of his uncompleted commissions. She became a warm friend of the philosopher, Arthur Schopenhauer, and the naturalist, Alexander von Humboldt, and made busts of them. During the years 1859–60 she spent several months in Hanover, engaged in making a colossal bust of King George V of Hanover. At this time, Friedrich Kaulbach made a famous portrait of her, and this, with her bust of the King, is now one of the most striking objects in the Museum of the province of Hanover.

In 1860 Elisabet Ney returned to her native town and remained there for three years, engaged in numerous works, largely busts and statues of historical personages of the province. As a result, Münster possesses the best array of her early work in public and private collections. During the summer of 1863 she made two visits to England. On Nov. 17, 1863, she was married to Montgomery in Madeira and then spent the following year in art travels in Egypt, Greece, and Italy. She returned to Munich early in 1865. After a few weeks, she left with her husband for Mentone and Rome and made a bust of Garibaldi during a year's sojourn in Italy. She returned with Montgomery to Munich in the spring of 1867 and rode the crest of a wave of unprecedented popularity. Among the many commissions that she received during the year were one from King Wilhelm I of Prussia for a bust of Bismarck, and busts of the chemists Justus von Liebig and Friedrich Wöhler for the Polytechnicum of Munich. In 1869 King Ludwig II of Bavaria had her make a statue of himself. She also received commissions for two classical figures to be cast in bronze for the Polytechnicum in Munich.

Although Elisabet Ney had been legally married to Montgomery in the office of the British consul at Madeira, she always, by an incomprehensible whim of hers, denied her marriage, even to her parents and closest friends, in the face of subsequent social ostracism in America and Europe. At Munich, in 1870, this insistence, coupled with her very close association with Montgomery, brought down upon her head the marked disapprobation of society, and finally ostracism. The result was that she determined to leave Europe and go to America, where her ideas might be "free," and so, at the end of December 1870, accompanied by Montgomery and a faithful servant, "Cencie," she left Munich. She made one of a company of free spirits who formed a colony at Thomasville, Ga. The colony later disintegrated and at the end of 1872 Ney and Montgomery traveled to Texas. Elisabet's indomitable and stiff-necked pride would not allow her to admit failure to her European friends, and hence she accepted banishment from cultured Europe and its artistic associations. In March 1873 Montgomery purchased a plantation, "Liendo," near Hempstead, Tex. For twenty years the sculptress was here isolated from all contact with the artistic world. In the meantime she bore two children, one of whom died. In 1892, after many years of deprivation, in furtherance of her lifelong, insatiable hunger for recognition as a sculptor, she moved to Austin, the capital of Texas. There, with the aid of Montgomery, she built a studio (now the "Elisabet Ney Museum"). About this time she received a com-

mission to make statues of Stephen F. Austin and Samuel Houston for the Texas Building at the World's Columbian Exposition at Chicago. When state-wide recognition of her gifts as a sculptor followed upon the completion of these statues, she executed a number of works, chiefly busts of Texans prominent in the history of the state. Three visits to Germany followed during the next ten years. Her first (1895) was in the nature of a triumphal return. Subsequent visits (1902, 1903) saw the completion of her most ambitious works, "Prometheus Bound" (now in the Bavarian royal castle at Linderhof) and the Albert Sidney Johnston Memorial, now in the state cemetery at Austin, Tex. Lorado Taft (*The History of American Sculpture*, 1924, pp. 214–15) said of her: "She is one of the best equipped of women sculptors. . . . Her sketches and compositions are admirable, as are her virile, simply handled heads of the forceful sons of Texas. . . . The details of the features are epitomized with great discrimination and with an easy mastery of form which is unknown to the majority of our sculptors."

Elisabet Ney was marked by an independence of spirit that broke everything to her will; this was especially true of her treatment of her husband and her surviving son. She possessed a haughtiness and uncalculating ambition that surmounted all personal and material obstacles, and this, together with a pride that could not bend, conspired to rob her of opportunities by means of which she might have risen to world-wide acclaim as a sculptor. The isolation of her twenty years at "Liendo," and her semi-isolation for another fifteen years at Austin, prevented the growth to be expected in one of her genius. Without constant friendly criticism her work was destined to show qualities of unevenness.

[Bride Neill Taylor, *Elisabet Ney, Sculptor* (1916); Eugen Müller-Münster, *Elisabeth Ney, die seltsamen Lebensschicksale der Elisabeth Ney und des Edmund Montgomery* (1931); Alfred von Mensi-Klarbach, *Vor und hinter den Kulissen der Welt- und Kulturgeschichte* (1925); I. K. Stephens, "Edmund Montgomery, The Hermit Philosopher of Liendo Plantation," *Southwest Rev.*, Jan. 1931; *Biographisches Jahrbuch und Deutscher Nekrolog*, 1907; *Der Grosse Brockhaus*, vol. XIII (1932); *Galveston Daily News*, July 1, 1907.]
S. W. G.

NG POON CHEW (Apr. 28, 1866–Mar. 13, 1931), Chinese editor, lecturer, was born in South China, 150 miles southwest of Shuang Hu, on the fourteenth day of the third moon, in the Chinese lunar calendar. He was the son of Ng Yip and Wong (Shee) Hok. Among Americans he was always addressed as if his family name were Chew instead of Ng (or Wu, as it is pronounced in the Mandarin dialect). In early years he was placed under the tutelage of a Taoist priest in the hope of entering the priesthood of that faith, but in 1879 an uncle, after spending eight years in California, returned to China with $800 Mexican. This seemingly fabulous sum, spread out on the table in eight sacks containing $100 each, so impressed the boy's imagination that he resolved in 1881 to go to San Francisco under the care of a relative. From there he proceeded to San José, where for several years he worked in the daytime and attended public school at night. Converted to Christianity in 1882, he resolved to utilize the pulpit to elevate the lot of his people. After some years of preparation in Occidental College, he entered San Francisco Theological Seminary in 1889, graduating in 1892. He was ordained the same year by the Presbytery of San Francisco and was appointed assistant pastor of the Chinese church of that city. In 1894 the Presbyterian Board of Foreign Missions appointed him to Los Angeles to look after the Chinese missions of southern California. In 1899 he resigned from the ministry in the hope of influencing his countrymen in secular as well as religious matters. Believing that his purpose could be accomplished through a newspaper, he persuaded friends to cooperate with him in establishing at San Francisco in 1899 the *Hua Mei Hsin Pao* (Chinese American Weekly). Although many prophesied that Chinese readers would be too few and that the venture would fail, the success was great enough to warrant the paper's becoming a daily in 1900, at which time its name was changed to *Chung Sai Yat Po* (Chinese Western Daily)—the first Chinese daily newspaper to be published in the United States. With the exception of one week during the San Francisco earthquake, this paper has appeared regularly ever since. Ng furthered the cause of Sun Yat-sen in China, not only by the policy of his paper, but by securing the release of that leader from the immigration office in San Francisco, and providing him with financial aid to proceed to London. During the last sixteen years of his life he lectured extensively on Chautauqua and Lyceum platforms, visiting every state in the Union, and crossing the continent for this purpose no less than eighty-six times. His keen sense of humor, his expansive good will, and his boundless optimism made him a very acceptable speaker. He did much to promote among Americans an appreciation of the best in Chinese culture, and among the Chinese a recognition of the superiority of western civilization on the material side. The University of

Pittsburgh in 1913 conferred upon him the honorary degree of Litt.D. He was a thirty-second-degree Mason, and the first Chinese in California to become a Shriner. An authority on all phases of the Chinese exclusion question, he did much to promote mutual understanding in this matter. For some years (1906–13) he was adviser to the Chinese consulate general of San Francisco, and from 1913 till his death, vice-consul in that city. He married, May 4, 1892, Tso Chun Fah, of San Francisco. At the time of his death he left, beside his widow, a son and four daughters, all engaged in professional or humanitarian work.

[*Who's Who in America*, 1930–31; *Gen. Assem. Presbyt. Ch., U. S. A., Reports of the Boards*, 1895; E. A. Wicher, *The Presbyt. Ch. in Cal., 1849–1927* (1927); *Chung Sai Yat Po*, Mar. 14, and 17, 1931; *San Francisco Examiner*, Mar. 14, 1931.]   A. W. H.

NIBLACK, ALBERT PARKER (July 25, 1859–Aug. 20, 1929), naval officer, was born in Vincennes, Ind. He was the fifth generation in descent from John Niblack of Scotland, who came to America in 1760 and settled in Salisbury, N. C. His father was William Ellis Niblack [*q.v.*]; his mother, Eliza Ann Sherman. Niblack had his early education in the public schools, and entering the United States Naval Academy at seventeen, was graduated four years later (1880). After two years on the South Pacific Station, he was sent to the Smithsonian Institution for instruction and then spent four years in survey and exploration in Alaska. Written during this period was his treatise, "The Coast Indians of Southern Alaska and Northern British Columbia," published in the *Annual Report of the Board of Regents of the Smithsonian Institution . . . 1888* (1890). In May 1887 he was instrumental in saving the crew of the *Ocean King*, which foundered off the northwest coast, and for this he received a letter of commendation. Varied duty afloat followed. In the years 1896–98 he was naval attaché in Berlin, Rome, and Vienna. His interest in writing continued, and in 1890 and again in 1896 he was the prize essayist of the United States Naval Institute. In the Spanish-American War he took part in the blockade of the Cuban coast and in the battle of Nipe Bay. On being ordered to the East, he assisted in the suppression of the Philippine insurrection. In 1900, at the time of the Boxer trouble, he served in the North China Expeditionary Force. Later he was in the Philippine Islands, where, under the United States navy hydrographic office, he acted as secretary to the naval commission and was personally charged with the surveys made for several of the naval stations. On Nov. 24, 1903, he was married to Mary A. Harrington of San Francisco.

After commanding several ships in the Pacific and the Atlantic, he served again as naval attaché, first for a year and a half in South America at Buenos Aires, Rio de Janeiro, and Santiago, and then for somewhat less than two years in Europe at Berlin and The Hague. He had been promoted captain in 1911, and in 1914 when he was in command of the battleship *Michigan* he took part in the occupation of Vera Cruz. Later he was ordered to Newport for the long course at the Naval War College, with which for some time he had had a close relation both as student and lecturer, and was graduated in December 1916. At the outbreak of the World War he was given command of the First Division and later of the First Squadron of Battleships of the Atlantic Fleet. In November 1917 he was given command of the Second Squadron, Patrol Force, of the Atlantic Fleet based on Gibraltar, and had this most important duty until after the signing of the armistice. It was estimated that more than one-fourth of the convoys which reached the Allies either rendezvoused at this point or passed through the straits. His force here consisted of forty-one ships and a personnel which averaged 314 officers and 4,660 men (Sims, *post*, p. 161). The American ships attending the convoys provided approximately seventy per cent. of the escorts between Gibraltar and the United Kingdom as well as twenty-five per cent. of those required for the Allied forces in the Mediterranean. Secretary Josephus Daniels said of his service: "Admiral A. P. Niblack . . . directed our forces at Gibraltar to the end of the war, with fine judgment and ability. He and his force became a tower of strength in that region, to the Allies as well as our own Navy" (*Our Navy at War*, 1922, pp. 117–18). Herbert Hoover, director-general of relief, wrote with like enthusiasm of his subsequent work when in 1919 he was commander of the United States forces operating in the Eastern Mediterranean, saying: "It would not have been possible to have secured any relief to these people but for your co-operation" (letter from Hoover to Niblack).

In the final years of his naval career Niblack was successively director of naval intelligence, Washington; naval attaché, London; commander of the United States naval forces in Europe, with the rank of vice-admiral; and commandant of the sixth naval district and navy yard, Charleston, S. C. He had been promoted to the grade of rear-admiral in 1918 and was retired in that grade in 1923 at the statutory age of sixty-four. In 1924 he became representative of the United States in the International Hydrographic Bureau, Monaco, and in 1927 was elected president for a term of five years. He died in Nice, France. His published work, in addition to the treatise mentioned and many articles that appeared in magazines, consisted of *Why Wars Come* (1922) and *Summary of Data on Coastal Signals, with Proposals for Their Unification* (Monaco, 1926). In recognition of his services in the World War and later he received many decorations.

[W. S. Sims, *The Victory at Sea* (1920); *Who's Who in America*, 1928–29; *Proc. U. S. Naval Inst.*, Nov. 1929; annual reports of the secretary of the navy; *Army and Navy Jour.*, Aug. 24, 1929; *N. Y. Times*, Aug. 21, 1929; data from the Navy Dept. and from private sources.]   C. S. A.

NIBLACK, WILLIAM ELLIS (May 19, 1822–May 7, 1893), congressman, judge, was the eldest of the seven children of Martha (Hargrave) Niblack and John Niblack, who was of Scotch-Irish descent and who, about 1817, removed from Kentucky to Dubois County, Ind., where he was married and where his son was born. After a boyhood on his father's farm William entered Indiana University but soon withdrew, and for the next few years he worked on the farm, taught school, assisted in managing a trading boat, and was assistant surveyor of Dubois County. During these years he studied law and on Apr. 25, 1845, he was admitted to the bar and began practice in Martin County, Ind. He married Belvina Reily in January 1848. She died the following April, and on Oct. 4, 1849, he married Eliza Ann Sherman of Cazenovia, N. Y. They had five children, one of whom was Albert Parker Niblack [*q.v.*]. This same year, 1849, he became a Democratic member of the Indiana House of Representatives, and in 1850 the party elected him to the state Senate. In January 1854 Gov. Joseph A. Wright appointed him as circuit judge to fill out the unexpired term of Alvin P. Hovey. He succeeded himself in the October election that year. In December 1855 he removed to Vincennes and in 1857 went to Congress from the Vincennes district to fill the seat of James Lockhart, who had died in September. He was a successful candidate for reelection in 1858 but declined to run in 1860. Knox County sent him to the state legislature in 1862.

In 1864 he became a member of the Democratic national committee on which he served until 1872. In the National Democratic Convention of 1864 he supported the nomination of McClellan on the platform of peace. On this platform he was reëlected to Congress in 1864, but the war was over before he took his seat. He served until 1875. In 1876 he was elected to the supreme court of Indiana. He suffered his first defeat in the election of 1888, and after the expiration of his term in 1889 he removed to Indianapolis, where he engaged in private practice until his death. He represented the thought of southern Indiana. He voted for the Lecompton constitution, because he believed the best remedy for slavery troubles was the organization of Kansas into a state and that the views of Buchanan on the validity of the Lecompton constitution were correct (see speech of Mar. 31, 1858, *Cong. Globe,* 35 Cong., 1 Sess., App., 1858, pp. 297–98). He was typical of that class of Northern Democrats who during the Civil War represented that paradoxical combination of union and peace but not Copperhead principles. During the Reconstruction period he supported Johnson and opposed the radical Reconstruction measures as too harsh and militaristic. Ever a strong Democrat and imbued with a highly legalistic mind, he continually opposed the encroachments on what he believed were state's rights.

[Papers in the possession of the family in Indianapolis; *Memorial on the Death of Judge William Ellis Niblack by the Ind. State Bar Asso. Mag. of 1893* (1893); G. I. Reed, *Encyc. of Biog. of Ind.,* vol. I (1895); J. G. Blaine, *Twenty Years in Cong.,* vol. II (1886); *Indianapolis Sentinel,* May 8, 1893.]

J. L. N.

NIBLO, WILLIAM (1789–Aug. 21, 1878), hotel and theatre manager, was born in Ireland and came to America in his youth. With his first apprenticeship to a coffee-house proprietor of 43 Pine Street he entered upon the career which made his name familiar through half a century of New York history. Hotel and theatre were often associated in those days, especially in the form of outdoor gardens with platform stages connected with hotels where guests and neighbors and their friends gathered in the evenings to listen to some simple and often topical entertainment, while they partook of light refreshments and discussed the news of the day. After he had conducted the Bank Coffee House for several years, Niblo decided to invest in the concert garden business as an outlet for both his ambitions and his products. In 1823 he leased the Columbian Gardens at Broadway and Prince Street on the site of the old circus and started summer night entertainments there, later developing this into the Sans Souci Theatre. In 1829 he reopened the place as Niblo's Garden. Leaving the old circus arena as it was, he built a small theatre which at once became so great a success that he soon built another, finer and larger than the first. By 1837 this was the fashionable entertainment center in New York life with such attractions as the Ravels (the famous

family of acrobats and rope dancers) and a vaudeville company headed by the elder Jefferson, with a dramatic season under the lead of John Sefton, a concert series, and a season of opera in which the outstanding production was *The Barber of Seville* with Fornasari.

Later Niblo's Garden passed through many changes and vicissitudes. The theatre burned in 1846 and was not rebuilt until 1849. The actual direction of the theatre passed through diverse hands, including such competent theatre managers as Henry Palmer and James J. Wallack. Niblo himself does not seem to have been in any more direct relation to the performances than that of lessee of the property. But his personality was strong and his popularity was great, and to him are generally credited the success and distinction of the entire venture, including the long procession of famous theatre folk who were attracted by the quality of the audience at Niblo's Garden and played there during Niblo's management. In 1850 William Florence made his first New York appearance there. Among the other performances there were Mathilda Heron in *Camille,* Charles Kean in *Hamlet* and *Macbeth,* Edwin Forrest in a series of his tragic impersonations, Henry Wallack, Henry and Thomas Placide, Anna Cora Mowatt, the author of *Fashion,* E. L. Davenport who made his first New York appearance there, J. H. Hackett in his first New York appearance as Falstaff in *The Merry Wives of Windsor,* Charlotte Cushman, Dan Rice, Dion Boucicault, Agnes Robertson, George Holland, and Adelina Patti; and in 1866, after Niblo had retired, *The Black Crook* which carried the fame of Niblo's Garden around the world. Although Niblo was not highly educated, he picked up a knowledge of literature and art and as he grew more affluent, became somewhat of a collector. After the death of Francis Lister Hawks [*q.v.*] he purchased the latter's American history library and presented it to the New York Historical Society. Niblo retired in 1861 and died in 1878. His wife, Martha (King) Niblo had died in 1851.

[See: T. A. Brown, *The Hist. of the N. Y. Stage* (1903), vol. I; G. C. D. Odell, *Annals of the N. Y. Stage,* vols. III–VII (1928–31); J. N. Ireland, *Records of the N. Y. Stage from 1750 to 1860,* vol. II (1867); *Appletons' Ann. Cyc.,* 1878; *Wm. Niblo: Seven Plates Illustrative of New York's Early Dramatic Hist.* (n.d.); *N. Y. Daily Tribune,* Aug. 22, 1878. The catalogue of the books in the Hawks library presented to the N. Y. Hist. Soc. occupies pages 47–166 of *A Memorial of Francis Lister Hawks, D.D., LL.D.* (1871), by E. A. Duyckinck.]

E. J. R. I.

NICHOLAS, GEORGE (1754?–June 1799), Virginia politician and Kentucky pioneer, brother of John, Wilson Cary, and Philip Norborne

Nicholas [*qq.v.*], was the eldest son of Robert Carter [*q.v.*] and Anne (Cary) Nicholas. Born at Williamsburg, he attended the College of William and Mary and entered the army on the outbreak of the Revolution, rising from the rank of captain to that of colonel. In 1778, at an officers' ball in Baltimore he met Mary Smith, daughter of John and sister to Robert and Samuel Smith of that city, a family notably conspicuous for its part in the political and commercial life of Maryland. Retiring from the army, he married her, studied law, and entered politics. In 1781 he removed from Hanover to Albemarle County with his mother and brothers, his father having died the year before. During 1781 he made his political début in the House of Delegates by moving an investigation into the conduct of Governor Jefferson during Arnold's invasion. The charges were later dropped and no ill feeling arose between the two men because of the incident (H. S. Randall, *The Life of Thomas Jefferson*, 1858, I, p. 351), Nicholas presently becoming one of Jefferson's leading supporters. In the Assembly he cooperated with Madison in the struggle for religious freedom in 1784. In 1787 he at first supported and then deserted him when he advocated the payment of British debts (*The Writings of James Monroe*, ed. by S. M. Hamilton, I, 1898, p. 178). During the same period he opposed the issuance of paper money by Virginia. He was a member of the Virginia convention of 1788 and was an ardent advocate of the adoption of the Federal constitution. During the debates on this subject, Nicholas and Patrick Henry hurled at each other certain implications regarding land speculations, which indicated that each had information concerning the investments of the other (Wm. W. Henry, *Patrick Henry*, 1891, II, pp. 355–56). Harry Innes [*q.v.*], whose friendship with Nicholas dated from their college days, had gone to Kentucky in an official capacity after the Revolution, and had become closely associated with James Wilkinson and others in land speculations and in trade with the Spanish at New Orleans. In 1790 Nicholas removed to Kentucky and became interested in the operations of these men. He was a member of the convention which, in 1792, drafted the first Kentucky constitution. One of the remarkable features of that instrument, for which Nicholas was said to be largely responsible, was a clause requiring all cases involving land titles to be tried before the supreme court of the state. Nicholas became the first attorney-general when Kentucky was admitted to statehood. In 1797 he was involved in the last phase of the Spanish Conspiracy (R. M. McElroy, *Kentucky in the Nation's History*, 1909, pp. 200–08) and in 1798 took a leading part in the framing and advocating of Jefferson's famous anti-Federalist resolutions of that year, thus becoming one of the leaders of the rising Republican party in Kentucky (*The Writings of Thomas Jefferson*, Memorial Edition, X, 1904, p. 104). He died, however, during the next year.

In personal appearance George Nicholas was stocky, blond, and bald. Taciturn in public, he is said to have been genial and humorous in private conversation. He must have been a man of great energy and restless enterprise. In Virginia his associations with Madison and Jefferson were entirely creditable to him, and his policy was enlightened as was theirs. In Kentucky his associations with Wilkinson and Innes were certainly devious. Though he probably had no treasonable intent in connection with the Spanish Conspiracy, it is certain that he worked in harmony with a group of land speculators and that he used his public position in order to promote his private interests. In most of his political activities he had the cooperation of his brother, Wilson Cary, who later became governor of Virginia.

[There is a good brief account of Geo. Nicholas in H. B. Grigsby, *The Hist. of the Va. Fed. Convention of 1788*, II (1891), 281–98. The biographies and published correspondence of Thos. Jefferson throw some light on his political career in Virginia. Humphrey Marshall's *Hist. of Ky.* (2 vols., 1824), and the papers of Harry Innes in the Lib. of Cong. furnish the best clues to his Kentucky connections. See also: Temple Bodley, ed., *Reprints of Littell's Pol. Trans. . . . and Letter of Geo. Nicholas* (1926); and Robt. Peter, *Transylvania Univ.* (1896), Filson Club Pubs., no. 11. In the Durrett Collection, Univ. of Chicago, there is a volume of letters, papers, and speeches in the handwriting of Geo. Nicholas.]   T. P. A.

NICHOLAS, JOHN (1756?–Dec. 31, 1819), member of Congress from Virginia, brother to George, Wilson Cary, and Philip Norborne Nicholas [*qq.v.*], and son of Robert Carter [*q.v.*] and Anne (Cary) Nicholas, was born in Williamsburg, Va. Almost nothing is known of his early life, but being the second son of the Treasurer of the Colony, he doubtless received every advantage that the little provincial capital afforded. It appears that he attended the College of William and Mary, studied law, and practised for a time in Williamsburg, but his career was interrupted by the outbreak of the Revolution, which occasioned the removal of his family to the comparative safety of an estate in Hanover County. Though at some time during his career John lost the use of one of his eyes, he appears to have continued his studies or his practice during the war, and to have taken no part in military operations. In 1781, on the death of his father, his family removed from Hanover to Albemarle County. It is not clear that John followed them to their new home, for we presently find him located in Stafford County, where he married Anne Lawson, daughter of Gavin Lawson, by whom he had eleven children. In 1793 he was elected to the Federal House of Representatives and, being thrice re-elected, served until 1801. He came to be recognized as one of the leading supporters of the Republican cause on the floor of the House. He was effective in debate, and his speech advocating repeal of the Sedition Act was published in 1799 as a Republican pamphlet and later included by Alexander Johnson in his collection of *Representative American Orations* (1884, I, 83–95). Nicholas appears to have suffered financially as a consequence of his public service, and in 1799 desired to give up his seat in Congress but consented to serve another term in the interest of the Republican cause. It was presumably due to this economic situation that he finally retired from public life in 1801 and two years later removed to Geneva, Ontario County, New York (Manning J. Dauer, "The Two John Nicholases," *American Historical Review,* January, 1940, 338–53). In his new home he engaged in agricultural pursuits and in 1806 was elected to the state senate, which place he held until 1809. From 1806 until 1819 he acted as judge of the court of common pleas of Ontario County. He died at his home in Geneva on Dec. 31, 1819, and was interred in Glenwood Cemetery. Little is known of his private life except that he was a devout member of the Episcopal Church.

[There is a meager account of John Nicholas in the *Biog. Dir. Am. Cong.* (1928); and another in Alexander Brown, *The Cabells and their Kin* (1895), pp. 200–01. See also: Louise P. du Bellet, *Some Prominent Va. Families* (n.d.), vol. II; *Va. Mag. of Hist. and Biog.,* July 1901; Orin Clark, *A Funeral Address, Delivered at the Interment of the Hon. John Nicholas . . . 1820* (n.d.); *Richmond Enquirer,* Jan. 15, 1820.]

T. P. A.

NICHOLAS, PHILIP NORBORNE (1775?– Aug. 18, 1849), Virginia jurist and politician, brother of George, John, and Wilson Cary Nicholas [*qq.v.*], was the youngest son of Robert Carter [*q.v.*] and Anne (Cary) Nicholas. He was born in Williamsburg, Va., and was named for Norborne Berkeley, Lord Botetourt, the governor of the Province. He attended the College of William and Mary, studied law, and in 1800 became attorney-general of Virginia (*The Writ-*

ings of James Monroe, ed. by S. M. Hamilton, III, 1900, p. 170). In 1804 he was made a director of the first bank to be established in Richmond, and for years was president of the Farmer's Bank of that city. In 1817 he was made a director of the Richmond branch of the Bank of the United States, of which institution his brother Wilson Cary was for a short while president. In 1823 he was made judge of the General Court of Virginia and retained this position until his death in 1849.

These activities stamp him as a substantial citizen rather than as a man of action and ideas. He spent his entire active life in Richmond, establishing his home on Shockoe Hill where John Marshall and other notable citizens had their residences (C. H. Ambler, *Thomas Ritchie,* 1913, p. 16). He was appointed on civic committees and presided over civic rites on important occasions when internal improvements were to be considered or when the death of a Jefferson or a Monroe was to be mourned. Though never a great political figure, he yet took a very active part in politics and was one of the guiding forces in the establishment of the Jacksonian party in Virginia. As early as 1800 he consulted with Jefferson on tactical political moves (*The Writings of Thomas Jefferson,* Memorial Edition, X, 1904, p. 163), and doubtless worked in concert with his brothers, George and Wilson Cary, for the promotion of the Jeffersonian cause in Virginia. He apparently devoted his time to his banking interests during the long rule of the Virginia Dynasty, but when this period came to an end, his noted brothers were dead, and he carried on the tradition of the family by taking a powerful, though quiet, part in the political transition that followed. Like most of the state-rights men of the Jeffersonian school in Virginia, he supported William H. Crawford for the presidency in 1824 (H. H. Simms, *The Rise of the Whigs in Virginia,* 1929, p. 16), but on Crawford's failure, he and Thomas Ritchie [*q.v.*], of the *Richmond Enquirer,* along with certain others who came to be known as the "Richmond Junta," decided to throw their support to Andrew Jackson. They carried their state for him and continued to control it in his interest. Now a thoroughgoing Jackson man, Nicholas wrote articles condemning nullification, and he appeared against Lieut. R. B. Randolph in the case of the personal attack upon Jackson by that young hot-spur. Though opposed to the sub-treasury, as a banker should have been, Nicholas remained faithful to Van Buren, as did his associates of the Junta. It was, in fact, in collaboration with Van Buren that the Virginia group had made the transition from the Crawford to the Jackson camp (C. H. Ambler, *op. cit.*, p. 106). On one of the very few occasions when Nicholas became a candidate for office, he was elected a member of the convention which framed Virginia's second constitution in 1829. He was married twice: his first wife was Mary Spear of Baltimore, Md., and his second, Maria Carter Byrd, of Clark County, Va.

[The works which deal with the Jackson movement in Virginia contain scattered references to Philip Norborne Nicholas. A little personal information is to be found in R. A. Brock, *Va. and the Virginians* (1888), I, 121–29; W. A. Christian, *Richmond, her Past and Present* (1912); Louise P. du Bellet, *Some Prominent Va. Families* (n.d.), II, 320–21; *Richmond Enquirer,* Aug. 21, 1849.] T. P. A.

NICHOLAS, ROBERT CARTER (Jan. 28, 1728–Sept. 8, 1780), colonial official and Revolutionary patriot, was the eldest son of Dr. George and Elizabeth (Carter) Burwell Nicholas. His mother was daughter to Robert, the famous "King" Carter, of Virginia, and widow of Nathaniel Burwell. His father, after having served as a surgeon in the British Navy, emigrated about 1700 from Lancashire to Williamsburg, Va. (Louise P. du Bellet, *Some Prominent Virginia Families,* n.d., II, pp. 310 ff.). Robert was educated at the College of William and Mary and presently took up the practice of law, becoming in time the recognized head of the provincial bar. Probably in 1751 he was married to Anne, daughter to Wilson and Sarah Cary of Virginia. In 1756 he was elected to represent York County in the House of Burgesses, and for years he took an active part in the proceedings of that body (*Journals of the House of Burgesses of Virginia,* 1752–55, 1756–58, ed. by H. R. McIlwaine, 1909, p. x). In 1765 he opposed Patrick Henry's Stamp Act resolves. At the same time he took a leading part in exposing the irregularities in the treasury, and on the death of Speaker John Robinson [*q.v.*] in 1766, Nicholas' friends were instrumental in inducing Governor Fauquier to consent to the separation of the speakership and the office of treasurer and the appointment of Nicholas to the latter post ("The Preston and Virginia Papers," *post,* I, p. 59; *Journals of the House of Burgesses of Virginia,* 1766–69, ed. by John P. Kennedy, 1906, pp. xv–xviii). Though opposing revolutionary measures, Nicholas did not favor unconditional submission to the British Parliament. In 1769 he helped to frame resolutions condemning the attitude of that body on the questions of taxation and the transportation of criminals for trial in England. By 1771 his other interests had become so pressing that he offered his unfinished legal business to Thomas Jefferson, but Jefferson was unable to accept it and it was turned over to Patrick Henry in 1773.

When news of the closing of the port of Boston reached Williamsburg, Jefferson, Henry, and their radical friends persuaded the conservative and religious Nicholas to offer a resolution which they had drafted setting aside a day of prayer and fasting (Lyon G. Tyler, *History of Virginia,* 1924, II, p. 121). A pamphlet criticizing this action and upholding the British policy was published anonymously, but it is believed to have been written by the attorney-general, John Randolph. Nicholas answered with another publication in which he defended the American cause and his own actions (*Considerations on the Present State of Virginia, Attributed to John Randolph—and Considerations on the Present State of Virginia Examined, by Robert Carter Nicholas,* ed. by Earl G. Swem, 1919). When Dunmore seized the supply of powder at Williamsburg in 1775, Nicholas helped to prevent a clash between the Governor and the outraged colonists led by Henry. It was during this anxious time that he opposed Henry's resolutions proposing to arm the colony for defense, but the measure having passed despite his efforts, he was placed upon the committee charged with its execution.

Alone of all the important men in the Virginia Assembly, Nicholas opposed the adoption of the Declaration of Independence, but he was a member of the committee appointed to draft a declaration of rights and a new form of government. In this capacity he opposed the assertion that "all men are by nature equally free and independent" as being the forerunner of civil convulsion (Kate Mason Rowland, *The Life of George Mason,* 1892, I, p. 240). This reluctant acceptance of the changing situation classified him as a stanch conservative Patriot, and he further entrenched himself with the conservatives when he became one of the leading defenders of the established Church against the liberals who worked for religious freedom. On the organization of the new state government, Nicholas, largely through the influence of Jefferson, was defeated by George Wythe in the contest for the speakership of the House of Delegates (J. H. Eckenrode, *The Revolution in Virginia,* 1916, p. 172). His duties as treasurer now came to an end, and in 1779 he was placed on the bench of the High Court of Chancery. In 1780 he was appointed on the committee charged with the construction of public buildings which were to be erected in Richmond, but he died within the year.

At the outbreak of hostilities in 1775, Nicholas removed his family from Williamsburg to "The Retreat," his estate in Hanover County. It was here that he died in 1780. After the invasion of

Cornwallis in 1781, his widow removed her family to a tract of land which her father-in-law had purchased in the piedmont county of Albemarle. Here her promising children grew up under the influence of Thomas Jefferson. Four of her sons, George, John, Wilson Cary, and Philip Norborne [*qq.v.*] took active parts in political life. Her daughter Elizabeth became the wife of Edmund Jennings Randolph [*q.v.*]. The conservative father of this family of Democrats was an unusual man in his time. A close friend to Governor Botetourt, an important member of the colonial régime, and a stanch defender of the established Church, there was yet much of puritanical austerity in his character. He exposed fraud in high places and administered the treasury with scrupulous honesty. He opposed most of the plans of the Revolutionists, but was trusted by them to aid in carrying out the very designs against which he had argued.

[Material is scattered through the works dealing with the Revolutionary history of Virginia, such as C. R. Lingley, *The Transition in Va. from Colony to Commonwealth* (1910); and J. H. Eckenrode, *The Revolution in Va.* (1916). The only good characterization is in Henry S. Randall, *The Life of Thomas Jefferson* (1858), I, 198–99. See also: Wm. Meade, *Old Churches, Ministers, and Families of Va.* (1857), vol. I; *Va. Mag. of Hist. and Biog.*, July 1901; R. A. Brock, *Va. and the Virginians* (1888), vol. I; H. B. Grigsby, *The Va. Convention of 1776* (1855); "The Preston and Va. Papers of the Draper Collection of MSS.," *Wis. Hist. Soc. Pubs., Calendar Series*, vol. I (1915); *Sons of the Revolution in Va. Quart. Mag.*, Apr. 1923.]   T. P. A.

NICHOLAS, WILSON CARY (Jan. 31, 1761–Oct. 10, 1820), congressman, United States senator, and governor of Virginia, brother of George, John, and Philip Norborne Nicholas [*qq.v.*] was the third son of Robert Carter [*q.v.*] and Anne (Cary) Nicholas. He was born at Williamsburg, Va., but removed with his parents to Hanover County in 1775. At an early age he became a student at the College of William and Mary but withdrew in 1779 to join the Revolutionary army. He became commanding officer of Washington's Life Guard, which post he held until the dissolution of the corps in 1783. During the period of his service in the army, his father had died and his mother had removed to Albemarle County. He now joined the family in the new abode, and shortly thereafter married Margaret Smith, daughter of John Smith, a prominent citizen of Baltimore. Another daughter of the house, Mary, had married his brother George. After his marriage, Wilson Cary Nicholas made his home at "Warren" in Albemarle. In 1784 he was elected to the House of Delegates and in that body disregarded his father's example and his mother's advice by supporting Madison in his stand for religious liberty. He also sup-

ported him in his effort to remove legal obstructions to the payment of British debts in accord with the treaty of 1783. He remained in the House of Delegates until 1789, serving meanwhile in the convention of 1788 and acting again in accord with Madison in championing the adoption of the Federal constitution. Like Jeffersonians in general, he was in thorough sympathy with the ideals of the French Revolution (*The Writings of James Madison*, ed. by Gaillard Hunt, vol. VI, 1906, p. 132). In most of his early political activities he cooperated with his elder brother George, who went with him to the convention of 1788.

From 1794 until 1799 Nicholas again served in the Assembly. In 1798 he and his brother George consulted with Jefferson in the framing of the famous anti-Federalist resolutions of that year. He then passed them on to his friend John Breckinridge for enactment by the Kentucky Assembly, while he himself championed those presented to the Virginia Assembly by Madison (D. R. Anderson, *William Branch Giles*, 1914, pp. 62–64). In 1799 he was elected to the United States Senate, where he quickly became a leader of the Jefferson forces. In 1804 he resigned in order to become collector of the port of Norfolk, but Jefferson still needed his help in Congress and in 1807 he was elected to the House of Representatives. He favored war as a result of the *Chesapeake* and *Leopard* affair but restively supported Jefferson's Embargo. In 1808 he was one of the organizers of Madison's candidacy for the presidency (*Ibid.*, pp. 123–24). Though elected for a second term in Congress, Nicholas resigned in 1809 because of ill health and retired for some years from active public life. In 1814, however, he was elected governor of Virginia and served during the final period of the War of 1812. As soon as this struggle was ended, he turned his attention to the problems of internal improvement and education, and, in his official capacity, collaborated with Jefferson in the foundation of the institution which presently became the University of Virginia (P. A. Bruce, *History of the University of Virginia*, I, 1920, p. 87). On his retirement from office he served for a short time as president of the Richmond branch of the Bank of the United States, but again his health failed and he was forced into his final retirement.

With his brother George he had been a heavy speculator in western lands, and for this or other reasons, his financial affairs became heavily involved in the panic year of 1819. His default on a twenty-thousand-dollar note which Jefferson had indorsed was the crowning blow which brought economic calamity upon his old friend and patron (H. S. Randall, *The Life of Thomas Jefferson*, 1858, III, p. 533). In 1820 Nicholas was stricken and died at the home of his son-in-law, Thomas Jefferson Randolph in Albemarle County, and he was buried in Jefferson's plot at "Monticello." He was a man of solid ability rather than one of brilliant parts; he was worker rather than creator. Throughout his life he was a devoted follower of his great political mentor. Nicholas' son, Robert Carter Nicholas, was United States senator from Louisiana; his daughter Jane married Thomas Jefferson Randolph, grandson of Jefferson.

[There are sketches of the life of Wilson Cary Nicholas in H. B. Grigsby, *Hist. of the Va. Fed. Convention of 1788*, II (1891), 299–310; in L. G. Tyler, *Hist. of Va.* (1924), II, 449; and in R. A. Brock, *Va. and Virginians* (1888), I, 121–29. There is considerable material concerning him in H. S. Randall, *The Life of Thos. Jefferson* (1858), and in Jefferson's published correspondence.] T. P. A.

NICHOLLS, FRANCIS REDDING TILLOU (Aug. 20, 1834–Jan. 4, 1912), Confederate general, governor and chief justice of Louisiana, was born at Donaldsonville, La., the fifth and youngest son of Louisa Hannah (Drake) Nicholls, the sister of Joseph Rodman Drake [q.v.], and Thomas Clark Nicholls, a member of the legislature and judge of the court of appeals. He was the descendant of Edward Church Nicholls who, when disinherited for refusing to become a Roman Catholic priest, emigrated from Cornwall, England, to Maryland and later removed to Louisiana. The boy received his preparatory training at Jefferson Academy in New Orleans, and then, more by accident than because of military taste, entered the United States Military Academy at West Point. He was graduated in 1855, assigned to a second-lieutenancy in the artillery, served in Florida in the Seminole campaign, and then was sent to the lonely outpost of Fort Yuma, Cal. The resignation of his commission in 1856 may have been due to overhearing the regimental physician predict his death unless he left that climate. He studied in the law school of the University of Louisiana, now of Tulane University, but, tempted by the offer of an exceedingly large fee, he left the law school before graduation, passed his examination, and won the case. He was married to Caroline Zilpha Guion, the daughter of George Seth Guion, on Apr. 26, 1860.

The outbreak of the Civil War found him a counselor-at-law in Napoleonville, practising with his brother Lawrence, and already attracting attention. Although he did not favor secession, when confronted with the necessity of a choice he chose to go with his state. He entered the Confederate army as captain of a company of infantry, the Phoenix Guards, that he and a brother raised in Ascension and Assumption parishes, but was promptly chosen as lieutenant-colonel of the 8th Louisiana Regiment. Ordered to Virginia he participated in the first battle of Manassas and saw service subsequently with Taylor's brigade in northern Virginia. In the spring of 1862, taking part in Stonewall Jackson's Valley campaign, he fought at Front Royal and Winchester, in which latter battle he was taken prisoner and sustained a wound that cost his left arm. By the following September, when he was exchanged, he had been commissioned colonel of the newly organized 15th Louisiana, but before he could join it he was promoted to the rank of brigadier-general. Although he had lost one arm, he was given command of the 2nd Louisiana brigade. This command he led gallantly in the battle of Chancellorsville, where his horse was shot from under him and his left foot torn off by a shell. He was recognized in Lee's report (*War of the Rebellion, post*, 1 ser. XXV, pt. 1, p. 803) and rewarded by Davis with the offer of a major-generalship, which he was too conscientious to accept since his days of active service at the front were ended. After his convalescence he was placed in command of the post at Lynchburg and on July 28, 1864, was made superintendent of the conscript bureau of the Trans-Mississippi Department, where he served until the close of the war.

He resumed his practice in Napoleonville, until his state again demanded his fighting services, this time in the political arena, for his friends nominated for governor at the Democratic convention in 1876 "all that is left of General Nicholls." His task was to rid the state of negro and Carpet-bag rule. One-armed and one-legged he stumped the state, inspiring courage and awakening enthusiasm. When the returning-board declared his Republican opponent, Packard, elected, the grim warrior ignored the decision, established a *de facto* government, and was ultimately recognized by the federal authorities after a period of dual governments. When a group of city politicians obtained control of his party and succeeded in calling a constitutional convention in 1879 that reduced his term to three years, he declined to be a candidate again and took up his profession in New Orleans. It was during this period of eight years of semi-retirement from public life that he was appointed by President Cleveland to the board of visitors for West Point. In the moral and economic crisis of 1888, while the Louisiana lottery company was bargaining for an extension of its charter by specious offers of revenue without taxation to a debt-ridden state, the people seeking a man with the requisite moral courage and political daring to lead the fight turned once more to him for their gubernatorial candidate. He was elected in the most bitter campaign of Louisiana's history and during his term of office, 1888 to 1892, succeeded in destroying the lottery.

His third period of service, which covered almost the entire remainder of his life, lay in the field of jurisprudence. In 1892 he accepted appointment as chief justice of the supreme court of Louisiana for a term of twelve years. In accordance with the provision of the constitution of 1898 that the judge senior in date of appointment should hold the chief post, a change he recognized as an effort to improve the system, he became associate justice upon his reappointment in 1904 and served until 1911 when ill-health compelled his retirement. He enjoyed the unusual honor of continuing on the pay-roll. In his nineteen years on the bench, he wrote voluminous reports, lucid and painstakingly elaborate, through which he molded Louisiana constitutional law. He spent the year after his retirement on his plantation near Thibodeaux. In the public service that was thrust upon him he served his state well and gained from his fellow citizens a degree of respect rarely accorded. It is significant of the modesty of the man that he died thinking that his sacrifice had hardly been worth the price he had paid, not because of his physical loss but because his services had been of so little worth to the Confederate cause.

[*Asso. of the Grads. of the U. S. Military Acad. Ann. Reunion . . . 1912* (1912) ; *Biog. Reg. of the Officers and Grads. of the U. S. Mil. Acad.*, Supp., vol. VIA, ed. by Wirt Robinson (1920) ; *Confed. Mil. Hist.*, ed. by C. A. Evans (1899), vol. X ; *War of the Rebellion: Official Records (Army)*, esp. 1 ser. XXVII, pt. 2, XXIX, pt. 2, XXXVII, pt. 1, XL, pt. 3, 2 ser. IV ; "The Nicholls Family in La.," *La. Hist. Quart.*, Jan. 1923 ; *Daily Picayune*, Jan. 5–7, 1912, and *Times-Democrat*, Jan. 5, 1912, of New Orleans ; *L'Abeille de La Nouvelle Orleans*, Jan. 6, 1912.]   E. L.

NICHOLLS, RHODA HOLMES (Mar. 28, 1854–Sept. 7, 1930), artist and educator, was born in Coventry, England. The daughter of the Rev. William Grome Holmes, a graduate of Oxford University and vicar of Little Hampton, and Marion (Cooke) Holmes, she was named Rhoda Carleton Marion Holmes. Governesses were her first teachers but as she developed a marked talent for art she was sent to London, to the Bloomsbury School of Art, where she won the Queen's Scholarship, a prize of sixty pounds for three years. She also studied in one of the schools of the Kensington Museum. Lured by the brilliant color of the South, she sacrificed two years of the Queen's prize to go to Italy, where she studied with Vertunni and Cammerano in Rome and became a member of the Circello Artistico Club, in which were gathered artists of many nationalities who criticized each other's work. Her own work immediately attracted attention and she exhibited in Rome, Turin, the Royal Academy in London, and elsewhere. She spent three years in South Africa on her brother's large ostrich farm, returning to England with many beautiful canvases of rich and brilliant colors in oil and water-color. While in Italy she met in Venice Burr H. Nicholls, an American painter. They were married in Lyminster, Sussex, England, in 1884 and they sailed for America almost immediately, where she at once won enthusiastic recognition. She was active as a teacher, her pupils coming from all parts of the country, especially for out-of-door study. For many years she was in charge of the water-color department at the William Chase School at Shinnecock, L. I. She also taught at the Art Students' League, in New York, and for many years conducted summer classes at Gloucester and Provincetown, Mass., or at Kennebunkport, Me. She was on the staff of the *Art Interchange* and the *Art Amateur* and was co-editor of *Palette and Brush*. Aside from her professional activities she was an early champion of the political emancipation of women.

Mrs. Nicholls was also known as an illustrator. Her work ranged all along the line of painting, water-color, wash drawings, crayons, and pastels. She had few rivals and her acute knowledge of drawing and genius for composition are apparent in all her work. She devised a method for water-color painting which came to be widely employed. By having a saturated blotting paper under her water-color paper she could work with more freedom and less speed because the paper could be kept wet indefinitely. A critic writing of the exhibition of the American Water-color Society, says : "In her two works 'Cherries' and 'A Rose,' Mrs. Rhoda Holmes Nicholls shows us a true water-color, executed by a master hand. The subject of each is slight, each stroke of her brush is made once and for all, with a precision and dash that are inspiriting, and you have in each painting the sparkle, the deft lightness of touch, the instantaneous impression of form and coloring that a water-color should have" (*International Studio*, March 1901, p. 80). Her water-colors are well known through their repeated reproduction. It is said that her picture "Those Evening Bells" for which she won the gold medal at the New York Prize Fund Exhibition in 1886, she sold for $100 to a publisher, who eventually realized $30,000 from the reproductions. She was a member of many art groups and won numerous awards, among them medals at the World's Columbian Exposition, 1893; Atlanta, 1895; Nashville, 1897; Buffalo, 1901; and St. Louis, 1904. She is represented in the principal museums and galleries. A special exhibition of her water-colors was given at the Corcoran Gallery of Art in Washington in 1924. She died at Stamford, Conn., having been a sufferer from arthritis for several years. A daughter, a son, and two grand-children survived her.

[Who's Who in America, 1926–27; Am. Art Annual, 1930; Mich. State Lib., Biog. Sketches of Am. Artists (1924); Art Digest, Sept. 1930; Special Exhibition of Water Colors by Rhoda Holmes Nicholls, Corcoran Gallery of Art, Washington, D. C. (1924); Hartford Daily Courant, Sept. 9, 1930; Evening Star (Washington), Feb. 17, 1924; N. Y. Times, Sept. 8, 1930.] H. W.

NICHOLS, CHARLES HENRY (Oct. 19, 1820–Dec. 16, 1889), physician, psychiatrist, was born at Vassalboro, Kennebec County, Me., the son of Caleb Nichols. He received his academic training in the schools of his native state and at the Friends' School of Providence, R. I. He studied medicine at the University of the City of New York and the University of Pennsylvania, receiving his degree from the latter institution in 1843, after which he practised for a short time at Lynn, Mass. From 1847 to 1849 he served Dr. Amariah Brigham [q.v.], one of the pioneers in mental medicine, at the New York State Lunatic Asylum, Utica, N. Y., and from 1849 to 1852 he was resident physician at the Bloomingdale Asylum, New York City.

Nichols is best known as the first superintendent of the Government Hospital for the Insane (now St. Elizabeth's Hospital) at Washington, D. C. In 1852 he was selected by President Fillmore to superintend and take charge of the establishment of that institution. An appropriation of $200,000 was made for the purchase of a site, consisting of 200 acres, and for the construction work required. Nichols prepared the plans for the original building and personally supervised the entire work, meeting the deficiency of this small appropriation by manufacturing the bricks out of the earth dug for the foundation. Architecturally the building was a modified type of the old Kirkbride style, and consisted of a central administrative portion, with wings on each side. Nichols' construction, differing from the older type in that the wings were in echelon, is said to have been twenty-five years in advance of its time, and was reproduced by many of the state hospitals and those of Australia and New-

foundland. A well-appointed lodge for the colored insane, probably the first distinct provision of the kind ever made for the people of that race, was attached to the institution. For a quarter of a century Nichols remained at St. Elizabeth's, erecting additional buildings, acquiring considerable additional land, and at the same time keeping the institution abreast of the most modern curative methods in the treatment of the insane. During the Civil War he acted as volunteer surgeon of the St. Elizabeth's General Army Hospital, and was present as one of General McDowell's staff at the battle of Bull Run.

In 1877 he resigned to accept the position of medical superintendent of the Bloomingdale Asylum in New York City, and when it was decided to build the new hospital at White Plains, he was sent to Europe to study the newest methods of hospital construction. He visited many foreign institutions and the ideas which he obtained were utilized to great advantage in his new construction program. He died shortly after his return to Bloomingdale, and is buried in Congressional Cemetery at Washington, D. C. For a number of years he was president of the Association of American Superintendents of Institutions for the Insane, and was an honorary member of the Medico-Psychological Association of Great Britain. He was one of the most eminent forensic psychiatrists of his time and appeared in many causae celebrae. Chiefly remembered perhaps is his testimony for the defense in the trial of the United States vs. Charles J. Guiteau, who assassinated President Garfield.

In appearance, Nichols was imposing. Well over six feet tall and broad in proportion, with a commanding presence, he was well fitted by nature to be a leader. The betterment of the conditions of the mentally ill occupied the greater portion of his life. No doubt his interest in this particular class of unfortunates was due to his upbringing among the Quakers, a sect which has supplied so many pioneers in the field of psychiatry. In 1860 he married Ellen G. Maury, daughter of John Maury, at one time mayor of Washington; they had one daughter, who died at an early age, and a son. His first wife having died June 12, 1865, he married in 1872 Sallie (Lathrop) Garlic of Pittsfield, Mass.

[Joint Select Committee to Investigate the Charities and Reformatory Institutions in the District of Columbia, pt. III (1898); H. M. Hurd and others, Institutional Care of the Insane in the U. S. and Canada, vol. IV (1917); Am. Jour. of Insanity, Jan. 1889, Jan. 1890; Report of the Government Hospital for the Insane, 1890; Report of the Proc. in the Case of the U. S. vs. Charles J. Guiteau (3 vols., 1882), pt. I; Jour. of Mental Sci., Apr. 1890; N. Y. Tribune, Dec. 18, 1889; Evening Star (Washington, D. C.), Dec. 17, 1889.] W. A. W.

NICHOLS, CHARLES LEMUEL (May 29, 1851–Feb. 19, 1929), physician, bibliophile, author, was the son of Dr. Lemuel Bliss and Lydia Carter (Anthony) Nichols, and grandson of Dr. Ezra and Waity Grey Nichols of Bradford, N. H. Born in Worcester, Mass., he was a "blue baby," whom only infinite care preserved through a precarious infancy for a long life of useful activities, distinguished attainments, and many beneficences. Graduating from Brown University in 1872 with first rank in chemistry, he stayed on at Brown for a year as assistant in that subject. The Cambria Iron Works offered him $10,000 a year as resident chemist; but, holding to his purpose to follow his father's footsteps, he graduated at Harvard Medical School in 1875, served a year as interne in Ward's Island Hospital in New York harbor, and returned to Worcester in 1876 to practise medicine, according to the homeopathic school, to which his father had belonged. A college classmate termed him "a very prince among physicians . . . his patients' physician, friend, and counsellor." His entire life was one of unselfish devotion to parents, family, church, college, and community (Kellen, *post,* pp. 9, 11). He was a founder and long president of the Worcester Associated Charities, president of county and state medical societies, founder of the Worcester Welfare Association, trustee of Brown University, director of the Worcester Free Library, trustee of Westboro Hospital, and an active member of many clubs in Worcester, Boston, Providence, and London. From 1887 to 1907 he lectured on medical history at the Boston University Medical School.

Once firmly established in his profession, he took up bibliography as a hobby, being afflicted with "the incurable disease, Biblio-mania," as he termed it. Elected in 1897 to membership in the American Antiquarian Society, he long served it as recording secretary, councillor, and finally, as president (1927-29). From 1917 he was a member of the Massachusetts Historical Society. These two organizations he enriched with generous gifts of books, historical manuscripts, money, and literary contributions, including printed memoirs of G. Stanley Hall, Albert J. Beveridge, Henry Vignaud, L. P. Kinnicutt, Nathaniel Paine, Franklin Pierce Rice, and Henry E. Huntington. His other publications include: *Bibliography of Worcester* (1899); *The Library of Rameses the Great* (1909), for the Club of Odd Volumes; *Some Notes on Isaiah Thomas and His Worcester Imprints* (1900); *Isaiah Thomas, Printer, Writer and Collector* (1912); *Notes on the Almanacs of*

Massachusetts (1912); *Justus Fox, a German Printer of the Eighteenth Century* (1915); *The Portraits of Isaiah Thomas* (1921); *The Various Forms of the Columbus Codex* (1926); *Samuel Salisbury, a Boston Merchant in the Revolution* (1926); *The Boston Edition of the Baskett Bible* (1927); *Checklist of Maine, New Hampshire and Vermont Almanacs* (1929).

He was twice married: first, in 1877 to Caroline Clinton Dewey, who had one daughter, and died in 1878; second, in 1884, to Mary Jarette Brayton, who died in 1910 leaving two sons and a daughter. In All Saints Church his children placed cloister windows, picturing subjects of his special interest: Gutenberg printing the Bible, Tyndale translating it, and the resulting Reformation.

[W. V. Kellen, *Charles Lemuel Nichols; a Tribute* (1929); L. C. Wroth, "Dr. Nichols of Worcester," *Brown Alumni Monthly,* May 1929; unpublished records of the Class of 1872, Brown University; *Proc. Am. Antiquarian Soc.,* 1929; *The Parish* (pub. by All Saints Church, Worcester), Feb. 24, Nov. 3, 1929; *Worcester Evening Gazette* and *Worcester Evening Post,* Feb. 19, 1929; *The Pastoral Staff* (Springfield, Mass.), Apr. 1929; *Boston Transcript,* Feb. 20, 1929.] F. W. A.

NICHOLS, CLARINA IRENE HOWARD (Jan. 25, 1810–Jan. 11, 1885), reformer, editor, publicist, was born in Townshend, Windham County, Vt., of English and Welsh ancestry. She was the daughter of Chapin and Birsha (Smith) Howard and the grand-daughter of Levi Howard or Hayward who removed to Townshend from Milford, Mass., about 1775. She became a teacher in public and private schools and is said to have founded a young ladies' seminary in Herkimer, N. Y., about 1835. On Apr. 21, 1830, at Townshend she was married to her first husband, Justin Carpenter. On Mar. 6, 1843, she was married, also at Townshend, to George W. Nichols who was the publisher of the *Windham County Democrat* at Brattleboro. His illness forced her, soon after their marriage, to take the financial and editorial control of his paper. It was in these columns that she began the work for woman's rights that marked the whole of her long career. She wrote editorials from 1843 to 1853, when the paper was discontinued. A series of articles, published in 1847 and addressed to the voters of Vermont, dealt with the property disabilities of women and were important in influencing the passage, in 1848, of the Vermont law to secure to a wife the real estate owned at marriage or thereafter acquired by gift, devise, or inheritance even against the debts of the husband, with the corollary right of disposing of her property by will as if "sole." In 1850 she began speaking for woman's suffrage in her native state, in New Hampshire, and in Massachusetts.

In September and October 1853 she traveled 900 miles in the state of Wisconsin as agent of the woman's state temperance society. As a result of her work and that of others, a law was passed by the Wisconsin legislature to secure to the wives of drunkards their own earnings along with the custody and earnings of their minor children.

In October 1854, with her two eldest sons, she joined a company of 225 emigrants to Kansas. She went directly to Lawrence and at once began lecturing and speaking on woman's rights. Her husband followed with another party but died a few months after his arrival. She returned to Vermont to settle his estate and, while in the East, lectured on Kansas and its problems. In the winter and spring of 1856 she also wrote for the *Herald of Freedom,* published at Lawrence, Kan., a series of articles dealing with women's legal disabilities. Upon her return to Kansas in 1857 with her daughter and her youngest son she went to Wyandotte County, where for some years she made her home. When in 1859 the constitutional convention for Kansas met at Wyandotte, she, knitting in hand, the only woman present, sat through its sessions, "watching every step of the proceedings, and laboring with members to so frame the Constitution as to make all citizens equal before the law" (*History of Woman Suffrage, post,* III, 704). After the Kansas woman's rights association was formed in 1859, as its representative she attended the session of the first state legislature at Topeka in 1860 and by invitation addressed both houses. For the two years preceding this legislative session she had spoken in the towns and hamlets of Missouri that lay along the Kansas border. In 1860 and 1861 she lectured in Wisconsin and Ohio. From December 1863 to March 1866 she was in Washington, D. C., writing in the military and revenue departments, and acting as matron in the home for colored orphans. She returned to Kansas in 1869 and two years later removed to Mendocino County, Cal. She died in Potter Valley. "A good writer, an effective speaker, and a preëminently brave woman," she was "gifted with that rarest of virtues, common sense." She "may be said to have sown the seeds of liberty in three states in which she resided," Vermont, Kansas, and California (*History of Woman Suffrage, post,* III, pp. 764–65).

[*Hist. of Woman Suffrage,* ed. by E. C. Stanton, S. B. Anthony, and M. J. Gage, esp. vols. I, III (1881–87); *Annals of Brattleboro,* ed. by M. R. Cabot, vol. I (1921); *Gazetteer . . . of Windham County, Vt.,* comp. by Hamilton Child (1884), p. 304; P. W. Morgan, *Hist. of Wyandotte County, Kan.* (1911), vol. I; records in office of secretary of state, Montpelier, Vt.; clipping from *Ukiah* (Cal.) *City Press,* Jan. 16, 1885, in library of the Kan. State Hist. Soc.]   L. K. M. R.

NICHOLS, ERNEST FOX (June 1, 1869– Apr. 29, 1924), physicist, teacher, college president, was born in Leavenworth, Kan., in the Reconstruction period following the Civil War. His father, Alonzo Curtis Nichols, a photographer especially interested in daguerreotypes, and his mother, Sophronia (Fox) Nichols, succumbed to the struggle against poverty and ill health while Nichols was yet a boy, and left him to the care of his maternal uncle, Gen. S. M. Fox, of Manhattan, Kan. His ancestry on both sides was American for many generations back, the family coming from English-Scotch stock which had settled in New England during the early part of the seventeenth century. A frail child, Nichols obtained his elementary education at home. His first institutional schooling was received at the Kansas State Agricultural College at Manhattan, from which he obtained the degree of B.Sc. in 1888. While there he attended an illustrated talk on experimental physics given in the college chapel by Professor Edward L. Nichols of Cornell University. This lecture so stimulated his interest in physics that he decided to devote himself to the study of that subject, and after a year of graduate study in Kansas he went to Cornell to undertake advanced work. The next four years he spent at Ithaca in study and in acquiring experimental technique in his chosen field of radiation. He was appointed associate professor of physics at Colgate University in the fall of 1892 and received the degree of M.Sc. from Cornell the following spring. At Hamilton he made the acquaintance of Katharine Williams West, whom he married on June 16, 1894. She and a daughter survived him.

His first published paper appeared on page 1, Volume I (July-August 1893) of the *Physical Review.* Although this contribution came from Colgate, the work which it described was done at Cornell during the summer of 1892. It consisted of an experimental study of the transmission spectra of a number of substances in the infra-red region extending as far as the wave length 3μ. For this investigation Nichols devised a weak-field galvanometer of such high sensitivity that he was able to measure currents of 10^{-10} amp. The difficulty of working with an instrument so susceptible to external disturbances led him to consider other methods of studying radiation and resulted in the later development of the Nichols radiometer, an instrument which he used in all his more important researches.

In 1894 Nichols obtained leave of absence from Colgate to go to Emil Warburg's laboratory in Berlin. The first task undertaken there was the adaptation of Sir William Crookes's radiometer to the measurement of energy in the infra-red spectrum. Aided by suggestions from Ernst Pringsheim, who had already studied this instrument, Nichols constructed a radiometer with blackened mica vanes hung by a quartz fiber the suspended parts of which weighed only 7 mg. (*Physical Review,* January-February 1897, p. 297). This instrument was so sensitive that a candle 6 meters away produced a deflection of 60 scale divisions. With it he investigated the reflecting powers of silver and of quartz up to 9μ, finding that silver became an almost perfect reflector for wave lengths between 4μ and 9μ and that quartz possessed such strong absorption bands between 8μ and 9μ that it exhibited the properties of metallic reflection.

In this investigation Nichols took his first step in bridging the unexplored region between the visible spectrum and the electro-magnetic waves of Heinrich Hertz, a task which he made one of the principal objectives of his life, and which he successfully completed only on the day of his death. The work under consideration extended the known spectrum from 3μ, to which point it had been brought by Heinrich Rubens, up to 9μ. Nichols' investigation of the absorption bands of quartz led him to develop with Rubens (*Physical Review,* January-February 1897) a new method of isolating a limited portion of the long-wave spectrum without the difficulties attendant upon the use of prisms or gratings. This method of "residual rays" consists in the successive reflection of radiation from surfaces of a substance like quartz which has a narrow absorption band at the wave length to be studied surrounded by regions of transparency. Radiation of the critical wave length is almost completely reflected, while that on either side passes through the surface. Using fluorite the investigators were able to study residual rays of a wave length of 30μ. To measure the wave length accurately, recourse was had to a diffraction grating of fine gold wires and a bolometer, use of the radiometer being precluded by the fact that no substance transparent to these long waves could be found of which to construct the window.

In later papers (*Physical Review,* August, September 1897), Rubens and Nichols studied the residual rays from rock salt and mica as well as those from quartz and fluorite. In these investigations a radiometer with a silver chloride window was used in place of a bolometer, as it had been found that silver chloride was sufficiently transparent to the long waves involved to make the radiometer a much more sensitive detector than the bolometer. The longest radiation investigated was that obtained by reflection from

rock salt, which was estimated to be not far from 50μ. Thus the known spectrum of heat rays was extended from the red end of the visible region to a wave length of a twentieth of a millimeter, approximately the thickness of a sheet of paper.

In addition to this extension of the spectrum, the September 1897 paper contained an experimental confirmation of the electromagnetic character of infra-red radiation. As a verification of James Clark Maxwell's electromagnetic theory of light, this work was second in importance only to the famous experiments of Hertz. The method consisted in measuring the radiation reflected from a glass plate covered by minute rectangular silver resonators. In accord with theory and with the results which Augusto Righi had obtained for short electrical waves, the reflection was found to be much greater when the lengths of the resonators approximated a whole number of half-wave lengths than when near an odd number of quarter-wave lengths.

On his return from Germany Nichols completed the requirements for the D.Sc. which was conferred upon him by Cornell in 1897. The following year he left Colgate to accept a professorship of physics at Dartmouth. Here he spent five of the most productive years of his life applying his radiometer to the investigation of important physical problems. His first research, carried out at the Yerkes Observatory during the summers of 1898 and 1900, consisted in the measurement of the relative heat received by the earth from the stars Vega and Arcturus and the planets Jupiter and Saturn. Several years before, Charles Vernon Boys had made a similar attempt with his radiomicrometer, but without success. The sensitivity of the radiometer used by Nichols in this work was sufficient to detect one fifty-millionth of the heat coming from a candle one meter distant, a sensitivity twenty-six times as great as that of Boys's instrument.

Nichols' next investigation, undertaken at Dartmouth with the collaboration of Gordon F. Hull (*Physical Review,* November 1901, *et seq.*), was the crowning achievement of his life. Maxwell had shown as early as 1873 that light, if electromagnetic in nature, should exert a pressure on an obstacle placed in its path, which is twice as great for a perfect reflector as for an ideal absorber. The minuteness of the predicted effect, however, had discouraged experimenters from attempting to detect it. Nichols, nevertheless, had planned as early as his Berlin days to make an effort to measure light pressure with the sensitive radiometer which he had designed. For this purpose the blackened vanes of the instrument were replaced by silvered vanes of high reflecting power and a series of preliminary experiments were made to find the pressure (16 mm. of Hg) at which the effect of the bombardment of gas molecules was a minimum. For gas action, although an advantage in the measurement of heat energy, would only mask the effect of light pressure in the present work. Since gas action increases with the time of exposure, this effect was further reduced by allowing the light to fall on the radiometer vane for a very short time, and measuring the pressure by the ballistic throw. The intensity of the incident light was determined at first by a bolometer, but later more accurately by means of the rise in temperature occasioned by its absorption. Not only was light pressure detected, but the theoretical formula connecting the pressure with the energy per unit volume was verified within a probable error of less than one per cent. Unknown to Nichols and Hull, Peter Lebedew in Moscow was working on the same problem at the same time, and through a strange coincidence the first complete reports of the two independent investigations appeared simultaneously in November 1901 in the *Physical Review* and in Drude's *Annalen der Physic*. Lebedew's results were in complete accord with those of Nichols and Hull, although his method differed in a number of important details.

In 1903 Nichols left Dartmouth to become professor of physics at Columbia University. Here he remained until 1909, with the exception of the winter of 1904–05, spent on leave of absence at Cambridge University, England. During this period he carried out further work on residual rays (*Physical Review,* October 1908), consisting particularly of exact measurements of wave length. Incidentally he showed the complete absence in sunlight, even at the altitude of Mt. Wilson Observatory, of long-wave radiation of the order of 50μ (*Astrophysical Journal,* July 1907).

In addition to being a brilliant investigator, Nichols combined the power of the artist with that of the scientist in devising demonstration experiments to illustrate his lectures and had the rare gift of inspiring his students with a love of productive scholarship. Moreover he exhibited the wise judgment, the eloquence of speech, and the sympathetic appreciation of the viewpoints of others characteristic of a successful administrator. Hence it was natural that the board of regents of Dartmouth College should turn to him in 1909 to fill the vacancy in the presidency caused by the retirement of W. J. Tucker. Although he realized that acceptance would halt his scientific activities, he served in

this position for seven years. At the end of that time he had established the college on a secure financial and scholastic basis and felt free to resign in order to accept a professorship of physics at Yale. But before he could resume research the United States entered the World War, and he spent the next two years in investigating schemes proposed by others to combat the submarine menace and in making contributions of his own. In 1920 he left Yale to become director of the Nela Research Laboratory in Cleveland, and a few months later he succeeded Richard Cockburn MacLaurin [q.v.] as president of Massachusetts Institute of Technology. Unfortunately he was stricken by a serious illness which made it necessary for him to resign from this position even before he had stepped into active service.

The remaining years of his life were spent at the Nela Laboratory in completing the exploration of the region between the longest known heat rays and the shortest known electrical waves which he had begun twenty-five years earlier. In the intervening time the gap had been shortened to the region from 0.4 mm. to 7.0 mm. This time he approached the unexplored territory from the long-wave length side, developing, in collaboration with James DeGraff Tear, a Hertzian oscillator consisting of a spark gap in kerosene between tungsten cylinders only 0.01 mm. apart. The receiver was a radiometer whose vanes carried minute platinum resonators which absorbed the waves to which they were tuned. With this apparatus fundamental wave lengths were obtained as short as 0.9 mm. and harmonics down to 0.22 mm. The work was completed in time for Nichols to report the complete closing of the gap between heat rays and electrical waves at the spring meeting of the National Academy of Sciences in 1924. In the middle of his paper, the speaker's heart stopped, and before medical aid could arrive he had passed away. Among other honors Nichols received the Rumford medal of the American Academy of Arts and Sciences in 1907, and was given honorary degrees by Dartmouth, Colgate, Clark, Wesleyan, Vermont, Pittsburgh, and Denison. He was chairman of the physics and engineering section of the National Academy of Sciences from 1917 to 1920, a member of the American Philosophical and many other societies, and a fellow of the American Physical Society.

[E. L. Nichols, "Ernest Fox Nichols," *Nat. Acad. Sci. . . . Biog. Memoirs,* vol. XII (1929); Philip Fox, "Ernest Fox Nichols," *Astrophysical Jour.,* Jan. 1925; Augustus Trowbridge, "Ernest Fox Nichols," *Science,*

May 9, 1924; *Electrical World.* May 10, 1924; *Light,* June 1924; *N. Y. Times,* Apr. 30, 1924.]   L. P.

NICHOLS, GEORGE WARD (June 21, 1831–Sept. 15, 1885), promoter of art education and music in Cincinnati, was born in the village of Tremont, Mount Desert, Me., the son of John and Esther Todd (Ward) Nichols. His father and grandfather were sea-captains. In 1835 the family moved to Boston, Mass., where George received a public-school education. He appears to have entered journalism promptly upon leaving school. Later he went to Kansas and was active in the political and military struggle which attended the organization of that state. In 1859 he spent some time in Europe, principally in Paris, where he studied painting under the direction of Thomas Couture, and upon his return was art editor on the New York *Evening Post,* writing also for magazines. On Apr. 25, 1862, he entered the Union army as a captain, and served at first on the staff of Frémont. Subsequently (1863), he was detailed to assist the provost-marshal general's department in Wisconsin, after which duty he was a recruiting officer until 1864, when he was made aide-de-camp on the personal staff of General Sherman. He accompanied Sherman on his march to the sea and was with him until the conclusion of the war. Upon his resignation he was brevetted lieutenant-colonel of volunteers.

From a full diary which he kept while in the service, Nichols immediately compiled a volume entitled *The Story of the Great March* (1865), which had a sale of 60,000 copies within a year, besides being reprinted in English newspapers and being translated (it is said) into Spanish, French, and German. Perhaps hoping to repeat this success—which, however, resulted from the fame of Sherman's exploits rather than from Nichols' literary skill—he utilized the same matter in the composition of a war-novel, *The Sanctuary* (1866). This artless story, conventional in motivation and stilted in language, attracted no widespread attention and was soon completely forgotten.

Shortly after the close of the war, Nichols went to Cincinnati with Sherman, and there met Maria Longworth, aunt of Nicholas Longworth, 1869–1931 [*q.v.*], whom on May 6, 1868, he married. From this time Cincinnati was his home, and he quickly made himself felt there as an energetic, commanding force, promoting the cultural development of the city. He had much to do with the founding of the School of Design, which was at first a part of the University of Cincinnati and was later transferred to the Art Museum. Convinced that a large and

profitable field awaited the employment of trained artists and craftsmen in industry, he busied himself in advancing the cause of art education. In 1877 he published *Art Education Applied to Industry,* and in 1878 *Pottery: How it is Made, its Shape, and Decoration.* These are straightwardly written and well-arranged manuals, on the whole skilfully adapted to their purpose. His most conspicuous and important service to the arts, however, lay in another direction. The Harmonic Society of Cincinnati under his presidency and management gave a series of concerts which were so successful as to suggest a more elaborate undertaking, and in 1872 the May Festival Association was organized with Nichols at its head. The first musical festival took place in 1873, and he continued to direct the affairs of the Association until 1880, during which time three festivals were held. Meanwhile, in 1879, with the aid chiefly of Reuben R. Springer [*q.v.*], he established the College of Music of Cincinnati and became its first president, a position which he held until his death from pulmonary tuberculosis. He was a born "promoter," with remarkable executive capacity, determination, and self-confidence, with the result "that his career often seemed to those about him too full of his own individuality for the most comfortable enjoyment of easy social friendship" (Cox, *post,* p. 25). Yet it may be said, in general, that Cincinnati owes its importance as a musical center very largely to his audacity and diligence.

[*Cincinnati Enquirer* and *Cincinnati Commercial Gazette,* Sept. 16, 1885; *Cincinnati Times-Star,* Sept. 15, 1885; *Circulars, Papers and Annual Meeting of the Ohio Commandery of the Military Order of the Loyal Legion During the Year 1885* (1887); J. D. Cox, in *Memorial Services in Honor of George Ward Nichols . . . Mar. 4, 1887* (1887); C. T. Greve, *Centennial Hist. of Cincinnati* (1904), vol. I; *The Biog. Cyc. and Portrait Gallery with an Hist. Sketch of the State of Ohio,* vol. IV (n.d.); *Harper's Weekly,* Sept. 26, 1885; local records, Town of Mount Desert, Me.]
R. S.

NICHOLS, JAMES ROBINSON (July 18, 1819–Jan. 2, 1888), chemist, son of Stephen and Ruth (Sargent) Nichols, was born at West Amesbury (now Merrimac), Mass., and died at Haverhill, Mass. His early life was spent on his father's farm, where he acquired an interest in agriculture and utilized his spare hours in study. At the age of eighteen he became associated with his uncle, Moses Nichols, who was a druggist in Haverhill. His desire for a formal education was not gratified; in fact the only academic connection he had was attendance on a course of lectures at the medical school of Dartmouth College in 1841–42. This connection was broken by illness and he did not graduate.

His work there, however, supplemented by numerous specific contributions to chemistry, pharmacy, and science in general, was recognized by the institution a quarter of a century later, and he was granted the degree of M.D. in 1867 and the honorary degree of M.A. He returned to the drug business in Haverhill in 1843, but left most of the work to assistants so that he could pursue his investigations in the laboratory. He gave considerable time also to studying chemistry, lecturing, and writing. After an extended tour through Europe, he gave up his drug business in Haverhill in 1857 and established in Boston the firm of J. R. Nichols & Company, for the manufacture of fine chemicals and medical preparations. Its property was destroyed by the great fire of 1872 and Nichols retired from the firm, but the business was resumed by his partners under the name of Billings, Clapp & Company. During his connection with the concern he made several trips to Europe in an effort to learn the process of manufacturing the finer chemicals, *e.g.*, those used in medicine, photography, dyeing, and painting, his aim being to supply these products which had previously been imported at considerable expense. He was responsible for the introduction of new chemical and pharmaceutical compounds, and of more economical methods for manufacturing them. Soda-water apparatus, the carbonic-acid fire extinguishers and the leatherboard industry, were the results of inventions which he made. An improved form of hot-air furnace of his devising had extensive use (*Popular Science News*, Feb. 1, 1888).

In July 1866 he founded the *Boston Journal of Chemistry and Pharmacy,* which was the first publication in the United States devoted to the exposition of chemistry in a popular but accurate way. The following year the name was changed to *Boston Journal of Chemistry* and remained as such until January 1881, when it was merged with a scientific periodical having a wider field, and was known first as the *Boston Journal of Chemistry and Popular Science Review,* and later, as *The Popular Science News and Boston Journal of Chemistry.* This journal, of which, under its various names, he was the editor-in-chief until his death, had a large circulation and exercised a marked influence on the growth of interest in the simpler aspects of chemistry. Besides numberless editorials and articles he wrote *Chemistry of the Farm and the Sea* (1867), *Fireside Science* (1872), *From Whence, What, Where?* (1882), the sixth edition (1883) being entitled *Whence, What, Where?* and *Science at Home* (1883). Always

interested in books, he founded the Merrimac Public Library in 1877, presented it with a large number of volumes, and continued his interest and help from year to year until his death.

His unbroken interest in agriculture led him in 1863 to buy a large tract of land in Haverhill. Here he built a summer home called "Winnekeni Castle" and tried out many experiments with chemical fertilizers. His investigations led to practical results of value which were freely given to farmers. In 1878 he was made a member of the state Board of Agriculture. From 1873 to 1878 he was president of the Vermont & Canada Railroad, and from 1873 until his death, a director of the Boston & Maine Railroad. In 1844 he married Harriet Porter and in 1851 Margaret Gale. His only son was associated with him in many enterprises.

[Information from a descendant; H. A. Kelly and W. L. Burrage, *Am. Medic. Biogs.* (1920); *Biog. Encyc. of Mass. of the Nineteenth Century,* vol. II (1883); *Haverhill Gazette,* and *Daily Evening Bulletin* (Haverhill), Jan. 3, 1888; *Popular Sci. News,* Feb. 1, 1888; *Boston Jour.,* and *Boston Herald,* Sept. 21, 1870.]

L. C. N.

NICHOLS, MARY SARGEANT NEAL GOVE (Aug. 10, 1810–May 30, 1884), author, reformer, and water-cure physician, was born in Goffstown, N. H., the daughter of William and Rebecca Neal. Her girlhood was spent in Craftsbury, Vt., her parents having moved to this village when she was a small child. She had little formal schooling but educated herself as completely as possible by wide reading. Books on anatomy and physiology held a special fascination for her, and in spite of ridicule she persisted in studying them. As a young woman she taught in a district school, contributed tales and verse to local papers, and believed that she was destined for some peculiar mission in the world. In 1831 she married Hiram Gove, of Weare, N. H. This marriage proved most unhappy. After the birth of a daughter in 1832, Mrs. Gove began to devote herself to a study of books on health, receiving help and encouragement from kindly physicians. About 1837 her husband removed to Lynn, Mass., and there she found opportunity to use her knowledge in teaching anatomy and physiology to young women. Her work aroused interest and she was invited to lecture in other New England towns. Opposed by her husband in her beliefs and way of life, she separated from him in 1840, and the same year assumed for a brief period the editorship of the *Health Journal and Advocate of Physiological Reform,* a periodical published in Worcester, Mass., setting forth the principles of vegetarianism.

Ill health and difficulty in obtaining the custody of her child darkened the next few years of her life, but she persevered in her chosen field and by 1844 had established herself in New York as a water-cure physician. From 1845 to 1853 she contributed extensively to the New York *Water-Cure Journal,* published *Lectures to Women on Anatomy and Physiology* (1846), *Experience in Water-Cure* (1849), and several novelettes. She was included by Poe in his account of *The Literati,* and became well known in reform circles for her advocacy of mesmerism, spiritualism, Fourierism, temperance, and dress reform. On July 29, 1848, divorced from her first husband, she married Thomas Low Nichols [*q.v.*]. One child was born of this marriage. From 1851 to 1853 they carried on a school in New York for the training of water-cure practitioners, both of them speaking and writing, meantime, for almost all the radical causes of the day. In 1853 they joined in editing *Nichols' Journal,* a monthly magazine, published in Cincinnati, Ohio, setting forth the theory of "individual sovereignty," especially the theory of freedom in love. In 1854 they published a volume called *Marriage: Its History, Character, and Results,* expounding the same ideas. Later Mrs. Nichols published *Mary Lyndon; or Revelations of a Life* (1855), a frank account of her own career.

When the Civil War broke out, Mrs. Nichols and her husband left America for England, where they spent the remainder of their lives. They established a hydropathic institution at Great Malvern and continued their efforts to spread knowledge of sanitary science. Mrs. Nichols contributed frequently after 1875 to the London *Herald of Health,* and was well known in English vegetarian and spiritualistic societies. During her later years she was a great sufferer, but the energy and will power that had carried her through many vicissitudes enabled her to continue her work almost to the last day of her life. She died in London in her seventy-fourth year, a dauntless crusader for many unpopular causes.

[In addition to *Revelations of a Life* see: Sarah J. Hale, *Biog. of Distinguished Women* (1876); files of the *Water-Cure Jour.,* 1845–54; E. A. Poe, *The Literati* (1850); *Nichols' Health Manual* (1887); *Dietetic Reformer and Vegetarian Messenger,* July 1884.]

B. M. S.

NICHOLS, THOMAS LOW (1815–1901), pioneer dietician, hydrotherapist, author, and editor, was a descendant of early English settlers in Massachusetts. He spent an uneventful boyhood in his native village, Orford, N. H., and some quiet years at the end of his life in France. Between these two periods he was engaged in ceaseless activity to bring about some radical social or sanitary reform. He began the study of medicine at Dartmouth College, abandoned it for journalism, served an apprenticeship on newspapers in Lowell and New York, and in 1837 became the editor and part proprietor of a political paper called the *Buffalonian.* This he edited with such vehemence that he was sentenced to four months' imprisonment for libel. His first book, *Journal in Jail* (Buffalo, 1840), is a lively egotistical account of this experience. The next fifteen years of his life he spent in New York City, advocating with voice and pen the ideas of Sylvester Graham on vegetarianism and the social theories of Fourier, Josiah Warren, and J. H. Noyes. On July 29, 1848, he married Mary S. Gove [see Nichols, Mary Sargeant Neal Gove], a water-cure physician, and after completing his medical course at the University of the City of New York (1850), joined her in founding a school for the training of water-cure practitioners. He published *Esoteric Anthropology* in 1853, *Marriage: Its History, Character, and Results,* written jointly with his wife, in 1854, and wrote voluminously for the *American Vegetarian and Health Journal* and for the *Water-Cure Journal.* When his views on social questions became too radical for these papers, he and his wife established, in 1853, *Nichols' Journal of Health, Water-Cure, and Human Progress.* In 1855 they removed to Cincinnati, where they continued their paper as *Nichols' Monthly* (1855–57), setting forth in it the doctrines of free love, spiritualism, health reform, and individual liberty. For a short time (1856–57) they conducted a water-cure and "School of Life" at Yellow Springs, Ohio. Soon after this they became converts to Catholicism, were received into the church, and for two years gave lectures on hygiene in Catholic institutions in the Mississippi Valley.

With the outbreak of the Civil War they left the United States. Nichols did not believe in the war and felt that he owed no duty to a "military despotism." Thereafter he made his home in England. In 1864 he published *Forty Years of American Life,* two volumes of vivid, well-written social history. From 1867 to 1875 he and his wife conducted a hydropathic institute at Great Malvern. There he wrote a widely popular little volume entitled *How to Live on Sixpence a Day* (1871). In 1875 he began the publication of the London *Herald of Health,* and continued as its editor until 1886, trying through its columns to raise the standard of health and to teach temperate living. He established a Sanitary Depot in London as a distributing center for his publications and for the health foods and sanitary appliances which he invented. He said little during his later years on the subject of his radical social theories but lectured frequently on food reform, which he had come to regard as the root of all questions. Of his later works *Eating to Live* (1881), *Dyspepsia* (1884), and *Nichols' Health Manual* (1887) are most important. The last years of his life were spent in complete retirement. He died at Chaumont-en-Vezin, France, at the age of eighty-five, widely known as a great pioneer of food reform.

[In addition to the *Jour. in Jail* and *Forty Years of Am. Life* see: *Nichols' Health Manual* (1887); files of the New York *Water-Cure Jour.*, *Nichols' Monthly*, the London *Herald of Health* and *Dietetic Reformer*.]

B. M. S.

NICHOLS, WILLIAM FORD (June 9, 1849–June 5, 1924), second Protestant Episcopal bishop of the diocese of California, was born in Lloyd, N. Y. His father, Charles Hubert, a business man, was of old colonial stock, his first American ancestor being Francis Nichols, one of the proprietors of Stratford, Conn. His mother, Margaret Emilia (Grant) of Hobart, Delaware County, N. Y., was of Scotch descent and vigorous Scotch character. At Dutchess County Academy and at the Poughkeepsie Collegiate School, from which he graduated in 1866 first in his class, William prepared for Trinity College, Hartford, Conn. His decision to enter the ministry, although reached only after long deliberation, was the normal outcome of his training and character. He entered the Berkeley Divinity School, Middletown, Conn., in the autumn of 1870. Through the latter part of his course and for three years after his graduation, he served as secretary to the bishop of Connecticut, Dr. John Williams [*q.v.*], who became a determinative influence in his life.

He was made deacon on June 4, 1873, and ordained priest exactly a year later. His first parish was St. James', West Hartford, with the care of Grace Church, Newington. On May 18, 1876, he married Clara Quintard, daughter of Edward Augustus Quintard of New York. To them two sons and three daughters were born. In 1877 he became rector of Christ Church, Hartford, and there his gifts as pastor and administrator were quickly revealed. From 1885 to 1887 he added the duties of professor of church history at Berkeley Divinity School. In 1887 he accepted the rectorship of St. James' Church, Philadelphia. The following year he declined an election as assistant bishop of Ohio; but when California elected him in February

1890 to a like position he accepted and was consecrated on June 24. Bishop William I. Kip [*q.v.*], then over eighty, placed the entire administration in Nichols' hands, and after the death of the former in April 1893, Nichols succeeded him. The area, still administered from San Francisco, was very large; churches were widely scattered; unity of action was difficult. Los Angeles and the southern part of the state were beginning to grow with unexampled rapidity. Nichols saw that for effective church work there must be a division of territory. Such a division was made in 1895 by the erection of the diocese of Los Angeles; and fifteen years later, the vast central valley of San Joaquin with the mountains to the east was in its turn separated from the parent diocese.

Bishop Nichols' episcopate was notable for many reasons other than the general growth of the Church. He founded in 1893 at San Mateo the Church Divinity School of the Pacific (moved in 1930 to Berkeley), acted as its dean for thirty years, and also served as professor of church history. From its foundation in 1907 in Berkeley he guided the work of the Deaconess Training School of the Pacific. He organized the Cathedral chapter of the diocese, and after the earthquake and fire of 1906 secured the gift of a strategic site and began the building of Grace Cathedral. He reorganized completely the administration of the diocese, established sound financial policies, and vastly increased its resources. Through his initiative there was established in 1904 the House of Churchwomen, an official body acting in collaboration with the Convention. After the earthquake and fire he rendered distinguished service not only through his leadership in rehabilitating parishes and rebuilding churches, but also as a member of the citizens' committee in general relief work. He was early associated with General Convention as assistant secretary of the House of Bishops, was deputy from Pennsylvania in 1889, and after he became bishop was a member of many important commissions and committees. In 1902 he went to the Hawaiian Islands to carry out the transfer of the property and jurisdiction of the Church of England there to the Protestant Episcopal Church. When provinces were organized by General Convention in 1915 he was elected first president of the Province of the Pacific (comprising the coast and adjacent mountain states), holding the office until failing health led to his resignation in 1921. He continued the administration of his diocese alone until 1919, when a coadjutor was elected, to whom the Bishop surrendered the heavier work.

He traveled extensively, twice going to Europe officially; first in 1884, as delegate to the Seabury Centenary at Aberdeen, and in 1897, as a member of the Lambeth Conference. In 1911 he went around the world, commemorating the journey in a considerable book of reminiscences—*Some World-Circuit Saunterings* (1913). Among his other publications were *On the Trial of your Faith* (pamphlet, 1895); *A Father's Story of the Earthquake and Fire in San Francisco April 18, 19, 20, 1906* (pamphlet, 1906); *Apt and Meet; Counsels to Candidates for Holy Orders at the Church Divinity School of the Pacific* (1909); *Days of My Age* (1923), an autobiography; *Memories Here and There of the Fourth Bishop of Connecticut* (pamphlet, 1924).

In churchmanship Nichols was commonly accounted conservative; but his mind was unusually alert to world movements of thought, he welcomed the advances of science, and his sympathies were broad; he belonged to no school. In character he was well poised, wise, judicious, slow in forming judgments, inflexible in carrying them out when formed.

[In addition to autobiography mentioned above, see D. O. Kelley, *Hist. of the Diocese of Cal. from 1849 to 1914* (1915); C. C. Tiffany, *A Hist. of the Protestant Episcopal Ch. in the U. S. A.* (rev. ed., 1898); W. S. Perry, *The Bishops of the Am. Ch. Past and Present* (1897); *Who's Who in America*, 1924–25; *San Francisco Chronicle*, June 6, 1924.]   E.L.P.

NICHOLSON, ALFRED OSBORNE POPE (Aug. 31, 1808–Mar. 23, 1876), United States senator and jurist, the son of O. P. Nicholson and Saachy Hunter, was born in Williamson County, Tenn. After graduation from the University of North Carolina in 1827, he attended lectures in Jefferson Medical College in Philadelphia. He never practised medicine, however; instead, he became editor of the Columbia, Tennessee, *Mercury,* and a member of the local bar. In 1829 he married Caroline O'Reilly. He was an able lawyer; in cooperation with R. L. Caruthers he prepared *A Compilation of the Statutes of Tennessee* (Nashville, 1836); and in 1851, on the appointment of Gov. William Trousdale, he served for a few months as chancellor for the Middle Division of Tennessee. He was prominently identified with the development of railroads in Tennessee, as a director of the Nashville & Chattanooga and other railroads, and as an able advocate of the granting by the state of financial aid in railroad construction. In 1847 he was president of the Bank of Tennessee. Like many young lawyers, Nicholson entered actively into political life. In 1833 he began a series of three consecutive terms in the Tennessee House of Representatives, and subsequently (1843–45), he was a member of the state Senate. In 1835 he gave temporary support to the presidential candidacy of Hugh Lawson White, but he soon returned to the Jacksonian camp, supported Van Buren's candidacy, and thereafter was a faithful and prominent worker in the Democratic party. Upon the death of Felix Grundy he was appointed by Gov. James K. Polk to serve a portion (1840–42) of Grundy's unexpired term in the United States Senate. He was an ardent supporter of Polk's presidential candidacy in 1844, and on the solicitation of the President-Elect he became editor of Polk's organ and the leading Democratic newspaper in Tennessee, the *Nashville Union*. As a reward for his effective services in this capacity during the state campaign of 1845, it was expected that he would be sent again to the United States Senate. Polk desired this and the Democratic legislative caucus nominated Nicholson, but a combination of the Whig minority with anti-administration Democrats prevented his election. Nevertheless, he was recognized soon as the leader of his party in Tennessee. He supported the presidential candidacy of Lewis Cass in 1848 and was the recipient of the famous "Nicholson Letter" in which Cass sought to explain his views on the Wilmot Proviso (W. L. G. Smith, *Fifty Years of Public Life: The Life and Times of Lewis Cass*, 1856, pp. 607–16). He was a member of the Tennessee delegation in both sessions of the Southern Convention that met in Nashville in 1850, but his influence in that body was conservatively against secession and in advocacy of the acceptance of the compromise measures of 1850. He became a close friend of President Pierce but refused a place in the cabinet. Instead, as a result of the President's influence, he assumed the editorship of the administration organ, the Washington *Daily Union* (though not very effectively), and was chosen public printer to the House of Representatives. In 1857 he was elected to succeed John Bell upon the expiration of the latter's senatorial term in 1859. By no means a "fire eating" secessionist, he gave his support to the Confederacy after Tennessee's withdrawal from the Union, and for this he was expelled from the Senate on July 11, 1861. After the Civil War he was one of the leaders of the majority in Tennessee that were disfranchised by the Radicals. He was an influential member of the constitutional convention of Tennessee in 1870 that completed the overthrow of the Radical régime. For the remaining years of his life, 1870–76, he was chief justice of the supreme court of his state. He died at Columbia, Tenn.

[W. S. Speer, *Sketches of Prominent Tennesseans* (1888), pp. 332–33; J. W. Caldwell, *Sketches of the Bench and Bar of Tenn.* (1898), pp. 227–30; Roy F. Nichols, *Franklin Pierce* (1931); J. T. Moore, *Tenn.: The Volunteer State* (1923), vol. II; *Biog. Dir. Am. Cong.* (1928); Philip M. Hamer, *Tenn.; A Hist.* (1933).]   P. M. H.

NICHOLSON, ELIZA JANE POITEVENT HOLBROOK (Mar. 11, 1849–Feb. 15, 1896), newspaper proprietor and poet, was born near Pearlington, in Hancock County, Miss., the daughter of William J. Poitevent and Mary A. (Russ) Poitevent. Her mother being an invalid, Eliza grew up under the care of an aunt near what is now Picayune, Miss. In July 1867 she was graduated from the Amite (Louisiana) Female Seminary. She began to write verses "while still almost a mere girl," contributing to New Orleans papers, and to the *Home Journal* and the *Ledger* of New York. Her first productions were published in a little sheet called the *South,* whose editor, J. W. Overall, gave her encouragement. Her verses appeared over the signature Pearl Rivers, a *nom de plume* most happily chosen, since the Pearl River ran close to her girlhood home, and in its valley she spent her most impressible years. Her poems attracted the attention of Col. A. M. Holbrook, editor of the New Orleans *Picayune,* and in the summer of 1870 poems by Pearl Rivers began to be a feature of the Sunday issue. Her career and that of the paper from that time were closely connected. It has been frequently stated that she became literary editor of the *Picayune* in 1874 at a weekly salary of $25, and that she and Holbrook were married a few months later. Actually, her poems began to appear after July 1870, and according to the legal records the marriage took place on May 18, 1872. Her position as "literary editor" seems to have meant that her verses were regularly printed on the front page of the *Picayune,* for she signed no book reviews or dramatic criticisms, although she did contribute some short prose narratives.

Holbrook sold the paper to a company of New Orleans merchants in January 1872. A selection from her newspaper verses was printed in 1873 entitled *Lyrics by Pearl Rivers.* The volume was warmly reviewed in the *Picayune* on Apr. 6, 1873, and was praised by many, including Paul Hamilton Hayne. In December 1874 Holbrook regained control of the *Picayune,* but his illness and death (January 1876) prevented him from putting the paper on its feet, so that his wife was left with a debt of $80,000 and a dubious title to the paper. About six months

after Holbrook's death George Nicholson acquired an interest in the paper. A native of Leeds, England, he had gone to New Orleans in 1842 and had worked up to the position of business manager of the *Picayune.* On June 27, 1878, Mrs. Holbrook and Nicholson were married. From that time on the affairs of the paper gradually improved, until it became a prosperous enterprise. Mrs. Nicholson took an intimate interest in her paper. She introduced a society column into the Sunday issue, an innovation which conservative New Orleans society regarded at first with mild dismay. She supported many public movements, particularly the efforts of Sophie B. Wright to improve public education. Her decisions were rapid and intuitive rather than cautious, but were usually lucky. She was the first woman in the South to become proprietor of an important newspaper.

The *Lyrics* of 1873 and three small pamphlets contain all her accessible poems, numbering about fifty in all. Her best poems deal with some phase of country life and are filled with memories of swamp maples in bud, wild briers, and partridge-calls. The ambitious dramatic monologues *Hagar* and *Leah,* in spite of some good lines, are rhetorical rather than passionate. The sincerity of her emotions is usually evident, though sometimes obscured by inadequate technique and expression. It was the feeling in her poems which appealed to her many readers. Although she was slight in build and unassuming in manner, she succeeded in leaving vivid impressions of her personality. She was particularly fond of travel. She died ten days after her husband, in an influenza epidemic, leaving two sons.

[Information from files of the *Picayune* and the New Orleans *Times;* J. H. Harrison, *Pearl Rivers, Publisher of the Picayune* (1932), pub. by the Dept. of Education, Tulane Univ.; *Biog. and Hist. Memoirs of La.* (1892), vol. II; *Lib. of Southern Lit.,* vol. IX (1909); *La. Hist. Quart.,* Oct. 1923; *Times-Democrat* (New Orleans), and *Daily Picayune,* Feb. 16, 1896.]   R. P. M.

NICHOLSON, FRANCIS (Nov. 12, 1655–Mar. 5, 1728), colonial governor, was born at Downholme Parke, near Richmond, in Yorkshire, England, on a part of the vast Bolton estate, but his parentage is not known. It has been suggested (Dalton, *post*) that he was a natural son of Lord St. John, later Duke of Bolton, who came into possession of the property shortly before Nicholson's birth. But more probably, he was the son or grandson of a certain Francis Nicholson, who had assisted the Earl of Sunderland, former owner of the estate, in arranging his children's inheritance in 1629 ("Yorkshire

Royalist Composition Papers," vol. I, *Yorkshire Archæological Society. Record Series,* vol. XV, 1893, pp. 56–57). In either case, the Duke of Bolton took an active interest in Nicholson's career. In his youth Nicholson served as page to his patron's wife. He entered the army in 1679 and spent a few years in Tangier, acting as courier and aide-de-camp to the governor. After returning to England with his regiment, he is said to have knelt during mass in the tent of James II on Hounslow Heath, though his later career shows him to have been a stanch Anglican. His long connection with the colonies began in 1686 with his appointment as captain of a company of foot sent to New England under Sir Edmund Andros [*q.v.*]. Soon afterward, Nicholson was sworn a member of the Council for the Dominion of New England, and in 1688 he was commissioned lieutenant-governor. Andros was at Pemaquid and Nicholson at New York when news came of the Revolution in England. The latter handled the local situation badly. His indiscreet remarks angered the followers of Jacob Leisler [*q.v.*], while the concessions which he made to popular feeling only resulted in his losing control of the fort. Eventually he decided to sail for England, ostensibly to report on the uprising but probably in reality to avoid imprisonment.

He was disappointed in his hope of returning to New York as governor, but the home officials showed their confidence in him by appointing him lieutenant-governor of Virginia, the absentee governor of which was the Roman Catholic, Lord Howard of Effingham. Nicholson now began what was probably his most successful administration. Always taking a broad, and even continental, view of colonial affairs, he made several trips to the interior to study frontier conditions. He also sent a personal agent through the northern colonies to report on the situation there. He encouraged the establishment of postal services within Virginia and between that province and New York. His most enduring service to Virginia was the support and financial assistance he gave to the commissary, the Rev. James Blair [*q.v.*], in the founding of the College of William and Mary. In 1692 Nicholson was replaced as chief executive by Sir Edmund Andros, who had succeeded Lord Howard as governor. But two years later Nicholson was back in America, this time as governor of Maryland. Here, as in every colony in which he served, he labored to advance the causes of the Anglican church and of education, the two matters closest to his heart. His activities in these directions were so exten-

sive as to lead to the report in England a few years later that he had established "two universities and 28 churches" in America (Narcissus Luttrell, *A Brief Historical Relation of State Affairs,* 1857, vol. V, 292). As far as education was concerned, the report was exaggerated, for Blair deserves most of the credit for the College of William and Mary, while the little King William's School at Annapolis (later St. John's College), which Nicholson helped to found, did not attain collegiate rank during the colonial period. Yet, everywhere he went, Nicholson encouraged the building of schools and churches, both by appeals to the assemblies for necessary legislation and by generous gifts from his own funds. He was largely responsible for the removal of the Maryland capital from St. Mary's to the more centrally located Annapolis. He was less successful in persuading the assemblies of Maryland and Virginia to aid in the defense of New York. The Maryland legislature did agree in 1694 to send £133 if he would advance the sum, but when he offered to repeat the loan a year later, the assembly refused to accept it. The last years of this administration were marred by a series of bitter personal quarrels, during which Nicholson's ungovernable temper destroyed much of his earlier popularity. But, on the whole, he showed more than average ability in office and his services were rewarded in 1698 by his promotion to the full governorship of Virginia.

His second term in this colony was far less successful than the first. His temper became more violent than before and led to his estrangement from Commissary Blair after the latter had read him a lecture on conduct. Nicholson's dictatorial behavior aroused the opposition of several leading councilors, who accused him of trying to dominate the Council. The charge was doubtless true, although his opponents, who represented the colonial aristocracy, were equally as guilty as the governor of attempting to dominate provincial affairs. Yet he managed to do much for the good of the colony. He was the leading spirit in the removal of the capital from Jamestown to Williamsburg and in the establishment there of adequate facilities for governmental offices. He greatly improved the provincial finances and succeeded, at least partially, in making the local administration more efficient. He continued his interest in intercolonial affairs and once went personally to New York to confer with Governor Cornbury on problems of mutual concern. His downfall came, not because of a hostile Assembly, for the House of Burgesses continued friendly to the end, but because of the little group of aristocratic councilors whom he had antagonized. He was recalled in 1705.

Of his life in England during the next four years we know little except that he was elected a fellow of the Royal Society in 1706. When a joint attack upon Canada and Port Royal was proposed in 1709, he volunteered to accompany its commander, Samuel Vetch [q.v.]. Although Nicholson had attained the rank of colonel several years before, his actual military experience was slight. But he was so active in organizing the northern colonies for the enterprise that their governors persuaded him to command the contingent which was to march northward from New York. However, the whole scheme fell through when the promised troops failed to arrive from England. Nicholson returned to that country with a request from Massachusetts to renew the attack upon Port Royal the following year. The British government agreed and Nicholson, now a brigadier-general, was made commander in chief of the expedition. With 400 marines and 1,500 colonial troops, he effected a bloodless conquest of Port Royal in October 1710, thus establishing British military supremacy on the Acadian peninsula. In 1711 another joint military and naval attack upon Quebec was proposed. Nicholson was given a commission as lieutenant-general in America and made commander of the troops which were to go by land from New York. But the shipwreck of part of Admiral Walker's fleet in the St. Lawrence led to the abandonment of the entire expedition. Late in 1713 Nicholson was named governor of Nova Scotia, but he spent only a few weeks there, for he also had a series of commissions to inquire into provincial finances, clandestine trade, prize money, and ecclesiastical affairs, throughout the northern colonies. As a sort of "Governour of Governours," he proved a failure, for his temperament irritated the other colonial executives. Governor Robert Hunter [q.v.] of New York, who did not sympathize with his high-church views and who directed his farce Androborus against him, called him "that eternall teazer," and declared that "for the present folks have no manner of occasion for mad men" (New York Colonial Documents, V, 400, 453). On the other hand, the Anglicans of Newbury, Mass., praised Nicholson as "that worthy patron of vertue and religion" (Calendar State Papers, Colonial . . . 1712–1714, 1926, p. 258). His various commissions were not renewed after the accession of George I and he retired to England. During the next few years the Board of Trade often called upon him for advice on colo-

nial matters, but he was never rewarded for his American services with knighthood as has commonly been supposed.

In 1720 he undertook his last colonial governorship, that of South Carolina, whose inhabitants had declared in favor of royal rather than proprietary control. Nicholson won the confidence of the colonists and his administration was relatively quiet. But he gained the hostility of the Charlestown merchants, chiefly by failing to oppose the issue of large quantities of paper money. Eventually they petitioned for his recall. He himself was failing in health and asked for a leave of absence which was granted. He sailed for England in 1725 and died there three years later without returning to the province. He never married though he is said to have courted a daughter of Major Burwell in Virginia, and to have threatened if she were married to another, to cut the throats of the bridegroom, the clergyman, and the justice of the peace giving the license (Perry, post, p. 90). At his death he left most of his estate to the Society for the Propagation of the Gospel in Foreign Parts, of which he had long been an ardent member.

Nicholson's long and varied career in America was very nearly unique. As governor or lieutenant-governor in five colonies and as supervising official or military organizer in several others on the continent, he was almost the only Englishman of his times who might be called a professional colonial governor. His usefulness was seriously impaired by his unrestrained temper which made it difficult for other officials to work with him. An Indian, who once saw him in a fit of rage, is said to have remarked that he was "born drunk." But despite this lack of self-control, his constructive energy, zeal for education and religion, and breadth of vision, entitle him to a high rank among colonial governors.

His Journal of an Expedition . . . For the Reduction of Port Royal (1711), first appeared in the Boston News Letter, Oct. 30–Nov. 6, 1710; it was reprinted, under a slightly different title, in Reports and Collections of the Nova Scotia Historical Society, vol. I (1879). He also published An Apology or Vindication of F. Nicholson, His Majesty's Governor of South-Carolina, from the Unjust Aspersions Cast on Him by Some of the Members of the Bahama-Company (1724).

[Official documents connected with Nicholson's career are given, in full or in abstract, in Calendar of State Papers, Colonial Series, America and West Indies, 1685–1721 (1899–1933); Jour. of the Commissioners for Trade and Plantations, 1704–28 (1920–28); Colls. of the N. Y. Hist. Soc., Publication Fund Ser., vol. I (1868); Colls. of the S.-C. Hist. Soc., I (1857),

228–93 ; E. B. O'Callaghan, *Docs. Relative to the Colonial Hist. of the State of N. Y.*, III–V (1853–55) ; A. M. Macmechan, ed., *Nova Scotia Archives,* II (1900). A sketch of Nicholson by Charles Dalton, in *George the First's Army, 1714–1727* (1912), II, 54–62 (1912), corrects some errors in the article in the *Dict. of Nat. Biography.* The best accounts of Nicholson's administrations are in H. L. Osgood, *The American Colonies in the Seventeenth Century,* III (1907), and *The Am. Colonies in the Eighteenth Century* (4 vols., 1924). See also W. S. Perry, *Papers Relating to the Hist. of the Church in Va.* (1870) ; H. R. McIlwaine, *Executive Journals of the Council of Colonial Va.,* vols. I–III (1925–28).]

L. W. L.

NICHOLSON, JAMES (*c.* 1736–Sept. 2, 1804), naval officer, was a member of a notable Maryland family, many of whose members have been officers of high rank in the navy. The immigrant, William Nicholson, who was born at Berwick-upon-Tweed in Scotland, settled at Annapolis early in the eighteenth century. His grandson, James Nicholson, was born in Chestertown, Md., the son of Joseph and Hannah (Smith) Scott Nicholson. Educated in England, he went to sea at an early age and was with the British fleet at the capture of Havana in 1762. In the following year, on Apr. 30, he married Frances Witter and became for a time a resident of New York City. Early in the Revolution, having moved to the Eastern Shore of Maryland, he offered his services to his native state and was appointed captain of the *Defence,* the chief vessel of the Maryland navy. In March 1776 he checked the advance up Chesapeake Bay of the sloop-of-war *Otter* and recaptured several prizes. On June 6 Congress appointed him captain in the Continental navy and later when it fixed the rank of the captains placed him at the head of the list. From Jan. 2, 1778, when Esek Hopkins [*q.v.*] was dismissed from the service, until the Continental navy was disbanded at the end of the Revolution, Nicholson was its senior officer. He successfully maintained his right to this rank against the claim of John Paul Jones [*q.v.*]. His first Continental command, the frigate *Virginia,* built at Baltimore, was not ready for sea until early in 1777.

In the meantime Nicholson and his crew had temporarily joined the army and participated in the battle of Trenton. Because of the close blockade of the Chesapeake maintained by the British, the *Virginia* was forced to remain idle until Mar. 30, 1778, when she sailed from Annapolis for the West Indies. Running on to a shoal the next day, within sight of two British men-of-war, the ship was captured, but Nicholson escaped in a boat, with the ship's papers. An inquiry into the loss of the *Virginia* instituted by Congress acquitted him of blame, and he was never brought before a court-martial. Somewhat earlier he had

been suspended by Congress for a brief period for writing a "contemptuous" letter to the governor of Maryland. As the number of captains was greatly in excess of the number of ships, Nicholson did not obtain another vessel until September 1779, when he was made commander of the frigate *Trumbull,* fitting for sea at New London, Conn. Late in May of the following year he sailed on a cruise and to the northwest of Bermuda fought with the Liverpool letter of marque *Watt,* 32 guns, one of the most hotly-contested actions of the Revolution. After an engagement of two hours and a half both vessels withdrew seriously disabled and with difficulty reached friendly ports. The Continental Board of Admiralty congratulated Nicholson on his gallantry.

In the spring of 1781, while he was temporarily in command of a fleet consisting of the privateer *Nesbit* and two other small vessels, Nicholson convoyed Lafayette's army from the head of Elk to Annapolis. In August he again went to sea on board the *Trumbull,* this time bound for Havana, having shipped an ill-assorted crew composed of British deserters. Dismasted in a storm, his vessel was overtaken by the British frigate *Iris,* 32 guns. When called to quarters, three-fourths of her crew, by reason of disaffection or cowardice, refused to fight. With the remaining fourth, Nicholson, aided by Lieuts. Richard Dale and Alexander Murray [*qq.v.*] fought his ship for an hour and a half until forced to surrender. His next command was the frigate *Bourbon,* but the war came to an end before she was ready for sea.

In 1785 Nicholson still regarded himself as liable for naval service, for in that year he asked Congress for permission to go to sea in command of a merchantman. A few years later he was living in New York as a retired naval captain in good circumstances and active in Republican politics and in the social life of the city. His house on William Street, one of the most valuable in the metropolis, was the headquarters for the followers of Burr and Jefferson. The "commodore," as he was now called, could always be counted upon to grace and dignify the ceremonies of state occasions. In April 1789 he commanded the decorated barge that transported Washington from New Jersey across New York harbor. He once had a tiff with Alexander Hamilton and the duel that threatened possessed considerable charm for him, now a choleric old man. He had eight children. One of his daughters married Albert Gallatin [*q.v.*]. His two brothers, Samuel [*q.v.*] and John, like himself, were captains in the Continental navy. In 1801 he sought and obtained from Jefferson the commissionership of loans for New York, a post that he was filling when he died.

[*Ancestry of Albert Gallatin . . . and Hannah Nicholson* (1916), revised by W. P. Bacon; G. W. Allen, *Naval Hist. of the Am. Revolution* (1913); Henry Adams, *The Life of Albert Gallatin* (1879); C. O. Paullin, *Out-Letters of the Continental Marine Committee and Board of Admiralty* (2 vols., 1914); *Jours. of the Continental Cong.*, 1776–82.]   C. O. P.

NICHOLSON, JAMES BARTRAM (Jan. 28, 1820–Mar. 4, 1901), bookbinder, fraternal official, was a son of John and Eliza (Lowry) Nicholson, both natives of Philadelphia, and a grandson of John Nicholson, a gunsmith who came from Scotland in 1755 and settled in that city, where, during the Revolutionary War, he manufactured firearms for the Continental Army. He is said to have designed the firelock, or musket, which was adopted by the Committee of Safety. James was born in St. Louis, Mo., while his parents were temporarily residing there.

In 1822 John and Eliza Nicholson returned to Philadelphia, which was henceforth James's home. At the age of twelve he was placed in a lawyer's office as errand boy; later he was similarly employed for a drygoods house and for a grocery. At sixteen he was apprenticed to a house carpenter, but because of poor health and ill treatment he left his master. The latter attempted to force his return, but it was decided that the terms of his indenture did not demand it, and he went into the shop of Weaver & Warnick, where he learned the trade of bookbinding. After completing his apprenticeship, in 1848 he joined in a partnership with James Pawson, an English binder, and under the style of Pawson & Nicholson began a business which was continued by descendants of the original partners until about 1911. Nicholson retired from active business in 1890, his house having become one of the leading binderies in this country. He was a thorough student of his craft, which he followed as a fine art, and in 1856 published *A Manual of the Art of Bookbinding,* the first practical manual of the subject by an American. Although it was founded upon John Hannett's *Bibliopegia* (1835), it went farther than that popular work and came to be regarded as the most nearly complete treatise yet published in America.

Nicholson was as prominently identified with the life of the Independent Order of Odd Fellows in the United States as he was with the bookbinding trade. He joined the Order in 1845, was elected Grand Sire of the Sovereign Grand Lodge in 1862, Grand Secretary of the Grand Lodge of Pennsylvania in 1866, and Grand Scribe of the Grand Encampment of Pennsylvania in 1869. He held this last office at the time of his death. His efforts as Grand Sire of the national lodge were largely responsible for the fact that "the Order issued intact from the chaos of the Civil War, the only Order of the kind in the whole country, it is said, which was not disrupted by that four year struggle between North and South" (*Public Ledger,* Philadelphia, Mar. 5, 1901). His own account of the experience was privately printed in 1896 as *I.O.O.F.: The Story of '65.* He gained a national reputation for oratory, and as Grand Scribe introduced reforms into the business of the Order regarding questions of dues and benefits by which he is said to have "conferred untold blessings" upon its members (*In Memoriam,* p. 15).

While addressing a meeting at Berwyn, Pa., in December 1892, he was stricken with paralysis, which rendered useless the right side of his body and caused his death in Philadelphia nine years later. He was married, Oct. 5, 1841, to Adelaide Broadnix, and they had three sons, two of whom carried on the business their father founded. Although Nicholson was buried in Odd Fellows Cemetery, Philadelphia, the Pennsylvania Grand Lodge, I.O.O.F., in 1917 erected a large bronze statue of him in Mount Peace Cemetery.

[Nicholson family MSS., and information from a son, the late C. G. Nicholson, Philadelphia; *In Memoriam: James B. Nicholson, Past Grand Sire of the Sovereign Grand Lodge . . . I.O.O.F. of Pennsylvania* (1901); *Public Ledger* (Phila.), Mar. 5, 1901.]   J. J.

NICHOLSON, JAMES WILLIAM AUGUSTUS (Mar. 10, 1821–Oct. 28, 1887), naval officer, born in Dedham, Mass., was the son of Nathaniel Dowse and Hannah (Gray) Nicholson. His father served as an officer of the navy in the War of 1812, and his grandfather, Capt. Samuel Nicholson [*q.v.*], in the Revolution. Appointed midshipman on Feb. 10, 1838, James saw his first active service on board the *Levant* of the West India Squadron. Later, after a cruise in the Mediterranean, he was for a time attached to the New York navy yard and then to the Philadelphia naval school. In 1844, when he was promoted to the grade of passed midshipman, he was ordered to the steamer *Princeton* on special service. After a tour of duty in the Pacific, he served as acting master in the home squadron. In 1852 he was advanced to a lieutenancy and in the following year was ordered to the *Vandalia,* one of the ships of Commodore M. C. Perry [*q.v.*] destined for service in Japanese waters. For several months he was stationed with a guard on shore at Shanghai, China, to protect the foreign settlement from contending

Nicholson

Chinese. From 1857 to 1860 he was on board the *Vincennes* of the African Squadron, assisting in the suppression of the slave trade.

In April 1861 Nicholson volunteered to assist in the relief of Fort Sumter and took part in the expedition thereto as an officer of the *Pocahontas*. He was serving as her executive officer a few months later when she engaged the Confederate batteries at Aquia Creek below Washington. In October he received his first command, the *Isaac Smith,* one of the ships of Flag Officer S. F. Du Pont [*q.v.*], and participated in the battle of Port Royal. In the following year he assisted in the capture of Jacksonville, Fernandina, and St. Augustine, Fla., and for a time commanded the last-named city, as well as the waters of St. John's River where he defeated a party of Confederate riflemen. After a period of service on ordnance duty at the New York navy yard, during which he was promoted commander from July 16, 1862, he joined the West Gulf Blockading Squadron and participated with his ship, the *Manhattan,* in the battle of Mobile Bay, engaging the forts and the Confederate ram *Tennessee.*

In 1865–66 Nicholson commanded the *Mohongo* of the Pacific station and was present at Valparaiso when that city was bombarded by a large Spanish fleet. He was promoted captain from July 15, 1866. After commanding the *Wampanoag* on her trial voyage and the *Lancaster* of the South Atlantic station, he attained the grade of commodore, taking rank from Nov. 8, 1873. From 1876 to 1880 he was commandant of the New York navy yard. In 1881 he was chosen to command the European station, with the rank of acting rear admiral. In June 1882, under orders from the Navy Department, he visited Alexandria, Egypt, and when that city was bombarded by a British fleet he rescued the archives of the American consulate and received the American and other refugees on board his ships. After the bombardment he reëstablished the consulate, and, landing a detachment of marines, rendered timely aid in extinguishing fires, burying the dead, and restoring order. For his services he was commended by the Navy Department, thanked by Great Britain and several other foreign governments, and presented with a gold medal by the king of Sweden. On Mar. 10, 1883, he was retired as rear admiral. He died at his residence in New York City, leaving a widow, Mary (Heap) Nicholson, and at least one son.

[*New-Eng. Hist. and Geneal. Reg.,* Oct. 1858, for name of mother; Record of Officers, Bureau of Navigation, 1832–88; *War of the Rebellion: Official Records (Navy),* 1 ser., vols. XII, XIII, XXI; *House Misc. Doc.*

No. 46, 47 Cong., 1 Sess., *Army and Navy Jour.,* Nov. 5, 1887; *Memorials of the Mass. Soc. of the Cincinnati* (1890).]
C. O. P.

NICHOLSON, JOHN (d. Dec. 5, 1800), comptroller general of Pennsylvania, land-company promoter, was born in Wales and with his brother Samuel emigrated to Philadelphia prior to the American Revolution.

In 1781 he was chosen one of the three commissioners of accounts of Pennsylvania. The following year (Apr. 13, 1782) the legislature abolished the commission and appointed John Nicholson comptroller general of the state, as "a person of known integrity, diligence and capacity." He was given Draconic powers to settle all accounts to which the state was a party and collect all debts, except taxes, due the state. His decisions could not be appealed from and became liens on the lands of all debtors. He could issue subpoenas and commit for contempt. By giving such far-reaching powers to one man, Pennsylvania was the first state to bring order into its financial affairs during the turmoil of the Revolution. When peace was finally proclaimed, the comptroller was also given, by an act of Apr. 1, 1784, the duties of issuing certificates for pay and for depreciation on pay to the disbanded militia. He handled over six million dollars in various forms of certificates. In 1785, in addition to being comptroller, he was appointed receiver general of taxes, and in 1787, escheator general to liquidate the estates of those attainted of treason. An attempt was made to remove him from office in 1790 but his services in settling the Revolutionary accounts of Pennsylvania with the new federal treasury could not be dispensed with. On this occasion he published *Address to the People of Pennsylvania Containing a Narrative of the Proceedings against John Nicholson* (1790). Three years later he was impeached by the Pennsylvania House for redeeming certain of his own state certificates instead of funding them in federal certificates. He was acquitted by the Senate in 1794 but resigned all his offices (Edmund Hogan, *The Pennsylvania State Trials,* vol. I, 1794).

After his resignation, Nicholson became the partner of Robert Morris [*q.v.*], the financier of the American Revolution, with whom, as early as 1780, he had been interested in a glass works. He was by now regarded as one of the wealthiest men of the day. The firm of Morris & Nicholson acquired seven thousand lots in the new Federal City (Washington) and built one-third of the structures which were standing there when it became the nation's capital. They also promoted the Asylum Company with a million acres on

504

the Susquehanna as a haven for French and Santo Dominican refugees. The North American Land Company, formed in 1795 by Morris, Nicholson, and James Greenleaf, had four million acres in various states, one-half in Georgia. The Pennsylvania Land Company, formed in 1797, was their final venture. Nicholson alone promoted the Pennsylvania Population Company in 1794, with a million acres, and the Territorial Company with lands in the South Western Territory in 1795. He did much to encourage settlers to move onto the new lands, promoted industries such as Hayden's Forge, the first of the Allegheny iron works, and had agents all over Europe to induce immigration.

The financial stringency which began in 1795 and the defeat of the Federalists in Pennsylvania in 1796 brought confusion into the affairs of the land speculators. Morris was arrested for debt in 1798, but Nicholson struggled on till 1800 when he joined his partner in the debtor's prison. Here he edited *The Supporter or Daily Repast.* When he died in December of that year, he left a wife, eight children, and debts amounting to more than four million dollars. The career of John Nicholson was very similar to that of Robert Morris. Both rendered invaluable financial assistance during the Revolution, both did much to develop and settle the new territories, and both were finally broken by being too sanguine of the rapid growth of the country.

[Henry Simpson, *The Lives of Eminent Philadelphians now Deceased* (1859); E. P. Oberholtzer, *Robert Morris* (1903); W. G. Sumner, *The Financier and Finances of the American Revolution* (2 vols., 1891); J. B. Anthony, *Report on Liens of the Commonwealth upon the Lands of John Nicholson and Peter Baynton* (1839); *First Report of the Commissioners . . . to Settle the Estates of John Nicholson and Peter Baynton* (1841); *Extracts from the Diary of Jacob Hiltzheimer* (1893), ed. by J. C. Parsons; A. C. Clark, *Greenleaf and Law in the Federal City* (1901); Franklin Ellis, *Hist. of Fayette County, Pa.* (1882); *Poulson's Am. Daily Advertiser,* Dec. 8, 1800.]   G. E. H.

NICHOLSON, JOSEPH HOPPER (May 15, 1770–Mar. 4, 1817), jurist, congressman, was born probably in Chestertown, Kent County, Md., the second child of Joseph Nicholson, Jr., and Elizabeth (Hopper) Nicholson, and a nephew of James and Samuel Nicholson [qq.v.]. Colonel Joseph Nicholson, his grandfather, was high sheriff of Kent County, and for many years colonel of the county militia. Joseph Nicholson, Jr., was a member of the council of safety, or committee of observation, which shared in the government of Maryland in 1776–77. Joseph Nicholson, Jr., provided his son with a good education. When the latter was twenty-three years old he married (Oct. 10, 1793) Rebecca Lloyd, the attractive second daughter of Col. Edward Lloyd,

1744–1796 [q.v.], of "Wye House," near Easton, Md., and of the Chase House, in Annapolis. Nicholson studied law, moved to Centerville, now in Queen Annes County, Md., and rapidly became one of the prominent men in his community.

From 1796 to 1798 he was a member of the Maryland House of Delegates. He served in Congress from 1799 to 1806, and during the session of 1801–02 gained renown by insisting, although he was dangerously ill, upon being carried into the House for seventeen successive days, to cast his ballot in favor of Jefferson in the contest between Burr and Jefferson for the presidency. Nicholson displayed great ability in the House and soon, with Nathaniel Macon [q.v.] of North Carolina and John Randolph [q.v.] of Roanoke, became one of its three leaders. Between Randolph and Nicholson a strong friendship developed. Nicholson, who acted as the right-hand man for his friend in the affairs of the House, shared many of his burdens, such as the conduct of the impeachment proceedings against Judge John Pickering, 1737–1805 [q.v.]. On May 13, 1803, Jefferson wrote to Nicholson and suggested that he take the necessary steps to arrange for the impeachment of Justice Samuel Chase [q.v.]; but Nicholson was a candidate for Chase's office, which, it appears to have been well understood, he was to receive if Chase was impeached. Accordingly at a hint from Macon that no candidate for the judge's office should be the leader in the proceedings, he passed the President's charge to Randolph. Nicholson sponsored many important measures in the House and his position was such that even Jefferson, according to Henry Adams, "was glad to conciliate Joseph Nicholson, next to Randolph, the most formidable 'old Republican' in public life" (*History, post,* III, 166–67). In 1805 the governor and council of Maryland unanimously chose him as fiscal agent to sell English funds held by the state and to reinvest the proceeds in American securities. He was a poor man with a wife and six children to support; his pay as a representative was only six dollars a day and not sufficient to meet his needs. When the governor and council first offered him a position as associate judge of the second judicial district of Maryland, which carried with it a salary of $1400 a year, he declined the offer, but when in March 1806 he was offered the chief judgeship of the sixth judicial district at $2200 a year, he accepted it. His letter of resignation was read to the House on Apr. 9, 1806, by the speaker. At once Randolph wrote him: "I was not in the House when your letter to the speaker was read but I got it from Beckly and paid it the willing tribute of my tears. God bless you, Nicholson" (quoted from Nicholson Manuscripts by Bond, *post,* p. 106).

Nicholson served as a judge of the Maryland court of appeals from 1806 until his death in 1817. In one of the earliest cases over which he presided he stated that "he had uniformly been of opinion, that it was improper for the court in the last resort, to assign their reasons for the final judgment. In the inferior court it was proper that they should give the reasons of their decision, because it afforded counsel an opportunity, when they came before the court of appeals, to show the fallacy of the reasoning of the court below, if it was fallacious. He had therefore, on this account, always given the reasons of the court in which he presided. But here there was no necessity of that kind, because the decision of the court of appeals became the law of the land, whether that or their reasoning was or was not correct; and where the reasoning was bad, it was too often blended with the decision of the court, and considered likewise as the law" (*Beatty* vs. *Chapline, 2 Harris & Johnson,* 7, 26). He deviated from this rule in only two or three instances and his longest opinion does not exceed a page and a half. As a circuit judge, however, he wrote full-length opinions, which reveal the ability for which he was so highly regarded by the bar and the public. In 1810 he became the first president of the important Commercial and Farmers' Bank of Baltimore, and during the War of 1812 raised at his own expense and commanded a company of artillery. He was present at the battles of Bladensburg and Fort McHenry. Francis Scott Key [*q.v.*] married Mary Tayloe Lloyd, a sister of Nicholson's wife; Nicholson, becoming acquainted with Key's poem, "The Star Spangled Banner," caused it to be published. His death was sudden; the mayor and city council of Baltimore attended his funeral in a body and the bar and judges of the court of appeals resolved to wear crepe in his honor until the end of the court's session. He was buried at "Wye House."

[Nicholson MSS., Lib. of Cong.; C. T. Bond, *The Court of Appeals of Md., A Hist.* (1928); Henry Adams, *John Randolph* (1883); *Hist. of the U. S. A.,* vols. I–IV (1889–90); W. C. Bruce, *John Randolph of Roanoke, 1773–1833* (1922); *Niles' Weekly Reg.,* Mar. 8, 1817; H. D. Richardson, *Sidelights on Md. Hist.* (1913); *Biog. Dir. Am. Cong., 1774–1927* (1928); *Sun* (Baltimore), Sept. 25, 1904; *American and Commercial Daily Advertiser* (Baltimore), Mar. 6, 1817; Nicholson Papers, Md. Hist. Soc.]   H. Ca—s.

NICHOLSON, SAMUEL (1743–Dec. 29, 1811), naval officer, was born in Maryland, the son of Joseph and Hannah (Smith) Scott Nichol-

son and the brother of James Nicholson [*q.v.*]. Regularly bred to the sea, he was active in the patriot cause during the first months of the Revolution. Obliged to go to London on private business, he remained there for a time without official duties. On visiting Paris he was employed by the American commissioners in the line of his profession and on Dec. 10, 1776, was commissioned captain in the Continental navy. When ordered to procure a vessel at French or English ports, he went to England and returned with the cutter *Dolphin,* which he purchased at Dover. In May, having armed and fitted out this vessel, he sailed as the junior commodore in a small fleet, of which Capt. Lambert Wickes [*q.v.*] was the senior officer. In June the fleet cruised to the northward of Ireland and in the Irish Sea and Nicholson shared in the success of the venture, which included the capture of eighteen prizes. One of them was a Scottish armed brig, which surrendered to the *Dolphin* after a half-hour's engagement.

On the completion of the frigate *Deane,* 34 guns, which was built for the American commissioners at Nantes, Nicholson was placed in command of her and ordered to America, where he arrived in May 1778. Early in the following year he cruised for upwards of four months, chiefly in the West Indies, and captured several prizes, one of which, the *Viper,* mounted 16 guns. In the summer of 1779 he made a successful cruise in company with the frigate *Boston,* during which eight prizes were taken, including the ships *Sandwich* and *Thorn,* each of 16 guns. The two frigates returned to Boston with 250 prisoners, among whom were several army and navy officers. Nicholson was congratulated on his success by the marine committee. He cruised rather fruitlessly off the coast of South Carolina in 1780 and in the West Indies in 1781. In the spring of 1782 he was again in the West Indies, and captured several prizes, one of which, the *Jackal,* 20 guns, was the last naval prize taken by a Continental vessel. On his return to the United States he was relieved of his command, for a reason now unknown, and in September 1783 he was tried by a court martial and honorably acquitted.

On June 4, 1794, Nicholson was commissioned captain in the new navy organized that year, taking rank next to its senior officer. His first duty was to superintend the construction of the frigate *Constitution* at Hartt's navy yard, Boston. On her completion in the summer of 1798 he went to sea and cruised off the Atlantic coast in search of French ships. He captured the British privateer *Niger,* mistaking her for a

Nicholson

Nicholson

French vessel, and was forced to release her. In the winter and spring of 1799 he cruised in the West Indies, but with little success, since the *Constitution* was too large to chase the smaller privateers. He captured the *Spencer,* but gave her up, under a misapprehension respecting his authority, because she was unarmed. On his return to Boston in May he was detached from his ship and henceforth until the end of the war was employed on shore. Retained by Jefferson under the peace establishment of 1801, he became the first superintendent of the navy yard at Charlestown, Mass., where he died, having been the senior officer of the navy since 1803. On Feb. 9, 1780, he was married in Trinity Church, Boston, to Mary Dowse, a niece of Sir John Temple. Four of his sons were naval officers; James W. A. Nicholson [*q.v.*] was a grandson. In 1901 the torpedo boat *Nicholson* was named for him.

[G. W. Allen, *A Naval Hist. of the Revolution* (1913); *Our Naval War with France* (1909); C. O. Paullin, *Out-Letters of the Continental Marine Committee and Board of Admiralty* (1914); E. E. Hale, and E. E. Hale, Jr., *Franklin in France,* vol. I (1887); *Ancestry of Albert Gallatin . . . and of Hannah Nicholson* (1916), revised by W. P. Bacon; *Repertory and Gen. Advertiser* (Boston), Dec. 31, 1811.] C. O. P.

NICHOLSON, SAMUEL DANFORD (Feb. 22, 1859–Mar. 24, 1923), mining operator, United States senator, was a native of Springfield, Prince Edward Island, Canada, the eldest of the thirteen children born to Donald M. and Catherine (McKenzie) Nicholson, sturdy Scotch settlers. His boyhood was spent on the island, where he attended village school and the Presbyterian kirk, and worked on his father's farm. At the age of nineteen he went to Bay City, Mich., and continued his schooling there while living with an uncle and earning his board and room. After working for a short time on a farm in Nebraska, in 1881 he moved to Colorado, reaching the booming mining camp of Leadville with twenty-five cents in his pocket. A tall, reddish-haired youth, he had a good physique, courage, and perseverance. He worked for several years as a mine laborer; then advanced to positions of foreman, superintendent, and manager of various mines, his most important position being that of president and manager of the Western Mining Company. Hard-earned savings he invested in mining prospects, the first of which proved failures. Further efforts met with better results, his leases of the Colonel Sellers, the Maid of Erin, and other mines bringing him good returns. Part of the mining profits he invested in banking and public-utility enterprises in Leadville and Denver. On Nov. 28, 1887, he married Anna Neary of Clifton Springs, N. Y.

Being so closely identified with silver mining,

he naturally became a leader among the Populists when that party championed free silver. He was elected mayor of Leadville on the Populist ticket in 1893, and reëlected in 1895. A miners' strike and other difficult local problems he handled with considerable executive ability. He was sent as delegate to the Populist National Convention of 1896. A zinc-bearing aragonite ore found in a mine under Nicholson's management was named for him, "nicholsonite." Its discovery was a boon to Leadville. After the decline of the Populists, Nicholson resumed his connection with the Republican party. He had close business relations with the American Smelting and Refining Company, controlled by the Guggenheims, and worked for the election of Simon Guggenheim to the United States Senate in 1906. Nicholson was an unsuccessful candidate for governor of Colorado at the Republican primaries in 1914 and 1916. During the World War he served as state chairman of the Liberty and Victory Loan campaigns, and of the Salvation Army drive, and was a member of the fuel administration for Colorado. In 1920 he was elected to the United States Senate on the Republican ticket. In that body he concerned himself more with local than national affairs, being especially active on the committee for mines and mining. He introduced a measure providing for a secretary of mining in the president's cabinet, but it failed of enactment. His senatorial career was cut short by death in 1923. He was survived by a son and a daughter.

[W. F. Stone, *Hist. of Colo.,* vol. III (1918); J. H. Baker and L. R. Hafen, *Hist. of Colo.* (1927), vol. V; *Samuel D. Nicholson. Memorial Addresses Delivered in the U. S. Senate . . . Mar. 9, 1924* (1925); *Biog. Dir. Am. Cong., 1774–1927* (1928); *Who's Who in America,* 1922–23; *Denver Post* and *Rocky Mountain News* (Denver), Mar. 25, 1923; data from associates and relatives.] L. R. H.

NICHOLSON, TIMOTHY (Nov. 2, 1828–Sept. 15, 1924), Quaker humanitarian, was born near Belvidere, N. C., the son of Josiah and Ann (White) Robinson Nicholson, and a descendant of Edmund Nicholson, who about 1660 settled in New England. Timothy's early boyhood was spent in a typical pioneer Quaker home on a farm which offered ample outlet for his boundless energy. After attending the local Friends academy, he entered Friends (now Moses Brown) School at Providence, R. I. On his return to North Carolina he was made principal of Belvidere Academy, which flourished under his six years' direction. On Nov. 8, 1853, he married Sarah N. White. He was appointed teacher in the preparatory department of Haverford College, Pa., in 1855 and in 1859 was made general superintendent of that institution. At the age of thirty-three he removed with his family to Rich-

507

mond, Ind., where he soon established himself in
the book business with a brother. At the time of
his death he was widely known in the book trade
as the Nestor of American booksellers.

It was in the field of human betterment, however, that he won state and national recognition.
In him was embodied the Quaker ruling passion
for social amelioration. With this social impulse
he combined the scientific spirit which gave directness and effectiveness to his work in the field
of reform. During the Civil War period he was
a leader among American Friends in administering relief to the colored freedmen in the South.
The work for which he was best known began in
1867 when he was appointed as a member of the
Indiana Yearly Meeting's committee on prison
reform. It was chiefly through the persistent
efforts initiated by this committee that the state
schools for delinquent boys and girls, the Woman's Prison, and later the Board of State Charities were established by state legislation. For
forty years Timothy Nicholson was a leader in
this work, both on and off the committee. From
1889 to 1908 he was a prominent member of the
state board. In 1901 he was elected president of
the National Conference on Charities and Corrections. He was an early advocate of temperance and prohibition legislation. His association with the educational development of his
state was long and intimate. In 1862 he was
appointed a trustee of Earlham College at Richmond, in which capacity he gave forty-nine years
of distinguished service. In 1868 he was appointed by the governor as a trustee of the state
normal school and served during the formative
years of that institution. He was indefatigable
in laboring for the furtherance of peaceful methods of settling disputes among nations.

In the Society of Friends he was a distinguished leader. He filled various offices of trust
in Indiana Yearly Meeting, of which he was for
some years presiding clerk. He was instrumental in promoting the General Conferences of
Friends, the first of which was held at Richmond
in 1887, which eventuated in 1902 in a national
organization, the Five Years Meeting of Friends
in America. Uniformly benign and courteous,
he was fearless and outspoken on occasion, especially when the cause of the unfortunate was involved. Once when criticism and reprimand of
a state official were required, the State Board of
Charities laid the unpleasant duty upon Timothy
Nicholson. Accepting it, he said: "Sometimes
we Friends have to use very plain language. But
when a duty like this is to be performed, I have
long ago learned first to dip my sword in oil in
order that it may heal as well as cut" (Wood-

ward, *post*, p. 111). His first wife died in 1865,
and on Apr. 30, 1868, he married her sister, Mary
White.

[Primary source material consists chiefly of 200–
page autobiographical sketch in MSS., private correspondence, and proceedings of social welfare organizations with which Nicholson was connected; see esp.
Proceedings of the Ind. State Conf. of Charities and
Corrections, 1892–1924. For secondary accounts see
W. C. Woodward, *Timothy Nicholson, Master Quaker*
(1927); Alexander Johnson, *Adventures in Social Welfare* (1923); *Am. Friend*, Sept. 25, 1924; *The Friend*,
Sept. 25, 1924; *Indianapolis Star*, Sept. 16, 1924; *The
Survey*, Oct. 15, 1924.]   W. C. W.

NICHOLSON, WILLIAM JONES (Jan.
16, 1856–Dec. 20, 1931), soldier, came of a family represented in many wars of the United
States. He was born in the city of Washington,
his father being Commodore Somerville Nicholson, United States Navy, and his grandfather,
Maj. Augustus Nicholson, first quartermaster of
the United States Marine Corps. His mother,
Hannah, was the daughter of Dr. William Jones,
a surgeon who took part in the battle of Bladensburg in the War of 1812. A brother, Reginald
Fairfax Nicholson, reached the grade of admiral,
United States Navy.

Young Nicholson attended the schools of the
Jesuit Fathers in Washington and later (1867–
68), the preparatory school of Georgetown College. In 1876, the 7th United States Cavalry
having become depleted of officers by reason of
the so-called "Custer Massacre," Nicholson was
appointed by President Grant a second lieutenant
in that regiment, in which he subsequently served
for some thirty-seven years. He shared hardships with his regiment in campaigns against
the Apaches, Nez Percés, and Sioux, culminating in the sanguinary battle of Wounded Knee
(1890). During the war with Spain, he served
on the staff of General Sanger as major and
chief ordnance officer, United States Volunteers.
Promoted through all the intermediate grades,
he reached the rank of colonel, Aug. 24, 1912.
Later, as a participant in General Pershing's
punitive expedition into northern Mexico, he
commanded the 11th Cavalry. With the outbreak
of the World War, he was commissioned brigadier-general, National Army, and commanded
first the training camp at Camp Meade and later
a similar one at Camp Upton. In 1918 the War
Department sent him overseas in command of
the 157th Brigade, 79th Division, composed in
large part of soldiers from Pennsylvania and
Maryland. He participated with marked distinction in the military operations of the Avocourt
sector, the Meuse-Argonne offensive, and the
Bois Belleu-Côte sector, until hostilities were
terminated by the Armistice. The most notable

achievement of his brigade was perhaps its leading part in the capture of Montfaucon.

In recognition of his record overseas, he was awarded the Distinguished Service Medal for "exceptionally meritorious and distinguished services," and the Distinguished Service Cross for "distinguished and exceptional gallantry at Bois de Beuge on September 29, 1918." The French Republic made him an officer of the Legion of Honor. Tall, wiry, active in his movements, affable and just in his relations with subordinates, but forceful in the administration of his brigade, he possessed to a marked degree the qualities of a successful leader of soldiers.

He was retired from active service as a colonel of cavalry Jan. 16, 1920, by operation of law, and seven years later was advanced to the grade of brigadier-general by special act of Congress. On Feb. 6, 1883, while a student officer at the Infantry and Cavalry School, from which he graduated, he was married to Harriette Fenlon of Leavenworth, Kan. His death occurred at Washington, D. C., from a stroke of paralysis, following a hunting trip some months before in the high altitudes of Colorado, and he was buried with military honors in Arlington National Cemetery. His widow, a son, and a daughter survived him.

[Information from Nicholson's family; sketches of his career in the *Evening Star* (Washington) and *Washington Post,* Dec. 21, 1931, and in the *Army and Navy Reg.* and *Army and Navy Jour.,* Dec. 26, 1931; *Who's Who in America,* 1930–31; military facts from War Department records, *U. S. Army Reg.,* 1931, and F. B. Heitman, *Hist. Reg. and Dict. U. S. Army* (1903).]

C. D. R.

NICHOLSON, WILLIAM THOMAS (Mar. 22, 1834–Oct. 17, 1893), inventor, manufacturer, son of William and Eliza (Forrestell) Nicholson, was born in Pawtucket, R. I., but shortly after his birth his father, a machinist, moved with his family to Whitinsville, Mass. Here the boy attended the common-schools, afterwards spending a year at the academy at Uxbridge, Mass. At the age of fourteen he began his machinist apprenticeship in Whitinsville, and upon completing it three years later, went to Providence, R. I., to obtain a more varied experience. After two or three years in various machine shops in that city, he entered in 1852 the shop of Joseph R. Brown [*q.v.*], where he remained six years— the last two as manager—meanwhile studying mechanics and mechanical drawing. In the spring of 1858 he established a general machine business of his own in partnership with Isaac Brownell. A year later he bought Brownell's interest and then enlarged his shop so as to manufacture a spirit level and an egg-beater, both of

which he patented in 1860. His plans were thwarted by the outbreak of the Civil War, but in due time the demand for war materials gave him the opportunity to manufacture special machinery for the production of small arms. For this work he took Henry A. Monroe into partnership, but in 1864 sold his interest in the ordnance work to his partner and turned his attention to the development of a machine for cutting files, an invention which he had long desired to perfect.

Two patents were granted to him for a file-cutting machine on Apr. 5, 1864, and shortly thereafter he organized the Nicholson File Company in Providence and began to devise the necessary machinery not only for cutting but also for forging and grinding files. Years were required to accomplish the purpose he had in mind, and meantime he completed forty inventions and produced four hundred different kinds of files. One of the most serious problems confronting him was the task of establishing a market for his product. Trade unions combined to prevent the use of, and consumers were disposed not to buy, files made by machinery, one of the many objections being that the machine-made file required more labor in use than the hand-made file. Nicholson, however, overcame all difficulties and lived to see his business grow to be the greatest of its kind in the world. He was president and general manager of his company from the time of its inception until his death. He served as an alderman of the City of Providence for three years and was a trustee of the Providence Public Library from the time of its organization. He was director in several Rhode Island public utilities and banks and was a member of the American Society of Mechanical Engineers. He married Elizabeth Dexter Gardiner at Smithfield, R. I., in 1857, and at the time of his death in Providence was survived by his widow and five children.

[*Machinist,* Oct. 26, 1893; *Trans. Am. Soc. Mech. Engrs.,* vol. XIV (1893); *Providence Daily Journal,* Oct. 18, 1893; *The Biog. Cyc. of Representative Men of R. I.* (1881); Caroline E. Robinson, *The Gardiners of Narragansett* (1919); information from Nicholson File Company, Providence; Patent Office records.]

C. W. M.

NICOLA, LEWIS (1717–Aug. 9, 1807), Revolutionary soldier, public official, editor, merchant, appears to have been born in France, of Huguenot stock, and to have been educated in Ireland (*Pennsylvania Magazine of History and Biography,* July 1922, p. 269). He had twenty-six years' experience as a military officer before migrating from Dublin to Philadelphia in or after 1766 (*A Treatise of Military Exercise,* p. 88).

A Ludwick Nichola, who lived in Berks County and was naturalized in Philadelphia Nov. 18, 1769, seems to be an earlier arrival. He may have practised surveying in his new homeland; it is certain that he set up as a wholesale and retail merchant in Philadelphia, maintained a circulating library, and edited *The American Magazine, or General Repository*, all before 1770. His magazine (nine numbers published, January–September 1769), "the least unsuccessful" of several similar attempts in the Colonies, 1760–74, sought to promote public progress as well as to entertain and instruct its readers. Elected to membership in one of Philadelphia's two scientific organizations (1768), Nicola was a negotiator of the merger (1769) by which the American Philosophical Society was formed, repeatedly served as one of the Society's curators, published the *Transactions* as a supplement to his magazine, and gave special emphasis to scientific news and articles (Richardson, *post*). In 1774 he was appointed a justice in Northampton County, Pa., where he had established a home for his wife and daughters.

During the Revolutionary War Nicola frequently displayed his aptitude for framing ingenious projects for public service. He published three military manuals for American use, *A Treatise of Military Exercise* (1776), and two translations from the French, *L'Ingénieur de Campagne: or Field Engineer* (1776), and *A Treatise, on the Military Service, of Light Horse and Light Infantry* (1777). Early in 1776 he was appointed barrack master of Philadelphia, and from December of that year to February 1782 was town major, commanding the "home guards." He also was active as a recruiting officer, and made an historically valuable map showing the effects of the British occupation of Philadelphia in 1777–78. Doubtless irked by Benedict Arnold's misrule in Philadelphia following the British evacuation, Nicola (May 1780) proposed the appointment of a military governor for the city, recommending himself for the post. The plan was not adopted but meanwhile Nicola had been appointed (June 1777) colonel of the invalid regiment recently established by Congress. With his utilization of invalid veterans, incapacitated for field service, Nicola combined the systematic instruction of fresh recruits. From the summer of 1781 to the spring or summer of 1783 Nicola was at the main cantonment of the Continental Army, on the Hudson, and here, in May 1782, wrote the most famous of his proposals, suggesting to Washington that a change of government to monarchical institutions was in order and recommending

that Washington become king, perhaps with a title modified to allay popular prejudice against monarchy. Due to the breaking down of government under the Congress of the Confederation similar sentiments were held by numerous persons, but Nicola was not their spokesman. Washington's reply, a stern rebuke, called forth agitated yet dignified apologies from Nicola (W. C. Ford, *The Writings of George Washington*, vol. X, 1891, pp. 23–25; Dunbar, *post*, appendix).

Nicola has been severely criticized for his monarchical propositions; however, they were kept secret at the time and subsequently (November 1783) he was brevetted brigadier-general, and from time to time was entrusted with positions of responsibility in Philadelphia. He was a member of the Pennsylvania Society of the Cincinnati, and was elected to its standing committee in 1784 but did not complete his term, it being announced (March 1785) that he had "removed to a distant part of the state," probably to Northumberland County where he held property. By 1788 he was again in Philadelphia, was made commandant of the Invalid Corps, and till 1793 served as keeper of Philadelphia's "model" workhouse. Subsequently he was brigade inspector of the Philadelphia militia (his name now appearing officially as Nicolas) and maintained, it is said, a broker's shop. In 1798 he removed to Alexandria, Va., where he died Aug. 9, 1807, aged ninety. Nicola frankly regarded public appointments as a means of livelihood where "private advantage" should "coincide with the public utility." He discharged his public trusts with much diligence.

[*Pa. Mag. of Hist. and Biography*, July 1922; Nicola's letters to Washington, May 1782, in MSS. Division, Lib. of Cong.; *The American Magazine*, Jan.–Sept. 1769, one of the best files of which is in the William L. Clements Lib., Univ. of Mich.; *Proc. Am. Phil. Soc.*, vols. XXVII (1889), LXVI (1927), p. 24; J. C. Fitzpatrick, *Calendar of the Correspondence of George Washington . . . with the Officers* (4 vols., 1915); *Proc. of the Pa. Soc. of the Cincinnati* (1785); *A Synopsis of the Records of the State Soc. of the Cincinnati of Pa.* (1909); Bureau of the Census, *Heads of Families at the First Census of the U. S.* (1908); J. C. Fitzpatrick, "The Invalid Regiment and Its Colonel," in *The Spirit of the Revolution* (1924); J. T. Scharf and Thompson Westcott, *Hist. of Philadelphia* (3 vols., 1884); *Mag. of Am. Hist.*, Nov. 1883, pp. 358–60; Justin Winsor, *Narrative and Critical Hist. of America*, vol. VI (1887); L. B. Dunbar, "A Study of 'Monarchical' Tendencies in the U. S., from 1776 to 1801," *Univ. of Ill. Studies in the Social Sciences*, March 1922, vol. X, no. 1; C. S. R. Hildeburn, *Issues of the Pa. Press, 1685–1784*, vol. II (1886), F. L. Mott, *A Hist. of Am. Magazines, 1741–1850* (1930); L. N. Richardson, *A Hist. of Early Am. Magazines, 1741–1789* (1931), pp. 153–56; obituary in *Poulson's Daily Am. Advertiser*, Aug. 13, 1807.]   L. B. D.

NICOLAY, JOHN GEORGE (Feb. 26, 1832–Sept. 26, 1901), private secretary and biographer of Lincoln, was an immigrant German-American in whose career one may read the triumph of American opportunity, aided by self-education, over the limitations of poverty, hardship, and physical frailty. He was born in the village of Essingen, near Landau, in the Rhenish Palatinate, Bavaria, the son of John Jacob and Helena Nicolay. The family, with its five children, sailed from Havre to New Orleans in 1838, lived for a time at Cincinnati, moved to Indiana, shifted to Missouri, and later settled in Pike County, Ill., where the father and brothers operated a flour mill for which John George acted as scribe and business interpreter. Thrown upon his own resources by the death of his parents, young Nicolay clerked for a year in a store at White Hall, Ill.; he then entered the establishment of the *Free Press,* published in the picturesque town of Pittsfield, county seat of Pike County, a New England town settled from Pittsfield, Mass., and surrounded by the primitive environment whose tang and flavor are preserved in John Hay's *Pike County Ballads.* From printer's devil and typesetter he became editor-proprietor of the paper in 1854. In 1851 the brilliant John Hay [see Hay, John Milton] of Warsaw, Ill., came to Pittsfield to prepare for college; Nicolay and Hay at once became chums, and they remained fast friends for life. Denied the college training for which he yearned, Nicolay found his education in the *Free Press* office, in type-setting, in editorial tasks, in reading the Bible "for recreation," and in the study of books. In 1856 he sold the *Free Press* and became a clerk for the secretary of state in Springfield. Now an ardent Republican, he became acquainted with Lincoln, whose private secretary he became upon Lincoln's nomination for the presidency. Nicolay obtained Hay's appointment as assistant secretary; and the two chums thus stepped together upon the escalator of fame.

Sharing a room in the White House, the secretaries enjoyed the intimate friendship of the President, whom in their own chitchat they lovingly termed the "Tycoon," or the "Ancient." Few men, indeed, were as close to Lincoln as Nicolay or so fully enjoyed his confidence. Sometimes his duties were more than secretarial, as when he attended the Republican convention at Baltimore in June 1864 to "watch proceedings," that is, to promote Lincoln's interests. Nicolay served as consul at Paris, 1865–69; in 1872 he became marshal of the Supreme Court of the United States, serving until 1887. For fifteen arduous years, 1875–90, he collaborated with Hay on the ten-volume biography entitled *Abraham Lincoln: A History* (1890). The plan

was conceived in 1861; and before they began to write Nicolay had spent six years in collecting and arranging the elaborate mass of Lincoln papers loaned by Robert Lincoln, and had blocked out the chapters. There was constant consultation; each chose the chapters he preferred; and the manuscript of each was passed to the other for criticism. Such is the literary blending of the final product that it is practically impossible by reading the text to distinguish the style of one author from that of the other. Prepared under the scrutiny of Robert Lincoln, and written by Republicans who were "Lincoln men all through" (Thayer, *post,* II, 33), the work is caustic in treating Lincoln's opponents; yet it stands as an impressive monument, not only because of the vastness of the undertaking, but also because of its enduring historical significance.

On June 15, 1865, Nicolay was married to Therena Bates of Pittsfield, Ill., who died in November 1885. His later years were spent in Washington where he died in 1901, survived by his daughter. A son had died in infancy. He was of slight build and frail health, and labored under the handicap of severe eye trouble. Beneath a grave exterior he revealed a charming vein of humor to his intimate friends. He was interested in music and drawing, and was an inventor of various mechanical devices. Literary labors and historical interests occupied his later years. With the collaboration of Hay he edited the works of Lincoln in two volumes (1894), subsequently enlarged and published in twelve (1905). His other writings include *The Outbreak of Rebellion* (1881), which was the initial volume of a series published by Scribner's entitled *Campaigns of the Civil War;* the article on Lincoln in the ninth edition of the *Encyclopaedia Britannica* (vol. XIV, 1882); *A Short Life of Abraham Lincoln* (1902); the Civil War chapters (XIV–XVI, XVIII) in the *Cambridge Modern History* (vol. VII, 1903); and numerous magazine articles.

[The above sketch is based largely upon manuscripts furnished by Nicolay's daughter, Miss Helen Nicolay. Fragmentary data are to be found in W. R. Thayer, *The Life and Letters of John Hay* (2 vols., 1915); *Letters of John Hay and Extracts from Diary* (3 vols., 1908); Helen Nicolay, *Personal Traits of Abraham Lincoln* (1912); Tyler Dennett, *John Hay: From Poetry to Politics* (1933). See also *Who's Who in America,* 1901–02; obituaries in *Washington Post* and *Evening Star* (Washington, D. C.), Sept. 27, 1901.]

J.G.R.

NICOLET, JEAN (1598–Nov. 1, 1642), French explorer, was the discoverer of Lake Michigan, Green Bay, and Wisconsin. He was a native of Cherbourg, France, whence his father, Thomas Nicolet, was carrier of the mail to Paris. His mother, Marguerite de la Mer, was from a neighboring town, both parents being of Norman ancestry. Jean was familiar with the sea and ships and was quick to respond when Samuel de Champlain, founder of New France, asked the lad to accompany him to the New World. It was Champlain's policy to bring over promising French youths and to place them among the Indians to learn their languages in order to become interpreters. They were also to learn the lore of the wilderness and to be able to explore the unknown hinterland. In Nicolet Champlain found the qualities he sought—persistence, steadfastness, love of the wilderness, and a talent for adventuring.

Nicolet was twenty years old when he landed in New France; the same year he went with some of the French-allied Indians to live on Allumette Island, high up on Ottawa River. There he dwelt for two years, learning the native language and Indian woodcraft, but, unfortunately, he never learned to swim. During his residence on Allumette Island he went on a peace mission to the Iroquois. On his return, Champlain sent him further from the colony to live among the Nipissing. In 1624 he was appointed their official interpreter, dwelling somewhat apart, much revered by the tribesmen. In 1633, after the English occupation, he returned to Canada and became official interpreter for the colony with headquarters at Three Rivers.

Jean Nicolet's name was practically unknown until the middle of the nineteenth century, when John G. Shea, studying the sources of early Canadian history, found in the *Jesuit Relations* an account of Nicolet's western journey and discovered that he was the first known visitor to Lake Michigan and Wisconsin. Shea dated his voyage west in 1639 (*History of the Discovery of the Mississippi River,* 1852, p. xx). Immediately, Western historians took up the subject, and published all that could be found about the man and his discoveries. Benjamin Sulte proved conclusively that the voyage took place in 1634, the year before Champlain's death. Nicolet's biographers give a short but vivid description of his voyage. He accompanied a mission flotilla to Huronia, where he secured a large canoe with seven Hurons to paddle it. Mounting Lake Huron, he passed the Straits of Mackinac, entered a deep bay on the west side of Lake Michigan, and there, near the bottom of Green Bay, found the tribe he was seeking, called the Winnebago or "Men of the Sea." He had hoped to find Orientals and discovered only a new tribe of Indians. With them he made a

treaty of alliance; hundreds came to see the "Manitou-iriniou"—that is, the "wonderful man." They feasted him and admired him and thought him descended from the gods.

How far Nicolet explored in this region is a matter of controversy. Probably he did not go far inland, for he returned to Huronia by the autumn. The next year he was again at his post at Three Rivers, which he never again left for western traveling. He was drowned during a storm on the St. Lawrence, calling to his companion as his boat overturned: "Sir, save yourself; you can swim, I cannot; as for me, I depart to God." Nicolet's biographers were the Jesuit missionaries who highly esteemed him and declared he was "equally and singularly loved" by both French and Indians. He was married at Quebec, Oct. 7, 1637, to Marguerite Couillard.

[R. G. Thwaites, *The Jesuit Relations and Allied Documents,* vols. XVIII (1898), XXIII (1898); *Early Narratives of the Northwest* (1917), ed. by L. P. Kellogg; Benjamin Sulte, in *Wis. Hist. Soc. Colls.,* vol. VIII (1879) and Henri Jouan, in vol. XI (1879); L. P. Kellogg, *The French Régime in Wis. and the Northwest* (1925).]
L. P. K.

NICOLL [See also Nicolls].

NICOLL, DE LANCEY (June 24, 1854–Mar. 31, 1931), lawyer, born at Shelter Island, L. I., belonged to a family prominent in New York for nearly three centuries. He was a son of Solomon Townsend Nicoll, a successful East India merchant, and of Charlotte Ann (Nicoll) Nicoll; and through both his parents was descended from Matthias Nicolls [*q.v.*], a London barrister who came to New York in 1664 as secretary of the Duke of York's commission. After attending various private schools, De Lancey Nicoll completed his college preparatory work at St. Paul's School, Concord, N. H. He was graduated from the College of New Jersey (Princeton) in 1874 and from the Columbia Law School two years later. After his admission to the bar in 1876 and a short apprenticeship in the offices of Clarkson N. Potter and of Julien T. Davies, he began practising in partnership with Walter D. Edmonds. In 1885, while still comparatively unknown at the bar, he was appointed assistant district attorney of New York County. A series of brilliant prosecutions brought him immediate recognition as an outstanding trial lawyer. Among others he convicted Frederick Ward, the partner of General Grant, of brokerage frauds; and four of the notorious "boodle" aldermen, or "combine of thirteen" (the rest having fled to Canada), of having accepted bribes to grant a street railway franchise on Broadway. In 1887 he was the unsuccessful candidate of independent Democrats and Republicans for district attorney; but three years later he was elected on the Tammany ticket. The duties of the office were administrative, and Nicoll was chiefly engaged in directing and advising a group of able assistants whom he had appointed.

At the close of his term he refused a renomination and resumed his practice. Among his clients were labor organizations, the New York *World,* the Interborough Rapid Transit Company, and the American Tobacco Company. Three cases which he argued before the Supreme Court of the United States were of unusual interest. In the Panama Libel case (*U. S.* vs. *Press Publishing Co.,* 219 *U. S.,* 1) which concerned the publication by the *World* of sensational exposures of scandals in the acquisition of the Canal Zone, Nicoll was pitted against the whole executive department of the government from the President down. Basing his defense chiefly on narrow legal grounds, but with some attention to the constitutional aspects of the case, he won a significant victory for a free press. In the case of *Hale* vs. *Henkel* (201 *U. S.,* 43), a contempt proceeding against an officer of a corporation for refusing to testify or to produce books and papers, Nicoll, though not sustained on several important points, established the principle that papers of corporations are not subject to indiscriminate subpoena by the courts. In defending the American Tobacco Company in anti-trust proceedings (*U. S.* vs. *American Tobacco Co.,* 221 *U. S.,* 106), he argued for a reasonable interpretation of the Sherman Act and perhaps suggested the "rule of reason" which the Supreme Court announced in another case and considerably extended in this case. After the decision, which went against his client, he successfully applied the "rule of reason" in the dismemberment of the company.

Besides utilizing the resources of precedent and legal principles, Nicoll showed great originality in the preparation and presentation of cases. He liked difficult cases and was at his best before judges who were unsympathetic toward his clients. In politics he was always a Democrat except in 1896, when he voted for McKinley. As a member of the state constitutional conventions of 1894 and 1915 he supported the short ballot and other genuine reforms but fought against specious proposals. He hated demagogues and professional altruists. In private life he was a brilliant wit and a rare friend. He married Maud Churchill of Savannah, Ga., on Dec. 11, 1890, and had a son and a daughter. Only the son survived him.

[J. S. Auerbach, *De Lancey Nicoll, An Appreciation* (1931), is an excellent presentation of Nicoll as a lawyer and as a man. Obituary sketches in the *N. Y. Herald Tribune* and the *N. Y. Times,* Apr. 1, 1931, give additional details, but need to be checked carefully. The published arguments in the Panama and American Tobacco cases show Nicoll's methods of presenting cases; and the *Revised Record* of the conventions of 1894 (5 vols., 1900) and of 1915 (4 vols., 1916), his opinions on public questions. See also for certain biographical details, *Who's Who in America,* 1930–31; *N. Y. County Lawyers' Asso. Year Book,* 1931.]

E. C. S.

NICOLL, JAMES CRAIG (Nov. 22, 1847– July 25, 1918), marine painter and etcher, the son of John Williams and Elizabeth Phillips (Craig) Nicoll, was a descendant of John Nicoll, a Scotchman who emigrated to America in 1711. Born in New York City, he attended the Quackenbos School there, then worked for two years in the studio of M. F. H. de Haas, the marine painter, who was his adviser and critic rather than his master, for Nicoll always insisted that he was not the pupil of any man or any school. He went out into the country frequently on sketching trips, with De Haas and with Kruseman van Elten. Very soon he began to specialize in marine and coast subjects, and from 1868, when he began to exhibit at the National Academy of Design, he was incessantly busy painting his favorite subjects all the way along the Atlantic coast from the Gulf of St. Lawrence to the tip of Florida. His ability to suggest the appearance of water in motion, the *sine qua non* of a marine painter, was beyond all question; his waves are surely rolling; but in respect of color his pictures are not especially noteworthy. There is, at times, a certain brilliance, but depth is lacking. Textures are skilfully indicated, as in pictures of the sea, rocks, sand, and sky; this is especially true of his water colors, which were perhaps better known and more popular than his oil paintings. His "On the Gulf of St. Lawrence" and "Foggy Morning, Grand Manan" were shown at the Centennial Exhibition, Philadelphia, in 1876, and he sent two water colors to the Paris Exposition of 1878. His "Squally Weather" belongs to the Metropolitan Museum, New York. He was among the earliest etchers in New York, and his etching, "In the Harbor," was praised for its understanding of the sea. The list of his honors comprises medals from Paris, New York, Boston, and New Orleans.

Nicoll was a man of executive ability. For nine years (1870–79) he served as secretary of the American Water Color Society, of which he was the founder; and later (1904–10) he was its president. For some years he was secretary of the National Academy of Design, of which he was elected a member in 1885. He was active in the affairs of at least a half-dozen other artistic organizations in New York. He acted as secretary of the Etching Club for several years, and was president of the Artists' Fund Society in 1887. He was also secretary of the international jury of awards for paintings at the World's Columbian Exposition of 1893 in Chicago. He married Cora Anna Noble, in New York, June 4, 1873, and they had four children, two sons and two daughters. He died at his summer home at Norwalk, Conn., in the seventy-first year of his age.

[*Am. Art News*, Aug. 17, 1918; *Am. Art Annual*, 1918; *Boston Transcript*, July 27, 1918; Frank Weitenkampf, *Am. Graphic Art* (1912); *Art Jour.* (N. Y.), Mar. 1875; *Metropolitan Museum of Art, Catalogue of Paintings* (1924); *Who's Who in America*, 1916–17, which is authority for date of birth; Ulrich Thieme and Felix Becker, *Allgemeines Lexikon der Bildenden Künstler*, vol. XXV (1931); W. L. Nicoll, *The Nicoll Family of Orange County, N. Y.* (copr. 1886).]

W. H. D—s.

NICOLLET, JOSEPH NICOLAS (July 24, 1786–Sept. 11, 1843), explorer and mathematician, erroneously called Jean, came in 1832 to the United States from France. He was born in Cluses, Savoy, of poor parents and passed his early years as a herdsman on the slopes of the Alps. A priest of the locality, having discovered that the boy was very intelligent, taught him to read and secured for him a scholarship in the college at Cluses. There he proved to be a mathematical prodigy and at the age of nineteen was teaching at Chambéry. Some years later he went to Paris, where he was naturalized and in 1817 became secretary and librarian at the Observatory, working with Pierre Simon Laplace. In 1821 he discovered a comet in the constellation of Pegasus. The next year he was made astronomical assistant at the bureau of longitude and was sent to measure an arc of latitude in southern France. He became professor of mathematics at the Collège Louis-le-Grand, for which he wrote *Cours de Mathématique à l'Usage de la Marine* (Paris, 1830). Having become involved in speculations in the Bourse during the Revolution of 1830, he determined to emigrate to the United States, where he had been invited to visit. Arriving in 1832 at New Orleans, he sought first the regions of the former French occupation. At St. Louis he became intimate with the Chouteau family, members of which encouraged his plans for exploration.

His first expedition occurred in 1836, when he ascended the Mississippi in the attempt to find its source. On July 26 he arrived at Fort Snelling, where he was cordially welcomed by the officers and encouraged in his purpose to continue to the headwaters of the Mississippi. Two months later he returned to Fort Snelling having had many adventures among the Chippewa, especially those of Leech Lake, whose chief he persuaded to accompany him to the fort. On Sept. 29, 1836, the Indian agent at the fort wrote Governor Dodge of Wisconsin: "Mr. Nicollet who has just returned (Sept. 27) from the sources of the Mississippi found the Chippewa of Leech Lake in great excitement; his situation was critical and unpleasant" (Indian Office files, Washington). The explorer spent the winter with the officers at the fort and the next year was invited by Secretary Poinsett to visit Washington. In 1838 he headed an official expedition for a survey of the upper Missouri. On this occasion he was accompanied by Lieut. John C. Frémont [*q.v.*], who joined him at St. Louis. Notwithstanding a slight physical frame, unsuited to the hardships of exploration, Nicollet's eager spirit urged him to continue his adventures. In 1839 he made a second survey up the Missouri in the steamboat *Antelope,* reaching Fort Pierre in seventy days. From this point he rode northward across the plains towards the sources of the Red River of the North, exploring as far as Devil's Lake in North Dakota. Upon his return to Washington he devoted his time to the preparation of a map of the region northwest of the Mississippi, dwelling with Ferdinand R. Hassler [*q.v.*], chief of the Coast Survey. He prepared also *Report Intended to Illustrate a Map of the Hydrographical Basin of the Upper Mississippi* (1843), published by the government after its author's death, which occurred at Washington.

Nicollet was an urbane, polished gentleman, with a superior mind. He was a musician as well as a mathematician and was a great favorite in social circles, particularly in New Orleans and St. Louis, where he felt at home among the residents of French descent. The Western states are indebted to him for his early surveys and his enthusiastic descriptions of primitive conditions. Minnesota has several place names in his honor.

[J. C. Frémont, *Memoirs of My Life* (1887); *Minn. Hist. Soc. Colls.*, vols. I (1872), VI (1894), VII (1893); *La Grande Encyc.*, vol. XXIV; *Globe* (Washington, D. C.), Sept. 11, 1843; Journals and Reports (MSS.) in Lib. of Cong.]

L. P. K.

NICOLLS, MATTHIAS (Mar. 29, 1626–Dec. 22, 1687?), provincial secretary of New York, jurist, was born at Plymouth, England, the son of the Rev. Matthias Nicolls and his wife, Martha Oakes. The family, whose name was variously spelled Nicolls, Nicoll, or Nicholls, had been established at Islip, Northamptonshire, since the fifteenth century. Following his education at Plympton grammar school and Lincoln's Inn, where he was admitted Nov. 27, 1649, Matthias took up the practice of law in London. In 1663 Samuel Maverick, who had been appointed one of the royal commissioners to investigate conditions in New England, secured for him the position of secretary to the commission (*Collections of the New York Historical Society,* Publication Fund Series, vol. II, 1870, p. 57). Together with his wife, the former Abigail Johns, and their two children, Nicolls accompanied the expedition to America in the following year. The principal member of the commission, Richard Nicolls [*q.v.*], to whom Matthias was not related, was also appointed governor of New York by the Duke of York and charged with the task of wresting that province from the Dutch. After the conquest, the new English governor named Matthias Nicolls secretary of the province, a position he held continuously until 1680 except for the short period of Dutch reoccupation in 1673–74. In his capacity as secretary he was a member of the council and served as presiding judge in the court of assizes. He also held a number of other offices. He was captain of a military company and was twice appointed mayor of New York City, 1671–72 and 1674–75. After the abolition of the court of assizes and the reorganization of the provincial judicial system in 1683 he became judge of the court of oyer and terminer and continued to act in that capacity during the remainder of his life. In 1683 he was also chosen speaker of the first assembly called in the province. Matthias Nicolls is best known, however, as the reputed principal author of the legal code known as the "Duke's Laws" promulgated by Governor Nicolls in 1665. Unquestionably the provincial secretary, with his legal training, had a large part in the drafting of the document, though his exact contribution cannot be determined. Many sections were drawn from codes of New England, since the inhabitants first affected by its provisions were those of Long Island and Westchester, a large proportion of whom had originally come from the Puritan colonies. Other sections of the code were simply adaptations of familiar English practices to the immediate circumstances of the province. The system of government established by this code served on the whole as a highly satisfactory and adequate arrangement during the transition period of the colony's history. (See A. E. McKinley, "The Transition from Dutch to English Rule in New York," *American Historical Review,* July 1901.)

Nicolls acquired a considerable tract of land at Cow Neck (now Manhasset), Long Island, where he established an estate. He is said to have had several children, but according to family tradition all except one daughter and one son, William [*q.v.*], were drowned in an accident in the East River near Hell Gate, the latter saving himself by swimming to the shore. According to family tradition, Nicolls died Dec. 22, 1687, but his name appears in a list of those appointed Apr. 16, 1688, to a special court of oyer and terminer in New York (*Calendar of Council Minutes, post,* p. 58), and letters of administration on his estate were not granted until 1693.

[*The Records of the Honorable Society of Lincoln's Inn,* vol. I, "Admissions" (1896), p. 261; *Docs. Rel. to the Col. Hist. of the State of N. Y.,* vols. III (1853), XIV (1883); I. N. P. Stokes, *The Iconography of Manhattan Island,* vols. IV, VI (1922, 1926); New York State Library, *Calendar of Council Minutes, 1668–1783* (1902); *N. Y. Hist. Soc. Colls.,* Pub. Fund Ser., XXV (1893), 219–20; B. F. Thompson, *Hist. of Long Island* (3rd ed., 4 vols., 1918); De Lancey Nicoll, *Matthias Nicolls 1626–1687* (address delivered before the Society of Colonial Dames of the State of New York, Jan. 21, 1915, privately printed); E. H. Nicoll, *The Descendants of John Nicoll of Islip, England* (n.d., Pref. 1894); and information supplied from family records by De Lancey Nicoll, Jr.] L. W. L.

NICOLLS, RICHARD (1624–May 28, 1672), the first English governor of New York, was the fourth son of Francis Nicolls, a barrister of Ampthill, Bedfordshire, and his wife Margaret, daughter of Sir George Bruce. The family was stanchly royalist, and in 1643 Richard took command of a troop of horse against the parliamentary forces. The words used in this connection on his epitaph, *"relictis musarum castris,"* have led writers to assert that he abandoned a university career to enter the army, but no record of his matriculation at either Oxford or Cambridge has been found. In 1663, however, Oxford conferred a doctorate of laws upon him (Anthony à Wood, *Fasti Oxonienses, The Second Part,* 1820, ed. by Philip Bliss, p. 275). Nicolls, together with two brothers, followed the Stuarts into exile, where he attached himself to the Duke of York, serving under the latter's command in the French army (*Documents Relative to the Colonial History of the State of New York,* III, 133). It was probably during this service that he gained the title of colonel by which he was always subsequently known. He was never knighted as sometimes has been said. Upon the Restoration, he became a groom of the bedchamber to the Duke of York.

In 1664, when Charles II determined to seize the Dutch colony of New Netherland and conferred the lands between the Connecticut and

Delaware rivers upon the Duke of York, the latter appointed Nicolls governor of the province about to be acquired. The king also made him the principal member of a commission of four men empowered to investigate the condition of affairs in New England, to hear complaints and appeals in the colonies of that region, and to bring them under closer control of the Crown. Nicolls and his associates, accompanied by three companies of troops and a squadron of four vessels, sailed from England in May. After spending a few weeks on the New England coast the squadron blockaded New Amsterdam on Aug. 18 (Aug. 28, new style) and shortly afterwards Nicolls sent a summons to Peter Stuyvesant [q.v.], the director general, to surrender. Stuyvesant favored resistance, but was opposed by the leading inhabitants when they learned that Nicolls offered liberal terms for submission to English authority. The capitulation took place without bloodshed on Aug. 29 (Sept. 8, new style), and subordinates of Nicolls soon effected the occupation of all other Dutch posts.

The new governor began at once the difficult task of organizing the administration in conformity with his instructions from the Duke of York. He wisely made the transition to English institutions of local government as gradual as possible and appointed many of the Dutch inhabitants to minor offices. Since many towns on Long Island had been settled by New Englanders, Nicolls promised them equal, if not greater, freedoms and immunities than any of his Majesty's colonies in New England (*Documents . . ., XIV, 561*). Nevertheless, the authority given to the Duke of York by his charter was extensive and he never intended that his governor should establish an elective legislature. In March 1664/65, Nicolls issued a legal code, known as the "Duke's Laws," which he had prepared with the assistance of the secretary, Matthias Nicolls [q.v.], and the court of assizes. The new code, which was largely drawn from the codes of Massachusetts and New Haven, was put in force at once in the English parts of the colony and was gradually extended to the Dutch communities as well. Some outspoken criticism arose among the Long Islanders at the absence of any provision for an assembly such as they had expected from Nicolls' earlier promises, but in spite of his arbitrary powers, he ruled so fairly and well that he gained almost universal respect and esteem.

He was so much occupied with the affairs of New York that he was able to devote little time to his duties as head of the royal commission to New England. After the other commissioners had met with some success in Plymouth, Rhode Island, and Connecticut, Nicolls joined them in Boston in May 1665. But the theocratic leaders of Massachusetts were so determined to preserve their system of control without interference that the royal appointees were able to accomplish nothing. The Massachusetts General Court defended its actions in an address to the king in which it charged all the commissioners except Nicolls with acting in a spirit of partisanship (*Records of the Governor and Company of the Massachusetts Bay,* vol. IV, pt. 2, 1854, p. 274).

Nicolls remained in office in New York until his resignation as governor, which took effect in August 1668. His departure was accompanied with every evidence of the high regard in which the colonists held him. Once more in England, he resumed his place as groom of the bedchamber to the Duke of York. On the outbreak of the Third Dutch War in 1672 he volunteered to serve in the fleet and was killed at the battle of Solebay. He was buried in Ampthill Church, where a monument was erected enclosing in its upper portion the cannon ball which had killed him, and bearing the words *"Instrumentum mortis et immortalitatis."*

[E. B. O'Callaghan, *Docs. Rel. to the Col. Hist. of the State of N. Y.,* vols. II, III (1858, 1853); and Berthold Fernouw, *Ibid.,* vol. XIV (1883); *Notes & Queries,* Mar. 14, 1857; Charles Wolley, *A Two Years Journal in New York* (1860), ed. by E. B. O'Callaghan which quotes Nicolls' epitaph; J. R. Brodhead, *Hist. of the State of N. Y.* (2 vols., 1853, 1871); sketch by E. H. Nicoll in *N. Y. Geneal. and Biog. Reg.,* July 1884; A. E. McKinley, "The Transition from Dutch to English Rule in New York," *Am. Hist. Rev.,* July 1901; manuscript correspondence of Nicolls, especially with Governor Berkeley of Va., in the Huntington Lib., San Marino, Cal.]   L. W. L.

NICOLLS, WILLIAM (1657–May 1723), colonial lawyer and politician, was born in England, the son of Matthias Nicolls [q.v.], the first secretary of the province of New York, and of Abigail (Johns) Nicolls. He probably accompanied his father to America in 1664, but went back to England in 1677 and spent two years in the army, seeing service in Flanders. Following his return to New York, he began the practice of law. He was appointed clerk of Queen's County in 1683 and became attorney general of the province in 1687. When the Leislerian revolt took place in 1689, he ranged himself at once on the side of the conservatives. In a private letter he forcefully though indiscreetly described the *de facto* lieutenant-governor as "that incorrigeable brutish coxcomb Leisler," and with reference to the party in control declared that "out of hell certainly never was such a pack of ignorant, scandalous, false (malitious), impudent, impertinent rascalls herded together" (*Documents . . ., post*, III, 662–63). The interception of this letter in January 1690 gave Leisler [*q.v.*] an excuse for the arrest and imprisonment of Nicolls. The latter remained in custody until the collapse of Leisler's administration in March 1691, with the arrival of Governor Sloughter, in whose instructions Nicolls was named a councillor. For the next seven years his star was in the ascendent. He was one of the prosecutors who brought about the conviction of Leisler and his associate Milborne. Governor Sloughter's successor, Fletcher, added to Nicolls' already large holdings in Suffolk County until his estate at Islip contained more than one hundred square miles. At various periods he also acquired large tracts of land on Shelter Island. In 1695 he was one of two agents sent to England to discuss measures for the colony's defense. On the voyage he and his colleagues were captured by the French, but ultimately were exchanged and reached London, where they made a strong plea for the total reduction of the French in Canada.

In 1698 Fletcher was replaced as governor by Richard Coote [*q.v.*], Earl of Bellomont, who was soon identified with the Leislerian party in colonial politics. Nicolls was one of the first to suffer, being suspended from the council on charges of having participated in Fletcher's profitable negotiations with pirates. The Board of Trade thought the evidence sufficiently conclusive to justify Nicolls' definite removal as councilor. Bellomont also accused him of bribery in the passage of an act injurious to the interests of New York City. Nicolls' political ambitions had now to be satisfied through the assembly rather than through the council. At first he contented himself merely with electioneering. Bellomont, who later admitted that he was "the most sensible man of the [anti-Leislerian] party, and the hottest," declared that in the election of 1698 Nicholls "rode night and day about the country with indefatigable pains" (*Documents*, IV, 783, 507). In 1701 he was chosen to represent Suffolk County in the assembly and came within one vote of election as speaker, but the Leislerian majority brought about his disqualification as a deputy on the ground that he was not a resident of Suffolk County although he was one of its most important freeholders. Thereupon he built a house upon his Islip estate and made it his permanent residence. In 1702 he was again chosen deputy and this time was the successful candidate for speaker. He held this office continu-

ously until 1718 when he resigned because of ill health, though he retained his seat as deputy during the remaining five years of his life. In his capacity as speaker he took an active part in the assembly's successful efforts to gain control of finance at the expense of the governor.

Nicolls was recognized as one of the ablest lawyers in the colony and participated in many important cases. Among these, besides the prosecution of Leisler and Milborne, were the trials of Nicholas Bayard [*q.v.*] for treason in 1702 and of the Rev. Francis Makemie [*q.v.*] in 1706 for preaching without the governor's license. In both cases Nicolls represented the defense and in both cases the accused were ultimately freed. In 1693 Nicolls married Anne, daughter of Jeremiah Van Rensselaer and widow of her cousin Kiliaen Van Rensselaer. His will, drawn up in 1719, mentions six sons and three daughters.

[E. B. O'Callaghan, *Docs. Rel. to the Colonial Hist. of the State of N. Y.*, vols. III, IV (1853–54), and *Doc. Hist. of the State of N. Y.*, vol. II (1849); *Jour. of the Votes and Proc. of the Gen. Assembly of the Colony of N. Y.*, vol. I (1764); B. F. Thompson, *Hist. of Long Island* (4 vols., 1918); J. R. Brodhead, *Hist. of the State of N. Y.*, vol. II (1871); Nicolls' will in *N. Y. Hist. Soc. Colls.*, Pub. Fund Ser., vol. XXVI (1894).]   L. W. L.

NIEDRINGHAUS, FREDERICK GOTTLIEB (Oct. 21, 1837–Nov. 25, 1922), manufacturer, congressman, was born in Lübbecke, Westphalia, the son of Frederick William and Mary (Siebe) Niedringhaus. His entire academic training was received before he left Germany. In 1855, with the other members of his family, he came to the United States, settling immediately in St. Louis. He first worked at a tinner's bench, making such common household articles as he could market in his immediate neighborhood. In 1862 his brother, William, became his partner. Until this time tinware vessels of all kinds had been made by soldering pieces together; the stamping of entire articles from single sheets of tin, then a new French process, had not as yet been introduced into the United States. Niedringhaus was instrumental in bringing to America a Frenchman who was familiar with this stamping process, and the new method was introduced by the Niedringhaus Brothers into their factory, which they incorporated in 1866 under the name of the St. Louis Stamping Company, with Frederick G. Niedringhaus as president. In addition to the new stamping process, which was a complete success from the beginning, Niedringhaus himself conducted a long series of experiments by which he tried baking many different kinds of chemicals on steel plates, and at length developed and introduced a method of enameling steel plates which added greatly to the cleanliness of cooking utensils and made them rust proof. The business grew so rapidly that new quarters had to be found. Accordingly, after a survey, a tract of farm land in Illinois, just across the river from St. Louis, was acquired, and a large group of influential investors were interested who assured adequate capital. When the plant was moved to its new location, the name of the concern was changed to the National Enameling & Stamping Company, but Niedringhaus continued as president until his retirement in 1908, after which he served as chairman of the board of directors. The new enameling process gave the name to Granite City, Ill., where the factory was established.

In 1888 Niedringhaus was elected to the Fifty-first Congress of the United States, from the eighth congressional district of Missouri. He served one term, Mar. 4, 1889–Mar. 4, 1891, and became a stanch supporter of protection, especially of the tin-plate industry. With his business well founded, with adequate protection by means of the tariff from outside competition, he turned his attention to the labor question within his own plant. At considerable expense to himself, he brought to the United States a colony of Welshmen and established them near his factory in Granite City, Ill. His other business connections were numerous. He was president of the Granite Realty & Investment Company, a director of the Blanke-Wenneker Candy Company, president of the St. Louis Press Brick Company, vice-president of the Granite City Gas Company, and a director of the Louisiana Purchase Exposition Company. He was a member of Grace Methodist Church, St. Louis, and was affiliated with several St. Louis clubs. His chief recreations were reading and walking. In 1860 he married Dena Key of St. Louis. Ten children were born to them. He died at his home in St. Louis, in his eighty-sixth year.

[*St. Louis Star, St. Louis Globe-Democrat,* and *St. Louis Post-Dispatch,* Nov. 26, 1922; Wm. Hyde and H. L. Conard, *Encyc. of the Hist. of St. Louis* (1899), III, 1643; *The Book of St. Louisans* (1912); *Who's Who in America, 1922–23.*]   **O. B.**

NIEMEYER, JOHN HENRY (June 25, 1839–Dec. 7, 1932), artist, teacher of drawing, was born in Bremen, Germany, a son of Charles Henry and Margareta Dorettea (Otto) Niemeyer. In his childhood his parents removed to the United States, settling in Cincinnati, where the boy grew up and was educated in the city schools. About 1858 he was living in Indianapolis and working in a sign painter's shop. In November 1860 he moved to New York City,

and later taught in a school in New Jersey until he had enough money to go to Europe. In 1866 he was in Paris, where he pursued his studies for about four years. At the École des Beaux Arts he worked under Jean Léon Gérôme and Adolphe Yvon. He also studied with Sébastien Cornu. His main work as a student, however, was done under Jacquesson de la Chevreuse, who was then carrying on the atelier of Ingres and the classical traditions of that master. Of all his teachers, de la Chevreuse influenced him most. During this time, Augustus Saint-Gaudens [*q.v.*], who had come to Europe to study, was supporting himself by cutting cameos in Paris. His evenings he spent with Niemeyer, who taught him what he himself had learned during the same day in the studio of de la Chevreuse. Saint-Gaudens in his greatness never forgot his youthful teacher. Later pupils who won renown were Frederic Remington and Bela Lyon Pratt [*qq.v.*].

After receiving three medals in the government schools, Niemeyer returned home in 1870, and in 1871 became professor of drawing in the Yale Art School. Here he remained until his retirement with the title emeritus in 1908, having in the interval been made Street Professor of Drawing. He came to be a great teacher of drawing, by some considered unsurpassed in the entire country. On the walls of the room in which he gave instruction he placed a quotation from Ingres, "Drawing is the probity of art." For some years he gave lectures on the fine arts at Smith College, and assisted in laying the foundations of the art school and collection there. He exhibited his canvases in the annual exhibitions of the National Academy of Design, of which he was made an associate member in 1905. He was also a member of the Society of American Artists and of the American Art Association of Paris. Competent critics, among them George De Forest Brush, considered his work unexcelled by any artist of his day in beauty and precision of line and perfection of modeling.

In the Graduates Club (New Haven), Niemeyer is represented by fine portraits of President Woolsey (a full-length, painted in 1876), Prof. Bernadotte Perrin, Prof. William Dwight Whitney, and Prof. Thomas R. Lounsbury. The Yale School of the Fine Arts owns his "Gutenburg Discovering Movable Types" (1872), a "Portrait of a Lady," and a number of his masterly drawings from the antique, dating from his student days in Paris. In his private collection were examples of the work of Julian Alden Weir and John H. Twachtman, both lifelong friends, and of John La Farge. One of Niemeyer's most admired canvases is his portrait of the late Theodore S. Gold, of Cream Hill, Cornwall. He was also notably successful in his portraits of Prof. Hubert Newton—a fine piece of characterization and composition and beautiful in color—and of Dr. John Slade Ely, sometime dean of the Yale School of Medicine. Niemeyer also executed some bas-reliefs, among them a large medallion of William M. Hunt (1883) and "Lilith Tempting Eve" (1883). Among his etchings is a notable portrait of President Woolsey of Yale. His self-portrait hangs in the dean's office of the Yale School of the Fine Arts.

He was married, July 10, 1888, to Anna Beekman Talmage, a daughter of the Rev. Goyn Talmage of Port Jervis, N. Y., and a niece of Rev. T. DeWitt Talmage [q.v.]. She was a woman of strong mentality and had a keen appreciation of the fine arts. After Niemeyer's retirement they spent much time abroad, especially in Paris, Normandy, and Brittany. He died in New Haven.

[G. D. Seymour, in *Yale Alumni Weekly*, Dec. 16, 1932; M. Q. Burnet, *Art and Artists of Ind.* (1921); *Am. Art Annual, 1923*; *Who's Who in America*, 1930–31; *New Haven Jour.-Courier*, Dec. 8, 1932.] G. D. S.

NIES, JAMES BUCHANAN (Nov. 22, 1856–June 18, 1922), Protestant Episcopal clergyman and archaeologist, was born at Newark, N. J., the son of Simon and Antoinette Fredrika (Landano) Nies. While he was still a boy, his family removed to New York City, where he began his education in the public schools. After attending Trinity College, Hartford, Conn., for a term, he studied successively at Columbia College, from which he received the degree of A.B. in 1882, and at the General Theological Seminary, from which he graduated in 1885. Ordered deacon that same year and priested in 1886, he was meanwhile in charge of a mission of Holy Trinity, Harlem. From 1886 to 1887 he was rector of St. John's, Tuckahoe, N. Y., with charge of St. John's, Upper New Rochelle, and then for five years (1887–92) vicar of Christ Chapel, Brooklyn. In the meantime he had done graduate work at Columbia and was awarded the degree of Ph.D. in 1888. From 1892 to 1898 he was rector of the Church of the Epiphany, Brooklyn. He then retired, on account of rheumatism, from the active ministry, except for two years (1905–07) when he served as rector of Christ Church, Sharon, Conn. Possessed of private means, he devoted himself to travel and archaeology. His chief interest lay in southern Italy, Greece, Egypt, and especially Palestine; but he also visited other regions, such as Lake Titicaca, Peru. On Sept. 3, 1891, he married Jeanie Dows, daughter of Alexander E. Orr of

Brooklyn, and after her death, having no children, he made his home in that city with his brother, Frederick Nies.

Deeply interested in the archaeology of the Holy Land, Nies sought successfully to organize systematic excavation there by his compatriots through endowment of the American School for Oriental Study and Research at Jerusalem, of which he was field-director in 1901. It was there that he died, having returned to erect for the School a building named in honor of his wife. He also bequeathed to it gifts valued at some $25,000, while to Yale University he left his rich collection of Babylonian clay tablets, together with $50,000 for their augmentation. He was a member of many learned societies, among them the American Association for the Advancement of Science, of which he was a fellow, and the American Oriental Society.

Nies wrote comparatively little, his published volumes being *Ur Dynasty Tablets* (Leipzig, 1920) and *Historical, Religious and Economic Texts and Antiquities* (volume II of *Babylonian Inscriptions in the Collection of James B. Nies*, New Haven, 1920). He also contributed a few articles to technical journals, among which may be mentioned "Kufic Glass Weights and Bottle Stamps" (*Proceedings of the American Numismatic and Archaeological Society*, 1902), and "A Pre-Sargonic Inscription on Limestone from Warka" (*Journal of the American Oriental Society*, June 1918). Although his published works were few, he rendered service of much importance by collecting material, by making research possible for others, and, above all, by his labors for the American School at Jerusalem. He possessed a remarkable, almost intuitive, talent for reading cuneiform, and his personality won the hearty cooperation of all associated with him. Theologically he belonged to the evangelical (Low Church) wing of his communion, but with liberal (Broad Church) tendencies.

[A. T. Clay, in *Bull. Am. Schools of Oriental Research*, Oct. 1922; *Who's Who in America*, 1922–23; *N. Y. Times*, June 20, 1922; information from a sister-in-law.] L. H. G.

NIES, KONRAD (Oct. 17, 1861–Aug. 10, 1921), poet, was born in Germany at Alzey in Rhenish Hesse, the third of the four sons of Franz and Katharina Margarethe (Breyer) Nies. His father was a prosperous baker. Nies attended the public school of his native town, was apprenticed for two years to a dry-goods merchant at Worms, and at the age of seventeen entered an actors' training school at Leipzig. He played for brief engagements in a stock company at Aachen and in guest performances at Chemnitz and Kaiserslautern, but even the roving life of a young actor could not satisfy his inveterate *Wanderlust*, and in August 1883 he emigrated to the United States, making his headquarters at first with his brother Philip at Newark, Ohio. For a short time he attended Doane Academy at Granville. Through his boyhood friend, Fannie Bloomfield (later Fannie Bloomfield-Zeisler), he secured introductions to various people in Chicago and Milwaukee and became a traveling representative of the Freidenker Publication Company. In Milwaukee he met Elisabeth Waldvogel, whom he married in 1887. She remained loyal to him throughout all the vicissitudes of his career and supported him by her labor when he himself was too ill to work. They had two children, a son and a daughter.

For a short time after his marriage Nies lived at Omaha, Nebr., where he began to edit a monthly publication of his own. In 1888 he became a teacher of German in the Newark, Ohio, high school, but his literary ambition soon took him to New York, where, during the years 1888–90, he continued his monthly, *Deutsch-Amerikanische Dichtung*, devoted to the cultivation of German literature in America. His first volume of verse, *Funken*, was published at Leipzig in 1891. He visited his home in Germany in the summer of 1892. Meanwhile he had developed tuberculosis of the larynx from which he sought relief in brief residences at Palenville, N. Y., and Orlando, Fla. In 1894–95 he visited the literary centers of Germany and Austria, became acquainted with many persons of note, but avoided the men and methods of the naturalistic movement. He lectured on "German Literature in America" in Berlin, Breslau, and Wiesbaden. Discontented, he returned to America and took over the direction of the Victoria Institute, a private school for girls in St. Louis. But he was not the man to stick to one task for any length of time. He began traveling again far and wide over the United States and Canada, lecturing and reading poetry wherever Germans resided in large numbers. He thus visited at least seventy-three cities on the North American continent, returning to some of them more than ten times. In this way he became known and liked everywhere. By his example and by inspiring others he hoped to keep alive the appreciation of German poetry among the Germans of America. Between 1900 and 1905 he published at St. Louis four short verse-dramas: *Deutsche Gaben* (1900), *Rosen im Schnee* (1900), *Im Zeichen der Freiheit* (1902), and *Die herrlichen Drei* (1905). While he was desperately ill again in 1900–02, his friends collected funds which enabled him to rest and travel abroad during 1905–07. He now published a second volume of poetry, *Aus Westlichen Weiten* (Leipzig, 1905). To this period belongs his ardent and, in the end, disillusioning, friendship with a young Russian noblewoman, Olga Khripounoff.

Partly because of his own shiftlessness his family life was wrecked, many friends estranged, and valuable connections severed. A modest inheritance from his mother, however, enabled him once more to unite with wife and children under one roof. He took up residence in San Francisco in 1909. For the peace of his soul he turned to spiritualism, theosophy, and later to the anthroposophy of Rudolf Steiner. The economic problem of his life he hoped to solve by founding a quasi-communistic colony in California, but the plan did not materialize. With the help of generous friends in Denver, Colo., he acquired a cottage on the southeastern slope of Mount Tamalpais, Marin County, Cal. There, in his "Waldnest," overlooking San Francisco Bay, he spent the last seven years of his life in solitude, poverty, and greatest simplicity. During these years he wrote some of his most mature poetry, *Welt und Wildnis* (Leipzig, 1921). This period of retirement was interrupted when Nies was called to become editor-in-chief of the *Colorado Herold* during the critical year 1916–17. It was his dearest hope that the country of his adoption would not take up arms against the country of his birth. Disappointment made him age rapidly and visibly. He died after a belated appendectomy in the German Hospital at San Francisco on Aug. 10, 1921.

Nies had a lovable, winning, even inspiring personality; yet he was irresponsible and unreliable in his dealings with many, including those nearest to him. He had a remarkable command of written and spoken German. He wrote English well, but spoke it with a noticeable accent. He was conservative in the selection of subject matter and form of his poetry. He achieved unusual mastery of the sonnet; he introduced the "quintine" as a stanza and rhyme-sequence into German literature. Nies's poetry is determined by his reactions to nature, love, friendship, and fatherland, by his struggle for self-mastery and his metaphysical longing. Some of his finest poems have been inspired by various aspects of American life and nature, notably the ballad, "Die Rache der Wälder," calling attention to the destruction of American forests. He was the most talented and accomplished of German poets who had made America their permanent home.

[G. A. Zimmermann, *Deutsch in Amerika* (2nd ed., 1894); G. A. Neeff, *Vom Lande des Sternenbanners*

(Heidelberg, 1905) ; *Daily Leader* (Davenport, Iowa), May 11, 1899 ; Amalie von Ende, "Konrad Nies, eine Dichterindividualität Deutschamerikas," *New Yorker Staatszeitung*, Mar. 9, 1902 ; *Denver Post*, Oct. 5, 1903 ; *Baltimore News* and *Evening Star* (Washington, D. C.), May 14, 1904 ; *Lit. Digest*, Feb. 24, 1906 ; *Springfield Union* (Springfield, Mass.), Jan. 26, 1914 ; *San Francisco Chronicle*, Aug. 12, 1921 ; editorial and letter by Ferdinand Freytag, *Nation* (N. Y.), Aug. 31, Oct. 5, 1921 ; Werner von Elpons, "Über Konrad Nies," *Die Neue Zeit* (ed. Oscar Illing, New Ulm, Minn., 1928) ; Ernst Jockers, "Deutschamerikanische Dichtung," *Auslanddeutsche : Mitteilungen des Deutschen Auslandinstituts* (Stuttgart, 1928; vol. XII, no. 10) ; C. R. Walther Thomas, "Konrad Nies, ein deutscher Dichter in Amerika," in manuscript ; Nies's papers, diaries, and letters.]   C. R. W. T.

NILES, HEZEKIAH (Oct. 10, 1777–Apr. 2, 1839), editor, was born at Jefferis' Ford, Chester County, Pa., whither his parents had gone for safety just before the battle of the Brandywine. His father, Hezekiah Niles, a plane-maker of Philadelphia, had married Mary Way of Wilmington, Del., and moved to the latter place. Both were of the Quaker faith, though the father was "disowned" a few years after going to Wilmington. Though definite record is lacking, it is probable that the younger Hezekiah attended the Friends' School in Wilmington. At seventeen he was apprenticed to Benjamin Johnson, a printer of Philadelphia, with whom he worked for three years, until 1797, when he was released because of his master's lack of funds. Niles's first writing was done in Philadelphia ; in 1794 he published in newspapers several essays favoring protection, and in 1796 arguments against Jay's Treaty. He married Ann, daughter of William Ogden, of Wilmington, May 17, 1798, and they had twelve children. She died in 1824, and two years later Niles married Sally Ann Warner, by whom he had eight children. At the time of his second marriage he was described by an acquaintance as "a short stout-built man, stooping as he walked, speaking in a high key, addicted to snuff, and with a keen gray eye, that lighted up a plain face with shrewd expression" (J. E. Semmes, *John H. B. Latrobe and His Times*, 1917, p. 184).

Upon returning to Wilmington in 1797 Niles assisted in publishing an almanac and did job printing. After two years he formed a partnership with Vincent Bonsal, but the partnership was dissolved because of losses incurred in the publication of *The Political Writings of John Dickinson* (2 vols., 1801). In 1805, following the failure of a short-lived literary magazine, the *Apollo,* Niles moved to Baltimore and became editor of the *Baltimore Evening Post.* This paper supported the Jeffersonian party in all of its policies ; it was sold in June 1811, and Niles immediately issued the prospectus for his *Weekly*

Register (later *Niles' Weekly Register*) which after seven years of publication had over 10,000 subscribers. This paper he edited and published until 1836, with the assistance of his son, William Ogden Niles, from 1827 to 1830, and on it his reputation is based. In these twenty-five years he made it the strongest and most consistent advocate of union, internal improvements, and protection to industry, in the country. Niles was probably as influential as any in the nationalist economic school which sponsored the American System after the War of 1812. He was the intimate associate of Mathew Carey and Henry Clay. He was a principal mover in the protectionist conventions at Harrisburg in 1827 and at New York in 1831 ; for the former he wrote the address to the people of the United States ; of the latter he was the chief secretary (*Niles' Weekly Register,* Aug. 11, Oct. 13, 1827 ; Nov. 5, 1831). In each instance he gave spirit and form to the work of the convention, and utilized, besides, his remarkable talents and opportunities as a propagandist in its behalf. His opinions and advocacies developed as he advanced. He opposed the recharter of the first Bank of the United States in 1811, believing it to be unconstitutional and a harmful monopoly. But he espoused the recharter of the second Bank of the United States in Jackson's administration, declaring that it had become a necessity to prosperity. In politics, Niles was a Jeffersonian until 1816 or 1817, when he described himself as a no-party man. On Jan. 10, 1824, he wrote: "I cannot believe that either [Jackson or Calhoun] will be elected, and should regret votes thrown away. I esteem both, personally and politically ; and though my private wish is rather for Mr. Adams, I shall be content to accept any other than Mr. Crawford" (Darlington Collection, *post*). When Jackson came into office in 1829, Niles differed sharply with his policies, and became a Whig.

Niles devoted many editorials to the institution of slavery, which he declared should be abolished, though gradually. While in Delaware he was an officer of the state abolition society. In his arguments for the protective tariff, he exerted himself with much ingenuity to win the agricultural interest to his side. His writing was characterized by vigor and decision. He was a tireless worker, and supplied statistical evidence where many in his group were content with eloquence. Besides a number of pamphlets, he published the *Principles and Acts of the Revolution in America* (1822). He never held national office, but in Wilmington was twice town clerk and twice assistant burgess ; in Baltimore he served two terms in the first branch of the city council. He was elected and reëlected (1818–19) grand high priest by the Masonic Order in Maryland. He was a leading figure in the Baltimore Typographical Society. He died in Wilmington.

[R. G. Stone, *Hezekiah Niles as an Economist* (1933); biographical notices in *Niles' National Register* (as it was then called), Apr. 6, 13, 1839; Philadelphia *North American*, Apr. 4, 1839; *Baltimore Patriot and Commercial Gazette*, Apr. 3, 1839; "Village Record, West Chester, Pa., Notae Cestrienses, No. 34," in *Genealogical Soc. of Pa. Colls.* The *Register* is the best source for his opinions and activities. See also Clay and Darlington collections in MSS. Div., Lib. of Cong.; E. T. Schultz, *Hist. of Freemasonry in Md.*, II (1855); J. S. Futhey and Gilbert Cope, *Hist. of Chester County, Pa.* (1881); Edward Stanwood, *Am. Tariff Controversies in the Nineteenth Century* (1903), vol. I.]
B. M.

NILES, JOHN MILTON (Aug. 20, 1787– May 31, 1856), editor, United States senator, postmaster general, was born into a family of moderate means residing in that part of Windsor, Conn., known as Poquonock. His parents, Moses and Naomi (Marshall) Niles, found it no easy task to rear their five children, and John, consequently, received no better education than could be gained from the common-schools of the period. As a young man of some ambition, he applied himself to a course of self-improvement, reading largely in the fields of history and politics. To his public career, he brought also a strong sense of moral uprightness, derived from his Puritan ancestors.

In 1817 he was admitted to the Hartford bar, and in the same year he founded the *Hartford Weekly Times,* a liberal paper, designed to further the cause of political reform in Connecticut. He was an ardent Republican, or Tolerationist, and when his party had secured a new state constitution in 1818, he hoped for still further democratic reforms, which were not soon realized. From 1821 to 1829 he was a judge of the Hartford County court; in 1826 he served one term in the state legislature; and a year later he was a candidate for the United States Senate, being defeated, however, because of his liberal views. He had, by 1827, become a leader of the Jacksonian party, which did not secure a strong hold on conservative Connecticut until 1833. He was made postmaster of Hartford in 1829. Six years later he was chosen by Gov. Henry W. Edwards [*q.v.*] to fill a vacancy in the Senate, caused by the death of Nathan Smith, and being subsequently elected he served until March 1839.

At the outset of his senatorial career, he displayed independence of judgment, refusing to vote immediately for the recognition of Texas, which annoyed his fellow Democrats very much (*Congressional Globe,* 24 Cong., 1 Sess., pp. 438–

39). Some of his other actions during the term were more pleasing to his constituents, especially his plea for a memorial to Nathan Hale, and several speeches in support of the sub-treasury (*Ibid.,* 24 Cong., 1 Sess., p. 145; 25 Cong., 1 Sess., pp. 44–45, 2 Sess., p. 179). Niles believed the latter institution would protect the interests of the laboring classes, whose cause strongly appealed to him. His speeches were not brilliant, but evidenced an accurate and discriminating mind. Because of his uncompromising democracy he was an object of loathing to Connecticut Whigs, who could hardly mention his name without adding vile and insulting epithets. After his first senatorial term he ran unsuccessfully for the governorship of Connecticut in the elections of 1839 and 1840, and was for a short time, May 25, 1840, to Mar. 3, 1841, postmaster general in Van Buren's cabinet. During his second term as senator, 1843–49, he was even less strictly partisan than before, although he held firmly to the doctrine of strict construction, and the belief that the activities of the federal government should be restricted to the smallest possible sphere. In 1844 he was stricken with a severe illness, which temporarily affected his mind, giving hope to his enemies that he might be removed from office on the ground of insanity, but to their discomfiture he recovered (*Ibid.,* 28 Cong., 1 Sess., pp. 564–65, 602). Shortly afterward his friends began to fear that his illness had actually altered his democratic principles, for he turned protectionist, and later showed himself very lukewarm in support of the Mexican War (*Ibid.,* 30 Cong., 1 Sess., pp. 328–29).

Leaving the Senate in 1849, he retired to a quiet horticultural life; he made a trip to Europe in 1851–52; and just before his death from cancer, in 1856, was about to found a new Hartford paper, the *Press,* as an organ of the newly formed Republican party. Throughout his life this quiet-demeanored man was kind-hearted and benevolent, although continual political strife threw over his behavior a cloak of diffidence, and often bitterness, which made him appear unsociable. He married, June 17, 1824, Sarah Robinson, widow of Lewis Howe, and after her death in 1842, he took for his second wife, Nov. 26, 1845, Jane Pratt, of Columbia County, N. Y. There were no children.

Niles combined considerable literary ability with his taste for politics; he edited the first American edition (1816) of *The Independent Whig,* and was either joint or sole author of other works, including *A Gazetteer of the States of Connecticut and Rhode-Island* (1819), *The Life of Oliver Hazard Perry* (1820), *The Con-*

necticut Civil Officer (1823), *A View of South America and Mexico* (1825), enlarged and republished under the title *History of South America and Mexico* (1838). He was interested in the Wadsworth Athenæum and the Connecticut Historical Society, leaving his personal library to the latter; he also bequeathed to the city of Hartford a large sum of money to be used as a charity fund. Niles could hardly be called a nationally prominent figure, but in Connecticut he was outstanding, not only because he was for over thirty years the power behind the local Democratic party, but because he refrained from the mean personalities of politics and dealt only with broad and worthy principles. He died in Hartford.

[H. R. Stiles, *The Hist. and Geneals. of Ancient Windsor, Conn.*, vol. II (1892); Green's *Connecticut Register;* files of the *Hartford Times* and the *Connecticut Courant; Biog. Dir. Am. Cong.* (1928); scattered letters in the Daggett Papers, Yale Univ. Lib.; Boardman collection of Conn. MSS., Conn. State Lib.; miscellaneous papers of the legislature in the office of the secretary of state.]　　　　　　　　　　　J. M. M.

NILES, NATHANIEL (Apr. 3, 1741–Oct. 31, 1828), inventor, theologian, preacher, politician, and man of business with a somewhat less happy dash of the poet, was born at South Kingston, R. I., the son of Samuel and Sarah (Niles) Niles and the grandson of Samuel Niles [*q.v.*]. His parents were cousins german. Like his father and grandfather, Nathaniel was sent to Harvard College but because of illness he left that institution after his first year. Later (1765), with his brother Samuel, he entered the College of New Jersey where he graduated in 1766. His many interests proved at first somewhat of a handicap; he could not decide upon his life work. For a time he studied medicine, then law, and finally turned to theology under the direction of Joseph Bellamy. Though he preached in several New England towns, he was never ordained. Shortly before the Revolution he settled in Norwich, Conn., where he married Nancy, the daughter of Elijah Lathrop, a prosperous trader and manufacturer. He entered Lathrop's factory and is said to have invented an improved type of wool card and to have discovered a new method of applying water power to the drawing of wire from bar iron. These inventions, however, seem to have left no mark upon American industry. Meanwhile he was preaching frequently at Norwich and elsewhere. Several of his sermons he published. He also found time for politics, serving in the Connecticut legislature for three sessions (1779–81). Toward the end of the Revolution he bought a large tract of land in Orange County, Vt., and in 1782 or 1783, he abandoned his business career to move with several friends

into the northern forest. They were the first settlers in what became the township of West Fairlee.

The rest of his strenuous life Niles spent in Vermont, preaching frequently, attending the sick when physicians were not available, writing on theology, but devoting himself primarily to the management of his land and to politics. His position as the largest proprietor in the neighborhood, his undoubted intelligence, his positive and democratic ideas, his forceful and aggressive character, all contributed to his success in politics. From 1784 to 1814, when at the age of seventy-three he retired to his farm, he was almost always in office, on occasion filling two positions simultaneously. For eight terms he sat in the lower house of the Vermont legislature. From 1784 to 1787 he was a member of the supreme court of the state; hence his title of judge by which he was called thereafter. For many years he was a member of the Council, a popularly elected executive and legislative body. From 1791 to 1795 he sat in the federal House of Representatives. He took a leading part in the state convention of 1791 which ratified the federal Constitution, and in another of 1814 which revised the fundamental laws of the state. Unlike most New England clergymen he was a Jeffersonian Democrat. Leading his party in Vermont, he fought against slavery and against banks; he gave vigorous support to the second war with England and as vigorous condemnation of the Hartford Convention. His influence, however, was not widespread for the Federalist triumph in Vermont in 1794 kept the state Democrats out of national office for many years.

In 1793 he was made trustee of Dartmouth College, a position he held until 1820. Characteristically he took his duties with the utmost seriousness. In temperament and in religious and political ideas he was in sharp contrast to President John Wheelock. He early became convinced that the college was suffering under the latter's direction and he soon headed the opposition in the board of trustees. When matters came to a crisis in 1815, he joined with his Federalist fellow members to oust the president and to defend the institution against the state authority. Besides his sermons he published numerous theological articles. His one attempt at poetry, an ode called *The American Hero,* was written in celebration of the battle of Bunker Hill. Set to music it gained wide popularity during the Revolutionary War. Posterity will not regret that thereafter Niles turned his talents to other fields. Despite weak health in his youth his physical and mental vigor was remarkable; even in extreme age he spent long hours renewing his knowledge of Latin. He left nine children, five of them by his second wife, Elizabeth Watson of Plymouth, Mass., whom he married on Nov. 22, 1787.

[J. A. Vinton, *The Vinton Memorial* (1858); F. M. Caulkins, *Hist. of Norwich, Conn.* (2nd ed., 1866); A. M. Hemenway, *The Vt. Hist. Gazetteer*, vol. II (1871); W. B. Sprague, *Annals of the Am. Pulpit*, vol. I (1857); J. M. Comstock, *A List of the Principal Civil Officers of Vt.* (1918); J. G. Ullery, *Men of Vt.* (1894); J. K. Lord, *A Hist. of Dartmouth Coll.* (1913); E. B. Huntington, *A Geneal. Memoir of the Lo-Lathrop Family* (1884); *Vt. Watchman and State Gazette* (Montpelier), Nov. 18, 1828.]   P. D. E.

NILES, NATHANIEL (Dec. 27, 1791–Nov. 16, 1869), diplomatist, was the son of Nathaniel Niles, 1741–1828 [q.v.], pioneer settler of Fairlee, Vt., dubbed by his contemporaries "the Athenian of the East Side of the Green Mountain." His mother, Elizabeth (Watson) Niles, daughter of Judge William Watson of Plymouth, Mass., if less famous than her husband was hardly less talented and devout. Judge Samuel Niles of Braintree, Mass., was Nathaniel's grandfather, and Dr. Samuel Niles, famous New England clergyman, his great-grandfather. The founder of the Niles family came from England soon after the Massachusetts colony was established. Graduating from the Harvard Medical School in 1816, Nathaniel practised medicine for several years in Boston and then went to Paris for further study. There he married an accomplished French woman, Mme. Rosella Sue, widow of Dr. Sue, physician to King Louis XVIII. When William C. Rives, American minister at Paris, resigned in 1830 to return to the United States, he left Niles in charge of the legation. Niles was officially appointed secretary of legation on Nov. 9, 1830, and remained until 1833, when a new chargé d'affaires replaced him. Losing interest in a medical career, he returned to America and sought another opening in the diplomatic service. On June 7, 1837, he was appointed special diplomatic agent to Austria-Hungary, to find a market for American tobacco and to induce the Austrians to lower the high barriers against American commerce. For more than a year he worked hard collecting information and negotiating with high officials, and when Henry A. P. Muhlenburg [q.v.], the new American minister, arrived at Vienna to take over his work in 1838, Niles was able to report substantial progress.

At Vienna the Count de Sambuy, Sardinian minister to Austria, suggested to Niles the desirability of forming diplomatic relations between Sardinia and the United States, which at this time had no relations with any of the Italian states. Niles reported the conversation to the State Department and was immediately given power to negotiate such a treaty, if it could be done within three months. He reached Turin in September 1838, and on November 26 a most-favored-nation treaty of commerce and navigation was signed. It was transmitted to the Senate, which voted for its ratification notwithstanding the fact that it had not been consulted as to the negotiations. This treaty stood until superseded in 1871 by the treaty with Italy following the union of the Italian states. In 1839 Niles left the foreign service, but went again to Sardinia as chargé d'affaires from Jan. 4, 1848, to Aug. 20, 1850. During this period he submitted two interesting projects to the State Department, one involving the building of a Panama canal, to be under international control, the cost of construction and maintenance to be borne by the chief maritime nations; the other, a scheme for the exchange, free of duty, between the United States and Italy, Switzerland, and other European countries, of cheap editions of the national literature of each country in the original language, the main object of which was to promote international good feeling through mutual understanding of national cultures. From 1850 until his death Niles's home was in New York City.

[Manuscript sources include: Nathaniel Niles Papers, 2 vols. (letters to Niles), U. S. Lib. of Cong., Division of MSS.; U. S. Dept. of State, "Diplomatic Correspondence," France, vols. XXV and XXVI, Austria, vol. I, Sardinia, vols. IV and V, Special Agents, vol. XII. Published sources include: *House Executive Document 40*, 23 Cong., 2 Sess.; *House Executive Document 229*, 26 Cong., 1 Sess.; *Senate Document 246*, 27 Cong., 2 Sess.; *Senate Document 118*, 29 Cong., 1 Sess.; *Senate Executive Document 1, House Executive Document 5*, 31 Cong., 1 Sess.; *Senate Executive Document 7*, 32 Cong., 1 Sess.; H. M. Wriston, *Executive Agents in Am. Foreign Relations* (1929); T. F. Harrington, *The Harvard Medic. School: A Hist., Narrative and Documentary* (1905), vol. III.]   I. L. T.

NILES, SAMUEL (May 1, 1674–May 1, 1762), clergyman, religious controversialist, and historian, was born on Block Island, between Narragansett Bay and Long Island, the son of Nathaniel and Sarah (Sands) Niles, and a grandson of John Niles who was in Dorchester, Mass., as early as 1634 and later moved to Braintree. Samuel attended school at Braintree, but in 1689 his education was interrupted. As he afterwards wrote: "the great spoil made on the island by the French, in their repeated visits, and particularly on my father's interest, occasioned my staying from school six years. . . . In this time I turned my hand to husbandry, and sometimes to handicraft. . . . After the space of six years thus employed I returned to school, so that by reason of this delay, I was near two-and-twenty years old when I entered into the college at Cambridge" (*Collections of the Massachusetts Historical Society,* 3 ser. VI, 274). There he received the degree of A.B. in 1699, the first Harvard degree granted to a Rhode Islander.

He then studied for the ministry, probably with the Rev. Peter Thacher [*q.v.*] of Milton, whose daughter Elizabeth he married on May 29, 1701. From 1702 until 1710 he engaged in difficult missionary work at Kingstown, R. I. In the latter year he removed to Braintree, where on May 23, 1711, he was ordained minister of the Second Church. His long pastorate there, which continued until his death, was a prosperous one. It is recorded that he administered baptism to 1,200 persons, and received 312 into the full communion of the church. His first wife died on Feb. 10, 1715/16, and in accordance with her death-bed request he married, Nov. 22, 1716, Ann Coddington of Newport, R. I., granddaughter of Gov. William Coddington [*q.v.*]. His third and last wife was Elizabeth (Adams), widow of the Rev. Samuel Whiting, to whom he was married on Dec. 22, 1737.

Niles took a prominent part in the religious controversies of the period. He was moderator of an Association of Ministers convened at Weymouth in January 1744, which attacked George Whitefield in a pamphlet entitled *The Sentiments and Resolutions of an Association of Ministers* . . . (1745). Niles himself published *Tristitiæ Ecclesiarum or, a Brief and Sorrowful Account of the Present State of the Churches in New England* (1745), deploring the effects of Whitefield's preaching; *A Vindication of Divers Important Gospel-Doctrines* (1752); and *The True Scripture Doctrine of Original Sin* (1757). Two years later Harvard awarded him an A.M. degree. The most important of his writings is "A Summary Historic Narrative of the Wars in New England with the French and Indians" (*Collections of the Massachusetts Historical Society,* 3 ser. VI, and 4 ser. V). A work in rhyme entitled *A Brief and Plain Essay on God's Wonder Working Providence for New England in the Reduction of Louisburg* (1747) and his "Summary Historic Narrative" have gained him a small place in the history of American literature. Niles was included by a contemporary, the Rev. John Barnard [*q.v.*], among prominent preachers who were all "men of learning, pious, humble, prudent, faithful and useful men in their day" (*Ibid.,* 1 ser. X, 170). That he was humble may be questioned, however. He had a talent for obstinacy. He refused to permit the new way of singing from notes to be introduced in his church at Braintree, held services in the parsonage rather than yield, and surrendered only when some of

his flock went over to the Episcopalians. The town of Braintree had to accept a most inconvenient boundary line because he refused to let the line cross his farm. He ordinarily rode a horse that no one else could and to him "were brought for breaking all the rebellious colts and young religious innovators of Braintree" (Shipton, *post,* IV, 490).

[*Colls. Mass. Hist. Soc.,* 1 ser. X (1809), 3 ser. VI (1837), 4 ser. V (1861); J. A. Vinton, *The Vinton Memorial* (1858); Wilkins Updike, *A Hist. of the Episcopal Ch. in Narragansett, R. I.* (2nd ed., 1907), vol. I; preface of Niles's *A Vindication* . . . (1752); C. K. Shipton, *Sibley's Harvard Grads.,* vol. IV (1933); diary of Niles containing his mother's lineage, a record of baptisms, and a history of Braintree during the time that he lived there, in the possession of Asa P. French of Randolph, Mass.]   H. M. N.

NIPHER, FRANCIS EUGENE (Dec. 10, 1847–Oct. 6, 1926), physicist, was born at Port Byron, N. Y., the son of Peter Nipher and Roxalana Powell Tilden. His paternal great-grandfather, Michael Niver, born in Württemberg, Germany, came to America in 1756 at the age of ten years, and later served in the Revolutionary War. On his mother's side, Nipher was of English descent through Nathaniel Tilden, who settled in Massachusetts in 1634, and who was a brother of one of the London merchants who fitted out the *Mayflower.* Peter Nipher, with his wife and three children, moved in 1863 to Iowa City, where the Nipher family owned a government grant of land. The principal purpose of the move was to enable the son Francis to take advantage of the educational opportunities offered at the State University of Iowa. Here he specialized in the natural sciences and mathematics, and in 1870 received the degree of Ph.B. For several years thereafter he served the same institution as instructor in the physics laboratory, at the same time continuing his studies as a candidate for the master's degree which was conferred in 1873. In the same year he married Matilda Aikens, of Atalissa, Iowa, who had been one of his students, and who, with their five children, survived him.

Called to the chair of physics at Washington University in 1874, Nipher began a career which continued without interruption until his retirement in 1914. Probably the greatest influence he exerted as a teacher was due to his insistence upon the inductive method of arriving at physical laws from actual observations and measurement, utilizing to an unusual extent the algebraic interpretation of graphs. It was as an original investigator, however, rather than as class-room or laboratory teacher, that he will be remembered. The variety of his interests is attested by the long list of his published papers, of which the most important are to be found in the *Transactions* of the Academy of Science of St. Louis. Among his important contributions are a series of reports on magnetic observations in Missouri, beginning with the summer of 1878 and continuing for four summers thereafter. This work led to the publication, in 1886, of a book entitled *Theory of Magnetic Measurements*. When electrical engineering began to develop as a major division of technology, Nipher was one of the first to offer courses of study in that branch of science. The course of lectures he developed culminated in 1895 in the publication of *Electricity and Magnetism: A Mathematical Treatise for Advanced Undergraduate Students*.

The measurement of wind pressure on stationary and moving structures engaged his attention for over ten years beginning in 1896, at the time of the disastrous St. Louis tornado. Nipher developed apparatus which made it possible to separate the static from the dynamic pressure head at any point of a structure, and when Washington University took possession of its new campus in 1905 the physics building was completely equipped with an elaborate apparatus exhibited at the Louisiana Purchase Exposition of 1904 and which was there awarded a gold medal for excellence of design. The apparatus, in modified form, was used to measure the frictional effect of railway trains upon the air, a paper on that subject appearing as Volume X, Number 10, of the *Transactions* of the Academy of Science of St. Louis. Other researches included a long series of original experiments on the properties of photographic plates. At the same time that this work was in progress, he contributed to the Academy of Science a series of interesting papers on the thermodynamics of gaseous nebulae. Later, in St. Louis and at his summer home in northern Michigan, he undertook a study of the causes of local variations of the earth's magnetic field. His last, and probably his most important, work was an experimental study of the nature of the electric discharge, the results of which appear in a series of five papers in the *Transactions* of the Academy of Science of St. Louis, summarized in a book, *Experimental Studies in Electricity and Magnetism* (1914). The last years of his life were spent in quiet retirement at his home in Kirkwood, Mo., where he died.

[*Who's Who in America*, 1926–27; *St. Louis Globe-Democrat*, Oct. 7, 1926; information from Nipher's daughter, Mrs. James C. Dawson; personal recollections.] A. S. L.

NISBET, CHARLES (Jan. 21, 1736–Jan. 18, 1804), Presbyterian clergyman and first president of Dickinson College, son of William and Alison Nisbet, was born at Haddington, Scotland. Graduating from the University of Edinburgh at the age of eighteen, he studied theology for six years at Divinity Hall, and in 1760 was licensed by the Presbytery of Edinburgh. After preaching for two years in Glasgow, on May 17, 1764, he was ordained by the Presbytery of Brechin and installed as pastor at Montrose. In 1766 he was married to Anne, daughter of Thomas Tweedie of Quarter, by whom he had four children. He possessed natural abilities of a high order, enhanced by an extraordinary memory. He soon rose to an influential position in the General Assembly of the Church of Scotland, participating freely in discussion as a champion of strict Calvinistic theology. In 1783 the College of New Jersey conferred upon him the degree of D.D.

Nisbet ardently defended the cause of the American Colonies in the Revolutionary struggle. This fact together with his renown as a scholar led Benjamin Rush and John Dickinson [*qq.v.*], in 1784, to offer him the presidency of Dickinson College at Carlisle, chartered in 1783. After considerable urging, he accepted the invitation and arrived in Philadelphia, June 9, 1785. The bright prospects with which he entered upon his duties were soon obscured. A lingering fever fastened upon his body, while the poverty, demoralization, and gloom of the postwar period depressed his spirit. Within a few months he resigned, intending to return to Scotland, but a strong prejudice of his own forbade his sailing in a vessel commanded by an Irish captain. In the ensuing delay his health so improved that he consented to an unanimous reelection, and served at his post with unabating vigor until his death eighteen years later. Simultaneously with his inauguration as president of Dickinson, he was chosen co-pastor of the Presbyterian church at Carlisle with Dr. Robert Davidson [*q.v.*].

As college president Nisbet lectured on logic, mental and moral philosophy, and belles-lettres, and in addition, for the accommodation of students for the ministry, he prepared and delivered a course of 418 lectures on systematic theology and twenty-two lectures on pastoral theology. In the solidity and variety of his erudition he excelled most of the learned men of his age; he was master of nine languages, ancient and modern, was versed in their literatures, and was equally distinguished for his acquirements in sacred and secular knowledge. His manner of speaking was calm and dignified, his style clear and direct; he appealed to intelligent and serious minds. He was a man of fixed habits and prejudices, outspoken in his opinions and inclined to caustic expression. According to Chief Justice Taney of the United States Supreme Court, who was a student under the Scotch divine, Nisbet's classes were warmly and affectionately attached to him. He was cheerful and animated, full of anecdote and classical allusion, seasoned with playful and lively wit. His sarcasm and wit were at times severe and cut deep. His lectures were written out and read slowly that the students might copy them. In his examinations he always preferred an answer in the student's own language, though it might not be as accurate; his object was to teach the student to study, to think, to reason, to form an opinion. He was anti-republican, had no faith in American institutions, did not believe in their stability. The class was good-natured about such utterances, but would not write them down; against such views from any other professor they would have rebelled (Samuel Tyler, *Memoir of Roger Brooke Taney*, 1872, p. 2).

Many of Nisbet's classroom lectures are preserved in manuscript in the Museum of Dickinson College. His publications, which were few, include a review of Wesley's system of doctrine, written in 1771, according to Nisbet's biographer, Miller (*post*), and published some years later in a periodical; his inaugural sermon at Dickinson, *The Relation Between Learning and Piety* (1785); *Address to the Students of Dickinson College* (1786) on the occasion of his reëlection to the presidency; a sermon, *The Usefulness and Importance of Human Learning* (1786). After his death, *Miscellaneous Writings* (1806) appeared.

Nisbet was of portly habit and florid complexion. In his youth he was remarkable for physical agility and endurance, frequently jogging twenty miles before breakfast as a morning exercise. Pneumonia terminated his earnest and active career and his body was interred in the Old Graveyard at Carlisle.

[W. B. Sprague, *Annals Am. Pulpit*, vol. III (1858); Samuel Miller, *Memoir of the Rev. Charles Nisbet, D.D., Late President of Dickinson Coll.* (1840); C. P. Wing, *A Hist. of the First Presbyt. Ch. of Carlisle, Pa.* (1877); Alfred Nevin, *Centennial Biog.: Men of Mark of Cumberland Valley* (1876); *Centennial Memorial of the Presbytery of Carlisle* (2 vols., 1889); G. R. Crooks, *Dickinson Coll.: The Hist. of a Hundred Years* (1883); J. H. Morgan, *Dickinson Coll.: The Hist. of One Hundred and Fifty Years* (1933); C. F. Himes, *Sketch of Dickinson Coll.* (1879); S. W. Parkinson, *Charles Nisbet, First President of Dickinson Coll.* (1908); H. C. King, *Hist. of Dickinson Coll.*, reprinted from the *Am. Univ. Mag.*, Feb., Mar., Apr., May 1897.]
L. C. P.

NISBET, EUGENIUS ARISTIDES (Dec. 7, 1803–Mar. 18, 1871), Georgia legislator and supreme court judge, congressman, was born in

Greene County, Ga., the son of Penelope (Cooper) and James Nisbet, a physician who removed from North Carolina to Georgia in 1791, was a member of the convention that framed the constitution of 1798, and for twelve years served on the board of trustees of the University of Georgia. He was the descendant of John Nesbitt, whose father had emigrated to America from the North of Ireland and who, himself, changed the spelling of his name to Nisbet and removed from Lancaster County, Pa., to Rowan County, N. C., about 1741. The boy received an excellent education at Powelton Academy, at South Carolina College (now the University of South Carolina), and at the University of Georgia, where he was graduated in 1821 with highest honors. He began to read law in the office of Judge Augustin S. Clayton but soon went to the law school established by Tapping Reeve and James Gould [*qq.v.*] at Litchfield, Conn. Returning to practise his profession, he obtained a special act of the legislature to admit him to the bar, since he was still under the legal age, an unusual procedure that provoked a spasm of opposition and brought him valuable publicity. He located at Madison in the Ocmulgee circuit, where, gifted in tongue, pen, and bearing, he met immediate success. On Apr. 12, 1825, he married Amanda Battle, his boyhood sweetheart. Of their twelve children, five boys and seven girls, nine reached maturity. He was a member of the General Assembly for eight terms, two in the House, 1827–29, and six in the Senate, 1829–32, 1834, 1835. He was a follower of Troup, and later, like many of the Troup adherents, he became successively a member of the State-Rights, Whig, and Know-Nothing parties. He was known at this time for his support of education and of all liberal movements and for his literary ability. He was offered the chair of belles-lettres in the University of Georgia, and, later, in Oglethorpe College, a Presbyterian institution at Midway, of which he was one of the founders.

In 1837 his growing practice led to his removal to the larger center of Macon. The following year he was elected to Congress on the Whig ticket and in 1840 was reëlected. He resigned before the expiration of his second term to assume the burden of a heavy debt for which, during his absence, his firm had become liable as surety. When the supreme court of Georgia was inaugurated in 1845, he, Joseph Henry Lumpkin, and Hiram Warner received the honor of selection as judges by the General Assembly. During the first difficult years of the existence of the court he contributed all the force of his vigorous mind. Of the opinions he wrote several are notable. In *William Culbreath* vs. *James M. Culbreath and Daniel C. Culbreath* (*7 Ga. Reports,* 64) he maintained, along a delicate line of reasoning, that there existed a well-defined distinction between ignorance of the law and a mistake in understanding the law and that the courts were bound to recognize such a difference; in *Wiley Mitchum* vs. *The State of Ga.* (11 *Ga. Reports,* 615) he held that a new trial should be granted because, in argument to the jury, counsel overstepped the rules of justice in commenting on facts not proven, and this opinion had the distinction of being used as the decision of another court without acknowledgment of the quotation (see *Green Bag, post,* p. 23). Resuming his law practice in Macon in 1853, he soon became, in cooperation with Benjamin Harvey Hill, a leader of the Know-Nothing party in Georgia. To the secession convention that assembled in Milledgeville on Jan. 16, 1861, he had been chosen as a delegate, though known as a Union man and an opponent of the Democratic majority in the state, and he proved an unexpected accession to the leadership of secession. On Jan. 18, he proposed a resolution that it was the right and duty of Georgia to secede from the Union and to cooperate with such of the other states as had done or would do the same for the purpose of forming a Southern Confederacy, and that a committee be appointed to report an ordinance to assert the right and fulfil the obligation of the state. Notwithstanding the opposition of Herschel V. Johnson, Benjamin H. Hill, and Alexander H. Stephens, the committee was appointed. Nisbet, as chairman, drafted the ordinance of secession that was prepared by the committee and presented to the convention. In 1861 he was his party's candidate against Joseph E. Brown but was unsuccessful. He declined election to the provisional Congress of the Confederacy and continued to practise in Macon until his death.

[Sketch by J. R. Lamar, in *Great Amer. Lawyers,* ed. by W. D. Lewis, vol. IV (1908) ; George White, *Hist. Colls. of Ga.* (1854) ; I. W. Avery, *The Hist. of the State of Ga.* (1881) ; L. L. Knight, *Georgia's Landmarks* (2 vols., 1913–14) ; W. J. Northen, *Men of Mark in Ga.,* vol. III (1911) ; B. T. Hartman, *A Geneal. of the Nesbit, Ross . . . Families of Pa.* (1929) ; *Green Bag,* Jan. 1892.]   J. H. T. M.

NITCHIE, EDWARD BARTLETT (Nov. 18, 1876–Oct. 5, 1917), teacher of the deaf and author of textbooks on lip-reading, was born in Brooklyn, N. Y., the son of Henry Evertson Nitchie and Elizabeth Woods Dunklee. At the age of fourteen he became almost totally deaf but he persisted in his efforts to obtain an education and attended successively the Adelphi Academy, Brooklyn, the Brooklyn Latin School, and Betts

Academy, Stamford, Conn. By occupying a front seat, using an ear-trumpet, and interviewing his instructors after class he managed not only to attain but to keep up high grades. He entered Amherst in 1895, made Phi Beta Kappa in his junior year, became editor-in-chief of the *Amherst Literary Magazine,* was "ivy poet" at Commencement, and was graduated in 1899 *magna cum laude.* In spite of his brilliant record he had difficulty in finding employment. After several unsuccessful attempts he studied lip-reading and essayed to teach it and to devise simpler and easier methods of acquiring it. His own personal experience taught him to lay "less stress on technicalities and phonetic analysis and the mechanical phases of speech and speech-reading, and more on the mental processes involved" (Wright, *post,* p. 787). He believed that lip-reading must be largely self-taught. With the advice and sympathy of Alexander Graham Bell he put the results of his studies into his first book, *Self-Instructor in Lip-Reading,* published in 1902. In 1903 he started the New York School for the Hard-of-Hearing, which after his death became the Nitchie School. He was a rarely sympathetic and understanding teacher. In the fourteen years before his death he taught 1,100 pupils, and owing to the simplicity of his methods 117 of them became teachers much sought after by lip-reading schools everywhere. His second book, *Lessons in Lip-Reading for Self Instruction,* was published in 1905, and the revised edition in 1909. In 1912 appeared *Lip-Reading Principles and Practice,* which became the standard textbook in most schools. He also published a pamphlet, *Lip-Reading Simplified* (n.d.).

In 1910 the Nitchie Alumni Association was formed to facilitate social intercourse and to award scholarships to deserving pupils without means, and this association expanded two years later into the Nitchie Service League. The program included recreation, instruction, and employment. Nitchie was largely responsible for breaking down the prejudice against deaf employees and for securing opportunities for them to earn their own living in occupations for which deafness was no serious bar. Two years later the organization became, at Nitchie's own suggestion, the New York League for the Hard-of-Hearing that there might be no misapprehension as to its purpose. This League was the parent of similar groups organized in many cities of the United States and Canada, united in a national federation, the membership composed mainly of the hard-of-hearing, but including many eminent otologists. Nitchie created a life-work out of his deafness. It gave him under-

standing and suggested courses of action. His fertility in devising social amusements for the deaf, such as lip-reading contests, was amazing. For three out of the last six years of his life his work was interrupted by ill-health, but as often as the doctor permitted he went back to his work. He made wonderful use of the small pittance of life allowed him. His pupils placed a memorial tablet in the Volta Bureau at Washington, and six of his teachers erected one in the Nitchie School. He had married, June 18, 1908, Elizabeth Logan Helm in New York. They had one son.

[Juliet D. Clark, "Edward Bartlett Nitchie: An Appreciation," *Volta Rev.*, Nov. 1917; tributes by Alice N. Trask and Elizabeth Brand in *Ibid.*, Dec. 1917; J. D. Wright, "In Memory of Edward Bartlett Nitchie," *Ibid.*, Dec. 1918; Elizabeth Helm Nitchie, "Edward Bartlett Nitchie," *Ibid.*, Jan. 1919; *N. Y. Times*, Oct. 6, 1917; information as to certain facts from Nitchie's widow and from the N. Y. League for the Hard-of-Hearing.] E. E. Ca—s.

NITSCHMANN, DAVID (Dec. 27, 1696–Oct. 8, 1772), bishop of the Renewed Unitas Fratrum or Moravian Church, was born at Zauchtenthal, Moravia, the son of George Nitschmann, a pious and well-to-do citizen, in the line of a family that had given leaders to the Ancient Unitas Fratrum for over a century. The son possessed a strain of evangelical enthusiasm that, at an early age, brought him into conflict with his environment and with the pious but conforming habits of his father. In 1722 he and four like-minded young men made the acquaintance of Christian David who had persuaded Count Nicholas von Zinzendorf to found a refuge for the persecuted remnant of the Ancient Brethren's Church on his estate at Berthelsdorf, Saxony. In May 1724 these five young men, outcasts from their homes, escaped by devious mountain passes to the Saxon haven and were present when the cornerstone of the first building of Herrnhut was laid. For a year Nitschmann remained in this growing asylum and learned the carpenter's trade. Then he visited his home as an evangelist and persuaded, among others, his invalid father and his uncle, also a David Nitschmann, to abandon their homes and enter the new community, and they were all present in 1727 when the Renewed Unitas Fratrum or Moravian Church was formed. On this trip, Nov. 12, 1726, he married Rosina Schindler.

Count Zinzendorf, recognizing the inherent power of the young man, promptly made use of him for the furtherance of evangelistic work. He was sent to various courts and centers in Europe, going as far as Denmark, Russia, and England. It was at David Nitschmann's instigation that the official center for Moravian work was placed at London, just at the moment when English supremacy in the trade world was becoming an assured fact. And it was this quiet, practical-minded carpenter who realized that the hopes of Herrnhut could be brought to fruition by attaching them to the power of England. In August 1732 he was sent with Leonard Dober to establish a mission among the black slaves of St. Thomas, W. I. This work having been accomplished he returned to Europe in 1733. In 1735 he was consecrated bishop.

Zinzendorf's plans for the evangelization of the North American Indians and for the unification of the migrant Germans of Pennsylvania opened with the attempt at Savannah, Ga., in 1735. Nitschmann arrived early in 1736 and ordained Anton Seifert (or Seiffert) as the first pastor of the Savannah group. This was the first ordination, by a Protestant bishop, in America. In March 1736 he went to Pennsylvania and then sailed for Europe to meet Zinzendorf in England. For the next two years he was constantly in motion from country to country seeking support for the Pennsylvania plan. In 1740, accompanied by his uncle, David Nitschmann the elder, he started for America to establish centers for the evangelization of the Indians. The Savannah settlement was abandoned and the entire company proceeded to Pennsylvania. Nitschmann bought five hundred acres at the confluence of the Lehigh River and the Monocacy Creek in Pennsylvania, and on this tract David Nitschmann the elder began, with the rest of the party, the erection of the town of Bethlehem. From this period on, the headquarters of the sect at Bethlehem was entirely in the hands of Nitschmann. He was unquestionably the founder of all the Moravian work in America, though his uncle, because he held title and directed most of the physical operation, has often mistakenly been called the founder of Bethlehem. In 1744 the administration of the American work was given to Bishop Augustus Gottlieb Spangenberg and Nitschmann started for Europe. His vessel was captured by a Spanish frigate and he was carried to St. Sebastian as a prisoner, not reaching Herrnhut until 1745. He renewed his organization work but before 1750 he had returned to America, and between this time and 1756 he was constantly in motion, making over forty journeys across the Atlantic. His last voyage took him to Pennsylvania in 1755. At the age of sixty-five he returned to Bethlehem where he lived in retirement until his death in 1772. His first wife having died in 1753, he later married Mary Barbara (Leinbach) Martin, widow of Frederick Martin.

[Manuscript materials include the "Autobiog. of David Nitschmann" (1765), the "Bethlehem Diary, 1740–72," and the certificate of consecration from Daniel Jablonsky, June 14, 1737, in the archives of the Bethlehem Church, as well as correspondence and diaries of itinerant workers, 1735–72. Published material includes: J. M. Levering, *Hist. of Bethlehem* (1896); Edmund deSchweinitz, "David Nitschmann, First Bishop of the Renewed Brethrens Church," in *Trans. Moravian Hist. Soc.*, vol. II (1886), section I, and *The Hist. of the Church Known as the Unitas Fratrum* (1885); Adelaide L. Fries, *The Moravians in Ga., 1735–40* (1905); L. T. Reichel, *The Early Hist. of the Church of the United Brethren Commonly Called Moravians in North America* (1888), and *Memorials of the Moravian Church* (1870); J. T. Hamilton, *A Hist. of the Church Known as the Moravian Church or the Unitas Fratrum* (1900) and *Moravian Missions* (2 vols., 1904).]   A. G. R.

NIXON, JOHN (Mar. 1, 1727–Mar. 24, 1815), Revolutionary soldier, was born in Framingham, Mass., the son of Christopher Nixon or Nickson and his wife, Mary Seaver. At the age of eighteen he enlisted in Capt. Ephraim Baker's company of Sir William Pepperell's regiment and served in the expedition of 1745 against Louisbourg. At the outbreak of the French and Indian War, he enlisted (Mar. 27, 1755) in Capt. Ebenezer Newell's Roxbury company and was commissioned lieutenant. Subsequently transferred to Capt. Jonathan Hoar's Concord company and promoted (Sept. 8) to be captain, he took part in the expedition against Crown Point. In the following year he served in the provincial force organized to capture Ticonderoga. In 1758 he was captain of a company in Colonel Ruggles' regiment at Half Moon, N. Y. He also saw considerable service in the closing years of the struggle. In the meantime he had acquired a farm in Sudbury and a wife, Thankful Berry, whom he married on Feb. 7, 1754. In the course of time ten children, five sons and five daughters, were born.

Family and fireside could not hold him back when the Revolution began. He commanded a company of minute-men in the fighting at Lexington and Concord of Apr. 19, 1775. His keen sense of discipline is illustrated by the fact that when he was ordered to hold his detachment in check and one of his men impatiently accused him of cowardice, he replied: "I should rather be called a coward by you, than called to account by my superior officer, for disobedience of orders" (Temple, *post*, p. 276). A week later, under authority of the Massachusetts Committee of Safety, he proceeded to raise a regiment. He was wounded in the battle of Bunker Hill and participated in the siege of Boston. On Jan. 1, 1776, he became colonel of the 4th Continental Infantry, and later moved with the army to New York. On Washington's recommendation, Congress elected him brigadier-general (Aug. 9).

He was placed in command of two regiments of infantry and a detachment of artillery on Governor's Island, and took part in the operations on the mainland subsequent to the capture of New York. In 1777 his brigade, as part of the northern army, participated in the movements resulting in the defeat of Burgoyne. On one occasion a cannon-ball passed so near to his head as to impair his sight and hearing on one side. He was detailed to escort the captive British from Saratoga to Cambridge, Mass. Granted a furlough of several months because of ill health, he took occasion to marry, on Feb. 5, 1778, his second wife, Hannah (Drury) Gleason, widow of a comrade-in-arms. Upon his return to the colors, he served on the court martial appointed to try General Schuyler. His health continuing poor, he resigned Sept. 12, 1780, receiving an honorable discharge. About 1806 he removed from Sudbury to Middlebury, Vt., where he died. Notwithstanding his soldierly bearing and firmness of character, he was a man of engaging manners, who in later years especially enjoyed recounting stories of his military career for the pleasure of his grandchildren.

[J. H. Temple, *Hist. of Framingham, Mass.* (1887); Peter Force, *Am. Archives* (9 vols., 1837–53); Wm. Barry, *A Hist. of Framingham, Mass.* (1847); S. A. Drake, *Hist. of Middlesex County, Mass.* (2 vols., 1880); A. S. Hudson, *The Hist. of Sudbury, Mass.* (1889); D. H. Hurd, *Hist. of Middlesex County, Mass.* (1890), II, 402; *Mass. Soldiers and Sailors of the Revolutionary War*, vol. XI (1903); F. B. Heitman, *Hist. Reg. of Officers of the Continental Army* (1914); J. M. Merriam, *Five Framingham Heroes of the Am. Rev.* (1925); *Hist. Mag.*, Dec. 1860, Jan. 1861; *Repertory* (Boston), Apr. 11, 1815.]   E. E. Cu—s.

NIXON, JOHN (1733–Dec. 31, 1808), Revolutionary patriot, merchant, financier, was born in Philadelphia, Pa., the son of Richard and Sarah (Bowles) Nixon, and on Apr. 17, 1735, at the age of two, was baptized in Christ Church. His father was a prominent shipping merchant and the proprietor of Nixon's Wharf on the Delaware River in Philadelphia. John received but little education except in his father's business, which he inherited in 1749. He early took a leading part in public affairs and in March 1756 was chosen lieutenant of the Dock Ward Company, a home-guard organization. In 1765 he was one of the signers of the non-importation agreement and from that time ranked as one of the leaders of the patriot cause in Philadelphia. The following year he was appointed a warden of the port, and in 1767 was one of the signers of the paper money issued by Pennsylvania.

He became a member of the first Committee of Correspondence in June 1774 and a deputy to the General Conference of the Province of Pennsylvania, July 15; he was a delegate to the Convention for the Province in January 1775; and in April of that year helped organize and was chosen lieutenant-colonel of the 3rd Battalion of Associators, known as the "Silk Stockings." On Oct. 20, 1775, he was made a member of the provincial Committee of Safety, serving and acting as president *pro tempore* whenever the president and vice-president, Benjamin Franklin and Robert Morris, were absent. He was also chairman of the committee on accounts of this organization. In May 1776 he commanded the defenses of the Delaware at Fort Island and in July was placed in command of the Philadelphia city guard. During this year he was also a member of the Continental navy board. On July 8, 1776, appointed by the sheriff of Philadelphia for the task, he had the distinction of publicly reading and proclaiming the Declaration of Independence to an assemblage of citizens, for the first time after its adoption. Immediately after this his Battalion of Associators was called upon to aid in the defense of Amboy, N. J. Six weeks later they returned to Philadelphia, where they remained until December when, Nixon having succeeded to the command of the organization, they joined General Washington in the campaign against Trenton and took part in the battle of Princeton, Jan. 3, 1777. He was a member of the committee to settle and adjust the accounts of the Committee and Council of Safety in 1778; and in 1779 was one of the auditors of public accounts, whose chief business was to settle and adjust the depreciation of the Continental currency. In the spring of 1780 he was one of the organizers of the Bank of Pennsylvania for the purpose of supplying the army of the United States with provisions and supplies. He contributed the sum of five thousand pounds sterling and was appointed as one of the two directors. In 1784 he became a director of the Bank of North America and in 1792 was elected its president, which post he held until his death. From 1789 to 1796 he was an alderman of the city.

Throughout his life Nixon maintained his interest in the business which his father had founded and at the time of his death was senior member of the firm of Nixon & Walker, shipping merchants. He was a member of and officer in numerous social and business organizations, was one of the managers of the Pennsylvania Hospital, 1768–72, and a trustee of the College of Philadelphia, 1789–91. In October 1765 he married Elizabeth Davis, who bore him four daughters and a son. He died in Philadelphia and was buried in St. Peter's Church Yard. Dignified and reserved in manner but noted for his kind-

ness, he was recognized as a man of honor, integrity, and decision.

[C. H. Hart, *Memoir of the Life and Services of Col. John Nixon* (1877), reproducing portrait by Gilbert Stuart, repr. from *Pa. Mag. of Hist. and Biog.*, vol. I (1877); Henry Simpson, *The Lives of Eminent Philadelphians Now Deceased* (1859); J. L. Chamberlain, *Universities and Their Sons: Univ. of Pa.*, vol. I (1901); J. T. Scharf and Thompson Westcott, *Hist. of Phila.* (1884), vol. I; E. P. Oberholtzer, *Phila., A Hist. of the City and Its People* (n.d.), vol. I; J. H. Campbell, *Hist. of the Friendly Sons of St. Patrick and of the Hibernian Soc.* (1892); Michael Hennessy, "Col. John Nixon," in *Hist. Mag. and Notes and Queries*, Dec. 1860, Jan. 1861; Lawrence Lewis, Jr., *A Hist. of the Bank of North America* (1882); W. W. Bronson, *The Inscriptions in St. Peter's Church Yard, Phila.* (1879), p. 14.]   J. H. F.

NIXON, JOHN THOMPSON (Aug. 31, 1820–Sept. 28, 1889), jurist, was born in Fairton, a small village about four miles from the county seat of Cumberland County, N. J. He was the son of Jeremiah S. Nixon and his wife Mary Shaw (Thompson). The Nixon family was one of the leading families of the county. After the usual preliminary education, John entered the College of New Jersey (now Princeton University) in 1837, graduating in 1841, and for a time was employed in teaching languages there. About 1843 he went to Staunton, Va., as a tutor in the family of Judge Isaac S. Pennybacker of the United States court for the western district of that state, and while so engaged he studied law and was admitted to the Virginia bar in 1844. The retirement from practice of a prominent lawyer of Bridgeton, N. J., brought him back to his native county as a partner of Charles E. Elmer. He was admitted to the New Jersey bar at the October term 1845 as an attorney and at the July term 1849 as a counselor.

On September 24, 1851, he married Mary H. Elmer, the daughter of Lucius Q. C. Elmer [*q.v.*], who in 1838 had rendered a great service to the bar and people of the state by compiling and publishing *A Digest of the Laws of New Jersey,* a compendium of the general statutory law then in force which came to be known as "Elmer's Digest." In 1852 Elmer was appointed to the state supreme court, and since the new constitution of 1844 had intervened and the arrangement of the revised statutes of 1847 was unsatisfactory, Nixon undertook the preparation of a second edition of Elmer's *Digest.* It appeared in 1855 with Elmer's name above Nixon's on the title-page, but was generally known as "Nixon's Digest." A third edition appeared in 1861, and a fourth in 1868, all compiled by Nixon but continuing to bear Elmer's name.

Meanwhile Nixon had diligently pursued the practice of his profession and had also entered the field of politics. He served in the New Jersey Assembly in 1849 and 1850, and in the latter year was speaker. In 1858 he was elected a representative in Congress from his district, and served for two terms, until Mar. 3, 1863. In 1864 he was elected a trustee of Princeton College and served as such until his death. He was also a trustee of Princeton Theological Seminary from 1883 until his death, and for many years was an active and valued participant in the councils of the Presbyterian Church. His judicial career began in April 1870 when President Grant appointed him judge of the district court of the United States for the district of New Jersey; and for nearly twenty years he handled the difficult specialties of admiralty, bankruptcy, and patents in a manner which caused his court to be sought out as a forum for important litigation, particularly in the field of patent law. His outstanding characteristics were indefatigable industry, thorough and profound knowledge of the law, sturdy honesty, a keen and delicate sense of honor, and a geniality without undue familiarity which endeared him to the bar and drew to his court a volume of business which ultimately wore him out. He carried an increasing load of work until failing eyesight in 1887 forced him to permit others to aid him. In the summer of 1889 he went to Maine for his vacation, but on the way home died at Stockbridge, Mass., Sept. 28. Three children survived him.

[*Gen. Cat. of Princeton Univ.* (1908); T. F. Fitzgerald, *State of N. J., Manual of the Legislature,* 1889; *N. J. Law Jour.,* Oct. 1889; *Rules of the Supreme Court of the State of N. J. . . . . 1885* (1885); Wm. Nelson, *Nelson's Biog. Cyc. of N. J.* (1913), vol. I; *Daily True American* (Trenton), Sept. 30, 1889; personal information from Nixon's grandson, J. N. Brooks of Trenton, N. J.]   C. W. P.

NIXON, WILLIAM PENN (Mar. 19, 1833–Feb. 20, 1912), journalist, derived from his ancestors two highly dissimilar strains. His father, Samuel Nixon, was the son of a famous Quaker preacher, a Virginian of English ancestry and an early protestant against human slavery; while from his mother, Rhoda Hubbard (Butler) Nixon, who was descended from Cherokee Indians, he may have acquired the quality of patient persistence which, coupled with a Quaker's devotion to the right as he saw it, made him a power in his profession. Born in Fountain City, Wayne County, Ind., he sought his education mainly in the schools adjacent to his home, going at fourteen years of age to Turtle Creek Academy, Warren County, Ohio, then entering Earlham College, Richmond, Ind. In 1854 (according to *Who's Who in America*) he was graduated at Farmers' (now Belmont) College

near Cincinnati, having interrupted his scholastic endeavors from time to time by months of teaching. A four-year course in law and graduation (LL.B.) at the University of Pennsylvania in 1857 completed his academic training.

Like many others destined to win later success in journalism, he embarked first upon the practice of law. In Cincinnati between 1860 and 1868 he attained a measure of success as an attorney, though his taste for politics, already apparent, interfered with a single-minded devotion to his profession. He was elected to the state legislature in 1864 and through reëlection served until 1868. In that year he joined his brother, Dr. O. W. Nixon, in the establishment of the *Cincinnati Daily Chronicle,* an evening newspaper. The position of financial editor, which he held at first, he soon abandoned for the post of publisher and general manager, and as such continued until 1872 when the paper was merged with the *Times.* He had, in the meantime, been married twice; in September 1861 to Mary Stites of Cincinnati, who died a year later, and on June 15, 1869, to Elizabeth Duffield of Chicago.

In 1872 Nixon went to Chicago, which was just beginning to be rebuilt upon the charred ruins of its great fire. Here he found that the chief Republican paper of the city and state, the *Chicago Daily Tribune,* was at odds with its party on the fundamental issue of the tariff, while an almost moribund paper, the *Inter Ocean,* was feebly attempting to make its way. In May 1872 he became business manager of the latter journal. After serving for a time in this capacity, he secured with his brother a controlling interest, and in 1875 became general manager and editor. Thenceforth until 1897 he gave his personal attention to every department of the paper.

Under his editorship the *Inter Ocean* was always what the politicians call a "reliably" Republican newspaper. The party platform was its sufficient guide in matters economic and political. Believing thoroughly, as he did, in the worth of the policy of protection to American industries, Nixon made the paper the most unfaltering advocate of that policy in the Middle West. It was generally believed that some beneficiaries of protection were among its owners, for the period was one in which newspaper management had not reached its present business stage, and the profits of many papers were based as much on their political associations as upon legitimate advertising receipts. The journals of that time were more scholarly, however, than the press of a later day—less sensational, more world-wide in their viewpoint—and Nixon's own editorial endeavors impressed these characteristics especially upon the *Inter Ocean*. In 1896 he was chosen delegate-at-large to the Republican National Convention. It was the year of the struggle over free silver, and those who recalled that he had printed "Coin's Financial School" in the *Inter Ocean* (greatly to the advantage of the paper's circulation) apprehended that he might not follow his party on that issue. But the life-long habit of regularity was not easily interrupted, and during the heated campaign he earnestly advocated the election of William McKinley. In December 1897 he was appointed collector of the port of Chicago, and reappointed in 1902. His paper passed into other hands, and his later years were spent in retirement.

In what was perhaps the stormiest period of Chicago's social and political development, Nixon displayed a quiet and kindly demeanor, an aversion to anything which savored of self-assertion or a desire for political domination. He went with his party with little endeavor to lead it, yet his influence was extended and in the main for good. He did not succeed in making his paper financially successful, but at least he made it eminently respectable and, within its own party, exceedingly influential. In all the progressive and esthetic public activities of the day he took a leading part, not merely as a journalist but as a public servant. He was a member of the Lincoln Park Board in 1896 and its president in 1897–98. For some time he was president of the Associated Press.

[Paul Gilbert and C. L. Bryson, *Chicago and Its Makers* (1929); *Who's Who in America*, 1908–09; *The Book of Chicagoans* (1911); A. T. Andreas, *Hist. of Chicago*, vol. III (1886); *Rev. of Revs.* (N. Y.), June 1895; clippings, etc., in files of Chicago Hist. Soc.; *Inter Ocean* (Chicago), Feb. 19, 21, 1912.] W.J.A.

NIZA, MARCOS de (d. Mar. 25, 1558), Franciscan missionary, author, and explorer, was born in Nice, in the duchy of Savoy. He went to Santo Domingo as a missionary in 1531 and from there to Peru. He is said to have been present at the capture and execution of the Inca, Atahualpa, and is credited with having founded the Franciscan province of Lima, with having written several works which deal with the conquest and native races of Ecuador and Peru (see Juan Velasco, *Historia del Reino de Quito*, 3 vols., 1841–44), and with having supplied Las Casas with information concerning the treatment of the Indians of Peru by the Spaniards. From Peru, Fray Marcos went to New Spain by way of Central America and soon was sent to the province of Nueva Galicia, of which Francisco Vazquez Coronado [*q.v.*] became governor in 1538. Fray Marcos was highly esteemed, and in 1539 became

vice-commissary-general of the Franciscan Order in New Spain. The following year he was elected provincial of the province of Santo Evangelio and held that office for three years.

By Viceroy Mendoza, he was sent in 1539 to investigate reports brought to New Spain in 1536 by Núñez Cabeza de Vaca [*q.v.*] concerning a high civilization in the present states of New Mexico and Arizona, and it is for this expedition that he is best known. A former negro slave who accompanied Núñez was selected as guide and went on in advance. Upon reaching one of the Zuñi pueblos in western New Mexico he was murdered by the inhabitants. Accordingly, Fray Marcos contented himself with viewing the pueblo from a safe distance, and returned to New Spain to report that he had seen a city that was "greater than the city of Mexico." Bandelier (*post*, p. 172) believes that he did not deliberately lie, reasoning that in the desert atmosphere the pueblo appeared larger from a distance than was the case; he argues, furthermore, that the comparison was with the newly founded Spanish town of Mexico, not with the old city which had been destroyed in 1521. Whatever his intentions, Fray Marcos' report was exaggerated and quickly spread over New Spain, with the result that Coronado was commissioned to conquer the region. When his spectacular expedition set out in 1540 the Franciscan went along as a guide. Zuñi proved to be disappointing and the prestige of Fray Marcos waned correspondingly; in fact, "such were the curses that were hurled upon him" by the disappointed treasure-seekers that he soon returned to New Spain. The chief result of the Coronado expedition which the earlier report of Fray Marcos had inspired was the military occupation by the Spaniards of the upper Rio Grande Valley for two winters.

On his northern expeditions the friar lost his health. The date of his death is disputed but according to Vetancurt (*post*) he died in the city of Mexico on Mar. 25, 1558.

[Niza's report appears in *Colección de Documentos Inéditos Relativos al Descubrimiento, Conquista y Colonización de las Posesiones Españolas en América y Oceanía*, III (1865), 325–69; with translation and notes by P. M. Baldwin, in *Hist. Soc. of N. Mex., Pubs. in Hist.*, vol. I (1926), and in translation, in *N. Mex. Hist. Rev.*, Apr. 1926. See also H. H. Bancroft, *Hist. of Ariz. and N. Mex.* (1889), pp. 27–68; A. F. Bandelier, in *Papers of the Archæological Institute of America*, V (1890), 106–78; H. E. Bolton, *The Spanish Borderlands* (1921), pp. 80–105; Fray Antonio de la Rosa Figueroa, "Promptuario General y Específico" (MS., Mexico, 1770; original MS. in García Collection, Univ. of Tex.); Woodbury Lowery, *The Spanish Settlements within the Present Limits of the United States, 1513–1561* (1901), pp. 260–336; G. P. Winship, "The Coronado Expedition, 1540–1542," in *Fourteenth Ann. Report, Bureau of Ethnology*, pt. I (1896), pp. 329–613; Agustín de Vetancurt, "Menologio Franciscano," *Teatro Mexicano*, IV (Mexico, 1871), 117–19.] C.W.H.

NIZZA, MARCOS de [See Niza, Marcos de, d. 1558].

NOAH, MORDECAI MANUEL (July 19, 1785–Mar. 22, 1851), lawyer, playwright, journalist, was born in Philadelphia, Pa., of Portuguese-Jewish ancestry. His father, Manuel M. Noah, a Jewish patriot of Charleston, S. C., is said to have served with General Marion and to have contributed a considerable sum to the Revolutionary cause. His mother, Zipporah Phillips Noah, was the daughter of Robert Phillips, a Jewish merchant of Philadelphia. Noah's early youth was spent in Charleston, S. C. At the age of ten, after the death of his mother, he was sent to live with his maternal grandfather in Philadelphia. Here, after a short period at school and after a brief apprenticeship to a carver and gilder, he was appointd a clerk in the auditor's office of the United States Treasury. Upon the removal of the national capital to Washington in 1800, Noah became a reporter at the sessions of the Pennsylvania legislature at Harrisburg, where he acquired his first experience in journalism, a profession which he was to follow, with few interruptions, for the rest of his life.

In early manhood Noah returned to Charleston, where he engaged in politics and possibly studied law. An ardent patriot, he advocated war with Great Britain and the maintenance of American rights on the high seas; many of his vigorous communications to the Charleston press bore the signature "Muley Malack." He had become interested in the theatre in Philadelphia, had published a play, and in 1812 wrote a melodrama, *Paul and Alexis,* adapted from *Le Pélerin blanc* (1802) of *Pixerécourt.* This, his first acted play, was afterward produced under the title *The Wandering Boys.*

In April 1813 Noah was appointed consul to Tunis, with a special mission to Algiers. He was instructed to negotiate for the release of some Americans held as prisoners by the Algerine pirates. On May 23, 1813, he sailed from Charleston, but his vessel being captured by the British, he was taken to England and detained two months. In October he arrived in Cadiz, where he contracted with Richard R. Keene, an American who had become a Spanish subject, to effect the release of the twelve Americans held for ransom by the Algerines. After being delayed in France and Spain for more than a year, Noah finally arrived in Tunis. On July 30, 1815, he received a letter from James Monroe, secretary of state, revoking his commission and hinting at irregularities in his accounts. Monroe's treatment of Noah was never satisfactorily ex-

plained, though his association with Keene, who had been accused of treason, was doubtless detrimental to his prestige. In January 1817, however, Noah received a letter from the Department of State which vindicated his conduct and returned several thousand dollars due him in the enterprise which resulted in the release of the American captives. He wrote a defense of his actions, published as *Correspondence and Documents Relative to the Attempt to Negotiate for the Release of the American Captives at Algiers* (1816), the substance of which was embodied in his *Travels in England, France, Spain, and the Barbary States* (1819). Returning to America in 1816, Noah entered the field of journalism in New York City. In 1817 he became editor of the *National Advocate,* a daily journal founded by the Tammany faction of the Democratic party. During this period of editorship which continued for almost ten years, Noah engaged in a project which he had cherished for many years. Always strongly attached to his own people, he desired to establish in America a colony for the oppressed Jews of all nations. Accordingly, in 1825, with imposing ceremonies, he laid the corner-stone of "Ararat, a City of Refuge" which he hoped to establish on Grand Island in the Niagara River. Though the project came to naught, it affords an interesting commentary upon an otherwise practical mind. Shortly upon his return to America Noah's patriotic impulses sought dramatic expression. His play, *She Would be a Soldier* (1819), based upon the battle of Chippewa, held the stage for many years. *The Siege of Tripoli,* first produced in 1820, later played in Philadelphia under the title *Yuseff Caramalli,* has not been preserved. *Marion, or the Hero of Lake George,* performed in 1821, a drama of the Revolution, uses the battle of Saratoga for background. His last play, *The Grecian Captive* (1822), though an adaptation from a French melodrama, is charged with patriotic sentiments.

In 1822 Noah was appointed sheriff of New York, an office which he held for less than a year, and, in 1823, he was admitted to the New York bar. In 1826 he married Rebecca Esther Jackson, by whom he had six sons and one daughter. In this same year he left the *National Advocate* and established the *New York Enquirer,* which, in 1829, was merged with the *Morning Courier* under the title *Morning Courier and New York Enquirer,* a paper which supported Jackson's first administration. In 1829 President Jackson appointed Noah surveyor of the Port of New York, but in 1833 Noah resigned this office, and the following year he founded the *Evening Star* to support the new Whig party. In 1841 Governor Seward appointed him associate judge of the New York court of sessions, an office which he resigned the following year. He then became successively editor of the *Union,* and *Noah's Times and Weekly Messenger.* The last-named paper he edited to the end of his life. *Gleanings from a Gathered Harvest* (1845) is a collection of his newspaper essays. He died of a stroke of apoplexy in his sixty-sixth year.

[See Simon Wolf, *Mordecai Manuel Noah, a Biog. Sketch* (1897) ; C. P. Daly, *The Settlement of the Jews in North America* (1893) ; L. F. Allen, "Founding of the City of Ararat on Grand Island by Mordecai M. Noah," *Buffalo Hist. Soc. Pubs.,* vol. I (1879) ; M. J. Kohler, "Some Early Am. Zionist Projects," *Am. Jewish Hist. Soc. Pubs.,* no. 8 (1900) ; G. H. Cone, "New Matter Relating to Mordecai M. Noah," *Ibid.,* no. 11 (1903) ; Noah's speech on the laying of the corner-stone of "Ararat" in *Ibid.,* no. 21 (1913) ; letters from the Van Buren papers relating to Noah, *Ibid.,* no. 22 (1914) ; Wm. Dunlap, *A Hist. of the Am. Theatre* (1832), pp. 380–84 ; A. H. Quinn, *A Hist. of the Am. Drama from the Beginning to the Civil War* (1923) ; Samuel Lockwood, "Major M. M. Noah," *Lippincott's Mag.,* June 1868 ; Anita L. Lebeson, *Jewish Pioneers in America, 1492–1848* (1931), useful for references ; *N. Y. Tribune,* Mar. 24, 1851.]
H. W. S—g—r.

NOAILLES, LOUIS MARIE, Vicomte de (Apr. 17, 1756–Jan. 5, 1804), French soldier, man of affairs, was born in Paris, France, the second son of Philippe, duc de Mouchy, and his man of affairs, was born in Paris, France, the Duc d'Arpajon. On Sept. 19, 1773, at the age of seventeen, he married his cousin, Louise de Noailles, a daughter of the Duc d'Ayen, whose sister later married Lafayette. It was rather as a "modern" and fashionable young man than as a crusader that Noailles welcomed the revolt of the American colonies. Lack of an independent income prevented his departure with Lafayette ; but as an officer in the French army he later took part in d'Estaing's campaign in the West Indies, commanded a trench with credit in the siege of Savannah, and arrived at Newport with Rochambeau in 1780 as colonel *en second* of the regiment of Royal-Soissonais. As the real commander of this regiment he took a distinguished part in the Yorktown campaign and was chosen to represent the French army in negotiating the terms of surrender with Cornwallis. He returned to France and served both in the Assembly of Notables of 1787 and in the Estates-General of 1789. He is forever associated with one of the most radical steps taken by the National Assembly. On the night of Aug. 4, 1789, Noailles in a brief and very effective speech proposed that the privileged orders take the first step toward the abolition of social and

economic privilege by giving up freely their antiquated feudal status. This speech started an orgy of verbal altruism, and before the night was over the *ancien régime* was abolished, at least on paper. Noailles attempted to serve as an officer in the new army but could not completely repudiate his blood and his upbringing. He left France in 1792, and his name was placed on the list of *émigrés*—a step which meant the confiscation of his property. After a brief stay in England he went to Philadelphia in 1793, probably for economic reasons. His second stay in America is perhaps more interesting, save to military and diplomatic history, than his first, for he built up a moderate fortune for himself in the Philadelphia business world. He became a partner in the banking house of Bingham & Company and seems to have speculated successfully on the stock exchange. With Robert Morris and John Nicholson [*qq.v.*] he promoted the Asylum Company, organized to buy and sell lands, especially in an attempt to provide a refuge for French *émigrés*. The colony was established in what is now Bradford County, Pa. In 1800, Noailles's French possessions were restored to him, and his name was erased from the list of *émigrés*. He did not, however, return to France. But having gone to Santo Domingo on business, he accepted a commission under Rochambeau, son of his former commander. He held Môle St. Nicolas against a large force of blacks and a blockading British squadron for five months, and then ran the blockade, escaping with his men to a Cuban port. Proceeding with a few men toward Havana on the schooner *Courrier,* he met an English corvette of seven guns, the *Hazard,* fooled her commander by his knowledge of English, and got close enough to board and capture her in one of the most romantic struggles in French naval history. He died of wounds received in this action, after having brought the *Hazard* to Havana as a prize.

Noailles was clearly a man of great personal charm and social flexibility. He was a brave and capable officer, and a good man of business. Living as he did in eighteenth-century France, he had the radical sympathies of the most active of his order. But there are no signs that he really thought out for himself the consequences of his devotion to liberty, novelty, and progress. He left his wife in France to be guillotined and never returned to see his sons. He was apparently somewhat vain, and shared with Lafayette a thirst for glory. Yet his speeches, his letters to the Robinsons, and his activities in Philadelphia reveal a man of common sense, to whom the ideas of 1776 and of 1789 were neither a faith nor a goal, but something to be accepted, and used, like a fashion.

[A. M. R. A. Noailles, *Souvenirs d'Amérique et d'Orient* (Paris, n.d.) ; Marquis de Castellane, "Gentilshommes démocrates : le Vicomte de Noailles," *Nouvelle Revue*, Sept. 1, 15, 1890 ; A. H. Wood, "The Robinson Family and their Correspondence with the Vicomte and Vicomtesse de Noailles," *Newport Hist. Soc. Bull.*, no. 42, Oct. 1922 ; C. A. Pontgibaud, *Mémoires du Comte de Moré* (Paris, 1898), of which an English edition, translated by R. B. Douglas, was published in Paris in 1897 ; Louise W. Murray, *The Story of Some French Refugees and Their "Azilum," 1793–1800* (2nd ed., 1917) ; J. B. P. J. Courcelles, *Histoire Généal. et Heraldique des Pairs de France*, vol. VIII (1827).]   C. B—n.

NOBILI, JOHN (Apr. 8, 1812–Mar. 1, 1856), Catholic missionary and educator, was born at Rome, where his father was a lawyer of repute. Trained in a Roman college, he entered the Society of Jesus in 1826, and after following the regular Jesuit course of study he taught in the Society's colleges at Rome, Loretto, Placentia, and Fermo. Ordained in 1843, he volunteered for the American missions and accompanied Father Pierre-Jean De Smet [q.v.] to the Rocky Mountains. Here in the wild regions of Oregon and of New Caledonia as far as Fort Stuart, this Roman, accustomed to the mild Italian climate, spent six years of terrible suffering from hunger and cold. Often reduced to a diet of herbs and of the flesh of dogs and wolves, he labored with desperate intensity as a missioner and as superior of the Oregon–Rocky Mountain missions among the Okanagans, Flatheads, and Kalispels, of whom he is said to have baptized about 1,500.

In 1849, because of failing health, he was ordered to California and assigned to duties in San Francisco, where he is said to have been the first priest to preach. He won the merited approval of its rough inhabitants in the severe cholera epidemic of 1850, during which he nursed the sick and comforted the dying. A year later, Bishop José S. Alemany [q.v.] assigned him to a mission at Santa Clara, where he opened a school for boys with the assistance of two lay teachers and a matron. The institution attracted attention because of its technical instruction in mining and grew rapidly as the population of the state increased. In 1855 the college was incorporated as a university with Nobili as president. A scholarly, urbane man of excessive zeal, with the aid of brother Jesuits expelled from Sardinia, he made this pioneer school unequaled on the Pacific Coast. His death, at a comparatively early age, was from lockjaw, occasioned by his stepping upon a nail.

[*The Metropolitan Cath. Almanac for the Year 1857*, p. 298 ; *N. Y. Freeman's Jour.*, Apr. 5, June 14, 1856 ;

Records of the Am. Cath. Hist. Soc., June 1906 ; H. M. Chittenden and A. T. Richardson, *Life, Letters, and Travels of Father Pierre-Jean De Smet, S. J.* (1905) ; J. W. Riordan, *The First Half Century of St. Ignatius Church and College* (1905) ; *San Francisco Daily Herald*, Mar. 3, 1856.]   R. J. P.

NOBLE, ALFRED (Aug. 7, 1844–Apr. 19, 1914), civil engineer, was born in Livonia, Wayne County, Mich. His father, Charles, and his mother, Lovina (Douw) Noble, were the descendants of several ancestors who saw military service in the American Revolution, and his grandfather, Norton Noble, was a soldier in the War of 1812. Alfred's early education in the public schools of his native town was interrupted when he was eighteen years of age by service in the Civil War. Enlisting in the 24th Michigan Volunteers, he participated between October 1862 and February 1865 in most of the important campaigns and battles of the Army of the Potomac. For two years, 1865–67, he was a clerk in the War Department at Washington, then entered the sophomore class at the University of Michigan, where he was graduated C.E. in 1870, despite an absence of a year and a half as recorder of the federal Lake survey. His first work after graduation was in connection with surveys of harbors on Lake Michigan, but from September 1870 until 1882 he was engaged in the improvement of navigation in the St. Mary's River between Lakes Superior and Huron and in the enlargement of the St. Mary's Falls Canal at Sault Ste. Marie, Mich. As assistant engineer, 1873–82, under Maj. Godfrey Weitzel [q.v.] he had an important part in the construction of the Weitzel Lock at the "Soo." In 1882 he became resident engineer of the Shreveport Bridge across the Red River, and then, 1883–86, was assistant engineer in charge of bridge construction on the Northern Pacific Railroad. Subsequently, he became resident engineer of the Washington Bridge, New York City (1886–87), under William R. Hutton ; of the Cairo Bridge over the Ohio River (1887–89), under G. S. Morison and E. L. Corthell [qq.v.] ; and of the Memphis Bridge over the Mississippi (1888–92), under Morison. Upon the completion of the last-named work he formed a limited partnership with Morison during which he was assistant chief engineer of bridges at Alton, Ill., Bellefontaine, Mo., and Leavenworth, Kan.

Upon the expiration of this partnership in 1894, he opened an office as consulting engineer in Chicago. In April 1895 he was appointed by President Cleveland a member of the Nicaragua Canal Commission, with Gen. William Ludlow and Commander Mordecai Thomas Endicott [qq.v.] as his colleagues. The commission visited many points in Central America with a view to the construction of an inter-oceanic canal, and in October 1895 submitted its final report. Thereafter, Noble was engaged in private practice, mostly as a consulting engineer, until appointed by the secretary of war to membership in the Deep Waterways Commission, to study ship-canal routes from the Great Lakes to the sea (1897–1900). By appointment of President McKinley, 1899–1903, he was member of the Isthmian Canal Commission, which was charged with determining the route of the Panama Canal. Subsequently President Theodore Roosevelt appointed him (1905) to the board of consulting engineers on the Panama Canal. Although a majority of this board favored the construction of a sea-level canal, Noble was one of those who held out strongly for a lock-canal, the type finally adopted. (See his statement before a Senate sub-committee, *The Isthmian Canal*, 1902; and his statement before the Senate Committee on Interoceanic Canals, *Investigation of Panama Canal Matters*, 1906, pp. 441–94.) In 1900 he served on a board of engineers to advise the state engineer of New York with regard to plans for the projected State Barge Canal. From 1901 to 1905 he and Ralph Modjeski were associated in the building of a bridge across the Mississippi at Thebes, Ill., Noble having special charge of the substructure. From 1902 to 1909 he was chief engineer of the East River division of the Pennsylvania Railroad, supervising important tunnel construction under the river and terminal improvements which included the foundations of the Pennsylvania Station, New York City. As consulting engineer, he was connected with the construction of the Galveston seawall, the New York rapid-transit subways, the Pearl Harbor (Hawaii) Dry Dock, the new Welland Canal and the new Quebec Bridge, the Catskill Aqueduct, and a number of important water-power developments.

Throughout his life, he contributed papers and studies to the Western and the American societies of civil engineers, and to the Chicago Academy of Sciences. He became president of the Western Society of Civil Engineers in 1897, of the American Society of Civil Engineers in 1903, and of the American Institute of Consulting Engineers in 1913. In 1910, he was awarded the John Fritz Medal of the American Institute of Mining Engineers "for notable achievements as a civil engineer," and in 1912, the Elliott Cresson Medal of the Franklin Institute "for distinguished achievement in the field of civil engineering." At the time of his death, follow-

ing a serious operation, he held a position in the front rank of his profession. He was survived by his wife, Georgia Speechly of Ann Arbor, Mich., whom he married May 31, 1871, and by one son, also a civil engineer.

[*Trans. Am. Soc. Civil Engineers*, vol. LXXIX (1915), containing memoir, bibliography, tributes, and reprints of numerous obituaries; W. F. Johnson, *Four Centuries of the Panama Canal* (1907); *Who's Who in America*, 1914–15; R. W. Raymond, in *Engineering Record* (N. Y.), Apr. 25, 1914; *Railway World*, May 1914; *N. Y. Times* and *N. Y. Herald*, Apr. 20, 1914.]
C. D. R.

NOBLE, FREDERICK ALPHONSO (Mar. 17, 1832–Dec. 31, 1917), Presbyterian and Congregational clergyman, was born in Baldwin, Me., the son of James and Jane (Cram) Noble. The characteristics of his parents—the father of Scotch descent, unremittingly industrious as farmer and cooper, a captain of militia, scornful of unrighteous living, gifted with effective speech in town-meetings; the mother tall, dignified, alert, hospitable—appear distinctly in their son, the first-born of twelve children.

Early determined to obtain an education, he worked his way through Kimball Union Academy, Meriden, N. H., and borrowed money for his college course at Yale, graduating in 1858. After two years at Andover Theological Seminary he entered Lane Seminary, Cincinnati, Ohio, from which he graduated in 1861. On Sept. 15, 1861, he married Lucy A. Perry of Dummerston, Vt. He was invited to supply the pulpit of the House of Hope Presbyterian Church, St. Paul, Minn., and there, July 16, 1862, he was ordained and installed pastor. The church had but sixty members and an indebtedness exceeding the value of its entire property. Under the leadership of the young pastor it grew steadily in membership and influence, and his eloquent patriotism made helpful contribution to the Union cause throughout the war. In 1867 he was called to the Third Presbyterian Church of Pittsburgh, Pa. He was already recognized as a vigorous writer and administrator: a progressive conservative, he became an advocate of woman's suffrage. From Pittsburgh he was called in 1875 to the First Church of Christ (Congregational), New Haven, Conn.

In 1879 he was recalled to the interior by a challenging invitation to Union Park Congregational Church, Chicago. The great fire of 1871 had left this church struggling with a crushing indebtedness and its future was problematical. Here Noble entered upon his largest work, achieving the apparently impossible in effecting the extinction of the debt, and organizing the church upon widely serviceable lines. In the meantime he advanced steadily to prominence among the recognized leaders in the Congregational body. Of impressive physique, a wide reader, a consecutive and practical thinker and convincing speaker, a sympathetic pastor, a sagacious counselor, a public-spirited citizen, a coworker in world-wide religious undertakings, he became during his twenty-two years at Union Park an outstanding example of statesmanship in the ministry. His dominating will and forthright utterance were tempered by his friendliness and just appreciation of others. He was a founder of the New West Education Commission and its president, 1879–98; a founder of the Chicago City Missionary Society; moderator of the National Congregational Council, 1898; president of the American Missionary Association, 1898–1900; and editor of *The Advance,* Chicago, 1886–88. He was also the author of *The Divine Life in Man* (1896), *Discourses on Philippians* (1897), *Our Redemption* (1898), *Typical New Testament Conversions* (1901), *The Pilgrims* (1907), *Spiritual Culture* (1914), besides pamphlets on civic, educational, and religious subjects.

In 1901 he closed his pastorate, continuing active in a general ministry. Mrs. Noble had died, June 7, 1895; and on July 1, 1897, he married Leila M. Crandon of Evanston, Ill. For several years he was much in New England. It had long been his custom to visit the Rangeley Lakes (Maine) in summer, and his had been the leading influence in the erection of a church-building and later a public library at Rangeley. After 1910 he made his home in Evanston.

[*Obit. Record Grads. Yale Univ.,* 1918; editorial and obituary in *The Congregationalist and Advance,* Jan. 17, 1918; *Who's Who in America,* 1916–17; a study of Noble's life and character by his son Frederic Perry Noble of Spokane, Wash. (1918, unpublished); *The Treasury* (New York), Jan. 1891.]

E. D. E.

NOBLE, JAMES (Dec. 16, 1783–Feb. 26, 1831), senator, was born in Clarke County, Va., the second of the fifteen children of Elizabeth Claire (Sedgwick) and Thomas Noble, a physician of Scotch descent. Toward the end of the century the family moved to Campbell County, Ky., where Thomas Noble had a grant of 210 acres on the Bank Lick. There James received the self-directed and informal education typical of the frontier. About the time of his marriage, on Apr. 7, 1803, to Mary Lindsay of Newport, Ky., he began to read law in the office of Richard Southgate of Newport. Some six or eight years later he removed to Indiana, where his two younger brothers, Noah and Lazarus, soon followed him and where his family continued to be important in Indiana politics for many years.

He was admitted to the bar and became one of the first lawyers in Lawrenceburg. There were, perhaps, other men who knew more law than he, but, as an orator who could appeal to the emotions of the crowd, he was unsurpassed. He was popular, ambitious, and a political opportunist.

When Franklin County was formed in 1810, he was appointed prosecuting attorney and thereafter made Brookville his home. In 1811 he became lieutenant-colonel of militia and the next year, when his regiment was called out to protect the frontiers of the county, he became colonel. In 1815 he operated a ferry across the Ohio from his lands in Switzerland County. On Apr. 25, 1815, Gov. Thomas Posey appointed him to fill an unexpired term as judge of the third circuit. The following year he was sent by the voters of Franklin County to represent them in the Indiana state constitutional convention. Legislative work was not new to him for he had served as clerk of the territorial House of Representatives as early as 1810. In the convention he was chairman of the committees on the legislative department, elections, and banks and banking companies, and was a member of the committees on the militia, judicial department, and school lands. Characteristically, he was one of the chief leaders of the convention and when forced to a vote usually carried his point. On Nov. 8, 1816, four days after the meeting of the first state legislature, to which he was a representative, he and Waller Taylor were elected as Indiana's first two senators. To this same office he was reëlected in 1821 and again in 1827. He fought for internal improvements and the development of the west, and he pushed along the bill in Congress to authorize the selling of the public lands in quarter sections. His work in Congress did not bar him from other activities. In 1820 he became a director of the Brookville branch of the Vincennes Bank, and, when that institution became involved in difficulties with the United States, he was assigned by the government to settle the affair, which he did to the satisfaction of all. He died in Washington, D. C.

["Executive Journ. of Ind. Territory," ed. by W. W. Woollen, D. W. Howe, and J. P. Dunn, *Ind. Hist. Soc. Pubs.,* vol. III (1900); *Journ. of the Convention of the Ind. Territory* (1816); *Ind. Hist. Colls.,* "Governors Messages and Letters. Messages . . . of Wm. Henry Harrison," ed. by Logan Esarey (1922), vol. II; *Ibid.,* "Messages of Jonathan Jennings, Ratliff Boon, and Wm. Hendricks" (1924); W. W. Woollen, *Biog. and Hist. Sketches* (1883); A. J. Reifel, *Hist. of Franklin County* (1915); Archibald Shaw, *Hist. of Dearborn County* (1915); L. M. Boltwood, *Hist. and Geneal. of the Family of Thomas Noble* (1878); state treasurer's account book for 1810 and manuscript, "Family Hist. of Noah Noble," by E. N. Carter, in Ind. State Lib. at Indianapolis; date of birth from letter of Mrs. Esther Noble Carter of Indianapolis, giving data copied from family Bible of Philip Sweetser.]

J. L. N.

NOBLE, JOHN WILLOCK (Oct. 26, 1831–Mar. 22, 1912), soldier, lawyer, secretary of the interior, was born at Lancaster, Ohio, the son of John and Catherine (McDill) Noble, Pennsylvania Presbyterians who had migrated early to Ohio. After attending the public schools of Cincinnati, he spent three years at Miami College, before his graduation with honors from Yale in 1851. The year following he received his law degree from the Cincinnati Law School but continued to study in the office of Henry Stanbery before his admission to the bar. In 1855 he moved to St. Louis, but, shortly becoming convinced that, as a Free-Soiler and a Republican, he could not succeed in the pro-slavery atmosphere there, he moved to Keokuk, Iowa, where from 1856 to 1861 he acquired an extensive practice and shared with Samuel Freeman Miller the leadership of the state bar. In August 1861 he enlisted in the 3rd Iowa Cavalry and during the Civil War served with distinction in every grade from lieutenant to colonel, seeing service in various western campaigns and in raids into the lower South. He also acted as judge-advocate-general of the Army of the Southwest. "For gallant and meritorious services" he was brevetted brigadier-general in 1865. On Feb. 8, 1864, he married Lisabeth Halsted, of Northampton, Mass., a woman of marked intellectual power and a leader in early social-welfare movements.

In 1865 Noble returned to St. Louis. His subsequent career was divided between professional and public interests. At the instance of his former teacher, Stanbery, he was appointed in 1867 United States district attorney for the eastern district of Missouri. During three years of hard work and of harder fighting Noble prosecuted with intelligence and thoroughness numerous violaters of the internal-revenue laws. The chief offenders were certain of the whiskey and tobacco interests and their corrupt and entrenched governmental allies, a notorious combination which defrauded the government of huge sums. Against this group, the forerunner of the Whiskey Ring, Noble fought with some success and set in operation forces which eventually exposed the ramifications of the system. In 1870 he resumed practice and won immediate success. His clients included large corporate and railroad interests of the Southwest. He was very effective both in trial and in appellate practice, despite a too frequent reliance upon oratory. He declined in 1872 the position of solicitor-general.

He was considered well qualified for the secretaryship of the interior to which Harrison named him in 1889 (*St. Louis Globe-Democrat,* Mar. 4, 1889). As an esteemed Grand Army man and as an exponent of the orthodox Republican view that the surplus collected largely under the tariff laws should properly be distributed in pensions, Noble favored a policy of great liberality and repeated in his reports many of the platitudes concerning the old soldier. He absolutely refused, however, to sanction the highly irregular and illegal administrative activities and rulings of "Corporal" James Tanner, the commissioner of pensions. A sharp difference arose over the policy of reratings, and the two men clashed frequently. Harrison supported Noble in the controversy, and Tanner, "insubordinate in the last degree," finally resigned (W. H. Glasson, *Federal Military Pensions in the United States,* 1918).

The pension act of 1890 received Noble's cordial approval, although its administration was beset with fraudulent claimants, political sentimentalists, and astute claim attorneys whom he found impossible to control. With reference to the timber lands, his practice was to dispose of the thousands of cases in the Land Office by a more liberal interpretation of the land laws in favor of the settler (*Report of the Secretary of Interior,* 1889, 1891). In this manner the cases were rapidly settled but probably many fraudulent claims received approval. In 1890 Noble strongly supported the views of the American Forestry Association and the Division of Forestry and was responsible for the introduction of the forest reserve sections in the revision of the land laws in 1891 (John Ise, *The United States Forest Policy,* 1920). Harrison acted immediately and withdrew for national forests millions of acres of valuable lands. The act of 1891 remains Noble's most significant achievement. At his retirement from office in 1893, the general administrative functions of the department were efficiently conducted. Politically, he was generally regarded as a follower of the president rather than of Blaine. He was austere and formal in his official relations but friendly and democratic in his personal contacts. Upon his return to St. Louis he reëntered his profession but found it difficult to regain his practice. Concerning his public life he ruefully declared, "I spent my whole fortune living up to the office. My house cost me more than my salary. . . . I thought I was doing well but when I came home I had no practice and came near starving" (I. H. Lionberger, "Glimpses of People and Manners in St. Louis," 1920). A mining interest provided

Noble

him with necessary resources. He was not again active in political affairs but remained an interested and benevolent figure at veterans' gatherings and college reunions. He died in St. Louis after a month's illness.

[L. D. Ingersoll, *Iowa and the Rebellion* (1866); B. E. Fernow, *A Brief Hist. of Forestry* (1907); I. H. Lionberger, "Glimpses of People and Manners in St. Louis" (1920); J. T. Scharf, *History of St. Louis City and County* (2 vols., 1883); D. L. McMurry, "The Bureau of Pensions during the Administration of President Harrison," *Miss. Valley Hist. Rev.*, Dec. 1926; annual reports of the secretary of the interior, 1889–92; *Who's Who in America*, 1912–13; *Obit. Record of Yale Grads.*, 1911–12.]   T. S. B.

NOBLE, SAMUEL (Nov. 22, 1834–Aug. 14, 1888), ironmaster, founder of the city of Anniston, Ala., was born in Cornwall, England, the son of James Noble and Jenifer Ward Noble. The family emigrated to Pennsylvania in 1837 and at Reading Samuel received an elementary education. More important, however, was the early training in ironmaking from his father; he was brought up in the atmosphere of the furnace and forge. When the family moved to Georgia in 1855, Samuel became the leading spirit of the firm of James Noble & Sons, whose plant consisted of a rolling-mill, foundry, and nailery in Rome, and a furnace in Cherokee County, Ala. Their business prospered and they expanded it to meet the needs of the Confederacy by building Cornwall Furnace in the same county to provide more iron for war materials. Both the furnace and the factory at Rome were destroyed by the Federal forces in 1864.

Noble typified in many ways the industrial pioneer of the post-war period who undertook the task of building a new South. Successful in enlisting capital from the North, he soon rebuilt the works at Rome. Meanwhile he was in search of larger ore deposits in the hill country of northeastern Alabama. After prospecting near Oxford he secured financial aid in New York with which to buy in Calhoun County extensive brown-ore properties and a large acreage of yellow pine for charcoal. On a visit to Charleston, S. C., he chanced to meet Gen. Daniel Tyler, a northern capitalist, who was so impressed by the young man's enthusiasm that he explored the ore fields in company with Noble. The result was the formation of the Woodstock Iron Company in 1872 with Gen. Tyler's son Alfred as president and Samuel Noble as secretary-treasurer and general manager. In April 1873 their charcoal blast furnace No. 1, of forty-ton capacity, was blown in and ran almost continuously for twenty years. It produced a high quality of car-wheel iron which found a ready market in the North. The steady demand for this iron en-

Noble

abled the company to survive the panic and depression of the mid-seventies, to construct furnace No. 2 in 1879, and to enlarge No. 1 the following year.

Meanwhile the town of Woodstock had been organized in July 1873 as Anniston, named for the wife of Gen. Tyler. Samuel Noble, dynamic spirit of the enterprise, with visions of the "model city of the South" (as it was later advertised), directed the policy of the company in laying out streets and parks, erecting schools, and providing lots for churches of every denomination. When the first boom of the eighties appeared, Anniston grew by leaps and bounds. During the period 1880–85 Noble and his associates organized the Clifton Iron Company at Ironaton where they built two forty-ton charcoal furnaces and enlarged an older one, the Jenifer. In Anniston a cotton-mill with 12,000 spindles was erected and the car-wheel works of Noble Brothers was moved thither from Rome. In 1883 the Woodstock Company, which had retained possession of all property, formally opened the city to the public and encouraged new industries. Noble, always a progressive ironmaster, acquired valuable coal properties and constructed two two-hundred-ton coke furnaces to make pig iron for the manufacture of cast-iron pipe, a pioneer enterprise embodied in the Anniston Pipe Works Company, organized in 1887.

That the progress of Anniston, social as well as economic, was always Noble's primary consideration, was evidenced in the schools, the Anniston Inn, and the first newspaper—the *Weekly Hot Blast*—which he founded. People of every sect and worthy cause were recipients of his gifts, and his employees, both white and colored, were devoted to him. He built the Episcopal church, of which he was the leading member. At the height of his achievements, when Anniston's industrial capital represented an investment of more than eleven million dollars, he died suddenly. Convinced that the southern iron industry needed a protective tariff, he consistently supported the Republican party. In 1861 he married Christine Stoeckel of Philadelphia, Pa., by whom he had one son and three daughters.

[A contemporary sketch of Samuel Noble and the early years of Anniston is found in *Northern Ala. Hist. and Biog.* (1888), pp. 112, 470–77, and in *Anniston, "The Model City of the South," A Description of Anniston* (1887). The *Memorial Record of Ala.* (1893), vol. I, contains a biographical sketch. An article in the *Anniston Star*, Mar. 6, 1924, is the report of an interview with Noble's sister, Miss Mary Noble, who provided most of the material on Noble in Ethel Armes, *The Story of Coal and Iron in Ala.* (1910). See also T. M. Owen, *Hist. of Ala. and Dict. of Ala. Biog.* (1921), vol. I, and the *Daily Reg.* (Mobile), Aug. 16, 1888.]   L. J. C.

NOEGGERATH, EMIL OSCAR JACOB BRUNO (Oct. 5, 1827–May 3, 1895), physician, was born in Germany, at Bonn on the Rhine. His father, Jacob John Noeggerath, professor of mineralogy at the University of Bonn, was an authority on subjects concerning mining and ore-refining, but his interests extended beyond his special field to literature and politics. He was apparently personally acquainted with Goethe and his home was a center for the dormant liberalism of the post-Napoleonic period. The maiden name of Emil's mother was Primavesi; her family was originally Italian. Emil Noeggerath began his medical education at the University of Bonn in 1848 and received the degree of M.D. in 1852. From Bonn he went to Berlin, started special work in gynecology, and in 1853 passed the official state examinations. He then visited Vienna, Prague, and Paris. Upon his return to Bonn he served as first assistant in the obstetrical clinic and in 1856 entered upon private practice in Neuwied on the Rhine.

The following year he came to America to accept a position on the faculty of a prospective medical school in St. Louis, Mo., but the plan was frustrated by the financial failure of the institution and he was forced to enter general practice in New York City. He soon gained a reputation for special abilities in gynecology and obstetrics and all his subsequent practice was in these specialties. He was associated with the German Hospital, Mount Sinai, and other prominent medical institutions, was one of the founders of the American Gynecological Society and of the New York Obstetrical Society, and professor of obstetrics and gynecology at the old New York Medical College. In 1885 his life-long ailment, tuberculosis, forced him to return to Germany, where he died in 1895. He had married a kinswoman, Rolanda Noeggerath, and had a daughter and three sons.

Noeggerath was probably one of the most talented American physicians of his time. He combined an acute sense of biological mechanism with an appreciation for the totality of the organism. In this characteristic he fused the old and new systems of medicine in a blend whose virtue was not appreciated until recent times. He was among the first to use pathology at the sick-bed itself in that he advised the microscopic examination of the uterine tissues removed by curettage. At a time of operative enthusiasm, he taught that conservative treatment must always be the method of choice. This attitude he assumed despite the fact that he was himself a brilliant surgeon and developed new operative methods. He deplored the development of virtuosity in

surgical technique at the cost of surgical diagnosis. For many years he stood alone in his belief that the cervical tear was an innoxious deformity and that the operations devised for its repair were needless and dangerous. He was interested in bacteriology at a time when this subject was still only an interesting biological curiosity. He developed a surgical aseptic technique for gynecological examinations which transcended the bounds of Lister's antisepsis. Again, it was many years before gynecologists appreciated the potential sources of infection which the examining finger or instrument represented and instituted the measures which Noeggerath had proposed.

His greatest work is his publication: *Die Latente Gonorrhoe im Weiblichen Geschlecht* (Bonn, 1872). In this brochure, which was written in the hours of relaxation from a busy practice, he stated and supported the following theses: 1) that gonorrhea is a chronic disease which retains its infective power long after the acute stage has passed; 2) that every male in such a latent stage will perforce infect the female with whom he cohabits; 3) that the disease can also produce a latent stage in the female from which it can be awakened by sexual activity, by parturition, or by simple mechanical interference, such as medical instrumentation; 4) that most of the inflammations of the genital tract in females are due to gonorrheal infection; 5) that sterility is often due to the same agent and that the male in many sterile unions is the deficient member. This book was published three years before Robert Koch made bacteriology an exact science and seven years before Neisser discovered the gonococcus. So fundamental are these theses that they have become commonplaces of medical knowledge today.

It is remarkable that a man of such talent and achievement should have made so little impression on his age that he was all but forgotten by medical historians. His critical mind aroused animosity among his American colleagues and the extramural scientific activities of a self-made specialist received a cold welcome at European universities. He thus never succeeded in founding a school of thought. Close upon the heels of his publications came the dramatic discoveries of the classical bacteriologists who were the fortunate possessors of Koch's golden key to discovery, and in the flush of the new era all previous work was forgotten.

[Paul Diepgen, "Emil Noeggerath," *Klinische Wochenschrift*, Oct. 1, 1927; F. H. Garrison, *An Intro. to the Hist. of Medicine* (4th ed., 1929); H. S. Reichle, "Emil Noeggerath (1827–1895)," in *Annals of Medic. Hist.*, Mar. 1928; Zinsser, "Emil Noeggerath,"

Münchener Medizinische Wochenschrift, Sept. 30, 1927; *Archiv für Pathologische Anatomie und Physiologie und für Klinische Medicin*, Mar. 9, 1896; J. Pagel, *Biographisches Lexikon hervorragender Ärzte des Neunzehnten Jahrhunderts* (1901); information concerning wife and children from a son, Prof. Carl Noeggerath, Univ. of Freiburg, Germany.]　　H. S. R.

NOGUCHI, HIDEYO (Nov. 24, 1876–May 21, 1928), bacteriologist, parasitologist, and immunologist, was born at Inawashiro in northern Japan, the son of a peasant, Sayosuke Kobiyama, and his wife, Shika Noguchi, who adopted her husband in order to give her son her family name. Owing to the poverty of his family and to a deformation of his left hand following a severe burn in infancy, he was, in childhood, so heavily handicapped that his opportunities for securing an education were threatened. Fortunately, his native ability was discovered by the principal of an academy, a certain Kobayashi, who made suitable arrangements for his schooling. A successful operation upon his hand by Dr. K. Watanabe, led the boy to decide upon medicine as a career. Serving at first as errand boy and apprentice to Watanabe and attending to the household affairs and medical practice of the latter during his absence because of the war between Japan and China, Noguchi (whose childhood name was "Seisaku," changed to "Hideyo" on the attainment of manhood) in 1894 entered the Tokyo Medical College where he graduated in 1897. He then became assistant to Surgeon-General Satow at the General Hospital, edited the hospital journal, and lectured on general pathology and oral surgery at the Tokyo Dental College. In September 1898 he joined Kitasato's staff at the Government Institute of Infectious Diseases and when bubonic plague broke out in China he was sent by the International Sanitary Board to New Chwang, and became physician-in-chief to the Central Bureau in charge of the hospital and the bacteriological laboratory. The plague dying out there, he was sent to Manchuria under a Russian medical commission but, on the development of the Boxer movement, he was recalled to Kitasato's Institute in Tokyo, where he wrote textbooks on pathology, bacteriology, and dentistry, and translated part of Hueppe's manual of hygiene into Japanese.

Early in 1899 Noguchi became acquainted with Simon Flexner, who, on his way to the Philippine Islands as a member of a Johns Hopkins Medical Commission, visited Kitasato's Institute. The young Japanese expressed the desire to go to America to study pathology and bacteriology, and though this was not strongly encouraged by Flexner, Noguchi, after earning the

money for the journey and receiving a promise from Kobayashi that his family would be looked after, went to Philadelphia at the end of 1899 and started work in the laboratory of pathology of which Flexner had just been made head at the University of Pennsylvania. After consultation with Dr. Silas Weir Mitchell, Noguchi was assigned to the study of immunity against snake-venoms, receiving support from the National Academy of Sciences and the Carnegie Institution of Washington. In this study, he investigated most carefully the problems relating to the hemolysins and agglutinins of snake venom and the protective sera. With his clarity of interest, his technical skill, and his prodigious industry he was able quickly to obtain brilliant results, which were published in a series of important articles, and, finally, in an illustrated volume on the subject, *The Action of Snake Venom upon Cold-blooded Animals,* brought out by the Carnegie Institution in 1904, a work that, in itself, established Noguchi's reputation as a keen observer and an experimenter of the first order.

In 1903, pending the transfer of his activities to the Rockefeller Institute of Medical Research, Noguchi, attracted by the immunochemical researches of Madsen and Arrhenius, worked in Copenhagen. On taking up work at the Rockefeller Institute after it opened in 1904, he applied Madsen's ideas to the study of the Wassermann reaction and devised a new and important method for the diagnosis of syphilis. As a result of this study, he was led into his most important researches upon methods for obtaining pure cultures of spiral organisms, modifying the method of Theobald Smith (in which a fragment of sterile rabbit's kidney was added to culture media). In these investigations, Noguchi displayed his extraordinary ability to adapt technical methods by means of subtle alterations to make them successful for varying purposes. Not only was he able to grow in pure culture the spiral organism that causes syphilis (previously demonstrated in the lesions of syphilis by Schaudinn) but he also obtained in pure culture a large variety of pathogenic spiral organisms as well as many saprophytic spiral forms. The isolation of the *Treponema pallidum* in pure culture made possible, too, the preparation of luetin, a soluble extract analogous to tuberculin, useful for the diagnosis of latent and of congenital lues. In 1913, with J. W. Moore, Noguchi demonstrated the presence of *Treponema pallidum* in the cerebral cortex of patients dead of general paralysis; the post-mortem recovery of this parasite in the central nervous system in both general paresis and tabes dorsalis settled once and for all the nature of the etiological agent in these two serious maladies.

His discovery of the great value of media containing rabbits' testis for the growth of the etiological agent of syphilis in large numbers and for freeing it from associated contaminating bacteria was further applied by him to the cultivation of the globoid bodies in poliomyelitis, to the study of Rocky Mountain spotted fever, and to the enrichment and purification of the virus of vaccinia (so as to free it from the miscellaneous bacteria of the bovine product). During the last ten years of his life Noguchi directed his investigations to the clearing up of the etiology of yellow fever, of Oroya fever, and of trachoma. As a result of his four expeditions to South America he concluded that the yellow fever there was due to infection with *Leptospira icteroides,* for he was able to isolate this organism from the blood of more than twenty per cent. of the patients called yellow fever by clinical experts. Later, the studies of Stokes and others indicated that the yellow fever of Africa is due to a filter-passing virus, and there is now doubt whether the South American yellow fever studied was another infectious disease (confused with yellow fever and due to *Leptospira*) or is the same as African yellow fever but complicated by an associated secondary or concomitant infection with *Leptospira.*

In his studies of the Oroya fever of Peru, Noguchi was able to grow Barton's rod-shaped bodies in special media and by animal experiments to prove that the general febrile process, Oroya fever, and the clinically widely different warty or verrugous local process, Verruga peruviana, are due to the same micro-organism, *Bartonella bacilliformis,* an infectious agent that entomologists have since shown is carried by nocturnal blood-sucking insects of the Phlebotomus class. The much-studied problem of the etiology of trachoma among American Indians was finally solved by Noguchi through a series of painstaking researches in which he eliminated successively many types of bacteria that live in or upon the conjunctiva of trachomatous patients until he was able to isolate one, *Bacterium granulosis,* that will produce the characteristic lesions in certain monkeys.

In 1927 Noguchi went to Africa to study the yellow fever there. He confirmed the findings of Stokes of the presence of a filterable virus and of the absence of *Leptospira,* but, just as he was ready to return, contracted yellow fever himself and died at Accra on May 21, 1928, thus succumbing to a disease of which Stokes had already become a victim and from which Young, who

was to have continued the experiments, also died eight days later. Physically, Noguchi was frail but he exhibited extraordinary powers of endurance. By disposition he was kindly, cheerful, and affectionate, and he was inspired by an intense desire to serve humanity in a practical way through discovery of the causes of disease. His originality, his capacity to formulate problems clearly, his power of inventiveness of new technical methods, his prodigious industry, his indomitable will, and his good fortune in establishing intimate and sympathetic associations in an environment that supplied him with adequate facilities for his work account for the achievements that made him, at the age of fifty-two, the outstanding figure in microbiology since Pasteur and Koch. He was the recipient of many honors from governments and learned societies and after his death the Order of the Rising Sun was conferred by his native country. He was survived by his wife, Mary Dardis, whom he had married on Apr. 10, 1912. His birthplace has been bought to be made into a shrine in which the records of his life and work will be permanently preserved.

[See: Gustav Eckstein, *Noguchi* (1931); *Japan Medic. World,* July 15, 1928; *Schweizerische medizinische Wochenschrift,* July 14, 1928; *Current Hist.,* July 1928; *Science,* June 28, 1929; *Sci. Monthly,* July 1928; *Bull. N. Y. Acad. of Medicine,* Sept. 1929; *N. Y. Times,* May 22, 1928.]   L.F.B.

NOLAN, PHILIP (*c.* 1771–Mar. 21, 1801), contraband trader, is said to have been born at Frankfort, Ky. (Hale, "The Real Philip Nolan," *post,* p. 282), though according to his own questionable declaration in 1794 (census report, Nacogdoches, Texas), he was a native of Belfast, Ireland, twenty-three years old. A reference to him by Gen. James Wilkinson [*q.v.*] as "a child of my own raising" (King, *post,* p. 92) and the fact that Nolan once referred to Wilkinson as "the friend and protector of my youth" (Wilkinson, *post,* II, App. 2) give some ground for the belief held by Spanish officials in Louisiana that he was reared in the General's family. As early as 1790 he was Wilkinson's agent in tobacco dealings at New Orleans. The following year he made the first of four trading ventures into Texas. Suspected as a spy in Mexico and cheated of his goods (according to his own account, *Ibid.*) he lived for a time among the Indians, but subsequently went back to the Spaniards, and having sold skins and caught a number of wild horses, returned in 1794 to Louisiana. From his second expedition (1794–96), to San Antonio, he took back 250 horses, selling some in Natchez and Kentucky, though he was legally entitled only to supply mounts for the Spanish cavalry in Louisiana. Sharing in the profits of his enterprises, Spanish officials both there and in Texas winked at his illicit trading, and he was even permitted to pasture his wild horses with the cavalry horses at San Antonio until they were gentle. He had corrals also and a "pasture" on the Trinity River, in East Texas.

At the beginning of his third expedition he fell in with Andrew Ellicott [*q.v.*], then on his way to survey the Southwestern boundary. Seizing the opportunity to obtain instruction in Ellicott's profession, he accompanied him as far as Natchez, and in the summer of 1797 set out with instruments and a passport from Governor Gayoso [*q.v.*] of Louisiana to explore and map for him the north Texas region. After his death it was said that he had intended to gather information for General Wilkinson to use in a projected conquest of Mexico (Deposition of Samuel P. Moore, 1810, Wilkinson, II, App. 3). After penetrating apparently as far south as the Rio Grande in the state of Tamaulipas, he returned with some 1,300 horses. Before his return the suspicions of Gayoso had been aroused and the Texan authorities warned to look out for Nolan, and after this expedition his license to do horse-trading was revoked. Accordingly, when he set forth the next year, it was with the avowed purpose of bringing into the United States horses from his "pasture" on the Trinity River, but it is evident that he planned to do other trading also. Gayoso's warnings against him now became effective, however, and a hundred men under Lieut. M. Musquiz were sent out from Nacogdoches to arrest him. In a skirmish between this force and Nolan's party near the present Waco, Nolan was killed. He had married on Dec. 19, 1799, Frances Lintot, daughter of Bernard Lintot, a merchant of Natchez. An only son, born after his father's death, died at the age of twenty-one.

The testimony of those who knew him shows Nolan to have been a man of magnetic personality, reputed to possess an exceptional knowledge of the Spanish frontier. Daniel Clark, 1766–1813 [*q.v.*], in a letter to Thomas Jefferson written in 1799, characterized him as "that extraordinary and enterprising Man . . . whom Nature seems to have formed for Enterprises of which the rest of Mankind are incapable" (*Quarterly of the Texas State Historical Association,* April 1904, pp. 309–10). William Dunbar [*q.v.*] attributed to him "energy of mind not sufficiently cultivated by education, but which under the guidance of a little more prudence might have conducted him to enterprises of the first magnitude" (*Ibid.,* p. 315). According to Professor

E. C. Barker, "Nolan's connection with Wilkinson, Jefferson's desire to get information from him concerning the habits of wild horses, and Clark's vague references to 'a man who will at all times have it in his Power to render important Services to the U. S.' (*Ibid.,* p. 310) have enveloped his smuggling adventures in an atmosphere of mystery and international intrigue which candid scrutiny of available sources tends to dispel."

[Information concerning Nolan, including manuscripts in the Nacogdoches and Bexar Archives and transcripts and photostats from Mexican archives, is collated in an unfinished master's thesis by Maurine T. Wilson, at the Univ. of Tex. The original *testimonios* taken in the examination of Nolan's companions in 1801 are in the Yale Univ. Lib. Much of the information in the foregoing sketch has been furnished by Professor E. C. Barker. Published sources include J. A. Quintero, "Philip Nolan and his Companions," in *The Texas Almanac,* 1868, pp. 60–64; E. E. Hale, "The Real Philip Nolan," in *Miss. Hist. Soc. Pubs.,* IV (1901), 281–329, in which he explains that the historical Nolan is not the prototype of "The Man Without a Country"; Grace King, "The Real Philip Nolan," in *La. Hist. Soc. Pubs.,* vol. X (1918); James Wilkinson, *Memoirs of My Own Times* (1816), vol. II, pp. 232–42 and Apps. 2, 3, 28; *Quart. Tex. State Hist. Asso.,* Apr. 1904; Dunbar Rowland, *Mississippi* (1907), II, 342–45; Henderson Yoakum, *Hist. of Tex.* (1855), I, 403–07. E. E. Hale, *Philip Nolan's Friends* (1876) is a novel based on the real Nolan's career.]   H. C. B.
E. R. D.

NOONAN, JAMES PATRICK (Dec. 15, 1878–Dec. 4, 1929), labor leader, was born in St. Louis, Mo., the son of Thomas P. Noonan and Bridget Kemmey. His father was a farmer in St. Louis County whose family came from Ireland and settled in Missouri in 1850. Young Noonan attended school until he was about thirteen but, left an orphan at an early age, he spent his boyhood mainly in manual labor of various kinds. On the outbreak of the Spanish-American War in 1898 he enlisted as a private and after his discharge the next year became an electric lineman in St. Louis. He married, at Clayton, Mo., Inez M. Mitchell on June 26, 1901. In the same year he joined the International Brotherhood of Electrical Workers and for the next twenty-eight years was identified with the history of that organization. At twenty-four he was president of his local union, the next year president of the Missouri and Illinois District Council, and in 1904 vice-president of the international organization with headquarters at Springfield, Ill. In this capacity Noonan served throughout the internal struggle of 1908 to 1913 which threatened to disrupt the union, and in 1917, when President Frank Joseph McNulty [*q.v.*] went on leave of absence, became acting president and two years later president, with headquarters after 1920 in Washington. He had an enormous capacity for work and was thorough and conscientious, a good fighter when the need arose but more often a skilled diplomat who won the respect of the employers who sat opposite him at the council table. Under his pacific and progressive leadership from 1919 to 1929 his organization made rapid progress toward solidarity and business efficiency. Meanwhile he was elected in 1922 fifth vice-president of the Building Trades Department of the American Federation of Labor, later a member of the National Board of Jurisdictional Awards for the Building Trades, and in 1924 a member of the executive council of the Federation. He was fifth vice-president of the American Federation of Labor and third vice-president of the Building Trades Department at the time of his death. As an authority on the effect of electric power on labor and labor organizations Noonan was made the only American labor delegate to the World Power Conference at London in 1924 and submitted a paper on "Labour's Part in Power Production" (*Transactions of the First World Power Conference*, London, 1925, vol. IV, pp. 1414–20). He was also appointed by Governor Pinchot a member of Pennsylvania's Giant Power Board and by Secretary of Commerce Hoover a member of the St. Lawrence Waterway Commission. He served on numerous committees, including the committee on seasonal operation in the construction industry of the President's Conference on Unemployment from 1921 to 1924. He was a member of the Elks and of the Congressional Country Club. His death resulted from burns received when he fell asleep while smoking in his Washington apartment, and his funeral in St. Louis where, because of the large amount of traveling required by his official duties, he kept his family home, was attended by several hundred members, many of them from distant points, of the International Brotherhood of Electrical Workers. A heavy-set man, broad-shouldered and almost completely bald but erect, alert, and energetic in his movements, Noonan owed his popularity to his friendliness, his personal charm, and his frank and candid manner of approaching all questions. But the qualities which kept him for many years an outstanding figure in the labor movement were his practical common sense, his honesty, his broad interests, and his ability to adapt himself to circumstances and opportunities.

[Obituaries were published in the *N. Y. Times,* and *St. Louis Globe-Democrat,* Dec. 5, 1929, in the *Jour. of Electrical Workers and Operators,* Dec. 1929 and Jan. 1930, and in other journals. Biographical material is also contained in M. A. Mulcaire, *The Internat. Brotherhood of Electrical Workers* (1923) ; the *Jour. of Electrical Workers and Operators;* the *Proc.* and the *Reports of Officers of the Internat. Brotherhood of Electrical Workers* from 1904 to 1929; and in the *Re-*

ports of Proc. of the . . . Ann. Conventions of the Building Trades Dept., Am. Federation of Labor from 1922 to 1930. Additional information has been secured from Noonan's son, Robert E. Noonan of St. Louis.]

H. S. W.

NORCROSS, ORLANDO WHITNEY (Oct. 25, 1839–Feb. 27, 1920), master-builder, second son of Jesse Springer and Margaret Ann (Whitney) Norcross and eighth in descent from Jeremiah Norcross, a proprietor in Watertown, Mass., as early as 1642, was born in Clinton, Me. Removing with his family to Salem, Mass., at the age of four, he attended the grammar schools there, but started to work at about thirteen because his father had joined the gold rush of 1849 and never returned. After following for several years his father's trade of carpenter, he enlisted as artificer July 5, 1861, in the company which became Company D, 1st Heavy Artillery, Massachusetts Volunteers. As road and bridge-builder during his three years with the Army of the Potomac, he was often under Confederate fire.

Honorably discharged in the summer of 1864, he formed a partnership, as building-contractor, with his elder brother James, who managed the clerical and financial affairs of the firm while Orlando directed the constructional work, to which he was always, heart and soul, devoted. After completing successfully their first large contract, the Leicester Congregational Church, the firm established permanent headquarters at Worcester, Mass., in 1868. The financial panic of 1873 yielded them an unexpected dividend, for building prices dropped substantially shortly after they had signed a contract for the erection of Trinity Church, Boston. This contract had other important results. Executed between 1872 and 1877, it brought young Norcross into personal contact with H. H. Richardson [*q.v.*], the eminent architect, who during fifteen years regarded him as his right-hand man on all matters of practical construction.

Norcross was quick to adopt new methods and materials. To him is to be credited the flat-slab construction of reinforced concrete, which he invented. His practical inventiveness and resourcefulness often put the technical judgments of engineers to rout, notably in the case of a stone arch at the Springfield, Mass., railway station. At West Point, the erection of the Battle Monument, a granite monolith 41.6 feet high, weighing eighty-one tons, at that time (1893) the largest polished shaft in the world, presented almost insuperable difficulties, over which, however, Norcross as usual triumphed. He came to be widely recognized as a leader in his field. In 1875 he was appointed by the Secretary of the Treasury as one of three commissioners to inspect the Chicago Federal Building. The first edition of Frank E. Kidder's *Architect's and Builder's Pocket-Book* (1885), known as the "contractor's Bible" for nearly half a century, was dedicated to him. His firm's important contracts included Custom House Tower and Harvard Medical School, Boston; Harvard Union, Cambridge; Rhode Island State Capitol; New York Public Library; Bank of Montreal; D.A.R. Building, Pan-American Building, Corcoran Art Gallery, and Masonic Temple in Washington, D. C.; Howard Memorial Library, New Orleans; and the Ames Memorial Monument of the Union Pacific Railroad at Sherman, Wyo.

To the financial side of his work Norcross was always indifferent, and in later years he suffered as a consequence. From early life he was devoted to books, seeking to atone by wide and constant reading for his lack of formal education. His absorption in work was proverbial. His Civil War experiences and abundant contacts with labor having impressed him keenly with the waste and suffering entailed by strong drink, he was always a firm temperance advocate. He was a disciple of nature and fond of tramping; he loved his home and shunned club life. He was a vestryman of two Episcopal churches and a trustee of Clark University, an office he, a self-educated man, particularly prized. He married in May 1870, Ellen Sibley of Salem, who bore him five children, of whom two sons died in infancy. At the age of eighty he was seized with apoplexy while on his way to business and died within a few hours. On his eighty-first birthday a bronze tablet bearing a bas-relief portrait of him was unveiled in the Worcester City Hall.

[T. H. Gage, *Memorial Address, Oct. 25, 1920* (n.d.); Charles Nutt, *Hist. of Worcester and Its People* (1919), vol. IV; *Who's Who in America,* 1918–19; *Record of the Mass. Volunteers 1861–65,* vol. I (1868); *Trans. Am. Soc. Mech. Engineers,* Feb. 1921; *Trans. Am. Soc. Civil Engineers,* vol. LXXXIV (1921); *Worcester Evening Gazette* and *Boston Transcript,* Feb. 27, 1920; *Sunday Telegram* (Worcester), Mar. 7, 1920.]
R. K. S.

NORDBERG, BRUNO VICTOR (Apr. 11, 1857–Oct. 30, 1924), mechanical engineer, the son of Capt. Carl Victor and Dores (Hinze) Nordberg, was born at Björneborg, Finland. His father, a prominent and successful shipbuilder, died while Bruno was still at the preparatory school, where he studied theology, history, and languages. When he entered the University of Helsingfors and discovered that his inclination was toward technical subjects, he found that his early schooling had given him little of value for his later career. Close association with Prof. Rudolf Kolster, a physicist at the University,

confirmed his desire to become an engineer, but it required his greatest efforts to build up the foundation in science and mathematics which had previously been neglected and at the same time to progress in his studies.

In 1879, about two years after his graduation, he came to the United States and obtained work in Buffalo. Four months later he pushed westward to Milwaukee, and there came upon the works of the E. P. Allis Company, where he found employment detailing Corliss engine parts. Soon thereafter he seized upon an opportunity to design a blowing engine, an achievement which revealed his unusual skill as a designer and engineer and resulted in his further advancement. In an endeavor to improve the economy of slide-valve engines, he designed a poppet valve cut-off governor, and in 1886, with the financial aid of friends, organized the Bruno Nordberg Company for the manufacture of such governors. The first shop was in small rented quarters.

Increased demand for Corliss engines led Nordberg to design such units, the first of which was built at the Wilkins Manufacturing Company of Milwaukee. In 1890 the need for enlarged quarters was felt and the Nordberg Manufacturing Company was organized, of which, during the years which followed, Nordberg served as president and chief engineer. An existing building was equipped with machinery, where governors, Corliss-valve, and poppet-valve engines were built. There followed the building of compressors, pumps, blowing engines, hoists, condensers, and heaters. The reputation of the Company grew rapidly and to it were referred all manner of difficult engineering problems. The economy of Nordberg's steam engines was soon recognized, and what became known as the Nordberg generative cycle was developed. This cycle is used at the present time (1934) in modern turbine plants.

Among the works of the company were the Champion Copper Company's compressor at Painesdale, Mich., and the pumps built for the Wildwood Water Works, Wildwood, Pa., both still known as record-holding plants. Nordberg's compound steam stamps were epoch-making in the milling operation of Northern Michigan Copper Mines. Hoists were improved with such rapid strides that the demand for them came from all metal mines. He designed the hoist for the Tamarack Mining Company, which remarkable piece of work was followed some years later by the famous hoist built for the No. 2 Shaft at the Quincy Mining Company, Hancock, Mich., the largest one so far built. The chemical industry profited by a great variety of special vacuum pumps and gas compressors which he devised. The company built the largest uniflow engine in the country for rolling-mill work, as well as some of the largest compressors for mining work. Nordberg's greatest work, however, was the building of the pneumatic hoisting system for the Anaconda Copper Company, Butte, Mont.

He had taken out some seventy United States patents before his death. In his private laboratory he was active in electrical and chemical experiments, and developed many new ideas. As early as 1890, he was awarded a gold medal by the French Academy for noteworthy inventions. His genius attracted to the Nordberg Manufacturing Company a class of men notable for their ability, and as his enormous capacity for work diminished, these men gradually took responsibilities from his shoulders. His hobby was sailing his yacht. He designed yachts and spent much of his spare time in making yacht models. His mechanical genius was reflected even in the fittings of his boats. On Sept. 24, 1882, he married Helena Hinze, and his married life was an inspiration to all with whom he came in contact. He had two sons, one of whom died at the age of thirty-four. Nordberg's death occurred in his sixty-eighth year, at Milwaukee.

[*Trans. Am. Soc. Mech. Engineers*, vol. XLVI (1925), repr. from *Mechanical Engineering*, Dec. 1924, portr.; *Engineering* (London), Nov. 21, 1924; Paul Langer, in *Zeitschrift des Vereines Deutscher Ingenieure*, Dec. 20, 1924; C. E. Holmbery, in *Finlands Svenska Tekniker* (Helsingfors, Finland), ed. by Jonatan Reuter, pt. 1, 1923; *History of Milwaukee County* (1895), II, 7; *Men of Progress of Wis.* (1897); *Who's Who in America*, 1924–25; *Milwaukee Sentinel*, Oct. 31, 1924.]   D. K.

NORDHEIMER, ISAAC (1809–Nov. 3, 1842), Orientalist, was born in Memelsdorf, Bavaria, to Meyer and Esther Natal (Strauss) Nordheimer. Six years spent in the Yeshiba (Rabbinical Academy) at Presburg under the renowned Talmudist Moses Sofer gave him a thorough grounding in Hebrew and Aramaic literature. Thereafter, at the Gymnasium in Würzburg and at the Universities of Würzburg and Munich he gained his classical education and his knowledge of cognate Semitic languages, receiving the degree of Ph.D. at Munich in 1834. In response to the urging of some American friends there, he left Germany for the Western world, landing in New York in 1835. His mastery of Hebrew obtained for him in 1838, Jew though he was and remained, the position of instructor in sacred literature at Union Theological Seminary, where all the other members of the faculty had to profess the Westminster Confession. Attempts were made to draw him into religious controversy, but when his interpretations were challenged, he studiously limited himself to grammatical issues and was able to avoid all theological questions. From 1839 to 1840 he was also acting professor of Hebrew in the faculty of science and letters of the University of the City of New York, and from 1840 till his death, professor of German and of Oriental languages. Never marrying, he lived with his sister Jeanette in the University building and gave himself unremittingly to his exacting toil, winning the esteem of students and colleagues both for his simple-hearted, childlike, affectionate nature, and for his devotion, enthusiasm, and skill as a teacher. The eminent Semitic scholar Edward Robinson [*q.v.*], in his report to the board of directors of Union Theological Seminary on June 28, 1842, testified to the great ability and fidelity with which Nordheimer instructed his classes, and to the very important aid which his labors gave to the reputation and best interests of the Seminary. By that time, however, Nordheimer, whose frame had always been frail, was exhausted by overwork, and four months later, at the early age of thirty-three, he died of tuberculosis. He was buried in the little Jewish cemetery on Twenty-first Street near Sixth Avenue, New York. His death destroyed the promise of the most brilliant Semitic grammarian of nineteenth-century America.

On his voyage to America he had conceived the idea of writing a textbook of Hebrew grammar according to the laws governing philology and the development of speech. He offered the completed manuscript of his first volume to the printer B. L. Hamlen in New Haven. Hamlen, pointing to shelves filled with copies of Hebrew grammars by Gesenius, Stuart, and Bush, for which there was virtually no demand, would not even look at it. To Nordheimer's plea that the original discoveries on every page of his volume would make it live, Hamlen replied coldly, "Your book also will die." Whereupon Nordheimer, pale with emotion, threw his manuscript on the counter, and said, "Den I will die wid my book." Touched by the depth of feeling of the gentle, curly-headed scholar, Hamlen relented, accepted the manuscript for examination, and on a favorable report, printed the book. This was *A Critical Grammar of the Hebrew Language* in two volumes (1838–41) on which Nordheimer's reputation is based. It is an original and penetrating piece of clear and profound scholarship, which attempts to show lexical and grammatical relations with Indo-European as well as with Semitic forms. Nordheimer's other writings were *A Grammatical Analysis of Selections from* the Hebrew Scriptures (1838); an elaborate review of Fürst's Hebrew concordance to the Bible, in the *Biblical Repertory and Princeton Review,* July 1839; "Hebrew Lexicography" (*American Biblical Repository,* April 1838); "The Philosophy of Ecclesiastes" (*Ibid.,* July 1838); "The Talmud and the Rabbies" (*Ibid.,* October 1839); and "The Rabbies and Their Literature" (*Ibid.,* July 1841). He issued a prospectus of a *Complete Hebrew and Chaldee Concordance to the Old Testament* in the year of his death.

[A. Rhine, in *The Jewish Encyc.* (1925), vol. IX; Henry Neill, in the *New Englander,* July 1874 (repr. for private circulation by William Nordheimer, London, 1906); G. L. Prentiss, *The Union Theol. Sem. in the City of N. Y.* (1889); C. R. Gillett, *Alumni Cat. of the Union Theol. Sem.* (1926); *Gen. Alumni Cat., N. Y. Univ.* (1906); "The Tomb of Nordheimer" (poem), in *Morning Courier and N. Y. Enquirer,* Nov. 17, 1842; Edward Robinson, *Bibliotheca Sacra: or Tracts and Essays* (1843).]
D. deS. P.

NORDHOFF, CHARLES (Aug. 31, 1830–July 14, 1901), journalist and author, was born in Erwitte, Westphalia, in the Kingdom of Prussia. When he was five years old his parents, Charles and Adelheid (Platé) Nordhoff, emigrated with him to the United States. After attending school in Cincinnati he was apprenticed at the age of thirteen to a printer. He served a year and then went to Philadelphia, where he worked as compositor on a newspaper. Enlisting in 1844 in the United States Navy he served three years and made, in that time, a voyage around the world. After the expiration of the term of his enlistment he spent several years on merchant vessels and in the New England fisheries. At the age of twenty-three he gave up seafaring and took up journalism as a profession. While employed as newspaper reporter he wrote a series of books inspired largely by his own experiences as a sailor. They were the three volumes, *Man-of-War Life* (1855), *The Merchant Vessel* (1855), and *Whaling and Fishing* (1856) that were later collected as *Nine Years a Sailor* (1857), and a fourth book, *Stories of the Island World* (1857). His life at sea not only provided the material for his first literary production, but, by hard physical training and by broadening his field of experience and quickening his powers of observation, it gave him an invaluable training for his later career as a newspaper correspondent. In 1857 Harper & Brothers engaged him as an editor and four years later he became managing editor of the New York *Evening Post.* During the Civil War he strongly advocated the Union cause both in the columns of his paper and in a number of books and pamphlets. He published *Secession*

is Rebellion (1860), *The Freedmen of South-Carolina* (1863), and *America for Free Working Men* (1865). He resigned from the *Post* in 1871 and spent the following two years in travel visiting California and Hawaii. In 1874 the *New York Herald* engaged him for its Washington correspondent, a position which he filled with great success until his retirement in 1890. In Washington "he won the friendship of the leading men of the day, and a high place among the political writers of the country. His letters were recognized as the authoritative presentation of the news, and the final word on the moral merits of a controversy. He . . . was not only one of the few correspondents in whom public men confided, but one of still fewer whom they consulted" (*Harper's Weekly, post,* p. 761). Some of his newspaper assignments led to rather important publications. His *Communistic Societies in the United States* (1875) was a valuable contribution to the social history of the United States. It was based on visits to a number of communities and on personal observation of their method of life. In *The Cotton States in the Spring and Summer of 1875* (1876), he set a high standard of impartiality for investigators of controversial political and economic questions. Holding no brief for party or section, his book records his own painstaking and systematic inquiries (see J. F. Rhodes, *History of the United States,* VII, 1906, p. 126). The strongly moral and religious trend of his thinking is displayed in two books written particularly for the instruction of his children and those of his friends. They are *Politics for Young Americans* (1875), which had considerable vogue as a school textbook, and *God and the Future Life* (1883). All of his writing was characterized by a direct and forceful style and by a preference for simple words and short sentences. His personality was like his writing, straightforward and downright. He spent the last years of his life in Coronado, Cal., partly because of his fondness for the region and partly because of the delicate health of his wife, Lida (Letford) Nordhoff. He died in San Francisco.

[*Harper's Weekly,* July 27, 1901; *Who's Who in America,* 1899–1900; *San Francisco Call,* July 15, 1901.]
P. W. B.

NORDICA, LILLIAN (May 12, 1859–May 10, 1914), prima donna, was born in Farmington, Me., the daughter of Edwin and Amanda (Allen) Norton, and the grand-daughter of a well-known revivalist preacher, familiarly known as "Camp-meeting John Allen." Her parents were talented and she was reared in a musical atmosphere. After studying with John O'Neill at the New England Conservatory of Music, she made her concert début at Madison Square Garden in New York City as the soprano soloist with Patrick Gilmore's band. In 1878, after two years of successful concert work, she accompanied Gilmore's band on a European tour in the same capacity and sang in London and in Liverpool, and at the Trocadéro in Paris. But in Germany her objection to open-air singing led her to sever her connection with Gilmore and study operatic rôles with the famous singing-master Antonio San Giovanni of Milan, who gave her the stage name by which she is known. On Apr. 30, 1879, she made her début as an operatic soprano as Brescia, in La Traviata, with immediate success. After singing in Genoa, Danzig, Königsberg, and Berlin, she first appeared as prima donna at the Grand Opera in Paris as Marguerite in Gounod's Faust, on July 21, 1882, scoring an instant success in a part in which her coloratura work was considered inimitable. That same year she married Frederick A. Gower, scientist and inventor, who accompanied her to the United States where, at the New York Academy of Music, she appeared for the first time in opera in America, Nov. 26, 1883, in the same rôle that had won her success in Paris. For a time she withdrew from the stage. Her marriage had not been happy and in 1886 when legal steps were being taken to secure a separation, Gower vanished into oblivion in a balloon.

She resumed her activity as a prima donna in 1887, appearing at the Covent Garden Theatre, London, where, until 1893, she continued as one of the stars of the London operatic season. In the latter year she first sang at the Metropolitan Opera House in New York as a member of an Italian company managed by Henry Eugene Abbey and Maurice Grau, and which included Melba, Calvé, Eames, Plançon, and the de Reszkés. But she was not content to remain an exponent of French and Italian operatic rôles. Her ambition was fixed upon Wagnerian opera, and after studying the rôle of Elsa with Julius Kniese and Cosima Wagner, she sang it at the Bayreuth Festspielhaus in 1894 with outstanding success. After further intensive study with Kniese at Bayreuth, she scored a triumph at the Metropolitan Opera House in New York, Nov. 27, 1895, when she sang Isolde to Jean de Reszké's Tristan. Thenceforward her successes in Germany, France, and England were achieved in Wagnerian rôles. In 1896 she married in Indianapolis, Ind., the Hungarian tenor, Zoltan Döme, from whom she was divorced in 1904. From that time on, with occasional intermissions, she sang at the Metropolitan Opera House until

1907. During the season of 1907–08 she was a member of Oscar Hammerstein's Manhattan Opera Company, but thereafter her operatic appearances were only occasional, and she devoted herself chiefly to extended concert tours. On July 29, 1909, she was married to the American banker George W. Young, in London, and only now and again made use of her repertory of forty operas, as when she sang Isolde and Brünnhilde in Paris (1910), and Isolde (1912) with the Boston Opera Company. Her last concert tour, which began in 1913, was to have taken her around the world. But as a result of exposure after the grounding of the Tasman on Bramble Cay in the Gulf of Papua in December 1913, she contracted pneumonia and died in Batavia, Java, on May 10 of the following year. Nordica was a singer rather than an actress. She had a voice rich in tone, notable coloratura range, and consummate artistic ability. She may be regarded as one of the very great Wagnerian sopranos. Lillian Nordica's Hints to Singers, containing also many letters written by Nordica and her mother, was published in 1923 by William Armstrong.

[In addition to Lillian Nordica's Hints to Singers see: Who's Who in America, 1912–13; Mabel Wagnalls, Stars of the Opera (1899); H. E. Krehbiel, More Chapters of Opera (1919); Anton Seidl, The Music of the Modern World (1895), vol. I; Wm. Armstrong, "Nordica: A Study," Music, Nov. 1900; Musical Courier, May 13, 1914; Musical Observer, June 1914; New Eng. Conservatory Mag. and Alumni Rev., June 1914; Foyer, June 1914; N. Y. Times, May 11, 1914; and the Robinson Locke Collection, N. Y. Pub. Lib.]
F. H. M.

NORELIUS, ERIC (Oct. 26, 1833–Mar. 15, 1916), Swedish Lutheran clergyman, was born at Hassela, Helsingland, Sweden. At the age of nine he underwent an intense religious awakening, and after his confirmation he secured his parents' grudging consent to study. In January 1849 he entered school at Hudiksvall, where he heard of the Rev. L. P. Esbjörn [q.v.] and his work in America. Norelius decided to emigrate, and arrived in New York on Oct. 31, 1850. He went to Princeton, Ill., and thence to Andover, Ill., to see Esbjörn, who sent him to Capital (Lutheran) University, Columbus, Ohio, where he studied from 1851 to 1856. He served a congregation at West Point, Ind., which sent him in the fall of 1855 to find a better location for a settlement, when he chose Red Wing and Vasa, Goodhue County, Minn. After another year in school, he was ordained in the fall of 1856 at Dixon, Ill., and entered upon a ministry at Vasa and Red Wing, which, with interruptions, covered a period of sixty years. In spite of recurrent hemorrhages of the lungs, he was a zealous pastor, an active missionary, and an indefatigable literary worker throughout his long life. At his death his congregations had expanded into fifteen parishes served by nine pastors.

In 1857 Norelius and Jonas Engberg began the publication at Red Wing of *Minnesota Posten,* a Swedish paper. At the end of 1858 this was merged with *Hemlandet,* the paper of Dr. T. N. Hasselquist [*q.v.*], of Galesburg, Ill., and issued from Chicago by the Publication Society. In 1877–78 he issued *Ev. Luthersk Tidsskrift* at Vasa. He contributed regularly to the secular and religious press, and in recognition of his work he was made editor of the Augustana Synod's official organ, the *Augustana,* but resigned after a year on account of ill health. In a reminiscent mood he wrote "Memories of Sixty Years at Vasa" (*My Church,* vol. I, 1915), and "A Pioneer Boy's First Christmas in America" (*My Church,* vol. XIII). He issued an historical handbook, *The Ev. Lutherska Augustana-synoden i Nord Amerika och dess Mission* (Lund, 1870), and *The Life and Work of Rev. J. Ausland* (Red Wing, 1878). His more pretentious publications are the large biographical work, *Dr. T. N. Hasselquist* (Rock Island, n.d.), and *De Svenska Lutherska Församlingarnas och Svenskarnes Historia i Amerika* (Rock Island, vol. I, 1890; vol. II, 1916).

Norelius founded an orphanage at Vasa in 1865 which he conducted for eleven years. More enduring was a private school, which he started in 1862 at Red Wing, Minn., and which later expanded into the present Gustavus Adolphus College, St. Peter, Minn. He witnessed the growth of his synod from the Ev. Lutheran Synod of Northern Illinois to the Scandinavian Augustana Synod (1860). Of this synod he was president twice, from 1874 to 1881, and from 1899 to 1911. At the end of his second term of office he declined reëlection on account of ill health. He was then made president emeritus. He also served as president of the Minnesota Conference of the synod for four years. In recognition of his services, the King of Sweden made him a Knight and later a Knight Commander of the Order of the North Star, first class.

[*Who's Who in America,* 1903–05; *My Church,* vol. II (1916); J. C. Jensson, *Am. Lutheran Biogs.* (Milwaukee, 1890); *Minneapolis Jour.,* Mar. 16, 1916.]
J. M. R.

NORMAN, JOHN (*c.* 1748–June 8, 1817), engraver and publisher, seems to have been born in England. The published London parish registers do not give his name among christenings, nor has any authoritative statement been found concerning his parentage and early training. In May 1774 he advertised himself in the *Pennsyl-*

vania Journal, Philadelphia, as "John Norman, Architect and Landscape Engraver, from London," offering assistance to "booksellers in any part of America" in preparing "frontispieces of any kind." A considerable record of his subsequent crude but prolific work has been amassed, though little has been discovered that concerns his personality. It is probable that he had a continuous struggle, echoes of which are noted in the distribution of his insolvent estate (25,285 in the probate records of Suffolk County, Mass.). Norman and Ward, "Engravers and Drawing Masters," advertised in the *Pennsylvania Journal,* Aug. 17, 1774, adding that "they have likewise opened an Evening Drawing School." The next year, Norman, styling himself "Architect-Engraver," made the copper-plate illustrations for Robert Bell's edition of *Swan's British Architect, or the Builders' Treasury of Staircases.* In 1776, from his shop in Second Street, near Spruce, he published *A Map of the Present Seat of War.* Apparently still in Philadelphia, about 1789 he engraved a portrait of General Washington, which appeared in *The Philadelphia Almanack for the Year of Our Lord 1780.*

In 1781 he was in Boston, and there engraved the title-piece and music of *The Psalm-singers' Amusement* (1781), by William Billings. Beginning two years later, in November 1783, the *Boston Magazine,* projected by gentlemen of historical tastes, several of whom subsequently formed the Massachusetts Historical Society, was issued by Norman & White "at their office in Marshall's Lane." With the magazine was printed at intervals a *Geographical Gazetteer of Massachusetts,* now prized by collectors. The publishing firm's name was changed to Norman, White & Freeman and then, in July 1784, presumably after a disagreement, Norman dropped out. He published in 1789 the first *Boston Directory,* in which his own address is given as 75 Newbury St. Others took over the directory, but Norman printed and sold *Weatherwise's Federal Almanack for the Year of our Lord 1790,* and in 1791 began his publication of *The American Pilot.* He continued for many years to engrave portraits which neither in his own time nor among later connoisseurs were universally esteemed. His plates made for *An Impartial History of the War in America between Great Britain and the United States* (2 vols., 1781–82) had a scathing criticism from the *Freeman's Journal* (Philadelphia), Jan. 26, 1795, the portraits of Samuel Adams, Henry Knox, and Nathanael Greene being pronounced especially bad. These and other Norman portraits are justly described by Weitenkampf (*post,* p.

64) as "a mixture of graver-work and stipple" foreshadowing the "'mixed manner' which in the middle of the 19th century degenerated into the production of a characterless, machine-made sauce."

Norman died of a slow fever and was buried on Copp's Hill. The records of the administration of his estate reveal that his wife's name was Alice and that his affairs were in bad shape. The inventory discloses a great mass of unsold publications and materials, together with household furniture on which a total valuation of $620.47 was placed.

[S. A. Green, "Remarks on the Boston Magazine, The Geographical Gazetteer of Mass., and John Norman, Engraver," published in *Proc. Mass. Hist. Soc.*, May 1904, corrected by C. H. Hart in "Some Notes Concerning John Norman," *Ibid.*, Oct. 1904. See also Frank Weitenkampf, *Am. Graphic Art* (1924) ; W. C. Ford, *Broadsides, Ballads, etc. Printed in Massachusetts 1639–1800* (1922) ; D. M. Stauffer, *Am. Engravers upon Copper and Steel* (1907) ; *A Descriptive Cat. of an Exhibition of Early Am. Engraving, at the Boston Museum of Fine Arts* (1904) ; *One Hundred Notable Am. Engravers* (N. Y. Pub. Lib., 1928) ; *Boston Daily Advertiser*, June 10, 1817.] F. W. C.

NORRIS, BENJAMIN FRANKLIN (Mar. 5, 1870–Oct. 25, 1902), journalist and novelist, known both in private life and in the literary world as Frank Norris, was born in Chicago, Ill., the son of Benjamin Franklin Norris and Gertrude (Doggett) Norris. His father, lame because of hip disease and consequently unfitted for the severe toil of a Michigan farm, became at the age of fourteen unpaid assistant to a village watchmaker, learned the trade, saw something of the world as itinerant clock-mender and pedler, prospered, and ultimately founded his own jewelry firm in Chicago. Frank's mother, born of mixed New England and Virginia ancestry on a Massachusetts farm, was before her marriage a teacher in the public schools of Chicago and an actress who had enjoyed considerable success on the professional stage. Of their five children, but two, Frank and a brother Charles, eleven years his junior, also destined to win distinction as a writer, survived the perils of infancy and childhood.

In 1884, largely on account of the health of the elder Norris, the family moved to California, residing first at Oakland and a year later in San Francisco. Frank was sent to a school for boys at Belmont, some twenty miles south of the city. In 1886 he was kept out of school for a time by a fracture of the left arm, and to relieve the tedium of its convalescence he went to a local artist for lessons in drawing. He showed such aptitude that his father resolved to give him the best opportunities for its development. In 1887 the parents took their two sons

first to London and then to Paris where Frank enrolled in the Atelier Julien. The family remained in Paris for more than a year and then returned to California, leaving the young artist to pursue his studies. But these studies came to an abrupt end in 1889 when the elder Norris, convinced, it is said, by the discovery of a serial romance with which Frank was entertaining his younger brother by mail, that his time in Paris was not being profitably employed, cabled him instructions to return home. The next year he definitely committed himself to literature rather than art by entering the University of California. In college he exercised his talents on student plays and class books, with an occasional story or poem. Having come under the influence of Zola, whom he read with the devotion of a disciple, he adopted realism as a creed and began the first chapters of a story of San Francisco to be later completed and published as *McTeague*. Prevented by unfulfilled requirements in mathematics from graduating with his class in 1894, he spent the next year at Harvard, as a special student in English, electing among others a course in English composition with Lewis E. Gates, who recognized and encouraged his literary ambition. Parts of *Vandover and the Brute* were written under this stimulus.

In the autumn of 1895 Norris went to South Africa with credentials from the *San Francisco Chronicle,* arriving just in time to become involved in Dr. Leander Starr Jameson's disastrous raid on Johannesburg. He was captured by the Boers and ordered to leave the country. A severe attack of African fever prevented him from doing so at once, and he was not able to return to San Francisco until the spring of 1896. There he was taken on the staff of a literary weekly known as the *Wave* and wrote diligently for its columns. "Moran of the Lady Letty," a tale of love and adventure at sea, based, it is said, upon material secured from a sailor in the coast guard, was written at this time. Within two years he was in New York City, where he was associated with *McClure's Magazine.* As correspondent for the same periodical he was in Cuba during the Santiago campaign and suffered there a severe recurrence of the African fever. Upon his recovery he returned to New York and in 1899 entered the service of Doubleday, Page & Company. He resumed his literary work, the quality of which speedily won him recognition as a novelist of unusual vigor and originality. *Moran of the Lady Letty* appeared in book form in 1898 and *McTeague* and *Blix* in 1899. *McTeague,* which some regard as his strongest work, is a tale of passion and violence, beginning in the office of a charlatan dentist in the older section of San Francisco and ending in the scorched distances of Death Valley. It is the stuff of romance realistically set forth in scenes new to most readers.

A less successful novel, *A Man's Woman,* a story of love and arctic exploration, followed in 1900, and then began a more ambitious undertaking, his "Epic of the Wheat." This was to consist of "The Octopus," a story of California and the growing of the wheat, "The Pit," a Chicago tale of wheat in the commerce of the world, and "The Wolf," which should show the wheat consumed as bread in some famine-stricken village of the old world. *The Octopus* appeared in 1901. It was a novel with a purpose, an ardent defense of the wheat-growers in their struggle against the dominating greed of the railroad trust, and through it ran the epic story of the life-giving wheat, impersonal and irresistible, in the end engulfing the odious figure of the railway agent. *The Pit* was posthumously issued in 1903, and as a novel and as a play enjoyed a great success. A collection of essays, *The Responsibilities of the Novelist,* was published in the same year and *Vandover and the Brute* in 1914.

Norris was married Jan. 12, 1900, to Jeannette Black of California, and one child, a daughter, was born to them. *Blix* is said to be in some degree the story of his own wooing and of his struggle for literary recognition. He died in a hospital in San Francisco of peritonitis following an operation for appendicitis. He had returned to California in 1902 and had purchased a ranch near Gilroy, intending to make it his home. A projected trip to India for material for "The Wolf" and a second trilogy, to deal with the battle of Gettysburg, were frustrated by his death, which brought to a close a life of real literary promise. His works were published in collected editions in 1903 and 1928.

[See Franklin Walker, *Frank Norris, A Biog.* (1932); Introduction by Kathleen Norris in 1925 edition of *Blix* and by Henry S. Pancoast in 1918 edition of *McTeague*; W. D. Howells, "Frank Norris," *North Am. Rev.,* Dec. 1902; editorial, "Memories of Frank Norris," in the *Bookman,* May 1914; C. C. Dobie, "Frank Norris, or Up from Culture," *Am. Mercury,* Apr. 1928; F. T. Cooper, *Some Am. Story Tellers* (1911); *San Francisco Chronicle* and *San Francisco Examiner,* Oct. 26, 1902.]   J.C.F.

NORRIS, EDWARD (d. Dec. 23, 1659), Congregational clergyman, is said to have been a native of Gloucestershire, England, and to have been either seventy or eighty years of age at his death. His name is often spelled Norice, and at least one of his extant letters is so signed. He may be identical with an Edward Norris who was probably the son of Edward Norris, vicar of Tetbury in Gloucestershire, was born in 1584, matriculated at Balliol College, Oxford, in 1599, was awarded the degree of B.A. by Magdalen Hall in 1606/7 and that of M.A. in 1609, and was rector of Anmer in Norfolk in 1624 (Joseph Foster, *Alumni Oxonienses,* 1891, vol. III, early series, p. 1076). It was said by a contemporary, John Traske, that he lived at Tetbury and Horsley, Gloucestershire, as a teacher of youth, as well as minister (Felt, *post,* I, 387). In 1635 he published *A Treatise Maintaining that Temporall Blessings Are to Bee Sought and Asked with Submission to the Will of God. Wherein Is . . . Also a Discovery of the Late Dangerous Errours of Mr. John Traske . . .* ; in 1637 he issued *Reply to John Traske's True Gospel Vindicated*; and in 1638, a second reply entitled *The New Gospel Not The True Gospel.* John Traske was an antinomian in London, and Norris mingles theological argument with coarse personal abuse. From these pamphlets it appears that his congregation had sailed for America about 1636, and that he had hoped to accompany them. Incidentally Norris shows no love for the "Jacobites or semi-separatists," believing evidently in remaining inside the establishment.

In July 1639 Norris and his wife, Eleanor, were in New England, where they became members of the Boston church. In September, in response to invitations, he obtained permission to move to Salem as assistant to Hugh Peter [*q.v.*]; and on Mar. 18, 1639/40, he was installed as teacher over the Salem church, almost all the ministers of the colony being present. He received one hundred acres of land and sixteen of meadow, and a salary of sixty pounds. In 1642 Norris wrote a defense of the standing council in answer to a pamphlet by Richard Saltonstall [*q.v.*]; in 1646 he preached the election sermon; in 1647 he was named first of the seven ministers commissioned to draw up a confession of faith; in 1651 he was joined with John Cotton and John Norton [*qq.v.*] to convince William Pynchon that his book, *The Meritorious Price of our Redemption* (1650), was heretical; in 1653 he urged the Commissioners of the United Colonies, by speech and letter, to prosecute vigorous war against the Dutch of New Amsterdam (the letter is quoted by Ebenezer Hazard in *Historical Collections,* vol. II, 1794, p. 255); in 1656 he received John Whiting as assistant in his ministry; in 1658 he was stricken speechless in the pulpit; and in May 1659 his death was so imminent that the town voted to pay the funeral expenses.

Norris is said to have been unusually tolerant, taking no part against the Gortonists or the

Baptists, and never adopting into his own church the Cambridge Platform. According to William Bentley (*post*), he was successful in opposing accusations of witchcraft in Salem in 1655, and his influence was against violent means toward the Quakers, though he died before the Quaker troubles were at their height. He diverted the fury of fanaticism by encouraging spinning in families, "he quieted alarms by inspiring a military courage, and in . . . a well directed charity, with a timely consent to the incorporation of towns around him, he finished in peace the longest life in the ministry which had been enjoyed in Salem" (Bentley, p. 259). Winthrop called him "a grave and judicious elder"; he was certainly an able and learned theologian; but he does not appear to have been so commanding a personality or so formative an influence on the institutions of New England as were some of his fellow clergymen.

[*Winthrop's Journal* (2 vols., 1908), ed. by J. K. Hosmer; John Eliot, *A Biog. Dict.* (1809); J. B. Felt, *The Ecclesiastical Hist. of New England* (2 vols., 1855–62); Sidney Perley, *The Hist. of Salem*, vol. II ((1926); William Bentley, "A Description and History of Salem," in *Colls. Mass. Hist. Soc.*, 1 ser. VI (1800); L. A. Morrison, *Lineage and Biogs. of the Norris Family in America* (1892); "Town Records of Salem, 1634–1659," in *Essex Inst. Hist. Colls.*, 2 ser. I (1868).]   H. B. P.

NORRIS, FRANK [see NORRIS, BENJAMIN FRANKLIN, 1870–1902].

NORRIS, GEORGE WASHINGTON (Nov. 6, 1808–Mar. 4, 1875), surgeon, was born in Philadelphia, Pa., the sixth son of Joseph Parker and Elizabeth Hill (Fox) Norris and a descendant of Isaac Norris, 1671–1735 [*q.v.*]. He was graduated from the University of Pennsylvania in 1827, with the degree of A.B., and in 1830 from the same institution as M.D. After serving from 1830 to 1833 as resident physician in the Pennsylvania Hospital, he went to Paris where he attended the lectures of Dupuytren, Velpeau, Roux, and Magendie. Returning to Philadelphia in 1835, he was in 1836 elected surgeon to the Pennsylvania Hospital and served that institution faithfully and with distinction until his resignation in 1863. In 1848 he was elected to succeed Dr. Jacob Randolph as professor of clinical surgery in the University of Pennsylvania and this post he resigned in 1857 upon his election as a member of the board of trustees of the university. He was married, in 1838, to Mary Pleasants Fisher, daughter of William W. Fisher. William Fisher Norris [*q.v.*] was their son. Of Norris's marriage his grandson has written: "Born a Quaker, he was thrown out of meeting for marrying a 'worldly'

woman, to wit, an Episcopalian, and thereafter always and regularly attended the Episcopal Church."

Norris is remembered as a sound and "conservative" surgeon. He was excellent in practical surgery and he trained many young men who became distinguished surgeons. He left a reputation for care and neatness in the dressing of wounds, and for insisting strenuously upon personal cleanliness in his assistants. He was gentle both in spirit and in touch, and was revered by many of his patients for his sympathy and kindness. He wrote comparatively little, but his few professional papers show careful preparation and thorough familiarity with the subjects. He took a lifelong interest in historical matters, and in 1886, some years after his death, his son published a volume from his pen entitled *The Early History of Medicine in Philadelphia*. He published *Practical Surgery* (1838), an edition of the work of Robert Liston; *A System of Practical Surgery* (1843), an edition of the work of Sir William Fergusson; and *A System of Surgery* (3 vols., 1847) an edition of G. F. South's translation of the work of M. J. von Chelius. In 1873, under the title *Contributions to Practical Surgery,* he published a collection of his more important "fugitive papers." Among these was the treatise, "On the Occurrence of Non-union after Fractures," which was very highly regarded at the time. His interest in the institutional life of Philadelphia may be inferred from his connection with the American Philosophical Society, the Historical Society of Pennsylvania (president, 1858–60), the Philadelphia Medical Society (vice-president, 1859), Academy of Natural Sciences of Philadelphia, the College of Physicians of Philadelphia (censor, 1848–1875, vice-president, 1864), and the Philadelphia Library Company. For a year, 1850–51, he was vice-president of the American Medical Association. He was consulting surgeon to the Children's Hospital of Philadelphia, and president of its board of managers, and for several years (1868–75) consulting surgeon to the Philadelphia Orthopædic Hospital.

[Wm. Hunt, "Memoir of George W. Norris, M.D.," *Trans. Coll. of Physicians of Phila.*, 3 ser. II (1876); T. G. Morton and Frank Woodbury, *The Hist. of the Pa. Hospital* (1895); H. A. Kelly and W. L. Burrage, *Am. Medic. Biogs.* (1920); the *Press* (Phila.), Mar. 6, 1875.]   A. P. C. A.

NORRIS, ISAAC (July 26, 1671–June 4, 1735), wealthy merchant and mayor of Philadelphia, official of the province of Pennsylvania, was born in London, England, the son of Thomas Norris or Norrice, a Quaker merchant, and Mary

(Moore) Norris. The family emigrated to Port Royal, Jamaica, about 1678 and Isaac served an apprenticeship in his father's business. In 1692 he was sent to Philadelphia to consider the prospects of removing to that city. On his return he found that his father had perished in the great earthquake of June 7, 1692, and that most of his other relatives had died. He went back to Philadelphia in 1693 and soon became a successful merchant. On Mar. 7, 1694, he was married to Mary Lloyd (1674–1748), a daughter of Thomas Lloyd [q.v.].

Norris was a member of the Assembly from 1699 to 1703 and again in 1705. In the years 1706–08 he visited England where he helped to rescue William Penn from a debtors' prison and played a leading part in settling the dispute between Penn and Philip Ford, Sr., and his son, over the proprietary rights to Pennsylvania. In return for these services he was appointed one of the five commissioners who acted as agents for the mortgage trustees and he was later named in Penn's will as a trustee of the province. He was an alderman of Philadelphia from 1708 to 1724 and was elected mayor in 1724. From 1709 to 1735 he served in the governor's council and, contrary to the usual custom, was also a member of the Assembly, 1710–13, 1715–16, 1718–20, 1734, and speaker in 1712 and 1720. He was likewise a justice of the Philadelphia county courts from 1715 to 1735 and a master in chancery for several years before his death. In 1731 he was chosen to succeed David Lloyd [q.v.] as chief justice of the supreme court but refused to serve. He attended the Indian conference at Albany in 1722 and was appointed a commissioner in the settlement of the boundary dispute with Maryland in 1734. He died in Germantown, Pa., June 4, 1735, survived by his wife and seven of his fourteen children.

Next to James Logan [q.v.], Norris was the chief representative of proprietary interests in Pennsylvania from 1708 until his death. John Penn wrote to him, May 1, 1732, acknowledging "the many and great obligations I am under to you for your constant good advice and friendly assistance for many years, both to my late Father and since his decease to us his children" (Norris Letter Books, II, 142). Norris's fortune was largely invested in real estate. In 1704 he and William Trent purchased from William Penn, Jr., a large tract of land on the Schuylkill River, including the site of Norristown, and, in 1712, he bought Trent's share of the property. He also owned the "Slate-roof House" in Philadelphia, celebrated as the residence of Penn on his second visit to Philadelphia, and a mansion,

"Fair Hill," in the Northern Liberties, where he lived from 1717 until his death. He was fond of books and his library was the nucleus of a collection that was later given to Dickinson College. A letter that he wrote to his son Isaac [q.v.] on the latter's visit to England in 1722 is interesting in this connection and also as an illustration of the workings of the Quaker conscience: "Thou may omit of my orders by thee, *The Arabian Nights Tales* and bring me Milton's *Paradise Lost*—octavo, large print" (Letter Books, II, 55).

[The Norris Papers in the Hist. Soc. of Pa. contain a copy of the journal kept by Norris on his visit to Philadelphia in 1692 and several letter books. There are also Norris letters in the Penn, Logan, and Pemberton collections. Some of his letters have been published in "Correspondence Between Wm. Penn and Jas. Logan," ed. by Edward Armstrong, in *Memoirs of the Hist. Soc. of Pa.*, vols. IX and X (1870–72). Other printed sources include: *Minutes of the Provincial Council of Pa.*, vols. II and III (1852); C. P. Keith, *The Provincial Councillors of Pa.* (1883); and J. W. Jordan, *Colonial Families of Philadelphia* (1911), vol. I.]

W. R. S.

NORRIS, ISAAC (Oct. 23, 1701–July 13, 1766), Philadelphia merchant, leader of the Quaker party and speaker of the Pennsylvania Assembly, was the son of Isaac Norris [q.v.] and Mary (Lloyd) Norris. He was born in Philadelphia and was educated at the Friends' school. In 1722 he spent a few months in England and in the years 1733–34 he made a longer visit to England and the Continent. He was a common councillor of Philadelphia, 1727–30, an alderman, 1730–42, a member of the Assembly of Pennsylvania, 1734–66, speaker of the Assembly, 1750–64, and a representative of Pennsylvania at the Indian Conferences held at Albany in 1745 and 1754. During his first term as speaker (1751), the old state house or Liberty bell was ordered from England and it was at his suggestion that the famous inscription was placed upon it: "Proclaim liberty throughout the land, unto all the inhabitants thereof."

Norris's militant pacifism is the pride of Quaker historians. In 1739, when Deputy-Governor George Thomas asked the Assembly to provide for the defense of the colony against the Spaniards, they replied that they had conscientious scruples and would put their trust in God and the mother country. In accordance with this decision, they refused to enact a militia law or to appropriate funds for military purposes. The quarrel, which was later complicated by a dispute over the right of the Assembly to tax the proprietary estates, lasted until the close of the Seven Years' War. Norris played so prominent a part in this conflict that the Quaker majority in the Assembly was frequently called the Norris party. He was selected to go to England with Benjamin Franklin in 1757 to represent the anti-proprietary faction, but, owing to ill health, was compelled to refuse. Although he continued to oppose the proprietors, he was not in sympathy with the petition sent to the King in 1764 asking for a change from proprietary to royal government. There is a difference of opinion as to whether he resigned the speakership at this time (May 1764) because of his health, which was undoubtedly poor, or because he disapproved the policy of the Assembly. It is possible that he was influenced to some extent by his son-in-law, John Dickinson [q.v.], who was associated with the proprietary party. He was again elected speaker by the new Assembly in the following October and again resigned after a few days' service. He retained his seat in the house, however, and was reëlected in 1765, but his health continued to fail and he died at his home, "Fair Hill," near Philadelphia, July 13, 1766.

The mercantile establishment of Norris & Company was one of the largest firms in Philadelphia. Norris managed it during the latter part of his father's life and became the senior partner after his father's death. He lived in the famous "Slate-roof House" in Philadelphia for several years, but in 1742 he removed to "Fair Hill" in the Northern Liberties, where he spent the remainder of his life (Logan Papers, XIII, 63–64). He was married to Sarah Logan, the eldest daughter of James Logan [q.v.], June 6, 1739. She died Oct. 13, 1744. He was survived by two daughters—Mary, who married John Dickinson, and Sarah, who died in 1769. With his father's books as a nucleus, he built up a large and well-selected library which in 1784 was given by his son-in-law to Dickinson College. He was interested in education and was a trustee of the Academy and College of Philadelphia from 1751 to 1755.

[Sources include the Norris and Logan Papers in the Hist. Soc. of Pa.; Votes and Proc. of the House of Representatives of Pa., 1752–76; The Jour. of Isaac Norris . . . During a Trip to Albany in 1745 (Philadelphia, 1867); J. W. Jordan, Colonial Families of Philadelphia (1911), vol. I; G. W. Norris, "Isaac Norris," Pa. Mag. of Hist. and Biog., vol. I, no. 4 (1877); C. P. Keith, The Provincial Councillors of Pa. (1883).]
W. R. S.

NORRIS, MARY HARRIOTT (Mar. 16, 1848–Sept. 14, 1919), author and educator, the daughter of Charles Bryan and Mary Lyon (Kerr) Norris, was born at Boonton, N. J. Before the opening of Vassar College in 1865 her parents decided to send their daughter there. She was prepared in a private school, where she was the only girl studying Latin and, in spite of the disapproval of her mother's friends, made

her entrance, taking with her the water-proof cloak and other modest equipment required in the pamphlet issued by the college. Her own account of the early days at Vassar, The Golden Age of Vassar (1915), reveals a life of frugality and hard work. Hannah Lyman, the first lady principal, said of her that she was "as greedy for learning as many people are for food" (Golden Age, ante, p. 30). In 1870 she was graduated with the A.B. degree. In 1872 she delivered the annual address at the Vassar Commencement. In 1873 she published her first fiction, Fräulein Mina; or, Life in a North American German Family, which was so successful that she continued to write and published more than a dozen books of transient popularity. Among them were School Life of Ben and Bentie (1874) of the Ben and Bentie Series, Dorothy Delafield (1886), and The Gray House of the Quarries (1898). In the writing of such stories she showed some descriptive and story-telling ability, much sentiment, and an orthodox religious outlook. She also contributed to periodicals and edited for use in schools George Eliot's Silas Marner (1890); Sir Walter Scott's Marmion (1891); Henry Wadsworth Longfellow's Evangeline (1896); Kenilworth by Sir Walter Scott (1899); Quentin Durward (1900).

In 1880 she founded a private school in New York City and was its principal until 1896. In 1898 she became the first regularly elected dean of women of Northwestern University. She held this position as well as that of assistant professor of English literature for only a year, as she had stipulated that only for so long could she withdraw herself from her literary and other activities. During that time she organized a students' self-governing association and started a library for the woman's hall. Another change in which she took pride was that during her year the young women almost entirely abandoned the custom "of appearing at breakfast in wrapper and dressing sacks," she wrote, "a custom I found almost universal in the Hall on my arrival there" (Wilde, post, p. 100). Her Tuesday morning chapel talks on religious themes and her Thursday evening talks on etiquette and personal hygiene were considered very helpful to the students. She was made an honorary member of the class of 1899 of the university. During her later years she resided at Morristown, N. J.

[Biog. material in The Golden Age of Vassar, ante; Who's Who in America, 1918–19, 1920–21; Men and Women of America (1910); A. H. Wilde, Northwestern Univ. (1905), vol. II.]
S. G. B.

NORRIS, WILLIAM (July 2, 1802–Jan. 5, 1867), locomotive builder, was the son of William and Mary (Schaefer) Norris and was born in Baltimore, Md., where his father had a dry-goods store. He was a descendant of Henry Norris who emigrated from England to Virginia in 1680. After graduating from St. Mary's College, Baltimore, Norris was associated in business with his father for a few years and in 1828, with his father's help, opened a whole-sale dry-goods store in Philadelphia. His father failed in business the following year and Norris was forced to close his store and look about for other work.

He had always been keenly interested in steam engines and he now designed and built a steam carriage with an upright boiler and wooden wheels, which he demonstrated on the streets of Philadelphia. This achievement brought about his meeting with Col. Stephen H. Long [q.v.], Corps of Engineers, United States Army, who was also interested in locomotive building, and in 1832 the two organized the American Steam Carriage Company, with Long as president and Norris as secretary. They began the construction of a locomotive, designed by Colonel Long, which was to use anthracite coal as fuel, but it proved a failure. A second engine, the "Black Hawk," was completed in 1833 and used first on the Philadelphia & Columbia Railroad and later on the Philadelphia & Germantown Railroad. This locomotive, however, was not entirely successful and all members of the company withdrew their interest, leaving Long and Norris alone. The two then built three anthracite-coal-burning locomotives for a New England railroad, which were completed in 1834, but while these were entirely successful they were soon relegated to sand and gravel trains, because "the coal fires required more attention from the enginemen than did fires of wood." About this time Norris bought Colonel Long's interest in the locomotive works and soon after completed the successful locomotive "Star" for the Philadelphia & Germantown Railroad. In 1835 he moved his shop from Kensington, Pa., to Bush Hill, Philadelphia, and there with six employees began the construction of another locomotive of his own design. The "George Washington," as it was called, was completed in 1836 for the Philadelphia & Columbia Railroad, and by its initial performance of hauling a train weighing 19,200 pounds to the top of an inclined plane in Philadelphia at a speed of fifteen miles per hour, with a boiler pressure of only sixty pounds, it brought world-wide fame to Norris as a locomotive designer and builder. The year after the successful demonstration of the "George Washington," Norris received an order for seventeen

similar engines from the Birmingham & Gloucester Railroad in England, and by 1855 his locomotive works had shipped one hundred engines to France, Austria, Prussia, Italy, Belgium, South America, and Cuba, besides constructing many engines for the railroads of the United States.

In 1841 Norris had formed a partnership with his brother Richard, but three years later he resigned from the company to take charge of the government locomotive shops near Vienna. He remained abroad five years and on his return to the United States he accepted the appointment of chief engineer of the eastern division of the Panama Railroad. When he again returned to the United States in 1855, he organized a company in New York City for the purpose of constructing a fast steamship of his own design, capable of making the voyage to England in six days. The company failed, however, and Norris was obliged to abandon his project before its completion. For his services abroad he received many valuable presents from the Emperor of Austria, Louis Philippe of France, and the Czar of Russia. His great interest outside of locomotive design was music, and when but fifteen years of age he was organist and choir leader of a church in Baltimore. He composed sacred music and on Feb. 8, 1841, produced in Musical Fund Hall, Philadelphia, at his own expense, Mozart's opera, The Magic Flute. Norris was married in Baltimore in 1825 to May Ann Heide. A son survived him.

[Henry Hall, *America's Successful Men of Affairs*, vol. II (1896); Zerah Colburn, *Locomotive Engineering and the Mechanism of Railways* (2 vols., 1871); *The Railway and Locomotive Hist. Soc., Bull. No. 10* (1925); *U. S. Mag. of Science, Art, Manufactures, Agriculture, Commerce, and Trade*, Oct. 1855; data from Am. Antiquarian Society.]   C. W. M.

NORRIS, WILLIAM FISHER (Jan. 6, 1839–Nov. 18, 1901), ophthalmologist, was born in Philadelphia, Pa., the son of George Washington Norris [q.v.], a prominent surgeon, and Mary Pleasants Fisher. He received his preparatory education at Ferris' private school in Philadelphia and then entered the University of Pennsylvania, receiving the degree of A.B. in 1857. In 1861 he received the degree of M.D. from the same institution and was appointed resident physician to the Pennsylvania Hospital, which institution he served for a period of eighteen months. He then (1863) entered the United States army as assistant surgeon and served until October 1865 when he resigned with the brevet rank of captain. The greater part of his army experience was in connection with the Douglas Hospital in Washington, D. C., where in conjunction with Dr. William Thomson he experimented considerably with photography and microphotography and demonstrated the feasibility of the photographic record for important medical and surgical cases which was subsequently utilized in the preparation of the elaborate *Medical and Surgical History of the War of the Rebellion.* This work probably led to his subsequent intensive study of ophthalmology.

In 1865, when he was twenty-six years of age, he went to Europe for this purpose and visited the clinics of Arlt, Jaeger, and Mauthner. It was this early contact with Vienna that shaped his subsequent career, and while he was there he carried on extensive studies in the histology and pathology of the cornea in collaboration with Stricker at the Pathologic Institute which were quite creditable. Upon his return to Philadelphia in 1870 he began the practice of ophthalmology. He was appointed lecturer in ophthalmology at the University of Pennsylvania and soon after this appointment, with Doctors Strawbridge and Ezra Dyer, was elected an attending surgeon to Wills Eye Hospital, Philadelphia. In 1871 in association with Dr. Horatio C. Wood and Dr. William Pepper he conceived the idea of the hospital of the University of Pennsylvania and in three years these men brought this idea to a successful issue by the construction of the hospital and the opening of its doors for the reception of patients. He was appointed clinical professor of ophthalmology at the University in 1873 and full professor of the same subject in 1876. In the interval between these appointments he was given the chair of honorary professor of ophthalmology, an unusual distinction. The yeoman work and accomplishment necessary for the creation of this hospital in the face of almost insuperable obstacles doubtless accounted for the great influence Norris wielded in connection with it since not only was he the ophthalmologist to the hospital during his lifetime but also president of the board of trustees over a long period. He was made a fellow of the College of Physicians in 1866, a member of the Academy of Natural Sciences in 1868, and a member of the American Ophthalmological Society in 1870. In 1877 he acted as vice-president of the Pathological Society and from 1894 to 1897 he was chairman of the section on ophthalmology of the College of Physicians of Philadelphia.

Norris' accomplishments in the literature of American ophthalmology began with his paper read before the American Ophthalmological Society in 1871 entitled "Paralysis of the Trige-

minus followed by Sloughing of the Cornea." It was followed by more than thirty papers, including the investigation of double staining in microscopic work, in collaboration with Dr. Edward O. Shakespeare, and that of the microscopic anatomy of the human retina with special consideration of the terminal loops of the rods and cones, in collaboration with Dr. James Wallace. The studies made early in his career covering hereditary optic atrophy, orbital growths, brain tumors, and tabes stamp him as a scientific investigator of merit. His major works include his contribution to James Tyson's *Treatise on Bright's Disease and Diabetes* (ed. 1881) and to John Ashhurst's *Principles and Practice of Surgery* (1871), and the section on medical ophthalmology in William Pepper's *System of Practical Medicine* (vol. IV, 1886). In collaboration with Charles A. Oliver he wrote *A Text-Book of Ophthalmology* (1893) and with the same associate he published *System of Diseases of the Eye* (4 vols., 1897–1900), a monumental work utilizing contributions from nearly all of the contemporary authorities in the world. Norris was married twice. His first wife was Rosa Clara Buchmann of Vienna, daughter of Hieronymus Buchmann, whom he met while a student in Vienna and married on July 4, 1873. She died in 1897. Three sons were born of this union. His second wife was Annetta Culph Earnshaw of Gettysburg, Pa., whom he married June 12, 1899, and who with two sons by his first marriage survived him. In 1901 Norris became the subject of recurring attacks of double pneumonia, complicated by a diabetes of long standing, and he died in November of that year.

[C. A. Oliver, *Memoir of Wm. Fisher Norris* (1901); *Trans. Am. Ophthalmol. Soc.,* vol. X (1905); *Trans. Coll. of Physicians of Phila.,* vol. XXIV (1902); J. L. Chamberlain, *Universities and Their Sons: Univ. of Pa.* (1901); *Alumni Reg., Univ. of Pa.,* Dec. 1881; *Phila. Medic. Jour.,* Nov. 23, 1901; *Univ. of Pa. Medic. Bull.,* Aug.–Sept. 1902; *Annals of Ophthalmol.,* Jan. 1902; *N. Y. Medic. Jour.,* Nov. 23, 1901; *Pub. Ledger* (Phila.), Nov. 19, 1901; communications from contemporaries.]   L. W. F.

NORSWORTHY, NAOMI (Sept. 29, 1877–Dec. 25, 1916), psychologist, educator, was born in New York of Devonshire stock. Her father, Samuel Bowden Norsworthy, a mechanical engineer with experience in the navy, brought his bride, Eva Ann Modridge, to the United States from England. To the mother's stern, Puritanic training was due Naomi Norsworthy's characteristic refusal to compromise with the second best, and her unswerving devotion to ideals. A delicate shyness was intensified by the social restrictions and seclusions involved in the family's adherence to the beliefs of the religious sect known as the Plymouth Brethren. A natural generosity was trained into unquestioning sharing of goods, home, time, personal interest with any who made worthy demand. The fun-loving, vivacious child developed into a radiant, sensitive, winsome woman whose charm was magnetic. Slender, dark, slightly over medium height, she appeared fragile; but an inner vitality was manifested by her restless, expressive hands and chiefly by her big, dancing brown eyes.

Educated in the public schools of Rutherford, N. J., she entered the state normal school at Trenton in 1893, where she was recognized as possessing a rare intellect with an unusual memory and a passion for clear thinking. Graduating in 1896, she taught a third grade in Morristown, N. J., till 1899, when she matriculated at Teachers College, Columbia University. The next year she was selected as student assistant in psychology. She received the degree of B.S. and higher diploma in 1901, and the degree of Ph.D. in 1904. Appointed on the staff of Teachers College as assistant in 1901, she rose through the ranks of tutor, instructor, assistant professor, to associate professor in 1912. Her doctor's dissertation, *The Psychology of Mentally Deficient Children* (1906), established the idea of feeblemindedness as a matter of degree of intelligence rather than of special type, in a period before the concept of mental age had become familiar. It was her fortune similarly to do pioneer work in other lines, though in none did she go very far. Thus in an article entitled "The Validity of Judgments of Character," contributed to *Essays, Philosophical and Psychological, in Honor of William James* (1908), she exemplified the use of the method of group ratings of personality traits. Later, she collaborated in planning the experimental teaching which preceded the formulation of the phrase "project method." Though she was joint author of the two books *How to Teach* (1917) and *The Psychology of Childhood* (1918), her reputation lay rather in her skill as a teacher than as a writer. Immediate disciple of Thorndike, McMurray, and Dewey, she combined, transmuted, and demonstrated their teachings, while evidencing rare gifts in guiding discussion and stimulating thought, whether on the public platform or in the classroom. Conscientious to an extreme degree, scorning superficiality, she inspired students with something of her own fearless truthfulness. Ever responsive, but with no sentimentality, her unofficial function at the college was adviser, counsellor, friend at large.

[Records on file at Teachers College; F. C. Higgins, *The Life of Naomi Norsworthy* (1918); *Teachers Coll. Record*, Jan. 1917; *Who's Who in America*, 1914–15;

Woman's Who's Who of America, 1914–15; personal recollections.]   M. T. W.

NORTH, EDWARD (Mar. 9, 1820–Sept. 13, 1903), educator, classicist, was a native of Berlin, Conn. His father, Reuben North, was a son of Col. Simeon North, 1765–1852 [*q.v.*]; his mother, Hulda (Wilcox), was the daughter of Daniel Wilcox, owner of a large landed property in East Berlin. Edward spent his early years in Berlin, but at the age of fifteen he went to Clinton, N. Y., to live in the family of his uncle, Simeon North, 1802–1884 [*q.v.*], president of Hamilton College. He was graduated at Hamilton in the class of 1841 with the rank of valedictorian. After a year as a private tutor in a family in Paterson, N. J., and a few months spent in a law office, he was appointed principal of the Clinton Grammar School, and soon thereafter, on Dec. 27, 1843, professor of ancient languages in Hamilton College. In 1862 he was made Edward Robinson Professor of Greek, and held this position until his resignation, Nov. 16, 1901, after fifty-seven years of service. The greater part of the college year 1871–72 he spent in Athens, holding a position as secretary under John M. Francis [*q.v.*], United States minister to Greece. After the death of President Henry Darling [*q.v.*], he was appointed acting president of Hamilton College, serving from Apr. 21, 1891, until November 1892.

During his active connection with the faculty he was preëminently a teacher, with a singular skill in interpreting the masterpieces of Greek poetry. In addition to his classroom duties he did a great amount of editorial work, preparing the copy for the annual catalogue under at least three presidents. For thirty-four years he contributed news items concerning graduates to the college literary magazine. It was he who first undertook to prepare accurate obituary records of deceased alumni. He had a wide acquaintance with the public and private schools of the state and many teaching appointments were made upon his recommendation. In 1864 he declined the principalship of the State Normal School at Albany. In 1865 he was president of the New York State Teachers' Association. From 1881 until his death he occupied a unique position as trustee of the college in which he was a professor. In his earlier years he appeared frequently as a lyceum lecturer. His classroom lectures were remembered by his students for their singular charm. A part of one of these was published in the *North American Review*, July 1857 (pp. 168–77). He took a deep interest in local history and tradition and contributed frequently to current publications. He was an elder in the

Presbyterian Church from 1865 until his death, and sat twice, 1870 and 1876, in the General Assembly. He married Mary Frances Dexter, daughter of Hon. S. Newton Dexter, of Whitesboro, N. Y., July 31, 1844. Her death occurred May 27, 1869. Simon Newton Dexter North [*q.v.*] was their son.

One of Edward North's marked traits was a love of nature and a sympathy with country life. His feeling of companionship with trees inspired some of the most characteristic utterances quoted in the memoir, *Old Greek,* compiled by his son. Other published works of his are: *Dedicatory Address for the Sunset Hill Cemetery, Clinton* (1857); *Uses of Music* (1858); *Memorial of Henry Hastings Curran* (1867).

[S. N. D. North, *Old Greek: An Old-Time Professor in an Old-Fashioned College; a Memoir of Edward North, with Selections from His Lectures* (1905); Dexter North, *John North of Farmington, Conn., and His Descendants* (1921); Catharine M. North, *Hist. of Berlin, Conn.* (1916); *Who's Who in America,* 1901–02; *N. Y. Times,* Sept. 14, 1903.]   E. F.

NORTH, ELISHA (Jan. 8, 1771–Dec. 29, 1843), physician, was born in Goshen, Conn. He was a lineal descendant of John North who emigrated from England in 1635 and settled in Farmington, Conn. His father was Joseph North of Goshen, who married Lucy Cowles of Farmington. Although Joseph North had no regular medical education, he became a local practitioner, and it was under his guidance that his son first began the study of medicine. Later, Elisha studied under Dr. Lemuel Hopkins [*q.v.*] of Hartford, one of the celebrated "Hartford Wits" and one of the most prominent physicians of his day. In the fall of 1793 he entered the University of Pennsylvania, where he spent the greater part of two years but did not graduate. He then returned to his native town and prepared to settle down to his life work. In 1797 he married Hannah, the daughter of Frederick Beach of Goshen. Three years later, shortly after vaccination had been introduced in America, he made a trip to New Haven to obtain as he says "some Vaccine Fluid," and during 1800 and 1801 the "business of vaccination" was extensively carried on by himself and Jesse Carrington in Goshen. In May 1801 North recognized the first example of kine-pox in the country and it was through his efforts that the first kine-pox used for vaccination purposes was introduced into the city of New York. In 1807 a new disease known as "Spotted Fever" came to North's attention. His experience with the condition was very extensive and his treatment unusually successful. In one year he treated sixty-five patients afflicted with this dread disease and lost only

one. Four years after the appearance of the disease he published his notable work on the subject, *A Treatise on a Malignant Epidemic Commonly Called Spotted Fever* (1811), and became thereby the author of the first volume on cerebrospinal meningitis to be found in medical literature.

In 1812 he was invited to remove to New London, Conn., an important seaport, where he established the first eye dispensary in the United States, at the same time carrying on a general medical practice. He was actively interested in medical society activities and in 1813 the Connecticut Medical Society conferred upon him the degree of M.D. Although possessed of a large clientele, he had pecuniary difficulties which led him to observe, "Judging from the lowness of medical fees in Connecticut, one would suppose that property regarded as a means of health, was held by the community in higher estimation than health itself." In 1829 he published in Connecticut papers several essays under the title "The Rights of Anatomists Vindicated" and signed Vesalius. In the same year he published a volume of 200 pages entitled *Outlines of the Science of Life; Which Treats Physiologically of Both Body and Mind,* a work showing wide acquaintance with current English literature on physiology; and in 1836, *The Pilgrim's Progress in Phrenology,* by "Uncle Toby." He was also the author of a number of essays in addition to those already mentioned. He lived to be seventy-three years of age and except for deafness in his latter years enjoyed splendid health. His life even to its close was devoted to study and to reading and writing. To him and his wife were born eight children.

[Dexter North, *John North of Farmington, Conn., and His Descendants* (1921); H. C. Bolton, "Memoir of Elisha North," in *Proc. Conn. Medic. Soc.,* vol. III, no. 4 (1887); W. R. Steiner, "Dr. Elisha North," in *Johns Hopkins Hosp. Bull.,* Oct. 1908; H. A. Kelly and W. L. Burrage, *Am. Medic. Biogs.* (1920).]   H. T.

NORTH, FRANK JOSHUA (Mar. 10, 1840– Mar. 14, 1885), scout and plainsman, second son of Thomas Jefferson and Jane Almira (Townley) North, was born in Ludlowville, Tompkins County, N. Y. Though named Frank Joshua, he rarely used his middle name. His early boyhood was spent in Richland County, Ohio. In the spring of 1856, the family moved on to the new settlement of Omaha, Nebraska Territory, and in 1858 to a still newer location, Columbus, on the Loup Fork of Platte River, Nebr. Through intimate association with the Pawnees, North learned their language and also the Indian sign language. In 1860, he drove a freight outfit to the Colorado gold fields. Returning to Nebraska, in 1861 he became clerk-interpreter at the Pawnee reservation on the Loup. In 1864, Gen. S. R. Curtis [q.v.], while organizing a campaign against the hostile Indians who had practically stopped overland stage travel and wagon traffic across the plains, took into service seventy-six Pawnee volunteers, with Joseph McFadden, a reservation employee who had formerly served under Gen. W. S. Harney, as captain of the company, and Frank North as lieutenant. North and two Pawnees were soon detached as scouts and guides for General Curtis and his escort to Fort Riley, Kan., the remainder of the Pawnees and Captain McFadden accompanying Gen. R. B. Mitchell farther west.

Curtis authorized North to enlist a regular Pawnee scout company as Civil War volunteers, and on Oct. 24, 1864, he was commissioned captain by Alvin Saunders, governor of Nebraska Territory. Early in 1865, the company was ordered on the Powder River Indian Expedition, under Gen. Patrick E. Connor [q.v.]. It participated in several skirmishes and the battle of Aug. 28, 1865, on Tongue River, Dakota Territory (now northwestern Wyoming). Later, North and some Pawnees were sent out to locate Col. Nelson Cole, whose force had missed Connor's main column and nearly perished in Montana from short rations and severe weather. This object was accomplished, and the entire expedition united at Fort Connor (later Fort Reno). Discharged in the spring of 1866, North returned to the Nebraska Pawnee reservation; but early in 1867 was authorized by Gen. C. C. Augur [q.v.], commanding the Department of the Platte, to organize and command, as major of cavalry, a battalion of four Pawnee companies, mainly for the protection of surveys and construction work on the Union Pacific Railroad against hostile Indians. On Aug. 17, part of his command won a running fight with the Cheyennes at Plum Creek, Nebr. The same general duties continued, with varying members of companies, until after the completion and opening of the railroad. Among later engagements was the battle of Summit Springs, Colorado Territory, July 11, 1869, where North and the Pawnee scouts led the charge into the hostile village of Tall Bull, renegade Cheyenne chief, whose defeat saved the frontier settlements in adjacent Colorado and Nebraska from attacks by that band.

North was afterwards guide-interpreter at Fort D. A. Russell, Wyo., and Sidney Barracks, Nebr., participating frequently in scouts and occasionally in scientific explorations. In August 1876 he was sent by Gen. P. H. Sheridan to the Indian Territory to enroll and bring up 100 Pawnee Indians (including many veterans of previous expeditions) for service with Gen. George Crook [q.v.] in the fall and winter campaign. This last Pawnee company assisted Col. R. S. Mackenzie [q.v.] in his round-up of Red Cloud and Red Leaf on Chadron Creek, Nebr., Oct. 23, and formed a part of the Powder River Expedition. On Nov. 25, 1876, North and his Pawnees led the attack on the village of Dull Knife's Northern Cheyennes in the Big Horn region of Wyoming. They also accompanied the command to and from the Belle Fourche River in search of Crazy Horse [q.v.] and his band. Returning to the line of the Union Pacific, they were mustered out of service at Sidney Barracks, Nebr., late in April 1877. For about five years Frank and Luther H. North were partners of William F. Cody [q.v.] in a ranch on the Dismal River, Nebr. In the fall of 1882, Frank North was elected to the Nebraska legislature from the Platte County district. Later he joined Cody's "Wild West" show, and led the Pawnees in exhibitions of Indian warfare. In the summer of 1884 he was severely injured at Hartford, Conn.; and although later he rejoined the troupe, he never fully recovered, and died at Columbus, Nebr., after returning from New Orleans in the spring of 1885. On Dec. 25, 1865, he married Mary L. Smith, and they had one daughter.

Frank North had no superior as frontiersman and guide in his day, which was somewhat later than that of James Bridger and Christopher Carson [qq.v.]; he was probably the best revolver shot then on the plains, having beaten "Wild Bill" (James Butler) Hickok [q.v.] and others in competition in 1873. He was the only leader of Indian scouts thoroughly acquainted with the language and customs of his men, who called him Pani La Shar ("Pawnee Chief"), by which name he is still remembered among the tribe. Though often exposed to dangers, he was never wounded in the service. He kept the Pawnees in discipline, ready for emergencies; during six campaigns under his leadership, only one Pawnee was killed in battle and a few wounded, though greatly superior numbers were encountered and defeated. North was never a regular army officer; he was employed by the Quartermaster's Department only for stated periods overlapping the several enlistments of Pawnee scouts, but his rank and title corresponded to those involving similar duties in the regular establishment.

[G. B. Grinnell, *Two Great Scouts and Their Pawnee Battalion* (1928) and *Pawnee Hero Stories and Folk-Tales* (1889; 1909); Robert Bruce, *The Fighting Norths and Pawnee Scouts* (1932); Dexter North, *The Caleb North Genealogy* (1930); *Trans. and Reports Nebr.*

State Hist. Soc., vol. II (1887); Omaha Daily Herald, Mar. 15, 1885; various histories of the Indian wars, 1864-77.]   R. B.

NORTH, SIMEON (July 13, 1765–Aug. 25, 1852), manufacturer of pistols and rifles for the United States government for more than fifty years, was born in Berlin, Conn., the fourth son of Jedediah and Sarah (Wilcox) North, and of the sixth generation in descent from John North, who came from England in 1635 and settled in Farmington, Conn. Like his father and grandfather, he began life as a farmer. On his sixteenth birthday, in 1781, he shouldered his gun and walked to Saybrook, where he attempted to enlist in the Continental Army, but he was rejected by the recruiting officer. In 1786 he married Lucy, daughter of Jonathan and Elizabeth Ranney Savage of Berlin, Conn. She died in 1811, after bearing him five sons and three daughters. His second wife, Lydia, whom he married Mar. 2, 1812, was the daughter of Rev. Enoch Huntington of Middletown, Conn. She bore him one daughter. In 1795 he began a business of making scythes in an old mill adjoining his farm, and on Mar. 9, 1799, he secured his first contract with the War Department for 500 horse-pistols to be delivered within one year. It is probable that previously he had made some pistols for private sales. Other government contracts followed, some of which were for pistols for the Navy Department. It is not definitely known whether it was North or the more famous Eli Whitney [q.v.] who first devised tools and machines for making separate parts and was, therefore, the first American manufacturer to make arms whose parts should be interchangeable one with the other, but it is quite certain that the system of interchangeable parts had its birth in the work of these two men, both engaged in manufacturing arms for the federal government. In North's contract for 20,000 pistols, dated Apr. 16, 1813, there was this provision which he himself had recommended: "The component parts of pistols are to correspond so exactly that any limb or part of one Pistol may be fitted to any other Pistol of the twenty thousand." The contract price per pistol was $7.00.

His work for the government was invariably well done. His last pistol contract was made Aug. 18, 1828; all subsequent contracts were for rifles and carbines. His first rifle contract was dated Dec. 10, 1823, and called for 6,000 rifles to be delivered at the rate of 1,200 a year for five years. He delivered them all in four years. The last order received by him from the government was dated Feb. 5, 1850, for 3,000 guns. In 1825 he made a multicharge repeating rifle capable of

firing ten charges without reloading. One of these weapons is now owned by the Winchester Repeating Arms Company of New Haven, Conn.

In 1811 North was elected lieutenant-colonel of the 6th Connecticut Regiment, but resigned the office in 1813, although the title "Colonel" clung to him. While he had not the advantages of college training, he had a well-disciplined mind, was well-informed, and kept abreast of the world's affairs by reading the New York papers. He indicated his appreciation of education by participating in the establishment of the first Berlin Academy which was incorporated in 1802. He was a man of stalwart and erect figure, tireless energy, genial temperament, quiet and modest manner. Although a generous supporter and regular attendant of the village Congregational church, he was not a member of any religious body. He brought up his children strictly in accordance with his own principles of personal honor, the dignity of conscientious labor, the need of square dealing with every one, and the necessity of self-reliance. His four older sons were associated with him in business, but the youngest, Simeon [q.v.], was sent to Yale, where he graduated as valedictorian of his class, was ordained to the ministry, and became president of Hamilton College.

[North's papers were destroyed after his death. S. N. D. North and Ralph North, Simeon North, First Official Pistol Maker of the United States (1913), is based on official records of the War and Navy Depts., which are copiously used. See also J. W. Roe, English and American Tool Builders (1916); Dexter North, John North of Farmington, Conn., and His Descendants (1921); Catharine M. North, Hist. of Berlin, Conn. (1916); death notice in N. Y. Daily Tribune, Sept. 6, 1852.]   J. W. L.

NORTH, SIMEON (Sept. 7, 1802–Feb. 9, 1884), educator, clergyman, was born in Berlin, Conn., the son of Col. Simeon North [q.v.] and Lucy (Savage) North. While his elder brothers, Reuben, James, Alvin, and Selah, were engaged with their father in manufacturing firearms, Simeon, the youngest, entered Yale College and was graduated in 1825 with the rank of valedictorian. After spending two years in the Yale Divinity School he was appointed tutor in Yale College in 1827. In 1829, having before him a choice between one of the best parishes in Connecticut and a professorship of ancient languages in Hamilton College, Clinton, N. Y., he chose the latter.

On arriving at the scene of his labors he found the fortunes of the college at their lowest ebb. Owing to internal dissensions ten of the trustees had resigned and the faculty consisted of the president, Henry Davis [q.v.], and the professor of chemistry, Josiah Noyes. Only nine students remained, and these were members of the lower classes. Nothing daunted, the young professor entered upon his duties and had the satisfaction of seeing the regular succession of graduating classes resumed, after an intermission of two years, and never again interrupted. After serving ten years as a teacher he was elected fifth president of the college, and held that office until 1857. In 1840 he was elected a trustee of Auburn Theological Seminary and served nine years. In May 1842 he was ordained to the ministry by the Oneida Association of Congregational Churches. Five years later he delivered the oration before the Yale chapter of Phi Beta Kappa: *Anglo-Saxon Literature* (1847). Other published addresses and discourses are *The College System of Education* (1839), his inaugural address; sermons at the funeral of his colleague and intimate friend, Professor Marcus Catlin (1849), and of his predecessor in the presidency, Dr. Henry Davis (1852). In 1879 he made his last contribution to the literature of the College in the form of a Half-Century Letter of reminiscence, marking the fiftieth anniversary of his election to the chair of ancient languages. The years following his resignation, 1857 to 1884, were spent at his home near the campus, where, as a trusted counselor of three succeeding presidents, he lived quietly, finding satisfaction in cultivating old friendships and in reading the classics, ancient and modern. His administration was marked by substantial additions to the equipment of the college, including the building of the Litchfield Astronomical Observatory, and the founding of the Maynard professorship of law and history, first held by Theodore W. Dwight [*q.v.*].

He married on Apr. 21, 1835, Frances Harriet Hubbard, daughter of Dr. Thomas Hubbard, professor of surgery in Yale Medical College. Her death occurred Jan. 21, 1881; their only son died in boyhood. Edward North [*q.v.*] was North's nephew.

[*Memorial of Rev. Simeon North, D.D., LL.D.* (1884), comp. by Edward North; S. N. D. North and R. H. North, *Simeon North, First Official Pistol Maker of the U. S.* (1913), ch. ii; C. M. North, *Hist. of Berlin, Conn.* (1916); *Doc. Hist. of Hamilton Coll.* (1922); *Obit. Record Grads. Yale Coll.*, 1884; Dexter North, *John North of Farmington, Conn., and His Descendants* (1921); *The Congreg. Year Book* (1885); *N. Y. Times*, Feb. 11, 1884.]   E. F.

NORTH, SIMON NEWTON DEXTER (Nov. 29, 1848–Aug. 3, 1924), editor and statistician, was born in Clinton, N. Y., the son of Edward [*q.v.*] and Mary Frances (Dexter) North. He was educated at Hamilton College, and as an undergraduate displayed ability in journalism which led to his employment, im-

mediately after graduation in 1869, as managing editor of the *Utica Morning Herald*. A few years later he acquired a financial interest in the paper, of which he remained editor until 1886. On July 8, 1875, he married Lillian Sill Comstock of Rome, N. Y., by whom he had two daughters and two sons. He was one of the first newspapermen to make use of the typewriter. In 1885 he was elected president of the New York State Associated Press, and in 1886 became editor and part owner of the *Albany Express*. When after two years the paper was sold, he was employed for a short time as an editorial writer on the *New York Press*. In 1889 he went to Boston to become secretary of the National Association of Wool Manufacturers. As editor of the association's quarterly *Bulletin,* he began the collection of wool prices and other statistics important to the industry. Much of his time was spent in Washington, however, where during the tariff revisions of 1894 and 1897 he presented before congressional committees the case for the domestic manufacturers. He also acted as clerk for a sub-committee of the Senate Finance Committee during the tariff discussions of 1894 and 1897 (letter, *Congressional Record,* 63 Cong., 1 Sess., pp. 1659ff.).

In 1903 he was appointed director of the United States Census, a position for which he was well qualified by previous experience. For the Tenth Census (1880) he had prepared an exhaustive study, *History and Present Condition of the Newspaper and Periodical Press of the United States* (1884); he was the author of a special report, "Wool Manufacture," in *Report of Manufacturing Industries ... at the Eleventh Census, 1890* (1895, pt. 3; also published as "A Century of American Wool Manufacture," in *Bulletin of the National Association of Wool Manufacturers,* September 1894–March 1895); and had been chief statistician for manufactures for the Twelfth Census. His appointment as director came at a critical period in the history of the census bureau. In response to the urging of economists and statisticians, Congress, by the act providing for the Census of 1900, had made the Bureau of the Census, placed in the Department of the Interior, substantially independent of the secretary. In 1903, however, the census bureau was transferred by executive order to the newly created Department of Commerce and Labor, and immediately differences of opinion arose between Director North and Secretary George Bruce Cortelyou. North opposed the Secretary's attempts to control the bureau on the ground that the director's authority as defined by statute could not be limited by executive orders. Legally, North's position appears to have been impregnable, but strategically he was at a great disadvantage in dealing with a cabinet member. He proceeded to reorganize and expand the work of the Bureau, but the administrative conflict, continually renewed, threatened to interfere with the plans for the Thirteenth Census, and finally President Taft, acting on a report from Secretary Charles Nagel, forced North to resign (*Evening Star,* Washington, May 26, June 1, 1909).

He was then sixty years old. Turning again toward editorial work, he spent a few months in Concord, N. H., associated with Messrs. Chandler, Rossiter, and others in building up the Rumford Press. In 1911 he returned to Washington to become assistant secretary of the Carnegie Endowment for International Peace, in which position he remained until 1921, when failing health caused his retirement. He died at the home of a daughter in Wilton, Conn., three years later.

North was a member of the United States Industrial Commission by appointment of President McKinley in 1898, and one of three commissioners sent to Germany by President Roosevelt in 1906 to investigate complaints regarding the administration of American customs laws. He was a prolific writer. His publications, in addition to those already mentioned, include "An American Textile Glossary" (*Bulletin of the National Association of Wool Manufacturers,* March 1893–September 1896); *Old Greek* (1905), a memoir of his father; *Simeon North, First Official Pistol Maker of the United States* (1913), in collaboration with Ralph H. North, a biography of his great-grandfather; and a large number of magazine articles of an historical or statistical nature. He edited *The American Year Book, 1910* (1911).

[W. F. Willcox, "The Development of the American Census Office Since 1890," *Pol. Sci. Quart.,* Sept. 1914; *Bull. Nat. Asso. of Wool Mfrs.,* Oct. 1924, with bibliog. of North's articles published in that journal; *Who's Who in America,* 1922–23; *Independent,* Apr. 15, 1909; Dexter North, *John North of Farmington, Conn., and His Descendants* (1921), which is authority for date of birth; W. L. Downing, *Thirty Years Post Graduate Record of the Class of 1869, Hamilton Coll.* (1899); *Hamilton Coll. Bull., Necrology,* Apr. 1925; *Evening Star* (Washington) and *N. Y. Times,* Aug. 4, 1924.]
P. W. B.

NORTH, WILLIAM (1755–Jan. 3, 1836), Revolutionary soldier, was born at Fort Frederic, Pemaquid, Me., the son of Capt. John North and his second wife, Elizabeth Pitson. After his father's death in 1763, William removed with his mother to Boston where he was educated and began training for a mercantile career. At the outbreak of the Revolution, he desired to accompany Arnold's expedition to Quebec but illness prevented. On May 9, 1776, he was "engaged" as second lieutenant in Col. Thomas Crafts's train of artillery. Subsequently he served as an officer in various regiments of Massachusetts infantry, including Col. Henry Jackson's, the 4th, and the 16th. In May 1779 he was appointed aide-de-camp to the Baron von Steuben [*q.v.*]. This was the beginning of a romantic friendship terminating only with Steuben's death. North accompanied the baron on his campaigns, assisted him in reorganizing the army, was adopted by him as a son, became one of his heirs and executors, erected a monument over his grave, and wrote a biographical sketch of him which was used by Steuben's biographer Friedrich Kapp.

After the war North served for a time as inspector of the army with the rank of major. On Oct. 14, 1787, he married Mary, daughter of James Duane [*q.v.*], mayor of New York City. He acquired an estate in Duanesburg, N. Y., and was the father of three sons and three daughters. In 1794, when war with England seemed imminent, he served on a commission to devise measures for strengthening the defenses of the state. He was several times elected to the assembly as a Federalist. In 1795, 1796, and 1810 he was honored with the speakership. Upon the resignation of John Sloss Hobart [*q.v.*] as United States senator, he was appointed by Governor Jay, during the recess of the legislature, to fill the vacancy. After taking his seat on May 21, 1798, he voted for the Alien and Sedition laws (though not for the Naturalization Act), for increases in the military and naval establishments, and for suspension of commercial relations with France. His experience as a soldier led to his appointment (sometimes as chairman) upon various committees charged with the consideration of military affairs, such as the arming of the militia and the expense of raising a regiment of artillerists and engineers.

On July 19, the last day of the executive session, he was nominated by President Adams to be adjutant-general of the provisional army, and the nomination was at once confirmed. He served in this capacity until June 1800, when he was honorably discharged. By concurrent resolution of Mar. 13–15, 1810, the New York legislature appointed him member of a commission to report upon the feasibility of a canal between Lakes Erie and Ontario and the Hudson River. He entered upon his duties in July, and after study of the project joined the other commissioners in framing a report which helped to pave the way for the building of the Erie Canal. He died in

New York City and was buried in Duanesburg. He was a man of strong prejudices who combined in rare fashion joviality of temper with zeal in the performance of duty.

[Letters of North among the Steuben Papers in N. Y. Hist. Soc.; Friedrich Kapp, *The Life of Frederick William von Steuben* (1859); J. W. North, *The Hist. of Augusta* (1870); J. B. Doyle, *Frederick William von Steuben and the Am. Rev.* (1913); J. D. Hammond, *The Hist. of Pol. Parties in the State of N. Y.* (4th ed., 2 vols., 1846); *Buffalo Hist. Soc. Pubs.*, vol. II (1880); *Mass. Soldiers and Sailors of the Rev. War* (16 vols., 1896–1907); F. B. Heitman, *Hist. Reg. of Officers of the Continental Army* (rev. ed., 1914); *National Intelligencer* (Washington, D. C.), Jan. 12, 1836.]   E. E. Cu—s.

NORTHEN, WILLIAM JONATHAN (July 9, 1835–Mar. 25, 1913), governor of Georgia, was, in the course of his varied life, teacher, farmer, legislator, editor, writer, and soldier. He was born in Jones County, Ga., the son of Peter and Louise Maria Louisa (Davis) Northen and a descendant of Edmund Northen of English descent who emigrated to Virginia probably in the middle of the seventeenth century. His father moved to Penfield, where Mercer University had been established, and became a steward of the college and treasurer of the Baptist Convention. There the boy was graduated in 1853. He taught a private school in Mt. Zion until 1856, when he became assistant principal of Mt. Zion High School near Sparta in Hancock County. In 1857, upon the retirement of Carlisle P. Beman, he was made principal. He married on Dec. 19, 1860, Martha Moss Neel, the daughter of Thomas Neel of Mt. Zion. They had two children. During the Civil War he was a Confederate private in a company commanded by his father. In 1871 he moved his school to Kirkwood near Atlanta and at the end of 1874 resigned his school and returned to Hancock County, where he became a farmer. Until 1890 he farmed with success, being especially interested in cattle breeding and in producing large proportions of butter fat. He mixed with his farming no small measure of politics; he became permanent president of the Hancock County Farmers' Club, president of the Georgia State Agricultural Society, 1886–90, and he was representative of the county in the General Assembly, 1877–78 and 1880–81, and state senator, 1884–85. He was active in efforts to educate farmers to improved methods and to crop diversification, was a leader in the boycott to prevent an advance in the price of the jute bagging used to cover cotton bales, and supported the attack on the monetary system. In 1890 he was elected governor as the candidate of the Democratic party with the support of the farmers of the Georgia State Agricultural Society and the

Farmers' Alliance. In 1892 he was reëlected for a second term against the Populist candidate. During his administration he advocated the interests of agriculture and urged the importance of such state undertakings as the geological survey, prison reform, and the improvement of the common-schools.

As ex-governor he continued to reside in Atlanta. He became manager of the Georgia Immigration and Investment Bureau, a position in which he was instrumental in bringing many desirable settlers into the state and, particularly, a group of Union veterans from Indiana who founded the town of Fitzgerald. He became editor of an extensive collection of biographical sketches published in six volumes from 1907 to 1912 under the title of *Men of Mark in Georgia* and himself wrote a number of the contributions. He published a seventh volume with uniform binding and title page in 1912 which, however, is not registered in the records of the copyright office and is not usually included in a description of the set. He took a prominent part in the councils of the Baptist Church, serving fourteen years as president of the Georgia Convention and three years as president of the Southern Baptist Convention. He was a trustee of Mercer University from 1869 to his death and held other positions of trust. On the death of Allen D. Candler he was appointed his successor as compiler of state records and edited in part *The Colonial Records of Georgia,* vol. XXII, pts. 1, 2 (1913). He maintained a constant and active interest in agriculture and education and was a strong advocate of prohibition. He was a frequent contributor to agricultural, educational, and religious journals. He was buried in Oakland Cemetery at Atlanta.

[Papers in the possession of his daughter, Annie B. Northen, Atlanta, Ga.; A. B. Caldwell, "William Jonathan Northen," *Men of Mark in Ga.*, IV (1908); L. L. Knight, *Reminiscences of Famous Georgians* (2 vols., 1907–08); and Georgia's *Landmarks* (2 vols., 1913–14); *Who's Who in America,* 1912–13; A. M. Arnett, *The Populist Movement in Ga.* (1922); *Atlanta Constitution,* Mar. 26, 1913.]   J. H. T. M.

NORTHEND, CHARLES (Apr. 2, 1814–Aug. 7, 1895), educator, was born at Newbury (now Newburyport), Mass., the descendant of Ezekiel Northend, who emigrated from Yorkshire, England, and settled in Newbury before 1691, and the son of John and Anna (Titcomb) Northend. His father, a studious, well-read man played an active part in the affairs of the town, serving as selectman and representative to the Massachusetts General Court. As a student in the public schools at Newbury and, later, at Dummer Academy at South Byfield during the period of his preparation for college, Charles

Northend achieved a reputation for scholastic accomplishment. He entered Amherst College in 1831 but was obliged, for financial reasons, to withdraw at the close of his sophomore year. Upon leaving college he was engaged as an instructor in Dummer Academy and remained there several terms. On Aug. 18, 1834, he was married to his cousin Lucy Ann Moody, the daughter of William and Abigail (Titcomb) Moody, of Newbury. They had three sons. In 1836 he accepted an appointment as principal of the First Grammar School in Danvers, Mass. Five years later he removed to Salem to take charge of the Epes Grammar School, in which position he served until 1852, when he returned to Danvers as superintendent of public schools. During this period he worked untiringly to improve conditions in the common schools. He organized teachers' associations and conducted institutes for the discussion of teaching problems. To his efforts were due many reforms in various phases of educational practice. The Essex County Teachers' Association recognized his contributions by electing him president for three successive terms, 1846, 1847, 1848. His success at Danvers attracted considerable attention throughout New England.

When the town was divided, in 1855, and his opportunities there were consequently curtailed, he was invited to New Britain, Conn., as school visitor, a position corresponding to that of assistant superintendent of public schools. He accepted this election in 1856 and devoted the remainder of his professional life to the New Britain school system. As in Massachusetts, he gave unsparingly of his time and energy to the cause of the common-school. From 1856 to 1866 he was an editor of the *Connecticut Common School Journal*. In 1878 he became an associate editor of the *New England Journal of Education* (later the *Journal of Education*). Among other activities, he delivered many addresses on educational topics before county, state, and national associations; and he became known as one of the most progressive superintendents of his time. The American Institute of Instruction elected him president for the year 1863–64. He became a member of the New Britain school board in 1872 and secretary in the following year. In 1879 he was elected superintendent of schools, a position which he held until his retirement in 1880. The last years of his life were spent in New Britain. Although he had withdrawn from public office, he continued his interest in educational affairs, brought out later editions of his books, and contributed articles to professional journals. He was a prolific writer of school-

books, some of which went through many editions. Among those best known are: *The Common School Book-Keeping* (1845), *The American Speaker* (1848), *Dictation Exercises* (1851), *The Teacher and the Parent* (1853), *The Teacher's Assistant* (1859), *Selections for Analysis and Parsing* (1864), *Gems for the Young* (1864), and *Entertaining Dialogues* (1876).

[*Amer. Jour. of Education*, June, Sept. 1865; Alfred Andrews, *Geneal. and Eccles. Hist. of New Britain* (1867); "The Northend Family," *Essex Institute Hist. Colls.*; vol. XII (1874); *Vital Records of Danvers, Mass.*, vol. II (1910); *Vital Records of Newbury, Mass.* (2 vols., 1911); *Hartford Courant*, Aug. 8, 1895.]

R. F. S.

NORTHROP, BIRDSEY GRANT (July 18, 1817–Apr. 27, 1898), educator, was born in Kent, Conn., the son of Thomas Grant and Aurelia (Curtiss) Northrop, and a descendant of Joseph Northrop who emigrated from England to Boston, Mass., in 1637, settling, two years later, at Milford, Conn. Since his grandfather, Amos Northrop, had attended Yale College, the boy wrote to the president of Yale, Jeremiah Day [q.v.], asking him "what school or schools are the best and most celebrated." "I wish," he added, "to attend a good school in a preparatory course for college" (*New England Magazine*, May 1900, p. 269). Presumably upon the advice of Dr. Day, but against the wishes of his father, the young man went to school in Ellington, Conn., and from there to Yale, from which he was graduated in 1841. He then entered the Yale Theological School and was graduated in 1845. During his college course he was troubled by ill health but, although he gave up study for a time, he was able to teach in Elizabethtown, N. J. In 1846 he married Harriette Eliza Chichester of Troy, N. Y. Five children were born to them.

In 1846 Northrop was called to the pastorate of the Congregational church at Saxonville, Mass., where he remained for ten years. In 1857 he resigned and was appointed agent of the Massachusetts State Board of Education, a position which he held until 1867, when he was appointed secretary of the Connecticut State Board of Education. He helped to inaugurate a free-school system in the state and to establish compulsory school attendance. After his resignation in 1883, he began to devote his energies to the establishment of Arbor Day, a project in which he had been actively interested since 1876, and to the improvement and beautifying of towns. To this latter activity is due much of the beauty of such towns as Barre, Great Barrington, and Lenox, Mass., Litchfield, New Milford, and Norfolk, Conn., and Geneseo, N. Y. In 1872 the government of Japan invited him to initiate a system of public education, but his duties kept him at home. Aside from his interest in the establishment of Arbor Day and village improvement societies, Northrop's great desire was to induce the United States government to return the Japanese indemnity exacted because of the Shimonoseki episode in 1863. In a bulletin issued from the "State House, New Haven, Conn.," dated Jan. 1, 1873, he gave a statement of the situation and sent out a petition for signatures, which was later presented to the Senate by Senator Joseph Hawley of Connecticut. The matter of the indemnity was before Congress at intervals for a number of years, but finally, in 1883, the whole amount paid by Japan was returned to be used for educational purposes. Northrop acted as the guardian of some of the first Japanese students who came to the United States. His advice in educational matters was frequently sought. It was after consultation with him that Daniel Hand [q.v.] gave over a million dollars to help the Southern freedmen. Charles Pratt [q.v.], who founded Pratt Institute, Brooklyn, N. Y., also consulted him. He was one of the original trustees of Smith College and was for some years a trustee of Hampton Institute. When he was nearly eighty years old he went to Japan and the Hawaiian Islands, giving many lectures, and in 1897 he went through the Southern states, lecturing and visiting numerous negro schools.

His publications, the titles of which suggest their character, include the following: *Education Abroad* (1873); *Lessons from European Schools* (1877); *The Legal Prevention of Illiteracy* (1878); *Village Improvement* (1878); *Schools of Forestry and Industrial Schools of Europe* (1878); *Tree Planting and Schools of Forestry in Europe* (1879); *Schools and Communism, National Schools and Other Papers* (1879); *Menticulture and Agriculture* (1881); *Rural Improvement* (1882); *Forests and Floods* (1885); *Arbor Day in Schools* (1892).

[A. J. Northrup, *The Northrup-Northrop Geneal.* (1908); *Obit. Record Grads. Yale Univ.*, 1898; *Semi-Centennial Hist. and Biog. Record of the Class of 1841 in Yale Univ.* (1892); E. B. Peck, "The Founder of Arbor Day," in *New England Mag.*, May 1900; *New Haven Evening Register*, Apr. 28, 1898.] A. B. M—h.

NORTHROP, CYRUS (Sept. 30, 1834–Apr. 3, 1922), second president of the University of Minnesota, was born on a farm near Ridgefield, Conn. His mainly peaceful and prosperous life divides itself roughly into three ample blocks: the period of nonage (1834–1857), the Yale professorship (1863–1884), and the presidential tenure, active and retired, lasting from 1884 to 1922.

Six years of fluctuation and uncertainty divide the first of these periods from the second.

He was a descendant of Joseph Northrop who emigrated from England in 1637 and two years later settled in Milford, Conn. His father's family, poor, industrious, thrifty, long-lived, God-fearing men, farmed the soil of Connecticut, without recorded interruption, from 1639 to the later nineteenth century. The elder Cyrus Northrop, father of the educator, married in 1822 Polly Bouton Fancher, whose ancestry, French on both sides, reached America in 1635 with John Bouton, Huguenot and refugee. It was only in Cyrus junior, the sixth and youngest child, that this devout and hardworking breed emerged from rusticity, a rusticity not incompatible with terms in the Connecticut legislature for two of the older brothers. Cyrus was sent to Williston Seminary in Easthampton, Mass., then at the zenith of its merited fame under Josiah Clark—first, for all time, among his teachers for the young Cyrus. To Yale College, in 1852, by a family decision which family poverty made touching and even heroic, the lad of eighteen betook himself. He graduated, third in his class, in 1857, and from the Yale Law School in 1859. Even at this early age his personality in conversation and his eloquence on the rostrum made impressions on practically everybody that were both instantaneous and ineffaceable.

In 1860 he was admitted to the bar. Two rasping years of small-town law practice in Norwalk and South Norwalk, Conn., in which fees were even rarer than clients, were alleviated by clerkships in the two houses of the state legislature, and ended by his acceptance of the editorship of the New Haven *Palladium,* a newspaper which opposed slavery and upheld Lincoln. His conduct of this paper was vigorous and inspiring, but fifteen months in its office showed him that the hopes of income on the strength of which he had married Anna Elizabeth Warren of Stamford, Conn., Sept. 30, 1862, were chimerical, and in 1863 he was led by "poverty" to accept the chair of rhetoric and English literature in Yale College. The fact marks a curious angle in his career. The young man predestined, as it seemed, to reach politics via law, actually drifted into instructorship by way of journalism. The new post was at once a step upward and a step aside.

Cyrus Northrop filled this post for twenty-one years with efficiency and with distinction. He mended his income by adding to his college work the collectorship of duties for the port of New Haven (1869–81), and he enlivened its routine by an unsuccessful canvass for a seat in Congress on the Republican ticket in 1867. In this snug academic harbor the man—not the teacher—was, in a sense, becalmed. Half the man was more than enough to perform his work efficiently; the other and richer half was unemployed. From this beguiling monotony he was released by an offer of the presidency of the University of Minnesota (1884) tactfully pressed upon his first unhesitating refusal and his slowly diminishing reluctance. Admirable teacher as he was, the classroom was both too large and too small to give scope for a personality which reached its perfection in the cabinet or on the rostrum. His gift was both public and intimate. He persuaded; he convinced; he impressed; he diverted; he controlled. It is impossible to trace here the steps (not to say the leaps and bounds) by which a small and shrinking institution of less than 300 students, subsisting on meager doles from an inconstant legislature, became in twenty-seven years a great and various body numbering its faculty by the hundred; its students by the thousand, and its income by the million. To this advance Cyrus Northrop contributed by judgment, address, resolution, fearlessness, and liberality. He helped even more perhaps by personifying the university in a form which dignified and magnified it in its own eyes and in the eyes of its constituents. He was not a thinker in education, not by instinct an innovator. Left to himself, he might have been content with an education predominantly classical and predominantly masculine; but he was never for a moment ungracious or uncordial to the movements which brought sciences and women to the front. He owed much of his success, both with communities and with individuals, to a humor which made a trifle or a nothing delectable by putting behind it the whole ironic weight of his majestic personality.

He retired from the presidency in 1911, at the age of seventy-seven. Pecuniary and domestic afflictions clouded his last years. He survived his three deeply loved children, of whom the eldest died in early childhood; the second, after an attack of scarlet fever, suffered from life-long mental infirmity; a third, Elizabeth, wife of Joseph Warren Beach, after years of tottering health, died in 1918, leaving two young sons, the president's only surviving descendants. He died of a ruptured heart, Apr. 3, 1922, and, three days later, was buried in the family lot in Lakewood Cemetery, Minneapolis. Throughout his life he was faithful to the Congregationalist Church, in which he had been born and to which, at nineteen, he had pledged his loyalty.

A volume of *Addresses, Educational and Patriotic* from his hand was published in 1910. An imposing auditorium on the campus of the University of Minnesota bears his name and protects his memory.

[A. J. Northrup, *The Northrup-Northrop Geneal.* (1908); *Yale Univ. Obit. Record*, 1922; O. W. Firkins, *Cyrus Northrop* (1925); *Minneapolis Jour.*, Apr. 4, 1922.]   O. W. F.

NORTHROP, LUCIUS BELLINGER (Sept. 8, 1811–Feb. 9, 1894), Confederate commissary-general, was born in Charleston, S. C., the son of Amos Bird Northrop and Claudia Margaret Bellinger. The Northrop family was well known in Charleston and was descended from Joseph Northrop, who emigrated from England and settled in Milford, Conn., in 1639. Lucius was graduated from West Point in 1831. He was made brevet second lieutenant of the 7th Infantry but in 1833 was transferred to the 1st Dragoons. He was stationed with this regiment in the West on Indian service and was for a time associated with Jefferson Davis. In 1834 he was promoted first lieutenant. During the Seminole War of 1839 in Florida he received a severe wound and was retired from the army on a permanent sick furlough. He then studied medicine at Jefferson Medical College, Philadelphia. Returning to Charleston, he was in 1848 dropped from the army for practising medicine on charity patients there. Later in the year, however, he was reinstated by Jefferson Davis, secretary of war, and was promoted captain. From 1853 to 1861 he practised medicine in Charleston. About 1841 he had married Maria Euphenia Joanna de Bernabeu, daughter of Juan Baptisto de Bernabeu, United States consul from Spain.

Shortly after the secession of South Carolina, Northrop resigned his commission and upon the urgent request of President Davis accepted the position of colonel and commissary-general in the Confederate army. He was entrusted with the enormous task of providing food for the Southern armies and also, after 1862, for all the Northern prisoners. Though at first his position was considered rather insignificant, as the food supply began to decrease it became quite important. Next to Bragg, and perhaps Benjamin, Northrop was deemed the special favorite of Davis, and soon he was bitterly criticized. Early in 1864, Senator Foote of Tennessee introduced a measure into the Confederate Senate for Northrop's removal, but it was defeated. Meantime, against the wishes of several officers, he had introduced a system by which he appointed state commissary agents and held them responsible directly to himself. He was accused of inadequately feeding Federal prisoners but in January 1865 the Confederate Senate acquitted him of the charge. On Jan. 18, 1865, J. B. Jones wrote that Northrop was "still held by the President, contrary to the wishes of the whole Confederacy" (*post*, II, p. 390). A month later, after the Confederate House of Representatives had passed a bill seeking his removal, Davis finally consented to take this step. After Lee's surrender, Northrop was arrested by Federal troops and imprisoned, but no charges were preferred against him and he was released in a few months.

After Bragg, Northrop was probably the most unpopular of Davis' appointees. The Confederate army officers thought him inefficient; Lee had little patience with him, and finally asked for his removal. Northrop was peevish, obstinate, condescending, and fault-finding. He was secretive, indirect, and inclined to regard every suggestion as interference. On the other hand, his work could hardly have been conducted without receiving criticism. He had to contend with the lack of sufficient funds and the necessity of buying with a depreciated currency, with the capture of supplies and the possession of productive country by the invading armies, and with the necessity of resorting to the hated methods of price-fixing and impressment. But during the last two years of the war, his worst trouble was with the transportation system. This was under control of the separate Quartermaster's Bureau. Even in January 1865 there were sufficient supplies in the lower South for Lee's army. Yet Northrop's urgent requests for the improvement of the railroad service were not sufficiently heeded. All in all, Northrop seems to have been a rather good, if "crusty, routine" executive, who was forced to resort to harsh methods. Upon his release from imprisonment after the war, he retired to a farm near Charlottesville, Va. He and Jefferson Davis now renewed their friendship. Northrop's letters to Davis reveal his bitterness toward Beauregard, J. E. Johnston, and others. In 1889 his wife died, and the next year he suffered a stroke of paralysis. He then entered the soldiers' home at Pikeville, Md., where he spent his few remaining years.

[There are a considerable number of Northrop papers in the N. Y. Pub. Lib. Printed sources include: *Confed. Mil. Hist.*, vol. I (1899); *War of the Rebellion, Official Records (Army)*; Dunbar Rowland, *Jefferson Davis, Constitutionalist* (10 vols., 1923), containing correspondence between Davis and Northrop; Northrop's article, "The Confederate Commissariat at Manassas," in *Battles and Leaders of the Civil War*, vol. I (1887); J. B. Jones, *A Rebel War Clerk's Diary* (2 vols., 1866); E. A. Pollard, *Southern Hist. of the*

War (1866), vol. II, pp. 477–83; G. C. Eggleston, *A Rebel's Recollections* (1875), pp. 203–09; A. J. Northrup, *The Northrup-Northrop Geneal.* (1908); the *Sun* (Baltimore), Feb. 10, 1894.]   R. D. M.

NORTON, ALICE PELOUBET [See Norton, Mary Alice Peloubet, 1860–1928].

NORTON, ANDREWS (Dec. 31, 1786–Sept. 18, 1853), a man of letters and a Biblical scholar of distinction, was born in Hingham, Mass., the youngest child of Samuel and Jane (Andrews) Norton, and a descendant of William, a brother of Rev. John Norton [*q.v.*]. He was graduated from Harvard College in 1804, pursued graduate studies for four years, preached for a brief period in Augusta, Me., taught for a year at Bowdoin College, in 1811 was appointed tutor at Cambridge, and in 1813 librarian of Harvard College and lecturer on the Bible. In 1819 he became Dexter Professor of Sacred Literature in the Harvard Divinity School. He resigned his professorship in 1830, but continued his literary and theological work at Cambridge until his death, which occurred twenty-three years later at his summer residence at Newport, R. I.

His most important work was his treatise on *The Evidences of the Genuineness of the Gospels*, of which the first volume was published in 1837, and the second and third volumes in 1844. This work, dealing with the history of the New Testament canon on the basis of a careful investigation of the evidence outside the Bible itself, was one of the earliest studies of Biblical literature from the critical point of view to be published in America. It antedates most of the New Testament criticism by nineteenth-century German scholars, who dealt primarily with questions of text and of internal evidence and to whom Norton owed less than he did to English writers. It ran through several editions in this country and in England (the latest being an abridged edition, Boston, 1867), brought him wide recognition as a scholar, and was an influential contribution to theological literature. In 1852 he published a volume entitled *Tracts on Christianity*, a collection of essays and discourses previously printed in various forms. After his death *Internal Evidences of the Genuineness of the Gospels* (1855), which among other things contained a critique of Strauss' *Life of Jesus*, and *Translation of the Gospels with Notes* (2 vols., 1856), appeared. He was actively concerned in the theological controversies of the time, in which, with a certain fastidiousness of thought and statement, he occupied the position of conservative Unitarianism. But, while he accepted the point of view of liberal

Christianity, he was disinclined to enter any associations formed on denominational lines. He established and wrote for the short-lived *General Repository and Review* (January 1812–October 1813), and contributed many reviews to the *Christian Examiner* and several to the *North American Review*. In 1833 he printed *A Statement of Reasons for not Believing the Doctrines of Trinitarians*. His address in 1839, *On the Latest Form of Infidelity*, was commonly interpreted as a reply to Emerson's famous *Divinity School Address* of the preceding year. By many persons who know nothing of Norton's substantial achievements its unfortunate title has been remembered to the disparagement of his just reputation.

In the field of general literature he played an influential part through the editing, with Charles Folsom, of *The Select Journal of Foreign Periodical Literature* (4 vols., 1833–34). He also edited *Poems by Mrs. Hemans* (1826–28). A volume of his own poems, *Verses*, was published in the year of his death. His poetry was of a reserved and formal type, reminiscent of the eighteenth century, but two of his hymns, "My God, I thank thee! may no thought E'er deem thy chastisements severe" (1809), and "Where ancient forests round us spread" (1833) are to be found in modern hymnbooks.

He was an independent and solitary thinker, but his learning enabled him to speak with an authority possessed by few American scholars of his generation, and his influence upon the literary and religious life of his time was constructive and beneficent, thanks to the clarity of his thought and the integrity of his character.

On May 21, 1821, he married Catharine, daughter of Samuel Eliot of Boston. They had six children, of whom four survived infancy. One of these, Charles Eliot Norton [*q.v.*], became a distinguished scholar, and another, Grace Norton, was well-known for her work on Montaigne. Andrews Norton lived in Cambridge at "Shady Hill," a mansion which he erected about the time of his marriage, and which, during the life of his son, became widely known as a center of influence in art and letters.

[William Newell, in *Christian Examiner*, Nov. 1853; W. B. Sprague, *Annals of the American Pulpit*, vol. VIII (1865); A. P. Peabody, *Harvard Reminiscences* (1888), pp. 73–78; S. A. Eliot, ed., *Heralds of a Liberal Faith* (1910), vol. II; *New-Eng. Hist. and Geneal. Reg.*, July 1859; Sara Norton and M. A. DeW. Howe, *Letters of Charles Eliot Norton* (2 vols., 1913.).]

H. W. F.

NORTON, CHARLES ELIOT (Nov. 16, 1827–Oct. 21, 1908), editor, author, teacher, was born in Cambridge, Mass., the fifth child and only surviving son of Andrews Norton [*q.v.*], then Dexter Professor of Sacred Literature in the Harvard Divinity School, and his wife, Catharine Eliot, daughter of Samuel Eliot of Boston. His parents made their home at "Shady Hill," an estate of some fifty acres in Cambridge, where their six children were born, and where Charles died. This home, with its simple but spacious and scholarly elegance, was the hospitable center of the life of the Nortons. Andrews had also a summer place in fashionable Newport. Charles made a retreat at the little town of Ashfield, in northwestern Massachusetts. Wherever domiciled he entered into the life of the place and was a factor in its civic betterment. By inheritance he was endowed with financial competence, scholarly tastes, and a pervasive moral sense. The thoroughness of his scholarship, and his ethical poise were accompanied by personal charm, qualities which combined to make a personality of rare and enduring influence.

Graduating from Harvard in 1846, at the age of nineteen, Norton spent three years with a Boston importing firm. To business he gave conscientious days: his evenings were spent in the congenial tasks of establishing night schools for men and boys in Cambridge and helping the almost blind Francis Parkman prepare for the press his *Oregon Trail*. In 1849, Norton went to India as supercargo. The business instinct of the Eliots, the ways and means of making money, he had not inherited; he was interested in commerce simply as an exchange of commodities. He spent a leisurely two years in Egypt, Italy, France, and England, indulging his bent in studying social conditions and making friendships. In Paris he met "the long-haired and sweet-visaged" George William Curtis [*q.v.*], fresh from his Nile experiences, and the two quickly began a lifelong association. In Florence he became on familiar terms with the Brownings. In England he enjoyed the Ascot races, and the literary society of the day.

Returning to Boston in 1851, Norton began on his own account a modest business in the East India trade. This faded out in 1855, leaving him free to indulge fully his propensity for a literary life. He began by editing the translations of the Gospels, discourses, and poems of his father, who had died in 1853. The doctors ordered Norton abroad in 1855, and with no reluctance he, accompanied by his mother and two sisters, went to Rome. His studies, observations, and opinions, embodied in *Notes of Travel and Study in Italy* (1860), came to be modified but never were essentially changed. He translated *The New Life of Dante Aligheri*

(1867, privately printed 1859) as a prelude to his prose rendering of *The Divine Comedy* (3 vols., 1891–92). In Switzerland he began the intimate friendship with Ruskin, recorded in the *Letters of John Ruskin to Charles Eliot Norton* (2 vols., 1904). James Russell Lowell joined the Nortons in Italy for mule rides, continuing a companionship which widened and deepened with their lives, as may be read in their published letters, those of Lowell in the two volumes Norton edited (1894); Norton's in the two volumes of his own letters. In England he met Thackeray, and was taken into companionship with the Pre-Raphaelites (*Letters,* I, 175). He visited his close friends, the Gaskells and the A. H. Cloughs.

Returning in 1857, Norton wrote articles and reviews for the *Atlantic Monthly,* just established with Lowell as its editor. He enjoyed companionship with its contributors—Lowell, Holmes, and Emerson especially. The impending Civil War engrossed him. Intimacy with the Middleton family of Charleston, S. C., whose summer home was at Bristol, R. I., gave him occasion to study slavery under its most favorable conditions, and to convince him that bad as that institution was for the blacks, it was even worse for the whites. John Brown's rash invasion of Virginia, his conviction, and his heroic death on the gallows, seemed to Norton to place Brown among the Covenanters and the Puritans, and, despite the wrongness of the means adopted, to "set up a standard by which to measure the principles of public men" (*Letters,* I, 201). He was undismayed by the prospect of war and had no fear for the result; but he looked forward "with the deepest sorrow and compassion to the retribution" the South was preparing for itself (*Ibid.,* I, 216). If his early confidence in Lincoln wavered at times, he was quick to readjust his judgment. As editor of the Loyal Publication Society broadsides, for three years he furnished local newspapers with copies of the most effective editorial writings of the day. In 1864, Lowell and Norton as editors made the *North American Review* convincingly loyal. On May 21, 1862, Norton married Susan Ridley Sedgwick, daughter of Theodore Sedgwick, 3rd, of Stockbridge and New York. After an ideal domestic life at "Shady Hill" and Ashfield, she died in February 1872, at Dresden, Germany, while the family (which included three sons and three daughters) were spending five years in Europe.

In March 1869, Norton met Thomas Carlyle, then seventy-four years old, at the latter's London home. Norton said Carlyle was "the Court-jester of the century," and that like all great talkers, he said much for immediate effect and forgot it as soon as said (*Letters,* I, 332–33). Again, Norton wrote of Carlyle: "Like Dante, his face was black with the smoke of Hell" (*Ibid.,* II, 147). Emerson and Norton directed to Harvard, Carlyle's gift of a large portion of his library, as a sort of reparation for his attacks on the United States. In 1882, Froude, as Carlyle's literary executor, published a garbled version of the intimate journals of Jane Welsh Carlyle, thereby creating a literary sensation. "I could not have believed, even of Froude, bad as I thought him," wrote Norton, "a capacity for such falseness, for such betrayal of a most sacred trust, for such cynical treachery to the memory of one who had put faith in him" (*Ibid.,* II, 135). The family appealed to Norton, and he edited Carlyle's letters, reminiscences, and two notebooks, together with the Carlyle-Emerson and the Goethe-Carlyle correspondence—in all eleven volumes (1883–91).

Norton's work as a teacher covered the years from 1873 to 1897, from his forty-sixth to his seventieth year. Called to service by his cousin, the youthful, innovating President Charles W. Eliot [*q.v.*], Norton began at Harvard the first continuous university instruction in the history of the fine arts as related to social progress, general culture, and literature (manuscript letter, Harvard Library). Eliot Norton wittily and aptly called his father's courses "Lectures on Modern Morals as Illustrated by the Art of the Ancients" (*Letters,* II, 8). All his gathered learning, his discriminating judgment, the results of close companionship with world-worthies, he lavished on the students who flocked to him. The quiet, pervasive charm that had endeared him to the Brownings, to Carlyle, Ruskin, Emerson, Curtis, Lowell, and Longfellow was exercised in his crowded classroom and was expanded in the rare companionship of his home, where he exemplified the attributes of a gentleman. The purchase and gift to the Harvard Library of his rare books, by his students; the creation of The Norton Fellowship in Greek Studies by one of his pupils, and by another the foundation of the Charles Eliot Norton Lectureship of Poetry are manifestations of a sway which came to be accounted by many as the determining influence in their lives. His book, *Historical Studies of Church-Building in the Middle Ages* (1880), is a treasure to practitioners of architecture as a fine art. Another book, *History of Ancient Art* (1891), was prepared by H. F. Brown and W. H. Wiggin from his lectures.

The range of Norton's activities in literature and life was great. He edited *The Poems of John Donne* (2 vols., 1895), *The Love Poems of John Donne* (1905), and *The Poems of Mrs. Anne Bradstreet* (1897), as well as the *Orations and Addresses of George William Curtis* (3 vols., 1894). The Archaeological Institute of America, the American School of Classical Studies at Athens and in Rome, and the movement to preserve Niagara Falls owe to him inspiration and effective support. His sympathies were fresh and catholic. One of the first (*Putnam's Monthly*, Sept. 1855) to recognize Walt Whitman, as combining "the characteristics of a Concord philosopher with those of a New York fireman" (*Letters*, I, 135), he was equally quick to see the merits of Kipling and to enjoy Mr. Dooley. (See *Rudyard Kipling; A Biographical Sketch*, 1899, and *Atlantic Monthly*, Jan. 1897.) The Chicago Fair of 1893 was to him a foretaste of "the ideal Chicago, which exists not only in the brain, but in the heart of some of her citizens. I have never seen Americans from whom one could draw happier auguries for the future of America, than some of the men whom I saw at Chicago" (*Letters*, II, 218).

In 1865, E. L. Godkin, F. L. Olmsted, J. M. McKim, Norton, and others founded the *Nation* as a critical journal to maintain standards in politics, literature and art, familiarly known as "the weekly day of judgment." During forty years of intimacy with Godkin, Norton gave to him active support morally, financially, and by reviews and criticisms in art and letters. During summers at Ashfield, Norton and Curtis, in 1879, started for the benefit of local charity, a series of annual dinners at which Choate, Howells, Moorfield Storey, Booker Washington, and others advocated reform of the tariff and the civil service, the promotion of negro education, and especially anti-imperialism. Stigmatized as mugwumps and party renegades, the speakers through the press found a nation-wide audience. With Curtis' death and Norton's failing health the dinners ceased in 1903.

The breadth of Norton's intelligence, the unflinching clearness of his reasoning, the intensity of his moral convictions aroused antagonisms which he neither sought nor avoided. Companionship with Chauncey Wright, Cambridge mathematician and philosopher, developed a philosophy of life which led him out of the creeds of his ancestors and into a position "almost solitary in my open profession of free-thinking" (*Ibid.*, II, 249), . . . "perplexed indeed by the mighty mystery of existence, and

of the universe and happy in the conviction that the chief lesson of life is that of love" (*Ibid.*, II, 364). To him God and immortality were inconceivable, but "the motives which impel an intelligent man . . . to virtuous conduct, are the strongest which can be addressed to a human being, because they appeal directly to the highest qualities of his human nature" (*Ibid.*). Thus to him came "a new sense of the value of life to the individual, and of his infinite unimportance to the universe; . . . he can be a help or a harm to his fellows, and that is enough" (*Ibid.*, II, 347). His religious opinions caused momentary hesitation as to his confirmation as professor, and always colored estimates of him.

Norton's advice to his students that they ponder the question as to their duty to enlist for the Spanish-American War aroused widespread criticism, and the vituperations of his classmate, Senator G. F. Hoar, which were afterwards regretted by the latter, also an anti-imperialist. His insistence on *ethos* as the fundamental element in beauty in art brought about conflict with the architect, Charles F. McKim, who in reality practised Norton's precepts, and whose life-work in the American Academy in Rome, was later united with Norton's in the School of Classical Studies in the Eternal City. At times he failed to perceive that the principles he advocated were the very ones which actuated artists to create works he criticized. So, too, in politics the critic in his censures often was unmindful of exigencies which statesmen might guide but could not control.

Recognition of Norton's influence and service came in honorary degrees from Cambridge and Oxford, as well as from Harvard, Yale, and Columbia; also in original membership in the American Academy of Arts and Letters, and in appointment as grand officer of the Order of the Crown of Italy for his Italian studies. In 1907 his eightieth birthday was marked by a group of letters from friends, expressing the esteem he had won for himself. Edith Wharton sent a sonnet, appropriately entitled "High Pasture" (*Harvard Graduates' Magazine*, Dec. 1907); and in 1913, G. E. Woodberry paid his tribute in a Phi Beta Kappa poem (*Ibid.*, Sept. 1913). President Eliot put the climax to Norton's career in sober, prophetic words (*Ibid.*, Dec. 1907, p. 222): "Thousands of Harvard students attribute to his influence lasting improvements in their modes of thought, their intellectual and moral interests, and their ideas of success and true happiness. His work and his training for it were both unique, and are not likely to be parallelled in the future."

[Sara Norton and M. A. DeW. Howe, *Letters of Charles Eliot Norton with Biographical Comment*, containing a list of his writings (2 vols., 1913), a permanent piece of literature; Jane Whitehill, ed., *Letters of Mrs. Gaskell and Charles Eliot Norton, 1855–1865* (1932); W. R. Thayer, in *Harvard Grads. Mag.*, Dec. 1908; E. T. Cook and Alexander Wedderburn, *Works of John Ruskin*, vol. XXXV (1908), Præterita, II, chs. 2–3; *Development of Harvard University, 1869–1929* (1930), ed. by S. E. Morison, ch. v; *Proc. Am. Academy of Arts and Letters*, no. IV, 1910–11 (1911); E. W. Emerson and W. F. Harris, *Charles Eliot Norton* (1912); Barrett Wendell, in *Atlantic Monthly*, Jan. 1909; W. D. Howells, in *No. Am. Rev.*, Dec. 1913; *Boston Evening Transcript*, Oct. 20, 21, 22, 1908.]
C. M.

NORTON, ELIJAH HISE (Nov. 21, 1821–Aug. 5, 1914), congressman, jurist, was born near Russellville, Logan County, Ky. His father, William F. Norton, was the son of Quakers, but he became a Baptist when he married Mary Hise. She was of sturdy Pennsylvania German stock, was a pronounced Baptist, "loved to talk, talked much and talked well." About 1817 they moved from Pennsylvania to Kentucky, where William F. Norton engaged in farming and salt merchandizing. Elijah Hise Norton, their son, obtained most of his preliminary education at Centre College, Danville, Ky. He then entered the law department of Transylvania University, graduated in 1842, was admitted to the bar, and practised law at Russellville for about two years. But the strong pioneer spirit of the times soon took control of him, and in 1845 he moved west, to settle in the promising Platte Purchase country of northwest Missouri. Here, at the town of Platte City, he hung his shingle over the door of a two-room log cabin and soon won recognition as a leading lawyer among a dozen competitors. Upon being elected county attorney, with a salary of $100, he felt sufficiently prosperous to marry on May 28, 1850, Malinda C. Wilson, the daughter of an older and prominent lawyer of Platte City. She died in 1873, leaving a family of seven children, and on Sept. 17, 1877, he married Missouri A. (Green) Marshall.

During the fifties Norton was looked upon as the leading anti-Benton Democrat of northwest Missouri. In 1852 he was elected circuit judge of the Platte Purchase district and ably fulfilled the duties of this office until 1860. He was then nominated and elected to the stormy Thirty-seventh Congress (1861–63), where he took a decided stand in opposition to secession, although he stated that he did not favor war to prevent it. He was defeated when he stood for reëlection to Congress in 1862. As a leading delegate to the state convention of 1861 to consider the relations of Missouri to the federal government, he labored stubbornly and effectively against the movement to take Missouri out of the Union. He was an outstanding member of the Missouri constitutional convention of 1875. The constitution then formulated and adopted was so permeated with his sound and statesmanlike proposals that it was subsequently not infrequently denominated the "Norton Constitution." It is still (1934) the fundamental law of the state.

When a vacancy occurred on the state supreme bench in 1876, Gov. C. H. Hardin [*q.v.*] appointed Norton to fill the place. Two years later he was elected to the office for the ensuing term and served until Dec. 31, 1888, when he declined renomination. He was chief justice in 1887–88. Among the scores of supreme-court decisions which he rendered, students of jurisprudence may read with profit his citations and conclusions in such cases as *State* vs. *Shock* (68 *Missouri*, 552), dissenting opinion; *Kitchen* vs. *St. Louis, Kansas City & Northern Railway Co.* (69 *Missouri*, 224); *St. Louis* vs. *St. Louis Gaslight Co.* (70 *Missouri*, 69); and *The Julia Building Association* vs. *The Bell Telephone Co.* (88 *Missouri*, 258). He was an able judge, though he did little to construct new bases of legal reasoning or re-direct the course of legal evolution. From 1890 until his death he lived on his large farm near Platte City. He was a successful farmer and business man.

[L. C. Krauthoff, *The Supreme Court of Mo.* (1891); R. P. C. Wilson, "Memorial Address upon Judge Elijah Hise Norton," *Proc.... Mo. Bar Asso.*, 1914; A. J. D. Stewart, *The Hist. of the Bench and Bar of Mo.* (1898); *Jour. and Proc. Mo. State Convention ... 1861* (1861); *Jour. Mo. Constitutional Convention of 1875* (2 vols., 1920), ed. by Isidor Loeb and F. C. Shoemaker; W. M. Paxton, *Annals of Platte County, Mo.* (1897); *A Hist. of Northwest Mo.* (1915), ed. by Walter Williams, vol. II; J. C. Maple and R. P. Rider, *Mo. Bapt. Biog.*, vol. III (1918); H. C. McDougal, *Recollections* (1910); *Mo. Hist. Rev.*, Oct. 1914; *Boonville Daily Advertiser*, Jan. 20, 22, 1877; *Jefferson Inquirer*, Sept. 25, 1852; *St. Joseph Gazette*, Aug. 6, 1914.]
H. E. N.

NORTON, JOHN (May 6, 1606–Apr. 5, 1663), Puritan clergyman, was born at Bishop's Stortford, Hertfordshire, England, the eldest son of William and Alice (Browest) Norton, and grandson of William Norton of Sharpenhow, Bedfordshire (*New-England Historical and Genealogical Register*, July 1859, pp. 225–30). The boy studied under Alexander Strange of Buntingford, and at fourteen proceeded to Peterhouse, Cambridge, where he received the degree of B.A. in 1623/4 and that of M.A. in 1627 (John and J. A. Venn, *Alumni Cantabrigienses*, vol. III, 1924; T. A. Walker, *Admissions to Peterhouse or S. Peter's College ... Cambridge*, 1912, p. 16). For a short time he was an usher at Stortford Grammar School and curate there. He then became private chaplain to Sir William

Masham of High Lever, Essex, and a determined foe of Antinomianism. It is said that his uncle offered him a good benefice and also that he was offered a fellowship at Cambridge but that he declined them both because of his growing Puritanism. Having married "a gentlewoman both of good estate and of good esteem" (Mather, *post*, I, 289), he took ship for New England in the fall of 1634, in company with Thomas Shepard [*q.v.*], but was turned back by a severe storm and did not make another attempt to embark for nearly a year. He reached Plymouth in New England in October 1635. Here he preached and was invited to remain, but he preferred to settle in Massachusetts Bay, and became "teacher" in the church at Ipswich. He was admitted as a freeman May 17, 1637, but was not ordained until Feb. 20, 1638.

At once upon his arrival, he took his place among the leaders of the colony. He had come just in time for the Antinomian controversy and in 1637 was an influential member of the Synod convened to adjust the differences arising from it. Incidentally, he is partly responsible for the loss of valuable papers connected with it. John Cotton's son, charged by his father with destroying all his papers, hesitated to do so and put the question as a point of conscience to Norton, who decided for their destruction (Hutchinson, *post*, I, 179, note). In 1646 Norton was chosen to go with Winthrop as a special agent to England, but the plan was abandoned. The same year he took a leading part in the Synod and in 1648 he was active in drawing up the famous Cambridge Platform. When John Cotton [*q.v.*] was dying, he suggested Norton as his successor in the pastorate of the First Church of Boston, and after his death (Dec. 23, 1652), Norton took his place. He had some thought of returning to England, however; the church at Ipswich was reluctant to dismiss him, and it was only after three years and a sharp dispute between the Ipswich and Boston churches as to which should have the benefit of his ministry that he was installed at Boston, July 23, 1656. Meantime, on Oct. 18, 1654, he had been appointed an Overseer of Harvard and a week later, with Richard Mather, had been chosen to offer the presidency of the College to Charles Chauncy [*q.v.*].

Norton took a prominent part in the persecution of the Quakers at the end of that decade, showing himself bigoted, narrow-minded, and tyrannical. In spite of the succeeding popular reaction, he was one of the few who held out firmly for the passage of laws inflicting the death penalty (Bishop, *post*, p. 101). In 1662 he accompanied Simon Bradstreet [*q.v.*] as agent to present the colony's petition to Charles II, an embassy which signally failed, owing in no small part to the Quaker persecution. On the return of Norton and Bradstreet the disgruntled elements in Massachusetts did not hesitate to say that their liberties had been sold out by the agents, and Norton lost much of his popularity with the reactionary party. It is said, though without much foundation, that the criticism hastened his death. He died suddenly of apoplexy just after preaching his Sunday morning sermon.

Norton was a learned man but with a narrow and technical mind, not at all comparable in humane outlook and breadth of vision to his predecessor, Cotton. He was a fairly prolific writer whose pen was at the service of the authorities. In 1645 he wrote a treatise in Latin on the government of the New England churches, in reply to inquiries from the Dutch clergy (*Responsio ad Guliel. Apollonii Syllogen, ad Componendas Controversias in Anglia*) which was published at London in 1648. With Cotton and Edward Norris [*q.v.*] he was appointed in 1651 to convince William Pynchon [*q.v.*] that his book, *The Meritorious Price of Our Redemption* (1650) was heretical. Norton's answer, *A Discussion of That Great Point in Divinity, The Sufferings of Christ* (1653), was published by order of the General Court, and for his labor in preparing it he received £20. The following year he published *The Orthodox Evangelist* (1654), an extremely technical exposition of the Puritan system of theology. Other works were *Abel Being Dead Yet Speaketh; or the Life and Death of . . . John Cotton* (1658); and *The Heart of N— England Rent at the Blasphemies of the Present Generation*, a bitter attack on the Quakers written by order of the General Court and published at Cambridge in 1659. His will disposed of an estate valued at the large sum of £2,095, of which his library of 729 volumes amounted to over £300 (*New-England Historical and Genealogical Register*, October 1857). The day of his installation in Boston he married a second wife. Her Christian name was Mary and she has sometimes been confused with the Mary Mason who married Norton's nephew, John Norton, in 1678 (*Ibid.*, July 1859, p. 229). Norton left numerous collateral relatives, but no children.

[Cotton Mather, *Magnalia Christi Americana* (ed. of 1853), I, 286ff.; A. W. M'Clure, *The Lives of John Wilson, John Norton, and John Davenport* (1846); W. B. Sprague, *Annals Am. Pulpit*, vol. I (1856); W. H. Whitmore, *A Geneal. of the Norton Family* (1859), repr. from *New-Eng. Hist. and Geneal. Reg.*, July 1859; N. B. Shurtleff, *Records of the Gov. and Company of the Mass. Bay*, vols. I–IV (1853–54); T. F. Waters, *Ipswich in the Mass. Bay Colony*, vol. I (1905); *Colonial Soc. of Mass. Pubs.*, vol. XXI (1920); Thomas Hutchinson, *The Hist. of the Colony of Mass. Bay.*, vol. I (1764); George Bishop, *New England Judged by the Spirit of the Lord* (1703).]	J. T. A.

NORTON, JOHN NICHOLAS (1820–Jan. 18, 1881), Protestant Episcopal clergyman, was born in Waterloo, N. Y., the son of George Hatley Norton and his wife, Maria Gault. The father, a Virginian and one of the founders of the Episcopal Church in Western New York, soon settled at Allen's Hill, in the township of Richmond, Ontario County, but his sons apparently were educated in Geneva. John Norton's *Allerton Parish* (1863) is the story of Allen's Hill; and his first book, *The Boy Who Was Trained Up To Be a Clergyman* (1853), is autobiographical. The hero's college is evidently Hobart (then Geneva) College, which Norton entered in 1838. His picture of college life a century ago has real value; it is sadly trustworthy. Much chapel and little religion seems to have been his impression, and yet his class produced two other able clergymen. Graduated in 1842, Norton went to the General Theological Seminary in New York and in 1845 was duly ordained and became assistant at St. Paul's, Rochester. In 1847 he became rector of the Church of the Ascension, Frankfort, Ky., where he was to spend nearly twenty-four years.

He found little to work upon, but he worked very hard; from a dozen families developed a large and prosperous congregation; a small building gave way to a fine church and that also had to be enlarged. He was as generous as he was indefatigable. When poor he gave away all he could, and later on with money at command he still gave all he could. He preached a peculiar type of sermon, but people of all sorts and ages heard him gladly. Objection was made to his use of very homely illustrations, stories that to some seemed undignified; but the people came. He had the instinct of the good teacher—to begin where his hearers had left off, on their plane, not his. He could fill a church with children. In the midst of his zealous service at Frankfort he married, in 1855, Mary Louisa Sutton, daughter of George Washington Sutton of Lexington. She was in deepest sympathy with her husband's work and she commanded considerable means. In 1870 Norton became associate rector of Christ Church, Louisville. Again he worked incessantly, gave money to almost any one who asked for it, went anywhere, saw anybody, wherever there was work for him to do. He found the negroes without a church, and built them one and maintained it.

As soon as his work at Frankfort was well under way, he had begun to publish. His *Sketches,*

Literary and Theological (1872) show an extraordinary range of interest. He subscribed, it appears, to innumerable magazines and newspapers, out of which he culled the stories that attracted so much attention in his sermons. He left to Hobart College a collection of several thousand pamphlets, which he had apparently had bound as he gathered them. His published sermons were very widely circulated, running sometimes into a dozen editions, and his lives of Episcopal bishops—some twenty biographies—were well known. His biographical work is very simple and unostentatious. The complexities of modern biography would doubtless have appalled him.

Norton had no doubts. Shy and retiring, he had entire courage; small and rather frail, he showed a most persistent and devoted diligence. He was a follower of the great Bishop Hobart in his high claims for his Church, but as he once remarked: "The member of an old and well-established family does not feel called upon to be forever proclaiming his pedigree." Having marked off boldly the inferior position of dissent, he proceeded with all diligence to serve the dissenter.

Among his published works not already mentioned are: *Full Proof of the Ministry* (1855); *Rockford Parish* (1856); *Short Sermons* (1858); *Life of Dr. Franklin* (1859); *Pioneer Missionaries; or, the Lives of Phelps and Nash* (1859); *Life of General Washington* (1860); *Lectures on the Life of David* (1860); *Life of Cranmer* (1863); *Life of Archbishop Laud* (1864); *The Lay Reader* (1870); *Milk and Honey* (1870); *Every Sunday* (1873); *Golden Truths* (1875); *The King's Ferry Boat* (1876); *Warning and Teaching* (1878); *Old Paths* (1880).

[*In Memoriam: John Nicholas Norton* (1881); *Churchman*, Feb. 5, 1881; *Louisville Commercial*, Jan. 19, 1881; information as to certain facts from a daughter, Mrs. Paul E. Johnson, Washington, D. C.]
M. H. T—k.

NORTON, JOHN PITKIN (July 19, 1822–Sept. 5, 1852), educator, agricultural chemist, was born in Albany, N. Y. His father, John Treadwell Norton, was a successful farmer and his mother, Mary Hubbard (Pitkin), was the daughter of Timothy Pitkin [*q.v.*], lawyer, statesman, and historian. John Treadwell, governor of Connecticut in 1809–11, was his great-grandfather. Of his own choice young Norton decided to become a farmer, to which plan his father agreed, but on the unusual condition that he should be broadly and thoroughly educated for that pursuit. Accordingly the boy spent his summers at work upon his father's farm, and his winters in a strenuous program of study in Albany, New York City, New Haven, and Boston, with some of the best masters of that day. He had little liking for the ordinary courses of study, particularly Latin and Greek, but manifested an absorbing interest in natural science which appears to have been first aroused by his study of mineralogy. He studied chemistry with the elder Silliman at Yale and in 1844 he went abroad, spending two years with Professor James F. W. Johnston at Edinburgh, and nine months with Professor Gerardus J. Mulder at Utrecht. While yet a student his ability as an analyst and his resourcefulness as an investigator attracted the favorable attention of his teachers.

In 1846 he was appointed professor of agricultural chemistry at Yale and, in association with the younger Benjamin Silliman [q.v.] who had at the same time been appointed professor of practical chemistry, he initiated that department of scientific education at Yale which was later to become the Sheffield Scientific School. The labors of the first years of this new school were severely taxing, particularly to Norton, who shortly assumed entire responsibility for the new enterprise because of the withdrawal of his colleague to accept a post of duty in another institution.

He was an indefatigable worker, compelled not only by an intense devotion to his chosen subject but also by a sense of duty to the public welfare. He always maintained an intelligent and sympathetic interest in the practical problems of the farmer, and his influence as an educator extended far beyond the walls of his classroom and laboratory. In addition to numerous articles of a popular character upon agricultural topics contributed to the agricultural press, he was the author of a number of scientific papers, among which may be cited his comprehensive prize study, "On the Analysis of the Oat," made in 1845 while he was a student at Edinburgh and published in the *Transactions of the Highland Agricultural Society of Scotland,* July 1846, and later in the *American Journal of Science and Arts,* May 1847; "The Potato Disease" (*American Journal of Science and Arts,* November 1846, July 1847); "Account of Some Researches on the Protein Bodies of Peas and Almonds, and a Body of Somewhat Similar Nature Existing in Oats" (*Ibid.,* May 1848); and another prize essay written in 1850, submitted to the New York State Agricultural Society and afterwards published under the title *Elements of Scientific Agriculture* (1850) as a textbook for schools.

On Dec. 15, 1847, he married Elizabeth P. Marvin of Albany, N. Y. They had two sons, one of whom died in infancy. Their home was a center of hospitality and it does not appear that in Norton's devotion to work he failed to enjoy the social activities of his community. He was possessed of an engaging personality into which entered the charm of cheerfulness, modesty, and quiet humor, blended with the dignity of culture. He was deeply religious and Christian motives controlled his life. With a future brilliant with promise of a highly useful career, he was stricken by illness which his overtaxed strength could not resist and died in Farmington, Conn., on Sept. 5, 1852. In his brief span of life he had come to be regarded as "the most practical agricultural writer and thinker of his time" (editor of the Albany *Cultivator,* quoted in *New Englander,* November 1852, p. 627), and had established a place for himself among the distinguished men of the age.

[*Am. Jour. Sci. and Arts,* Nov. 1852; Wm. A. Larned, in *New Englander,* Nov. 1852, and *Biog. Sketch of John Pitkin Norton* (1852); *Memorials of John Pitkin Norton* (1852), printed for private distribution; A. P. Pitkin, *Pitkin Family of America: A Geneal. of the Descendants of William Pitkin* (1887); Elizabeth A. Osborne, *From the Letter-Files of S. W. Johnson* (1913); R. H. Chittenden, *Hist. of the Sheffield Scientific School of Yale Univ.* (1928), vol. I; private correspondence with Norton's son, the late John T. Norton.]
E. M. B.

NORTON, MARY ALICE PELOUBET (Feb. 25, 1860–Feb. 23, 1928), teacher of home economics, daughter of Rev. Francis Nathan Peloubet [q.v.] and Mary Abby (Thaxter) Peloubet, was born at Gloucester, Mass., in a parsonage home of simple living. Named Mary Alice, she rarely made use of her first name. She was descended from Joseph Alexander de Chabrier de Peloubet, who came from Perigord, France, to the United States in 1803. In 1882 she received the degree of A.B. from Smith College; and on June 6 of the following year she was married, at Natick, Mass., to Lewis Mills Norton, of the chemistry department of the Massachusetts Institute of Technology. He died in 1893, and she faced a struggle to support her five children. Ellen H. Richards [q.v.], home-economics pioneer, became her counselor and directed her into a life of further study, teaching, and lecturing until she herself was recognized as one of the leaders in the home-economics movement. She held positions as teacher or lecturer in home economics at Lasell Seminary, 1893–99; the Hartford School of Sociology, 1894; the Boston Young Women's Christian Association School of Domestic Science, 1895–1900; the Boston Cooking School, 1898–1900; the High School at Brookline, Mass., where she was also supervisor of grammar-school work, 1896–1900; the Chicago Institute, 1900–01; the

University of Chicago, where she was assistant professor in home economics in the School of Education, 1901–04, and assistant professor in household administration, 1904–13. She was dietitian, 1913–14, of the Cook County, Ill., public institutions. During the summers of 1900 to 1905 and 1915 to 1917, she served as director of the Chautauqua, N. Y., School of Domestic Science.

She was one of the founders of the American Home Economics Association (1908), which developed from annual conferences held at Lake Placid, N. Y., beginning in 1899. At these conferences she was a constructive contributor on the subjects of teacher training and home economics in colleges. She was secretary of the Association, 1915–18, and editor of the *Journal of Home Economics,* 1915–21. During the World War she served as an editor for the United States Food Administration (1917–18) and was with the war-savings division of the treasury department (1919), where she helped to issue *Thrift Leaflets.* In 1921 the American Home Economics Association raised a sum of money to pay the salary of a professor of home economics at the Constantinople Women's College, and Mrs. Norton consented to occupy this position in a country where housework was considered a menial occupation suitable only for servants or peasants. She remained for over two years, making a survey of the elementary schools of the city, acquiring equipment, building up a permanent department, and giving lectures to the nurses' training class in the American Hospital at Stambul.

After her return from Constantinople, she substituted as head of the home-economics department of Indiana University (1924–25). Thereafter she made her home in Northampton, Mass., and carried on a study for the Institute for the Coördination of Women's Interests at Smith College. Shortly before her death her Institute bulletin, *Cooked Food Supply Experiments in America* (1927), was published. Her life was so full of changing activities that her writing was confined to articles and bulletins on home-economics subjects. Considering the many professional demands on her time and her personal economic problems (she provided college education for all her five children), the number of her civic and educational interests is remarkable. In addition to membership in many professional societies, she was a more or less active member of the American Association of University Women, the Religious Education Association, the College Political Equality League, the Drama League, the Chicago Women's Club,

the League of Women Voters, the Foreign Policy Association, and the Women's International League of Peace and Freedom.

[*Cat. of Officers, Grads., and Non-Grads. of Smith Coll.* (1925); *Who's Who in America,* 1928–29; *Woman's Who's Who of America,* 1914–15; Joseph Peloubet, *Family Records of Joseph Alexander de Chabrier de Peloubet* (1892); "In Memory of Alice Peloubet Norton," *Jour. of Home Economics,* Sept. 1928; *Boston Transcript,* Feb. 25, 1928.]   S. G. B.

NORTON, WILLIAM EDWARD (June 28, 1843–Feb. 28, 1916), marine painter, was born in Boston, Mass., the son of Daniel and Mary (Carr) Norton and a descendant of a family of shipbuilders. His father was a sailmaker and his mother was descended from George Carr, ship's carpenter of the *Mayflower.* Norton was educated in the public schools of Charlestown. From the time he could hold a pencil he began to draw, and when he was about ten he made a drawing of the statue of Gen. Joseph Warren on Bunker Hill which so impressed one of the members of the school board that he advised the boy to go to the Lowell Institute, but his parents would not allow him to do so. On leaving school he went to work in an office on Rowe's Wharf, Boston, where at odd moments he made sketches of the stevedores, the horses, the shipping and docks; then he went to sea on a merchant ship for a long voyage before the mast. Two episodes gave him standing with the tough company in the forecastle: he whipped "Dutch Louis" for attempting to bully him, and while off watch he drew lifelike sketches of his shipmates, their rude quarters, and various scenes on the deck. On his return to Boston he found employment as a house and sign painter. He now entered the night classes of the Lowell Institute, where he came under the excellent instruction of George Hollingsworth, studying perspective, light and shade, and color. He also studied anatomy both in the Lowell Institute and at the Harvard Medical School, where he made over five hundred drawings in the dissecting room. His daylight hours were devoted to house and sign painting, and, later, to fresco work and decorating; the early hours of the evening he gave to study; and from nine o'clock to midnight, in the paint shop of his employer, he often painted sea pictures with house paints, which he sold for trifling sums to his fellow workmen.

At the age of twenty-one he ventured to open a studio in Boston, and George Inness [*q.v.*] gave him counsel and encouragement. After two more voyages before the mast, in 1877 he found himself in London, where he remained for about a year, then went to Paris for further training under Antoine Vollon and Jacquesson de la

Chevreuse and in the École des Beaux-Arts. During the ensuing three years he visited Italy and other European countries, then opened a studio in London, where he continued to live until 1902. He exhibited three pictures at the Royal Academy in 1878, and was for about twenty years a constant and regular exhibitor there as well as at the Paris Salon and many other places. A number of his sea pieces were sent to the American exhibitions, and four cash prizes with three or four gold medals were among his honors. His picture of "The English Channel" is owned by the Boston Chamber of Commerce; his "Fight of the Alabama and the Kearsarge" belongs to the Historical Society of Portland, Me.; his "Fish Market, Dieppe, France" is in the Public Library of Malden, Mass., and his "Crossing the Grand Banks" is in the Abbot Hall collection at Marblehead, Mass. Other good examples of his work are owned by the Boston Art Club, the Boston Athletic Association, Essex Hall at Salem, Mass., and the Black Heath Art Club of London. His paintings of sailing vessels are spirited and full of movement. Nothing could be more thoroughly suggestive of the atmosphere and color of the ocean and the old-time clipper-ships than his mid-Atlantic compositions. His work has sailor-like qualities and could never have been done by a landsman.

On Sept. 23, 1868, he married Sarah D. Ryan of Grand Manan, N. B., who died in 1904. They had two daughters. Norton's death occurred in New York in 1916.

[F. T. Robinson, in *Art Interchange*, Feb. 1894; *N. Y. Herald*, June 20, 1909; *N. Y. Times*, Feb. 29, 1916; *Boston Transcript*, Mar. 1, 1916, Jan. 30, 1920; *Am. Art News*, Mar. 4, 1916; Cat. of exhibition at Vose Gallery, Boston, Jan.–Feb. 1920; *Am. Art Annual*, vol. XIII (1916); *Who's Who in America*, 1914–15; Ulrich Thieme and Felix Becker, *Allgemeines Lexikon der Bildenden Künstler*, vol. XXV (1931).] W. H. D—s.

NORWOOD, ROBERT WINKWORTH (Mar. 27, 1874–Sept. 28, 1932), Episcopal clergyman, was born at New Ross, Nova Scotia, the son of Rev. Joseph William Norwood and Edith Matilda (Harding). After coming to the United States he dropped his middle name. Joseph William Norwood had come to New Ross as rector of Christ Church (of the Church of England in Canada) after having been a sea captain, a soldier in the Union Army in the Civil War, and a missionary to the coast of Africa. Robert had a particular devotion to his father, and an admiration for his father's life and ministry; therefore, after going to school at Coaticock Academy in Quebec and studying at Bishops College, Lennoxville, Que., and at Kings College, Wind-

sor, N. S., he determined to enter the same calling, and was ordained deacon and priest of the Church of England in Canada in 1897 and 1898 respectively. On Sept. 12, 1899, while he was missionary in charge of St. Andrew's Church, Neil's Harbour, Cape Breton, he married Ethel McKeen. A few months later, his father, who was then rector of St. Luke's Church, Hubbards, N. S., was taken ill, and Robert went there as curate to carry on the work. In this early ministry in Hubbards he revealed the characteristics which always afterwards marked him—an unusual sensitiveness to all beauty, and a warm and friendly approach toward people which, beginning in his contacts with the fisher-folk of his Nova Scotia coast, broadened afterward to include persons of every kind. Subsequently, he became successively rector of Trinity Church, Bridgewater, N. S. (1901–07); All Saints' Church, Springhill (1908–10); assistant rector, Trinity Church, Montreal (1910–12); and rector of Memorial Church, London, Ont. (1912–17). In 1917 his life entered a new chapter with his removal from Canada to the United States to become rector of St. Paul's Memorial Church at Overbrook, Pa.

In 1925 when Dr. Leighton Parks resigned the rectorship of St. Bartholomew's Church in New York City, Norwood was called to succeed him. In Overbrook his preaching had drawn overflowing congregations, not only from his own community but from other suburbs of Philadelphia and the city itself. In New York his magnetism proved equally great. He had a musical voice, unusual dramatic vividness in utterance and gesture, and the gift of putting his thought into flashing pictorial form. Moreover, he was one of those rare persons who possess a mystical experience. In his look and in his message he conveyed to his congregation the sense of a man who was in touch with an invisible world. Both in his theology and in his impatience of ecclesiastical restraints he belonged to the liberal group in the Protestant Episcopal Church. He insisted upon interpreting truth not in terms of old formulas but of new experience, and he was a leader in efforts for close coöperation with other Christian churches, and for a better understanding, also, of the non-Christian religions. As tangible evidence of his ministry he left behind him at St. Bartholomew's a great community house and many enrichments of the church's structure, including the completion of its dome.

His religious thinking, as expressed in his published Lenten sermons—*The Steep Ascent* (1928), *His Glorious Body* (1930), and *Increasing Christhood* (1932), and in his life of Paul, entitled *The Heresy of Antioch* (1928), and in his life of Christ, entitled *The Man Who Dared to Be God* (1929)—was not systematic nor profound. Like his teaching, it was intuitive, impulsive, and poetic. He always liked to be regarded as primarily a poet—a poet of the goodness of life. His published poems include *His Lady of the Sonnets* (1915); *The Witch of Endor* (1916); *The Piper and the Reed* (1917); *The Modernists* (1918); *The Man of Kerioth* (1919); *Bill Boram* (1921), which is a description of the Nova Scotian country and people among whom he had grown up; *Mother and Son* (1925); and *Issa* (1931), a final volume, introspective and intimate in self-revelation. All these books are marked by a strong religious note. Measured by purely poetic standards, they are notable for their lyrical spontaneity and their colorful imagination.

[C. D. G. Roberts, "The Poetry of Robert Norwood," introduction to *Issa*; W. R. Bowie, "The Ministry of the Poet," introduction to *Increasing Christhood*; *The Churchman*, Oct. 8, Nov. 12, 1932; *The Canadian Theosophist* (Hamilton, Ont.), Oct. 15, 1932; A. D. Watson, *Robert Norwood* (Toronto, 1923); J. D. Logan and D. G. French, *Highways of Canadian Literature* (Toronto, 1924); *Canadian Poets*, ed. by J. W. Garvin (Toronto, 1926); *Who's Who in America*, 1932–33; *Publisher's Weekly*, Oct. 8, 1932; *N. Y. Times*, Sept. 30, 1932.]　　　W. R. B.

NOSS, THEODORE BLAND (May 10, 1852–Feb. 28, 1909), educator, was born on a farm at Waterloo, Juniata County, Pa., the son of George and Isabella (Coulter) Noss. His maternal grandfather, the Rev. John Coulter, was a prominent Presbyterian minister. Young Theodore attended the rural schools and helped in the work of his father's farm, store, and tannery. In 1868 the family moved to Strasburg, Va. At the age of nineteen he began teaching in a district school near Hagerstown, Md. He entered the Cumberland Valley State Normal School at Shippensburg, Pa., and was graduated in 1874. For some years thereafter he taught in the Shippensburg public schools; in Dickinson Seminary, Williamsport, where he was principal of the preparatory department; and in the Pittsburgh Female College. He was graduated from Syracuse University in 1880 and received there the degrees of A.M. (1882) and Ph.D. (1884). He made four trips to Europe for study, spending a total of approximately three years in residence at the universities of Vienna, Berlin, Jena, and Paris. On May 17, 1883, he was married to Mary B. Graham, of Monongahela, Pa. They had two children.

In 1883 Noss became principal of the Southwestern State Normal School, at California, Pa., of which he had previously been vice-principal,

and remained there until his death twenty-six years later. This long period of identity with one institution, which he built up to high standing, brought him a national reputation as a progressive educator. He was an active member of the National Education Association and in 1898–99 served as president of its normal department. He was a frequent contributor to educational journals and was in demand for the platforms of teachers' institutes. His special field of scholarship was educational psychology. On his European tours he became impregnated with the doctrines of Froebel, Herbart, and Pestalozzi, which he endeavored to adapt to American normal-school practice. Much of his time abroad was spent observing the technique of the Continental schools, especially those for training teachers. In his own school he insisted upon the admission of only the best-qualified students and also upon a maximum of personal attention to the needs of the individual. Intense moral earnestness was the outstanding trait of his character. During his administration more than 1,500 young persons were graduated from the institution, all of whom felt deeply the impress of his personality.

Noss's published works include *Outlines of Psychology and Pedagogy* (1890) and *Child Study Record* (1900). He was general editor of *The School Year Books* (Chicago, 1898–1907), a series of manuals of methods for elementary grades, and he compiled *The Chapel Hymnal* (1900), a collection of standard hymns and reading for use in schools which reached twelve editions. He was throughout his life a devoted layman of the Methodist Episcopal Church, serving as lay delegate to its General Conference in 1896. He was also an active leader in local community movements. He died of pneumonia at the Auditorium Hotel, Chicago, while on his way to a session of the National Education Association. At the largely attended memorial services held in the chapel of the Normal School at California, Pa., William Jennings Bryan, a friend of long standing, led the eloquent tributes. In May 1930 the new Theodore B. Noss Demonstration School, built by alumni of the Normal School, was dedicated to his memory.

[*Who's Who in Pa.* (2nd ed., 1908); *California (Pa.) Sentinel*, Mar. 10, 1909; the *Normal Rev.* (California, Pa.), Mar. 1909; *The Syracusan* (Syracuse, N. Y.), Apr. 1909; *Christian Advocate* (Pittsburgh), May 13, 1909; *Alumni Record and Gen. Cat. of Syracuse Univ., 1872–1910*, vol. III (1911), pt. I; Pittsburgh newspapers at the time of Noss's death; personal notes supplied by Mrs. Theodore B. Noss, Athens, Ohio.]　　　K. M. G.

NOTT, ABRAHAM (Feb. 5, 1768–June 19, 1830), jurist and member of Congress from

578

South Carolina, was born at Saybrook, Middlesex County, Conn. He was the second son of Deacon Josiah Nott and Zerviah Clark and the grandson of Abraham Nott, a prominent Congregational clergyman. He received his early education from the Rev. John Devotion of Westbrook Parish in Saybrook and, with the intention of becoming a minister, entered Yale College. He graduated from that institution in 1787, but finding in himself no distinctly religious convictions he felt that it would be sacrilegious for him to enter the pulpit. As he was not in good health, in 1788 he went to a plantation on Sapelo River, McIntosh County, Ga., where he found employment as a tutor in the family of the father of George M. Troup, the future governor being one of his pupils. The next year he removed to South Carolina where he studied law in the office of Daniel Brown, another Yale graduate, at Camden, and was admitted to the bar in Charleston in 1791. After his admission to the bar he settled at Union Court House where he practised law for three years. In August 1794 he was married to Angelica Mitchell and moved to a plantation on the Pacolet River where he continued the practice of his profession.

Nott was a Federalist member of the Sixth Congress (1799–1801). In the momentous struggle for the presidency in 1800 he at first voted for Aaron Burr but finally abstained from voting and thus assisted in the election of Jefferson. In the fall of 1804 he moved to Columbia, S. C., where he practised his profession with distinct success until 1810 when he was elected as a Law Judge to succeed Samuel Wilds. In 1816 the South Carolina legislature initiated a constitutional amendment giving to itself the power to fix the time and meetings of the Constitutional Court of the state and, in anticipation of the ratification of the amendment by the people, proceeded to enact a law ordering the judges to clear the dockets at Charleston and Columbia. Nott, together with his associates, declared this law unconstitutional on the ground that it was passed before the authority to enact it had been completely established. This decision, especially one of its statements, "that which was conceived in sin must be brought forth in iniquity," aroused a storm of protest and almost resulted in his removal from the court. In 1817 the salaries of the judges of the state were increased and when he resigned in order to obtain the benefit of the increase by reëlection he was returned to his position by a very narrow majority. He recovered his popularity, however, and in 1824 when the court of appeals was organized he was placed at its head by an overwhelming vote. In

this position he remained for the rest of his life and doubtless hastened his death by his industry in the discharge of his duties. He contracted tuberculosis in January 1830 and died on June 19 of the same year at the home of his friend, Dr. Davis H. Means, in Fairfield District, while on the way to his plantation in Union District. He is buried in the First Presbyterian Churchyard in Columbia. Nott's opinions both in law and equity bear comparison with those of any judge in the state. In the courtroom he enjoyed anecdotes and frequently "broke the tedium of an argument by some playful, witty, question." He was small and somewhat unimposing in person, but his face was well-featured and highly intellectual. His two sons, Henry Junius and Josiah Clark Nott [qq.v.], also had distinguished careers.

[Biog. Dir. Am. Cong. (1928); J. B. O'Neall, Biog. Sketches of the Bench and Bar of S. C. (1859), vol. I; F. B. Dexter, Biog. Sketches of the Grads. of Yale Coll., vol. VI (1907); Charleston Courier, June 25, 30, 1830.]   J. W. P.

NOTT, CHARLES COOPER (Sept. 16, 1827–Mar. 6, 1916), jurist, was born at Schenectady, N. Y., the son of Joel B. and Margaret Cooper Nott. His paternal ancestors were of early Connecticut stock but for two generations the family life had been interwoven with that of Union College of which Nott's grandfather, Eliphalet Nott [q.v.], had been president, and in which his father was professor of chemistry. It was but natural that the boy's education, uneventful in its earlier phases, should culminate in his graduation from the college in 1848. For two years thereafter he studied law in Albany and was admitted to the bar in 1850. He then moved to New York City where he practised successfully until the outbreak of the Civil War. He was a fairly active Republican and in 1860 was one of the committee responsible for bringing Lincoln to New York to deliver his Cooper Institute speech. A friendship between the two men began at this time. Shortly thereafter Nott secured from Lincoln the manuscript of his address which, with Cephas Brainerd, he published with notes in September 1860. After the outbreak of the war he entered the Union army under an appointment by General Frémont as captain in the Frémont Hussars. He later served in the 5th Iowa Cavalry and in the New York volunteers. He finally became colonel of the 176th New York Regiment. In June 1863 he was captured at Brashear City, La., and remained a Confederate prisoner for thirteen months. He did not see further active service and emerged from prison seriously impaired in health. He returned to the practice of law in New York.

The entire course of Nott's later life was determined by his appointment by President Lincoln as judge of the United States Court of Claims on Feb. 22, 1865. He remained a member of that tribunal for forty years, retiring Dec. 31, 1905, and from the time of his promotion by President Cleveland in 1896 he served as chief justice. When Nott took office the Court of Claims was still in its formative period and his life was spent in aiding in the establishment of a system of jurisprudence under which the claims of a contractual or business nature of the citizen against the federal government might be recognized and enforced. The record of his labors is found in opinions spread through forty-eight volumes of the *Cases Decided in the Court of Claims*. No small part of Nott's service to the Court lay in his reporting of its decisions. From 1867, when the publication of regular reports began, until 1914, Nott served as reporter. Until 1872 he was aided in this labor by Judge Samuel H. Huntington and from that date on by his brother-in-law, Archibald Hopkins. This long series of his reports is broken only in 1882–83 when his illness necessitated a year's absence from all official duties.

During his adult years Nott was a fairly voluminous contributor to the press and to more substantial publications. Much of his writing was done anonymously in the form of editorials and reviews. His longer works include: *A Treatise on the Mechanics' Lien Laws of the State of New York* (1856); *Sketches of the War* (1863); *Sketches in Prison Camps* (1865); *The Seven Great Hymns of the Mediæval Church* (1865); and *The Mystery of the Pinckney Draught* (1908). Nott was married on Oct. 22, 1867, to Alice Effingham Hopkins, the daughter of Mark Hopkins [*q.v.*], president of Williams College. Of this marriage there were born a son and a daughter. He died at the home of his son in New York City on Mar. 6, 1916.

[See *Who's Who in America*, 1914–15; *N. Y. Times*, *N. Y. Herald*, Mar. 7, 1916.] R. E. C.

NOTT, ELIPHALET (June 25, 1773–Jan. 29, 1866), college president, Presbyterian clergyman, inventor, was born in Ashford, Conn., the son of Stephen and Deborah (Selden) Nott. His father proved himself a failure in each of his undertakings, but his mother was a woman of superior culture. She instructed the boy in the rudiments, and he prepared for college under the supervision of his brother Samuel [*q.v.*], pastor of the Congregational church at Franklin, Conn. At sixteen, he taught in the district school at Franklin. A year later, he became principal of the Plainfield Academy, and studied Latin, Greek, theology, and mathematics with the Rev. Dr. Joel Benedict, pastor of the local Congregational church. In 1795 he entered Rhode Island College (Brown University), and without completing a full year there, was admitted to the degree of master of arts upon passing a special examination. On June 26, 1796, he was licensed to preach by the New London Congregational Association. In the following month, July 4, 1796, he married Sarah Maria, eldest daughter of Joel Benedict.

Commissioned by the Domestic Missionary Society of Connecticut, he set out for the wilderness of upper New York State, and in the fall became pastor of the Presbyterian church at Cherry Valley. Here he founded an academy which he conducted successfully while discharging the obligations of his pastoral office. His reputation as a preacher grew, and in 1798 he removed to Albany, where, on Oct. 13, he was ordained and installed as pastor of the First Presbyterian Church. At Albany, he established himself as a peculiarly gifted preacher, learned, eloquent, and convincing, and was soon considered one of America's greatest pulpit orators. Among the most celebrated of his published sermons was *A Discourse . . . Occasioned by the Ever to be Lamented Death of General Alexander Hamilton* (1804), delivered at the invitation of the Common Council of Albany. His interest in education expressed itself in his persistent efforts to reform the antiquated public-school system of Albany. As a result of his recommendations, first outlined in March 1803, the Albany Academy was finally incorporated, in 1813. On Mar. 11, 1804, his wife died, and on Aug. 3, 1807, he married Gertrude (Peebles) Tibbitts, widow of Benjamin Tibbitts of Troy. After her death, early in 1840, he married Urania E. Sheldon of Utica, Aug. 8, 1842.

Meanwhile, in 1804, he had succeeded Jonathan Maxcy [*q.v.*] as president of Union College, Schenectady, of which he had been a trustee since 1800. He found the college laboring under a heavy debt, while its income was far less than its necessary expenditures. His executive abilities were manifest at once in his admirable, far-sighted program. The state legislature responded to his appeal, Mar. 30, 1805, by authorizing four lotteries for the purpose of raising the sum of $80,000 for the college, and the following year Nott secured a loan of $15,000 from the state to defray pressing current expenses. Eight years later, when the drawing finally took place, the college realized but $76,000. By this time, there was an urgent need for a larger sum, and again Nott appealed to the legislature, which on Apr. 13, 1814, made an additional grant of $200,000, to be raised in the same manner. After waiting eight years without results, Nott took upon himself the management of the lotteries, and with such success that he was able to extricate the college from its embarrassments. By heroic personal efforts, he placed the endowment fund upon a secure basis. The building program went forward satisfactorily, the college developed rapidly from within, and achieved a high reputation for the excellence of its instruction. His form of control enabled the students to enjoy a larger measure of self-government than was customary in American colleges at that time. Among his innovations was the introduction of the scientific course as an alternative to the traditional classical curriculum.

His interest was not confined to the affairs of the college; as early as 1811, in baccalaureate addresses, he advocated the abolition of slavery; he often served as moderator in church trials; the religious revival of 1838 inspired some of his most memorable sermons, which added further to his reputation as a preacher. He was president of the American Association for the Advancement of Education at its second meeting, held in 1850 at Philadelphia. As an instructor of youth, he saw the dangers of intemperance, and became one of the most active and influential advocates of temperance in his time. His addresses on the subject, *Ten Lectures on the Use of Intoxicating Liquors* (1846), *Lectures on Temperance* (1847), *Lectures on Biblical Temperance* (1863), were published and circulated widely. Another of his publications which went through numerous editions was *Counsels to Young Men on the Formation of Character* (1840). His *Miscellaneous Works* had appeared in 1810. In addition to his prodigious labors as an educator, he experimented with the properties of heat. The results of his research are recorded in some thirty patents, granted for applications of heat to steam boilers and generators. Among his inventions was the first base-burning stove for the use of anthracite coal.

Nott's extraordinary influence over men—exemplified in his influence over the New York legislature—led him sometimes to accomplish his purposes by indirect means that laid him open to the accusation of double-dealing (Francis Wayland, quoted in Francis and H. L. Wayland, *A Memoir of the Life and Labors of Francis Wayland*, 1867, I, 90–92). In 1851, after a legislative inquiry concerning the financial condition of Union College, he was accused, in many newspapers, of misappropriating college funds. Upon examining the books of the institution, an Assem-

bly commission reporting in February 1852 completely vindicated him of all charges of dereliction. As a fitting sequel to this unpleasant affair, he donated in 1854 to the endowment fund $600,000 of his own fortune. His active career was terminated by a paralytic stroke, which forced him, in 1859, to relinquish some of the duties of his office. He presided at commencements, however, until 1862. At his death, in 1866, he had been president of Union for sixty-two years, an unprecedented period in the annals of higher education in America.

[Cornelius Van Santvoord and Tayler Lewis, *Memoirs of Eliphalet Nott* (1876); *Am. Jour. of Educ.*, Mar. 1863; H. L. Ellsworth, *A Digest of Patents Issued by the U. S. from 1790 to Jan. 1839* (1840); G. P. Schmidt, *The Old Time College President* (1930); J. T. Backus, *Address at the Funeral of the Rev. Dr. Nott* (1866); *Albany Evening Journal*, Jan. 29, 1866.]
R. F. S.

NOTT, HENRY JUNIUS (Nov. 4, 1797–Oct. 9, 1837), educator, author, was the son of Judge Abraham Nott [*q.v.*], and Angelica (Mitchell) Nott, and a brother of Josiah Clark Nott [*q.v.*]. He was born in Union District, S. C. His schooling was obtained at the Columbia Academy, from which he entered the sophomore class of the South Carolina College in 1810. Graduating in December 1814, he studied law in the office of William Harper, was admitted to the bar in 1818, and formed a partnership with David J. McCord [*q.v.*]. The firm did not enjoy a very large practice. The partners published two volumes of law reports, which have been considered valuable, although the reports of cases were very brief. Nott's health failing, he sailed for Europe in 1821, where he spent the next three years in study, for the most part in France and Holland. In the former country he met and married a French woman. On Dec. 7, 1824, he was elected professor of the elements of criticism, logic, and the philosophy of language in his alma mater, and for thirteen years he held the chair with marked success. Maximilian LaBorde [*q.v.*], who knew him, says of him in his *History of the South Carolina College:* "Perhaps no one ever filled the department with more ability" (p. 211). He adds that he was remembered as occupying a place among the most brilliant professors: "He had great enthusiasm in the cause of letters, was well fitted for presenting it in its most inviting and entertaining aspects, and very apt, therefore, to awaken a love for it in the bosom of others" (p. 213). When the South Carolina College was reorganized in 1835, he alone of the professors was retained; he served during that year as chairman of the faculty.

Nott was a frequent contributor to the *South-*

ern Review. His *Novellettes of a Traveller; or, Odds and Ends from the Knapsack of Thomas Singularity, Journeyman Printer* (2 vols., 1834) is the only other work that came from his pen. It was received with enthusiasm at the time and was regarded as "full of fun"; but the modern reader finds in it little merit. The sketch of Singularity is a dull narrative of his by no means interesting adventures. Of the other tales the "Dwarf's Duel" may still engage the attention of the reader. On Oct. 7, 1837, Nott left New York for Charleston on the unfortunate steamer *Home*. The vessel was wrecked two days later off the coast of North Carolina. He could have saved his life, according to all accounts, but he perished with his wife rather than survive her. He left one daughter.

[J. B. O'Neall, *Biog. Sketches of the Bench and Bar of S. C.* (1859), vol. II ; E. J. Scott, *Random Recollections of a Long Life* (1884) ; G. A. Wauchope, *The Writers of S. C.* (1910) ; the *Charleston Courier*, Oct. 13, 14, 17, 19, 20, 1837 ; *Morning Herald* (N. Y.), Oct. 18, 19, 1837.]   E. L. G.

NOTT, JOSIAH CLARK (Mar. 31, 1804– Mar. 31, 1873), physician, ethnologist, was born at Columbia, S. C., the son of Abraham Nott [*q.v.*] and Angelica Mitchell, and the brother of Henry Junius Nott [*q.v.*]. He graduated from South Carolina College in 1824 and began his medical education in Columbia under the preceptorship of Dr. James Davis. In 1825 he entered the College of Physicians and Surgeons in New York City but a year later moved to Philadelphia and graduated in medicine from the University of Pennsylvania in 1827. He remained at the University for two years as demonstrator in anatomy and then began private practice in Columbia. In 1835 he went abroad and for a period of several months studied in Paris. Upon his return he settled in Mobile, Ala., and during the course of his long active practice in that city became one of the leading surgeons of the South and Southwest. He took an active part in the formation of the Mobile Medical Society in 1841 and in framing an act to revise the Alabama state law regulating the practice of medicine. During 1857 and part of 1858 he served as professor of anatomy at the University of Louisiana. Returning to Mobile in 1858, he helped to found the Medical College of Alabama, to which he was appointed professor of surgery. During the Civil War he served in the Confederate army. He moved to Baltimore in 1867 and to New York City the following year, where he became a charter member of the New York Obstetrical Society. Forced to retire because of ill health, he went to Aiken, S. C., in 1872, and soon afterward to Mobile. He died at Mobile on his birth-

day, Mar. 31, 1873, his death being registered as due to "laryngeal phthisis." He had married, in 1832, Sarah Deas, daughter of James Deas of Columbia, S. C. There were eight children from this union, four of whom died from yellow fever during the Mobile epidemic of 1853. One son died from exposure and fatigue after the battle of Shiloh and another was killed in action at Chickamauga.

Besides participating actively in civic affairs and caring for a large general and consultation practice, Nott wrote extensively on a variety of medical and scientific subjects including yellow fever, surgery, hypnotism, and ethnology. In a paper published in 1844 (*New Orleans Medical Journal*, May–July 1844), he stressed the importance of a knowledge of the anatomy and physiology of the nervous system as a background for treating certain types of cases. He reported in this paper the case of the removal of the coccyx of a patient who was suffering from severe lumbar pains, stating that he knew of no similar operation on record. In 1866 he published *Contributions to Bone and Nerve Surgery*, which was intended for young practitioners. Written in a confident, authoritative style, the book describes the pathology of bone and joint injuries sustained in the war and outlines proper methods of surgical treatment. He had expressed his belief in "animal magnetism" or "magnetic influences" in 1846 ("A Lecture on Animal Magnetism," *Southern Journal of Medicine and Pharmacy*, May 1846), citing as examples of this phenomenon several persons hypnotized by himself, and recommending mesmerism as a form of treatment for ill-defined nervous disorders. He was also interested in ethnology and in 1854, with George R. Gliddon, he published *Types of Mankind*, a volume of more than seven hundred pages, which ran through ten editions. The authors attempted to prove that each of the different races of man sprang from a fixed type, "permanent through all recorded time"—a doctrine later contradicted by the Darwinian theory. *Indigenous Races of the Earth*, by the same authors, followed in 1857.

Nott is perhaps best known for his views regarding yellow fever which have been discussed by Walter Reed and several other investigators. (See the *New Orleans Medical and Surgical Journal*, March 1848, March 1854.) Making use of his own observations in Mobile and those made elsewhere, among the conclusions he reached were the following: that the spread of yellow fever cannot be explained by any of the laws governing gases, vapors, and emanations, but that the disease has an inherent power of propagation independent of atmospheric conditions; that yellow fever is a clinical entity, distinct from malaria and intermittent fevers; and that yellow fever must be caused by an insect or some lower form of animal life. He mentioned mosquitoes only casually along with other flying insects. There is no reason to believe that he had any conception that the virus is carried by the mosquito as an intermediate host. He apparently recognized, however, that the cause of yellow fever is a living organism—a doctrine well in advance of the theories accepted by the majority of physicians in the middle of the nineteenth century.

[W. H. Anderson, memoir in *Trans. Am. Medic. Asso.,* vol. XXIX (1878); C. B. Partlow, Address delivered at the unveiling of the portrait of Josiah Clark Nott at the medical school of the Univ. of Ala., Univ. Ala., Oct. 3, 1930; *Am. Jour. of Obstetrics,* May 1913; H. R. Carson, *Yellow Fever* (1931); "Yellow Fever," *Senate Document 822,* 61 Cong., 3 Sess.]   G. H. R.

NOTT, SAMUEL (Jan. 23, 1754–May 26, 1852), clergyman, for seventy years pastor of the Congregational church in what is now Franklin, Conn., was the son of Stephen and Deborah (Selden) Nott, the grandson of Rev. Abraham Nott, minister of the Second Ecclesiastical Society of Saybrook, and a descendant of John Nott who came to America from Nottingham, England, about 1640 and settled in Wethersfield, Conn. At the time of Samuel's birth his father was keeping a small store in that portion of Saybrook which is now the town of Essex, Conn. Later he was a tanner in East Haddam, and after 1772, a farmer in Ashford, Conn. He never prospered and Samuel's youth was one of poverty. At the age of eight he was apprenticed to a blacksmith. He worked at this trade for four years and at a half dozen others in the years that followed. His schooling was meager, but he was a bright, ambitious, resourceful boy. Having taught a district school with some success, he determined to get a college education, and in 1774 began his preparation under Rev. Daniel Welch of Mansfield, Conn. Two years later he entered Yale College. During his course there he did considerable teaching, for which he seemed to have special aptitude, and at the end of his junior year took over the school in New Haven formerly taught by Joel Barlow [*q.v.*]. During his senior year and for some months after his graduation in 1780 he studied theology under the younger Jonathan Edwards [*q.v.*]. He was licensed to preach by the New Haven Association of Ministers on May 29, 1781, and for a short time supplied the Presbyterian church in Bridgehampton, L. I. Called to the Second Parish in Norwich, Conn., Norwich West Farms, now Franklin, he was ordained there on Mar. 18, 1782. A month before, Feb. 14, he had married Lucretia, daughter of Josiah and Abigail Taylor of Mansfield, Conn., by whom he had eleven children.

His abilities, character, and especially the extraordinary length of his pastorate gave him in time an almost unique ecclesiastical position in eastern Connecticut. On Mar. 13, 1832, he preached a half-century sermon, *Reasons for Ministerial Fidelity*; ten years later he preached and published, *The Sixtieth Anniversary Sermon*. During 1844, when he was ninety years of age, he received fifty-four members into his church. It was not until he was ninety-five that a colleague pastor was called. His home was an educational institution. Between two and three hundred young men came there for instruction: some were fitted for college, and a few were given a theological training. He took his younger brother, Eliphalet [*q.v.*], into his family and instructed him for some years. When they were grown, two of his daughters conducted a school for young ladies in the parsonage. He also secured the nucleus of a public library and was for years school visitor. Outside his parish he was esteemed as one well versed in practical affairs, an excellent administrator, and an exceptional presiding officer. For eighteen years he was a director of the Missionary Society of Connecticut, and he also served as president of the Connecticut Bible Society and of the Norwich Foreign Missionary Society. His death in his ninety-ninth year was caused by burns received when his dressing gown caught fire from a stove in his room. Seventeen of his sermons were published.

[W. B. Sprague, *Annals Am. Pulpit*, vol. II (1857); F. B. Dexter, *Biog. Sketches Grads. Yale Coll.,* vol. IV (1907); Cornelius Van Santvoord and Tayler Lewis, *Memoirs of Eliphalet Nott* (1876); *Conn. Quart.,* Apr.–June and July–Sept. 1897; *Hartford Courant,* May 31, 1852.]   H. E. S.

NOTZ, FREDERICK WILLIAM AUGUSTUS (Feb. 2, 1841–Dec. 16, 1921), educator, was born at Lehrensteinsfeld in the Weinsberg district of Württemberg, the eldest child of the Lutheran pastor, Gottlieb Notz, and his wife, Wilhelmina Louisa Burger. He received his early schooling in the Lateinschule at Leonberg and the Königliche Gymnasium at Stuttgart and was admitted in 1855 to the Klosterschule at Maulbronn, where he came under the decisive influence of Wilhelm Bäumlein, equally noted as classical scholar and pedagogue. He matriculated in the Evangelische Stift of the University of Tübingen in 1859, studied philosophy, theology, and classical philology under Ferdinand

Christian Baur, Johann Tobias Beck, Gustav Öhler, Wilhelm Sigismund Teuffel, and Karl Ludwig Roth, won the Freiherr von Palm prize with an essay on Roman history in the regal period, and took his doctor's degree in 1863 with a dissertation on the same subject. Having passed the theological examinations, he remained at the University for another year, was appointed vicar to his father, became a tutor in a noble family, and in 1866 came to the United States as tutor in a family living at Darien, Ga.

He decided to remain in America and, having established relations with Lutheran officials in the East, became professor of German in Pennsylvania (Gettysburg) College in 1868. The next year he accepted a professorship in Muhlenberg College, where the theological atmosphere was better suited to his own rigorous orthodoxy, and took part in the founding of the American Philological Association. He was secretary of the German-American Press Association in 1870 and president of the German School Association of Pennsylvania in 1871, began his career as an industrious writer for Lutheran periodicals in America and Germany, and in the summer of 1871 was pulpit supply in Philadelphia for his Tübingen friend, Adolph Spaeth. Meanwhile he had become interested in the work of C. F. W. Walther [q.v.] in the West. At first Walther wanted him for a professorship at St. Louis but, with his usual eye for strategy, decided instead to send him to Wisconsin to build up the educational work of the Wisconsin Synod. Accordingly, Notz became professor of Greek and Hebrew in Northwestern University (now College) at Watertown, Wis., and remained there for forty years, retiring because of impaired health in 1912. For many years he was "inspector" of the school, which in its organization, curriculum, and methods of instruction was modeled on the plan of a German Gymnasium.

His influence extended far beyond the sphere of the school itself. He was a member of the board of official visitors and later of the board of regents of the University of Wisconsin and gave valuable aid to various Lutheran educational institutions. In person he was the very embodiment of the German schoolmaster, genuinely learned, and with an inordinate respect for every detail, but mitigating the rigors of instruction and discipline with a wholesome South German humor. He was one of the chief opponents in 1889–90 of the notorious Bennett Law. His one separate publication was a German translation of Johann Conrad Dietrich's *Institutiones Catecheticae* (1876; 2nd ed., 1896). He was

married June 20, 1875, to Juliana Friederike Schulz of Watertown, by whom he had two sons and three daughters. He spent his last years in Milwaukee, where he died in his eighty-first year.

[This article is based chiefly on material supplied by Notz's son, William Frederick Notz. See also: J. C. Jensson, *Am. Luth. Biogs.* (1890); *Milwaukee Sentinel*, Dec. 17, 1921; *Lehre und Wehre*, Jan. 1922.]
G. H. G.

NOYAN, GILLES-AUGUSTIN PAYEN de (1697–Feb. 26, 1751), French officer in Louisiana, was born in France, the second son of Pierre Payen de Noyan, a naval officer, and Catherine Jeanne Le Moyne, sister of Bienville and Iberville [qq.v.]. It is probable that he received some sort of military training under his father and uncles. He came to Louisiana in 1717 or 1718, with the rank of lieutenant, and saw his first important service in 1719, when Bienville sent him, with a troop of Indians, to relieve Chateaugué in the recently captured Pensacola. Noyan arrived just after the Spanish had retaken the fort; presumably he took part in the second seizure by the French a month later. He next served for a year in command at New Orleans, and was given charge of a company of infantry. When Bienville was removed from office and recalled to France, Noyan appeared before the Superior Council to defend him, and in 1726 with his younger brother was dismissed from service and possibly recalled to France. If so, he soon returned, and through the years of Bienville's absence acted as his uncle's agent, showing much activity in disposing of his lands. Upon Bienville's reappointment to his old post in 1732, he showed his appreciation of his nephew's service by obtaining for him the position of adjutant at Mobile, and a year later transferred him to a similar post at New Orleans.

Bienville's great task for the next years was to stiffen the Choctaws' resistance to their old enemies, the Chickasaws, and the English behind them. Noyan was entrusted with diplomatic missions to the Choctaw chiefs, and on occasion took command in war raids. He was severely wounded in the campaign of 1736, but recovered to carry on his activities. Three years later he was sent up the Mississippi to find suitable headquarters and explore the country preparatory to an attack upon the Chickasaws by the combined French and Indian forces from Louisiana and Illinois. After months of inactivity at Fort Assomption on the Chickasaw Bluffs, ascribed to heavy rains and lack of pack animals, the expedition returned with nothing achieved, and Noyan, who had spent much for the campaign to his own impoverishment, was blamed for the selection of an impossible route.

He was made *lieutenant du roi* in 1741, and sat frequently as a member of the Superior Council of Louisiana; in 1748 he was for a time acting governor. He married, May 1, 1735, Jeanne Faucon Dumanoir, daughter of the agent for the Company of the Indies, and widow of Jean Baptiste Massy. His eldest son, Jean Baptiste Noyan, was executed in 1769, with his father-in-law, Nicholas Lafrénière, for protests against the Spanish régime.

Noyan is often confused with his brothers, Pierre-Jacques [*q.v.*], who rendered notable service at Detroit, and Pierre-Bénoit, who also served in Canada and Louisiana and died in France in 1766.

[Archives des Colonies, esp. C 13, A 5:303; F 3, 24:112; D 2 C, 4; D 2 C, 50; D 2 C, 51:105 (transcripts in Lib. of Cong.) give important unpublished material. Printed sources are: N. M. Surrey, *Calendar of MSS. in Paris Archives . . . Relating to . . . the Mississippi Valley* (2 vols., 1926–28), for date of death see II, 1173; *La. Hist. Quart.*, Oct. 1919, July, Oct. 1920, Apr. 1921, Apr. 1923, Jan. 1925, Jan. 1927–July 1928, Jan. 1929–Oct. 1932; F. A. A. de LaChesnaye-Desbois, *Dictionnaire de la Noblesse*, XV (1869), 535; Bénard La Harpe, *Journal Historique de . . . la Louisiane* (1831); Dunbar Rowland and A. G. Sanders, *Mississippi Provincial Archives, 1729–1740; French Dominion*, vol. I (1927); Grace King, *Jean Baptiste Le Moyne, Sieur de Bienville* (1892); Charles Gayarré, *Hist. of La.* (4th ed., 1903), vols. I, II; B. F. French, *Hist. Colls. of La.*, vol. V (1853).]   H. C. B.

NOYAN, PIERRE-JACQUES PAYEN de (Nov. 3, 1695–c. 1763), French-Canadian officer, was born at Montreal, the eldest son of Pierre Payen de Noyan and Catherine Jeanne Le Moyne. Allied through his mother to Bienville and Iberville [*qq.v.*] in Louisiana, and to the Longueuils in Canada, he and his younger brothers were fairly predestined to the colonial service. Whatever his early training may have been, he appeared in 1721 as commandant at Fort Frontenac (now Kingston, Ont.), and from that time on, in spite of persistent ill health, was constantly active along the Great Lakes. A few years later he visited Niagara, reporting on English relations to the Iroquois, and he took part in Lignery's expedition to the Sioux country in 1728, gaining a first-hand knowledge of the region. This he embodied in two memoirs, dated 1730 (*post*), which were favorably recommended to the attention of the French ministry by the intendant Hocquart. He urged, as a means of keeping the English from the Lakes, the better regulation of trade with the Indians, strict control of the traders, and the establishment of permanent settlements. Not only the fur trade, but the growing of wheat to supply the needs of the posts, the building of boats on the Lakes, and the development of copper and lead mines in the region deserved attention. He advocated in addition to these projects, an attack upon the Fox Indians to put the fear of the French into that tribe and their allies, the Iroquois. In full confidence of his own ability and disinterestedness, he asked for the command at Detroit, a request which was not granted until 1738. In the meantime he was appointed to Michilimackinac, but on the ground of his ill health was sent to Point à Chevalure (the later Crown Point), instead. When finally he went to Detroit, he had some success in establishing "Police, Order, and Love for Agriculture" among its inhabitants, but his greatest service was in keeping the Indians firmly attached to the French.

He complained of lack of support from the governor and made himself disliked by a prolonged dispute with other officers over the methods of paying the troops. He was succeeded by Céloron de Blainville [*q.v.*] in 1742, and with the reputation of "a man of talent, who has governed well," returned to Lower Canada. His influence among the Iroquois, by whom he had been adopted, was of great service as the last struggle with England drew near. He commanded again at Crown Point (Fort St. Frédéric), at Three Rivers, and in 1758 was sent to Fort Frontenac. Here, with a garrison of fifty men, he was wholly unable to withstand an attack by a force of 3,000 under Col. John Bradstreet [*q.v.*], to whom he surrendered on Aug. 27. Permitted to go to Montreal on parole, he was soon exchanged for Col. Peter Schuyler. It was said that Governor Vaudreuil had sacrificed Noyan to cover his own neglect to raise adequate forces.

Noyan's active career was now over. He went to France, and in 1761 was put on trial, with the intendant Bigot and others, for maladministration in Canada, but after a year's imprisonment, he was set free with a judicial admonition and a light fine (*Jugement rendu dans l'affaire du Canada*, 1763). Beyond this point nothing has been found concerning his life or death.

Noyan married Louise Catherine d'Aillebout, widow of Jean Baptiste Charly, on Nov. 17, 1731. He is said to have been a poet, something of a physician, possessed of a sharp wit which made enemies, and a high sense of his own merit. He has frequently been confused with his brother Gilles-Augustin [*q.v.*].

[Aegidius Fauteux, *La Famille d'Aillebout* (1917); Cyprien Tanguay, *Dictionnaire Généalogique des Familles Canadiennes*, vol. VI (1889); F. A. A. de LaChesnaye-Desbois, *Dictionnaire de la Noblesse*, XV (1869), 535; E. B. O'Callaghan, *Docs. Rel. to the Colonial Hist. of . . . N. Y.*, vols. V, IX, X (1855–58); Noyan's memoirs of 1730 and other material in *Hist. Colls. . . . Mich. Pioneer and Hist. Soc.*, vol. XXXIV (1905) and *Wis. Hist. Soc. Colls.*, vol. XVII (1906); *Mémoires sur le Canada, depuis 1749 jusqu'à 1760* (1838); F. H. Severance, "An Old Frontier of France," *Buffalo Hist. Soc. Pubs.*, vols. XX–XXI (1917); *Collection des Manuscrits du Maréchal de Lévis*, vol. VII (1895); Alex. Jodoin and J. L. Vincent, *Histoire de Longueuil et de la Famille de Longueuil* (1889).]   H. C. B.

NOYES, CROSBY STUART (Feb. 16, 1825–Feb. 21, 1908), journalist, was born on a farm in Minot, Me. He was a grandson of Nicholas and Rachel (Hill) Noyes and descended from Nicholas Noyes who came from England in 1633 and later settled at Newbury, Mass. Though frail of body, after a day's work in the fields Crosby Noyes would make a ten-mile trip on foot to borrow books from a neighbor. He spent much of his boyhood in Lewiston, Me., where he made and mended harness and worked in a cotton-mill to earn money with which to gain an education. Later he taught school. From early boyhood he wrote and published. At fifteen he issued a diminutive four-page weekly, the *Minot Notion,* written by hand and devoted to the "promotion of science, literature and the fine arts." Not much later he wrote a dialect sketch relating the unhappy experiences of "A Yankee in a Cotton Factory," first printed in the *Yankee Blade* of Boston. Some of his juvenile productions were reprinted in *The Harp of a Thousand Strings* (1858), pieces by American humorists. In December 1847, in quest of a milder climate and a more promising opening in the field of journalism, he went to Washington, D. C., arriving with less than two dollars in his pocket. His first employment was in a bookstore and as route agent for a newspaper; he also ushered in a theater. Soon he found employment on the weekly *Washington News* and began to send news and descriptive letters and character sketches to the *Lewiston Evening Journal,* the *Yankee Blade,* the *Spirit of the Times* (New York), and the *Saturday Evening Post* (Philadelphia), receiving an average of one dollar per column. In 1855 he traveled in Europe, following Bayard Taylor's example in *Views Afoot* and describing his experiences in a series of letters which were published in the *Portland* (Me.) *Transcript.* On his return late in 1855 he became a reporter on the Washington *Evening Star,* a four-page paper established in 1852. He covered sporting events, political meetings, debates in Congress, church affairs. During the Civil War he enjoyed acquaintance with Lincoln and Stanton and official announcements were frequently made through the *Star,* as a trustworthy newspaper.

After the war Washington's population decreased so greatly that the owner of the *Star*

decided to sell it. Noyes had become assistant editor and was practically manager, also. Offered, in 1867, a forty-eight-hour option to buy the paper at the seemingly extravagant price of $100,000, he promptly organized a company, of which Alexander R. Shepherd [*q.v.*] was a member, bought the *Star,* and became its editor-in-chief. He decided to devote the paper to local welfare and succeeded also, according to a fellow editor, in making it "the most influential newspaper in Washington . . . which shapes more legislation than any other paper in the United States" (quoted in the *New York Tribune,* Feb. 22, 1908, p. 7). He advocated equitable municipal finances, enlargement of park areas, reclamation of the Potomac flats, and other projects that paved the way for the development of the capital city. He kept the *Star* independent in politics, praising or rebuking policies and acts, not parties. He was a conservative, not from cowardice, but from reserve, and so was the more effective when he went into action. He loathed coarseness, obscenity, and "yellow journalism," and his policy succeeded in winning devoted local esteem for the *Star* and in making it one of the most conspicuously prosperous of American newspapers. In 1904 he read a paper on "The Journalistic Outlook" before the World's Press Parliament at St. Louis and in June 1907, a particularly able and vigorous paper, "Journalism Since Jamestown," before the National Editorial Association at the Jamestown Tercentennial Exposition. He traveled widely, visiting practically all civilized and some semi-civilized countries, and sent a stream of letters to the *Star.* He gathered an extensive collection of Japanese prints, original drawings, and illustrated books which he presented in 1906 to the Library of Congress. He endowed a chair in Bowdoin College. He served as an alderman of Washington for two terms, from 1863, but after that foreswore public office, except on boards of charitable institutions. He was tall and slender in build, and modest almost to the point of shyness. The respect and affectionate regard accorded him alike by humble citizens and by statesmen were attested by the outpouring at the memorial meeting held in the National Theater, Washington, Apr. 5, 1908. In 1856 he married Elizabeth S. Williams of Maine. Of their sons, Theodore W. Noyes succeeded his father as editor of the *Star,* and Frank B. Noyes became president of the Evening Star Newspaper Company and in 1900 of the Associated Press.

[*Crosby Stuart Noyes, 1825–1908* (n.d.), a memorial pamphlet containing speeches and a biographical sketch; *Evening Star,* Washington, D. C., Feb. 22, 1908; *Washington Post,* Feb. 22, 1908; *N. Y. Tribune,* Feb. 22,

1908; G. T. Little, *Geneal. and Family Hist. of the State of Me.*, vol. IV (1909); H. E. and H. E. Noyes, *Geneal. Record of Some of the Noyes Descendants of James, Nicholas and Peter Noyes* (1904), vol. I.]

G. F. B.

NOYES, EDWARD FOLLANSBEE (Oct. 3, 1832–Sept. 4, 1890), governor of Ohio and minister to France, was born at Haverhill, Mass., the son of Theodore and Hannah (Stevens) Greely Noyes; he was a descendant of James Noyes who emigrated about 1633 with his brother Nicholas, the ancestor of John Humphrey Noyes [q.v.], and settled in Newbury, now Newburyport, Mass., where he was an influential clergyman for a quarter of a century. Left an orphan at three, Edward Follansbee Noyes spent his boyhood with his grandfather and his guardian in New Hampshire. A four years' apprenticeship to a printer was followed by study at the academy in Kingston and at Dartmouth College, where he was graduated in 1857. Visiting a classmate the following winter in Cincinnati he remained to study law and graduated from the law school of Cincinnati College in 1858. A law practice in that city was interrupted by his entering the Union Army in July 1861 as a major in the 39th Ohio Infantry. He served under Frémont and on the staff of Pope in Missouri. Becoming a colonel and participating in operations in Mississippi and Tennessee, he was designated by his superior commander as being "as efficient and faithful as he is brave and determined" (*War of the Rebellion: Official Records, Army*, 1 ser., XVII, pt. I, p. 186). Near Nickajack Creek, Ga., on July 4, 1864, a musketball entering his left ankle necessitated amputation. Later he was assigned to command at Camp Dennison, Ohio, and was brevetted brigadier-general. Resigning in April 1865 he became city solicitor and then probate judge of Hamilton County.

In 1871 his war record and the favor of prominent politicians and of Liberal Republicans won him the Republican nomination for governor by acclamation. Although he was elected by a decisive majority, his administration was undistinguished. He was renominated in 1873, but charges of personal corruption, jealousy among state leaders, general financial distress, and the aggressive opposition of William Allen [q.v.] combined with the scandals of the Grant régime to elect by a narrow plurality the first Democratic governor in almost twenty years. At the Republican National Convention of 1876, as chairman of the Ohio delegation, he made the speech placing Hayes in nomination, but its effect was largely lost because of Ingersoll's brilliant presentation of Blaine's candidacy (J.

B. Foraker, *Notes of a Busy Life*, 1916, I, 97). An over-night adjournment, however, made possible shrewd maneuvering by Noyes and others that resulted in Hayes's nomination. The candidate preferred Noyes for national committee chairman, but Zachariah Chandler was selected. After the fall elections he became a visiting statesman, going to Louisiana and then to Florida, where he presented the Republican case before the canvassing board. He was appointed minister to France by Hayes but visited the United States in 1878 to testify before the House committee as to his conduct in Florida. The evidence indicated that he made no promises to members of the canvassing board until after their work had been completed (*House Miscell. Docs. No. 31*, 45 Cong., 3 Sess., vols. IV, V, 1879). As minister he assisted in negotiations for the international monetary conference of 1878, received French assurances that no protectorate over Liberia was intended, and visited Africa in the interests of American commerce. He was an American representative at the Paris conference on industrial property in 1880.

Returning to Cincinnati in 1881 he encountered difficulty in reëstablishing his law practice. He was elected to the superior court at Cincinnati in 1889. A year later he died suddenly on the street. He was survived by his wife, Margaret Wilson (Proctor) Noyes, to whom he had been married on Feb. 15, 1863, and by their one son.

[*The Biog. Encyc. of Ohio* (1876); Whitelaw Reid, *Ohio in the War* (1868), vol. I; C. R. Williams, *The Life of Rutherford Birchard Hayes* (2 vols., 1914); R. C. McGrane, *William Allen* (copr. 1925); H. E. and H. E. Noyes, *Geneal. Record of Some of the Noyes Descendants* (1904), vol. II; *Papers Relating to the Foreign Relations of the U. S.*, 1877–81; *Cincinnati Commercial Gazette*, Sept. 5, 1890; the spelling of the middle name follows that in *Geneal. Record, ante* and in *Gen. Cat. of Dartmouth Coll.*, ed. by C. F. Emerson (1910–11).]

F. P. W.

NOYES, GEORGE RAPALL (Mar. 6, 1798–June 3, 1868), Unitarian clergyman, professor of Oriental languages at Harvard, was a native of Newburyport, Mass., a son of Nathaniel and Mary (Rapall) Noyes and a descendant of Nicholas Noyes who settled in Newbury in 1635. George's parents intended him for the ministry but were able to do little toward his education. Nevertheless he entered Harvard at sixteen, supporting himself largely by teaching for three winters at Bradford, Bolton, and Lexington, having as his pupil in the last-named place Theodore Parker [q.v.]. After his graduation in 1818 he taught for a year at Framingham Academy and entered the Harvard Divinity School the year following. He had been reared in the strictly orthodox Old South Presbyterian

Church of Newburyport, whose pastor, Dr. Daniel Dana, had given him much help and encouragement during his school and college course, but in the liberal atmosphere of Harvard he outgrew the theology of his earlier environment and prepared to enter the Unitarian ministry. After graduating from the Divinity School in 1822, he remained at Harvard for five years longer engaged in Biblical studies, serving at the same time as teacher and college tutor. In 1827 he was ordained and became pastor of the Unitarian church at Brookfield, Mass., where he remained till 1834, when he assumed the pastorate of the more important church at Petersham. During his ministry, which was faithfully and successfully performed, he continued his Biblical studies and published *An Amended Version of the Book of Job* (1827) and *A New Translation of the Book of Psalms* (1831). These, together with a number of scholarly articles on Biblical and theological subjects which appeared chiefly in the *Christian Examiner*, revealed him as one of the ablest Biblical scholars of his day and led to his dual appointment in 1840 as Hancock Professor of Hebrew and Oriental Languages and Dexter Lecturer on Biblical Literature and Theology in the Harvard Divinity School. These positions he held for the remainder of his life.

Noyes published translations of the entire Old Testament except the historical books, but the work which probably constitutes his most secure title to remembrance is his translation of the New Testament (1869), based on the text of Tischendorf. Completed during the last months of his life, it was not published till after his death. It is characterized by faithfulness to the original, clearness, simplicity, and dignity, and is often rated as one of the best ever made. Like his other scriptural translations, however, it is somewhat lacking in the poetic and imaginative qualities.

For nearly thirty years Noyes was a leading spirit in the teaching and administration of the Harvard Divinity School and a formative influence in the lives of generations of students in a time of theological ferment and transition. He was thoroughly familiar with German scholarship and a pioneer in the United States in the critical study of the Bible, early reaching conclusions which have long since become widely accepted, but were then branded as heretical. He was entirely reverent and conservative in temper but his intellectual honesty was so great that he often went counter to his own predilections in his logical following of the critical method. That he had the courage of his convictions

is shown by his publication, at a time when it made him liable to prosecution for blasphemy under an old statute, of a statement that he found no prediction in the Prophets of Jesus as the Messiah ("Christology of the Old Testament," *Christian Examiner,* July 1834).

On May 8, 1828, Noyes was married to Eliza Wheeler Buttrick of Framingham, Mass. Of their five children to grow to maturity, four sons were graduates of Harvard.

[S. A. Eliot, *Heralds of a Liberal Faith* (1910), vol. III, contains a good account of the life of Noyes, with a full bibliography of his works. Other sources are: H. E. and H. E. Noyes, *Geneal. Record of Some of the Noyes Descendants of James, Nicholas and Peter Noyes* (1904), vol. I; *Vital Records of Framingham, Mass.* (1911); A. P. Peabody, *Harvard Reminiscences* (1888); Sarah A. Emery, *Reminiscences of a Nonagenarian* (1879), pp. 116–18; *Christian Examiner,* July 1868; *Monthly Jour. of the Am. Unitarian Asso.,* Sept. 1868; *Christian Register,* June 6, 13, and 20, 1868; *Boston Transcript,* June 5, 1868.]   F.T.P.

NOYES, HENRY DRURY (Mar. 24, 1832–Nov. 12, 1900), ophthalmologist, was born in New York City, the son of Isaac Reed Noyes, a merchant, and his wife, Sarah Flint (Drury), both natives of Massachusetts. He was descended from James Noyes who emigrated from England in 1633. After taking the degree of A.B. from the University of the City of New York in 1851 and that of A.M. in 1854, he graduated from the College of Physicians and Surgeons of New York City in 1855. An interneship in the New York Hospital followed from 1855 to 1858, after which he studied in England, France, and Germany under the masters who founded ophthalmology. He returned to New York in 1859 and began to practise, being at once appointed to the position of assistant surgeon to the New York Eye and Ear Infirmary. He evidently filled this position faithfully and well for in November 1864 he was elevated to the office of full surgeon, and to executive surgeon in 1873. These responsibilities gave full scope to his unusual executive powers. He was particularly active in developing the Infirmary to one of the world's best special hospitals. He was elected first secretary of the American Ophthalmological Society in 1864, was first president of the American Otological Society (1868–73), and later (1879–84) served as president of the American Ophthalmological Society. His genius for organization soon became recognized and respected, and he was appointed to the chair of ophthalmology and otology at Bellevue Hospital Medical College, serving from 1868 until 1892, when the department was divided and he become professor of ophthalmology. His incumbency of this post lasted until his death.

Noyes was one of the first in the United States

to employ cocaine as a local anesthetic for eye operations. He kept abreast of the literature of his specialty and made many valuable contributions to a wide variety of subjects. In 1881 he published *A Treatise: Diseases of the Eye,* in Woods' Library of Standard Medical Authors, and in 1890 revised and expanded it into *A Text-Book on the Diseases of the Eye.* The list of his published papers numbers nearly one hundred. As his writings indicate, he was particularly interested in the surgical aspects of ophthalmology and was unusually skillful in operative procedures, but like so many men of attainments, he had interests so broad as to embrace many fields beyond the medical horizon.

He married Isabella Beveridge of Newburgh, N. Y., in 1859, soon after his return from his European studies. She died some ten years later, and in 1870 he married Anna M. Grant, likewise of Newburgh. He died at his summer home in Mount Washington, Mass., survived by his wife, two daughters, and a son. Two children had died in childhood.

[C. A. Wood, *The Am. Encyc. and Dict. of Ophthalmology,* vol. XI (1917); H. E. and H. E. Noyes, *Geneal. Record ... of James, Nicholas and Peter Noyes* (2 vols., 1904); *Archives of Ophthalmology,* Jan. 1901; *Jour. Am. Medic. Asso.,* Nov. 24, 1900; *Medic. News,* Nov. 17, 1900; *Medic. Record,* Nov. 17, 1900; *Ophthalmic Record,* Dec. 1900; *Trans. Am. Ophthalmological Soc.,* vol. IX (1902); *Trans. Am. Otological Soc.,* vol. VII (1901); *N. Y. Times,* Nov. 14, 1900; information as to certain details from friends and relatives.]
J. N. E.

NOYES, JOHN HUMPHREY (Sept. 3, 1811–Apr. 13, 1886), social reformer, founder of the Oneida Community, was born in Brattleboro, Vt., the descendant of Nicholas Noyes who with a brother, James, the ancestor of Edward Follansbee Noyes [*q.v.*], emigrated from England about 1633 and settled in Newbury, now Newburyport, Mass. His father, John Noyes, graduated from Dartmouth College, developed agnostic views that caused him to abandon his study of theology, attained unusual success in business, and was a member of Congress. His mother Polly (Hayes) Noyes, an aunt of Rutherford B. Hayes [*q.v.*], was a woman of strong character who devoted much attention to the religious education of her nine children, the eldest of whom became the mother of Larkin Mead, William R. Mead [*qq.v.*], and Elinor, the wife of William Dean Howells [*q.v.*]. As a boy, John Humphrey Noyes was thoughtful and was said to be passionate and violent when provoked. Strongly built and fond of outdoor life, he was the leader of his playmates. When he was ten, the family removed to Putney but he was sent back to Brattleboro to prepare for Dartmouth

College, which he entered at the age of fifteen. He was diligent in his studies and graduated in 1830 with high honors. For a year he devoted himself to the study of law at Chesterfield, N. H., in the office of Larkin G. Mead. At this time New England was experiencing a great "religious awakening." Having been "converted" at last, he abandoned his legal studies and began to prepare himself for the ministry. In the autumn of 1831 he entered the Theological Seminary at Andover. His burning zeal found the attitude of the students there too worldly, and after a year he transferred to the Theological Department at Yale College. There he became associated with a group of revivalists and with them organized a free church. Sharing the current reaction against the Calvinistic doctrine of human depravity, he became convinced that it was possible in this life to attain perfect holiness. He also developed a unique view of the second coming of Christ, fixing it not in the future but in the past, in 70 A.D.

Perfectionist and adventist beliefs received wide-spread acceptance during the intense religious excitement of the early 1830's, but he, with remarkable exegetical ingenuity, combined both views and from them derived religious sanction for an audacious social experiment. After his announcement, in February 1834, that he had attained a state of perfection or sinlessness, he was deprived of his license to preach, was requested to withdraw from the college, and was dismissed from the free church. For a few years he led a wandering life, during which he visited groups of perfectionists in New York and Massachusetts and also endeavored to interest reformers such as William Lloyd Garrison and Lyman Beecher in his new theology. Discouraged finally with the difficulty of welding together the scattered and somewhat disreputable perfectionist groups, in 1836 he returned to his home in Putney. There he gathered his family and their friends and expounded to them his views, which he later gathered together in *The Berean* (1847). From this "Bible School" developed a society known as the Bible Communists whose aim was to spread by means of its publications the gospel of perfectionism. Communism was adopted as for expediency rather than on principle, for his converts were well-to-do people, and he was more interested in changing their ideas than in improving their economic condition. As early as 1834 he became convinced that monogamic marriage was not compatible with perfectionism and in his famous "Battleaxe Letter" of 1837 he asserted his belief in promiscuity or free love (*Bibliotheca Sacra, post,* p.

Noyes

186). Later, in the letter in which he proposed marriage to Harriet A. Holton, he stated his radical views, which, however, did not prevent their marriage in 1838. Complex marriage, or promiscuity within the bounds of the community, was first practised in the Putney community in 1846. A storm of indignation arose in the neighborhood, which was not abated by the claims of miraculous healing powers put forth by the community. He was arrested on a charge of adultery, but he broke bail and fled to central New York. Thither the Bible Communists followed him and established in 1848 the Oneida Community.

For a period of thirty years he was undisturbed in his social and economic experiments. In these years he set forth his religious and sociological views in various publications. Of these several are notable, *Bible Communism* (1848), *Male Continence* (1848), *Scientific Propagation* (c. 1873), and *Home Talks* (1875). In 1870 he published a study of communistic experiments, *History of American Socialisms*. His genius for organization and his dominating personality made Oneida Community the most successful of all American Utopias. When in 1881 the Community was reorganized as a business corporation, its property was found to be worth $600,000. By a rather harsh discipline Noyes enforced on his followers birth control and stirpiculture. The number of children to be born each year was predetermined and their parents were selected so as to produce the best possible offspring. In his character the extreme views of the reformer were strangely combined with the astuteness of the opportunist. In 1879, recognizing imminent decline of his personal leadership and sensing the growing strength of outside opposition, he proposed to the Community the formula under which it abandoned its peculiar sex relations. The members then married legally among themselves. By emigration to Canada he put himself beyond the reach of legal action. He died at Niagara Falls, Ontario.

[*Religious Experience of John Humphrey Noyes* (1923) and *John Humphrey Noyes: The Putney Community* (1931) both ed. by G. W. Noyes; autobiog. material in writings, esp. *American Socialisms, ante,* and *Dixon and His Copyists* (1874); Charles Nordhoff, *Communistic Societies of America* (1870); W. A. Hinds, *American Communities,* rev. ed. (1902); Gilbert Seldes, *The Stammering Century* (1928); B. B. Warfield, "John Humphrey Noyes and his 'Bible Communists,'" *Bibliotheca Sacra,* Jan.–Oct. 1921.]
P. W. B.

NOYES, LA VERNE (Jan. 7, 1849–July 24, 1919), inventor, manufacturer, the son of Leonard R. and Jane (Jessup) Noyes, was born on his father's farm in Genoa, Cayuga County, N. Y. He was descended from James Noyes who emigrated from England and in 1633 became pastor of the Congregational church in Newbury, Mass. When La Verne Noyes was five years old his parents journeyed west to Springville, Linn County, Iowa, and there undertook the conversion of wild prairie land into a farm and home. In this arduous labor the boy did his part, but prepared for college as well, and entered Ames Agricultural College, now Iowa State College, Ames, Iowa, in 1868. The year before his graduation in 1872 he was assistant in the department of physics. His duties involved particularly the design and construction of much of the equipment used in the classroom and this experience, coupled with his earlier mechanical training on the farm in repairing machinery and tools, stimulated his genius for invention. After graduation he returned to his home where he again assisted his father and for a time had charge of the sale of farm implements in the village store at Marion, near by. He thus had opportunity to perceive the shortcomings of the existing farm machinery and to note the direction in which it needed improvement. In 1874, when twenty-five years old, he established a business in Batavia, Ill., for the manufacture of haying tools and carried it on successfully for about five years. Among the improvements he perfected during this time was a horse hay fork, patented June 22, 1878.

He was married, May 24, 1877, to Ida Elizabeth Smith of Charles City, Iowa. In 1879 he moved to Chicago and established a plant for the manufacture of a wire dictionary holder which he had first devised at the request of his wife. This undertaking was extremely profitable almost from the start, and gave him the opportunity to continue his inventive work in farm machinery. Thus in the succeeding decade he sold manufacturing rights to twelve patented inventions, including tractor wheels (Aug. 4, 1885), a harvester reel (Aug. 4, 1885), a sheaf carrier for self-binding harvesters (Nov. 13, 1888), and a cord-knotter for grain binders (Feb. 19, 1889). About 1886 he began giving serious attention to the possibilities of improving the windmill. After three years of experimentation resulting in the invention of numerous improvements, he organized the Aërmotor Company in Chicago and began the manufacture of steel windmills, which reduced the cost of wind power to one-sixth of what it had been previously. The business grew so rapidly that it required the enlargement of the manufacturing plant until it covered some ten acres. Besides his "air motors," he manufactured specially

590

designed steel towers for his windmills and for electric power lines and wireless stations, gasoline engines, and water-supply goods. He was particularly interested in the utilization of his air motor for the generation of electric power.

While his business absorbed much of his attention, he was engaged in many enterprises for the public good. He worked for the organization of the Department of Commerce and Labor; and was one of the first advocates of the creation of the Interstate Commerce Commission. He was president of the Illinois Manufacturers' Association for two years and also of the board of trustees of the Chicago Academy of Sciences and of many other educational and charitable institutions. He made generous gifts to his alma mater, Iowa State College, and to a number of charities in Chicago, but his two outstanding philanthropies were gifts to the University of Chicago: first, the Ida Noyes Hall, a social center for women, erected as a memorial to his wife, who died in 1912, and second, the La Verne Noyes Foundation for the education of honorably discharged soldiers of the World War and their descendants. He died in Chicago in his seventy-first year.

[Although Noyes' name frequently appears as La Verne W., the middle initial is not perpetuated in the title of his estate or in that of the La Verne Noyes Foundation. Sources include: T. W. Goodspeed, "La Verne Noyes," in *Univ. Record* (Univ. of Chicago), Oct. 1918, and *Univ. of Chicago Biog. Sketches*, vol. I (1922); Alumni Records, Iowa State College; *The Alumnus of Iowa State College*, vols. VIII (1912–13), X (1914–15), XIII (1917–18); *Descendants of Rev. William Noyes* (1900); H. E. and H. E. Noyes, *Geneal. Record of Some of the Noyes Descendants of James, Nicholas, and Peter Noyes* (1904), vol. II; *The Book of Chicagoans* (1917); *Who's Who in America*, 1918–19; *Chicago Daily News*, July 24, 1919; Patent Office records. Preferred form of name and date of marriage have been confirmed by Estate of La Verne Noyes, Chicago.]   C. W. M.

NOYES, WALTER CHADWICK (Aug. 8, 1865–June 12, 1926), jurist, was born in Lyme, Conn., to Richard and Catherine (Chadwick) Noyes. He was the sixth lineal descendant of the Rev. Moses Noyes to own and occupy the lands set apart to the Reverend Noyes as the minister in charge of the church established by the first settlers of the town of Old Lyme. He was a grand-nephew of Chief Justice Morrison R. Waite [*q.v.*]. After attending private schools Noyes went to Cornell University for a year (1884–85) and then entered upon the study of law in the office of Samuel Parks in New London, Conn. He studied also in the office of Judge Augustus Brandegee, one of the leading lawyers and political leaders of the state. After his admission to the bar he practised in New

London for many years in association with Judge Brandegee and his son, Frank B. Brandegee [*q.v.*], in the firm of Brandegee, Noyes & Brandegee. In 1895 Noyes became judge of the court of common pleas of New London County, a post which he held for twelve years. In 1904 he became president of the New London Northern Railroad Company. In 1907 he was appointed by President Roosevelt as United States circuit judge of the second judicial circuit. This made him a member *ex officio* of the United States circuit court of appeals in New York. During his tenure of the federal bench he participated in many important cases. These included a number of cases in patent law in which he became expert. He also participated in the famous Patten cotton corner case as well as in the proceedings against the American Tobacco Company.

In 1913 Noyes drew nation-wide attention to himself by resigning from the bench with the statement that his judicial salary of $7,000 was too low for the comfortable maintenence of his family and the education of his children (*New York Times*, June 6, 7, 1913). Much editorial comment on low judicial salaries ensued. Noyes resumed private practice in New York City where he at once assumed a position of importance at the bar. His practice was largely corporate in character and was highly lucrative. It included much business which brought him before the United States Supreme Court. He became general counsel for the Delaware & Hudson Company and he was peculiarly successful in the administration of important receiverships assigned to him. Perhaps the most conspicuous of these was that of the Rock Island Company in the management of which he was able to recover a substantial amount accruing to the benefit of bonds previously thought worthless. He served as chairman of the Connecticut corporation which operated the street and interurban railways of the state from 1914 until they were returned to the New York, New Haven & Hartford Railroad in 1925. Among his more notable cases in the United States Supreme Court was that of *The Kronprinzessin Cecilie* (224 *U. S.*, 12), in which he successfully argued that the abandonment of a voyage in reasonable anticipation of war did not entitle shippers to damage for breach of contract. In 1909–10 he served as a representative of the United States at the third international conference on maritime law at Brussels at which two treaties were negotiated. He published two legal works: *A Treatise on the Law of Intercorporate Relations* (1902, 1909) and *American Railroad Rates* (1905).

On Oct. 22, 1895, Noyes was married to Luella Shapley Armstrong; they had three daughters and one son. He always maintained the ancestral home in Lyme, Conn., as a country residence, although after his appointment to the federal bench it ceased to be the main family residence. It was known as "Indian Rock Farms." His death occurred in New York on June 12, 1926, after an illness of three months.

[See *Who's Who in America*, 1926–27; *Case and Comment*, Dec. 1911; Henry E. and Harriette E. Noyes, *Geneal. Record of Some of the Noyes Descendants of James, Nicholas, and Peter Noyes* (1904), vol. II; *N. Y. Times*, June 14, 1926.]   R. E. C.

NOYES, WILLIAM CURTIS (Aug. 19, 1805–Dec. 25, 1864), New York lawyer, was born in Schodack, N. Y., the son of George and Martha (Curtis) Noyes and a descendant of James Noyes who came to New England in 1633. He received a common-school and academy education, and at the age of fourteen years entered as a student the law office of Welcome Esleeck of Albany. He completed his studies in the office of Storrs & White of Whitesboro, was admitted to the bar as attorney in 1827 and as counselor in 1830. He practised law successively in Rome and Utica and became district attorney of Oneida County before his thirtieth year. In 1838 he removed to New York and rapidly advanced to the front ranks as an advocate.

Lacking a college education, he possessed the capacity to educate himself. He gradually built up a remarkable library, valued at $60,000, consisting of about five thousand law books and two thousand general works, all of which he bequeathed to Hamilton College on his death. He possessed a taste for miscellaneous reading and was a profound student of the law. His success as an advocate was enhanced by his exhaustive researches into the law and facts of his cases. He reduced his briefs to writing, memorized his speeches, and delivered them as though unpremeditated. In the "Huntington case" his masterly analysis of moral insanity secured the conviction of Huntington, a Wall Street broker on trial for forgery, who had set up a plea of insanity. Another notable suit was the Rose Will case (4 *Abbott's Court of Appeals Decisions*, 108), in which Noyes ably presented the history and doctrine of charitable uses. His greatest triumph occurred in the suit of the *Mechanics' Bank* vs. *New York & New Haven R.R. Co.* (13 *N. Y. Reports*, 599). In this trial in the New York court of appeals Noyes defended the stockholders of the railroad against the claim that they should be deprived of their holdings without compensation, because the transfer agent of the railroad had issued fraudulent stock to a third party.

Although he was sincerely interested in public affairs and politics, he was never a politician in the ordinary sense. Originally a Whig, he became a Republican upon the dissolution of the former party (1856). He was defeated for the office of state's attorney general in 1857, though running ahead of the party ticket. As a stanch Republican, he publicly attacked the Kansas-Nebraska Bill and Fugitive Slave Law. He was a delegate to the Peace Conference in Washington (1861), where he labored to harmonize conflicting views between the sections. His unionist convictions are summed up in the title of an address, which he delivered in 1862 to support the Emancipation Proclamation: *One Country! One Constitution! One Destiny!* In 1857, with Alexander W. Bradford and David Dudley Field he was appointed to codify the state laws, and in this work engaged chiefly in the revision of the penal code, which he completed just before his death. Though the code was rejected in New York, it was adopted at a later date by several western states. Noyes was a consistent Christian and philanthropist. For years he supported a home missionary without hinting of it to others. He was on the executive committee of the American Temperance Union, and was chosen president of the New England Society three days before he died. He was twice married, first to Anne Tracy, who bore him three children, and second to Julia A. Tallmadge, to whom two children were born. He was survived by one daughter of each marriage.

[H. E. Noyes and H. E. Noyes, *Geneal. Record of . . . James, Nicholas and Peter Noyes* (1904), vol. II; 43 *Barbour's Supreme Court Reports* (N. Y.), 649–73; S. W. Fisher, *William Curtis Noyes, a Baccalaureate Discourse* (1866); *Am. Ann. Cyc. . . . 1864* (1865); David McAdam and others, *Hist. of the Bench and Bar of N. Y.*, vol. I (1897); C. A. Alvord, printer, *Library of William Curtis Noyes* (1860); Charles Warren, *A Hist. of the Am. Bar* (1911); *N. Y. Herald*, Dec. 27, 1864; letters from Noyes to G. C. Verplanck, Apr. 18, 1840 and 1842, Mar. 31, 1846, Nov. 21, 1859 (MSS.), N. Y. Hist. Soc.]   A. L. M.

NUGENT, JOHN FROST (June 28, 1868–Sept. 18, 1931), United States senator, was born at LaGrande, Ore., the son of Edward and Agnes P. (Frost) Nugent. He grew up at Silver City, Idaho, where, after attending the public schools until the age of fifteen, he entered the mines and soon became a superintendent, having charge of several different workings in Idaho and, for a time, a mine in Australia. Returning to Idaho, he became court reporter for the third judicial district, of which his father was judge. At the same time he studied law, was admitted to the bar in 1898, and began practice at Silver City.

He was elected prosecuting attorney for Owyhee County for four terms, and was chairman of the county Democratic central committee for two terms. He then moved to Boise, where on May 15, 1895, he married Adelma Ainslie, by whom he had one son. He was associated with Clarence S. Darrow in 1907 in the defense of William D. Haywood [q.v.], George A. Pettibone, and Charles H. Moyer, officials of the Western Federation of Miners, against the charge of complicity in the assassination of former Gov. Frank Steunenberg. These defendants were accused in a confession of Harry Orchard (Alfred E. Horsley), the slayer, but were acquitted.

Idaho political control, at the time Nugent began his public career, was in the hands of Fred Thomas Dubois, who had been territorial representative in Congress, and later became the first senator from Idaho. Dubois was first a Republican, and opposed the Mormons and espoused free coinage of silver. He bolted the party in 1896 on the latter issue, and became a Democrat after election to the Senate for the term 1901–07. This shift in allegiance lost him strength in Idaho, and Nugent, as chairman of the state Democratic central committee, fought to oust him from leadership, completing the work by opposing Dubois' proposed anti-Mormon plank in the Democratic National Convention in 1908. Gov. Moses Alexander, in whose election Nugent had been most instrumental, appointed him United States senator in January 1918, to fill the unexpired term of James H. Brady. In the election of November 1918, the Non-Partisan League routed the Democrats in Idaho, but Nugent defeated former Gov. Frank R. Gooding for the Senate for the remainder of the term, receiving much League support. He defended the reconstruction policies of President Wilson and espoused American adherence to the League of Nations. Nugent resigned from the Senate, effective Jan. 14, 1921, President Wilson having appointed him, Dec. 20, 1920, a member of the Federal Trade Commission. In 1926 he ran unsuccessfully for the Senate. Retiring from the Federal Trade Commission in 1927, he practised law in Washington, D. C., until his death, which occurred in that city.

Nugent was a handsome man, with regular features and forceful presence. He was an excellent public speaker, took an active interest in fraternal organizations, and used his aptitudes to acquire an enthusiastic political following. He not only shone in campaign meetings, but proved himself an adroit political manager, and remained Democratic leader of his state from 1908 to 1920.

[Biog. Dir. Am. Cong. (1928); Who's Who in America, 1930–31; C. S. Darrow, The Story of My Life (1932); Boise Capital News, Sept. 18, 1931; Idaho Daily Statesman (Boise), Sept. 19, 1931.]

B. M.

NÚÑEZ CABEZA DE VACA, ALVAR (c. 1490–c. 1557), Spanish colonial official and explorer, was born in Jerez de la Frontera, Spain, toward the close of the fifteenth century and died (evidently at Seville) probably in 1556 or between that year and 1559. His father, Francisco de Vera, was a member of the municipal council of Jerez, and his paternal grandfather, Pedro de Vera Mendoza, one of the conquerors of the Canaries and their governor. His mother, Teresa Cabeza de Vaca, was descended from that shepherd, Martín Alhaja, who was ennobled and given the name Cabeza de Vaca by Sancho, King of Navarre, for showing the Christians a pass through the mountains by placing a cow's head at its entrance and thus enabling them to win the battle of Las Navas de Tolosa (June 11, 1212) from the Moors. Instead of bearing his father's name, Alvar was named for a maternal ancestor who was captain of the fleet of Jerez. In 1511 and 1512 he fought in Italy, in 1520 against the comuneros in Spain, and still later in Navarre against the French.

On Feb. 15, 1527, he was appointed treasurer and alguacil mayor of the expedition of Pánfilo de Narváez [q.v.] which set out to conquer and settle Florida. While wintering in Cuba, he and another officer were sent with two ships to get provisions at Trinidad, but both ships were lost in a sudden hurricane. Shortly afterward he was made commander of Narváez's fleet at Jagua, Cienfuegos Bay. When the expedition reached the coast of Florida in April 1528, he vainly advised Narváez not to abandon the fleet. After the costly overland march to Apalache, when the remnant of the expedition embarked on Sept. 22, 1528, in five rude boats made near the site of the present St. Marks, he was given command of one of them. Two only of the boats finally came through stress of weather to a small desolate island off the coast of Texas, dubbed Mal Hado (Bad Luck) by the men. The eighty survivors, succored for the moment by the wretched Indians of the island, were soon reduced by hunger, cold, and disease to fifteen, who were enslaved by the Indians and separated one from another.

In February 1530, Cabeza de Vaca escaped to a friendly tribe and became a trader, bartering articles from the coast for others from the interior. Once a year he returned to Mal Hado to try to persuade a Spaniard, Lope de Oviedo, to escape with him, and in 1532 succeeded, but shortly after, Oviedo, fainthearted, turned back. In 1534, Cabeza de Vaca and three others—Andrés Dorantes, Alonso del Castillo, and the latter's black slave Estavanico—took refuge among the Avavares or Coahuiltecas, among whom they plied the art of the medicine man with success. At last, in the spring of 1535, they set out in earnest on their long trek westward, traveling triumphantly from tribe to tribe, healing as they went. Their route led them across the continent, through what is now southern Texas and northern Mexico. In March 1536 they came to the Sinaloa River, and on July 23, to Mexico City, where they were met by Cortes and Mendoza. In 1537, despite the wishes of Mendoza, who desired to employ him in other expeditions, Cabeza de Vaca returned to Spain. Finding that the Florida expedition which he wished to obtain for himself had been given to Hernando de Soto [q.v.], he remained inactive for about two years.

On Mar. 18, 1540, he was commissioned to lead an expedition to the Rio de la Plata region in South America. Its most noteworthy incident was the thousand-mile march from the Brazilian mainland opposite Santa Catalina Island to Asunción, Paraguay, during which for the first time Europeans gazed upon the falls of the Iguazú. On Apr. 25, 1544, festering dissatisfaction among some of his men came to a head; he was arrested and held in close confinement for some months, and then sent back to Spain to be tried on certain definite charges, some of which seem to have been trumped up. Reaching Seville in August 1545, he was kept in prison until Mar. 18, 1551, when he was sentenced to deprivation of all offices and titles, permanent banishment from the Indies, and exile to Oran for five years. Later in that year his exile to Oran was repealed, and on Sept. 15, 1556, being ill, he was given a royal grant of 12,000 maravedis.

In *La Relacion que Dio Alvar Nuñez, Cabeça de Vaca de lo Acaescido enlas Indias* (Zamora, 1542), Cabeza de Vaca, first of all Europeans, described the opossum and the American bison and gave information of the Texas Indians. He also brought the first reports of the Pueblo Indians, although he did not see their towns. His reports led directly to the Coronado expedition and to the martyrdom of Fray Marcos de Niza [q.v.]. Cabeza de Vaca was sane, capable, adaptable, honest, and sincere. His narrative may contain some exaggerations and some inaccuracies, but he was no lover of the marvelous. He was thoroughly imbued with the religious faith of his day and his success in healing he attributed to divine intervention. Working alone, or almost alone, with the Indians, he was resourceful and successful, but with men of his own race, he ran almost immediately into difficulties, although he inspired devotion in not a few.

[Sources for the Florida expedition are the *Relacion* of 1542, of which notable English translations are Buckingham Smith, *Relation of Alvar Nuñez Cabeça de Vaca* (1871) and Fanny R. Bandelier, *The Journey of Alvar Nuñez Cabeza de Vaca* (1905); the account sent to the Audiencia of Santo Domingo, probably written jointly by Cabeza de Vaca and Dorantes in 1536 or 1537 and utilized by Oviedo in his *Historia General y Natural delas Indias* (Madrid), III (1853), 579–618; a short summary relation, perhaps given to the king by Cabeza de Vaca in 1537 (MS. in Archivo de Indias), reproduced in *Coleccion de Documentos Inéditos Relativos al Descubrimiento . . . de América*, XIV (1870), 265 ff.; and a letter of Feb. 11, 1537, written to the king by Viceroy Mendoza (MS. in Archivo de Indias, 2-2-2/5). Sources for the South American expedition are the *Comentarios*, perhaps dictated in part by Cabeza de Vaca, in *La Relacion y Comentarios del Gouernador Aluar Nuñez Cabeça de Vaca* (1555) and translated into English in Luis L. Dominguez, *The Conquest of the River Plate, 1535–1555* (Hakluyt Soc., 1891); Ulrich Schmidel's narrative of 1567, translated in Dominguez, *ante*; and Francisco López de Gómara, *La Historia General de las Indias* (1554). The best life of Cabeza de Vaca is Morris Bishop, *The Odyssey of Cabeza de Vaca* (1933), containing numerous references to other works. Andrés Bellogin García, *Vida y Hazanas de Alvar Núñez Cabeza de Vaca* (Madrid, 1928) has much to commend it but must be used with discretion. See also A. F. Bandelier, in *Hemenway Southwestern Archæological Expedition* (1890), pp. 24–67; Woodbury Lowery, *The Spanish Settlements* (1911); R. B. Cunningham Graham, *The Conquest of the River Plate* (1924); Enrique de Gandía, *Historia de la Conquista del Rio de la Plata y del Paraguay* (1932).]   J. A. R.

NUNÓ, JAIME (Sept. 8, 1824–July 17, 1908), conductor, composer, impresario, was born in San Juan de las Abadesas, Spain. He studied music in Barcelona under Mateo Ferrer, director of the cathedral choir, and at ten was admitted to the choir. After singing and studying there for six years he undertook the direction of an orchestra at Sabadell and conducted other small orchestras. He also composed religious music. In 1851 he became a Spanish army bandmaster and was sent to Cuba to establish military bands in the regiments there on duty. In 1853 the Mexican dictator, Antonio Lopez de Santa Anna, then in exile in Havana, met Nunó and was so impressed by his ability that on his recall to Mexico as president that same year, he took Nunó with him as general band inspector of the Mexican army. Soon afterward Nunó was appointed one of the two directors of the new National Conservatory of Music in Mexico city. In 1855, when Santa Anna was again overthrown, Nunó, like most of his protégés and partisans, fled the country, and in 1856 was active in the United States, managing tours for Italian opera singers, acting as orchestra conductor for Sigismund Thalberg, then concertizing in America, and afterward conducting both French and Italian opera in Havana. From 1863 to 1869 he directed opera troupes in Cuba, the United States, Mexico, and Central America, and on June 12, 1864, when the Emperor Maximilian made his state entry into Mexico city, Nunó assisted as bandmaster in the welcome given him. In 1869 he settled in Buffalo, N. Y., as a teacher of singing. For four years, 1878–82, he was in Rochester as organist and choirmaster at the cathedral, then he returned to Buffalo and for a time conducted the Buffalo Symphony Orchestra. During these years he wrote many sacred compositions. He died in Bayside, L. I., where he was spending the summer, at the age of eightyfour. He was survived by a wife and two children.

Nunó's outstanding achievement was the writing of the Mexican national hymn, to a poem by Francisco Gonzalez Bocanegra. Henri Herz, the pianist, touring Mexico in 1849, was surprised to find that the country lacked a national hymn. He offered to set to music a competitively selected poem, and did so. Neither his setting nor the one by Bottesini, composed to Bocanegra's verses (which won a prize offered by Santa Anna in 1853) won popular recognition, however, and in 1854 the Mexican government officially adopted Nunó's "Himno Nacional Mejicano"—already unofficially a favorite. On Sept. 15, 1854, it was given an inaugural performance in the Teatro de Santa Anna in Mexico city with a display of the national flag, speeches, and a salute of cannon. In 1901, Mexican visitors to the Pan-American Exposition in Buffalo discovered Nunó in that city. As a result he was invited to Mexico to conduct the singing of his hymn at the ninety-first anniversary of Mexican independence (Sept. 16, 1901). It was performed by a large chorus of school children in Mexico city, and Nunó, after depositing a wreath of flowers on the poet Bocanegra's tomb, was crowned with a golden chaplet and accorded a great ovation.

[See: Enrique de Olavarría y Ferrari, *Historia del Himno Nacional y Biografía de Don Jaime Nunó* (1901); "El Himno Nacional Mexicano," in *Anales del Museo Nacional de Arqueologia, Historia y Etnografía*, vol. XXII, no. 1; *Musical America*, July 25, 1908; *La Gaceta Comercial*, Sept. 5, 12, 13, 14, 1901; *Buffalo Express, N. Y. Times*, July 19, 1908.]

F. H. M.

NURSE, REBECCA (1621–July 19, 1692), victim of the Salem witchcraft delusion, was born in Yarmouth, England, the daughter of William Towne and Joanna (Blessing), and

was baptized Feb. 21, 1621. It is not known when she came to America, but she married Francis Nurse, a tray-maker, who lived in Salem, Mass., for forty years after 1638. He then purchased a farm in Salem Village (the present Danvers) and removed thither with his wife and eight children. The Nurse family were involved in various local squabbles and had acquired some enemies who took advantage of the witchcraft frenzy which started in this community in 1691. By absenting themselves from meeting out of disgust at the commotions raised by "possessed" wenches of Danvers, they attracted unfavorable attention and Rebecca was denounced. Although she was feeble, ill, and seventy years old, and although thirty-eight respectable citizens testified that "her life and conversation were according to her profession" and had given no cause to be suspected, she was arrested and examined, Mar. 24, 1692, in the presence of her four accusers. She repeatedly denied her guilt: "I can say before my Eternal Father, I am innocent, and God will clear my innocency"; but the wenches counteracted this by throwing fits timed to her every movement. She was indicted on June 2; a jury of women examined her and found what the majority believed to be a mark of the devil. Two of the women, however, dissented, and Goody Nurse petitioned for another examination, a plea which the court evidently disregarded. At her trial, June 29, the jury at first returned a verdict of "not guilty," but the judges demanded if they had well considered one expression of the prisoner's, how when she was confronted with one Goody Hobbes, a confessing witch, Mrs. Nurse had muttered, "She is one of us." The jury retired for further debate, returned to ask the accused what her remark had meant, and, upon receiving no answer from her, reversed their verdict. She later explained that she had only meant that she and Goody Hobbes had been held in prison together, and that "being something hard of hearing and full of grief" she had not been aware of the jury's question. Governor Phips granted her a reprieve, whereupon her accusers renewed their outcry and certain gentlemen of Salem prevailed upon him to recall his order. On July 3 Rebecca Nurse was solemnly excommunicated by her church and on July 19 was executed at Gallows Hill. With the rapid reaction of the colony from the excesses of the delusion, her innocence speedily became apparent; in 1712 the very pastor who had cast her out of the church had the congregation by a formal and public act cancel the excommunication.

[The documents concerning Rebecca Nurse are found in W. E. Woodward, *Records of Salem Witchcraft, Copied from the Original Documents* (2 vols., 1864), and in *The Hist. Colls. of the Topsfield Hist. Soc.*, vol. XIII (1908), pp. 39–58; see also C. W. Upham, *Salem Witchcraft; With an Account of Salem Village* (2 vols., 1867); and C. S. Tapley, *Rebecca Nurse, Saint but Witch Victim* (1930).]   P.M.

NUTHEAD, WILLIAM (c. 1654–1695), printer of Virginia and Maryland, was probably of English birth and professional training. His name occurs for the first time in colonial records in a minute of the Governor and Council of Virginia, dated Feb. 21, 1683, in which it appears that, sponsored by John Buckner, Gentleman, of Gloucester County, he had set up a press at Jamestown and printed, without license, several papers and two sheets of the acts of assembly of November 1682. From Buckner's testimony before the Council, it became clear that in this instance the printer had acted prematurely. Because of the official dislike of "the liberty of a presse," Nuthead and his sponsor were thereupon required to give bond jointly that nothing else should be printed until the royal pleasure were known. In response to the Council's immediate representations, the king's orders of Dec. 14, 1683, forbade that any person in Virginia "be permitted to use any press for printing upon any occasion whatsoever," and it was not until the coming to Williamsburg of William Parks [q.v.] in 1730 that the press was reëstablished in Virginia. None of the papers or trial sheets of the acts printed by Nuthead at Jamestown is known to have survived, and his record as an American printer would consist of what has been said above if the government of the neighboring province of Maryland had not been more liberal in its policy than the Virginia Council at the time of this critical situation in his affairs. In the appropriation act of the Maryland Assembly of October 1686, three years after the inhibition of the Jamestown press, occurred the item: "To Wm. Nutthead Printer five Thousand five Hundred & fifty pounds of Tobaccoe." It is uncertain whether Nuthead had come to Maryland immediately after the stopping of his Virginia press, or whether this entry represents his first association with the government of that province. If the payment had been made for services rendered, however, it would mean that he had been at work in St. Mary's City for a year at least at the time of passage of the money act of October 1686. It is certain that he remained there from that time until his death in 1695. His name, with the designation "printer," appears in land records in 1686 and 1687; he was reproved by the Council in 1693 for actions that seemed to show partiality to the party of the dispossessed Proprietary; and in the same year he was engaged by that body for a service of some delicacy. In October 1694 he signed an address protesting the removal of the capital from St. Mary's City to Annapolis. Nuthead died sometime before Feb. 7, 1694/5, on which day his widow Dinah, who later received the Governor's license to print in his place, asked to be appointed administratrix of his estate. Only a single imprint from the Maryland press of Nuthead remains—*The Address of the Representatives of Their Majestyes Protestant Subjects, in the Provinnce of Maryland Assembled,* Aug. 26, 1689—but he is known to have printed a week or two earlier the more extensive *Declaration* of the same body. Among his accounts, moreover, was found a list of sums owed him by various persons and officials, which suggests a moderate activity of his press during the years of his Maryland residence. Nuthead set up in Jamestown the earliest press in this country south of Massachusetts. Because of this fact and because of his persistence in the operation of his later Maryland press in spite of poverty and governmental interference, he has place in typographical history with Stephen Day [q.v.] of Massachusetts and William Bradford [q.v.] of Pennsylvania.

[W. W. Hening, *Statutes at Large . . . of Va.* (2nd ed., 1823), II, 517–18; *Calendar of State Papers, Col. Ser., America and West Indies, 1681–1685* (1898); records in Land Office, Annapolis, Md.; *Archives of Md.*, vols. VIII (1890), XIII (1894), XIX (1899), XX (1900); L. C. Wroth, *A Hist. of Printing in Colonial Md., 1686–1776* (1922).]   L.C.W.

NUTTALL, THOMAS (Jan. 5, 1786–Sept. 10, 1859), botanist and ornithologist, the son of Jonas Nuttall, was born in humble circumstances at Settle in Yorkshire. He was apprenticed to a printer and later entered the printing shop of an uncle in Liverpool. He seems to have been of a studious nature and lost no spare moment that was available for reading and study. In 1808 he emigrated to Philadelphia. He had apparently given some attention to the study of mineralogy before leaving England and must have had a general interest in nature, but it remained for the Philadelphia botanist Benjamin Smith Barton [q.v.] to introduce him to the pleasure found in the study of plants. He at once began collecting and investigating the native flora, extending his explorations southward from the valley of the Delaware and the pine barrens of New Jersey, through the Delaware-Maryland peninsula, to Virginia and the lowlands of North Carolina, and later to Mississippi and Florida. Embracing every opportunity for distant exploration, he went in 1809–11 with

John Bradbury, a Scotch naturalist, up the Missouri River beyond the Mandan Indian villages; in 1818–20, explored along the Arkansas and Red rivers in Arkansas, Louisiana, and Indian Territory; and in 1834–35, accompanied the Wyeth Expedition to the mouth of the Columbia River, in company with John K. Townsend [q.v.], the ornithologist, returning by himself through California and thence to the Hawaiian Islands and around Cape Horn.

After the first of these expeditions he was elected a fellow of the Linnæan Society of London (1813), a member of the American Philosophical Society (1817), and a correspondent of the Academy of Natural Sciences of Philadelphia (1817), in whose rooms he studied his botanical collections. His outstanding contributions to botany are: *The Genera of North American Plants, and a Catalogue of the Species, to the Year 1817* (1818), the greater part of the type of which he set with his own hands; his continuation (vols. IV–VI, 1842–49) of *The North American Sylva* of F. A. Michaux [q.v.]; numerous descriptions of new species and reports on collections, published in the *Journal of the Academy of Natural Sciences,* the *Transactions of the American Philosophical Society,* and Silliman's *American Journal of Science*; and a little treatise entitled *An Introduction to Systematic and Physiological Botany* (1827). In 1821 he published *A Journal of Travels into the Arkansa Territory, during the Year 1819,* with appendices dealing with the history of the Indian tribes and meteorological observations.

In 1822 he accepted a call to be curator of the Botanical Garden of Harvard University, where he remained for ten years, giving a few lectures on botany but devoting most of his time to the culture of rare plants. He resigned to accompany the Wyeth expedition to the Pacific Coast. While in Cambridge, his attention seems to have been turned more actively to ornithology, which had always attracted him to a certain degree, and in 1832 he published *A Manual of the Ornithology of the United States and Canada.* Upon this book and one paper, "Remarks and Inquiries Concerning the Birds of Massachusetts" (*Memoirs of the American Academy of Arts and Sciences,* n.s. I, 1833), rests his entire ornithological reputation. So great, however, was the need of such a work as his *Manual,* with only the expensive folios of Wilson and Audubon available, that it brought him a great and deserved reputation, and the first ornithological club in America was named in his honor. The *Manual* is well written, as were all of his works, and the preface and numerous notes show a remarkable famili-

arity with the literature of ornithology, while the pages are replete with original observations. One of the unique features is the painstaking effort to record the songs of birds by the syllabic method.

Several papers on mineralogy and a period devoted to the study of shells further illustrate the breadth of Nuttall's learning and his ability to turn from one field to another, maintaining in all the high quality of his writings. A paper which he read in December 1820 before the Philadelphia Academy of Natural Sciences, "Observations on the Geological Structure of the Valley of the Mississippi" (*Journal,* January 1821), in which he found the Secondary formations of Iowa to resemble the mountain limestone of Derbyshire, was the first attempt in America to correlate, by means of the fossils contained therein, geological formations widely separated geographically. It antedated by nearly fifteen years the similar work of Samuel George Morton [q.v.], who is generally considered the pioneer of American paleontology. (See Keyes, *post.*)

How Nuttall subsisted during his residence in Philadelphia his friends never knew; yet he is reported to have saved a certain sum of money. He was disorderly in his dress and excessively economical, living the life of a recluse, with few friends besides the botanists with whom he associated at the Academy. In 1842 an uncle bequeathed to him his estate, "Nutgrove," near Liverpool, on condition that he live there during nine months of the year for the remainder of his life, and he returned to England. While the estate did not yield a great income, it enabled him to devote his time to the cultivation of exotic plants, especially rhododendrons. He made one visit to Philadelphia in 1847–48, and plunged at once into his favorite work at the Academy, describing the collections brought from the Far West by Dr. William Gambel. He was never married and died on his estate in 1859.

[Elias Durand, "Biog. Notice of the Late Thomas Nuttall," *Proc. Am. Phil. Soc.,* vol. VII (1861); autobiographical sketch in Preface to vol. IV (1842) of *The North American Sylva*; F. L. Burns, "Miss Lawson's Recollections of Ornithologists," *The Auk,* July 1917; J. W. Harshberger, *The Botanists of Phila.* (1899); *Proc. Linnæan Soc. of London,* 1859; *Pop. Sci. Mo.,* Mar. 1895, with complete bibliography; *Ibid.,* Jan. 1909; C. R. Keyes, *Ibid.,* Feb. 1914; G. E. Osterhout, in *Plant World,* Apr. 1907.]   W.S.

NUTTING, CHARLES CLEVELAND (May 25, 1858–Jan. 23, 1927), ornithologist and marine zoologist, son of the Rev. Rufus and Margaretta Leib (Hunt) Nutting, was born at Jacksonville, Ill. Later, the family moved to Indianapolis, where Nutting received his high-school education. One of his teachers was David Starr Jordan [*q.v.*], who encouraged him in his natural taste for scientific studies and undoubtedly influenced the direction of his future career. Appointment of the father to the chair of Greek at Blackburn University brought the Nuttings to Carlinville, Ill., where Charles graduated in 1880 with the degree of A.B. and was awarded that of A.M. in 1882. The Presbyterian collegiate environment was a strong factor in his life and manifested itself in his open disapproval of Sunday scientific work by members of the parties he headed, and in his narratives.

Having developed a desire for travel, he opened correspondence with Spencer F. Baird [*q.v.*], which resulted in a commission from the Smithsonian Institution to investigate Nicaragua and Costa Rica where, in 1881 and 1882, he collected birds and antiquities. On Aug. 10, 1886, he married Lizzie B. Hersman, of Hersman, Ill., and a month later went to Iowa City as professor of zoology and curator of the museum in the State University of Iowa. His classes were small at first, and his teaching duties light, thus allowing him to devote his major effort to museum development, which was always his favorite enterprise. He was a natural collector, a good taxidermist for his day, and he had the ability to interest others in his projects. A trip to the Bahamas with his wife in 1888 gave him his first intimate acquaintance with marine life. Up to this time he had been particularly interested in ornithology, but now his tastes seemed to turn in the direction of the coelenterates. In 1889 his first serious paper, "Contribution to the Anatomy of Gorgonidae," appeared as an *Iowa University Bulletin.*

The death of his wife, after the birth of a daughter, early in 1891, was a heavy bereavement. In seeking distraction, he made a trip with two of his students to the muskeg country of the Saskatchewan district, where the party secured a considerable collection of birds. His "Report on Zoological Explorations on the Lower Saskatchewan River" (*Iowa University Bulletin*) appeared in 1893. In that year he organized and headed a party of twenty-three, mostly students, which chartered a ninety-ton schooner and made a three months' cruise for the purpose of studying the natural history of the Bahamas and adjacent seas. After his return he published "Narrative and Preliminary Report of Bahama Expedition," which also appeared as a *Bulletin* in 1895. It attracted wide and favorable attention, and brought him into communication with many influential zoologists. In 1895 he studied at the marine laboratories of Plymouth and

Naples, further enlarging his professional acquaintance. On June 16, 1897, he married M. Eloise Willis of Iowa City, by whom he had two sons. He went on the Hawaiian cruise of the U.S.S. *Albatross* in 1902 as a civilian member of the scientific staff, and was so impressed by the bird rookeries on Laysan Island that he became fired with the idea of reproducing the scene in a cyclorama for the museum—a plan carried out years later.

At the request of many students, he organized and directed another trip to the West Indies in 1918, but this time the steamer route was used and the work confined principally to shore and littoral stations on Barbados and Antigua. The scientific results, however, were of considerable interest (*Barbados-Antigua Expedition: Narrative and Preliminary Report,* 1919). His last enterprise of this nature was to lead a small party from the University of Iowa faculty to Fiji and New Zealand in 1922, an account of which trip he published under the title *Fiji-New Zealand Expedition* (1924). Meanwhile, he had been busy studying marine invertebrates and had brought out an important series of reports, *American Hydroids* (1900–15), and a mass of shorter articles, many of the later ones of a controversial nature in support of his views on evolution. At the end of this academic year he retired from his administrative duties as curator and departmental head but continued teaching until a few days before his death, which came suddenly in an attack of angina pectoris.

Nutting was a man of forceful character and manners, energetic in organizing and executing projects in which he was interested. His passion for collecting was a great aid to him in his museum development, while his industry, attention to detail, and aptitude in drawing fitted in well with his taxonomic studies. He was a good teacher, a man of strong religious convictions, and although his health had been failing visibly for many years he maintained his interests and his activity to the end.

[J. M. Cattell and D. R. Brimhall, *Am. Men of Science* (1921); *Science,* Feb. 11, 1927; *Who's Who in America,* 1926–27; personal association for forty-two years, and information as to certain facts from Mrs. Chas. C. Nutting.]   H. F. W.

NYE, EDGAR WILSON (Aug. 25, 1850–Feb. 22, 1896), "Bill" Nye, journalist, humorous writer and lecturer, was born at Shirley, a hamlet of Piscataquis County, Me. His parents, Franklin and Elizabeth Mitchell (Loring) Nye, were farming people of good New England stock, the father descended from Benjamin Nye who settled at Lynn, Mass., in 1635. Poverty prompted their removal to the new West in the migration which poured into Wisconsin after its admission as a state. On the St. Croix River in 1852 they took up, as Bill Nye has recorded, "one hundred and sixty acres of beautiful ferns and bright young rattlesnakes" (*Century*, November 1891, p. 60). Edgar's boyhood was spent in the typically American surroundings of a bush farm. The Nyes built themselves a cabin of basswood logs, and a year later, were able to add to it the luxury of a glass window. Bill Nye himself tells us that he went to school between Indian massacres. Later on his parents were able to send him for a time to an academy at River Falls. His studies, though much broken into by "vacations" during which he worked out by the month, were turned towards the law. For a time he worked in the law office of Bingham & Jenkins in Chippewa Falls, sleeping on the premises at night and keeping his blankets in the office safe. After an interlude of teaching school, in a final effort to achieve admission to the bar he removed to the county seat of Burnett County, which "consisted at that time only of a boarding-house for lumber men, surrounded by the dark-blue billows of a boundless huckleberry patch" (*Ibid.*, November 1892, p. 156). Here Bill Nye had his first taste of journalism, conducting for two weeks a newspaper housed in a log hovel. He left Wisconsin in 1876, drifted westward to Wyoming Territory, and brought up at the new settlement of Laramie City, ever after associated with his name. An informal examination by a "committee of kindly but inquisitive lawyers" admitted him to the bar. But he never practised. His legal status merely served to obtain him the position of justice of the peace. "The office was not a salaried one," he wrote, "but solely dependent upon fees. . . . So while I was called Judge Nye and frequently mentioned in the papers with great consideration, I was out of coal half the time, and once could not mail my letters for three weeks because I did not have the necessary postage" (*Ibid.*, November 1891).

Neither the bench nor the bar was destined to be his vocation in life. Soon after his arrival at Laramie and even before he had been elected a justice of the peace, he had done some casual work on a local paper, the *Laramie Daily Sentinel*. He seems to have acted as reporter and writer of anything and everything at a salary of fifty dollars a month. His connection with the *Sentinel* brought to him an offer from the *San Francisco Chronicle* to accompany, as a reporter, General Custer's ill-fated expedition against Sitting Bull (1876). Nye explains with characteristic drollery that a difficulty about getting his trunk checked in time to catch the right train deprived him of the opportunity offered. He varied his work as reporter and justice of the peace by random contributions to other western journals, such as the *Cheyenne Daily Sun* and the *Denver Tribune*. During this period he married (Mar. 7, 1877) Clara Frances Smith of Chicago, by whom in due course of time he had two sons and two daughters.

In 1881, with the aid of Judge Jacob Blair, his associate and friend from his first arrival, he started the famous *Laramie Boomerang* with which his memory has ever since been connected. Nye edited this paper for about three years. His droll comments and *obiter dicta*—before the days of the "columnist"—and his humorous yarns of frontier life brought the *Boomerang* a continental reputation, though its editor assures us that he made no money out of it. Many of Nye's "pieces" which were collected to form his books appeared first in the *Boomerang*. The first collection, *Bill Nye and Boomerang* (1881), was followed in short order by *Forty Liars and Other Lies* (1882) and *Baled Hay* (1884). Meanwhile he had served as postmaster of Laramie from August 1882 until October 1883, when he resigned. His health had broken, and from time to time for the rest of his life he suffered from meningitis, the disease which eventually caused his death. Advised to seek a lower altitude, he went first to Greeley, Colo., then back to Wisconsin, buying a farm in Hudson, near the home of his parents. In 1886 he moved East and early in the following year accepted a position on the staff of the New York *World*, from which time on his name and his writings obtained a national circulation.

In 1885 he had appeared in a new and entirely successful rôle as a public lecturer. To vary his entertainment, at first too monotonously funny to be sustained, he united in 1886 with James Whitcomb Riley, thus forming a combination of gravity and gayety whose merit justified its success. For the rest of his life his services were in constant demand on the platform. He appeared with Riley until January 1890, and subsequently with Alfred P. Burbank and with William Hawley Smith. For some time he lectured under the management of James Burton Pond [*q.v.*], the famous lyceum organizer. In 1891 he moved his home to Arden, N. C., where after repeated periods of ill health he died five years later.

Edgar Wilson Nye's place in American literature belongs among that brilliant and distinctive group of the middle and later nineteenth century, represented chiefly by Mark Twain and Artemus

Ward, who first made American humor a distinct and truly national branch of literature. His work, like that of all the school, is often disfigured by the haste of its casual production and by its frequent reliance upon the cheap devices of verbal form. But the real merit of it lies in its essential point of view—broad, kindly, and human, and reflecting the new American analysis of traditional and conventional ideas. In addition to the volumes already mentioned, many others appeared both before and after his death. With Riley he wrote *Nye and Riley's Railway Guide* (1888). His most ambitious books were *Bill Nye's History of the United States* (1894) and *Bill Nye's History of England* (1896). He was also the author of two plays: *The Cadi*, based on his experience as postmaster of Laramie, which had moderate success, and *The Stag Party*, completed under pressure shortly before his last illness, which was a failure.

[Nye left two fragmentary chapters of autobiography in the *Century*, Nov. 1891 and Nov. 1892, while *Bill Nye, His Own Life Story* (1926), comp. by his son, F. W. Nye, is largely autobiographical. J. B. Pond, *Eccentricities of Genius* (1900), contains two delightful chapters upon Nye as a lecturer. See also G. H. Nye and F. E. Best, *A Geneal. of the Nye Family* (1907); Stephen Leacock, "American Humour," *Nineteenth Century*, Aug. 1914; "Letters of Riley and Bill Nye," *Harper's Mag.*, Mar. 1919; J. L. Ford, "A Century of American Humor," *Munsey's Mag.*, July 1901; Robert Ford, *Am. Humorists* (1897); F. B. Beard, *Wyoming* (1933), vol. I; *World* (N. Y.), Feb. 23, 1896; *N. Y. Times*, Feb. 23, 1896.] S. L.

NYE, JAMES WARREN (June 10, 1814–Dec. 25, 1876), governor of Nevada Territory, United States senator, was the son of James and Thankful (Crocker) Nye and a descendant of Benjamin Nye who emigrated from England to settle in 1635 at Lynn, Mass. Born at De Ruyter, Madison County, N. Y., James grew up amidst the severe limitations of poverty. He secured secondary schooling at Homer Academy, however, and then studied law in Hamilton, N. Y., where he practised for some years. He was surrogate of Madison County, 1844–47, and judge of the county court, 1847–51. In 1848, running for Congress as a Free-Soil or "Barnburner" Democrat, he was defeated by the Whig candidate, William Duer. In 1851 he removed to Syracuse, continuing to enjoy a successful practice. Six years later, in 1857, he became one of the police commissioners of the metropolis under an act of that year amending the city charter.

When Fort Sumter was fired upon, Nye became an enthusiastic supporter of Lincoln, using his remarkable gift as a stump orator in behalf of the administration, and he was soon appointed governor of the newly created territory of Nevada. Upon arrival in Carson City, Nev., July

8, 1861, he was confronted with the difficult task of organizing the territory. The bulk of the population was included in what had been Carson County, Utah Territory. Without friction, Nye absorbed the government of the old county into that of the new territory, and guided the latter swiftly into the position of an effective governmental organization, a task the more difficult because the $30,700 a year in greenbacks, voted by Congress for support of the territory, was worth hardly more than half its face value.

When in 1864 Nevada was advanced to statehood, and Nye County, newly created, was named for him, Nye logically became a candidate to represent the new state in the United States Senate and was elected in company with William M. Stewart [*q.v.*]. The two cast lots in the state Senate for the long term, Nye drawing the short term. Reëlected to the Senate in 1867 after a hot contest with Charles E. DeLong, he served with honor on important committees, always stanchly loyal to the Republican party which had sent him to Washington. He concluded his term on Mar. 3, 1873, having been defeated for reelection by John Percival Jones [*q.v.*]. This was his last political office. About two years later he sailed from San Francisco for New York, apparently in good health, but during the voyage he lost his mind, and after living many months under this cloud he died on Dec. 25, 1876, at White Plains, N. Y.

Nye was of medium height, weighed nearly two hundred pounds, but was well built, with small hands and feet. His dancing black eyes, expressive features, and shoulder-length snow-white hair gave him in his later years a striking appearance, while his genial humor, quick repartee, and natural gift for oratory gave him power in social as well as in political life. The name "Gray Eagle" was bestowed upon him in recognition of his abundant life and vitality. The friend of Captain Jim of the Washoe Indian tribe as well as of President Lincoln, he swapped stories with both. He was a prolific user of Bible quotations, though not always in anecdote of the choicest character. In Fabius, N. Y., he had married Elsie Benson, and they had two children.

[G. H. Nye and F. E. Best, *A Geneal. of the Nye Family* (1907); *Frank Leslie's Illus. Newspaper*, Mar. 20, 1858, Sept. 14, 1872; *Hist. of Nev.* (1881), ed. by Myron Angel; H. H. Bancroft, *Hist. of Nev., Colo., and Wyo.* (1890); *Biog. Dir. Am. Cong.* (1928); *Daily Territorial Enterprise* (Virginia City, Nev.), Dec. 29, 1876; *N. Y. Times*, Dec. 28, 1876; *Daily Alta California*, May 24, 27, 1875, Dec. 29, 1876, Jan. 19, 1877.] J. E. W.

OAKES, GEORGE WASHINGTON OCHS (Oct. 27, 1861–Oct. 26, 1931), editor, was born in Cincinnati, Ohio, the son of Julius Ochs [*q.v.*] and Bertha (Levy) Ochs. In 1865 the family moved to Knoxville, Tenn., where George attended public and private schools and earned a little money by delivering newspapers. In the fall of 1876, he entered East Tennessee University (later the University of Tennessee). On the completion of his junior year in 1879 he joined his family in Chattanooga. He won the highest distinction in his class in mathematics and Greek in his sophomore and junior years, and when his class graduated in 1880, on account of his high record during his three years, he was awarded the B.A. degree along with the other graduates. Some two years before, his elder brother, Adolph S. Ochs, had become owner of the *Chattanooga Daily Times,* and after leaving college George began his journalistic career as a reporter on this paper. In two years' time he was made city editor; a year later, news editor; and in 1884, managing editor. This position he occupied until late in the eighties, when he assumed charge of the *Tradesman,* a semimonthly industrial magazine controlled by the *Times,* returning to the latter as general manager in 1896 when Adolph Ochs purchased the *New York Times.*

During these years he took a lively interest in public affairs and served locally in various official capacities. In 1891 he was appointed police commissioner. A delegate to the National Democratic Convention the following year, he delivered a speech in support of Cleveland and was active in his interests during the campaign that followed. On Oct. 10, 1893, he was elected mayor of Chattanooga and assumed office Oct. 16; he was reëlected in 1895, and served until October 1897. His administration was characterized by such economy and business efficiency that the city debt was practically wiped out and a low tax rate maintained, although new school buildings were erected and a park system and city hospital established. In 1895 he served as vice-president of the National Municipal League. During the Bryan campaign of 1896 the *Chattanooga Times* supported John M. Palmer, the candidate of the Gold Democrats, much to the annoyance of local politicians, some of whom demanded that Ochs resign as mayor. After the completion of his second term as mayor, he served as president of the board of education. He was active in the establishment of the earliest public library in the city and became its president. In 1891 he made the first of numerous trips to Europe, during which he recorded his experiences in a series of letters which were published in the *Chattanooga Times.*

In 1900 his brother Adolph placed him in charge of the publication of a daily edition of the *New York Times* at the Paris Exposition Universelle. He carried through the project with great success and for his services was made a Chevalier of the Legion of Honor. Upon his return to the United States he became general manager of the Philadelphia *Times,* which his brother had purchased on May 5, 1901. The following year the *Public Ledger* was acquired and merged with the *Times* and Ochs was made publisher and general manager. This publication became the reform newspaper of Philadelphia and was in part responsible for the election of Rudolph Blankenburg [*q.v.*] as mayor. On Jan. 30, 1907, he married Bertie Gans of Philadelphia, by whom he had two sons. In 1912, Cyrus H. K. Curtis bought the *Ledger* from Adolph Ochs, and George remained as publisher. Finding himself out of sympathy with Curtis's policies and methods he resigned at the end of 1914.

In the summer of 1915 he went to New York at the invitation of his brother to become editor of the *New York Times Current History* (after February 1916, *Current History*) and of the *Mid-Week Pictorial,* also an auxiliary of the *Times.* With the former he was associated for the remainder of his life. It was founded to record impartially the economic, political, and military developments growing out of the World War, and at the close of the war it was continued as a journal of significant happenings throughout the world.

Greatly embittered against the Germans by the events of the war, he determined that he would not hand down to his descendants a name of German origin, and early in 1917 he was given permission by the Philadelphia court of common pleas to change his name to George Washington Ochs Oakes. He was too old to be accepted for service in the war and was unwilling to accept a "swivel-chair position with a commission"; but he enlisted as a private in the New York militia. Few did more to develop public opinion on the issues of the struggle than did he. In New York he abstained from political activities, but was a member of numerous civic and social organizations.

He was a sagacious editor, a man of delightful personality, and had an unquenchable interest in things of the mind. He had nearly completed the requirements for the degree of Ph.D. at Columbia at the time of his death. Perhaps his most marked characteristic was his tolerance. Himself conservative, orthodox in economic beliefs, and austere in morals, he welcomed and sought for *Current History* all shades of thought. After his death selections from his voluminous writings, arranged and edited by William M. Schuyler, were published under the title, *The Life and Letters of George Washington Ochs-Oakes.*

[In addition to the above, see *Current Hist.,* Dec. 1931; *N. Y. Times,* Oct. 27, 28, 1931; *Chattanooga Times,* Oct. 27, 1931; *Am. Hebrew,* Oct. 30, 1931.]

A. B. H.

OAKES, THOMAS FLETCHER (July 15, 1843–Mar. 14, 1919), railroad executive, was born in Boston, Mass., the son of Francis Garaux and Caroline Comfort (Paige) Oakes, and a descendant of Nathaniel Oak who emigrated to Massachusetts, probably from Wales, about 1660. He was educated in the public schools and under private tutors. When he was twenty years of age he began work with a firm of contractors engaged in the construction of the Kansas Pacific Railroad, the eastern division of the Union Pacific. From this company he entered the service of the railroad itself in 1865 as purchasing agent and assistant treasurer. For the following six years he was general freight agent. He was then elected vice-president and after serving in this capacity for seven years he was appointed general superintendent. During this period James F. Joy of Detroit, with the aid of Boston capitalists, was endeavoring to build up a transcontinental system out of the Michigan Central, the Chicago, Burlington & Quincy, the Kansas City, Fort Scott & Gulf, and other shorter lines, but after the panic of 1873 the system disintegrated and the western lines were shifted from one group to another. Oakes had attracted the attention of the Boston owners by his ability, and in 1879 he was asked to become general superintendent of the Kansas City, Fort Scott & Gulf and the Kansas City, Lawrence & Southern Railroad companies, which with their branches made up about six hundred miles. He had occupied this position only a year when in May 1880 he was asked by Henry Villard to take the managership of the Oregon Railway & Navigation Company, which had been organized shortly before. Villard was at this time obtaining control of the Northern Pacific Railroad Company, and with the company just mentioned he practically monopolized both the north and south shores of the Columbia River as well as the navigation of the stream itself. When Villard became president of the Northern Pacific in June 1881, Oakes was elected director and vice-president, in which position he remained until his election as president in 1888.

As vice-president Oakes was in charge of the operating and construction departments, and also of the traffic and land departments, acting as executive officer to the president. When he assumed these duties the eastern division of the Northern Pacific had pushed west as far as Dickinson, Dakota Territory, while the western division stopped at Sprague, Washington Territory. The gap remaining to be built to connect these termini was about a thousand miles and embraced the most difficult portions of the work on the main line, including the crossing of the mountains and the building of two long tunnels. Yet in a little over two years he not only completed this work but built an additional thousand miles. He also reorganized the system of operation and increased its effectiveness. The panic of 1893 affected the Northern Pacific very severely, and in that year Oakes resigned the presidency and was appointed general receiver, in which capacity he acted from 1893 to 1895. After his retirement from this work he resided in Concord, Mass., but for several years maintained a connection with the banking firm of Taylor, Cutting & Company at 7 Wall Street, New York. He died at Seattle, Wash., where he had spent the last years of his life. His wife was before her marriage Abby Rogers Haskell of Gloucester, Massachusetts. They had five children, four of whom survived him.

[Biographical data concerning Oakes are meager. See *Who's Who in America,* 1910–11; *The Biog. Directory of Railway Officials of America,* 1913; *Railway Age,* Mar. 21, 1919; E. V. Smalley, *Hist. of the Northern Pacific Railroad* (1883); R. E. Riegel, *The Story of the Western Railroads* (1926); H. L. Oak, *Oak-Oaks-Oakes: Family Reg.* (1906); the *Post-Intelligencer* (Seattle, Wash.), Mar. 14, 1919. Information as to certain facts was supplied by Oakes's son, Prescott Oakes.]

E. L. B.

OAKES, URIAN (*c.* 1631–July 25, 1681), colonial poet, clergyman, and college president, was born in England, probably in London, in 1631 or 1632, and was brought to Cambridge, Mass., by his parents, Edward and Jane Oakes, about the year 1640. He received the degree of B.A. at Harvard with the class of 1649 and was named fellow of the college in the charter of 1650. The annual Cambridge almanac for 1650 was prepared by Oakes, who filled the blank spaces with an outline history of the world. On the title-page appears the epigram "Parvum parva decent; sed inest sua gratia parvis," the first three words (Horace, *Ep.* I, vii, 44) being a playful allusion to the author's diminutive stature. Returning to England after three years' tutoring of Harvard students, he became minister of Tichfield, Hants. Silenced by the Act of Uniformity in 1662, he became for a time headmaster of the Southwark Grammar School (John Oldmixon,

The British Empire in America, 1741 ed., I, 219) ; and then, when the persecution of dissenters had abated, organized a Congregational church at Tichfield. Eventually the Church of Cambridge, Mass., gave him a call, which he accepted in 1671.

Oakes had a high reputation in his day for social qualities, classical wit, and elegant Latinity (see example in *Magnalia,* Bk. IV, chap. vi). He is best remembered for his one published poem, the *Elegie* on Thomas Shepard, which, in the opinion of Moses C. Tyler "reaches the highest point touched by American poetry" in the colonial era (*post,* II, p. 16). His prose style was flexible, energetic, and dignified. As official orator on notable occasions, he lent the vigor of his English and grace of his delivery to the service of the orthodox cause; for unlike many New-England divines who had sojourned in the old country, Oakes stanchly supported early New-England principles, and frankly regarded "an unbounded Toleration as the first born of all Abominations" (*New-England Pleaded With,* 1673, p. 54). With Increase Mather and two other divines, he was appointed a censor of the Massachusetts press (*Proceedings of the Massachusetts Historical Society,* 2 ser. IX, 1895, p. 444) ; but his respect for authorities did not extend to those of Harvard College. Out of disappointment, perhaps, at not being offered the presidency after the death of Charles Chauncy, Oakes became ringleader of those who wrecked the promising administration of Leonard Hoar [*q.v.*]. After Hoar had been driven out, Oakes twice declined to be his successor; but while continuing his duties to the Cambridge church, he consented to be "acting President." Jasper Danckaerts' depressing picture of the unshepherded Harvard student body (*Journal,* 1913, ed. by B. B. James and J. F. Jameson, pp. 266–68) was during Oakes's "acting," or rather inactive, presidency of five years. Only twenty-two students—fewer than at any similar period in the college history—were graduated; but these included Cotton Mather, John Leverett, and the two Brattles; and Oakes did get a much-needed new building, the first Harvard Hall, completed. Upon being again elected president, Feb. 9, 1679/80 (correct date in *Colonial Society of Massachusetts, Publications,* XV, p. clii) and being voted a salary of £50 and a new President's Lodge, Oakes consented to be formally installed; but before having much opportunity to mend matters, he died.

[Contemporary estimates may be found in John Sherman's preface to Oakes's *Soveraign Efficacy of Divine Providence* (1682) ; in *A Poem Dedicated to the Memory of . . . Mr. Vrian Oakes* (Boston, 1682), Cotton Mather's first published work, reprinted in *Proc. Mass. Hist. Soc.,* 2 ser. XII (1899), and in the same author's *Magnalia Christi Americana,* Bk. IV, chap. v. J. L. Sibley, *Biog. Sketches of Grads. of Harvard Univ.,* I (1873), 173–85, is uncritical, but has a bibliography of Oakes's published writings ; M. C. Tyler, in *A Hist. of Am. Lit. During the Colonial Time* (rev. ed., 1897), II, 15–18, 163–67, is even more eulogistic than contemporaries. Josiah Quincy, *The Hist. of Harvard Univ.* (1840), I, 34–38, is somewhat severe. Oakes's elegy on Shepard (Cambridge, 1677) has been reprinted in *Elegies and Epitaphs* (1896), ed. by J. F. Hunnewell, and there are selections in Tyler, *op. cit.* The unique copy of his *Almanack for the Year of our Lord 1650* is in the H. E. Huntington Library ; but it will be found in Charles L. Nichols, *A Coll. of Photographic Reproductions of Mass. Almanacs, 1646–1700.* The records of his college administration are in *Colonial Soc. of Mass. Pubs.,* vols. XV and XVI (1925). A feeble elegy on Oakes by Daniel Gookin, Jr., is printed *Ibid.,* XX (1920), 248–52.]

S.E.M.

OAKLEY, ANNIE (Aug. 13, 1860–Nov. 3, 1926), markswoman, was born in a log-cabin in Patterson Township, Darke County, Ohio, the sixth of the eight children of Jake Mozee and his wife Susanne, and was named Phoebe Anne Oakley Mozee. Her parents had emigrated to Ohio from Pennsylvania. When she was four years old her father died as the result of exposure in a blizzard, and until her mother's remarriage made a home for her Annie suffered to the full the hardships of the unfriended orphan. When nine years old she began to shoot rabbits and quail and was, almost from the start, a dead shot. In the course of five years she paid off the mortgage on the farm with game that she shipped by stagecoach to the Cincinnati market and gained a local reputation as a markswoman. A year or so later she was taken to Cincinnati to shoot a match with Frank E. Butler, a vaudeville performer, and defeated him by one point. Butler fell in love with the girl, kept up a correspondence with her for several years, married her, and, when his partner fell sick, used her as an assistant in his act. On the stage her girlish charm and inerrant shooting won her instantaneous success; she became the feature of the act, and Butler, with a self-effacement almost unbelievable in an actor, became her assistant and personal manager. While trouping with Sells Brothers Circus they played New Orleans when Buffalo Bill was there with his Wild West Show, and, liking the friendly spirit of his outfit, they joined it the next spring (1885) at Louisville. Nate Salsbury, Cody's perspicacious manager, lost no time in making Annie Oakley a star, and for seventeen years, with but one interruption, she was one of the chief features of the show. Rifle or shotgun in hand, she seemed to become a shooting machine. At thirty paces she would slice a playing-card held with the thin edge toward her, hit dimes tossed in the air, or shatter a cigarette held in her husband's lips. A playing-card flung in the air she would perforate a half-dozen times before it fluttered to the ground; to this day theatrical passes, meal tickets, and complimentary tickets of all kinds are known as "Annie Oakleys," because of the punch-marks in them. In the course of her career she smashed more glass balls than any one else that ever lived. In one contest, with a .22 rifle, she broke 943 out of 1000. In a single day she made a record of 4772 out of 5000. In England and on the continent of Europe she was almost as great a favorite as in the United States. Queen Victoria was especially charmed by her, and the Crown Prince of Germany (later William II) insisted, to the consternation of everyone but himself and the markswoman, that she shoot a cigarette from his lips. In 1901 she was severely injured in a railroad wreck, and for a time her career seemed at an end. She recovered, however, and, though partially paralyzed for a while, made some of her most sensational records during the next two decades. For a number of years her home was at Nutley, N. J. Later she lived at Pinehurst, N. C., and in Florida, and frequently returned to her native county. Herself childless, she supported and educated some eighteen orphan girls. To the last her favorite reading was in the New Testament. In 1903 she brought suit against more than fifty newspapers for printing a libelous article on her and won all but a few of them. She died at Greenville, Ohio, in her sixty-seventh year and was buried at Brock, near her birthplace. Her husband died three weeks later.

[C. R. Cooper, *Annie Oakley—Woman at Arms* (1927) is based on the autobiographical notes and scrap-books that Mrs. Butler gave to Fred Stone, the comedian, but the material has been carelessly used. See also F. E. Wilson, *Hist. of Darke County, Ohio* (1914), I, 348–52, and the *N. Y. Times*, Nov. 5, 6, 14, 24, Dec. 28, 1926. Many American newspapers printed editorials and extended biographical notices of her at the time of her death.] G. H. G.

OAKLEY, THOMAS JACKSON (Nov. 10, 1783–May 11, 1857), jurist, was born in Beekman, Dutchess County, N. Y., the son of a Revolutionary officer and farmer, Lieut. Jesse Oakley, and Jerushah (Peters) Oakley. He was graduated from Yale in 1801, studied law in Poughkeepsie, and practised there after his admission to the bar in 1804. In 1808 he was married to Lydia S. Williams, the daughter of Robert Williams, a Federalist lawyer of Poughkeepsie. Through his father-in-law's influence he was appointed surrogate of Dutchess County (1810) but lost this position a year later by a party reversal. As a Federalist member of the Thirteenth Congress (1813–15) he was a critic

of the administration and of the War of 1812. From 1816 to 1820 he was a member and Federalist leader of the state Assembly. He supported the Erie Canal project, the bill for founding the state library, and was counsel for the defendant in the impeachment trial of Judge W. W. Van Ness, in which the latter was acquitted. In 1819 he succeeded Martin Van Buren to the office of attorney-general of the state but was removed in 1821 for political reasons. Associated with Thomas A. Emmet and opposed by Daniel Webster and William Wirt, he represented New York state in *Gibbons* vs. *Ogden* (9 *Wheaton*, 1). Because of his able arguments in this case and in others before the Supreme Court, he rose to the front ranks as an advocate. He represented the claimants, Astor and Fowler, in a case which involved a large tract of land in Putnam County, confiscated during the Revolution because of Tory ownership, and he was conspicuous in litigation in New York state between landlords and their tenants which eventually degenerated into the anti-rent disturbances. In 1826 he was elected as a Clinton Democrat to the Twentieth Congress but resigned in 1828 to become a judge of the superior court of New York City. He remained on the bench until his death, becoming chief justice in 1847. As a judge he was noted for his impartiality, his quick grasp of the controlling factors of a case, and his clear and direct charges to the jury. He was a member of the Kent Club, an organization composed of leading lawyers and judges who met on Saturday nights for legal and scientific discussions after which "reports of champagne bottles were preferred to law reports" (Allan Nevins, ed., *The Diary of Philip Hone*, 1927, I, p. 396). He was a member of the Calvary Church and for many years an active member of the diocesan conventions of the Protestant Episcopal Church. After the death of his first wife in 1827 he was married, on Mar. 29, 1831, to Matilda Caroline Cruger. Four children by the second marriage survived him. In private life he was simple in habits, approachable and unostentatious. On the bench he was punctual, rigorous, and formal. He had a majestic bearing and spoke easily with "but little rhetoric or gesticulation."

[F. B. Dexter, *Biog. Sketches of the Grads. of Yale Coll.*, vol. V (1911); "In Memoriam," 24 *Superior Court* (City of N. Y.) *Reports*, pp. xv–xxii; Charles Warren, *A Hist. of the Am. Bar* (1911); David McAdam and others, *Hist. of the Bench and Bar of N. Y.*, vol. I (1897); M. B. Flint, *A Peters Lineage* (n.d.); H. W. Reynolds, ed., *The Records of Christ Church, Poughkeepsie, N. Y.*, vol. II (1919); D. R. Fox, *The Decline of Aristocracy in the Politics of N. Y.* (1918); the *Green Bag*, Sept. 1892; *N. Y. Herald*, May 13, 1857.] A. L. M.

OATES, WILLIAM CALVIN (Nov. 30, 1835–Sept. 9, 1910), Confederate soldier, congressman, governor of Alabama, was born in Pike (now Bullock) County, Ala. His father's ancestors, of Welsh descent, had settled in South Carolina before the Revolutionary War, and his father, William Oates, had moved into Alabama some years before the birth of his son. His mother, Sarah (Sellers) Oates, had an Irish and French heritage. The family lived in extreme poverty, and Oates for only a few months at rare intervals was able to attend a country school. When he was sixteen years old he went to the Southwest, where he made a precarious living as a painter and a carpenter. Returning to Alabama, he taught a few months, attended school for a few months, and taught again. In this way he graduated from the Lawrenceville academy and financed himself while he studied law at Eufaula. He was admitted to the bar in 1858 and began practice in Abbeville in 1859, supplementing his small income by editing a Democratic newspaper. He raised a company of infantry for the Confederate army in 1861. It became a part of the 15th Alabama Infantry, and he served as its captain until 1863 when, having commanded the regiment at Sharpsburg (Antietam), he received the rank of colonel upon the recommendation of General Hood. He held the extreme right of the Confederate line during the assault on Little Round Top at the battle of Gettysburg, and, when his regiment had been transferred to the west, he took part in the battles of Chickamauga and Lookout Mountain. In 1864, he was assigned to command the 48th Alabama Infantry and returned to Virginia. He was wounded at Brown's Ferry and lost his right arm at Fussell's Mill near Petersburg in August 1864. At that time he had been recommended for promotion to the rank of brigadier-general.

In 1865 he resumed his law practice and entered politics. He was a delegate to the National Democratic Convention in 1868, served in the Alabama House of Representatives from 1870 to 1872, and in 1875 was chairman of the judicial committee in the state constitutional convention. He was elected to Congress from the 3rd district in 1880, reëlected six times, and resigned in 1894, when he was elected governor of his state. In Congress he was the only member of the Alabama delegation to support Cleveland in his demand for the repeal of the Sherman Silver Purchase Act. In 1890, when the Farmers' Alliance was strong, he bitterly opposed the sub-treasury scheme and led the hard-money forces of the state. His gubernatorial campaign of 1894 against Reuben F. Kolb [*q.v.*] was one of the most exciting in the history of the state after the Reconstruction period. As "the one-armed hero" of Henry County he stumped the state for sound money and succeeded in carrying the election by a good majority. His two years in office were not years of achievement. It was not an easy time to be the governor of an agricultural state, when prices were low, money scarce, and taxes hard to collect. The state could not borrow money, and part of the time salaries were unpaid. In 1897 he was a candidate for the nomination of his party to the United States Senate, an honor that he had refused seven years earlier, but the Silver men were in the saddle and gave the nomination to Gen. Edmund W. Pettus. Made brigadier-general of volunteers by President McKinley, he served through the Spanish-American War at Camp Meade, Pa., where he commanded three different brigades. He served as a delegate-at-large to the state constitutional convention in 1901, where he acted as chairman of the committee on the legislative department and of the committee on suffrage and elections. He was one of the few men who opposed the soldier and grandfather clauses and demanded an equal standard of fitness for members of both races who should be granted suffrage (*Speeches . . . in the Constitutional Convention . . . 1901*, n.d.). The last years of his life were spent in the practice of law at Montgomery and in writing. He published "Gettysburg—the Battle on the Right" in *Southern Historical Society Papers* (Oct. 1878) and "Industrial Development of the South," *North American Review* (Nov. 1895). He also published *Speeches of Hon. W. C. Oates in the House of Representatives, 1880 to 1894* (n.d.), and wrote his recollections of the Civil War, *The War between the Union and the Confederacy* (1905). He was survived by his wife, Sallie (Toney) Oates, to whom he had been married on Mar. 28, 1882.

[T. M. Owen, *Hist. of Ala. and Dict. of Ala. Biog.* (1921), vol. IV; J. B. Clark, *Populism in Ala.* (1927); J. Sparkman, "The Kolb-Oates Campaign of 1894" (Univ. of Ala. thesis, 1924); *War of the Rebellion: Official Records (Army)*, 1 ser., XIX, XXVII, XXX–XXXII; *Montgomery Advertiser*, Sept. 10, 1910.]
H. F.—r.

OATMAN, JOHNSON (Apr. 21, 1856–Sept. 25, 1922), gospel hymn writer, was born near Medford, N. J., and died at the home of his daughter in Norman, Okla. His parents were Johnson Oatman and Rachel Ann Cline. He learned to sing with his father, was educated at Herbert's Academy, Vincentown, and at the New Jersey Collegiate Institute, Bordentown, now the Bordentown Military School. He joined the Methodist church, was licensed as a local preacher, and was ordained deacon by Bishop Stephen M. Merrill at Burlington on Mar. 24, 1895, but he did not enter the itinerant ministry. For a while he was in business with his father at Lumberton, N. Y., later conducting the business of a life-insurance company at Mount Holly. On July 21, 1878, he was married to Wilhelmina Ried of Lumberton, with whom he lived until her death in 1909. A son and two daughters were born to them. Failing health in 1893 compelled Oatman to retire from his business and he then settled at Ocean Grove. The summer meetings at this resort were congenial to his religious nature and with returning health and strength, and encouraged by his surroundings, he found what proved to be the outlet for his spiritual nature. It was not his desire to take charge of a church, but to do his preaching through songs. His first gospel song, "I am walking with my Master," was written in 1892 and was set to music by John R. Sweney, who published it the following year. Encouraged by the latter he began to feel that his real work in life was to spread the gospel through his songs and he began to express in verse the emotions and sentiments of his own life. "When our Ships come sailing home," inspired by his stay near the ocean, was also set to music by Sweney, and was one of the favorites of its author, but it did not become so popular as some of his other hymns. "No, not one," has appeared in more recent hymn books than any other of his songs. Written in 1895, it was copied into thirty-five different collections within a single year, and it has been translated into many languages. "Count your Blessings" was likewise incorporated into many hymnals, and "Higher Ground" and "Sweeter than all" were widely sung. He wrote the words of at least seven thousand hymns which have been set to music by such composers as J. Howard Entwisle, Adam Geibel, A. J. Showalter, Charles H. Gabriel, George C. Hugg, and William J. Kirkpatrick.

[J. H. Hall, *Biog. of Gospel Song and Hymn Writers* (1914); C. H. Gabriel, "The Singers and Their Songs," *Epworth Herald*, Apr. 10, 1915; *Minutes, N. J. Conf., Meth. Episc. Ch.*, 1886; *Minutes of Ann. Conferences of the Meth. Episc. Ch.*, 1895; the *Music Teacher and Home Mag.*, June 1924; information as to certain facts from Oatman's daughter, Mrs. Frederick F. Blachly, Washington, D. C.]   Γ. J. M.

OBER, FREDERICK ALBION (Feb. 13, 1849–May 31, 1913), ornithologist, was born in Beverly, Mass., the eldest child of Andrew Kimball and Sarah Abby (Hadlock) Ober. On his father's side he was descended from Richard Ober who emigrated from Abbotsbury, Eng-

land, to the Salem colony and settled in Mackerel Cove, later Beverly, on a grant of land from the King. From early childhood he was interested in natural history, but the lack of funds prevented him from getting far in his schooling. Before he reached manhood he had stuffed and mounted a collection of local birds which interested Alexander Agassiz of the museum at Harvard University. Later his collection was bought by the university and that gave young Ober the means to begin his life work. In 1872–74, having a connection with *Forest and Stream* and the Smithsonian Institution, he collected birds in Florida and explored the Lake Okechobee region. He wrote several articles on his experiences for *Forest and Stream* under the pen name of Fred Beverly. Later (1876–78, and 1880) he collected extensively in the Lesser Antilles, discovering twenty-two species of birds new to science, two of which were named after him—a flycatcher, *Myiarchus oberi,* and an oriole, *Icterus oberi.* The results of the first Antilles expedition were published under the title "Ornithological Exploration of the Caribee Islands" in the *Annual Report of the Board of Regents of the Smithsonian Institution . . . for the year 1878* (1879). He subsequently made several trips to Mexico, and still later to Spain, northern Africa, South America, and again to the West Indian islands. He served as United States commissioner for the Columbian Exposition at Chicago, having supervision of the ornithological exhibits. The government awarded him a diploma and bronze medal for his services.

Ober was a prolific writer and made use of his knowledge of Mexico and the West Indies in books of travel and adventure and historical tales. In his Heroes of American History Series he published the biographies of ten early explorers. Perhaps best known is his *Guide to the West Indies* (1908) of which a third edition was published in 1920. In 1908 Ober entered the real-estate business in Hackensack, N. J., and remained there until his death. He was married three times. When he was twenty-one years old he was married to Lucy Curtis of Wenham, Mass., but she died within a few months. In the early nineties he married Jean MacCloud of New Hampshire, and she died within a couple of years. His travels in out-of-the-way places were partly attempts to assuage his grief. In 1895 he married Nellie MacCartny of Cambridge, Mass., who survived him about a year. She left two children. Ober's lasting work, with which his name will always be connected, was his zoölogical exploration of the Lesser Antilles.

Oberholtzer

[Who's Who in America, 1912–13; Forest and Stream, June 7, 1913; the World (N.Y.), June 2, 1913; information as to certain facts from Ober's relatives.] H. F—n.

OBERHOLTZER, SARA LOUISA VICKERS (May 20, 1841–Feb. 2, 1930), author, leader in movement for school savings, was born in Uwchlan, Chester County, Pa., the daughter of Paxson and Ann (Lewis) Vickers. Her father's ancestors were Quakers who came from England to Eastern Pennsylvania about the time of William Penn's second visit to Philadelphia. Her great-grandfather and grandfather, Thomas and John Vickers, were owners of earthenware potteries in Chester County. She was educated by private tutors, at the Friends' Boarding School, and at the Millersville State Normal School. On Jan. 1, 1862, she married John Oberholtzer of Chester County, who became a merchant in Philadelphia. Having from an early age shown considerable literary talent, she contributed articles to magazines and other periodicals and published hymns, letters of travel, pamphlets, and several volumes of verse, including *Violet Lee* (1873); *Come for Arbutus* (1882); *Daisies of Verse* (1886); and *Souvenirs of Occasions* (1892). She was also the author of *Hope's Heart Bells* (1884), a novel of Quaker life in Pennsylvania. She wrote the "Burial Ode" for the funeral services of Bayard Taylor at Longwood, verses for the dedication of the monument at Antietam Bridge, and many other commemorative poems. While John Greenleaf Whittier was engaged in anti-slavery work in Philadelphia he formed a close friendship with her that lasted until his death.

Mrs. Oberholtzer devoted much time to social and philanthropic as well as literary activities. Organizing the Anti-Tobacco Society in 1881 and the Longport Agassiz Microscopical Society in 1884, she served as president of both organizations for several years. She was president of the Pennsylvania Woman's Press Association, 1903–05, and took a prominent part in the World's and in the National W.C.T.U. Becoming interested in 1888 in methods of thrift teaching used in the public schools of Europe, especially in France and Belgium, she became an ardent advocate of school savings banks. She wrote letters, articles, and pamphlets, spoke in nearly every state in the union urging women's organizations to promote the idea and teachers to undertake the work, and labored with banks and trust companies to persuade them to receive the small deposits. For many years she edited *School Savings,* published from 1907 until 1923 under the name of *Thrift Tidings,* a periodical devoted to the promotion of the project. She saw the movement develop until in 1929 there were 15,598 schools using the system in forty-six out of the forty-eight states, with 4,222,935 depositors, while it had the support of legislators, teachers, and bankers. Mrs. Oberholtzer died at her home in Philadelphia and was survived by two sons.

[Who's Who in America, 1920–21; J. S. Futhey and Gilbert Cope, Hist. of Chester County, Pa. (1881); Woman's Who's Who of America, 1914–15; W. E. Albig, A Hist. of School Savings Banking (1930), a pamphlet published by the Am. Bankers Asso.; N. Y. Times, Feb. 4, 1930; information as to certain facts from Mrs. Oberholtzer's son, E. P. Oberholtzer of Philadelphia.] A.L.L.

O'Brien

O'BRIEN, EDWARD CHARLES (Apr. 20, 1860–June 21, 1927), merchant, diplomat, was born in Fort Edward, N. Y., the son of James O'Brien, a well-to-do Irish farmer, and Mary (Walsh) O'Brien. Following his education in the public schools and in the Granville (N.Y.) Military Academy, he engaged for several years in the flour-commission business in Plattsburg, N. Y. The transportation phase of this business turned his attention toward deep waterways, foreign commerce, and maritime shipping, and these were to remain his major interests through life. He served as disbursing clerk in the United States House of Representatives during the Fifty-first Congress (1889–91). In 1892 and 1893 he was United States commissioner of navigation, and, as chief of the Bureau of Navigation of the Treasury Department, he won recognition for his satisfactory handling of the Norwegian and Swedish tonnage rate case. In 1895 he was appointed by Gov. Levi P. Morton commissary-general of the state of New York with the rank of brigadier-general. He resigned three months later to become commissioner of docks of New York City under Mayor Strong. During his four years in office he accomplished extensive dock improvements, acquired for the city over four million square feet of additional wharfage space by securing permission from the War Department to extend the pier head line farther into the North River, and constructed the city's first six recreation piers. Appreciation of his activities in behalf of inland deep waterways, particularly with regard to a proposed ship canal connecting the Great Lakes with the Hudson River, was shown in his appointment as chairman of the opening session of the first annual convention of the International Deep Waterways Association at Cleveland in September 1895. Following his retirement to private life in 1898 he organized and became president of the International Express Company, and of the Cuban and Pan-American Express Company.

In March 1905 O'Brien was appointed envoy extraordinary and minister plenipotentiary of the United States to Uruguay and Paraguay by President Roosevelt. During his four years' residence in Montevideo and Asunción he negotiated and signed a naturalization convention between the United States and Uruguay (Aug. 10, 1908), and an arbitration convention between the United States and Paraguay (Mar. 13, 1909). He was dean of the diplomatic corps at Asunción when the Paraguay revolution of July 2, 1908, occurred. With great coolness and diplomacy, and with the cooperation of his colleagues, he succeeded through his friendly offices in bringing about a cessation of hostilities, risking his life several times during the two days of heavy street fighting. He was afterward thanked by both the successful revolutionists and the defeated government leaders for his service in preventing a much greater loss of life and property than that which actually occurred. He resigned from the diplomatic service in 1909 and subsequently engaged in many enterprises connected with the development of South American ports and internal communications, and Latin-American trade with the United States, at the same time neglecting no opportunity to promote understanding and good will between the South American countries and the United States. At the time of his death he was visiting Montevideo on business connected with the construction of a motor highway joining the capitals of Uruguay and Argentina. He was buried in Troy, N. Y. He had never married.

[*Proc. First Ann. Convention, Internat. Deep Waterways Asso.*, 1895; *Municipal Affairs* (N. Y.), Sept. 1897; U. S. Bureau of Navigation, *Reports of the Commissioner of Navigation*, 1892, 1893; *Papers Relating to the Foreign Relations of the U. S.*, 1908; *Who's Who in America*, 1920–21; *Who's Who in N. Y. City and State* (3rd ed., 1907); *N. Y. Times*, June 22, 1927.]   I. L. T.

O'BRIEN, FITZ–JAMES (*c.* 1828–Apr. 6, 1862), journalist and author, son of James and Eliza O'Driscoll O'Brien, was born in County Limerick, Ireland, where his father was an attorney-at-law. His characteristic exaggerations and the destruction of records in Ireland have deprived us of accurate knowledge of his early years. He received an excellent education, but not, as is often asserted, at Trinity College, Dublin. At an early age he evinced a certain facility in writing verse and he seems to have determined upon a literary career. When he was about twenty-one he settled in London and during the course of two years, there and in Paris, he is said to have spent his inheritance of £8,000. Francis Wolle has recently established that before he came to America O'Brien had contributed at least twenty-seven poems, one story, and twelve articles to English and Irish periodicals. He came to America, probably early in 1852, with letters of introduction to George Pope Morris and others. Through them he was quickly welcomed into New York's literary and Bohemian circles where he became a conspicuous figure. He contributed poems, short stories, and articles to a number of periodicals, the *American Whig Review, Putnam's Magazine, Harper's Weekly, Vanity Fair,* and the *Atlantic Monthly,* but his most important literary association was that of regular contributor to *Harper's Magazine.* From time to time he contributed to the *Evening Post* and the *New York Times,* and for the latter he was once an editorial writer. For James W. Wallack he wrote several plays which gained some popular favor; one of these, *A Gentleman from Ireland,* was presented successfully as late as 1895. He adapted a play for Joseph Jefferson, who was the manager and principal actor at Laura Keene's Theatre, and he once traveled for a short time as literary assistant to H. L. Bateman who was directing a professional tour of Matilda Heron, the actress.

There have been several efforts to arouse public interest in O'Brien as "a neglected genius" and "an enchanted Titan," but they have met with indifferent success. The best of his voluminous poetry is hardly more than clever, spirited verse, and the most effective of his short stories, said to have "electrified" the reading public of the late fifties, have lost the greater part of their appeal. He possessed a facile talent but was hasty and careless in his work. Like many another gifted Irish writer, he was too impatient and undisciplined to cultivate his promising talent. Like several other flickering lights of American literature, he was more significant as a personality than as an author. He was one of the most colorful figures of that Bohemian society that flourished at Windust's, the old Hone House, and Pfaff's in the New York of his day. But the Bohemian "orgies" which afforded him pleasure were confined to late hours, the foaming flagon, and boisterous hilarity. His florid complexion, dark-blue eyes, tiny chin, his heavy, brown cavalry mustache, and his checkered tweed suit were a familiar and welcome sight in those gay and restless circles. He tried to lead the life of a poet and gentleman, retiring with the rising sun and breakfasting at two in the afternoon. During his first six years in New York he lived surrounded by all the trappings of a man of means—an elegant apartment, a large library, and a costly wardrobe. But, beginning in 1858, as a result of that convivial improvidence which marked his career, his waking hours were haunted by waiting landladies, who gradually acquired, in the course of his peregrinations, all his worldly goods. While at times he partially solved his domestic problem by moving into the rooms of such friends as Thomas Bailey Aldrich and William Winter, he was often reduced to the point where he had neither pen, ink, nor paper. The chief distresses of this proud and combative spirit were occasioned by the painful discrepancy between a gentleman's tastes and a hack-writer's income.

Upon the outbreak of the Civil War, O'Brien quickly joined the 7th Regiment of the New York National Guard. When the regiment returned to New York he became active for a time in gathering recruits for a volunteer regiment to be called the McClellan Rifles, but this failed. In January 1862 he was taken on the staff of Gen. Frederick W. Lander. The next month for his gallantry at the battle of Bloomery Gap, he received special and honorable mention, but on Feb. 16 he received a shoulder wound in a skirmish with the enemy which was improperly treated and he died of tetanus on Apr. 6 at Cumberland, Md.

[*Poems and Stories of Fitz-James O'Brien*, collected and edited, with a sketch of the author by Wm. Winter (Boston, 1881) contains reminiscences by O'Brien's friends and reprints contemporary comment on his death. It is the best source of information; later articles have added virtually nothing to this publication. Prof. Francis Wolle of the University of Colorado has supplied information about his early career abroad. See also: R. H. Stoddard, "The Best of the Bohemians," *Critic*, Feb. 26, 1881; Paul Fatout, "An Enchanted Titan," *South Atlantic Quart.*, Jan. 1931; Albert Parry, *Garrets and Pretenders: A Hist. of Bohemianism in America* (1933); *War of the Rebellion: Official Records* (*Army*), 1 ser. V, p. 406; *N. Y. Times*, Apr. 7, 9, 10, 1862.]
         F. M—n.

O'BRIEN, FREDERICK (June 16, 1869–Jan. 9, 1932), journalist, author, was born in Baltimore, the son of William James and Catherine (McCarthy) O'Brien, and a grandson of an Irish immigrant, John O'Brien, who settled in Baltimore in 1820. His father was a lawyer, a Democrat in the national House of Representatives from 1873 to 1877, and in his later years a judge of the city orphans' court. He died in 1905 a highly regarded citizen and magistrate. Of his four sons two had respectable, commonplace careers in business and law, and a third became a Jesuit and a monsignor, but in Frederick the conventional middle-class pattern was crossed with a thread of waywardness. After a few years (1882–85) at Loyola College, where

he read Herman Melville to more effect than the prescribed books, he shipped out of Baltimore as a common sailor and returned with memories of adventures in Brazil, Venezuela, and Trinidad. When the study of law grew unbearably irksome, he went to sea again—this time to Liverpool on a cattle-boat—trudged the sidewalks of the London East End between the boards of a "sandwich," got back to the United States on a freighter, and until 1894 was a hobo and casual laborer. Then he happened into reporting for the Marion, Ohio, *Mirror*, at $8.00 a week, but soon went over to its rival, Warren Gamaliel Harding's *Star*, at $9.00 a week.

For the next twenty-five years, with respites devoted to globe-trotting, he was a newspaperman, likeable, competent, but hardly distinguished. After serving various papers in New York and San Francisco, he was news editor of the Honolulu *Advertiser*, 1900–01; editor and publisher of the Manila *Cablenews*, 1902–09; and manager of the Riverside, Cal., *Enterprise* and the Oxnard *Courier*, 1910–13. He had been married, May 26, 1897, to Gertrude, daughter of Wakefield Gale Frye of Belfast, Me. They had no children and ultimately separated, O'Brien disappearing among the islands of the South Seas to loaf and invite his soul indefinitely. He returned, however, in wartime, was connected with the California railroad commission and the United States food administration, edited the *Manilla Times* for a few months after the Armistice, and then set out on his second trip around the globe.

His first book, *White Shadows in the South Seas* (1919), was an account of his sojourn in the valley of Atuona, on Hivaoa, in the Marquesas. It was published just in time to strike what was virtually a new reading public, weary of war and of the discipline of military life, baffled by the complexities of contemporary society, and eager to escape, in imagination, to the only half-ruined paradise of O'Brien's romantic narrative. The astounding success of *White Shadows* called forth a number of imitators, helped to revive interest in the work of Herman Melville, Charles Warren Stoddard, and Robert Louis Stevenson, and ensured a ready market for O'Brien's subsequent books, magazine articles, and lectures. *Mystic Isles of the South Seas* (1921) dealt with his travels and experiences on Tahiti and Moorea, and *Atolls of the Sun* (1922) with Paumotu or the Low Archipelago. Like the earlier work, they were written in fluent journalese, showed marked sympathy not only for the native races but for individual natives, and were well laden with anecdote and adventure and a tolerant attitude toward the world in general. O'Brien himself lived the last years of his life at Sausalito on San Francisco Bay. Genial, unpretentious, and reticent about himself, he had friends throughout the world, but perhaps no intimates. He died of a heart ailment, after an illness of six months. His body was cremated, with none of his relatives present, and the ashes strewn on the ocean.

[*Who's Who in America*, 1930–31; J. J. Ryan, *Hist. Sketch of Loyola Coll., Baltimore, 1852–1902* (copr. 1903); E. F. Barker, *Frye Geneal.* (1920); Frederick O'Brien, "The Author of 'White Shadows,'" *Bookman*, Dec. 1920; *The Literary Spotlight* (1924), ed. by John Farrar; *Sun* (Baltimore), Nov. 14, 1905, Jan. 10, 1932; *San Francisco Chronicle*, Jan. 10, 11, 1932; *N. Y. Times*, Jan. 10, 12, 1932.]   G. H. G.

O'BRIEN, JEREMIAH (1744–Sept. 5, 1818), naval officer, was born in Kittery, Me., the eldest son of Morris and Mary (Hutchins) Cain O'Brien. Early in life Morris O'Brien followed the tailoring trade, first in his native city of Dublin, Ireland, and later in the towns of Kittery and Scarborough, Me. In 1765 he moved to Machias, Me., then a frontier town recently settled, and, aided by his sons, engaged with much success in lumbering, the main industry of the settlement. At the outbreak of the Revolution he and his family eagerly espoused the cause of the patriots. On June 2, 1775, there arrived at Machias the Boston sloops *Unity* and *Polly*, convoyed by the schooner *Margaretta*, under the command of Midshipman James Moore of the Royal Navy, for the purpose of obtaining a cargo of lumber for the use of the British army. Determined to prevent the shipping of the lumber, Jeremiah O'Brien with about forty volunteers, including his five brothers, armed with guns, swords, axes, and pitchforks, seized the *Unity*, and after a considerable chase, on June 12 engaged and captured the *Margaretta*, 4 guns, with a loss of seven men on each side. Midshipman Moore was mortally wounded. O'Brien exhibited much enterprise and daring in this "Lexington of the seas," the first naval engagement of the war. By a resolution, dated June 26, 1775, the Massachusetts General Court thanked him and his compatriots for their courage and good conduct.

Under the orders of the Machias Committee of Safety, O'Brien took command of the *Unity*, renamed the *Machias Liberty* and armed with the guns of the *Margaretta*. When, a few weeks after his first fight, the British naval schooner *Diligent* with her tender *Tapnaquish* appeared off Machias, he, with the aid of another vessel, captured the two British ships without firing a gun. In August 1775 the General Court, recognizing his ability, placed him in command of the *Machias Liberty* and the *Diligent*, thus taking these vessels into the service of the state, the first ships of the Massachusetts navy. O'Brien cruised intermittently with his small fleet, taking a few prizes, until it was put out of commission in the fall of 1776. He next became a privateersman and in 1777 went to sea in command of the ship *Resolution* and captured the British ship *Scarborough* off Cape Negro. Continuing in this service he was captured in 1780 with his vessel, the *Hannibal*, and was confined first in the Jersey prison ship at New York and later in Mill Prison, England, where he suffered considerable hardship. Escaping, he returned to America and in 1781 commanded successively the *Hibernia* and the *Tiger*.

After the Revolution O'Brien lived a retired life at Machias until 1811 when President Madison appointed him collector of customs for the Machias district, a position he held at the time of his death. He was married, to Elizabeth Fitzpatrick, but appears to have left no descendants. In 1900, in recognition of his valuable services in the Revolution, Secretary of the Navy John D. Long named one of the torpedo boats, then under construction, after this gallant officer.

[A. M. Sherman, *Life of Capt. Jeremiah O'Brien* (1902), and *The O'Briens of Machias, Me.* (1904); *Memorial of the Centennial Anniversary of the Settlement of Machias* (1863); G. W. Allen, *Naval Hist. of the Am. Revolution* (1913); G. W. Drisko, *Narrative of the Town of Machias* (1904); *Boston Daily Advertiser*, Sept. 26, 1818.]   C. O. P.

O'BRIEN, MATTHEW ANTHONY (May 1804–Jan. 15, 1871), Roman Catholic preacher and missionary, son of John and Grace (Meagher) O'Brien, was born in the village of Bawn, County Tipperary, Ireland, where his father managed to rear a family of thirteen children from the profits of a distillery. Trained in a local hedge school and at Nenagh, the boy was poorly educated when in April 1826 he sailed on an immigrant ship for Quebec. From Canada, he managed to work his way to Savannah, Ga., and thence to New Orleans, where he had maternal uncles. Apparently, he had a desire to enter the priesthood, because he tramped and labored on boats for his passage until he reached Bardstown, Ky., where he presented himself to Bishop Flaget [*q.v.*], who urged that he become a lay brother in view of his age, irregular education, and aptitude for a trade. This he did in 1827, but the institute at Bardstown failed and was dissolved, whereupon he was enrolled at St. Rose's, Springfield, Ky. This time ill health thwarted his hopes, but he found a friend in an Irish priest, William Byrne, who had established St. Mary's College, Marion County, Ky. Here, from 1829 to 1835, he taught elementary subjects and was tutored in the classics by the rector and by the Jesuit Fathers who took over the institution. At length he was prepared to enter the Dominican seminary of St. Rose's, where he subscribed to the final vows of the Dominicans on Sept. 8, 1837, and was ordained by Bishop R. P. Miles [q.v.] in 1839. As submaster and master of novices, he continued his studies and reading. There was little expectation that he would develop into a preacher because of his awkward bearing, diffidence, piercing voice, and wretched memory, but he made an ideal novice-master because of his sound common sense, sincere piety, and marked tact. Hence, in 1842, he was assigned to a similar position at St. Joseph's House of Studies in Perry County, Ohio. Not until 1844 was he given a parish—that of St. Patrick's on Rush Creek near by, a German and Irish settlement, where he built a new church, and as procurator for his order superintended its general construction work. His controversy with a Protestant divine, Thomas Harper, and his missionary tours made him a familiar character in Kentucky, Tennessee, and Ohio.

Soon after returning from a short vacation in Ireland, O'Brien was elected American provincial of the Dominicans, Oct. 30, 1850. While St. Rose's remained his center, he was engaged in establishing St. Joseph's College, which died with the Civil War, in building a number of churches, schools, and convents, including St. Dominic's in Washington, D. C., and in promoting vocations for his own order as well as for the Dominican sisterhoods. He brought the Dominicans to the seaboard and won popularity for the order as he preached missions from the Gulf states to New England. Moreover, he became a magnetic if not a brilliant or erudite preacher, whose heartfelt sermons, interspersed with homely illustrations and unvarnished truths, appealed not only to the lowly but challenged critical scholars like J. A. McMaster and Orestes Brownson [qq.v.]. At the end of his term he became prior and pastor at St. Rose's, where he remained from 1854 until ordered to organize a Dominican parish in London, Ontario, in 1861. Two years later, he was recalled to work among the soldiers in Kentucky and to compromise warborn hostilities among the people. He himself was no violent Northern partisan.

As a visiting preacher, O'Brien continued to win attention and incidentally made his share of converts. There were few bishops who were not friends and admirers of the friar and few centers from New York to the Mississippi where he was unknown, stationed as he was at St. Vincent Ferrer's in New York and St. Louis Bertrand's in Louisville. A temperance advocate and a reformer, he had the courage to invade the gambling dens of New Orleans and attack that protected vice. At sixty-six, aged far beyond his years, he fell a victim to pneumonia in Louisville and was buried in the community cemetery at St. Rose's in Kentucky.

[V. F. O'Daniel, *An American Apostle: Matthew A. O'Brien, O. P.* (1923), a detailed, accurate, panegyric; B. J. Webb, *The Centenary of Catholicity in Ky.* (1884); *Freeman's Journal* (N. Y.), Feb. 4, 1871; *Louisville Commercial*, Jan. 17, 1871.]   R. J. P.

O'BRIEN, RICHARD (*c.* 1758–Feb. 14, 1824), mariner, United States consul-general to Algiers, was born in Maine and died in Washington, D. C. In his later years he spelled his name as given above, but during much of his life used the spelling, O Bryen. He was a son of William O Bryen and Rebecca Crane, who were married in 1757 and a few years later went with their four children to Ireland. The father died soon thereafter, leaving his family destitute. Richard, in order to visit his relatives in America, became apprenticed to a sea-captain, and until 1785 led a seafaring life. His formal schooling in consequence of these circumstances was slight; and, according to his own testimony, his reading in youth was limited to a primer, a collection of Aesop's Fables, an arithmetic, the Bible, and a few newspapers (O'Brien to J. L. Cathcart, Nov. 12, 1794, Despatches: Tripoli, II, State Department). The effects of this deficiency O'Brien deplored in later life, although native ability and devotion to the task of becoming a skilful navigator offset them to some extent. During the American Revolution he engaged in privateering and for a time served as a lieutenant on board the brig *Jefferson*. At the end of the war he became master of the ship *Dauphin*, owned by two Philadelphia merchants, but while sailing near Lisbon on July 30, 1785, was captured by Algerine pirates. During the period of his captivity he carried on an extensive correspondence with prominent Americans regarding Algerine affairs; then, when peace was made between the United States and Algiers in September 1795 and he was released, he conveyed a copy of the treaty to Lisbon to be countersigned by the United States' peace commissioner, David Humphreys [q.v.]. From Lisbon O'Brien went to London for funds to put the treaty into operation; then returned to Algiers in March 1796; and in June sailed to the United States to transact further business relative to the treaty. The following October he was commissioned to conclude a treaty of peace with Tripoli, and within less than a month had successfully performed the task. In July 1797 he was appointed consul-general to Algiers, in which capacity he served creditably until November 1803. On Mar. 25, 1799, he married Elizabeth Robeson, an Englishwoman, who prior to her marriage had been a maidservant in the household of J. L. Cathcart [q.v.], in America and for a time in Algiers (Cathcart, *Tripoli, post*, pp. 51, 52).

While the United States was at war with Tripoli, O'Brien found living in Barbary more and more irksome, and frequently expressed a desire to return to America. In November 1803 he was relieved by Col. Tobias Lear [q.v.]. For a time thereafter O'Brien aided Commodore Preble in negotiating with the Pasha of Tripoli; then, in December 1804, he returned to the United States. He settled in Philadelphia temporarily, and in 1808 became a member of the Pennsylvania legislature, serving one term in the lower house. In 1810 he established residence on a farm near Carlisle, Pa., and there spent the greater portion of his remaining years.

[*Am. State Papers: Foreign Relations*, vols. I–II (1832–33); Correspondence of J. L. Cathcart (MSS.), in the *N. Y. Pub. Lib.*; Despatches: Algiers, Tripoli, Tunis, etc. (1793–1805), in Archives of Dept. of State, Washington; autobiographical letter in *New-Eng. Hist. and Geneal. Reg.*, Jan. 1896; J. L. Cathcart, *Tripoli, First War with the U. S.* (1901); *Daily National Intelligencer* (Washington, D. C.), Feb. 16, 1824.]
R. W. I.

O'BRIEN, WILLIAM SHONEY (*c.* 1826–May 2, 1878), capitalist, operator of Nevada silver mines, was born in Queen's County, Ireland, of humble parentage. He came to America before reaching his majority and took out citizenship papers in the New York marine court on Nov. 3, 1845. For a time he considered going to Texas to seek his fortune, but chose to remain in New York, where he found a job in a store. When gold was discovered in California, however, he was one of the first of the "argonauts" to go. He sailed in the ship *Tarolinta* around the Horn and arrived in San Francisco on July 6, 1849, an event which was yearly celebrated by the passengers of the ship as long as O'Brien lived. In San Francisco he was glad to earn a few dollars by helping to discharge the cargo of the vessel and also to accept a pair of boots, whose donor he unsuccessfully sought in later years. In 1850 he went to Poor Man's

Gulch on Feather River to mine, and there met James C. Flood, his later partner. In the fall of 1851 he returned to San Francisco, where until May 1854 he was a partner successively of Col. W. C. Hoff and Capt. W. J. Rosener in operating mercantile lines.

He then joined James C. Flood in the proprietorship of the Auction Lunch Saloon on Washington Street near Sansome, which during the next twelve years was increasingly patronized by mining men and stock-dealers. From these customers the partners obtained advantageous mining information and thus were able to become successful stock-brokers. They also became interested in several mines in the Grass Valley region and in 1866 felt justified in selling their saloon and concentrating upon the mines. The previous year, with J. M. Walker and John William Mackay [q.v.] they had obtained control of the Hale and Norcross mine on the Comstock lode in Nevada, and here they got their first real start on the road to wealth. In combination with Mackay and with James G. Fair [q.v.], who joined them in 1868, they purchased the Consolidated Virginia and the California mines. Soon thereafter the "Big Bonanza" was struck, from which by January 1875 each of the four had derived a princely fortune. In that year they opened the Nevada Bank of San Francisco, with a capital of $5,000,000 which was subsequently increased to $10,000,000.

O'Brien did not live long to enjoy his good luck. Bright's disease, induced by too generous living, killed him within three years. He died at San Rafael, whither he had been taken in hopes of relief, and was buried in a previously prepared mausoleum in Calvary Cemetery, San Francisco, after a pontifical requiem mass at St. Mary's Cathedral. He was never ostentatious of his fortune and although he bought an elegant private residence he remained more or less foreign to his new surroundings. He was noted for his geniality, being called "the jolly millionaire." He was a life member of the Society of California Pioneers and also of the Exempt Firemen California Engine Company Number 4, whom he had served as foreman in 1855–56, when he was given a silver trumpet. Except for the ownership of his mining stock, his partnership with Flood had been dissolved before his death. His vast fortune, with the exception of $100,000 for charities, went to his two sisters and their children.

[*Daily Alta California* (San Francisco), Sept. 3, 1856, Jan. 13, 1877, May 8, 1878, Oct. 20, 1878; Alonzo Phelps, *Contemporary Biog. of California's Representative Men* (1881); Hugh Quigley, *The Irish Race in Cal. and on the Pacific Coast* (1878); *The Exempt Firemen of San Francisco, Their Unique and Gallant*

Record (1900); Rollin Daggett Scrapbook, I, 118, in Cal. State Library.] J. E. W.

O'CALLAGHAN, EDMUND BAILEY (Feb. 28, 1797–May 29, 1880), physician, historian, was born in Mallow, near Cork, Ireland, the youngest of a large family. His education included courses at Dublin, Paris, and Quebec, and he was admitted to the practice of medicine in Canada in 1823. His tastes were literary, however, and he became editor of the *Vindicator* at Montreal in 1834. After a year in the Canadian parliament (1836) he participated in Papineau's revolution of 1837, and found it necessary to flee the country. It would have been easy for him to return later, but he chose to remain in Albany, N. Y., where he resumed the practice of medicine and was for a time treasurer of the Albany County Medical Society. At the same time his literary proclivities were manifested. Interest in the anti-rent agitation led him to a study of the Dutch land grants and thence into early New York history. During the years 1842–44 he contributed poetry and historical articles to *The Northern Light,* a monthly published at Albany in the interest of the working class. In these articles was revealed a casual acquaintance with the mass of Dutch records, at that time undamaged by fire, in the office of the secretary of state. O'Callaghan's interest deepened. His early linguistic studies helped him to master Dutch and to produce the *History of New Netherland* (2 vols., 1846–48). This was a much needed antidote for Irving's burlesque *Knickerbocker* and won immediate commendation. Happily the state of New York realized its opportunity and induced the medical practitioner to give all his time to editing the old records, and for twenty-two years (1848–70) this native of Ireland and fugitive from Canada revealed to New Yorkers their Dutch beginnings. The man's energy was prodigious, as is evidenced by the scores of volumes published during those years, and scholars of three generations later marvel at the breadth of knowledge and the accuracy of workmanship shown by the sharp-eyed collator. The volumes most prized by all research students are *The Documentary History of the State of New York* (4 vols., octavo, 1849–51; 4 vols., quarto, 1850–51), and *Documents Relative to the Colonial History of the State of New York* (vols. I–XI, 1853–61). The second series was continued by Berthold Fernow [*q.v.*], who edited *Documents Relating to the Colonial History of the State of New York* (vols. XII–XV, 1877–87).

Amiability and a fund of Irish wit stood O'Callaghan in good stead with legislators. During his state service he became familiar with the colonial records of the metropolis down the river, had indeed translated some of the minutes of the New Amsterdam burgomasters. His translation was used later by Fernow in *The Records of New Amsterdam, 1653–74* (7 vols., 1897). Finally in 1870 Mayor A. Oakey Hall induced him to change his residence and undertake the editing of the common-council minutes of New York City. In two years' time the editorial work was completed and under the direction of C. A. Alvord [*q.v.*] the press work had begun (see fifteen volumes, two completely bound and the rest ready for binding, in the custody of the New York Historical Society), but Comptroller Andrew H. Green [*q.v.*], in the course of his financial reforms after the corrupt reign of the "Tweed ring," halted the publication, leaving the work to be done all over again a generation later (see *Minutes of the Common Council of the City of New York,* 8 vols., 1905). Other noteworthy publications by O'Callaghan include: *A List of Editions of the Holy Scriptures, and Parts Thereof, Printed in America Previous to 1860* (1861); *Journal of the Legislative Council of the Colony of New York . . . 1691 . . . 1775* (2 vols., 1861); *The Register of New Netherland, 1626 to 1674* (1865); *Calendar of Historical Manuscripts in the Office of the Secretary of State, Albany* (2 vols., 1865–66); *Laws and Ordinances of New Netherland, 1638–1674* (1868).

O'Callaghan was twice married: first, to Charlotte Augustina Crampe, who died in 1835, a native of Ireland who was brought to Canada in childhood; and second, May 9, 1841, to Ellen Hawe of Albany. There was one child by each marriage, but both died in infancy.

[J. J. Walsh, "Edmund Bailey O'Callaghan, of New York," with portrait, *Records Am. Cath. Hist. Soc.,* Mar. 1905; J. G. Shea, "Edmund Bailey O'Callaghan," *Mag. of Am. Hist.,* July 1880; *N. Y. Hist. Soc. Quart. Bull.,* Oct. 1923; *Hist. Mag.* (N. Y.), Apr., May 1873; letters (MSS.) in N. Y. Hist. Soc., N. Y. Pub. Lib., and Lib. of Cong.; information regarding marriages from Francis Shaw Guy, "Edmund Bailey O'Callaghan: His Position in American Historiography" (thesis in preparation at Catholic University); Wm. Schroeder, in H. A. Kelly and W. L. Burrage, *Am. Medic. Biogs.* (1920).] A. E. P.

O'CALLAGHAN, JEREMIAH (1780–Feb. 23, 1861), Roman Catholic priest and writer, was born in County Cork, Ireland, one of fifteen surviving children of Jeremiah and Mary (Twohig) O'Callaghan, pious farmers. Educated for the priesthood, he was ordained in 1805 by Dr. William Coppinger, Bishop of Cloyne and Ross, and appointed to curacies on the Island of Cape Clear and at Aghnakishey. At the latter place, a controversy raged concerning the righteousness of taking interest, especially usurious interest, and O'Callaghan became a fanatic on the subject. Holding cobbeen-men and brokers responsible for the economic ills of the land, such as rack-rents and tithes, he denounced the tacit acceptance of usury by the Church in Ireland and made war upon the interest-takers in the vicinity. When his preaching involved him in difficulty, he applied for a decision to his bishop, who in 1818 transferred him to Ross Carbery, and when he got into trouble again, censured him for not remaining silent on the question of usury.

For more than a decade thereafter, although he carried an *exeat* guaranteeing that he was "of good fame and conversation, under no excommunication," he was something of a wanderer. He went to the College of Picpus in Paris and served at Soissons; returning to Cork in 1820, he opened a classical school at Ross Carbery. Three years later he emigrated with high hopes to New York, but despite the intercession of his friend, John Power [*q.v.*], Bishop Connolly, who did not relish his anti-capitalistic views, refused to place him. Neither was he accepted by Archbishop Maréchal [*q.v.*] of Baltimore, nor by Bishop Plessis of Quebec. In Montreal, he wrote *Usury, or Interest, Proved to be Repugnant to the Divine and Ecclesiastical Laws, and Destructive to Civil Society,* for which an irregular publisher was procured in New York. The volume appeared in 1824 and sold readily. The author maintained that the attack on trusteeism which it contained saved the church in New York $3,000 per annum. William Cobbett [*q.v.*] republished the work (1825, 1828) without the author's knowledge and forwarded him the profits. Cobbett also included a eulogy of O'Callaghan's work in his *History of the Protestant "Reformation" in England and Ireland* (2 vols., 1824–27), which was republished in Rome under the censor. O'Callaghan's book caused no sensation in the Sacred Congregation. Rome ordered him to make peace with his bishop, but the latter would not relent. Neither was O'Callaghan accepted in London, despite the shortage of priests; for a time he gained a livelihood by tutoring in Cobbett's household. In 1830, he returned to New York where Power, now vicar general, recommended him to Bishop Fenwick [*q.v.*], who accepted him for the diocese of Boston.

Assigned to Vermont, O'Callaghan did such noble service that he is referred to by local historians as the "apostle of Vermont," where "his influence and pastoral zeal radiated far and wide for nearly a quarter of a century" (Byrne, *post,*

II, 467). He traveled enthusiastically through the frontier settlements of French Canadians and Irish emigrants and gathered scattered congregations; he built the first Catholic church in Vermont at Burlington, and rebuilt an enlarged structure after an incendiary fire in 1838; he organized schools and Sunday Schools. Continuing to be a vigorous controversialist, he published *A Critical Review of Mr. J. K. Converse's Calvinistic Sermon* (1834); *The Creation and Offspring of the Protestant Church; also the Vagaries and Heresies of J. H. Hopkins, Protestant Bishop, and Other False Teachers* (1837); *The Hedge around the Vineyard* (1844); *Atheism of Brownson's Review, Unity and Trinity of God, Divinity and Humanity of Christ Jesus; Banks and Paper Money* (1852); and *Exposure of the Vermont Banking Companies* (1854). He renounced none of his views, but republished his *Usury* in 1834 and again in 1856, when he included an account of Jackson's war against the second United States Bank and a reprint of his "Exposure" of banking in Vermont. Removing to Holyoke, Mass., in 1854, he organized a congregation and built St. Jerome's Church. Here, worn out by missionary labors and intellectual harassments, he died seven years later and was buried in his church, where a monument was erected to his memory by loyal parishioners.

[Memoir in *Usury,* etc. (ed. of 1828 and subsequent eds.); William Byrne, *Hist. of the Cath. Church in the New Eng. States* (2 vols., 1899); *Cath. Encyc.,* vol. XV (1912); James Fitton, *Sketches of the Establishment of the Church in New England* (1872); W. S. Rann, *Hist. of Chittenden County, Vt.* (1886); J. R. Jackson, *Hist. of Littleton, N. H.* (1905), vol. II; Zadock Thompson, *Hist. of Vermont* (1842), pt. II, pp. 201–02; E. P. Walton, *The Hist. of the Town of Montpelier, Vt.* (1882), ed. by A. M. Hemenway.]

R. J. P.

OCCIDENTE, MARIA DEL [See Brooks, Maria Gowen, *c.* 1794–1845].

OCCOM, SAMSON (1723–July 14, 1792), Indian clergyman and missionary, was born at Mohegan, near New London, Conn., and reared, according to his own account, "in heathenism" until he was between sixteen and seventeen years of age, when he was influenced by the exhortations of the Rev. James Davenport [*q.v.*], an evangelist of the "Great Awakening," to adopt the religion of his white neighbors. From 1743 to 1747 he was a docile and reasonably intelligent pupil of the Rev. Eleazar Wheelock [*q.v.*], of Lebanon, being the first of the Indians to be trained by that clergyman. Prevented by weakness of the eyes from taking a college course, in 1749 Occom became schoolmaster and minister to the Montauk tribe, on the eastern tip of Long Island, receiving £20 a year from the London

Society for the Propagation of the Gospel, but supporting himself mainly by labors as a farmer, fisherman, cooper, and bookbinder. In the autumn of 1751 he married Mary Fowler, a Montauk Indian, by whom he had ten children. His success among the Indians attracted much attention and in 1759, despite his lack of theological training, he was ordained by the Long Island Presbytery. In 1761 he was sent by Dr. Wheelock on a mission to the Oneida tribe in New York and repeated the journey in the two years following. He left Montauk in 1764 for a home in his native Mohegan and at the end of the following year he accompanied Rev. Nathaniel Whitaker [q.v.], of Norwich, on a journey to England to secure money for Wheelock's Indian Charity School.

Under the patronage of George Whitefield and his followers, including the second Earl of Dartmouth, the mission was an immediate success. An Indian preacher with the garb, mannerisms, and habits of thought of the Puritan divine was a novelty in England, and Occom attracted much attention. He conducted himself with great propriety, modesty, and dignity, winning for himself many friends. In the two years of their stay the envoys collected in England and Scotland over £12,000. Upon his return in 1768 Occom was disinclined to enter upon the missionary work among the Iroquois which Wheelock wished him to undertake, and was strongly opposed to his patron's plan to use the fund collected for the establishment of Dartmouth College; as a result the relations between the two men came to an end. Subsequently he acted as an itinerant preacher to the New England tribes and fell into extreme poverty and occasional intemperance. In 1773 he formed the plan of securing a grant of land from the Oneida tribe, upon which a selected group of New England Indians might settle and there live, undisturbed by encroachments of the whites. The movement was interrupted by the Revolution, but it was resumed in 1784, and Brothertown was established in the next year. Occom finally removed from Connecticut to that region in 1789 and spent the remainder of his life as pastor and adviser of his people.

His appearance was dignified, his voice pleasant, his fluency in English sufficient to enable him to preach without notes, while in the Indian language his brethren esteemed him a great orator. He paid little attention to the dogmas of theology, but centered his efforts upon the emphasis of rules of personal conduct with the citation of simple and pertinent illustrations. His *Sermon Preached at the Execution of Moses*

Paul, an Indian, a moving plea for temperance delivered in New Haven in 1772, was published and went through nineteen editions. He composed a number of hymns, the best known of which is "Awaked by Sinai's Awful Sound," and published an Indian hymnal, *A Choice Selection of Hymns* (1774), which attained three editions. He was a sturdy and uncompromising leader of his people in resisting white encroachment upon Indian lands, an activity which brought upon him great unpopularity in Connecticut, and which was successful in preserving to his followers their possessions in New York.

[Samuel Buell, *A Sermon Preached at Easthampton, Aug. 29, 1759, at the Ordination of Mr. Samson Occum* (1761), contains a biographical sketch. See also W. D. Love, *Samson Occom and the Christian Indians of New England* (1899); M. G. Humphreys, *Missionary Explorers Among the Am. Indians* (1913); L. B. Richardson, ed., *An Indian Preacher in England* (1933), letters of Occom and Whitaker; J. K. Lord, *A Hist. of Dartmouth Coll.* (1913); L. B. Richardson, *Hist. of Dartmouth Coll.* (2 vols., 1932). The greater part of Occom's manuscript diary is in the library of Dartmouth Coll., with a smaller portion in the collections of the Conn. Hist. Soc.]   L. B. R.

OCCONOSTOTA [See Oconostota, d. 1785].

OCHS, JULIUS (June 29, 1826–Oct. 26, 1888), merchant, promoter of civic welfare, was born at Fürth, in the Kingdom of Bavaria, Germany, where for generations his ancestors had lived. He was the son of Lazarus and Nannie (Wetzler) Ochs. Lazarus Ochs was a man of education and ability; he spoke several languages fluently, and was an authority on rabbinical law. Julius had his father's linguistic gifts and, having received his preliminary schooling at the Hyman-Schwabacher Institute, Fürth, was proficient at an early age in the classics and able to converse in German, English, French, and Italian. When he was thirteen years of age he went to Cologne, where he pursued further studies and, permitted access to the military post there, acquired knowledge which later stood him in good stead. By scholastic ability and taste he seemed destined for a professional career, but at the death of his father he was apprenticed by an elder brother to a bookbinder at Frankfurt-am-Main. Dissatisfied with his lot, he walked 600 miles to Bremen, embarked for New York, at which port he arrived in the summer of 1845, and then made his way to Louisville, Ky., where a brother and two sisters, who had emigrated earlier, were living.

His knowledge of languages attracting attention, he was soon engaged to teach in the Female Academy at Mount Sterling, Ky. Circumstances again conspired to thrust him into business, however, for in a short time the institution met with financial difficulties and was unable to pay salaries. While he was in Mount Sterling the Mexican War began and young Ochs enlisted in a company formed there, of which he was made sergeant and drill master. Its services were not required, however, and he returned to Louisville. During the next dozen years he was associated with various business enterprises, spending much of his time in the South, where his contacts with slavery made him an ardent abolitionist. In Nashville, Tenn., on Feb. 28, 1855, he was married to Bertha, daughter of Joseph Levy. A resident of Cincinnati during the Civil War, he took an active part in local military affairs, organizing in 1861 a company, known as "Julius Ochs Company," which became a part of Lieut.-Col. A. E. Jones's Independent Battalion of Ohio Volunteers and did guard duty in the state. Ochs served both as captain and as adjutant to Colonel Jones. In 1864, having removed to Knoxville, Tenn., he again enlisted, and was an officer in a regiment organized to protect the city from anticipated attack. He continued to reside in Knoxville until 1878 when he went to Chattanooga to become treasurer of the *Chattanooga Times,* which his twenty-year-old son, Adolph, had recently acquired.

Julius Ochs was a man of incorruptible integrity, firm but kind, devoted to the faith of his fathers, yet tolerant, active in public affairs and philanthropically inclined. While living in Knoxville, he was a delegate to the state convention which nominated William G. Brownlow [*q.v.*] for governor and campaigned in his behalf. From 1868 to 1872 he was justice of the peace and member of the Knox County court. As a delegate to the national convention of Liberal Republicans in 1872 he supported Horace Greeley for the presidency. He was one of the commissioners who built the first bridge across the Tennessee at Knoxville. For the little group of Jews in Knoxville he acted as rabbi. At Chattanooga he organized the first humane society there, helped to establish Erlanger Hospital, and was chaplain of the G. A. R. post. Here, too, he was influential in building up a prosperous Jewish congregation, of which he acted as rabbi, and a synagogue erected in 1927 bears the name, Julius and Bertha Ochs Memorial Temple. He was a lover of music and composed some light operas, among them, *The Megilah; or The Story of Esther,* for performance by Sabbath-school children. He died at Chattanooga, where he was buried with distinguished honors. He was survived by three daughters and three sons, the latter all prominent in the journalistic world,

Adolph Simon, publisher of the *New York Times,* George Washington [see Oakes, George Washington Ochs], and Milton Barlow.

[*Official Roster of the Soldiers of Ohio in the War of the Rebellion,* vol. I (1893) ; William Rule, *Standard Hist. of Knoxville, Tenn.* (1900) ; *Chattanooga Times,* June 13, 1927 ; G. W. O. Oakes, *Julius Ochs* (1927).]

H. E. S.

OCHSNER, ALBERT JOHN (Apr. 3, 1858–July 25, 1925), surgeon, was the son of Henry and Judith (Hottinger) Ochsner, Swiss pioneers who settled at Sauk City, Wis. The family claimed direct descent from the great physician Vesalius. Albert was born in Baraboo, the county seat where his father was serving as county treasurer. He was educated in the common schools of Sauk City and Baraboo, and took the degree of B.Sc. at the University of Wisconsin in 1884. After graduation from Rush Medical College, Chicago, in 1886, and an internship in the Presbyterian Hospital, 1886–87, he took post-graduate work in Vienna and Berlin. He returned to Chicago in 1889 and in 1891 he became chief surgeon of Augustana Hospital, a position he occupied for the rest of his life. Throughout his subsequent career he was connected with medical instruction, first as instructor in histology at Rush Medical College, later as associate professor in surgery. In 1900 he was appointed to the professorship of clinical surgery at the University of Illinois College of Medicine, which he filled for twenty-five years. Though he spoke in a halting manner, without fluency, his words commanded a hearing given to few surgeons of his time. For a quarter of a century his Augustana clinic was one of the outstanding surgical clinics of the country. He was one of the first to remove tonsils as a part of the operation for removal of tubercular glands of the neck, to remove carious teeth as prevention of rheumatism, and to emphasize care of diet in peritonitis and appendicitis and the value of complete rest in septic infections. More than any other Chicago surgeon, he created a school of surgery to carry on his traditions. In addition to his work at Augustana he was chief surgeon at St. Mary's Hospital from 1896 to 1925.

Besides being a frequent contributor to periodical literature, Ochsner was the author of a number of books. Most noteworthy of these are *A Handbook on Appendicitis* (1902), *Clinical Surgery* (1902), *Organization, Management and Construction of Hospitals* (1907), and *The Surgery and Pathology of the Thyroid and Parathyroid Glands* (1910), written in collaboration with R. L. Thompson. He edited *Surgical Diagnosis and Treatment,* which was published in four volumes (1920–22). He was a fellow

Ockerson

and one-time president of the American College
of Surgeons, a fellow of the Royal Society of
Surgeons of Ireland, and of the Royal Microscopical Society of London. He was given the
honorary degree of LL.D. from the University
of Wisconsin in 1909. During the World War
he served in the army in the grade of major. A
man of amiable disposition, he yet had strong
convictions and was a fearless crusader without thought of compromise in any cause he espoused. He was married on Apr. 3, 1888, to
Marion H. Mitchell of Chicago. He died of
coronary thrombosis, after a few days' illness,
and was buried alongside his parents in the
churchyard cemetery at Honey Creek, Wis.

[*Proc. Inst. of Medicine of Chicago,* vol. VI (1926);
Trans. Southern Surgic. Asso., vol. XXXVIII (1926);
Medic. Jour. and Record, Aug. 19, 1925; *Chicago Trib-
une,* July 26, 1925.]   J. M. P.

OCKERSON, JOHN AUGUSTUS (Mar. 4,
1848–Mar. 22, 1924), engineer, was born in the
province of Skane, Sweden, the son of Jans and
Rose (Datler) Akerson. When he was two years
old, the family, together with a group of relatives and friends, emigrated to America with
Chicago as their destination. On the trip overland from New York, both parents and the eldest
son died of cholera. John was brought up by
relatives who settled near Elmwood, Ill., and
received his early training in the Elmwood public schools. After coming to America, the family
Anglicized the spelling of their name to Ockerson, conforming to the Swedish pronunciation.
In the spring of 1864, when only sixteen, the boy
enlisted in the 132nd Illinois Infantry, but was
mustered out after less than six months' service.
In January 1865, he again enlisted, this time in
the 1st Minnesota Heavy Artillery, with which
he served until the end of the Civil War.

In 1869 he entered the civil-engineering course
at the University of Illinois, graduating in 1873.
Upon leaving the University he became principal assistant engineer in the federal Great
Lakes Survey, for which he had been recorder
during a college vacation, and for five years was
engaged in hydrographic, topographic, and triangulation surveys, including the survey for the
famous jetties at the mouth of the Mississippi
constructed by James Buchanan Eads [*q.v.*].
When the Mississippi River Commission was
established in 1879 by act of Congress, Ockerson
was appointed its principal assistant engineer
in charge of surveys and physical examinations
from the source of the river to the Gulf. Nine
years later, when the work of the Commission
temporarily slackened because appropriations
were reduced, he left the service for a short

period to engage in a mining venture in Colorado. He returned to his old position in 1890,
however, and occupied it until 1898, when he
was appointed to a membership on the Commission, which he held until his death. His expert
technical knowledge of all the problems connected with river improvement made him at
once a leading member of that body and toward
the end of his period of service he was the dominant figure on the Commission, usually heading
its most important committees.

In his later years, Ockerson was internationally recognized as a leading authority on river and
harbor improvement, navigation, and related
problems, and developed a large consulting practice at home and abroad. One of his greatest individual achievements, undertaken in 1910, was
the construction of levees to control the flood
waters of the Colorado River, which threatened
to overflow into the Salton Sea. This was not
only an engineering achievement of the first magnitude, but since some of the construction and
much of the hauling of materials had to be done
in Mexican territory, was a task involving many
delicate problems in international diplomacy and
required administrative skill of a very high order. For the successful completion of this work,
Ockerson received personal commendation from
President Taft. He was the delegate from the
United States to four International Congresses
on Navigation (1900, 1905, 1908, 1912) and
received many honors and decorations from foreign governments. In 1912 he was elected to
the presidency of the American Society of Civil
Engineers. His numerous contributions to technical literature were mostly in the form of official reports issued in connection with his work
for the Mississippi River Commission. An especially elaborate report, on the opening and
maintaining of navigation channels in rivers by
hydraulic dredging, based as it was on original
observation and experiment, will stand as one
of the greatest contributions to this important
field: "Dredges and Dredging of the Mississippi
River" (*Transactions of the American Society
of Civil Engineers,* vol. XL, 1898).

Ockerson was twice married: on Nov. 3, 1875,
to Helen M. Chapin, who died in March 1886,
and on June 4, 1890, to Clara W. Shackelford,
who survived him. His was an outstanding personality; he possessed a powerful and commanding physique and unusual dignity and charm of
manner. He was a gifted and persuasive talker
on the platform or in private, and one of the
most beloved as well as most highly respected
members of his profession. He died at his home
in St. Louis after an apoplectic stroke.

[*Trans. Am. Soc. Civil Engineers*, vol. LXXXVIII (1925); *Who's Who in America*, 1924–25; *Illinois Alumni News*, May 1924; *St. Louis Globe-Democrat*, Mar. 23. 1924; personal reminiscences.]   J. I. P.

O'CONNOR, JAMES (Sept. 10, 1823–May 27, 1890), Roman Catholic bishop of Omaha, was born at Cobh, Ireland, where he received his early schooling. At about sixteen years of age, he accompanied his brother, Michael [*q.v.*], who had just accepted the rectorship of the Seminary of St. Charles Borromeo, Philadelphia, to that city, and began his studies for the priesthood in the seminary. Sent to Rome, he completed his work in theology at the Propaganda and was ordained, Mar. 25, 1848, by Cardinal Franzoni. Returning to America, he served as a missionary priest under his brother, then bishop of Pittsburgh, until 1857, when he was named to the rectorship of St. Michael's Seminary. In addition to the duties of this office, he acted as vicar-general during the bishop's absence in Europe (1859–60). In 1862 he was relieved of his assignment at the seminary by Bishop Michael Domenec, and accepted the rectorship of the Seminary of St. Charles Borromeo, which he retained until June 1872, when he was transferred to the pastorate of St. Dominic's Church, Holmesburg, Pa. Four years later he was appointed second vicar-apostolic of Nebraska and consecrated as titular bishop of Dibona at the Philadelphia seminary by Patrick J. Ryan [*q.v.*], coadjutor-bishop of St. Louis, on Aug. 20, 1876.

Bishop O'Connor's jurisdiction, which included Nebraska, Wyoming, Montana, and the Dakotas, grew rapidly with the development of the Union Pacific and Burlington railroads, and in 1885, Omaha was made a see, with O'Connor as first bishop, his diocese covering Nebraska and Wyoming. A man of simple habits and marked ability, he won the frontiersmen and retained their good will. Approachable, he ruled his priests with tact, never disturbing any "man who does an honest day's work." Foreseeing the importance of Omaha and cleverly distinguishing permanent from boom towns, he judiciously invested in church properties. Through the generosity of Edward Creighton [*q.v.*] and his wife Mary, he established a college in Omaha (1879), which, under Jesuit control, became Creighton University. He introduced into the diocese the Franciscan Fathers, Poor Clares, Sisters of Mercy, Religious of the Sacred Heart, Sisters of Providence, and Benedictines, thus ensuring a parochial school system. Along with Katherine Drexel of Philadelphia and Archbishop Ryan, he established the Sisters of Divine Providence (1889), for missionary work among negroes and Indians. About the same time, he aided in organizing the Catholic Mutual Relief Society of America. A director of the Irish Catholic Colonization Association, he was deeply concerned with the Irish colony of General O'Neil and John McCreary in Greeley County, Nebr., which centered around the town of O'Connor. During his episcopate the original diocesan area, which had twenty-seven priests and 23,000 Catholics, developed into five bishoprics with 210 priests and about 300,000 people; the city of Omaha, which in 1876 had two churches and 2,000 Catholics, had in 1890 nine churches, including the cathedral, and 20,000 parishioners. Of literary remains O'Connor left little, save several articles in the *Catholic Quarterly Review*. At the time of his death the *Daily World-Herald* (May 28, 1890) depicted him, editorially, as follows: "A scholar, liberal, though churchly, ambitious yet not arrogant, broadly charitable, actively beneficent, daring yet not aggressive, he stood for the best that can be represented by the churchman in this country."

[*Cath. Encyc.*, XI (1911), 249; A. A. Lambing, *Hist. of the Cath. Ch. in the Dioceses of Pittsburg and Allegheny* (1880); R. H. Clarke, *Hist. of the Cath. Ch. in the U. S. with Biog. Sketches of the Living Bishops*, vol. II (1890); *Hist. of the State of Nebraska* (1882); *Appletons' Ann. Cyc. for the Year 1890* (1891); L. B. Palladino, *Indian and White in the Northwest* (1894); *Sadliers' Catholic Directory*, 1891; *Records Am. Cath. Hist. Soc.*, vol. III (1891); *Omaha Daily Bee*, May 28, 1890; *Daily World-Herald* (Omaha), June 5, 1890.]   R. J. P.

O'CONNOR, MICHAEL (Sept. 27, 1810–Oct. 18, 1872), Roman Catholic prelate, was born near Cork, Ireland, and received his preliminary schooling in Cobh. At the age of fourteen years, he was sent to college in France and then to the Propaganda, Rome, where he was a fellow student of the later Cardinal Cullen of Dublin, F. P. Kenrick [*q.v.*], and M. J. Spalding [*q.v.*], and gained distinction in theology, languages, and mathematics. Ordained June 1, 1833, he was awarded a doctorate in divinity the following year and then taught in the Propaganda and in the Irish College. Employed as a linguist, he became intimately acquainted with Gregory XVI. Returning to Ireland, he was a curate in Fermoy and chaplain of the Presentation Convent at Doneraile. About 1839 he accepted Bishop Kenrick's offer of the rectorship of the Seminary of St. Charles Borromeo, Philadelphia. In addition to teaching, he found time to serve stations at Norristown and Westchester and to build St. Francis Xavier's Church in Fairmont.

Transferred to Pittsburgh as vicar-general and rector of St. Paul's Church, which had 4,000 communicants (1841), he built a school and founded a Catholic literary institute (1843). While he was in Rome petitioning that he be allowed to join the Society of Jesus, he was named first bishop of Pittsburgh at the request of the American bishops, and was consecrated in the Irish College by Cardinal Franzoni on Aug. 15, 1843. Obtaining financial aid from the Leopold Verein, seminarians from Maynooth, and a colony of sisters of Our Lady of Mercy from Carlow, Bishop O'Connor returned to Pittsburgh in 1844 and inaugurated a period of diocesan development in keeping with the rapid growth of Western Pennsylvania. Within a decade, when the diocese of Erie was carved from that of Pittsburgh, churches and chapels had increased from thirty-three to eighty-two, priests from sixteen to sixty-four, and communicants from 25,000 to 50,000, of whom one-third were Germans; Boniface Wimmer [q.v.] had established the foundation of his Abbey of St. Vincent's at Beatty; a chapel had been erected for colored people (1844); and The Catholic had been established (1844) as a diocesan organ. In addition many educational and philanthropic activities had been put into operation. A cathedral was completed in 1855, for which the bishop procured Pietro Gagliardi's "Crucifixion" when in Rome the previous year. He brought the Passionist Order to the United States, with its establishment in Pittsburgh. During the Know-Nothing excitement, Bishop O'Connor courageously went his way, though he advised his priests to lay aside their clerical garb in order to avoid annoyances.

On the division of the diocese, O'Connor, with characteristic self-effacement, accepted the poorer see of Erie (1853), and Rev. Joshua A. Young was named to Pittsburgh. As a result of popular demand, however, Bishop O'Connor returned to Pittsburgh and Young took Erie. Worn out by his labors, O'Connor sought rest in a tour of Europe and Palestine (1856), and returned more determined than ever to change the mitre for the garb of the religious. Leaving his brother, Father James O'Connor [q.v.], as administrator, he went to Rome with his petition in 1859, and the following year his resignation was accepted (see valedictory, The Catholic, June 18, 1860). He thereupon entered the Jesuit novitiate at Gorheim, Sigmaringen, in Germany, and two years later, Dec. 23, 1862, made his solemn profession in Boston. After teaching for a year in Boston College, he was named socius to the provincial of Maryland, with residence at Loyola College, Baltimore. Always interested in the negroes, he founded St. Francis Xavier Church in Baltimore, and even asked to be sent as a missionary among the slaves of Cuba. This request was denied. In 1871 he returned from a visit to England, with a group of Josephites who were dedicating themselves to the colored missions. Finally, after ten years as a Jesuit missionary during which he traveled from Maine to Louisiana, and into Cuba and Canada, he retired to Woodstock, Md., where on his death he was buried in the Community cemetery.

[R. H. Clarke, Lives of the Deceased Bishops of the Cath. Ch. in the U. S. (1888), III, 560–82; A. A. Lambing, A Hist. of the Cath. Ch. in the Dioceses of Pittsburg and Allegheny (1880); J. J. O'Shea, The Two Kenricks (1904); Cath. Encyc., XII (1911), 122 f.; M. E. Herron, Sisters of Mercy in the U. S. (1929); J. G. Shea, Hist. of the Cath. Ch. in the U. S. (1890–92), vols. III, IV; Felix Ward, The Passionists (1923); N. Y. Freeman's Jour., Jan. 25, Feb. 5, Mar. 26, 1859; Biog. Sketch of Fr. Michael O'Connor, S. J. (Woodstock College Press, 1873); Pittsburgh Commercial and Sun (Baltimore), Oct. 19, 1872; material contributed from the Society's archives at Woodstock, Md.]
R. J. P.

O'CONNOR, WILLIAM DOUGLAS (Jan. 2, 1832–May 9, 1889), journalist, author, civil servant, friend and champion of Walt Whitman, was born in Boston and was of Irish stock with an admixture of Scotch. In his youth he read widely in several literatures and studied art, intending to make it his career, but on coming of age he turned journalist and was employed on the Boston Commonwealth in 1853 and on the Philadelphia Saturday Evening Post, 1854–59. In 1856 he married Ellen M. Tarr of Boston, whose sympathy and helpfulness were his lifelong good fortune. Their happiness was marred only by the death of their two children. O'Connor was gaining a reputation as a journalist and literary man when he was summarily dismissed from the Post for writing too favorably about John Brown of Osawatomie. His rejoinder, concocted in his enforced leisure, was a vivid, vehement Abolitionist novel, Harrington (1860), which is still readable. The rest of his life he spent in the government service in Washington as corresponding clerk of the Light House Board, 1861–73; chief clerk, 1873–74; librarian of the Treasury Department, 1874–75; clerk in the Revenue Marine Division (with which the Life Saving Service was connected), 1875–78; and assistant general superintendent of the Life Saving Service, 1878–79. He wrote the annual reports of the Service, giving to them, and especially to the narrative portions, a literary quality seldom encountered in such documents. Years later Sumner Increase Kimball [q.v.] published a volume of extracts from them, Heroes of the

Storm (1904), as a tribute to his old friend and adjutant.

The most significant episode in O'Connor's life was his friendship with Walt Whitman, which began with a casual meeting in the office of Thayer & Eldridge, publishers, in Boston, in June 1860. When the poet came to Washington, penniless and friendless, in December 1862, it was O'Connor who came to his assistance, gave him shelter, and found him employment. Of all his services to Whitman, the most famous was the publication of *The Good Gray Poet* (1866), an eloquent philippic against James Harlan [*q.v.*], who, as secretary of the interior, had dismissed the poet from his clerkship. In "The Carpenter" (*Putnam's Magazine,* January 1868) O'Connor made his friend the hero of a tale in which he appears, unnamed, as a mystic savior of mankind. After O'Connor's death three of his stories were republished, with a preface by Whitman, as *Three Tales: The Ghost, The Brazen Android, The Carpenter* (1892). Of his poems the most ambitious was "To Fanny" (*Atlantic Monthly,* February 1871), remarkable for its metrical finesse.

O'Connor was strikingly handsome, graceful, and magnetic, and had the highly combustible temperament of a romantic Irishman of genius: eloquent, high-minded, impetuous, and chivalrous. As the result of a dispute over the merits of negro suffrage, Whitman and he quarreled and were partially estranged from 1872 to 1882; but when Whitman was again in need of a defender O'Connor was at his side, and their friendship remained close until the end. O'Connor was also an ardent Baconian and the author of two pamphlets on the subject: *Hamlet's Notebook* (1886) and *Mr. Donnelly's Reviewers* (1889). In Washington his home was the meeting place of a group of intellectuals that included John Burroughs, Spencer Fullerton Baird, and other men of note. He died in Washington, of paralysis, after a long illness.

[*Appletons' Ann. Cyc.,* 1889; Ellen M. Calder (Mrs. W. D. O'Connor), "Personal Recollections of Walt Whitman," *Atlantic Monthly,* June 1907; S. I. Kimball's introduction to *Heroes of the Storm* (1904); Horace Traubel, *With Walt Whitman in Camden* (3 vols., 1906–14); W. S. Kennedy, *The Fight of a Book for the World* (1926); Clara Barrus, *Whitman and Burroughs, Comrades* (1931); *Evening Star* (Washington), May 10, 1889.]   G. H. G.

O'CONOR, CHARLES (Jan. 22, 1804–May 12, 1884), lawyer, born in New York City, was the son of Thomas and Margaret (O'Connor) O'Connor and the great-grandson of Charles O'Connor who wrote a history of Ireland. In 1839–40, upon visiting Ireland and discovering that his ancestors spelled the name with one "n," he adopted that form. Thomas O'Connor incurred the disapproval of the British authorities by engaging in the Irish rebellion of 1798 and found it wise to emigrate to New York in 1801. He earned a precarious living by writing editorials for the local press, and after his marriage to the daughter of Hugh O'Connor, and the birth of Charles, was able to give his son scarcely any educational advantages. The mother died in 1816, after which Charles was apprenticed to a tar and lampblack manufacturer. At the end of a year he began his legal education as errand boy in Henry Stannard's office, from which he graduated to the office of Stephen P. Lemoine and finally into the office of Joseph D. Fay, where he served as clerk and law student. He was admitted to the bar in 1824, and at the age of twenty, with a capital of only $25, opened his own law office. This was the inauspicious beginning of a career in which he became nationally famous.

Politically O'Conor was a Democrat, with an aspiration for public office, to which, however, he never attained. He attributed his failure to win political recognition to the fact that he was a Roman Catholic and the son of an Irish emigrant. He was nominated for the office of lieutenant-governor of New York in 1848 but was not elected; and in 1872, at the Louisville Convention, he was nominated for president of the United States by the "Straight-out" Democrats. His popularity among Southern Democrats was due to his belief in slavery as a "just, benign and beneficent" institution, and to his firm conviction, often expressed, that there was no constitutional warrant for coercing seceding states. After the Civil War he served as senior counsel for Jefferson Davis when he was under indictment for treason, and along with Horace Greeley went surety for his bail bond. He held only two semi-political offices. In 1846 he was elected a member of the New York state constitutional convention, and in 1853 he was appointed United States district attorney for the southern district of New York, an office in which he served with distinction for fifteen months. He was for ten years treasurer of the New York Law Institute, and in 1869, its president; and he served also as vice-president of the New York Historical Society. Five institutions of learning conferred upon him the doctorate of law. Late in life he retired from practice, built a house on the Island of Nantucket, and there, surrounded by his library of 18,000 volumes, spent his last years.

O'Conor's fame is due almost entirely to his phenomenal success as a lawyer. It was literally true that his life was in his cases, so that they constitute his true biography. He was not a law reformer, did not believe in codification, and opposed it, says David Dudley Field, "with might and main." The papers in his principal cases, bound and bequeathed by him to the New York Law Institute, fill 100 volumes. They cover a period of fifty years. One of the earliest is the case of *Bowen* vs. *Idley* (1 *Edwards Chancery Reports*, 148), in which succession to property depended upon establishing the parentage of an illegitimate child. His most famous cases were probably the following: two cases involving the status of slaves temporarily brought into free states—*Jack* vs. *Martin* (12 *Wendell*, 311; 14 *Wendell*, 507) and *Lemmon* vs. *People* (20 *N. Y.*, 562, see article on William M. Evarts); four testamentary cases, the Parish and Jumel will cases, the Roosevelt Hospital case (43 *N. Y.*, 254), and *Manice* vs. *Manice* (43 *N. Y.*, 303); the Tilden-Hayes election contest; the Tweed cases; and the Forrest divorce case. He was a master of the law of uses and trusts, and of the law of wills, and seemed equally at home in commercial and corporation law, a fact evidenced by his conduct of the North American Trust & Banking Company cases (15 *N. Y.*, 9); and of the case of *Ogden* vs. *Astor* (4 *Sandford*, 311). This latter case involved intricate commercial dealings between Ogden and the two Astors, John Jacob and William B., running over a period from 1816 to 1850.

The two cases which brought him most fame were the Tweed litigation and the Forrest divorce suit. In the former of these he represented the state of New York, as special deputy attorney-general. The chief counsel opposed to him was David Dudley Field [*q.v.*]. Although these suits resulted in the dissolution of the "Tweed ring," they did not, in the judgment of O'Conor, give to the law an interpretation necessary to protect the public from corruption in office. His view of the result is expressed in the title given by him to a collection of documents which he published in 1875: *Peculation Triumphant: Being the Record of a Four Years' Campaign against official Malversation in the City of New York. A. D. 1871 to 1875.*

Twenty years before the Tweed cases, O'Conor, by his brilliant conduct of the Forrest divorce case, had established himself as the ablest member of the New York bar. In 1837, Edwin Forrest, the tragedian, married Catherine N. Sinclair in England. In 1849, after having made their home in New York for several years, they agreed upon a permanent separation. Subsequently Forrest unsuccessfully sought a leg-

islative divorce in Pennsylvania, and then cross-suits for divorce were brought by both in New York. O'Conor appeared for Mrs. Forrest in a trial which lasted from Dec. 16, 1851, to Jan. 26, 1852, and resulted in a decree of absolute divorce with alimony. Justice Benjamin R. Curtis said at the time that O'Conor's management of the case was "the most remarkable exhibition of professional skill ever witnessed in this country" (Curtis, *post*, p. 167). The validity of the divorce and the award of alimony were bitterly contested by Edwin Forrest through legal proceedings which were finally decided against him on last appeal in 1862. Twenty-five years after the original suit, it was charged in the New York papers that, far from acting for Mrs. Forrest without compensation, O'Conor had in fact kept most of the awarded arrears of alimony for himself, contrary to an actual understanding with his client, and contrary to a public belief which he had allowed to go uncorrected. The venerable counselor, then seventy-two years old, himself presented these charges to the Association of the Bar of the City of New York and demanded an investigation. A committee was appointed which, after examination of evidence, reported that the charges were without foundation.

O'Conor was married in 1854 to Cornelia (Livingston) McCracken, the daughter of Francis A. Livingston and the widow of L. H. McCracken. Their married life was unhappy and they agreed to live apart. Physically O'Conor was tall and spare, and possessed of a physique which for strength, said Joseph H. Choate, seemed to be made of gutta-percha and steel springs. He was renowned as a pedestrian and in his long walks from Wall Street to Washington Heights, wearing an ill-fitting suit of black broadcloth and a rusty high hat, was the counterpart of the early stage lawyer. He had piercing gray eyes, a finely chiseled Irish face, and a square chin fringed with a white beard.

[H. E. Gregory, "Chas. O'Conor," in *Great Am. Lawyers*, vol. V (1908), ed. by W. D. Lewis; John Bigelow, "Some Recollections of Chas. O'Conor," *Century Mag.*, Mar. 1885; Irving Browne, "Chas. O'Conor," the *Green Bag*, Jan., Feb., 1895; J. C. Walsh, "Chas. O'Conor," *Jour. Am. Irish Hist. Soc.*, vol. XXVII (1928); Theron G. Strong, *Landmarks of a Lawyer's Lifetime* (1914); *Address of Chas. O'Conor to the Bar Asso. of the City of N. Y.* (1876); *Superior Court of the City of N. Y.: Catharine N. Forrest, Respondent, against Edwin Forrest, Appellant* (1855); B. R. Curtis, *A Memoir of Benjamin Robbins Curtis* (1879), vol. I; *N. Y. Times*, May 14, 1884.]

F. C. H.

OCONOSTOTA (d. 1785), Cherokee chief, lived at Great Echota, the Overhill town of sanctuary on the south side of the Little Tennessee River in what is now Monroe County, Tenn. His name was spelled in various ways, such as Ouconnastote or Occonostota, and he was often called Great Warrior. In 1756, while DeBrahm was building the ill-fated Fort Loudoun five miles away from his home, Oconostota, with Attakullaculla, organized an expedition to divert possible French interference. Three years later he led thirty-two Cherokee to Charleston in order to offer satisfaction for the ravages of the young warriors who, outraged at the treatment they received in Virginia on their way home from helping the Americans in the expedition against Fort Duquesne, had attacked the straggling frontier settlements. When his delegation was repulsed by Gov. William Henry Lyttelton [q.v.] against the advice of Lieut.-Gov. William Bull [q.v.], seized, and, in violation of its safe-conduct, was imprisoned at Fort Prince George, he himself was released through the efforts of Attakullaculla. Under such circumstances he signed an agreement to reëstablish peace and to consider his imprisoned companions as hostages, but neither he nor any other Cherokee ever showed any evidence of considering himself bound by that agreement. Instead he devoted all his energies to repaying treachery with equal treachery. During the attack on Fort Prince George early in 1760, he gave the signal to shoot down Lieutenant Cotymore as he emerged from the stockade in answer to an invitation to parley. When his forces proved unable to take the fort and to rescue his companions, whom he did not yet know to have been massacred immediately after the murder of Cotymore, he led the Cherokee against the frontier settlements. A little later he appeared in command of the Indians before Fort Loudoun and was responsible for the massacre of its defenders upon their surrender.

As it became evident that he could not overcome the white forces he seems to have reconciled himself to the situation, at least for the moment. It is probable that he went to England in 1762 with Timberlake's party in which Outacity [q.v.] cut so picturesque a figure (*Journals of the House of Burgesses, 1761–65*, p. xvii). He was the leader of the Cherokee and made the principal speech for the treaty of peace with the Iroquois at Johnson Hall in 1768. In the negotiations with Richard Henderson [q.v.] at Sycamore Shoals in 1775 he opposed the sale of Cherokee lands with great eloquence (for his speech see James Phelan, *History of Tennessee*, 1888, pp. 18–19), but in the end he seems to have signed the deed, although after his death his signature was denied by the Cherokee (Ramsey,

post, p. 120; *American State Papers: post*, p. 42). During the Revolution he fought on the side of Great Britain. Defeated, driven to a retreat in the mountains, helpless at seeing his lands ravaged by war and overrun by settlers, he made his peace with the state governments. In 1782, old and broken, he resigned his leadership to his son, Tuksi, the Terrapin, from whose uncertain grasp, however, it at once passed to the Tassel, a chief friendly to the newly organized states.

[*A Short Description of the Province of S. C. . . . Written in . . . 1763* (1770), repr. in B. R. Carroll, *Hist. Colls. of S. C.* (1836), vol. II; Alexander Hewat, *An Hist. Account of . . . S. C.* (1779), II, 201–54; J. H. Wynne, *A General Hist. of the British Empire* (1770), II, 273–82; "DeBrahm's Account," *Early Travels in the Tenn. Country* (1928), ed. by S. C. Williams, p. 193; E. B. O'Callaghan, *Docs. Rel. to the Col. Hist. of . . . N. Y.*, vol. VIII (1857); John Haywood, *The Civil and Pol. Hist. of Tenn.* (1823), App., pp. 488–500; *Journals of the House of Burgesses of Va., 1758–61* (1908), *1761–65* (1907), p. xx, *1770–72* (1906); *Cal. of Va. State Papers* (1875–93), I, 380, 602, III, 171, 234, 398, 527, IV, 54; J. G. M. Ramsey, *The Annals of Tenn.* (1853), pp. 50–61, 117–215; date of death from *Am. State Papers: Indian Affairs*, vol. I (1832), p. 42, and *Cal. of Va. State Papers*, IV, 54.]

K. E. C.

ODELL, BENJAMIN BARKER (Jan. 14, 1854–May 9, 1926), governor of New York, was born at Newburgh, N. Y., the eldest son of Benjamin Barker and Ophelia (Bookstaver) Odell and a descendant of William Odell who emigrated from England and settled in Fairfield, Conn., about 1644. His father was in business at Newburgh and, attaining prominence in politics, served for several terms as mayor. At eighteen, after attending the public schools and the Newburgh academy, the son joined the freshman class of Bethany College in West Virginia but transferred to Columbia College (Columbia University), where he excelled in athletics. He left before graduation, however, to enter business. Beginning on an ice-delivery route in Newburgh owned by his father, he engaged in the work with zest, quickly developed initiative, and succeeded in winning new customers. In a few years he had greatly widened his acquaintance, so that when he began to take an interest in politics he already had a large circle of personal friends in and about Newburgh. He was able, without great difficulty, to replace local Democratic majorities with Republican.

When thirty years of age he was made a member of the Republican state committee, and for twenty-five years thereafter he was a power to be reckoned with in the party councils. In 1894, without seeming to have personal ambition in the matter, he was persuaded to take the nomination for Congress in the Newburgh district and was reëlected, but his service at Washington was without distinction. His interest in state politics, however, was stronger than ever. Before the end of his second term in Congress he was made chairman of the Republican state executive committee. When the war with Spain gave prominence to Theodore Roosevelt, Odell was quick to suggest him as the Republican candidate for governor. The victory of the Republican nominee in a doubtful year, 1898, enhanced the state chairman's prestige among the party chieftains. In 1900 Odell himself was named for the governorship and in the McKinley-Roosevelt sweep of that year had no difficulty in carrying the state by a large majority. On entering office he promised a business man's administration. His first efforts were directed toward economies in the state government and in this he made marked headway. He understood and decried the wasteful organization and working of state bureaus. Most of the hostile criticism in his first term had to do with his retention of the party chairmanship while serving as governor. In 1902 he was nominated for a second term and was elected by a greatly reduced plurality. In his administration the state policy of indirect taxation was carried to the point where direct taxation practically ceased. Even his political opponents conceded his efficiency in office. He was called the most successful governor since Tilden (J. L. Heaton, *The Story of a Page,* 1913, pp. 178, 188).

He was the first of the so-called "machine" Republicans to defy the boss rule of Thomas C. Platt. He made appointments without consulting Platt and after the expiration of his second term as governor he continued his independent attitude as chairman of the Republican state committee. He was a thorough-going realist in politics; his whole success was based on his capacity to analyze and predicate actualities. In that, too, he was like Tilden. After his return to unofficial life his career as a party leader was uneven. Having declared himself in favor of Frank S. Black to succeed Chauncey M. Depew in the United States Senate, he felt compelled to withdraw his support from that movement and to acquiesce in Depew's reëlection in January 1905. The insurance investigation of 1905 and 1906 upset his plans and gave Hughes the Republican nomination. Thereafter Odell never scored an important success; in 1910 he announced his retirement from politics. He was married first, in 1877, to Estelle Crist, who was drowned in the Hudson River in 1888; and second, in 1891, to Linda (Crist) Traphagen, the

widowed sister of his first wife. She, with two sons and a daughter, survived him.

[*Public Papers of Benjamin B. Odell* (4 vols., 1907); C. W. Thompson, *Party Leaders of the Time* (1906), pp. 104–08, 399–411; *Official New York from Cleveland to Hughes,* ed. by C. E. Fitch (1911), vol. I; *Who's Who in America,* 1924–25; H. F. Gosnell, *Boss Platt and his N. Y. Machine* (1924); *The Autobiog. of Thomas Collier Platt,* ed. by L. J. Lang (1910), p. 460; *Portrait and Biog. Record of Orange County, N. Y.* (1895); *Pedigree of Odell of U. S. and Canada* (1894), comp. by Rufus King; Robert Bolton, *The Hist. of . . . Westchester* (1881), vol. II; *N. Y. Herald,* Dec. 28, 1902; *N. Y. Tribune,* Jan. 3, 14, 22, May 6, 1906; *N. Y. Times,* May 10, 1926; Odell's testimony in *Barnes vs. Roosevelt* on May 2, 1915, 3 *N. Y. Supreme Court Reports, Appellate Division,* 4th Department, 1826–36.]   W. B. S.

ODELL, JONATHAN (Sept. 25, 1737–Nov. 25, 1818), Loyalist, was born in Newark, N. J. His father, John, was descended from William Odell who came from England to Concord, Mass., in 1639 or earlier and some five years later settled at Fairfield, Conn.; his mother, Temperance, was a daughter of the Rev. Jonathan Dickinson [*q.v.*], first president of the College of New Jersey, now Princeton University. Young Odell was graduated from the College of New Jersey in 1759, was educated as a physician, and served as a surgeon in the British army. While stationed in the West Indies he left the army to go to England, where he studied for the ministry, being made deacon Dec. 21, 1766, in the Chapel Royal, St. James's Palace, and ordained priest in January 1767. During his stay in England he exhibited a talent for poetry. In July 1767 he was inducted by Gov. William Franklin [*q.v.*] into the office of missionary to St. Ann's Church (afterward St. Mary's) in Burlington, N. J., under the Society for the Propagation of the Gospel. In the same capacity he also served a church at Mount Holly. On July 25, 1771, as a side issue to help sustain his family, he began to practise medicine at Burlington. He married Anne, daughter of Isaac De Cou of Burlington, May 6, 1772. On Nov. 8, 1774, he was elected a member of the New Jersey medical society.

With the outbreak of the Revolution, Odell was found a strong partisan on the side of the Crown. On June 4, 1776, verses of his assailing the American position were sung by British prisoners then confined in the Burlington jail. This circumstance brought upon him much condemnation by the public and his case came up before the Provincial Congress. On July 20 he was ordered to be placed on parole whereby he should keep within a circle of eight miles from the Burlington County courthouse and on the east side of the Delaware River. He kept this parole till December, when he took refuge in Governor Franklin's house, and on Dec. 18 escaped to New York City. Later, Oct. 3, 1778, the grand jury of Burlington County brought in an inquisition against him for treason. He remained within British lines until the close of the war and was held in such esteem as to be intrusted with an important rôle in the negotiations between Benedict Arnold and British headquarters. From the beginning of the secret correspondence, in 1779, Odell acted as André's go-between, meeting the messengers, deciphering the letters received, and, under various pseudonyms, corresponding with Arnold's agent. At the same time he had the approval of Headquarters in writing and publishing sharp essays and satirical verses in Rivington's *Royal Gazette* and other newspapers. These stinging verses engaged much attention on both sides, and were among the most influential published during the period. Many of them were collected by Joel Munsell [*q.v.*] in *The Loyal Verses of Joseph Stansbury and Doctor Jonathan Odell* (Albany, 1860). Less poetic than Stansbury [*q.v.*], seldom showing playfulness or humor, Odell has been described as possessing "invincible tenacity, a deathless love, a deathless hate," while the same critic says that no one on the Loyal side "approaches Odell either in passionate energy of thought or in pungency and polish of style" (Tyler, *post*, II, 129, 80). Few public men in New Jersey escaped the lampoons of his verse or his prose. He became chaplain of a regiment of Pennsylvania Loyalists, translated French and Spanish papers, and was assistant secretary to the Board of Directors of Associated Loyalists. On July 1, 1783, he became assistant secretary to Sir Guy Carleton, then commander-in-chief of the British forces. He accompanied Carleton to England soon after the evacuation of New York, taking with him his wife and three children. In 1784, however, he returned to the Loyalist province of New Brunswick, Canada.

The Doctor had been greatly beloved by his Burlington congregation despite his attitude toward the war, and upon settling in New Brunswick he became registrar and clerk of the province, with a seat in the executive council, at a salary of £1,000. He continued in the former office until 1812, when he was succeeded by his only son, William Franklin Odell, godson of Gov. William Franklin. The younger Odell held the office for thirty-two years, dying in 1844. Jonathan Odell died at Fredericton, N. B., in 1818. His wife survived him, remaining in Fredericton until her death in 1825.

[E. M. Woodward and J. F. Hageman, *Hist. of Burlington and Mercer Counties, N. J.* (1883), pp. 76–77; E. A. Jones, "The Loyalists of New Jersey," *N. J. Hist. Soc. Colls.*, X (1927), 155; Lorenzo Sabine, *Biog. Sketches of Loyalists of the Am. Rev.* (1864), II, 122–23; G. M. Hills, *Hist. of the Church in Burlington* (1876); *Archives of the State of N. J.*, 2 ser. II (1903), 543; F. B. Lee, *N. J. as a Colony and as a State* (1902), II, 299–305; *Winslow Papers, A.D. 1776–1826* (1901), ed. by W. O. Raymond; J. W. Lawrence, *The Judges of N. B. and Their Times* (n.d.), ed. by A. A. Stockton; *New-Eng. Hist. and Geneal. Reg.*, Jan. 1892, pp. 20–21; M. C. Tyler, *The Lit. Hist. of the Am. Rev.* (1897), II, 97–129; information from the Sir Henry Clinton Papers in the Wm. L. Clements Lib., through the courtesy of Miss Jane Clark.]
A. V.–D. H.

ODENHEIMER, WILLIAM HENRY (Aug. 11, 1817–Aug. 14, 1879), Episcopal bishop, was born in Philadelphia, the son of John W. and Henrietta (Burns) Odenheimer. He received his early education at St. Paul's College, Flushing, L. I., under Dr. W. A. Muhlenberg [*q.v.*], graduated at the University of Pennsylvania in 1835, and at the General Theological Seminary in 1838. He was made deacon Sept. 2, 1838, and ordained priest Oct. 3, 1841, by Bishop Henry U. Onderdonk. Upon admission to the diaconate he became assistant rector of St. Peter's Church, Philadelphia, where in 1841 he succeeded William Heathcote De Lancey [*q.v.*] as rector, remaining in this position until his elevation to the episcopate. St. Peter's Church became during his rectorship one of the most flourishing parishes in the community. He was among the first of Episcopal clergymen in America to establish in his parish a daily service and a weekly celebration of the Holy Communion, practices which have long since become common. So effective was his administrative work, as well as his ministry to his people, that he became known as the "model parish priest." During his rectorship he made two journeys to Europe, one of which, in 1852, was extended to include a visit to the Holy Land. On his return he delivered a series of lectures in St. Peter's on his travels, which formed the basis of a volume, *Jerusalem and Its Vicinity*, published in 1855.

Elected bishop of New Jersey, May 27, 1859, he was consecrated in St. Paul's Church, Richmond, Va., Oct. 13, 1859, during the session of the General Convention in that city. He carried on the work of his diocese with marked ability, combining distinguished scholarship with unusual administrative capacity. He was twice elected assistant secretary to the House of Bishops. During his episcopate the diocese, which included the entire state of New Jersey, grew so rapidly that it became necessary to divide the territory into the Diocese of New Jersey and the Diocese of Northern New Jersey

Odin

(later the Diocese of Newark). Bishop Odenheimer was elected to the latter, thus becoming its first bishop. Soon after his removal to the northern diocese in November 1874, his convention granted him a leave of absence for six months because of failing health. This period he spent in England. Though he returned improved in health, he suffered for the remainder of his life through physical infirmity, but carried on his work with energy and courage.

While he was of gentle disposition, both his sermons and his charges to his convention were marked by forthrightness. His published works include: *The True Catholic No Romanist* (1843); *Thoughts on Immersion* (1843); *The Origin and Compilation of the Prayer Book* (1844); *Bishop White's Opinions* (1846); *The Young Churchman Catechized* (2 parts, 1846, 1859); *The Private Prayer Book* (1851); *The Devout Churchman's Companion* (1853); *The Clergyman's Assistant in Reading the Liturgy* (1847); *The Sacred Scriptures, the Inspired Record of the Glory of the Holy Trinity* (1862); *The Church's Power in Her Controversy with Anti-Christ* (1865); *Canon Law* (1868). In 1881 his widow published a volume of his sermons, with a memoir. The essay on Canon Law, written for the alumni of the General Theological Seminary, was the first contribution on the subject of church law published for the Protestant Episcopal Church in the United States. Odenheimer edited *The Celebrated Treatise of Joach. Fortius Ringelbergius, De Ratione Studii* (1847), translated from the Latin, and, in collaboration with Frederic M. Bird, published *Songs of the Spirit* (1871). He died at Burlington, N. J., survived by his wife, Anne D. R. (Shaw), and by two daughters.

[*Sermons by the Rt. Rev. Wm. H. Odenheimer, with an Introductory Memoir* (1881); W. S. Perry, *The Bishops of the Am. Church* (1897); H. G. Batterson, *The Am. Episcopate* (3rd ed., 1891); *The Churchman*, Aug. 23, 30, 1879; *Newark Daily Advertiser*, Aug. 16, 1879. Names of mother and wife obtained from newspaper files at Hist. Soc. of Pa., through the courtesy of Rev. E. M. Jefferys.]

G. E. S.

ODIN, JOHN MARY (Feb. 25, 1801–May 25, 1870), Roman Catholic prelate, was born at Ambierle, France. Although he was the seventh child of a family of ten, his parents, Jean and Claudine Marie (Seyrol) Odin, were able to send him to classical schools at Roanne and Verrière and, later, to colleges at L'Argentière and Alix. Deeply religious, he entered the Sulpician seminary at Lyons, where he became interested in the American missions. He answered the appeal of Bishop Louis G. V. Dubourg [q.v.] for volunteers and accompanied

him in 1822 to New Orleans. Immediately he was sent to the Lazarist seminary at the Barrens, Mo., where he studied theology under Dr. Joseph Rosati [q.v.]. Joining the priests of the Mission, he was ordained May 4, 1823. As a missionary to Arkansas, as an instructor in theology, and as director of the seminary at the Barrens, Father Odin gained renown for both zeal and scholarship. In 1833, he was selected by Bishop Rosati as his theologian at the Second Provincial Council of Baltimore, which commissioned him to take its decrees to Rome. For two years he carried on a crusade in behalf of the western missions, seeking money and recruits in the Continental seminaries. On his return to the United States, he was assigned to Cape Girardeau, where he opened a school and attended outlying stations.

In 1839 Odin, as the Vice-Prefect Apostolic of Bishop John Timon [q.v.], departed for Texas, where he was destined to serve for a score of years as a simple missionary, journeying on horseback among the Comanche and Tonakanie tribesmen, visting Catholic communities, tracing isolated co-religionists, repairing Spanish missions, building churches and chapels in far-flung settlements, fostering colonization, and training disciples. In 1841 he refused the coadjutorship of Detroit, since Timon insisted that a bishop could easily be found for Detroit while Texas might wait long for another apostle. Tactful in handling politicians and empresarios who solicitously gave him attention because of his colonizing activities, he obtained the restoration of the old Spanish church properties, including the Alamo. In 1842 Texas was erected into a vicariate-apostolic with Odin as administrator under the title of Bishop of Claudiopolis; he was consecrated on Mar. 6, by Archbishop Antoine Blanc [q.v.]. Three years later, while in Europe, he secured the services of a number of French, German, and Irish priests, as well as material assistance from Belgium, the Society of the Propagation of the Faith at Lyons, and the Leopoldine Society of Vienna. He returned in time to attend the Sixth Provincial Council, which, in view of the political situation, urged that Texas be made a bishopric. Such action was taken and Rome appointed Odin to the see of Galveston in 1847. Convinced of the need of schools, he appealed to the religious communities for aid. The Ursulines from New Orleans established a convent and academy at Galveston (1847); the Ladies of the Incarnate Word came to Brownsville (1852); the Oblates of Mary Immaculate appeared in 1849 and soon founded the College of the Immaculate Conception; the

625

Brothers of Mary established St. Mary's College, long known as the French school, at San Antonio (1852), with other academies at Brownsville, Brazoria, and Laredo; the Conventual Franciscans busied themselves with the care of German and Polish settlers (1852); and the Benedictines revived the mission of San José (1860). Tender in the treatment of priests and people, devoted to the exiled Mexicans, appreciative of Protestant good will, and ready to minimize the Know-Nothing persecutions, Odin was esteemed as a saintly man and a loyal Texan. It was with regret that he accepted promotion to the archbishopric of New Orleans (Feb. 15, 1861) and withdrew from his well-ordered diocese.

No longer young but still indomitable, Odin continued to work energetically in the New Orleans of Civil War days. A Southern adherent of moderate views, he managed to survive the militarism of General Butler and General Banks and to meet the problems of physical and spiritual reconstruction. That he did so with boldness his printed pastorals indicate. In 1867 he journeyed to Rome in the interest of his diocese; two years later, despite feeble health, he attended the Vatican Council, where he obtained the appointment of Napoleon J. Perché [q.v.] as his coadjutor with the right of succession. Worn out, he sought relief from the sessions of the Council in his native village, where he died, his body being buried in the shrine at which he had worshipped as a child.

[R. H. Clarke, Lives of the Deceased Bishops of the Cath. Church in the U. S., vol. II (1888); Cath. Encyc., XI (1911), 208; J. G. Shea, A Hist. of the Cath. Church in the U. S., vol. IV (1892); Vie de Mgr. Jean-Marie Odin (Paris, 1896), translated in part in Annals Cong. of the Miss., vols. II, III (1895–96); M. A. Fitzmorris, Four Decades of Catholicism in Texas, 1820–1860 (1926); C. G. Deuther, The Life and Times of Rt. Rev. John Timon (1870); Records of the Am. Cath. Hist. Soc., June 1903, Sept. 1904; N. Y. Freeman's Jour., June 8, 1861, Sept. 26, 1863, Feb. 27, 1864, July 9, 16, 1870; Morning Star and Cath. Messenger (New Orleans), June 26, 1870.] R. J. P.

O'DONNELL, THOMAS JEFFERSON (June 2, 1856–June 11, 1925), lawyer, lived and died in the fighting spirit of his Irish forebears. His father, Michael, and his mother, Amy Winifred O'Connell, the latter a relative of the great Irish liberator, Daniel O'Connell, came to America from Ireland in search of political liberty and economic opportunity. Their son Thomas Jefferson, one of ten children, was born in Mendham Township, Morris County, N. J. The boy, who was educated in the local public school and in William Rankin's academy in Mendham, attracted attention in the community by his mental ability and oratorical powers. Soon after he

was graduated from the academy in 1873 he was made sub-editor of the Morris Republican of Morristown; four years later he founded the Morris County Chronicle. During his journalistic days he acted as correspondent for the Sun and the New York Herald and published a handbook history of Morristown. From 1876 to 1878 he read law in the offices of Frederick A. De Mott and of George T. Werts of Morristown. In 1879 he moved to Denver, Colo., and there spent the remainder of his life in the practice of law. Alert, tenacious, independent, and fearless, he became one of the most noted trial lawyers of the Rocky Mountain region. He was at his best when representing some unfortunate person against whom was arrayed, unjustly in his opinion, the power of the State, or of wealth, or of a hostile press. He was one of the organizers of the Denver Bar Association and its president in 1894, president of the Colorado Bar Association in 1916–17, and for many years one of the most active members of the American Bar Association.

Active in politics, O'Donnell was a power in the Democratic party in his adopted state and a delegate to the national conventions of the party of 1892, 1896, and 1904. At the first of these conventions he violently objected to President Cleveland's currency and financial policies, opposed his renomination, and on the adjournment of the convention returned to Colorado to join with other disaffected Democrats in a bolt of the party ticket. He was chairman of the convention of Colorado Democrats in 1892 which indorsed the candidacy of the Populist leaders, James B. Weaver and James G. Field. In the Democratic National Convention of 1896 he represented Colorado on the steering committee of the silver forces which dominated the session. He was several times a candidate for public office but never won an election. In 1883 he received the Democratic nomination for county judge in Denver; in 1890 he was defeated as a candidate for a seat in the House of Representatives; in 1911 he was one of the unsuccessful contestants for the United States senatorship before a deadlocked state legislature in which ninety-two ballots were taken in a vain attempt to fill a vacancy; and in 1912 he was defeated in the state primary election by John F. Shafroth for the Democratic nomination for United States senator.

An uncompromising fighter by nature, and a master of denunciation and invective, he naturally made enemies who struck back at him whenever opportunity presented itself in a political campaign. Through the midst of acrimonious personal and party contests, he continued to serve the public in various non-partisan capacities; he was a member of Denver's charter convention in 1903; was vice-president and active head of the Colorado commission to the St. Louis Exposition in 1904; a member of the National Conference of Commissioners on Uniform State Laws; and an ardent champion of the Allied and American cause in the World War, in which he took a leading part in relief and patriotic organizations. He was married, on Oct. 24, 1881, to Kathrine Dwyer of St. Louis who with three of their five children survived him.

[See *Who's Who in America*, 1924–25; T. H. Hood, "Thomas J. O'Donnell," *Report of the Colo. Bar Asso.*, vol. XXVIII (1925); W. F. Stone, *Hist. of Colo.*, vol. III (1918); J. C. Smiley, *Semi-Centennial Hist. of the State of Colo.* (1913), vol. II; *Rocky Mountain News* (Denver), June 12, 1925; *Denver Bar Asso. Record*, July 1926.]
C. B. G—z.

O'DONOVAN, WILLIAM RUDOLF (Mar. 28, 1844–Apr. 20, 1920), sculptor and painter, son of James Hayes and Mary Bright O'Donovan, was born in Preston County, Va. (now W. Va.). In his eighteenth year he entered the Confederate army, in which he served until the close of the Civil War as a member of the Staunton Artillery. Though little is known about his education, apparently in art he was self-taught. In the early seventies he settled in New York City, where he was to pass a half-century of active professional life. He established a studio and soon became favorably known for his portrait busts and bas-reliefs of eminent citizens. At the National Academy of Design he exhibited in 1874 his bust of Peter Gilsey; in 1876, that of J. A. Kennedy, ordered by the Odd Fellows as a cemetery memorial; in 1877, that of the painter Thomas Le Clear. In 1878 he showed portrait busts of his artist friends William H. Beard, Winslow Homer, and William Page. On the strength of the "Page" he was made an associate member of the Academy; a group of New Yorkers presented the work to that body, which still possesses it. O'Donovan was an artist who as a painter felt the coloring of his subject, while as a sculptor he sought to express absolute truth of characterization, yet with details so subordinated as to preserve unity. Evidently his ideals in sculptural portraiture were fully abreast of the times, perhaps even in advance of them. Among his sitters were Walt Whitman, Theodore Tilton, E. C. Stedman, Alexander S. Drake, the painters Arthur Quartley and Thomas Eakins, Gen. Daniel E. Sickles, Gen. James Grant Wilson, and Judge Charles P. Daly. A well-known bronze portrait bust is that of Gen. Joseph Wheeler, an old friend of the sculptor. Made in 1899, it was some years

later given by Henry Clews and others to the National Gallery of Art, Washington, D. C. His Dr. Talcott Williams was shown at the San Francisco Exhibition in 1915.

O'Donovan's early monumental works include a colossal statue of Father Matthew, the bronze statue of John Paulding, chief captor of André, for the André Capture Monument, Tarrytown, N. Y. (1881), and a soldier's monument for Lawrence, Mass. In collaboration with his friend Thomas Eakins, primarily a painter, but also a sculptor and an expert in the anatomy of the horse, he modeled the two life-size equestrian high reliefs of Lincoln and of Grant, cast in bronze, and placed in 1894 on the piers of the Soldiers' and Sailors' Memorial Arch, Prospect Park Plaza, Brooklyn, N. Y. No pains were spared to make these reliefs historically accurate; weeks were spent in trying to find as a model a horse similar to Grant's favorite mount (Cleveland Moffett, *Munsey's,* vol. V, pp. 419–32). A statue of Washington by O'Donovan is in Caracas, Venezuela; another crowns the shaft of the Battle Monument, Trenton, N. J. (1893); yet another, said to be a copy from Houdon's original, is a feature of the Peace Monument, Newburgh, N. Y. (1882). His statue of Archbishop Hughes is in St. John's College, Fordham, N. Y. For the Oriskany Battle Monument, Oriskany, N. Y., he made two anecdotic bas-reliefs (see description and illustrations in the *Magazine of American History,* August 1884). Cornell University at Ithaca, N. Y., has his memorial tablet to Bayard Taylor.

O'Donovan had a broad interest in art. He was among the half-dozen founders of the famous Tile Club (1877); in 1909 he served on the decorations' committee of the Hudson-Fulton Commission. He often expressed himself by painting landscapes. In 1919 an exhibition of his landscape studies, in tempera, praised for their poetic quality, was held at Cottier's, New York City. He was married to Mary Corcoran of New York in 1893. He died of "old age" at Flower Hospital, New York City.

[*Who's Who in America*, 1918–19; "A Sculptor's Method of Work," *Art Jour.* (N. Y.), Feb. 1878; Clara E. Clement Waters and Lawrence Hutton, *Artists of the Nineteenth Century* (1907); *Cat. of the Works of Art Belonging to the City of N. Y.* (1909), pp. 207, 208; Sadakichi Hartmann, *A Hist. of Am. Art* (1932), vol. II; *Am. Art News*, Apr. 24, 1920; *N. Y. Times*, Apr. 21, 1920.]
A. A.

O'DWYER, JOSEPH (Oct. 12, 1841–Jan. 7, 1898), physician, the first successfully to employ intubation for asphyxia in diphtheria, was born in Cleveland, Ohio. His parents moved to the vicinity of London, Ontario, where he received a common-school education and commenced the study of medicine in the office of a Dr. Anderson. Having served two years of apprenticeship, he matriculated at the College of Physicians and Surgeons, New York, where after two terms (four months each) he was graduated in 1866. His graduation thesis dealt with pyemia. On competitive examination he was appointed resident physician to the Charity (now City) Hospital on Blackwell's Island. During an epidemic of cholera there, he contracted the disease. When another cholera epidemic developed in New York City, he was among the volunteers who went to Hart's Island to care for the patients. He again contracted the disease and a little later, typhus.

Following two years' service on Blackwell's Island, he took up private practice and married Catherine Begg. They had eight sons, four of whom died of "summer complaint," victims of the infected milk of the period. In 1872 he was appointed to the staff of the New York Foundling Asylum. Diphtheria was the scourge of institutions for children at that time and in many cases death occurred from asphyxia: the false membrane, from which diphtheria in its Greek etymology is named, choking up the tiny larynx. O'Dwyer experimented with many ways of keeping the larynx open. Intubation proved successful, after he had worked long to devise a satisfactory tube. He saved the lives of many children and reported his results to the New York Academy of Medicine. Specialists in children's diseases who heard his paper declared that his idea was not new, that it had been tried unsuccessfully by the ancient Greeks and by the French in the modern time, and that it had been condemned by the Academy of Medicine in Paris. All agreed that intubation was infeasible, since the larynx would not tolerate a foreign body. Extremely sensitive, O'Dwyer was much hurt by this reception of the report of his years of labor, and for several days would not leave his house. He continued his work, however, and physicians who visited the Foundling Asylum were soon convinced of the life-saving value of intubation. Dr. Abraham Jacobi [q.v.], the distinguished children's specialist, shared in the first objection to O'Dwyer's report, but later, as president of the Academy of Medicine, he recanted and highly praised O'Dwyer's work because of his successful solution of all the problems connected with it. Others were soon won over. O'Dwyer showed that his tube could also be used with great benefit for adults suffering from constriction of the larynx. By special invitation he discussed the subject at the annual meeting of the British Medical Association in

Bristol, England, July 1894, in a paper published in the *British Medical Journal,* Dec. 29, 1894, under the title, "Intubation in the Treatment of Chronic Stenosis of the Larynx." Dr. W. P. Northrup, well-known children's specialist, praised O'Dwyer's "genius as an inventor, his achievement in adding a great operation to the equipment of the profession, thus making the most conspicuous real contribution to medical progress within the last fifty years" (*Medical Record,* New York, Mar. 12, 1898).

He was also among the first to recognize the value of diphtheria serum as a remedy, though there were many skeptics in the medical profession in the early years of its use, and the success of this remedy would mean inevitably lessened need for intubation. In his later years he was occupied with special research on the treatment of pneumonia. His results were bringing encouragement when a brain abscess put an end to his career. His first publication on intubation, "Intubation of the Larynx," appeared in the *New York Medical Journal,* Aug. 8, 1885; other articles include "Intubation in Laryngeal Stenosis Caused by Diphtheria," *American Lancet,* December 1893; "The Present Status of Intubation in the Treatment of Croup," *New York Medical Journal,* Mar. 10, 1894; and "The Evolution of Intubation," *Transactions of the American Pediatric Society,* vol. VIII (1896).

[W. P. Northrup, in *Archives of Pediatrics,* Jan. 1898; J. J. Walsh, *Makers of Modern Medicine* (1907); Roswell Park, in *Janus* (Amsterdam), May–June 1898; Abraham Jacobi, in *Pediatrics,* Feb. 1, 1898; G. McNaughton, in *Brooklyn Medic. Jour.,* June 1898; H. von Ranke, in *Münchener Medizinische Wochenschrift,* Mar. 15, 1898; G. Variot, in *Journal de clinique et de thérapeutique infantiles* (Paris), Feb. 24, 1898; H. A. Kelly and W. L. Burrage, *Am. Medic. Biogs.* (1920); N. Y. Tribune, Jan. 8, 1898.]   J. J. W.

OEHMLER, LEO CARL MARTIN (Aug. 15, 1867–Nov. 3, 1930), musician, composer, was born in Pittsburgh, Pa., the son of German-American parents—Rudolph Christian Oehmler and his wife, Elizabeth (Foerster). Oehmler was musically inclined from boyhood. At six he began his first lessons in music and continued them under local instructors until 1885, when he finished a course in the Western University of Pennsylvania (now University of Pittsburgh). He then went to Germany, and for a while studied at the conservatory at Schwartzburg Sondershausen under Paul E. M. Gruenberg (violin), Ritter (piano), and Adolph Schutze (composition). Later he went to the Stern Conservatory at Berlin and worked with Émile Sauret, Keyser, and Heinrich Ehrlich, and, in composition, with Robert Radecke. While in Germany he became interested in Heinrich Ger-

mer's piano methods, which fact influenced both the teaching and editorial work of his later career. About 1891 he returned to the United States and spent the next sixteen years teaching and concertizing in Pittsburgh and nearby cities. Among his pupils during these years was the young Charles Wakefield Cadman, destined to become one of the leading American composers of his time. In 1907 Oehmler moved to Pasadena, Cal., where he lived until his death. On Dec. 25, 1911, he married Lillian Katharine Heche of Pomona, Cal., one of his pupils in piano, violin, and harmony.

As a composer, Oehmler's contribution was valuable chiefly for the large quantity of teaching pieces he produced. Altogether his printed works numbered over three hundred. His most ambitious published composition was a sonata for violin and piano, issued in Germany. For the same instrumental combination he wrote "Elegy," "Saltarella," "Romanczco," "Gypsy's Serenade," and "Sandman's Lullaby." For piano alone he composed a "Cleopatra Suite," "California Romance," "Indian Tomahawk Dance," "Moonlight in the Forest," "Autumn Nocturne," "Reverie Romantique," "Purple Sunset." His songs included "When You I Beheld," "Ae Fond Kiss," "A Sailor's Life for Me," "Sleep Little Birdie," "God, My Father, Lend Thine Aid," and "Jesus, Lead Me to Thy Side."

Oehmler was of a romantic nature, a lover of sentiment, generous, cordial, with a gift for telling humorous anecdotes. He enjoyed the pursuit of several hobbies—nature study, painting, versification, and retouching photographs. He was both a pianist and violinist, playing the violin with warmth and vigor. He enjoyed robust health until the year before his death, when he suffered his first stroke of apoplexy. A second stroke followed a year later, and his death occurred within a few months.

[Material for this sketch has been furnished chiefly by Mrs. Leo Oehmler; for printed sources see *Who's Who in America,* 1930–31; *The International Blue Book,* 1926; *The Etude,* June 1919; *Musical America,* Nov. 25, 1930; *N. Y. Times,* Nov. 5, 1930.]
J.T.H.

OEMLER, ARMINIUS (Sept. 12, 1827–Aug. 8, 1897), physician, agriculturist, and promoter of the oyster industry in Georgia, was born at Savannah, Ga., son of Augustus Gottlieb and Mary Ann (Shad) Oemler, daughter of Maj. Solomon Sigismond Shad of Revolutionary fame. Augustus was born in Hettstedt, Germany, son of a Lutheran pastor, a direct descendant of Nicholas Oemler, who married Martin Luther's sister, and to whom Luther dedicated his translation of the Bible. He came to America when he was about eighteen and settled in Savannah, Ga. He was a pharmacist, botanist, and entomologist, and from him Arminius inherited his scientific tastes. His mother died when he was eight years old. He first attended school at the Chatham Academy in Savannah, but when he was about twelve his father took him to Germany. During 1846 to 1848 he was a student at the Dresden Technische Bildungsanstalt. After graduating with honors he returned to Savannah and began the study of medicine in the office of Dr. Stephen N. Harris, continuing it at the University of the City of New York, from which he received the degree of M.D. in 1856. He then began to practise in Savannah. On Apr. 10, 1856, he married Elizabeth P. Heyward, daughter of John and Constantia Pritchard Heyward of Charleston and Grahamsville, S. C. To them were born six children, three boys and three girls. Oemler practised medicine for only a short time, since the strain on his sympathies affected his health. He was advised to lead an outdoor life and decided to take up farming. When the Civil War broke out he joined the Confederate army and was made captain of the Second Company of DeKalb Riflemen. He was soon afterwards placed in the engineering corps under Major McCreary and assigned to the duty of making topographical maps, being stationed at the fortifications of Savannah. He made the first map of Chatham County.

After the close of the war he went to live on his plantation ("The Shad"), Wilmington Island, near Savannah, where he engaged in truck farming. He was among the first to introduce scientific diversified farming into the South and was president of the Chatham County, Georgia, Fruit and Vegetable Growers Association. His book entitled *Truck Farming at the South,* published first in 1883, was for many years the chief authority on the subject, later editions being published in 1888, 1900, and 1903. An article by him on "Truck Farming" appeared in *Report of the Commissioner of Agriculture,* 1885. He also wrote for the *American Agriculturist* and *Meehan's Monthly.* For several years he was inspector of fertilizers in Savannah. In his scientific investigations he anticipated by two years the discovery, made in 1888 by Hellriegel and Wilfarth in Germany, of the presence of nitrogen-fixing bacteria in the nodules of leguminous plants. In a letter to the United States Department of Agriculture, May 30, 1886, he expressed the conviction that such bacteria exist. In reply, the chemist of the Department wrote him as follows: "Your idea . . . that clover or cow-peas or any kind of plant might possibly be a source of utilizing the free nitrogen of the air must be regarded at the present time as untenable" (Letter in possession of family). This reply discouraged Oemler from further experiments along this line and thus he lost the credit which otherwise might have been his for this important discovery. His broad scientific knowledge is further attested by the fact that he was well known among American entomologists of his day as a keen entomological observer.

With his son Augustus he launched on Wilmington Island the first commercial oyster packing plant in the South. After six years' investigation of the oyster industry he presented his findings in an essay entitled "The Life History, Propagation, and Protection of the American Oyster," which he read before the Georgia Historical Society, Mar. 4 and Apr. 1, 1889, in the interest of a proposed bill for the protection and development of the oyster industry of Georgia. This presentation of facts was largely instrumental in influencing the legislature to enact the "Georgia Oyster Law" (1889). At the World's Fisheries Congress in 1893 he read a paper on the "Past, Present, and Future of the Oyster Industry of Georgia" (*Bulletin of the United States Fish Commission for 1893*, 1894). Through his various public-spirited activities he contributed much both to this industry and to the agricultural development of the South. He died at the Savannah Hospital after a brief illness caused by an apoplectic stroke, and was buried at Wilmington Island.

[Most of the information in the foregoing sketch is taken from Oemler family records; see also obituary in *Savannah Morning News,* Aug. 9, 1897, which is incorrect in some particulars.]   C. R. B.

OERTEL, JOHANNES ADAM SIMON (Nov. 3, 1823–Dec. 9, 1909), artist, Episcopal clergyman, was born in Fürth, Bavaria, the son of Thomas Friedrich Oertel, a metal-worker, and Maria Magdalena (Mennensdörfer) Oertel. Dedicated from childhood to the church, he began in his thirteenth year to study with a Lutheran clergyman, expecting to become a foreign missionary. He revealed such talent for drawing, however, that his preceptor urged him to study art. Accordingly, he became the pupil of J. M. Enzing-Müller, an engraver, with whom he spent some time in Munich, where he was much influenced by the painting of Wilhelm von Kaulbach. In 1848 he came to the United States and settled at Newark, N. J., where he was soon joined by his parents and two brothers. Here he gave lessons in drawing and in 1851 married Julia Adelaide Torrey. She became the mother

of four children, and until her death in 1907 was the "balance wheel" of her husband's life.

In the winter following his marriage Oertel made sketches for a series of four great paintings which should illustrate the redemption of mankind. Thereafter he looked upon the completion of these pictures as the major purpose of his life, and most of his work, during more than fifty years of moving from place to place, was undertaken in an effort to secure means for accomplishing it. From 1852 to 1857 he made steel-engravings for banknotes, painted portraits, and even colored photographs. In 1857–58 he designed the decorations for the ceiling of the House of Representatives in the Capitol at Washington; a few months of 1862 he spent with the Army of the Potomac, gathering material for several war paintings. In the sixties, at Westerly, R. I., he painted a picture first called "Saved, or an Emblematic Representation of Christian Faith," which came to be widely known in chromo reproductions under the title "Rock of Ages." An amazing number of photographs and lithographs after the original were sold, bringing to the publisher a handsome income in royalties, but through a flaw in the copyright, the artist was deprived of all profits after the first few years.

He had been confirmed in the Protestant Episcopal Church in 1852 and at Westerly occasionally acted as lay reader. In 1867, upon the urging of his rector, he was admitted to deacon's orders by Bishop T. M. Clark. Two years later he moved to Lenoir, N. C., where he assumed charge of a rural church and two mission stations—being ordained priest in 1871—and founded a school for girls. Here he remained until 1876. Later he was rector of another church at Morganton, N. C., for eighteen months; and after a year in Florida he lived for various periods at Washington, D. C., Sewanee and Nashville, Tenn., and St. Louis, Mo., where in 1889–91 he was instructor in fine arts at Washington University. He always looked upon religious art as his chief vocation, however, and his paintings and ecclesiastical wood carving were his principal means of support. The former are to be seen in churches in New York, Glen Cove, L. I., Lenoir, N. C., St. Louis, Mo., Jackson, Tenn., Emmorton and Belair, Md., and Washington, D. C., in many instances accompanied by elaborate wood carvings from his hand. An especially notable work was his altar and reredos for the Church of the Incarnation, Washington.

The last eighteen years of his life were spent near Washington, D. C. For a while he took charge of the church at Emmorton, Md., during the illness of its rector, his friend. In 1895, his sons having relieved him of the necessity for gaining a livelihood, he began at last to paint the first picture in his "Redemption" series: "The Dispensations of Promise and the Law." This was followed by "The Redeemer," "The Dispensation of the Holy Spirit," and "The Consummation of Redemption." The last of the four was completed in 1902. In 1897 he had declined an offer of $10,000 for the first painting, because he was unwilling to break the series, which he ultimately gave to the University of the South. There, in 1902, he received at the hands of Bishop Gailor the degree of D.D. Thenceforth he lived with a son at Vienna, Va., where he painted prolifically in his characteristic vein until the end. In 1906–07 he produced the paintings and designed the woodwork for the reredos of the Cathedral at Quincy, Ill. He died at Vienna at the age of eighty-six.

Oertel's draftsmanship was excellent from the beginning. At the outset of his painting career his delineation of form was far superior to his use of color; frequently his canvases were done in monochrome. In his later years, however, notably in the "Redemption" series and in the work for the Cathedral at Quincy, he used color with striking results. Always having a didactic purpose, his pictures sometimes include symbolic detail at the cost of artistic effect. Nevertheless, his composition is forceful and his rendering of the human figure and of animals thoroughly able. The University of the South has a number of his works besides the "Redemption" series; "The Walk to Gethsemane" is in the National Gallery at Washington; "It is Finished," "The Church Militant," and "The Burial of Moses" are at Washington Cathedral.

[J. F. Oertel, *A Vision Realized: A Life Story of Rev. J. A. Oertel* (1917); C. E. Fairman, *Art and Artists of the Capitol* (1927); D. M. Stauffer, *Am. Engravers Upon Copper and Steel* (1907); W. H. Holmes, *Smithsonian Inst., The Nat. Gallery of Art; Cat. of Colls.*, vol. I (1922); *Boston Transcript*, July 30, 1907; *Churchman*, Dec. 25, 1909; *Evening Star* (Washington), Dec. 10, 1909.]   W. H. D—s.

O'FALLON, BENJAMIN (Sept. 20, 1793– Dec. 17, 1842), Indian agent and trader, born in Kentucky, probably at Lexington (Parish, *post*, p. 260, note), was the son of Dr. James O'Fallon [*q.v.*] and Frances Eleanor (Clark), the youngest sister of William and George Rogers Clark [*qq.v.*]. Dr. O'Fallon died soon after Benjamin was born and the infant came under the guardianship of his uncle William Clark, who resided at St. Louis. Here the boy was reared and attended a school conducted by a Mr. Fay.

In 1816 Benjamin wrote from St. Louis to his brother John [*q.v.*] that he had sold his mill establishment and was about to set out to trade with the Sioux because his pride would not permit him to do business on so small a scale as he had done in St. Louis (O'Fallon papers, Missouri Historical Society). He became Indian agent at Prairie du Chien and in 1817 made treaties between the United States and the Otos and Poncas. In 1819 he was appointed Indian agent for the Upper Missouri, acquiring the title of major. Under his jurisdiction were the Pawnees, Otos, Missouris, and Omahas. With his deputy and interpreter, John Dougherty, he joined the Yellowstone Expedition led by Maj. Stephen H. Long [*q.v.*] at St. Charles and accompanied it to Council Bluffs, where he made his headquarters. The expedition was designed for the several purposes of protecting the growing fur trade, controlling the Indian tribes, and lessening the influence which the British trading companies were believed to exert upon them, but it failed to get sufficient appropriation from Congress to complete its work. The copies of Major O'Fallon's speeches at the councils with the Indians at Engineers Cantonment quoted by Major Long (R. G. Thwaites, *post*, vols. XIV–XVII) show that he was an orator of no mean ability and that he possessed a remarkable knowledge of Indian customs, habits, and characteristics. During the winter of 1821 O'Fallon acted as a guide for a group of Pawnees who visited the chief cities of the Eastern states, performing for the curious. On his return to Council Bluffs he resumed his duties as "Father" to the tribes. While at St. Charles, in November 1823, he married Sophia Lee, who bore him six children. In 1825 he signed fifteen treaties between the United States and Indian tribes in the Upper Missouri country. He resigned his position as agent in 1827 and returned to St. Louis. The following year he was named presidential elector for General Jackson from Missouri. He retired to Jefferson County, where he died fourteen years later. O'Fallon had become one of the principals of the Missouri Fur Company and to him is due the comparative friendliness of the Western tribes with that company. Honest and courageous, his bravery reaching the point of foolhardiness, he was efficient in the discharge of his duties, though he occasionally lost control of his temper. His memory is perpetuated in the West by O'Fallon's Creek in Montana, which was named in his honor by Gov. William Clark on the Lewis and Clark Expedition, while Benjamin was yet a boy. It is believed that O'Fallon's Bluff, seventeen miles west of North Platte on the Overland Trail, was named for him also, although the statement has been made that it was named for a hunter who was killed there.

[O'Fallon MSS. in the Mo. Hist. Soc.; records in the office of Indian affairs, Department of Interior, Washington; J. S. Morton, Albert Watkins and G. L. Miller, *Illustrated Hist. of Nebr.*, II (1906), 140; M. A. Leeson, *Hist. of Mont.* (1885); R. G. Thwaites, ed., *Early Western Travels*, vol. XI–XII, XIV–XVII (1905); Thomas James, *Three Years Among the Indians and Mexicans* (1916), ed. by W. B. Douglas; *Am. State Papers: Indian Affairs*, vol. II (1834); J. C. Parish, "The Intrigues of Dr. James O'Fallon," *Miss. Valley Hist. Rev.*, Sept. 1930.]   F. W. S.

O'FALLON, JAMES (Mar. 11, 1749–1794?), physician, Revolutionary soldier, political adventurer, and dabbler in foreign intrigue in the troublous days of James Wilkinson, George Rogers Clark, and Citizen Genêt [*qq.v.*], was born in Ireland, the son of William and Anne (Eagan) Fallon, or O'Fallon. As a youth he traveled extensively on the Continent, and studied medicine at the University of Edinburgh. In 1774 he came to North Carolina and became interested in public affairs as well as in the practice of his profession. The committee of safety of Wilmington caused him to be jailed in January 1776, for inflammatory writings. He served in the Revolution, at first with troops, but later as senior surgeon.

At the close of the war he removed to Charleston, S. C., where he was involved in politics as secretary of an extreme anti-Loyalist organization, first known as the Smoking Society, later converted into the Marine Anti-Britannic Society. Up to this time he had been known as James Fallon. He now added the prefix and was henceforth James O'Fallon. In 1788 he unsuccessfully approached Spanish officials with a project for the promotion of a Spanish colony in northern Florida. Having been appointed general agent of the South Carolina Yazoo Company in 1790, he left Charleston for Kentucky to arrange for colonizing a tract of land near the mouth of the Yazoo River, which had been granted to the company by the state of Georgia. He associated himself with James Wilkinson and opened a remarkable correspondence with Esteban Rodriguez Miró [*q.v.*], Spanish governor at New Orleans, in which he insisted that the intention of the company was to separate from the United States and form an independent government allied to Spain. In Kentucky he began to gather colonists and organize a battalion for military defense. Wilkinson supported him at first but soon discredited him with Miró, and undermined him in Kentucky and Charleston. Miró pretended acquiescence in O'Fallon's plans but secured a promise from the Choctaw and

Chickasaw to attack any colonial venture in the Yazoo country. Meantime, in September 1790, O'Fallon had written to President Washington giving him a more patriotic version of the company's plans and asking for the cooperation of the United States. He took the occasion to divulge the activities of Wilkinson and his associates, and suggested that he (O'Fallon) could be of much use to the United States as a spy. During the winter he joined forces with George Rogers Clark, to whom he gave the command of his battalion, and in February 1791, he married the General's younger sister, Frances Eleanor Clark. His letters to Miró took on a more threatening cast, and his military plans assumed the aspect of offensive rather than defensive preparations.

A proclamation by Washington in March 1791, warning the West against O'Fallon, proved disastrous to his immediate plans. He dropped into the background and practised medicine in and about Louisville, but continued his intrigues and was instrumental in securing the appointment of George Rogers Clark by the French government as commander of troops in Genêt's projected attack upon Louisiana in 1793. About this time, however, he broke with Clark, and his wife separated from him, taking with her the two children, John and Benjamin [*qq.v.*]. His death apparently occurred during the first three months of 1794. Although his failures were constant, his audacity gave him prominence in the international contest for the Mississippi Valley. Wilkinson himself rightly characterized O'Fallon as possessed of talent but lacking in the judgment necessary for great enterprises.

[Manuscript material is available in the Spanish archives (see *Descriptive Catalogue of the Documents Relating to . . . the U. S. in the Papeles Procedentes de Cuba . . . at Seville*, 1916), and in various collections in the United States, notably that of the State Historical Society of Wisconsin. Contemporaneous printed matter is found in *The Colonial Records of N. C.*, vol. X (1890), *The State Records of N. C.*, vol. XIV (1896), the newspapers of S. C. and Ky., and *An Extract from the Minutes of the S. C. Yazoo Company* (1791). A sketch of O'Fallon is given in an introduction by L. P. Kellogg to a letter from Thomas Paine to James O'Fallon, in the *Am. Hist. Rev.*, Apr. 1924. Incidental accounts are contained in C. H. Haskins, "The Yazoo Land Companies," in *Papers of the Am. Hist. Asso.*, vol. V (1891), pt. 4; in Charles Gayarré, *Hist. of La.* (4th ed., 1903), vol. III; and in A. P. Whitaker, *The Spanish-American Frontier* (1927). For family history see W. H. English, *Conquest of the Country Northwest of the River Ohio . . . and Life of George Rogers Clark* (1896), II, 1151. The most extended treatment is J. C. Parish, *The Intrigues of Doctor James O'Fallon* (n.d.), reprinted from the *Mississippi Valley Hist. Rev.*, Sept. 1930.]   J. C. P.

O'FALLON, JOHN (Nov. 17, 1791–Dec. 17, 1865), soldier, merchant, and philanthropist, was born near Louisville, Ky. His father, Dr. James

O'Fallon

O'Fallon [*q.v.*], a native of Ireland, had married in 1791 Frances Eleanor Clark, a sister of the two celebrated brothers, George Rogers Clark and William Clark [*qq.v.*], and of the union were born two children, John and Benjamin [*q.v.*]. The education of the two boys was looked after by their uncle, William Clark, whose correspondence with John, then in school, contains the following advice: "I must recommend you to court the company of men of learning, sober, sedate and respectable characters. You will not only gain information from them but respectability and influence" (O'Fallon papers, Missouri Historical Society).

Having been a student in Kentucky, first at an academy in Danville and later at an incipient college near Lexington, young O'Fallon entered in 1811 upon a military career. He served as a private (as did also his cousin, George Croghan [*q.v.*], the future hero of Fort Stephenson) in Gen. William Henry Harrison's campaign of that year against the Indians. Wounded severely in the battle of Tippecanoe, he went for convalescence to St. Louis, where he entered the service of his uncle William, at that time superintendent of Indian affairs in the West. During the War of 1812 he was in turn ensign, second lieutenant, first lieutenant, and captain; he also became private secretary to General Harrison, his acting deputy adjutant-general at Fort Meigs, and his regular aide-de-camp. "I live," the young soldier wrote to his mother in January 1813, "with Gen. Harrison, who manifests a strong attachment to me and expresses every confidence" (*Ibid.*). Later, when, in the heat of political controversy, attempts were made to belittle Harrison's military record, the General appealed to O'Fallon, asking him to write from his intimate personal knowledge for publication a letter in which the actual facts regarding Harrison's participation in the battles of Tippecanoe, Fort Meigs, and the Thames should be truthfully set forth. This request O'Fallon complied with in a remarkable letter, dated St. Louis, Feb. 26, 1840, in the course of which he observes: "I doubt whether there is another living who has possessed equal opportunities with myself of forming a correct opinion of Gen. Harrison's military character. I served under him during the greater part of the period he was in active service, near his person, commencing with the Tippecanoe expedition and continuing to its termination; . . . I can safely say that I never in my life saw a braver man in battle, one more collected, prompt, and full of resources than Gen. William Henry Harrison" (Scharf, *post*, I, 348).

O'Ferrall

Having been in command at Malden, which Canadian post he delivered to the British at the end of the War of 1812, O'Fallon in 1818 resigned at Mackinaw his commission in the army, prospects of promotion being slender, and went to St. Louis with the ambition, which he frankly avowed, of making a fortune in business. In this endeavor he eminently succeeded, becoming in turn Indian trader, army contractor, and merchant on a large scale. Within a year of his arrival in the West, he wrote to his mother that he was making money "at the rate of $1000 a month." Shrewd real-estate investments added largely to his means and in the end he became one of Missouri's wealthiest citizens. His reputation for personal integrity was widespread, and this, together with his well-known business acumen and great private fortune, gave him a position of unique influence in the community. He was president of the St. Louis branch of the United States Bank during the entire period of its existence, and president also of the Mississippi & Ohio Railroad and of the North Missouri Railroad. His benefactions were constant and included liberal gifts to O'Fallon Polytechnic Institute, St. Louis and Washington universities, and to churches of various denominations, especially his own, the Methodist Episcopal Church South. "The fact is," wrote Abel Rathbone Corbin to him in 1851, "you have done so much for religion, scientific and public purposes that it is difficult to make out a list of beneficiaries; not a fire-company, not a library association, not a church, not anything but appeals to Col. O'Fallon in their hour of need" (Scharf, *post*, I, 353). John O'Fallon was twice married: in 1821 to Harriett Stokes, an Englishwoman; and, on Mar. 15, 1827, to Ruth Caroline Sheets of Maryland. He died in St. Louis, survived by four sons and one daughter.

[O'Fallon papers in Mo. Hist. Soc. (St. Louis) and in the Draper Collection, State Hist. Lib. (Madison, Wis.); J. T. Scharf, *Hist. of St. Louis City and County* (1883), I, 344–54; Richard Edwards and M. Hopewell, *Edwards's Great West and Her Commercial Metropolis* (1860); W. H. English, *Conquest of the Country Northwest of the River Ohio 1778–1783 and Life of George Rogers Clark* (1896), vol. II; J. F. Darby, *Personal Recollections* (1880); Alfred Pirtle, *The Battle of Tippecanoe* (1900), being Filson Club Pubs., no. 15; Logan Esarey, "Messages and Letters of William Henry Harrison" (1922), being *Ind. Hist. Colls.*, vols. VII, IX; *Daily Mo. Democrat* (St. Louis), Dec. 18, 22, 1865.]

G. J. G.

O'FERRALL, CHARLES TRIPLETT (Oct. 21, 1840–Sept. 22, 1905), congressman, governor of Virginia, the son of John and Jane Green (Lawrence) O'Ferrall, was born in Frederick County, Va. At the age of fifteen he was appointed clerk *pro tempore* of the circuit court of Morgan County, Va. (now W. Va.). At sev-

633

enteen he was elected clerk of the county court and held this position until the outbreak of the Civil War. When Virginia seceded, he followed her, in spite of the strong union sentiment in his county. Joining the 12th Virginia Cavalry, he rose rapidly to the rank of captain. With this organization he participated in the Valley campaign of 1862, in the second battle of Manassas, and in the cavalry engagements of June 1863 at Brandy Station, Aldie, and Upperville. He was severely wounded in the last engagement. Upon his recovery, he reëntered the service in December 1863 as a major in a battalion that became part of the 23rd Virginia Cavalry, and he fought with this regiment in the Valley of Virginia until the end of the struggle, attaining finally the rank of acting colonel of cavalry. On Feb. 8, 1865, he was married to Annie E. (McLain) Hand, and at the close of the war, engaged in business at Staunton, Va. In the autumn of 1868 he entered the law class of Washington College, under the presidency of Robert E. Lee.

Graduating in 1869, he located at Harrisonburg, Va., and represented Rockingham County in the House of Delegates for two terms, 1871–72, and 1872–73. He was elected to the legislature as an opponent of the funding bill that provided for the funding of all the former state debt except the third to be assumed by West Virginia. Nevertheless, he remained a Democrat in the party struggles with the Readjusters over the adjustment and the settlement of the ante-bellum state debt. From 1874 to 1880, he was judge of the county court of Rockingham County. On Jan. 12, 1881, he was married to his second wife, Jennie (Knight) Danforth. In 1882 he was nominated for Congress by the Democrats, carried the contested election to Congress, where a Readjuster, John Paul, had obtained the seat, and, after a delayed contest in Congress, was allowed the seat. He served from May 5, 1884, to Dec. 28, 1893, when he resigned. As a member of the committee of commerce in 1886 he advocated the proposed interstate commerce act, yet condemned those "always ready to engage in idle clamor against railroad monopolies" (*Congressional Record*, 49 Cong., 1 Sess., p. 7293); a strict constructionist, he favored federal aid for public education on the ground that the federal government, having freed the negroes, should assist in their education (*Ibid.*, 49 Cong., 2 Sess., pp. 1165–70). In regard to the tariff and the silver issue, he supported the policies of President Cleveland and voted to repeal the Sherman Silver Act of 1890. As governor of Virginia from

1894 to 1898, he made a determined effort to wipe out lynching, and, during the first two years of his term, largely because of his vigilance and free use of the militia, he was successful. In his last two years, however, his administration was marred in this respect by three lynchings. He proposed in one of his messages that the locality where mob violence occurred should be forced to pay into the school fund two hundred dollars per thousand population, and that the local officials should be removed from office and also be liable for damages to the relatives of the victim (*Rockbridge County News*, Dec. 12, 1895). This proposed legislation, however, was not enacted. Refusing to support Bryan in 1896 upon the silver platform and thereby losing favor with the dominant element in the Democratic party, at the expiration of his gubernatorial term he retired from public life, wrote his reminiscences, *Forty Years of Active Service* (1904), and practised law in Richmond until his death.

[C. T. O'Ferrall, *Forty Years of Active Service* (1904); L. G. Tyler, *Men of Mark in Va.*, vol. V (1909); *Who's Who in America*, 1903–05; *Times-Dispatch* (Richmond), Sept. 23, 1905.]   W. G. B.

OFFLEY, DAVID (d. Oct. 4, 1838), merchant, diplomat, and consul, member of a Philadelphia Quaker family, first appears as lieutenant and quartermaster in a regiment of volunteers enrolled when war with France was impending in 1799. In 1811 he went with a cargo of merchandise to Smyrna in Asia Minor, founding there the first American commercial house in the Levant. Feeling against England was bitter in the United States when he left, and he imported this antagonism into Turkey, where the lack of a treaty made American trade dependent upon British protection. Formerly American goods had paid the same duties as British, but recently the Turkish government had doubled the rate because New England captains had indiscreetly passed the Dardanelles without proper papers. Influenced by ardent nationalism, Offley erroneously attributed this to English intrigues and suspected that it lacked the Sultan's approval. When he refused to pay the increased duties, his property was seized, and he carried the case to Constantinople. Four months of negotiation and the judicious expenditure of several thousand dollars in bribes produced little result until he threatened to present a petition directly to the Sultan. A spirit of accommodation was then suddenly discovered and an agreement made which was practically a private treaty. The duty on American goods was fifteen per cent. more than that of nations

Offley

having treaties, but the added expense was no greater than the cost of foreign protection. Returning to Smyrna, he was mortified to find other Americans unwilling to risk their goods under this arrangement. Trade was suspended during the war with England, but in 1815 he induced his countrymen to abandon British protection by agreeing to be responsible personally for any losses. In 1816 he gained the favor of Husrev Pasha, Turkish minister of marine, under whose powerful protection American trade prospered for fifteen years.

Settled in Smyrna with an Armenian wife and handling most of the growing American trade, Offley became wealthy enough to play successfully the part of unofficial ambassador, greatly respected by natives and foreigners. In 1823 his services were rewarded by appointment as consular commercial agent. Meanwhile Secretary John Quincy Adams, convinced of the need for a formal treaty, sent out several secret agents, and in 1826 sponsored a meeting between Husrev Pasha and Commodore John Rodgers of the American Navy. Greatly impressed by Offley's knowledge of the people and manners of Turkey, Rodgers took him along as adviser, but nothing definite came of the interview. Husrev kept suggesting a direct negotiation at Constantinople to Offley, who urged it upon the American government, feeling certain that success would be easy while Turkey was embarrassed by the Greek Revolution and war with Russia. In 1828 he and Commodore William M. Crane were commissioned to negotiate, but several months of labor in the capital were rendered fruitless by insufficient funds and foreign influence. A year later he was appointed on another commission with Commodore James Biddle and Charles Rhind. Since Offley was widely known, Rhind went alone to Constantinople and secretly concluded a most-favored-nation treaty on May 7, 1830. When the other commissioners arrived to add their signatures, Rhind disclosed a secret article against which they protested violently. Refusal to sign would have wrecked the whole negotiation. After an acrimonious quarrel they unwillingly signed and distributed the customary presents to the Ottoman negotiators. In 1832 Offley was raised to the rank of consul, a position he held at Smyrna until his death. A man of great vigor, keen judgment, wide knowledge of Turkey and the Turks, he was the founder of American commerce in the Levant, for he bestowed freely upon his countrymen the advantages won by his own liberal expenditure, energy, and bold diplomacy.

Oftedal

[Many of Offley's official letters are printed in *House Document 250, 22* Cong., 1 Sess., and in *Senate Document 200, 25* Cong., 3 Sess. These may be supplemented by MSS. in the volume "Negotiations with Turkey" in the State Dept. Archives and letters among the Rodgers Papers in the Lib. of Cong. A report by Charles Folsom in the Navy Dept. Archives, Captains Letters, 1820, vol. III, no. 27, gives his own account of Smyrna trade to 1820. See also C. O. Paullin, *Diplomatic Negotiations of Am. Naval Officers* (1912), chap. v, and H. M. Wriston, *Executive Agents in Am. Foreign Relations* (1929), *passim*.] W. L. W., Jr.

OFTEDAL, SVEN (Mar. 22, 1844–Mar. 30, 1911), Lutheran clergyman, theologian, was born in Stavanger, Norway, the son of Svend L. and Gunhild (Stokke) Oftedal. After training in the Stavanger Latin school, he entered Christiania University in 1862 and graduated in theology in 1871, his stay there having been interrupted by two years of travel in southern Europe. He continued his studies for a year in Paris, where he formed a life-long friendship with Georg Sverdrup [*q.v.*], later his colleague for thirty years. Married in 1873 to Marie L. Gjertsen, he emigrated with her to the United States, where he became professor of theology at Augsburg Seminary, Minneapolis, Minn. In June 1874 he was elected president of the board of trustees, which position he held, except for one year, until his death.

Educationally, his conviction was that ministers should be trained in a religious, not a secular college, but that they should be educated so that they would not become a caste estranged from the men of every-day life and the priesthood of general believers. Ecclesiastically, he favored the congregationed church polity, viewing the local church as the body of Christ, and the group-church, or synod, as a human organization. He formulated these beliefs in a spirited, personal declaration of independence, *Aaben Erkläring* (1874). This document, enthusiastically received by many as a manifesto against a Romanizing tendency at work among the Norwegian Lutherans in America, was hotly contested for years, especially in the "Declaration of the Thirty," presented in 1882 by fourteen ministers and sixteen laymen, members of the Norwegian Lutheran Conference, of which also Oftedal was a member. He weathered the storm; but in 1893 it blew up again, this time in the United Norwegian Lutheran Church, into which the Conference and two other church bodies had merged three years before. On this occasion the educational issue was added to the ecclesiastical. The new body would give no guarantees that the college department of Augsburg Seminary would be continued as an integral department of the school, though the agreement had been that the institution was to be the training school for ministers in the new body. A conflict between the Church board and that of Augsburg arose, and the latter with Oftedal as president, was sued, losing in a lower court, but winning before the supreme court in 1898. The clash of issues and the resulting litigation and newspaper comments created ill feeling and even the questioning of Oftedal's honesty, though he had labored more than anybody else for the economic support of the school.

In teaching theology, Oftedal aimed more at the practical than at the theoretical. He defended lay preaching, and attached little value to doctrinal and ecclesiastical formularies. Among German theologians he found much to admire in Michael Baumgarten; among the French, Godet attracted him. He wrote and lectured equally well in English and Norwegian; he was also thoroughly familiar with the classics and at home in the languages of southern Europe, including modern Greek, which he spoke with ease. He was an able preacher and some of his published sermons may be found in *Aand og Liv* (Minneapolis, 1898). From 1877 to 1883 he edited, with Sverdrup, a newspaper, *Folkebladet*; and continued to be a leading contributor to its columns till his death. From 1875 to 1881 he was joint editor of *Kvartalskrift for den norsk lutherske Kirke i Amerika,* a theological periodical; from 1885 to 1890, joint editor of *Lutheraneren,* and from 1890 to 1893 of *Kirkebladet.* For ten years, from 1878, he was a member of the Minneapolis board of public education, being for four years its president; he was also member of the public-library commission from 1886 to 1896, and is known as the father of the Minneapolis branch library and branch high school. As he had been a leader in the Conference, so he was the leader among the "Friends of Augsburg," a group which was an informal successor to the merged Conference, and in 1897 was organized into the "Lutheran Free Church," which rallied to the support of Augsburg Seminary. He retired as professor at the age of sixty, and went to Greece, but in 1907, at the death of Georg Sverdrup, was again drafted into service by the Seminary, his work now being of a supervisory nature solely. In 1908 King Haakon VII of Norway made him Knight of the first class in the Order of St. Olaf. A lifelong enemy of dogmatism and clericalism, he did not permit the formidable opposition that beat upon him to bend his physical frame or sour his outlook on life. At his death, shortly after his sixty-seventh birthday, he was survived by his wife and four children.

[H. B. Hudson, *A Half Century of Minneapolis* (1908); J. C. Roseland, *Am. Lutheran Biogs.* (1890); *Who's Who Among Pastors in All the Norwegian Lutheran Synods of America, 1843–1927* (1928); Lars Lillehei, *Augsburg Seminary and the Lutheran Free Church* (1928); *Minneapolis Jour.,* Mar. 31, 1911; *In the District Court of the State of Minn. . . . Fourth Judicial District . . . : In the Matter of the Application of Nils C. Brun . . . Affidavits of Sven Oftedal . . . and Others* (1907); *Minn. ex rel. Nils C. Brun and Others* vs. *Sven Oftedal and Others* (72 Minn. Reports, 498).]   J.O.E.

OGDEN, AARON (Dec. 3, 1756–Apr. 19, 1839), soldier, lawyer, United States senator, governor of New Jersey, steamboat operator, was born at Elizabethtown (now Elizabeth), N. J., where his ancestor, John Ogden, had been a pioneer settler in 1664 after emigrating from Hampshire, England, to Long Island in 1640. Aaron was the son of Robert, at one time speaker of the colonial House of Assembly, and Phebe (Hatfield) Ogden. At sixteen he was graduated from the College of New Jersey (later Princeton) in the class of 1773 with "Light-Horse Harry" Lee and a year behind Aaron Burr, a boyhood companion. For three years he taught school, first at the Nassau Hall Grammar School and then at Barber's Grammar School in his native town. He had an active military career in the Revolution. His first exploit, with some Elizabethtown volunteers, was the capture of a British supply ship off Sandy Hook. From Nov. 26, 1776, until 1783, he was a "regular" officer in the 1st New Jersey, a line regiment of which his brother Matthias was finally colonel. Aaron rose from first lieutenant to brigade major, serving all the way from Brandywine to Yorktown, where he led the van of Hamilton's regiment in storming a redoubt. He bore to Clinton Washington's proposal to exchange André for Arnold. At the close of the war he studied law with his brother Robert, becoming successively attorney, counselor, and sergeant-at-law.

In the years between the two wars with England, he was reckoned as one of the leaders of the New Jersey bar. He had "strong analytical and logical powers of mind," unusual industry and thoroughness, and considerable effectiveness as an orator, revealing intimate acquaintance with the classics. The title of "colonel" which was generally attached to him came from the French war scare between 1797 and 1800 when he commanded the provisional 15th Infantry and was lieutenant-colonel of the 11th Infantry, as well as deputy quartermaster-general of the army. For a number of years he was clerk of Essex County. A prominent Federalist, he was chosen United States senator in 1801 to fill the remaining two years of an unexpired term. He served as one of the commission which, in 1807, discussed the boundary between New York and New Jersey. His principal activity, however, was legal. He resided in Elizabethtown, where on Oct. 27, 1787, he had married Elizabeth, daughter of Judge John Chetwood. She bore him two daughters and five sons. In the fall of 1812, Ogden was elected governor of New Jersey on a peace ticket, but a year later the war party rallied and elected William S. Pennington. Madison nominated Ogden major-general in 1813, intending probably to give him a command in Canada. He declined the appointment, however, saying that he preferred to remain in command of the state militia for defense purposes.

The war period marked a turning point in Ogden's career. He turned from the law to a steamboat venture which wrecked his fortune. In 1811 he built the steamer *Sea Horse,* with engines designed by Daniel Dod, to run between Elizabethtown Point and New York City. In 1813, however, the New York legislature, upholding the Fulton-Livingston monopoly, barred his boat from New York waters. The New Jersey legislature's attempts at reprisal were unsuccessful, so in 1815 Ogden submitted to the monopoly and paid heavily for a ten-year monopoly of steamboat navigation between his native town and New York. That soon brought him into conflict with the rival line of the irascible Georgian, Thomas Gibbons [q.v.]. Both men were stubborn fighters and the monopoly case was fought from the New York courts, where Ogden was successful, to the United States Supreme Court, which in 1824 reversed the decision, giving the occasion for Marshall's celebrated opinion. The expensive litigation wrecked the fortune which Ogden had accumulated in law. His only satisfaction came when Gibbons came to his home with a challenge for a duel, whereupon Ogden won five thousand dollars in a trespass suit. In 1829 Congress created specially for him the post of collector of customs at Jersey City, which was thereafter his home. He was soon imprisoned for debt in New York, but, thanks apparently to Burr, the New York legislature rushed through a bill prohibiting the debt imprisonment of Revolutionary veterans. Ogden continued as collector until his death. He was a man of powerful physique and massive features, with an expression fully as truculent as that of his antagonist Gibbons.

[Ogden's *Autobiography* (1893) is a brief sketch, chiefly military, written for his children. See also: W. O. Wheeler, *The Ogden Family in America* (1907), and accompanying genealogical chart; L. Q. C. Elmer, *The Constitution and Government . . . of N. J., with . . . Reminiscences of the Bench and Bar* (1872); E. F. Hatfield, *Hist. of Elizabeth, N. J.* (1868); S. D. Alexander, *Princeton Coll. during the Eighteenth Century* (1872), p. 168; *Gen. Cat. of Princeton Univ., 1746-1906* (1908), pp. 9, 19, 97; F. B. Heitman, *Hist. Reg. of Officers of the Continental Army* (1914); L. H. Stockton, *A History of the Steam-Boat Case* (1815); and the *Newark Daily Advertiser,* Apr. 20, 1839. For his litigation see: 17 *Johnson,* 488; 6 *Wheaton,* 448; 9 *Wheaton,* 1; and 2 *Southard,* 598, 987.]   R.G.A.

OGDEN, DAVID (1707-1798), lawyer, judge, Loyalist, was born in Newark, N. J., the son of Josiah Ogden, chief founder of Trinity Episcopal Church at Newark, and his first wife, Catharine Hardenbroeck. He was descended from John Ogden who emigrated to Long Island from Hampshire, England, in 1640, and in 1664 settled in Elizabethtown, N. J. In 1728, ranking second in his class, he was graduated from Yale College. He read law in New York City but practised in Newark, where he soon exhibited distinguished ability and independence. From 1744 until 1750 he was prominent with James Alexander and Robert Hunter Morris, in matters of proprietary titles, which had caused various riots in three counties of the state. The rioters claimed title from the Indians and ejectment suits and various indictments followed. By 1751, when he was appointed one of His Majesty's Council for the Province of New Jersey, he was considered "at the head of the Bar in his native State." For a period of twenty-four years he served with great acceptability as a member of the Council, most of the time at the head of it. In the dispute in 1760 between Robert Hunter Morris and Nathaniel Jones, as to which one was entitled to be chief justice, he was the main counsel for Morris, whose cause succeeded. In 1761 he was one of several commissioners to try the cases of pirates. By 1764, in which year he was made sergeant-at-law, the threats of an American Stamp Act made him suggest a meeting of the colonies to see if the act could be averted. To the Congress which met in New York City Nov. 28, 1765, he went as a delegate from New Jersey. He disagreed wholly with the measures there taken and withdrew from the deliberations. In 1770, owing to the feeling against him because of his leanings toward the English Crown, his stables and out-buildings were burned.

Until 1772 he had practised law both in New Jersey and in New York City and was counsel for the East Jersey Proprietors, besides acting as a member of Council. But in that year, on May 18, he was appointed associate justice of the New Jersey supreme court and went upon the bench as the second justice in that court. He acted in this capacity until deprived of the office in 1776. On Jan. 5, 1777, although no warrant had been issued against him, he feared arrest and made his escape with two sons to New York City. The next day a regiment of Continental troops went to his house in Newark and plundered it of most of his valuable effects. In June 1778 the remainder of his personal property and most of his real estate, consisting of twenty-three pieces of property in Newark and other parts of the state, were confiscated and sold for the benefit of the state. He valued these possessions at £15,231 sterling; his aggregate losses totaled £18,528 sterling. While in New York City he became a member of the Board of Refugees and devised a plan of government for such time as the American colonies should submit to Great Britain; a time, he said, "certain and soon to happen." In November 1783, the war being over, he sailed with his son Peter for England, where he asked for compensation for his loss of property and salary, printing a pamphlet stating his claims. He also acted as agent for other Loyalists seeking remuneration for losses. The British government awarded him £9,415 for property and salary losses, and because of his previous distinguished position, gave him a pension of £200 per year. On returning from England in 1790 he settled at Whitestone, Long Island. His wife, who had been Gertrude Gouverneur, daughter of Isaac Gouverneur and Sarah Staats, had died in 1775, during his residence in Newark. He died at Whitestone between May 19, 1798, the date of his will, and Aug. 6 of that year, when it was probated. He had eleven children. His son, Isaac, lawyer and Loyalist, after serving as clerk of the New Jersey supreme court, went to Canada and gained distinction there as a judge of the Court of Queen's Bench. Nicholas, also Loyalist, obtained a lucrative office in Nova Scotia. Abraham adhered to the American cause and became the first appointed United States attorney for New Jersey. Samuel [q.v.], also a patriot, removed to Pennsylvania, where he became active in the politics of the state. His daughter Sarah married Nicholas Hoffman of New York City and was the mother of Josiah Ogden Hoffman [q.v.].

[E. A. Jones, *The Loyalists of N. J. in the Revolution* (1927); R. S. Field, *The Provincial Courts of N. J., with Sketches of the Bench and Bar* (1849); W. H. Shaw, *Hist. of Essex and Hudson Counties, N.J.* (1884), vol. I; W. O. Wheeler, *The Ogden Family in America* (1907); F. B. Dexter, *Biog. Sketches of the Grads. of Yale Coll.*, vol. I (1885); Lorenzo Sabine, *Biog. Sketches Loyalists of the Am. Revolution* (2 vols., 1864); the *Green Bag*, Aug. 1891; *N.-Y. Hist. Soc. Colls.*, vol. VIII (1876).]   A. V–D. H.

OGDEN, DAVID BAYARD (Oct. 31, 1775–July 16, 1849), lawyer, was born at Morrisania,

N. Y., the eldest of the twelve children of Samuel [q.v.] and Euphemia (Morris) Ogden. He received the degree of A.B. from the University of Pennsylvania in 1792; read law with his uncle Abraham Ogden; and was admitted to the New Jersey bar as attorney in 1796, becoming a counselor three years later. Desiring a wider scope for his legal career, he moved in 1803 from Newark to New York City, where he thereafter made his home. He married Margaretta Ogden, the daughter of his legal preceptor, and had eight children. Facilitated by family prestige and legal ability, he quickly gained social prominence and a flourishing practice. His chief fame arose from his practice before the Supreme Court. With a great fund of legal learning, he was able to present his cases with remarkable directness and simplicity of statement. Marshall said of him that "when he stated his case, it was already argued" (Warren, *post*, p. 304). His first appearance before the Supreme Court was apparently on Feb. 4, 1812, in *Fitzsimmons et al.* vs. *Ogden et al.* (*7 Cranch, 2*). He was one of the counsel for the defense, in which his uncle, Gouverneur Morris, was concerned. He appeared again in 1815 (*9 Cranch, 244*); four times in 1817; and eight times in 1818. From that time on until his final case in 1845, he was in constant demand and received some of the heaviest fees of any lawyer in the country.

The most celebrated case in which Ogden participated was *Cohens* vs. *Virginia* in 1821 (*6 Wheaton, 264*). Ogden, Pinkney, and Wirt supported Cohens while Webster represented Virginia. The case involved the jurisdiction of the Court. Ogden declared: "It is no objection to the exercise of the judicial powers of this court, that the defendant in error is one of the states of the Union.... We deny, that since the establishment of the national constitution, there is any such thing as a sovereign state, independent of the Union" (p. 346). Such federalist views naturally appealed to Marshall and were reflected in his decision. In *Sturges* vs. *Crowninshield* in 1819 (*4 Wheaton, 122*) and *Ogden* vs. *Saunders* in 1824 and 1827 (*12 Wheaton, 212*), both involving bankruptcy laws, Ogden was on the losing side, but his logic was impressive. One of the most difficult cases was that of *John Inglis, Demandant,* vs. *The Trustees of the Sailor's Snug Harbour* in 1830 (*3 Peters, 99*). In 1837 he successfully supported the constitutionality of a municipal regulation of passengers on vessels coming to New York from foreign ports or ports of other states in *City of New York* vs. *Miln* (*11 Peters,*

102). Two years later, in *Bank of Augusta* vs. *Earle* (13 *Peters*, 519), his arguments for the plaintiff did much to secure a decision which facilitated the interstate influence of corporations. His final appearance was in December 1845, when with Webster he supported the plaintiff in *Smith* vs. *Turner,* concerning the right of New York to tax passengers on ships arriving from foreign ports (7 *Howard*, 283).

Unlike most of his prominent colleagues at the bar, Ogden held no important public office, though he ran unsuccessfully for Congress in 1828. He was a Federalist and then a Whig. He sat in the New York Assembly in 1814 and again in 1838. Supported by Thurlow Weed, he was surrogate of New York County from 1840 to 1844, though Weed described him shortly before as "confiding even to credulity and as guileless as a child, but when roused . . . intellectually strong" (*The Life of Thurlow Weed,* vol. I, p. 408). William Kent called him a "good, pompous kind of man" (*Ibid.,* vol. II, p. 73), while his obituary stressed his kindness and urbanity, amenity of manners, kind and conciliating conduct at the bar, and his benevolence of heart. He was for years a trustee of Columbia and was a devoted Episcopalian. He died on Staten Island.

[In addition to the Supreme Court reports see: W. O. Wheeler, *The Ogden Family in America* (1907); Jas. Parker, *Hist. Sketches . . . of the Protestant Episc. Ch. in N. J.* (1889); Charles Warren, *A Hist. of the Am. Bar* (1911); *The Life of Thurlow Weed* (2 vols., 1884), ed. by H. Weed and T. W. Barnes; A. J. Beveridge, *The Life of John Marshall,* vol. IV (1919); C. M. Fuess, *Daniel Webster* (1930), vol. II; *Niles' Weekly Reg.,* Oct. 18, Nov. 15, 1828; E. A. Werner, *Civil List . . . of the Colony and State of N. Y.* (1889); *N. Y. Commercial Advertiser, N. Y. Herald,* July 18, 1849. Although the *Gen. Alumni Cat.* of the Univ. of Pa. gives Ogden's middle name as Boonton, it appears in the *Columbia Univ. Alumni Reg.* (1932) as Bayard, and his son is mentioned in Wheeler, *op. cit.,* as David Bayard Ogden, Jr.]   R. G. A.

OGDEN, FRANCIS BARBER (Mar. 3, 1783–July 4, 1857), engineer, consul, was born at Boonton, N. J., son of Gen. Matthias and Hannah (Dayton) Ogden, and a descendant of John Ogden who emigrated from Hampshire, England, to Long Island about 1640 and in 1664 settled in Elizabethtown, N. J. Matthias was a man of marked intelligence and natural ability and had gained his title of General through his distinguished services in the Revolution. Following the war, he had resumed his occupation of tanner and currier in Boonton, and there young Ogden obtained his primary education and grew to manhood. He had shown from early youth a keen interest in mechanics and as he matured this interest was confined more and more to studies and experiments with the steam engine

as a propelling power for boats. That such should have been the case was natural enough, since the most important experimental work on the steamboat was being done almost at his door by John Stevens, Nicholas Roosevelt, Daniel Dod, and Robert Fulton [*qq.v.*]—men whom Ogden probably knew well. His uncle, too, Aaron Ogden [*q.v.*], governor of New Jersey, had established a stagecoach line from Bristol, N. J., to Elizabeth, N. J., and in 1811 had constructed the steamboat *Sea Horse* to carry his stage passengers from Elizabeth to New York. There seems little doubt, in view of his interest, that Francis had much to do with this steamboat, both in its construction and operation. In 1812 Ogden entered the army and remained in the service until after the battle of New Orleans (1815), in which he saw action as aide-de-camp under Gen. Andrew Jackson.

Following the war, he returned to Boonton to resume his studies, and in 1817 went to England, presumably to be near the great master James Watt. In Leeds he designed and built for steamboat service a low-pressure condensing engine with two cylinders in which the steam worked expansively and the cranks were adjusted at right angles. In 1830 he was appointed United States consul at Liverpool, by President Jackson, and continued in the consular service until his death twenty-eight years later. During this time he remained keenly interested in steam navigation and sometime in the 1830's he formed the acquaintance of John Ericsson [*q.v.*], who had just devised his screw propeller. Ogden at once saw the probable value of this invention and confident of its success, placed money at the disposal of Ericsson for the building of an experimental boat, which, on its completion, the latter named the *Francis B. Ogden.* In addition, Ogden succeeded in bringing Ericsson's invention to the attention of the British Admiralty and in staging a demonstration of its capabilities, with the aid of the new craft. Little interest was manifested, but later Ogden brought about the meeting of Ericsson and Capt. Robert F. Stockton [*q.v.*], as a result of which Ericsson built the screw-propelled tug-boat *Robert F. Stockton,* demonstrated it to officials of the United States Navy, and a few years later, designed and superintended the construction of the U. S. S. *Princeton,* the first screw-propelled steam war vessel ever built. Meanwhile, in 1840, Ogden was made consul at Bristol, England, by President Van Buren. He remained at this post to the day of his death and was buried there. In 1837 he married Louisa Pownall of Liverpool, who survived him.

[W. O. Wheeler, *The Ogden Family in America* (1907); G. H. Preble, *A Chronological Hist. of the Origin and Development of Steam Navigation* (1883); J. H. Morrison, *Hist. of Am. Steam Navigation* (1903); R. H. Thurston, *A Hist. of the Growth of the Steam Engine* (3rd ed., 1893).]   C. W. M.

OGDEN, HERBERT GOUVERNEUR (Apr. 4, 1846–Feb. 25, 1906), cartographer and topographer, the son of Morgan Lewis and Eliza Glendy (McLaughlin) Ogden and great-grandson of Rev. Uzal Ogden [*q.v.*], was born in New York City. A descendant of John Ogden who came to America in 1640 and finally settled in New Jersey, he numbered also among his ancestors Francis Lewis [*q.v.*], signer of the Declaration of Independence. Ogden was educated in the grammar schools of New York City, at Rugby Institute, Washington, D. C., and under private tutors. He became a clerk in the office of the register of wills in Washington, serving in this capacity until Apr. 22, 1863, when he was appointed aid in the United States Coast and Geodetic Survey, with which he remained connected up to the time of his death. During the Civil War he was assigned to detached service and was engaged in the construction of the defenses of Washington (1863), under Gen. John G. Barnard [*q.v.*] of the corps of engineers. From November 1863 to May 1864 he saw duty on the North Atlantic blockade at Beaufort, Hatteras Inlet, N. C., and was on the gunboat *Commodore Hull* as volunteer watch officer when the Confederates besieged New Bern, N. C. In 1865 he went with the Nicaraguan expedition, and five years later served as topographer with the first naval exploring expedition to the Isthmus of Darien. He was promoted to sub-assistant in the Coast and Geodetic Survey, Jan. 1, 1869, and on Jan. 1, 1872, was made assistant.

In the regular course of his duties he eventually directed nearly every branch of the work. He was given charge of the engraving division in 1880, which position required an extensive and varied knowledge of chart construction and publishing. On Nov. 1, 1898, he was made inspector of hydrography and topography. Under his direction three editions of the *United States Coast Pilot* (1899, 1903, 1904), covering the coast of the United States and Alaska, were published. "Of the thousands who traverse our coasts in ships few are aware of the extent their safety depends on the integrity and completeness of his charts" (D. B. Wainright, *post*, p. 227). His best-remembered service was his work in connection with the boundary of Alaska and British Columbia. In 1893 he carried on original explorations and made maps, on the basis of which the present international boundary in southeastern Alaska was determined. His memory is perpetuated there by the names Mount Ogden, and Ogden Passage—an important Alaskan waterway on the southwestern coast of Chichagof Island.

From Sept. 4, 1890, till his death he served on the United States Board of Geographic Names. His interest led him to catalogue 2,400 names of places in southeastern Alaska, and these comprise 72 per cent. of those listed by Marcus Baker [*q.v.*] in his Geographic Dictionary of Alaska (1906), a work with which Ogden was for some time connected. Among his publications are an article under the title "Map" in *Johnson's Universal Cyclopaedia* (vol. V, 1897) and "Geography of the Land," in the *National Geographic Magazine* (vol. I, no. 2, 1889). He was a fellow of the American Association for the Advancement of Science and a member of several other learned societies. On May 28, 1872, he married Mary A. Greene of Brooklyn, N. Y., by whom he had five children. He died at Fortress Monroe, Va.

[W. O. Wheeler, *The Ogden Family in America* (1907); *Who's Who in America*, 1906–07; D. B. Wainright, "Herbert Gouverneur Odgen," *Proc. Washington Acad. of Sci.*, Dec. 24, 1908; *Fifth Report of the U. S. Geographic Board 1890 to 1920* (1921); records of U. S. Board of Geographic Names; records in Office of U. S. Coast and Geodetic Survey; *Evening Star* (Washington), Feb. 27, 1906.]   F. W. S.

OGDEN, PETER SKENE (1794–September 1854), fur trader and explorer, youngest son of Isaac and Sarah (Hanson) Ogden, was born at Quebec, Canada, and died at Oregon City, Oregon. His parents, following events of the Revolution, removed from Newark, N. J., by way of England to Canada. Isaac Ogden, the son of David Ogden [*q.v.*], served many years as judge in the admiralty and other courts in Canada and his son in turn was schooled for the legal profession. Breaking away from social and cultural environment at home, Peter Skene, when near the age of majority, decided to enter active service in the fur trade, which was then the most lucrative business in Canada. He began as clerk in the North West Company and was stationed at Isle à la Crosse, but about 1818 he was transferred to the Columbia district beyond the Rocky Mountains and there spent the remainder of his life. With the merger in 1821 of the North West Company with the older and larger Hudson's Bay Company he remained with the latter company and at his death was at the head of the business in the district.

In Canada and in the Oregon Country the fur trader was by force of circumstances an ex-

Ogden

of the annual hunting and trading expedition
sent to the so-called Snake Country to make contact with the Indian tribes and compete with
American traders from St. Louis. It was a life
of hardship, danger, and exposure which took
him into almost every valley in southern Idaho
and eastern Oregon and also to the head of Jefferson River in Montana. In this connection he
was one of the first white men to visit the region
of Great Salt Lake (where the city of Ogden
was named in his honor) and actually the first
to traverse the valley of the Humboldt River,
first charted as Ogden's River, in northern
Nevada; and his journals contain the first known
mention of the name Shasta in northern California. From that service he was transferred to
the trade in ships along the northwest coast of
British Columbia and Alaska in competition with
the Russians from Sitka. About 1836 he was
sent to take charge of the difficult district known
as New Caledonia on the Fraser River and remained there nearly six years. Beginning with
1844 his station was Fort Vancouver, the headquarters of the entire trade on the Columbia.

Ogden was a man of unusual force of mind
and personal charm. His associates at Fort
Vancouver were Dr. John McLoughlin and
James Douglas, afterward Sir James Douglas,
prominent in Oregon and British Columbia his-
tory, and he was especially trusted by Gov.
George Simpson of the Hudson's Bay Company.
In 1844, returning from a year's leave in Canada
and England, he was assigned to escort to the
Columbia two British army officers, Warre and
Vavasour, who were sent incognito to examine
the Columbia with reference to defense by British troops in the event of war with the United
States for the possession of Oregon. Later
Ogden was in command at Vancouver upon the
arrival of the American officers and men after
the treaty of 1846 and his urbane conduct and
tact prevented possible friction then. His acquaintance with early travelers and settlers in
Oregon was very wide, and the Indians knew
him as a man of fair dealing but of authority.
This made it possible for him singly to rescue
the fifty or more women and children held as
captives by the Cayuse tribe following the massacre of Marcus Whitman in November 1847
near Walla Walla, Wash. He was twice married, each time to a native woman, as was the
custom with many of the officers in the fur trade.

Ogden was familiar with many Indian dialects
and the Chinook jargon and spoke French as
readily as English. By his voyageurs he was
known as "M'sieur Pete." He enjoyed literature

and wrote a small book entitled *Traits of American Indian Life and Character,* published anonymously in London in 1853. He left considerable
property and Sir George Simpson was his executor.

[For biographical details see T. C. Elliott, "Peter
Skene Ogden, Fur Trader," in *Quart. Ore. Hist. Soc.,*
Sept. 1910, and W. O. Wheeler, *The Ogden Family in
America* (1907). Ogden's journals of his expedition
into the Snake Country were published in the *Quart.
Ore. Hist. Soc.,* Dec. 1909, June, Dec. 1910.]

T. C. E.

OGDEN, ROBERT CURTIS (June 20, 1836–
Aug. 6, 1913), merchant, and promoter of education, was born at Philadelphia, Pa., a son of
Jonathan and Abigail (Murphey) Ogden. His
father was a descendant of Richard Ogden, who
in the seventeenth century settled at Stamford,
Conn., and at Fairfield, N. J. His mother came
of Scotch Presbyterian stock from County Antrim, Ireland. All of Robert's formal schooling
was obtained before his fourteenth year, chiefly
at a city academy that prepared students for the
University of Pennsylvania. At fourteen he was
working in a dry-goods store and in 1852, when
Jonathan Ogden removed to New York as a
partner in the clothing house of Devlin & Company, the son went with him and continued his
apprenticeship to trade. Within a few years he
had been admitted as a junior partner in the
Devlin firm, had married on Mar. 1, 1860, Ellen
Lewis, a young woman of Welsh descent, and
had established a home in Brooklyn. His part
in the Civil War was mainly confined to a month
of soldiering with the 23rd Regiment of the New
York National Guard in the defense of Pennsylvania towns threatened by Lee's invasion in 1863.

Ogden's earliest contacts with the South were
formed on a journey during the opening months
of 1861 as an agent of his clothing house. After
peace came, the work of his friend Samuel C.
Armstrong [q.v.] in founding and conducting
Hampton Institute in Virginia had a profound
influence upon his life and ideals. He saw that
Armstrong was giving his life to the problem of
negro education and the example inspired him
to devote his own abilities to some like form of
public service. His business and his growing
family, however, made financial demands that
could not be ignored or postponed, and a series
of bad years in the seventies made his position
precarious. In 1879, when his situation in New
York had grown almost impossible, John Wanamaker invited him to become an associate in his
Philadelphia retailing enterprises. Ten years
later, upon Wanamaker's joining President Harrison's cabinet, Ogden took over the management of the entire business, which remained in

641

his hands, much to Wanamaker's satisfaction, until the close of the Harrison administration in 1893. At the age of sixty he returned to New York to open the Wanamaker store in that city. Then followed more than ten strenuous years in which activities and exertions such as usually fall to the lot of younger men were required of him in the rapid expansion of the business.

Meanwhile, as a trustee of Hampton, Ogden had never lost interest in Southern education, but the schooling of the white population was taking a more central place in his thought. He was fortunate in his contacts with progressive Southern school men and with several Southern-born men of influence who lived and worked in the North. Cooperating heartily with both groups, he was able, through annual conferences held in Southern cities, to enlist the effective support of public opinion for ambitious educational programs. In the opening years of the twentieth century this "Ogden movement," as it was called, was an effective factor in the educational revival that swept over the Southern states. Ogden headed the Southern Education Board which vigorously promoted campaigns for increased school taxes and higher standards of supervision for both white and negro schools, and lengthening of terms, and later sponsored farm demonstration work in many communities. He was also a member of the General Education Board and was instrumental in dispensing large funds for Southern education. His kindliness and humor made him an irresistible campaigner. Encountering much opposition in the early years, he continually gained support until the time came when few Northerners were so favorably known in the South.

As old age approached, Ogden developed heart trouble and in 1907 felt compelled to retire from business. Within three years his wife died. He was still president of the Hampton board of trustees, a trustee of Tuskegee Institute, and a director of Union Theological Seminary. He had long been an elder in the Presbyterian Church, especially active in Sunday-school work, and was a leader of the liberal element in that denomination. He died at his summer home in Kennebunkport, Me., survived by two daughters.

[The authorized biography of Ogden, entitled *An Unofficial Statesman*, was written by Philip W. Wilson (1924). See also: *A Life Well Lived* (1914), a collection of memorial addresses on the life of Ogden by Francis G. Peabody, S. C. Mitchell, and William H. Taft; H. A. Gibbons, *John Wanamaker* (2 vols., 1926); Albert Shaw, "An Ogden Memorial," *Am. Rev. of Revs.*, Nov. 1915; the *Southern Workman*, Sept. 1913; F. G. Peabody, *Education for Life: The Story of Hampton Institute* (1918); *The Gen. Educ. Board: An Account of its Activities, 1902–14* (1915); *Southern Educ. Board: Activities and Results, 1904–10* (1911); *Report of the Commissioner of Education for the Year 1903* (1905), vol. I; *N. Y. Times*, Aug. 7, 1913.]

W. B. S.

OGDEN, SAMUEL (Dec. 9, 1746–Dec. 1, 1810), iron founder and land promoter, was the son of David [*q.v.*] and Gertrude (Gouverneur) Ogden and was born in Newark, N. J. While two brothers of Samuel adopted the profession of law and gained position, he engaged in business, chiefly the manufacture of iron, which had some years before enlisted the attention of the Ogdens of Newark. In the War of Independence his iron works at Boonton, Morris County, figured with other prominent concerns as affording supplies of ammunition for the American troops and material for the fortifications on the Hudson River. In 1781 he advertised nail manufacture "in all its branches"; and later, it is said, he built the forge at Hopewell, N. J. In spite of his contributions to the American cause and his rank as colonel in the patriot militia, general knowledge that his father and three of his brothers were stout Loyalists sometimes bred doubts of his steadfastness. A memorandum sent to Gov. George Clinton of New York in 1781, purporting to give names of persons in the secret service of the King, conveys the charge that Samuel Ogden of "Boon Town" furnished a rendezvous for a very active Loyalist, "when on his Rout to Sussex and Other ways in Jersey" (*Public Papers of George Clinton*, VII, 1904, p. 492). The weight of the accusation is relieved by the circumstance that the accuser had rendered aid to the enemy and was recommending himself for pardon by alleged disclosures. No conclusion need be drawn from the recorded fact that Ogden quarreled with the mettlesome William Livingston, New Jersey's war governor.

In the period following the war Samuel Ogden had important land transactions in Northern New York. Most of the area of the state was forest, held by the Six Nations. By a series of treaties from 1789 to 1795 aboriginal titles were extinguished and lands thrown open in northern New York. Ogden made his first investment on the St. Lawrence River in 1792, obtaining a tract in "mile squares," which was to become the town of Oswegatchie, St. Lawrence County. Immediate settlement was impossible because the frontier posts from Niagara to Oswegatchie were retained by the British. Persons in Canada procured leases within Ogden's tract from Oswegatchie Indians and under the guns of the fort stripped the trees from the soil. Ogden was soon in York (now Toronto) and in Quebec, protesting to Lord Dorchester, the governor-general, and to Simcoe, the lieutenant-governor of Upper Canada, in behalf of his property rights. He appointed as a resident agent Nathan Ford, a man who counts largely in the pioneer history of the region. The strife did not cease however until British troops were withdrawn from the posts by the Jay treaty, and one more treaty was framed to settle Indian claims.

The activity in sales and improvements which ensued is impressive. The foundation of the city of Ogdensburg at the mouth of the Oswegatchie River was laid by Samuel Ogden. Samuel's brother, Abraham, had purchased with others of the family a tract that later became the town of Madrid; and along the river enterprising communities sprang up during the first three decades of the nineteenth century. Samuel Ogden married Euphemia Morris, sister of Gouverneur and Lewis Morris [qq.v.], on Feb. 5, 1775. They had twelve children, one of whom was David Bayard Ogden [q.v.]. The latter years of his life were spent in New York City.

[F. B. Hough, *A Hist. of St. Lawrence and Franklin Counties, N. Y.* (1853); Gates Curtis, ed., *Our County and Its People: Memorial Record of St. Lawrence County, N. Y.* (1894); *A Hist. of Morris County, N. J.* (2 vols., 1914); W. O. Wheeler, *The Ogden Family in America* (1907); *Public Papers of Geo. Clinton* (10 vols., 1899–1914), ed. by Hugh Hastings; *N. Y. Evening Post*, Dec. 4, 1810.]   R. E. D.

OGDEN, THOMAS LUDLOW (Dec. 12, 1773–Dec. 17, 1844), lawyer, was descended from John Ogden, who emigrated from England to Southampton, Long Island, in 1640, later settling in Elizabethtown, N. J. Thomas' grandfather, Judge David Ogden [q.v.], was an influential Loyalist, and after the Revolution prosecuted Loyalist claims in English courts. His son, Abraham, Thomas' father, was a distinguished lawyer, surrogate of Morris County, N. J., and after his removal to Newark, was appointed United States attorney for that district (1791–98) by George Washington. Ogden was born probably in Morristown, N. J. Here, in the winter of 1776–77, Washington spent much time with the Ogden family, and according to family tradition, young Thomas often rode mounted on the saddle in front of Washington, on the General's tours of inspection of the army. It is recorded also that during the progress of a playful duel between the two, the button flew off the boy's foil, and Washington received a small flesh wound in the hand. Owing to the Loyalist sentiments of David Ogden, a rumor of attempted assassination got abroad, but was soon dissipated. In 1788 Thomas entered Columbia College, and four years later delivered his graduation oration, "On the Rising Glory of America."

He studied law with his father and Richard Harison and was admitted to the New York bar in 1796. In the same year he was married, on Jan. 23, to Martha Hammond, and formed a law partnership with his elder brother, David. Later, he was associated in practice with Alexander Hamilton. He became one of the most active corporation lawyers in New York City, specialized in trusts and will and equity jurisprudence, and served as counsel for prominent families in the city. He was eminently successful when, as temporary counsel for the Holland Land Company, which owned a three-million-acre tract of land in the western part of the state, he secured through political influence at Albany the passage of a law which the corporation had desired for twenty years. This law enabled it "to re-enter lands sold under the foreclosure of mortgages" and allowed the transfer of lands to aliens on equal terms with natives.

Outside his professional life, his interests and activities centered around religious and philanthropic enterprises. He was vestryman or warden of Trinity Church, New York, from 1807 to 1844, and for many years was "an able and and judicious delegate" to special councils of the Episcopal Church. He was one of the founders and vice-presidents of an Episcopal society for promoting religion and learning in New York, and a trustee of the General Theological Seminary; was trustee of Columbia College, 1817–44, and served in the same capacity for Sailors' Snug Harbor. The vigorous support which he gave a treaty which in his opinion offered the Indians a chance to "be saved from extinction and become a civilized people," further illustrates his breadth of interest (Ogden to Verplanck, manuscript collection, New York Historical Society). Socially prominent, he was vice-president of the banquet at the city hall in honor of Washington Irving's return to America (1832) and committeeman of the public dinner for Chancellor Kent (1843). He is described as a modest, courteous, public-spirited gentleman of the old school. He had seven sons and four daughters.

[W. O. Wheeler, *The Ogden Family in America* (1907); David McAdam and others, *Hist. of the Bench and Bar of N. Y.*, vol. I (1897); J. A. Scoville, *The Old Merchants of N. Y.*, 3rd ser. (1865); *The Diary of Philip Hone* (2 vols., 1889, ed. by Bayard Tuckerman); P. D. Evans, "The Holland Land Company," *Buffalo Hist. Soc. Pubs.*, vol. XXVIII (1924); C. H. Haswell, *Reminiscences of an Octogenarian* (1896); Wm. Berrian, *An Hist. Sketch of Trinity Church New-York* (1847); *Proc. Relating to the Organization of the Gen. Theol. Sem. of the Protestant Episcopal Church* (1854); MSS. in N. Y. Hist. Soc.; *N. Y. Jour. and State Gazette*, May 7, 1791; *N. Y. Commercial Advertiser*, Dec. 19, 1844; *N. Y. Spectator*, Dec. 21, 1844; *N. Y. Daily Tribune*, Dec. 20, 1844.]   A. L. M.

OGDEN, UZAL (1744–Nov. 4, 1822), clergyman, controversialist, was born in Newark, N.

J., the son of Uzal Ogden and Elizabeth Charlotte (Thébaut), daughter of Gabriel Lewis Thébaut of Antigua. On his father's side he was descended from John Ogden of Hampshire, England, who having emigrated to America about 1640, settled in Elizabethtown, N. J., in 1664. The elder Uzal was a merchant of Newark and one of the founders of Trinity Church in that city. As early as 1770 the younger Ogden seems to have interested himself in missionary work in Sussex County and was instrumental in forming the parish of Newtown (now Newton). He pursued theological studies under the Rev. Dr. Thomas B. Chandler [q.v.], rector of St. John's Church, Elizabethtown, and in the summer of 1773 went to England, where, on Sept. 21, he was ordained by the Bishop of London. Upon his return, he continued his missionary work in Sussex County. In April 1779 he was invited to minister occasionally to the needs of Trinity Church, Newark, of which his father was warden, and in November 1785 he was asked to become its rector, but did not accept until 1788, having in the meantime served as assistant rector of Trinity Church, New York. By his intellectual gifts and forceful personality he soon rose to leadership.

On Aug. 16, 1798, he was elected, by a substantial vote, the first bishop of New Jersey. The usual certificate was signed for presentation to the General Convention, which met at Philadelphia in June 1799; that body, however, refused to consent to his consecration, ostensibly because of doubts as to the regularity of his election, and referred the matter back to a future convention of the diocese. A special convention, meeting in October 1799, affirmed that the previous election had been regular in every respect. The matter was again considered by the General Convention held at Trenton, Sept. 8–12, 1801, which held to its previous action, and New Jersey did not have a bishop till some fourteen years later. Behind the refusal to consent to Ogden's consecration lay, probably, a wide-spread objection to his churchmanship, based upon his reputation for laxity in doctrine and disregard for the order of the Episcopal Church. Nothing was urged against his personal character (Hills, *post,* pp. 714, 286–93).

In 1803 he had trouble with his Newark congregation. The matter was brought before a special diocesan Convention in 1804, which requested that he resign on a pension from Trinity Church. Ogden refused and on May 9, 1805, the standing committee, with the aid and consent of Bishop Moore of New York, suspended him from the exercise of any ministerial duties in

New Jersey. On Oct. 15, 1805, the Presbytery of New York received him as a member of that body and he remained such until his death. He never had a stated charge but preached as he found opportunity. In 1776 he married Mary, daughter of Samuel Gouverneur, who died in 1814, having had six children. Ogden's death occurred in Newark, in 1822, and four years later the city received by bequest from his estate four thousand dollars for poor orphaned children. He published numerous pamphlets and sermons and a two-volume treatise, *Antidote to Deism: The Deist Unmasked* (1795), refuting Thomas Paine's *Age of Reason.*

[W. O. Wheeler, *The Ogden Family in America* (1907); W. B. Sprague, *Annals Am. Pulpit,* vol. IV (1859); *Jours. of the Conventions of the Protestant Episcopal Ch. in N. J.,* 1785–1815 (1890); G. M. Hills, *Hist. of the Ch. in Burlington, N. J.* (2nd ed. 1885); N. Y. *Evening Post,* Nov. 5, 1822.]   H. S.

OGDEN, WILLIAM BUTLER (June 15, 1805–Aug. 3, 1877), railroad executive, was born in Walton, Delaware County, N. Y., the son of Abraham and Abigail (Weed) Ogden and a descendant of John Ogden who settled in Elizabethtown, N. J., in 1664. He was educated in the public schools and planned to study law, but when he was only fifteen his father suffered a paralytic stroke and the boy was compelled to devote himself to the management of his father's interests, which consisted of property in what was then an undeveloped country. William devoted himself to the improvement and sale of this land, and in this work showed the executive and financial ability which marked his later career. In 1834 he was elected to the New York legislature on a platform advocating the construction of the New York & Erie Railroad by state aid, which was obtained in 1835. In that year, Charles Butler, a New York capitalist, who had married Ogden's sister, urged his brother-in-law to move to Chicago to take charge of his real-estate interests there. Accordingly, Ogden went to Chicago and laid out a tract for subdivision. With characteristic energy he held an auction at which he sold one-third of the property for more than one hundred thousand dollars or enough to cover the original cost. He then established a land and trust agency and made purchases of land on his own account; in 1843 he formed a partnership with William E. Jones. His success in business and the rise in the value of his real estate later created for him a large fortune.

When Chicago was incorporated as a city in 1837 Ogden was elected its first mayor on the Democratic ticket. The population of the town was only 4,179, and the first problem was the improvement of the streets, which were in a bad condition, and the building of bridges to connect the three parts of the city. After his term as mayor Ogden served many years on the city council and was instrumental in having bridges and many miles of improved streets built. Ogden avenue was named after him. He next devoted himself to the construction of railways east and west from Chicago. One of the first roads projected was the Galena & Chicago Union Railroad which was to run to the then important lead mines. A charter was obtained in 1836 but the panic of the following year prevented the continuation of work, though the charter was kept alive. In 1846 Ogden was elected president of the company. By 1849 the road was built with strap rails to the Des Plaines River, a distance of ten miles, and in April of that year the first locomotive started west from Chicago on the line. Thereafter Ogden devoted himself entirely to railroad development. In 1853 he was chosen one of the directors of the Pittsburg, Ft. Wayne & Chicago Railroad Company, and when the road was made insolvent by the panic of 1857 he was appointed general receiver in 1859 and restored it. He presided over the National Pacific Railway Convention of 1850, held to advocate the building of a transcontinental railroad. In 1857 he became president of the Chicago, St. Paul & Fond-du-Lac Railroad, which later became part of the Chicago & Northwestern. He logically became president of the latter road in 1859 and continued in that office until 1868. When the Union Pacific was organized Ogden was elected its first president in 1862 in order to give prestige to the project. But subscriptions to the needed $2,000,000 capital were not forthcoming until Congress doubled the land grant, when the military character of the road was emphasized by the election in 1863 of Gen. J. A. Dix to the presidency. Ogden also served as president of the Illinois & Wisconsin Railroad, of the Buffalo & Mississippi, and of the Wisconsin & Superior Land Grant Railroad.

Ogden's executive ability was called into service in many lines of civic enterprise. He was the first president of Rush Medical College, a charter member of the Chicago Historical Society, and president of the Board of Trustees of the University of Chicago. When the Merchants Loan & Trust Company was organized in 1857 he was one of its first directors. When the slavery question arose he allied himself with the Free-Soil party and in 1860 was elected by the Republicans to the Illinois Senate, but he split with the party over the Emancipation Proclamation and retired from politics. In 1866 he

purchased an estate at Fordham Heights, just outside of New York City, where he made his home until his death. Late in life, on Feb. 9, 1875, he married Maryanne Arnot, daughter of John and Mary (Tuttle) Arnot, of Elmira, N. Y. He was a man of commanding presence, whose most striking characteristic was his self-reliance. He contributed liberally to educational and charitable institutions, and his name was given to the Ogden Graduate School of Science at the University of Chicago which a bequest from his estate helped to found.

[References to Ogden's life and services are found in a great many scattered references, of which the following are the best: A. T. Andreas, *Hist. of Chicago* (3 vols., 1884–86); I. N. Arnold, *Wm. B. Ogden and Early Days in Chicago* (Fergus Hist. Ser., no. 17, 1882); *The Biog. Encyc. of Ill. of the Nineteenth Century* (1875); D. W. Wood, ed., *Chicago and its Distinguished Citizens* (1881); *Yesterday and Today: A Hist. of the Chicago and North Western Railway System* (3rd ed., 1910); T. W. Goodspeed, *The Univ. of Chicago Biog. Sketches*, vol. I (1922).] E. L. B.

OGILVIE, JAMES (d. Sept. 18, 1820), teacher and lecturer, was born in Aberdeen, Scotland, and emigrated to Virginia at the age of nineteen. He opened an academy at Milton, in Albemarle County, where he taught the entire curriculum, from grammar and geography to literature, ethics, natural philosophy, and political economy. Later, he moved to Richmond and there, as at Milton, had for pupils the sons of the most prominent families. With the maturer students he employed the lecture, or "expostulatory and explanatory" method, admirably suited to his emotional temperament, his high enthusiasm, and his *flair* for oratory. Another innovation of his was the "semi-annual academical examinations and exhibitions; at which, his pupils exhibited specimens of their proficiency and skill in composition and elocution" (see his *Philosophical Essays,* Supplementary Narrative, pp. ii, iii). On these public occasions he delivered sample orations of his own. Their enthusiastic reception encouraged him to plan a weekly course of orations for the people of the vicinity. President Thomas Jefferson attended one of these and was so favorably impressed that he sent Ogilvie an elegant edition of the works of Cicero and later gave other evidences of interest and regard. Popular applause proving far more stimulating and gratifying to his eccentric, if not psychopathic, mind, than the drudgery of teaching, which even a liberal use of opium did not relieve, he conceived the plan of abandoning teaching altogether and devoting himself exclusively to public lecturing.

Accordingly, in 1809 he closed his school and

put his plan into execution. Marked success in his new undertaking was outrun by a still greater ambition, and forthwith he conceived the idea of establishing in all the American colleges professorships of rhetoric, and of having erected in each of the large cities a spacious and magnificent hall for the exhibition of oratory. In pursuance of this idea, after delivering orations in many cities, he arrived in Columbia, S. C., and was invited by President Jonathan Maxcy [q.v.] of the South Carolina College to deliver three orations in the chapel of that institution. Their success was phenomenal. In March 1815 he returned to the college and gave oratorical lectures for the remainder of the session. During this time he delivered an oration before the legislature, making an impassioned plea for the establishment of a professorship of oratory at the college. "In vain! The feelings of his respectable auditors, after venting themselves in a loud and protracted plaudit, evaporated 'into thin air'" (Ibid., p. lxvi). This and other bitter disappointments suffered during seven years of struggle to win support for his project convinced him that further efforts would be futile, unless he could manage to acquire a "permanent and extended celebrity, as a philosophical writer." The need of a greater prestige than would be accorded even the best elocutionist and the urgings of an ever-mounting ambition called for the display of "other and higher qualifications and accomplishments, than those of a popular declaimer."

Despite misgivings as to his philosophical competency and the handicap of his reputation as an elocutionist, he set to work, therefore, to win fame as a philosopher. In a few months the three essays, which were to bring the much hoped-for renown, were completed, and these together with "Copious Notes ... A Supplementary Narrative [autobiographical], with an Appendix," he published in one volume, Philosophical Essays, at Philadelphia, in 1816. The second essay, "On The Nature, Extent, and Limits of Human Knowledge, so far as it is Founded in the Relation of Cause and Effect, and Concerns Mind and Matter"—the only one that could possibly lay claim to the term philosophical—was a restatement of Hume's skepticism. The few reviews the book received condemned both its substance and its style. In 1820 he embarked for London on his way to Scotland, to prosecute his claim to the earldom of Findlater. During his stay in London he was invited to lecture before a distinguished audience, but the effort (owing perhaps to the effect of opium) was a dismal failure. His claim to the earldom was not en-

tertained, and in September 1820 he committed suicide at Aberdeen.

["Recollections of James Ogilvie, Earl of Finlater, By One of his Pupils," Sou. Literary Messenger, Sept. 1848; William Crafts, "The Late Mr. Ogilvie, the Orator," A Selection in Prose and Poetry from the Miscellaneous Writings of W. Crafts (1828), pp. 277–81; Sou. Literary Messenger, Jan. 1852, p. 8; Analectic Mag., Dec. 1816; North Am. Rev., Mar. 1817; Blackwood's Edinburgh Mag., Feb. 1825; J. P. Little, Hist. of Richmond (1933); Joseph Irving, The Book of Scotsmen (1881); Dict. of Nat. Biog.]   J. M—e.

OGILVIE, JOHN (1724–Nov. 26, 1774), a clergyman of the Church of England, prominent for twenty-five years in the Province of New York, was of Scotch descent, born, it is commonly assumed, in New York City, his first known residence. He graduated from Yale College in 1748, and having officiated as a lay reader in Norwalk and Ridgefield, Conn., went abroad for Episcopal ordination. With him he carried a letter to the Bishop of London from Rev. Henry Barclay, then rector of Trinity Church, New York, but formerly in charge of the Albany mission, which states: "I have engaged the bearer hereof, Mr. John Ogilvie, to undertake the mission to Albany and the Mohawk Indians, if your Lordship shall find him duly qualified for Holy Orders. . . . I look upon him as the best qualified for the Indian Mission of any person I could have found on account of his speaking the low Dutch language, which I found very useful to me, both on account of its conformity to the Indian in pronunciation as well as the service I was thereby enabled to do a considerable number of the Dutch inhabitants who are entirely destitute of religious instruction" (Joseph Hooper, A History of St. Peter's Church in the City of Albany, 1900, p. 86). Ogilvie was duly ordained by the Bishop of London and on June 30, 1749, licensed by him to officiate in the Plantations, his appointment to the mission at Albany having been approved by the Society for the Propagation of the Gospel in Foreign Parts.

Returning to America, he commenced his labors in the spring of 1750, taking charge of St. Peter's Church and beginning his ministry to the Mohawks. He found the work both among the Indians and at Albany much demoralized because of the border warfare that until recently had been going on, and reorganized it with great success. His ability, sound judgment, social qualities, and unselfish devotion to his calling gave him a high place in the esteem of the people; St. Peter's flourished, and in 1751 the church edifice was rebuilt with a "handsome Steeple, and a very good Bell," and all the "proper ornaments." He acquired a knowledge of the Mohawk language and his activities among the

Indians were as successful as those among the English. About 1755 he married Susanna Catharine, daughter of Lancaster Symes, Jr., of New York. They had a daughter and a son, George, who became an Episcopal clergyman. The Earl of Loudoun, impressed by Ogilvie's "great pains in the performance of his duties," appointed him, probably in 1756, chaplain to the 62nd or Royal American Regiment of Foot, and in 1759 he accompanied Sir William Johnson on the expedition against Fort Niagara. At the end of the year he was hard at work again in Albany. In 1760 his missionary zeal carried him as far west as Oswego. His work as chaplain had been of such an order that General Amherst commanded him to accompany the army of occupation to Canada. From Montreal he sent to the Society for the Propagation of the Gospel a detailed account of the state of religion there, thus helping to prepare the way for the establishment of the Church of England in Canada.

After the treaty of peace in February 1763, Ogilvie did not resume his work at the Albany mission, and in the autumn of 1764 was appointed an assistant minister of Trinity Church, New York. Here he labored with characteristic fidelity and achieved considerable popularity as a preacher. In 1769 there was published *The Order for Morning and Evening Prayer . . . Collected and Translated into the Mohawk Language Under the Direction of the late Rev. Mr. William Andrews, the Late Rev. Dr. Henry Barclay and the Rev. Mr. John Oglivie* [sic]. That same year, Apr. 17, his first wife having died, Ogilvie married Margaret (Marston) Philipse, daughter of Nathaniel Marston, Jr., and widow of Philip Philipse of New York. On Friday, Nov. 18, 1774, while he was officiating in St. George's Chapel, he suffered a cerebral hemorrhage and died Nov. 26, in his fifty-first year. Mrs. Anne Grant wrote of him, "His appearance was singularly prepossessing; his address and manners entirely those of a gentleman. His abilities were respectable, his doctrine was pure and scriptural, and his life exemplary . . . add to all this a talent for conversation, extensive reading, and a thorough knowledge of life" (*Memoirs of an American Lady,* 1808, II, 93–94). An elegy on his death appeared in *Rivington's New York Gazetteer* for Jan. 5, 1775.

[F. B. Dexter, *Biog. Sketches Grads. Yale Coll.,* vol. II (1896) contains a comprehensive bibliography. See also Hooper, *ante,* who gives an excellent account of Ogilvie's Albany career; Chas. Inglis, *A Sermon . . . Occasioned by the Death of John Ogilvie, D.D.* (1774); Morgan Dix, *A Hist. of the Parish of Trinity Ch. in the City of N. Y.,* pt. I (1898); *Colls. N. Y. Hist. Soc. . . . 1870,* Pub. Fund Ser., III (1871), 250–52, 262–63.]
H. E. S.

OGLE, SAMUEL (*c.* 1702–May 3, 1752), colonial governor of Maryland, was born in Northumberland County, England, where the Ogle family had become prominent as early as the eleventh century. The son of Samuel Ogle of Bousden, who represented Berwick-on-Tweed in the House of Commons, and of his second wife, Ursula, the daughter of Sir Robert Markham and the widow of Lord Altham, he was a captain of cavalry in the British army, when in 1731 he sailed for Annapolis, Md. He arrived on Dec. 2, and five days later was sworn in as proprietary governor of the province, in which his predecessor, Benedict Leonard Calvert, the brother of the lord proprietor, had failed to procure the cooperation of the popular branch of the General Assembly. Tobacco, the staple crop, was yielding small returns for labor, and the boundary dispute with the Penns was so serious that the lord proprietor visited the province and from Dec. 18, 1732, to July 11, 1733, administered the government in person. From the latter date until Aug. 23, 1742, Ogle was again governor, and he served a third term from Mar. 16, 1747, until his death.

As governor, he made it his first care not to show a disregard for any faction, and he was somewhat successful in his efforts to win the support of the leaders of the opposition by promises of lucrative offices. He issued effective proclamations for the apprehension and punishment of persons guilty of inciting mob violence for the destruction of tobacco plants. By accepting a compromise he brought to a close the dispute over the question of the extension of the English statutes to Maryland, a question that since 1722 had been a chief source of discord between the governor and the Assembly. He ably defended the interests of Maryland in a petty border warfare arising from the boundary dispute with Pennsylvania. He met his first and only serious defeat as governor, when in 1739 he attempted to force the passage of a bill for continuing the levy of a tobacco duty for the purchase of arms and ammunition. Disputes over other money bills contributed to a deadlock, and to break this the lord proprietor appointed his own brother-in-law, Thomas Bladen, to succeed Ogle. When Bladen proved to be incompetent, Ogle was restored and from his restoration until his death he was popular. Acting on his recommendations the Assembly, at its first session of his third term, not only passed an acceptable bill for the purchase of arms and ammunition but also passed a bill for the inspection of tobacco and the limitation of officers' fees. The limitation of fees removed a large source of discord between the executive and legislative branches. The inspection of tobacco was the salvation of the tobacco industry and contributed to the successful floating of a paper currency.

In 1741 he married Anne, the daughter of Benjamin Tasker, through whom he came into possession of "Belair," an estate of 3600 acres in Prince George's County twenty miles west of Annapolis. The house was a fine specimen of architecture, and the estate was laid out with a deer park of perhaps six hundred acres, a race track, kennels, and a bowling green. Here and on the highways in a four-in-hand coach with outriders, he maintained the traditions of the English gentleman. He was a lover of sport and took a prominent part in the organization of the Maryland Jockey Club. At his death in Annapolis he was characterized as a man of ability and understanding, whose conversation was affable and instructive but never assuming. He had five children; among them Benjamin, who was governor of Maryland from 1798 to 1801.

[*Archives of Md.*, esp. vols. XXV, XXVIII, XL, XLII (1905–23); "The Calvert Papers," no. 2, *Md. Hist. Soc. Fund Pub.* no. 34 (1894); N. D. Mereness, *Md. as a Proprietary Province* (1901); J. M. Hammond, *Colonial Mansions of Md. and Del.* (1914); *Md. Gazette*, May 7, 1752; H. A. Ogle, *Ogle and Bothal* (1902), pp. 211–13.]   N. D. M.

OGLESBY, RICHARD JAMES (July 25, 1824–Apr. 24, 1899), governor of Illinois and senator, was born in Oldham County, Ky., the son of Jacob and Isabella (Watson) Oglesby. His father was a farmer, owned a few slaves, and was a member of the Kentucky legislature. In 1833 his parents, two brothers, and a sister died of the cholera and the family property was sold, including the slaves. He maintained that it was the sale of these slaves, especially of Uncle Tim, whom he later bought and freed, that made him an abolitionist. An uncle took the orphaned boy to Decatur, Ill., where he attended the district school a few months before be began his struggle for a livelihood as farmer, rope-maker, and carpenter. He studied law in the office of Silas W. Robbins of Springfield, was admitted to the bar in 1845, and practised his profession at Sullivan, Ill., until the outbreak of the Mexican War. During the war he served as first lieutenant in the 4th Illinois Volunteers, participating in the battles of Vera Cruz and Cerro Gordo. After the war he resumed his law practice and attended a course of lectures at the law school in Louisville. In 1849 he went to California to dig for gold and returned to his profession at Decatur in 1851. Five years later he went abroad for twenty months' travel in Europe, Egypt, and the Holy Land.

On his return to Decatur he entered politics. He had been a Whig and had served as a Scott elector in 1852 but joined the Republican party upon its formation. In 1858 he ran for Congress on the Republican ticket and was defeated by only a small majority in a strong Democratic district. In 1860 he was elected to the state Senate, but he served only one term, resigning at the outbreak of the Civil War to become colonel of the 8th Illinois Volunteers. He served as brigade commander under Grant at Fort Henry and Fort Donelson and was severely wounded at the battle of Corinth. In April 1863 he returned to the army and was promoted to the rank of major-general. He resigned in May 1864. In November 1864 he was elected governor of Illinois on the Republican ticket. He was an ardent advocate of Lincoln's war policies; however, later he denounced Johnson bitterly and sent a formal demand to Washington for action against him. During his administration, Illinois ratified the Thirteenth and the Fourteenth Amendments and repealed her "Black Laws." Further enactments provided for a home for the children of deceased soldiers, a school for the feeble-minded, the location of the Illinois industrial college at Urbana, and the construction of a southern Illinois penitentiary. At the end of his term he returned to his law practice, but in 1872 he was again the Republican nominee for governor, the party realizing that he was the only Republican who could carry the state. There was an understanding, however, that the lieutenant-governor should succeed to the governorship immediately after inauguration and that Oglesby in turn should receive election to the United States Senate. A few days after his inauguration, therefore, he was elected to succeed Lyman Trumbull. As senator, he served as chairman of the committee on public lands and on the committees of Indian affairs, pensions, and civil service. As a member of the pensions committee, he was an earnest champion of the soldiers' interests. He retired at the end of his term in the Senate. In 1884 the Republican party nominated him governor by acclamation, and he was elected, the first man in Illinois to receive that honor three times. During this administration his general policies were carried out in laws providing for a soldiers' and sailors' home, a home for juvenile delinquents, and the creation of various pension funds. In 1889 he retired to his home at "Oglehurst," Elkhart, Ill. In 1891 he was nominated for the Senate, but he failed of election.

The last years of his life were spent in comparative quiet. He was married twice: to Anna

Oglesby

White in 1859 and, after her death in 1868, to Emma (Gillet) Keyes in 1873. He was a fine-looking man with a bluff, friendly manner that appealed to the people. This, added to his wit and good humor, his sincerity and enthusiasm, and his ability to speak to the people in the vernacular, made him an excellent stump speaker, and as such he acquired considerable fame. He believed in the people and in their ability to govern themselves; in return, he was dearly beloved by them, to whom he was known as "Uncle Dick."

[Correspondence in possession of Ill. State Hist. Lib., Urbana, and of his son, John G. Oglesby, Elkhart; J. M. Johns, *Personal Recollections of Early Decatur* (1912); *The Bench and Bar of Ill.*, ed. by J. M. Palmer (1899), vol. II; *The Biog. Encyc. of Ill.*, ed. by Charles Robsen (1875); G. B. Raum, *Hist. of Ill. Republicanism* (1900); John Moses, *Ill., Hist. and Statistical*, vol. II (1892); A. C. Cole, *The Era of the Civil War* (1919); E. L. Bogart, *The Industrial State* (1920); *Ill. State Register* (Springfield), Apr. 25, 1899.]   E. B. E.